Lecture Notes in Artificial Intelligence   4188

Edited by J. G. Carbonell and J. Siekmann

Subseries of Lecture Notes in Computer Science

T0189809

Petr Sojka   Ivan Kopeček
Karel Pala (Eds.)

Text, Speech
and Dialogue

9th International Conference, TSD 2006
Brno, Czech Republic, September 11-15, 2006
Proceedings

Series Editors

Jaime G. Carbonell, Carnegie Mellon University, Pittsburgh, PA, USA
Jörg Siekmann, University of Saarland, Saarbrücken, Germany

Volume Editors

Petr Sojka
Masaryk University
Faculty of Informatics
Department of Computer Graphics and Design
Botanická 68a, 602 00 Brno, Czech Republic
E-mail: sojka@informatics.muni.cz

Ivan Kopeček
Karel Pala
Masaryk University
Faculty of Informatics
Department of Information Technologies
Botanická 68a, 602 00 Brno, Czech Republic
E-mail: {kopecek,pala}@informatics.muni.cz

Library of Congress Control Number: 2006931937

CR Subject Classification (1998): I.2.7, I.2, H.3, H.4, I.7

LNCS Sublibrary: SL 7 – Artificial Intelligence

ISSN   0302-9743
ISBN-10   3-540-39090-1 Springer Berlin Heidelberg New York
ISBN-13   978-3-540-39090-9 Springer Berlin Heidelberg New York

Springer is a part of Springer Science+Business Media

springer.com

© Springer-Verlag Berlin Heidelberg 2006
Printed in Germany

Typesetting: Camera-ready by Petr Sojka from source files by respective authors,
             Scientific Publishing Services, Chennai, India
                  SPIN: 11846406   06/3142   5 4 3 2 1 0

Preface

The annual Text, Speech and Dialogue Conference (TSD), which originated in 1998, is now coming to the end of its first decade. During this time almost 400 authors from 36 countries have contributed to the proceedings. TSD constitutes a recognized forum for the presentation and discussion of state-of-the-art technology and recent achievements in the field of natural language processing. It has become an interdisciplinary forum, interweaving the themes of speech technology and language processing. The conference attracts researchers not only from Central and Eastern Europe but also from other parts of the world. Indeed, one of its goals has always been to bring together NLP researchers with different interests from different parts of the world and to promote their mutual cooperation.

This volume contains the proceedings of the Ninth TSD Conference, held in Brno, Czech Republic in September 2006. Following the review process, 87 papers were accepted out of 175 submitted, an acceptance rate of 49.7%. The number of the submissions this year was the highest so far. We would like to thank all the authors for the efforts they put into their submissions and the members of the Program Committee and reviewers who did a wonderful job helping us to select the most appropriate papers. We are also grateful to the invited speakers for their contribution. Their talks provided insight into important issues, applications and techniques related to the conference topics.

Special thanks are due to the members of the Local Organizing Committee for their tireless effort in organizing the conference. Dagmar Janoušková and Dana Komárková carried the main administrative burden and contributed in many other ways to the preparation of the conference. The TeXpertise of Petr Sojka resulted in the production of the volume that you are holding in your hands.

We hope that you benefitted from the event and that you also enjoyed the social program prepared by the Organizing Committee.

July 2006   Ivan Kopeček, Karel Pala

Organization

TSD 2006 was organized by the Faculty of Informatics, Masaryk University, in cooperation with the Faculty of Applied Sciences, University of West Bohemia in Plzeň. The conference Webpage is located at http://www.tsdconferences.org/tsd2006/

Program Committee

Jelinek, Frederick (USA), *General Chair*

Hermansky, Hynek (USA), *Executive Chair*

Agirre, Eneko (Spain)

Baudoin, Geneviève (France)

Černocký, Jan (Czech Republic)

Ferencz, Attila (Romania)

Gelbukh, Alexander (Mexico)

Guthrie, Louise, (UK)

Hajičová, Eva (Czech Republic)

Hlaváčová, Jaroslava (Czech Republic)

Hovy, Eduard (USA)

Kopeček, Ivan (Czech Republic)

Krauwer, Steven (The Netherlands)

Kunzmann Siegfried (Germany)

Matoušek, Václav (Czech Republic)

Nöth, Elmar (Germany)

Ney, Hermann (Germany)

Oliva, Karel (Austria)

Pala, Karel (Czech Republic)

Pavesić, Nikola (Slovenia)

Petkevič, Vladimír (Czech Republic)

Psutka, Josef (Czech Republic)

Pustejovsky, James (USA)

Rothkrantz, Leon (The Netherlands)

Schukat-Talamazzini, E. Günter (Germany)

Skrelin, Pavel (Russia)

Smrž Pavel (Czech Republic)

Vintsiuk, Taras (Ukraine)

Wilks, Yorick (UK)

Zakharov, Victor (Russia)

Referees

Iñaki Alegria, Ben Allison, Lukáš Burget, Oliver Bender, Jan Bungeroth, Pavel Cenek, Thomas Deselaers, Nerea Ezeiza, Nestor Garay-Vitoria, Christian Gollan, Mark A. Greenwood, František Grezl, David Guthrie, Sasa Hasan, Georg Heigold, Aleš Horák, Sanaz Jabbari, Sergej Krylov, Arantza Díaz de Ilarraza, Jonas Lööf, David Martinez, Pavel Matejka, Arne Mauser, Brian Mitchell, Olga Mitrofanova, Yoshihiko Nitta, Ilya Oparin, Nino Peterek, Christian Plahl, Joe Polifroni, German Rigau, Pavel Rychlý, Kepa Sarasola, Petr Sojka, Daniel Stein, Igor Szöke, Zygmunt Vetulani, David Vilar.

Organizing Committee

Dana Hlaváčková *(administrative contact)*, Aleš Horák, Dagmar Janoušková *(Accounting)*, Dana Komárková *(Secretary)*, Ivan Kopeček *(Co-chair)*, Karel Pala *(Co-chair)*, Adam Rambousek *(Web system)*, Pavel Rychlý, Petr Sojka *(Proceedings)*.

Supported by:

International Speech Communication Association, South Moravia Gas Company.

Table of Contents

I Invited Papers

Learning by Reading: An Experiment in Text Analysis 3
Eduard Hovy (ISI, University of Southern California, USA)

Depth of Feelings: Alternatives for Modeling Affect in User Models 13
Eva Hudlicka (Psychometrix Associates, Blacksburg, USA)

II Text

The Lexico-Semantic Annotation of PDT 21
Eduard Bejček, Petra Möllerová, Pavel Straňák (Charles University, Prague, Czech Republic)

Czech Verbs of Communication and the Extraction of Their Frames 29
Václava Benešová, Ondřej Bojar (Charles University, Prague, Czech Republic)

Featuring of Sex-Dependent Nouns
in Databases Oriented to European Languages 37
Igor A. Bolshakov (National Polytechnic Institute, Mexico City, Mexico), Sofia N. Galicia-Haro (National Autonomous University of Mexico (UNAM), Mexico City, Mexico)

On the Behaviors of SVM and Some Older Algorithms
in Binary Text Classification Tasks 45
Fabrice Colas (Leiden University, The Netherlands), Pavel Brazdil (University of Porto, Portugal)

A Knowledge Based Strategy for Recognising Textual Entailment 53
Óscar Ferrández, Rafael M. Terol, Rafael Muñoz, Patricio Martínez-Barco, Manuel Palomar (University of Alicante, Spain)

Paragraph-Level Alignment of an English-Spanish Parallel Corpus of
Fiction Texts Using Bilingual Dictionaries* 61
Alexander Gelbukh, Grigori Sidorov, José Ángel Vera-Félix

Some Methods of Describing Discontinuity in Polish and Their
Cost-Effectiveness 69
Filip Graliński (Adam Mickiewicz University, Poznań, Poland)

Exploitation of the VerbaLex Verb Valency Lexicon
in the Syntactic Analysis of Czech 79
*Dana Hlaváčková, Aleš Horák, Vladimír Kadlec (Masaryk University,
Brno, Czech Republic)*

Hungarian-English Machine Translation Using GenPar................. 87
András Hócza, András Kocsor (University of Szeged, Hungary)

Combining Czech Dependency Parsers................................. 95
*Tomáš Holan and Zdeněk Žabokrtský (Charles University, Prague,
Czech Republic)*

Processing Korean Numeral Classifier Constructions
in a Typed Feature Structure Grammar............................. 103
*Jong-Bok Kim (Kyung Hee University, Seoul, Korea), Jaehyung Yang
(Kangnam University, Korea)*

Parsing Head Internal and External Relative Clause Constructions in
Korean 111
Jong-Bok Kim (Kyung Hee University, Seoul, Korea)

A Hybrid Model for Extracting Transliteration Equivalents from
Parallel Corpora 119
*Jong-Hoon Oh (NICT, Republic of Korea), Key-Sun Choi (KAIST,
Republic of Korea), Hitoshi Isahara (NICT, Republic of Korea)*

Sentence Compression Using Statistical Information About Dependency
Path Length 127
*Kiwamu Yamagata, Satoshi Fukutomi, Kazuyuki Takagi, Kazuhiko
Ozeki (The University of Electro-Communications, Tokyo, Japan)*

Transformation-Based Tectogrammatical Analysis of Czech............. 135
Václav Klimeš (Charles University, Prague, Czech Republic)

The Effect of Semantic Knowledge Expansion
to Textual Entailment Recognition 143
*Zornitsa Kozareva, Sonia Vázquez and Andrés Montoyo (Alicante
University, Spain)*

Segmentation of Complex Sentences 151
*Vladislav Kuboň, Markéta Lopatková, Martin Plátek (Charles
University, Prague, Czech Republic), Patrice Pognan (CERTAL
INALCO, Paris, France)*

Enhanced Centroid-Based Classification Technique by Filtering
Outliers 159
*Kwangcheol Shin, Ajith Abraham, SangYong Han (Chung-Ang
University, Seoul, Korea)*

Multilingual News Document Clustering: Two Algorithms Based on
Cognate Named Entities 165
*Soto Montalvo (URJC, Spain), Raquel Martínez (UNED, Spain),
Arantza Casillas (UPV-EHU, Spain), Víctor Fresno (URJC, Spain)*

A Study of the Influence of PoS Tagging on WSD 173
*Lorenza Moreno-Monteagudo, Rubén Izquierdo-Beviá, Patricio
Martínez-Barco, Armando Suárez (Universidad de Alicante, Spain)*

Annotation of Temporal Relations Within a Discourse 181
Petr Němec (Charles University, Prague, Czech Republic)

Applying RST Relations to Semantic Search 189
*Nguyen Thanh Tri, Akira Shimazu, Le Cuong Anh, Nguyen Minh Le
(JAIST, Ishikawa, Japan)*

Data-Driven Part-of-Speech Tagging of Kiswahili 197
*Guy De Pauw (University of Antwerp, Belgium), Gilles-Maurice de
Schryver (Ghent University, Belgium), Peter W. Wagacha (University
of Nairobi, Kenya)*

Hand-Written and Automatically Extracted Rules for Polish Tagger 205
Maciej Piasecki (Wrocław University of Technology, Poland)

Effective Architecture of the Polish Tagger 213
*Maciej Piasecki, Grzegorz Godlewski (Wrocław University of
Technology, Poland)*

Synthesis of Czech Sentences from Tectogrammatical Trees 221
*Jan Ptáček, Zdeněk Žabokrtský (Charles University, Prague, Czech
Republic)*

ASeMatch: A Semantic Matching Method 229
*Sandra Roger (University of Alicante, Spain & University of Comahue,
Argentina), Augustina Buccella (University of Comahue, Argentina),
Alejandra Cechich (University of Comahue, Argentina), Manuel Sanz
Palomar (University of Alicante, Spain)*

Extensive Study on Automatic Verb Sense Disambiguation in Czech 237
Jiří Semecký, Petr Podveský (UFAL MFF UK, Czech Republic)

Semantic Representation of Events: Building a Semantic Primes
Component 245
Milena Slavcheva (Bulgarian Academy of Sciences, Sofia, Bulgaria)

Cascaded Grammatical Relation-Driven Parsing
Using Support Vector Machines 253
Songwook Lee (Dongseo University, Busan, Korea)

Building Korean Classifier Ontology Based on Korean WordNet......... 261
Soonhee Hwang, Youngim Jung, Aesun Yoon, Hyuk-Chul Kwon (Pusan National University, Busan, South Korea)

Exploiting the Translation Context for Multilingual WSD 269
Lucia Specia, Maria das Graças Volpe Nunes (Universidade de São Paulo, Brazil)

Post-annotation Checking of Prague Dependency Treebank 2.0 Data 277
Jan Štěpánek (ÚFAL UK Prague, Czech Republic)

Language Modelling with Dynamic Syntax 285
David Tugwell (University of St Andrews, Scotland, UK)

Using Word Sequences for Text Summarization 293
Esaú Villatoro-Tello, Luis Villaseñor-Pineda, Manuel Montes-y-Gómez (National Institute of Astrophysics, Optics and Electronics, Mexico)

Exploration of Coreference Resolution: The ACE Entity Detection and Recognition Task 301
Ying Chen, Kadri Hacioglu (University of Colorado at Boulder, USA)

Parsing with Oracle 309
Michal Žemlička (Charles University, Prague, Czech Republic)

III   Speech

Evaluating Language Models Within a Predictive Framework: An Analysis of Ranking Distributions 319
Pierre Alain, Olivier Boëffard, Nelly Barbot (Université de Rennes 1, France)

Another Look at the Data Sparsity Problem 327
Ben Allison, David Guthrie, Louise Guthrie (University of Sheffield, UK)

Syllable-Based Recognition Unit to Reduce Error Rate for Korean Phones, Syllables and Characters 335
Bong-Wan Kim, Yongnam Um, Yong-Ju Lee (Wonkwang University, Korea)

Recognizing Connected Digit Strings Using Neural Networks 343
Łukasz Brocki, Danijel Koržinek, Krzysztof Marasek (Polish-Japanese Institute of Information Technology, Warsaw, Poland)

Indexing and Search Methods for Spoken Documents 351
*Lukáš Burget, Jan Černocký, Michal Fapšo, Martin Karafiát, Pavel
Matějka, Petr Schwarz, Pavel Smrž, Igor Szöke (Brno University of
Technology, Czech Republic)*

Analysis of HMM Temporal Evolution for Automatic Speech
Recognition and Verification...................................... 359
*Marta Casar, José A.R. Fonollosa (Universitat Politècnica de
Catalunya, Barcelona, Spain)*

Corpus-Based Unit Selection TTS for Hungarian 367
*Márk Fék, Péter Pesti, Géza Németh, Csaba Zainkó, Gábor Olaszy
(Budapest University of Technology and Economics, Hungary)*

Automated Mark Up of Affective Information in English Texts 375
*Virginia Francisco, Pablo Gervás (Universidad Complutense de Madrid,
Spain)*

First Steps Towards New Czech Voice Conversion System 383
*Zdeněk Hanzlíček, Jindřich Matoušek (University of West Bohemia,
Plzeň, Czech Republic)*

Are Morphosyntactic Taggers Suitable to Improve Automatic
Transcription? 391
Stéphane Huet, Guillaume Gravier, Pascale Sébillot (IRISA, France)

Fast Speaker Adaptation Using Multi-stream Based Eigenvoice in
Noisy Environments 399
Hwa Jeon Song, Hyung Soon Kim (Pusan National University, Korea)

Phonetic Question Generation Using Misrecognition 407
*Supphanat Kanokphara, Julie Carson-Berndsen (University College
Dublin, Ireland)*

Speech Driven Facial Animation Using HMMs in Basque 415
*Maider Lehr (University of the Basque Country, Spain), Andoni Arruti
(VICOMTech Research Centre, Donostia - San Sebastián, Spain),
Amalia Ortiz, David Oyarzun, Michael Obach (University of the Basque
Country, Spain)*

Comparing B-Spline and Spline Models for F0 Modelling 423
*Damien Lolive, Nelly Barbot, Olivier Boëffard (University of Rennes 1,
France)*

Environmental Adaptation with a Small Data Set of the Target
Domain 431
*Andreas Maier, Tino Haderlein, Elmar Nöth (University of Erlangen
Nüremberg, Germany)*

Current State of Czech Text-to-Speech System ARTIC 439
*Jindřich Matoušek, Daniel Tihelka, Jan Romportl (University of West
Bohemia, Pilsen, Czech Republic)*

Automatic Korean Phoneme Generation Via Input-Text Preprocessing
and Disambiguation 447
*Mi-young Kang, Sung-won Jung, Hyuk-Chul Kwon, Aesun Yoon (Pusan
National University, Busan, South Korea)*

Robust Speech Detection Based on Phoneme Recognition Features 455
France Mihelič, Janez Žibert (University of Ljubljana, Slovenia)

Composite Decision by Bayesian Inference in Distant-Talking Speech
Recognition 463
*Mikyong Ji, Sungtak Kim, Hoirin Kim (Information and
Communications University, Daejeon, Korea)*

Speech Coding Based on Spectral Dynamics 471
*Petr Motlíček (IDIAP, Switzerland & Brno University of Technology,
Czech Republic), Hynek Hermansky (IDIAP, Switzerland & Brno
University of Technology, Czech Republic & EPFL, Switzerland),
Harinath Garudadri, Naveen Srinivasamurthy (Qualcomm Inc., San
Diego, USA)*

Detecting Broad Phonemic Class Boundaries from Greek Speech
in Noise Environments 479
*Iosif Mporas, Panagiotis Zervas, Nikos Fakotakis (University of Patras,
Greece)*

A System for Information Retrieval from Large Records of Czech
Spoken Data 485
*Jan Nouza, Jindřich Žďánský, Petr Červa, Jan Kolorenč (TU Liberec,
Czech Republic)*

A Structure of Expert System for Speaker Verification 493
*Aleš Padrta, Jan Vaněk (University of West Bohemia in Pilsen, Czech
Republic)*

Automatic Online Subtitling of the Czech Parliament Meetings 501
*Aleš Pražák, J. V. Psutka, Jan Hoidekr, Jakub Kanis, Luděk Müller,
Josef Psutka (University of West Bohemia in Pilsen, Czech Republic)*

Character Identity Expression in Vocal Performance
of Traditional Puppeteers 509
Milan Rusko, Juraj Hamar (Comenius University, Bratislava, Slovakia)

A Dissonant Frequency Filtering for Enhanced Clarity of Husky Voice
Signals 517
Sangki Kang, Yongserk Kim (Samsung Electronics Co., Korea)

Post-processing of Automatic Segmentation
of Speech Using Dynamic Programming............................ 523
*Marcin Szymański, Stefan Grocholewski (Poznań University of
Technology, Poland)*

Diphones vs. Triphones in Czech Unit Selection TTS 531
*Daniel Tihelka, Jindřich Matoušek (University of West Bohemia in
Pilsen, Czech Republic)*

Silence/Speech Detection Method Based on Set of Decision Graphs...... 539
*Jan Trmal, Jan Zelinka, Jan Vaněk, Luděk Müller (University of West
Bohemia in Pilsen, Czech Republic)*

Prosodic Cues for Automatic Phrase Boundary Detection in ASR 547
*Klára Vicsi, György Szaszák (Budapest University for Technology and
Economics, Hungary)*

Dynamic Bayesian Networks for Language Modeling.................. 555
*Pascal Wiggers, Leon J. M. Rothkrantz (Delft University of Technology,
The Netherlands)*

IV   Dialogue

Feature Subset Selection Based on Evolutionary Algorithms for
Automatic Emotion Recognition in Spoken Spanish and Standard
Basque Language 565
*Aitor Álvarez, Idoia Cearreta, Juan Miguel López, Andoni Arruti,
Elena Lazkano, Basilio Sierra, Nestor Garay (University of the Basque
Country, Spain)*

Two-Dimensional Visual Language Grammar 573
*Siska Fitrianie, Leon J.M. Rothkrantz (Delft University of Technology,
The Netherlands)*

Are You Looking at Me, Are You Talking with Me:
Multimodal Classification of the Focus of Attention 581
*Christian Hacker (University of Erlangen-Nuremberg, Germany),
Anton Batliner (University of Erlangen-Nuremberg, Germany), Elmar
Nöth (University of Erlangen-Nuremberg, Germany)*

Visualization of Voice Disorders Using the Sammon Transform.......... 589
*Tino Haderlein, Dominik Zorn, Stefan Steidl, Elmar Nöth (University
of Erlangen-Nuremberg, Germany), Makoto Shozakai (Asahi Kasei
Corp.), Maria Schuster (University of Erlangen-Nuremberg, Germany)*

Task Switching in Audio Based Systems 597
*Melanie Hartmann, Dirk Schnelle (Darmstadt University of Technology,
Germany)*

Use of Negative Examples in Training the HVS Semantic Model 605
*Filip Jurčíček, Jan Švec, Jiří Zahradil, Libor Jelínek (University of
West Bohemia in Pilsen, Czech Republic)*

Czech-Sign Speech Corpus for Semantic Based Machine Translation 613
*Jakub Kanis (University of West Bohemia), Jiří Zahradil (SpeechTech),
Filip Jurčíček (University of West Bohemia), Luděk Müller (University
of West Bohemia)*

Processing of Requests in Estonian Institutional Dialogues: Corpus
Analysis 621
*Mare Koit, Maret Valdisoo, Olga Gerassimenko (University of
Tartu, Estonia), Tiit Hennoste (University of Helsinki, Finland and
University of Tartu, Estonia), Riina Kasterpalu, Andriela Rääbis,
Krista Strandson (University of Tartu, Estonia)*

Using Prosody for Automatic Sentence Segmentation of Multi-
party Meetings 629
*Jáchym Kolář (ICSI, Berkeley, USA and University of West Bohemia
in Pilsen, Czech Republic), Elizabeth Shriberg (ICSI, Berkeley, USA
and SRI International, Menlo Park, USA), Yang Liu (ICSI, Berkeley,
USA and University of Texas at Dallas, USA)*

Simple Method of Determining the Voice Similarity and Stability by
Analyzing a Set of Very Short Sounds 637
*Konrad Lukaszewicz, Matti Karjalainen (Helsinki University of
Technology, FInland)*

Visualization of Prosodic Knowledge Using Corpus Driven MEMOInt
Intonation Modelling 645
*David Escudero Mancebo, Valentín Cardeñoso-Payo (University of
Valladolid, Spain)*

Automatic Annotation of Dialogues Using n-Grams 653
*Carlos D. Martínez-Hinarejos (Universidad Politécnica de Valencia,
Spain)*

PPChecker: Plagiarism Pattern Checker in Document Copy Detection ... 661
*NamOh Kang (Chung-Ang University, South Korea), Alexander
Gelbukh (National Polytechnic Institute, Mexico), SangYong Han
(Chung-Ang University, South Korea)*

Segmental Duration Modelling in Turkish   669
*Özlem Öztürk (Dokuz Eylul University, Izmir, Turkey), Tolga Çiloğlu
(Middle East Technical University, Ankara, Turkey)*

A Pattern-Based Methodology for Multimodal Interaction Design   677
Andreas Ratzka, Christian Wolff (University of Regensburg Germany)

A Pattern Learning Approach to Question Answering Within the
Ephyra Framework   687
*Nico Schlaefer, Petra Gieselmann (University Karlsruhe, Germany),
Thomas Schaaf, Alex Waibel (Carnegie Mellon University, Pittsburgh,
USA)*

Explicative Document Reading Controlled by Non-speech Audio
Gestures   695
*Adam J. Sporka (Czech Technical University in Prague, Czech
Republic), Pavel Žikovský (Academy of Performing Arts in Prague,
Czech Republic), Pavel Slavík (Czech Technical University in Prague,
Czech Republic)*

Hybrid Neural Network Design and Implementation on FPGA
for Infant Cry Recognition   703
*I. Suaste-Rivas, A. Díaz-Méndez, C.A. Reyes-García (Instituto
Nacional de Astrofísica Óptica y Electrónica, México), O.F.
Reyes-Galaviz (Instituto Tecnológico de Apizaco, México)*

Speech and Sound Use in a Remote Monitoring System for Health
Care   711
*Michel Vacher, Jean-François Serignat, Stéphane Chaillol, Dan Istrate,
Vladimir Popescu (CLIPS-IMAG, Grenoble, France)*

Author Index   719

Part I

Invited Papers

Learning by Reading: An Experiment in Text Analysis

Eduard Hovy
(with collaborators Hans Chalupsky, Jerry Hobbs, Chin-Yew Lin, Patrick Pantel,
Andrew Philpot, and students Rutu Mulkar and Marco Pennacchiotti)

Information Sciences Institute, University of Southern California
4676 Admiralty Way
Marina del Rey, CA, USA
hovy@isi.edu

Abstract. It has long been a dream to build computer systems that learn automatically by reading text. This dream is generally considered infeasible, but some surprising developments in the US over the past three years have led to the funding of several short-term investigations into whether and how much the best current practices in Natural Language Processing and Knowledge Representation and Reasoning, when combined, actually enable this dream. This paper very briefly describes one of these efforts, the Learning by Reading project at ISI, which has converted a high school textbook of Chemistry into very shallow logical form and is investigating which semantic features can plausibly be added to support the kinds of inference required for answering standard high school text questions.

1 Context and Background

From almost the beginnings of Artificial Intelligence, it was clear that automated systems require knowledge to reason intelligently, and that for multi-purpose, wide-domain, robust reasoning, the amount required is nontrivial. Experience, especially with expert systems during the 1970s, illustrated just how hard it is to acquire enough of the right knowledge, and how difficult it is to formalize that knowledge in ways suitable for supporting reasoning. Naturally, then, the dream arose to enable systems to read text and learn by themselves. But this dream has never been realized. In fact, as research in Knowledge Representation and Reasoning (KR&R) and Natural Language Processing (NLP) progressed, the two areas diverged, to the point where today they are more or less entirely separate, with unrelated conferences, journals, and research paradigms.

A few years ago, three research groups, funded by Vulcan Inc., participated in an audacious experiment called Project Halo: to (manually) convert the information contained in one chapter of a high school textbook on Chemistry into knowledge representation statements, and then to have the knowledge representation system take a standard high school Advanced Placement (AP) exam. Surprisingly, two of the three systems passed, albeit at a relatively low level of performance. The project engendered wide interest; see (Friedland et al., 2003).

Over the past year, DARPA has funded five groups in the US to conduct pilot studies that investigate the feasibility of building fully Learning by Reading (LbR) systems. The largest, Project Möbius, is a consortium of some 20 researchers from numerous institutions. Its goal

Petr Sojka, Ivan Kopeček and Karel Pala (Eds.): TSD 2006, LNAI 4188, pp. 3–12, 2006.

is to design a general framework for LbR systems in the future, and to advise DARPA on the wisdom of funding a new program in this area. Typical questions include: How feasible is fully automated LbR? What are the different phases/components/steps of LbR? What are the current levels of capability of the component technologies, and where are the major bottlenecks and failure points? What kind of research would best further the dream of LbR? What sorts of results could one expect after five years?

The remaining four projects proceed independently but report back to Möbius. All are smaller, 9-month efforts, and each focuses on one or more specific aspects of the general LbR problem:

- A project jointly at Boeing and SRI, led by Peter Clark of Boeing, focuses on the mismatch between English sentences and their equivalent knowledge representations propositions, with the methodology of building manually the representations for a carefully selected extract of 5 pages from the Chemistry textbook.
- A project at Northwestern University, led by Ken Forbus, concentrates on the processes of self-guided inference that occurs after new information is read. Called *introspection* or *rumination*, these processes work in parallel with the reading, and serve as a source of expectations, questions, and background checking. This project focuses on a few selected sentences from the Chemistry textbook, and the thoughts that may arise from them.
- A project at CYC Corp., led by Michael Witbrock, addresses the problem of learning the meaning of new, unknown, words in context. Starting with the knowledge already inside their very large ontology and reasoning system Cyc, researchers develop methods to apply inferences in order to build up likely interpretations of a sentence and from these hypothesize the meaning of the unknown word.
- The fourth project is the subject of this paper. Located at ISI, we are investigating how much can be done by combining traditional and statistical NLP methods, and what kinds of KR&R are absolutely required, at which points in the process. We have parsed the whole Chemistry textbook, have developed methods to convert the parses into shallow logical form, and are investigating the what types of -semantics should be added to support the reasoning required for question answering.

In this paper we briefly outline the architecture and general aspects of ISI's LbR project, which will finish in August, namely about three months after the time of writing this paper.

2   The Text

The text is *Chemistry: The Central Science* (9th ed.), by Brown, LeMay, Bursten, and Burdge, which is intended for senior high-school students. The publishers have kindly made an electronic version available to the projects, to be used for research purposes only.

The book contains 313590 words (12722 different words). Of this, nouns comprise 146825 / 9279 tokens/types, verbs 28627 / 1387 tokens/types, and adjectives and adverbs together 35775 / 2795. The most frequent 50 nouns cover 67.2% of all noun tokens in the book; the most frequent 50 verbs cover 92.4% of the verb tokens, and the most frequent 50 adjectives/adverbs cover 83.7%. This is relatively good news: should one have to hand-construct core meanings of (most of) these words before the systems starts to read, it will suffice to treat only the most frequent 200 nouns (covering 96.1% of all noun tokens), 50 verbs, and 50 adjectives/adverbs.

3   The Learning by Reading Architecture and Modules

3.1   System Architecture

Given the very short time available—9 months from start to finish—the project is necessarily very incomplete; we decided to focus on just selected areas of interest and to simplify or ignore many of the interesting questions we encountered. Since our strength lies in language processing technology, we focus on the NLP areas, with the intent to discover how little KR&R we needed, and how shallow semantics is possible, to still produce something interesting. We therefore consciously sidestep the many complex phenomena involved in semantic understanding, as opposed to syntactic parsing, including in particular wordsense disambiguation, coreference and anaphora resolution, quantification, negation, complex NP structure and modification, discourse structure, and so on.

One might ask: if you ignore all this, what's the point? And indeed, designing some kind of evaluation, or at least some criteria by which one can measure and/or describe the validity and utility of the outcome, is a significant challenge, as we discuss in Section 4. Nonetheless, it is extremely interesting and quite instructive to proceed under these very strong simplifications, and to then discover what phenomena of semantics are in fact required for a practical application of LbR (as opposed to what phenomena have received a lot of attention from researchers), as well as to investigate whether there are simple and robust methods to derive these phenomena using modern techniques.

The overall system architecture is shown in Figure 1. The system was built in three 3-month stages: stage 1 covered textbook analysis, background knowledge structures, and syntactic parsing; stage 2 covered conversion of parse structures into shallow logical form, creation of notations for selected semantic phenomena, and building of inferences / transformation rules to create these representations; stage 3 covers instantiation of the final output for into a KR&R system and experiments with question answering.

3.2   The Skeletal Ontology

No human would dream of reading a book like this without any knowledge whatsoever of English words. Since we had only 9 months for the project, we decided to extract from our large general-purpose term taxonomy/ontology Omega (Philpot et al., 2005) just the terms used in the book, with their inheritance structure, verb case frame information, and selected other relationships such as partonyms and synonyms. (The largest part of Omega, the Middle Model, was derived by combining WordNet 2.1 (Fellbaum et al., 1998) with Mikrokosmos (Mahesh, 1996) and adding to it a variety of additional information, notably the verb frame structures of Framenet (Baker et al., 1998), Lexical-Conceptual Structures (Dorr and Habash, 1991), and the PropBank frame (Palmer et al, 2005). The LbR 'ontology' we derived consists of 10371 terms, of which 6117 were already in Omega (the remaining terms were multi-word phrases, unknown proper names, etc.).

In a technical book such as this, complex NPs pose a serous problem for understanding. No current NLP engines do an adequate job of analyzing their internal structure. To avoid this problem, and to fill in the rather large gap in the ontology due to these terms, Pantel applied his Mutual Information-based method (see for example (Pantel, 2005; Pantel and Ravichandran, 2004) for similar word on noun clusters and concept formation) to identify

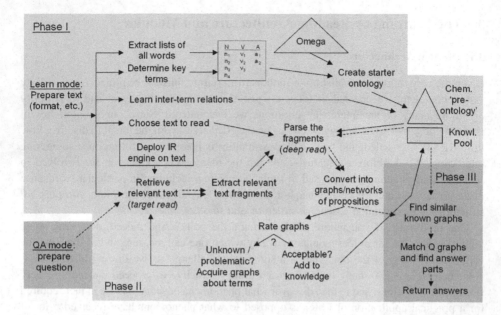

Fig. 1. ISI's Learning by Reading system architecture. The top region was completed in stage 1; the middle region in stage 2, and the bottom (left and right) region in stage 3.

bigrams, trigrams, and longer strings of nouns that occur unusually frequently in this corpus compared to general English. We obtained several thousand multi-word terms, including (starting with highest mutual information) *practice exercise, Solution Analysis, equilibrium constant, periodic table, boiling point, equilibrium constant, partial pressures,* and so on, which we added to the ontology through simple automated matching of the final noun, which we assumed was the head in all cases.

Although each term in the book is represented in the skeletal ontology, this does not mean much is actually known about the concept. The system knows in all cases the English forms of a word (plural, past tense, etc.), its purported taxonomic location (according to Omega, which is not specialized for Chemistry), and the frame structure of some of the verbs. It does not however have the words in the textbook disambiguated by sense: to the system, for example, the noun *water* might mean the normal fluid we drink, a sea or lake, or any of several other meanings. (Our initial assumption that words would tend to be monosemous because we are dealing only with a single domain turned out not to hold; even in Chemistry, many words have different senses. For example, "water" might refer to the substance in general, to its formula in an equation, or to a specific instance of it as being discussed in an experiment,

3.3   Information Retrieval

We identified the need to support three modes of reading: *skimming*; general sentence-by-sentence processing, as one normally reads a book (which we called *deep reading*); and *targeted reading*, in which one focuses on a specific term and reads fragments about it from all over the text. As described in Section 3.6, we used skimming to extract relations from the book using statistical methods. In contrast, as discussed in Sections 3.4 and 3.5, targeted reading is required during more typical reading, both to find details about some term that may be lacking crucial information and to answer questions (Section 3.7). To enable targeted reading, Lin deployed over the textbook an instance of the Lucene information retrieval package (Lucene 2005), and built a small web-based interface for it, by which one can explore the book manually as well. This IR system and its interface we called Scout.

3.4   Parsing and Conversion to Hobbs Normal Form

We decomposed the conversion of natural language text into logical form into a series of steps. In this process we used our Basic Element package, built at ISI earlier this year for automated summarization evaluation (Hovy et al., 2006), which can be downloaded from http://www.isi.edu/~cyl/BE. The purpose of the package is to convert sentences of text into a list of relation-head-modifier triples and then to compare the lists obtained from automated text summarizers to the lists produced from gold-standard human summaries.

For LbR, we required just the triples. Using the package, we applied both Charniak's parser (Charniak, 2000) and MINIPAR (Lin, 1994) to the whole book, and for technical reasons chose the former. Using the BE package tree-decomposition rules, Lin converted the entire book's contents into so-called flat form. Next using a set of conversion rules written manually by Lin, each flat form statement was converted into what we call Hobbs Normal Form (HNF), which is a list of clauses, one per triplet, combined using logical AND, that expresses the dependency structure of the sentence in quasi-logical format. During this process, Lin also replaced the syntactic relations Subject and Object with the appropriate case frame roles obtained from Omega, using a process trained on the PropBank corpus. A brief example of a heading is shown in Figure 2.

This process has not been fully optimized, and still contains quite a few easily fixed errors (as well as some unfortunately not so easily fixed). Of the 12394 sentences in the book, 51.7% contain some kind of known error, including 2219 verbs without arguments (broken parse trees), 2621 cases in which some argument (case frame role) has been wrongly duplicated within a sentence, and 752 auxiliary verbs with main verb. Some of these errors can be ignored for later purposes; many of them can be fixed by inserting additional tree-cutting rules. Parsing the whole book took 39 minutes on a standard PC; creating the basic element triples took 340 minutes; and converting into HNF took an additional 15 minutes.

```
0201-1.fr.txt:# 2.1/1 The/2 Atomic/3 Theory/4 of/5 Matter/6
0201-1.fr.txt:
0201-1.fr.txt:  [ X4 :type Theory/NN/theory
0201-1.fr.txt:        :#NN-CD 2.1/CD/2.1<* ( X1 )
0201-1.fr.txt:        :#NN-NNP The/NNP/the<* ( X2 )
0201-1.fr.txt:        :#NN-JJ Atomic/JJ/atomic<* ( X3 )
0201-1.fr.txt:        :#NN-NN Matter/NN/matter<OF ( X6 ) ]
0201-1.fr.txt:
0201-1.fr.txt: @@@LF 2.1' (e1,x1) & the'(e2,x2) & nn'(e3,x2,x1)
                & atomic'(e4,x1) & theory'(e5,x1) & of'(e6,x1,x3)
                & matter'(e7,x3)
```

Fig. 2. Input sentence, Basic Element triples, and HNF

3.5   From Hobbs Normal Form to Limited Semantics

HNF is our starting point en route to semantics. This notation is a simplified variant of the logical form developed over almost a decade by Jerry Hobbs (Hobbs, forthcoming). Our implementation avoids numerous complex problems, including wordsense disambiguation, quantifier and negation scoping, complex NP structure, and other issues. Nonetheless, it provides a starting point into which we could systematically add representations of the kinds of logical phenomena required to answer questions in the Chemistry domain. Guided by analysis of the text and questions, Hobbs and Mulkar implemented a set of abductive inference rules that takes as input HNF and returns a set of possible 'deeper' interpretations of them, in which some particular semantic phenomenon has been addressed each time. At the time of writing, the phenomena for which rules were created include:

- Determiner interpretation: insertion of $\forall$ and $\exists$ quantifiers (without scope)
- Plural handling: insertion of sets to represent aggregations, plus skolem variables to represent their individual item(s). These sets are denoted by S variables in the HNF

An example will be helpful. Consider the sentence

All atoms of a given element are identical.

After parsing and basic element conversion, the flat logical form is

$all(s,e1)$ & $atom'(e1,x)$ & $plural(x,s)$ & $of'(e2,x,y)$ & $given(y)$
& $element'(e3,y)$ & $identical1'(e4,s)$ & $MainAssertion(e4)$

Here each e variable expresses an eventuality, each s variable a set (as introduced by a plural), and each x or y a specific instance. After application of the determiner inference rule and canonicalization of symmetric predicates, we obtain

$FORALL(x,e1,e4)$ & $atom'(e1,x)$ & $of'(e2,x,y)$ & $element'(e3,y)$ & $identical1'(e4,s)$

and after recursively collecting the properties of x, the final result is an axiom in chemical theory:

$(\forall x)[atom(x1)$ & $atom(x2)$ & $of(x1,y)$ & $of(x2,y)$ & $element(y) \rightarrow identical2(x1,x2)]$

The engine performing this transformation is a simplified version of the abductive theorem prover TACITUS (Hobbs, 1986). It combines weight scores, originally assigned to inferences, in order to obtain numerical goodness scores for each derived result, and then ranks them accordingly.

Since each rule handles a different semantic phenomenon, the rules have to be written by hand. How many such rules will eventually be required, and will the rule set eventually grow unmanageable? This is impossible to estimate, but Hobbs is optimistic. In a passage of 7 clauses selected for its high content, for example, all clauses are of form $(\forall x)[Subject(x) \rightarrow (\exists y) VP(x, y)]$

The density of occurrence of the principal phenomena we have so far encountered in the book (which has a relatively homogeneous style of exposition) suggests that a relatively small number of rules/phenomena will do a lot of the work in translating sentences into content theory axioms.

3.6 Skimming to Obtain Relations

In a completely separate stream of work, Pantel and Pennacchiotti investigated the extraction of axioms from the text using the statistical text harvesting paradigm. In (Pennacchiotti and Pantel, 2006; Pantel and Pennacchiotti, 2006) they report the results. Their harvester, called Espresso, uses weak supervision to learn lexical patterns that typically signal relations of interest, and then applies these relations to extract all likely instances of the relation from the book. These extractions are then reformulated as HNF axioms and added to the system's knowledge.

Espresso follows in the pattern-based extraction paradigm of Hearst (1992), Berland and Charniak (1999), Ravichandran and Hovy (2002), Fleischmann et al. (2003), and Girju et al. (2003). The patterns themselves are not manually built, but are learned from the text after a small set of seed instances is given by the user, following the general design of Ravichandran and Hovy. The most reliable patterns are identified using pointwise mutual information, and the overly general ones are discarded. The resulting patterns are applied throughout the textbook, to deliver a set of instances of the relation. Once instances have been collected, pointwise mutual information is again used to prefer the ones best associated with the most (reliable) patterns.

Espresso was applied to the Chemistry textbook, in which the relations of particular interest (because they provide useful axioms in the domain) are *is-a*, *part-of*, *react-with*, and *produces*, as in *HCl is-a strong acid, atom part-of molecule, hydrogen-gas reacts-with oxygen-gas*, and *ammonia produces nitrous oxide* respectively. After quality filtering, Espresso produced 200 *is-a* instances (with average precision of 85.0%), 111 *part-of* (precision 60.0%), 40 *reacts-with* (precision 85.0%), and 196 *produces* (precision 72.5%).

The resulting instance expressions were then reformulated as axioms as follows:

R is-a S becomes $R(x) \Diamond S(x)$
R part-of S becomes $(\forall x)R(x) \Diamond (\exists y)[S(y) \& part-of(x,y)]$

3.7 Answering Questions: Inferences in Powerloom[1]

Given the modules described above, not much more is required to answer questions. The parser's grammar has to be extended to handle question syntax, and a rudimentary question typology is required, along the lines of the QA typology described in (Hovy et al., 2002).

Most important, however, is the inclusion of a reasoning system to apply learned inferences to newly-acquired propositions or questions in order to derive appropriate connections with the existing knowledge. For this purpose we use Powerloom (Chalupsky and Russ, 2002), a knowledge representation and reasoning system that has been widely distributed and used in numerous projects over the past decade. All axioms and semantic propositions derived from HNF are asserted into Powerloom, which is responsible for their interconnection and maintenance.

The process of asserting semantic propositions into Powerloom, performed by Chalupsky, makes very clear how much is taken for granted in the textbook as background knowledge, either of Chemistry or of English in general. For example, for the sentence *each element*

---

[1] This work is still underway at the time of writing and hence this section does not include many details.

composed of extremely small particles called atoms the shallow semantic representation, derived from HNF and asserted to Powerloom, is

```
(ASSERT
 (FORALL (?E34 ?E35 ?x)
  (=> (AND
   (subject ?E34 ?E35)
   (element' ?E35 ?x))
  (EXISTS (?E62 ?E63 ?s1 ?e10 ?y ?e4 ?e9 ?e3 ?e5 ?a ?z ?e11 ?s2 ?e6)
   (AND
   (asserted ?E62 ?E63)
   (compose' ?E63 ?x ?s1)
   (plural ?e10 ?y ?s1)
   (small' ?e4 ?y)
   (extremely ?e9 ?e4)
   (particle' ?e3 ?y)
   (call' ?e5 ?a ?y ?z)
   (plural ?e11 ?z ?s2)
   (atom' ?e6 ?z))))))
```

With this knowledge, Powerloom is able to answer question 1 but not question 2:

1. *Is each element composed of particles?*
2. *Is each element composed of atoms?*

because it does not know that the relation *call'* denotes object identity—that it, it does not know the meaning of the word "called".

Probably the most problematic aspect of this project is the fact there exists no set of axioms that define the meanings of general English words, even to the rudimentary level required for the simplest questions. This lack places a serious limitation on the amount of text a short-term project such as this can handle. Fortunately, as mentioned in Section 2, one need not define more than a few hundreds nouns, verbs, adjectives, and adverbs in order to cover most of the book.

4   Evaluation

It remains unclear exactly how one should evaluate a Learning by Reading system such as this. The general QA paradigm used in Halo and planned for Möbius—obtain a set of AP exam questions, apply them to the system before reading and then again to the system after reading, and compare the results—is somewhat inappropriate because in a 9-month period one simply cannot build enough of the system, and include enough background knowledge in the form of axioms, to be able to understand enough text for a real-world exam.

We therefore plan two approaches to evaluation. First, we are investigating the kinds of questions the system can be expected to handle, and are building a typology of the question types, arranged by complexity of reasoning. This typology will range from the simplest questions (being able to answer *Is it true that X?* after having been given proposition X), to formula-oriented computations (such as balancing equations), to the most complex ones (involving deeper inference with several axioms, obtained from several places in the text). If possible, we will try to estimate the frequencies of these types in typical AP exams, in order to estimate how much of each type of background knowledge (definitions of English; formula reasoning; simple and complex inference; etc.) will be required of a full-blown LbR system.

Second, we are assembling a set of questions about material about which the system will have been given the necessary background knowledge. We will apply these questions three times, at levels of increasing complexity:

1. Baseline: just in English, using the Scout IR engine on the untreated English text;
2. No inference: after the system has read the text and asserted its knowledge and axioms in Powerloom, but without inference allowed;
3. With inference: after the system has read and ingested the text, with Powerloom inference enabled.

We will apply the same two relatively transparent evaluation metrics at each level, the first counting just how much relevant material/propositions have been found, and the second counting how many exact and correct answers have been found. (We are curious to learn the results, and hope that they show that inference is useful, in other words, that pure text-level IR is not enough for Chemistry.)

These two approaches to evaluation do not constitute a real evaluation, but will be informative in helping to understand just how far one can expect a Learning by Reading system of this (language-oriented) type to go, and in just what kinds of areas it falls short.

References

1. Baker, C.F., C.J. Fillmore, and J.B. Lowe. 1998. The Berkeley FrameNet Project. *Proceedings of the COLING/ACL conference*, 86–90.
2. Berland, M. and E. Charniak. 1999. Finding Parts in Very Large Corpora. *Proceedings of the conference of the Association for Computational Linguistics (ACL-99)*, 57–64.
3. Chalupsky, H. and T.A. Russ. 2002. WhyNot: Debugging Failed Queries in Large Knowledge Bases. *Proceedings of the Fourteenth Innovative Applications of Artificial Intelligence conference (IAAI-02)*, 870–877.
4. Charniak, E. 2000. A Maximum-Entropy-Inspired Parser. *Proc. of NAACL '00 conference*.
5. Dorr, B.J. and N. Habash. 2001. Lexical Conceptual Structure Lexicons. In Calzolari et al. (eds), ISLE-IST-1999-10647-WP2-WP3, *Survey of Major Approaches Towards Bilingual/Multilingual Lexicons*.
6. Fellbaum, C. (ed.). 1998. *WordNet: An On-line Lexical Database and Some of its Applications*. MIT Press.
7. Fleischmann, M., E.H. Hovy, and A. Echihabi. 2003. Offline Strategies for Online Question Answering: Answering Questions before They are Asked. *Proceedings of the conference of the Association for Computational Linguistics (ACL-03)*, 1–7.
8. Friedland, N. et al., 2003. http://www.projecthalo.com/halotempl.asp?cid=30.
9. Girju, R., A. Baldulescu, and D. Moldovan. 2003. Learning Semantic Constraints for the Automatic Discovery of Part-hole Relations. *Proceedings of HLT-NAACL-03 conference*, 80–87.
10. Hearst, M. 1992. Automatic Acquisition of Hyponyms from Large Text Corpora. *Proceedings of the COLING-92 conference*, 539–545.
11. Hobbs, J.R. 1986. Overview of the TACITUS Project. *Computational Linguistics* 12(3).
12. Hobbs, J.R. (forthcoming) *Discourse and Inference*.

13. Hovy, E.H., U. Hermjakob, C.-Y. Lin, and D. Ravichandran. 2002. Using Knowledge to Facilitate Pinpointing of Factoid Answers. *Proceedings of the COLING-2002 conference.* Available at `http://www.isi.edu/natural-language/projects/webclopedia/Taxonomy/taxonomy_toplevel.html`.

14. Hovy, E.H., C.-Y. Lin, L. Zhou, and J. Fukumoto. 2006. Automated Summarization Evaluation with Basic Elements. 2006. *Proceedings of the LREC conference.*

15. Lin, D. 1994. Principar — An Efficient, Broad-Coverage, Principle-Based Parser. *Proceedings of the COLING/ACL conference*, 42–48.

16. Lucene. 2005. Open Source software `http://lucene.apache.org/java/docs/`.

17. Mahesh, K. 1996. Ontology Development for Machine Translation: Ideology and Methodology. New Mexico State University CRL report MCCS-96-292.

18. Palmer, M., D. Gildea, and P. Kingsbury. 2005. The Proposition Bank: A Corpus Annotated with Semantic Roles, *Computational Linguistics*, 31(1).

19. Pantel, P. and D. Ravichandran. 2004. Automatically Labeling Semantic Classes. *Proceedings of the HLT-NAACL-04 conference.*

20. Pantel, P. 2005. Inducing Ontological Co-occurrence Vectors. *Proceedings of the conference of the Association for Computational Linguistics (ACL-05).*

21. Pantel, P. and Pennacchiotti, 2006. Espresso: Leveraging Generic Patterns for Automatically Harvesting Semantic Relations. *Proceedings of the conference of the Association for Computational Linguistics (COLING/ACL-06).*

22. Pennacchiotti, M. and P. Pantel. 2006. A Bootstrapping Algorithm for Automatically Harvesting Semantic Relations. *Proceedings of the ICOS-06 conference.*

23. Philpot, A., E.H. Hovy, and P. Pantel. 2005. The Omega Ontology. *Proceedings of the ONTOLEX Workshop* at the International Joint Conference on NLP. Jeju Island, Korea.

24. Ravichandran, D. and E.H. Hovy. 2002. Learning Surface Text Patterns for a Question Answering System. *Proceedings of the conference of the Association for Computational Linguistics (ACL-02)*, 41–47.

Depth of Feelings:
Alternatives for Modeling Affect in User Models

Eva Hudlicka

Psychometrix Associates, 1805 Azalea Drive, Blacksburg, VA, USA
evahud@earthlink.net

Abstract. Neuroscience and psychology research has demonstrated a close connection between cognition and affect, and a number of emotion-induced effects on perception, cognition, and behavior. The integration of emotions within user models would therefore enhance their realism and fidelity. Emotions can also provide disambiguating information for speech recognition and natural language understanding, and enhance the effectiveness of dialogue systems. This paper discusses the motivation and alternatives for incorporating emotions within user models. The paper first identifies key model characteristics that define an analytical framework. The framework provides a basis for identifying the functional and architectural requirements on one hand, and alternative modeling approaches on the other, thereby laying the groundwork for a set of model development guidelines. The paper then describes examples of existing models for two core affective processes, cognitive appraisal and emotion-induced effects on cognition, within the context of the analytical framework.

1 Introduction

Over the past two decades, emotion researchers in psychology and neuroscience have made great strides in identifying the pervasive role of emotion in adaptive behavior and social interaction, developing theories regarding the mechanisms mediating cognitive-affective interactions, and elucidating the neural circuitry of affective processes [1]. Emotion research demonstrates that cognitive and affective processes function in parallel, in a closely-coupled manner [2]. Affective factors (emotions and personality traits) can profoundly influence perception, cognition, and behavior, via a variety of biases and heuristics. Affective factors also influence social interaction, facilitating communication and coordination through facial expressions, speech quality and content, non-verbal cues, and behavioral choices.

Motivated both by theoretical and practical considerations, the potential benefits of including emotions in user models and cognitive and agent architectures are being recognized [3,4]. In many cases, the motivation is to *elucidate the mechanisms of affective processes* and cognitive-affective interactions, and their role in adaptive and social behavior [5,6]. In other cases, *emotions are included to improve human-computer interaction,* by enhancing the realism of user models and believability of synthetic agents. Variety of applications benefit from affective user models, including: *tutoring and education, decision-support systems*, and *assistive technologies*, where affective user models support recognition of, and adaptation to, users' emotions (e.g., customized pedagogical strategies, affect-adaptive user interfaces); *dialogue and recommender systems*, where affective user models enhance effectiveness by matching the speech content and quality to the user's emotional states [7]; *autonomous synthetic agents and robots*, where affective user models enhance believability by enabling behavioral variability and affective expressiveness (e.g., facial expressions).

Petr Sojka, Ivan Kopeček and Karel Pala (Eds.): TSD 2006, LNAI 4188, pp. 13–18, 2006.
© Springer-Verlag Berlin Heidelberg 2006

In spite of the surge of interest emotion models, there are as yet no systematic guidelines for their development. The purpose of this paper is to lay the groundwork for the definition of such guidelines. The paper first provides a brief review of relevant emotion research (section 2), introduces a framework for analyzing computational models of emotions, by defining their key characteristics, requirements, and available modeling alternatives (section 3), and concludes with a description of existing models of two core affective processes: *emotion generation via cognitive appraisal* and *the effects of emotions on cognitive processing* (section 4).

2   Emotion Research Background

Definitions and Terminology. Psychologists draw a distinction between stable *traits* and transient *states*. *Emotions* are mental states that involve evaluations of current situations (internal or external; past, present or future) with respect to the agent's goals, beliefs, values and standards. Emotions thus reflect self- and survival-relevant evaluations of the state of the world, the self or other agents.

Emotional states can be differentiated on the basis of *duration, degree of specificity, cognitive complexity, and universality. Affective states* represent the least differentiated evaluations (positive vs. negative), and similarly undifferentiated behavioral responses (approach vs. avoid). *Emotions* proper reflect more differentiated evaluations, and are often divided into *basic* (e.g., joy, sadness, anger, fear, disgust), and *complex* (e.g., pride, shame, guilt, and jealousy) [8]. As emotions increase in complexity, so does their cognitive component, and associated potential for individual and cultural variability, in both the triggering stimuli and the behavioral repertoire. *Moods* are similar to emotions in terms of affective content (e.g., sad, happy, jealous), but differ in terms of the triggering conditions (less specific, less awareness of stimulus), duration (hours, days or longer), and behavioral specificity (more diffuse and generalized behaviors).

Multi-modal Nature of Emotion. Emotional states are *multi-modal phenomena*, with manifestations across four distinct modalities [9]: *physiology* (e.g., increased heart rate); *behavior* (e.g., smile vs. frown, fight vs. flee); *cognition* (specific effects on cognition such as positive mood facilitating recall of positive thoughts, anxiety-linked threat bias); and *distinct subjective feelings.* Different emotions, moods and affective states have distinct 'signatures' across these modalities; e.g., simple fear has significant and distinct physiological and behavioral components, but a limited cognitive component, whereas pride has a complex and significant cognitive component but a limited and non-specific physiological component.

Cognitive Appraisal. Appraisal is the process whereby current stimuli (internal and external; real or imagined; past, present or future) are mapped onto an *affective state, emotion* or *mood* [10,11,12]. Early theories focused on *descriptive* characterizations, identifying taxonomies of triggers, emotions, and the mappings among them. The triggers (or elicitors) can be characterized in terms *domain-specific stimuli* (e.g., snarling large dog induces fear; birthday cake induces joy), or in terms of domain-independent characteristics of the stimuli (termed *appraisal dimensions* or *appraisal variables*), such as novelty, desirability, and responsible agent [11]. Particular combinations of appraisal variables then trigger specific emotions.

More recent appraisal theories emphasize the *mechanisms* mediating these mappings [12]. These *process theories* attempt to identify the structures and processes mediating cognitive appraisal. The processes are frequently divided into *automatic (*generating rapid, high-level initial assessments), and *deliberate* (generating more differentiated emotions). The increased complexity of cognition in the deliberate appraisal allows for more variability and individual idiosyncracies in the elicitors-to-emotion mappings. Many appraisal theories also include an assessment of the individual's coping potential, which influences the type of emotion generated (e.g., being accosted by a burglar may trigger anger or fear, depending on the coping potential).

Emotion Effects on Cognition. Emotions, moods and personality traits exert a variety of effects on the structures and processes mediating cognitive functions. At the *fundamental cognitive processing* level, these include effects on *attention* (anxiety-linked attention narrowing and threat bias), *working memory* (anxiety-linked reduction in working memory capacity), and *memory* (mood congruent recall) [13,14]. These then result in observed effects in higher cognitive functions, *including situation assessment and expectation generation* (anxiety-linked threat bias), *goal selection* (trait- and mood-linked self focus), and *problem solving* (mood-linked strategy choice, focus on details (negative) vs. 'big picture' (positive).

States (emotions, moods) exert transient effects on cognitive or perceptual processes, while *traits* exert their influence via more stable structures (e.g., content and organization of long-term memory schemas), but also influencing the emotion dynamics (e.g., sensitivity, and ramp-up and decay rates of emotion intensities).

3   Framework for Affective Model Analysis and Comparison

The model characteristics below define an orienting framework which provides a basis for the systematic analysis of the functional and architectural requirements on one hand, and the available theories, data and modeling approaches on the other.

The first four characteristics are the model *objective* (e.g., explore mechanisms of affective biases vs. generate affect-matched dialogue), *task domain* (e.g., speech generation, tutoring agent)*focus* (e.g., emotion generation via appraisal vs. affective biases), and *scope* (e.g., the set of specific emotions modeled and the associated elicitors) These constrain the applicable theories, empirical data and modeling approaches, suggesting the appropriate level of abstraction, and the methods and criteria for validation (e.g., human data on matched empirical studies used for mechanism elucidation vs. heuristic evaluations of 'believability' for evaluating affective agents). While not conceptually intriguing, the choices made here can have a large impact on the overall effort and success. Considerable effort can be saved by selecting tasks with well-defined ontologies, relevant emotions with well-established elicitors and behavioral expressions, and appropriate level of model resolution (e.g., generation of facial expressions in a synthetic agent may not require a process model of cognitive appraisal).

Theoretical framework, selected on the basis of both focus and scope above, guides the model development by suggesting the specific structures and processes necessary to implement the selected phenomena. Affective processes and phenomena vary in their degrees of theoretical support, with *cognitive appraisal theories* being the most extensively developed. Existing theories define taxonomies of stimuli and emotions [15]; emotion elicitors and elicitor-to-emotion mappings; sequence of steps or stages within this process [10,11]; functions included in the appraisal process (e.g., assessment of coping [10]); and the functions calculating the intensity and decay of specific emotions, and those determining how multiple emotions are combined (e.g., what emotion results from an event producing both sadness and relief?).

Theoretical foundations of *emotion effects on cognition* and the mechanisms of particular biases are not as well developed as the appraisal theories, though some do exist (e.g., Bower's spreading activation model of mood-congruent recall [14]). The lack of well-developed theoretical basis for many affective phenomena poses a challenge, requiring the modeler to use available empirical data (e.g., anxiety-induced interpretive threat bias) and theory 'fragments', and filling-in the gaps through 'educated guesses' regarding the causal pathways and internal structures.

Model resolution is influenced by the *modeling objective (e.g.,* for applied user models black-box models may be adequate); *data availability* (e.g., available data may only support low levels of resolution); and *existing theories* (e.g., lack of theories regarding detailed mechanisms limits the level of resolution). Models lie on a spectrum, bounded by *input/output models* (also black box, shallow, or performance models), and detailed *process models* (also deep models). Within a given architecture, different functions and phenomena can be modeled at different levels of resolution.

Architecture structure is determined by the theoretical framework and the resolution level, which define the specific modules and the data and control flow among them. Affective user models and cognitive-affective architectures typically include modules that correspond to specific cognitive or affective processes (e.g., appraisal, expectation generation, goal management), as well as 'purely' cognitive processes such as attention, different types of memories (sensory; working; long-term including declarative, procedural, episodic), which are necessary to provide the cognitive infrastructure within which the affective processes are modeled. Some architectures do not localize affective processes within dedicated modules, but consider them as emergent properties arising from complex information processing [16]. Execution control ranges from sequential 'see-think-do' models (or 'see-think-feel-do'?) to parallel distributed models, with no centralized control; the latter frequently using blackboards for communication and process coordination (e.g., [17]).

Empirical data required to build (and validate) models vary, depending on the choices above. Black-box models have less demanding data requirements than process-oriented models, which may require data about internal mental structures and processes that are difficult or impossible to obtain with current empirical methods. The data come from empirical studies (e.g., [13,14]), and from knowledge elicitation, and task and protocol analysis with subjects and users.

Type and complexity of cognitive structures are a function of the selected theoretical framework, the level of abstraction, and the available empirical data, as well as the overall model objective, which determine the specific constructs represented in a particular model (e.g., situations, expectations, goals, plans), the processes that operate on them (e.g., problem-solving, learning, planning), and the memory types (e.g., declarative, episodic). For example, appraisal models necessarily require representation of the *actual* and the *desired states* of the world and self. Appraisal models that include coping require explicit representation of the anticipated consequences, and appropriately detailed models of the agent's own capabilities within the context. Future oriented emotions (e.g., hope, anxiety) or past oriented emotions (e.g., regret) require the explicit representation of time.

Representational and inferencing formalisms Process models typically use symbolic formalisms, most frequently rules and belief nets, the latter providing a mechanism for uncertainty management. Black-box models use a variety of approaches to implement the elicitor-emotion or emotion-effects mappings, including rules and belief nets, but also vector spaces and connectionist models.

4 Models of Cognitive Appraisal and Emotion Effects

This section describes existing models of two core affective processes, *emotion generation via cognitive appraisal* and *the effects of emotions on cognition,* within the context of the analytical framework described above.

Modeling Emotion Generation Via Cognitive Appraisal. Cognitive appraisal is the most frequently modeled aspect of affective processing. In computational terms, the objective is to map the emotion elicitors (patterns of task-specific stimuli or abstract appraisal dimensions) to the resulting emotions, or to dimensions such as valence and arousal, within the context of a specific set of agent's goals and beliefs. These mappings have been the basis of a range of *'black box' appraisal models* (e.g., [11]). More recent mechanistically-oriented theories (e.g., [12]) lend themselves to computational implementations of *process models,* which attempt to emulate the structures and processes mediating appraisal. The detailed taxonomies of stimuli and emotions developed by Ortony et al. [15] are widely used as basis for appraisal models; e.g., Reilly's EM [18], Gratch and Marsella's EMA [17], the former focusing in addition on the functions calculating intensity, decay, and integration of multiple emotions; the latter on coping and emotion dynamics. Scherer's stimulus evaluation checks [11] and Lazarus' [10] theories provide basis for the dynamic aspects of appraisal, outlining the sequence of stages within the process. Smith and Kirby's mechanism-oriented theories are increasingly used as basis for process models of appraisal (e.g., [17,20]).

Modeling Emotion Effects on Cognition. Models of emotion effects on cognition are less common, and more challenging, due to lack of theories and difficulties obtaining the required internal data. In computational terms, the objective is to map a particular emotion (or emotion mix) onto changes in specific characteristics of cognitive structures and processes (e.g., attention and working memory speed, capacity and bias). Particular challenges occur when multiple, possibly opposing, effects must be combined.

Hudlicka's MAMID cognitive-affective architecture [20] implements a generic methodology [19,21] for modeling multiple, interacting effects of emotions and traits on a range of cognitive processes, including appraisal. The methodology enables the modeling of a number of affective biases, within the context of decision-making in simulated environments. The underlying assumption of the approach is that a broad range of interacting emotion effects can be represented in terms of distinct configurations of a small number of architecture parameters. These parameters control processing within individual architecture modules, influencing their speed, capacity, and content biases (e.g., threat- or self-bias). These low-level 'micro effects' are eventually manifested in differences in observable behavior associated with different emotions. MAMID is a domain-independent architecture, originally demonstrated within the context of a peacekeeping scenario, and recently transitioned to a search-and-rescue team task.

5 Conclusions

The frequent love-hate relationship that characterized academic emotion research until the 1980's was echoed in the early AI and cognitive science work. Attitudes toward emotion models were frequently of the all-or-nothing variety: either summarily rejected as infeasible, irrelevant or both, or uncritically embraced as essential for adaptive, intelligent behavior. As affective modeling research matures, these attitudes are giving way to more balanced views, and the need arises for systematic guidelines for affective model development. The analytical framework presented above aims to provide a basis for such guidelines.

References

1. Davidson, R.J., Scherer, K.R., Goldsmith, H.H.: *Handbook of Affective Sciences*. NY: Oxford. (2003).
2. LeDoux, J.: Cognitive-Emotional Interactions: Listen to the Brain. In *Cognitive Neuroscience of Emotion*, Lane, R.D. & Nadel, L. (eds). NY: Oxford. (2000).
3. Picard, R.: *Affective Computing*. Cambridge, MA: MIT. (1997).
4. Hudlicka, E.: To Feel or Not To Feel: The Role of Affect in HCI. *International Journal of Human-Computer Studies*, 59 (1-2), (2003) 1–32.
5. Fellous, J-M, and Arbib, M.: *Who Needs Emotions?* NY: Oxford. (2005).
6. Trappl, R., Petta, P., Payr, S.: *Emotions in Humans and Artifacts*. Cambridge, MA: MIT. (2002).
7. de Rosis, F.: *International Journal of Human-Computer Studies*, 59 (1-2), (2003).
8. Ekman, P., Davidson, R.J.: *The Nature of Emotion*. NY: Oxford. (1994).
9. Clore, G.L. & Ortony, A.: Cognition in Emotion: Always, Sometimes, or Never? In *Cognitive Neuroscience of Emotion*, Lane, R.D. & Nadel, L. (eds). NY: Oxford. (2000).
10. Lazarus, R.S.: *Emotion and Adaptation*. NY: Oxford. (1991)
11. Scherer, K.R.: Appraisal Considered as a Process of Multi-level Sequential Checking. In *Appraisal Processes in Emotion*. Scherer, K., Schorr, A., Johnstone, T. (eds.). NY:Oxford. (2001).
12. Smith, C.A., Kirby, L.: Consequences require antecedents: Toward a process model of emotion elicitation. In *Feeling and Thinking: The role of affect in social cognition*, Forgas, J.P. (ed.). NY: Cambridge. (2000).
13. Mineka, S., Rafaeli, E., Yovel, I.: Cognitive biases in emotional disorders: Information processing and social-cognitive perspectives. In Davidson, R.J., Scherer, K.R., Goldsmith, H.H. (eds.), *Handbook of Affective Sciences*. Oxford. (2003).
14. Bower, G.H.: Mood and Memory. *American Psychologist*, 36, (1981) 129–148.
15. Ortony, A., Clore, G.L., Collins, A.: *The Cognitive Structure of Emotions*. NY: Cambridge. (1988).
16. Sloman, A.: How many separately evolved emotional beasties live within us? In *Emotions in Humans & Artifacts*, Trappl, R., Petta, P., Payr, S. (eds.). Cambridge, MA: MIT. (2003).
17. Gratch,, J., Marsella, S.: A domain independent frame-work for modeling emotion. *Journal of Cognitive Systems Research*, 5(4), (2004) 269–306.
18. Reilly, W.S.N.: Modeling What Happens Between Emotional Antecedents and Emotional Conse-quents. In *Proceedings of ACE 2006*. Vienna.
19. Hudlicka, E.: This time with feeling: Integrated Model of Trait and State Effects on Cognition and Behavior. *Applied Artificial Intelligence* (2002) 16:1–31.
20. Hudlicka, E.: Two Sides of Appraisal: Implementing Appraisal and Its Consequences within a Cognitive Architecture. In *AAAI Spring Symposium, Architectures for Modeling Emotion*, TR SS-04-02. Menlo Park, CA: AAAI Press. (2004).
21. Hudlicka, E.: *Modeling Emotion in Symbolic Cognitive Architectures*. AAAI Fall Symposium, TR FS-98-03. Menlo Park, CA: AAAI Press. (1998).

Part II

Text

"**Text**: a book or other written or printed work, regarded in terms of its content rather than its physical form: *a text which explores pain and grief.*"

NODE (New, Oxford Dictionary of English), Oxford, OUP, 1998, page 1998, meaning 1.

The Lexico-Semantic Annotation of PDT: Some Results, Problems and Solutions

Eduard Bejček, Petra Möllerová, and Pavel Straňák

Institute of Formal and Applied Linguistics,
Charles University, Prague, Czech Republic
{bejcek, mollerova, stranak}@ufal.mff.cuni.cz

Abstract. This paper presents our experience with the lexico-semantic annotation of the Prague Dependency Treebank (PDT). We have used the Czech WordNet (CWN) as an annotation lexicon (repository of lexical meanings) and we annotate each word which is included in the CWN. Based on the error analysis we have performed some experiments with modification of the annotation lexicon (CWN) and consequent re-annotation of occurrences of selected lemmas. We present the results of the annotations and improvements achieved by our corrections.

1 Introduction

In the Prague Dependency Treebank (PDT; see [1,2]), the annotation can be viewed as an iterative analysis of text in the following sequence: raw text — tokenized text — morphologically analysed and lemmatised text — surface syntax (analytical layer) — deep syntax including verb valencies, topic-focus articulation and other features (tectogrammatical layer). It is not just enrichment of the original text with additional information or rather explication of grammatical information contained in the text. The tectogrammatical layer includes all the information needed to generate the surface structure without using the original text or the other layers. For technical reasons lexico-semantic annotations have been added to the morphological level.

Lexico-semantic annotation (if the process is manual, done by humans) or *tagging* (if it is automatic, performed by a machine) means assigning a semantic tag from an a priori given set to *each* relevant lexical unit in a text. Lexical units which we deal with during this process are lemmas of words;[1] the relevant ones are those of the autosemantic parts of speech, namely all nouns, adjectives, verbs, and adverbs.

In this paper, symbol $T_p(l)$ denotes a set of *possible semantic tags* which can be assigned to lemma l and $\chi \subset T_p(l)$ is a set assigned.

The purpose of lexico-semantic annotation or tagging is to distinguish between different meanings a semantically ambiguous lemma has in different contexts.

---

[1] The lemmas at the syntactical level of the PDT form a set of *tectogrammatical lemmas*, which is different from the set of lemmas at the morphological level [3]. However (despite lexico-semantic analysis being placed only after the syntactical level), we currently use the lemmas produced by morphological analyser for various practical or technological reasons.

Petr Sojka, Ivan Kopeček and Karel Pala (Eds.): TSD 2006, LNAI 4188, pp. 21–28, 2006.

2   The Project Goal

The original goal was to provide training data for word sense disambiguation. For this purpose two annotators begun to annotate in parallel[2]the files of PDT 1.0 [2] with synsets from Czech WordNet. Later it was decided to aim for complete lexico-semantic annotation of PDT, thus enriching it with word sense information. To this day each annotator has processed 34,231 sentences consisting of 431,447 words. Because not all words occurring in the text exist in CWN, 148,774 instances (i.e. words) of 7972 lemmas were actually annotated. Since the morphological layer of PDT 2.0 consists of approximately 2 million words, we have annotated over 20% of PDT 2.0.

3   Annotation Using the Czech WordNet

The CWN consists of 28,392 synsets (including nouns, adjectives, verbs, and adverbs) [4]. We use it to obtain the set of possible semantic tags $T_p(l)$ for each relevant lemma. In the process of annotation, each annotated lemma is assigned the best tag from this set.

Table 1. List of the exceptions ordered by their preference

Incorrect Reflexivity
Missing Positive Sense
Missing Negative Sense
Incorrect Lemma
Figurative Use
Proper Name
Unclear Word Meaning in the Text
Unclear CWN Sense
Missing More General Sense
Missing Sense
Other Problem

The annotators must always assign exactly one synset or exception[3] to each relevant word (i.e. $|\chi| = 1$). In case annotators believe that one synset cannot be assigned, they can either mark the occurrence as vague (Exception 8) or they can say they are missing more general sense in the CWN (Exception 10). These two exceptions are equivalent to situations when we know that $|\chi| = 1$, but we cannot identify χ, and when we know that $|\chi| > 1$, respectively. These exceptions were assigned very rarely and agreed on in 20 and 0 cases, respectively. From this we can conclude that allowing $|\chi| > 1$ would give us nothing and could only hurt interannotator agreement, because $T_p'(l)_{|\chi|>1} = \mathcal{P}(T_p(l)_{|\chi|=1})$.

Annotators are instructed to try to assign a uniliteral synset first. Only if no uniliteral synset is usable, they examine the multiliteral synsets (if present). If and only if no synset

---

[2] We have used double blind annotation to be able to create a gold standard data by imploying a corrector (=third annotator).

[3] In contrast to SemCor [5] and other similar projects (see Section 8).

from $T_p(l)$ can be assigned, the annotators choose one of the exceptions given in Table 1 (for details see [6]).

4   Annotation Statistics

4.1   Summary of the Data Distribution

In terms of lexical semantics, only *autosemantic* words (nouns, adjectives, verbs, and adverbs)[4] can be the subject of semantic tagging. There were 70% such words in the annotated text. However, only words present in the CWN were annotated because they have at least one possible tag to be assigned. 35% of all words fullfiled this condition but only 24% were ambiguous (i.e. had more than one possible tag). This implies that only about 1/2 of all autosemantic words in a given text can be subject of automatic word sense disambiguation and only 1/3 are really ambiguous (according to the CWN). Detailed counts are given in the Table 2.

69% of annotated words were nouns, 21% were verbs, and 10% were adjectives. Since the CWN version we worked with does not contain any adverbial synsets, no adverbs were annotated.

Only 67% of nouns, 26% of adjectives, and 49% of verbs occur at least in one synset and thus could be processed by annotators. Now let us see how difficult this work was.

As described in section 3, there are three types of semantic tags used for annotation: uniliteral synsets, multiliteral synsets, and exceptions. A typical annotated word had 3 possible uniliteral and 6 multiliteral synsets in the set of possible tags $T_p(l)$. Considering only those words with more than one possible tag, they have 3.8 uniliteral synsets and 8 multiliteral ones. Multiliteral synsets appeared almost exclusively in the tag sets of nouns.

4.2   Inter-annotator Agreement

All kinds of linguistic annotation are usually performed by more than one annotator. The reason is to obtain more reliable and consistent data. In order to learn this reliability we can measure inter-annotator agreement, a relative number of cases when selections of the annotators were identical. This number gives also evidence of how difficult the annotation is. Manually annotated data is often used to train systems for automatic assigning relevant tags (tagging). Inter-annotator agreement gives an upper bound of accuracy of such systems.

Table 3 shows the inter-annotator agreement measured from various points of view. Basic agreement on selection of uniliteral synsets was 61.5%. If we consider both uniliteral and multiliteral synsets the inter-annotator agreement increases only by 0.2%. Overall inter-annotator agreement on all possible types of tags is 74.6% – 1/4 of all processed words are not annotated reliably. This number varies depending on POS: verbs were significantly more difficult to assign a correct uniliteral synset.

Generally speaking, the inter-annotator agreement is relatively low but it does not necessarily imply that annotators had problems to distinguish word meanings. They rather had problems to select the most suitable options that would correspond to their opinion.

---

[4] Numerals are sometimes considered autosemantic words too, but usually they are not the subject of semantic annotation.

According to the CWN, some words occurring in the annotated texts had up to 18 senses. Surprisingly, the inter-annotator agreement does not depend on the degree of ambiguity. It ranged from 15% to 80% regardless of the number of possible tags. We can conclude that the size of word tag sets is probably not what causes the low inter-annotator agreement.

5 Discussion on Semantic Tags and the Inter-annotator Agreement

There are two basic situations when the annotators can hardly generate the desired results, i.e. choose both the same synset: a) if they for some reason do not understand the meaning of the word to be annotated in the text, or b) if they understand the text and the word meaning, but they are unable to choose the desired meaning from proposed $T_p(l)$.

If we wanted to tackle the first source of non-agreement, we could allow the annotators to choose more than one synset, to address the vagueness of meaning. Such a change would however result in much bigger $T_p(l)$. Our experience shows us that if the choices are too many, the annotators make more mistakes and the work is slow and therefore expensive. Because $T_p(l)$ would be enlarged for every word, but the vague contexts are very rare, we have decided against this option.

6 Corrections

When we have analysed the inter-annotator agreement and the exception annotations, we have found that significant number of non-agreements is caused by several highly frequent lemmas that are not treated well in the CWN (see 6).

The inter-annotator agreement on a synset (i.e. both annotators assigned the word the same synset) was 61.5%. In 25.7% at least one annotator assigned an exception and in the remaining 12.8% both annotators assigned a synset but they disagreed. This gives us 38.5% of non-agreement.

The non-agreement here means anything but the agreement of both annotators on assigning the same synset to a word. We have split the non-agreements into 2 classes:

a) At least one annotator assigned a synset (i.e. disagreement on synset or synset / exception disagreement)
b) Both annotators assigned an exception (i.e. agreement or disagreement on exception)

The analysis of the synsets for words with frequent non-agreement showed that the annotators had

Table 2. Word counts in annotated text

All words	431 447	100.0%	
Autosemantic words	300 725	69.7%	100.0%
Annotated words	148 744	34.5%	49.5%
Ambiguous words	101 703	23.6%	33.8%

Table 3. Inter-annotator agreement (in %) on selection of the same: uniliteral synset (U); uniliteral or multiliteral synset (UM); uniliteral or multiliteral synset or exception (UME)

POS	U	UM	UME
N	65.6	66.0	74.1
V	44.8	44.8	75.4
A	67.0	67.0	76.1
All	61.5	61.7	74.6

1. Either little or no information for choosing correct synset from a range of choices (synsets were missing definitions and examples), so they basically had to choose randomly, or
2. The correct meaning of the word was not in CWN (missing synset).

We have decided to try and correct the non-agreement cases in two rounds:

1. Have a corrector (3rd annotator) look at the choices of both annotators in cases of a) and try to decide whether one of them is right. In cases where 2 of 3 agree we would consider the word successfully annotated.
2. In cases of b) and in cases from the first round where the corrector can't find a reason to agree with 1st or 2nd annotator we would:
   – Check all the meanings (synsets) of a word in CWN, merge, divide, add or clarify the synsets as needed to give annotators a clear guideline for decision.
   – Re-annotate the occurrences of the corrected lemma.

For our experiment we have taken the lemmas with the frequency of non-agreement ≥ 200. This resulted in 25 lemmas as given in Table 4 and marked by circles in Figure 1.

Lemmas with Error annotations (sorted by freq.)

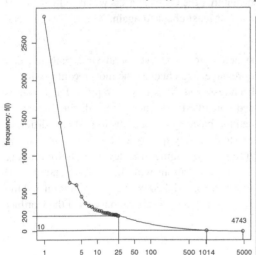

Fig. 1. Corrected lemmas

Table 4. Lemmas with highest non-agreement frequency

Lemma	Agr.	Non-agr.	Total
čas (time)	41	242	283
část (part)	23	238	261
cena (price)	85	642	727
člověk (human)	326	267	593
dát (to give)	17	332	349
den (day)	159	236	395
dobrý (good)	252	217	469
dostat (to get)	20	261	281
fax (fax)	49	212	261
místo (place)	136	274	476
mít (to have)	0	2853	2853
moci (to can)	9	1435	1444
návrh (offer)	49	229	278
podnik (business)	20	458	478
práce (work)	193	215	408
právo (law)	29	201	230
řada (row)	16	216	232
říkat (say)	1	212	213
rok (year)	1629	611	2240
stát (to stand)	152	369	521
stát (state)	136	318	454
svět (world)	59	236	295
systém (system)	32	212	244
uvést (to state)	38	284	322
vysoký (high)	282	200	482

First Round of Corrections. For each lemma we have taken all cases of non-agreement where at least one annotator chose a synset and extracted all the occurrences from the original files. Each occurrence had a context of at least 20 words on each side.

These lists of snippets were further divided to group similar cases in order to simplify the work of the corrector (3rd annotator). The division was as shown in Table 5 according to choice of annotators.

Most of the possible list were empty, only 6 in average existed for each lemma. Each of the resulting lists was added a choice of annotator A and B respectively to each lemma occurrence.

The corrector then had at most three options:

1. agree with A (if he chose a synset)
2. agree with B (if he chose a synset)
3. don't agree with either A or B

First two options meant the word was considered successfully annotated, the third one added this occurrence to those already prepared for the second round.

The corrector was also able to add notes to the word in general or to each occurrence separately for use in the second round.

Although the corrector agreed with A or B sometimes, each lemma of our chosen 25 was in the end sent into the second round. This meant that the CWN synsets will be edited and all the occurrences will have to be re-annotated or at least checked again. Nevertheless crucial data for editing CWN ware gathered.

Second Round of Corrections. First the notes from the 1st round were gathered and compared to the CWN we have been using. We have also checked the most recent version of CWN in order to see if the problems have been resolved. Various Czech printed dictionaries as well as the Princeton WordNet were also consulted. The new sense distinctions were kept as simple as possible. We have identified the basic synset and distinguished a different meaning (created a synset) only if we were able to precisely specify a difference. This in many cases resulted in merging existing CWN synsets. At the same time new synsets for missing senses were sometimes added. For these cases the annotations with the exception number 10 (missing sense) proved valuable. Each synset was also enriched by the sort definition and the example sentence (usually from our data). For editing the synsets we have used the wordnet browser and editor VisDic [4].

7   Results of Corrections

After the CWN was modified we have started the re-annotation of the data with the new synsets. Although this part has not yet been finished, we can calculate the result. When all the occurrences of our 25 lemmas will be successfully annotated, the improvements of annotated data will be as shown in Table 6.

We have corrected 25 of 4,738 lemmas for which there are cases of non-agreement. We gave gained 10,971 new words annotated with the synsets. This means that by correcting 0.5% of problematic lemmas we have gained 7.4% improvement with respect to annotated words.

Table 5. Classes of files according to annotators' choices (A and B are original annotators)

Table 6. Annotation with uniliteral synset (U) (in %)

A	B
uniliteral-x	uniliteral-y
uniliteral	multiliteral
multiliteral	uniliteral
multiliteral-x	multiliteral-y
exception	uniliteral
exception	multiliteral
uniliteral	exception
multiliteral	exception

POS	U
N	70.3 (+4.7)
V	63.6 (+18.8)
A	69.7 (+2.7)
All	68.9 (+7.4)

It is also interesting to look at the sentences that are fully disambiguated with respect to our CWN. This means that in such sentence all the annotated words are annotated correctly: before our corrections there were 5,111 sentences fully disambiguated, after the corrections it is 6,941 sentences. This means 35.8% improvement with respect to data that can be used for "all words" word sense disambiguation.

Corrections took aproximatelly 320 hours to the corrector who decided on the changes to CWN and annotated the data and 215 hours to the programmer who created the annotation data sets and scripts, implemented changes to CWN and processed the data as needed.

8 Summary

To our best knowledge, there are three similar projects: English SemCor [5], cf. also [7], Spanish Cast3LB [8] and recent Basque corpus annotation [9]. All of these efforts are smaller[5] and they differ in important methodological aspects; most prominently, both Spanish and Basque projects use transversal annotation (word-type by word-type) and they (as well as SemCor) allow arbitrary subset of $T_p(l)$ (i.e. $\chi : |\chi| > 1$) to be assigned as the final tag. We have implored linear process, because, as we have explained earlier in Section 2, we wanted to obtain training data for all words WSD. As for allowing $|\chi| > 1$, we put forward our reasons against it in Section 3.

Our semantic annotation of the PDT has two major applications:

1. Lexico-semantic tags are a new kind of labels in the PDT and will become a substantial part of a complete resource of training data, which can be exploited in many fields of NLP.

   We have shown above that the recent corrections improved significantly the number of sentences that are fully lexico-semantically annotated with respect to our current annotation lexicon.

2. The process of annotation provides a substantial feedback to the authors of the CWN and significantly helps to validate and improve its quality. In process of the corrections we have also begun improving CWN on our own.

---

[5] Basque: cca 300,000, Cast3LB: 125,000 vs. PDT: cca 2,000,000 tokens.

Acknowledgments

This work has been supported by grant 1ET201120505 of Grant Agency of the Czech Republic, and project MSM0021620838 of the Ministry of Education.

References

1. Hajič, J., Vidová-Hladká, B., Hajičová, E., Sgall, P., Pajas, P., Řezníčková, V., Holub, M.: The current status of the prague dependency treebank. In Matoušek, V., Mautner, P., Mouček, R., Taušer, K., eds.: TSD2001 Proceedings, LNAI 2166, Berlin Heidelberg New York, Springer-Verlag (2001) pp. 11–20.
2. Hajič, J., Hajičová, E., Pajas, P., Panevová, J., Sgall, P., Vidová-Hladká, B.: Prague dependency treebank 1.0 (Final Production Label) (2001) Published by Linguistic Data Consortium, University of Pennsylvania.
3. Hajič, J., Honetschläger, V.: Annotation lexicons: Using the valency lexicon for tectogrammatical annotation. Prague Bulletin of Mathematical Linguistics (2003) 61–86.
4. Smrž, P.: Quality Control for Wordnet Development. In Sojka, P., Pala, K., Smrž, P., Fellbaum, C., Vossen, P., eds.: Proceedings of the Second International WordNet Conference—GWC 2004, Brno, Czech Republic, Masaryk University (2003) 206–212.
5. Landes, S., Leacock, C., Tengi, R.I.: Building semantic concordances. In Fellbaum, C., ed.: WordNet, An Electronic Lexical Database. 1st edn. MIT Press, Cambridge (1998) 199–216.
6. Hajič, J., Holub, M., Hučínová, M., Pavlík, M., Pecina, P., Straňák, P., Šidák, P.M.: Validating and improving the Czech WordNet via lexico-semantic annotation of the Prague Dependency Treebank. In: LREC 2004, Lisbon (2004).
7. Stevenson, M.: Word Sense Disambiguation: The Case for Combinations of Knowledge Sources. CSLI Studies in Computational Linguistics. CSLI Publications, Stanford, California (2003).
8. Navarro, B., Civit, M., Martí, M.A., Marcos, R., Fernández, B.: Syntactic, semantic and pragmatic annotation in cast3lb. Technical report, UCREL, Lancaster, UK (2003).
9. Agirre, E., Aldezabal, I., Etxeberria, J., Izagirre, E., Mendizabal, K., Pociello, E., Iruskieta, M.Q.: Improving the basque wordnet by corpus annotation. In: Proceedings of Third International WordNet Conference, Jeju Island (Korea) (2006) 287–290.

Czech Verbs of Communication
and the Extraction of Their Frames*

Václava Benešová and Ondřej Bojar

Institute of Formal and Applied Linguistics
ÚFAL MFF UK, Malostranské náměstí 25, 11800 Praha, Czech Republic
{benesova, bojar}@ufal.mff.cuni.cz

Abstract. We aim at a procedure of automatic generation of valency frames for verbs not covered in VALLEX, a lexicon of Czech verbs. We exploit the classification of verbs into syntactico-semantic classes. This article describes our first step to automatically identify verbs of communication and to assign the prototypical frame to them. The method of identification is evaluated against two versions of VALLEX and FrameNet 1.2. For the purpose of frame generation, a new metric based on the notion of frame edit distance is outlined.

1 Introduction

The main objective of this paper is to present first experiments with an automatic extension of VALLEX, a valency lexicon of Czech verbs. Czech verbs were included in the lexicon on the basis of their frequency in the Czech National Corpus (CNC[1]) to achieve maximal corpus coverage. VALLEX nowadays covers around 66% of verb occurrences; 23% of verb occurrences belong to few frequent auxiliary verbs, esp. *být, bývat (to be)*. (See Table 1.) The remaining 10% occurrences belong to verbs with low corpus frequency. It would not be economical to continue manual development of VALLEX for the remaining entries because the distribution of verbs closely follows Zipf's law and there are about 28k verbs needed just to cover our particular corpus.

In order to cover the missing verbs, we have experimented with the possibility of automatic generation of frames based on corpus evidence. Our experiment exploits the classification of verbs into semantic classes, a piece of information which is already available in VALLEX. For the time being, we have focused on a single class: verbs of communication, the so called *verba dicendi*.

In our contribution, we first provide a basic description of VALLEX 1.x, including its classification of verbs. The examined class of verbs of communication is described in a greater detail. Next, we describe and evaluate the proposed automatic method to identify verbs of communication. Finally, we estimate the usefulness of the identification of this class in the task of automatic creation of VALLEX entries.

---

* The work reported in this paper has been supported by the grants GAAV ČR 1ET201120505, LC536 and GAČR No. 405/04/0243.

[1] http://ucnk.ff.cuni.cz/

Petr Sojka, Ivan Kopeček and Karel Pala (Eds.): TSD 2006, LNAI 4188, pp. 29–36, 2006.

Table 1. Coverage of VALLEX 1.0 and 1.5 with respect to the Czech National Corpus

	VALLEX 1.0				VALLEX 1.5			
	Occ.	[%]	Verb lemmas	[%]	Occ.	[%]	Verb lemmas	[%]
Covered	8.0M	53.7	1,064	3.6	8.0M	65.6	1,802	6.1
Not covered but frequent	4.1M	27.9	20	0.1	3.5M	23.4	4	0.0
Not covered, infrequent	2.7M	18.3	28,385	96.3	1.6M	10.9	27,663	93.9
Total	14.8M	100.0	29,469	100.0	14.8M	100.0	29,469	100.0

1.1 VALLEX, Valency Lexicon of Czech Verbs

VALLEX uses the Functional Generative Description [1] as its theoretical background and is closely related to the Prague Dependency Treebank (PDT, [2]). VALLEX is fully manually annotated, which sets limits on the growth rate. On the other hand, manual annotation ensures attaining data of high quality. The first version of VALLEX 1.0 was publicly released in 2003 and contained over 1,400 verb entries[2]. The set of covered verbs was extended to about 2,500 verb entries in VALLEX 1.5, an internal version released in 2005. (See also Table 2.) The second version, VALLEX 2.0 (almost 4,300 entries) based on the so-called alternation model (see [3]), will be available in autumn 2006.

VALLEX 1.0 and 1.5 consist of verb entries containing a non-empty set of valency frames. Under the term *valency*, we understand the ability of a verb to bind a range of syntactic elements. A valency frame is assigned to a verb in its particular meaning/sense and is captured as a sequence of frame slots. Each slot stands for one complement and consists of a functor (a label expressing the relation between the verb and the complement), its morphemic realization and the type of complement.

1.2 Verb Classes in VALLEX

Verb classes were introduced to VALLEX primarily to improve data consistence because observing whole groups of semantically similar verbs together simplifies data checking.

At present, classification of verbs into semantic classes is a topical issue in linguistic research (cf. Levin's verb classes [4], PropBank [5], LCS [6,7], FrameNet [8]). Although we consider these approaches to be very stimulative from the theoretical point of view, we decided to use our own classification for the reason of differences in the theoretical background and in the methods of description.

However, we must emphasize that building verb classes and their description in VALLEX is still in progress and the classification is not based on a defined ontology but is to a certain extent intuitive. VALLEX classes are built thoroughly from below. When grouping verbs together, we give priority mostly to syntactic criteria: the number of complements (FGD classifies them into inner participants, the so-called *actants*, and *free modifications* roughly corresponding to adjuncts), their type (mainly obligatory or optional), functors and their morphemic realizations.

---

[2] The term *verb entry* refers to a VALLEX entry which distinguishes homographs and reflexive variants of the verb. The term *verb lemma* refers to the infinitive form of the verb, excluding the reflexive particle.

As displayed in Table 2, VALLEX now defines about 20 verb classes (communication, mental action, perception, psych verbs, exchange, change, phase verbs, phase of action, modal verbs, motion, transport, location, expansion, combining, social interaction, providing, appoint verb, contact, emission, extent) that contain on average 6.1 distinct frame types (disregarding morphemic realizations and complement types).

Table 2. Basic statistics about VALLEX 1.0 and 1.5

	VALLEX 1.0	VALLEX 1.5
Total verb entries	1,437	2,476
Total verb lemmas	1,081	1,844
Total frames	4,239	7,080
Frames with a class	1,591 (37.5%)	3,156 (44.6%)
Total classes	16	23
Avg. frame types in class	6.1	6.1

1.3 Verbs of Communication

The communication class is specified as the set of verbs that render a situation when 'a speaker conveys information to a recipient'. Besides the slots ACT for the 'speaker' and ADDR for the 'recipient', communication verbs are characterized by the entity 'information' that is expressed on the layer of surface structure as a dependent clause introduced by a subordinating conjunction or as a nominal structure.

On the one hand, the entity 'information' is the property that relates these verbs to verbs of some other classes (mental action, perception and psych verbs). On the other hand, the inherence of the 'recipient' distinguishes the verbs of communication from the aforementioned other classes. However, in a small number of cases when the addressee which represents the 'recipient' does not appear explicitly in valency frame (*speak, declare, etc.*), this distinctive criterion fails.

On the basis of our observations, the verbs of communication can be further divided into subclasses according to the semantic character of 'information' as follows: simple information (verbs of announcement: *říci (say), informovat (inform)*, etc.), questions (interrogative verbs: *ptát se (ask), etc.*) and commands, bans, warnings, permissions and suggestions (imperative verbs: *poručit (order), zakázat (prohibit), etc.*).The dependent clause after verbs of announcement is primarily introduced by the subordinating conjunction *že (that)*, interrogative by *zda (whether), jestli (if)* and imperative verbs by *aby (in order to), at' (let)*. We recognize some other distinctions between these three subclasses but their description goes beyond the scope of this paper.

2 Automatic Identification of Verbs of Communication

In the present section, we investigate how much the information about valency frame combined with the information about morphemic realization of valency complement can contribute to an automatic recognition of verbs of communication. For the sake of simplicity, we use the term *verbs of communication* to refer to verbs with at least one sense (frame) belonging to the communication class.

2.1 Searching Corpus for Typical Surface Patterns

Our experiment is primarily based on the idea that verbs of communication can be detected by the presence of a dependent clause representing the 'information' and an addressee representing the 'recipient'.

This idea can be formalized as a set of queries to search the corpus for occurrences of verbs accompanied by: (1) a noun in one of the following cases: genitive, dative and accusative (to approximate the ADDR slot) and (2) a dependent clause introduced by one of the set of characteristic subordinating conjunction (*že*, *aby*, *at'*, *zda* or *jestli*) (to approximate the slot of 'information').

We disregard the freedom of Czech word order which, roughly speaking, allows for any permutation of a verb and its complements. In reality, the distribution of the various reorderings is again Zipfian with the most typical pattern (verb+ADDR+subord) being the most frequent. In a sense, we approximate the sum with the first, maximal, element only. On the other hand we allow some intervening adjuncts between the noun and the subordinating clause.

2.2 Evaluation Against VALLEX and FrameNet

We sort all verbs by the descending number of occurrences of the tested pattern. This gives us a ranking of verbs according to their 'communicative character', typical verbs of communication such as *říci* (say) appear on top. Given a threshold, one can estimate the class identification quality in terms of a confusion matrix: verbs above the threshold that actually belong to the class of verbs of communication (according to a golden standard) constitute *true positives* (TP), verbs above the threshold but not in the communication class constitute *false positives* (FP), etc.

A well-established technique of the so-called ROC curves allows to compare the quality of rankings for all possible thresholds at once. We plot the *true positive rate* ($TPR = TP/P$ where P is the total number of verbs of communication) against *true negative rate* ($TNR = TN/N$, N stands for the number of verbs with no sense of communication) for all thresholds.

We evaluate the quality of class identification against golden standards from two sources. First, we consider all verbs with at least one frame in the communication class from VALLEX 1.0 and 1.5 and second, we use all possible word-to-word translations of English verbs listed in FrameNet 1.2[3] Communication frame and all inherited and used frames (For an explanation, see [9,10]; the English-to-Czech translations were obtained automatically using available on-line dictionaries). As the universum (i.e. $P + N$), we use all verbs defined in the respective version of VALLEX and all verbs defined in VALLEX 1.5 for the FrameNet-based evaluation.

Figure 1 displays the *TPR/TNR* curve for verbs suggested by the pattern V+N234+subord. The left chart compares the performance against various golden standards, the right chart gives a closer detail on contribution from different subordinating conjunctions.

The closer the curve lies to the upper right corner, the better the performance is compared to the golden standard. With an appropriate threshold, about 40% to 50% of verbs of communication are identified correctly while 20% of non-communication verbs are falsely

---

[3] http://framenet.icsi.berkeley.edu/

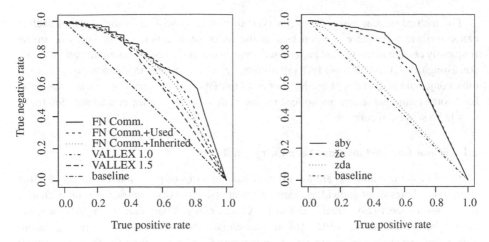

Fig. 1. Verbs of communication as suggested by the pattern V+N234+subord, evaluated against VALLEX and FrameNet (left) and evaluated against VALLEX 1.0 for three main contributing subordinating conjunctions (*aby*, *že*, *zda*) independently (right)

marked, too. We get about the same performance level for both VALLEX and FrameNet-based evaluation. This confirms that our method is not too tightly tailored to the classification introduced in VALLEX.

The right chart in Figure 1 demonstrates that the contribution of different subordinating conjunctions is highly varied. While *aby* and *že* contribute significantly to the required specification, the verbs suggested by the pattern with *zda* are just above the baseline of not suggesting any verb. (The conjunctions *at'* and *jestli* had too few occurrences in the pattern.)

2.3 Weak Points of Patterns

From the very beginning, we eliminated the nominal structures (which can also express 'information') from the queries in order to avoid verbs of exchange as *give, take*, etc. In a similar vein, the queries were not able to identify sentences with verbs of communication where some of the searched complements were not realized on the layer of surface structure. Therefore, some verbs which belong to the communication class remained undiscovered.

On the contrary, the fact that conjunctions *aby* and *že* are homonymous lowers the reliability of the queries. We tried to eliminate the number of incorrectly chosen verbs by a refinement of the queries. (For instance, we omitted certain combination of demonstratives plus conjunctions: *tak, aby (so that), tak, že (so that)*, etc.) A further problem is represented by cases when the identified dependent clause is not a member of the valency frame of the given verb but depends on the preceding noun.

3   Frame Suggestion

One of our foreseen tasks is to generate VALLEX frame entries for new verbs based on corpus data. This is a well-established research topic (see [11] for a survey) but most experiments were conducted with focus on surface frames only, making the experimental setting comparably easier.

The method of searching corpus for typical patterns described in the previous section can contribute to frame extraction task in the following manner: for all verbs occurring frequently enough in the typical pattern, we propose the most typical 'communication frame' consisting of ACT, ADDR and PAT (all obligatory). For each verb independently, we assign only conjunctions discovered by the queries to the PAT. Every verb of communication can have some additional senses not noticed by our method but at least the communication frame should be suggested correctly.

3.1 Frame Edit Distance and Verb Entry Similarity

Methods of frame extraction are usually evaluated in terms of precision and recall of either frames as wholes or of individual frame elements (slots). These metrics are unfortunately too rough for the richly structured VALLEX-like frames. Therefore, we propose a novel metric, *frame edit distance* (FED). The metric estimates the number of edit operations (insert, delete, replace) necessary to convert a hypothesized frame to a correct frame. In the current simple version of the metric, we assign equal costs to all basic edit operations (fixing the obligatoriness flag, adding or removing allowed morphemic forms), only the functor is considered as fixed. In order to change the functor, one pays for complete destruction of the wrong slot and complete construction of the correct slot. We consider charging more for slot destruction than for slot construction in future versions of the metric because we prefer methods that undergenerate and produce safer frames to methods that suggest unjustified frames.

As described above, VALLEX is organized as a set of verb entries each consisting of a set of frames. Given a verb lemma, the set of its VALLEX entries and a set of entries produced by an automatic frame suggestion method, we can use FED to estimate how much of editing work has been saved. We call this measure *entry similarity* or *expected saving* (ES) and define it as follows:

$$ES = 1 - \frac{\min FED(G, H)}{FED(G, \emptyset) + FED(H, \emptyset)}$$

where G denotes the set golden verb entries of this base lemma, H denotes the hypothesized entries and $\emptyset$ stands for a blank verb entry. Not suggesting anything has ES of 0% and suggesting the golden frames exactly has ES of 100%.

3.2 Experimental Results with Verb Entry Similarity

Table 3 displays the ES of four various baselines and the result obtained by our method. When we assume that every verb has a single entry and this entry consists of a single

Table 3. Expected saving when suggesting frame entries automatically

Suggested frames	ES [%]
Specific frame for verbs of communication, default for others	38.00 ± 0.19
Baseline 1: ACT(1)	26.69 ± 0.14
Baseline 2: ACT(1) PAT(4)	37.55 ± 0.18
Baseline 3: ACT(1) PAT(4) ADDR(3,4)	35.70 ± 0.17
Baseline 4: Two identical frames: ACT(1) PAT(4)	39.11 ± 0.12

frame with the ACT slot only, ES estimates that about 27% of editing operations was saved. Suggesting ACT and PAT helps even better (Baseline 2, 38%), but suggesting a third obligatory slot for ADDR (realized either as dative (3) or accusative (4)) is already harmful, because not all the verb entries require an ADDR.

We can slightly improve over Baseline 2 if we first identify verbs of communication automatically and assign ACT PAT ADDR with appropriate subordinating conjunctions to them, leaving other verbs with ACT PAT only. This confirms our assumption that verbs of communication have a typical three-slot frame and also that our method managed to identify the verbs correctly.

Our ES scores are relatively low in general and Baseline 4 suggests a reason for that: most verbs listed in VALLEX have several senses and thus several frames. In this first experiment, we focus on the communication frame only, so it still remains quite expensive (in terms of ES) to add all other frames. In Baseline 4, we suggest a single verb entry with two core frames (ACT PAT) and this gives us a higher saving because most verbs indeed ask for more frames.

4 Conclusion

We briefly described the classification of verbs in VALLEX and we proposed and evaluated a corpus-based automatic method to identify verbs of communication. The performance of our method was tested not only on VALLEX data but also on an independent verb classification as available in the FrameNet.

We introduced a novel metric to capture the effort to construct VALLEX verb entries and to estimate how much effort an automatic procedure can save. Having assigned a prototypical frame of communication to the verbs that were automatically identified in the previous step, we achieved a little improvement over the baseline, although not statistically significant.

We conclude that the automatic identification of communication verbs proposed performs satisfactorily. However, to employ this step in an automatic generation of verb entries for new verbs, the method must not be restricted to a single class and suggest also other frames for other verb senses. Otherwise, only very little of lexicographic labour is saved.

References

1. Sgall, P., Hajičová, E., Panevová, J.: The Meaning of the Sentence in Its Semantic and Pragmatic Aspects. D. Reidel Publishing Company, Dordrecht (1986).
2. Hajič, J.: Complex Corpus Annotation: The Prague Dependency Treebank. In Šimková, M., ed.: Insight into Slovak and Czech Corpus Linguistics, Bratislava, Slovakia, Veda, vydavateľstvo SAV (2005) 54–73.
3. Lopatková, M., Žabokrtský, Z., Skwarska, K.: Valency Lexicon of Czech Verbs: Alternation-Based Model. In: Proceedings of LREC 2006, ELRA (2006) 1728–1733.
4. Levin, B.: English Verb Classes and Alternations. University of Chicago Press, Chicago (1993).
5. Palmer, M.e.a.: The Proposition Bank: An Annotated Corpus of Semantic Roles. Computational Linguistics 31 (2005) 71–106.
6. Jackendoff, R.: Semantic Structures. The MIT Press, Cambridge, MA (1990).
7. Dorr, B.J., Mari, O.B.: Multilingual Generation: The Role of Telicity in Lexical Choice and Syntactic Realization. Machine Translation 11 (1996) 37–74.

8. Baker, C.F., Fillmore, C.J., Lowe, J.B.: The Berkeley FrameNet project. In Boitet, C., Whitelock, P., eds.: Proceedings of the Thirty-Sixth Annual Meeting of the Association for Computational Linguistics and Seventeenth International Conference on Computational Linguistics, San Francisco, California, Morgan Kaufmann Publishers (1998) 86–90.

9. Fillmore, C.J., Wooters, C., Baker, C.F.: Building a large lexical databank which provides deep semantics. In: Proceedings of the Pacific Asian Conference on Language, Information and Computation, Hong Kong (2001).

10. Fillmore, C.J.: FrameNet and the Linking between Semantic and Syntactic Relations. In Tseng, S.C., ed.: Proceedings of COLING 2002, Howard International House (2002) xxviii–xxxvi.

11. Korhonen, A.: Subcategorization Acquisition. Technical Report UCAM-CL-TR-530, University of Cambridge, Computer Laboratory, Cambridge, UK (2002).

Featuring of Sex-Dependent Nouns in Databases Oriented to European Languages*

Igor A. Bolshakov[1] and Sofia N. Galicia-Haro[2]

[1] Center for Computing Research (CIC)
National Polytechnic Institute (IPN), Mexico City, Mexico
`igor@cic.ipn.mx`
[2] Faculty of Sciences
National Autonomous University of Mexico (UNAM)
Mexico City, Mexico
`sngh@fciencias.unam.mx`

Abstract. It is argued that human-denoting nouns in European languages forming pairs like English steward vs. stewardess, or Spanish jefe vs. jefa 'chief', or German Student vs. Studentin 'student', or Russian moskvič vs. moskvička 'Muscovite' may be featured in factographic databases conjointly as Sex-Dependent Nouns?a special part of speech. Each SDN has two forms, maybe coinciding, selected when necessary by the sex of the denoted person. SDN notion ensures a kind of universality for translation between various languages, being especially convenient in languages with gender of nouns implied by sex. We base our reasoning on Spanish, French, Russian, German, and English examples.

1 Introduction

European languages have numerous pairs of human-denoting nouns that are the same in meaning but differ in the sex of their bearer. The semantics of these pairs covers at least the following groups:

1. Profession, occupation or official position (in English: *steward* vs. *stewardess*; in Spanish: *jefe* vs. *jefa* 'chief'; in Russian: *učitel'* vs. *učitel'nica* 'teacher'; in German: *Student* vs. *Studentin* 'student'; in French: *directeur* vs. *directrice* 'director');
2. Nationality or confession (in English: *Frenchman* vs. *Frenchwoman*; in Spanish: *católico* vs. *católica* 'Catholic'; in Russian: *nemec* vs. *nemka* 'German'; in French: *suédois* vs. *suédoise* 'Swede');
3. Dwelling locality (in French: *parisien* vs. *parisienne* 'Parisian'; in Spanish: *madrileño* vs. *madrileña* 'dweller of Madrid'; in Russian: *sibirjak* vs. *sibirjačka* 'Siberian'; in French: *sévillan* vs. *sévillane* 'Sevillian');
4. Main feature of personality (in English: *madman* vs. *madwoman*; in Spanish: *histérico* vs. *histérica* 'hysteric'; in Russian: *durak* vs. *dura* 'stupid'; in French: *délinquant* vs. *délinquante* 'delinquent').

---

* Work done under partial support of Mexican government (CONACyT, SNI, SIP–IPN). Many thanks to Steve Legrand for the proofreading of the manuscript.

Petr Sojka, Ivan Kopeček and Karel Pala (Eds.): TSD 2006, LNAI 4188, pp. 37–44, 2006.

Because of the same meaning, the pair counterparts are considered synonymous. Morphologically, they usually have the same root, and the repertoire of sex-forming suffixes is rather limited (about a dozen suffix pairs, depending on language).

In contrast to the pairs, there exist many nouns of the mentioned groups whose dependence of sex is not expressed explicitly. The same form is used, but their co-reference relationships in context are expressed by sex-dependent personal pronouns, e.g., *he is a teacher* vs. *she is a teacher*.

Meanwhile, in languages with grammatical gender (e.g., of Romance or Slavic families) such nouns are of masculine or feminine gender for males and females respectively. The sex as a semantic feature is expressed by means of the morpho-syntactic category of gender of dependent articles (Sp. *el estudiante$_{MALE}$* vs. *la estudiante$_{FEMALE}$* 'the student'), dependent adjectives (Sp. *nuevo estudiante$_{MALE}$* vs. *nueva estudiante$_{FEMALE}$* 'new student') or syntactically related predicatives (Sp. *estudiante$_{MALE}$ está cansado* vs. *estudiante$_{FEMALE}$ está cansada* 'student is tired'; Rus. *vrač$_{MALE}$ skazal* vs. *vrač$_{FEMALE}$ skazala* 'physician said').

The Sex-Dependent Nouns are already described in the works [1, 2, 3] of general linguistics. In [3] two different viewpoints are compared. One of them considers SDN pairs as members of the same lexeme, and this is usual for many modern Spanish and French dictionaries. E.g., the French pair *fou* vs. *folle* 'insane' appears in the same dictionary entry as inflectional forms of the same entity. Hence it is admitted that such nouns get inflectional forms of each sex according to the specific gender?the way adjectives or participles do.

The contrary viewpoint considers *fou* and *folle* as two different lexemes linked by a derivational relation. Hence, the sex is included in the semantic description of each lexeme. Russian lexicography always prefers this viewpoint, whereas Romance language lexicographies adopt it only in cases when the difference betweeen the two forms is rather significant, e.g. for *actor/actriz* 'actor/actress' in Spanish.

In this paper, we argue for the first viewpoint and suggest the introduction of a new part of speech, i.e., Sex-Dependent Nound (SDNs), for use in computational linguistics. SDNs are especially applicable to languages with gender. In these languages, they are similar to adjectives, the number and gender of which have the same word-forming characteristics. Both number and gender of SDNs are semantically loaded: they reflect the number of persons and their sex. Hence, they both should be recognizable when analyzed as a meaning unit in the semantic representation of the analyzed text. In synthesis, the sex feature is used for the selection of target word form from the pair (if the forms are different) and for correct agreement of words referentially related with the target.

We base our considerations on Spanish, French, Russian, German, and English languages, revealing few differences in properties of SDNs in various languages.

2 Sex-Dependent Nouns in Spanish

The number of SDNs in Spanish is tremendously high, i.e. several thousands. The Anaya dictionary contains ca. 3600 nouns of this type, i.e. 18% of the total nouns. The most common morpho-classes of SDN formation are shown in Table 1 (Ø is empty string).

The most common are the morpho-classes 1 to 3, both broadly spread and actually productive. Indeed, the modern Spanish easily admits new female forms for profession and positions now occupied equally by women. The forms *jefa* 'she-chief', *ingeniera* 'she-engineer', *doctora* 'she-doctor', *profesora* 'she-professor' or *secretaria* 'she-secretary' are quite usual, while *oficiala* 'she-officer' and *presidenta* 'she-president' are already admitted in speech and TV (*La socialista Michelle Bachelet será la primera presidenta de Chile* 'The socialist Michelle Bachelet will be the first president$_{FEMALE}$ of Chile').

Table 1. Some morpho-classes of SDN formation in Spanish

Morpho-class	Endings		Examples		Translation
	masc	fem	masc	fem	
1	o	a	ruso	rusa	Russian
2	Ø	a	doctor	doctora	doctor
3	e	a	jefe	jefa	chief
0	ista	ista	tesista	tesista	defender of thesis
0	nte	nte	estudiante	estudiante	student
4	a	isa	poeta	poetisa	poet
0	i	i	iraqui	iraqui	Iraqi
5	or	triz	actor	actriz	actor/actress
6	e	esa	alcalde	alcaldesa	mayor
7	e	ina	héroe	heroína	hero/heroine

Class 0 is very numerous in Spanish and corresponds to endings used for both masculine and feminine forms. The sex is expressed in this class only morpho-syntactically. Following are several examples of class 0: *artista* 'artist', *turista* 'tourist', *camarada* 'comrade', *comerciante* 'merchant', *compatriota* 'compatriot', *cónyuge* 'spouse', *estudiante* 'student', *hereje* 'heretic', *indígena* 'aborigine', *idiota* 'idiot', *intérprete* 'interpreter', *mártir* 'martyr', *patriota* 'patriot', *rival* 'rival', *suicido* 'suicide', *testigo* 'witness', *soprano* 'soprano', etc.

In addition to the semantic groups given in the introduction, we may also consider SDN in the groups denoting in Spanish close relatives (*hermano* vs. *hermana* 'brother/sister', *hijo* vs. *hija* 'son/daughter', *esposo* vs. *esposa* 'husband/wife', *etc.*) and highly generic nouns of both sexes (*niño* vs. *niña* 'little boy/girl', *muchacho* vs. *muchacha* 'boy/girl', etc.). However, the gender formation by means of suppletion (total changing of the root) is also frequent in these groups (*padre* vs. *madre* 'father/mother', *yerno* vs. *nuera* 'son-in-law/daughter-in-law', *caballero* vs. *dama* 'gentleman/lady').

Together with the mentioned 'standard' SDNs, there exist also more rare cases:

– Only masculine form exists and it is equally applicable for men and women, e.g., *miembro* 'member': *Miguel, el miembro más antiguo de la academia* 'Miguel, the oldest member of the academy'; *la recién nacida es el séptimo miembro de la familia* 'the$_{FEM}$ new born$_{FEM}$ is the seventh$_{MASC}$ family member$_{MASC}$').
– Feminine form is well-known, while the masculine one, even if exists, is not used, e.g., *institutriz* 'preceptress'. This is valid for professions considered mainly feminine.
– Only feminine form exists and it is equally applicable for men and women, e.g., *persona* 'person'.
– Only masculine form exists and it is aplicable only for men, e.g. *el político* 'politician' (*Ramón Corral, el político sonorense* 'Ramon Corral, the politician from Sonora')

or *el ordenanza* 'courier'. The corresponding notion for women can be formed in a descriptive manner, e.g., *functionaria de politica* 'politic functionary$_{FEM}$' to some degree corresponds to the masculine *político*. Note that a feminine morphological counterpart can exist for such masculine nouns, but not as a feminine role in a SDN: *la politica* means 'policy', *la ordenanza* means 'standing order'. Cf. also non-SDN pairs *el cura* 'priest' vs. *la cura* 'care'; *el papa* 'Pope' vs. *la papa* 'potato'.

- The SDN forms coincide and are broadly used, but the feminine form has an additional semantic burden. E.g., for SDNs *guardia* 'guard', *guía* 'guide', *policía* 'policeman/woman', *vista* 'custom employee', *vocal* 'jury member', and *trompeta* 'trumpet player', the feminine forms mean also 'guard corps', 'guide-book', 'police corps', 'eyesight', 'vowel', and 'trompet' relatively.

3   Sex-Dependent Nouns in French

French, like other Romance languages, has two genders. The most common morpho-classes of SDN formation are listed in 2. The morpho-class 1 is very productive.

Table 2. Some morpho-classes of SDN formation in French

Morpho-class	Endings		Examples		Translation
	masc	fem	masc	fem	
0	Ø	Ø	*artiste*	*artiste*	artist
1	Ø	e	*artisan*	*artisane*	craftsman
2	Ø	ine	*tsar*	*tsarine*	Tsar
3	Ø	sse	*suisse*	*suissesse*	Swiss
4	eur	rice	*créateur*	*créatrice*	creator
5	eur	euse	*chanteur*	*chanteuse*	singer
6	eur	eresse	*demandeur*	*demanderesse*	claimant
7	ien	ienne	*historien*	*historienne*	historian
8	f	ve	*veuf*	*veuve*	widow/er

However, unlike Spanish, French does not easily admit feminine forms for professions and positions now equally occupied by women [4]. Hence, the same form is frequently used for men and women, e.g., *professeur* 'professor', *médecin* 'physician', *écrivain* 'writer', *otage* 'hostage', *témoin* 'witness'. (Nevertheless, Canadian dialect accepts some feminine forms, e.g., *professeur* vs. *professeure* 'professor'.

Gender formation by means of suppletion is broader in French, for example: *steward* 'steward' vs. *hôtesse de l'air* 'stewardess', *frère* 'brother' vs. *sœur* 'sister'.

Among peculiar pairs, let us first mention those with only one gender serving for both sexes: *la vedette* 'actor/actress', *le capitaine* 'captain', *le savant* 'scientist', *le mannequin* 'he/she model', *le clown* 'he/she clown'. Some forms can be only applied to men, e.g. *le politique* 'politician' (*la politique* means 'politics'). Cf. also the non-SDN pairs *le vigile* 'night watchman' vs. *la vigile* 'abstinence'; *le médecin* 'physician' vs. *la médecine* 'medicine'.

4   Sex-Dependent Nouns in Russian

Some broadly spread and productive Russian morpho-classes of SDN are given in the lines 0 to 10 of Table 3.

Table 3. Some morpho-classes of SDN formation in Russian

Morpho-class	Endings		Examples		Translation
	masc	fem	masc	fem	
0	Ø	Ø	doktor	doktor	doctor
1	Ø	ka	belorus	beloruska	Byelorussian
2	Ø	ša	vaxter	vaxterša	janitor
3	ec	ka	japonec	japonka	Japanese
4	ec	jka	avstriec	avstrijka	Austrian
5	ec	ica	pevec	pevica	singer
6	ec	janka	kitaec	kitajanka	Chinese
7	l'	l'nica	žitel'	žitel'nica	dweller
8	ik	ica	učenik	učenica	pupil
9	k	čka	uzbek	uzbečka	Uzbek
10	in	ka	armjanin	armjanka	Armenian
11	er	risa	akter	aktrisa	actor/actress
12	Ø	esa	kloun	klounesa	clown

SDNs with such morphological formation cover in Russian at least several hundred pairs?nearly completely the semantic classes 2 to 4 given in the introduction. Meanwhile, for the class 1 modern Russian exhibits staunch conservatism. One cannot freely use in texts the female version of many profession or position titles if they are not accepted by official and literary professionals. This is especially valid if a loan word is in question. As a result, such frequent 'masculine' words as *vrač* 'physician', *doktor* or *professor* are uniquely possible for titling and addressing a woman professional. There exist also *vračixa, doktorša, professorša*, etc., but they may be used only in a colloquial manner. The pairs *director* vs. *direktrisa* 'director', *kritik* vs. *kritikesa* 'critique' can be used in texts, but the feminine forms have a slight ironic flavor, i.e. they are not neutral and, officially, they are not accepted. Additionally, the colloquial female morphological counterparts of high-leveled positions like *ministerša* or *general'ša* are still interpreted as minister's or general's wife.

This feature of Russian is not valid in some other Slavic languages. For example, both forms of the pair {*doktor, doktorka*} in Czech are stylistically neutral and may be used officially.

The Russian bureaucratic tradition is so strong that even with words *geroinja* 'heroine' and *stroitel'nica* 'she-constructor' available, Russian woman may be officially honored only as *Geroj Rossii* 'Hero of Russia' or *Zaslužennyj Stroitel'* 'Honorable He-constructor'.

Nevertheless, the laws of Russian morpho-syntax require expressing the sex of professionals by means of words that agree with the given noun. Hence in the middle of the 20th century the semantically-induced agreement with syntactically related words has appeared in speech and then in paper.

Currently, the agreement with predicates like *vrač*$_{MALE}$ *skazal/utomlen vs. vrač*$_{FEMALE}$ *skazala/utomlena* 'physician said/is tired' has become usual and is considered stable, but for dependent adjectives the situation is different. For example, in modern press one can meet the word combination *moloden'kaja glavnyj redaktor* 'young editor-in-chief$_{FEMALE}$', literally 'youngish$_{FEM}$principal$_{MALE}$ editor'. The first adjective gives the personal feature of the woman and it has feminine gender, while the second adjective, together with the noun, forms her official masculine title not changeable to feminine one because of the literary tradition. Even more intricate situation may be observed when a SDN is a part of compose predicate: *ona byla xorošim redaktorom* 'she was a good$_{MALE}$ editor$_{MALE}$'.

Thus, many Russian SDNs of the class 1 have the same forms for both sexes but differ morpho-syntactically. For this reason, the peculiarities of a SDN in agreement (if any) should be expressed in dictionaries, e.g., as a short list of official title-forming adjectives valid for the given noun.

Among peculiarities, let us first mention professions which are considered mainly female: *šveja* 'seamstress', *kuxarka* 'she-kook', *dojarka* 'milkmaid', *balerina* 'balet she-dancer'. When necessary, the corresponding masculine counterpart is expressible approximately by means of suppletion (*portnoj* 'tailor', *povar* 'kook') or in a descriptive manner (*master doenija* 'milking master', *tancor baleta* 'dancer of balet'). Among professions that have been considered purely masculine for many years, there exist, e.g., *mexanik* 'mechanic' (its morphological feminine counterpart *mexanika* means 'mechanics'), *kuznec* 'blacksmith' (its morphological counterpart *kuznica* means 'smithy'), and *mašinist* (its morphological counterpart *mašinistka* means 'she-typist' and the latter does not have its own SDN counterpart!). If necessary, the masculine form can be applied to a woman, with corresponding morpho-syntactic changes in the context.

5 Sex-Dependent Nouns in German

The main and prevalence class of morphs in the formation of the SDN is {∅, *in*}, e.g., *Architekt* vs. *Architektin* 'architect'; *Verkäufer* vs. *Verkäuferin* 'shop assistant'; *Pazifist* vs. *Pazifistin* 'pacifist'. The masculine version of some nouns is applicable to women, even though there exists the feminine form: *Frau Doktor Opfermann ist Professor (Professorin) an der Universität* 'the lady doctor$_{MASC}$ Opfermann is professor$_{MASC/FEM}$ in the university'.

Again, there exist nouns whose two possible genders do not give a SDN: *der*$_{MALE}$ *Leiter* 'manager' vs. *die*$_{FEM}$ *Leiter* 'stairs'; *der*$_{MALE}$ *Junge* 'boy', *das*$_{NEU}$ *Junge* 'puppy' (NEU means the neuter gender).

6 Sex-Dependent Nouns in English

English does not have genders, and the pairs distinguishing sexes like *Englishman/Englishwoman, actor/actress, steward/stewardess, avitor/aviatrix, widower/widow, hero/heroine, executor/executrix*, are rather few. Therefore, the introduction of the SDN notion seems excessive in this language.

However, the label *SDN* at a noun of semantic groups given in the introduction could designate that the noun has sex-dependent personal pronouns and, while translated to Romance or Slavic languages, it has thereby a unique counterpart of the same class, with specific forms chosen depending on the sex indication.

7 Universal Featuring of SDNs

We suggest universal featuring of Sex-Dependent Nouns to be used in various machine dictionaries. An SDN item should include a title name, a class of sex formation, and a short list of peculiarities (if these exist). It is also necessary to indicate, for both elements of a pair, their own classes of declension. In Romance languages these classes reflect only the manner of forming numbers; in Slavic languages they reflect formation of numbers and cases. Below we ignore the declension classes.

Following are some examples of dictionary items with provisory class numbers and two resulting forms. These forms are only given to clarify that the title element coincides with the masculine form and permits to generate the feminine form using the number of the given class.

- For Spanish: TESISTA (sdn, 0) {*tesista, tesista*} 'defender of thesis'; RUSO (sdn, 1) {*ruso, rusa*} 'Russian'; DOCTOR (sdn, 2) {*doctor, doctora*} 'physician'; JEFE (sdn, 3) {*jefe, jefa*} 'chief'.
- For French: RUSSE (sdn, 0) {*russe, russe*} 'Russian'; CHANTANT (sdn, 1) {*chantant, chantante*} 'singer'; INSTITUTEUR (sdn, 4) {*instituteur, institutrice*} 'teacher'.
- For Russian: KOLLEGA (sdn, 0) {*kollega, kollega*}; DOKTOR (sdn, 0) {*doktor, doktor*}; REDAKTOR (sdn, 0; *glavnyj* 'principal', *vypuskajuščij* 'issuing') {*redaktor, redaktor*}; BELORUS (sdn, 1) {*belorus, beloruska*} 'Byelorussian'; PEVEC (sdn, 5) {*pevec, pevica*} 'singer'.
- For German: KÜNSTLER (sdn, 1) {*Künstler, Künstlerin*} 'artist'; LEHRER (sdn, 1) {*lehrer, lehrerin*} 'teacher'.
- For English: DOCTOR (sdn, 0) {*doctor, doctor*}; STEWARD (sdn, 1) {*steward, stewardess*}.

8 Applications and Conclusions

SDNs seem to be especially relevant for multilanguage factographic databases where official human features should be recorded in a universal and easily translatable form, as well for automatic translation in general and for text generation. The value of SDNs is quite evident for translation from English to Romance, Slavic or some other Germanic languages. For example, to correctly translate the Eng. *teacher* to Spanish or to German, the program should extract sex feature of a denoted person from a record of the same database or from context and then select from the pair {*maestro, maestra*} or {*Lehrer, Lehrerin*} respectively. In the reverse direction, when source language (say, Spanish) shows grammatical gender of a person, the way to conserve the complete information in English includes storing separately the sex indication observed.

Another value of SDNs is in language learning. It is known [4,5,6] that acquisition of grammatical genders in a second language is affected by the morpho-syntactic features of gender in the native language. A dictionary containing SDNs could be then effectively help learning.

Therefore, we suggest introducing a new part of speech: Sex-Dependent Nouns. Each SDN has two forms selected when different by the sex of the denoted person. Our considerations are based on facts of Spanish, French, Russian, German, and English, and, with all differences exposed, they support our proposal. A database with the new POS entries could help in translation, text generation and language learning.

References

1. Mel'čuk, Igor. Course de morphologie général. Vol. III. Montréal /Paris, Les Presses de l'Université de Montréal / C.N.R.S. (1995).
2. Mel'čuk, Igor. Course de morphologie général. Vol. IV. Montréal /Paris, Les Presses de l'Université de Montréal / C.N.R.S. (1997).
3. Mel'čuk, Igor. Un FOU/une FOLLE: un lexème ou deux? Lexique, syntaxe et sémantique. Mélanges offertes à Gaston Gross à l'occasion de son soixantième anniversaire. BULAG, No. hors série (2000) 95–106.
4. Rousseau, J. "Madame la ministre": la féminisation des noms en dix questions. Sité du Centre International d'Etudes Pédagogiques (1998) 1–28.
5. Sabourin, L. L1 effects on the processing of grammatical gender in L2. In: S. Foster-Cohen and A. Niznegorodcew (Eds.). EUROSLA Yearbook, Vol. 1 Amsterdam, John Benjamins (2001) 159–169.
6. Sabourin, L., L.A. Stowe, G.J. de Haan. Transfer effects in learning a second language grammatical gender system. Second Language Research, V. 22, No. 1 (2006) 1–29.

On the Behavior of SVM and Some Older Algorithms in Binary Text Classification Tasks

Fabrice Colas[1] and Pavel Brazdil[2]

[1] LIACS, Leiden University, THE NETHERLANDS
fcolas@liacs.nl
[2] LIACC-NIAAD, University of Porto, PORTUGAL
pbrazdil@liacc.up.pt

Abstract. Document classification has already been widely studied. In fact, some studies compared feature selection techniques or feature space transformation whereas some others compared the performance of different algorithms. Recently, following the rising interest towards the Support Vector Machine, various studies showed that the SVM outperforms other classification algorithms. So should we just not bother about other classification algorithms and opt always for SVM?

We have decided to investigate this issue and compared SVM to kNN and naive Bayes on binary classification tasks. An important issue is to compare optimized versions of these algorithms, which is what we have done. Our results show all the classifiers achieved comparable performance on most problems. One surprising result is that SVM was not a clear winner, despite quite good overall performance. If a suitable preprocessing is used with kNN, this algorithm continues to achieve very good results and scales up well with the number of documents, which is not the case for SVM. As for naive Bayes, it also achieved good performance.

1 Introduction

The aim of using artificial intelligence techniques in text categorization, is to build systems which are able to automatically classify documents into categories. But as the feature space, based on the set of unique words in the documents, is typically of very high dimension, document classification is not trivial. Various feature space reduction techniques were suggested and compared in [1,2]. A large number of adaptive learning techniques have also been applied to text categorization. Among them, the k nearest neighbors and the naive Bayes are two examples of commonly used algorithms (see for instance [3] for details). JOACHIMS applied the Support Vector Machine to document classification [4]. Numerous classifier comparisons were done in the past [5,4,6,7].

Some published comparative studies evaluate classifier performance on complex classification tasks by calculating the mean performance across a large number of classes. Some algorithms like the SVM are by default binary classifiers. Therefore, if we have a problem with more than two classes, we need to construct as many classifiers as there are classes (*one versus all* strategy). It is thus not fair to compare a single naive Bayes or kNN classifier to n SVM classifiers (for n classes). This is why we have decided to compare classifiers on *one against one* binary tasks. Moreover, a study of FÜRNKRANZ [8] showed that a *round robin* approach using a set of binary classifiers, performs at least as well as a one versus all

Petr Sojka, Ivan Kopeček and Karel Pala (Eds.): TSD 2006, LNAI 4188, pp. 45–52, 2006.

approach. Binary problems involve also smaller amounts of data, which means that the classifiers are faster to learn. The properties of the train set have much influence on the classifier learning abilities. Therefore, focusing on binary classification tasks allows one to carefully control the nature of train sets. Finally, directly studying multi-class classification tasks tends to obscure the particular behaviors of the classifiers on some classes which may be of interest.

In this comparative study based on binary classification tasks, we seek answers to the following questions. *Should we still consider old classification algorithms in text categorization or opt systematically for SVM classifiers ? What are the strengths and weaknesses of the SVM, naive Bayes and kNN algorithms in text categorization on a set of binary problems ? Are there some parameter optimization results transferable from one problem to another ?* Before giving the answers to the above questions, our experimental settings and evaluation methodology are described. Then, our parameter optimization results are presented. These optimized versions of the classifiers are then used in the subsequent comparative study.

2   Data, Classifiers and Evaluation Methodology

2.1   Document Collection

For our experiments we used the well known 20newsgroups dataset composed of 20000 newsgroup emails (removed email headers and no stemming) and the ohsumed-all dataset composed of 50216 medical abstracts categorized into 23 cardio vascular disease categories (no stemming). We chose to study the set of *one against one* binary classification tasks on these datasets. Thus, $\frac{20(20-1)}{2} = 190$ classification tasks on 20newsgroups and 162 out of $\frac{23(23-1)}{2} = 253$ on ohsumed-all were studied, which makes a total of 352 classification tasks.

2.2   Algorithms

In this paper, two well known classifiers are compared to the SVM, namely kNN and naive Bayes. These two classifiers were chosen because of their simplicity and their generally good performance reported in document classification. With respect to the SVM, the PLATT's SMO implementation was used as well as another derived from SVMLight. They are available in libbow [9] library.

2.3   Evaluation Methodology

As previous studies have shown that classifier performance is affected by the train set size and the feature set size, we have decided to examine these issues in detail. First, we have compared the classifiers for an increasing train set size. For this purpose we have adopted a sub-sampling strategy which involves creating train sets of increasing size, but with equal number of cases from each class. When the examples of one of the classes gets exhausted, the train set is augmented using the documents of the other class. Thus we were giving to both classes the same chance to be learned as well for small samples.

We have also examined the classifier behavior when the dimension of the feature space was increased. The ordering of the set of attributes was done using the *Information Gain*. We chose this heuristic for its simplicity and its good performance, as presented in [1,2].

A classical 10-fold cross validation was used to estimate classifier performance. We chose the macro averaged F_1 measure $MF_1 = \frac{2 \times MPrecision \times MRecall}{MPrecision + MRecall}$ [10], where the $MPrecision$ and the $MRecall$ measures are the averages of the precision and the recall computed on the basis of the two confusion matrices (in one, a class is considered positive and the other negative ; in the other the assignment is interchanged). Finally, we recorded the global processing time in seconds (the sum of the training and the testing time).

3 Experimental Results

3.1 Parameter Optimization Results

We ran some preliminary experiments on 20newsgroups to find the best parameter values. The train set size was set to its maximum value of 1800^3 documents, whereas all the features were selected. Three binary classification tasks were chosen[4]. The results are presented in the following.

Support Vector Machines. Various parameters of SVM were considered in the attempt to optimize the performance of this algorithm. The parameter C (relative importance of the complexity of the model and the error)was varied and various kernel functions were tried as well. None of those lead to interesting improvements in terms of performance (MF_1) or processing time. So, the default value $C = 200$ and a *linear* kernel are used. This choice for a *linear* kernel is consistent to previous results [6,7].

While varying the ϵ parameter controlling the accepted error, we have found that ϵ has no influence on MF_1 as long as its value was smaller or equal to 0.1. However, the processing time could be reduced by a factor of four in the best case, when the largest value of ϵ was used. Fig. 1 (A) shows the dependence of the processing time of the SVM classifier on the number of features for different values of ϵ. Fig. 1 (B) is similar, but portrays the dependence of the processing time on the number of documents. Our hypothesis is that the resolution of the optimization problem is simplified, when an acceptable optimal hyper plane is bounded by a larger error ϵ. The processing time is then consequently reduced. Therefore, it seems that no high precision is needed to train SVM on these 20newsgroups's binary classification tasks.

k **Nearest Neighbors.** The search for the best number of neighbors (k) involved 3 problems. The study was then repeated for each problem using 10-fold cross validation. So in total, each problem was characterized by 30 measures. We have used pairwise t-test (95% confidence interval) to determine whether one setting was significantly better than another. If one setting proved to be better, a victory point was attributed. In case of tie, no point was given.

Large values of k lead to good performance. This can be explained by the way how the similarity measure is computed. The contribution towards the class score of the neighbors is weighted by their similarity to the test point. Therefore, the farthest neighbors have little effect on the class score. Our experiments have shown $k = 49$ to be the best number of

---

[3] A binary task involves 2×1000 documents. Considering that 10-fold cross validation is used, each training set includes 1800 documents and the test set 200.

[4] alt.atheism vs. talk.religion.misc, comp.sys.ibm.pc.hardware vs. comp.sys.-mac.hardware, talk.politics.guns vs. talk.politics.misc

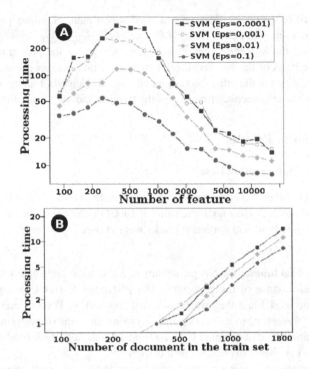

Fig. 1. Processing time of the SVM classifier on `alt.atheism` vs. `talk.religion.misc`, for several values of ϵ, given an increasing number of features (**A**) and an increasing number of documents in the train set (**B**).

nearest neighbors. The subsequent comparative study is based on the 49-NN. In fact, this optimal k value (49) is interestingly quite close to the one in [6] (45) with completely different experimental settings (`Reuters-21578`, classification task seen as a single multi-class problem). We also included 1-NN as a rival against which any other classifier should perform better.

To achieve good performance with kNN, the feature space should be transformed to a new one. A transformation Φ involves the number of occurences of the ith term tf_i, the *inverse document frequency* defined as the ratio between the total number of documents N and the number of documents containing the term df_i, and a normalization constant κ making $\|\Phi\|_2 = 1$. Any transformation was found to be suitable but not the *binary* transformation (value 1 or 0) which degraded the performance. It is consistent with a previous study [11]. Depending whether a particular word is (or is not) present, the *inverse document frequency* should be systematically applied because, as it is well known, it decreases the importance of common words occurring in numerous documents. The normalization do not affect the performance. In all subsequent experiments we have adopted `ntn.lnc` transformation which achieved good results. The feature space transformation for the documents in the train set is $\Phi_{\mathrm{ntn}}(tf_i) = tf_i log(\frac{N}{df_i})$ whereas the transformation for the documents in the test set is $\Phi_{\mathrm{lnc}}(tf_i) = \frac{log(tf_i)}{\kappa}$.

3.2   Comparisons for Increasing Document and Feature Sizes

The aim of our experiments was to examine the classifier learning abilities for an increasing number of documents in the train set (learning curves), and also, how the performance is affected by the number of attributes. In the study involving learning curves, *all the features* were selected. Similarly, when the behaviors for an increasing number of features were studied, the train set was composed of its maximum size, containing as many documents of both classes.

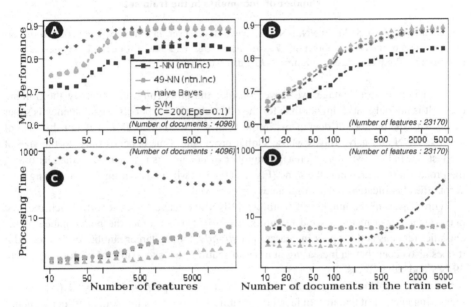

Fig. 2. Performance (**A, B**) and processing time (**C, D**) of the naive Bayes, 49-NN, 1-NN and SVM on the task: `Bacterial Infections and Mycoses` and `Disorders of Environmental Origin` (`Ohsumed-All`, C01-C21), given an increasing number of features (**A, C**) and of documents (**B, D**).

First of all, we observed that the parameters related to the experimental set-up (sample selection, feature space, feature subset selection, classifier parameters) had a *larger* impact on the performance than the choice of individual classifiers. In fact, if suitable parameters of the set-up are chosen and if the parameter settings of the classifiers get correctly optimized, then the differences between the algorithms are not very large. This is illustrated in Fig. 2 (B) which shows very similar MF_1 performance of the 49-NN, naive Bayes and SVM algorithms on a *typical* binary classification task given an increasing train set size.

Fig. 3 illustrates that 49-NN and naive Bayes often start with an advantage on SVM when the train sets are composed of a small number of documents, but as the number of documents increases, the difference diminishes. When the whole train set is used, as described previously, the performance of the SVM are most of the time very similar to 49-NN and naive Bayes. However, it is rare to have SVM achieve better performance for the largest train set.

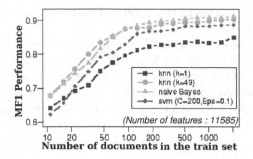

Fig. 3. Performance of SVM, 49-NN, 1-NN and naive Bayes given an increasing number of documents in the train set on the classification task : `Virus Diseases` vs. `Female Genital Diseases and Pregnancy Complications` (`Ohsumed-All` dataset, C02-C13).

SVM is in a disadvantage, when we consider the processing time (mostly the training time). It is not only much higher than for the other algorithms, but also, its tendency is super linear with the number of documents in the train set (see Fig. 2 (D)). It is not the case of 49-NN, 1-NN and naive Bayes whose global processing time depends only on the size of the test set. Indeed, when an increasing number of documents is provided to the classifiers, the processing time remains the same (Fig. 2 (D)). But when comparing the processing time across the classification tasks, differences are observed[5].

With respect to the number of features, 49-NN and naive Bayes tend to reach the best performance on a medium sized feature space. Most of the time, the performance of the classifier remains at the top, or increases *very slightly*, for any larger number of features. But it does also occur that an increasing number of features leads to a drop of performance with 49-NN and naive Bayes.

As for the SVM, we systematically observed a *wave pattern* (see Fig. 2 (A)) for an increasing number of features. In fact, large feature spaces do not imply the best performance for the SVM. It is somewhat surprising, since SVM is often regarded as an algorithm that deals well with very large number of features. It appears that naive Bayes and 49-NN do this better. On the other hand, SVM is the top ranking classifier for small feature space (see left part of Fig. 2 (A)). This advantage on very small feature space may result in a gap of performance as high as 25% with 49-NN and naive Bayes on some tasks. Furthermore, these SVM classifiers built using a small feature space have often a comparable quality to others built using a very large one. The SVM optimality criterion is only met when the number of documents in the train set is sufficiently large. Thus, having a small feature space where documents might not be linearly separable with a large train set place SVM close to its condition of optimality.

Considering the processing time, both naive Bayes and kNN are affected by the number of features (Fig. 2 (C)). The training time of the SVM is particularly high, especially for small feature space. Indeed, the search for the optimal hyper plane of the SVM may require very large training time in these conditions. With extended feature space, the learning task is much faster. This behavior is probably a result of the very high dimension of the word vector space, where data points become linearly separable.

---

[5] This is due to the fact that the size of the classification tasks are different.

Related Works.   Our results disagree somewhat with previous comparative studies. For example in [5], PLATT's SVM SMO algorithm was presented to outperform naive Bayes. But only 50 features were selected for naive Bayes. It is a very restricted feature set size, considering that the best performance occurs with larger number of features. On the other hand, SVM was used with 300 features, which may not be far from the optimal setting. Indeed, we can confirm that SVM outperformed any other classifier for such small feature space.

Other studies [6,7] found naive Bayes to perform worse than SVM and kNN. The number of features selected in [6] seem consistent with our results (2000 for naive Bayes, 2415 for kNN and 10000 for SVM). However, the experimental conditions were rather different. Indeed, Reuters-21578 was used. But the document frequency per class varies widely. About 33% of the categories have less than 10 documents, whereas the most common 2 categories have more than 2000 documents each. So, Reuters-21578 is probably not the best choice for doing reliable classifier comparisons since many factors related to dataset properties may affect the comparisons.

Moreover, comparisons were done on multi-class classification tasks [6,7] or on the averaged performance of the set of *one against all* classification tasks [5,7]. But as explained earlier, comparing a single multi-class naive Bayes (or kNN) to n SVM classifiers (n the number of categories) is definitively not fair for naive Bayes (or kNN).

4   Conclusion

When investigating the best parameter settings for the SVM, the *linear* kernel was found to be the best choice together with a large value of ϵ. This is consistent with previous works. However, a surprising result is a relatively good performance of SVM with small or medium size feature space. Regards kNN, the optimal number k is interestingly close to the ones used in other work.

Both kNN, naive Bayes and SVM achieve very similar performance if suitable parameter settings are used. These results are in agreements with a recent study [12] showing that the set-up parameters have a more important affect on performance than the individual choice of a particular learning technique. Therefore, one should keep considering kNN and naive Bayes as possible options because they are fast, simple and well understood. Regards SVM, perhaps it can handle better complex classification tasks, but it remains to be seen how we can identify them. Moreover, the cost to train SVM is a clear weakness.

However, results highly depend of the adopted methodology and we have focused here on binary classification tasks. For this purpose, new experiments should be carried out to explain why naive Bayes behave so well on *one against one* classification tasks in opposite of *one against all* tasks. Also, one would like to know why a *wave pattern* occurs when the number of features is increased for SVM. Moreover, if we are interested to recommend a classifier with suitable parameter settings, we should have a good way of characterizing the given documents and develop a good meta-learning strategy for achieving that.

Acknowledgements

The Portuguese Pluri-annual support provided by FCT and funding under the FCT project SUMO is gratefully acknowledged. This work has also been partially supported by the

Netherlands Bioinformatics Centre (NBIC) through its research programme BioRange. Finally, The first author wishes to express his gratitude to LIACC-NIAAD where this work was initiated.

References

1. Rogati, M., Yang, Y.: High-performing feature selection for text classification. In: 11th International Conference on Information and Knowledge Management. (2002) 659–661.
2. Yang, Y., Pedersen, J.O.: A comparative study on feature selection in text categorization. In: 14th International Conference on Machine Learning. (1997) 412–420.
3. Mitchell, T.M.: Machine Learning. McGraw-Hill (1997).
4. Joachims, T.: Making large-scale support vector machine learning practical. In: Advances in Kernel Methods: Support Vector Machines. (1998).
5. Dumais, S., Platt, J., Heckerman, D., Sahami, M.: Inductive learning algorithms and representations for text categorization. In: 7th International Conference on Information and Knowledge Management. (1998) 148–155.
6. Yang, Y., Liu, X.: A re-examination of text categorization methods. In: 22nd International Conference on Research and Development in Information Retrieval. (1999) 42–49.
7. Zhang, T., Oles, F.J.: Text categorization based on regularized linear classification methods. Information Retrieval (2001) 5–31.
8. Fürnkranz, J.: Pairwise classification as an ensemble technique. In: 13th European Conference on Machine Learning. (2002) 97–110.
9. McCallum, A.K.: Bow: A toolkit for statistical language modeling, text retrieval, classification and clustering. http://www.cs.cmu.edu/~mccallum/bow (1996).
10. Yang, Y.: An evaluation of statistical approaches to text categorization. Information Retrieval (1999) 69–90.
11. McCallum, A., Nigam, K.: A comparison of event models for naive bayes text classification. AAAI-98 Workshop on Learning for Text Categorization (1998).
12. Daelemans, W., Hoste, V., Meulder, F.D., Naudts, B.: Combined optimization of feature selection and algorithm parameters in machine learning of language. In: 14th European Conference of Machine Learning. (2003) 84–95.
13. Yang, Y.: A scalability analysis of classifiers in text categorization. In: 26th International Conference on Research and Development in Information Retrieval. (2003).

A Knowledge Based Strategy for Recognising Textual Entailment*

Óscar Ferrández, Rafael M. Terol, Rafael Muñoz, Patricio Martínez-Barco,
and Manuel Palomar

Natural Language Processing and Information Systems Group
Department of Software and Computing Systems
University of Alicante, Alicante, Spain
{ofe, rafamt, rafael, patricio, mpalomar}@dlsi.ua.es

Abstract. This paper presents a knowledge based textual entailment approach comprising two stages. The first stage consists of inferring the logic forms for both the text and the hypothesis. The logic forms are obtained by analysing the dependency relations between words. The second stage carries out a comparison between the inferred logic forms by means of WordNet relations. This comparison aims at establishing the existence of an entailment relation. This approach has been evaluated within the PASCAL Second RTE Challenge and achieved 60% average precision.

1 Introduction

A well-known problem in Natural Language Processing (NLP) is the existence of a wide variety of expressions stating the same meaning. An automatic method that can determine how two sentences relate to each other in terms of semantic relations or textual entailment would be very useful for robust NLP applications.

Textual entailment has been recently defined as a common solution for modelling language variability [1]. Textual entailment is defined as a relation holding between two natural language expressions, a text (T) and an entailment hypothesis (H) that is entailed by T. The following example is a true entailment.

T: His family has steadfastly denied the charges.
H: The charges were denied by his family.

Many NLP applications need to recognize when the meaning of one text can be expressed by, or inferred from, another text. The textual entailment phenomenon captures broadly the reasoning about this language variability. Recognising this phenomenon is, without doubt, a complex task and great obstacle for NLP applications. For example, in a Question Answering (QA) system the same answer could be expressed in different syntactic and semantic ways, and a textual entailment module could help a QA system in identifying the forecast answers that entail the expected answer. Similarly, in other applications such us Information Extraction a textual entailment tool could help by discovering different variants expressing

---

* This research has been partially funded by the Spanish Government under project CICyT number TIC2003-07158-C04-01.

Petr Sojka, Ivan Kopeček and Karel Pala (Eds.): TSD 2006, LNAI 4188, pp. 53–60, 2006.

the same concept. In multi-document summarization, it could use to identify redundant information among the most informative sentences and, therefore, eliminate duplicates. In general, a textual entailment tool would be profitable for a better performance of many NLP applications.

The PASCAL RTE (Recognising Textual Entailment) Challenge [2] introduces a common task and evaluation framework for textual entailment, covering a broad range of semantic-oriented inferences needed for practical applications. This task is therefore suitable for evaluating and comparing semantic-oriented models in a generic manner. Participants in the evaluation exercise are provided with pairs of small text snippets (one or more sentences in English), which the organizers term Text-Hypothesis (T-H) pairs. Participating systems have to decide for each T-H pair whether T indeed entails H or not, and their results are then compared to the manual annotation.

In this paper we present a system based on knowledge for solving the textual entailment phenomenon, as opposed to other authors who solve the problem of textual entailment by means of machine learning techniques. Our system attempts to recognise textual entailment by determining if the text and the hypothesis are related by deriving logic forms from the text and the hypothesis, and by finding relations between their predicates using WordNet.

The rest of the paper is organized as follows. The next section presents a brief background of textual entailment. The architecture of our system is provided in Section 3, evaluation and performance analysis are presented in Section 4, and the conclusions and future work are drawn in Section 5.

2   Background

The recognition of the textual entailment phenomenon is a novel task within the NLP field. The research community has a strong interest in the RTE task. A clear example of this interest is the organization of several Workshops such as the PASCAL Challenge Workshops[1] and the ACL Workshop on Empirical Modeling of Semantic Equivalence and Entailment[2]. The RTE task has an important potential in support of other NLP applications.

We may distinguish two main different approaches adopted by researchers in order to solve the RTE task. On the one hand, there are approaches based on knowledge techniques, which normally use linguistic resources and, on the other hand, approaches using machine learning and statistical methods to induce specific entailment relations.

Normally, the approaches based on machine learning and statistical methods apply statistical measures over large textual collections or obtain a pool of suitable features for future integration into a machine learning algorithm. For example, Glickman and Dagan [3] propose a general probabilistic setting that formalises the notion of textual entailment. Bos and Markert [4] present a decision tree trained using features obtained by shallow and deep NLP methods. Another research effort in was carried out by Zanzotto et al. [5]. They investigate the prototypical textual forms that describe entailment relations, calling them *textual entailment patterns*. These patterns are analysed by both analysing large textual collections and applying statistical measures relevant for the task.

---

[1] http://www.pascal-network.org/Challenges/RTE/
[2] http://acl.ldc.upenn.edu/W/W05/

On the other hand, the approaches based on knowledge techniques are characterized by applying lexical resources: representing text with logic forms, generating dependency trees and analysing semantic similarity measures are some of the knowledge-based methods employed so far. Akhmatova [6] describes a system based on syntax-driven semantic analysis and uses the notion of atomic proposition as main element for entailment recognition. Herrera et al. [7], converts texts into dependency. These trees are compared with a simple matching algorithm, and the lexical entailment relations obtained using WordNet. Another work on dependency trees is reported by Kouylekov and Magnini [8]. The authors use a tree edit distance algorithm applied to the dependency trees of the texts.

Although there are many approaches that rely on statistical and machine learning methods, the main trend towards solving the textual entailment phenomenon is to provide the systems with knowledge resources. This is due to the fact that RTE is dependent on a deep semantic understanding of the text. Therefore, establishing suitable parameters for the machine learning algorithms, during the training and test phases, is hard to achieve. Moreover, using semantic resources such as WordNet seems appropriate for the detection of semantic relations between two fragments of text.

3   System Architecture

Our present work focuses on the development of a textual entailment system based on knowledge techniques. Our system consists of two main components: the first one derives the logic forms and the other one computes the similarity measures between logic forms. The former embodies various advanced natural language processing techniques that derive from the text and the hypothesis the associated logic forms. The latter component realizes a computation of similarity measures between the logic forms associated with the text and the hypothesis. This computational process provides us with a score illustrating the similarity of the derived logic forms. Depending on the value of this score, we will decide if the two logic forms (text and hypothesis) are related or not. If the logic forms are related then the entailment between the text and the hypothesis is true. Otherwise, there is no entailment relation holding between the texts.

An overview of our system is depicted in Figure 1. The following sections will describe in detail the main components of our system.

3.1   Derivation of the Logic Forms

The logic form of a sentence is derived through an analysis of dependency relationships between the words of the sentence. Our approach employs a set of rules that infer several aspects such as the assert, its type, its identifier and the relationships between the different asserts in the logic form. This technique is clearly distinguished from other logic form derivation techniques such as Moldovan's [9] that constructs the logic form through the syntactic tree obtained as output of the syntactic parser. Our logic form, similar to Moldovan's logic form, is based on the logic form format defined in the eXtended WordNet [10].

As an example, the logic form "*story:NN(x14) of:IN(x14, x13) variant:NN (x10) NNC(x11, x10, x12) fly:NN(x12) and:CC(x13, x11, x6) emergency:NN(x5) NNC(x6, x5, x7) rescue:NN(x8) NNC(x7, x8, x9) committee:NN(x9) who:NN(x1) save:VB(e1, x1, x2) thousand:NN(x2) in:IN(e1, x3) marseille:NN(x3)*" is automatically inferred from the analysis of

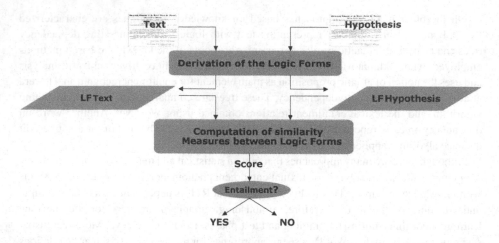

Fig. 1. System architecture

dependency relationships between the words of the sentence *"The story of Variant Fly and the Emergency Rescue Committee who saved thousands in Marseille"*. In this format of logic form each assert has at least one argument. The first argument is usually instantiated with the identifier of the assert and the rest of the arguments are identifiers of other asserts related to it. For instance, the assert *"story:NN(x14)"*, has the type noun *(NN)* and the identifier $x14$; the assert *"NNC(x11, x10, x12)"*. has the type complex nominal *(NNC)*, and its identifier is $x11$. and the other two arguments indicate the relationships to other asserts: $x10$ and $x12$.

3.2   Computation of Similarity Measures Between Logic Forms

This section presents the method employed by our system in order to obtain a similarity score between the logic forms. This method is focused on initially analysing the relation between the logic form predicates corresponding to the verbs of the text and the hypothesis respectively. Then. if there is any relation between the two verbs, the method will analyse the relations between the logic form predicates of the words depending on the two verbs. All the weights provided by the analysis of these relations are summed and then normalized, thus obtaining the final normalized-relation score. This method is described by the pseudo-code below.

```
simWeight = 0
Tvb = obtainVerbs(T)
Hvb = obtainVerbs(H)
for i = 0 ... size(Tvb) do
    for j = 0 ... size(Hvb) do
        if calculateSim(Tvb(i),Hvb(j)) ≠ 0 then
            simWeight += calculateSim(Tvb(i),Hvb(j))
            Telem = obtainElem(Tvb(i))
            Helem = obtainElem(Hvb(j))
            simWeight += calculateSim(Telem,Helem)
```

end if
   end for
end for
if simWeight > threshold **then**
   return *TRUE*
else
   return *FALSE*
end if

In order to calculate the similarity between the predicates (*calculateSim(x,y)*), two approaches have been implemented: one based on WordNet relations and another one based on Lin's measure [11]. Both of them are based on WordNet hierarchy, and they are described in detail below. A Word Sense Disambiguation module was not employed in deriving the WordNet relations between any two predicates. Only the first 50% of the WordNet senses were taken into account. The threshold, above which one can consider that the text entails the hypothesis, has been obtained empirically using the development data.

Approach Based on WordNet Relations. In the WordNet lexical database [12], a synset is a set of concepts that express the same meaning. A concept is defined as the use of one word in one determined context (sense). Thus, this task deals determining if two different concepts are related through the composition of different WordNet relations: hypernymy, hyponymy, entailment, similarity, meronymy and holonymy. The length of the path that relates the two different concepts must be lower or equal than 4 synsets. A weight has been assigned to each one of the WordNet relations: 0.8 for the hypernymy relationship, 0.7 for the hyponymy and entailment relationships, 0.9 for the similarity relationship, and 0.5 for the meronimy and holonymy relationships. Then, the weight of the path between two different concepts is calculated as the product of the weights associated to the relations connecting the intermediate synsets. This technique is different from the SpreadWeights algorithm [13], even though derived from it.

Approach Based on Lin's Measure. In this case, the similarities were computed using Lin's similarity measure [11] as implemented in WordNet::Similarity[3] [14]. WordNet::Similarity is an open source software package developed at the University of Minnesota. It allows the user to measure the semantic similarity or relatedness between a pair of concepts, as well as between a pair of words. WordNet::Similarity provides three measures of relatedness and six measures of similarity based on the WordNet lexical database. The similarity measures are based on analysing the WordNet *is-a* relations.

The similarity measures of WordNet::Similarity are divided into two groups: path-based and information content-based. For our experiments, we have chosen an information content-based similarity measure called Lin's similarity measure.

Lin's similarity measure augments the information content of the least common subsumer (LCS[4]) of the two concepts with the sum of the information content of the concepts themselves. The Lin's measure scales the information content of the LCS by this sum.

---
[3] http://www.d.umn.edu/~tpederse/similarity.html
[4] LCS is the most specific concept that two concepts share as an ancestor.

4 Evaluation

In order to evaluate our system for the textual entailment task, we used the corpus provided by the PASCAL Second Recognising Textual Entailment Challenge[5]. The organizers of this challenge provide participants with development and test corpora, both of them with 800 sentence pairs (text and hypothesis) manually annotated for logical entailment. It consists of four subsets, which correspond to typical success and failure settings in different applications such as Information Extraction (IE), Information Retrieval (IR), Question Answering (QA) and Multi-document summarization (SUM). Within each application setting the annotators selected both positive entailment examples (annotated YES) as well as negative examples (annotated NO), where entailment does not hold (50%-50% split). The organizers have also established two measures for evaluating the systems. The judgments returned by the systems will be compared to those manually assigned by the human annotators. The percentage of matching judgments will provide the *accuracy* of the run, i.e. the fraction of correct responses. As a second measure, an *Average Precision* measure will be computed. This measure evaluates the ability of systems to rank all the pairs in the test set according to their entailment confidence, in decreasing order from the most certain entailment to the least certain. *Average precision* is a common evaluation measure for system rankings. More formally, it can be written as follows:

$$Average\_Precision = \frac{1}{R}(\sum_{i=1}^{n} E(i)\frac{\#\_correct\_up\_to\_pair\_i}{i}) \tag{1}$$

where n is the number of the pairs in the test set, R is the total number of positive pairs in the test set, $E(i)$ is 1 if the i-th pair is positive and 0 otherwise, and i ranges over the pairs, ordered by their ranking.

For evaluating our system we consider appropriate to carry out two different runs. Both runs were based on deriving the logic forms from the text and the hypothesis. However, our *LINrun* computes the similarity measures between logic forms by means of Lin's similarity measure, whereas the *WNrun* uses our approach based on WordNet relations. The results obtained by the PASCAL RTE2 evaluation script for the development and test data are shown in Table 1.

Table 1. Results obtained by the PASCAL RTE2 evaluation script

			overall	IE	IR	QA	SUM
development	LINrun	Accuracy	0.5462	0.5421	0.5440	0.5722	0.5260
	WNrun	Accuracy	0.5273	0.5510	0.5345	0.4677	0.5686
test	LINrun	Accuracy	0.5563	0.4950	0.5800	0.6100	0.5400
		Average Precision	0.6089	0.5722	0.6159	0.6431	0.6215
	WNrun	Accuracy	0.5475	0.4750	0.5850	0.6150	0.5150
		Average Precision	0.5743	0.5853	0.6113	0.5768	0.5589

As we can deduct from Table 1, the run using Lin's similarity measure achieves better results than the approach based on WordNet relations, both when tested on development, as

---

[5] http://www.pascal-network.org/Challenges/RTE2/

well as test data. This slight loss of accuracy is due to the fact that our WordNet relations approach (see Section 3.2) attempts to establish an objective semantic comparison between the logic forms rather than an entailment relation. Nevertheless, Lin's similarity measure, although not a pure entailment measure, seems to adapt good to the RTE task.

5   Conclusions and Future Work

This paper presents a system that deals with the textual entailment phenomenon. Our system derives the logic forms for the text/hypothesis pair and computes the similarity between them. The similarity is computed using two different measures: Lin's similarity measure and WordNet relation-based similarity measure. A score is therefore obtained, showing the semantic similarity between two logic forms. Although our system does not provide a specific entailment score, we found it challenging to evaluate it with the resources provided by Textual Entailment competition. We have achieved promising results for the RTE task, and the next step is to focalize our system for recognising only textual entailment.

As future work, we intend to perform a deeper study about the most suitable WordNet relations for recognising textual entailment. It is possible only hyponymy, synonymy and entailment relations between words belonging to the text and the hypothesis are more suitable for the entailment phenomenon. On the other hand, we are also interested in testing how other NLP tools can help in detecting textual entailment. For example, using a Named Entity Recognizer could help in detecting entailment between two segments of text.

References

1. Dagan, I., Glickman, O.: Probabilistic Textual Entailment: Generic Applied Modeling of Language Variability. In: PASCAL Workshop on Learning Methods for Text Understanding and Mining, Grenoble, France (2004) 26–29.
2. Dagan, I., Glickman, O., Magnini, B.: The PASCAL recognising textual entailment challenge. In: Proceedings of the PASCAL Challenges Workshop on Recognising Textual Entailment, Southampton, UK (2005) 1–8.
3. Glickman, O., Dagan, I.: A Probabilistic Setting and Lexical Cooccurrence Model for Textual Entailment. In: Proceedings of the ACL Workshop on Empirical Modeling of Semantic Equivalence and Entailmen, Ann Arbor, Michigan (2005) 43–48.
4. Bos, J., Markert, K.: Combining Shallow and Deep NLP Methods for Recognizing Textual Entailment. In: Proceedings of the PASCAL Challenges Workshop on Recognising Textual Entailment, Southampton, UK (2005) 65–68.
5. Zanzotto, F.M., Pazienza, M.T., Pennacchiotti, M.: Discovering Entailment Relations Using "Textual Entailment Patterns". In: Proceedings of the ACL Workshop on Empirical Modeling of Semantic Equivalence and Entailment, Ann Arbor, Michigan (2005) 37–42.
6. Akhmatova, E.: Textual Entailment Resolution via Atomic Propositions. In: Proceedings of the PASCAL Challenges Workshop on Recognising Textual Entailment, Southampton, UK (2005) 61–64.
7. Herrera, J., Peñas, A., Verdejo, F.: Textual Entailment Recognition Based on Dependency Analysis and WordNet. In: Proceedings of the PASCAL Challenges Workshop on Recognising Textual Entailment, Southampton, UK (2005) 21–24.
8. Kouylekov, M., Magnini, B.: Recognizing Textual Entailment with Tree Edit Distance Algorithms. In: Proceedings of the PASCAL Challenges Workshop on Recognising Textual Entailment, Southampton, UK (2005) 17–20.

9. Moldovan, D., Rus, V.: Logic Form Transformation of Wordnet and its Applicability to Question-Answering. In: Proceedings of 39th Annual Meeting of the Association for Computational Linguistics, Toulouse, France (2001).
10. Harabagiu, S., Miller, G., Moldovan, D.: WordNet 2 - A Morphologically and Semantically Enhanced Resource. In: Proceedings of ACL-SIGLEX99: Standardizing Lexical Resources, Maryland (1999) 1–8.
11. Lin, D.: An Information-Theoretic Definition of Similarity. In: Proceedings of the 15th International Conference on Machine Learning. (1998) 296–304.
12. Miller, G.: WordNet: An on-line lexical database. In: International Journal of Lexicography 3, 4. (1990) 235–312.
13. Moldovan, D., Novischi, A.: Lexical Chains for Question Answering. In: Proceedings of the 19th international conference on Computational linguistics - Volume 1, Taipei, Taiwan (2002) 1–7.
14. Pedersen, T., Patwardhan, S., Michelizzi, J.: WordNet::Similarity - Measuring the Relatedness of Concepts. In: Proceedings of the 19th National Conference on Artificial Intelligence, San Jose, CA (2004).

Paragraph-Level Alignment of an English-Spanish Parallel Corpus of Fiction Texts Using Bilingual Dictionaries*

Alexander Gelbukh, Grigori Sidorov, and José Ángel Vera-Félix

Natural Language and Text Processing Laboratory
Center for Research in Computer Science
National Polytechnic Institute
Av. Juan Dios Batiz, s/n, Zacatenco, 07738, Mexico City, Mexico
`sidorov@cic.ipn.mx`
`http://www.Gelbukh.com`

Abstract. Aligned parallel corpora are very important linguistic resources useful in many text processing tasks such as machine translation, word sense disambiguation, dictionary compilation, etc. Nevertheless, there are few available linguistic resources of this type, especially for fiction texts, due to the difficulties in collecting the texts and high cost of manual alignment. In this paper, we describe an automatically aligned English-Spanish parallel corpus of fiction texts and evaluate our method of alignment that uses linguistic data-namely, on the usage of existing bilingual dictionaries-to calculate word similarity. The method is based on the simple idea: if a meaningful word is present in the source text then one of its dictionary translations should be present in the target text. Experimental results of alignment at paragraph level are described.

1 Introduction

Current development of corpus linguistics and machine learning methods in text processing leads to increasing importance of text corpora, from raw texts to texts marked up with certain additional linguistic information: phonetic, morphological, syntactic, word senses, semantic roles, etc. The simplest form of such marks is linguistic information on the text itself: e.g., part of speech marks on the words. A more interesting kind of marks relates elements of the text to some external source: some another text, multimedia items [12], multimodal streams [15], pragmatic situation, etc. In spite of great importance of such information, there exist few corpora offering it.

In this paper we are interested in a specific kind of corpora with such external information: aligned parallel texts, i.e., texts that express the same information in two different languages, with the structural parts (units) of these texts that are mutual translations explicitly related to each other by the markup. The procedure of establishing such relation is called alignment. There are various levels of alignment depending on what is considered a unit:

– Document: we just know that two documents express the same information in two different languages (in case of very short texts, such as news messages or paper abstracts, this can be directly useful);

---

* Work done under partial support of Mexican Government (CONACyT, SNI) and National Polytechnic Institute, Mexico (SIP, COFAA, PIFI).

- Paragraph: it is indicated which paragraphs are mutual translations;
- Sentence: similarly, but the information is given for individual sentences;
- Phrase (such as noun phrase) or word.

A unit in a parallel text can have one, several, or no counterparts: for example, a sentence can be translated by several ones; some words can be omitted, etc. This makes alignment of parallel texts quite a difficult task. Such situation is especially frequent in fiction texts, which we discuss in this paper.

An obvious source of parallel texts is Internet. Unfortunately, texts presented in Internet are difficult to process: they may contain pictures, special formatting, HTML tags, etc. Often the texts are in PDF format and during their conversion into plain text format the information about paragraph boundaries is lost. Rather extended preprocessing, often manual, is necessary for these texts. We will not discuss here this process, as well as the problem of automatic search of parallel texts in Internet.

The importance of aligned parallel corpora is closely related to the presence of structural differences between languages. On the one hand the differences make the alignment task very difficult, but on the other hand, they can be exploited for automatic extraction of information on various linguistic phenomena-for example, for word sense disambiguation. An obvious application of parallel corpora is machine translation [1], from dictionary compilation to example-based machine translation.[1] Examples of other applications are automatic extraction of data for machine learning methods, bilingual lexicography [8,13], and language teaching.

There are two major classes of alignment methods: those based on statistical data and those using additional linguistic knowledge.[2] This distinction is not related to methods of processing but to types of information involved.

Statistical methods usually exploit the expected correlation of length of text units (paragraphs or sentences) in different languages [5,9] and try to establish the correspondence between the units of the predicted size. The size can be measured in words or characters. Linguistic-based methods, on the other hand, use linguistic data for establishing the correspondence between structural units.

Statistical methods work well for texts when very literal translation is necessarily, like texts of laws or technical manuals. For fiction texts, where the structure of the original and the translation can vary significantly, it is more desirable to use linguistic methods, though they require more thorough processing. Linguistic methods can also be used for alignment at word level, though they require not only dictionaries, like the method described in this paper, but also some additional syntactic information or syntactic heuristics. For example, translation of an adjective should not be too far from the translation of the noun it modifies, etc.

The idea of application of dictionaries to alignment problem is not new [2,10,11,13]; of recent works the paper [4] can be mentioned. Still, it is not as popular as statistical methods-probably due to the fact that the dictionaries are not so easily available. Usually, as we have mentioned above, the experiments on parallel texts are conducted using specialized texts, like texts of Canadian or European parliament, legal texts, or programming help files. The

---

[1] Perhaps the most famous example of application of parallel texts is deciphering of Egyptian hieroglyphs based on the parallel texts of Rosetta stone.

[2] Similarly to, say, word sense disambiguation [6] and many other language processing tasks.

problem we are dealing with in this paper is how a method based on a bilingual dictionary method performs for fiction texts.

The main idea behind this method is that if a meaningful word is present in one text then one of its dictionary translations should be present in the other text. So, even if some words are omitted, the presence of the translation of other words allows for alignment at least at the level of paragraph or sentence. The situation is more complicated at the word level, because, as we mentioned, it requires not only lexical information from the dictionaries, but also syntactic information.

The paper is organized as follows. First we describe the English-Spanish parallel corpus compiled for fiction texts of significant size. Then we present a method of alignment based on the use of bilingual dictionaries. Finally, we discuss the experiments on evaluation of automatic alignment conducted at paragraph level.

2 Preparation of the Parallel Corpus

We began with preparation of a bilingual corpus, i.e., with compilation and preprocessing of parallel texts. Generally speaking, a corpus can contain texts of different genres, like fiction, newspaper articles, technical manuals, etc. In our case, we chose fiction genre because it is the most non-trivial case of translation. Sometimes, fiction texts present the situations that are difficult for automatic processing: for example, if one of the texts contains a joke, it is possible that the other text will contain a joke that has nothing in common with the original. I.e., the fiction translation is not literal.

On the other hand, there are many fiction texts in Internet, while variety of possible parallel texts of other genres is lower.

We included the following titles in our corpus: *Alice's adventures in wonderland, Through the looking-glass, The adventures of Sherlock Holmes, The turn of the screw, The jungle book, Frankenstein, Dracula, Advances in genetics,*[3] *Five weeks in a balloon, From the earth to the moon, Michael Strogoff, Twenty thousand leagues under the sea* by Lewis Carroll, Arthur Conan Doyle, Henry James, Rudyard Kipling, Mary Shelley, Bram Stoker, Ubídia, Abdón, and Jules Verne, correspondingly, with their Spanish equivalents. The texts were originally in PDF format and were preprocessed manually for elimination of special format elements, Internet links, and for restoration of paragraph boundaries. The size of corpus is more than 11.5 MB. The corpus size might seem too small, but this is a parallel corpus, for which the data are very difficult to obtain. Our corpus is freely available upon request for research purposes.

3 Alignment Based on Bilingual Dictionaries

Our task is alignment of structural units (parts) of texts, such as paragraphs and sentences. We do not consider words for the moment because of the lack of syntactic information necessary for this type of alignment. Note that the correspondence of paragraphs and sentences in the source and target texts is not necessarily one-to-one; see an example in Table 1.

We use lemmatization of words. For Spanish, we apply the morphological analyzer AGME [14] that allows for analysis of grammar forms of 26,000 lexemes, i.e., more than a million grammar forms; for English we use a similar morphological analyzer [6] based

---

[3] This is a fiction text, not a scientific text.

Table 1. Example of alignment of paragraphs with pattern 2-to-1

Spanish	Literal English translation	Real English text
Luego, al percatarse	*After this, when she*	*When she saw my*
de mi gesto	*noticed my*	*baffled look, she*
estupefacto,	*surprised gesture,*	*corrected herself: "My*
corrigió:	*she corrected herself:*	*grandmother."*
— No. Es mi abuela.	*"No, this is my grandmother."*	

on the morphological dictionary of WordNet with about 60,000 lexemes. Thus, all words in the pair of texts are normalized before we begin any further processing. We do not resolve morphological homonymy; instead, we consider the presence of homonymic lemmas as a source of possible translations. It is justified by the fact that often the only difference between morphological homonyms is their part of speech, i.e., semantically they are similar (*work* vs. *to work*). Also, often a word can be translated into the other language using a different part of speech. It may be even useful in future work to search the translations of all related words of different parts of speech—at least in some cases. If the morphological analyzer does not succeed with analysis of a word then we treat it as a literal string and search for exact matching in the other text. This is useful, for example, for proper names.

We filter out all auxiliary words, i.e., if at least one morphological homonym is an auxiliary word (preposition, article, conjunction, or pronoun) then we do not consider it for further comparison. This corresponds to the use of a stop word list, but in our case we rely on morphological analyzers to determine whether the word should be considered or not. It is justified by the very high frequency of this type of words, so that they can be present practically in any sentence or paragraph.

3.1 Similarity Measure

Dictionary-based methods use some similarity measure. Sometimes it is a global optimization, as in [10], and sometimes local, as in [4]. We used the simplest local measure. The main idea of the implemented method is that if a meaningful word appears in a sentence or paragraph of the source text, then one of its possible translations given in a bilingual dictionary should appear in the corresponding part of the target text. It is not always so, because a word can be translated by several words, omitted, or substituted by a far synonym that does not appear as a translation variant in the dictionary.

In the future it is interesting to analyze the cases of absence of translation. For example, we expect that many such cases occur due to the presence of idiomatic expressions. This may allow for automatic extraction of such expressions. In case of translation of a word using non-idiomatic word combination, it is natural to expect that at least one word in this word combination would be its dictionary translation.

These considerations allow for introducing a measure of similarity between two structural units for a pair of parallel texts. We use as the measure of similarity a coefficient similar to the well-known Dice coefficient:

$$Similarity = \frac{2x}{y+z} \times \begin{cases} \frac{1}{K} & \text{if } K \geq 1, \\ K & \text{if } K < 1, \end{cases}$$

where y is the size in words of the source text unit, z is the size of the target text unit, x is the number of intersections of the two units counted as the presence of any dictionary translation of a source text word in the target text unit; $K = y \times k/z$, k is an expected coefficient of correspondence of the number of words in source and target texts: namely, $k = Z/Y$, where Z and Y are the total number of words in the target and the source text, correspondingly. This measure differs from the traditional Dice coefficient in the parameter K, which penalizes the units with too different sizes.

For the current version of the algorithm we used Spanish-English dictionary with about 30,000 entries. In the future, we plan to use English-Spanish dictionary as well, because it is not guaranteed that the dictionaries are symmetric. We will use the average value of similarity calculated with both dictionaries.

3.2 Algorithm

Currently we use an *ad hoc* alignment algorithm that passes through the units of the source text and analyzes three immediately available units from the target text, i.e., we search only the alignment patterns 1-to-1, 1-to-2, 1-to-3, 2-to-1, and 3-to-1 paragraphs. It is not a complete scheme, but it serves for evaluation of quality of the results of our dictionary-based method of alignment. Other patterns are extremely rare and in fact did not occur in our experiments with paragraphs. In the future, we plan to use a genetic algorithm for searching for the global alignment optimum, as in [7] for word sense disambiguation. Other possibilities are to use dynamic programming [5] or simulated annealing [3].

For improvement of the performance of the algorithm we also implemented an anchor points technique. Anchor points are short units with very high similarity. They serve for limiting the effect of cascaded errors during alignment, since the algorithm restarts after each anchor point. With this, if an error occurs, it will not affect alignment of the whole text. The algorithm performs two passes. First, it searches for anchor points, and then it processes the units between the anchor points.

The algorithm implements the following processing: it takes a unit from the source text (Spanish in our case), calculates the similarity of the patterns 1-to-1, 1-to-2, 1-to-3, 2-to-1, and 3-to-1 taking into account two subsequent units from the source text and three current units from the target text (English). Then it selects the pattern with the best similarity score and continues from the next available units in the source and target texts.

4 Experimental Results

The results of an experiment for 50 patterns of paragraphs of the text *Dracula* are presented in Table 2. The precision of the method in this experiment was 94%. Here we dealt with non-literal translations of the fiction texts.

An example of an error of our method is presented in Table 3. The paragraph is rather small that makes the correct solution less probable. Usually, the larger is the unit, the more probable it is to obtain correct similarity. It is so because it is more probable to find a word and its translation.

The paragraph in Table 3 would present difficulties for statistical methods as well, because the size of the English unit is 21 words, while the size of the Spanish one is only 11 words. There are only three words that have translations given in the dictionary or direct

Table 2. Alignment results for 50 patterns of paragraphs

Patterns found	Correct	Incorrect
1–1	27	0
1–2	8	2
1–3	6	0
2–1	7	0
3–1	2	1

Table 3. Alignment results for 50 patterns of paragraphs

English text	Spanish text	Literal translation
"Suppose that there should turn out to be no such person as Dr. Fergusson?" exclaimed another voice, with a malicious twang.	*>Y si el doctor Fergusson no existiera? —preguntó una voz maliciosa.*	*"And if Doctor Fergusson does not exist?" asked a malicious voice.*

string matching: *voice, malicious, Fergusson*. There are 9 meaningful words in the English paragraph and 6 in the Spanish paragraph. The words that are presented as translations but do not have correspondence in the dictionary are: *ask* and *exclaim*. In order to detect that it is something related, we should use, for example, some additional dictionary with marked-up hyponymic relations, such as WordNet. The other words are really different, though they carry the same meaning: *turn out to be no such person = not exist*. A grammatical way of expression of conditional mode is used in Spanish, while in English a special construction appears: *suppose that there should exist* vs. Spanish *existiera*.

This is a representative case of the most difficult situation consisting in non-literal translation of a short unit. The situation is worse if there are several subsequent units of this type because the possibility of wrong alignment increases. We expect that adding more dictionary information (synonyms, hyponyms), syntactic information, and genetic algorithm as optimization technique will alleviate this problem.

5 Conclusions and Future Work

We have presented an English-Spanish parallel corpus of fiction texts of considerable size freely available for researchers and discussed a dictionary-based method of alignment as applied to fiction texts. The experiment conducted at the paragraph alignment level shows that the dictionary-based method has high precision (94%) for non-literal translations.

In the future, we plan to implement a better alignment algorithm based on genetic algorithm with global optimization. Another direction of improvement of the method is the use of other types of dictionaries with synonymic and homonymic relations, such as WordNet. Also, the method can beneficiate from weighting the distance between a word and its possible translation, especially in case of the large units, because some words can occur in a unit as translation of the other word and not the one we are looking for.

It is also interesting to analyze the influence of the special treatment of morphological homonyms. As to alignment at the word level, we plan to try some additional syntactic heuristics. As a possible application, we plan to analyze the cases of absence of translations, as discussed above.

References

1. Brown, P. F., Lai, J. C., and Mercer, R. L. 1991. Aligning Sentences in Parallel Corpora. In: *Proceedings of the 29th Annual Meeting of the Association for Computational Linguistics*, Berkeley, California, pp. 169–176.
2. Chen, S. 1993. Aligning sentences in bilingual corpora using lexical information. In: *Proceeding of ACL '93*, pp. 9–16.
3. Cowie, J., J. A. Guthrie, L. Guthrie. Lexical disambiguation using simulated annealing. In *Proc. of the International Conference on Computational Linguistics*, 1992, 359–365.
4. Kit, Chunyu, Jonathan J. Webster, King Kui Sin, Haihua Pan, Heng Li. 2004. Clause alignment for Hong Kong legal texts: A lexical-based approach. *International Journal of Corpus Linguistics* 9:1. pp. 29–51.
5. Gale, W. A., and Church, K. W. 1991. A program for Aligning Sentences in Bilingual Corpora. In: *Proceedings of the 29th Annual Meeting of the Association for Computational Linguistics*, Berkeley, California.
6. Gelbukh, Alexander, and Grigori Sidorov. 2003. Approach to construction of automatic morphological analysis systems for inflective languages with little effort. *Lecture Notes in Computer Science*, N 2588, Springer-Verlag, pp. 215–220.
7. Gelbukh, Alexander, Grigori Sidorov, SangYong Han. 2005. On Some Optimization Heuristics for Lesk-Like WSD Algorithms. *Lecture Notes in Computer Science*, Vol. 3513, Springer-Verlag, pp. 402–405.
8. McEnery, A. M., and Oakes, M. P. 1996. Sentence and word alignment in the CRATER project. In: J. Thomas and M. Short (eds), *Using Corpora for Language Research*, London, pp. 211–231.
9. Mikhailov, M. 2001. Two Approaches to Automated Text Aligning of Parallel Fiction Texts. *Across Languages and Cultures*, 2:1, pp. 87–96.
10. Kay, Martin and Martin Roscheisen. 1993. Text-translation alignment. *Computational Linguistics*, 19(1):121–142.
11. Langlais, Ph., M. Simard, J. Veronis. 1998. Methods and practical issues in evaluation alignment techniques. In: *Proceeding of Coling-ACL-98*.
12. Li, Wei, Maosong Sun. Automatic Image Annotation based on WordNet and Hierarchical Ensembles. In: A. Gelbukh (Ed.) Computational Linguistics and Intelligent Text Processing. Proc. of CICLing 2006. *Lecture Notes in Computer Science* N 3878, Springer, pp. 551–563.
13. Meyers, Adam, Michiko Kosaka, and Ralph Grishman. 1998. A Multilingual Procedure for Dictionary-Based Sentence Alignment. In: *Proceedings of AMTA '98: Machine Translation and the Information Soup*, pages 187–198.
14. Velásquez, F., Gelbukh, A. and Sidorov, G. 2002. AGME: un sistema de análisis y generación de la morfología del español. In: Proc. *Of Workshop Multilingual information access and natural language processing of IBERAMIA 2002 (8th Iberoamerican conference on Artificial Intelligence)*, Sevilla, España, November, 12, pp. 1–6.
15. Villaseñor Pineda, L., J. A. Massé Márquez, L. A. Pineda Cortés. Towards a Multimodal Dialogue Coding Scheme. In: A. Gelbukh (Ed.) *Computational Linguistics and Intelligent Text Processing*. Proc. of CICLing 2000. IPN, Mexico, pp. 551–563.

Some Methods of Describing Discontinuity in Polish and Their Cost-Effectiveness

Filip Graliński

Adam Mickiewicz University,
Faculty of Mathematics and Computer Science,
ul. Umultowska 87, 61-614 Poznań, Poland
filipg@amu.edu.pl

Abstract. The aim of this paper is to present some methods of handling discontinuity (and freer word order in general) within a medium-level grammatical framework. A context-free formalism and the "backbone" set of rules for verbal phrases are presented as the background for this paper. The main result consists in showing how discontinuous infinitive phrases and discontinuous noun phrases (interrogative phrases included) can be theoretically covered within the introduced formalism and similar grammatical frameworks. The second result reported in this paper is the cost-effectiveness analysis of introducing discontinuity rules into a medium-level grammatical framework: it turns out that attempting to cover some types of discontinuity may be unprofitable within a given grammatical framework. Although only examples from the Polish language are discussed, the described solutions are likely to be relevant for other languages with similar word order properties.

1 Introduction

In languages such as Polish, Russian, Finnish, Turkish or Latin, the word order is relatively free. Therefore, parsing such languages for practical applications (machine translation, question answering, grammar checking, etc.) requires, at least to some extent, the ability to handle free order of constituents (e.g. free subject-verb-object order) and their discontinuity.

The aim of this paper is to present some methods of dealing with free word order phenomena within a medium-level grammatical formalism, a formalism occupying a middle position on a continuum extending from shallow parsing formalisms to more sophisticated (and computationally more expensive) types of grammars such as HPSG or Lexical-Functional Grammar. Another objective is to try to delimit the extent of discontinuity that can successfully be handled within medium-level formalisms. Although all the solutions proposed in this paper are expressed within a specific grammatical formalism, the described methods should be applicable in any context-free grammatical formalism in which *tree operations* (see Section 1.1) are provided (e.g. in a DCG encoded in Prolog).

In Section 1.1 the grammatical framework addressed herein is presented. In Section 1.2 the rules of the VP backbone are introduced, whereas in central Sections 2 and 3 some types of discontinuity (resp. discontinuous infinitive clauses and discontinuous noun phrases) are discussed. Some remarks about other types of discontinuities are expressed in Section 4. Although only examples from Polish are given, the described solutions are likely to be relevant for other languages with similar word-order characteristics, e.g. other Slavonic languages.

Petr Sojka, Ivan Kopeček and Karel Pala (Eds.): TSD 2006, LNAI 4188, pp. 69–77, 2006.

When handling discontinuity in practice, one should be concerned not only with what could be done, but also with what is cost-effective, as discontinuity is relatively infrequent in Polish and false detection of discontinuity may result in particularly inaccurate and misleading interpretations of the input text. In Section 5 some preliminary experiments with real-world texts are presented.

1.1 Grammatical Framework

In this subsection, we briefly present the grammatical framework referred to in Sections 2 and 3. The framework as such (named *TgBGs* for *Tree-generating Binary Grammars*) was introduced in [6] and [7]. The formalism was partially inspired by the ideas given in [2], [3], and [5].

To introduce the grammatical framework, let us consider the following sample rule for noun phrases (for the incorporation of an adjective phrase):

```
np → ap np@ : la(modif) :
   ap.Case == Case && ap.Num == Num && ap.Gender == Gender
```

A grammar rule is composed of three parts separated by colons: a *production* (np → ap np@ in the above example), a *tree operation* (la(modif)), and an *attribute expression* (ap.Case == Case && ap.Num == Num && ap.Gender == Gender). A production is a unary or binary CFG-like rewriting rule. In addition, a symbol may be marked with an @ sign – by default the *attributes* (see below) of the newly formed node are copied from the node referred to by such a symbol. (If no symbol is marked with @, the values of the attributes are equal to 0 by default.) In the above example, the production states that an adjective phrase (ap) with a noun phrase (np on the right) constitute a noun phrase (np on the left) and that the attributes of the node representing the noun superphrase will be copied from the node representing the noun subphrase.

Syntax trees derived within the proposed framework are composed of symbols different than those of productions – production symbols form a "scaffolding" which could be discarded after parsing. Arcs connecting category nodes in a syntax tree are labelled with *syntactic roles*, such as *head*, *obj* (object), *subj* (subject), *modif* (modifier).

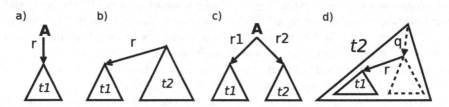

Fig. 1. Basic tree operations: (a) unary new node, (b) left attachment, (c) binary new node, (d) left insert

The shape of a syntax tree is determined with unary or binary (parametrised) tree operations associated with productions. For example, a binary tree operation $la(r)$ (t_1, t_2) (*left attachment*) specifies to attach tree t_1 to tree t_2 and label the arc connecting the root of t_1 and the root of t_2 with syntactic role r (see Figure 1b). The following basic tree operations are referred to in this paper: **identity** (id), **unary new node** of category A with syntactic role r $(nn(A, r)$; see Figure 1a), **binary new node** of category A with roles r_1 and r_2 $(nn(A, r_1, r_2)$; see Figure 1c), **left attachment** with syntactic role r $(la(r)$; see Figure 1b), **right attachment** with syntactic role r $(ra(r); ra(r)(t_1, t_2) = la(r)(t_2, t_1))$, **left insert** with syntactic role r into the daughter of role q $(li(q, r)$; see Figure 1d), **right insert** with syntactic role r $(ri(r); ri(q, r)(t_1, t_2) = li(q, r)(t_2, t_1))$.

Generally speaking, nn operations are used to introduce new tree nodes, with la/ra operations it is possible to construct flat syntax trees, and with li/ri – discontinuous ones.

Nodes of syntax trees may be augmented with *attributes* having atomic values (numbers and symbols starting with a lower-case letter). Attribute expressions are used to check conditions (e.g. agreement conditions) and to set values for attributes of new nodes. Standard C operators (assignment =, equality ==, negation !, AND operator &&, OR operator ||) are used in attribute expressions. Attribute names start with an upper-case letter. Attributes of the existing nodes are referenced with a dot (e.g $ap.Case$), whereas attributes of the newly created node are referred to in a direct manner (e.g. $Case$).

1.2 VP Backbone

The sentence structure is relatively flexible in Polish – generally speaking, any order of subject, verb and object is possible (though SVO is the most frequent order) [4].

In this subsection, a backbone of rules describing VPs is presented. We start with the verb (VP head), then attach constituents (subject, object, adverbial phrases, etc.) to the right of the verb and after all the right constituents are attached, we start attaching VP constituents on the left side. (A subject is assumed to be a constituent of a VP.) This way of specifying rules could be viewed as inducing head-driven parsing. Note that with the fixed direction (first the right constituents, then the left ones) spurious ambiguities are avoided.

The rules of the VP backbone are as follows:

rvp → v@ : nn(VP, head)
creating a new VP node with a verb (v) as its head

rvp → rvp@ advp : ra(modif)
attaching an adverbial phrase (advp) on the right

rvp → rvp@ np : ra(subj) :
  np.Case == nom && np.Gender==Gender && np.Num==Num
  && np.Person==Person && !SubjFilled && SubjFilled = r
  attaching the subject on the right; nom stands for nominative;
  SubjFilled is checked (!SubjFilled) and set (SubjFilled = r) to
  ensure that at most one subject is attached; (it is assumed that clauses of
  a conjunction are calculated from left to right – as in C)

rvp → rvp@ np : ra(obj) :
  np.Case == ObjCase && !ObjFilled && ObjFilled = r
  && ObjNum = np.Num && ObjGender = np.Gender
  attaching the nominal object; ObjCase is the required case of the object
  (usually accusative); the number (ObjNum) and gender (ObjGender) of
  the object is stored to be used later for discontinuous objects

```
lvp → rvp@ : id
```
all the right VP constituents have been attached; switching to the left side

```
lvp → advp lvp@ : la(modif)
```
attaching an adverbial phrase on the left

```
lvp → np lvp@ : la(subj) :
    np.Case == nom && np.Gender==Gender && np.Num==Num
    && np.Person==Person && !SubjFilled && SubjFilled = 1
```
attaching the subject on the left

```
lvp → np lvp@ : la(obj) :
    np.Case == ObjCase && !ObjFilled && ObjFilled = 1
    && ObjNum = np.Num && ObjGender = np.Gender
```
attaching the object on the left

```
vp → lvp@ : id
```
now the VP is completed

```
s → vp : nn(S, head) : Tense != inf
```
finally the S (sentence) node is introduced for finite VPs

2 Handling Discontinuous Infinitive Clauses

An infinitive clause used in sentences with Polish verbs such as *chcieć* (*want*), *lubić* (*like*), etc. may be discontinuous. For example, consider various permutations of sentence *Adam chce reperować drukarkę* (*Adam wants to repair a printer*, lit. *Adam(nom) wants to-repair printer(acc)*). Let us denote the subject *Adam*, the main verb *chce*, the verb in infinitive *reperować* and the object *drukarkę* by respectively S, V, V_i and O. Assuming that we want to treat the infinitive VP $(O + V_i)$ as a constituent of the main VP[1], $SOVV_i$ is discontinuous (whereas e.g. $SVOV_i$ or SVV_iO are continuous).

2.1 The VV_i Order

Now we are going to extend VP backbone presented in Section 1.2 to cover sentences like $SOVV_i$. Let us start with a general rule for attaching an infinitive clause on the right:

```
lvp → rvp@ vp : ra(infobj) : Obj == inf && vp.Tense == inf
```

(`Obj` attribute is set to `inf` for verbs taking an infinitive clause as their object.) Note that we assume that an infinitive clause closes the main VP on the right (i.e. no other constituents can follow it), since `lvp` rather than `rvp` was used on the left-hand side of the production. In practice this seems to be a reasonable approximation except that VV_iS order is not covered. (This order can be handled by temporarily attaching the subject to the verb in infinitive and re-attaching it later to the main verb; note that this would require the introduction of a new tree operation for re-attaching a node.)

---

[1] Note that if VV_i were to be treated as a complex predicate, $SVOV_i$ or $OVSV_i$ would be discontinuous.

In order to cover OVV_i order, the above rule should be augmented as follows:

```
lvp → rvp@ vp : ra(infobj) :
  Obj == inf && vp.Tense == inf
  &&
  ((vp.ObjFilled && ObjFilled = r)
    || (Obj = vp.Obj && ObjSource = inf))
```

The expression `(vp.ObjFilled ...) || (... ObjSource = inf)` can be read as an if-else-then statement[2]: if an object has already been attached to the infinitive clause (`vp.ObjFilled ...`), then set `ObjFilled` attribute (`ObjFilled = r`). Otherwise, set the expected object of the infinitive as the expected object of the main verb (`Obj = vp.Obj`) and set the special attribute `ObjSource` to remember that the object will, in fact, belong to the infinitive clause rather than the main VP.

Finally, an additional rule for attaching objects is needed:

```
lvp → np lvp@ : li(infobj,obj) :
  ObjSource == inf
  && np.Case == ObjCase && !ObjFilled && ObjFilled = 1
```

This way, the syntax tree depicted in Figure 2 will be generated for sentence *drukarkę chce reperować* (*(he/she) wants to repair the printer*, lit. *printer(acc) wants to-repair*). Note that this tree is discontinuous – the discontinuity was introduced with the `li(infobj,obj)` tree operation.

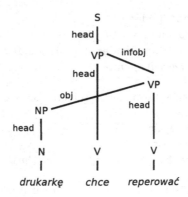

Fig. 2. A syntax tree for sentence *drukarkę chce reperować*

The proposed solution should also work for verb chains (e.g. *chce móc reperować* = *wants to be able to repair*), although some minor modifications in attribute expressions are necessary (in order to distinguish $VV_i V_i$ from VV_i).

---

[2] "Short-circuit" semantics of `||` and `&&` is assumed (as in C).

2.2 The $V_i V$ Order

This order seems to be much less frequent than VV_i. For instance, Google search engine returned 2480000 and 184 results (May 2006) for *chce kupić* (lit. *wants to-buy*) and *kupić chce* respectively. The following rule covers the $V_i V$ order:

```
lvp → vp lvp@ : la(infobj) :
  Obj == inf && !ObjFilled && vp.Tense == inf
```

However, the $V_i VO$ order (as opposed to $V_i OV$ and $OV_i V$) cannot be covered in the manner analogous to the manner in which OVV_i was handled. This asymmetry is a result of the fixed order in which VP constituents are attached (first the right constituents, then the left ones) – it is not possible to attach the object on the right when the infinitive clause has not been incorporated into the VP yet. This is an important limitation of the proposed solution.

3   Handling Discontinuous Noun Phrases

Consider a VP composed of a verb and a noun phrase containing an adjective, e.g. *reperuje nową drukarkę* (*(he/she) is repairing a new printer*). Let us denote the verb (*reperuje*), the noun (*drukarkę*) and the adjective (*nową*) by resp. V, N and A. There are two discontinuous configurations: *AVN* (*nową reperuje drukarkę*) and *NVA* (*drukarkę reperuje nową*).

3.1   The *AVN* Order

Discontinuous objects of this type can be handled with the following rule:

```
lvp → ap lvp@ : li(obj,modif):
  ObjFilled == r && ap.Case == ObjCase
  && ap.Num == ObjNum && ap.Gender == ObjGender
  the ap symbol refers to an adjective phrase
```

In a similar manner analogous discontinuous subjects can be captured:

```
lvp → ap lvp@ : li(subj,modif):
  SubjFilled == r && ap.Case == nom
  && ap.Num == lvp.Num && ap.Gender == lvp.Num
```

The `ObjFilled` (`SubjFilled`) is tested to determine if it is equal to `r` in order to (1) ensure that there is an object (subject) and to (2) exclude spurious interpretations in case of continuous *ANV* order. Note that any number of adjective phrases can be attached this way.

Not all discontinuous noun phrases can be covered in this manner, for example noun phrases with "government" numerals (e.g. *siedem mam drukarek* = *I have seven printers*, lit. *seven(acc) I-have printers(gen)*) cannot be handled this way because the numeral changes the case of the noun. However, discontinuous NPs with "agreement" numerals (e.g *dwie mam drukarki* = *I have two printers*, lit. *two(acc) I-have printers(acc)*) can be straightforwardly described with rules similar to the rules given above for NPs with adjectives.

3.2 The *NVA* Order

As was the case with $V_i VO$ / OVV_i (see Section 2), the *NVA* order cannot be handled in the same way as *AVN*. One possible solution would be to attach the adjective phrase to rvp and then force attaching the noun phrase on the left (thus temporarily breaking the order of attaching VP constituents). This solution has the following disadvantages: (1) additional rules for attaching object/subjects ought to be introduced, (2) no adverbial phrase (nor any other VP constituent) can be placed between the noun and the verb.

4 Other Types of Discontinuity

Polish analytical future forms are, to some extent, similar to constructions with infinitive phrases. Handling analytical future forms within a TgBG was discussed in [7][3]. Note that it was assumed there that the auxiliary verb is not the head of the VP – the motivation behind it was to take advantage of the fact that in one type of the analytical future (e.g. *będzie robił*) the main verb agrees with the subject. Also discontinuous interrogative prepositional phrases are described in [7].

5 Cost-Effectiveness of Handling Discontinuity

It has been established in the previous sections that at least some types of discontinuity can be handled within a medium-level grammatical formalism. Now let us address the question of whether it is cost-effective to do so in practice. It should be noted that the frequency of discontinuity is not very high in Polish[4] and false positives may occur (discontinuity may be detected where there is none). What is more, such false positives may be very confusing in further processing, e.g. in machine translation.

The following simple experiment with a text corpus[5] may be carried out: parse a corpus, check how many times the given type of discontinuity was detected and count false positives – if the percentage of false positives is too high or the number of discontinuities is very low, the rule for the given type of discontinuity is probably useless in the context of the given parser and type of texts.

In a preliminary experiment the corpus of the *Frequency dictionary of contemporary Polish* [1] was parsed with the parser of the POLENG machine (Polish-to-English) translation system [8] enhanced with some of the elements of the grammatical formalism described in this paper.

The following types of discontinuity were checked: discontinuous infinitive clauses (*iVP*; see Section 2), discontinuous interrogative noun phrases (*iNP*, e.g. *jaką ... drukarkę = which ... printer*; this a special and highly important case of discontinuous NPs discussed in Section 3), discontinuous interrogative prepositional phrases (*iPP*; e.g. *o jakiej ... drukarce*

---

[3] Let us note here that in a similar manner discontinuous conditional tense (*by ... zrobił*) can be covered.

[4] Derwojedowa [4, p. 68] reports that of 4839 Polish sentences (a subset of the corpus of *Frequency dictionary of contemporary Polish* [1]) 8% contained a construction that was classified as discontinuous.

[5] A raw corpus was used as no large tree bank exists for Polish.

= *about which ... printer*; see [7] for the theoretical discussion of this type of discontinuous construction). The results are given in Table 1: A is the number of sentences with the given discontinuity detected by the parser[6], $A\%$ is their percentage relative to the number of sentences in the corpus (42056), F is the number of false positives and $F\%$ is their percentage relative to A.

Table 1. Various types of discontinuity detected in the corpus

	A	%	F	%
iVP	435	1.034%	70	16.1%
iNP	49	0.117%	25	51.0%
iPP	3	0.007%	0	0.0%

The number of detected discontinuous infinitive phrases is significant and the percentage of false positives is probably acceptable. In contrast, the number of detected discontinuous interrogative noun phrases is lower and more than half of them are false positives. It should be concluded that in the context of the given parser, covering discontinuous interrogative NPs brings more harm than profit.

6 Conclusion

It was shown in this paper that discontinuity can be – at least to some extent – covered within a medium-level context-free grammatical formalism. Unfortunately, the cost-effectiveness of handling some types of discontinuity may be low for a given parser.

Only cases when a phrase is separated with a verb have been discussed in this section. There are (probably less frequent) other types of discontinuity in Polish, for example a noun phrase can be separated with a noun (e.g. *na suchego przestwór oceanu*). Handling such types of discontinuity within a medium-level formalism needs further research.

References

1. Kurcz I., Lewicki A. et al.: Słownik frekwencyjny polszczyzny współczesnej (1990).
2. Holan T., Kuboň V. et al.: Two Useful Measures of Word Order Complexity. COLING-98 Workshop "Processing of Dependency-Based Grammars" (1998).
3. Sylvain K, Nasr A., Rambow O.: Pseudo-Projectivity: A Polynomially Parsable Non-Projective Dependency Grammar. http://citeseer.ifi.unizh.ch/586031.html (1998).
4. Derwojedowa M.: Porządek linearny składników zdania elementarnego w języku polskim. Elipsa, Warszawa (2000).
5. Nasr A., Rambow O.: A Simple String-Rewriting Formalism for Dependency Grammar. Proceedings of the COLING-98 Workshop "Recent Advances in Dependency Grammar" (2004).

---

[6] The syntactical interpretation with the highest score was chosen for each sentence. The scores are assigned by the parser according to various heuristics.

6. Graliński F.: A Simple CF Formalism and Free Word Order. 2nd Language & Technology Conference, Proceedings. (2005) 172–176.
7. Graliński F.: A Simple CF Formalism and Free Word Order. Archives of Control Sciences Lecture Notes in Computer Science, Vol. 15. Institute of Automatic Control, Silesian University of Technology, Gliwice (2005) 541–554.
8. Jasssem K.: Przetwarzanie tekstów polskich w systemie tłumaczenia automatycznego POLENG, Wydawnictwo Naukowe Uniwersytetu im. Adama Mickiewicza, Poznań (in press) (2006).

Exploitation of the VerbaLex Verb Valency Lexicon in the Syntactic Analysis of Czech

Dana Hlaváčková, Aleš Horák, and Vladimír Kadlec

Faculty of Informatics, Masaryk University Brno
Botanická 68a, 602 00 Brno, Czech Republic
{hlavack, hales, xkadlec}@fi.muni.cz

Abstract. This paper presents an exploitation of the lexicon of verb valencies for the Czech language named VerbaLex. The VerbaLex lexicon format, called *complex valency frames*, comprehends all the information found in three independent electronic dictionaries of verb valency frames and it is intensively linked to the Czech WordNet semantic network.

The NLP laboratory at FI MU Brno develops a deep syntactic analyzer of Czech sentences, the parsing system `synt`. The system is based on an efficient and fast head-driven chart parsing algorithm. We present the latest results of using the information contained in the VerbaLex lexicon as one of the language specific features used in the tree ranking algorithm for the Best Analysis Selection algorithm, which is a crucial part of the syntactic analyser of free word order languages.

1 Introduction

The ambiguity level in the syntactic analysis of free word order languages suffers from the exponential explosion of the number of resulting derivation trees. The main reasons for this combinatorial grow arise on several levels of the sentence building process (prepositional attachment, verb argument resolution, non-projectivity, ellipsis, anaphoric relations, etc.). A traditional solution for these problems is presented by probabilistic parsing techniques aiming at finding the most probable parse of a given input sentence. This methodology is usually based on the relative frequencies of occurrences of the possible relations in a representative corpus. "Best" trees are judged by a probabilistic figure of merit. Our experiments show, that in the case of really free word order languages (like Czech) the probabilistic measures are not able to cover the complexity of the sentence syntax. That is why we need to exploit the knowledge of the language specific features as described in [1].

The basic sentence frame is driven by the lexical characteristics of its predicative construction based on the set of possible verb valencies of the particular verb (see e.g. [2]). We have implemented the technique of discovering the possible verb valencies from the resulting ambiguous packed shared forest (stored in the parsing chart). This enables us to work with verb valencies in two directions: a) using the VerbaLex valency lexicon to prune impossible combination regarding the particular verb, and b) automatically process large corpora for discovering possible verb valencies that are missing in the lexicon. These valencies are then offered to the linguistic expert for addition to VerbaLex. Similar approach has been described in [3], in which a partial parsing outputs were used for obtaining the verb subcategorization information. Our approach includes a full parsing of Czech sentence, which increases the credibility of the verb frame information.

Petr Sojka, Ivan Kopeček and Karel Pala (Eds.): TSD 2006, LNAI 4188, pp. 79–85, 2006.

2   The VerbaLex Valency Lexicon

This paper presents an exploitation of the lexicon of verb valencies for the Czech language named VerbaLex [4]. VerbaLex was created in 2005 and it is based on three valuable language resources for Czech, three independent electronic dictionaries of verb valency frames.

The first resource, Czech WordNet valency frames dictionary, was created during the Balkanet project and contains semantic roles and links to the Czech WordNet semantic network. The other resource, VALLEX 1.0 [5], is a lexicon based on the formalism of the Functional Generative Description (FGD) and was developed during the Prague Dependency Treebank (PDT) project. The third source of information for VerbaLex is the syntactic lexicon of verb valencies denoted as BRIEF, which originated at FI MU Brno in 1996 [6].

The resulting lexicon, VerbaLex, comprehends all the information found in these resources plus additional relevant information such as verb aspect, verb synonymy, types of use and semantic verb classes based on the VerbNet project [7]. The information in VerbaLex is organized in the form of *complex valency frames* (CVF). All the valency information in VerbaLex is specified regarding the particular verb senses, not only the verb lemmata, as it was found in some of the sources. The current work on the lexicon data aims at enlarging the lexicon to the size of about 16.000 Czech verbs. The VerbaLex lexicon displays syntactic dependencies of sentence constituents, their semantic roles and links to the corresponding Czech WordNet classes. An example of such verb frame is presented in the Figure 1.[1]

The complex valency frame in VerbaLex is designed as a sequence of elements which form a "pattern"[2] for obligatory sentence constituents that depend on the verb. There are two types of information displayed in CVF. The constituent elements of valency frames cover both syntactic level and lexical semantic level (represented by two-level semantic roles). The default verb position 'VERB' as the centre of the sentence is marked on the syntactic level. The pattern of sentence constituents are situated in left and right positions in accordance with the complementarity needed by the verb. The constituent elements of frame entries are entered as pure pronominal terms, e.g. kdo (who), co (what), or prepositional phrase pattern (with the lemma of the preposition) followed by the number of the required grammatical case of the phrase.

> *opustit*:4/*leave office*:1 (give up or retire from a position)
> frame: AG<person:1>$_{\text{who1}}^{\text{obl}}$ VERB ACT<job:1>$_{\text{what4}}^{\text{obl}}$
> example: opustil zaměstnání / he left his job

This way of notation allows to differentiate an animate or inanimate subject or object position. The types of verbal complementation are precisely distinguished in the verb frame notation.

If a verb requires a completion with adjective or adverb, this fact is written as the adjectival or adverbial lemma and part of speech tag from WordNet semantic network – [a] or [b].

> *cítit se*:1/*feel*:5 (have a feeling or perception about oneself in reaction to someone's behavior or attitude)

---

[1] This is a slightly enhanced version of CVF that splits the attribute values to *verb attributes* and *frame attributes*.

[2] A list of necessary grammatical features such as the grammatical case or the the preposition.

Princeton WordNet: dress:2, clothe:1, enclothe:1, garb:1, raiment:1, tog:1,
garment:1, habilitate:2, fit out:2, apparel:1
definition: provide with clothes or put clothes on

VerbaLex Synset: obléci:1_{pf}, oblékat:1_{impf}, obléknout:1_{pf}, ustrojit:1_{pf}, strojit:1_{impf}
=def: provide with clothes or put clothes on
=canbepassive: yes
=meaning: 1
=class: dress-41.1.1

Complex valency frames:

1. obléci:1, oblékat:1, obléknout:1
   -frame: AG<person:1>$^{obl}_{who1}$ VERB
   PAT<person:1>$^{obl}_{to\_whom3}$ ART<garment:1>$^{obl}_{what4}$
   -synonym: ustrojit:1, strojit:1
   -example: *maminka oblékla dítěti kabát / the mother put a coat
   on her child*
   -attr: use: prim, reflexivity=obj_dat, mustbeimperative=no

2. obléci:1, oblékat:1, obléknout:1, ustrojit:1, strojit:1
   -frame: AG<person:1>$^{obl}_{who1}$ VERB
   PAT<person:1>$^{obl}_{whom4}$ ART<garment:1>$^{obl}_{in+sth2}$
   -synonym:
   -example: *maminka oblékla dítě do kabátu / the mother dressed
   her child in a coat*
   -attr: use: prim, reflexivity=obj_ak, mustbeimperative=no

Fig. 1. An example of a VerbaLex verb frame

frame: AG<person:1>$^{obl}_{who1}$ VERB ATTR<[a]>$^{obl}_{which1}$
example: *cítil se bezvýznamný / he felt insignificant*

cítit se:2/*feel*:4 (seem with respect to a given sensation given)
frame: AG<person:1>$^{obl}_{who1}$ VERB MAN<[b]>$^{opt}_{how}$
example: *cítil se špatně / he felt badly*

A verb valency with an infinitive construction is marked by abbreviation 'inf' and link to the verbal literal from Princeton WordNet. A subordinate clause complementation is specified by the lemma of the subordinating conjunction.

začít:1/*begin*:1 (take the first step or steps in carrying out an action)
frame: AG<person:1>$^{obl}_{who1}$ VERB ACT<|v|>$^{obl}_{inf}$
example: *začal stavět dům / he began to build a house*

popřít:1/*disclaim*:1 (renounce a legal claim or title to)
frame: AG<person:1>$^{obl}_{who1}$ VERB COM<statement:1>$^{obl}_{that}$
example: *popřel, že ho zná/he disclaimed that he knows him*

The type of valency relation can be obligatory 'obl' (must be present) or optional 'opt'. With this notation format it is possible to generate two (or more) frames from one basic frame.

The basic frame

děsit:1/*frighten*:1 (cause fear in)

frame: AG <person:1> $^{obl}_{who1}$ VERB PAT <person:1> $^{obl}_{whom4}$

ACT <act:2> $^{opt}_{with\_what7}$

example: děsil ho hrozbami / he frightened him with threats

contains the potential frame:

frame: AG <person:1> $^{obl}_{who1}$ VERB PAT <person:1> $^{obl}_{whom4}$

example: děsil ho / he frightened him

Other details of the complex valency frame notation (e.g. the way of selection of the two-level semantic roles that link the constituents to the wordnet hypero-hyponymical hierarchy) are described in [4].

3 The Syntactic Analyzer synt

The NLP laboratory at FI MU Brno develops a deep syntactic analyzer of Czech sentences, the parsing system synt [8]. The system uses the meta-grammar formalism, which enables to define the grammar with a maintainable number of meta-rules. These meta-rules are produced manually by linguists. The rules are then translated into context-free rules supplemented with additional contextual constraints and semantic actions. Efficient and fast head-driven chart parsing algorithm is used for the context-free parsing. The result of the context-free parsing process – a chart – is stored in the form of a packed shared forest. To apply the constraints and to compute the semantic actions, we build a new *forest of values* instead of pruning the original chart. We use this multi-pass approach, because all described functions are implemented as plug-ins that can be modified as needed or even substituted with other implementations. For example, we compared four different parsing algorithms which use identical internal data structures. The parsing system is aimed at analyzing the sentence not only at the surface level, but it also covers the logical analysis of the sentence by means of the Transparent Intensional Logic (TIL) [9].

4 The Verb Frames and Syntactic Analysis

In the case of a syntactic analysis of a really free word order language as the Czech language is, we need to exploit the language specific features for obtaining the correct ordering of the resulting syntactical analyzes. So far the most advantageous approach is the one based upon valencies of the verb phrase – a crucial concept in traditional linguistics.

The part of the system dedicated to exploitation of information obtained from a list of verb frames is necessary for solving the prepositional attachment problem in particular. During the analysis of noun groups and prepositional noun groups in the role of verb valencies in a given input sentence one needs to be able to distinguish free adjuncts or modifiers from obligatory valencies. The wordnet classes together with the surface features in complex valency frames are directly used for setting up a set of heuristic rules that determine whether a noun group found in the sentence serves here as a free adjunct or not. The heuristics are based on the lexico-semantic constraints derived from the VerbaLex links to the EuroWordNet hypero-hyponymical hierarchy.

4.1   Automatic Extraction of Verb Frames from the Packed Shared Forest

The verb frame extraction (VFE) process in the `synt` system is controlled by the metagrammar semantic actions. As we have described in the Section 3, we build a forest of values to represent a result of the application of contextual constraints. The VFE actions are then executed on a different level (see [8]) than the "usual" actions, which allows us to apply VFE actions on the whole forest of values.

First of all, we find all noun groups covered by the particular context-free rule. Then compatible groups[3] are processed by the VFE action. Notice, that this step suffers from a possible exponential time complexity because we work with the derivation trees and not with the packed forest. On the other hand our experiments show (see the Table 1) that in the average case this is not a problem.

If the analyzed verb has a corresponding entry in VerbaLex, we try to match the extracted frame with frames in the lexicon. When checking the valencies with VerbaLex, the dependence on the surface order is discharged. Before the system confronts the actual verb valencies from the input sentence with the list of valency frames found in the lexicon, all the valency expressions are reordered. By using the standard ordering of participants, the valency frames can be handled as sets independent on the current position of verb arguments. However, since VerbaLex contains an information about the *usual* verb position within the frame, we promote the standard ordering with increasing or decreasing the respective derivation tree probability.

We have measured the results of the first version of the automatic verb frame extraction on 4117 sentences from the Czech corpus DESAM [10]. We have selected sentences which are analysed on the rule level 0, i.e. sentences, which do not contain analytically difficult phenomena like non-projectivity or adjective noun phrase. Even on those sentences the number of possible valency frames can be quite high (see the Table 1). However, if we work with intersections of those possible valency frames, we can get a useful reduction of the number of resulting derivation trees – see the examples described in the next Section.

4.2   Examples

The projection of the extracted valency frames to the corresponding VerbaLex entry can be used as effective pruning tool for decreasing the number of successful derivation trees. As an example of such pruning, we can have a look at the sentence

Pokud *uchazeči kurs rekvalifikace úspěšně absolvují*, budou mít jistě uplatnění v zaměstnání.

If *the candidates successfully complete the retraining course*, they will certainly assert themselves in their job.

The valency frame for the verb 'absolvovat' from VerbaLex:

absolvovat:1/*complete*:1 (come or bring to a finish or an end)

$AG <person:1>^{obl}_{who1}$ $VERB\ KNOW <course:1>^{obl}_{what4}$

---

[3] Compatible in the term of derivation, i.e. groups within the same derivation tree.

Table 1. The results of verb frame extraction from the corpus DESAM

Number of sentences:	
count	**4117**
Number of words in sentence:	
minimum	2.0
maximum	68.0
average	16.8
median	**15.0**
Number of discovered valency frames:	
minimum	0
maximum	37080
average	380
median	**11**
Elapsed time:	
minimum	0.00 s
maximum	274.98 s
average	6.86 s
median	**0.07 s**

There are 132 trees for that sentence in the parsing system `synt`. Due to the free word order the sequence of sentence parts is

subject (uchazeči/candidates) – *object* (kurs/course)
– *verb* (absolvují/complete).

According to the valency frame the subject is a noun in nominative and the object is a noun in accusative. It is evident, that those elements cannot form a nominal phrase. This constriction reduces the number of trees to 24.

Another example is displayed in the following sentence:

Havel se radil s představiteli justice a vnitra o posílení práva.
Havel consulted with representatives of judiciary and home office on the consolidation of the legal system.

The valency frame for the verb 'radit se' from VerbaLex is:

radit se:1/*consult*:1 (get or ask advice from)
AG <person:1> $_{\text{who}}^{\text{obl}}$1 VERB SOC <person:1> $_{\text{with_whom}}^{\text{opt}}$7
ENT|ABS <entity:1,abstraction:1> $_{\text{about_what}}^{\text{opt}}$6

The number of `synt` trees for this sentence is 2672. The part of sentence with the preposition 's' (with) and a noun in instrumental and the part of sentence with preposition 'o' (on) and a noun in locative are necessarily prepositional nominal phrases. The application of such limits in `synt` allows a significant reduction of the number of trees to 18.

5 Conclusions

We have presented the results of exploitation of automatic verb frame extraction for Czech as a language specific feature used for pruning the packed shared forest of results of syntactic analysis with the synt parser. A necessary tool for this, the VerbaLex lexicon of valency frames that is being built at FI MU Brno, is also described.

The preliminary results of the exploitation of VerbaLex in the syntactic analysis of Czech are very promising and the precision of the analysis grows significantly. We believe that with enlarging the lexicon to a representative number of Czech verbs the synt system will be able to detect the correct derivation tree in many cases which were unsolvable so far.

Acknowledgments

This work has been partially supported by Czech Science Foundation under the project 201/05/2781 and by Grant Agency of the Academy of Sciences of CR under the project 1ET400300414.

References

1. Horák, A., Smrž, P.:   Best analysis selection in inflectional languages.   In: Proceedings of the 19th international conference on Computational linguistics, Taipei, Taiwan, Association for Computational Linguistics (2002) 363–368.
2. Trueswell, J., Kim, A.: How to prune a garden-path by nipping it in the bud: Fast-priming of verb argument structures. Journal of Memory and Language (1998) 102–123.
3. Gamallo, P., Agustini, A., Lopes, G.P.: Learning subcategorisation information to model a grammar with co-restrictions. Traitement Automatique de la Langue **44** (2003) 93–117.
4. Hlaváčková, D., Horák, A.: Verbalex – new comprehensive lexicon of verb valencies for czech. In: Proceedings of the Slovko Conference, Bratislava, Slovakia (2005).
5. Žabokrtský, Z., Lopatková, M.: Valency Frames of Czech Verbs in VALLEX 1.0. In Meyers, A., ed.: HLT-NAACL 2004 Workshop: Frontiers in Corpus Annotation. (2004) 70–77.
6. Pala, K., Sevecek, P.: Valence českých sloves (Valencies of Czech Verbs). In: Proceedings of Works of Philosophical Faculty at the University of Brno, Brno, Masaryk University (1997) 41–54.
7. Dang, H.T., Kipper, K., Palmer, M., Rosenzweig, J.: Investigating regular sense extensions based on intersective levin classes. In: Proceedings of Coling-ACL98, Montreal CA (August 11–17, 1998) http://www.cis.upenn.edu/~mpalmer/.
8. Horák, A., Kadlec, V.:   New meta-grammar constructs in Czech language parser synt.   In: Proceedings of Text, Speech and Dialogue 2005, Karlovy Vary, Czech Republic, Springer-Verlag (2005) 85–92.
9. Horák, A.: The Normal Translation Algorithm in Transparent Intensional Logic for Czech. Ph.D. thesis, Faculty of Informatics, Masaryk University, Brno (2002).
10. Pala, K., Rychlý, P., Smrž, P.: DESAM — annotated corpus for Czech. In: Proceedings of SOFSEM '97, Springer-Verlag (1997) 523–530 Lecture Notes in Computer Science 1338.

Hungarian-English Machine Translation Using GenPar

András Hócza and András Kocsor

Department of Informatics, University of Szeged,
H-6720 Szeged, Árpád tér 2., Hungary
hocza@inf.u-szeged.hu, kocsor@inf.u-szeged.hu
http://www.inf.u-szeged.hu

Abstract. We present an approach for machine translation by applying the GenPar toolkit on POS-tagged and syntactically parsed texts. Our experiment in Hungarian-English machine translation is an attempt to develop prototypes of a syntax-driven machine translation system and to examine the effects of various preprocessing steps (POS-tagging, lemmatization and syntactic parsing) on system performance. The annotated monolingual texts needed for different language specific tasks were taken from the Szeged Treebank and the Penn Treebank. The parallel sentences were collected from the Hunglish Corpus. Each developed prototype runs fully automatically and new Hungarian-related functions are built in. The results are evaluated with BLEU score.

1 Introduction

Machine translation (MT) is the application of computers to the translation of texts from one natural language to another. The practical reason for attempting this is that in many fields people have to read documents and have to communicate in languages they do not know and a good quality MT system could provide a quick solution for this problem.

Today's state of the art in MT has been defined by statistical machine translation (SMT) systems. The main goal of the 2005 SMT workshop [3] was to build a publicly available toolkit for experimenting with tree-structured translation models. The GenPar toolkit was published by organizers of the workshop to allow one to retarget the toolkit to new language pairs.

In this paper we present a Hungarian-English application of the GenPar toolkit by creating new prototypes and using available data sources from various treebanks. The manually POS-tagged and syntactically parsed Hungarian and English texts needed for preprocessing was derived from the Szeged Treebank [4] and from the Penn Treebank [9]. The Hungarian-English parallel sentences for testing the GenPar toolkit were collected from the Hunglish Corpus [16].

This paper is organized as follows. In Section 2 the difficulties of parsing the Hungarian language are described. Section 3 provides a review of related works and a brief discussion of efforts made by Hungarian researchers. Section 4 then introduces the GenPar toolkit. Section 5 presents the details of our experiences, the data sources used, language-specific modules and test results. Lastly, conclusions and suggestions for future study are given in Section 6.

Petr Sojka, Ivan Kopeček and Karel Pala (Eds.): TSD 2006, LNAI 4188, pp. 87–94, 2006.

2   Difficulties of the Hungarian Language

The Hungarian language is customarily defined as an agglutinative, free word order language with a rich morphology. These properties make a full analysis of it difficult, compared to Indo-European languages. Machine translation is based on syntactic parsing, but unambiguous marks for the automatic recognition of phrase boundaries do not exist in Hungarian.

Another problem is the high morphological and syntactic diversity of the Hungarian language. Many words with same stem have up to 100 word forms. The (almost) free word order significantly raises the number of possible patterns and schemas, and this decreases the effectiveness of statistical machine learning methods applied. Especially the realization of inflections is a problem because the linguistic information that is stored in word order in English are expressed with endings in Hungarian A simple example of the inflection problem is showed in Figure 1.

Lekapcsolnád a lámpát? → Would you turn off the lights?
le- → off
kapcsol- → turn
ná- → would (hi or shi)
d → you
a → the
lámpa- → lamp (→ light-s)
t (lámpa → lámpát) → (accusative)

Fig. 1. An example of the ending problem in Hungarian-English translation

In the Hungarian language - because of the free word order - more phrase structures exist than in the English language. Therefore the realization English-Hungarian machine translation seems to be an easier problem than the Hungarian-English one, because the translator tool needs to store much less phrase syntax cases for English and it is easier to recognize and find a possible translation.

3   Related Works

The best SMT systems are driven by translation models that are weighted finite-state transducers (WFSTs) [11,7]. These methods go beyond the original IBM MT models [2] by allowing multi-word units (phrases) in one language to be translated directly into phrases in another language. The phrase-based variety of WFSTs memorizes the translations of word n-grams rather than just single words. Translating strings of multiple words as a unit is beneficial in two ways. First, the translations of individual words are more likely to be correct when they are translated together and have the same context. Second, phrases can capture local variations in word order, making the decoder's job easier.

English-Hungarian MT tools, like MetaMorpho [13] have been developed which combines the advantages of example-based and rule-based MT. MetaMorpho has achieved good results compared to well-known MT systems (e.g. SYSTRAN, PROMPT, SDL). There is ongoing work on Hungarian-English machine translation [15], but up till now there was no good-quality MT tool available for this problem.

One important task is a comparison of the performance of MT systems. Over the past few years, several automatic metrics for MT evaluation have been introduced, largely to reduce the human cost of iterative system evaluation during the development cycle [12,8,10]. All are predicated on the concept of n-gram matching between the sentence hypothesized by the translation system and one or more reference translations—that is, human translations for the test sentence. Although the motivations and formulae underlying these metrics are all different, ultimately they all produce a single number representing the goodness of the MT system output over a set of reference documents. This method is used mainly for determining whether a given system modification has a positive impact on the overall translation performance. For example unigram precision and recall statistics tell us something about the performance of an MT system's internal translation dictionaries, but nothing about reordering. However these metrics cannot provide a precise comparison of MT systems unless conditions (e.g. reference sentences) are exactly the same when tests are performed.

The BLEU metric [12] is probably the best known Machine Evaluation for MT. Essentially, the algorithm looks for n-gram coincidences between a candidate text (the automatically produced translation) and a set of reference texts (the human-made translations). The value of N is typically between 1 to 4 (BLEU-4) and its value is always a number between 0 and 1. This value tells us how similar the candidate and reference texts are. In fact, the closer the value is to 1, the more similar they will be.

4   About GenPar

The GenPar (Generalized Parsing) package is an object-oriented software toolkit for generalized parsing. The design is based on the architecture laid down by [10]. In an ordinary parser, the input is a string, and the grammar ranges over strings. A given method applies generalizations of ordinary parsing algorithms that allow the input to consist of string tuples and/or the grammar to range over string tuples. Such inference algorithms can perform various kinds of analysis on parallel texts, also known as multitexts. Figure 2 shows some of the ways in which ordinary parsing can be generalized.

The grammar development of GenPar focuses on multitext grammar (MTG), which is an abstract generalization of context-free grammar (CFG) to the synchronous case [10]. In this way, MTGs generate tuples of parse trees that are isomorphic up to the reordering of sibling nodes and deletion. Figure 3 shows a typical representation of a multidimensional tree that might be generated by an MTG.

The main goal of the 2005 SMT workshop [3] was to build a publicly available toolkit for experimenting with tree-structured translation models. The GenPar toolkit was published by organizers of workshop to allow one to apply the toolkit to new language pairs. The design of GenPar has two goals:

- **Flexibility:** The toolkit should support many parser variants, and should be easily configurable into one of them at run time.
- **Extensibility:** It should be easy to add new features and new functions.

To satisfy the above requirements, the parser was decomposed into different components and each type of component was defined by an object class family. This decomposition helps

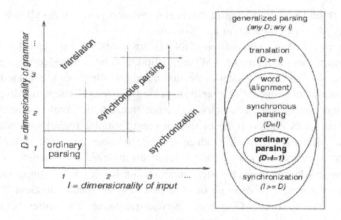

Fig. 2. Generalizations of ordinary parsing [10]

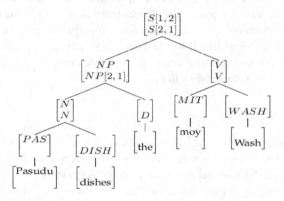

Fig. 3. Short example of 2D multitree [10]

the parser to support more variations and to be easily configured on demand. It also makes the parser more easily extendible.

GenPar provides an integrated prototype system to save the toolkit users a lot of effort of system integration. Hence it is easy to retarget the toolkit to new language pairs. Each prototype contains the software modules and configuration files necessary for training, testing, and evaluation with a particular language pair. A default directory structure and execution order are shows in Figure 4.

With the GenPar toolkit, prototypes are provided for three different language pairs: Arabic-English, French-English and English-English. These prototypes give an overview of all of the modules. The code distributed with GenPar is suffient to run all but the preprocess modules. The default configuration of the sandbox is to use previously preprocessed data sets that were shipped with the software. However, the preprocessing modules are necessary for applying the system on new data sets, but the installation guide describes how to obtain and install the additional modules. These language-specific modules are tokenization, lemmatization, POS-tagging and syntactic parsing.

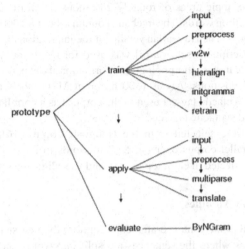

Fig. 4. Default execution [3]

The example prototypes contain not just different language pairs but different execution orders as well. The following languages have different properties:

- **English:** is tokenized, POS-tagged and syntactically parsed in each prototype using the formalism of Penn Treebank.
- **Arabic:** is tokenized and lemmatized in a different way because of the properties of language. POS-tagging and syntactic parsing are done based on the reduced formalism of the Penn Arabic Treebank
- **French:** is POS-tagger and syntactic parser were not used hence these texts are unparsed.

5 Experiences

In this section the Hungarian-English application of GenPar will be described that used datasources and preparation of language-specific modules. The results of applied GenPar prototypes for Hungarian-English machine translation are also described.

5.1 Evaluation Domains

One of the most notable of all, the Penn Treebank project [9] produced skeletal parses on top of an initial POS tagging containing rough syntactic and semantic information on about 2.5 million words of American English. The syntactic parsing of the texts included the annotation of predicate-argument structures.

In order to perform well and learn from the various Natural Language Processing tasks, an adequately large corpus had to be collected to serve as the training database. A relatively large corpus of Hungarian texts of various types was collected, and later called the Szeged

Treebank [4]. It has six topic areas of roughly 200 thousand words each, meaning a text database of some 1.2 million words. The treebank contains about 82,000 POS-tagged and full syntactic parsed sentences. The Hungarian version of the internationally acknowledged MSD (Morpho-Syntactic Description) schema [5] was used for the encoding of the words. The MSD encoding schema can store morphological information about part-of-speech determined attributes on up to 17 positions. About 1800 different MSD labels are employed in the annotated corpus. The syntactic tag-set used in the corpus has a correlation with many other internationally accepted syntactic tag-sets.

Parallel sentences were selected from the Hunglish Corpus [16], a sentence-aligned Hungarian-English parallel corpus of about 54.2 m words in 2.07 m sentence pairs. The corpus was manually collected in eight topic areas and was aligned with automatic methods.

5.2 Language Specific Modules

The input texts of GenPar are sentence-aligned. Therefore the first step of preprocessing is the tokenization process where the sentences are split into words and punctuation marks. The Hungarian tokenization task was similar as English tokenization was implemented in the original prototypes. The Ratnaparkhi's POS-tagger [14] was used for both languages and it was trained on parts of the Szeged Treebank and Penn Treebank. The Hungarian texts were lemmatized in some prototypes in order to decrease stored word-forms in the word-to-word alignment model of GenPar. This method determines the stem of words by using parts of speech information and the stem-dictionary gathered from the Szeged Treebank. English texts are not lemmatized in all prototypes. The syntactic parsing of English texts was performed by Dan Bikel's parser [1], and the actual data for training was derived from 2–21 sections of the Penn Treebank. The Hungarian texts were syntactically parsed with the PGS parser [6] that was trained on the Szeged Treebank.

5.3 Results

The evaluation was performed on 5k training and 500 test sentence pairs selected from the Hunglish Corpus. The results are not suitable for comparing its performance with other MT systems because the "goodness" of translation is related to the rate of unknown words, word-forms and word order of syntactic structures. On the other hand it is a harder task to learn something from training only, an MT system can be prepared more by people for the translation of general or special texts, e.g. using a dictionary. Hence the BLEU metric was used to determine which modification has a positive impact on the performance.

New prototypes were created from existing ones to run on GenPar with different preprocessing steps and the models were evaluated on test sentences. **Prototype 1** was performed like the French-English one where the source language was unparsed. The results were quite poor; probably the 5500 sentences are not enough for the parser to recognize the occurrence of word-forms. **Prototype 2** tries to reduce the number of word-forms in word-to-word alignment model of GenPar by lemmatization. **Prototype 3** is the same as Prototype 2, but the Hungarian texts are POS-tagged. The results are worse than with Prototype 2, because GenPar has to store the morpho-syntactic category of words and this increases the uncertainty. **Prototype 4** uses each available preprocessing step for Hungarian including syntactic parsing. The results of experiences with prototypes are shown in Table 1.

Table 1. The BLEU score for different prototypes

	BLEU-4	1-gram	2-gram	3-gram	4-gram
Prototype 1	0.033	0.343	0.094	0.059	0.035
Prototype 2	0.114	0.457	0.197	0.106	0.068
Prototype 3	0.085	0.374	0.134	0.076	0.049
Prototype 4	0.191	0.521	0.275	0.186	0.135

6 Summary and Future Work

In this paper, we showed how the GenPar toolkit could be applied to Hungarian-English machine translation. New language-specific modules and prototypes were developed in GenPar. In order to perform Hungarian-English machine translation, manually POS-tagged and syntactically parsed Hungarian and English texts were gathered from the Szeged Treebank and from the Penn Treebank and parallel sentences were collected from the Hunglish Corpus. The BLEU metric was used to determine the effects of modifications on translation performance. In the future we plan to investigate more methods for improving the performance of GenPar on Hungarian-English and we will utilize our experiences in our MT methods.

References

1. Bikel, D.: A distributional analysis of a lexicalized statistical parsing model. In Proceedings of the 9th Conference on Empirical Methods in Natural Language Processing (EMNLP), Barcelona, Spain (2004).
2. Brown, Peter F., Stephen A. Della Pietra, Vincent Della J. Pietra, and Robert L. Mercer.: The mathematics of statistical machine translation: Parameter estimation. Computational Linguistics (1993), 19(2):263–312, June.
3. Burbank, A., Carpuat, M., Clark, S., Dreyer, M., Fox, P., Groves, D., Hall, K., Hearne, M., Melamed, I. D., Shen, Y., Way, A., Wellington, B., Wu, D.: Final Report of the 2005 Language Engineering Workshop on Statistical Machine Translation by Parsing, November.
4. Csendes, D., Csirik, J., Gyimóthy, T., Kocsor, A.: The Szeged Treebank. In Proceedings of the 8th International Conference on Text, Speech and Dialogue, TSD 2005, Karlovy Vary, pp. 123–131.
5. Erjavec, T. and Monachini, M., ed.: Specification and Notation for Lexicon Encoding. Copernicus project 106 "MULTEXT-EAST", Work Package WP1 - Task 1.1 Deliverable D1.1F (1997).
6. Hócza, A., Felföldi, L., Kocsor, A.: Learning Syntactic Patterns Using Boosting and Other Classifier Combination Schemas, in Proceedings of the 8th International Conference on Text, Speech and Dialogue, TSD 2005, Karlovy Vary, pp. 69–76.
7. Kumar, S., Byrne, W.: A weighted finite-state transducer implementation of the alignment template model for statistical machine translation. In Proceedings of the Human Language Technology Conference and the North American Association for Computational Linguistics (HLT-NAACL), pages 63–70, Edmonton, Canada (2003)
8. Lin, Chin-Yew and Och, Franz Josef: Automatic evaluation of machine translation quality using longest common subsequence and skip-bigram statistics. In Proceedings of the 42nd Annual Meeting of the ACL (2004), pp. 606–613.
9. Marcus, M., Santorini, B., Marcinkiewicz, M.: Building a large annotated corpus of English: the Penn Treebank. in Computational Linguistics (1993), vol. 19.

10. Melamed, I. D., and Wei Wang: Statistical Machine Translation by Generalized Parsing. Technical Report 05-001, Proteus Project, New York University (2005).
11. Och, Franz Josef and Hermann Ney: Discriminative training and maximum entropy models for statistical machine translation. In Proceedings of the 40th Annual Meeting of the Association for Computational Linguistics (ACL), Philadelphia (2002), July
12. Papineni, K., Roukos, S., Ward, T., Zhu, W. J.: BLEU: a method for automatic evaluation of machine translation. In Proceedings of the 40th Annual Meeting of the ACL (2002), pp. 311–318,
13. Prószéky, G., Tihanyi, L.: MetaMorpho: A Pattern-Based Machine Translation Project. 24th 'Translating and the Computer' Conference, 19–24, London, United Kingdom (2002).
14. Ratnaparkhi, A.: A linear observed time statistical parser based on maximum entropy models. In Proceedings of the 2nd Conference on Empirical Methods in Natural Language Processing (EMNLP), Providence, Rhode Island (1997).
15. Tihanyi, L., Csendes, D., Merényi, Cs., Gyarmati, Á.: Technical report of NKFP-2/008/2004 (2005).
16. Varga, D., Németh, L., Halácsy, P., Kornai, A., Trón, V., Nagy, V.: Parallel corpora for medium density languages. In Proceedings of the Recent Advances in Natural Language Processing 2005 Conference, pp. 590–596.

Combining Czech Dependency Parsers*

Tomáš Holan and Zdeněk Žabokrtský

Faculty of Mathematics and Physics, Charles University
Malostranské nám. 25, CZ-11800 Prague, Czech Republic
{tomas.holan, zdenek.zabokrtsky}@mff.cuni.cz

Abstract. In this paper we describe in detail two dependency parsing techniques developed and evaluated using the Prague Dependency Treebank 2.0. Then we propose two approaches for combining various existing parsers in order to obtain better accuracy. The highest parsing accuracy reported in this paper is 85.84 %, which represents 1.86 % improvement compared to the best single state-of-the-art parser. To our knowledge, no better result achieved on the same data has been published yet.

1 Introduction

Within the domain of NLP, dependency parsing is nowadays a well-established discipline. One of the most popular benchmarks for evaluating parser quality is the set of analytical (surface-syntactic) trees provided in the Prague Dependency Treebank (PDT). In the present paper we use the beta (pre-release) version of PDT 2.0,[1] which contains 87,980 Czech sentences (1,504,847 words and punctuation marks in 5,338 Czech documents) manually annotated at least to the analytical layer (a-layer for short).

In order to make the results reported in this paper comparable to other works, we use the PDT 2.0 division of the a-layer data into training set, development-test set (d-test), and evaluation-test set (e-test). Since all the parsers (and parser combinations) presented in this paper produce full dependency parses (rooted trees), it is possible to evaluate parser quality simply by measuring its accuracy: the number of correctly attached nodes divided by the number of all nodes (not including the technical roots, as used in the PDT 2.0). More information about evaluation of dependency parsing can be found e.g. in [1].

Following the recommendation from the PDT 2.0 documentation for the developers of dependency parsers, in order to achieve more realistic results we use morphological tags assigned by an automatic tagger (instead of the human annotated tags) as parser input in all our experiments.

The rest of the paper is organized as follows: in Sections 2 and 3, we describe in detail two types of our new parsers. In Section 4, two different approaches to parser combination are discussed and evaluated. Concluding remarks are in Section 5.

---

* The research reported on in this paper has been carried out under the projects 1ET101120503, GAČR 207-13/201125, 1ET100300517, and LC 536.

[1] For a detailed information and references see http://ufal.mff.cuni.cz/pdt2.0/

Petr Sojka, Ivan Kopeček and Karel Pala (Eds.): TSD 2006, LNAI 4188, pp. 95–102, 2006.

2   Rule-Based Dependency Parser

In this section we will describe a rule-based dependency parser created by one of the authors. Although the first version of the parser was implemented already in 2002 and its results have been used in several works (e.g. [2]), no more detailed description of the parser itself has been published yet.

The parser in question is not based on any grammar formalism (however, it has been partially inspired by several well-known formal frameworks, especially by unification grammars and restarting automata). Instead, the grammar is 'hardwired' directly in Perl code. The parser uses tred/btred/ntred[2] tree processing environment developed by Petr Pajas. The design decisions important for the parser are described in the following paragraphs.

One tree per sentence. The parser outputs exactly one dependency tree for any sentence, even if the sentence is ambiguous or incorrect. As illustrated in Figure 1 step 1, the parser starts with a flat tree – a sequence of nodes attached below the auxiliary root, each of them containing the respective word form, lemma, and morphological tag. Then the linguistically relevant oriented edges are gradually added by various techniques. The structure is connected and acyclic at any parsing phase.

No backtracking. We prefer greedy parsing (allowing subsequent corrections, however) to backtracking. If the parser makes a bad decision (e.g. due to insufficient local information) and it is detected only much later, then the parser can 'rehang' the already attached node (rehanging becomes necessary especially in the case of coordinations, see steps 3 and 6 in Figure 1). Thus there is no danger of exponential expansion which often burdens symbolic parsers.

Bottom-up parsing (reduction rules). When applying reduction rules, we use the idea of a 'sliding window' (a short array), which moves along the sequence of 'parentless' nodes (the artificial root's children) from right to left.[3] On each position, we try to apply simple hand-written grammar rules (each implemented as an independent Perl subroutine) on the window elements. For instance, the rule for reducing prepositional groups works as follows: if the first element in the window is an unsaturated preposition and the second one is a noun or a pronoun agreeing in morphological case, then the parser 'hangs' the second node below the first node, as shown in the code fragment below (compare steps 9 and 10 in Figure 1):

```
sub rule_adj_noun($) {
  my $win = shift;
  if (adjectival($win->[0]) and noun($win->[1])
      and ($win->[0]->{p_ordinal} or
        (agr_case($win->[0],$win->[1]) and
          agr_number($win->[0],$win->[1]) and
          agr_gender($win->[0],$win->[1]))))) {
    return hang($win->[0],$win->[1]);
    } else {  return 0 }
}

sub rule_prep_noun($) {
```

---

[2] http://ufal.mff.cuni.cz/~pajas/tred/index.html
[3] Our observations show that the direction choice is important, at least for Czech.

```
my $win = shift;
if (preposition($win->[0])
   and nominal($win->[1])
   and not $win->[0]->{p_saturated}){
      $win->[0]->{p_saturated}=1;
      return hang($win->[1],$win->[0]);
} else {  return 0 }
}
```

The rules are tried out according to their pre-specified ordering; only the first applicable rule is always chosen. Then the sliding window is shifted several positions to the right (outside the area influenced by the last reduction, or to the right-most position), and slides again on the shortened sequence (the node attached by the last applied rule is not the root's child any more). Presently, we have around 40 reduction rules and – measured by the number of edges – they constitute the most productive component of the parser.

Interface to the tagset. Morphological information stored in the morphological tags is obviously extremely important for syntactic analysis. However, the reduction rules never access the morphological tags directly, but exclusively via a predefined set of 'interface' routines, as it is apparent also in the above rule samples. This routines are not always straightforward, e.g. the subroutine `adjectival` recognizes not only adjectives, but also possessive pronouns, some of the negative, relative and interrogative pronouns, some numerals etc.

Auxiliary attributes. Besides the attributes already included in the node (word form, lemma, tag, as mentioned above), the parser introduces many new auxiliary node attributes. For instance, the attribute `p_saturated` used above specifies whether the given preposition or subordinating conjunction is already 'saturated' (with a noun or a clause, respectively), or special attributes for coordination. In these attributes, a coordination conjunction which coordinates e.g. two nouns pretends itself to be a noun too (we call it the effective part of speech), so that e.g. a shared attribute modifier can be attached directly below this conjunction.

External lexical lists. Some reduction rules are lexically specific. For this purpose, various simple lexicons (containing e.g. certain types of named entities or basic information about surface valency) have been automatically extracted either from the Czech National Corpus or from the training part of the PDT, and are used by the parser.

Clause segmentation. In any phase of the parsing process, the sequence of parentless nodes is divided into segments separated by punctuation marks or coordination conjunctions; the presence of a finite verb form is tested in every segment, which is extremely important for distinguishing interclausal and intraclausal coordination.[4]

Top-down parsing. The application of the reduction rules can be viewed as bottom-up parsing. However, in some situations it is advantageous to switch to the top-down direction, namely in the cases when we know that a certain sequence of nodes (which we are not able to further reduce by the reduction rules) is of certain syntactic type, e.g. a clause delimited on one side by a subordinating conjunctions, or a complex sentence in a direct speech delimited from both sides by quotes. It is important especially for the application of fallback rules.

---

[4] In our opinion, it is especially coordination (and similar phenomena of non-dependency nature) what makes parsing of natural languages so difficult.

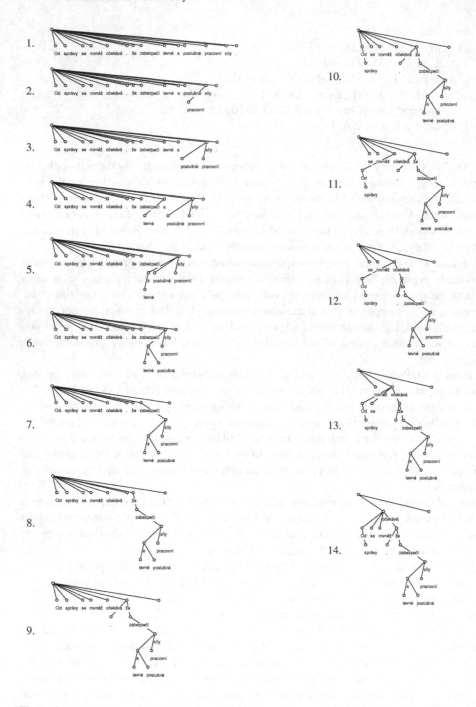

Fig. 1. Step-by-step processing of the sentence *'Od správy se rověž očekává, že zabezpečí levné a poslušné pracovní síly.'* (The administration is also supposed to ensure cheap and obedient manpower.) by the rule-based parser.

Fallback rules. We are not able to describe all language phenomena by the reduction rules, and thus we have to use also heuristic fallback rules in some situations. For instance, if we are to parse something what is probably a single clause and no reduction rules are no longer applicable, then the finite verb is selected as the clause head and all the remaining parentless nodes are attached below it (steps 11–14 in Figure 1).

Similar attempts to parsing based on hand-coded rules are often claimed to be hard to develop and maintain because of the intricate interplay of various language phenomena. In our experience and contrary to this expectation, it is possible to reach a reasonable performance (see Table 1), speed and robustness within one or two weeks of development time (less than 2500 lines of Perl code). We have also verified that the idea of our parser can be easily applied on other languages – the preliminarily estimated accuracy of our Slovene, German, and Romanian rule-based dependency parsers is 65–70 % (however, the discussion about porting the parser to other languages goes beyond the scope of this paper).

As for the parsing speed, it can be evaluated as follows: if the parser is executed in the parallelized ntred environment employing 15 Linux servers, it takes around 90 seconds to parse all the PDT 2.0 a-layer development data (9270 sentences), which gives roughly 6.9 sentences per second per server.

3   Pushdown Dependency Parsers

The presented pushdown parser is similar to those described in [3] or [4]. During the training phase, the parser creates a set of premise-action rules, and applies it during the parsing phase. Let us suppose a stack represented as a sequence $n_1 \ldots n_j$, where n_1 is the top element; stack elements are ordered triplets $<form, lemma, tag>$. The parser uses four types of actions:

- read a token from the input, and push it into the stack,
- attach the top item n_1 of the stack below the artificial root (i.e., create a new edge between these two), and pop it from the stack,
- attach the top item n_1 below some other (non-top) item n_i, and pop the former from the stack,
- attach a non-top item n_i below the top item n_1, and remove the former from the stack.[5]

The forms of the rule premises are limited to several templates with various degree of specificity. The different templates condition different parts of the stack and of the unread input, and previously performed actions.

In the training phase, the parser determines the sequence of actions which leads to the correct tree for each sentence (in case of ambiguity we use a pre-specified preference ordering of the actions). For each performed action, the counters for the respective premise-action pairs are increased.

During the parsing phase, in each situation the parser chooses the premise-action pair with the highest score; the score is calculated as a product of the value of the counter of the given pair and of the weight of the template used in the premise (see [5] for the discussion

---

[5] Note that the possibility of creating edges from or to the items in the middle of the stack enables the parser to analyze also non-projective constructions.

about template weights), divided by the exponentially growing penalty for the stack distance between the two nodes to be connected.

In the following section we use four versions of the pushdown parser: L2R – the basic pushdown parser (left to right), R2L – the parser processing the sentences in reverse order, L23 and R23 – the parsers using 3-letter suffices of the word forms instead of the morphological tags.

The parsers work very quickly; it takes about 10 seconds to parse 9270 sentences from PDT 2.0 d-test on PC with one AMD Athlon 2500+. Learning phase takes around 100 seconds.

4   Experiments with Parser Combinations

This section describes our experiments with combining eight parsers. They are referred to using the following abbreviations: McD (McDonnald's maximum spanning tree parser, [6]),[6] COL (Collins's parser adapted for PDT, [7]), ZZ (rule-based dependency parser described in Section 2), AN (Holan's parser ANALOG which has no training phase and in the parsing phase it searches for the local tree configuration most similar to the training data, [5]), L2R, R2L, L23 and R32 (pushdown parsers introduced in Section 3). For the accuracy of the individual parsers see Table 1.

We present two approaches to the combination of the parsers: (1) Simply Weighted Parsers, and (2) Weighted Evaluation Classes.

Simply Weighted Parsers (SWP). The simplest way to combine the parsers is to select each node's parent out of the set of all suggested parents by simple parser voting. But as the accuracy of the individual parsers significantly differ (as well as the correlation in parser pairs), it seems natural to give different parsers different weights, and to select the eventual parent according to the weighted sum of votes. However, this approach based on local decisions does not guarantee cycle-free and connected resulting structure. To guarantee its 'treeness', we decided to build the final structure by the Maximum Spanning Tree algorithm (see [6] for references). Its input is a graph containing the union of all edges suggested by the parsers; each edge is weighted by the sum of weights of the parsers supporting the given edge. We limited the range of weights to small natural numbers; the best weight vector has been found using a a simple hill-climbing heuristic search.

We evaluated this approach using 10-fold cross evaluation applied on the PDT 2.0 a-layer d-test data. In each of the ten iterations, we found the set of weights which gave the best accuracy on 90 % of d-test sentences, and evaluated the accuracy of the resulting parser combination on the unseen 10 %. The average accuracy was 86.22 %, which gives 1.98 percent point improvement compared to McD. It should be noted that all iterations resulted in the same weight vector: (10, 10, 9, 2, 3, 2, 1, 1) for the same parser ordering as in Table 1. Figure 2 shows that the improvement with respect to McD is significant and relatively stable.

When the weights were 'trained' on the whole d-test data and the parser combination was evaluated on the e-test data, the resulting accuracy was 85.84 % (1.86 % improvement compared to McD), which is the best e-test result reported in this paper.[7]

---

[6] We would like to thank Václav Novák for providing us with the results of McD on PDT 2.0.

[7] Of course, in all our experiments we respect the rule that the e-test data should not be touched until the developed parsers (or parser combinations) are 'frozen'.

Table 1. Percent accuracy of the individual parsers when applied (separately) on the PDT 2.0 d-test and e-test data.

	McD	COL	ZZ	AN	R2L	L2R	R23	L23
d-test	84.24	81.55	76.06	71.45	73.98	71.38	61.06	54.88
e-test	83.98	80.91	75.93	71.08	73.85	71.32	61.65	53.28

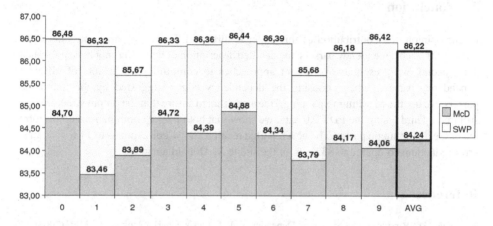

Fig. 2. Accuracy of the SWP parser combination compared to the best single McD parser in 10-fold evaluation on the d-test data.

Weighted Equivalence Classes (WEC). The second approach is based on the idea of partitioning the set of parsers into equivalence classes. At any node, the pairwise agreement among the parsers can be understood as an equivalence relation and thus implies partitioning on the set of parsers. Given 8 parsers, there are theoretically 4133 possible partitionings (in fact, there are only 3,719 of them present in the d-test data), and thus it is computationally tractable.

In the training phase, each class in each partitioning obtains a weight which represents the conditional probability that the class corresponds to the correct result, conditioned by the given partitioning. Technically, the weight is estimated as the number of nodes where the given class corresponds to the correct answer divided by the number of nodes where the given partitioning appeared.

In the evaluation phase, at any node the agreement of results of the individual parsers implies the partitioning. Each of the edges suggested by the parsers then corresponds to one equivalence class in this partitioning, and thus the edge obtains the weight of the class. Similarly to the former approach to parser combination, the Maximum Spanning Tree algorithm is applied on the resulting graph in order to obtain a tree structure.

Again, we performed 10-fold cross validation using the d-test data. The resulting average accuracy is 85.41 %, which is 1.17 percentage point improvement compared to McD. If the whole d-test is used for weight extraction and the resulting parser is evaluated on the whole e-test, the accuracy is 85.14 %.

The interesting property of this approach to parser combination is that if we use the same set of data both for the training and evaluation phase, the resulting accuracy is the upper bound for of all similar parser combinations based only on the information about local agreement/disagreement among the parsers. If this experiment is performed on the whole d-test data, the obtained upper bound is 87.15 %.

5 Conclusion

In our opinion, the contribution of this paper is threefold. First, the paper introduces two (types of) Czech dependency parsers, the detailed description of which has not been published yet. Second, we present two different approaches to combining the results of different dependency parsers; when choosing the dependency edges suggested by the individual parsers, we use the Maximum Spanning Tree algorithm to assure that the output structures are still trees. Third, using the PDT 2.0 data, we show that both parser combinations outperform the best existing single parser. The best reported result 85.84 % corresponds to 11.6 % relative error reduction, compared to 83.98 % of the single McDonald's parser.

References

1. Zeman, D.: Parsing with a Statistical Dependency. PhD thesis, Charles University, MFF (2004).
2. Zeman, D., Žabokrtský, Z.: Improving Parsing Accuracy by Combining Diverse Dependency Parsers. In: Proceedings of the 9th International Workshop on Parsing Technologies, Vancouver, B.C., Canada (2005).
3. Holan, T.: Tvorba závislostního syntaktického analyzátoru. In: Sborník semináře MIS 2004. Matfyzpress, Prague, Czech Republic (2004).
4. Nivre, J., Nilsson, J.: Pseudo-Projective Dependency Parsing. In: Proceedings of ACL'05, Ann Arbor, Michigan (2005).
5. Holan, T.: Genetické učení závislostních analyzátorů. In: Sborník semináře ITAT 2005. UPJŠ, Košice (2005).
6. McDonald, R., Pereira, F., Ribarov, K., Hajič, J.: Non-Projective Dependency Parsing using Spanning Tree Algorithms. In: Proceedings of HTL/EMNLP'05, Vancouver, BC, Canada (2005).
7. Hajič, J., Collins, M., Ramshaw, L., Tillmann, C.: A Statistical Parser for Czech. In: Proceedings ACL'99, Maryland, USA (1999).

Processing Korean Numeral Classifier Constructions in a Typed Feature Structure Grammar

Jong-Bok Kim[1] and Jaehyung Yang[2]

[1] School of English, Kyung Hee University, Seoul, 130-701, Korea
jongbok@khu.ac.kr
[2] School of Computer Engineering, Kangnam University, Kyunggi, 449-702, Korea
jhyang@kangnam.ac.kr

Abstract. The syntactic and semantic complexity of the so-called numeral classifier (Num-Cl) constructions in Korean challenges theoretical as well as computational linguists. We provide a constraint-based analysis of these constructions within the framework of HPSG with the semantic representations of MRS (Minimal Recursion Semantics) and reports its implementation in the LKB (Linguistic Knowledge Building) system.

1 Basic Data and Issues

One of the most salient features of languages like Korean is the complex behavior of numeral classifiers.[1] There exist at least three different environments where the numeral-classifier (Num-CL) expression can appear:[2]

(1) a. Genitive-Case (GC) Type:
      sey myeng-uy haksayng-i   o-ass-ta
      three CL-GEN student-NOM come-PST-DECL
      'Three students came.'
  b. Noun Initial (NI) Type:
      haksayng sey myeng(-i) o-ass-ta
      student   three CL-NOM come-PST-DECL
  c. Noun-Case (NC) Type:
      haksayng-i   sey myeng-i o-ass-ta
      student-NOM three CL-NOM come-PST-DECL

In the GC type, the Num-CL appears with the genitive case marking, preceding the modifying NP. In the NI type, the Num-CL sequence follows a caseless N, whereas in the NC type both the head noun and the following Num-CL are case-marked.

---

[1] Our thanks go to anonymous reviewers for the comments and suggestions. This work was supported by the Korea Research Foundation Grant funded by the Korean Government (KRF-2005-042-A00056).

[2] The abbreviations used for glosses and feature attributes in this paper are as follows: CL (CLASSIFIER), CONJ (CONJUNCTION), COP (COPULA), COMP (COMPLEMENTIZER), DECL (DECLARATIVE), GEN (GENITIVE), LBL (LABEL), LTOP (LOCAL TOP), NOM (NOMINATIVE), PNE (PRENOMINAL ENDING), PST (PAST), RELS (RELATIONS), SEM (SEMANTICS), SPR (SPECIFIER), SYN (SYNTAX), TOP (TOPIC), etc.

Petr Sojka, Ivan Kopeček and Karel Pala (Eds.): TSD 2006, LNAI 4188, pp. 103–110, 2006.
© Springer-Verlag Berlin Heidelberg 2006

The foremost difficulty in parsing these constructions comes from the NC type in which the Num-CL floats away from its antecedent:

(2) **pemin-i**   cengmal **sey myeng-i/*-ul** te   iss-ta
     criminal-NOM really   three CL-NOM/ACC more exist-DECL
     'There are three more criminals.'

Within a system where no movement is allowed, it is not an easy task to correctly link the Num-CL to its remote antecedent.

In order to build a computationally feasible Korean grammar that can yield deep-parsing results, the grammar needs to form these three types of numeral classifier constructions and obtain semantics appropriate for each type. This paper shows that a typed feature structure grammar, HPSG, together with Minimal Recursion Semantics (MRS), is well-suited in providing the proper syntax and semantics of these three types of constructions.[3]

2   Data Distribution

We have inspected the Sejong Treebank Corpus to figure out the distributional frequency of Korean numeral classifiers in real texts. From the corpus of total 378,689 words (33,953 sentences), we identified 694 occurrences of numeral classifier expressions and identified the top 8 most frequently-used classifiers:

(3)

CL Type	Frequency	Examples
pen	158	oycwul han pen 'outgoing one CL'
salam	103	swunkem han salam 'policeman one CL'
kaci	70	yuhyung twu kaci 'type two CL'
myeng	56	kkoma han myeng 'child one CL'
kay	50	pang two kay 'room two CL'
mali	27	say han mali 'bird one CL'
cang	25	pyenci han cang 'letter one CL'
tay	20	cenhwa twu tay 'phone two CL'

Of the 694 examples, we identified 86 GC examples, 104 NI examples, and 36 NC examples. The remaining 468 examples consist of 365 anaphoric usages and 103 miscellaneous usages(e.g, ordinal, appositive usages).[4] As expected, the NI type occurs more often than the other two types. The NC patterns are relatively rare partly because the Sejong Corpus we inspected consists mainly of written texts. However, the statistics clearly show these three categories are legitimate constructions and should be taken into consideration if we want to build a robust grammar for Korean numeral-classifiers. This research limited its scope to these three main types.

---

[3] Minimal Recursion Semantics, developed by [1], is a framework of computational semantics designed to enable semantic composition using only the unification of type feature structures. See [1] and [2]. The value of the attribute SEM(ANTICS) in our system represents a simplified MRS.

[4] Examples like *sey myeng-i o-ass-ta* 'three CL-NOM come-PST-DECL' are anaphoric usages in the sense that the antecedent of the Num-CL is within the given context.

3 Implementing an Analysis

3.1 Forming a Numeral-Classifier Sequence and Its Semantics

The starting point of the analysis is forming the well-formed Num-CL expressions. Syntactically, numeral classifiers are a subclass of nouns (for Japanese see [3]). However, unlike common nouns, they cannot stand alone and must combine with a numeral or a limited set of determiners:[5] *(twu) kay 'two CL' (Numeral), *(yeleo/myech) kay 'several CL' (Quantifier), and *(myech) kay 'how many' (Interrogative). Semantically, there are tight sortal constraints between the classifiers and the nouns (or NPs) they modify. For example, *pen* can classify only events, *tay* machinery, and *kwuen* just books. Such sortal constraints block classifiers like *tay* from modifying thin entities like books as in *chayk twu tay 'book two-CL'. Reflecting these syntactic and semantic properties, we can assign the following lexical information to numerals (*num-det*) and classifiers (*cl-n*) within the feature structure system of HPSG and MRS.[6]

(4)

a.
$$
\begin{bmatrix}
\textit{num-det} \\
\text{ORTH} \langle \text{sey} \rangle \\
\text{SYN} \mid \text{HEAD} \begin{bmatrix} \text{POS } \textit{det} \\ \text{NUM} + \end{bmatrix} \\
\text{SEM} \begin{bmatrix} \text{HOOK} \begin{bmatrix} \text{INDEX } i \\ \text{LTOP } h2 \end{bmatrix} \\ \text{RELS} \left\langle \begin{bmatrix} \text{PRED } \textit{card\_rel} \\ \text{LBL } h2 \\ \text{ARG0 } i \\ \text{CARG 3} \end{bmatrix} \right\rangle \end{bmatrix}
\end{bmatrix}
$$

b.
$$
\begin{bmatrix}
\textit{cl-n} \\
\text{ORTH} \langle \text{myeng} \rangle \\
\text{SYN} \begin{bmatrix} \text{HEAD} \begin{bmatrix} \text{POS } \textit{noun} \\ \text{CLTYPE} + \end{bmatrix} \\ \text{VAL} \mid \text{SPR} \left\langle \begin{bmatrix} \text{NUM} + \\ \text{INDEX } i \end{bmatrix} \right\rangle \end{bmatrix} \\
\text{SEM} \begin{bmatrix} \text{HOOK} \begin{bmatrix} \text{INDEX } i \\ \text{LTOP } h1 \end{bmatrix} \\ \text{RELS} \left\langle \begin{bmatrix} \text{PRED } \textit{person\_rel} \\ \text{LBL } h1 \\ \text{ARG0 } i \end{bmatrix} \right\rangle \end{bmatrix}
\end{bmatrix}
$$

The feature structure in (4a) represents that there exists an individual x whose CARG (constant argument) value is "3". The feature NUM is assigned to the numerals as well as to determiners like *yele* 'several' and *myech* 'some' which combine with classifiers. Meanwhile, (4b) indicates that syntactically a classifier selects a NUM element through the SPR, whereas semantically it belongs to the ontological category *person_rel*. The feature CLTYPE differentiates classifiers from common nouns. Assuming that only [NUM +] elements can combine with the [CLTYPE +], we can rule out unwanted forms such as *ku myeng 'the CL'. In addition, unlike quantifier determiners *motun* 'all' as in *ku motun haksayng* 'the all student', nothing can intervene between the NUM and CL. Our grammar captures these

---

[5] A limited set of common nouns such as *salam* 'person', *kulus* 'vessel', *can* 'cup', *khep* 'cup', and *thong* 'bucket' can also function as classifiers.

[6] The value of LBL is a token to a given EP (elementary predicate). The feature HOOK includes externally visible attributes of the atomic predications in RELS. The value of LTOP is the local top handle, the handle of the relations with the widest scope within the constituent. See [1] for the exact functions of each attribute.

multi-word like properties by treating the Num-CL sequence as a multiword (*mw*) expression formed by the following rule:[7]

(5)   Num-CL Rule:

$$\left[\,num\text{-}cl\text{-}mw\,\right] \mapsto \begin{bmatrix} num\text{-}det \\ \text{NUM} + \end{bmatrix}, \text{[CLTYPE +]}$$

When this rule is incorporated in our existing grammar and implemented in the LKB system[8], we then generate a right syntactic structure with the following MRS representation:

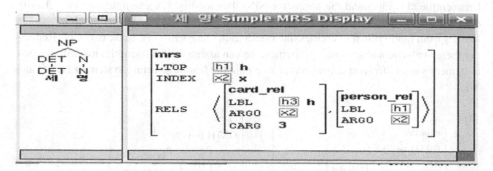

As represented here *sey myeng* 'three CL' forms a simple NP with the meaning that there are three individuals 'x2' which ontologically belongs to *person_rel*.

3.2   Genitive Case Type

Following [5], we assume the attachment of GEN case particle *-uy* to a nominal will add the information on GCASE (grammatical case) as well as the specification on the MOD feature:

(6)
$$\begin{bmatrix} num\text{-}cl\text{-}gen \\ \text{ORTH } \langle \text{sey myeng-uy} \rangle \\ \text{SYN} \begin{bmatrix} \text{HEAD} \begin{bmatrix} \text{POS } noun \\ \text{CASE} \mid \text{GCASE } gen \\ \text{MOD } \langle \text{NP}_j \rangle \end{bmatrix} \end{bmatrix} \\ \text{SEM} \mid \text{RELS} \left\langle \begin{bmatrix} \text{PRED } card\_rel \\ \text{LBL } h2 \\ \text{ARG0 } i \\ \text{ARG1 } 3 \end{bmatrix}, \begin{bmatrix} \text{PRED } person\_rel \\ \text{LBL } h1 \\ \text{ARG0 } i \end{bmatrix}, \begin{bmatrix} \text{PRED } part\text{-}of\_rel \\ \text{ARG0 } i \\ \text{ARG1 } j \end{bmatrix} \right\rangle \end{bmatrix}$$

---

[7] The type *num-cl-mw* is a subtype of *hd-spr-ph* formed by the combination of a head and its specifier.

[8] The current Korean Resource Grammar has 394 type definitions, 36 grammar rules, 77 inflectional rules, 1100 lexical entries, and 2100 test-suite sentences, and aims to expand its coverage on real-life data. The LKB, freely available with open source (http://lingo.stanford.edu), is a grammar and lexicon development environment for use with constraint-based linguistic formalisms such as HPSG. cf. [4].

Unlike the simple expression *sey myeng*, the GEN marked expression *sey myeng-uy* adds an additional constraint: the MOD value indicates that the expression that the *num-cl-gen* modifies must be a nominal expression whose index value is associated with it through *part-of_rel*. Unlike the determiners, the GEN-marked NP functions as a modifier to a completely saturated NP as in *John-uy ku chinkwu* 'John-GEN the friend' or *ku John-uy chinkwu* 'the John-GEN friend'. In capturing such an NP property, our grammar introduces the Head-MOD rule (generating *hd-mod-ph*) that allows the combination of an adnominal element and its head, generating an appropriate syntactic structure and semantic representations.

3.3   NI (Noun-Initial) Type

The cleft sentences in (7) indicate that unlike in the NC type, in the NI type the head noun forms a strong syntactic unit with a following Num-CL:

(7) a. ku sensayngnim-ul mos ka-key   ha-n kes-un
         that teacher-ACC   not go-COMP do   thing-PNE

         [haksayng   sey myeng]-i-essta.
         three-CL-GEN student-COP-PAST

         'What made the teacher not leave were five students.'
     b. *ku sensayng-nim-ul moskakey han kes-un [haksayng-i sey myeng-i]-ess-ta.

In addition, there exist various examples indicating that the NI type behaves like a synthetic compound or multiword expression. For example, the N and the following Num-CL sequence cannot be separated at all:[9]

(8) haksayng (*ku) sey   myeng-i   o-ass-ta
     student   the   three CL-NOM come-PST-DECL
     'Three students came.

Such a tight syntactic cohesion supports the idea that the NI sequence is another multi-word expression formed by a rule like the following:

(9) NI Compound Formation Rule:

$$\begin{bmatrix} cn\text{-}num\text{-}cl\text{-}mw \\ \text{HEAD} \mid \text{MOD} \langle \; \rangle \end{bmatrix} \rightarrow \begin{bmatrix} cn \\ \text{INDEX } i \end{bmatrix}, H \begin{bmatrix} num\text{-}cl\text{-}mw \\ \text{CLTYPE } + \\ \text{INDEX } i \end{bmatrix}$$

The resulting type *cn-num-cl-mw*, unlike *num-cl-mw*, has an empty MOD value, indicating that it can function not as a modifier but as an argument. This formation rule will eventually license the combination of *haksayng* 'student' with *sey myong* as a multiword expression, generating the following structure and MRS for (8):

---

[9] A long pause between the two improves the example, but such an example can be taken to be an NC type.

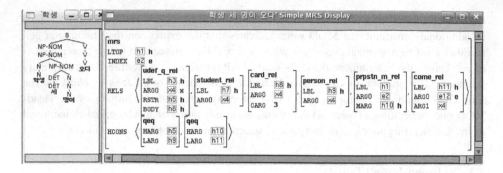

As represented in the structure, the common noun *haksayng* 'student' combines with the *num-cl-mw* expression *sey myeng* in accordance with the formation rule in (9). They both have the same index value with their own semantic contributions as given in the RELS values. The NP then functions as the ARG1 of the *come_rel* relation which projects a propositional message (*prpstn_m_rel*).

3.4   Noun-Case Type

The NC type allows the NOM or ACC-marked NP to be followed by the identical case-marked NUM-CL (called FQ here) which even can float away from the NP as noted in (2). There exist several supporting phenomena indicating that the FQ modifies the following verbal expression. One phenomenon is the substitution by the proverb *kule-* 'do so'. As noted in (10), unlike the NI type, only in the NC type, an FQ and the following main verb can be together substituted by the proverb *kulay-ss-ta*:

(10)   a.   namca-ka   [sey myeng o-ass-ko],   yeca-to   kulay-ss-ta
           man-NOM three CL   come-PST-CONJ woman-also do-PST-DECL.
           'As for man, three came, and as for woman, the same number came.'
       b.   *[namca sey myeng-i] o-ass-ko, yeca-to [kulay-ss-ta]

This means that the FQ in the NC type is a VP modifier, though it is linked to a preceding NP.

The question then is how to link an FQ with its appropriate antecedent. There exist several constraints in identifying the antecedents. When the floating quantifier is case-marked, it seems to be linked to an argument with the same case marking. However, a complication arises from examples in which either the antecedent NP or the FQ are marked not with a case marker, but a marker like a TOP:

(11)   a.   haksayng-tul-i/un   sakwa-lul   sey kay-lul   mekta
           student-PL-NOM/TOP apple-ACC three CL-ACC eat
           'As for the students, they ate three apples.'
       b.   sakwa-lul haksayng-tul-i/un sey kay-lul mekta

This implies that a surface case marking cannot be a sole indicator for the linking relation, and that we need to refer to grammatical functions. Regardless of its location, however, we can observe that the NOM-marked FQ is linked to the subject whereas the ACC-marked FQ is linked to the object. This observation is reflected in the following lexical information:

(12)

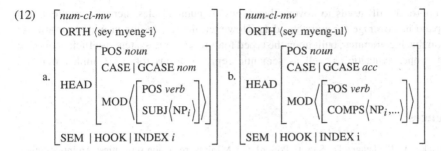

As given in the lexical information, the case-marked *num-cl-mw* functions as a specifier to a verbal expression, but quantifies over an argument with the same case value.

(13)

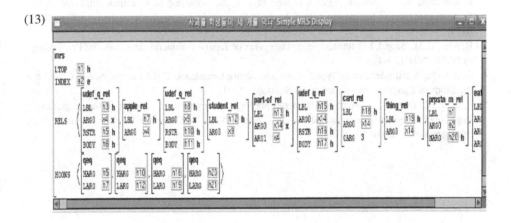

As given in (12), the NOM-marked *num-cl-mw* thus modifies a verbal element whose SUBJ has the same index value, whereas the ACC-marked *num-cl-mw* modifies a verbal element which has at least one unsaturated COMPS element whose INDEX value is identical with its own INDEX value. What this means is that the NOM or ACC marked *num-cl-mw* is semantically linked to the SUBJ or COMPS element through the INDEX value. As given in (13), this system provides a right MRS for (11b). The output MRS links the ARG0 value of *apple_rel* with the ARG0 value of the CL *thing_rel*.

4 Future Work and Conclusion

Our grammar has been implemented in the HPSG for Korean. In testing its performance and feasibility for parsing numeral classifier constructions, we used 100 sentences from the identified 226 sentences (GC, NI, and NC type) extracted from the Sejong corpus as noted in section 2, and 100 grammatical and 50 ungrammatical sentences extracted from the literature. As noted before, the grammar successfully constructed three main types of Num-CL constructions together with appropriate semantic representations. One strong merit of this analysis, as we have seen, is that it can capture the syntactic and semantic aspects of the NC type in which the NP and the FQ are not adjacent but in remote positions.

Our approach still needs to cover other types of numeral classifier constructions and then expand its coverage for authentic data. However, the test results provide a promising indication that the grammar, built upon the typed feature structure system, is efficient enough to build proper syntactic as well as semantic representations for the complex numeral classifiers.

References

1. Copestake, A., Flickenger, D., Sag, I., Pollard, C.: Minimal recursion semantics: An introduction. Manuscript (2003).
2. Bender, E. M., Flickinger, D. P., Oepen, S.: The grammar matrix: An open-source starter-kit for the rapid development of cross-linguistically consistent broad-coverage precision grammars. In Carroll, J., Oostdijk, N., Sutcliffe, R., (Eds.): Proceedings of the Workshop on Grammar Engineering and Evaluation at the 19th International Conference on Computational Linguistics, Taipei, Taiwan (2002) 8–14.
3. Bender, E. M., Siegel, M.: Implementing the syntax of Japanese numeral classifiers. In: Proceedings of IJCNLP-04. (2004).
4. Copestake, A.: Implementing Typed Feature Structure Grammars. CSLI Lecture Notes. Center for the Study of Language and Information, Stanford (2001).
5. Kim, J. B., Yang, J.: Projections from morphology to syntax in the korean resource grammar: implementing typed feature structures. In: Lecture Notes in Computer Science. Volume 2945. Springer-Verlag (2004) 13–24.

Parsing Head Internal and External Relative Clause Constructions in Korean

Jong-Bok Kim

School of English, Kyung Hee University, Seoul, 130-701, Korea
jongbok@khu.ac.kr

Abstract. Korean displays various types of relative clauses including head internal and external relative clauses (HIRC and HERC). In particular, the treatment of HIRC has received less attention from computational perspectives even though it is frequently found in both text and spoken languages. This paper shows that a typed feature structure grammar of HPSG (together with the semantic representations of Minimal Recursion Semantics) offers us a computationally feasible and applicable way of deep-parsing both the HIRC and HERC in the language.

1 Introduction

In terms of truth conditional meanings, there is no clear difference between (Korean) HIRCs like (1a) and HERCs like (1b).[1]

(1) a. Tom-un [sakwa-ka cayngpan-wi-ey iss-nun   kes]-ul   mekessta
         Tom-TOP apple-NOM tray-TOP-LOC   exist-PNE KES-ACC ate
         'Tom ate an apple, which was on the tray.'
     b. Tom-un [_ cayngpan-wi-ey iss-nun   sakwa]-ul mekessta.
         Tom-TOP   tray-TOP-LOC   exist-PNE apple-ACC ate
         'Tom ate an apple that was on the tray.'

Both describe an event in which an apple is on the tray and Tom's eating it.[2] Yet, there exist several intriguing differences between the two constructions. One crucial difference between the HIRC and HERC comes from the fact that the semantic object of *mekessta* 'ate' in the HIRC example (1a) is the NP *sakwa* 'apple' buried inside the embedded clause. It is thus the subject of the embedded clause that serves as the semantic argument of the main predicate [1,2].

We can treat the HERC as a modifier structure in which a sentence with a gap modifies a nominal. In terms of semantics, we then just need to link the gap with the nominal. However, complication arises in the HIRC since the head is inside the sentential element. In the analysis of such HIRCs, of central interest is how we can associate the internal head of the HIRC

---

[1] I thank Chung Chan, Peter Sells, and Jaehyung Yang for their helpful comments. My thank also goes to anonymous reviewers for the comments. This work was supported by the Kyung Hee Alumni Research Award in the year of 2005.
[2] This paper adopts the following abbreviations: ACC (ACCUSATIVE), COMP (COMPLEMENTIZER), LOC (LOCATIVE), NOM (NOMINATIVE), PNE (PRENOMINAL), TOP (TOPIC), etc.

Petr Sojka, Ivan Kopeček and Karel Pala (Eds.): TSD 2006, LNAI 4188, pp. 111–117, 2006.
© Springer-Verlag Berlin Heidelberg 2006

clause with the matrix predicate so that the head can function as its semantic argument. This paper provides a constraint-based analysis to these two different types of relative clauses within the framework of HPSG (Head-driven Phrase Structure Grammar) and implements it in the existing HPSG grammar for Korean using the LKB (Linguistic Building Knowledge) system to check the computational feasibility of the analysis proposed.

2   Syntax and Semantics of the HERC

Unlike English, Korean employs no relative pronouns like *who* or *which*. In addition, the predicate of the relative clause preceding the head noun is marked with a morphological marker depending on the type of tense information.[3]

(2) Tom-i   _ $_i$ ilk-nun/un/ul   chayk$_i$
      Tom-NOM   read-PRES.PNE/PST.PNE/FUT.PNE book
      'the book that Tom reads/read/will read'

The prenominal markers in (2) in a sense function both as a relative pronoun and tense marker. As also expected, the language also allows relativization from an embedded clause:

(3) John-i   [Mary-ka   _ $_i$ mekessta-ko] malha-n sakwa$_i$
      John-NOM Mary-NOM   ate-COMP   say-PNE apple
      'the apple that John said Mary ate yesterday'

The key point of our treatment of relative clauses includes the lexical constraints on the *v-rel-mod* verb heading the relative clause, a gap-introducing rule, and a grammar rule licensing the combination of a nominal head with a relative clause. The lexical constraints on the *v-rel-mod* will add the feature MOD, guaranteeing that a *v-rel-mod* element marked with a prenominal ending will modify a nominal element through the head feature MOD. The gap-introducing rule ensures the relative clause to be an incomplete sentence with one missing gap. As specified in the following feature description in the LKB (Linguistic Knowledge Building System), the rule allows any of the elements in the SUBJ or COMPS to be introduced as a GAP element:[4]

```
binary-start-gap-rule-1 := binary-sg &
[ SYN.VAL [ SUBJ <>,
            COMPS <>,
            GAP <! #2 !> ],
  ARGS < #1 & [ SYN [ HEAD [ CASE.GCASE nom, PRD - ],
                      VAL [ SUBJ <>, COMPS <> ] ] ],
          [ SYN.VAL [ SUBJ < #1 >,
                      COMPS < #2 > ] ] > ].
```

---

[3] These three basic kinds of tense-sensitive prenominal markers can be extended to denote aspects when combined with tense suffixes.

[4] The LKB, freely available with open source (http://lingo.stanford.edu), is a grammar and lexicon development environment for use with constraint-based linguistic formalisms such as HPSG. cf. [3].

This GAP value is passed upto the tree until it meets its filler to generate a long distance dependency like (3). For example, the word *mek-ess-ta-ko* 'eat-PST-DECL-COMP' selects two arguments. However, its COMPS can be realized as a GAP element according to the gap introducing rule described in the above. The *v-rel-mod* word *malha-n* has the information that it modifies a nominal element. In addition, the relative-clause modifying rule given in the below will terminate this GAP value when the index value of the GAP is identical with the modified nominal element:

```
head-rel-mod-rule := binary &
[ SYN.VAL.GAP <! !>
   ARGS < ph-ex & [ SYN.VAL [ MOD < #1 & [ SYN.HEAD.POS noun,
                                            SEM.INDEX #2 ] >,
                              GAP <! [ SEM.INDEX #2 ] !> ] ],
           syn-st & #1 & [ SYN.VAL [ GAP <! !>,
                                     ... ] ] > ].
```

As indicated in the first element of the ARGS value, the relative clause modifies a nominal element whose index value is identical with that of the GAP's value.

Equipped with these three fundamental mechanisms, the grammar allows us to parse the syntactic as well semantic structures of relative clause constructions. For example, on Fig. 1 you see what the grammar obtains within the system.[5] Leaving aside other semantic relations, we can at least observe that the ARG2 value of *eat_rel*, x2, is coindexed with the ARG0 value of *apple_rel*. The grammar can correctly parse relative clauses as well as generate proper a MRS meaning representation.

3   Syntactic and Semantic Aspects and HIRC

There exist several syntactic differences between HERC and HIRC. For example, in the HIRC, there is also a tight syntactic coherence between the nominal head and the adnominal clause headed with *kes*. Nothing can intervene between the two:

(4) *[sakwa-ka cayngpan-wi-ey iss-nun   cak-un   kes]-ul   mekessta
      apple-NOM tray-TOP-LOC   exist-PNE small-PNE KES-ACC ate
      '(intended) (He) ate a small apple, which was on the tray.'

A tight syntactic relation between the clause and the noun *kes* can also be found from the fact that unlike canonical nouns, it must combine with the preceding adnominal clause:

---

[5] Minimal Recursion Semantics, developed by [4], is a framework of computational semantics designed to enable semantic composition using only the unification of type feature structures. The value of the attribute SEM we used here represents simplified MRS, though it originally includes HOOK, RELS, and HCONS. The feature HOOK represents externally visible attributes of the atomic predications in RELS (RELATIONS). The value of LTOP is the local top handle, the handle of the relations with the widest scope within the constituent. See [4] and [5] for the exact functions of each attribute.

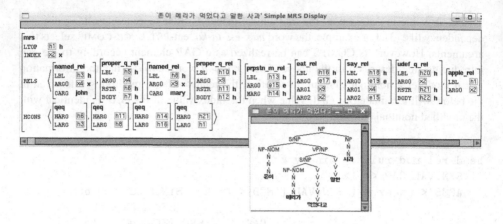

Fig. 1. Parsed structures and MRS for sentences like (3)

(5) Na-nun *(kangto-ka unhayng-eyse nao-nun)   kes-ul   capassta
    I-TOP   robber-NOM bank-from   come-out-PNE KES-ACC caught
    'I arrested the robber who was coming out of the bank.'

The HIRC example in (5) indicates that the adnominal HIRC clause as well as its predicate is an obligatory element. The observations imply that the pronoun *kes* selects an adnominal clause as its complement.

Another fact concerning the status of the HIRC comes from stacking: whereas more than one HERC clause can be stacked together, only one HIRC clause is possible:

(6) a. *kyongchal-i [**kangto-ka   unhayng-eyse nao-nun**]
       police-NOM   [robber-NOM bank-from   come.out-PNE]
       [ton-ul   hwumchi-in] **kes**-ul   chephohayssta
       money-ACC steal-PNE   KES-ACC arrested
       '(int.) The police arrested a thief coming out of the bank, stealing money.'
    b. kyongchal-i [_ **unhayng-eyse nao-nun**]
       police-NOM [bank-from   come.out-PNE]
       [ton-ul   hwumchi-in] **kangto**-lul   chephohayssta
       money-ACC steal-PNE   robber-ACC-ACC arrested
       '(int.) The police arrested a thief coming out of the bank, stealing money.'

This contrast implies that the adonminal clause in the HIRC has the canonical properties of a complement clause: *kes* combines with its complement clause, forming a *hd-comp-ph* (*head-complement-ph*).

One thing to note here is that HIRCs are syntactically very similar to DPCs (direct perception constructions). HIRCs and DPCs both function as the syntactic argument of a matrix predicate. But, in the HIRC (7a), the internal argument *John* within the embedded clause functions as its semantic argument. Meanwhile, in (7b) it is the embedded clausal complement that functions as the semantic argument of the matrix predicate:

(7) a. Mary-nun [John-i   talli-nun kes]-ul   **capassta**.
     Mary-TOP John-NOM run-PNE KES-ACC caught
     'Mary caught John who was running.'

   b. Mary-nun [John-i   talli-nun kes]-ul   **poassta**.
     Mary-TOP John-NOM run-PNE KES-ACC saw
     'Mary saw John running.'

The only difference between (7a) and (7b) is the matrix predicate. This difference induces the meaning difference. When the matrix predicate is an action verb such as *capta* 'catch', *chepohata* 'arrest', or *mekta* 'eat' as in (7a), we obtain an entity reading. But as in (7b) we will have only an event reading when the matrix predicate is a type of perception verb such as *po-ta* 'see', *al-ta* 'know', and *kiekhata* 'remember'.

The key point in our analysis is thus that the interpretation of *kes* is dependent upon the type of matrix predicate, in the sense that the matrix predicate affects the interpretation of the pronoun *kes*. The lexical entries in our grammar involve not only syntax but also semantics. For example, the verb *cap-ta* 'catch' in (8a) lexically requires its object to refer to a *ref-ind* (referential-index) whereas the verb *po-ta* 'see' in (8b) selects an object complement whose index is *indiv-ind* (individual index) whose subtypes include *ref-ind* and *event-ind*, indicating that its object can be either a referential individual or an event.

(8)

a.
$$\begin{bmatrix} \langle\text{cap-ta 'catch'}\rangle \\[4pt] \text{SYN} \mid \text{VAL} \begin{bmatrix} \text{SUBJ} \langle\text{NP}_i\rangle \\ \text{COMPS} \langle\text{NP}_j\rangle \end{bmatrix} \\[12pt] \text{SEM} \mid \text{RELS} \left\langle \begin{bmatrix} \text{PRED } catch\_v\_rel \\ \text{ARG0 } e1 \\ \text{ARG1 }_i [ref\text{-}ind] \\ \text{ARG2 }_j [ref\text{-}ind] \end{bmatrix} \right\rangle \end{bmatrix}$$

b.
$$\begin{bmatrix} \langle\text{po-ta 'see'}\rangle \\[4pt] \text{SYN} \mid \text{VAL} \begin{bmatrix} \text{SUBJ} \langle\text{NP}_i\rangle \\ \text{COMPS} \langle\text{NP}_j\rangle \end{bmatrix} \\[12pt] \text{SEM} \mid \text{RELS} \left\langle \begin{bmatrix} \text{PRED } see\_v\_rel \\ \text{ARG0 } e1 \\ \text{ARG1 }_i [ref\text{-}ind] \\ \text{ARG2 }_j [ind\text{-}ind] \end{bmatrix} \right\rangle \end{bmatrix}$$

These lexical entries will then project an identical syntactic structure for (7a) and (7b), represented together here in (9):

(9)

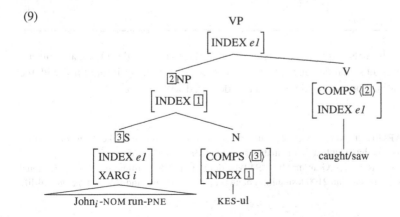

As represented in the structure, in both constructions *kes* selects the adnominal S as its complement and forms a *hd-comp-ph*. The resulting NP will then serve the complement of the main verb *caught* and *saw*. However, semantically, due to the lexical entries in (8a), the object of *caught* is linked to the external argument (XARG) *robber* whereas that of *saw* in (8b) is linked to the event denoted by the S.[6] The type of predicate thus determines whether the INDEX value of *kes* will be identified with that of the S or that of its XARG, as presented in the lexical entries:

(10)

a.
$$\begin{bmatrix} \langle kes \rangle \\ \text{SYN} \begin{bmatrix} \text{HEAD} \mid \text{POS } noun \\ \text{VAL} \mid \text{COMPS } \langle \text{S[INDEX } e1] \rangle \end{bmatrix} \\ \text{SEM} \mid \text{HOOK} \mid \text{INDEX } e1 \end{bmatrix}$$

b.
$$\begin{bmatrix} \langle kes \rangle \\ \text{SYN} \begin{bmatrix} \text{HEAD} \mid \text{POS } noun \\ \text{VAL} \mid \text{COMPS } \langle \text{S} \begin{bmatrix} \text{XARG } i \end{bmatrix} \rangle \end{bmatrix} \\ \text{SEM} \mid \text{HOOK} \mid \text{INDEX } i \end{bmatrix}$$

Our grammar, in which lexical information tightly interacts with the other grammatical components, ensures that the perception verb *saw* combines with the NP projected from (10a) whereas the action verb *caught* with the NP projected from (10b). Otherwise, the grammar will not satisfy the selectional restrictions of the predicates.

Incorporating this in our Korean grammar,[7] we implemented the analysis in the LKB and obtained the following two parsed trees and MRSs for (7a) and (7b), respectively:

(11)

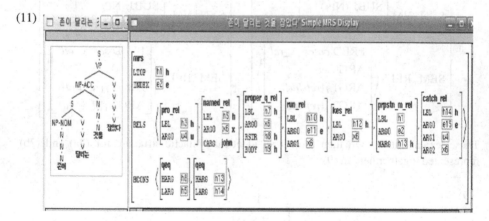

Leaving aside the irrelevant parts, we can see that the two have the identical syntactic structures but different semantics. In the former, the ARG0 value of *kes* is identified with the *named_rel* (for 'John') but the one in the latter is identified with *run_rel*.

---

[6] The feature XARG refers to the external argument in control constructions like *John tries to run*. The XARG of *run* is thus identical to the matrix subject *John*. See [5] for details.

[7] The current Korean Resource Grammar has 394 type definitions, 36 grammar rules, 77 inflectional rules, 1100 lexical entries, and 2100 test-suite sentences, and aims to expand its coverage on real-life data.

(12)

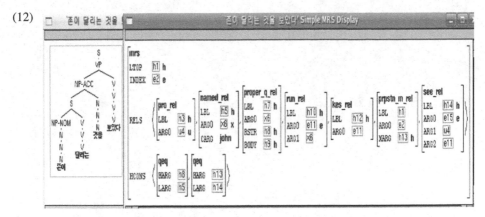

The analysis thus provides a clean account of the complementary distribution between the HIRC and DPC. That is, according to our analysis, we obtain an entity reading when the index value of *kes* is identified with that of the external argument. Meanwhile, we have an event reading when the index value is structure-sharing with that of the adnominal S. This analysis, thus, correctly predicts that there exist no cases where two readings are available simultaneously.

4 Discussion and Conclusion

The analysis we have presented so far, part of the typed-feature structure grammar HPSG for Korean aiming at working with real-world data, has been implemented into LKB to test its performance and feasibility.

We first inspected the Sejong Treebank Corpus (33,953 sentences), selected canonical types of the HERC and HIRC constructions, and then checked if the grammar can parse them both in terms of syntax and semantics. We hope to have shown that the grammar has been quite successful in producing the appropriate syntactic and semantic structures for both HERC and HIRC. Of course, issues remain of extending the coverage of our grammar to parse more real-time data and further identify the other constructional types of relative clauses.

References

1. Kim, Y. B.: Relevance in internally headed relative clauses in korean. Lingua **112** (2002) 541–559.
2. Chung, C., Kim, J. B.:   Differences between externally and internally headed relative clause constructions. In: Proceedings of HPSG 2002, CSLI Publications (2003) 3–25.
3. Copestake, A.: Implementing Typed Feature Structure Grammars. CSLI Lecture Notes. Center for the Study of Language and Information, Stanford (2001).
4. Copestake, A., Flickenger, D., Sag, I., Pollard, C.: Minimal recursion semantics: An introduction. Manuscript (2003).
5. Bender, E. M., Flickinger, D. P., Oepen, S.: The grammar matrix: An open-source starter-kit for the rapid development of cross-linguistically consistent broad-coverage precision grammars. In: Carroll, J., Oostdijk, N., Sutcliffe, R., (Eds.): Proceedings of the Workshop on Grammar Engineering and Evaluation at the 19th Int. Conference on Computational Linguistics, Taipei, Taiwan (2002) 8–14.

A Hybrid Model for Extracting Transliteration Equivalents from Parallel Corpora

Jong-Hoon Oh[1,2], Key-Sun Choi[2], and Hitoshi Isahara[1]

[1] Computational Linguistics Group, NICT, 3-5 Hikaridai, Kyoto 619-0289 Japan
{rovellia, isahara}@nict.go.jp
[2] Computer Science Division, EECS, KAIST, Daejeon 305-701 Republic of Korea
kschoi@cs.kaist.ac.kr

Abstract. Several models for transliteration pair acquisition have been proposed to overcome the out-of-vocabulary problem caused by transliterations. To date, however, there has been little literature regarding a framework that can accommodate several models at the same time. Moreover, there is little concern for validating acquired transliteration pairs using up-to-date corpora, such as web documents. To address these problems, we propose a hybrid model for transliteration pair acquisition. In this paper, we concentrate on a framework for combining several models for transliteration pair acquisition. Experiments showed that our hybrid model was more effective than each individual transliteration pair acquisition model alone.

1 Introduction

Transliteration, "phonetic translation" or "translation by sound", is frequently used for translating a foreign word of one's language into Korean. "Transliteration pairs (TPs)" are word pairs that are composed of a transliteration and its origin foreign word. "Transliteration equivalent" refers to a set of transliteration pairs that originate from the same foreign word. Note that most Korean transliterations generally originate from English words. For example, a set composed of the English word *data* and its Korean transliterations 'de-i-ta', 'de-i-teo', and 'de-ta' is a transliteration equivalent. The mixed use of various transliterations and their origin English word causes severe word mismatch problems in IR (information retrieval) [1]. When a user query and document text use different transliterations and when a user query uses Korean transliteration and a document contains English word or vice versa, simple word matching is not suitable for retrieving documents. Transliteration equivalents can help an IR system to solve the word mismatch problems caused by transliterations. Moreover, transliterations are one of the main sources for out-of-vocabulary (OOV) problems [2].

Several studies on transliteration pair acquisition (TPA) have been proposed. The studies are usually composed of two steps – TP candidate extraction and validation. Depending on the validation method, they can be roughly classified into the **phonetic conversion model (PCM)** [1,3] or the **phonetic similarity model (PSM)** [4,5]. The PCM uses a *"string comparison after phonetic conversion"* strategy. The phonetic conversion in a PCM transforms words of one language into phonetically equivalents of another language. Once two words in the TP candidate are written in the same language, the PCM then validates the TP candidates by a string comparison between the two words. This model is effective

Petr Sojka, Ivan Kopeček and Karel Pala (Eds.): TSD 2006, LNAI 4188, pp. 119–126, 2006.

when correct transliterations can be acquired through phonetic conversion. However, a string similarity measure enables a PCM to acquire TPs even if the phonetic conversion produces wrong transliterations. The PSM directly compares words written in two different languages. This model differentiates phonetic similarity between two phonetic units[1] in different languages depending on their phonetic characteristics. This makes it possible for the PSM to calculate phonetic similarity in a more sophisticated manner than the string similarity measure of the PCM.

Although each model on average has achieved good performance, both models incur errors when extracting transliteration pairs. They do not always make the same error because of each model's particular characteristics. Thus, combining the models could enhance a system's performance by exploiting their strengths. To date, however, there has been little literature regarding a framework that can accommodate two models at the same time. Moreover, there is little concern for validating TP candidates using up-to-date corpora, such as web documents. Web documents, as a knowledge source to validate relevant TPs, enable a TPA system to filter out non-relevant TPs by investigating their occurrence in web documents.

To address these problems, we propose a hybrid model for TPA. In this paper, we concentrate on modeling three TP candidate validation models, – called the PCM, PSM, and corpus based similarity model (CSM) – and a framework for combining all three models. This paper is organized as follows. Section 2 describes the parallel corpora that we used. Section 3 describes our method. Section 4 deals with the experiments. Section 5 discusses the results in detail. Section 6 contains our conclusion and future work.

2   Preparing Parallel Corpora

Ideally, large amounts of sentence aligned bilingual parallel corpora are necessary for a TPA task. However, such large-scale parallel corpora are not readily available. Therefore, we choose, as an alternative method, to use E-K bilingual technical dictionaries as the E-K parallel corpora. There were two reasons why we selected bilingual technical dictionaries as a source of TPs. First, over 40% of the Korean technical terms in scientific domains contain transliterations [6]. Second, we can easily obtain parallel corpora from the bilingual dictionaries because the bilingual technical dictionaries contain English technical terms and their Korean counterparts. Note that there are several Korean translations for one English technical term according to domains and translation methods. We constructed parallel sentences from bilingual technical dictionaries with Korean translations $(kt_{i1}, \cdots, kt_{in})$ that corresponded to a single English technical term (et_i) like $ps_i = (es_i, ks_i)$ where $ks_i = \{kt_{i1}, \cdots, kt_{in}\}$ and $es_i = et_i$.

3   A Hybrid Model for Transliteration Pair Acquisition

Our method is composed of two steps. First, our system extracted TP candidates. Second, the TP candidates were validated using three validation models (PSM, PCM, and CSM), each of which was represented as a similarity model between e_p and k_q, like Sim_{PSM}, Sim_{PCM}, and Sim_{CSM}. In this section, we denote $tp_{pq} = (e_p, k_q)$ as a TP candidate,

---

[1] A phonetic unit refers to a chunk of graphemes, which can be mapped into a phoneme.

where $e_p = e_{p1}, \cdots , e_{pm}$ is composed of m English graphemes and $k_q = k_{q1}, \cdots , k_{qn}$ is composed of n Korean graphemes.

3.1 TP Candidate Extraction

Our approach for extracting a TP candidate is to use phonetic similarity with the assumption that at least the first and last part of a Korean word and an English word in the relevant TPs will be phonetically similar to each other [1,3,4,5,6]. As a result, our strategy retrieves Korean transliteration candidates by finding the first and the last Korean syllable each of which contains Korean graphemes that are phonetically similar to the first and the last English grapheme of a given English word. Then, we can extract $tp_{pq} = (e_p, k_q)$ when it satisfies formula (1) and the length constraints ($m < 2 \times n$ and $n < 2 \times m$). The length constraints prevents the unnecessary extraction of TP candidates from redundant TP candidates, which are often redundant due to a length difference between e_p and k_q. Our method extracts single word TP candidates as well as multi-word TP candidates. Let $mtp_{sr} = (e_s, k_r)$ be a multi-word TP candidates, $e_s = ew_{s_1}, .., ew_{s_l}$ be composed of l English words, and $k_r = kw_{r_1}, .., kw_{r_l}$ be composed of l Korean words. mtp_{sr} can be extracted when both e_s and k_r appear in parallel sentences and there are $tp_{ew_{s1}kw_{r1}}, \cdots , tp_{ew_{sl}kw_{rl}}$.

$$P(k_{q1}, k_{q2}|e_{p0}, \cdots , e_{p3}) \times P(k_{qn-1}, k_{qn}|e_{pm-2}, \cdots , e_{pm+1}) > \theta_1 \tag{1}$$

3.2 Three Validation Models

PSM. The PSM ($Sim_{PSM}(e_p, k_q)$ in formula (2)) can be represented as the conditional probability, $P(k_q|e_p)$, like formula (3). We estimated $P(k_q|e_p)$ with kc_{qi}, which was a chunk of Korean graphemes that corresponded to e_{pi}. We can simplify $P(kc_{q1}, \cdots , kc_{qm}|e_{p1}, \cdots , e_{pm})$ into the products of $P(kc_{qi}|e_{p(i-2,i+2)})$ with the assumption that kc_{qi} is dependent on $e_{pi-2}, \cdots , e_{pi+2} = e_{p(i-2,i+2)}$.

$$Sim_{PSM}(tp_{pq}) = Sim_{PSM}(e_p, k_q) = \sqrt[m]{P(k_q|e_p)} \tag{2}$$

$$P(k_q|e_p) = P(kc_{q1}, \cdots , kc_{qm}|e_{p1}, \cdots , e_{pm}) = \prod P(kc_{qi}|e_{p(i-2,i+2)}) \tag{3}$$

PCM. TP candidates were validated using the PCM through *phonetic conversion followed by string comparison*. For phonetic conversion, we automatically transliterated an English word into a Korean word using formula (4). Formula (3) was used for estimating $P(K|e_p)$ to compare PCM and PSM in the same condition. Let $TR(e_p)$ be a Korean string of e_p transliterated by formula (4). The string similarity ($SS(e_p, k_q)$) between e_p and k_q can then be defined as formula (5), where $LD(k_q, TR(e_p))$ is the number of edits (*deletions*, *insertions*, and *substitutions*) required to transform k_q into $TR(e_p)$. Note that we choose the minimum of $SS(e_p, k_q)$ and $SS(k_q, e_p)$ as $Sim_{PCM}(e_p, k_q)$ in formula (6) because $SS(e_p, k_q)$ and $SS(k_q, e_p)$ were asymmetric.

$$K^* = \arg\max P(K|e_p) \tag{4}$$

$$SS(e_p, k_q) = \frac{length(k_q) - LD(k_q, TR(e_p))}{length(k_q)} \tag{5}$$

$$Sim_{PCM}(tp_{pq}) = Sim_{PCM}(e_p, k_q) = \min(SS(e_p, k_q), SS(k_q, e_p)) \tag{6}$$

CSM. TP candidates were validated using the CSM based on *corpus frequencies* ($C(e_p)$, $C(k_q)$, and $C(tp_{pq})$) and *web frequencies* ($W(k_q)$ and $W(tp_{pq})$). The philosophy under-lined in the CSM is that relevant TPs will appear more frequently in documents than non-relevant TPs. In formula (7), $Sim_{CSM}(e_p, k_q)$ is composed of two parts; $CS_m(k_q)$ is used for validating whether k_q is a correct Korean word used in the real world, and $CS_t(tp_{pq})$ is used for validating whether e_p and k_q are used as TPs in documents. To obtain $W(tp_{pq})$, a phrasal search, where a phrase is composed of e_p and k_q, was used as a query in a search engine. The web documents retrieved by the phrasal search usually contained a transliter-ation and its corresponding source language word as a translation pair in parentheses, like 'kol-lin' (*choline*) and 'kol-lin' [*choline*]. Therefore, we could rely on the web frequency de-rived from the phrasal search method to validate TP candidates and to test whether e_p and k_q were TPs.

$$Sim_{CSM}(tp_{pq}) = Sim_{CSM}(e_p, k_q) = \sqrt{CS_m(k_q) \times CS_t(e_p, k_q)} \tag{7}$$

$$CS_m(k_q) = \frac{C(k_q) + W(k_q)}{\sum_r C(k_r) + \sum_r W(k_r)} \tag{8}$$

$$CS_t(e_p, k_q) = \frac{C(e_p, k_q) + W(tp_{pq})}{C(e_p) + C(k_q) + \sum_j W(tp_{pj}) + \sum_i W(tp_{iq})}$$

TP Validation Using Three Validation Models. We validated TP candidates by combining the three validation models. Let mtp_{sr} be a multi-word TP candidate composed of l English words and Korean words ($e_s = ew_{s1}, \cdots, ew_{sl}, k_r = kw_{r1}, \cdots, kw_{rl}$). We then validated multi-word TP candidates using the product of $Sim(ew_{si}, kw_{ri})$ and threshold value θ_2 in formula (9). Single-word TP candidates were validated in a similar manner like that in formula (10). Note that $Sim(ew_{si}, kw_{ri})$ in formula (9) and $Sim(e_p, k_q)$ in formula (10) were calculated by formula (11)

$$Sim(mtp_{sr}) = \sqrt[l]{\prod Sim(ew_{si}, kw_{ri})} > \theta_2 \tag{9}$$

$$Sim(tp_{pq}) = Sim(e_p, k_q) > \theta_2 \tag{10}$$

$$Sim(e_p, k_q) = \sqrt[3]{Sim_{PCM}(e_p, k_q) \times Sim_{PSM}(e_p, k_q) \times Sim_{CSM}(e_p, k_q)} \tag{11}$$

4   Experiments

To evaluate our proposed method, we used several bilingual technical dictionaries, which contained over 1,400,000 English-Korean translation pairs and covered more than 20 scientific domains, including computer science, biology, and so on. We automatically generated about 514,200 parallel sentences, each of which contained a single English technical term, using the dictionaries. We then manually annotated transliteration pairs in the parallel sentences. The results were evaluated using precision (P), recall (R), and F-value. Precision is the proportion of the number of relevant TPs to the total number of extracted TPs. Recall is the proportion of the number of extracted TPs to the total number of TPs in the gold standard. The F-value is defined as $(2 \times P \times R)/(P + R)$. To train TP candidate extraction (formula (1)), PSM (formula (2)), and phonetic conversion in PCM (formula (4)), we used an English-Korean transliteration lexicon that contained 7,000 entries [7]. Two tests were conducted to investigate the effects of θ_1 and the contribution of each validation model to the overall performance.

4.1   Effects of θ_1

We tested the effects of θ_1 by setting θ_1 as 0.5, 0.1, 0.01, 0.001, and 0.0001. Table 1 lists the effects of θ_1 on TP candidate extraction. Here, STPC and MTPC represent the number of single-word TP candidates and multi-word TP candidates. As θ_1 is decreased to 0.0001, our system showed a higher recall but lower precision rate. The smaller θ_1 enabled more relevant TP candidates along with more non-relevant TP candidates to be extracted, thus a higher recall but lower precision rate was achieved. Note that TP candidate extraction significantly affected recall rate (θ_1 determined the upper bound of the recall rates for TP validation); while TP candidate validation significantly affected precision rate (the goal of TP candidate validation was to increase precision rate without a great loss to the recall rate). Therefore, we should consider a trade-off between the precision and recall rates derived from θ_1. To investigate the trade-off, we also examined the effects of θ_1 on overall TPA performance. We validated TP candidates extracted using various setting of θ_1.

Table 2 lists the experimental results evaluated using the F-value. The results suggest that a TPA system with a $\theta_1 = 0.5$ and $\theta_1 = 0.1$ cannot achieve high performance due to a low recall rate. However, our system showed about 87%~88% (F-value) when $\theta_1 \leq 0.01$, because a $\theta_1 \leq 0.01$ resulted in a relatively high recall rate (over 86% recall, see Table 1).

Table 1. Effects of θ_1 on TP candidate extraction

	$\theta_1 = 0.5$	$\theta_1 = 0.1$	$\theta_1 = 0.01$	$\theta_1 = 0.001$	$\theta_1 = 0.0001$
STPC (n)	182,042	234,604	285,923	362,848	449,543
MTPC (n)	12,361	18,608	23,436	31,001	39,072
Recall (%)	53.73	74.37	86.39	91.82	93.27
Precision (%)	82.94	82.37	69.76	51.16	37.56
F-value (%)	65.18	78.17	77.19	65.71	53.55

Table 2. Effects of θ_1 on transliteration pair acquisition (evaluated using F-value)

θ_2	$\theta_1 = 0.5$	$\theta_1 = 0.1$	$\theta_1 = 0.01$	$\theta_1 = 0.001$	$\theta_1 = 0.0001$
0.1 (%)	66.6	79.9	81.5	76.0	69.5
0.3 (%)	68.0	82.0	87.2	88.3	88.1
0.5 (%)	61.0	74.0	78.2	79.2	79.1

4.2 Contribution of Each Validation Model

To investigate the effects of each validation model on TPA performance, we tested TP validation performance using various combinations of validation models – a single model (PCM, PSM, and CSM), a combination of two models (PCM+PSM, PCM+CSM, and PSM+CSM), and three models together (ALL). In this section, we set θ_1 as 0.001 because it showed the best result in Table 2. Figure 1 shows the evaluation results. Although PCM and PSM were based on phonetic similarity, they showed different distributions[2] due to the different strategies used for calculating phonetic similarity. However, there was no significant difference in performance between PCM and PSM. Unfortunately, CSM showed the worst performance among the three models (71.33% as a maximum when $\theta_2 = 0.15$) because of its sharp decrease in recall rate as θ_2 is increased to 1. The main reason for the low recall in CSM was that we could not retrieve web documents ($W(tp_{ij}) = 0$) for relevant TPs. However, a hybrid model between CSM and the other models enhanced system performance because the CSM has different characteristics (corpus based similarity) from both PSM and PCM (phonetic similarity). Due to the combined characteristics, the ALL model showed the best performance (88.31% in $\theta_2 = 0.3$). In summary, our hybrid model increased performance by about 5~23% as compared to the individual PCM, PSM, and CSM.

5 Discussion

Let $tp_{ij} = (e_i, k_j)$ and $tp_{ik} = (e_i, k_k)$ be TP candidates where k_j and k_k are the same string except for one or two syllables, and $|e_i|$, $|k_j|$, and $|k_k|$ be the length (the number of graphemes) of e_i, k_j, and k_k, respectively. If $tp_{ij} = (e_i, k_j)$ is a relevant TP and $tp_{ik} = (e_i, k_k)$ is an irrelevant TP, our transliteration validation process would have difficulties in distinguishing relevant TPs between tp_{ij} and tp_{ik}, especially when the $|k_j|$ and $|k_k|$ are long. The PCM and PSM rely on $|e_i|$, $|k_j|$, and $|k_k|$ to normalize phonetic similarity. This results in the PCM and PSM being insensitive to the phonetic difference between e_i and k_j or between e_i and k_k when the $|k_j|$ and $|k_k|$ are long. Moreover, we rarely retrieved web documents using the phrasal search method when the $|k_j|$ and $|k_k|$ are long, thus the CSM can not distinguish relevant TPs from irrelevant TPs in the case. The rigid constraint in the TP candidate extraction can be one possible solution. However, it leads to a low recall. To address the problem, therefore, we need a more sophisticated algorithm in TP validation. We plan to address such problems to improve TPA performance in the future.

We compared our PCM with the previous works based on PCM [1,3]. Because the previous works used phonetic conversion, we applied the same E-K transliteration method

---

[2] PCM showed the best performance in $\theta_2 = 0.7$ (83.26%) while PSM showed the best performance in $\theta_2 = 0.3$ (84.26%)

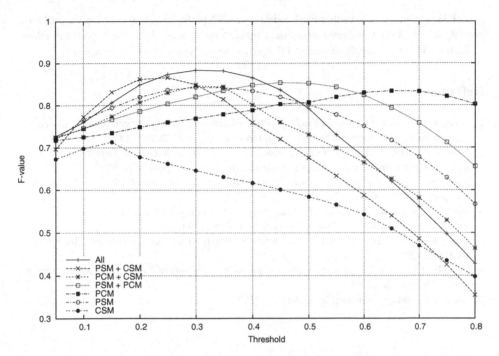

Fig. 1. Performance based on PCM, PSM, and CSM

as ours described in formula (4). Then their own string similarity measures, such as dice coefficient [3] and KODEX [1], were applied. The results suggest that there was no significant difference in performance between our PCM and previously reported PCMs, although precision and recall differed from each other [3]. Although we did not directly compare our PSM and previously reported PSMs [4,5], we can infer that there may be no significance difference in performance because the information source for phonetic similarity in our PSM and the previous PSMs, which significantly affects performance, is similar to each other. Totally, our method improved TPA performance because of the combined effects of the PCM, PSM, and CSM.

6   Conclusion

We described a hybrid model for TPA. Our method extracted TPs through TP candidate extraction and TP candidate validation. In TP candidate extraction we took advantage of phonetic similarity between English graphemes and Korean graphemes for the first and last syllables. For TP candidate validation, we used three individual TP candidate validation models and a hybrid model that combined all three individual models. Experiments showed that the hybrid model was more effective than each individual TP candidate validation

---

[3] KODEX showed the highest precision but the lowest recall rate because its binary decision for TP validation. The dice coefficient and our PCM showed similar precision and recall rates.

model. However, we need further work to improve TPA performance. To address the problem described in Section 5, we need to devise a more sophisticated algorithm for TP candidate validation. We plan to apply extracted TP equivalents to cross-language applications.

References

1. Kang, B.J., Choi, K.S.: Two approaches for the resolution of word mismatch problem caused by English words and foreign words in Korean information retrieval. IJCPOL **14** (2001).
2. Fujii, A., Tetsuya, I.: Japanese/English cross-language information retrieval: Exploration of query translation and transliteration. Computers and the Humanities **35** (2001) 389–420.
3. Tsujii, K.: Automatic extraction of translational Japanese-Katakana and English word pairs from bilingual corpora. IJCPOL **15** (2002) 261–279.
4. Brill, E., Kacmarcik, G., Brockett, C.: Automatically harvesting Katakana-English term pairs from search engine query logs. In: Proc. of NLPRS 2001. (2001) 393–399.
5. Bilac, S., Tanaka, H.: Extracting transliteration pairs from comparable corpora. In: Proc. of NLP2005. (2005).
6. Oh, J.H., Choi, K.S.: A statistical model for automatic extraction of Korean transliterated foreign words. IJCPOL **16** (2003).
7. Nam, Y.S.: Foreign dictionary. Sung An Dang (1997).

Sentence Compression Using Statistical Information About Dependency Path Length

Kiwamu Yamagata, Satoshi Fukutomi, Kazuyuki Takagi, and Kazuhiko Ozeki

The University of Electro-Communications, Tokyo 182-8585, Japan
http://www.oz.ice.uec.ac.jp/

Abstract. This paper is concerned with the use of statistical information about dependency path length for sentence compression. The sentence compression method employed here requires a quantity called inter-phrase dependency strength. In the training process, original sentences are parsed, and the number of tokens is counted for each pair of phrases, connected with each other by a dependency path of certain length, that survive as a modifier-modified phrase pair in the corresponding compressed sentence in the training corpus. The statistics is exploited to estimate the inter-phrase dependency strength required in the sentence compression process. Results of subjective evaluation shows that the present method outperforms the conventional one of the same framework where the distribution of dependency distance is used to estimate the inter-phrase dependency strength.

1 Introduction

Most of text summarisation methods reported so far are based on the idea of extracting important parts from the original text [1]. Those methods are classified from the view point of extraction unit. If *sentence* is employed as extraction unit, then the summarisation problem is how to extract a specified number of significant sentences from a text to make a shorter text. If *word* or *phrase* is adopted as extraction unit, then the problem is how to extract a specified number of significant words or phrases from a sentence to compose a shorter sentence. The latter is often referred to as *sentence compression* or *sentence compaction*, the topic of this paper.

Oguro et al. presented a Japanese sentence compression method [2], and conducted subjective evaluation for the quality of compressed sentences [3]. In their method two functions are defined to evaluate the *goodness* of a subsequence of phrases extracted from a sentence: one to measure the degree of information retention in the subsequence of phrases, and the other to measure its grammatical naturalness. The functions are linearly combined to make a single function to evaluate the overall goodness of the subsequence of phrases. Sentence compression is done by searching for a subsequence of phrases of given length that maximises the evaluation function. In the definition of the function to measure the grammatical naturalness, a quantity called *inter-phrase depedency strength* is required. In their work this was estimated from a large corpus without taking into account the relationship between an original sentence and its compressed version. In the present work we estimate the inter-phrase dependency strength through statistics of *dependency path length* using a corpus containing original sentences and corresponding compressed sentences. Results of subjective evaluation are presented to show the effectiveness of the present method.

Petr Sojka, Ivan Kopeček and Karel Pala (Eds.): TSD 2006, LNAI 4188, pp. 127–134, 2006.

2   Framework of Sentence Compression

Let us give a brief overview of the framework of sentence compression [2] employed in this work. A Japanese sentence is a sequence of phrases $w_0 w_1 \ldots w_{M-1}$, where a phrase w_k consists of a string of content words followed by a string of (possibly 0) function words. To compress the sentence, a subsequence of phrases $w_{k_0} w_{k_1} \cdots w_{k_{N-1}}$ is extracted in such a way as to preserve the original information and the grammatical naturalness as much as possible. It is assumed that we can determine the significance $q(w)$ of each phrase w. So a function $f(k_0, k_1, \ldots, k_{N-1})$ to measure the degree of information retention in the subsequence is defined as

$$f(k_0, k_1, \ldots, k_{N-1}) = \sum_{n=0}^{N-1} q(w_{k_n}). \tag{1}$$

Also a function $g(k_0, k_1, \ldots, k_{N-1})$ to evaluate the grammatical naturalness is defined on the basis of the assumption that we can determine the inter-phrase dependency strength $p(w_i, w_j)$, which is a measure of plausibility for w_i to modify w_j. We can determine a dependency structure on a phrase sequence by specifying a function $s(n)$ that maps a modifier phrase index k_n to that of the modified phrase $k_{s(n)}$. So the quantity

$$\sum_{n=0}^{N-2} p(w_{k_n}, w_{k_{s(n)}}) \tag{2}$$

should reflect the plausibility of the dependency structure represented by the function s. If the phrase sequence $w_{k_0} w_{k_1} \cdots w_{k_{N-1}}$ has a dependency structure with a large value of Eq.(2), it is considered grammatically natural. Thus the function $g(k_0, k_1, \ldots, k_{N-1})$ is defined as

$$g(k_0, k_1, \ldots, k_{N-1}) = \max_s \sum_{n=0}^{N-2} p(w_{k_n}, w_{k_{s(n)}}), \tag{3}$$

where s runs over all the possible dependency structures on the phrase sequence. By linearly combining these two functions, the overall evaluation function h is defined as

$$h(k_0, k_1, \ldots, k_{N-1}) = \alpha f(k_0, k_1, \ldots, k_{N-1}) + (1 - \alpha) g(k_0, k_1, \ldots, k_{N-1}), \tag{4}$$

where $\alpha (0 \leq \alpha \leq 1)$ is a parameter to adjust the balance of contribution from f and g. Thus the sentence compression problem can be formulated as a mathematical problem of finding a subsequence of phrases $w_{k_0} w_{k_1} \cdots w_{k_{N-1}}$ of a given sentence $w_0 w_1 \cdots w_{M-1}$ that maximises the function $h(k_0, k_1, \ldots, k_{N-1})$. This problem can be solved efficiently by an algorithm similar to a dependency structure parser [2].

3   Inter-phrase Dependency Strength and Phrase Significance

3.1   Dependency Path Length

As stated in the preceding section, the inter-phrase dependency strength for every pair of phrases in the original sentence is necessary for sentence compression. We tried to estimate this quantity by analysing both original sentences and corresponding compressed sentences in the training corpus. First an original sentence is parsed, and a dependency structure tree as in Fig. 1 is constructed by using a morphological analyser [4] and a dependency structure analyser [5]. A subsequence of phrases $w_{k_0} w_{k_1} \cdots w_{k_N}$ of a sentence $w_0 w_1 \ldots w_{M-1}$ is said to be a *dependency path* connecting w_{k_0} and w_{k_N} if w_{k_n} depends on (modifies in a wide sense) $w_{k_{n+1}}$ for $n = 0, \ldots, N - 1$. Note that the dependency path connecting two given phrases is unique on a dependency structure if there is one. The number N is called the *dependency path length* [6] between w_{k_0} and w_{k_N}, denoted by $\mathrm{DPL}(w_{k_0}, w_{k_N})$. If there is no dependency path connecting w_m and w_n, we define $\mathrm{DPL}(w_m, w_n) = \infty$. In Fig. 1 for example,

$$\mathrm{DPL}(\text{kono, eikyoude}) = 2,$$
$$\mathrm{DPL}(\text{eikyoude, unkyuushita}) = 1,$$
$$\mathrm{DPL}(\text{taifuuno, kakusenga}) = \infty.$$

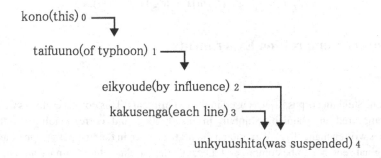

Fig. 1. Dependency structure tree for a Japanese sentence "kono taifuuno eikyoude kakusenga unkyuushita (*By the influence of this typhoon, each line was suspended*)"

3.2 Inter-phrase Dependency Strength

To avoid statistical sparseness, phrases are classified according to their morphological construct [7]. Modifier phrases and modified phrases are classified in different ways. The class of a phrase w is denoted by $C_k(w)$ or $C_u(w)$ depending on whether w is a modifier phrase or a modified phrase, respectively. There are about 200 modifier phrase classes, and about 100 modified phrase classes. For every pair of phrases w_m and w_n with $\mathrm{DPL}(w_m, w_n) \neq \infty$ in original sentences, we consider a triplet

$$(C_k(w_m), C_u(w_n), \mathrm{DPL}(w_m, w_n)). \tag{5}$$

We say that a triplet as in Eq.(5) in origial sentences *survives* the compression if it appears with $\mathrm{DPL}(w_m, w_n) = 1$ in the compressed sentences, that is, w_m and w_n appear in direct modifier-modified relation in compressed sentences. Then the *survival rate* $S(t)$ of a triplet t is defined as

$$S(t) = \frac{\text{the number of surviving tokens for } t}{\text{the number of tokens for } t \text{ in the training data}}. \tag{6}$$

Based on $S(t)$, the inter-phrase dependency strength $p(w_m, w_n)$ between w_m and w_n is estimated as

$$p(w_m, w_n) = \begin{cases} \log S(t), & \text{if DPL}(w_m, w_n) \neq \infty; \\ -\infty, & \text{if DPL}(w_m, w_n) = \infty, \end{cases} \quad (7)$$

where $t = (C_k(w_m), C_u(w_n), \text{DPL}(w_m, w_n))$.

3.3 Phrase Significance

The significance $q(w)$ of each phrase w was estimated by the method described in [7]. That is, phrases were classified into about 60 classes, and the survival rate $R(C(w))$ of each phrase class $C(w)$ was calculated by using original sentences and corresponding compressed sentences in the training corpus. Also TF-IDF(w) was calculated for the main content word in w appearing in an original sentence by using the background newspaper articles that appeared on the same day as the sentence appeared. Finally, the phrase significance $q(w)$ was estimated as

$$q(w) = \log R(C(w)) + \log \text{TF-IDF}(w). \quad (8)$$

4 Sentence Compression Experiments

4.1 Corpus

A Mainichi Shinbun corpus [8] was used in the experiments. This corpus contains newspaper articles appeared in Mainichi Shinbun in fiscal 2002 and corresponding 54-character summaries written manually. We extracted the first sentence in the first paragraph of an article as an original sentence to be compressed, because the 54-character summary attached to the article can be regarded as its compressed version in most cases [7]. The data was divided into three parts as in Table 1.

Table 1. Division of Mainichi Shinbun Corpus (2002) into training data and evaluation data. Training Data I is used for estimating the inter-phrase dependency strength and the phrase significance. Training Data II is used to calculate TF-IDF for terms appearing in the Evaluation Data. In the Evaluation Data, one sentence was extracted from each article.

Training Data I: 28423 articles from May 2002 to March 2003
Training Data II: 2778 articles in April 2002
Evaluation Data: 50 sentences extracted from 50 articles in April 2002

4.2 Experimental Conditions

We have compared the following three methods:

- Conventional Method
  The inter-phrase dependency strength $p_c(w_m, w_n)$ was estimated by the distribution of dependency distance as described in [3].

- Present Method

  The inter-phrase dependency strength $p(w_m, w_n)$ was estimated as described in subsection 3.2.
- Combined Method

  The combined quantity $p(w_m, w_n) + p_c(w_m, w_n)$ was used for the inter-phrase dependency strength.

In all cases, the phrase significance was estimated by the method reviewed in subsection 3.3. The parameter α was fixed at 0.5.

The *compression rate* is the ratio of the number of phrases in a compressed sentence to that in its original sentence. Each original sentence was compressed at three compression rates: 70%, 50%, and 30%.

5   Subjective Evaluation

5.1   Subjects and Evaluation Criteria

10 subjects were employed to evaluate the quality of compressed sentences. To each subject, 450 compressed sentences (50 original sentences × 3 methods × 3 compression rates) were presented to evaluate from three points of view: information retention, grammatical naturalness, and overall impression. The original sentence corresponding to each compressed sentence was also presented. Evaluation was done by scoring compressed sentences in 6 marks: 0 (very poor) through 5 (very good). Subjects were given instructions as to what each mark means.

5.2   Results

Fig. 2 (left and right) and Fig. 3 (left) show the evaluation score averaged over all the compressed sentences at each compression rate and all the subjects.

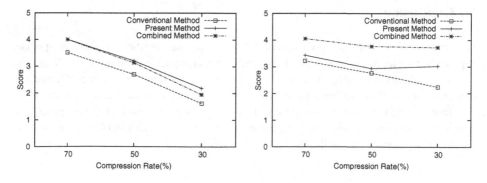

Fig. 2. Evaluation score for information retension (left) and grammatical naturalness (right) averaged over all the test sentences and all the subjects

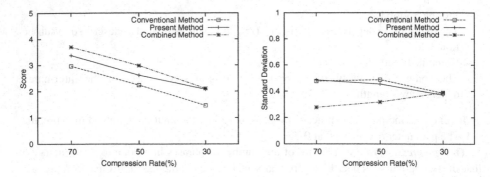

Fig. 3. Evaluation score for overall impression averaged over all the test sentences and all the subjects (left), and the standard deviation of the evaluation score over the subjects (right)

In all cases, the present method outperformed the conventional one. By combining the present method with the conventional one, grammatical naturalness was further improved. It is noted in Fig. 2 (left) that even though we have only changed the method for estimating the inter-phrase dependency strength, intending to improve the grammatical naturalness, the information retention score was also improved. This suggests that the original information is retained not only in each single phrase, but also in each pair of phrases. In the combined method, the grammatical naturalness score was kept almost constant with the change of the compression rate as seen in Fig. 2 (right). The tendency of the evaluation score to fall off with the compression rate was similar in the information retention and in the overall impression as seen in Fig. 3 (left). This means that the overall quality of compressed sentences is heavily influenced by the degree of information retention. It is worth noting in Fig. 3 (right) that the standard deviation of the overall impression score over the subjects was smaller in the combined method than in other two methods; the scores for sentences compressed by the combined method were comparatively stable over the subjects.

6   Conclusion

In a framework of sentence compression based on phrase significance and inter-phrase dependency strength, a new method of estimating the inter-phrase dependency strength was presented. The results of subjective evaluation showed that the new method outperformed the conventional one. By combining the new method with the conventional one, the performance was further improved. Our future work includes automatic correction of phrase ending in compressed sentences to improve the grammatical naturalness. The use of survival rate for n-tuples of phrases ($n \geq 3$) will also be worth pursuing.

Acknowledgments

This work was supported in part by the Japan Society for the Promotion of Science, Grant-in-Aid for Scientific Research (C) (16500077).

References

1. Okumura, M., Nanba, H.: Automated text summarization: A survey. Journal of Natural Language Processing **6** (6) (1999) 1–26.
2. Oguro, R., Ozeki, K., Zhang, Y., Takagi, K.: An efficient algorithm for Japanese sentence compaction based on phrase importance and inter-phrase dependency. Proc. TSD2000 (LNAI1902) (2000) 65–81.
3. Oguro, R., Sekiya, H., Morooka, Y., Takagi, K., Ozeki, K.: Evaluation of a Japanese sentence compression method based on phrase significance and inter-phrase dependency. Proc. TSD2002 (LNAI2448) (2002) 27–32.
4. JUMAN: http://www.kc.t.u-tokyo.ac.jp/nl-resource/juman.html
5. KNP: http://www.kc.t.u-tokyo.ac.jp/nl-resource/knp.html
6. Fukutomi, S., Takagi, K., Ozeki, K.: Aligning phrases in original text and its summary using concept distance and inter-phrase dependency. Proc. 67th Annual Meeting of IPSJ **2** (2005) 119–120.
7. Morooka, Y., Esaki, M., Takagi, K., Ozeki, K.: Summarization of newspaper articles using important sentence extraction and sentence compression. Proc. 10th Annual Meeting of Natural Language Processing Society (2004) 436–439.
8. Mainichi Sinbunsha: Mainichi Shinbun zenbun-kiji oyobi 54-moji database. (2002).

Appendix (Example of Compressed Sentences)

Original Sentence

31-nichi (*31st*)/ gogo (*afternoon*)/ shichi-ji (*7 o'clock*)/ 40-pun-goro (*about 40 minutes*)/ ibarakiken-toukaimura-no (*in Tokai village, Ibaraki prefecture*)/ nihon-genshiryoku-hatuden-toukai-dai2-hatudensho-de (*at the Toukai 2nd Plant of Japan Nuclear Power Generation*)/ gaibu-kara-no (*from outside*)/ denryoku-kyoukyuu-ga (*electric power supply*)/ shunkanteki-ni (*for a moment*)/ tomatta (*stopped*)/ tame (*because*),/ genshiro-ga (*nuclear reactor*)/ jidou-teishi-shita (*automatically stopped*)./
(*At the Toukai 2nd Plant of Japan Nuclear Power Generation in Tokai village, Ibaraki prefecture, the nuclear reactor automatically stopped at about 7 o'clock 40 mimutes p.m. on the 31st due to a momentary failure of electric power supply from outside.*)

Conventional Method

70% 40-pun-goro (*about 40 minutes*)/ ibarakiken-toukaimura-no (*in Tokai village, Ibaraki prefecture*)/ nihon-genshiryoku-hatuden-toukai-dai2-hatudensho-de (*at the Toukai 2nd Plant of Japan Nuclear Power Generation*)/ gaibu-kara-no (*from outside*)/ denryoku-kyoukyuu-ga (*electric power supply*)/ tomatta (*stopped*)/ tame (*because*), / genshiro-ga (*nuclear reactor*)/ jidou-teishi-shita (*automatically stopped*)./

50% ibarakiken-toukaimura-no (*in Tokai village, Ibaraki prefecture*)/ nihon-genshiryoku-hatuden-toukai-dai2-hatudensho-de (*at the Toukai 2nd Plant of Japan Nuclear Power Generation*)/ gaibu-kara-no (*from outside*)/ denryoku-kyoukyuu-ga (*electric power supply*)/ shunkanteki-ni (*for a moment*)/ genshiro-ga (*nuclear reactor*)/ jidou-teishi-shita (*automatically stopped*)./

30% ibarakiken-toukaimura-no (*in Tokai village, Ibaraki prefecture*)/ nihon-genshiryoku-hatuden-toukai-dai2-hatudensho-de (*at the Toukai 2nd Plant of Japan Nuclear Power Generation*)/ gaibu-kara-no (from outside)/ denryoku-kyoukyuu-ga (*electric power supply*)/

Combined Method

70% ibarakiken-toukaimura-no (*in Tokai village, Ibaraki prefecture*)/ nihon-genshiryoku-hatuden-toukai-dai2-hatudensho-de (*at the Toukai 2nd Plant of Japan Nuclear Power Generation*)/ gaibu-kara-no (*from outside*)/ denryoku-kyoukyuu-ga (*electric power supply*)/ shunkanteki-ni (*for a moment*)/ tomatta (*stopped*)/ tame (*because*)/ genshiro-ga (*nuclear reactor*)/ jidou-teishi-shita (*automatically stopped*)./

50% ibarakiken-toukaimura-no (*in Tokai village, Ibaraki prefecture*)/ nihon-genshiryoku-hatuden-toukai-dai2-hatudensho-de (*at the 2nd Plant of Japan Nuclear Power Generation*)/ gaibu-kara-no (*from outside*)/ denryoku-kyoukyuu-ga (*electric power supply*)/ tomatta (*stopped*)/ genshiro-ga (*nuclear reactor*)/ jidou-teishi-shita (*automatically stopped*)./

30% ibarakiken-toukaimura-no (*in Tokai village, Ibaraki prefecture*)/ nihon-genshiryoku-hatuden-toukai-dai2-hatudensho-de (*at the Toukai 2nd Plant of Japan Nuclear Power Generation*)/ genshiro-ga (*nuclear reactor*)/ jidou-teishi-shita (*automatically stopped*)./

Transformation-Based Tectogrammatical Analysis of Czech

Václav Klimeš

Institute of Formal and Applied Linguistics, Faculty of Mathematics and Physics
Charles University, Prague
klimes@ufal.mff.cuni.cz

Abstract. There are several tools that support manual annotation of data at the Tectogrammatical Layer as it is defined in the Prague Dependency Treebank. Using transformation-based learning, we have developed a tool which outperforms the combination of existing tools for pre-annotation of the tectogrammatical structure by 29% (measured as a relative error reduction) and for the deep functor (i.e., the semantic function) by 47%. Moreover, using machine-learning technique makes our tool almost independent of the language being processed. This paper gives details of the algorithm and the tool.

1 Introduction

There are several reasons for developing a tool performing annotation at the tectogrammatical layer, sometimes called "layer of deep syntax". Annotation of a sentence at this layer is closer to meaning of the sentence than its syntactic annotation and thus information captured at the tectogrammatical layer is crucial for machine understanding of a natural language. This can be used in areas such as machine translation and information retrieval, however it can help other tasks as well, e.g. text synthesis. Last but not least, the tool can be employed by annotators creating tectogrammatical representation (which then can be used for training tools performing the noticed tasks) to ease their work.

In Sect. 2, we introduce the structure and content of the Prague Dependency Treebank, which was used for training and testing of our tool; we characterize our training and testing data; and briefly describe the transformation-based toolkit used in our tool. The evaluation method is given in Sect. 3. Other tools performing partial tectogrammatical annotation are introduced in Sect. 4. The core of the article—the algorithm used by our tool—together with its results is described in Sect. 5. Finally, Sect. 6 contains some closing remarks.

2 Used Resources

2.1 The Prague Dependency Treebank and Layers of Its Annotation

The Prague Dependency Treebank (PDT), currently in version 2.0 [3], is a long-term research project, whose aim is a complex, linguistically motivated (manual) annotation of a small part of the Czech National Corpus.[1] It is being annotated at three layers: morphological, analytical (surface syntax), and tectogrammatical. The Functional Generative Description theory [7]

---

[1] http://ucnk.ff.cuni.cz

Petr Sojka, Ivan Kopeček and Karel Pala (Eds.): TSD 2006, LNAI 4188, pp. 135–142, 2006.

has been the main guidance for annotation principles and rules of PDT. A collection of newspapers, an economical weekly and a popular scientific magazine have been selected as the textual material for the PDT.

On the *morphological* layer, the morphological lexical entry (represented by a *lemma*) and values of morphological categories (a *morphological tag*, shortly *m-tag*, i.e. the combination of person, number, tense, gender, verbal voice, ...) are assigned to each word.

At the second and third (*analytical and tectogrammatical*) layer of the PDT, a sentence is represented as a rooted tree. Edges represent relation of dependency (also called "immediate subordination" in some other theories) between two nodes: the governor and the dependent.[2]

Every token (word, punctuation) from the original text becomes a node at the analytical (surface-syntactic) layer, shortly *a-layer*, of annotation and a label called an *analytical function*, shortly *s-tag*, is assigned to every node, describing the type of surface dependency relation of the node to its parent. The original word order position of the corresponding token is also kept as a separate attribute.

The tectogrammatical layer [4], shortly *t-layer*, captures the deep (underlying) structure of a sentence. Nodes represent only autosemantic words (i.e. words with its own meaning); synsemantic (auxiliary) words and punctuation marks can only affect values of attributes of the autosemantic words which they belong to. On the other hand, (new) nodes may be created for several reasons, usually as filling of ellipses, e.g., when the rules of valency so "dictate". For the sake of filling ellipses, nodes can also be copied.[3] At this layer, not less than 39 attributes (labels) can be assigned to nodes. One of the most important ones is the *(deep) functor*, shortly *f-tag*, capturing the tectogrammatical function of a child relative to its parent, i.e. the type of the modification.

Special f-tags are used for child–parent relations that are of a technical nature, such as for capturing coordination and apposition constructions.

2.2   Training and Test Data

In PDT, there are 833,357 tokens in 49,442 sentences annotated at the tectogrammatical layer. About one tenth of this volume are development test data, another tenth are evaluation test data and the rest are training data. All the data are annotated manually. Unless stated otherwise, our tool is trained on all the training data. All tests are performed on all the development test data.

2.3   fnTBL

For the machine learning part of our tool, we have chosen the fnTBL toolkit [6], the fast implementation of transformation-based learning mechanism [2]. Although we consider our choice to be good, the toolkit is aimed at classification tasks only and is not capable to process

---

[2] Usually, instead of 'dependent–governor', we denote pair of adjacent nodes as 'child–parent' since not all the edges correspond to the relation of dependency in the linguistic sense—some of them have rather technical character, e. g. edges adjacent to nodes representing punctuation marks.

[3] We want to stress that even if all nodes in a subtree exist on both the a-layer and t-layer, their relative position at these layers may differ.

tree structures. How we have overcome these drawbacks is described at the appropriate places.

The rules which the toolkit tries to learn are specified by *rule templates* which have to be designed manually before the learning can start. A rule template, in our case, is a subset of the possible names of features together with the name of a feature which bears information about the class the sample belongs to (since it is possible to perform more classification tasks at once). A rule is an instance of a template: particular values are assigned to all the features. The rule is interpreted such that a sample belongs to a given class if the given features have the given values.

3 Evaluation

Since two tectogrammatical trees constructed over the same sentence do not necessarily contain the same number of nodes, the first step of evaluation must be the *alignment* of nodes, i.e. a node from one tree will be paired with a node from the other tree and each node can be part of at most one such pair. Only after such alignment attributes of the paired nodes can be compared. We have developed an alignment procedure which is the basis for all the evaluations presented here (its description is beyond the scope of this paper).

We define *precision*, P, for any attribute assignment to be the number of pairs where both nodes agree in the value of the attribute divided by the total number of nodes in the test (= the automatically created) annotation; and we define *recall*, R, as the number of pairs with the correct value of the attribute divided by the total number of nodes in the "gold standard" annotation. We also define *F-measure*, F, in the usual way as the equally weighted harmonic mean of precision and recall.

When we want to compare the *structure*, we have to slightly modify this approach. We define a node to be correctly placed if the node and its parent are aligned and the counterpart of the parent of the node in question is the parent of the counterpart of the node in question.[4] Then, when comparing structure, the numerator of the fractional counts from the paragraph above is the number of correctly placed nodes.

We use the subscript s for reporting the evaluation of the structure, e.g. P_s means precision in structural annotation. Similarly we use the subscript t for f-tags.

4 Tools Performing the Tectogrammatical Annotation

Historically, there exist three tools performing partial annotation at the t-layer. They were all developed to reduce the human work needed to annotate the PDT. The first tool ever used in the annotation process, preannotating the t-layer on the basis of manual a-layer annotation, is AR2TR [1]. Its algorithm has been manually written. It determines the value of f-tags in clear-cut cases and those of several other attributes (e.g. verbal and sentence modalities and aspect); deletes most nodes of synsemantic words and fills the corresponding attributes of their parents accordingly; and reattaches nodes in certain cases and thus adjusts the tree structure.

---

[4] Informally, the "same" node in both trees has to depend on the "same" parent.

The output of the AR2TR is the input of a decision-tree based tool for the assignment of f-tags called AFA [8]. It was intended to use once the tectogrammatical structure is correctly determined, and the annotators reported that it made their work easier even in this initial phase, though.

The third tool [5], using a valency lexicon to add nodes and correct f-tags of valency members, was developed near the end of the main annotation process of PDT and thus was not used broadly by annotators. When these three tools are applied in the given order to the manually annotated data at the a-layer, the result is $P_s = 86.4\%$, $R_s = 82.9\%$, $F_s = 84.6\%$ and $P_t = 74.1\%$, $R_t = 71.1\%$, $F_t = 72.6\%$.[5]

5   The Algorithm

The input of our tool are data manually annotated at the analytical layer.

Since the tectogrammatical annotation is very complex (see above) and since machine-learning methods are not suitable for the determination of *all* the attributes, we aimed to determine the tectogrammatical structure and assignment of f-tags only.

The fnTBL toolkit is not capable of processing tree structures. Thus, when we want to pass features of the parent, children etc. of a node to the toolkit, we have to pass them as if they were features of the node. The biggest disadvantage of this procedure is that the toolkit cannot employ the tree structure in its actual state—it remains the same during the whole training or classification process and can be modified as late as when the process is finished.

Not only for this reason, we split the processes of training and classification into several phases. After each phase of training, a set of trees being processed is modified according to the rules used by this phase. The modified trees then serve as the input to the next phase. After careful analysis of the data we have split the process into three phases; their description and intended aim follows.

1. Deletion of nodes (synsemantic words or majority of punctuation) and assignment of f-tags to the remaining nodes;
2. relocations of nodes (mainly rhematizers and phrases having different structure on the a-layer and the t-layer), copying of nodes (filling ellipses), and creation (insertion) of "inner" nodes (again, filling ellipses); assignment of f-tags of copied or newly created nodes;
3. creation of leaf nodes (missing valency modifications) and assignment of their f-tags.

5.1   Phase 1

The aim of this phase of tectogrammatical parsing is to delete nodes which have no place at the t-layer and to assign f-tags to those nodes remaining.

Assignment of f-tags to nodes is an elementary classification task. It can easily accommodate also the deletion of nodes by assigning a special f-tag value meaning "deleted" to the node in question. However, when a node being deleted has children, one of them should take its place and become the new parent of its siblings. We call this node *successor*. That is why

---

[5] We should say too that the AFA was trained on the data of PDT 1.0 and we could expect slightly better performance if it is trained on PDT 2.0.

we have enriched rule templates by another type: deleting the parent of a node together with appointing this node as the successor of its parent. Both types of rule templates have to exist, since the second type cannot cause the deletion of leaf nodes.

A node is being deleted if a single rule of any type states so. If a node has children and its successor is not appointed, it is deleted only if it has the only child[6]—and this child becomes its successor. Otherwise the node is retained.

For both types of rules we have used only features of the node in question and of its parent.[7] Namely we worked with their lemmas, s-tags and the values of individual positions of their m-tags. However, the resulting number of features was too high to be kept in memory even for rules with low number of features. To evade this we have developed an automatic adaptive procedure which reduces templates. All the templates are used for training the rules on a small part of data; then, the number of instances of each template is counted in the resulting rule file. Templates with at least two instances are written into a new template file— and the rule file is completely discarded. These new templates are used for training on the whole data. We call this technique *template reduction*. Even with this technique employed, rule templates can contain maximum of three features with the condition that when there are exactly three features, they have to belong to different nodes.

The described set of rule templates gives the following precision, recall and F-measure of structure assignment: $P_s = 87.1\%$, $R_s = 76.2\%$, $F_s = 81.3\%$. The same figures for f-tag assignment are $P_t = 85.9\%$, $R_t = 75.2\%$, $F_t = 80.2\%$. When we tried to prefer somehow the features which we regarded as more important (i.e. lemma, s-tag, and part of speech) in templates, results were at best as good as those given above. Template reduction thus proved to be the best option.

5.2 Phase 2

The aim of this phase of parsing is the relocation and copying of nodes and the insertion of new inner nodes. F-tags of these new nodes should also be assigned.

After the analysis of the data and some experimenting, we find that the transformations this phase should perform are considerably complex and therefore we decided to describe each of them with a single formula as a subtree-to-subtree transformation. Besides relocation of nodes, a transformation can capture creation or deletion of a node or the process of copying an existing node. An example of a (real) complex transformation, on which the mechanism can be explained, is

A(B(C(D),E(F,G)))->A(B(D(C),a(F,G,b)))+Adv+Atr+AuxC+ExD+ExD;CPR+@|A

Each node is denoted with a letter and its children follow it in parentheses. Siblings on the left side of a transcription follow their surface order. The whole transformation is recorded along its node B. Since these pieces of information does not need to fully characterize C and following nodes, their s-tags, serving for their identification, are attached (after the last parenthesis). A lowercase letter denotes a copy of the node with uppercase variant of the same letter; for such nodes their f-tags or a special value @ meaning "the same f-tag as the original node has" are attached (after the semicolon). Similarly, a new node (not occuring in the example) is denoted with an asterisk and its f-tag is attached (after the colon). When a

---

[6] Which is not planned to be deleted as well

[7] Memory was the limiting factor.

node is deleted,[8] its successor node is given as well (after the |-sign). The transformation is the smallest possible, i.e. besides nodes being created, deleted, copied, or moved, only nodes required in order for the original and resultant structures to be trees are involved.

Although it would be best if fnTBL had access to features of all the nodes involved in it, variable and possibly high number of the nodes needs a compromise solution. After exploring the most frequent transformations occurring in the data, we decided to use features of five groups of nodes: the node in question (B), its parent (A), its children, its left siblings and its right siblings. Attributes from all the layers, namely lemma, m-tag, s-tag, and f-tag are chosen as features; and where there are more nodes in a group, the respective values are merged into one string and considered to be atomic. This way we got 20 feature types. However, even with templates containing at most five features the computation did not fit into memory even for a part of the training data. We thus threw out several feature types—we chose only lemmas of children, left siblings, and right siblings for their sparseness. We also had to reduce number of templates by eliminating those containing more that two features of any group. The set of templates obtained in this way has been reduced in the same way as in the previous phase with only one modification: since the number of resulting templates was low, all templates whose instance occurred in the rule file were selected.

Under the described conditions, the result of structure assignment was $P_s = 91.4\%$, $R_s = 80.3\%$, $F_s = 85.5\%$ and that of f-tag assignment $P_t = 85.9\%$, $R_t = 75.5\%$, $F_t = 80.4\%$.[9]

5.3   Phase 3

The aim of this phase is to create leaf nodes missing in the surface form of a sentence and fill in their (tectogrammatical) attributes. These nodes typically correspond to "missing" obligatory valency slots.

If we could determine the valency frame of a word in its occurrence, adding missing obligatory valency slots would be direct. However, we can hardly learn valency frames from a corpus, since a certain valency member which is sometimes present and sometimes not may indicate on one hand the only valency frame with the member being optional, or on the other hand that two frames, first one with the member being obligatory and the second one without it at all. That is why we make decisions about obligatoriness of a valency member one by one: each f-tag corresponds to one feature which states whether (or, in case of free modifications, how many times) a member with the f-tag should occur by an occurrence of a word. From the 67 f-tags, only 27 have been chosen—those occurring at least twice in the training data at nodes new at t-layer having no children, i.e. by potential valency members.

The set of features used in templates consists of a lemma (valency is the property of a word), part of speech (several characterizations can be made even for whole parts of speech, e.g. a verb usually has its actor), verbal voice (it affects valency frame of verbs), and negation (negation of verb is expressed by an extra node being child of the verb). Every rule template consists of either lemma or part of speech; and optionaly of either voice or negation.

However, things may be complicated by errors in assignment of f-tags done in the first phase: if a wrong f-tag is assigned to a valency member, an extra error can occur by

---

[8] This is given implicitely: it occurs on the left side, but not on the right side

[9] The result in f-tag assignment is almost the same as after the previous phase, because f-tags were assigned just to (a few) new nodes in this phase.

creating a superfluous node with the correct f-tag. To avoid it, we created rule templates able to correct an f-tag as well. Corrections are recorded by the node being altered and the following information is used in the features: lemma of the word whose valency frame we are interested in and f-tag and morphemic realization[10] of the valency member. Besides them we added voice of the parent word (for the reason stated above) and lemma of valency member (hopefully useful in identification of phrases). Every rule template contains lemma and either functor or morphemic realization of a valency member. It can also contain its lemma and/or voice of the parent.

A morphemic realization bears roughly the same information as that used in traditional description of valency frames: lemmas of all nouns, prepositions, and conjunctions being auxiliary words; and part of speech and case (if the word exhibits it) of the synsemantic word.

When applying changes suggested by fnTBL, f-tags are repaired first, then the number of valency members is determined, those missing in a tree are created and their f-tags are set. When there is an extra node, it is not deleted.

Since the total number of templates is low, there is no need to reduce them. After this phase, the result of structure assignment is $P_s = 90.2\%$, $R_s = 87.9\%$, $F_s = 89.0\%$ and that of f-tag assignment $P_t = 86.5\%$, $R_t = 84.3\%$, $F_t = 85.4\%$. These are the final evaluation figures for our tool on the PDT 2.0 test data.

When m-layer and a-layer of training and test data are analyzed automatically, the result of structure assignment is $P_s = 77.5\%$, $R_s = 76.6\%$, $F_s = 77.1\%$ and that of f-tag assignment is $P_t = 78.2\%$, $R_t = 77.3\%$, $F_t = 77.8\%$. The used parser [9] achieves accuracy 84.2% on PDT 2.0.[11]

6 Closing Remarks

We have shown that our tool substantially outperforms the accuracy of tectogrammatical annotation made by the set of formerly employed partial tools. However, trying the tool out on a new language can be useful and remains to be done (given the resources being created at LDC, our Institute and other places, we hope to be able to do similar experiments on English and later on Arabic).

This research was supported by the grant of the Grant Agency of the Czech Republic No. 405/03/0913 and the grant of the Grant Agency of Czech Academy of Sciences No. T10147016.

References

1. Alena Böhmová: Automatic Procedures in Tectogrammatical Tagging. In *The Prague Bulletin of Mathematical Linguistics 76*. Charles University, Prague, 2001.
2. Eric Brill: A Simple Rule-Based Part-of-Speech Tagger. In *Proceedings of 3rd Conference on Applied Natural Language Processing*, pp. 152–155. Trento, Italy, 1992.

---

[10] Called also "subcategorization information"

[11] The training and test data used for analytical parsing are, however, supersets of the respective sets used for tectogrammatical analysis.

3. Jan Hajič, Eva Hajičová, Jaroslava Hlaváčová, Václav Klimeš, Jiří Mírovský, Petr Pajas, Jan Štěpánek, Barbora Vidová Hladká, Zdeněk Žabokrtský: *Prague Dependency Treebank 2.0*, CD-ROM, Linguistic Data Consortium, 2006. In press. http://ufal.mff.cuni.cz/pdt2.0/

4. Eva Hajičová, Jarmila Panevová, Petr Sgall: *A Manual for Tectogrammatic Tagging of the Prague Dependency Treebank*. ÚFAL/CKL Technical Report TR-2000-09. Charles University, Prague, 2000.

5. Václav Honetschläger: Using a Czech Valency Lexicon for Annotation Support. In V. Matoušek, P. Mautner: *Proceedings of the 7th International Conference on Text, Speech and Dialogue*, pp. 120–126. Springer-Verlag, Berlin Heidelberg New York, 2003.

6. Grace Ngai, Radu Florian: Transformation-Based Learning in the Fast Lane. In *Proceedings of NAACL 2001*, pp. 40–47. Pittsburgh, PA, 2001.

7. Petr Sgall, Eva Hajičová, Jarmila Panevová: *The Meaning of a Sentence in Its Semantic and Pragmatic Aspects*. Academia – Kluwer, Praha – Amsterdam, 1986.

8. Petr Sgall, Zdeněk Žabokrtský, Sašo Džeroski: A Machine Learning Approach to Automatic Functor Assignment in the Prague Dependency Treebank. In R. M. Rodríguez, C. Paz Suárez Araujo (eds.): *Proceedings of the 3rd International Conference on Language Resources and Evaluation*, volume 5, pp. 1513–1520. European Language Resources Association, 2002.

9. Ryan McDonald, Fernando Pereira, Kiril Ribarov, and Jan Hajič: Non-projective dependency parsing using spanning tree algorithms. In *Proceedings of the Human Language Technology / Empirical Methods in Natural Language Processing conference (HLT-EMNLP)*, Vancouver, British Columbia, 2005.

The Effect of Semantic Knowledge Expansion to Textual Entailment Recognition

Zornitsa Kozareva, Sonia Vázquez, and Andrés Montoyo

Departamento de Lenguajes y Sistemas Informáticos
Universidad de Alicante, Spain
{zkozareva, svazquez, montoyo}@dlsi.ua.es

Abstract. This paper studies the effect of semantic knowledge expansion applied to the Textual Entailment Recognition task. In comparison to the already existing approaches we introduce a new set of similarity measures that captures hidden semantic relations among different syntactic categories in a sentence. The focus of our study is also centred on the synonym, antonym and verb entailment expansion of the initially generated pairs of words. The main objective for the realized expansion concerns the finding, the affirmation and the enlargement of the knowledge information. In addition, we applied Latent Semantic Analysis and the cosine measure to tune and improve the obtained relations. We conducted an exhaustive experimental study to evaluate the impact of the proposed new similarity relations for Textual Entailment Recognition.

1 Introduction

The web is the largest text repository, where millions of people share and consult information daily. Given a natural language query, present search engines identify and return relevant documents to the query. However, the relevant information may be present in different forms and a search about "tropical fruit" may return a document where "mango" appears. Although neither "tropical" nor "fruit" appear, the document is still relevant because "mango" is a type of tropical fruit. Other Natural Language Processing (NLP) applications have to handle language variabilities in order to avoid redundant information or to find the correct answer which may be represented in indirect way. Therefore, to improve their performance, a textual entailment (TE) module [1] is needed.

This directed researchers toward the development of diverse approaches of TE recognition such as logic forms [2], WordNet similarities [3,4,5], edit distance between parsing trees [6] among others [7].

At present, the already existing semantic similarity TE approaches, measure the word similarity among noun-noun, verb-verb, adjective-adjective and adverb-adverb pairs. In this work, we focus our study on word similarity relations among different syntactic categories. We measure the degree of contribution of such pairs to the recognition of textual entailment. In order to strengthen the similarity between the two texts, we expand the already obtained word pairs with their synonyms, antonym and verb entailment relations.

Additionally, we measure the semantic similarity between two texts using Latent Semantic Analysis (LSA) and the cosine measure. Instead of using the traditional word frequency approaches, we propose to measure similarity through the usage of relevant domains [8].

Petr Sojka, Ivan Kopeček and Karel Pala (Eds.): TSD 2006, LNAI 4188, pp. 143–150, 2006.
© Springer-Verlag Berlin Heidelberg 2006

The paper is organised in the following way. Section 2 describes the motivation of our work and the utilized resources for our TE approach. Section 3 shows the experiments which we conducted to establish the robustness of the proposed method. Finally, we conclude in Section 4 and mention some work in progress.

2   Motivation and Resource Description

Recent textual entailment (TE) approaches [4,9,5] that rely on semantic information use only relations between words of the same syntactic category. However, we realise that word pairs from different syntactic categories also give relevant information. Thus, the main goal of our approach focuses on the study of the effect of semantic similarity between different syntactic categories such as verb-noun, adjective-noun, among others.

Additionally, we propose a new semantic similarity approach where the cosine and LSA are employed and examined. These measures identify the semantic distance and hidden relations between the text (T) and the hypothesis (H). The relatedness of the sentences is determined with the resource of relevant domains, rather than using the traditionall word frequency methods. The next subsections present the resources we utilized in our approach.

2.1   Inter-syntactic Relations

Already existing works measure the semantic similarity between words of the same syntactic category. These systems do not take advantage of inter-syntactic relations[1]. In our study we find out that pairs of different syntactic categories are very indicative and can lead to a better textual entailment recognition. For example, in order to determine that *"He died of blood loss"* and *"He died bleeding"*, infer the same meaning, we need to use inter-syntactic relations. The previous approaches take into account only word pairs of the same syntactic category, so they cannot determine that *blood-N* and *bleeding-V* are semantically related. In this example *blood* and *bleeding* are the most relevant word pairs for the two texts and they infer that the entailment relation between the two sentences holds. Therefore, one of our main purposes in this investigation work is to apply the inter-syntactic relations which extract this kind of information.

To measure the semantic similarity between two sentences, first the parts of speech tags [10] are determined. From them, we took the four most significant word groups: verbs, nouns, adjectives and adverbs. The similarity between the different syntactic word pairs is determined with the WordNet::Similarity package [11].

For each word pair[2], the *lin* and *path* similarity measures are applied. The reason of their usage is due to the different word senses and similarity scores that the WordNet::Similarity assigns. For example, the word pair "bank-money" with the measure of *lin* disambiguates the words with the senses bank#3–money#2 and establishes their similarity as 0.46. While the measure of *path* disambiguates the words as bank#8–money#2 with 0.14 similarity. In this example the first measure is more indicative.

---

[1] Noun-verb, verb-noun, adjective-noun, noun-adjective, adverb-noun, noun-adverb, adjective-verb, verb-adjective, adverb-verb, verb-adverb

[2] A word pair consists of a word from the first sentences which is called the text and a word from the second sentence called the hypothesis

2.2 Sentence Expansion

To the previously extracted word pairs (noun–verb, noun–adjective, verb–adverb, etc), a synonym, antonym and verb entailment expansion is applied. For this expansion we use the WordNet[3] lexical resource.

The purpose of the word expansion is to provide to the original text (T) and hypothesis (H) sentences more relevant semantic information. The synonym expansion includes words that have the same meaning in the same context (arm–weapon). The antonym extracts words with opposite meaning (high–low). Verb entailment looks for verbs whose action can not be done unless the previous is accomplished (breathe–inhale, divorce–marry).

We come across some limitations associated to these expansions – the increase of computational cost and the degree of relevance for the new word pairs. The first obstacle is due to the large amount of possible combinations. The other is related to the appearance of a great number of synonyms that can transform the entailment relation from positive to negative and vice versa.

In order to reduce the noise of knowledge expansion, we used word sense disambiguation [11]. All words in T-H sentences are disambiguated and then expanded through WordNet. For example, for the pair bank-money, instead of including all synonyms related to all possible senses, we considered only the synonyms associated to senses bank#3–money#2 according to the measure of *lin*, and the senses bank#8–money#2 according to the measure of *path*.

2.3 Latent Semantic Analysis

LSA [12] has been applied in different NLP tasks. LSA consists in the construction and usage of a term-document matrix which describes the occurrences of terms in documents where each row corresponds to one term and each column corresponds to one document.

For our approach, we modify the space model of LSA. Instead of representing the columns as documents, we represent them as domains. These domains are extracted from the WordNet domain resource [13]. Thus, a new conceptual space with words and domains is obtained. This new space establishes the relevance among the words and the domains.

We use LSA technique to measure the similarity between two sentences. First, we obtain for each sentence the different constituents (noun, verb, adjective and adverb). Then, we apply the LSA over the words of the text T and the words of the hypothesis H. Thus, two different sets are obtained. These new sets contain a list of related words ordered by their similarity. The final step is to normalise the number of words that coincide between the T and the H.

Moreover, we use LSA in another approximation. Instead of using our conceptual space over terms and domains, we construct a new space, where the corpus is represented by the set of text sentences in the experimental data. Later, we use this new LSA space to determine the similarity between the T and H sentences. In the LSA experiments, we also study the effect of lemmatized and non lemmatized text.

2.4 Cosine Measure

In our work, the cosine measure is used to establish the semantic relevance between T and H sentences. The most known usage of the cosine measure is taking the frequency of the words

---

[3] http://wordnet.princeton.edu/

from the text and the hypothesis. In this work, we introduce a new interpretation of the cosine measure. Instead of word frequency, we consider Relevant Domains (RD).

The RD resource contains automatically extracted word-domain pairs, ordered by their association ratio. For each word in T/H, the set of RD is determined. Once this information is obtained, the T/H vectors are constructed and their similarity is measured with the formula (1).

$$\cos(T, H) = \frac{T \cdot H}{|T| \, |H|} = \frac{\sum_{i=1}^{n} T_i \cdot H_i}{\sqrt{\sum_{i=1}^{n} T_i^{\,2}} \cdot \sqrt{\sum_{i=1}^{n} H_i^{\,2}}} \tag{1}$$

The values of the cosine vary from 0 to 1, where a 1 indicates that T and H are very similar and 0 indicates that T and H have different meanings.

3   Experiments and Evaluation

This section concerns the experimental evaluation of the significance of the different knowledge representations which are described in the previous section.

All experiments are conducted with the Support Vector Machine (SVM) [14] algorithm. We selected this machine learning approach, because of its ability to manage high data scarcity problems and multidimensional attribute space.

3.1   Data Set

For our experiments, we use the development and test data sets provided by the Second Recognising Textual Entailment Challenge (RTE 2)[4]. The examples in these data sets have been extracted from real Information Extraction, Information Retrieval, Question Answering and Text Summarization applications.

The development set consists of 800 text-hypothesis pairs, used as training examples. The other set of 800 text-hypothesis pairs is used for testing. The provided data sets are for the English language. The performances of the different knowledge representation sets are evaluated with the RTE2 evaluation script[5]. According to the script, systems are ranked and compared by their accuracy scores.

3.2   Experiment with Knowledge Expansion

The experiment knowledge expansion section presents two aspects – the contribution of the inter-syntactic word pairs and the effect of synonym, antonym and verb entailment relation expansions for the recognition of Textual Entailment.

We start our experiment with the measurement of the similarity for words of the same syntactic category. This approach is similar to the one presented in [5]. Next, we expand the initial noun, verb, adjective and adverbs pairs with their synonyms and verb entailment, as previously described in subsection 2.2. The obtained results are shown in Table 1.

---

[4] http://www.pascal-network.org/Challenges/RTE2/
[5] http://www.pascal-network.org/Challenges/RTE2/Evaluation/

In this table, we show the results for the development and the test data sets, so that a general overview of the behaviour of the knowledge features can be obtained. Without the expansion, the development set obtains 60.12% accuracy, while after the expansion, the performance increases with 0.53%. For the test set the performance improves with 1.38%.

Table 1. Results for the knowledge expansion experiments

sets	Acc.	IE	IR	QA	SUM
devWithoutExp	60.12	54.00	61.00	59.00	66.50
devWitExp	60.75	53.50	58.00	61.50	70.00
devAllAttr	59.62	**57.50**	60.00	57.50	63.50
devExpARNVent	61.38	55.50	60.50	62.00	67.50
devExpARNV_NpCd	59.62	50.50	59.00	59.00	70.00
testWithoutExp	54.25	50.00	55.50	47.50	64.00
testWitExp	**55.63**	52.00	56.50	57.00	57.00
testAllAttr	53.50	**52.50**	53.50	53.00	55.00
testExpARNVent	53.75	48.00	54.50	54.50	58.00
testExpARNV_NpCd	**55.37**	52.50	57.50	56.50	55.00

Considering the general scope of TE resolution, the performance of the already existing systems varies from 49% of accuracy as a minimum to 60% of accuracy as a maximum [7]. Therefore 1.38% of improvement can be considered as significant for a Textual Entailment system.

Once we demonstrated that the inclusion of synonym and verb entail expansion aided the TE recognition, we added the antonym and all inter-syntactic category information. In Table 1 this experiment is denoted with *AllAttr*. This information decreased the performance for the development and test data sets. The low performance is due to the antonym relations and to the accumulated noise introduced by the expansion of the inter-syntactic word groups. Additionally, not all sentence pairs express negative fact or event, therefore there is no need to measure the antonym relation for each sentence. The synonym and antonym attributes contradict each other, therefore they sparse the example vector space of the SVM and hamper the classification of the employed machine learning algorithm.

An observation related to the *AllAttr* experiment concerns the performance of the Information Extraction (IE) task. Compared to the other sets, IE obtains 57.50% of accuracy. This shows that the inter-syntactic information is significant and important for the IE task, rather than to the other NLP tasks.

In order to confirm that the limitations of the *AllAttr* set are caused by the antonyms, we conduct an experiment where only the synonym expansion and verb entail information is included. For the development set, this combination obtains the highest accuracy of 61.38%. In addition, we add two more attributes: proper names and numbers. With them the performance of the development data decreases to 59.62%, however, the test data obtains 55.37%. This accuracy is the second highest score for the test data.

In this experimental subsection, we show that the expansion of synonym and verb entailment improves the score for the test data with around 1%. We also discover that the inter-syntactic relations are very informative for the IE task. In conclusion, we can affirm that semantic knowledge expansion has a positive effect over the performance of a TE system.

3.3   Experiment with LSA and the Cosine Measure

In respect to the previous experiments, in this section we study how entailments can be resolved using the LSA and the cosine measure. For all experiments, the results are shown in the Table 2.

Table 2. Results for the LSI and cosine measures

sets	Acc.	IE	IR	QA	SUM
devLSI_Lema	49.38	52.50	48.50	49.00	47.50
devLSI_NoLema	53.37	50.50	54.00	49.00	60.00
devCosine	54.25	50.50	48.00	57.00	61.50
devLSI_Lema_Cosine	53.63	52.50	50.00	50.00	62.00
devLSI_NoLema_Cosine	53.63	52.50	50.00	50.00	62.00
devBexpCosine	60.75	53.50	58.00	61.50	70.00
devBexpLSI_Lema_Cosine	63.38	55.50	63.50	62.50	72.00
devBexpLSI_NoLema_Cosine	61.50	57.00	60.00	61.00	68.00
testLSI_Lema	53.37	51.00	53.50	51.00	58.00
testLSI_NoLema	53.00	48.00	55.00	50.00	59.00
testCosine	54.00	46.50	56.50	56.00	57.00
testLSI_Lema_Cosine	52.38	47.00	54.50	52.50	55.50
testLSI_NoLema_Cosine	52.88	46.50	53.50	53.00	58.50
testBexpCosine	**55.63**	52.00	56.50	57.00	57.00
testBexpLSI_Lema_Cosine	52.88	51.50	55.00	51.50	53.50
testBexpLSI_NoLema_Cosine	**56.13**	53.50	57.00	58.00	56.00

The experimental setup starts with the observation of the performance of the LSA with and without a lemmatizer. For the development data, the accuracy score increases with 4% in favour of the non lemmatized sentences, while for the test set the accuracy increase only with 0.37%. From the four different NLP tasks, the lemmatizer affects the performance of the information retrieval and summarisation.

The next experiments represent the different combinations of LSA, the cosine and the feature set with the synonym and verb entailment expansion. When only the LSA and cosine are combined the accuracy for the test set is decreased, because both measures depend only on the information of the relevant domains. However, combined with the expanded features, the final performance increases.

The best score for the whole Textual Entailment experiment are obtained after the combination of the LSA without a lemmatizer, the cosine, the synonym and verb entailment expansion. For the test data, this score is 56.13%. In comparison with the initial approach where simply the similarity of words from the same syntactic category are considered, the improvement is 2%. This shows that the incorporation of various semantic knowledge sources is beneficial and can help a semantic textual entailment module.

4 Conclusions and Work in Progress

The main contributions of this paper are related to the study of new semantic knowledge resources for the recognition of Textual Entailment.

First, we study the effect of word similarity across different syntactic categories. We discover that inter-syntactic information is very important for the text entailment recognition of the IE task.

On a second place, we take into account the word pair expansion with synonym, antonym and verb entailment relations. Such expansion lead to 1% of improvement compared to a system which does not use knowledge expansion. The performance of our system is lowered by the introduced noise of the newly incorporated irrelevant words. Although we used a word sense disambiguation method, by which words whose word senses do not correspond to the initial words are discarded, the experiments show that the computational time is highly increasing and the obtained knowledge is still noisy. At the moment, we are developing a method to discard and reduce these irrelevant word pairs, by the help of the LSA and the cosine measure.

Furthermore, we propose a novel approach to establish the semantic similarity of two sentences. For this approach we use the LSA and cosine measure, where the source of information is the relevant domain recourse, instead of the traditional word frequency methods. In addition, we have done different experiments, where the role of word lemmatization for the textual entailment recognition is demonstrated.

Finally, the combination of different semantic knowledge resources is explored. Among all experiments, the inclusion of synonym expansion, the verb entailment, the LSA and cosine measure yielded the highest score.

In conclusion, we can say that the effect of semantic knowledge expansion is significant for the textual entailment recognition. Following the development of our approach, the 2% improvement that is reached is significant, considering the global performance of the already existing systems.

In the future, in order to avoid the dispersion introduced by the expanded word pairs, we want to work with noun phrases. This will diminish the word similarity combinations. With the same intention, LSA will be used to determine the most relevant synonym pairs.

Acknowledgements

This research has been funded by the Spanish Government under project CICyT number TIC2003-07158-C04-01 and PROFIT number FIT-340100-2004-14, and by the Valencia Government under project GV04B-276.

References

1. Dagan, I., Glickman., O.: Probabilistic textual entailment: Generic applied modeling of language variability. In: PASCAL Workshop on Learning Methods for Text Understanding and Mining, 2004.
2. Akhmatova, E.: Textual entailment resolution via atomic propositions. In: Proceedings of the PASCAL Challenges Workshop on Recognising Textual Entailment, 2005.

3. Herrera, J., Peñas, A., Verdejo., F.: Textual entailment recognition based on dependency analysis and wordnet. In: Proceedings of the PASCAL Challenges Workshop on Recognising Textual Entailment, 2005.
4. Jijkoun, V., de Rijke, M.: Recognizing textual entailment using lexical similarity. In: Proceedings of the PASCAL Challenges Workshop on Recognising Textual Entailment, 2005.
5. Kozareva, Z., Montoyo, A.: Mlent: The machine learning entailment system of the university of alicante. In: Proceedings of the PASCAL Challenges Workshop on Recognising Textual Entailment, 2006.
6. Kouylekov, M., Magnini, B.: Recognizing textual entailment with tree edit distance algorithm. In: Proceedings of the PASCAL Challenges Workshop on Recognising Textual Entailment, 2005.
7. Dagan, I., Glickman, O., Magnini., B.: The pascal recognising textual entailment challenge. In: Proceedings of the PASCAL Challenges Workshop on Recognising Textual Entailment, 2005.
8. Vázquez, S., Montoyo, A., Rigau, G.: Using relevant domains resource for word sense disambiguation. In: IC-AI. (2004) 784–789.
9. Corley, C., Mihalcea., R.: Measures of text semantic similarity. In: Proceedings of the ACL workshop on Empirical Modeling of Semantic Equivalence, 2005.
10. Schmid, H.: Probabilistic part-of-speech tagging using decision trees. In: Proceedings International Conference on New Methods in Language Processing., Manchester, UK (1994) 44–49.
11. Pedersen, T., Patwardhan, S., Michelizzi, J.: Wordnet::Similarity - measuring the relatedness of concepts. In: AAAI. (2004) 1024–1025.
12. Landauer, T., Dumais, S.: A solution to plato's problem: The latent semantic analysis theory of acquisition. In: Psychological Review. (1997) 211–240.
13. Magnini, B., Cavaglia, G.: Integrating Subject Field Codes into WordNet. In: Proceedings of LREC-2000, Second International Conference on Language Resources and Evaluation. (2000) 1413–1418.
14. Collobert, R., Bengio., S.: Svmtorch: support vector machines for large-scale regression problems. The Journal of Machine Learning Researc (2001).

Segmentation of Complex Sentences*

Vladislav Kuboň[1], Markéta Lopatková[1], Martin Plátek[2], and Patrice Pognan[3]

[1] ÚFAL MFF UK, Prague
{lopatkova, vk}@ufal.mff.cuni.cz
[2] KTIML MFF UK, Prague
martin.platek@mff.cuni.cz
[3] CERTAL INALCO, Paris
mcertal@wanadoo.fr

Abstract. The paper describes a method of dividing complex sentences into segments, easily detectable and linguistically motivated units that may be subsequently combined into clauses and thus provide a structure of a complex sentence with regard to the mutual relationship of individual clauses. The method has been developed for Czech as a language representing languages with relatively high degree of word-order freedom. The paper introduces important terms, describes a segmentation chart, the data structure used for the description of mutual relationship between individual segments and separators. It also contains a simple set of rules applied for the segmentation of a small set of Czech sentences. The segmentation results are evaluated against a small hand-annotated corpus of Czech complex sentences.

1 Introduction

It is quite obvious that the syntactic analysis of long and complicated natural language sentences is more difficult than the analysis of short sentences. A parsing success depends among other things also on the length of the input sentence. This has been shown very often in the past, let us mention for example [1,2] for rule-based syntactic analyzers and [3] for stochastic parsing of Czech.

There are also multiple solutions to the problem of bridging the gap between results of morphological analysis (or tagging) and a full-scale rule-based syntactic analysis or stochastic parsing. Let us mention for example the idea of cascaded parsing used in [4,5] or [6]. The advantage of working with a cascade of specialized parsers instead of having one very complex general parser is quite obvious – the complexity of the task is substantially reduced and the parsing process is speeded up.

The use of chunking[1] is also quite frequent. The identification of chunks prior to parsing helps to decrease the parsing complexity, the only problem being the correct identification of chunks – if it is done only on the basis of very limited local context (bigrams or trigrams), it may be misleading with regard to the context of the whole sentence.

Very interesting approach to dividing the parsing process into several relatively independent but mutually closely related parts has been introduced in the XDG theory of D. Duchier

---

* This paper is a result of the project supported by the grant No. 1ET100300517.
[1] Very comprehensive explanation of this notion can be found for example at
http://nltk.sourceforge.net/tutorial/chunking/

Petr Sojka, Ivan Kopeček and Karel Pala (Eds.): TSD 2006, LNAI 4188, pp. 151–158, 2006.
© Springer-Verlag Berlin Heidelberg 2006

and others, see [7]. We think that the idea presented in this paper may be exploited especially in connection with similar approaches.

This paper describes a method how to estimate the structure of clauses (their span and mutual relationships) solely on the basis of results of morphological analysis of an input sentence and very strict syntactic rules concerning punctuation.

Although the method presented in this paper had been designed for the syntactic analyzers of Czech, it is rather useful for a whole group of related and typologically similar languages. Some papers (e.g. [8]) indicate that the punctuation is important even for languages of a different type. It is not true that the information allowing to divide the complex sentence into individual clauses or segments is not important and that every stochastic parser will provide it for free in the parsing process – the substantially lower results (almost 10% difference) reported for Czech compared to English for identical parsers (see [3,9]) support the claim that even stochastic parsers have difficulties to cope with free-word order languages.

2   Describing a Structure of a Complex Sentence

The basic idea underlying our method is an assumption that every morphologically analyzed sentence already contains a lot of more or less reliable information that may be directly used for the benefit of more effective and precise syntactic parsing. We exploit Czech grammars (esp. [10]) as well as previous linguistic observations (see [11]).

The most important information we are looking for is the information about the mutual relationships between individual clauses, the span of embedded clauses etc. Let us call this type of structural information a **clause structure** of the (complex) sentence. At the beginning it is important to stress that we suppose neither that our method will be able to provide an unambiguous clause structure for every sentence nor that an unambiguous clause structure exists for every sentence. The aim is to create as precise an approximation of the clause structure as possible.

2.1   Important Notions

In the sequel an input sentence is understood to be a sequence of lexical items $w_1 w_2 \ldots w_n$. Each item w_i ($1 \leq i \leq n$) represents either a certain lexical form of a given natural language, or a punctuation mark, quotation mark, parenthesis, dash, colon, semicolon or any other special symbol which may appear in the written form of a sentence. All items are disjunctively divided into two groups – ordinary words and separators.

Let us call the words or punctuation marks which may separate two clauses (or two sentence members) **separators**. It is quite clear that there are at least three relatively easily distinguishable types of separators – opening ones, closing ones and mixed ones, those, which typically close the preceding clause or its part and open the following one. A typical opening separator is e.g a subordinating conjunction or a relative pronoun, a closing one is a full stop, question mark or exclamation mark at the end of a sentence, mixed separators are for example commas or coordinating conjunctions.

It is often the case that two clauses are separated by more than one separator (e.g. comma followed by *že* [that]), in some cases even combined with non-separators (emphasizing adverbs, prepositions, etc.). In such a case it would be more convenient to consider the whole sequence as a single item – let us call it a **compound separator**.

Let $S = w_1 w_2 \ldots w_n$ be a sentence of a natural language. A **segmentation of a sentence** S is a sequence of sections $D_0 W_1 D_1 \ldots W_k D_k$, where particular section W_i $(1 \leq i \leq k)$ represents so called **segment**, i.e. a (maximal) sequence of lexical items $w_j w_{j+1} \ldots w_{j+m}$ not containing any separator, and section D_i $(0 \leq i \leq k)$ represents a (compound) separator composed of items $w_q w_{q+1} \ldots w_{q+p}$. The section D_0 may be empty, all other sections D_i $(1 \leq i \leq k)$ are non-empty. Each item w_i for $1 \leq i \leq n$ belongs to exactly one section D_j if it is a member of a (compound) separator; in the opposite case, w_i belongs to exactly one W_j. A pair $D_{i-1} W_i$ (where D_{i-1} is an opening or mixed (compound) separator) is called an **extended segment**.

The section D_0 is usually empty for sentences which start with a main clause. D_0 is typically nonempty if a complex sentence starts with a subordinated clause, as e.g. in the sentence *Když jsem se probudil, zavolal jsem policii.* [When I woke up, I called the police.]. D_k represents the final punctuation mark at the end of a sentence.

The segmentation of a particular sentence can be represented by one or more **segmentation charts** that describes the mutual relationship of individual sections with regard to their coordination or subordination.

Each separator is represented by at least one node. If an opening separator represented by a node D_i has a subordinating function, a copy of the node D_i' is placed directly under a node D_i in the chart and it is connected by a dotted arrow with the original node D_i. The closing separator may by also represented by a "raised" copy of a node D_i. Let us demonstrate example of a segmentation chart on the Czech complex sentence *Zatímco neúspěch bývá sirotkem, úspěch mívá mnoho tatínku, horlivě se hlásících, že zrovna oni byli u jeho početí.* [While failure is usually an orphan, the success tends to have many fathers, claiming eagerly that particularly they were present at its conception.], see Fig. 1.

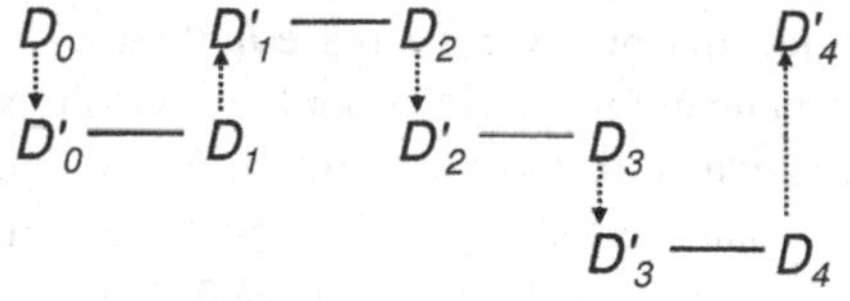

Fig. 1. Example of segmentation chart

D_0 - *Zatímco* [While]

W_1 - *neúspěch bývá sirotkem* [failure is usually an orphan]

D_1 - ,

W_2 - *úspěch mívá mnoho tatínku* [the success tends to have many fathers]

D_2 - ,

W_3 - *horlivě se hlásících* [claiming eagerly]

D_3 - , *že* [that]

W_4 - *zrovna oni byli u jeho početí* [that particularly they were present at its conception]

D_4 - .

There is more than one chart in case that the segmentation of a sentence is ambiguous. It may happen if a separator is ambiguous – e.g. the Czech word form *jak*, which may be both a noun or a subordinating conjunction – or if a separator does not clearly indicate the relationship between both segments it separates, as e.g. comma.

In order to be able to present a basic set od rules for creating segmentation chart it is necessary to introduce a couple of new notions, at least informally.

A **subordination flag** is assigned to particular extended segment either if this segment contains any word form with one of the following morphological tags (for conjunctions, pronouns, and numerals, see [12]) or if it contains one of the listed pronominal adverbs:

- tag="J,.*" representing a subordinating conjunction;
- tag="P.*" representing a interrogative/relative pronoun, where the second position in the tag contains any of the following characters:
  - 4 (*jaký, který, čí, ...*),
  - E (*což*),
  - J (*jenž, již, ...*),
  - K (*kdo, kdož, kdožs*),
  - Q (*co, copak, cožpak*),
  - Y (*oč, nač, zač*);
- tag="C.*" representing numerals, where the second position in the tag is either
  - ? (*kolik*),
  - u (*kolikrát*) or
  - z (*kolikátý*);
- tag="D.*" for pronominal adverbs
  - adverbs (jak, kam, kde, kdy, proè)

For the sake of an easier explanation of mutual relationships of individual nodes of a segmentation chart in vertical direction we would like to introduce the notion of **chart layers**. In informal terms, a top layer of the chart (layer 1) corresponds to a main clause of the sentence and the numbers identifying layers increase in the top-down direction. The lower layers (layers with higher numbers) represent subordinated clauses. If a clause contains an embedded clause (fully embedded, that is the main clause is divided into two non-empty parts), the "tail" of the main clause is located in the same layer as its "head"; the same holds also for subordinated clauses with more deeply embedded clauses.

2.2   General Principles of Building Segmentation Charts

The process of building segmentation charts is relatively straightforward. In accordance with the principles presented above, the first step is always the morphological analysis of the input sentence. On the basis of its (typically ambiguous) results we will divide the sentence into segments, taking into account the number and position of all separators and (compound) separators in the sentence.

The next step, drawing segmentation charts relevant for a given input sentence, is slightly more complicated due to the ambiguity concerning especially closing separators (mainly commas), which are generally highly ambiguous. Not only they can simply raise, lower or directly connect the following section at the same layer, they may even raise the following section several layers (in case of closing a deeply embedded subordinated clause). If there is such an ambiguous separator anywhere in the sentence, it is necessary to create more segmentation charts, each with an edge going in a different direction.

2.3   Basic Set of Rules

In order to demonstrate how the process of building the segmentation chart works, we present here a basic set of rules for Czech:

1. **Sentence start:** If the first (extended) segment does not have a subordination flag the edge representing the first segment starts at the topmost (1st) layer of the chart and continues straight to the right. Otherwise the edge for first segment starts at the 2nd layer.
2. **Comma:** If the comma is NOT followed by an item with a subordination flag, the next segment goes either straight to the right (this represents for example a comma separating two coordinated items inside a single clause) OR it jumps one or more layers (this is a highly ambiguous situation representing an end of an nested subordinated clause) upwards.
3. **Comma followed by an item with a subordination flag:** In this case the next segment moves downward.[2]
4. **Coordinating expression:** Coordinating conjunction or any other coordinating expression preserves a layer, even though it might be followed by an extended segment with subordination flag.
5. **Full stop, question mark, exclamation mark:** These characters represent an end of the sentence, therefore the last node of the segmentation chart always jumps to the 1st layer of the chart (the layer of the main clause).
6. **Opening quotation marks:** Opening quotation marks are considered to be a separator only when they are at the start of the sentence or when they are combined with other separators (comma, semicolon etc.) – in such a case the next segment jumps one layer down.
7. **Closing quotation marks:** They are a separator only if they follow opening quotation marks, which are considered being a separator as well – in such a case the next segment jumps one or more layer up.

3   Evaluation

The evaluation of our method turned out to be more complicated than we have originally envisaged. We have assumed that the richly syntactically annotated Prague Dependency Treebank[3] will provide large enough set of sentences, but it turned out that this assumption has been wrong.

The problem is the annotation – there are too many syntactic phenomena for which it is extremely difficult, if not impossible, to find a general consensus about annotation. A huge number of decisions has to be made concerning the annotation of complex linguistic phenomena like coordination, verbal complexes, the proper place of prepositions etc.

---

[2] There are some exceptions to this general rule, which may be handled by a set of conditions capturing those specific constructions allowing to go either right or to move the next segment upwards. Such a construction may be found for example in the sentence *Řekl, že byl, jaký byl, ŽE je, jaký je a že bude, jaký bude.* [(He) said that (he) was who (he) was, that (he) is who (he) is and the (he) is going to be who (he) is going to be.]

[3] http://ufal.mff.cuni.cz/pdt2.0/

This inevitably leads to difficulties when someone tries to search the corpus for an information which had not been accounted for at the moment of the annotation scheme design. Let us demonstrate this on a very simple example – nothing is probably more easy to determine as a single unit than a pair of parenthesis inside a sentence. Unlike punctuation signs, the parenthesis unambiguously show the beginning and the end of a text inserted into clause. It is therefore quite natural to expect this easily detectable segment to be annotated in one way.

It turned out that this is not the case of the analytical level of PDT. After an examination of a small sample of the treebank we have found as many as 7 different ways how the parenthesis (and their content) were annotated in a certain context. Let us show at least two of those cases, both even located in the same sentence (see particular subtrees in Fig. 2): *Před několika dny vypukl další skandál (privatizace Čokoládoven v Modřanech), v němž byl do role hlavního viníka opět obsazen Fond národního majetku (FNM) a jeho předseda Tomáš Ježek.* [Yet another scandal erupted few days ago (a privatization of Čokoládovny in Modřany), in which the main role was played by a National Property Fund (NPF) and its chairman Tomáš Ježek.]

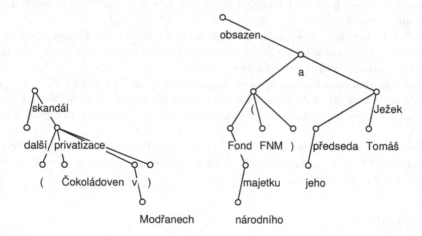

Fig. 2. Two types of parenthesis annotation in PDT

Not only the annotation of a content of both parenthesis differs, but even the mutual position of both types of parenthesis in the tree is different. It is quite clear that the transformation of sentences from PDT would require a lot of manual effort in order to provide a good testing material for our method.

These considerations led us to a decision to annotate manually a small sample of text not according to the standard of PDT, but according to the definition of the segmentation chart. Two articles from a daily newspapers Lidové noviny and Neviditelný pes[4] (LN, resp. NP in Table 1) containing political commentaries have been selected and manually annotated as a test set.

---

[4] http://pes.eunet.cz

The table below shows the degree of ambiguity of segmentation charts created automatically using the set of rules presented above, i.e. very local rules which do not presuppose understanding the sentence meaning.

Table 1. Degree of ambiguity of segmentation charts

	number of			number of charts					
	sentences	tokens	segments	1	2	3	4	5	more
LN	33	553	78	28	2	1	1	1	-
NP	15	334	57	12	3	-	-	-	-
total	48	887	135	40	5	1	1	1	-

Even though the test set is relatively small, the table clearly shows that the simple rules presented above provide a very good starting point and that in the average case the segmentation charts are almost unambiguous when a real text is concerned. It is of course possible to find very elaborated examples of sentences where our simple rules fail produce high number of segmentation charts, but the further refinement of those simple rules may improve even that. The most important result of the test was the 100% coverage of our method—not a single correct segmentation chart has been omitted by our algorithm.

4   Conclusion

The method presented in this paper shows that (at least for a language displaying inflectional morphology similar to that of Czech) it is possible to draw a chart reflecting the mutual position of clauses or their parts (segments) in complex sentences without applying the full-fledged syntactic parsing of the whole sentence first. The method is based on the identification of separators and their classification. The subsequent steps in the parsing process (which are not covered by this paper) may then decide, on one hand, which of the charts is not valid (in case that there are several variants of charts as an output of our method), and, on the other hand, exploit the charts for faster and more effective syntactic analysis of complex sentences. The evaluation of the method presented in the paper indicates that the segmentation may really help, the ambiguous segmentation charts are more or less rare.

The results achieved so far encourage further research in two areas. The first area concerns further development of more precise segmentation rules, the second one might concern the step from segmentation charts towards the chart reflecting the mutual position of clauses, not only segments.

References

1. Oliva, K.: A Parser for Czech Implemented in Systems Q. In: Explizite Beschreibung der Sprache und automatische Textbearbeitung, MFF UK Praha (1989).
2. Kuboň, V.: Problems of Robust Parsing of Czech. Ph.D. Thesis, MFF UK, Prague (2001).
3. Zeman, D.: Parsing with a Statistical Dependency Model. Ph.D. Thesis. MFF UK, Prague (2004).

4. Abney, S: Partial Parsing via Finite-State Cascades. In: Journal of Natural Language Engineering, Vol. 2, No. 4 (1995) 337–344.
5. Ciravegna, F., Lavelli, A.: Full Text Parsing using Cascades of Rules: An Information Extraction Procedure. In: Proceedings of EACL'99, University of Bergen (1999).
6. Brants, T.: Cascaded Markov Models. In: Proceedings of EACL '99, University of Bergen (1999).
7. Debusmann, R., Duchier, D., Rossberg, A.: Modular grammar design with typed parametric principles. In: Proceedings of FG-MOL 2005, Edinburgh (2005).
8. Jones, B.E.M.: Exploiting the Role of Punctuation in Parsing Natural Text, In: Proceedings of the COLING '94, Kyoto, University of Kyoto (1994) 421–425.
9. Hajič, J., Vidová-Hladká, B., Zeman, D.: Core Natural Language Processing Technology Applicable to Multiple Languages. The Workshop 98 Final Report. Center for Language and Speech Processing, Johns Hopkins University, Baltimore (1998).
10. Šmilauer, V.: Učebnice větného rozboru. SPN, Praha (1958).
11. Holan, T., Kuboň, V., Oliva, K., Plátek, M.: On Complexity of Word Order. In: Les grammaires de dépendance – Traitement automatique des langues, Vol. 41, No 1 (2000) 273–300.
12. Hajič, J.: Disambiguation of Rich Inflection (Computational Morphology of Czech). UK, Nakladatelství Karolinum, Praha (2004).

Enhanced Centroid-Based Classification Technique
by Filtering Outliers

Kwangcheol Shin, Ajith Abraham, and SangYong Han*

School of Computer Science and Engineering,Chung-Ang University
221, Heukseok-dong, Dongjak-gu, Seoul 156-756, Korea
kcshin@archi.cse.cau.ac.kr, ajith.abraham@ieee.org, hansy@cau.ac.kr

Abstract. Document clustering or unsupervised document classification has been used to enhance information retrieval. Recently this has become an intense area of research due to its practical importance. Outliers are the elements whose similarity to the centroid of the corresponding category is below some threshold value. In this paper, we show that excluding outliers from the noisy training data significantly improves the performance of the centroid-based classifier which is the best known method. The proposed method performs about 10% better than the centroid-based classifier.

1 Introduction

Since late 1990s, the explosive growth of Internet resulted in a huge quantity of documents available on-line. Technologies for efficient management of these documents are being developed continuously. One of representative tasks for efficient document management is text categorization, also called as classification. Given a set of training examples assigned each one to some categories, the task is to assign new documents to a suitable category. A fixed collection of text is clustered into groups or clusters that have similar contents. The similarity between documents is usually measured with the associative coefficients from the vector space model, e.g., the cosine coefficient.

A well-known text categorization method is kNN [1]; other popular methods are Naïve Bayesian [3], C4.5 [4], genetic programming [10], self organizing maps [11] artificial neural networks [9] and SVM [5]. Han and Karypis [2] proposed the Centroid-based classifier and showed that it gives better results than other known methods.

In this paper, we show that removing outliers from the training categories significantly improves the classification results obtained by using the Centroid-based method. Our experiments show that the new method gives better results than the Centroid-based classifier.

The paper is organized as follows. In Section 2, some related work is presented followed by the details of the proposed method in Section 3. Experiment results are presented in Section 4 and some Conclusions are given towards the end.

2 Related Work

Document representation. In both categorization techniques considered below, documents are represented as keyword vectors according to the standard vector space model with *tf-idf*

---

* Corresponding author.

Petr Sojka, Ivan Kopeček and Karel Pala (Eds.): TSD 2006, LNAI 4188, pp. 159–163, 2006.
© Springer-Verlag Berlin Heidelberg 2006

term weighting [6,7]. For definition purposes, let the document collection contains total N different keywords. A document d is represented as an N-dimensional vector of term weight t with coordinates

$$w_{td} = \frac{f_{td}}{\max f_{td}} \log \frac{n_t}{N}, \tag{1}$$

where f_{td} is the frequency of the term t in the document d and n_t is the number of the documents where the term t occurs. The similarity between two documents d_i and d_j is measured using the cosine measure widely used in information retrieval—the cosine of the angle between them:

$$s(d_i, d_j) = \cos(\theta(d_i, d_j)) = \frac{d_i^T d_j}{||d_i|| \, ||d_j||}, \tag{2}$$

where θ is the angle between the two vectors and $||d||$ is the length of the vector.

kNN classifier [1]: For a new data item, k most similar elements of the training data set are determined, and the category is chosen to which a greater number of elements among those k ones belong; see Figure 1, left.

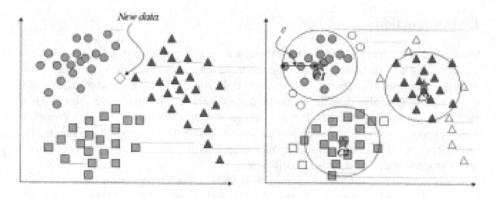

Fig. 1. Example of classification

Centroid-based classifier [2]: Given a set Si documents — the ith training category, its center is defined as its average vector:

$$\vec{C_i} = \frac{1}{|S_i|} \sum_{\vec{d} \in S_i} \vec{d} \tag{3}$$

where $|Si|$ is the number of documents in the category. For a new data item the category is chosen that maximizes the similarity between the new item and the center of each category. This was reported as the best known classifier so far [2].

3 Proposed Method

We observed that the training data items that are far away from the center of its training category tend to reduce the accuracy of classification. Our hypothesis is that those items merely represent noise and not provide any useful training examples and thus decrease the classification accuracy. Thus we exclude them from consideration; see Figure 1, right. Specifically, at the training stage we calculate the center Ci of each category Si using (2). Then we form new categories by discarding the outliers:

$$S_i' = \{d \in S_i : Sim(d_k, \vec{C}_i) > \varepsilon\} \qquad (4)$$

in the next section we discuss the choice of the threshold ε. After refining training data, we recalculate the center of each category:

$$\vec{C}_i' = \frac{1}{|S_i'|} \sum_{\vec{d} \in S_i'} \vec{d} \qquad (5)$$

And finally the Centroid-based classifier is applied to get the results.

4   Experimental Results

To evaluate the efficiency of the proposed method, we used two different datasets. First one is the 20-newsgroup dataset which has many noisy data and the other is the popular Reuter-21578 R10 dataset which doesn't have noisy data.

4.1   20-Newsgroup Dataset

At first, we use the 20-newsgroup dataset to evaluate performance of the proposed method. The dataset has 20 categories of roughly 1000 documents each. We used MC [8] program to build the document vectors. We implemented our modified Centroid-based classification and compared with the Centroid-based classification and kNN method with $k = 5$. As illustrated

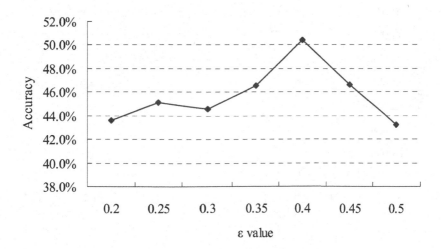

Fig. 2. Different accuracy according to ε value for 80% of 20-newsgroup data

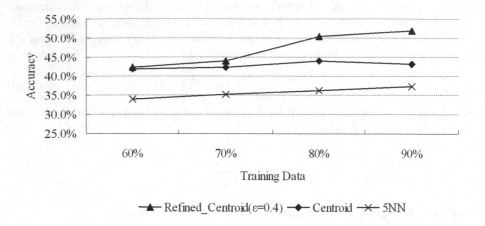

Fig. 3. Test results

in Figure 2, the proposed method provides the best performance with $\varepsilon = $ g.4. Figure 3 shows how the classification accuracy is affected due to the percentage of training dataset over total dataset. We obtained 9.93% improvement over the original Centroid-based classification and 32.11% over 5NN. Improvements clearly show that the proposed method worked very well for the noisy dataset.

4.2   Reuter-21578 R10 Dataset

We also applied our method to the popular Reuter-21578 R10 dataset, which has 10 categories and each category has different number of data. Because of being categorized by human indexers, it doesn't have noise data. Figure 4 illustrates that for noiseless dataset, like Reuter-

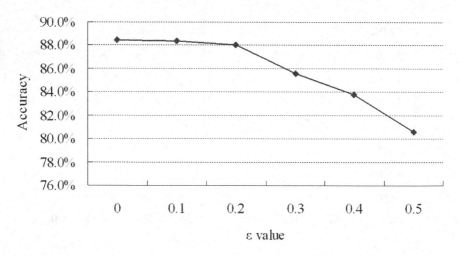

Fig. 4. Performance (accuracy) of the algorithm for different ε values for 60% of Reuter-21578 R10 dataset

21578 R10, the performance is not improved when compared to the Centroid-based classification approach (note: it is same with Centroid-based classification when we set 0 to ε).

5   Conclusion

We have presented an improved Centroid-based classifier. The improvement consists in removing outliers from the categories of the training dataset. Our method shows almost 10% better accuracy for noisy dataset than the original Centroid-based classifier, which was reported in [2] as the most accurate text categorization method. In the future, automatic choice of the threshold value ε is to be considered

Acknowledgments. Work supported by the MIC (Ministry of Information and Communication), Korea, under the Chung-Ang University HNRC-ITRC (Home Network Research Center) support program supervised by the IITA (Institute of Information Technology Assessment).

References

1. W.W. Cohen and H. Hirsh, Joins that generalize: Text Classification using WHIRL. In Proc. of the Fourth Int'l Conference on Knowledge Discovery and Data Mining, 1998.
2. E. Han and G. Karypis, Centroid-Based Document Classification: Analysis and Experimental Results, Principles of Data Mining and Knowledge Discovery, p. 424–431, 2000.
3. D. Lewis and W. Gale. A sequential algorithm for training text classifiers, In SIGIR-94, 1994.
4. J. Ross Quinlan. C4.5: Programs for Machine Learning. Morgan Kaufmann, San Mateo, CA, 1993.
5. V. Vapnik. The Nature of Statistical Learning Theory. Springer, 1995
6. G. Salton and. M. J. McGill, *Introduction to Modern Retrieval*. McGraw-Hill, 1983.
7. R. Baeza-Yates, and B. Ribeiro-Neto. *Modern Information Retrieval*. Addison-Wesley, 1999.
8. Dhillon I. S., Fan J., and Guan Y. Efficient Clustering of Very Large Document Collections. *Data Mining for Scientific and Engineering Applications*, Kluwer, 2001.
9. MacLeod, K. *An application specific neural model for document clustering*. Proceedings of the Fourth Annual Parallel Processing Symposium, vol. 1, p. 5–16, 1990.
10. Svingen, B. *Using genetic programming for document classification*. FLAIRS-98. Proceedings of the Eleventh International Florida Artificial Intelligence Research, p. 63–67, 1998.
11. Hyotyniemi, H. *Text document classification with self-organizing maps*. STeP '96 - Genes, Nets and Symbols. Finnish Artificial Intelligence Conference, p. 64–72, 1996.
12. Lam, Wai and Low, Kon-Fan *Automatic document classification based on probabilistic reasoning: Model and performance analysis*. Proceedings of the IEEE International Conference on Systems, Man and Cybernetics, Vol. 3, p. 2719–2723, 1997.

Multilingual News Document Clustering:
Two Algorithms Based on Cognate Named Entities

Soto Montalvo[1], Raquel Martínez[2], Arantza Casillas[3], and Víctor Fresno[1]

[1] GAVAB Group, URJC
{soto.montalvo, victor.fresno}@urjc.es
[2] NLP&IR Group, UNED
raquel@lsi.uned.es
[3] Dpt. Electricidad y Electrónica, UPV-EHU
arantza.casillas@ehu.es

Abstract. This paper presents an approach for Multilingual News Document Clustering in comparable corpora. We have implemented two algorithms of heuristic nature that follow the approach. They use as unique evidence for clustering the identification of cognate named entities between both sides of the comparable corpora. In addition, no information about the right number of clusters has to be provided to the algorithms. The applicability of the approach only depends on the possibility of identifying cognate named entities between the languages involved in the corpus. The main difference between the two algorithms consists of whether a monolingual clustering phase is applied at first or not. We have tested both algorithms with a comparable corpus of news written in English and Spanish. The performance of both algorithms is slightly different; the one that does not apply the monolingual phase reaches better results. In any case, the obtained results with both algorithms are encouraging and show that the use of cognate named entities can be enough knowledge for deal with multilingual clustering of news documents.

1 Introduction

Multilingual Document Clustering (MDC) involves dividing a set of n documents, written in different languages, into a specified number k of clusters, so that the documents that are similar to other documents will be in the same cluster. Meanwhile a multilingual cluster is composed of documents written in different languages, a monolingual cluster is composed of documents written in one language.

MDC has many applications. The increasing amount of documents written in different languages that are available electronically leads to develop applications to manage that amount of information for filtering, retrieving, and grouping multilingual documents. MDC tools can make easier tasks such as Cross-Lingual Information Retrieval, the training of parameters in Statistics Based Machine Translation, or the Alignment of parallel and non parallel corpora, among others.

MDC systems have developed different solutions to group related documents. On the one hand, the strategies employed can be classified in two main groups: the ones which use translation technologies, and the ones that transform the document into a language-independent representation. One of the crucial issues regarding the methods based on

Petr Sojka, Ivan Kopeček and Karel Pala (Eds.): TSD 2006, LNAI 4188, pp. 165–172, 2006.

document or features translation is the correctness of the proper translation. Bilingual resources usually suggest more than one sense for a source word and it is not a trivial task to select the appropriate one. Although word-sense disambiguation methods can be applied, these are not free of errors. On the other hand, methods based on language-independent representation also have limitations. For instance, those based on thesaurus depend on the thesaurus scope. Numbers or dates identification can be appropriate for some types of clustering and documents; however, for other types it could not be so relevant and even it could be a source of noise.

MDC is normally applied with parallel [12] or comparable corpus ([1,2,6,7,10,13]). In the case of the comparable corpora, the documents usually are news articles. Considering the approaches based on translation technology, two different strategies are employed: translate the whole document into an anchor language, or translate only some features of the document. Some authors, for example [7], use machine translation techniques to translate the whole document, while others apply the same techniques to translate selected features [10]. On the other hand, authors like [1] translate some selected features of the document consulting a bilingual dictionary. Some approaches first carry out a monolingual clustering in each language, and then they find relations between the obtained clusters generating the multilingual clusters. Other approaches start with a multilingual clustering to look for relations between the documents of all the involved languages. In [2] the authors select different features to carry out some experiments with both approaches.

The strategies that use language-independent representation try to normalize the content of the documents in a language-neutral way; for example: by mapping text contents to an independent knowledge representation, or by recognizing language independent text features inside the documents. Both approaches can be employed isolated or combined. The first approach involves the use of existing multilingual linguistic resources, such as thesaurus, to create a text representation consisting of a set of thesaurus items. In [13] the authors present an approach based on using the multilingual thesaurus *Eurovoc*. The second approach involves the recognition of independent elements. In [6] is presented an approach that exploits the presence of common words among different languages for solving cross language text categorization. In [5] use as document features the named entities as well as the publication date of the document to carried out the multilingual clustering. In this case the MDC is applied in order to align a comparable corpora to obtain a similarity multilingual thesaurus. However, in [4] the author affirms that the NEs themselves are not suitable to be used as features in document clustering. In [12] the authors present a method based on Relevant Expressions (RE). Others works ([9,14]) combine recognition of independent text features with mapping text contents to a thesaurus.

This paper presents an approach for MDC in comparable corpora. We have implemented two algorithms, both of heuristic nature, that use as unique evidence for clustering the identification of cognate named entities between both sides of the comparable corpora. None of the revised works use as unique evidence for clustering the identification of cognate named entities between both sides of the comparable corpora. One of the main advantages of this approach is that it does not depend on multilingual resources such as dictionaries, machine translation systems, thesaurus or gazetteers. In addition, no information about the right number of clusters has to be provided to the algorithms. The applicability of the approach only depends on the possibility of identifying cognate named entities between the languages involved in the corpus. It could be particularly appropriate for news corpus, where named entities play an important role. The main difference between the two algorithms consists of whether a monolingual clustering phase is applied or not. This allows to determine when is more appropriate the application of the monolingual and multilingual phases, or even if a monolingual phase is needed.

In Section 2 we present our approach for MDC and the two algorithms. Section 3 describes the corpora, as well as the experiments and the results. Finally, Section 4 summarizes the conclusions and the future work.

2   MDC by Cognate NE Identification

We propose an approach based only on cognate Named Entities (NE) identification. The NE categories that we take into account are: PERSON, ORGANIZATION, LOCATION, and MISCELLANY. Other numerical categories such as DATE, TIME or NUMBER are not considered in this work. We think they are less relevant regarding the content of the document. In addition, they can lead to group documents with few content in common.

The approach has two main phases: cognate NE identification which is common to the two algorithms, and clustering. Both phases are described in detail in the following subsections.

2.1   Cognate NE Identification

This phase is shared by the two algorithms. It consists of two steps:

1. Detection and classification of the NEs in each side of the corpus separately. In our case we used a corpus with morphosyntactical annotations and the NEs identified and classified.
2. Identification of cognates between the NEs of both sides of the comparable corpus.

In order to identify the cognates between NEs 4 steps are carried out:

– Obtaining two lists of NEs, one for each language.
– Identification of entity mentions in each list. For instance, "Ernesto Zedillo", "Zedillo", "Sr. Zedillo" will be considered as the same entity after this step since they refer to the same person. This step is only applied to entities of PERSON category. The identification of NE mentions, as well as cognate NE, is based on the use of the Levensthein edit-distance function (LD). This measure is obtained by finding the cheapest way to transform one string into another. Transformations are the one-step operations of insertion, deletion and substitution. The result is an integer value that is normalized by the length of the longest string. In addition, constraints regarding the number of words that the NEs are made up as well as the order of the words are applied.
– Identification of cognates between the NEs of both sides of the comparable corpus. It is also based on the LD. In addition, also constraints regarding the number and the order of the words are applied. First, we tried cognate identification only between NEs of the same category (PERSON with PERSON, ...) or between any category and MISCELLANY (PERSON with MISCELLANY, ...). Next, with the rest of NEs that have not been considered as cognate, a next step is applied without the constraint of being to the same category or MISCELLANY. As result of this step a list of corresponding bilingual cognates is obtained.

– The same procedure carried out for obtaining bilingual cognates is used to obtain two more lists of cognates, one per language, between the NEs of the same language.

2.2 Clustering

The two algorithms proposed for the clustering of multilingual news documents are of heuristic nature. Both, in an iterative way, decide the number of clusters.

Bilingual at the End Algorithm (BEA). BEA consists of 3 main phases: (1) first monolingual clusters creation, (2) monolingual relocation of documents, and (3) bilingual relocation of documents. This algorithm is based on a previous one described in [8].

1. First monolingual clusters creation. Documents in each language are processed separately. News of the same language that have more cognates in common than a threshold are grouped into the same cluster. In addition, at least one of the cognates have to be of a specific category. In this work we have fixed this category to be PERSON. After this phase all documents are assigned to some cluster. Notice that some cluster could have only a document since this one does not comply with the grouping conditions. After this phase two sets of clusters are obtained, one per language. The number of clusters obtained in this phase will be the top limit; the next phases could reduce it.
2. Monolingual relocation of documents. In this phase the documents in each language are processed separately as well. Each document is located in the cluster that contains the most similar document regarding the number of cognates in common, but only if that number is greater than a threshold. No constraint regarding the NE category is applied. This is an iterative process until no document is relocated. As result of this phase, the number of clusters in each set could be reduced because of the relocation.
3. Bilingual relocation of documents. Finally, both sets of monolingual clusters are merged into one. This process is not carried out by the union of the whole clusters, but by the relocation of documents. The process is similar to the previous one, but with the documents and clusters of both languages.

Bilingual Algorithm (BA). BA consists of 2 main phases: (1) first bilingual clusters creation, and (2) bilingual relocation of documents.

1. First bilingual clusters creation. This phase is similar to the first phase of BEA but comparing news documents of different languages. After this phase only one set of clusters is obtained.
2. Bilingual relocation of documents. This phase is similar to the third phase of BEA. Therefore, documents are compared among them irrespective of the languages. This is why no later phase is needed.

The thresholds of both algorithms can be customized in order to permit and make the experiments easier. In addition, the parameters customization allows the adaptation to different type of corpus or content. In Section 3.2 the exact values we have used are described.

3   Evaluation

We wanted not only determine whether our approach was successful for MDC or not, but we also wanted to compare if the application of the multilingual comparison only at the end or from the beginning influences the results.

3.1   Corpus

A Comparable Corpus is a collection of similar texts in different languages or in different varieties of a language. In this work we compiled a collection of news written in Spanish and English belonging to the same period of time. The news are categorized and come from the news agency EFE compiled by HERMES project (http://nlp.uned.es/hermes/index.html). That collection can be considered like a comparable corpus.

We used two subsets of that collection. In order to test the MDC results we have carried out a manual clustering with each subset. Three persons read every document and grouped them considering the content of each one. The first subset, call $S1$, consists on 63 news, 35 in Spanish and 28 in English. It consists on 8 multilingual and 2 monolingual clusters. The second one, $S2$, is composed of 136 news, 71 in Spanish and 65 in English. It consists on 24 multilingual and 2 monolingual clusters.

In the experimentation process the first subset, $S1$, was used to train the parameters and threshold values; with the second one the best parameters values were applied.

3.2   Experiments and Results with MDC by Cognate NE

The quality of the results is determined by means of an external evaluation measure, the F-measure [11]. This measure compares the human solution with the system one. The F-measure combines the precision and recall measures:

$$F(i, j) = \frac{2 \times Recall(i, j) \times Precision(i, j)}{(Precision(i, j) + Recall(i, j))}, \tag{1}$$

where $Recall(i, j) = \frac{n_{ij}}{n_i}$, $Precision(i, j) = \frac{n_{ij}}{n_j}$, n_{ij} is the number of members of cluster human solution i in cluster j, n_j is the number of members of cluster j and n_i is the number of members of cluster human solution i. For all the clusters:

$$F = \sum_i \frac{n_i}{n} max\{F(i)\} \tag{2}$$

The closer to 1 the F-measure value the better MCD performance.

The threshold for the LD in order to determine whether two NEs are cognate or not is 0.2, except for entities of ORGANIZATION and LOCATION categories which is 0.3 when they have more than one word. In the first clusters creation phase of both BEA and BA algorithms, one of the constraint refers to the category of at least one of the cognates in common. We realized that this constraint mainly influences in the number of clusters obtained in this phase. However, it has little impact in the resulting clustering after the relocation phases. Therefore, we have fix this category to be PERSON in this experiments. Regarding the thresholds of the phases of both algorithms, after training the thresholds with the collection $S1$ we concluded:

- In BEA algorithm two thresholds are needed: one for the first phase (TH1) and the other for the second and third phases (TH2). The second threshold has more impact in the result than the first one. In fact, with a low value for TH2 (2) the best results are obtained. It seems that using a TH1 relatively high (7, 8, 9) leads to a good first grouping that makes second and third phases more effective. However with lower values for TH1 good f-measure results are obtained as well.
- BA algorithm also needs two thresholds, one per phase. It performs the best clustering with both high and low values for TH1 but with low or medium values for TH2. It seems to be more independent of the threshold values.

Table 1 shows the 10 best results of the application of BEA and BA algorithms to subset $S2$. We run the algorithms with the best parameter set obtained of the experimentation with $S1$. This set was the best set for $S2$ collection as well. The fifth column represents: the number of multilingual clusters of the algorithm result, the number of clusters calculated, and the number of clusters of the human solution. Although none of the results got the exact number of clusters, it is remarkable that the resulting values are close to the right ones.

Table 1. MDC results with the BEA and BA Algorithms for cognate NE approach and $S2$ subset

Alg.	$TH1$	$TH2$	F-measure	Mult./Calcul./Total
BEA	7	2	0.8796	23/30/26
	8	2	0.8708	19/31/26
	9	2	0.8708	19/31/26
	10	2	0.8708	19/31/26
	4	2	0.8600	18/29/26
	5	2	0.8600	18/29/26
	6	2	0.8600	18/29/26
	7	4	0.8594	17/42/26
	3	2	0.8569	18/28/26
	8	4	0.8506	17/43/26
BA	2	3	0.8831	22/33/26
	2	2	0.8831	22/33/26
	2	1	0.8831	22/32/26
	2	0	0.8831	22/32/26
	8	3	0.8770	24/36/26
	8	2	0.8770	24/36/26
	8	1	0.8770	24/35/26
	8	0	0.8770	24/35/26
	2	4	0.8750	22/36/26
	2	5	0.8750	22/36/26

(Table header: Step Thresholds | Results | Clusters)

4   Conclusions and Future Work

We have described a novel approach for Multilingual Document Clustering based only on cognate named entities identification. One of the main advantages of this approach is that it does not depend on multilingual resources such as dictionaries, machine translation systems, thesaurus or gazetteers. The only requirement to fulfill is that the languages involved in the corpus have to allow the possibility of identifying cognate named entities. Another advantage of the approach is that it does not need any information about the right number of clusters. In fact, the algorithm calculates it according with the threshold values of the algorithm.

We propose two algorithms that follow our approach. The main difference between them is whether a previous monolingual clustering phase is applied or not. We have tested the two algorithms with a comparable corpus of news written in English and Spanish, obtaining encouraging results. The one that does not apply a monolingual phase obtains slightly better clustering results. This approach could be particularly appropriate for news articles corpus, where named entities play an important role. Even more, when there is no previous evidence of the right number of clusters. Future work will include the compilation of more corpora, the incorporation of machine learning techniques in order to obtain the thresholds more appropriate for different type of corpus.

Acknowledgements

We wish to thank the anonymous reviewers for their helpful and instructive comments. This work has been partially supported by MCyT TIN2005-08943-C02-02.

References

1. B. Mathieu, R. Besancon and C. Fluhr: "Multilingual Document clusters discovery". *RIAO'2004* (2004) 1–10.
2. H-H. Chen and C-J. Lin: "A Multilingual News Summarizer". *Proceedings of 18th International Conference on Computational Linguistics*, (2000), 159–165.
3. G. Karypis: "CLUTO: A Clustering Toolkit". *Technical Report: 02-017*. University of Minnesota, Department of Computer Science, Minneapolis, MN 55455 (2002).
4. W. Gang: "Named Entity Recognition and An Apply on Document Clustering". *MCSc Thesis*. Dalhousie University, Faculty of Computer Science, Canada (2004).
5. M. García, F. Martínez, L.A. Ureña y M.T. Martín: "Generación de un tesauro multilingue a partir de un corpus comparable aplicado a CLIR". *Procesamiento de Lenguaje Natural*, vol(28), (2002) 55–62.
6. A. Gliozzo and C. Strapparava: "Cross language Text Categorization by acquiring Multilingual Domain Models from Comparable Corpora". *Proceedings of the ACL Workshop on Building and Using Parallel Texts*, (2005), 9–16.
7. L.J. Leftin: "Newsblaster Russian-English Clustering Performance Analysis". *Columbia computer science Technical Reports* (2003).
8. S. Montalvo, R. Martínez, A. Casillas and V. Fresno: "Multilingual Document Clustering: an Heuristic Approach Based on Cognate Named Entities". To be published in *COLING-ACL 2006* (2006).
9. B. Pouliquen, R. Steinberger, C. Ignat, E. Käsper and I. Temikova: "Multilingual and cross-lingual news topic tracking". *Proceedings of the 20th International Conference on Computational Linguistics*, (2004), 23–27.
10. A. Rauber, M. Dittenbach and D. Merkl: "Towards Automatic Content-Based Organization of Multilingual Digital Libraries: An English, French, and German View of the Russian Information Agency Novosti News". *Third All-Russian Conference Digital Libraries: Advanced Methods and Technologies*, Digital Collections Petrozavodsk, RCDI'2001, (2001).

11. C.J. van Rijsbergen: "Foundations of evaluation". *Journal of Documentation*, vol(30), (1974), 365–373.
12. J. Silva, J. Mexia, C. Coelho and G. Lopes: "A Statistical Approach for Multilingual Document Clustering and Topic Extraction form Clusters". *Pliska Studia Mathematica Bulgarica*, vol(16), (2004), 207–228.
13. R. Steinberger, B. Pouliquen and J. Scheer: "Cross-Lingual Document Similarity Calculation Using the Multilingual Thesaurus EUROVOC". *CICling'2002*, (2002), 415–424.
14. R. Steinberger, B. Pouliquen and C. Ignat: "Exploting multilingual nomenclatures and language-independent text features as an interlingua for cross-lingual text analysis applications". SILTC (2004).

A Study of the Influence of PoS Tagging on WSD*

Lorenza Moreno-Monteagudo, Rubén Izquierdo-Beviá, Patricio Martínez-Barco,
and Armando Suárez

Departamento de Lenguajes y Sistemas Informáticos.
Universidad de Alicante. Spain
{loren, ruben, patricio, armando}@dlsi.ua.es

Abstract. In this paper we discuss to what extent the choice of one particular Part-of-Speech (PoS) tagger determines the results obtained by a word sense disambiguation (WSD) system. We have chosen several PoS taggers and two WSD methods. By combining them, and using different kind of information, several experiments have been carried out. The WSD systems have been evaluated using the corpora of the lexical sample task of SENSEVAL-3 for English. The results show that some PoS taggers work better with one specific method. That is, selecting the right combination of these tools, could improve the results obtained by a WSD system.

1 Introduction

There are several approaches to WSD based on machine learning techniques. Among others, maximum entropy [1,2,3] and support vector machines [4] are found, both of them supervised methods using feature vectors. Commonly, some of these features are words, lemmas, PoS tags, etc. The performance reached by these methods depends on all this information, and therefore on the way it is obtained, that is, the tools that are used.

In [5] three different PoS taggers were evaluated for a WSD system[1]. She found that the best results in her WSD system were achieved with the most accurate PoS tagger. However, the results of the WSD system did not reflect the stand-alone accuracy of the rest of PoS taggers. Our aim is to study how these tools, different kinds of PoS taggers and WSD methods, work together. At this point, we are more interested on determining if there exist differences when these tools are combined in different ways, than on the final precision achieved.

The rest of this paper is organized as follows: we first summarize the corpus and the PoS taggers we have used for the experiments (sections 2 and 3 respectively). Next, in section 4, the experiments are described. Section 5 discusses the results obtained with the different experiments, and, finally, in section 6 some conclusions and further work are shown.

2 Source Corpora

As said before, we have used the SENSEVAL-3 lexical sample corpus [6] for our experiments. This corpus consists of examples from the British National Corpus[2]. The examples have

---

* This paper has been supported by the Spanish Government under projects CESS-ECE (HUM2004-21127-E) and R2D2 (TIC2003-07158-C04-01).

[1] The experiment was undertaken with the training Dutch Senseval-2 data.

[2] http://www.natcorp.ox.ac.uk

Petr Sojka, Ivan Kopeček and Karel Pala (Eds.): TSD 2006, LNAI 4188, pp. 173–179, 2006.
© Springer-Verlag Berlin Heidelberg 2006

been manually annotated with senses using WordNet 1.7.1 for adjectives and nouns, and Wordsmyth[3] for verbs. The lexical sample task deals with annotating 57 words with their senses. There are 20 nouns, 32 verbs and 5 adjectives with an average number of senses of 5.8, 6.31 and 10.2 respectively. Only fine grained senses have been considered.

3   Description of the Part-of-Speech Taggers

In this section we summarize the different PoS taggers we have used for the experiments. They are the following: SVMTool [7], Freeling [8], TreeTagger [9], Brill's Tagger [10] and Ratnaparkhi's MaxEnt tagger [11]. Table 1 reflects their main features: the learning method they use, precision published by the authors, if they obtain the lemma, and the corpora used for training.

Table 1. Description of PoS taggers

PoS tagger	Method	Prec.	Lemma	Corpora
SVMTool	Support Vector Machines	97.16		Wall Street Journal
Freeling	Hidden Markov Models	95.0	✓	Wall Street Journal
TreeTagger	Decision Trees	96.36	✓	PennTreebank
Brill	Rules	94.9		PennTreebank Brown Corpus
Ratnaparkhi	Maximum Entropy	96.6		Wall Street Journal

4   Experiments

The experiments have been designed in order to analyze the behaviour of two WSD methods when combined with different PoS taggers and different types of information. In table 2 the different elements combined are specified: WSD method, PoS tagger, lemmatizer (we have used Freeling and TreeTagger to get the lemma) and kind of information used in the WSD systems. SVMLight[4] [12] and MxE[13] have been chosen as WSD systems based on SVM and maximum entropy respectively. The set of features defined for the WSD systems are:

- word, PoS tag, lemma and stem at positions 0 (target word), ± 1, ± 2, ± 3
- words, PoS tags and lemmas of collocations at positions $(-3, -2)$, $(-2, -1)$, $(-1, 0)$, $(0, +1)$, $(+1, +2)$, $(+2, +3)$

Three types of experiments have been defined, depending on the information used. So, *Experiment 1* uses words and PoS tags, *Experiment 2* adds lemmas and the last one, *Experiment 3*, uses words, PoS tags, lemmas and stems[5]. The reason for defining a third experiment using stems, when we already have lemmas, is to find out if the information provided by both sources is complementary, improving the final WSD results.

---

[3] www.wordsmyth.net

[4] Referred as SVM in tables. Available at svmlight.joachims.org

[5] The stemmers are available at http://www.unine.ch/info/clef and http://www.unine.ch.

Throughout these experiments the relation between a PoS tagger and the WSD results can be analyzed. Additionally, by adding lemmas and stems, we can study whether this influence lessens when more information, apart from PoS tags, is used. These three experiments have been carried out for each WSD method and PoS tagger, and considering each lemmatizer when necessary. That is for *Experiment 2* and *Experiment 3* with all the PoS taggers except for Freeling and TreeTagger.

Table 2. Different components to define experiments

Method	PoS tagger	Lemmatizer	Information
MxE	SVMTool	Freeling	Word
SVM	Freeling	TreeTagger	PoS
	TreeTagger		Lemma
	Brill tagger		Stem
	Ratnaparkhi		

5 Results

Results[6] for all the experiments have been arranged in different tables.

Table 3 shows the overall results organized by experiment and WSD method. For each experiment-WSD method, the accuracy obtained by the different PoS tagger-lemmatizers is shown. We also show the differences between the best and worst result in the last column. Significant differences, according to the *z'-test* [14] have been highligthed. So, we can study in what way the final result of the WSD system depends on the PoS tagger used. By experiments two and three we can determine if this "dependency" becomes weaker when more information (lemmas and stems) is added.

An interesting point is that SVM gets always the best result when combined with TreeTagger and the worst one with Freeling. This seems to verify the importance of choosing the right combination of PoS tagger and WSD method. Another important aspect is that the results converge when more information is used (*Experiment 3*), as it is shown by the *Dif.* column. However, this is not the case for MxE where there is not a "favourite" PoS tagger.

Moreover, the lemma information provided by Freeling or TreeTagger affects differently to each WSD method. As *Experiment 2* shows, both methods seem to work better with TreeTagger than with Freeling. However, when stems are introduced, *Experiment 3*, SVM perfoms better with TreeTagger, while MxE does it with Freeling. Additionally, TreeTagger is the best PoS tagger when used with SVM, but the worst one when combined with MxE. Besides this, Freeling is the best PoS tagger for MxE and the worst one for SVM. A reason for this different behavior could be on the nature of the WSD methods themselves and the way PoS taggers behave. While SVM is based on learning the linear discriminant, MxE learns probability models. Furthermore, errors made by PoS taggers may not be so systematic, meaning that one particular PoS tagger could not always make the same mistakes on the same kind of words. If so, MxE seems to be more affected by this kind of "noise" than SVM.

---

[6] Accuracy (correct clasifications/number of test examples) is used for all the experiments since coverage is always 100%.

Table 3. Average results by experiment, WSD method, PoS tagger and lemmatizer

Exp.	WSD	PoS tagger	Lemmatizer	Acc.	Dif.
Exp1	SVM	TreeTagger		67.72	**1.34**
		SVMTool	-	66.84	
		Ratnaparkhi	-	66.81	
		Brill	-	66.43	
		Freeling	-	66.38	
	MXE	Ratnaparkhi	-	64.88	0.94
		Brill	-	64.68	
		SVMTool	-	64.58	
		TreeTagger	-	64.45	
		Freeling	-	63.95	
Exp2	SVM	TreeTagger	TreeTagger	67.85	**1.04**
		SVMTool	TreeTagger	67.39	
		SVMTool	Freeling	67.22	
		Brill	TreeTagger	67.19	
		Brill	Freeling	67.11	
		Freeling	Freeling	67.01	
		Ratnaparkhi	TreeTagger	66.99	
		Ratnaparkhi	Freeling	66.81	
	MXE	TreeTagger	TreeTagger	65.97	0.58
		SVMTool	TreeTagger	65.90	
		Ratnaparkhi	TreeTagger	65.90	
		Brill	Freeling	65.85	
		Brill	TreeTagger	65.77	
		SVMTool	Freeling	65.62	
		Ratnaparkhi	Freeling	65.49	
		Freeling	Freeling	65.39	
Exp3	SVM	TreeTagger	TreeTagger	67.65	0.56
		Ratnaparkhi	TreeTagger	67.37	
		SVMTool	TreeTagger	67.29	
		Brill	TreeTagger	67.29	
		Brill	Freeling	67.22	
		SVMTool	Freeling	67.17	
		Ratnaparkhi	Freeling	67.11	
		Freeling	Freeling	67.09	
	MXE	Freeling	Freeling	66.56	0.66
		Ratnaparkhi	Freeling	66.28	
		Brill	Freeling	66.23	
		SVMTool	Freeling	66.18	
		Brill	TreeTagger	66.08	
		Ratnaparkhi	TreeTagger	66.00	
		SVMTool	TreeTagger	65.97	
		TreeTagger	TreeTagger	65.90	

The fact is that, in our case, the selection of one PoS tagger is not a trivial matter, even though the results show slight differences from one PoS tagger to another.

We have also arranged the results under word category, in order to find out if they depend on it. That is, if the results depend on the way PoS taggers behave with different word categories: adjectives, nouns and verbs. Table 4 shows these results for *Experiment 3*. This experiment has been chosen as an example of the differences found in all the tests.

Table 4. Results for Experiment 3 organized by category

PoS	WSD	PoS tagger	Lemmatizer	Acc.	Dif.
N	SVM	TreeTagger	TreeTagger	66.46	0.83
		Ratnaparkhi	Freeling	66.35	
		Ratnaparkhi	TreeTagger	66.24	
		SVMTool	Freeling	66.13	
		SVMTool	TreeTagger	66.08	
		Brill	Freeling	66.08	
		Brill	TreeTagger	66.08	
		Freeling	Freeling	65.63	
	MXE	SVMTool	Freeling	65.25	0.83
		Freeling	Freeling	65.02	
		Ratnaparkhi	Freeling	64.91	
		Brill	Freeling	64.86	
		Ratnaparkhi	TreeTagger	64.64	
		SVMToo	TreeTagger	64.58	
		Brill	TreeTagger	64.47	
		TreeTagger	TreeTagger	64.42	
V	SVM	TreeTagger	TreeTagger	69.97	0.86
		Freeling	Freeling	69.77	
		SVMTool	TreeTagger	69.72	
		Brill	TreeTagger	69.72	
		Ratnaparkhi	TreeTagger	69.67	
		Brill	Freeling	69.57	
		SVMTool	Freeling	69.41	
		Ratnaparkhi	Freeling	69.11	
	MXE	Freeling	Freeling	68,96	1.06
		Ratnaparkhi	Freeling	68.45	
		Brill	TreeTagger	68.40	
		Brill	Freeling	68.35	
		TreeTagger	TreeTagger	68.20	
		Ratnaparkhi	TreeTagger	68.15	
		SVMTool	TreeTagger	68.10	
		SVMTool	Freeling	67.90	

Studying the corpus we find much less adjectives (around 4%) than verbs (50%) and nouns (46%), which means that errors on adjectives are more evident. This is why we do not show the results obtained for adjectives, since we think they cannot be taken into account.

An interesting point is that the ranking of PoS taggers for each WSD method is different for each category. This shows that the selection of a PoS tagger for a WSD system does not only depend on the WSD method selected, but also on the lexical category. Consequently, we could possibly use the best PoS tagger for each category and then integrate the results in the WSD system.

6 Conclusions and Future Work

In this paper the way of combining different NLP tools has been explored, in order to achieve the best results in a specific task. In this case, the influence of using a PoS tagger with a WSD system has been studied. Slight differences, even of a few tenths, can be of great importance in a WSD task[7], specially when less information is used. In these cases it is necessary to pay more attention when selecting one PoS tagger. We have shown that some of the differences are significant ones.

Additionally, some tools seem to combine "better" with some other tools (TreeTagger shows a tendency to work better with SVM). So, depending on the WSD method, a different PoS tagger should be used. We are now studying each individual case in order to determine what kind of errors each PoS tagger makes. As the results show, not only the accuracy reported by the authors should be considered when choosing a PoS tagger. Moreover, the WSD method itself, indeed the combination of both, WSD method and PoS tagger, should be taken into consideration, since not the highest PoS tagger precision leads to the best results in WSD (in fact, TreeTagger does not have the highest reported precision).

For future work we expect to get further studying the aspects to be taken into consideration when combining these tools. An interesting question could be adding more features to the WSD systems from different sources, such as parsing, domains, bags of words... Besides this, we are considering gathering the information provided by several tools of the same type (for example different PoS taggers) to build up the set of features, determining in which way their individual errors affect the final results. Finally, we want to apply this type of experiments to other WSD methods, languages and NLP tasks.

References

1. Lau, R., Rosenfeld, R., Roukos, S.: Adaptative statistical language modeling using the maximum entropy principle. In: Proceedings of the Human Language Technology Workshop, ARPA. (1993).
2. Berger, A.L., Della Pietra, S.A., Della Pietra, V.J.: A maximum entropy approach to natural language processing. Computational Linguistics 22 (1996) 39–71.
3. Ratnaparkhi, A.: Maximum Entropy Models for Natural Language Ambiguity Resolution. Ph.D. thesis, University of Pennsylvania, Philadelphia (1998).
4. Vapnik, V. In: The Nature of Statistical Learning Theory. Springer (1995).
5. Gaustad, T.: The importance of high quality input for wsd: an application-oriented comparison of part-of-speech taggers. In: Proceedings of the ALTW 2003, Melbourne, Australia (2003) 65–72.
6. Mihalcea, R., Chklovski, T., Kilgarriff, A.: The Senseval-3 English lexical sample task. In Mihalcea, R., Edmonds, P., eds.: Senseval-3: Third International Workshop on the Evaluation of Systems for the Semantic Analysis of Text, Barcelona, Spain, Association for Computational Linguistics (2004) 25–28.
7. Giménez, J., Márquez, L.: SVMtool: A general pos tagger generator based on support vector machines. In: Proceedings of LREC 2004, Fourth International Conference on Language Resources and Evaluation, Workshop, Lisbon, Portugal (2004).

---

[7] Best two results for English at Senseval-3, lexical sample, are 72.9 and 72.6.

8. Carreras, X., Chao, I., L.Padró, Padró, M.: Freeling: An open-source suite of language analyzers. In: Proceedings of LREC 2004, Lisbon, Portugal (2004).

9. Schmid, H.: Probabilistic part-of-speech tagging using decision trees. In: Proceedings of NemLap-94, Manchester, England (1994) 44–49.

10. Brill, E.: A simple rule-based part of speech tagging. In: Proceedings of the 3rd Annual Meeting of the ACL, Trento, Italy (1992).

11. Ratnaparkhi, A.: A maximum entropy model for part-of-speech tagging. In Brill, E., Church, K., eds.: Proceedings of the Conference on Empirical Methods in Natural Language Processing. Association for Computational Linguistics, Somerset, New Jersey (1996) 133–142.

12. Joachims, T.: Learning to Classify Text Using Support Vector Machines. Kluwer Academic Publishers (2002).

13. Suárez, A., Palomar, M.: A maximum entropy-based word sense disambiguation system. In Chen, H.H., Lin, C.Y., eds.: Proceedings of the 19th International COLING. (2002) 960–966.

14. Dietterich, T.G.: Approximate statistical test for comparing supervised classification learning algorithms. Neural Computation **10** (1998) 1895–1923.

Annotation of Temporal Relations Within a Discourse

Petr Němec

Institute of Formal and Applied Linguistics
Faculty of Mathematics and Physics
Charles University
Malostranské náměstí 25, 118 00 Praha, Czech Republic
nemec@ufal.mff.cuni.cz

Abstract. In this paper we present an annotation scheme that captures general temporal relations between events expressed in a discourse. The proposed scheme aims to naturally extend the existing tectogrammatic annotation of the Prague Dependency Treebank and represents a step towards capturing the cognitive (ontological) content of a discourse. The existence of such an annotation will allow the training and testing of algorithms for automatic extraction of temporal relations which, in turn, contributes to various NLP tasks such as information retrieval and machine translation. 233 sentences of Czech translations of the Wall Street Journal (Penn Treebank) have been annotated so far. We also present statistics on the distribution of respective temporal relations based on this preliminary annotation data as well as the performance of a grammar-based algorithm.

1 Introduction

In this paper we present an annotation scheme that captures temporal relations between events[1] expressed in a discourse. The scheme aims to capture all the (evident or inferable) temporal relations within the discourse as formulated in the utterances of the respective speakers. The primary purpose of such an annotation is the possibility to train and test a system for automatic retrieval of temporal information. Such a system can be used in variety of applications such as machine translation (where the knowledge of the proper sequence of events expressed in a sentence makes it possible to select a correct tense in target languages with rich tense system such as English), information retrieval, and natural language understanding in general.

Although the scheme itself is language independent and can be used to annotate plain texts, it is particulary convenient to link the temporal annotation with the existing level of tectogrammatic annotation within the framework of the Prague Dependency Treebank (PDT). The tectogrammatic representation (TR) of a sentence captures its deep-syntax properties and relations as a tectogrammatical tree structure (TGTS). A TGTS is a dependency tree, the nodes of which represent the autosemantic words of the sentence. Each node is labelled with an inflectionally reduced word-form called the lemma and a functor that describes the deep syntactic valency relationship to its governor (parent node). Additionally, the nodes are labelled with grammatemes that capture further morphological and semantic information

---

[1] We will use the term *event* to refer to any type of time anchored entity, e.g. activity, accomplishment, state etc.

Petr Sojka, Ivan Kopeček and Karel Pala (Eds.): TSD 2006, LNAI 4188, pp. 181–188, 2006.

corresponding to the autosemantic words such as tense, aspect, gender, number, mood, verb and sentential modality etc. The textual coreference information is captured as well. For a detailed description of the TGTS annotation scheme see [1]. The temporal annotation can thus be viewed as a natural extension to the PDT framework.

The crucial reason for annotating TGTSs rather than plain texts is that in the next stage we would like to use the vast information contained in TGTSs to actually build the mentioned system for automatic retrieval of temporal information. Specifically for Czech, there exists an algorithm developed by Panevová [5] that identifies the relative ordering of events expressed by finite verbs of a sentence. It is based purely on the knowledge of sentence structure and morphology of the verbs. Of course, it identifies only a subset of all existing relations – these provided by the grammar. There are many other relations inferred and it is the identification of these that represents the challenge. Nevertheless, the availability of TGTS representation of a sentence makes it possible to use the described grammar-based algorithm straightforwardly (as all the required information is captured by the TR) and we believe that the information it provides (such as coreference) can also help in determining the "non-grammatical" relations. As there is already a parser to TGTS available, this approach does not exclude analysis of plain texts.

We annotate the Czech translation TGTSs of portion of Wall Street Journal. The corresponding sections have been previously translated and annotated at the tectogrammatical level for purposes of machine translation [2]. The reason for this decision (in contrast to annotating the original PDT data) was twofold: First, we expect the resulting automatic temporal information retrieval system to be integrated into this machine translation framework so this allows us to directly evaluate the contribution to the existing machine translation system. Second, we expect that the "non-grammatical" part of the system will be very hard to create as it requires substantial of context and world knowledge. Because of that, it is better to start with a fairly restricted semantic domain which is the case of Wall Street Journal. Currently, the preliminary set of 233 sentences (corresponding to the development testing data of the machine translation system) is annotated.

The paper is structured as follows: Section 2 introduces the basic principles of the formalism. Section 3 lists the defined temporal relations. Section 4 provides statistics on the annotated data together with the performance of the mentioned grammar-based algorithm. Section 5 compares our work to a similar project and Section 6 concludes the paper.

2 Basic Principles

In accordance with Novák [4] we recognize start time point anchor E_s and end time point anchor E_e of each event (activity, accomplishment, state etc.) E expressed in a discourse. E_s anchors the beginning of the event whereas E_e anchors the time the event is finished. The cited work provides convincing evidence for such unified treatment of various "event types" (in opposition to e.g. distinctions made by Steedman in [6]). If an event E takes place in one single time point, we take $E_s = E_e$.

These anchors are interpreted as time points on the real time axis regardless of the event modality, i.e., regardless of whether the event taking place is asserted, negated, desired, hypothesized etc. In any of these cases, the (asserted, negated etc.) event is anchored within real time by the speaker.

The set of all the anchor pairs and the set of time-of-speech points (one for each discourse utterance) together form the *temporal space* of a discourse. Consider the following Example[2] 1:

1. *A consortium of private investors operating as BPH Funding Co. said yesterday that it could eventually make a $300 million cash bid.*
2. *Today it announced that it no longer considers the possibility.*

There are two time-of-speech points (*1.tos, 2.tos*) and start and end points for the events expressed by the words *operating* (*op.s, op.e*), *said* (*say.s, say.e*), *make* (*mk.s, mk.e*), *announced* (*anc.s, anc.e*), and *considers* (*cnsd.s, cnsd.e*).

The task of the temporal annotation of a discourse is to identify its temporal space and to determine relations between these points.

The decision on which expressions denote an event may not be entirely straightforward. Basically, verbs and deverbative substantives and adjectives are subject to annotation.

3 Annotated Relations

We recognize two types of relations between the respective time points: the relative ordering relations and specific determination relations (that anchor the time points by means of time expressions). We describe both types in the following subsections.

The annotation of all the binary inter-sentential relations is very difficult as their number is potentially the square of the number of all the time points within the discourse. It is unfeasible for a human annotator to consider all of them. In practice, we annotate all the potential relations crossing the adjacent sentence boundary, i.e. when annotating a sentence we also consider all the time points of the previous one.

3.1 Relative Ordering Relations

The following relative ordering relations (corresponding to weak partial ordering) may hold between two time points p and q: precedence ($p \prec q$), precedence-or-equality ($p \preceq q$), antecedence ($p \succ q$), antecedence-or-equality ($p \succeq q$), equality ($p = q$). For the Example 1 (in Section 2) the smallest possible set of relative ordering relations would be as follows:

- $1.tos \prec 2.tos$ (sentence order)
- $op.s \prec 1.tos \prec op.e$
- $say.s = say.e \prec 1.tos$ (*said* expresses a single time point event)
- $1.tos \prec mk.s = mk.e$ (*make* takes place in the future if at all)
- $anc.s = anc.e \prec 2.tos$
- $cnsd.s \prec anc.s \prec cnsd.e$

These relations correspond to the information provided by the grammar. Nevertheless, more relations can be inferred with various level of confidence:

---

[2] Although the annotation has been performed on the Czech data we will present only the identical English examples where possible.

- $op.s \prec say.s$ (the consortium was probably operating as BPH Funding before it made a statement yesterday)
- $op.s \preceq cnsd.s$ (the same for considering the offer)
- $say.s \prec anc.s$ (follows from the absolute temporal determinations)
- $op.s \prec 2.tos \prec op.e$ (the state of affairs is true even in the time-of-speech of the other sentence)
- $cnsd.s \prec 1.tos \prec cnsd.e$ (the same)

The complete annotation of relative ordering of the respective events is the transitive closure of the entered relations (e.g. from $a \prec b \prec c$ the $a \prec c$ relation is inferred).

3.2 Specific Determinations

Values of some time points are determined by functions of other time points or are even specified absolutely. For example, in the sentence (Example 2)

Last year we spent our holiday in Austria and it was very similar to our vacation in Germany in February 1980.

the event of spending the holiday in Austria is determined as a function (last year) of the time-of-speech point whereas the event of spending the holiday in Germany has been positioned absolutely to the interval of February 1980. Note that although we may not know the value of speech time of the utterance we still understand the sentence and should be able to annotate it.

To capture this kind of information we have developed an apparatus based on the operators and functions described below[3]. It represents content of the expressions such as "last Friday", "beginning of the next month", "the middle of 80s" etc. Moreover, it allows for a construction of an efficient algorithm for the computation of partial ordering of these expressions on the real time axis.

Let us present type convention for these functions and operators first:

- t_point is a concrete point on the real time axis. It may be an event time point variable or it can be specified directly (e.g. 21.1.1980 23:55:00).
- $t\_interval$ is a concrete closed interval on the real time axis, e.g. the time period between two time points including the points. It may also be specified directly, e.g. 21.1.1980 represents the entire day interval.
- t_range is any amount of time (e.g. two seconds, four months etc.).
- t_entity_type is one of the following constants: $year, month, day, hour, minute, second$.
- t_entity is a name of a day or month.
- t_part is one of the following constants (representing vague language expressions): $beginning, end, middle$.

We may now list the operators and functions (the type of arguments and result follow after the colon):

---

[3] Using these operators and functions we have been able to capture all the absolute time determinations within the annotated data. However, we do not claim that this list is sufficient to capture all absolute time specifications. Its extension may be needed in the future.

- $\cup, \cap, \backslash (Interval_1, Interval_2) : (t\_interval, t\_interval) \rightarrow t\_interval$
- $+, -(Range_1, Range_2) : (t\_range, t\_range) \rightarrow t\_range$
- $shift(Point, Distance, InPast) : (t\_point, t\_range, boolean) \rightarrow t\_point$
- $entityRange(EntityType, Number) : (t\_entity\_type, R^+) \rightarrow t\_range$
- $span(Point, EntityType) : (t\_point, t\_entity\_type) \rightarrow t\_interval$
- $find(Point, Entity, Index) : (t\_point, t\_entity, integer) \rightarrow t\_interval)$
- $part(Interval, Part) : (t\_interval, t\_part) \rightarrow t\_interval$

$\cup, \cap$, and $\backslash$ are the standard interval union, disjunction, and intersection operators.

$+$ and $-$ are the addition and subtraction operators on time ranges respectively

$shift$ returns the time point that succeeds or precedes (depending on the value of $InPast$) $Point$ by $Distance$.

$entityRange$ function returns the time range represented by $Number$ time entities of type $EntityType$, e.g. $entityRange(year, 2)$ returns time range of two years.

The $span$ function returns the concrete time interval of the time entity of type $EntityType$ that contains the time point $Point$, e.g. $span(1_s, month)$ returns the interval of the month containing time point 1_s.

The $find$ function finds the $Index$-th occurence of $Entity$ succeeding or preceding(if $Index$ is negative) $Point$. For example, $find(1_s, Monday, -2)$ returns the interval of the Monday before the last Monday before 1_s.

The $part$ function returns the $Part$ of $Interval$, e.g. $part(February\ 1980, beginning)$ corresponds to the (vague) expression "beginning of the February 1980".

These functions and operators may be arbitrarily composed to form the resulting expression. A time point can then be positioned inside (outside) the interval specified by this expression. E.g. the starting point $sp.s$ of $spend$ from Example 2 can be positioned to "last year" as follows

$$sp.s \in span(shift(tos, entityRange(year, 1), yes), year)$$

where tos is the time of speech. The same mechanism can be used to specify absolute distance between two time points etc.

3.3 Special Modifiers

Some discourse expressions do not express a single event taking place in a single interval of time. In case the event is recurrent as in *"Last month, I used to wake up every morning and run 10 miles."* it is not enough to mark each of the two events separately as the connection between them would be lost. Instead, we introduce the notion of a *plan*: the two events are annotated as usual except that they are declared to be part of one particular box – the plan. The plan itself has a start time point and end time point (plan boundaries) which denote the interval of plan's validity (in the example, these are directly specified as the start and end of the "last month"). Repeat period (of $time\_range$ type) of the plan may also be specified (one day in our example).

Other special situation is when the event occurs separately for each actor in distributive readings such as *"Each company built its own headquarters in Boston."*. This is indicated in the annotation by a special marker. The two cases may co-occur as in *"Many people wake up every morning..."*. In this case the plan is marked as distributive as well.

4   Empirical Results

In this section we present some empirical results based on the annotated data. The primary purpose is to provide an idea of the distribution of respective annotated entity and relation types. We also present the performance of the Panevová's algorithm described in [5] that determines the relative ordering of finite verbs (and time of speech points) based solely on their grammatical properties[4]. The performance of the algorithm may be viewed as a baseline for further experiments.

The set consists of **233** sentences containing **804** annotated events (represented by 632 verbs, 120 substantives, and 52 adjectives) and 33 plans, i.e. there are 2*804 + 2*33 + 233 = **1907** time points in total. In addition, there are 88 specific determinations (time expressions) present.

There are **5637** annotated relation in total – the table lists their distribution (TOS stands for time of speech, PB for plan boundary).

	TOS	Verbs	Substantives	Adjectives	PB
TOS	221 (3.92%)	X	X	X	X
Verbs	944 (16.75%)	2698 (47.86%)	X	X	X
Subst.	139 (2.47%)	703 (12.47%)	211 (3.74%)	X	X
Adj.	83 (1.47%)	230 (4.08%)	29 (0.51%)	90 (1.60%)	X
PB	45 (0.80%)	179 (3.18%)	12 (0.21%)	2 (0.04%)	51 (0.90%)

Running the algorithm yielded accuracy of **80.80%** and coverage [5] of **42.47%**. There are various interesting types of errors produced by the algorithm (some of them mentioned in [5] itself) but space limitations prevent us from presenting them here.

5   Related Work

To annotate temporal expressions the TIMEX2 [3] annotation scheme was developed yielding the TIDES corpus [7]. The goal of this project could be characterized as the identification and precise formalization of the temporal expressions describing a time specification (not a event) occurring in the text. This is similar to our "specific determinations" as described Section 3.2. The difference consists in the fact the under TIMEX2 all such expressions (including indexical expressions – functions of time of speech or event) get resolved into a calendric expression - they get "extensionalized". On the other hand, our compositional functional approach preserves their "intension" (which makes it possible to annotate them even if the absolute time of speech is unknown) while ensuring the effective determination of their absolute value if possible. However, the crucial difference between TIMEX2 and our

---

[4] The algorithm can be briefly stated as follows: the morphological tense of a finite verb (head of a clause A) determines its relation – precedence, overlap (i.e. at least one one common time point), antecedence – with the verb of the dominating clause B (or time of speech point if A is the main clause) if A represents an object of B. Otherwise, let C be the nearest clause dominating (possibly indirectly) A that is an object of its dominating clause D. Then the morphological tense of A determines its relationship to D or to the time of speech if there is no such clause C.

[5] The ratio of the number of relations considered by the algorithm and the total number of relations.

annotation scheme consists in their respective primary purposes: our annotation scheme aims at capturing deep temporal information – namely the identification and relative order of the events expressed in the discourse. TIMEX2 focuses on fast and simple extraction of temporal expressions from documents.

6 Conclusion and Future Work

We have designed an annotation scheme that allows to capture large amount of temporal information contained in a discourse and annotated a preliminary set of data. This set can be readily used as a (development) test data for any automatic temporal information retrieval system. We have also presented statistical results based on this small set together with the performance results of a purely grammar-based algorithm. We were able to capture all the temporal phenomena we considered relevant by means of our annotation scheme.

In our opinion, the main problem with the annotation consist in the inability to annotate all the relations within a discourse and the necessity to restrain to relations within one utterance or at most between two adjacent utterances.

For the purposes of statistical training, larger data have to be annotated. This may also reveal potential problems within the current annotation scheme as well as the necessity to enrich it.

In summary, the presented work represents a preliminary attempt to annotate a discourse for deep temporal relations that will be worked on in the future.

Acknowledgements

The development of the presented work has been supported by the following organizations and projects: the LC536 grant of the Ministry of Education of the Czech Republic, Information Society Project No. 1ET201120505 of the Grant Agency of the Academy of Sciences of the Czech Republic, Grant No. 0530118 of the National Science Foundation of the USA, and Grant No. 352/2006 of the Grant Agency of Charles University. Any opinions, findings, and conclusions or recommendations expressed in this material are those of the author and do not necessarily reflect the views of the respective grant agencies.

References

1. Böhmová, A., Hajič, J., Hajičová, E., Vidová Hladká, B.: The Prague dependency treebank: Three-level annotation scenario. In Anne Abeille, editor, In Treebanks: Building and Using Syntactically Annotated Corpora. Dordrecht, Kluwer Academic Publishers, The Netherlands. 2002.
2. Hajič, J., Čmejrek, M., Dorr, B., Ding, Y., Eisner, J., Gildea, D., Koo, T., Parton, K., Radev, D., Rambow, O.: Natural language generation in the context of machine translation. Technical report, Center for Language and Speech Processing, Johns Hopkins University, Baltimore. Summer Workshop Final Report. 2002.
3. Mani, I., Wilson, G., Sundheim, B., Ferro, L.: Guidelines for Annotating Temporal Information. In Proceedings of HLT 2001, First International Conference on Human Language Technology Research, J. Allan, ed., Morgan Kaufmann, San Francisco, 2001.

4. Novák, V.: Towards Logical Representation of Language Structure. The Prague Bulletin of Mathematical Linguistics 82. 2004.
5. Panevová, J., Benešová, E., Sgall, P.: Čas a modalita v češtině. Charles University. 1971.
6. Steedman, M.: The Productions of Time: Temporality and Causality in Linguistic Semantics. Draft 4.1, October. 2002.
7. Tides Temporal Corpus, Spanish and English dialogs.
   http://www.nist.gov/speech/tests/ace/phase2/resource/index.htm.

Applying RST Relations to Semantic Search

Nguyen Thanh Tri, Akira Shimazu, Le Cuong Anh, and Nguyen Minh Le

School of Information Science
Japan Advanced Institute of Science and Technology
1-1 Asahidai, Nomi, Ishikawa, 923-1292, Japan
{t-thanh, shimazu, cuonganh, nguyenml}@jaist.ac.jp

Abstract. This paper proposes a new way of extracting answers to some kinds of queries based on Rhetorical Structure Theory (RST). For each type of question, we assign one or more rhetorical relations that help extract the corresponding answers. We use ternary expressions which are successfully applied in the well-known question answering system START to represent text segments, index documents and queries. The cosine measure is used in the matching process. The experiment with RST Discourse Treebank shows that the results of ternary-expression-based indexing are better than those of keyword-based indexing.

1 Introduction

Current key word based search engines have successfully served users for many years. These systems rely on key words and return pages in which the typed key words appear. Therefore users have to read through (up to thousands of) pages to find what they want. In order to overcome this problem, semantic search (a content-based search method) is proposed. One recent approach, applied to the World Wide Web (WWW), is Semantic Web. The mainstream of Semantic Web is to enable computers to understand data by adding some more information (called *metadata*) into Web pages, as in Simple HTML Ontology Extension (SHOE) [7]. Web pages that SHOE can process must include additional terms and concepts according to SHOE specification. In Distributed Open Semantic Elaboration platform (DOSE) [5], authors use the concept vector model, which is based on the classical vector space model. Another search engine which explores the semantics of XML tags in order to give better results is XML search (Xsearch) [10].

Though above methods give better results, they still return results in the form of pages. There are various types of questions, e.g, "Why didn't Mr. Bush need to wait for a law?" to which users want to have a direct answer (in form of a sentence or a passage) rather than pages containing the answers.

This study proposes a novel method for extracting answers (not pages) to some kinds of questions from documents by exploiting the structure of documents. The structure of documents includes the characteristic that one text span can be an answer to a question related to the adjacent text span. The structure of documents can be represented by Rhetorical Structural Theory (RST) proposed by Mann and Thompson [3]. In their proposal a document is represented in form of a tree, in which there are relations between adjacent text spans. Each relation has a specified meaning and some relations are clue for extracting answers to some types of questions.

Petr Sojka, Ivan Kopeček and Karel Pala (Eds.): TSD 2006, LNAI 4188, pp. 189–196, 2006.

The rest of this paper is organized as follows: Sect. 2 describes how RST can be used for finding and extracting answers as well as the way to index documents and retrieve answers. Sect. 3 gives details about implementation, and comparison with a similar system in which keywords are used instead of T-expressions. Finally, Sect. 4 concludes the paper.

2   Method for Semantic Search

This section gives details about how we apply RST to finding and extracting some kinds of questions, the method of representing text segments and the method of matching questions.

2.1   Rhetorical Relation Exploration

Rhetorical Structure Theory (RST) [3], proposed by Mann and Thompson, defined a set of 23 rhetorical relations. This model represents the structure of a text in the form of a hierarchical tree (called rhetorical tree) that labels relations between adjacent text spans, such as clauses (lowest level), sentences, or paragraphs. There is a relationship between adjacent spans (spans having the same parent), e.g., SOLUTIONHOOD, ELABORATION and PURPOSE. The smallest text spans are called elementary discourse units. Spans (or nodes) are either nucleus or satellite within a relation. A span is a nucleus if it is more important than the other, otherwise it is a satellite. For example, the sentence "because the car broke down, John was late for the meeting" can be divided into two text spans: "because the car broke down"(denoted as SP1) as the satellite, "John was late for the meeting" (denoted as SP2) as the nucleus, and there is a rhetorical relation "NON-VOLITIONAL CAUSE" between them.

The rhetorical structure of this sentence is represented in Fig. 1. Internal nodes consist of larger text segments, such as a sentence, a paragraph or a section, and the root node spans the entire document. Each rhetorical relation has a specified meaning. For example, the NON-VOLITIONAL CAUSE relation specifies the cause of the situation presented in one text span is stated in the other. Therefore, span SP1 is a candidate as an answer to the question "Why was John late?" which relates to the situation stated in SP2. In general, SP2 consists of smaller text spans. When the question is related to one child node of SP2, how to extract the answer is a problem. Fortunately, according to Marcu, "*If a rhetorical relation R holds between two text spans of the tree structure of a text, that relation also holds between the most important units of the constituent spans*" [4]. Hence, if the question is related to one of the most important descendants of span SP2, then SP1 is still a candidate as an answer.

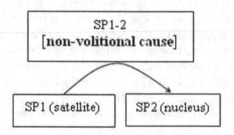

Fig. 1. The structure of the text

The process of constructing the discourse tree of a document can be automatic as presented in [4,8,11].

2.2 Rhetorical Relation Application

RST relation can be applied to extracting answers to a question of a specific type. As discussed in Sect. 2.1, the span SP2 has a NON-VOLITIONAL CAUSE relation with span SP2, so if given a question "Why was John late?", then the span SP1 is a candidate as an answer. This is the idea how to apply rhetorical relations to finding and extracting the answers to questions. The types of question given in the Text Retrieval Conference (TREC) [6] are divided into 3 types: list questions, definition questions and factoid questions. These are all factual questions and the answers can be directly extracted from the sentences that match the questions. There can be more types of questions:

- *How to* questions: e.g., "How can I recover space after installing updates?". SOLUTION-HOOD relation indicates the situation presented in nucleus is a solution to the problem stated in satellite. PURPOSE relation indicates that satellite presents a situation to be realized through the activity in nucleus. Thus, SOLUTIONHOOD and PURPOSE relations are clues for extracting answers.
- *Suggestion* questions: e.g., "What should I do about compilation error in V6.1.b10?". For this type of question, SOLUTIONHOOD relation gives a possible solution and is suitable for extracting answers.
- *Why* questions: e.g., "Why didn't Mr. Bush need to wait for a law?". CONDITION, VOLITIONAL CAUSE, NON-VOLITIONAL CAUSE and PURPOSE all are related to causal relation, therefore they are clues for extracting answers.
- *Yes/no* questions: e.g., "Did John buy a car?"

The question types and corresponding helpful rhetorical relations are listed in Tab. 1. Other types irrelevant to rhetorical relations are not listed. In order to use rhetorical relations for extracting answers, we need to construct the rhetorical structure of documents and then index documents in such a way that the rhetorical structure of documents remains. The technique for indexing is mentioned in Sect. 2.3. The method for retaining rhetorical structure of documents is described in Sect. 3. After these steps, we have a knowledge base for answering questions. In answering mode, the system operates as the algorithm described in Fig. 2, where $Answers$.add($span,d$) means to add text belonging to $span$ in the document d to the answer list. The method for matching the question against the knowledge base is described in Sect. 2.3.

2.3 Indexing Documents and Matching Questions

This section gives details on how we represent text segments, index documents and match questions. We borrow the sentence representation style used by natural language Question

Table 1. The question types and corresponding rhetorical relations

Question types	Rhetorical relations
How to	SOLUTIONHOOD, PURPOSE
Suggestion	SOLUTIONHOOD
Why	VOLITIONAL CAUSE, NON-VOLITIONAL CAUSE and PURPOSE

```
Search(Question q) {
1    Identify the type of question q;
2    Identify a set of rhetorical relations R corresponding to this question type;
3    if (is_empty(R)) {
4       return "This type of question is not supported!";
5    }else{
6       Match the question q against the knowledge base;
7       if (no matches found) return "Not found!"; else {
8       for (each match m){
9          for (each relation r in R){
10            Find a span sp₂ (in the rhetorical structure of a document d containing
12            the match m) having the relation r with the span sp₁ which contains
11            the match m (or one of its most important constituents contains the
12            match m);//As depicted in Fig 3.
13            if (found) Answers.add(sp₂, d);
14          }
15       }
16    }
17    return Answers;
18 }
19}
```

Fig. 2. The search algorithm

and Answering system START (SynTactic Analysis using Reversible Transformation) [1], which is successful in answering a series of questions by using this representation style.

Indexing and answering in START: A sentence, in START, is divided into kernel sentences which usually contain one verb. A kernel sentence is represented by a *ternary expression* (T-expression) which is a triple of *<subject relation object>*, where relation is an infinitive verb, a preposition or some *special* words (e.g., describe_relation). Other information of the sentence (such as tense, voice, negation, auxiliary verbs and adverbs) is stored in another place called *history*. For complex sentences, START allows any T-expression to take another T-expression as its subject or object. For example, the sentence "John Adams discovered Neptune" is represented as <"John Adams" discover Neptune>.

In answering mode, START converts questions into T-expressions and performs the search against its knowledge. For example, if given the above fact, START creates the T-expression <"John Adams" discover Neptune> and stores it in its knowledge base. Then if a user asks the question "Who discovered Neptune?", it converts the question into the T-expression <$who discover Neptune>, where $who serves as a matching variable. This T-expression is matched against the knowledge base, in this case, $who is matched with "John Adams", then START uses the T-expression <"John Adams" discover Neptune> with its history to restore the sentence "John Adams discovered Neptune" as the answer.

Indexing in our system: We propose a new way of indexing based on T-expressions. The idea is to *group* T-expressions of a sentence (or a text segment) together so that we can use *cosine* measure to calculate the similarity of a text segment and a question as described in the next section. The method for grouping T-expressions of the same text segment is mentioned in Sect. 3. We use T-expressions for the indexing and matching processes, not for the purpose of generating answers. When a span is found to be an answer, all the text segments belonging to this span are collected and returned.

Matching in our system: We use cosine measure for scoring the similarity between a question and a text segment. Suppose a question q is converted into T-expressions $(tq_1, tq_2, \ldots, tq_n)$ and a text segment s is converted into T-expressions $(ts_1, ts_2, \ldots, ts_l)$. In general cases, n and l are not equal, thus we have to normalize them to be the same size. Let m be the total of unique T-expressions of q and s. Let $(tc_1, tc_2, \ldots, tc_m)$ be the vector of unique T-expressions of q and s. Then s and q can be represented as vectors of size m $(t_1, t_2, \ldots, t_m)$, where $t_i = 1$ if T-expression tc_i is present in its T-expression list, otherwise $t_i = 0$. If one T-expression of the question q contains a variable, we must treat that T-expression differently from ordinary T-expressions in comparison. When two T-expressions are the same except for a variable, they are regarded as being matched. For example, if there is a T-expression <$who be worker>, this T-expression and T-expressions like <John be worker> and <James be worker> (in the knowledge base) are said to be matched. Finally, the cosine between the question q and the text segment s is defined as follows:

$$\cos(q, s) = \frac{\sum_{k=1}^{m} t_k(q) t_k(s)}{\sqrt{\sum_{k=1}^{m} t_k(q)^2 \sum_{k=1}^{m} t_k(s)^2}}$$

where $t_k(s)$, $t_k(q)$ are the presence of the kth element of T-expressions of the text segment s and question q correspondingly.

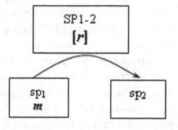

Fig. 3. Finding an expected span

This method provides the flexibility for matching process and users have an option to adjust the threshold to filter the result with respect to a degree of similarity in the range (0, 1].

There can be history (tense, negation, auxiliary verbs and adverbs) attached to a T-expression. In the matching process we must consider this issue. For yes/no questions, we just measure the similarity between the question and a sentence without considering negation and tense because a match is always an answer. For example, if we have the fact "John bought a new car in June", and the question is any one of "Did John buy a car in June?", "Didn't John buy the car in June" or "Has John bought a car?" that sentence is still the answer. For other types of questions, if the question and a sentence do not match regarding the negation or tense, we will not consider that sentence to be a candidate as an answer. For example, given a question "File access is denied. How to fix this problem?" it is incorrect to match the T-expressions of "File access is denied" with the T-expression of the fact "File access is not denied". We do not take adverbs into account because they do not affect the precision of answers.

3   Implementation and Evaluation

We used the RST Discourse Treebank [9] for testing because the task of building RST trees of documents is outside the scope of this study, and there are some studies on this issue [4,8,11]. This Treebank contains a subset of documents from the Wall Street Journal which are annotated according to RST theory. We used database management system

Table 2. The results of T-expression-based and keyword-based systems. The final column is the average answer per question

Question type	#questions	Precision		Recall		Ave. answer	
		T-expr	Keyword	T-expr	Keyword	T-expr	Keyword
Why	64	0.864	0.689	0.968	0.938	1.16	1.36
How to	91	0.801	0.739	0.978	0.967	1.21	1.35
Suggestion	25	0.952	0.778	0.800	0.840	0.84	1.08
Factual	259	0.806	0.306	0.984	0.857	1.22	2.79

MySQL[1] for storing data. A tree can be represented by parent-child relation, so the technique for grouping T-expressions of the same sentence and retaining RST structure is implemented using MySQL. The module of converting sentences into T-expressions is a rule-based system. We firstly use the Charniak parser[2] (whose F-score is 90%) to parse sentences, and secondly the T-expressions are built based on the output of Charniak parser. Starting from a set of basic conversion rules from a sequence of part-of-speech (POS) tags to T-expressions, e.g., "$Noun_1+(Preposition+Noun_2)$" is converted into $< Noun_1\ Preposition\ Noun_2 >$, complex sequences of POS tags are recursively processed at the lowest level. For example: for $Noun_1+(Preposition_1+$
$(Noun_2 + (Preposition_2 + Noun_3)))$, after having generated $< Noun_2$
$Preposition_2\ Noun_3 >$, the head noun $Noun_2$ is kept for generating $< Noun_1$
$Preposition_1\ Noun_2 >$. The complexity of this module is that of Charniak parser because the conversion time of a parsed sentence into T-expressions can run in real time. The precision, recall and F-score of this module are 92%, 90% and 91%, respectively.

We built another similar system, which uses keywords instead of T-expressions for base line evaluation. We created a question set consisting of 91 *how to*, 64 *why*, 25 *suggestion* and 259 *factual* questions. In keyword-based system, we set the threshold for cosine measure to 0.30 for factual questions and 0.20 for other questions, while in the T-expression-based system we set the threshold to 0. Non-factual questions have corresponding rhetorical relations to filter the results while factual questions do not. In order to reduce the number of answers returned to factual questions, we set a higher threshold for factual questions in the keyword-based system. The results are shown in Tab. 2.

The limitations that make the system fail to find answers in some situations are:

- When a question relates to more than one adjacent text segments of a sentence and T-expressions of the question are different from those of related text segments, the matching process will fail.
- The question does not match an important constituent of a span which has the expected relation with the span containing the answer.
- The module for converting a question into T-expressions incorrectly adds a matching variable in some situations.
- Questions contain proper names which are replaced by pronouns in the knowledge base.
- Questions are expressed in different ways from the original sentences used to build the knowledge base.

---

[1] The software is available at http://www.mysql.com

[2] The source code is available at http://www.cs.brown.edu/people/ec/

A possible solution to relieve some limitations is to build T-expressions from the original sentences (by concatenating text segments of the same sentence), and perform co-reference on original documents to resolve pronouns.

By representing text segments in T-expressions, we can support for entailment relation. From one text segment we can entail another one which omits some adjectives. For example, from the text segment "John bought a new car" is converted into <John buy car> and <new describe_relation car>, so we can infer the text segment which has the T-expression <John buy car> by omitting the T-expressions having describe_relation relation.

Another possible improvement is to generate finer-grained T-expressions. In the current implementation, the sentence "John and Jane bought a new car" is converted into two T-expressions <"John Jane" buy car> and <new describe_relation car>. If we convert the above sentence into three T-expressions: <John buy car>, <Jane buy car> and <new describe_relation car>, then we can answer a question that is written in a different order, such as "Did Jane and John buy a new car?".

4   Conclusion

This study proposes a method for finding and extracting answers to some kinds of questions based on the rhetorical structure of documents. We exploit the characteristics of document structure in which one segment of text can be an answer to a question related to the adjacent text segment. According to each question type, we identify related rhetorical relations which help in finding answers. T-expressions are used to index documents and cosine measure is used in the matching process. Comparison of the two experimental systems shows that the results of the T-expression-based system are better that those of keyword-based one.

We currently consider only five rhetorical relations, other ones are still valuable for further study.

Though the relation definitions of Mann and Thompson are only one well-known case, we may define any kind of relations that help answer an arbitrary type of question.

In a future study, we intend to apply an ontology, such as WordNet, in the matching process in order to be able to answer questions that have different linguistic expressions but the same meaning as some facts.

References

1. Boris Katz, 1988. *Using English for Indexing and Retrieving*, Proceedings of the 1st RIAO Conference on User-Oriented Content-Based Text and Image Handling.
2. Charles Clark, et al. 2000. *Question Answering by Passage Selection*, The 9th Text REtrieval Conference (TREC 2000), pp. 229–235.
3. William Mann, Sandra Thompson. 1987. *Rhetorical Structure Theory: A theory of text organization*, In L. Polanyi, (Ed.) Discourse structure (pp. 85–96). Norwood/NJ: Ablex.
4. Daniel Marcu. 2000. *The Rhetorical Parsing of Unrestricted Texts: A Surface-Based Approach*, Computational Linguistics, Vol. 26, Issue 3, pp. 395–448.
5. Dario Bonino, et al. 2003. *DOSE: a Distributed Open Semantic Elaboration Platform*, The 15th IEEE International Conference on Tools with Artificial Intelligence, Sacramento, California.
6. Ellen Voorhees. 2003. *Overview of TREC 2003*, The Twelfth Text REtrieval Conference (TREC 2003), pp. 1–13.

7. Jeff Heflin and James Hendler. 2000. *Searching the Web with SHOE*, In Artificial Intelligence for Web Search. Papers from the AAAI Workshop, WS-00-01. AAAI Press, Menlo Park, CA, pp. 35–40.
8. Huong Le Thanh. 2004. *Investigation into an approach to automatic text summarization*, Doctoral dissertation, Middlesex University.
9. Lynn Carlson, et al. 2003 *Building a discourse-tagged corpus in the framework of Rhetorical Structure Theory*, In Current Directions in Discourse and Dialogue, pp. 85–112, Jan van Kuppevelt and Ronnie Smith eds., Kluwer Academic Publishers.
10. Sara Colhen, et al. 2003. *XSearch: A semantic search engine for XML*, The 29th International Conference on Very Large Databases (VLDB).
11. Tadashi Nomoto. 2004. *Machine Learning Approaches to Rhetorical Parsing and Open-Domain Text Summarization*, Doctoral Dissertation, Nara Institute of Science and Technology.

Data-Driven Part-of-Speech Tagging of Kiswahili

Guy De Pauw[1], Gilles-Maurice de Schryver[2,3], and Peter W. Wagacha[4]

[1] CNTS - Language Technology Group, University of Antwerp, Belgium
guy.depauw@ua.ac.be
[2] African Languages and Cultures, Ghent University, Belgium
gillesmaurice.deschryver@ugent.be
[3] Xhosa Department, University of the Western Cape, South Africa
[4] School of Computing and Informatics, University of Nairobi, Kenya
waiganjo@uonbi.ac.ke

Abstract. In this paper we present experiments with data-driven part-of-speech taggers trained and evaluated on the annotated Helsinki Corpus of Swahili. Using four of the current state-of-the-art data-driven taggers, TnT, MBT, SVMTool and MXPOST, we observe the latter as being the most accurate tagger for the Kiswahili dataset. We further improve on the performance of the individual taggers by combining them into a committee of taggers. We observe that the more naive combination methods, like the novel plural voting approach, outperform more elaborate schemes like cascaded classifiers and weighted voting. This paper is the first publication to present experiments on data-driven part-of-speech tagging for Kiswahili and Bantu languages in general.

1 Introduction

It is well-known that Part-of-Speech (POS) taggers are crucial components in the development of any serious application in the fields of Computational Linguistics (CL), Natural Language Processing (NLP) or Human Language Technology (HLT). While great strides have been made for (major) Indo-European languages such as English, Dutch and German, work on the Bantu languages is scarcely out of the egg. The Bantu languages - of which there are roughly five to six hundred - are basically agglutinating in nature, are characterized by a nominal class system and concordial agreement, and are spoken from an imaginary line north of the Democratic Republic of the Congo all the way down to the southern tip of the African continent.

A particularly active region with regard to work on POS taggers for the Bantu languages is South(ern) Africa, but so far the projects have unfortunately not gone much beyond the development of (proposed) tagsets and, in some cases, prototype modules for morphological analysis. In this regard, the EAGLES tagset was adjusted for Setswana [1], a different tagset and suggestions to venture into Transformation-Based Tagging were presented for isiXhosa [2], yet another tagset and a combination of rule-based symbolic tagging and statistical tagging were offered as a corpus-processing tool for Sesotho sa Leboa [3,4], and a prototype finite-state morphological analyzer was developed for isiZulu [5,4].

For Kiswahili — a Bantu language spoken by up to fifty million people in East Africa (which makes it one of the most widely spoken African languages) — the situation is markedly different. Close to two decades of work at the University of Helsinki resulted in a

Petr Sojka, Ivan Kopeček and Karel Pala (Eds.): TSD 2006, LNAI 4188, pp. 197–204, 2006.

relatively large corpus, the Helsinki Corpus of Swahili (HCS) [6], which has been thoroughly analyzed and carefully annotated using a two-level finite-state formalism, with morphological disambiguation carried out using a Constraint Grammar Parser [7]. The POS tag information in HCS allows one to use supervised learning techniques to build data-driven POS taggers and to perform a quantitative comparative evaluation of the available techniques. The latter is exactly the purpose of this paper.

2   An Annotated Corpus of Kiswahili: HCS

Lexical ambiguity in Kiswahili is limited, making POS tagging relatively straightforward, but still far from trivial, as illustrated in the following example:

(1) *paka*	*alianguka*	*ndani*	*ya*	*maji*
cat	fell	inside	of	water
noun	**verb**	**adverb**	adjective	**noun**
	verb	noun	**preposition**	

To tackle this disambiguation problem, we investigate the applicability of existing data-driven POS taggers. These methods have in common that they require a large amount of annotated data to induce the word class disambiguation task. For the experiments we used the POS tag annotated part of the aforementioned HCS as our training material.

After some general data clean-up and disposal of duplicate sections, we had a corpus of 3,656,821 words (169,702 sentences) available. To obtain a reasonable spread in language usage, we randomized the sentences in the corpus, so that the tagger would not be biased towards a particular type of text during training. Given the expansive size of the corpus, full 10-fold cross validation experiments were not feasible. We therefore randomly divided the corpus into a 80% training set (2,927,846 words), a 10% validation set (362,866 words) on which the optimal parameters of the algorithms could be established, and finally a 10% blind test set (366,109 words) for evaluation on unseen text.

3   Data-Driven Taggers

The last 15 years have witnessed corpus-based methods making tremendous headway in providing accurate and robust POS taggers. Many of these tools have since been made publicly available, so that they can relatively easily be applied to new languages when annotated corpora become available. In this section, we briefly introduce the taggers used for the experiments.

TnT (Trigrams'n'Tags): Hidden Markov Modeling   One of the most common approaches to data-driven POS tagging is using Hidden Markov Models (HMMs). A very sophisticated HMM tagger is the Trigrams'n'Tags (TnT) tagger[1] [8]. It improves on previous HMM approaches through the use of well established smoothing methods and its more sophisticated processing of unknown words, capitalized words and sentence boundaries.

---

[1] TnT is available from http://www.coli.uni-saarland.de/~thorsten/tnt/

MXPOST: Maximum Entropy Modeling Maximum entropy modeling has consistently been achieving top performance on a variety of NLP tasks. The maximum entropy tagger, MXPOST[2] [9], is typically able to beat most other POS taggers in a direct comparison [10]. Like most other taggers, it uses lexical information about the word to be tagged, contextual features (preceding, following tags) and morphological features (prefix, suffix letters).

MBT: Memory-Based Learning With its emphasis on symbolic processing and its inherent robustness to exceptions, Memory-Based Learning (MBL) is particularly well suited for NLP classification tasks. The Memory-Based Tagger (MBT)[3] [11] induces two taggers from the training data: one for known words and one for unknown words, the former using contextual clues, while the latter also uses orthographical features.

SVMTool: Support Vector Machines Support Vector Machines (SVMs) have been successfully applied to a wide range of classification tasks [12], but only recently has an SVM-based POS tagging tool become available: SVMTool[4] [13], which functions as a set of pre- and postprocessing scripts for SVM-Light [14]. SVMTool has been shown to outperform TnT on English data [13], but has so far not been extensively compared to other methods and on other datasets.

4 Experiments: Individual Tagger Performance

In this section, we outline the performance of the individual data-driven taggers trained and evaluated on the Kiswahili dataset. The training, validation and test sets outlined in Section 2 were kept constant for all of the experiments, allowing for a systematic and direct comparison between the tagging methods.

In a first phase, algorithmic parameters and information source are optimized on the basis of the validation set. The taggers obtained from this training and optimization phase are subsequently used to tag the held-out test set. The accuracy of the respective taggers is calculated by comparing the output of the taggers to the gold-standard annotation provided by HCS.

The average per-word lexical ambiguity in the Kiswahili dataset is quite favorable, with only an average of 1.3 possible tags per word. This figure indicates that (on the basis of the HCS tagset) there is not a lot of lexical ambiguity in Kiswahili. Roughly 3% of the words (about 12,000 words) in the validation set, as well as the test set, are unknown, meaning that they do not occur in the training set.

The limited lexical ambiguity is further illustrated by the high score achieved by the baseline method: a simple statistical unigram method, which assigns to each of the known words in the test set the tag it has been most often associated with in the training set. For unknown words, it assigns the tag most frequently associated with unknown words in the validation set (PROPNAME). This baseline method already achieves more than 97% accuracy on known words (Table 1), but does not handle unknown words very well with a score of only 18.59%.

---

[2] MXPOST is available from ftp://ftp.cis.upenn.edu/pub/adwait/jmx/jmx.tar.gz
[3] MBT is available from http://ilk.uvt.nl/software.html
[4] SVMTool is available from http://www.lsi.upc.es/~nlp/SVMTool/

Table 1. Accuracy scores on blind test set (366K words) and approximate CPU times for the individual taggers

Tagger	Accuracy Scores			CPU Time	
	Known Words	Unknown Words	Total	Train	Tag
Baseline	97.01%	18.59%	94.50%	4s	1s
TnT	98.00%	91.66%	97.79%	9s	4s
MBT (default)	98.39%	90.59%	98.14%	3m	20s
MBT (optimal)	98.46%	91.61%	98.25%	6m	8m
SVMTool	98.48%	91.30%	98.24%	±80h	15s
MXPOST	98.61%	93.32%	98.44%	±5h	90s

Table 1 indicates that the **TnT** tagger by far exhibits the most efficient processing times of all data-driven taggers[5]. Despite an exhaustive optimization phase on the validation set (which still revealed the default settings to perform the best), the performance of the TnT tagger trails in direct comparison to the other taggers. It nevertheless establishes a significant increase compared to the baseline tagger, particularly with respect to unknown words.

The default **MBT** uses a context of two disambiguated tags to the left of the word to be tagged and one ambiguous tag to the right. Table 1 shows that the default MBT performs quite well for known words, but is lacking for unknown words. We subsequently performed extensive optimization experiments during which we established the ideal information source and optimal algorithmic parameters. For known and unknown words, this equaled to three tags before and after the word to be tagged. For unknown words, we also took into account five prefix and suffix letters and information on capitalization, hyphenation and numerical characters within the word. While this optimization had a significantly positive effect on the accuracy of the tagger, particularly on the processing of unknown words, it has a detrimental effect on CPU time during classification.

Typical for SVM-based methods, **SVMTool** has a laborious training phase, but very attractive efficiency properties during classification. The training phase of the SVMTool tagger is rather problematic with a processing time of several days, which rendered optimization experiments unfeasible. Table 1 therefore presents the accuracy scores on the test set using the default radial basis kernel. As expected however, tagging time is very favorable and SVMTool's performance is easily able to match that of the optimized MBT. Its lower performance on processing unknown words means it achieves a barely significantly lower score than MBT, but we are confident that further optimization experiments can at least level the field.

In direct comparison with other data-driven taggers, the **MXPOST** tagger further establishes its state-of-the-art status. The default settings of MXPOST were confirmed as performing the best during optimization experiments on the validation set, except for the number of iterations (we used 500 iterations during training instead of the default 200). Table 1 illustrates that MXPOST is able to achieve the highest accuracy, with a particularly impressive accuracy score for unknown words. Compared to the baseline tagger, MXPOST achieves an error reduction rate of 72% (54% on known words, 92% on unknown words).

---

[5] Approximate CPU time was measured on a dual 64bit AMD Opteron 2.44GHz system with 6GB RAM.

Data analysis showed that most taggers are able to resolve ambiguity well. The MXPOST tagger for instance has an accuracy of more than 94% on ambiguous words. Interestingly however, both TnT and MBT beat MXPOST when it comes to unambiguous words, which means MXPOST makes slightly more mistakes on words that should not be considered ambiguous. MXPOST seems to avoid overfitting the training data, by a more loose definition of lexical ambiguity, while the other 3 taggers tend to choose the single tag associated with the word in the lexicon.

The most common mistake made by all taggers is the tagging of a preposition (PREP) as an agentative particle (AG-PART) and vice versa. This accounts for almost 20% of all tagging errors. Other common mistakes include the tagging of a noun as a verb and the tagging of a proper name as a noun.

5 Experiments: System Combination

While some studies [15] suggest that classifier bias can be minimized given an exhaustive search through algorithmic parameters and information source, in practice most data-driven taggers exhibit quite different tagging behavior given the same data set. In the system combination experiments, we try to exploit these differences by combining the output of the taggers to create a type of tagging committee that agrees on a tag for a word. Data analysis indeed shows that only 97.23% of the time do the taggers all predict the same tag. 96.75% of the time do the taggers agree on a tag which matches the correct tag. Furthermore, only 0.5% of the time, do the taggers all agree on the same erroneous tag.

These figures indicate that there is enough disagreement between the individual taggers to obtain a considerable increase using system combination. This type of system combination is again performed in two processing steps: first we use the four data-driven taggers to tag the validation set and test set. We then create a new dataset with 6 columns: the word, the four tagger predictions and the gold-standard tag. The upper bound performance of any given combination method can be found on the last line of Table 2. If we were to have an oracle which, given the four possible predicted tags, always chooses the correct one, we could obtain a tagging accuracy of 99.44%.

Table 2. Results of system combination experiments

Method	Known Words	Unknown Words	Total
MXPOST	98.61%	93.32%	98.44%
Majority Voting	98.53%	93.12%	98.36%
Weighted Voting	98.59%	93.68%	98.42%
Plural Voting	98.72%	92.72%	98.56%
MXPOST+LLU	98.79%	93.32%	98.61%
Cascaded Classifier	98.63%	93.37%	98.46%
Oracle	99.52%	96.85%	99.44%

The first combination method we consider, simple majority voting, chooses for each word the tag that is most often predicted by the taggers. Ties are resolved randomly. This combination method improves on all of the individual taggers, except MXPOST. Apparently, many of the correct tags suggested by MXPOST are outvoted by the other taggers. To counter this effect, we implemented two more refined voting methods: weighted voting and plural voting. Interestingly, weighted voting in which the weight of each classifier's vote is equal to its observed accuracy on the validation set, again fails to yield a performance increase.

We also experimented with a more naive voting method, plural voting, in which we attribute MXPOST four votes, MBT and SVMTool three votes and TnT two votes. These values were manually chosen on the basis of their performance on the validation set. Plural voting achieves a higher accuracy on the test set than any of the individual taggers. To our knowledge, plural voting has not yet been attempted as a system combination technique. It is therefore interesting to observe that this very naive combination method outperforms the more sophisticated weighted voting method.

We previously observed that MXPOST makes more mistakes on unambiguous words than the other taggers, but is better at handling ambiguous words. Since ambiguity information is available before tagging, we are able to propose a combined system, where MXPOST tags ambiguous and unknown words and a simple lexicon lookup approach handles unambiguous words. This almost trivial combination method yields a substantial performance increase with an overall tagging accuracy of 98.61% (MXPOST+LLU in Table 2).

A last combination method takes the output of the taggers and transforms them into instances that can be used as training material for a machine learning algorithm, with the gold-standard tag as the class to be predicted. The tagged validation set was used to create a training set for a memory-based classifier which classified the instance base generated from the test set. The output tags were then considered as the final tag proposed by the tagger committee. Table 2 shows that the cascaded classifier is indeed able to improve on any of the individual taggers with an overall accuracy of 98.46%. Interestingly however, this combination method underperforms compared to the more naive combination methods.

The best system combination method (MXPOST+LLU) achieves an error reduction rate of more than 11% compared to the best individual tagger. While this increase in accuracy is not as dramatic compared to those observed for other languages and datasets [10], it nevertheless establishes further proof that system combination is able to overcome the individual taggers' bias to a significant extent. Moreover, given the upper-bound accuracy obtained by the oracle, there is still ample room for improvement for other system combination methods, especially for the disambiguation of unknown words.

6   Future Work and Conclusion

In this paper we presented experiments with data-driven part-of-speech taggers trained and evaluated on the annotated Helsinki Corpus of Swahili. We selected four of the current state-of-the-art data-driven taggers, TnT, MBT, SVMTool and MXPOST, and observed the latter as being the most accurate tagger for this dataset. In another set of experiments, we further improved on the performance of the individual taggers by combining them into a committee of taggers. Surprisingly, we observed the more naive combination methods, like the novel plural voting approach, outperform more elaborate schemes like cascaded classifiers and weighted voting.

This paper presents the first direct comparison of data-driven taggers on this particular data set. We are confident that significant increases in tagging accuracy can still be obtained through various stages of algorithmic optimization and more refined system combination methods. The results of SVMTool in particular can undoubtedly be improved through the selection of a more appropriate kernel and a thorough validation phase. Furthermore, the inclusion of other data-driven tagging methods such as CRF++, WPDV [10] or Transformation-Based Tagging [16] might also improve the performance of the system combination methods.

Future work will include learning curve experiments to determine how much data is minimally needed to obtain optimal performance. Thorough data analysis is further needed to investigate the way the taggers handle morphological issues in Kiswahili. Affixation is an important indicator of word class in Kiswahili and all of the data-driven taggers used in the experiments only cover this aspect indirectly on the level of the grapheme. Perhaps a more rigid morphologically inspired approach to part-of-speech tagging, where morphological analysis functions as a preprocessing step, might provide a significant performance increase. Despite the limitations of the taggers presented in this paper, we nevertheless hope that the results presented herein can function as a first benchmark for future research on data-driven part-of-speech tagging of Kiswahili, and Bantu languages in general.

References

1. van Rooy, B., Pretorius, R.: A word-class tagset for Setswana. Southern African Linguistics and Applied Language Studies **21(4)** (2003) 203–222.
2. Allwood, J., Grönqvist, L., Hendrikse, A.P.: Developing a tagset and tagger for the African languages of South Africa with special reference to Xhosa. Southern African Linguistics and Applied Language Studies **21(4)** (2003) 223–237.
3. Prinsloo, D.J., Heid, U.: Creating word class tagged corpora for Northern Sotho by linguistically informed bootstrapping. In: Proceedings of the Conference on Lesser Used Languages & Computer Linguistics (LULCL 2005), Bozen/Bolzano, Italy (2005 (to be published)).
4. Taljard, E., Bosch, S.E.: A comparison of approaches towards word class tagging: disjunctively vs conjunctively written Bantu languages. In: Proceedings of the Conference on Lesser Used Languages & Computer Linguistics (LULCL 2005), Bozen/Bolzano, Italy (2005 (to be published)).
5. Pretorius, L., Bosch, S.E.: Computational aids for Zulu natural language processing. Southern African Linguistics and Applied Language Studies **21(4)** (2003) 267–282.
6. Hurskainen, A.: HCS 2004 – Helsinki Corpus of Swahili. Compilers: Institute for Asian and African Studies (University of Helsinki) and CSC (2004).
7. Hurskainen, A.: Disambiguation of morphological analysis in Bantu languages. In: Proceedings of the Sixteenth International Conference on Computational Linguistics (COLING-96), Copenhagen, Denmark (1996) 568–573.
8. Brants, T.: TnT – a statistical part-of-speech tagger. In: Proceedings of the Sixth Conference on Applied Natural Language Processing (ANLP 2000), Seattle, WA, USA (2000) 224–231.
9. Ratnaparkhi, A.: A maximum entropy model for part-of-speech tagging. In: Proceedings of the Conference on Empirical Methods in Natural Language Processing, Somerset, NJ, USA (1996) 133–142.
10. van Halteren, H., Zavrel, J., Daelemans, W.: Improving accuracy in word class tagging through combination of machine learning systems. Computational Linguistics **27(2)** (2001) 199–230.
11. Daelemans, W., Zavrel, J., van den Bosch, A., van der Sloot, K.: MBT: Memory Based Tagger, version 2.0, Reference Guide. ILK Research Group Technical Report Series 03-13, Tilburg (2003).
12. Wagacha, P., Manderick, B., Getao, K.: Benchmarking Support Vector Machines using StatLog Methodology. In: Proceedings of Benelearn 2004, Machine Learning Conference of Belgium and the Netherlands, Brussels, Belgium (2004) 185–190.

13. Giménez, J., Màrquez, L.: SVMTool: A general POS tagger generator based on Support Vector Machines. In: Proceedings of the 4th International Conference on Language Resources and Evaluation (LREC 2004), Lisbon, Portugal (2004) 43–46.
14. Joachims, T.: Making Large-scale SVM Learning Practical. In Schölkopf, B., Burges, C., Smola, A., eds.: Advances in Kernel Methods – Support Vector Learning. MIT Press, Boston, MA, USA (1999) 41–56.
15. De Pauw, G., Daelemans, W.: The role of algorithm bias vs information source in learning algorithms for morphosyntactic disambiguation. In: Proceedings of the Fourth Conference on Computational Natural Language Learning (CoNLL 2000), Lisbon, Portugal (2000) 19–24.
16. Brill, E.: A simple rule-based part-of-speech tagger. In: Proceedings of the Third Conference on Applied Natural Language Processing (ANLP '92), Trento, Italy (1992) 152–155.

Hand-Written and Automatically Extracted
Rules for Polish Tagger

Maciej Piasecki

Institute of Applied Informatics, Wrocław University of Technology,
Wybrzeże Wyspiańskiego 27, Wrocław, Poland
maciej.piasecki@pwr.wroc.pl

Abstract. Stochastic approaches to tagging of Polish brought results far from being satisfactory. However, successful combination of hand-written rules and a stochastic approach to Czech, as well, as some initial experiments in acquisition of tagging rules for Polish revealed potential capabilities of a rule based approach. The goals are: to define a language of tagging constraints, to construct a set of reduction rules for Polish and to apply Machine Learning to extraction of tagging rules. A language of functional tagging constraints called JOSKIPI is proposed. An extension to the C4.5 algorithm based on introducing complex JOSKIPI operators into decision trees is presented. Construction of a preliminary hand-written tagging rules for Polish is discussed. Finally, the results of the comparison of different versions of the tagger are given.

1 Introduction

The statistical approach of [1] to tagging of Polish brought results far from being satisfactory. However the accuracy of statistical tagger for Czech, another inflective language, has been significantly improved after combination with hand-written rules [2]. Experience collected during experiments in acquisition of tagging rules for Polish [3] on the basis of Genetic Algorithms revealed potential capabilities of a rule based approach but showed also that the inefficient extraction algorithm had to be changed. This work follows this path. Similarly to [2], we want to combine hand-written rules with Machine Learning, but as in [3], we tend to base the whole tagging process on the rules. Our claim is that rules written in a symbolic language with high expressive power are a much better solution for tagging inflective languages than solutions relying on stochastic models.

The first goal is to define a symbolic language for expressing *tagging constraints*, in the sense similar to [4], i.e. constraints that must be preserved in all natural language expressions, or at least often enough. Such constraints must have local character and be verifiable without extensive parsing. But the main goal is to apply this language as a common tool for supporting automatic extraction of rules and expressing hand-written rules. We want to be able to express in this language both: simple constraints that are parts of automatically extracted rules and complicated premises of hand-written rules of tags reduction. Finally, we are going to present an algorithm for rules extraction and a preliminary set of hand-written rules for Polish.

Petr Sojka, Ivan Kopeček and Karel Pala (Eds.): TSD 2006, LNAI 4188, pp. 205–212, 2006.
© Springer-Verlag Berlin Heidelberg

2   JOSKIPI Language

The proposed language of constraints has a lot in common with its direct ancestors, namely [4,5], and [6]. The difference is in its primary application. As the intended Machine Learning algorithm for the extraction of rules should produce highly efficient rules on the basis of large corpus, we put the main stress on defining constraints working in a functional style. Such constraint, used as a part of extracted rules, should take context as input, check its state and return some information describing the state. Partial information delivered by component constraints is combined by the logic of the extracted rule. The intended algorithm was C4.5 [7]. Moreover, this work remotely inherits some ideas from Hermjakob and its work on parser learning [8].

A language called JOSKIPI (the acronym of a Polish name meaning 'the language of the description of the state in the IPI PAN Corpus' [9]) is proposed. The core of JOSKIPI is a set of predefined *operators* of the three main classes:

1. *simple operators* — atomic, return a set of symbolic values or strings,
2. *test operators* — compound, return a boolean value,
3. *conditional operators* — compound, include an operator and a test operator, the value of the operator is returned on the condition that the test is fulfilled.

The work of simple operators is closely related to the structure of a token description in the IPI PAN Corpus (further IPIC) XML format presented below:
```
<tok> <orth>token</orth>
<lex><base>base_form₁</base><ctag>tagₙ</ctag></lex>
...
<lex><base>base_formₙ</base><ctag>tagₙ</ctag></lex> </tok>
```
Moreover, a *positional tag* in IPIC is a sequence of values:
```
<ctag>gramm_class:cat_val₁:...:cat_valₖ</ctag>
```
The first value encodes one of the 32 *grammatical classes* (a more finer-grained division than parts of speech), e.g. *adjective, ad-adjectival adjective*, or *non-past form*. The following positions correspond to *grammatical categories* (12 in total), e.g. gender, aspect, or vocalicity, appropriate for the given grammatical class. For a given class each category is determined by position. An IPIC tag is considered to be *a structure of attributes* in JOSKIPI.

Simple operators allow for reading the state of a specified token. The *position* of the token can be directly specified by an *offset* from the *centre of the context*, e.g. `orth[-1]` returns a *string* (a sequence of characters) — a token first to the left from the centre. The centre of the context is always the token being currently disambiguated. A position can also be specified by a *variable*[1], e.g. `base[$P]` returns a *set of strings*. The size of the returned set is one if the token in the position stored in `$P` is non-ambiguous according to its base form. Other simple operators return sets of symbolic values of other attributes of tags assigned to the pointed token, e.g. grammatical class, case, number, gender etc. If there is no token in the pointed position or the pointed token does not possess the given attribute in any of its tags, the *empty value* `none` is returned. Names of the simple operators follow exactly the mnemonics used in the query language of IPIC. Filtered simple operators allow for reading values from attributes of tags fulfilling specified condition, e.g. `catflt(0,{nom,acc},{nmb})` reads

---

[1] Only variables over positions exists in JOSKIPI.

the number of the token 0 from its tags with case values in the given set, when there are no such tags the operator returns `none`.

Test operators construct compound expressions. There are five subclasses:

1. *sets comparison*: `equal(`o_1,o_2`)`, `inter(`o_1,o_2`)`, `in(`o_1,o_2`)`, where o_i can be an operator or a constant value, e.g. `equal(pos[0],pos[-2])`, where `pos` returns a set of grammatical classes, or `in(case[1], {nom, gen, acc})`;
2. *logical conjunctions*: `and`, `or`, and `not`, where the last one means *not or* when applied to more than one argument,
3. *search*: `llook(`pos_{st},pos_{end}`,$Var,`*test*`)` and `rlook`, where positions can be variables or constants (e.g. the begin and the end of a sentence), `$Var` is an obligatory iterator, both operators look for the first token fulfilling *test*, set `$Var` to its position and return `true`, otherwise return `false`;
4. *condition fulfilment over a sequence*: `only(`pos_{st},pos_{end}`,$Var,`*test*`)` and a similar `atleast`;
5. and *agreement*: `agrpp(`pos_1,pos_2`,{`*mask*`},`n`)` and `agr` with the same syntax, where *mask* is a set of names of attributes and/or values, `agrpp` checks agreement between a pair of tokens, while `agr` over a sequence, e.g. `agrpp(0,-1,{pl,gnd,gen},3)` checks *possible* agreement the two tokens: 0 and -1 on gender but only for tags with *number=pl* and *case=gen*.

Search operators setting some variables, when used in combination with other operators, can construct complex conditions over a large sequences of tags. The agreement operators add also a lot to the large expressive power of JOSKIPI.

Conditional operators, of the scheme: `op ? test`, combine any operator with a test operator and return `none` when the test is not fulfilled, e.g.
`cas[$Cs]?rlook(1,end,$Cs, not(equal(cas[$Cs],{none}) ))`

JOSKIPI has been implemented directly in C++ in order to achieve high efficiency. Especially, the implementation of `agr` had to be very careful, as in a sequence of tokens each can have many tags and the number of possible paths of agreement across the tags is huge. Instead of searching, the problem was considered as to be a *Constraint Solving Problem*.

3   Preliminary Rules

In JOSKIPI reduction rules have the following scheme:
`delete(` *test_{del}* `) # ` p ` :- ` *test_{app}*, where *test_{del}* and *test_{app}* are any test operators and p is the priority of the rule.

The value of *test_{app}* decides about applicability of the rule. If the rule is applicable, then *test_{del}* is evaluated for each tag of the 0 token i.e. the 0 token is presented several times to *test_{del}* as possessing only one tag. Tags for which *test_{del}* returns `true` are deleted from the 0 token. In order to protect against errors in IPIC (or text), if all tags are removed by a rule, then all are restored.

The staring point for the construction of our set of rules was the work of Rudolf [6] and a few rules in [3]. Unfortunately, Rudolf's rules are expressed in natural language, and in this form most of them are very imprecise and can be only guidelines. From the 17 rules presented in [6] only one (pp. 95 in [6]), presented below, survived in its original form in tests on IPIC:

```
delete(equal(pos[0],{fin})) # 150 :-
and( inter(pos[0],{fin}), equal(pos[1],{fin}) )
```

The above rule states that an ambiguous token cannot be a verb non-past form (fin) if followed by another non-past form. Oliva and Petkevič [10] claim that this rule is universal for all Slavic languages and our research supports this hypothesis, as it produces no errors tested on IPIC.

However, the other variant of this rule, where an unambiguous fin precedes a token which can be fin, have had to be refined:

```
delete(equal(pos[0],{fin})) # 140 :-
and( inter(pos[0],{fin}), equal(pos[-1],{fin}),
not( and( in(orth[-2],{"jest","znaczy"}),equal(orth[-3],{"to"})
) ) )
```

The additional constraints protect a little outdated constructions of the type *to znaczy* fin (gloss. *it means* fin) appearing several times in IPIC.

Inspired by [6] we tried to explore all cases of obligatory agreement in Polish and formulated a *preliminary set of tagging rules for Polish*. The set is called 'preliminary' as the work was time consuming, and we concentrated on very efficient and general rules first. The number of rules completely tested is 24. The work on rules is performed according to the following scheme:

1. An initial naive version of a rule is formulated.
2. The rule is tested on IPIC with the help of a special *Rule Debugger* tool.
3. *Rule Debugger* records positions of all cases in which a tag selected by a human was deleted by the rule.
4. The recorded exceptions are analysed in IPIC with the help of a constructed editor called *Manufakturzysta*. The errors are immediately corrected in IPIC.
5. If the rule produces some exceptions, it is refined and the process is repeated.

As we have no space for a detailed presentation of the rules, only the main groups of rules are described (all used in tests, Sec. 5).

Separation of two non-past forms — the two members of this group have been already presented. The other rules of this group block the occurrence of two verbs in non-past forms even if there are one or two *particle-adverbs* (qub) between the two tokens. However, if we add adverbs, we will encounter too many errors (i.e. mistakenly deleted tags).

Case after preposition — only tags agreeing in case with a preposition are left after the preposition. This almost always working rule had to be divided into several at least. Firstly, potential possessive pronoun *jego* (*his*) had to be treated separately. Secondly, numerals in dates or currencies break this rule (separate rules needed). Thirdly, genitive case can always appear as the indicator of possessive construction. And finally, adjective after preposition needs separate complicated rule taking into account some collocations.

Token "z"/"z" as preposition — cannot be a preposition if there is no following token with instrumental case as it is claimed in [6]. We added genitive case to the list and a collocation *z tak*.

Genitive case after numerals — in the preliminary set only a rule for indefinite numerals like *mało* (*little*) or *mnóstwo* (*plenty*) (being adverbs in IPIC) has been formulated. A set of rules for main numerals is in development.

Plural number after numeral — works well for nouns except cases of names of units, but adjectives in IPIC include ordinals which complicates the picture.

Agreement of relative pronoun "który" (which/who) *and noun in number and gender* — mainly works with the additional condition of the presence of ',', but anyway produces some small error rate.

4   Operator Based Learning

Large workload on manual construction of rules was predicated before we started, and from the very beginning we wanted to extract the bulk of rules automatically. As the application of rules should be efficient, we were looking for some simple form. Encouraged by the positive results in [8], as the first attempt, we decided to extract rules in the form of Decision Trees (DTs) by the C4.5 algorithm [7]. The rules of both types were applied in the reductionistic tagger described in [11]. The tagger works in three phases. During each phase a partial disambiguation is performed: firstly *grammatical class*, secondly *number and gender* and thirdly *case*. Most of the other attributes are dependent on those four, with the exception of: *aspect* in case of non-past forms of verbs ('present tense', third person) and *accentability* and *post-prepositionality* in the case of 3rd person pronouns.

DTs are constructed not for the whole phases but for *ambiguity classes*, following [12]. An ambiguity class is a set of tokens possessing the same set of possible values of some tag attribute or attributes, e.g. {adj fin subst} is an example of ambiguity class of the first phase. There are 143 DTs constructed: 61 (1st phase), 48, and 34. DTs encode from several to many thousands of rules.

The general idea for encoding more sophisticated rules by DTs is that each node of DT corresponds to the application of some JOSKIPI operator. During learning all operators of DT are applied in advance for example tokens and the returned values are stored as sequences. The sequences are next passed to the implementation of C4.5 as learning examples. Created DTs encodes identifiers of operators in their nodes. During tagging our implementation of DT while is entering some node requests from the environment application of the appropriate operator to the current context. After the value is returned, our DT compares the returned value with values assigned to the branches leaving the node. One of the branches is chosen and DT traverses to the next node corresponding to the next operator. The important limitation of this mechanism is that operators in DTs work independently. A highly expressive mechanism of joining by position variables is not avaible. But the operator encoded in the nodes can be of any complexity.

Each DT is specified by a JOSKIPI expression called a *pattern*:

```
ambiguity_class_specification # a_sequence_of_operators ,
```

where the specification of an ambiguity class is written as a set of mnemonics of possible values. The backbone of each DT is a set of simple operators called a *standard vector*, e.g. for DTs of the first phase the standard vector includes:

```
pos[-3]...pos[1] pos[2] cas[-3]...cas[2]
gnd[-3]...gnd[2] nmb[-3]...nmb[2]
```

We have been extending patterns with more complex operators for each DT individually. Firstly by manual inspection of members of the given ambiguity class in IPIC, we tried to identify some distinguishing features, e.g. `equal(orth[0],{"kiedy"})` in the pattern for `{conj qub}` points to the behaviour of the specific word, for which DT should build some specific rules. Secondly, we tried to formulate some relaxed linguistic constraints concerning agreement or some common word order, e.g. whether there is a particle *się* somewhere to the left and between it and the centre there are only tokens of some specified classes. Such constraints were tested by building pseudo-rules and running them by *Rule Debugger* on IPIC and next analysing the exceptions. Finally, the statistics of a set of learning examples generated by some preliminary version of a pattern was analysed. We could see how promising are the different versions of operators for C4.5. For example, we formulated an conditional operator checking whether two sequences of tokens agreeing on case, number and gender that are joined by a conjunction have a common case value. Mostly the operator returns `none`, but in some situations its boolean values are nicely correlated with a choice of some class. Unfortunately, for C4.5 this happens to rarely to include this operator in the given DT.

An example of a more complex operator (but a shorter one) is an operator looking for an adjective somewhere to the right which agrees with the 0 token:

```
!AdjPRight
or( and( inter(pos[1],adj,ppas,pact),
agrpp(0,1,cas,gnd,nmb,3) ),
and( rlook(2,end,$Adj,inter(pos[$Adj],{adj,ppas,pact})),
agrpp(0,$Adj,{cas,gnd,nmb},3),
only(1,$-1Adj,$Q,inter(pos[$Q],{adv,qub}) ) )
)
```

There are 11 operators of similar complexity applied in DTs of the first phase (grammatical class). The most sophisticated, but extensively used by C4.5 is the operator testing whether the 0 token can be a potential subject of some verb in the context. DTs of the second phase (number and gender) utilise several simpler operators and 8 complex. DTs of the third phase (case) use 10 complex operators, and a lot of simpler ones. Obviously, for each phase a version of a standard vector is defined.

5   Results and Conclusions

The tagger using the rules and DTs based on JOSKIPI operators achieved the accuracy of 92.55% (84.75% for ambiguos words). However, it must be emphasised that in addition to the simplifications disscussed in Sec. 4, the tagger does not distinguish *nouns* from *gerunds* on the other base than number, gender and case. All tokens *noun/gerund* ambiguous, if not disambiguated on the basis of the three attributes, are assigned two tags at the end. The accuracy of the tagger has been evaluated in ten-fold test on the learning part IPIC (LIPIC) including 885 669 tokens. All cases in which the set of tags assigned by the tagger has a non-empty intersection with the set assigned by a human were counted as proper decisions. In order to analyse what is the influence of hand-written rules and of the use of sophisticated operators in DTs, we prepared and tested 4 different versions of the tagger (Tab. 1)[2]:

---

[2] The results reported earlier were increased due to a programmer error in the test.

- *a full tagger* (T): hand-written rules and all types of operators in DTs,
- *a tagger without hand-written rules* (T-HR) but still DTs are constructed with the use of complex operators,
- *a tagger without hand-written rules and complex operators in DTs* (T-HR-C) in which DTs are constructed on the basis of standard vectors plus some simple operators checking existence of some particular words in the fixed positions,
- and *a tagger applying hand-written rules, but not using complex operators in DTs* (T+HR-C).

Table 1. Comparison of the accuracy [%] of different versions of the tagger

tagger	all tokens	all max.	all min.	ambiguous	amb. max.	amb. min.
T	**92.55**	93.04	91.98	**84.75**	86.12	83.4
T-HR	**91.60**	92.03	90.97	**82.70**	83.27	81.94
T-HR-C	**91.43**	91.86	90.76	**82.54**	83.16	81.38
T+HR-C	**91.75**	91.94	91.48	**82.8**	83.31	82.39

In Tab. 1 we can observe, that switching off both: the hand-written rules and the complex operators decreases significantly the accuracy. The mutual relation between both changes is less clear, as the decrease of accuracy in the case of T-HR-C is marginal in comparison to T-HR. But the tagger T+HR-C shows that the lack of the complex operators in DTs is as important, as the lack of the hand-written rules! The small difference between T-HR and T-HR-C can be the result of construction by DTs some general rules with the help of the complex operators. Such rules can express some important linguistic constraints. The complex operators are often used in the top parts of DTs.

The preliminary set of rules is very small, but very significant, see the result of T-HR. The rules when applied to LIPIC activated for 76 543 tokens and removed 187 895 tags. The tagger leaves at average **1.03 tags per token** (initially 2.87). The estimated speed of the full tagger is about 4000 tokens per second on the PC 512 MB RAM 2.41 GHz.

The accuracy is lower than [2], but it seems to be significantly improved in comparison to the previous Polish taggers [1,3]. Further work must be done on enlarging the set of hand-written rules. We plan also to look for an algorithm of extraction of more expressive rules based on JOSKIPI than DTs.

Acknowledgement. This work was financed by the Ministry of Education and Science projects No 3 T11C 003 28 and No 3 T11C 018 29.

References

1. Łukasz Dębowski: Trigram morphosyntactic tagger for Polish. In Mieczysław A. Kłopotek, Wierzchoń, S.T., Trojanowski, K., eds.: Proceedings of Intelligent Information Processing and Web Mining. Proceedings of the International IIS:IIPWM'04 Conference held in Zakopane, Poland, May 17–20, 2004. Springer Verlag (2004) 409–413.
2. Hajič, J., Krbec, P., Květoň, P., Oliva, K., Petkevič, V.: Serial combination rules and statistics: A case study in czech tagging. In: Proceedings of The 39th Annual Meeting of ACL, Morgan Kaufmann Publishers (2001) 260–267.

3. Piasecki, M., Gaweł, B.: A rule-based tagger for Polish based on Genetic Algorithm. [13].
4. Karlsson, F., Voutilainen, A., Heikkil a, J., Anttila, A., eds.: Constraint Grammar: A Language-Independent System for Parsing Unrestricted Text. Mouton de Gruyter, Berlin and New York (1995).
5. Květoň, P.: Language for grammatical rules. Report TR-2003-17, ÚFAL/CKL MFF UK, Prague (2003).
6. Rudolf, M.: Metody automatycznej analizy korpusu tekstów polskich. Uniwersytet Warszawski, Wydz. Polonistyki (2004).
7. Quinlan, J.: C4.5: Programms for Machine Learning. Morgan Kaufmann (1993).
8. Hermjakob, U.: Learning Parse and Translation Decisions From Examples With Rich Context. PhD thesis, University of Texas, Austin (1997).
9. Przepiórkowski, A.: The IPI PAN Corpus Preliminary Version. Institute of Computer Science PAS (2004).
10. Oliva, K., Petkevič, V.: Morphological and syntactic tagging of slavonic languages. Lecture Notes for Empirical Linguistics and Natural Language, Fall School, Sozopol (2002).
11. Piasecki, M., Godlewski, G.: Reductionistic, Tree and Rule Based Tagger for Polish. [14].
12. Márquez, L.: Part-of-speech Tagging: A Machine Learning Approach based on Decision Trees. PhD thesis, Universitat Politécnica de Catalunya (1999).
13. Mieczysław A. Kłopotek, Wierzchoń, S.T., Trojanowski, K., eds.: Proceedings of Intelligent Information Processing and Web Mining, 2005. Advances in Soft Computing. Springer, Berlin (2005).
14. Mieczysław A. Kłopotek, Wierzchoń, S.T., Trojanowski, K., eds.: Proceedings of Intelligent Information Processing and Web Mining 2006. Advances in Soft Computing. Springer, Berlin (2006).

Effective Architecture of the Polish Tagger

Maciej Piasecki and Grzegorz Godlewski

Institute of Applied Informatics, Wrocław University of Technology,
Wybrzeże Wyspiańskiego 27, Wrocław, Poland
maciej.piasecki@pwr.wroc.pl

Abstract. The large tagset of the IPI PAN Corpus of Polish and the limited size of
the learning corpus make construction of a tagger especially demanding. The goal of
this work is to decompose the overall process of tagging of Polish into subproblems
of partial disambiguation. Moreover, an architecture of a tagger facilitating this
decomposition is proposed. The proposed architecture enables easy integration of
hand-written tagging rules with the rest of the tagger. The architecture is open
for different types of classifiers. A complete tagger for Polish called TaKIPI is
also presented. Its configuration, the achieved results (92.55% of accuracy for all
tokens, 84.75% for ambiguous tokens in ten-fold test), and considered variants of the
architecture are discussed, too.

1 Introduction

If a tagset is very large and a learning corpus is quite small, then the problem of tagging
becomes very demanding. This is the case of Polish and the largest corpus of Polish, namely
IPI PAN Corpus (henceforth IPIC) [1]. In IPIC, there are 4179 theoretically possible tags,
but only 1642 of them occur in the manually disambiguated part of 885 669 tokens. Probably
it was the data spareness, which was the main cause of low accuracy of statistical tagger
of Dębowski [2] constructed on the basis of IPIC. However, a positional IPIC tag is a
sequence of symbols describing different morpho-syntactic features of a token. Thus, if a
tag is a sequence, then we can assume that subsequences of elements of tags appear in
IPIC with greater frequency than the whole tags. Starting with this assumption, the goal
of this work is to decompose the overall process of tagging of Polish into subproblems of
partial disambiguation. Next, we want to define an architecture of a tagger facilitating this
decomposition.

Moreover, as it was shown in [3], [4] and [5], the introduction of hand-written rules can
improve accuracy of a tagger for inflective languages like Czech or Polish. That is why, we
did our best to make the proposed architecture open for integration of hand-written tagging
rules with the rest of a tagger.

2 Task

In the IPIC XML format every tag is written in the following form:

```
<lex><base>base form</base>
<ctag>gram_class:cat_val₁:...:cat_valₖ</ctag></lex>,
```

Petr Sojka, Ivan Kopeček and Karel Pala (Eds.): TSD 2006, LNAI 4188, pp. 213–220, 2006.
© Springer-Verlag Berlin Heidelberg

where `gram_class` is a grammatical class[1], e.g. *noun, main numeral* or *impersonal*, cat_val$_i$ is a value of some grammatical category, e.g. *gender, case, number* etc., $k \in \langle 0, 12 \rangle$ is the number of categories for the given class.

In our approach, a IPIC tag is represented as a structure: $\langle class = name,$ $cat_1 = value, \ldots, cat_k = value \rangle$. All class names and category values are encoded as binary numbers with one bit per name/value, what makes operations on structures more efficient. We will call the elements of this structure *tag attributes*, or simply *attributes*, where it should not cause confusion.

According to the assumed representation of tags, the morfo-syntactic analyser Morfeusz [6] assigns to each token a list of structures, i.e. tags. In this paper, we call these structures simply *tags*. The overall task of the tagger is to choose the proper ones for each token, ideally one. We want to decompose this task into several steps. During the subsequent steps the subsequent groups of attributes are disambiguated, i.e. the values for them are chosen from the possible ones. The possible values are those that are present in the set of tags assigned to the given token by Morfeusz.

3 Architecture

The architecture of our tagger, called TaKIPI (Polish acronym for *The Tagger of IPIC*) is presented in Fig. 1.

The process starts with morpho-syntactic processing of input text (*Reader*). Division into tokens (tokenisation) and assignment of tags is done mainly by Morfeusz, but previously all strings between two spaces are presented to *Abbreviation Recogniser*, implemented as a transducer. If a string is recognised, then its full description, potentially ambiguous i.e. a set of tags, is taken from the *dictionary of abbreviations*, and the token is not further analysed by Morfeusz.

Pre-sentencer, a simple set of rules derived from [2], recognises boundaries of sentences, but in the case of a recognised dot-ended abbreviation, *Pre-sentencer* postpones making decision. The final decision is made by *Sentencer* on the basis of the results of tagging, e.g. in this phase it is already decided whether "*im.*" is[2]: "*im*:ppron3 '.':interp", (i.e. 3rd person pronoun and punctuation) or the abbreviation of a form of *imię* (*name*).

The rest of TaKIPI works on chunks of the input text roughly corresponding to the sentences[3] defined by *Pre-sentencer*. This main loop is not presented in Fig. 1 (for the sake of clarity). If an occurrence of an abbreviation postpones the final decision, then a block of several sentences is further processed in one iteration.

Following the approach of [3] we apply *hand-written rules* (see Sec. 4) before application of other classifiers. The rules can delete some tags.

Initial probabilities for tags are calculated by *Unigram Classifier* on the basis of frequencies of: ⟨token,tag⟩, stored in the *unigram dictionary*. The probabilities for the pairs not observed in the learning data, but possible according to the morphological analysis, are

---

[1] One of 32 possible in IPIC, grammatical classes express more fine grained division than parts of speech.

[2] In the examples, we present only selected attributes of tags, mostly only the class.

[3] This is done due to the assumptions underlying the manual disambiguation.

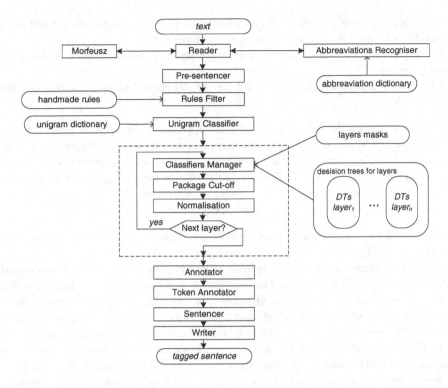

Fig. 1. The architecture of the tagger

calculated by smoothing (inspired by [7], where w_k is a token, t_i one of its possible tags, and K is the number of possible tags):

$$p(t_i|w_k) = \frac{freq(t_i|w_k) + \lambda}{freq(w_k) + \lambda K} \text{ where } \lambda = (K-1)/K \tag{1}$$

The core of the tagging process is divided in our architecture into several subsequent phases, corresponding to *serial combination* of [3]. During each phase some tags can be deleted according to the performed partial disambiguation. The set of all possible tag attributes is divided into several *layers*. Attributes of the same layer are disambiguated during the same phase of tagging. The definitions of layers and their order are stored in the sequence of *masks of layers*.

During each phase, tags are distinguished only on the basis of values of attributes of the corresponding layer. Moreover, a token can be ambiguous in some layers, and non-ambiguous in the others. A subset of tags of the given token such that all its members have identical values of attributes of the given layer is called a *package* of tags. During each phase, the tagger choose the best package according to the current probabilities of tags, and eliminates all packages except the best one — *Package Cutoff*.

Each phase of tagging begins with subsequent application of *classifiers* to each token in the sentence. More than one classifier can be applied to any token, as it often happens. Only tokens that are ambiguous with respect to the current layer are processed. The architecture is open for many types of classifiers. The only constraint is that a classifier should update the probabilities of tags. The way of calculating probabilities is free.

In the present version of TaKIPI there are three layers: *grammatical class*, *number and gender*, and *case*.

The other grammatical categories of IPIC are mostly dependent on the above. The only exceptions are:

- *aspect* in the case of non-past forms of verbs in present tense and third person, that are described by Morfeusz as being ambiguous in aspect (in each case the base form is the same), e.g. *razi* (*dazzles*, or *offends*), *pozostaje* (*stays*, *remains*), *napotyka* (*encounters*),
- *accentability* and *post-prepositionality* in the case of personal pronouns in third person, e.g. *on* (*he*) possesing four different combinations of values {*accented, non-accented*} × {*post-prepositional, non-post-prepositional*}.

As the differences in the above cases are very subtle and are based mainly on semantics, we do not disambiguated the attributes in these cases.

Another significant simplification assumed in TaKIPI is that we do not try to distinguish substantives (nouns, in IPIC: `subst`) from gerunds (IPIC: `ger`) on the other basis than number, gender and case. All tokens `subst/ger` ambiguous, if not disambiguated on the basis of the three attributes, are assigned two tags at the end. Except the cases described above, TaKIPI returns one tag per one token. Detailed statistics are presented in Sec. 6.

In the present version TaKIPI only classifiers based on the algorithm of Induction of Decision Trees (DT) called C4.5r8 [8], where "r8" is the 8th code release [9], are applied. However, the DT classifiers have been converted to classifiers returning probability of positive decision — selected value for some attribute, and negative decision — smoothed non-zero probability of other values. In the application of DT to tagging and their use as probabilistic classifiers we follow the main line of [7].

For each leaf of DT, the probability of its decision is calculated on the basis of the number of examples attached to this leaf during tree construction. The probability is smoothed according to the algorithm presented in [7]: (t is decision, $t|X$ — examples with the decision t in the given leaf, $\|X\|$ — all examples in the given DT, K — the number of possible decisions in the given DT):

$$p(t|X) = \frac{f(t|X) + \lambda}{\|X\| + \lambda K}, \text{ where } \lambda = (K - 1)/K \tag{2}$$

As in [7], instead of building one big classifier for a phase, we decided to decompose the problem further into the *classes of ambiguity* [7]. Each class corresponds to one of many possible combinations of values of layer attributes, e.g. there is only one attribute in the first layer, namely grammatical class, and different classes of ambiguity on the first layer are different combinations of grammatical classes observed in tokens of the learning data. Examples of classes of ambiguity are: {`adj`, `subst`}, {`adj`, `conj`, `qub`, `subst`} (where `qub` = *particle-adverb*), or {`sg`, `m1`, `m2`, `m3`} (of the second layer: number singular, but all male genders possible).

The number of examples for different classes of ambiguity varies in large extent. For some classes, e.g. {`gen`, `acc`} (the third layer of case) there are thousands of examples, for some only few, e.g. {`acc`, `voc`}. Following [7], we apply a kind of a *backing off* technique, in which an *inheritance relation* between ambiguity classes is defined. The inheritance relation is simply a set inclusion relation between sets of values defining ambiguity classes, e.g. the *'superclass'* {adj fin subst} (where fin = *verb non-past form*) is in inheritance relation with {adj fin}, {adj subst}, etc. Construction of DT for a particular ambiguity class supports accurate choice of components of learning vectors for DT. We deliver to the given DT information specific for the given linguistic problem, e.g. concerning the distinction between nominative and genitive case. Typically, 'superclasses' have fewer examples than its 'subclasseses', but the merged class is the sum of both. From the linguistic point of view, the choice of a learning vector for merged classes is not so essential to the problem, but still there are often some common morpho-syntactic features of the examples belonging to the merged classes.

Thus, TaKIPI works on the basis of a collection of DTs divided into groups assigned to layers. *Classifiers Manager* selects the proper set of DTs for each token which is ambiguous according to the current layer. Each DT multiplies the probabilities of tags in the token with the probabilities of a decision. Next, after processing of all tokens, only the package with the best maximal probability is left by *Package Cut-off*. At the end of the loop, probabilities in each token (only the winning package) are normalised. The process is repeated for each layer.

4 Learning

For the description of hand-written rules and learning examples the same language has been used, namely JOSKIPI [10], similar in its expressive power to [11] and [12]. The applied hand-written rules come from [10], as well.

As already noted, the manually disambiguated part of IPIC (further called Learning IPIC, or LIPIC) consists of only 885 669 tokens, including punctuation and 11 576 tokens unknown to Morfeusz. On the basis of an analysis of a part of LIPIC of about 655 000 tokens, we identified all possible ambiguity classes for all layers. We selected some ambiguity classes, called *supported classes*, that are sufficiently supported by examples (a heuristic criterion of having size about 100 examples) or are necessary according to the inheritance structure, i.e. the lack of linguistically reasonable superclass. Sets of learning examples are generated only for supported classes, but according to the inheritance hierarchy each token belonging to one of the non-supported classes is the source of learning examples added to the sets for its superclasses. We tested several depths of inheritance finally choosing the depth equal to 0 (see Sec.5) as giving the best results.

A *learning example* is a sequence of values produced by a sequence of *operators* defined in JOSKIPI for the given ambiguity class. Operators are functions taking the state of the context of some token and returning a value. There are three main classes of operators constructed from JOSKIPI primitives [10]:

1. *simple operators* — read some tag attribute and return a set of values (singletons for non-ambiguous attributes),
2. *test operators* — evaluate some logical condition and return a boolean value, a string — some token, or a set of strings — (ambiguous) base form;
3. *conditional operators* — an operator plus a test operator, return the *empty value* when the test is not fulfilled, otherwise the value of the operator.

Simple operators can read any attribute of any token. The token can be either specified by a distance from the centre or found by JOSKIPI operators `llook` and `rlook` according to some logical test. A test can be a simple equality test, a relation between sets of values, a test of a possibility of morfo-syntactic agreement or fulfilment of some constructed complex condition in some part of the context (the test can pertain to any part of a sentence). A complex condition can utilise a mechanism of variables over positions of tokens. An example of a complex operator used in learning can be a test checking whether there is some potential subject of a sentence somewhere to the left of the token being disambiguated. Operators do not cross the sentence boundaries. It is worth to notice that similar operators are used as premises of hand-written rules.

Generation of learning examples for the first layer is done in one go for all ambiguity classes of this layer by sequentially setting the centre of the context in subsequent ambiguous tokens and applying operators of the appropriate ambiguity classes. For the next layers the process is identical, except the initial preparation of the learning data. During tagging, DTs (or generally classifiers) of the second layer are applied to tokens partially disambiguated. During learning, we have to create a similar situation. This is achieved by learning partial taggers for subsequences of layers up till the 'full tagger'. Before preparation of learning examples for the k layer, a partial tagger for $k - 1$ layers is applied and the attributes of all $k - 1$ layers are disambiguated. This gradual learning appeared to be superior in comparison to an 'ideal' disambiguation based on manual disambiguation of LIPIC.

Construction of DTs by C4.5 algorithm is completely independent from generation of the examples, and is done by application of the C4.5 software [9].

5   Variations and Parameters

We tested several values of *pruning confidence level* for DTs [9] achieving the best results with an individual value for each DT. The range is from almost 100% (no prunning) to less than 1% (many branches pruned). A sequence of operators for each DT has been chosen on the basis of a heuristic analysis of results.

Many important variants of tagger's architecture were tested. The level of inheritance between ambiguity classes varied from 2 to 0. It expresses how many levels we are going up the hierarchy looking for superclasses matching a given token. The value 0 means that only the classes on the first matching level are taken for the given token (i.e. the exact class if exist, otherwise all in the minimal distance in the hierarchy). Values greater than 0 enlarge the set of superclasses applied. The value 1 during learning and tagging resulted in the best accuracy—during tagging each token is classified by DTs learned from similar contexts.

We tried to apply a mechanism of iterative improvement. Learning sequence of *operators* were extended with additional operators reading the attributes of winning tags in the context. DTs were applied several times during one phase in several iterations. In this version, the cut-off and the normalisation were applied after each iteration. But the results were lower. Probably, the number of different combinations of values increased and situations in the context did match the learned examples too often.

A similar problem appeared when we tried to iterate across different permutations of packages of tags generated with respect to the given layer. Generation of permutations was repeated in one phase several times with cut-off and normalisation after each iteration of all permutations. However, the achieved results were significantly lower. Once again, traversing of DT stopped very often inside the tree, not reaching any leaf. In that case, it is very hard to successfully estimate the probability.

We also tested the repeated application of *Unigram Classifier* before each phase, but it appeared, that it is much better to keep the probabilities established in the previous phase.

Finally, the version without application of the hand-written rules was tested, but the accuracy was worse by 0.95% (2.05% for ambiguous tokens).

6   Evaluation and Conclusions

The accuracy of TaKIPI has been evaluated in ten-fold test on LIPIC. In LIPIC some tokens are assigned more than one tag when human could not make a decision on the basis of sentential context. As our tagger tends to assign one tag per token, except the cases described in Sec. 3, we counted all cases in which the set of tags assigned by the tagger has a non-empty intersection with the set assigned by a human as proper decisions. However, the tagger leaves on average **1.03 tags per token** (initially 2.87). TaKIPI processes about 4000 words per sec. on PC, 512 MB RAM, 2.41GHz. The results are presented in Tab. 1[4].

Table 1. Accuracy [%] of the tagger evaluated on the IPI PAN Corpus

layer	all tokens	all max.	all min.	ambiguous	amb. max.	amb. min.
all	**92.55**	93.04	91.98	**84.75**	86.12	83.40
1 (gram. class ≈ POS)	**98.80**	98.83	98.71	**91.64**	91.85	91.04
2 (1 + nmb, gnd)	**95.90**	96.09	96.61	**87.40**	87.86	87.06

Comparison with 90.4% reported by Dębowski [2] is difficult, as his tagger always leaves the best one tag, and was tested on a very small part of LIPIC. However, the accuracy of TaKIPI seems to be better. Also some informal manual comparison of the results of both taggers revealed better accuracy of TaKIPI. More important is that in many practical applications, e.g. in Machine Translation, the worst errors are the ones made in grammatical classes (POS). With respect to 31 classes recognised by TaKIPI the average error of 8.36% in relation to *ambiguous tokens* can be acceptable in some applications. Moreover, the open architecture defines many possibilities for future improvements.

Acknowledgement. This work was financed by the Ministry of Education and Science projects No 3 T11E 005 28 and No 3 T11C 003 28.

References

1. Przepiórkowski, A.: The IPI PAN Corpus Preliminary Version. Institute of Computer Science PAS (2004).
2. Dębowski Ł.: Trigram morphosyntactic tagger for Polish. In Kłopotek, M.A., Wierzchoń, S.T., Trojanowski, K., eds.: Intelligent Information Processing and Web Mining. Proceedings of the International IIS:IIPWM'04 Conference, Zakopane, Poland. Springer Verlag (2004) 409–413.

[4] The results reported earlier were increased due to a programmer error in the test.

3. Hajič, J., Krbec, P., Květoň, P., Oliva, K., Petkevič, V.: Serial combination rules and statistics: A case study in czech tagging. In: Proceedings of The 39th Annual Meeting of ACL, Morgan Kaufmann Publishers (2001) 260–267.

4. Rudolf M.: Metody automatycznej analizy korpusu tekstów polskich: pozyskiwanie, wzbogacanie i przetwarzanie informacji lingwistycznych. PhD thesis, Uniwersytet Warszawski (2003).

5. Piasecki, M., Gaweł, B.: A rule-based tagger for Polish based on Genetic Algorithm. [13].

6. Woliński, M.: Morfeusz — a practical tool for the morphological analysis of polish. [14].

7. Márquez, L.: Part-of-speech Tagging: A Machine Learning Approach based on Decision Trees. PhD thesis, Universitat Politécnica de Catalunya (1999).

8. Quinlan, J.: C4.5: Programms for Machine Learning. Morgan Kaufmann, San Mateo (1993).

9. Quinlan, R.: Ross Quinlan's Personal Homepage. http://www.rulequest.com/Personal/c4.5r8.tar.gz (2005).

10. Piasecki, M., Godlewski, G.: Reductionistic, Tree and Rule Based Tagger for Polish. [14].

11. Karlsson, F., Voutilainen, A., Heikkil a, J., Anttila, A., eds.: Constraint Grammar: A Language-Independent System for Parsing Unrestricted Text. Mouton de Gruyter, Berlin and New York (1995).

12. Květoň, P.: Language for grammatical rules. Report TR-2003-17, ÚFAL/CKL MFF UK, Prague (2003).

13. Kłopotek, M.A., Wierzchoń, S.T., Trojanowski, K., eds.: Intelligent Information Processing and Web Mining — Proceedings of the International IIS: IIPWM'05 Conference, Gadańsk, Poland. Advances in Soft Computing. Springer, Berlin (2005).

14. Kłopotek, M.A., Wierzchoń, S.T., Trojanowski, K., eds.: Intelligent Information Processing and Web Mining — Proceedings of the International IIS: IIPWM'06 Conference, Zakopane, Poland. Advances in Soft Computing. Springer, Berlin (2006).

Synthesis of Czech Sentences from Tectogrammatical Trees*

Jan Ptáček and Zdeněk Žabokrtský

Institute of Formal and Applied Linguistics, Charles University
Malostranské náměstí 25, 118 00 Prague, Czech Republic
{ptacek, zabokrtsky}@ufal.mff.cuni.cz

Abstract. In this paper we deal with a new rule-based approach to the Natural
Language Generation problem. The presented system synthesizes Czech sentences
from Czech tectogrammatical trees supplied by the Prague Dependency Treebank 2.0
(PDT 2.0). Linguistically relevant phenomena including valency, diathesis, conden-
sation, agreement, word order, punctuation and vocalization have been studied and
implemented in Perl using software tools shipped with PDT 2.0. BLEU score metric
is used for the evaluation of the generated sentences.

1 Introduction

Natural Language Generation (NLG) is a sub-domain of Computational Linguistics; its
aim is studying and simulating the production of written (or spoken) discourse. Usually
the discourse is generated from a more abstract, semantically oriented data structure. The
most prominent application of NLG is probably transfer-based machine translation, which
decomposes the translation process into three steps: (1) analysis of the source-language text
to the semantic level, maximally unified for all languages, (2) transfer (arrangements of the
remaining language specific components of the semantic representation towards the target
language), (3) text synthesis on the target-language side (this approach is often visualized
as the well-known machine translation pyramid, with hypothetical interlingua on the very
top; NLG then corresponds to the right edge of the pyramid). The task of NLG is relevant
also for dialog systems, systems for text summarizing, systems for generating technical
documentation etc.

In this paper, the NLG task is formulated as follows: given a Czech tectogrammatical tree
(as introduced in Functional Generative Description, [1], and recently elaborated in more
detail within the PDT 2.0 project[1,2]), generate a Czech sentence the meaning of which
corresponds to the content of the input tree. Not surprisingly, the presented research is
motivated by the idea of transfer-based machine translation with the usage of tectogrammatics
as the highest abstract representation.

In the PDT 2.0 annotation scenario, three layers of annotation are added to Czech
sentences: (1) *morphological layer* (m-layer), on which each token is lemmatized and
POS-tagged, (2) *analytical layer* (a-layer), on which a sentence is represented as a rooted

---

* The research has been carried out under projects 1ET101120503 and 1ET201120505.

[1] http://ufal.mff.cuni.cz/pdt2.0/

[2] In the context of PDT 2.0, sentence synthesis can be viewed as a process inverse to treebank
annotation.

Petr Sojka, Ivan Kopeček and Karel Pala (Eds.): TSD 2006, LNAI 4188, pp. 221–228, 2006.

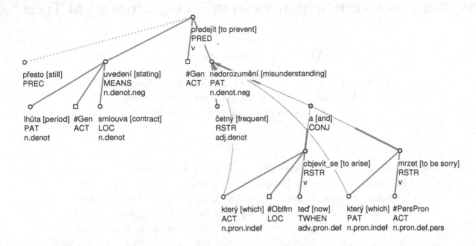

Fig. 1. Simplified t-tree fragment corresponding to the sentence *'Přesto uvedením lhuty ve smlouvě by se bylo předešlo četným nedorozuměním, která se nyní objevila a která nás mrzí.'* (But still, stating the period in the contract would prevent frequent misunderstandings which have now arisen and which we are sorry about.)

ordered tree with labeled nodes and edges corresponding to the surface-syntactic relations; one a-layer node corresponds to exactly one m-layer token, (3) *tectogrammatical layer* (t-layer), on which the sentence is represented as a deep-syntactic dependency tree structure (t-tree) built of nodes and edges (see Figure 1). T-layer nodes represent auto-semantic words (including pronouns and numerals) while functional words such as prepositions, subordinating conjunctions and auxiliary verbs have no nodes of their own in the tree. Each tectogrammatical node is a complex data structure – it can be viewed as a set of attribute-value pairs, or even as a typed feature structure. Word forms occurring in the original surface expression are substituted with their t-lemmas. Only semantically indispensable morphological categories (called grammatemes) are stored in the nodes (such as number for nouns, or degree of comparison for adjectives), but not the categories imposed by government (such as case for nouns) or agreement (congruent categories such as person for verbs or gender for adjectives). Each edge in the t-tree is labeled with a functor representing the deep-syntactic dependency relation. Coreference and topic-focus articulations are annotated in t-trees as well. See [2] for a detailed description of the t-layer.

The pre-release version of the PDT 2.0 data consists of 7,129 manually annotated textual documents, containing altogether 116,065 sentences with 1,960,657 tokens (word forms and punctuation marks). The t-layer annotation is available for 44 % of the whole data (3,168 documents, 49,442 sentences).

2   Task Decomposition

Unlike stochastic 'end-to-end' solutions, rule-based approach, which we adhere to in this paper, requires careful decomposition of the task (due to the very complex nature of the task, a monolithic implementation could hardly be maintainable). The decomposition was not trivial to find, because many linguistic phenomena are to be considered and some of them may interfere with others; the presented solution results from several months of experiments and a few re-implementations.

In our system, the input tectogrammatical tree is gradually changing – in each step, new node attributes and/or new nodes are added. Step by step, the structure becomes (in some aspects) more and more similar to a-layer tree. After the last step, the resulting sentence is obtained simply by concatenating word forms which are already filled in the individual nodes, the ordering of which is also already specified.

A simplified data-flow diagram corresponding to the generating procedure is displayed in Figure 2. All the main phases of the generating procedure will be outlined in the following subsections.

2.1 Formeme Selection, Diatheses, Derivations

In this phase, the input tree is traversed in the depth-first fashion, and so called *formeme* is specified for each node. Under this term we understand a set of constraints on how the given node can be expressed on the surface (i.e., what morphosyntactic form is used). Possible values are for instance simple case *gen* (genitive), prepositional case *pod+7* (preposition *pod* and instrumental), *v-inf* (infinitive verb),[3] *že+v-fin* (subordinating clause introduced with subordinating conjunction *že*), *attr* (syntactic adjective), etc.

Several types of information are used when deriving the value of the new *formeme* attribute. At first, the valency lexicon[4] is consulted: if the governing node of the current node has a valency frame, and the valency frame specifies constraints on the surface form for the functor of the current node, then these constraints imply the set of possible formemes. In case of verbs, it is also necessary to specify which diathesis should be used (active, passive, reflexive passive etc.; depending on the type of diathesis, the valency frame from the lexicon undergoes certain transformations). If the governing node does not have a valency frame, then the formeme default for the functor of the current node (and subfunctor, which specifies the type of the dependency relations in more detail) is used. For instance, the default formeme for the functor ACMP (accompaniment) and subfunctor `basic` is *s+7* (with), whereas for `ACMP.wout` it is *bez+2* (without).

It should be noted that the formeme constraints depend also on the possible word-forming derivations applicable on the current node. For instance, the functor APP (appurtenance) can be typically expressed by formemes *gen* and *attr*, but in some cases only the former one is possible (some Czech nouns do not form derived possessive adjectives).

2.2 Propagating Values of Congruent Categories

In Czech, which is a highly inflectional language, several types of dependencies are manifested by agreement of morphological categories (agreement in gender, number, and

---

[3] It is important to distinguish between infinitive as a formeme and infinitive as a surface-morphological category. The latter one can occur e.g. in compound future tense, the formeme of which is not infinitive.

[4] There is the valency lexicon PDT-VALLEX [3] associated with PDT 2.0. On the t-layer of the annotated data, all semantic verbs and some semantic nouns and adjectives are equipped with a reference to a valency frame in PDT-VALLEX, which was used in the given sentence.

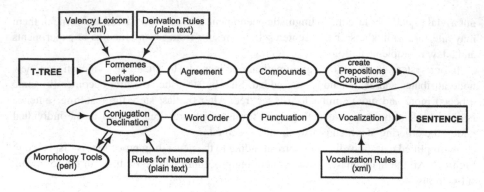

Fig. 2. Data-flow diagram representing the process of sentence synthesis

case between a noun and its adjectival attribute, agreement in number, gender, and person between a finite verb and its subject, agreement in number and gender between relative pronoun in a relative clause and the governor of the relative clause, etc.). As it was already mentioned, the original tectogrammatical tree contains those morphological categories which are semantically indispensable. After the formeme selection phase, value of case should be also known for all nouns. In this phase, oriented agreement arcs (corresponding to the individual types of agreement) are conceived between nodes within the tree, and the values of morphological categories are iteratively spread along these arcs until the unification process is completed.

2.3   Expanding Complex Verb Forms

Only now, when person, number, and gender of finite verbs is known, it is possible to expand complex verb forms where necessary. New nodes corresponding to reflexive particles (e.g. in the case of reflexiva tantum), to auxiliary verbs (e.g. in the case of complex future tense), or to modal verbs (if deontic modality of the verb is specified) are attached below the original autosemantic verb.

2.4   Adding Prepositions and Subordinating Conjunctions

In this phase, new nodes corresponding to prepositions and subordinating conjunctions are added into the tree. Their lemmas are already implied by the value of node formemes.

2.5   Determining Inflected Word Forms

After the agreement step, all information necessary for choosing the appropriate inflected form of the lemma of the given node should be available in the node. To perform the inflection, we employ morphological tools (generator and analyzer) developed by Hajič [4]. The generator tool expects a lemma and a positional tag (as specified in [5]) on the input, and returns the inflected word form. Thus the task of this phase is effectively reduced to composing the positional morphological tag; the inflection itself is performed by the morphological generator.

2.6   Special Treatment of Definite Numerals

Definite numerals in Czech (and thus also in PDT 2.0 t-trees) show many irregularities (compared to the rest of the language system), that is why it seems advantageous to generate their forms separately. Generation of definite numerals is discussed in [6].

2.7   Reconstructing Word Order

Ordering of nodes in the annotated t-tree is used to express information structure of the sentences, and does not directly mirror the ordering in the surface shape of the sentence. The word order of the output sentence is reconstructed using simple syntactic rules (e.g. adjectival attribute goes in front of the governing noun), functors, and topic-focus articulation. Special treatment is required for clitics: they should be located in the 'second' position in the clause (Wackernagel position); if there are more clitics in the same clause, simple rules for specifying their relative ordering are used (for instance, the clitic *by* always precede short reflexive pronouns).

2.8   Adding Punctuation Marks

In this phase, missing punctuation marks are added to the tree, especially (i) the terminal punctuation (derived from the `sentmod` grammateme), (ii) punctuations delimiting boundaries of clauses, of parenthetical constructions, and of direct speeches, (iii) and punctuations in multiple coordinations (commas in expressions of the form *A, B, C and D*).

Besides adding punctuation marks, the first letter of the first token in the sentence is also capitalized in this phase.

2.9   Vocalizing Prepositions

Vocalization is a phonological phenomenon: the vowel *-e* or *-u* is attached to a preposition if the pronunciation of the prepositional group would be difficult without the vowel (e.g. *ve výklenku* instead of **v výklenku*). We have adopted vocalization rules precisely formulated in [7] (technically, we converted them into the form of an XML file, which is loaded by the vocalization module).

3   Implementation and Evaluation

The presented sentence generation system was implemented in ntred[5] environment for processing the PDT data. The system consists of approximately 9,000 lines of code distributed in 28 Perl modules. The sentence synthesis can also be launched in the GUI editor tred providing visual insight into the process.

As illustrated in Figure 2, we took advantage of several already existing resources, especially the valency lexicon PDT-VALLEX [3], derivation rules developed for grammateme assignment [8], and morphology analyzer and generator [4].

We propose a simple method for estimating the quality of a generated sentence: we compare it to the original sentence from which the tectogrammatical tree was created during

---

[5] http://ufal.mff.cuni.cz/~pajas

the PDT 2.0 annotation. The original and generated sentences are compared using the BLUE score developed for machine translation [9] – indeed, the annotation-generation process is viewed here as machine translation from Czech to Czech. Obviously, in this case BLEU score does not evaluate directly the quality of the generation procedure, but is influenced also by the annotation procedure, as depicted in Figure 3.

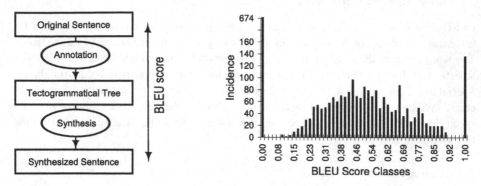

Fig. 3. Evaluation scheme and distribution of BLEU score in a development test sample counting 2761 sentences

It is a well-known fact that BLEU score results have no direct common-sense interpretation. However, a slightly better insight can be gained if the BLEU score result of the developed system is compared to some baseline solution. We decided to use a sequence of t-lemmas (ordered in the same way as the corresponding t-layer nodes) as the baseline.

When evaluating the generation system on 2761 sentences from PDT 2.0 development-test data, the obtained BLEU score is **0.477**.[6] Distribution of the BLEU score values is given in Figure 3. Note that the baseline solution reaches only 0.033 on the same data.

To give the reader a more concrete idea of how the system really performs, we show several sample sentences here. The O lines contain the original PDT 2.0 sentence, the B lines present the baseline output, and finally, the G lines represent the automatically generated sentences.

(1)   *O*: Dobře ví, o koho jde.
      B: vědět dobrý jít kdo
      G: Dobře ví, o koho jde.

(2)   *O*: Trvalo to až do roku 1928, než se tento problém podařilo překonat.
      B: trvat až rok 1928 podařit_se tento problém překonat
      G: Trvalo až do roku 1928, že se podařilo tento problém překonat.

(3)   *O*: Stejně tak si je i adresát výtky podle ostrosti a výšky tónu okamžitě jist nejen tím, že jde o něj, ale i tím, co skandál vyvolalo.

---

[6] This result seems to be very optimistic; moreover, the value would be even higher if there were more alternative reference translations available.

B: stejně tak být i adresát výtka ostrost a výška tón okamžitý jistý nejen jít ale i skandál vyvolat co
G: Stejně tak je i adresát výtky podle ostrosti a podle výšky tónu okamžitě jistý, nejen že jde o něj, ale i co skandál vyvolalo.

(4) *O*: Pravda o tom, že žvýkání pro žvýkání bylo odjakživa činností veskrze lidskou – kam paměť lidského rodu sahá.
B: pravda žvýkání žvýkání být odjakživa činnost lidský veskrze paměť rod lidský sahat kde
G: Pravda, že žvýkání pro žvýkání bylo odjakživa veskrze lidská činnost (kam paměť lidského rodu sahá).

4 Final Remarks

The primary goal of the presented work – to create a system generating understandable Czech sentences out of their tectogrammatical representation – has been achieved. This conclusion is confirmed by high BLUE-score values. Now we are incorporating the developed sentence generator into a new English-Czech transfer-based machine translation system; the preliminary results of the pilot implementation seem to be promising.

As for the comparison to the related works, we are aware of several experiments with generating Czech sentences, be they based on tectogrammatics (e.g. [10,11,12]) or not (e.g. [13]), but in our opinion no objective qualitative comparison of the resulting sentences is possible, since most of these systems are not functional now and moreover there are fundamental differences in the experiment settings.

References

1. Sgall, P.: Generativní popis jazyka a česká deklinace. Academia (1967).
2. Mikulová, M., Bémová, A., Hajič, J., Hajičová, E., Havelka, J., Kolářová, V., Lopatková, M., Pajas, P., Panevová, J., Razímová, M., Sgall, P., Štěpánek, J., Urešová, Z., Veselá, K., Žabokrtský, Z., Kučová, L.: Anotace na tektogramatické rovině Pražského závislostního korpusu. Anotátorská příručka. Technical Report TR-2005-28, ÚFAL MFF UK (2005).
3. Hajič, J., Panevová, J., Urešová, Z., Bémová, A., Kolářová-Řezníčková, V., Pajas, P.: PDT-VALLEX: Creating a Large-coverage Valency Lexicon for Treebank Annotation. In: Proceedings of The Second Workshop on Treebanks and Linguistic Theories, Vaxjo University Press (2003) 57–68.
4. Hajič, J.: Disambiguation of Rich Inflection – Computational Morphology of Czech. Charles University – The Karolinum Press, Prague (2004).
5. Hana, J., Hanová, H., Hajič, J., Vidová-Hladká, B., Jeřábek, E.: Manual for Morphological Annotation. Technical Report TR-2002-14 (2002).
6. Ptáček, J.: Generování vět z tektogramatických stromů Pražského závislostního korpusu. Master's thesis, MFF, Charles University, Prague (2005).
7. Petkevič, V., ed.: Vocalization of Prepositions. In: Linguistic Problems of Czech. (1995) 147–157.
8. Razímová, M., Žabokrtský, Z.: Morphological Meanings in the Prague Dependency Treebank 2.0. LNCS/Lecture Notes in Artificial Intelligence/Proceedings of Text, Speech and Dialogue (2005).
9. Papineni, K., Roukos, S., Ward, T., Zhu, W.J.: Bleu: a Method for Automatic Evaluation of Machine Translation. Technical report, IBM (2001).

10. Panevová, J.: Random generation of Czech sentences. In: Proceedings of the 9th conference on Computational linguistics, Czechoslovakia, Academia Praha (1982) 295–300.
11. Panevová, J.:   Transducing Components of Functional Generative Description 1.   Technical Report IV, Matematicko-fyzikální fakulta UK, Charles University, Prague (1979) Series: Explizite Beschreibung der Sprache und automatische Textbearbeitung.
12. Hajič, J., Čmejrek, M., Dorr, B., Ding, Y., Eisner, J., Gildea, D., Koo, T., Parton, K., Penn, G., Radev, D., Rambow, O.:   Natural Language Generation in the Context of Manchine Translation. Technical report, Johns Hopkins University, Baltimore, MD (2002).
13. Hana, J.: The AGILE System. Prague Bulletin of Mathematical Linguistics (2001) 147–157.

ASeMatch: A Semantic Matching Method*

Sandra Roger[1,2], Augustina Buccella[2], Alejandra Cechich[2], and Manuel Sanz Palomar[1]

[1] Natural Language Processing and Information Systems Group
Department of Software and Computing Systems, University of Alicante, Spain
{sroger, mpalomar}@dlsi.ua.es
[2] GIISCO Research Group, Department of Computing Sciences
University of Comahue, Argentina
{sroger, abuccel, acechich}@uncoma.edu.ar

Abstract. Usually, syntactic information of different sources does not provide enough knowledge to discover possible matchings among them. Otherwise, more suitable matchings can be found by using the semantics of these sources. In this way, semantic matching involves the task of finding similarities among overlapping sources by using semantic knowledge. In the last years, the ontologies have emerged to represent this semantics. On these lines, we introduce our ASeMatch method for semantic matching. By applying several NLP tools and resources in a novel way and by using the semantic and syntactic information extracted from the ontologies, our method finds complex mappings such as $1 - N$ and $N - 1$ matchings.

1 Introduction

Integration of different information sources is a widely referenced subject in the literature. These sources can be heterogeneous databases, internet pages or even texts that must be combined to obtain information from one simple interface. However, integration is not a straightforward task and several problems have to be faced such as dealing with semantic heterogeneity.

Several proposals have emerged aiming at providing different solutions to integration problems. In particular, we are interested in those defining automatic or semi-automatic methods to find similarities between ontologies. The last emerged proposals [1,2,3] take advantage of the information ontologies provide and new information extracted from semantic resources like WordNet [4]. Unfortunaltely, they do not represent the solution to the matching problems, since they only allow to find some missing relationships in the ontologies.

The work presented here is a continuation of the approach reported in [5,6], in which we have proposed a layered architecture and a method to deal with semantic heterogeneity problems. In our work, an ontology is a 4-tuple $O = < C, DT, SP, R >$ where C is a set of classes, DT is a set of datatype properties, SP is a set of special properties and R is a set of restrictions. By using semantic resources and taking into account the structure of the ontologies and their syntactic and semantic relationships, our method allows to find several

---

* This research has been partially funded by the Spanish Government under project CICyT number TIC2003-07158-C04-01 by the Valencia Government under project number GV04B-268, and by the University of Comahue under the project 04/E059 and 04/E062.

Petr Sojka, Ivan Kopeček and Karel Pala (Eds.): TSD 2006, LNAI 4188, pp. 229–235, 2006.

correct mappings. But there are still undiscovered mappings, called *complex mappings*, where $1 - N$ and $N - 1$ matches are involved. Focusing on them, the ASeMatch method finds these complex mappings by means of the application of several Natural Language Processing (NLP) tools and resources in a novel way.

The way how NLP tools are used by our method is the focus of this paper. It paper is organized as follows: Section 2 describes the Architectural Components of our approach. Then, Section 3 presents a case study showing how our method works. Section 4 briefly describes some proposals widely referenced in the literature denoting their main characteristics together with advantages and disadvantages with respect to our proposal. Conclusions and future work are addressed afterwards.

2   Architectural Components of ASeMatch

Our method receives *two ontologies* as input and generates a set of *equality axioms* as output. These axioms are like mappings providing information about what elements of one ontology are similar to elements of the another one.

Three main components have been defined in our arquitecture:

- **Parser and Instantiation Component**, which parses the ontology's codes loaded by the user in order to create two *Object Structures* (OS's) – the *Similarity Searcher Component*, which extracts the provided information and use it to find similarities; and the
- **Similarity Searcher Component** which is in charge of calculating the similarity values between the OS's and generating the equality axioms as a result of the whole process. Finally, the
- **Linguistic Component**, that is further explained in the next section.

2.1   Linguistic and Similarity Searcher Components

The ASeMatch method is based on the information extracted from the ontologies. This information is translated to OS's representing classes, properties, and restrictions ontologies provide. All of the elements of an ontology are represented by these OS's, thus, they represent a valid instantiation of the ontologies. NLP tools, in particular the "multiconcept" definition (MCR)[7], is used in order to find the *complex mappings*. This definition is an extension of the "multiword" concept defined in [7].

Definition 1 (Multiconcept). *Let E_P^s an OS element and $E_{P_1}^t, E_{P_2}^t, \ldots, E_{P_n^t}$ other OS elements, E_P^s is a multiconcept of $E_{P_1}^t, E_{P_2}^t, \ldots, E_{P_n^t}$ ($[E_P^s] \approx_{mc} [E_{P_1}^t, E_{P_2}^t, \ldots, E_{P_n}^t]$) if E_P^s semantically equivalent $\bigcup_i E_{P_i}^t$.*

Two elements are semantically equivalent if the application of our method returns a value that exceeds a certain threshold determined empirically. Our extended MCR definition is able to find mappings between one element of an OS and one or more elements of another OS and viceversa. This extension allows a more refined comparison than the multiword recognition proposed by [7] (only over labels). In this first stage of our work, the MCR is applied only to DT properties (E_P).

ASeMatch consists of three main phases: 1) Linguistic Analysis of the Labels, 2) Contextualization, and 3) Computation of Similarity Values. The application of all of them determines whether two elements are *semantically equivalent*.

1) Linguistic Analysis of the Labels. In this phase, the OS is translated into a new OS in which all words in labels are analyzed syntactically. To do so, the labels are tokenized (by using OnToken[1]) and FreeLing[2] is used as lemmatizer, PoS tagger and syntactic analyzer. Finally, WordNet[3] (WN) is used in the Word Sense Disambiguation process.

2) Contextualization. In this phase, we contextualize the interpretation of the OS elements. The combination of two contexts is used to represent the elements: 1) SContext embeds the structural context of the elements, and 2) HContext takes into consideration the hypernymy and hyponymy relation that occur among elements.

The first context is built using the elements that are *near* to the analyzed element. The *near(E)* function depends on the OS elements (DT, SP or class). For example, if E is a DT properties, the *near* function considers only the DP properties of its class as well as the corresponding SP properties. When E is an SP property, the *near* function considers the DT properties of the classes related by E. Finally, if E is a class, *near* considers both the class related to E through SP properties as well as their DP properties.

The second context (HContext) is obtained by extracting the chain of hypernyms and hyponyms for each sense analysed element. Synsets are also taken into account in the disambiguation process.

This process involves two main tasks. The first task consists of intersecting all hypernyms and hyponyms chains that correspond to all the senses of the analyzed elements. If the resulted intersection set contain more than one chain, a second disambiguation process is performed by using the SContext.

3) Computation of the Similarity Elements: Finding similarities is a very complex activity because in general it is complex to determine fully automatically all mappings between two models. The similarity functions we propose in this paper determine mapping candidates associated with probability values. These values give a degree of similarity among the elements of two OS's. Four main similarity functions are used depending on the OS's elements, DT, check restrictions, SP, and class similarity functions as follows.

Datatype Similarity Function: MCR is applied in this function. That is, not only structural information is taken into account but also contextual information is required to find complex mappings. To do so, three auxiliary functions are used and we will show in Section 3, by using an example, how this function works:

- *Textual entailment recognition(entail(label(dt$_1$) , label(dt$_2$)))* of DT properties labels: The *entail* function is used to perform this task. This function uses information extracted from WN relations such as synonyms, holonyms, hypernyms, and hyponyms involved in the Contextualization phase (HContext and SContext).
- *Datatype compatibility*: This a straightforward function because it only compares the data types of the two DT properties. For example, string to string or string to integer. The function returns 1 when both data types are equal. If there exists a logical

---

[1] developed by the University of Comahue.

[2] http://garraf.epsevg.upc.es/freeling/index.php

[3] http://wordnet.princeton.edu/

conversion between a data type and another, the result of the function is extracted from a compatibility table, otherwise it is equal to 0.

- *MCR* (Definition 1): This task uses the two last functions to find subsume relationships. That is, when a set of DT properties subsume to another.

Check Restriction Similarity Function: The check restriction function compares the restrictions applied to the SP properties. Only when both properties have the same restrictions the function returns 1, otherwise it returns a percentage according to the number of restrictions that are the same. Besides, a compatibility table is used to map restrictions with similar meanings. For example, if one property is defined as functional and another has a "no more than one" cardinality restriction, the similarity value between them is equal to 1 because both denote the same meaning.

Special Property Similarity Function: In this function we compare the SP properties belonging to common classes. The comparison is similar to the DT similarity function, but the DT compatibility is not calculated and it is replaced by the *check restriction* function to check SP property restrictions. As SP properties relate classes, this function compares not only the domain classes but also the range classes. This comparison generates the analysis of the DT and SP properties of these range clases. Therefore, our method is recursive and it will stop when all classes have been compared.

Class Similarity Function: Finally, we must compare the classes. Two comparisons are used in this function, *label* and *structural*. The *label* comparison compares the labels of classes by using the *entail* function like in the property functions. *Structural* comparison uses the results of the special and datatype functions in order to analyze the set of similar properties of the involved classes. To do so, we use the function (1) [8]:

$$sim_{att}(x, y) = \frac{|\mathcal{X} \cap \mathcal{Y}|}{|\mathcal{X} \cap \mathcal{Y}| + \alpha(x, y) | \mathcal{X}/\mathcal{Y}| + (1 - \alpha(x, y)) | \mathcal{Y}/\mathcal{X}|} \tag{1}$$
$$for\ 0 \leq \alpha \leq 1$$

where x and y are concepts and $\mathcal{X}$ and $\mathcal{Y}$ correspond to description sets of x and y (in this case "properties"). The function (1) is based on Tversky's model [9], in which the α function identifies the most common superclass between two concepts and calculates their depth in a hierarchy. If the depth of two concepts is the same, the value of this function is equal to 0.5.

As SP properties provide more information than DT properties, we divide the function (1) into two new weighted functions. Thus, we can increase the value of the SP property's weight to enhance this knowledge. Then, the function (1) is now as follows:

$$sim_{class}(c_1, c_2) = w_{special-properties} \times sim_{special-properties}(c_1, c_2) + \\ + w_{datatype-properties} \times sim_{datatype-properties}(c_1, c_2)$$

Besides, this function takes into account the 1-N and N-1 matches obtained in the comparison of the properties. That is, if there are 1-N or N-1 matches (found by the MCR process), the set of DT properties of an OS found as part of one DT property of another OS is considered like only one property. Thus, to consider these complex matches the function (1) has no need to change.

3   A Motivating Example

In order to illustrate how the ASeMatch method works, we have extracted two ontologies named *"Talk-ont"*[4] ($\mathcal{O}_1$) and *"Talk"*[5] ($\mathcal{O}_2$) from repositories on the Web. We have made some changes to both of them in order to show the main aspect of our proposal, the *MCR*. Figure 1 and 2 shows a part of the ($\mathcal{O}_1$) and ($\mathcal{O}_2$) ontology respectively.

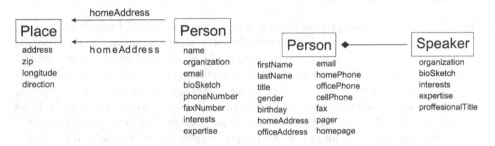

Fig. 1. A reduced version of the ontology Talk-ont ($\mathcal{O}_1$)

Fig. 2. A reduced version of the ontology Talk ($\mathcal{O}_2$)

Following our approach, we begin the similarity process by mapping the class *Person*(P) of ($\mathcal{O}_1$) and the class *Speaker* (S) of ($\mathcal{O}_2$). In order to determine their similarity, our method begins comparing the DT properties of these classes to other classes related to them by means of SP properties. As the class S is a subclass of the class *Person* of $\mathcal{O}_2$, the evaluation process will consider the DT properties of *Person* as DT properties of S as well. For example, *firstName* and *lastName* of *Person* will be also considered during the evaluation of S.

Now, let us see how ASeMatch compares *Name* of P and the *FirstName* property of the *Person* class. First of all, the method analyses the labels syntactic and morphologically, and disambiguation process is performed resulting in the selection of the *noun* category for the *Name* property. Following, the syntactic analysis determines that *first* is an adjective and *Name* is also a noun. In these cases, the method should compare the following pairs (*name, name*), (*name, first*). As *firstName* is defined by WN, the pair *(name, first name)* is compared too. Then, the "textual entailment recognition" of the previous labels determines that *name* subsumes *first name*; and a similar result is obtained by the analysis of the labels *name* and *last name*. In both cases, the type compatibility value results 1, since the type is the same for the three involved DT properties. Then, the MCR takes into account this result and the structural information to compute its functions. In this case, the *near* function (section 3) considers the classes P and Place, the DT properties of both classes, and the SP properties homeAddress and officeAddress of $\mathcal{O}_1$; and the classes S and Person of $\mathcal{O}_2$ along with their DT properties. Depending on the similarity value resulting from the comparison, and considering that there are only one DT property referring *name* in P, and there are two DT properties in S; then our method determines that [*name*] $\approx_{mc}$ [*firtName, lastName*].

---

[4] http://daml.umbc.edu/ontologies/talk-ont
[5] http://daml.umbc.edu/ontologies/ittalks/talk

The DT properties *organization, bioSketch, interests, email* and *expertise* of $\mathcal{O}_1$ are semantically equivalent to the corresponding DT properties of $\mathcal{O}_2$; and *faxNumber* is semantically equivalent to *fax* of $\mathcal{O}_2$. Finally, *homePhone, officePhone* and *cellPhone* of $\mathcal{O}_1$ are little similar to *phoneNumber* of $\mathcal{O}_2$. Besides, as there is a reference for *cell Phone* in WN, that is hyponym of phone, the similarity value between *cellPhone* and *phoneNumber* will be still greater.

4   Related Work

Several semantic matching proposals are found in the literature [1,2,3]. Particularly, the work in [2] presents a semantic matching algorithm based on graph-like structures. The approach contains two levels – the element and structure levels. Firstly, the labels are tokenized and lemmatized in order to obtain atomic words. A semantic resource, in this case EuroWordNet, is queried to obtain the senses of these words. Secondly, the element level is applied determining the semantic relations holding between pairs of atomic concepts of labels. To do so, the senses are extracted from EuroWordNet. Using sense filtering techniques [7] one sense can be selected as relevant instead of another one. Finally, the structure level is performed producing a set of semantic relations between concepts at nodes.

CtxMatch [7] is a model based schema/ontology matcher which computes mappings (namely a set of point-to-point) between schema/ontology elements. CtxMatch is an algorithm that encodes the meaning of each node in a formal language and computes a mapping between elements by comparing their meaning using a linguistic process. CtxMatch consists of three main phases: 1) linguistic analysis of the labels – in this phase the tokenization, PoS-tagging, and multiconcep recognition are realized; 2) contextualization – here a recognition of multi-level multiconceps, sense filtering, and sense composition are produced; and 3) computation of the logical relation – this phase receives the logic forms and calculates logical relations by using a SAT solver.

The work presented in [1] proposes an algorithm for ontology matching, named ASCO. This algorithm uses instances, concepts, relations, and the structure of hierarchy of concepts/relations that can be extracted from ontologies. Three main steps are used by this proposal: linguistic matching, structural matching and mapping generation. The first one uses a set of similarity functions to compare names, labels and descriptions of classes. In particular, in the description part, information retrieval techniques are used to determine if two classes are similar. Besides, to find synonyms, WordNet is required. Then, only one result is produced by combining all last results. If this value exceeds a threshold a mapping between these classes is added. The second step, structural mapping, analyzes the concepts in a hierarchy by building a graph structure and compares them by using graph similarity techniques [10].

The work presented in [3] proposes a methodology for ontology merging. The main idea of this proposal is to reconcile a large number of closely related, domain specific ontologies. The scenario is a large number of small ontologies. Two types of information are used to compare the ontologies: syntactic and semantic. The syntactic information analyses the names of the classes by using string-matching techniques. The semantic information uses WordNet to find synonyms. Thus, this step can find mappings which would not have been found using the syntactic information.

The implicit information obtained from both the context and the linguistic process is the main difference between our method and the approaches cited here. This information allows to find more correct mappings even those involving 1-N and N-1 matches. In general, the approaches take advantage of all information ontologies provide but they only deal with 1-1 matches such as person=human. By extending the filtering techniques proposed by [7], our method is able to find complex matches such as those presented in this paper. Therefore, in our ASeMatch method all the information that can be extracted from the ontologies is combined with NLP tools in order to find more suitable matchings.

5   Conclusions and Future Works

Using richer semantic resources with PLN tools is crucial to improve semantic heterogeneity problems. In this paper, we have presented an approach to semi-automatically enrich the semantic matching between two ontologies by finding complex mappings such as those involving $1-N$ and $N-1$ matchings.

The advantage of our proposal is clear: we improve the semantic matching between two ontologies by adding linguistic techniques and the MCR definition. However, our matching process still needs improvement to be able to compare other elements of the ontologies, such as classes; and aspects like performance and complexity should be analyzed. We are currently working on an implementation of our method in order to evaluate these aspects.

References

1. Le, B.T., Dieng-Kuntz, R., Gandon, F.: On ontology matching problems for building a corporate semantic web in a multi-communities organization. In: ICEIS 2004 Software Agents and Internet Computing. (2004) 236–243.
2. Giunchiglia, F., Yatskevich, M., Giunchiglia, E.: Efficient semantic matching. In: Gómez-Pérez, A., Euzenat, J., Eds.: ESWC 2005. Volume LNCS 3532, Springer-Verlag (2005) 272–289.
3. Stephens, L., Gangam, A., Huhns, M.: Constructing Consensus Ontologies for the Semantic Web: A Conceptual Approach. In: World Wide Web: Internet and Web Information Systems. Number 7, Kluwer Academic Publishers (2004) 421–442.
4. Richardson, R., Smeaton, A.: Using wordnet in a knowledge-based approach to information retrieval. Technical Report CA-0395, Dublin City Univ., School of Computer Applications, Dublin, Ireland (1995).
5. Buccella, A., Cechich, A., Brisaboa, N.R.: A federated layer to integrate heterogeneous knowledge. In: VODCA '04 First Int. Workshop on Views on Designing Complex Architectures, Bertinoro, Italy, Electronic Notes in Theoretical Computer Science, Elsevier Science B.V (2004) 101–118.
6. Buccella, A., Cechich, A., Brisaboa, N.R.: A three-level approach to ontology merging. In: MICAI '05: Fourth Mexican International Conference on Artificial Intelligence, Monterrey, México, LNCS 3789 of Springer-Verlag (2005) 80–89.
7. Magnini, B., Speranza, M., Girardi, G.: A semantic-based approach to interoperability of classification. hierarchies: Evaluation of linguistic techniques. In: Proceeding of COLING 2004, Geneva, Switzerland (2004).
8. Rodríguez, M.A., Egenhofer, M.J.: Determining semantic similarity among entity classes from different ontologies. IEEE Transactions on Knowledge and Data Engineering 15 (2003) 442–456.
9. Tversky, A.: Features of similarity. Psychological Review 84 (1977) 327–352.
10. Dieng, R., Hug, S.: Comparison of personal ontologies represented through conceptual graphs. In: Proceedings of the ECAI '98 – 13th European Conference on Artificial Intelligent, Brigthon, UK (1998) 341–345.

Extensive Study on
Automatic Verb Sense Disambiguation in Czech

Jiří Semecký and Petr Podveský

Institute of Formal and Applied Linguistics
Malostranské náměstí 25, 11800 Prague, Czech Republic
semecky@ufal.mff.cuni.cz, podvesky@ufal.mff.cuni.cz

Abstract. In this paper we compare automatic methods for disambiguation of verb senses, in particular we investigate Naïve Bayes classifier, decision trees, and a rule-based method. Different types of features are proposed, including morphological, syntax-based, idiomatic, animacy, and WordNet-based features. We evaluate the methods together with individual feature types on two essentially different Czech corpora, VALEVAL and the Prague Dependency Treebank. The best performing methods and features are discussed.

1 Introduction

Verb sense disambiguation (VSD) is an interesting and challenging problem of assigning the right sense to a given verb according to context. VSD aims at selecting the right sense using surrounding words or, perhaps, a thorough analysis of larger context. Verbs are usually central elements of sentences, therefore, the key aspect in determining the meaning of the whole sentence is a proper analysis of the verb sense. A verb can have several senses, for example in Czech the verb *dodat* can mean *to supply* or *to add*. VSD can also help in improving other NLP tasks, such as machine translation, information retrieval, etc.

Previous experiments on VSD have been already reported in the literature, e.g. [1] and [2] studied English VSD; initial experiments on Czech VSD have been also published [3]. Related problems are studied in the Curpus Pattern Analysis project http://nlp.fi.muni.cz/projekty/cpa/ and in [4].

In this paper we focus on automatic VSD methods. We propose novel elaborate features and employ them in standard automatic classifiers. We evaluate our approach on two corpora.

The paper is divided as follows. Section 2 introduces the corpora and lexicons that we used in our experiments. Section 3 describes the proposed features in detail. Section 4 covers the machine learning methods which we used for VSD. In Section 5, we summarize and evaluate achieved results.

2 Data

In this section we describe corpora which were used throughout our experiments. We worked with two corpora VALEVAL and the Prague Dependency Treebank 2.0. Verb senses are not directly annotated in the corpora, instead, the verbs are annotated with valency frames. The valency lexicon which was used for annotation of VALEVAL was VALLEX version 1.0 [3].

Petr Sojka, Ivan Kopeček and Karel Pala (Eds.): TSD 2006, LNAI 4188, pp. 237–244, 2006.

Table 1. Corpora statistics after parsing and cleaning

	# unique verbs	# annotated running verbs	Ø running verbs per verb	Ø senses per running verb
VALEVAL	109	7,779	71.4	4.58
PDT	1,636	67,015	41.0	14.8

The valency frame annotation of PDT corpus was done according to valency lexicon PDT-VALLEX. Verb valency frames are closely related to verb senses. In addition, in the valency lexicons, different verb senses even with the same configuration of syntactical constituents are labeled with two different frames. For example the verb *chovat* with accusative object have in Czech two different meanings: *cuddle*, and *breed*. In both valency lexicons, the two meanings are described by two different frames. As there is no straightforward procedure to determine the verb reflexivity, Verbs with reflexive particles are assumed to be variants of the main verb.

VALEVAL. VALEVAL contains randomly selected sentences from the Czech National Corpus [5]. 109 representative verbs were chosen to form VALEVAL. For each verb, 100 sentences were selected from the Czech National Corpus to constitute VALEVAL. For more details about the verb selection, see [6].

The corpus was independently annotated by three annotators. The inter-annotator agreement of all three annotators was 66.8%, the average pairwise match was 74.8%. Sentences on which the three annotators disagreed were double-checked by an expert who determined the correct annotation. Sentences with an obvious mistake were corrected.

To prepare the data for subsequent feature extraction, we automatically parsed the sentences using Charniak's syntactic parser [7]. The parser was trained on the Prague Dependency Treebank [8]. Some sentences could not be parsed due to their enormous length. Such long sentences were excluded from our corpus yielding the total number of 7,779 parsed sentences. In the parsed corpus, a verb occured 71.4 times in average, ranging from a single occurrence to 100 occurrences. The average number of senses per verb was 4.58, the average was computed over the corpus.

Prague Dependency Treebank 2.0 (PDT). PDT is a large corpus of manually annotated Czech data with linguistically rich information. PDT is based on the theory of Functional Generative Description [9]. It contains three layers of annotation – morphological, analytical, and tectogrammatical. We worked only with the tectogrammatically annotated part of the corpus. It contains about 800 thousand words. The verb frame annotation was done according to the PDT-VALLEX lexicon.

We automatically parsed PDT using the MST parser [10] trained on PDT using deleted interpolation. The tectogrammatical annotations were done only by one annotator, therefore the PDT data may be more biased than VALEVAL corpus. We excluded verbs which were only present either in the training set or in the testing set. This resulted in 67,015 annotated verbs occurences. For training we used the *train* portion of PDT which was comprised of 58,304 sentences. For testing we used so-called *dtest* portion which had 8,711 sentences. The number of unique verbs was 1,636. There were 41.0 occurrences of verb in average, ranging from two occurrences (one in each part of data) to 11,345 occurrences (for the verb *být*).

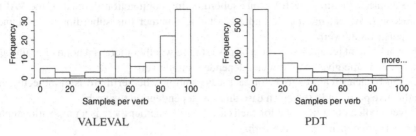

Fig. 1. Distributions of the number of samples per lemma

Table 1 summarizes the basic statistics of the corpora. Figure 1 shows distribution of the number of verb occurences in VALEVAL and PDT corpora respectively.

3   Features

Features are essential to any automatic classification method. Each occurrence of a verb in a context is described by a vector of features. Based on this feature vector, a verb sense is assigned. Features reflect various information about the context of a verb. We worked only with features with context confined to the actual sentence. No information behind sentence boundary was considered. We experimented with five types of features, namely morphological features, syntax-based features, idiomatic features, animacy features, and WordNet-based features. In the following paragraphs, we thoroughly describe each group of features.

3.1   Morphological Features

Morphological features are reliably estimated, and easy to obtain. Czech positional morphology [11] uses tags with 15 positions, out of which we used first 12 positions. Each position expresses one morphological category: part of speech, detailed part of speech, gender, number, case, possessor's gender, possessor's number, person, tense, grade, negation and voice. Categories which are not relevant for a given word are assigned a special void value.

We introduced one feature for each possition of the current verb tag. Moreover, we added tag features for two preceding words, and two following words. Thus we obtained 60 morphological features (5 words times 12 features).

3.2   Syntax-Based Features

We believe that syntax can capture deeper relation crucial to sense disambiguation, therefore we added the following features based on syntax:

- Two boolean features stating whether there is a pronoun *se* or *si* dependent on the verb.
- One boolean feature stating whether the verb depends on another verb.
- One boolean feature stating whether there is a subordinate verb dependent on the verb.

- Six boolean features, each for one subordinating conjunction defined in the VALLEX lexicon (*aby, at', až, jak, že* and *zda*) stating whether this subordinating conjunction depends on the verb.
- Seven boolean features, one for each case stating whether there is a noun or a substantive pronoun in the given case directly dependent on the verb.
- Seven boolean features, one for each case stating whether there is an adjective or an adjective pronoun in the given case directly dependent on the verb.
- Seven boolean features, one for each case stating whether there is a prepositional phrase in this case dependent on the verb.
- 69 boolean features, one for each possible combination of preposition and case stating whether there is the given preposition in the given case directly dependent on the verb.

All together we proposed 100 syntax-based features.

3.3 Idiomatic Features

Idiomatic constructions can alter verb sense. We extracted a single boolean feature for each idiomatic expression defined in the VALLEX lexicon. We set the value of the corresponding feature to *true* if all words of the idiomatic expression occurred anywhere in the sentence contiguously. Features corresponding to idiomatic expressions which did not occure in the sentence were set to *false*. In total we obtained 118 idiomatic features.

3.4 Animacy

We partially determined animacy of nouns and pronouns in the sentence using information from lemmatization and morphological analysis. We introduced seven boolean features, one for each case, stating whether there is an animate noun or pronoun in this case syntactically dependent on the verb. Moreover, we introduced another seven boolean features stating the same information for animate nouns and pronouns anywhere in the sentence. Together we obtained 14 features for animacy.

3.5 WordNet Features

Dependency of a certain lemma or a certain type of lemma on a verb can imply its particular sense. We described the type of a lemma in terms of WordNet [12] classes.

In the first step, we used the definition of WordNet top ontology [13] to obtain a tree-like hierarchy of 64 classes. Then, for each lemma captured in the definition of the top ontology, we used the WordNet **Inter-Lingual-Index** to map English lemmas to the Czech EuroWordNet [14], extracting all Czech lemmas belonging to the top level classes. We ended up with 1,564 Czech lemmas associated to the WordNet top-level classes. Moreover, if a lemma was mapped to a class, it belonged also to all the predecessors of the class.

In the second step, we used the relation of **hyperonymy** in the Czech EuroWordNet to determine the top-level class for other nouns as well. We followed the relation of hyperonymy transitively until we reached a lemma assigned in the first step. As we worked with the lemmas instead of synsets, one lemma could be mapped to many top-level classes.

For each top level class we created one feature telling whether a noun belonging to this class is directly dependent on the verb, and one feature telling whether such noun is present anywhere in the sentence. This resulted into 128 WordNet class features.

Table 2. Types of features. The column "#Used features" indicates the number of features used in the decision trees. The column "Relative weight" indicates the weight based on the feature occurrences in the decision trees.

Feature type	#Features	VALEVAL		PDT	
		#Features used	Relative weight [%]	#Features used	Relative weight [%]
Morphological	60	27	35.92	44	45.37
Syntax-based	100	23	46.28	39	30.76
Idiomatic	118	3	0.85	16	1.20
Animacy	14	8	5.25	9	3.12
WordNet	128	44	11.70	92	19.55
Total	**420**	**105**	**100**	**200**	**100**

4 Methods

To disambiguate verb senses, we tried several machine learning methods: Naïve Bayes classifier, decision trees, and a rule-based method.

Naïve Bayes is a straightforward probabilistic classifier based on an assumption that features are independent of each other. We did not expect this classifier to perform very well but rather use it for a direct comparison.

Decision tree is an algorithm based on the *divide and conquer* principle. It finds the most discriminative feature, and divides the training data into groups according to feature's possible values. The procedure is applied recursively for each group which results in a tree of decisions. Nodes of the tree represent tests on feature values.The decision tree divides the feature space into disjunctive parts. We tried two different implementations of the decision tree algorithms, namely Christian Borgelt's implementation of decision trees [15] (using information gain ratio as the attribute selection measure), and the comercial toolkit C5.0 [16], which implements an improved version of the C4.5 algorithm.

The rule-based classifier generates a set of independent *if-then* rules. Conditions of the rules may overlap, in which case the rules have to compete to reach the verdict. We used rule-based classifier implemented in the C5.0 toolkit which constructs the rules from the decision trees. Therefore, the results of the two methods are strongly correlated. However, the final classifier might differ from the C5.0 decision tree classifier.

5 Results

5.1 Baseline of Frame Disambiguation

As a baseline we chose the most common frame according to the relative frequency. The baseline is computed individually for each verb. For VALEVAL corpus, we computed the baseline using 10-fold cross-validation. Then, we weighed baselines of individual verbs by the relative frequency as observed in the Czech National Corpus. The weighted baseline was 60.7%.

For PDT, we acquired the most common frame from the training data and measured the baseline on the testing data. The baseline was 73.2%.

5.2 Evaluation

We tested performance of classifiers on both corpora using each feature type separately. We also experimented with different combinations of feature types. Table 3 states accuracy for VALEVAL and PDT corpus, respectively. The table shows that the syntactic features performed best among individual feature types. Morphological features turned out to be the second best. On VALEVAL, we achieved the best with the full feature set. On PDT, the best accuracy was achieved using combination of morphological, syntax-based and idiomatic features.

For VALEVAL it was 77.06% over the baseline of 60.7%. For PDT it was 79.28% over the baseline of 73.2%.

To compare individual features, we computed scores which represent importance of the features in the constructed decision trees. We summed the number of applications of features weighted by the 0.5-based exponent of the level in which they occurred (i.e. 1 for root, 0.5 for the first level, 0.25 for the second level, . . .). Table 4 shows the features with the highest weights on PDT corpus. Syntax-based features were used most often for important decisions. From the total amount of 420 features, 105 features were used in VALEVAL corpus, and 200 features were used in PDT corpus. Details can be seen in Table 2.

6   Conclusion

We have compared performance of different machine learning methods for automatic verb sense disambiguation on two qualitatively and quantitatively different corpora. We have investigated performance of various feature types describing local context of annotated verbs. Syntax-based features have shown to be the most effective of all feature types.

Table 3. Accuracy [%] of the frame disambiguation task for PDT corpus. Columns in the table correspond to individual disambiguation methods – Naïve Bayes classifier (NBC), Borgelt's implementation of decision trees (dtree), C5 decision trees (C5-DT), and C5 rule-based classifier (C5-RB).

Type of features	VALEVAL				PDT			
	NBC	dtree	C5-DT	C5-RB	NBC	dtree	C5-DT	C5-RB
baseline	60.7				73.2			
Morphological (M)	61.62	59.81	65.66	66.48	74.42	75.26	75.73	75.86
Syntax-based (S)	69.98	69.34	70.70	70.68	78.64	78.76	79.08	79.04
Animacy (A)	52.87	59.86	62.62	62.49	71.61	72.82	73.50	73.53
Idiomatic (I)	60.89	60.21	60.86	61.03	73.77	73.71	73.55	73.54
WordNet (W)	45.32	53.62	60.95	59.67	68.97	71.53	72.52	72.68
M + S	63.52	60.25	68.81	68.97	76.16	76.13	78.85	78.96
M + I	61.65	59.81	67.66	67.96	74.39	75.31	76.09	76.23
M + W	62.03	59.87	67.58	66.26	74.70	75.15	74.92	75.34
S + W	59.37	60.85	70.94	70.86	76.00	77.41	78.10	78.28
M + S + I	63.52	60.25	68.00	70.07	76.40	76.23	79.19	79.28
M + S + A	63.13	58.19	70.64	69.37	76.21	75.94	78.92	79.08
M + S + W	64.80	60.28	76.69	77.03	76.44	76.01	78.37	78.91
M + S + I + W	64.78	60.28	76.86	77.16	76.55	76.10	78.82	79.20
M + S + A + W	64.59	58.36	76.35	77.03	76.25	75.93	78.21	78.72
M + S + A + I + W	64.58	58.36	77.06	77.21	76.47	76.02	78.58	79.08

Table 4. Features most often chosen in the decision trees on PDT

Feature type	Feature description	Weight
Syntax-based	Presence of reflexive particle *se* dependent on the verb	291.0
Syntax-based	Presence of noun or a subst. pron. in dative dep. on the verb	64.6
Syntax-based	Presence of reflexive particle *si* dependent on the verb	61.7
Morphological	Detailed part of speech of the word following the verb	56.8
Syntax-based	Presence of preposition *do* with genitive dependent on the verb	39.8
Morphological	Detailed part of speech of the word two possitions after the verb	36.6
Syntax-based	Presence of noun or a subst. pron. in accusative dep. on the verb	36.3
Syntax-based	Presence of preposition in dative dependent on the verb	35.1
Syntax-based	Presence of noun or a subst. pron. in nominative dep. on the verb	34.6
Syntax-based	Presence of preposition *na* with accusative dependent on the verb	32.1

Acknowledgement

The research reported in this paper has been partially supported by the project of Information Society No. 1ET101470416, the grants of the Grant Agency of the Charles University No. 372/2005/A-INF/MFF and 375/2005/A-INF/MFF, and the grant MSM0021620838.

References

1. Dang, H.T., Palmer, M.: The Role of Semantic Roles in Disambiguating Verb Senses. In: Proceedings of ACL, Ann Arbor MI (2005).
2. Ye, P.: Selectional Preferenced Based Verb Sense Disambiguation Using WordNet. In: Australasian Language Technology Workshop 2004, Australia (2004) pp. 155–162.
3. Lopatková, M., Bojar, O., Semecký, J., Benešová, V., Žabokrtský, Z.: Valency Lexicon of Czech Verbs VALLEX: Recent Experiments with Frame Disambiguation. In: 8th International Conference on TSD. (2005) pp. 99–106.
4. Král, R.: Jaký to má význam? Ph.D. thesis, Masaryk University (2004).
5. Kocek, J., Kopřivová, M., Kučera, K., eds.: Czech National Corpus - introduction and user handbook (in Czech). FF UK - ÚČNK, Prague (2000).
6. Bojar, O., Semecký, J., Benešová, V.: VALEVAL: Testing VALLEX Consistency and Experimenting with Word-Frame Disambiguation. Prague Bulletin of Mathematical Linguistics **83** (2005).
7. Charniak, E.: A Maximum-Entropy-Inspired Parser. In: Proceedings of NAACL-2000, Seattle, Washington, USA (2000) pp. 132–139.
8. Hajič, J.: Building a Syntactically Annotated Corpus: The Prague Dependency Treebank. Issues of Valency and Meaning (1998) pp. 106–132.
9. Sgall, P., Hajičová, E., Panevová, J.: The Meaning of the Sentence in its Semantic and Pragmatic Aspects. Academia, Prague, Czech Republic/Reidel Publishing Company, Dordrecht, Netherlands (1986).
10. McDonald, R., Pereira, F., Ribarov, K., Hajic, J.: Non-Projective Dependency Parsing using Spanning Tree Algorithms. In: Proceedings of HLT Conference and Conference on EMNLP, Vancouver, Canada, ACL (2005) pp. 523–530.
11. Hajič, J.: Morphological Tagging: Data vs. Dictionaries. In: Proceedings of ANLP-NAACL Conference, Seattle, Washington, USA (2000) pp. 94–101.
12. Fellbaum, C.: WordNet An Electronic Lexical Database. The MIT Press (1998).

13. Vossen, P., Bloksma, L., Rodriguez, H., Climent, S., Calzolari, N., Roventini, A., Bertagna, F., Alonge, A., Peters, W.: The EuroWordNet Base Concepts and Top Ontology. Technical report (1997).
14. Pala, K., Smrž, P.: Building Czech Wordnet. Romanian Journal of Information Science and Technology **7** (2004) pp. 79–88.
15. Borgelt, C.: A Decision Tree Plug-In for DataEngine. In: Proceedings of 2nd Data Analysis Symposium, Aachen, Germany, MIT GmbH (1998).
16. Quinlan, J.R.: Data Mining Tools See5 and C5.0 (2005) http://www.rulequest.com/see5-info.html.

Semantic Representation of Events:
Building a Semantic Primes Component

Milena Slavcheva

Bulgarian Academy of Sciences
Institute for Parallel Information Processing
Linguistic Modeling Department
25A, Acad. G. Bonchev St., 1113 Sofia, Bulgaria
milena@lml.bas.bg

Abstract. This paper describes a system of semantic primes necessary for the large-scale semantic representation of event types, encoded as verbal predicates. The system of semantic primes is compiled via mapping modeling elements of the Natural Semantic Metalanguage (NSM), the Semantic Minimum - Dictionary of Bulgarian (SMD), and the Role and Reference Grammar (RRG). The so developed system of semantic primes is a user-defined extension to the metalanguage, adopted in the Unified Eventity Representation (UER), a graphical formalism, introducing the object-oriented design to linguistic semantics.

Keywords: event types, metamodel, verbal predicates.

1 Introduction

The systematic semantic representation of events, encoded as verbal predicates in natural language, requires the definition of that layer of the metamodel inheritance structure, which is necessary for building the specified semantic descriptors of the lexically encoded predicates, that is, the descriptors that constitute the genuine entries in a semantic lexicon. This paper presents a user-defined extension to the semantic metalanguage, adopted in the Unified Eventity Representation (UER) [4], a graphical formalism, introducing the object-oriented system design to linguistic semantics. The extension fosters the systematic semantic representation of verbal predicates in Bulgarian, providing for the specification of the generalized EVENTITY FRAME diagrams built for certain semantic verb classes [5]. A system of semantic primes is developed which serves modeling elements belonging to the dynamic core (i.e., state-machines) and the static periphery (i.e., PARTICIPANT CLASSES) of the EVENTITY FRAMES of verbal predicates. The system of semantic primes is compiled via mapping modeling elements belonging to extensively worked out semantic resources. The basic source for compiling the inventory of the semantic primes is a Semantic Minimum Dictionary (SMD) [3], which provides the semantic nucleus of the lexical system in Bulgarian. The categorization of semantic primes provided in the Natural Semantic Metalanguage (NSM) [2] is reformulated and adapted to the UER conceptual representation. Basic modeling principles are borrowed from the logical structure of predicates and the hierarchy of semantic roles of Role and Reference Grammar (RRG) [6,7]. The extended metalanguage is tested in the semantic representation of causative and decausative verb pairs,

Petr Sojka, Ivan Kopeček and Karel Pala (Eds.): TSD 2006, LNAI 4188, pp. 245–252, 2006.

whose generic EVENTITY FRAME TEMPLATES [5] are specified through the inclusion of the respective layer in the metamodel.

2 Basic Modeling Elements

The central concept of the UER framework is defined as an *eventity* [4] and is represented by an EVENTITY FRAME diagram, which contains a *dynamic core* and a *static periphery*. The dynamic core is a state chart depicting the state-transition system of the conceptualized actions. The static periphery includes representation of the participants, their properties and relations. The participants' specifications refer to PARTICIPANT CLASSES whose properties are described in sets of ATTRIBUTES [4]. Figure 1 provides a generic EVENTITY FRAME diagram (an octagon container) of a prototypical causative verbal predicate from which a decausative counterpart is derived. The rectangles in the upper part of the octagon belong to the static periphery of the EVENTITY FRAME and provide information for the two prominent participants, whose semantic roles are specified as Agent and Patient respectively, and whose ontological categories (the PARTICIPANT TYPES) are Individual and Ineventity respectively. The PARTICIPANT TYPES are referenced to the present UER participant ontology[4]. In the lower rectangle of the Agent compartment the eligible participant is specified as "animate" - that is the value of the ATTRIBUTE named *ani* which is of the data type Animacy. The PARTICIPATE ASSOCIATIONS (relating the PARTICIPANT CLASSES to the dynamic core, notated by a dashed line) are specified via STEREOTYPES (<<do>> and <<undergo>>) as the two prototypical semantic roles (i.e., macroroles, role archetypes) *proto-agent* (*actor*) and *proto-patient* (*undergoer*). The dynamic core (the dashed-outline rectangle with rounded corners) depicts the state-machines and the causation interaction (via the cause-SIGNAL) between the prominent participants, each one of which has its own SWIMLANE (indicated by the solid vertical line separating the dashed-outline rectangle with rounded corners). The left SWIMLANE belongs to the Agent, and its state-machine is interpreted as follows. At some point in time the Agent, being in an unspecified Active Simple State (ASS) sends a cause-SIGNAL, notated by the solid arrow crossing the borderline and entering the right SWIMLANE belonging to the Patient. The cause-SIGNAL triggers a transition of the second participant from an unspecified source state to a parameterized target state which in this case is generalized as being a Passive Simple State (PSS). The dash-outline rectangle in the upper right corner of the octagon indicates that the EVENTITY FRAME is a TEMPLATE which has a parameter to be bound.

Generic EVENTITY FRAME diagrams are provided for several semantic classes of verbs as a step in the initial semantic distribution of verbal predicates [5]. However, in order to build a real-world lexical semantic application, it is necessary to specify the semantic descriptors by integrating some sort of an expanded system of semantic primes into the UER architecture.

3 Sources of Semantic Primes

The Natural Semantic Metalanguage (NSM) is a well-known framework attempting to provide a small list of universal semantic primes, arranged in categories. The NSM list of semantic primes is not directly usable due to the following reasons: 1) it is too small; 2) it is

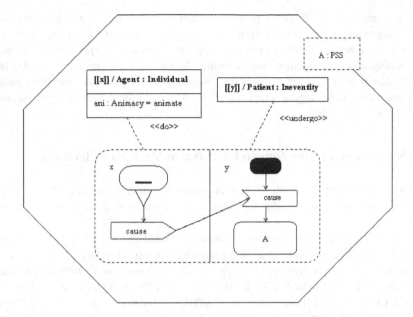

Fig. 1. Generic transitive EVENTITY FRAME

a static list of predefined semantic words; 3) the sematic words are organized in categories which do not fit the underlying conceptual categorization of the UER.

The Semantic Minimum Dictionary (SMD) consists of 905 semantic words, selected as the result of iterated mapping of lists of free word associations and taxonomies [3]. The semantic words are organized according to two principles: 1) the semantic words are ordered alphabetically and supplied with natural language definitions composed so that to include only semantic words of the SMD inventory itself; 2) the semantic words are organized in lexical-semantic fields.

The advantages of the SMD in view of the present semantic representation are: 1) it is declared to include the necessary and sufficient semantic units of the core of the lexical system of Bulgarian; 2) it is dynamic because, on one hand, it can serve as a dynamic supplier of inventories of semantic primes for different applications, and on the other hand, it, itself, can be expanded in a principled way.

The disadvantages of the SMD for the present semantic representation are the following: 1) the categorization of the semantic words does not fit the UER conceptual organization: it has to be adjusted; 2) it is necessary to further formalize the semantic dictionary so that to incorporate it in the UER framework.

Role and Reference Grammar (RRG) provides a system of lexical decomposition of verbal predicates combined with an *Aktionsart*-based classification of verbal predicates, represented in logical structures of the form

1) **predicate'**(x) or (x,y)
2) **BECOME predicate'**(x) or (x,y) [6]

At the same time, the RRG is a provider of semantic roles viewed as relational elements augmenting, with variable granularity, the predicate-argument structure of eventities.

While it can be viewed as a theoretical supporter of basic concepts in the UER, as well as a supplier of specifying modeling elements, the RRG has its drawbacks: 1) it is highly configurational in view of the semantic decomposition of the predicates and the positioning of the arguments in the logical structures; 2) at the same time the inventory of elementary predicates is too arbitrary.

4   User-Defined Extensions to UER Basic Modeling Elements

The UER provides the top-level of the metamodel inheritance structure. The user-defined extensions, necessary for specific applications, are introduced at the lower levels of the metamodel.

Let us consider the basic modeling elements included in the EVENTITY FRAMES in view of their possible augmentation with specifying semantic elements.

SIMPLE STATES are basic eventity types in the UER metamodel inheritance structure, which are subdivided into PASSIVE SIMPLE STATES (PSS) and ACTIVE SIMPLE STATES (ASS). The ACTIVE SIMPLE STATES are further subdivided into ACTIVITY STATES and ACT STATES depending on the concept of durative or transient action respectively. In Figure 1 the STATES are parameterized or unspecified and are used in a generalized semantic description. If we would like to describe an extensive subset of specific verbal predicates, we have to provide names and properties for the STATES according to our naive conception of the world [1]. The definition of new STEREOTYPES is a UER mechanism for subtyping and specification of characteristics of the UER constructs. It should be noted, that a number of stereotypes and keywords are already predefined in the UER [4], but a further specification of feature clusters is desirable for the systematic large-scale semantic representation of verbal predicates. Thus through the mapping of NSM categories, SMD semantic words and RRG logical predicates, classes of semantic primes are defined as libraries supplying the STATE and TRANSITION objects. The mapping can be summarized as follows.

The NSM categories of **Mental predicates**; **Speech**; **Actions, events, movements**; **Existence and possession**; **Life and death** are mapped onto the relevant SMD elements, drawn from the inventory of 159 semantic words in the form of verbs (e.g., *take, put, say, move, feel, perceive*, etc.), and also from the rest semantic words which serve as non-verbal predicates.

The NSM categories of **Evaluators**, **Descriptors** and **Space** are mapped onto the SMD supply of semantic elements consisting of the sum of 96 semantic words in the form of adjectives (e.g., *full, empty, wet, dry, clean, dirty*, etc.) and 31 semantic words in the form of adverbs (e.g., *up, down, in, out*, etc). The semantic elements name STATES and their PROPERTIES.

The RRG logical structures provide a semantic decomposition system, whose significance is twofold. On one side, basic semantic predicates can be borrowed (e.g., BECOME, SEMELFACTIVE) or defined by analogy (e.g., BEGIN, END), on the other side, decomposed semantic predicates are provided which enhance the system of nesting of eventities modeled in the UER by the inclusion of subcore eventities in the dynamic core of eventities.

For instance, a great number of STATES are related to **Psyche**, which can be subtyped in the STEREOTYPES **Mind** and **Emotion**, having their PROPERTIES in the form '{*'name'* '=' *value-expression* '}'. The rectangle below represents the CLASS notation for **Psyche**.

```
<<metaclass>>
Psyche
```

The next combination of rectangle compartments is the CLASS notation of the **Emotion** STEREOTYPE of **Psyche**.

```
<<stereotype>>
Emotion
Properties
mood:Enumeration
isIntense:Boolean
```

An ENUMERATION is a user-defined primitive data type. The next combination of rectangle compartments is the CLASS notation for the ENUMERATION of **Mood**, which is a PROPERTY of **Emotion**.

```
<<enumeration>>
Mood
joy
pleasure
calmness
sadness
anguish
```

The rest of this section presents the user-defined extensions to the other basic modeling elements.

The NSM **Substantives** are represented in the UER PARTICIPANT TYPES. The SMD semantic words usable in this category are the names of the semantic fields (e.g. *man, body, nature*, etc.) The semantic elements borrowed from the SMD are incorporated as the bottom-level elements in a participant ontology whose top-level hierarchy is predefined in the UER. When necessary semantic words from the full inventory of substantives can be selected as PARTICIPANT OBJECTS.

The NSM **Determiners** and **Similarity** categories are represented in the UER AT-TRIBUTES, ASSOCIATIONS and CONSTRAINTS, which model the relations among eventity participants. The respective SMD semantic words fill in the set of this category (e.g., *whole, separate, mutual*, etc).

The NSM categories of **Quantifiers** and **Intensifier, augmentor** are represented by PROPERTIES and CONSTRAINTS employed in UER modeling elements. The respective SMD semantic words for this category are selected (e.g., *only, more, enough*, etc.).

The NSM **Time** category corresponds to the UER EVENTS as triggers of TRANSITIONS or actions of the OBJECTS. The relevant set of semantic primes is filled in by the SMD inventory of semantic words in the form of adverbs (e.g. *before, after, early, late*, etc.)

250   M. Slavcheva

The NSM category of **Logical concepts** is represented by UER STEREOTYPES which apply to different modeling elements, for example, to EVENTS, STATES or TRANSITIONS. The semantic primes are drawn from a set of SMD sematic words like *must, can*, etc.

The NSM **Taxonomy, partonomy** category is represented by the AGGREGATION relationship between eventity participants, that is, relations like meronomy, attachment, possession. The relation is represented by the corresponding UER graphical notation including PROPERTY specifications.

RRG provides a hierarchy of thematic relations of the predicate arguments ranging from verb-specific semantic roles (e.g., *Speaker, Dancer, Thinker, Heard, Located*) to the two semantic macroroles *actor* and *undergoer* (which represent the STEREOTYPES of the PARTICIPATE ASSOCIATION in the UER eventity models (cf. Figure 1). The middle layer of abstraction contains five thematic relations (i.e., *Agent, Effector, Location, Patient, Theme*), which are positioned on a continuum, depending on the degree of "agent-ness", "volition" of the eventity participants.

Figure 2 represents an EVENTITY FRAME diagram of the OPRAZNJA-eventity ('TURN EMPTY'-eventity). The *Instigator* semantic role of the left participant is the supertype of the volitional **Agent** or non-volitional **Effector**, either of which can be instantiated [4]. The **Agent** and the **Effector** occupy the last and the last-but-one position respectively at the "agentivity" end of the continuum of thematic relation classes.

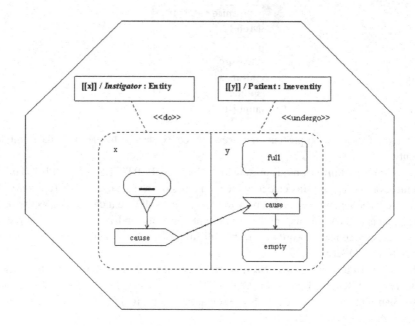

Fig. 2. Specified causative EVENTITY FRAME - OPRAZNJA-eventity

Figure 3 represents the EVENTITY FRAME diagram of the OPRAZNJA SE-eventity ('EMPTY-BY-ITSELF'-eventity). It models the decausative verbal predicate derived from the causative verbal predicate depicted in Figure 2.

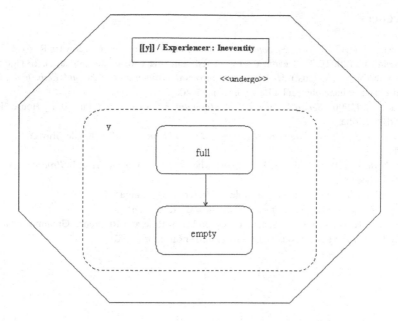

Fig. 3. Specified decausative EVENTITY FRAME - OPRAZNJA SE-eventity

In the derived decausative, the **Patient** becomes the focus of the activity: it becomes the only prominent participant and its prototypical semantic role is transformed to that of an **Experiencer**. On the RRG continuum of thematic relations, the **Experiencer** role occupies a middle position between the Agent and Patient extremities.

5   Discussion and Further Development

The UER formalism provides the possibility to capture variable granularity of the semantic description. The UER metamodel with its multiple layers of abstraction guarantees the deployment of a type hierarchy and makes use of the distinction between type and instance. The generalization mechanism is a fundamental one and allows the user to adjust the granularity of the linguistic modeling depending on the application requirements. Thus user-defined extensions to the semantic modeling constructs can be developed, which are necessary for the systematic semantic representation of language objects in real-world applications.

At present the user-defined extension to the UER semantic metalanguage has been applied in building specific EVENTITY FRAME diagrams of 120 pairs of causative and decausative Bulgarian verbal predicates. Using the inventory of semantic primes described in the previous sections, difficulties arise in the decision-making related to the granularity of semantic primes naming SIMPLE STATES, as well as to the nesting of subeventities in the state-machines. The next step is to expand the set of semantic descriptors of events utilizable in knowledge-driven systems.

References

1. Apresjan, J. D. (1974). *Lexical Semantics*. Nauka Publishing House, Moscow (in Russian).
2. Goddard, C. (2002). The search for the shared semantic core of all languages. In Goddard, C. and Wierzbicka, A. (eds.) *Meaning and Universal Grammar. Theory and Empirical Findings*. Amsterdam/Philadelphia: John Benjamins, pp. 5–40.
3. Kasabov, I. (1990). *Semantic Dictionary - Minimum*. Sofia University Publishing House "Kliment Ohridski", Sofia.
4. Schalley, A. C. (2004). *Cognitive Modeling and Verbal Semantics*. Mouton de Gruyter, Berlin - New York.
5. Slavcheva, M. (2006). Semantic Descriptors: The Case of Reflexive Verbs. In *Proceedings of LREC 2006*, Genoa, Italy.
6. Van Valin, R. D., Jr. A Summary of Role and Reference Grammar. http://linguistics.buffalo.edu/research/rrg.html.
7. Van Valin, R. D., Jr. (2002). Semantic Macroroles in Role and Reference Grammar. Manuscript, http://linguistics.buffalo.edu/research/rrg.html.

Cascaded Grammatical Relation-Driven Parsing Using Support Vector Machines

Songwook Lee

Division of Computer and Information Engineering, Dongseo University,
san69-1 Jurye-Dong, Sasang-Gu, Busan, 617-716, Korea
leesw@dongseo.ac.kr

Abstract. This study aims to identify dependency structure in Korean sentences with the cascaded chunking strategy. In the first stages of the cascade, we find chunks of NP and guess grammatical relations (GRs) using Support Vector Machine (SVM) classifiers for every possible modifier-head pairs of chunks in terms of GR categories as subject, object, complement, adverbial, and etc. In the next stage, we filter out incorrect modifier-head relations in each cascade for its corresponding GR using the SVM classifiers and the characteristics of the Korean language such as distance, no-crossing and case property. Through an experiment with a tree and GR tagged corpus for training the proposed parser, we achieved an overall accuracy of 85.7% on average.

1 Introduction

Dependency structure representing head-modifier relations with grammatical relations (GRs) in sentences is useful for most text analysis systems in applications such as information retrieval, information extraction, text summarization, and question answering.

For identifying dependency structure in a Korean sentence, we are faced with two kinds of problem: one problem is 'which phrase is the head of a modifier in a sentence?' and the other is 'which type of relation does exist between a given modifier and the head of it?' There have been many works for identifying modifier-head relation with GRs in sentences. Brant et al. (1997) train cascaded Hidden Markov Models to tag words with their GRs. They model GR determination as a tagging problem of POS. The tagger for GRs works with lexical and contextual probability measures depending on the category of the mother node. Argamon et al. (1998) apply memory-based learning to noun phrase (NP) chunking and subject/object identification with only POS features and Buchholz et al. (1999) add steps to the GRs assignment cascade. They chunk sentences into several phrases, then label several types of GRs between pairs of words in the sentence. They use POS tag and lexical information as features and achieve better result with NP chunks and verb phrase (VP) chunks than without chunks. Blaheta et al. (2000) assume a richer input representation consisting of labeled trees produced by a tree-bank grammar parser, and use the tree-bank again to train a further procedure that assigns GR tags to syntactic constituents in the trees. Carroll et al. (2002) set the threshold on the output of probabilistic parser to extract GRs that form part of all analyses licensed by the grammar with high precision at the cost of recall.

Most previous works discover main chunks of sentences and their heads, and determine GRs such as subject, object, adjunct relations between verbs and heads of other chunks.

Petr Sojka, Ivan Kopeček and Karel Pala (Eds.): TSD 2006, LNAI 4188, pp. 253–259, 2006.

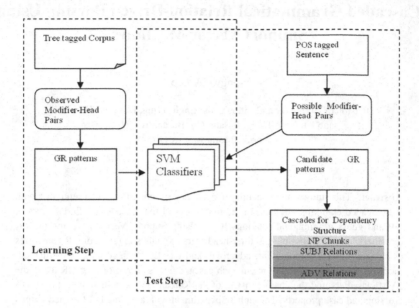

Fig. 1. The system architecture

However, Lee (2004) proposes a method which first tries to find every possible grammatical relation and then tries to find correct relations by using resolved GRs information for identifying subject-verb, object-verb, and adverbial-verb relations in sentences. They use probabilities of the GRs given NPs and VPs in sentences, and the characteristics of Korean such as distance, no-crossing and case property. However, Lee's model deals with only NP-VP relations.

We expand Lee (2004)'s shallow parsing method in dependency structure analysis by the cascaded chunking strategy and use Lee's method in each cascade to deal with all dependency relations. Details will be explained in Section 2. In each cascade, SVM classifier is used for its corresponding GR. SVM is automatically trained with a tree-tagged corpus.

2   System Architecture

Figure 1 illustrates the system architecture. The system consists of learning step and test step. In the learning step, every pair of a head-modifier relation is extracted from a tree-tagged corpus. The GRs of all extracted pairs of head and its modifier were manually tagged with seven types. Table 1 represents the types of GR which we deal with. These pairs construct GR patterns which are used for training SVM classifiers. Details about training SVM classifiers will be explained in Section 4.

In the test step, when a part of speech (POS) tagged sentence is given as an input, the system generates every possible combination pair of modifier-head regardless of its correctness. Let us denote the output of SVM classifier for a GR r given modifier m and head h as $SVM_r(m, h)$. The GR of every pair is determined with $arg_r max SVM_r(M_i, H_j)$ from a given every pair of $m - h$ in a sentence. In most cases, the $arg_r max SVM_r(M_i, H_j)$

Table 1. Types of Grammatical Relations

Type of GRs	Description of relation	Example
NP-chunk	Adnominal - NP	Han saram (a man)
SUBJ	Subjective	John-i na-o-da (John comes)
COMP	Complement	Mul-i doi-ess-da (became water)
OBJ	Objective	John-eul bo-ass-da (saw John)
ADV	Adverbial	Hak-gyo-e-seo na-o-da (come from school)
VPCONJ	VP - Aux. VP VP - VP (Complex verb) Conjunctive VP-VP	Ha-go sip-da (want to do) Dal-ryeo ga-da (run and go) Deo-wueo-seo ma-syeoss-da (drink (something) because (it) is hot)
ADNP	Adnoun Phrase - NP	Na-o-neun geos-eul (something that (someone) come)

Head Mod	John-i	Hakgyo-eseo	Nao-neun	Geos-eul	Bo-assda
Abeoji-neun (father)			Subj		Subj
John-i (John)	-	Subj		Subj	
Hakgyo-eseo (out of a school)	-	-	Adv		Adv
Nao-neun (coming)	-	-	-	ADNP	
Geos-eul (that)	-	-	-	-	Obj
Bo-assda (saw)	-	-	-	-	-

"Abeoji-neun John-i Hakgyo-eseo nao-neun geos-eul bo-assda."
Father saw that John was coming out of a school.

Fig. 2. Types of Grammatical Relations

is positive, however when all the features of an input data are unknown, it may be negative. We also exclude the candidates which have negative SVM output for the target GR. These pairs with GR information are called candidate GR patterns as illustrated in Fig. 2.

We must devise a method which can discriminate between correct and wrong relation from candidate GR patterns. We apply Lee (2004)'s shallow parsing method in dependency structure analysis by the cascaded chunking strategy. In the next Section 3, we will explain how to find correct relation in each cascade.

3 Cascades for Dependency Structure

In this section, we explain how to find the correct relations from candidate GR patterns in sentences. Our strategy is to identify each type of GRs independently on each cascaded stage. Thus, we consider only one type of GR among NP-chunk, SUBJ, COMP, OBJ, ADV, ADNP, and CONJVP in each corresponding cascade so we have seven cascades as many as the number of GR types. The type of GR which a cascade deals with is called target GR. We select modifier-head pairs which produce maximal weight considering language

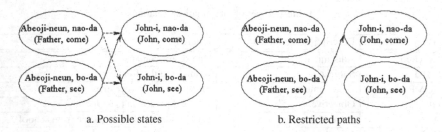

a. Possible states   b. Restricted paths

Fig. 3. An example of **possible states** and **restricted paths** by no-crossing property and case property for the subject cascade

characteristics such as no-crossing property, case property, and distance between words. The following more detailed explanations of this algorithm are executed on each type of GR. It is modified from Lee (2004)'s algorithm to handle every dependency relation.

Let us denote target GR as tgr, the weight function of tgr relations R_{tgr} in a sentence, given $M_1, \ldots, M_m$ and $H_1, \ldots, H_t$, could be Equation (2) by assuming that a relation appears in a candidate modifier and a head independent of the relations in the preceding or succeeding candidates. The H_k means one of $H_1, \ldots, H_t$ which is related with k-th candidate M_k (Lee 2004).

$$R_{tgr}(M_1, \ldots, M_m, H_1, \ldots, H_t) \approx \prod_{k=1}^{m} SVM_{tgr}(M_k, H_k)$$
$$\cdot f(M_k, H_k, M_{k-1}, H_{k-1}) \cdot P(d|r_k = tgr) \qquad (1)$$

$$f(M_k, H_k, M_{k-1}, H_{k-1}) = \begin{cases} 0, \text{ iff } (loc(H_k) = loc(H_{k-1}) \text{ and } H \in \text{ verb}), \\ \quad \text{or } loc(M_k) < loc(H_{k-1}) < loc(H_k) \\ 1, \text{ otherwise} \end{cases} \qquad (2)$$

We can find the correct relations for tgr if we find a sequence of (M_k, H_k) pairs which maximizes equation (2). Every pairs must meet the property that $loc(M_k) < loc(H_k)$ because Korean is a head-final language ($loc()$ denotes the location of an argument appeared in a sentence). Actually, there are cases of postposed phrases in the spoken Korean language, but usually they do not occur in written texts. Figure 3.a shows an example of the possible states of the subject cascade for a given sentence. Our goal is to find the most likely path which maximizes Equation (2).

However, the dotted paths in Figure 3.a must be excluded, because those violate the no-crossing property that no GR should cross each other and violate the case property that one verb can not have duplicated complements. We can exclude those paths by Equation (3). In Equation (3), '$loc(H_k) = loc(H_{k-1})$ and H is a verb' is for the case property and '$loc(M_k) < loc(H_{k-1}) < loc(H_k)$' is for the no-crossing property.

Figure 3.b shows the states and paths restricted by no-crossing property and case property. Then, we need to find the most likely paths among the restricted paths. We can easily find most likely path maximizing Equation (3) by applying the Viterbi algorithm. Because there is only one path in Figure 3.b, it is obvious that *Abeoji-neun*(Father) is the subject of *bo-da*(see) and *John-i*(John) is the subject of *nao-da*(come).

Additional context, the distance between a modifier and a head will also influence the likelihood of the modifier having relation with the head. It has been reported that distance is a crucial variable when deciding whether two words are related. We attempt to reflect it with $P(d|r_t = tgr)$ by which the distribution of distance given a particular GR can be considered. In this case, there may exist zero probability in a long distance. If $P(d|r_t = tgr)$ is zero, we smooth it with the first non-zero probability $P(d - i|r_t = tgr)$ for $i = 1$ to $d - 1$.

We estimate $SVM_{tgr}(M_k, H_k)$ by using the SVM, which will be explained in Section 4.

4   Training Support Vector Machines

To determine the GR of modifier-head, we use the output of a corresponding SVM classifier which is a learning approach for solving two-class pattern recognition problems introduced by Vapnik (1995). SVM is based on the Structural Risk Minimization principle for which the error-bound analysis has been theoretically motivated.

To make feature vector, we train SVM classifiers by using the head word of modifier, its functional word, and the head word of head as features. POS tags of all lexical items are also used as features. The dimension of a feature vector is determined by summing up the vocabulary size for each feature. Whether each feature is present or not is represented by the binary values '1' or '0' on its corresponding domain. That is, an observed data token is indicated as a point in the vector space. Consequently, each point is supposed to have the value '0' in most dimensions, while it is assigned the value '1' only in as many dimensions as the total number of feature sets. The GR between an NP and VP at each point is utilized as a positive example for the relevant specific GR classifier. It is, at the same time, utilized as a negative example for GR classifiers of any other categories.

Because we found that the kernel of SVM does not strongly affect the performance of our problem through many experiments, we concluded that our problem is linearly separable. Thus we will use the linear kernel only. As the SVM is a binary class classifier, we construct seven classifiers since we have seven types of GR. Each classifier constructs a hyperplane between one class and other classes. We use SVM^{light} system for our experiment (Joachim 1998).

Because our purpose is to find correct relations which maximize Equation (3) in each cascade, mapping it to sigmoid in order to make its value to be ranged from 0 to 1 is not necessary.

5   Experiments

We used the tree and POS tagged corpus of Korean Information Base which is annotated as a form of phrase structured tree (Lee et al. 1997). It consists of 11,932 sentences, which corresponds to 145,630 eojeols. An *eojeol* is a syntactic unit composed of one lexical morpheme with multiple functional words optionally attached to it. We regard an *eojeol* consisting of a main verb and auxiliary-verbs as a single main-verb *eojeol*. In case of a complex verb, we take into account only the first part of it. The total number of extracted pairs of head and its modifier is 120,830 and the GR of each pair was manually tagged. These pairs are used for training SVM classifiers.

Table 2. Accuracy of the proposed system

Test set	Method	Avg. P	Avg. R	Avg. F1
A	Cascaded	85.9	85.3	**85.7**
	Non-cascaded	82.0	81.5	81.8
B	Cascaded	86.3	85.4	**85.9**
	Lee et al.'s Model	86.1	82.7	84.4

To evaluate our results, we used the average precision/recall measure a sentence. Precision is the percentage of predicted relations that are actually correct and recall is the percentage of correct relations that are actually found. For convenient comparison of only one value, we represent the F1-measure that is $2 * P * R/(P + R)$ (Rijsbergen 1997). To compare with other methods, we prepared two types of test set. Test set A consists of 475 unseen POS tagged sentences (5,056 *eojeols*, averaging 10.6 *eojeols* per sentence) and is is prepared for comparison with a non-cascaded method. Test set B is composed of 195 sentences (1,743 eojeols, averaging 8.9 eojeols per sentence) and it is for comparison with Lee et al. (1997)'s model.

Table 2 shows the accuracy of our proposed model applied to two test sets. Experiments with test set-A compare the proposed cascaded methods and non-cascaded method. The non-cascaded method calculates Equation (3) not for head-modifier candidates but for every possible word pair having one of all GRs. The non-cascaded method is different from the cascaded method in that it deals with all types of GR at once whereas the cascaded method deals only one type of GRs at its corresponding cascade. As illustrated in Table 2, the proposed cascaded method outperformed non-cascaded method about 4.8% with test set-A.

Experiments with test set-B describes the results of dependency structure identification using our proposed model compared to other probabilistic models which have been used in full parsing. Lee et al. (1997)'s model was trained with about 30,000 tree-tagged sentences and used lexical co-occurrence information extracted from the training corpus. Since the output of Lee et al. model is not a dependency structural form but phrasal structural, we convert phrasal structure to dependency structure for this comparison. Comparison was done on 195 sentences of the test set (1,743 *eojeols*, averaging 8.9 *eojeols* per sentence). As shown in Table 3, the accuracy of our model is slightly higher than that of Lee et al.'s model. Lee et al.'s model is one of the state-of-art parsers in Korean. These results show that the proposed model can perform as Lee et al.'s full parser does. Consequently, we can conclude that the ambiguities of dependency structures can be solved efficiently with the cascades for GR as our method proposes.

One of most critical errors occurs when the candidate GR patterns has a wrong candidate. Regardless of whether our model considers language characteristics or not, these errors occur because our model utilizes the statistical information of GR given modifier and its head. Most errors can be attributed to sparse data problem.

6 Conclusions and Future Works

In this paper, we proposed a cascaded model for identifying dependency structure by using GR information. In identifying the relation of modifiers and their heads, we built a statistical model which independently finds subject-verb, object-verb, adverbial-verb, and etc. relations. Statistical information for GRs was automatically acquired from a tree-tagged corpus and used for training SVM classifiers.

In a series of experiments, we acquired an overall accuracy of 85.7% in identifying dependency relations in sentences on average. The proposed model utilized the statistical information of GRs between a modifier and its head to resolve the structural ambiguity. We showed that the structural ambiguity could be resolved efficiently with the GR information and the characteristics of Korean language, such as no-crossing property, the case property, and the distance feature.

More data needs to be collected in the future for more reliable verification and further performance improvement. We will try to combine with other technique such as word sense disambiguation to improve our system.

Acknowledgements. This work was supported by Korea Research Foundation Grant funded by Korea Government (MOEHRD, Basic Research Promotion Fund) (KRF-2005-003-D00349).

References

1. Brants, T., Skut, W. and Krenn, B. (1997). Tagging grammatical functions. In Proc. of the 2nd Conference on EMNLP, pp. 64–74.
2. Argamon, S., Dagan, I. & Krymolowski, Y. (1998). A memory-based approach to learning shallow natural language patterns. In Proc. of the 36th Annual Meeting of the ACL, pp. 67–73.
3. Buchholz, S., Veenstra, J. & Daelemans, W. (1999). Cascaded GR assignment. In Proc. of the Joint Conference on EMNLP and Very Large Corpora, pp. 239–246.
4. Blaheta, D. and Charniak, E. (2000). Assigning function tags to parsed text. In Proc. of the 1st Conference of the NAACL, pp. 234–240.
5. Carroll, J. and E. Briscoe (2002). High precision extraction of grammatical relations. In Proc. of the 19th International Conference on Computational Linguistics, pp. 134–140.
6. Joachims, T. (1998). Text Categorization with Support Vector Machines: Learning with Many Relevant Features. In Proc. of European Conference on Machine Learning, pp. 137–142.
7. Lee, S., Seo, J. and Jang, T. Y. (2003). Analysis of the grammatical functions between adnoun and NPs in Korean using Support Vector Machines. Natural Language Engineering, Cambridge University Press, Vol. 9, No. 3, pp. 269–280, Sept.
8. Lee, K. J., Kim, J. H., & Kim, G. C. (1997). An Efficient Parsing of Korean Sentence Using Restricted Phrase Structure Grammar, Computer Processing of Oriental Languages, Vol. 12, No. 1, pp. 49–62.
9. Viterbi, A. J. (1967). Error bounds for convolution codes and an asymptotically optimal decoding algorithm. IEEE trans. on Information Theory, 12:260–269.
10. Vapnik, V. N. (1995). The Nature of Statistical Learning Theory. Springer, New York.
11. Lee, K. J., Kim, J. H., Choi, K. S. and Kim, G. C. (1996). Korean syntactic tagset for building a tree annotated corpus. Korean Journal of Cognitive Science, 7(4):7–24.
12. Rijsbergen, C.J.van. (1979). Information Retrieval. Butterworth, London.
13. Lee, S. (2004). A statistical model for identifying grammatical relations in Korean sentences, IEICE transactions on Information and Systems, Vol. E87-D, No. 12, pp. 2863–2871, Dec. 2004.
14. Lee, S. & Seo, J. (2004). Grammatical relations identification of Korean parsed texts using support vector machines, In Proc. of TSD 2004, Lecture Notes in Artificial Intelligence, Vol. 3206, pp. 121–128, Sept.

Building Korean Classifier Ontology
Based on Korean WordNet

Soonhee Hwang[1], Youngim Jung[1,2], Aesun Yoon[1,3], and Hyuk-Chul Kwon[1,2]

[1] Pusan National University, Korean Language Processing Laboratory, Research Institute of
Computer Information and Communication
[2] Pusan National University, Department of Computer Science Engineering
[3] Pusan National University, Department of French
Jangjeon-dong Geumjeong-gu, 609-735 Busan, S. Korea
{soonheehwang, acorn, asyoon, hckwon}@pusan.ac.kr

Abstract. Being commonly used in most languages, the classifier must be reexamined using semantic classes from ontology. However, few studies have dealt with the semantic categorization of classifiers and their semantic relations to nouns, which they quantify and characterize in building ontology. In this paper, we propose the semantic recategorization of numeral classifiers in Korean and present the construction of a classifier ontology based on large corpora and KorLex 1.5 (Korean WordNet). As a result, a Korean classifier ontology containing semantic hierarchies and the relations of classifiers was constructed. This is the first Korean classifier ontology, and its size is appropriate for natural language processing. In addition, each of the individual classifiers has a connection to nouns or noun classes that are quantified by the classifiers.

1 Introduction

In this paper, we propose the semantic recategorization of numeral classifiers in Korean and construct a classifier ontology – containing semantic hierarchies and semantic relations to noun ontology – based on large corpora and KorLex Noun 1.5 (Korean WordNet). The classifier is considered to be universal in most languages, and is used mainly in Asian languages such as Chinese, Japanese and Korean. These languages have typically different classifiers, whose properties depend on their use.

The paper is structured as follows. In Section 2, we examine the related studies on the characteristics of classifiers, including Korean classifiers, in more detail. In Section 3, we present the scope and data of this work, and suggest a semantic classification of classifiers by integrating semantic properties and contextual features extracted from large corpora. In Section 4, hierarchies of classifiers are generated, and each classifier is connected to nouns or noun classes based on Korean linguistic knowledge and KorLex; then, the constructed classifier ontology is evaluated. Conclusions and future work follow in the final Section 5.

2 Related Work

Languages vary considerably in the kinds of classifiers and their categories of classification. In Section 2, related work on the characteristics of classifiers, including Korean classifiers, is investigated.

Petr Sojka, Ivan Kopeček and Karel Pala (Eds.): TSD 2006, LNAI 4188, pp. 261–268, 2006.

2.1   Characteristics of Classifiers

All languages are reported to have classifiers, but some languages are more appropriately called 'classifier language' than others. For example, Thai, Japanese or Korean are typical 'classifier languages,' whereas English or French are not. Especially in Asian Languages, such as Chinese, Japanese and Korean, most nouns are quantified by a numeral-classifier structure, which is quite different from English, in which numerals quantify directly nouns to form measure phrases [Allan (1977:286)].

Related previous work has concentrated on (1) typological surveys and classification of classifiers [Allan (1977), Lyons (1977:227, 316-317)]; (2) describing classifiers according to their meaning [Downing (1993)]; (3) semantic analysis for various classifiers [Huang & Ahrens (2003), Matsumoto (1993)]; and (4) application of classifiers' categories in NLP, using an ontology for generating numeral classifiers [Bond & Paik (2000)]. Besides, related work in the domain of NLP has been done mainly on the analysis of numeral classifiers and noun-classifiers for Chinese, Japanese and Thai, but not any for Korean.

2.2   Korean Classifiers

As for the classification of Korean classifiers, it has been largely limited to typological classification and semantic analysis. Traditionally, classifiers have been divided into two types, mensural and sortal. In Korean, numeral classifiers are a subset of nouns, namely dependent nouns. The main difference distinguishing classifiers from prototype nouns is that the former cannot be used alone. Most Korean nouns require a numeral classifier when they are quantified[1] as shown in (1)[2].

(1) a. *2-jang-ui jongi*   b. *jongi 2-jang*
     2-CL-AND paper   paper 2-CL
     "**2 sheets** of paper"   "paper **2 sheets**"

Morphologically, Korean classifiers are suffixed to numerals. The quantified phrase, consisting of a numeral and a classifier, occurs in pre-NP position with an adnominal case marker (genitive) "*-ui*" as in (1a), or in post-NP position without "*-ui*", as in (1b). In the latter case the quantifier noun phrases appear "floating" as adverbial phrases just before the verb [4]. Each classifier tends to be determined by the semantic properties of co-occurring nouns with classifiers. For example, the nouns that can be used with the classifier "*gadag* (strand)" are "*kkeun* (cord)", "*sil* (yarn)", and "*seon* (wire)", among others. All of these objects are long and thin. In this paper, the hypothesis that the choice of the appropriate classifier depends on the semantic features of the noun they modify is adopted.

3   Semantic Analysis of Korean Classifiers

As shown in Section 2, classifiers vary according to the language, and can be determined using the semantic features of co-occurring nouns. In the present section, the scope and data

---

[1] Some of nouns can be used, in place of classifiers, in the role of classifiers.

[2] We use the following abbreviations: ACC = accusative; AND = adnominal; CL = classifier; PAST = past; TOP = topic.

of this work are presented, and a semantic analysis of Korean classifiers is conducted for their recategorization considering semantic properties and contextual features extracted from large corpora.

3.1 Scope and Data

In order to analyze Korean classifiers and their semantic features, and to build Korean classifier ontology, we extracted examples of classifiers and nouns characterized and quantified by the classifiers from large corpora and *Standard Korean Dictionary*. The corpus was made up of articles from daily newspapers, texts from middle school text books, scientific papers, literature texts, or law documents, of which size is 7,778,848 words. 450,000 examples containing target classifiers and their adjacent words are extracted, and are used for analysis of semantic features of representative Korean classifiers.

3.2 Recategorization of Korean Classifiers

Most nouns show selectional restrictions for classifiers. Korean has typically five major types of classifiers: mensural, to measure the amount of some entity (*-sentimiteo*, "cm"); group, referring to a collection of members (*-ssang*, "pair"); event, used to quantify abstract events (*-dae* "shot"); sortal classifying the kinds of the quantified noun phrase (*-myeong*, "CL of counting people"); and taxonomic, restricting quantified noun phrases to generic kinds (*-gae* "CL of counting items").

Since classifiers are assigned according to the noun, the representative features for classifier prediction in ontology must be noun features. We present the classification of Korean classifiers in Table 1.

Mensural-CL[3] is for the measuring of the amount of an entity, and composed of two-subtypes, time and space. Around the semantic class of entity, three CL can be categorized: Group, Sortal, and Taxonomic-CL. Group-CL refers to a collection of members, and can be further classified by the features, [+/-fixed number] and [+/-pair]. Sortal-CL classifies the kind of the quantified noun phrase they collocate with, and can be divided into 2 sub-classes by [+/-living thing]. Taxonomic-CL limits the noun phrase to be interpreted as a generic kind. It can be further divided by the features [+/-shape][4], and in more detail, [+long], [+round], [fat], etc. Event-CL quantify abstract events. We can first classify this class into at least 2 kinds by its most salient features, [+/-time], e.g., [+event] & [+attribute], and it can be divided further.

3.3 Semantic Relations Between Classifiers and Nouns

In order to locate the classifiers, it is important to clarify the nature of the semantic categories and the organization of a set of co-occurring nouns with classifiers.

---

[3] For the classification of mensural-CL, we only focused on the classes of time & space, unique to Korean. The classification of the other standardized classes such as metric unit, monetary unit, etc., follows the hierarchy of KorLex.

[4] The sub-categorization of the class by [+shape] can be represented in two ways. The one concerns the major dimensional subcategories of long, flat, and round. The other concerns the following groups: saliently one-dimensional, two-dimension, and three-dimensional.

Table 1. Classification of Korean Classifiers by Semantic Features

Types	Description	Semantic Class	Subcategory	Semantic Features				Example
		Time	-					*nyeon* (year)
[1] Mensural-CL	measure the amount of some entity	Space	Length	-				*cm* (centimeter)
			Area	-				*majigi* (patch of field)
			Weight	-				*geulaem* (gram)
			Volume	-				*liteo* (liter)
[2] Group-CL	refer to a collection of members		Group	[+group]	[+fixed number]	[+pair]		*ssang* (pair)
						[-pair]		*chug* (bunch of)
					[-fixed number]			*beol* (battery)
[3] Sortal-CL	classify the kind of the quantified noun phrase	Concrete things	Individual	[+living thing]	[+animacy]	[+human being]		*myeong* (CL of counting people)
						[-human being]		*mali* (CL of counting animals)
					[-animacy]	[+plant]		*songi* (CL of counting flowers or fruits)
				[-living thing]	-			*gwon* (CL of counting books)
[4] Taxonomic-CL	restrict the noun as a generic kind			[+living thing]	[+shape]			*gyeob* (layer)
					[-shape]	[+function]		*jongryue* (kind)
[5] Event-CL	quantify the abstract events	Abstract events	Abstract events	[+time]	[+event]		[+action]	*bal* (CL of counting shots)
							[+repetition]	*beon* (CL of repetitive work)
				[-time]	[+attribute]	-		*deunggeub* (magnitude)

(2) *na-neun chaeg-eul du-**gwon** ilgeotda.*
I-TOP book-ACC two-**CL** read-PAST
'I read two books.'

A classifier for "bound objects" as in (2), "*gwon*," is selected to indicate the quantity of books. The selection of the classifier being based on the properties of the quantified objects, we can say that each classifier shows its specific semantic restrictions on the objects being counted. The classifier "*gwon*" must appear only with all of the bound objects, for example, books, magazines, theses, and others.

4   Building Classifier Ontology

In Section 4, a semi-automatic procedure for building Korean classifier ontology based on lexical information extracted from large corpora and lexical relations in KorLex Noun 1.5[5] is illustrated. Then, the constructed Korean classifier ontology is evaluated.

4.1   Extraction and Selection of Classifiers

In Korean, an agglutinative language, where content word and function morphemes come in one word, the word shows a variety of inflected variants in texts. For the correct extraction of

---

[5] Currently, KorLex (Korean WordNet) 1.5 is composed up of nouns, verbs, adjectives and adverbs. KorLex Noun 1.5 contains 58,656 synsets, and 41,368 word senses.

classifiers and co-occurring nouns from corpora, content word should be lemmatized through morphological analysis [11]. Through the morphological analysis, proper nouns, titles of books, films or events embedding Arabic numerals were deleted from the sample list (e.g. 5.1 *gyeonggijang* (5.1 Stadium)). Classifiers observed in corpora with high frequency and registered in the *Standard Korean Dictionary* were selected as the candidates. In the result, 572 classifiers were selected and analyzed in building our ontology.

4.2 Generation of Hierarchies of Classifiers

According to the semantic properties and Korean classifiers analyzed in Section 3.2, the hierarchies of the five types of classifiers are generated differently as follows.

(1) **Hierarchies of classifiers that are purely dependent nouns:** Classifiers that are syntactically dependent on adjectives are widely used in Asian languages, but they are absent in English. In addition, most of those classifiers are native to a particular language, and so the unique hierarchy of Korean classifiers must be generated. As described in this paper, hierarchies of Korean classifiers were generated based on expert Korean linguistic knowledge, as shown in Table 1.

(2) **Hierarchies of classifiers converted from nouns:** As explained in [4], some Korean nouns function as classifiers and every noun representing a container has the possibility to be used as a classifier. The bilateral semantic features of these classifiers are reflected in the ontology. The hierarchies are generated by semi-automatic intersection of the KorLex Noun hierarchies and the Classifier ontology.

(3) **Hierarchies of mensural classifiers including universal measurement units and currency units:** These have already been established in KorLex Noun 1.5. Thus the hierarchies for mensural classifiers can be generated automatically.

4.3 Generation of Relation Between Noun and Classifier Ontology

In order to reexamine the semantic features of classifiers in a more systemic way, nouns co-occurring with classifiers were collected from the corpora and mapped to KorLex Noun's hierarchy. We assume that once the semantic categories of nouns are obtained, they can attribute the semantic characteristics of classifiers co-occurring with them. The process of categorization of nouns based on the lexical hierarchy in KorLex is described by taking a sortal classifier, '*mali*', and its co-occurring nouns as examples, as follows.

Step 1: Creating inventories of lemmatized nouns that are quantified by each classifier and nouns that are not combined with the classifier. Nouns quantified by *mali* "*mali*(+)", nouns not combined by *mali* "*mali*(-)" are collected and clustered as follows:

> ***Mali*(+)** – {*nabi* (butterfly1[6]), *gae* (dog1), *go-yang-i* (cat1), *geomdung-oli*
> (scoter1), *mae* (hawk1), *baem* (snake1)}
> ***Mali*(-)** – {*saram* (human2), *gong* (ball6)}.

Step 2: Mapping words to the KorLex synsets and listing all common hypernyms of the synset nodes.

---

[6] Numbers after the English words such as '1' in 'butterfly1' and '6' in 'ball6' indicate sense IDs in Princeton WordNet Noun database.

Step 3: Finding the Least Upper Bound (LUB) of synset nodes mapped from the inventory. Here, *Mucheogchudongmul* (invertebrate1), *pachunglyu* (reptile1), *jolyu* (bird1), *yugsigdongmul* (carnivore1) are selected as LUBs automatically. Selected LUBs are applied as a semantic category for the cluster of contextual features.

Step 4: Connecting the LUBs to the classifier *mali* in Korean Classifier Ontology, as shown in Figure 1.

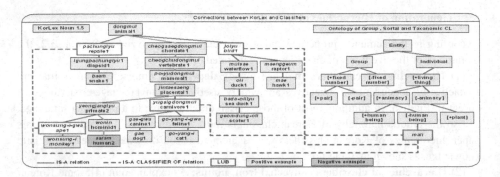

Fig. 1. Connection between Classifiers and Nouns of KorLex Noun 1.5

4.4   Results and Discussion

With the exploitation of the mapping algorithm based on the KorLex hierarchy shown in Section 4.3, each classifier are connected to individual noun or noun classes categorized semantically. Table 2 illustrates the five types of Korean classifiers and semantic classes of nouns.

As we have assumed that the co-occurring nouns can attribute the semantic properties of classifiers, the sense granularity of noun classes differ from each other depending on the types of the classifiers. For instance, mensural classifiers and taxonomic classifiers can quantify a wide range of noun classes; however, they can seldom characterize the semantic features of nouns co-occurring with them. On the other hand, sortal and event classifiers can combine with only a few specific noun classes such as 'bird1' and 'gun1' respectively. Group classifiers take nouns that form a unit by conjoining plural items. Five hundred and twenty-seven (572) Korean classifiers semantically reexamined compose our Korean Classifier ontology and semantic relations ("Is-a Classifier of") between the classifier and nouns in KorLex. The size of the ontology is applicable to NLP applications, considering the size classifier inventories created by the previous work. [2,3] generated a few classifiers from the Japanese *Goitai-kei* thesaurus. According to [9], 427 Chinese classifiers were managed as sufficient in size for studying the Mandarin classifier systems comprehensively.

5   Conclusions and Further Work

In this paper, the semantic recategorization of Korean numeral classifiers was presented, and the construction of classifier ontology was accomplished by means of the semantic features of their related nouns. The hypothesis that the appropriate classifier is selected based on the

Table 2. Semantic classes of nouns quantified by Korean classifiers

Types	Classifiers	Nouns quantified by the classifier	Semantic class of Nouns
Mensural	*cm* (centimeter)	Not specified	entity1
Group	*beol* (battery3)	*te-ipeu* (tape2), *peulinteu* (print4)	device1
		yangbog (business suit1)	clothing1
		os (clothing1), *yunipom* (uniform1)	
Sortal	*mali* (CL of counting animals except human beings)	*nabi* (butterfly1), *beol* (bee1)	invertebrate1
		gae (dog1), *go-yang-i* (cat1)	carnivore1
		geomdung-oli (scoter1), *mae* (hawk1)	bird1
		baem (snake1), *badageobug* (turtle1)	reptile1
		seolyu (paper5), *sinbal* (footwear2)	artifact1
Taxonomic	*jongryue* (kind)	*boheom* (insurance1)	insurance1
		jipye (paper money1), *menyu*(menu1)	communication2
Event	*bal* (CL of counting shots)	*jiloe* (land mine1), *yeonmagtan* (smoke bomb1), *so-itan* (incendiary2)	explosive device1
		gonggichong (air gun1), *gwonchong* (pistol1), *gaseuchong* (gas gun1)	gun1
		chongtan, chong-al (bullet1), *siltan* (ball cartridge1), *hampo* (naval gun1)	weaponry1
		lokes (rocket1), *misa-il* (missile1)	rocket1

semantic features of quantified nouns was verified by mapping the classifiers' co-occurring nouns to KorLex's nouns. As future work, first, establishing refined classificatory standards for the classifiers such as sortal-CL, taxonomic-CL, and event-CL will continue. Second, the event-CL the classificatory criteria of which were not presented clearly owing to its sparse data will be investigated in depth. Finally, we will study the application method of the suggested CL-ontology to e-Learning, especially in the domain of foreign language education, requiring sophisticated and easy-to-use learning support systems.

Acknowledgement

This work was supported by a National Research Laboratory Grant (Laboratory title: Korean Language Processing Lab. Project Number: M10203000028-02J0000-01510).

References

1. Allan, K.: Classifiers. Language 53(2) (1977) 285–311.
2. Bond, F., Paik, K.: Classifying correspondence in Japanese and Korean. In: 3rd Pacific Association for Computational Linguistics Conference: PACLING-97 (1997) 58–67.
3. Bond, F., Paik, K.: Reusing an ontology to generate numeral classifiers. In: Proceedings of the 18th Conference on Computational Linguistics (2000) 90–96.
4. Chae, W.: A Study on Numerals and Numeral Classifier Constructions in Korean, Linguistics Study 19–1 (1983) 19–34.

5. Downing, P.: Pragmatic and semantic constraints on numeral quantifier position in Japanese. Linguistics 29 (1993) 65–93.
6. Fellbaum, C. (ed.): WordNet - An electronic lexical database. MIT Press, Cambridge (1998).
7. Guo, H., H. Zhong: Chinese Classifier Assignment using SVMs. In: the Fourth SIGHAN Workshop on Chinese Language Processing (2005)
    `http://www.cs.sunysb.edu/~huguo/papers/ChineseClassifier.pdf`.
8. Hovy, E.: Methodologies for the Reliable Construction of Ontological Knowledge. In: Proceedings of ICCS 2005, (2005) 91–106.
9. Huang, C.R., K. Ahrens: Individuals, kinds and events: classifier coercion of nouns. Language Sciences 25 (2003) 353–373.
10. Jung, Y.I., Yoon, A.S., Kwon, H.C.: Disambiguation Based on WordNet for Transliteration of Arabic Numerals for Korean TTS. LNCS 3878 (2006) 366–377.
11. Kwon, H.C., Kang, M.Y., Choi, S.J.,: Stochastic Korean Word-Spacing with Smoothing Using Korean Spelling Checker, Computer Processing of Oriental Languages 17 (2004) 239–252.
12. Lyons, J.: Semantics 1. Cambridge University Press, Cambridge (1979).
13. Matsumoto, Y.: Japanese numeral classifiers: a study of semantic categories and lexical organization. Linguistics 31(4) (1993) 667–713.
14. Nirenburg, S., Raskin, V.: Ontological semantics, MIT Press, Cambridge (2004).
15. Sowa, J.F.: Knowledge Representation. Brooks Cole Publishing Co., Pacific Grove, CA (2000).

Exploiting the Translation Context for Multilingual WSD

Lucia Specia and Maria das Graças Volpe Nunes

Departamento de Ciências de Computaçao e Estatística -
ICMC - Universidade de São Paulo,
Caixa Postal 668, 13560-970 São Carlos, Brazil
{lspecia, gracan}@icmc.usp.br

Abstract. We propose a strategy to support Word Sense Disambiguation (WSD) which is designed specifically for multilingual applications, such as Machine Translation. Co-occurrence information extracted from the translation context, i.e., the set of words which have already been translated, is used to define the order in which disambiguation rules produced by a machine learning algorithm are applied. Experiments on the English-Portuguese translation of seven verbs yielded a significant improvement on the accuracy of a rule-based model: from 0.75 to 0.79.

1 Introduction

Word Sense Disambiguation (WSD) in multilingual applications is concerned with the choice of the most appropriate translation of an ambiguous word given its context. Although it has been agreed that multilingual WSD differs from monolingual WSD [4] and that WSD is more relevant in the context of a specific application [13], little has been done on the development of WSD modules for particular applications. WSD approaches generally focus on application independent monolingual contexts, particularly English. In the case of Machine Translation (MT), the application we are dealing with, WSD approaches usually apply traditional sense repositories (e.g., WordNet [7]) to identify the monolingual senses, which are then mapped into the target language translations. However, mapping senses between languages is a very complex issue.

One of the reasons for this complexity is the difference in the sense inventories of the languages. We recently evidenced this for English-Portuguese [11], showing that many English senses can be translated into a unique Portuguese word, while some English senses need to be split into different translations, conveying sense distinctions that only exist in Portuguese.

In addition to the differences in the sense inventory, the disambiguation process can vary according to the application. For instance, in monolingual WSD the main information source is the context of the ambiguous word, that is, the surrounding words in a sentence or text. For MT purposes, however, the context may also include the translation in the target language, i.e., words in the text which have already been translated.

This strategy has not been explored specifically for WSD, although some related approaches have used similar techniques for other purposes. For example, a number of approaches to MT, especially the statistics-based approaches, make use of the words which have already been translated as context, implicitly accomplishing basic WSD during the translation process [1]. Some approaches for monolingual WSD use techniques which are

Petr Sojka, Ivan Kopeček and Karel Pala (Eds.): TSD 2006, LNAI 4188, pp. 269–276, 2006.

similar to ours to gather co-occurrence evidence from corpora in order either to carry out WSD [6], or to create monolingual sense tagged corpora [2]. Other monolingual related approaches explore the already disambiguated or unambiguous words by taking into account their senses in order to disambiguate a given word [5].

In this paper we investigate the use of the translation context, that is, the surrounding words which have already been translated, as knowledge source for WSD. We present experiments on the disambiguation of seven verbs in English-Portuguese translation. The target language contextual information is based on the co-occurrence of the possible translations of the ambiguous word with a number of translated words, queried as n-grams in the web, using Google®. The resultant rank of translation is then used to reorder the set of rules produced by a machine learning approach for WSD. In such approach, multiples rules, pointing to different translations, can be applied to disambiguate certain cases, and thus the order in which the rules are applied plays and important role. The original approach relies on the order given by the machine learning algorithm, but we show that additional information to support the selection of the most appropriate rule for each case can improve the disambiguation accuracy.

In what follows we first briefly describe our approach for WSD (Section 2). We then present our strategy to gather information about the translation context from the web (Section 3) and the way this strategy is used in our WSD approach, with some experiments and the results achieved (Section 4).

2   A Hybrid Relational Approach for WSD in MT

In [9] we present an approach for WSD which exploits knowledge-based and corpus-based techniques and employs a relational formalism to represent both examples and linguistic knowledge. The relational representation is considerably more expressive than the attribute-value format used by all the algorithms traditionally applied to generate WSD models. The major advantages of such formalism are: it avoids sparse-ness in data, and it allows the use of the two types of evidence (examples and linguistic knowledge) during the learning process.

In order to explore relational machine learning in our WSD approach we use Inductive Logic Programming (ILP) [8]. ILP employs techniques of both Machine Learning and Logic Programming to build first-order logic theories from examples and background knowledge, which are also represented by means of first-order logic clauses. We implemented our approach using Aleph [12], an ILP system which provides a complete relational learning inference engine and various customization options. We use seven groups of syntactic, semantic, and pragmatic knowledge sources (KSs) as background knowledge: KS_1: Bag-of-words of 5 lemmas surrounding the verb; KS_2: Part-of-speech (POS) tags of content words in a 5 word window surrounding the verb; KS_3: Subject and object syntactic relations with respect to the verb under consideration; KS_4: Context words represented by 11 collocations with respect to the verb; KS_5: Selectional restrictions of verbs and semantic features of their arguments; KS_6: Idioms and phrasal verbs; KS_7: A count of the overlapping words in dictionary definitions for the possible translations of the verb and the words surrounding it in the sentence.

Some of these KSs were extracted from our sample corpus, while others were automatically extracted from lexical resources[1]. The majority of these KSs have been traditionally

---

[1] Michaelis and Password English-Portuguese Dictionaries, LDOCE, and WordNet.

employed in monolingual WSD, while other are specific for MT ($K S_6$ and $K S_7$). Additionally, our repository of senses is also specific for MT: instead of disambiguating the English senses and then mapping them into the Portuguese corresponding translations, we disambiguate directly among Portuguese translations. Thus, our sample corpus is tagged with the translation of the ambiguous verbs under consideration, while our set of possible translations for each verb is given by bilingual dictionaries: Michaelis and Password English-Portuguese Dictionaries.

Based on the background knowledge and on examples of disambiguation, Aleph's inference engine induces a set of symbolic rules. The resultant set of rules depends strongly on the order in which the training examples are given to the inference engine. Usually, to classify (disambiguate) new cases, the rules are applied in the order they are produced, and all the cases covered by a certain rule are assessed as correctly or incorrectly classified and removed from the test set. Although there can be other rules which will classify the same case, they are ignored. In what follows first present our experiment on acquiring co-occurrence information about the translation context, which will be used to reorder the set of rules.

3   Acquiring the Translation Context Information

We explore the translation context information through the analysis of the co-occurrence frequencies of sets of Portuguese words which have already been translated and each possible translation of the verb under consideration. This is obtained by querying the web (via Google's API[2]) with these sets of words. In principle, any subset of the words already translated to the target language could be used as context. However, words in certain positions are much more important than others. In order to identify a relevant contextual structure, we first ran a series of experiments with different structures, which we briefly describe in Section 3.2, after presenting our experimental setting.

3.1   Experimental Setting

In our experiments we are using the same set of words as in our WSD approach: seven highly frequent and ambiguous verbs previously identified as problematic for English-Portuguese MT systems: "to come", "to get", "to give", "to look", "to make", and "to take". Since we do have at our disposal a good quality English-Portuguese MT system, we use a sentence aligned parallel corpus - produced by human translators - to provide the translation context. In order to experiment with different query structures, we selected 100 English sentences for each of the seven verbs (a total of 700 sentences) from the parallel corpus Compara [3], which comprises fiction books. We used a version of this corpus in which the translations of the ambiguous verbs have already been (automatically) annotated. For each occurrence of a verb, this corpus contains the English sentence, annotated with such translation, and the corresponding Portuguese sentence, as the example shown in Fig. 1.

Our translation context strategy requires a list with all the possible translations of each verb. This list was extracted from bilingual dictionaries (e.g., DIC Prático Michaelis®), amounting to the numbers shown in Table 1. They include translations of both phrasal and non-phrasal usages of the English verbs.

---

[2] http://www.google.com/apis/

> tomar - I will take my medicines tonight, as prescribed by the doctor.
> Vou tomar meus remédios hoje à noite, conforme indicado pelo médico.

Fig. 1. Example of English-Portuguese parallel sentence in our corpus

Table 1. Our set of verbs and their number of possible translations in the corpus

Verb	Translations	Verb	Translations
come	226	look	63
get	242	make	239
give	128	take	331
go	197		

In order to assess the efficiency of our strategy, by embedding the resultant contextual information into our WSD approach (Section 4), we consider the set of test examples already used in our previous experiments with that approach: around 50 sentences for each ambiguous verb, also extracted from Compara. It is worth mentioning that these sentences are not part of the training example set: a rule-based model for each verb was produced by Aleph based on a training corpus of around 150 examples, and evaluated on an independent test corpus of around 50 examples.

3.2 Discovering the Most Useful Kind of Contextual Information

In our experiments we consider the use of the translation context in a hypothetical rule-based transfer MT system which first translates all the unambiguous words in the sentence and then each ambiguous word, using the WSD module. We assume that all the other words in the sentence will have already been translated, remaining only the verb to be disambiguated. In fact, since we are using the parallel corpus to provide the translation context, any combination of words in the target sentence, except the ambiguous one, could be used as context. In order to find out a suitable set of words, we experimented with different n-grams and bags-of-words, all including each of the possible translations of the ambiguous verb. As described in [10], after experimenting with the six types of query for a small number of words, we chose the two presenting the most promising results (examples are given in Table 2):

(a) trigrams with the 1st two words to the right of the verb;

(b) bags-of-words with all the content words already translated in the sentence, requiring any subset of the words to be in the results.

Given the parallel corpus as exemplified in Fig. 1, for each sentence, we created queries with the contextual words and each of the possible translations of the verb under consideration, and then submitted each query to Google. For example, assuming that the verb "to take" has only three possible translations, "tomar" (consume, ingest), "pegar" (buy, select), and "levar" (take someone to some place), the queries that will be built for the example sentence are shown in Table 2 (the translation each query represents is in bold face). The relevant information returned by Google is the number of hits for each query.

Table 2. Example of queries and their respective number of hits in Google

Type	Queries	Hits
(a)	"**tomar** meus remédios"	228
	"**pegar** meus remédios"	17
	"**levar** meus remédios"	8
(b)	(**tomar** AND (remédios OR hoje OR noite OR conforme OR indicado OR médico))	3,500,000
	(**pegar** AND (remédios OR hoje OR noite OR conforme OR indicado OR médico))	2,290,000
	(**levar** AND (remédios OR hoje OR noite OR conforme OR indicado OR médico))	1,770,000

3.3 Results

In Table 3 we show the accuracies that would be achieved by our strategy based on the translation context if it was used as unique information source for WSD. We also show the potential of this strategy to be used as additional information source, supporting a WSD approach. We first show the accuracy of the baseline using the most frequent translation in the set of 100 sentences per verb: 0.43, on average. We assumed the most frequent translation to be the one given first by the dictionary Password.

In the third to fifth columns of Table 3 we present the accuracies obtained in our experiments using queries of the type (a). The third column shows the percentage of sentences for which the query with the maximum number of hits contained the actual translation of the verb in that sentence. The other two columns show the percentages of sentences for which the query with the actual translation was included among the top 3 and top 10 positions, respectively, according to the number of hits. The sixth to eighth columns show the corresponding accuracies for queries of the type (b).

In general, the results were considerably better for queries of the type (a). The problem with queries of the type (b) is that long sentences produce queries consisting of many words and these are too general to accurately identify the sense of the verb. On average, the accuracy

Table 3. Accuracies: baseline, queries of the types (a) and (b)

Verb	Baseline	Qr.(a) 1st Choice	Qr.(a) 1st-3rd Choice	Qr.(a) 1st-10th Choice	Qr.(b) 1st Choice	Qr.(b) 1st-3rd Choice	Qr.(b) 1st-10th Choice
come	0.4	0.4	0.4	0.8	0.2	0.2	0.2
get	0	0.4	0.7	0.7	0	0	0.2
give	0.8	0.5	0.7	0.8	0.4	0.8	1
go	0.4	0.5	0.9	1	0	0	0
look	0.4	0.6	0.9	1	0.4	0.4	0.4
make	0.8	0.3	0.6	1	0	0	1
take	0.2	0.8	1	1	0	0.2	0.4
Aver.	0.43	0.50	0.74	0.90	0.14	0.23	0.46

Example: Quincas Borba took him everywhere. They slept in the same room.
Translation: Quincas Borba levava-o para toda parte, dormiam no mesmo quarto.
Rules: [Rule 19] = has_sense(A, tomar) IF has_collocation(A, col_11, in).
       [Rule 33] = has_sense(A, levar) IF has_bag(A, him).
       [Rule 48] = has_sense(A, puxar) IF has_collocation(A, col_2, propernoun).
Google queries: " <verb translation> para toda"
Google rank: ir 216 - levar 129 - dar 87 - fazer 56 ...
Rule chosen: [Rule 33], translation = levar –> correct

Fig. 2. Example of application of our strategy to reorder the disambiguation rules

of the strategy for the first choice with queries of the type (a) (0.5) outperforms the baseline considering the most frequent sense. However, as previously mentioned, our goal is to use the information provided by this strategy as additional evidence to our WSD approach, which already uses many other knowledge sources. In what follows we present a proposal to use this information in our WSD approach: given the set of rules that can be applied to classify a certain example, we choose the most appropriate rule according to the co-occurrence information.

4   Using Contextual Information to Reorder WSD Rules

As previously mentioned, in the rule-based models produced by ILP systems, multiple rules can cover the same example(s). We propose a strategy to employ contextual information acquired as explained in Section 3 to choose the most appropriate rule. Essentially, instead of applying each rule in the order it appears in the theory and using it to classify all the examples covered, we take each test example individually and, given all the rules covering that example, we select the most appropriate rule according to the score of the translation pointed out by the rule in the rank provided by Google for the translation context of that example (for queries of the type (a)). For example, in Fig. 2 we show the three rules covering one example of the verb "to take", which was correctly disambiguated as "levar". In this case, the correct translation was not the best scored in the rank provided by Google: it came in second, but since there was not a rule for the top translation ("ir"), "levar" was chosen.

We experimented with this strategy in the set of rules produced by our WSD approach for each of the verbs based on 150 training examples, and tested on around 50 examples per verb (cf. Section 3.1). This set of rules was produced by Aleph after adjusting several parameters and trying out different search, induction and evaluation methods (as described in [9]), and was considered a satisfactory disambiguation model. In Table 4 we first show the accuracy of our WSD approach without the translation context information, i.e., applying the rules in their original order. We then show the accuracy of the WSD model with the rule reordering, based on the translation context information. In the last column we present the percentage of examples for which multiple rules could be applied. The fact that a high percentage of examples is covered by multiple rules is very common in ILP-based models, and thus a strategy for choosing the best rule can make a crucial difference. As we can see, the strategy based on the translation context significantly improved the average accuracy of the WSD model.

Table 4. Accuracy of the WSD approach with and without the translation context information

Verb	Without translation context	With translation context - query (a)	% Examples with multiple rules
come	0.82	0.82	0.33
get	0.51	0.61	0.33
give	0.96	0.96	0.51
go	0.73	0.82	0.69
look	0.83	0.80	0.34
make	0.74	0.79	0.33
take	0.66	0.69	0.38
Aver.	0.75	0.79	

5   Conclusions

We described a strategy to support WSD in MT which is specific to this application: it uses co-occurrence information about the translation context. In order to gather this information, after experimenting with 700 sentences containing seven highly ambiguous verbs by searching Google with all the possible translations of the ambiguous verbs, with different queries formulated as bags-of-words and n-grams, we chose the most promising type of query: trigrams containing two words to the right of the verb. We then embedded the ranking of co-occurrence information provided by Google in our WSD approach by using the scores to reorder multiple rules covering the same example. The use of this very simple strategy yielded a significant improvement on the average accuracy of the WSD model. More complex strategies, also based on the translation context information, could yield even better results and will be investigated in future work.

References

1. Dagan, I. and Itai, A.: Word Sense Disambiguation Using a Second Language Monolingual Corpus. Computational Linguistics, 20 (1994) 563–596.
2. Fernández, J., Castilho, M., Rigau, G., Atserias, J., and Turmo, J.: Automatic Acquisition of Sense Examples using ExRetriever. Proceedings of the LREC, Lisbon (2004) 25–28.
3. Frankenberg-Garcia, A., and Santos, D.: Introducing COMPARA: the Portuguese-English Parallel Corpus. Corpora in translator education, Manchester (2003) 71–87.
4. Hutchins, W.J. and Somers H.L.: An Introduction to Machine Translation. Academic Press, Great Britain (1992).
5. Lesk, M.: Automated Sense Disambiguation Using Machine-readable Dictionaries: How to Tell a Pine Cone from an Ice Cream Cone. Proceeding of SIGDOC, Toronto (1986) 24–26.
6. Mihalcea, R. and Moldovan, D.I.: A Method for Word Sense Disambiguation of Unrestricted Text. Proceedings of the 37th Meeting of the ACL, Maryland (1999).
7. Miller, G.A., Beckwith, R.T., Fellbaum, C.D., Gross, D., and Miller, K.: WordNet: An On-line Lexical Database. International Journal of Lexicography, 3(4) (1990) 235–244.
8. Muggleton, S.: Inductive Logic Programming. New Generation Computing, 8(4) (1991) 295–318.
9. Specia, L. A Hybrid Relational Approach for WSD - First Results. To appear in the COLING/ACL 06 Student Research Workshop. Sydney (2006).

10. Specia, L., Nunes, M.G.V., Stevenson, M.: Translation Context Sensitive WSD. To appear in the 11th Annual Conference of the European Association for Machine Translation, Oslo (2006).
11. Specia, L., Castelo-Branco, G., Nunes, M.G.V., Stevenson, M.: Multilingual versus Monolingual WSD. Workshop Making Sense of Sense, EACL, Trento (2006).
12. Srinivasan, A.: The Aleph Manual. Technical Report. Computing Laboratory, Oxford University (2000).
13. Wilks, Y. and Stevenson, M.: The Grammar of Sense: Using Part-of-speech Tags as a First Step in Semantic Disambiguation. Natural Language Engineering, 4(1) (1998) 1–9.

Post-annotation Checking of
Prague Dependency Treebank 2.0 Data

Jan Štěpánek

Institute of Formal and Applied Linguistics
Charles University in Prague, Faculty of Mathematics and Physics
Malostranské náměstí 25, 118 00 Praha 1, Czech Republic
stepanek@ufal.ms.mff.cuni.cz

Abstract. This paper describes methods and tools used for the post-annotation checking of Prague Dependency Treebank 2.0 data. The annotation process was complicated by many factors: for example, the corpus is divided into several layers that must reflect each other; the annotation rules changed and evolved during the annotation process; some parts of the data were annotated separately and in parallel and had to be merged with the data later. The conversion of the data from the old format to a new one was another source of possible problems besides omnipresent human inadvertence. The checking procedures are classified according to several aspects, e.g. their linguistic relevance and their role in the checking process, and prominent examples are given. In the last part of the paper, the methods are compared and scored.

1 Introduction

The annotation of a corpus is always a complex task. In the case of Prague Dependency Treebank 2.0 (PDT) [1], the situation was even more complicated: the corpus contains not only a morphological annotation (linear), but also a syntactic (i. e. structural) one which is much more complex than a simple linear annotation. The structure of PDT reflects the structure of Functional Generative Description (see [2]) that proposes (besides the morphological layer) two structural layers, surface and deep syntax.

The main source of errors is the human lack of concentration, but there are other factors: the annotation is divided into several layers that are interlinked by references according to stand-off annotation principles, thus a change at one layer may produce an error at a different one. Moreover, annotation rules changed and evolved during the annotation process, possibly turning valid data into invalid ones, as they were not re-annotated every time a rule changed.

Other possible sources of errors were conversions from old one-purpose formats to the new XML-based format (see [3]), merging the data with parallel annotation (topic-focus articulation, coreference, valency frames), etc. The tools originally used just for basic checking of the data validity showed to be suitable for deeper corrections based on linguistically motivated invariants.

2 Tools

The main tool used for the PDT data processing was Tree Editor TrEd [4]. TrEd is written in the scripting language Perl and has several advantages to other and previously used tools:

Petr Sojka, Ivan Kopeček and Karel Pala (Eds.): TSD 2006, LNAI 4188, pp. 277–284, 2006.

– Since it is written in Perl, TrEd can be run under diverse operating systems (MS Windows, Linux etc.).
– Perl is an interpreted language. Therefore, Perl itself can be used to write "macros" — pieces of code that use the libraries for data processing that can be run from within the editor.
– TrEd is open-source and well documented, which means good accessibility and flexibility.

Besides the tree editor, there exists a "console" version of the data processor, called btred. It can search and/or change the data with all the benefits of TrEd, but without calling the graphical user interface. However, the corpus is too large to be processed by it, one file by one: it takes hours to traverse all the files, which makes debugging almost impossible. For that purpose, the distributed version ntred was developed and became the main tool for the post-annotation checking. Many minor tools were used in the checking process as well, mainly scripts in Perl and bash.

3   Classification of Checking Procedures

The checking procedures (CP's) can be classified according to two main aspects:

1. **Purpose of the procedure.** The CP's were divided into four sets.
    (i) The first set, called "find", contained 469 procedures that just searched for suspicious data, i. e. positions with probable occurrences of sought errors. The output of such a procedure was processed either by a procedure from the second set, if it was possible to handle the problem without human assistance, or by a human annotator.
    (ii) The second set, called "fix", comprehended 135 procedures that were able to change the data and repair errors.
    (iii) The third set, called "check", contained 196 procedures similar to those in the find set, but they included lists of exceptions for rare cases where the supposed invariant did not hold. All procedures from the check set were expected to report no errors when run on the whole data.
    (iv) The last set, called "misc", contained a variety of procedures that behaved in a different way than those in the first three sets.
2. **Layer of the data concerned.** PDT data are divided into four layers[1]. The "lowest" layer contains just the original source text and hence needed almost no CP's. The "core" layers, morphological (m), analytical (a) and tectogrammatical (t), contain human annotation and were subject to more CP's. Many types of errors were found by classifying the output of a procedure that was searching for identical surface strings with differing annotations (cf. [5]). An additional group of CP's dealt with the data format and other low-level features of the treebank data that could be possibly broken.

In Subsections 3.1, 3.2, 3.3, and 3.4, examples of checked invariants are given, assorted by the concerned layer. Dependencies between particular procedures are not presented in this paper due to lack of space.

---

[1] Most of the CP's concerned more than one layer. They have been classified according to the group they used the most.

CP's can be classified in many ways: e.g. by their "universality" (special to PDT, useful for any dependency treebank, any treebank, any corpus), aspect of language typology (special to Czech, useful for flective languages, Indo-European languages, all languages), etc.

3.1 Low-Level Checking Procedures

Low-level CP's have no linguistic relevance; they concern the data format, annotation scheme, or data representation. They condition any other, more sophisticated queries, therefore they had the highest priority.

Number of files: Number of files had to be the same all the time. Lower number typically indicated an accidentally deleted file.

File format: All the files had to be loadable by btred. This procedure was used to detect corrupted files.

Attribute values: Some of the attributes have only limited sets of possible values. For some attributes, the sets changed during the annotation process as some new values were added or some values were merged.

Uniqueness of identifiers: Identifiers had to be unique over the whole data. This procedure was complicated by the cluster architecture of ntred, because even if the identifiers had been unique at each server, there still could have been duplicities among different servers.

Reference validity: All the references were expressed as links to identifiers. This procedure verified that all referenced units really existed. As in the previous case, the cluster architecture made the procedure harder.

Hidden added nodes: "Added" nodes were created by the annotators on the t-layer, typically for omitted valency participants or ellipsis. "Hidden" nodes, on the other hand, corresponded to surface auxiliary words that were not represented as nodes on the t-layer. While hiding a node, all its children were hidden, too. That way added nodes might get accidentally hidden.

Inter-layer linking: There were 35 CP's in the find set dealing with inter-layer links. For illustration, note that in the t-representation of the sentence *"They know that she had to go home"*, there is only one node *"go"* corresponding to all the a-nodes *"that"*, *"had"*, *"to"*, and *"go"*. Not only modal verbs and conjunctions were handled this way, but also prepositions and other auxiliary words.

In the released data there exists no a-node with no link from the t-layer (with some exceptions as punctuation etc.).

Some errors in the inter-layer linking were caused by the "copying" process on the t-layer: if a word was missing in the sentence, but it was expressed in the previous context, the annotator could "copy" the node so it was no longer missing (cf. *"Peter bought flowers and Andrew cakes."* — the node for *"buy"* would be copied). Not all the links to lower layers from the original node should be preserved at the copied node, though.

Wrong sentence segmentation: The source text was segmented by a program that might make some errors. Several heuristics were used to determine such cases: a preposition without a word in the corresponding case, a sentence ending with a non-typical character or starting with a lowercase letter.

Word segmentation: Problems of word segmentation were similar to the problems of sentence segmentation. For example, a number representing date (*"6. 11."*) could be tokenised as a number with decimal point (*"6.11"*) followed by a dot. Therefore, all numbers with a decimal point that could be transformed to dates had to be checked manually.

3.2   Morphological Checking Procedures

Local case without a preposition: In Czech, every word in local case must have a preposition. This CP could take advantage of both the a-layer and t-layer.

Agreement of adjectival attribute: Attribute in adjective has to agree in case, gender and number with its parent. The a-layer could be used to find attributes.

Rule based error detection: All the data were tested by the rule based disambiguation program [6]. Marked errors were corrected manually.

3.3   Analytical Checking Procedures

Coordination: Coordination, apposition (and mathematical operations on the t-layer) were annotated in a special way: the coordinating conjunction is captured as a child of the node on which all the coordinated words depend. The words become children of the conjunction node with a special attribute is_member, while common dependent nodes are captured as children of the conjunction without the member attribute (see Figure 1: C denotes conjunctions, M denotes the member attribute, dashed arrows represent the actual dependency relations).

Special functions to find parents and children in such constructions were provided, but they worked well only if there were no errors in the annotations of the constructions.

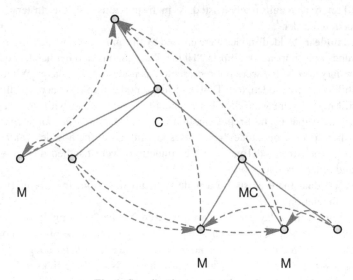

Fig. 1. Coordination construction scheme

Parent of an attribute: An attribute can have only a limited set of parents: nouns, some pronouns and numerals. Many exceptions exist to this rule, though, as almost any word can function as a name (e. g. *"the new Wash and Go"*).

Prepositions and conjunctions: Prepositions and conjunctions can be detected either by their morphological tag, or by their analytical function. If these two indicators do not agree, there is probably an error.

3.4   Tectogrammatical Checking Procedures

Predicative complement: Predicative complement (a participant called "doplněk" in Czech) depends on two words: on a verb and its child (subject or object). Since the annotation scheme of PDT does not allow for "double dependencies", there were special rules how to deal with complements. The rules were different for a-layer and t-layer, but the realization had to be in accord.

Lists of forms: For almost every functor there exists a limited set of possible forms[2]. This CP listed all forms of all functors so that the rare cases could be checked by a human annotator.

New and cancelled functors: During the annotation process, some of the functors were cancelled, because they were found too specific and indistinguishable from some others. Similarly, some others were added, because an old functor was found too broad and general.

Valency: Valency frames were captured as links to a valency lexicon. The CP had to verify that all the valency slots are filled with nodes of the prescribed form. Note that Actor is believed a part of a valency frame. Free time and place adverbials were checked via the "List of forms" procedure.

Coreference: Coreference was represented by a link to the antecedent of a node. For some kinds of nodes, coreference was obligatory, which was consequently verified by the CP.

Relative and content clauses: Restrictive relative clauses starting with some pronouns can be distinguished from content clauses either by the functor of their head verb, or by the agreement between the pronoun and the parent of the sentence (restrictive) or by the agreement between the pronoun and its parent (content). These two aspects had to be in accord.

Topic-focus articulation: CP's for topic-focus articulation (TFA) [7] made a special group of its own with almost thirty members. Due to the connection to deep word order, any change in the data that added new nodes or moved existing ones could damage the correctness of the TFA annotation.

CP's verified several invariants (every sentence must have a focus; topic is typically on the left side, while focus on the right and so on). Projectivity of trees was also checked by TFA related CP's because of its relation to deep word order.

Another area checked by TFA CP's were rhematizers – words that emphasise a part of a sentence and mark the focus or contrastive topic.

Annotators' comments: Annotators were allowed to write comments in a special attribute. Some of the comments had standard values and were amenable to be processed by a procedure, others had to be checked manually. All the comments had to be read and solved before the data were ready for release.

Grammatemes: Grammatemes correspond to morphological categories, but express their "semantic" values (e. g. *"trousers"* is plural morphologically, but its grammateme of number may be singular). Grammatemes were annotated manually only partially, most of them were generated by a program. The program was able to indicate some errors of various kinds if it was not able to assign any grammateme. For example, agreement between subject and predicate was checked when assigning grammatemes.

Names of people: All personal names were marked by a special attribute. Morphological information as well as capitalisation were used in heuristics with manual corrections.

---

[2] By form we mean morphological categories *and* auxiliary words (prepositions and conjunctions).

Direct speech: All heads of a direct speech were marked by a special attribute. This attribute was used by CP's for valency annotation, because some verbs allow participants only in direct speech.

4   Quantitative Analysis of Changes at the t-Layer

Some of the errors and changes in the data could have destructive character (e. g. deleting nodes). Therefore, older versions of the data were kept for later reconstruction.[3] A special tool was created to compare particular versions of the data, showing the progress of the post-annotation checking process. The principle is shown in Figure 2: first, the number of changes between neighbouring versions of the data was counted for various categories of the annotation (shown as the diff arrow, k_i corresponds to the number of changes for a category). Finally, the numbers of changes were summed for all the categories (sum arrow).

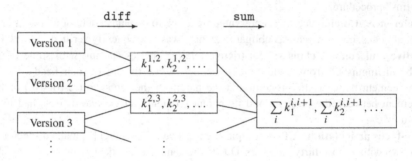

Fig. 2. Diagram for obtaining the number of changes

The resulting numbers had to be further corrected to give a realistic picture. Final numbers are presented in Table 1 (the numbers are rounded, the influence of some factors was only estimated). The = sign indicates that the value in the "all" column is the same as the value in the "relevant" column – i. e. all the nodes were relevant for the category. Numbers in parentheses are somehow "imprecise", because the total number of nodes was changing all the time and it is not clear how to count the percentage. The @ sign means that the annotation of the category was merged to the data very lately, so the number of differences is close to the number of changes.

The last column corresponds to $k_i^{1,25}$, since there were 25 versions of the data[4]. The number of differences is always smaller than the number of changes: for some nodes, a category could change several times. The subtraction does not represent redundant work, though — it rather indicates that some parts of the data were really problematic and changed several times.

---

[3] Only the tectogrammatical data were subject to this procedure because they changed most and most often.

[4] For some categories, the first version of the data could not be used, because the annotation was merged to the data in a later version.

Table 1. Number of changes

Category	Changes	% all	% relevant	Differences
New nodes	20 200	=	(2.4)	17 900
Deleted nodes	11 500	=	(1.4)	9 100
Form	2 300	=	0.3	700
Lemma	13 000	=	1.5	8 900
Tag	29 600	=	4.0	22 800
a-structure	5 000	=	0.6	3 000
Analytical function	4 500	=	0.5	2 900
t-structure	38 900	4.1	5.6	32 600
Functor	37 300	5.2	5.5	32 000
Hidden	2 900	=	0.3	1 600
Unhidden	6 300	=	0.7	4 000
Coordination-like constructions	11 300	1.2	42.5	5 600
Links to a-layer	54 200	6.0	42.1	42 400
Coreference – links	6 300	0.7	13.4	@
Coreference – type	5 400	0.6	11.5	@
Topic-focus articulation	27 200	3.0	6.3	@
Deep word order	51 400	=	5.6	@

It is interesting (but not surprising) that numbers inside "super-categories", indicated by horizontal lines, are similar, while numbers from different super-categories vary. The only exception is m-tag: the reason lies in its information value, because the tag contains information about several morphological categories (gender, number, tense etc.).

5 Conclusion

The total number of changes is 361,136 (some lines in Table 1 are missing). This number shows that the checking procedures did have their reason – not only they corrected annotation errors, but they also helped to keep the data in accordance with changing rules and to pick the preferred annotation in ambiguous cases.

Iterative running of a set of checking procedures seems to be a good tool not only to guarantee the data validity and quality, but also a good tool to measure the import of the procedures, to monitor the evolvement of the data, and to find the problematic areas of the annotation.

Finding a general way to generate checking procedures is almost impossible. Corpora differ in language, data formats, set of described phenomena, and theoretical framework. Comparing differing annotations of identical source data segments can give some hints on where to search for errors. Attention should be paid to building the annotation guidelines and tools, so that the chance of a mistake is decreased – mainly in the areas of higher-level relations that are not easily presented to annotators. Relations between layers of annotation are the prominent example; moreover, they can be expediently used to find annotation errors.

Acknowledgements

This paper was written with the support of the grant GA AV ČR 1ET101120503 (Integration of language resources in order to extract information from natural language texts).

References

1. Hajič, J., Mikulová, M., Bémová, A., Hajičová, E., Havelka, J., Kolářová-Řezníčková, V., Kučová, L., Lopatková, M., Pajas, P., Panevová, J., Razímová, M., Sgall, P., Štěpánek, J., Urešová, Z., Veselá, K., Žabokrtský, Z.: The Prague Dependency Treebank 2.0. CD-ROM (in preparation) http://ufal.mff.cuni.cz/pdt2.0/.
2. Sgall, P.: Generativní popis jazyka a česká deklinace [Generative Description of Language and Czech Declension]. Academia, Prague, Czech Rep. (1967).
3. Pajas, P., Štěpánek, J.: A Generic XML-Based Format for Structured Linguistic Annotation and Its Application to Prague Dependency Treebank 2.0. Technical Report TR-2005-29, ÚFAL MFF UK, Prague, Czech Rep. (2005).
4. Hajič, J., Vidová-Hladká, B., Pajas, P.: The Prague Dependency Treebank: Annotation Structure and Support. In: Proceedings of the IRCS Workshop on Linguistic Databases, Philadelphia, USA, University of Pennsylvania (2001) 105–114.
5. Dickinson, M.: Error detection and correction in annotated corpora. PhD thesis, The Ohio State University (2005).
6. Květoň, P.: *Rule based morphological disambiguation*. PhD thesis, in print (2006).
7. Sgall, P., Hajičová, E., Panevová, J.: The Meaning of the Sentence in Its Semantic and Pragmatic Aspects. Academia, Prague, Czech Rep. (1986).

Language Modelling with Dynamic Syntax

David Tugwell

School of Computer Science, University of St Andrews, Scotland, UK

Abstract. In this paper we introduce a system for the robust analysis of English using the apporach of Dynamic Syntax, in which the syntactic process is modelled as the word-by-word construction of a semantic representation. We argue that the inherent incrementality of the approach, in contrast with the essentially static assumptions of standard generative grammar, has clear advantages for the task of language modelling. To demonstrate its potential we show that this syntactic approach consistently outperforms a standard trigram model in word recovery tasks on parsable sentences. Furthermore, these results are achieved without recourse to hand-prepared training data.

1 Introduction

Generative grammars have typically founded on a base of static syntactic structures, which abstract away from the time-flow of language understanding, while capturing the incrementality of language has been left as a task for the processor. The central assumption of Dynamic Syntax is that grammars can and should mirror this time-flow of language directly by building structure word-by-word through the string. A corollary of this assumption is that syntactic structure is now no longer necessary and may be dispensed with.

Arguments for Dynamic Syntax have hitherto been mostly theoretical, arguing that it provides more precise characterizations of a range of syntactic phenomena (for example, non-constituent coordination [1] and anaphora binding effects [2]) or has superior properties from a language-theoretic perspective [3]. In this paper, we argue that this realignment of the relation between grammar and parser offers great potential for wide-coverage practical syntactic models to be used in a range of language engineering tasks. In particular, we argue that the incrementality of the construction of meaning not only allows the model to be psycholinguistically plausible, but also provides an ideal platform for incremental language modelling. Conversely, building a language model serves a crucial function in itself for it provides an objective and powerful evaluation metric, something that generative grammar has largely been lacking.

2 Dynamic Syntax

A dynamic grammar describes a set of triples (w_i, S_j, S_k), where w_i is a word of the vocabulary, S_j some state, and S_k a state that can follow from S_j given w_i. A derivation of the string $w_1 \dots w_n$ can thus be represented:

$$S_0 \xrightarrow{w_1} S_1 \xrightarrow{w_2} S_2 \dots\dots\dots S_{n-1} \xrightarrow{w_n} S_n \tag{1}$$

Petr Sojka, Ivan Kopeček and Karel Pala (Eds.): TSD 2006, LNAI 4188, pp. 285–292, 2006.

We assume that states represent the growing meaning, or information content, of the sentence and that S_n is therefore the final interpretation of the string. Since there is no bound on the length of sentences and therefore, on the amount of information they contain, the set of states will not be finite. Formally the model can be seen as a Markov model with a countably infinite number of states. Chomsky's argument [4] as to the insufficiency of *finite-state* Markov models for syntactic description does not apply.

2.1   Example Derivation

Let us consider the derivation of a simple example (1).

(1) The chicken walked across the road.

Let us suppose that we wish to represent the semantic content of this sentence as the following unordered collection of information about four conceptual constituents *s, x, p, y*:

situation(s) & past(s) & walk_v(s) & arg1(s,x) & goal(s,p)
& chicken(x) & definite(x) & singular(x)
& path(p) & across(p) & arg1(p,y)
& road_n(y) & definite(y) & singular(y)

Conceptual representations of this type[1] have always been prone to the accusation of arbitrariness – which distinctions should we make, what should we represent and how? However, if the system is open to objective evaluation, as will be shown to be the case here, then we immediately have a handle on the problem. For any enhancements to the representation, or new distinctions made, we can test to see if there is a corresponding improvement in performance.

Let us further suppose that our grammar will build the interpretation word by word as shown in Fig. 1.

State	Word	Constituent Stack $\longrightarrow$		
S_0		s situation		
S_1	the	s	x definite	
S_2	chicken	s	x chicken_n, sg	
S_3		s subject:x		
S_4	walked	s past, walk_v, arg1:x		
S_5	across	s goal:p	p path, across	
S_6	the	s	p	y definite
S_7	road	s	p	y road_n, sg
S_8		s	p arg1:y	y
S_9		s	p	
S_{10}		s		

Fig. 1. Derivation of sentence (1)

---

[1] Drawing on work in [5] and [6].

The diagram shows only the new information added at each state – the state itself contains all the information added in the sentence so far. We also assume that as the constituents are constructed they are placed on a *constituent stack*[2]. This stack is to be equated with the parsing stack employed by a processor, but here it is an integral component of the grammar.

The initial state S_0 consists of a constituent s containing the information that it is a *situation*.[3] At the next state S_1, with the input of the first word *the*, we create a new constituent x with the information that it is *definite* and this is placed above s on the stack. At the next state S_2, additional information is added to constituent x, namely that its head is the noun lexeme *chicken*. This constituent is removed from the stack at S_3 and attached as *subject* of the situation s. This *syntactic* relation between constituents was not in our semantic interpretation, but is found to be necessary for the construction of sentences. The transition between S_2 and S_3 does not correspond to an input word in the string and may be termed a *postlexical* transition. Such transitions may operate at any time, depending only on the current state of the interpretation. The derivation is complete when we have a single complete *situation* on the stack.

The use of the parsing stack by the dynamic grammar represents a major shift in the relation between grammar and parser compared to that in standard generative approaches. In the dynamic system, the objects manipulated by grammar and parser are identical. However, the grammar and the parser that uses it are still kept distinct – sentences can accord with the grammar but still be unprocessable due to memory constraints or garden-pathing. The grammar only provides possible transitions, and the parser is left to decide which path or paths to pursue at any point. The claim is that this redistribution simplifies the relation between grammar and processor and also simplifies both components: the grammar no longer needs syntactic structures, the parser simply uses the states defined by the grammar as parse states.

2.2 Transition Rules

The grammar consists of the lexicon and a set of transition rules: lexical and postlexical, corresponding to the two types of transition. Transition rules may be broadly equated with the grammatical constructions of Construction Grammar [7], conceived as separate and independently-learned operations to construct meaning.

Lexical rules may be represented in the following form:

Lex	Conditions on lexical entry of input word
S	Conditions on current interpretation state
S+1	Information added to form next state

Lexical rule schema

The lexical conditions are typically membership of a particular wordclass, but rules could also be restricted to a particular lexical item. Conditions on the current state of the

---

[2] Pictured on its side, with top to the right.

[3] The representation is simplified by omitting variables where they are recoverable from the constituent itself.

interpretation will generally relate to the constituent that is currently on top of the parse stack (referred to as the *active constituent*). The information added is generally the semantic information in the lexical entry of the word. Post-lexical rules will typically place conditions on the top two elements on the parse stack.

3 Current Implementation

The current system analyses unrestricted English, based on a set of hand-written transition rules.[4] Lexical information is derived from a lemmatized version of the POS-tagged 100m word British National Corpus (BNC). Semantic information about individual lexemes, such as prepositions, has been hand-coded into the lexicon. Probability estimates for the derivation are calculated at each state on the basis of lexeme frequencies from the BNC, estimated transition rule probabilities, and collocation probabilities derived from the BNC (see below).

The grammar covers a wide-range of constructions, including movement of all types (*wh*-movement, the various types of relative clause, exclamatives, *it*-clefts, pseudoclefts, extraposition), control constructions (raising, object and subject control), coordination (including non-constituent and unlike-constituent coordination) and many others. However, only 53% of sentences of less than 30 words receive a complete derivation, though this figure increases to 87% if we include sentences where the parser reaches the end of the string but none of the derivations are complete.

3.1 Using Corpus Information

In a previous project [8], grammatical relations (or *gramrels*) between words were extracted from the BNC using regular expressions and Mutual Information (MI) scores were calculated for these. Binary relations, relating two lexemes, include Subject, Object, Modifier, Coordination, Possessor and their inverses. Unary relations relate just to an individual lexeme and are largely propensities to take a range of complement types (finite, infinitive, gerundive etc). There is also three-way relation between a lexeme, the prepositional head of a PP modifying it and the noun head of the complement of the PP. The MI scores for gramrels are added directly into the probability metric (expressed logarithmically) of the state where the gramrel is found to hold.

So, in the derivation of sentence (1) the system incorporates the MI scores in Fig. 3 at S_4 and S_8 respectively.

Gramrel	MI
(Subject, *walk_v*, *chicken_n*)	2.0
(PP, *walk_v*, *across*, *road_n*)	4.0

Fig. 2. Gramrels used in sentence (1)

The depth of syntactic analysis means that grammatical relations can be recovered and used even when the elements of the relations are widely separated as in (2).

---

[4] Currently around 160 lexical and 90 post-lexical rules.

(2) Which problems did the boys seem to want to talk about?

The analysis of raising, subject control and *wh*-movement constructions allows the following gramrels to be used in choosing the desired derivation.

Gramrel	MI
(Inf-Comp, *seem_v*)	2.7
(Inf-Comp, *want_v*)	2.9
(Subject, *want_v*, *boy_n*)	1.0
(Subject, *talk_v*, *boy_n*)	1.2
(PP, *talk_v*, *about*, *problem_n*)	5.1

Fig. 3. Gramrels used in sentence (2)

The incrementality of the construction of meaning in dynamic syntax ensures that gramrel information is used as soon as possible.

Consider a sentence with "VP coordination" such as (3).

(3) The dogs barked and howled.

Employing a typical phrase structure approach would not allow us to establish that *dog* was the subject of *barked* until the whole coordinate VP was constructed, that is, at the final word *howled*, when the NP could be combined with it to complete the S.[5] In the analysis of coordination in dynamic syntax the string *the dogs barked* is here analysed as it would be if it was an independent sentence and the gramrel (Subject, *bark_v*, *dog_n*) is used at *barked*. Not only is this in line with psycholinguistic evidence on the incrementality of interpretation, it also benefits an incremental language model.

3.2   Control Structure

Given that the grammar itself produces and operates on "parse states", the only task relegated to the processor is to decide which derivation path or paths to pursue at each stage in the parse. At present we employ a beam-search with no backtracking, so that after each word has been processed and the lexical and postlexical rules performed, the system retains those states with the n-highest scores.

It is our experience that the beam that we need for wide-coverage parsing with dynamic syntax is considerably narrower than for similar coverage with a static constituency-based grammar. In the following evaluations the maximum beam used was 100.

4   Language Modelling

Syntactic theories have seldom been developed in systems open to objective evaluation. As the system and the syntax it embodies is still in an early period of development, evaluation is more important for development than for comparison with alternative approaches. However,

---

[5] And, of course, the VP could be indefinitely long, as in *The dogs barked, howled, yelped... and wailed*, resulting in an indefinitely long wait.

it is also useful to show the potential of the dynamic approach and compare its performance with alternative established technologies, which we do here.

It has already been shown [9,10] that syntactic models can outperform standard n-gram techniques in the task of language modelling, which corresponds to how well the model predicts the language. It would also be of great interest to see how a linguistically-motivated model compares with this baseline. Conversely, from the perspective of system development this fundamental measure of model performance is likely to be of most use in evaluating and measuring improvements to the model.

4.1 Word Recovery Task

However, the dynamic system is not a complete probabilistic model, and normalizing it in a reliable way would involve issues of considerable complexity. We decided therefore to employ an approximation method. We remove a word from a sentence, randomly generate a set of $n - 1$ competitors,[6] and get the system to rank the resulting n strings. In the language teaching community this task is known as cloze testing with a fixed choice of words and is held to be an accurate indicator of all-round linguistic ability.

The results were compared with a trigram model trained on the same data, the 100m word BNC.[7] We used the *one count* method of Chen and Goodman ([11]) as this offered close to optimal performance given the size of the training corpus.[8] Since the BNC has been used extensively for development of the system over a number of years, it was not possible to designate any of the corpus as test data. Therefore we used a section of the Hector corpus, a comparable mixed corpus of British English, as test data. This was already divided into sentences.

The results presented below are for those sentences (less than 30 words in length) where some result was returned by the parser (even if the derivation was not complete). This figure includes 72% of sentences of this length.

The results in Fig. 4 show both average number of errors (ie. higher-rated substitutions) per word and the percentage of correct guesses (ie. words where there was no higher-rated substitution) for different sizes of substitution sets.

The results clearly show that the dynamic model makes fewer errors overall, but the trigram model recovers more first place scores. Looking at the results in detail, the dynamic model is generally better on the less frequent words, as it captures collocation relations outside the window of trigrams and also makes use of grammatical zeroes. The trigram model, in contrast, is far stronger on frequent words and frequent sequences. In future work we aim to capture more of this local context by estimating a greater range of gramrels.[9]

---

[6] The set of competitors was generated randomly in proportion to word frequency. So frequent words were more likely to be included, but were only included once.

[7] Direct comparison of the two systems is made difficult by the differing expectations of format – following standard practice to keep the trigram model compact capitalization and punctuation is removed, with only an end of sentence tag used. The dynamic system on the other hand benefits from having texts with standard orthography and punctuation. Each system was given the words in its preferred form, therefore, although the task was only to recover the words, not the punctuation.

[8] Chen and Goodman's *all count* offers fractionally better performance, but is more time-consuming to implement. The marginal improvement would not effect the general findings.

[9] Interpolating the two models is likely to be a good strategy if we are seeking the best score at present.

Word Set	Trigram errors/word	Dynamic errors/word	Trigram correct	Dynamic correct
5	0.62	0.41	72.5%	72.5%
10	1.17	0.77	62.1%	62.1%
20	2.68	1.69	56.0%	40.6%
50	5.72	4.55	50.0%	34.4%
100	8.33	7.94	40.9%	30.1%

Fig. 4. Dynamic Syntax vs. Trigram, word recovery task, parsable sentences (< 30)

It should be noted that these are results for word recovery given the total context of the sentence. For many applications, such as speech recognition, word recovery given only the left context might be a more useful score. We are presently working on a range of scores given varying degrees of context.

5 Further Developments

As the syntax develops, aided by feedback from performance on the word recovery task, the performance and coverage should continue to increase. Since we have a relatively full linguistic model, building a deep representational semantic structure for input strings, it also presents a wealth of opportunities for using this information to improve performance, including capturing anaphoric relations between constituents and using richer semantic representations.

In order to counter the inevitable problem of data sparseness when computing gramrels for less frequent words, we are experimenting with using thesaural categories – a ranked near neighbours list has been calculated for all lexemes in the BNC using the same collocational information. In the absence of a gramrel score we will back off to a score calculated from the gramrels of its near neighbours and see if this gives an improvement in performance.

6 Conclusion

We have demonstrated that an unsupervised system based on a linguistically-motivated dynamic syntax grammar and information automatically extracted from a corpus can produce a language model that can consistently outperform a standard trigram model. It is to be hoped that this is the starting point for a succession of evaluated dynamic syntax models that can extract increasing amounts of information from a corpus to provide better language models and drive down the error rate on word recovery.

In the longer term, the usability of such full linguistic models for this task offers the prospect of combining the theoretical linguistic goal of building predictive and explanatory linguistic models with the practical goal of providing the best language model. A further advantage of the dynamic approach is that its incrementality of interpretation is consistent with psycholinguistic evidence, which allows the prospect of collaboration with the field of sentence processing.

References

1. Milward, D.: Dynamic Dependency Grammar. Linguistics and Philosophy. **17** (1994) 561–605.
2. Kempson, R., Meyer-Viol, W., Gabbay, D.: 2001. *Dynamic Syntax: the flow of language understanding*. Oxford: Blackwell.
3. Hausser, R.: Complexity in Left-Associative Grammar, Theoretical Computer Science. **106** (1992), 283–308.
4. Chomsky, N.: 1957. *Syntactic structures*. The Hague: Mouton.
5. Schank, R. C.: *Conceptual information processing*. 1975. Amsterdam: Elsevier.
6. Jackendoff, R.: *Semantic structures*. 1990. MIT Press.
7. Goldberg, A. E.: *Constructions: a construction grammar approach to argument structure*. 1995. Chicago: University of Chicago Press.
8. Kilgarriff, A., Tugwell, D.: Sketching words. In Marie-Héléne Corréard (ed.), Lexicography and Natural Language Processing: A Festschrift in Honour of B.T.S. Atkins. pp. 125–137. EURALEX.
9. Chelba, C., Jelinek, F.: Exploiting syntactic structure for language modeling. In: Proceedings of 36th ACL and 17th COLING (1998), 225–231.
10. Roark, B.: Probabilistic top-down parsing and language modeling. Computational Linguistics **27(2)** (2001), 249–276.
11. Chen, S. F., Goodman J.: An empirical study of smoothing techniques for language modeling, In: Proceedings of 34th ACL (1996), 310–318.

Using Word Sequences for Text Summarization

Esaú Villatoro-Tello, Luis Villaseñor-Pineda, and Manuel Montes-y-Gómez

Language Technologies Group, Computer Science Department,
National Institute of Astrophysics, Optics and Electronics (INAOE), Mexico
{villatoroe, villasen, mmontesg}@inaoep.mx

Abstract. Traditional approaches for extractive summarization score/classify sentences based on features such as position in the text, word frequency and cue phrases. These features tend to produce satisfactory summaries, but have the inconvenience of being domain dependent. In this paper, we propose to tackle this problem representing the sentences by word sequences (n-grams), a widely used representation in text categorization. The experiments demonstrated that this simple representation not only diminishes the domain and language dependency but also enhances the summarization performance.

1 Introduction

Current information technologies allow the creation and storage of massive amounts of data. In this context, document summaries are becoming essential. People can explore and analyze entire document collections just by looking at their summaries [1].

Text summarization is the task concerning the automatic generation of document summaries. It aims to reduce documents in length and complexity, while preserving some of their essential information [2]. Despite there are different types of summaries and approaches for their generation, today the most popular summarization systems focus on the construction of extractive summaries (extracts created by selecting a set of relevant sentences of the input text) by machine-learning techniques [3].

One central problem in machine-learning summarization is the representation of sentences. There have been used several surface-level features in order to represent them. Most of these features are "heuristically motivated", since they tend to emulate the manual creation of extracts. In a pioneering work by Kupiec *et al.* [2] sentences were represented by their position and length, the presence of cue phrases and their overlap with the document title. More recent works [1,4] enlarged these features incorporating information such as the occurrence of proper names and the presence of anaphors.

The "heuristically motivated" features allow producing very precise extracts. Nevertheless, they have the major disadvantage of being highly related to a target domain. This condition implies that when moving from one domain to another, it may be necessary to redefine or even eliminate some features. For instance, cue phrases, which are particular for each domain, require being modified, while the overlap with the title, which has no sense in all topics, may be eliminated.

In order to increase the domain (and language) independence of machine learning summarizers, we propose eliminating all kind of "heuristically motivated" attributes and substitute them by word-based features. In particular, we consider the use of word sequences

Petr Sojka, Ivan Kopeček and Karel Pala (Eds.): TSD 2006, LNAI 4188, pp. 293–300, 2006.

(so-called n-grams) as sentence features. Our goal is to develop a more flexible and competitive summarization method. In other words, we aim to boost the summarization flexibility without reducing the quality of the output summaries.

It is important to mention that simple word-based representations are common in many text-processing tasks. However, n-grams have been applied without much significant success. In this way, one relevant contribution of this work is the study of the application of word-based representations in text summarization, and the evaluation of the impact of using word sequences as sentence features. In our knowledge, this is the first attempt on using word sequence features for broad-spectrum text summarization.

The rest of the paper is organized as follows. Section 2 introduces the proposed feature scheme. Section 3 describes the experimental setup. Section 4 presents some experimental results on the use of word sequences as features for text summarization. Finally, section 5 depicts our conclusions and future work.

2   Word-Based Features

As we mentioned, the machine-learning approach for text summarization focuses on the creation of extracts by the selection of relevant sentences from the input texts. To pursue this approach it is necessary to establish the sentence features, the classification method and a training corpus of document/extract pairs.

Traditional methods for supervised text summarization use "heuristically motivated" features to represent the sentences. Our proposal is to consider word-based features in order to increase the summarization flexibility by lessening the domain and language dependency. In particular, we propose using n-grams (sequences of n consecutive words) as sentence features. Thus, in our model each sentence is represented by a feature vector that contains one boolean attribute for each n-gram that occurs in the training collection. Specially, we only consider sequences up to three words, i.e., from 1-grams to 3-grams.

Word-based representations have been widely used in several text-processing tasks. In particular, in text categorization the bag-of-words (1-grams) representation corresponds to the leading approach [5]. However, there are numerous studies on the effect of generalizing this approach by using word sequences as document features [6,7,8]. These studies indicate that the use of word n-grams does not considerably improve the performance on text categorization.

Despite of the unfavorable results in text categorization, we believe that the use of n-grams can be helpful in text summarization. This hypothesis is supported in the following two facts:

On the one hand, sentences are much smaller than documents, and consequently the classifier would require more and more detailed information to distinguish between relevant and irrelevant instances. For instance, in text categorization, the merely presence of the word earthquake may indicate that the document at hand is about this phenomenon. Nevertheless, it may not be enough to select the informative sentences. In text summarization, n-grams such as "earthquake-left" or "earthquake-of-magnitude" are more pertinent.

On the other hand, some recent works on text summarization make use of n-grams to evaluate the quality of summaries [9,10]. These works have shown that the n-gram correspondences between handwritten and automatically produced summaries are a good indicator of the appropriateness of the extracts.

Our proposal differs from these works in that it directly employs the n-grams to construct the summaries, i.e., it uses the n-grams to select the relevant sentences. Therefore, it represents the first attempt on using word sequence features in text summarization, and consequently the first evaluation on their impact in the quality of the extracts.

3 Experimental Setup

3.1 Corpora

We used two different corpora in our experiments, one of them in Spanish and the other in English. Both corpora consist of newspaper articles, but the first one only includes news about natural disasters, while the other considers different kinds of topics such as politics, economics and sports. Table 1 resumes some statistics about the corpora.

Table 1. Corpora Statistics

Data Set	Language	Domain	Number of Sentences	Relevant Sentences
DISASTERS	Spanish	Natural Disasters News	2833	863 (30%)
CAST	English	General News	4873	1316 (27%)

The *Disasters* corpus consists of 300 news reports collected from several Mexican newspapers. Each sentence of the corpus was labeled using two basic tags: relevant and non-relevant. In order to avoid subjectivity on the tagging process, annotators were instructed to mark as relevant only the sentences containing at least one concrete fact about the event. For instance, the date or place of the disaster occurrence, or the number of people or houses affected.

On the other hand, the *CAST* (Computer-Aided Summarization) corpus consists of 164 news reports. In contrast to the Disasters corpus, it includes news about different topics such as politics, economics and sports. It sentences were also annotated as relevant and non-relevant. Both corpora maintain a similar distribution of relevant sentences. More details on the *CAST* corpus can be found in [11].

3.2 Classifier

The Naïve Bayes classifier has proved to be quite competitive for most text processing tasks including text summarization. This fact supported our decision to use it as main classifier for our experiments. It basically computes for each sentence s its probability (i.e., a score) of been included in a summary S given the k features $F_j; j = 1..k$. This probability can be expressed using Bayes' rule as follows [2]:

$$P(s \in S | F_1, F_2, ..., F_k) = \frac{P(F_1, F_2, ..., F_k | s \in S) P(s \in S)}{P(F_1, F_2, ..., F_k)}$$

Assuming statistical independence of the features:

$$P(s \in S | F_1, F_2, ..., F_k) = \frac{\prod_{j=1}^{k} P(F_j | s \in S) P(s \in S)}{\prod_{j=1}^{k} P(F_j)}$$

where $P(s \in S)$ is a constant and $P(F_j | s \in S)$ and $P(F_j)$ can be estimated directly from the training set by counting occurrences.

3.3 Baseline Configuration

In order to define the baseline configuration we made an exhaustive study of previous supervised methods for text summarization. Particularly, we searched for common features across the different methods as well as for *domain independent* features. The following paragraphs briefly describe our main findings.

Kupiec *et al.* [2] used five different attributes, but only three of them were domain independent, namely, the position and length of the sentence, and the presence of proper names.

Chuang *et al.* [1] evaluated the representation of sentences by 23 different features. However, only a small subset of them were domain independent. For instance, it used the similarity with the document title and the term frequencies.

Neto *et al.* [4] used 13 features in their summarization system. Only four of them were domain independent: the centroid value of the sentence, its length and position, as well as the similarity with the title and the presence of proper names.

We implemented a baseline summarization method using the following features: the position and length of sentences, its centroid value and its similarity with the document title, and the presence of proper names. All these features are domain and language independent, and thus they may be applied to both corpora.

In addition, we also included the presence of numeric quantities. This feature was added because both data sets are news articles and they tend to use numeric expressions to explain the facts.

4   Experimental Results

In this paper, we have proposed the use of word-based features in order to develop a more flexible and competitive summarization method. This section presents the results of two initial experiments. The first experiment considers the representation of sentences by simple bag-of-words. Its purpose is to demonstrate that word-based features are domain and language independent and that its performance is comparable to that of traditional approaches. The second experiment applies word sequences as sentence features. Its goal is to evaluate their impact on text summarization.

In both experiments, the performance of classifiers was measured by the accuracy, precision and recall, and the evaluation was based on a cross-validation strategy.

4.1   First Experiment: Single Words as Features

In this experiment, single-word features represented sentences. Since the original feature space had a very high dimensionality, we needed to apply the information gain technique in order to select a subset of relevant features. Table 2 shows the number of features considered in this experiment for both data sets.

Table 3 presents the results obtained in this experiment. It is important to notice that (*i*) the proposed representation produced a similar performance for both data sets, indicating that it

Table 2. Number of single-word features

	Original Features	Selected Features
DISASTERS	8958	530
CAST	10410	612

Table 3. Evaluation of single-word features

	Baseline Configuration			Single-Word Features		
	accuracy	*precision*	*recall*	*accuracy*	*precision*	*recall*
DISASTERS	74.94	87.89	78.89	84.82	91.72	87.12
CAST	68.08	74.36	80.44	79.76	88.67	84.39

is domain and language independent, and that (ii) the proposed representation outperformed the baseline method, in both precision and recall.

4.2 Second Experiment: Word Sequences as Features

Here, we represented sentences by word sequences (n-grams). Specifically, we considered sequences up to three words, i.e., from *1*-grams to *3*-grams. Like in the previous experiment, we used the information gain technique to reduce the feature space and to select a subset of relevant features. Table 4 shows the number of features considered in this experiment for both data sets.

Table 4. Number of word sequence features

	Original Features				Selected Features
	1-grams	*2-grams*	*3-grams*	*All*	*All*
DISASTERS	8958	34340	53356	96654	2284
CAST	10410	52745	72953	136108	2316

Table 5 describes the results obtained in this experiment. They indicate that the use of n-gram features enhanced the classification precision, while maintaining the recall rate. This behavior is a direct cause of using features that are more detailed. This kind of features allows a better distinction between relevant and non-relevant sentences. In particular, they allow treating difficult cases.

Table 5. Evaluation of word sequence features

	Single-Word Features			Word sequence features		
	accuracy	*precision*	*recall*	*accuracy*	*precision*	*recall*
DISASTERS	84.82	91.72	87.12	86.16	95.53	86.09
CAST	79.76	88.67	84.39	84.54	96.48	84.53

4.3   A Practical Example

This section illustrates the summarization based on word sequence features. In particular, table 6 shows a news article from the CAST corpus and it corresponding calculated extract (in bold font).

Table 6. A document and it corresponding extract

Sentence ID	Relevance Assessments	Sentences
1	×	USA: U.S. June trade gap narrows sharply as imports drop.
2	×	U.S. June trade gap narrows sharply as imports drop.
3	×	Glenn Somerville.
4	×	WASHINGTON 1996-08-20.
5	✓	**The U.S. trade gap narrowed dramatically in June as imports of merchandise and petroleum plunged from May levels, the Commerce Department said on Tuesday.**
6	✓	**The monthly deficit dropped 23.1 percent to $8.11 billion from a revised $10.55 billion in May much lower than the $9.4 billion shortfall that Wall Street economists had forecast for June.**
7	✓	June exports eased a slight 0.3 percent to $69.71 billion while imports dropped 3.3 percent to $77.82 billion.
8	✓	**Amid the big overall improvement in June trade, China emerged for the first time as the nation with which the United States has the largest bilateral shortfall.**
9	×	The deficit with China climbed 8.8 percent to $3.33 billion in June, surpassing the $3.24 billion deficit with Japan that was up 3.6 percent from May.
10	×	**Commerce noted that exports of American-made goods to China declined for a fourth straight month in June, which is likely to fuel trade tensions between the two countries.**
11	✓	**Steady improvement in shrinking the deficit with Japan was the main reason that China became the leading deficit nation in June, Commerce officials said.**
12	×	The second-quarter deficit of $10.5 billion with Japan was the smallest quarterly deficit in five years, the department said.
13	×	Previously, the department said the overall May trade deficit was $10.88 billion but it revised that down to a $10.55 billion gap.
14	✓	**The United States typically runs a surplus on its trade with other countries in services like travel and tourism that partly offsets big merchandise trade deficits.**
15	✓	In June, the merchandise deficit fell 13.9 percent to $14.46 billion from $16.79 billion in May.
16	×	Lower imports of new cars and parts, especially from Japan and Germany, helped shrink the merchandise trade gap.
17	×	The surplus on services climbed 1.6 percent to $6.34 billion from $6.25 billion in May.
18	×	Analysts said beforehand that an influx of tourists bound for the Olympic Games in Atlanta would boost the services surplus.
19	×	The cost and volume of all types of petroleum products fell in June after a sharp May runup.
20	×	The cost of petroleum imports declined to $5.33 billion in June from $5.93 billion while the volume fell to 291,866 barrels from 305,171 in May.
21	×	Foreign sales of civilian aircraft declined in June by $117 million to $1.54 billion.
22	×	Exports of industrial supplies and materials were off $138 million to $12.32 billion.
23	×	Imports of autos and parts from all sources dropped sharply by $689 million to $10.79 billion in June.
24	×	Computer imports were down $413 million to $4.24 billion and semiconductor imports decreased $291 million to $2.87 billion in June.
25	×	In bilateral trade, the deficit with Western Europe fell 7.1 percent to $761 million and the shortfall with Canada was down 2.2 percent to $2.42 billion.
26	×	In trade with Mexico, the U.S. deficit shrank 6.4 percent to $1.49 billion amid signs the Mexican economy was recovering from a deep recession and grew solidly in the second quarter this year.
27	×	The deficit with oil-producing OPEC countries dropped 26.9 percent in June to $1.40 billion from $1.91 billion in May.

It is important to notice that each sentence of the article has associated a manual relevance judgment ($\checkmark$ for relevant sentences and $\times$ for non-relevant ones), and that the summarization procedure could identify most of the relevant sentences and just misclassified three sentences (7, 10 and 15). The generated extract contains six sentences, achieving a compression rate of 22%, and a precision and recall of 0.83 and 0.71 respectively.

5   Conclusions

This paper proposed the use of word-based features in text summarization. Specifically, it considered the use of word sequence (n-gram) features. Its goal was to increase the domain (and language) independence of machine-learning summarizers, and to develop a more flexible and competitive summarization method.

The main contributions of this paper were the following two:

On the one hand, it represented, in our knowledge, the first attempt on using word-based features for broad-spectrum text summarization. In this line, our conclusion was that these features are as appropriate for text summarization as they are for text categorization. In our experiments, they outperformed the baseline method, in both precision and recall. In addition, they were appropriated for both domains and both languages.

On the other hand, this paper presented an evaluation of the impact of using word sequences (n-grams) as sentence features in text summarization. In contrast to text categorization, where the application of n-grams has not improved the classification performance, our results confirmed that the n-grams are helpful in text summarization. In particular, these results indicated that the n-gram features enhanced the classification precision, while maintaining the recall rate. Our general conclusion in this line is that n-gram features are adequate for fine-grained classification tasks.

Acknowledgements. This work was done under partial support of CONACYT (scholarship 189943, project grants 43990 and U39957-Y). We also thank SNI-Mexico and INAOE for their assistance.

References

1. Chuang T. W., and Yang J. (2004). Text Summarization by Sentence Segment Extraction Using Machine Learning Algorithms. In *Proceedings of the ACL '04 Workshop*. Barcelona, España, 2004.
2. Kupiec, J., Pedersen J. O., and Chen, F. (1995). A Trainable Document Summarizer. In *Proceedings of the 18th ACM-SIGIR Conference on Research and Development in Information Retrieval*. Seattle, pp. 68–73, 1995.
3. Hovy, E. (2003) Text Summarization. In Mitkov R. (Ed). *The Oxford handbook of Computational Linguistics*. Oxford, NY, 2003.
4. Neto L., Freitas A. A., and Kaestner C. A. A. (2004). Automatic Text Summarization using a Machine Learning Approach. In *Proceedings of the ACL-04 Workshop*. Barcelona, España, 2004.
5. Sebastiani F. (1999) Machine Learning in Automated Text Categorization. In *ACM Computing Surveys*, Vol. 34, pp. 1–47, 1999.
6. Bekkerman R., and Allan J. (2003). Using Bigrams in Text Categorization. *Technical Report IR-408*. Departement of Computer Science, University of Masschusetts, USA, 2003.

7. Canvar W. B., and Trenkle J. M. (1994). N-Gram-Based Text Categorization. In *Proceedings of the third Annual Symposium on Document Analysis and Information retrieval*. Nevada, Las Vegas, pp. 161–169, 1994.
8. Fürnkranz J. (1998). A Study Using n—gram Features for Text Categorization. *Technical report OEFAI-TR-98-30*. Austrian Institute for Artificial Intelligence, Wien, Austria, 1998.
9. Lin C., and Hovy E. (2003). Automatic Evaluation of Summaries Using N-gram Co-occurrence Statistics. In *Proceedings of the Human Technology Conference 2003*. Edmonton, Canada, 2003.
10. Banko M., and Vanderwende L. (2004). Using N-grams to Understand the Nature of Summaries. In *Proceedings of HLT/NAACL 2004*. Boston, MA., 2004.
11. Hasler L., Orasan C. and Mitkov R. (2003): Building better corpora for summarisation. In *Proceedings of Corpus Linguistics 2003*, Lancaster, UK, pp. 309–319, 2003.

Exploration of Coreference Resolution:
The ACE Entity Detection and Recognition Task

Ying Chen and Kadri Hacioglu

Center for Spoken Language Research, University of Colorado at Boulder, USA

Abstract. In this paper, we consider the coreference resolution problem in the context of information extraction as envisioned by the DARPA Automatic Content Extraction (ACE) program. Given a set of entity mentions referring to real world entities and a similarity matrix that characterizes how similar those mentions are, we seek a set of entities that are uniquely co-referred to by those entity mentions. The quality of the clustering of entity mentions into unique entities significantly depends on the quality of (1) the similarity matrix and (2) the clustering algorithm. We explore the coreference resolution problem along those two dimensions and clearly show the tradeoff among several ways of learning similarity matrix and using it while performing clustering.

1 Introduction

Availability of large annotated corpora and advances in machine learning techniques have enabled Information Extraction (IE) to become an active research area. The detection and recognition of entities as unique objects that belong to the physical world are the initial but crucial steps in many NLP applications including question answering, summarization etc. Here we present a detailed exploration of an entity detection and recognition (EDR) system that has been developed as a part of a system that participated in the ACE 2005 Evaluation.

The EDR system consists of two steps; first, it detects all mentions of entities occurring in raw text (mention detection) and, then, resolves all different mentions of an entity into an object that uniquely represents that entity (coreference resolution). The coreference resolution can be considered as a clustering problem; given a set of objects to be clustered and a similarity matrix among pairs of objects to guide the clustering algorithm. We mainly focus on how to determine the similarity matrix and how to use it. Assuming that the correct mentions are available with the ideal similarity matrix (it just tells the pair of objects are similar or not), the coreference resolution is trivial by taking connected sets of mentions as unique entities. However, the estimated similarity matrix are usually far from perfect and, to mitigate that, one needs to exploit relatively advanced clustering algorithms, for example, an agglomerative or correlation clustering algorithm. Intuitively, a better estimation of similarity matrix reduces the burden on clustering and an advanced clustering strategy reduces the burden on the accurate estimation of similarity matrix. In this paper, we explore the tradeoff between those phenomena for entities occurring in English and Chinese languages.

Our framework for the exploration of the coreference resolution problem consists of two case studies; (1) advanced similarity matrix estimation (or learning) with simpler clustering, and (2) simpler similarity matrix estimation (or learning) with advanced clustering. Here, we consider the similarity matrix estimation as a link classification problem and the output of the classifier is used to estimate the similarity matrix. In our exploration, we try to improve

Petr Sojka, Ivan Kopeček and Karel Pala (Eds.): TSD 2006, LNAI 4188, pp. 301–308, 2006.

the classification, and hence the similarity matrix estimation, by extending our classification models from mention-level to entity-level. Similarly, we vary the complexity of the clustering algorithm by using different linkage and clustering schemes. It is interesting to note that the linkage schemes in clustering can also be considered as the adaptation schemes for the similarity matrix as we proceed in clustering. We clearly demonstrate that exploitation of this coupling between classification and clustering is very important to overcome the problems of inaccurate similarity matrix estimation and improve the overall system performance.

2 Related Work

In this section we focus on and describe related work based on data-driven approaches, and exclude those that are rule-based. There are several supervised or unsupervised machine learning (ML) methods that can be applied to coreference resolution. Usually, coreference resolution is cast as a classification problem in the supervised ML framework (Soon et al., 2001; Ng and Cardie, 2002) and as a clustering problem in the unsupervised machine learning framework (Cardie and Wagstaff, 1999). Here, in contrast, we consider coreference resolution as a clustering problem with similarity matrix learning, either supervised or unsupervised. The outputs of the pairwise classifier, such as in (Soon et al., 2001), can be used to construct the similarity matrix. Alternatively, the ad-hoc distance metric defined over the feature representation of each reference (or mention) in an unsupervised ML framework can be used to construct a similarity matrix. Therefore, both approaches differ only in similarity matrix learning and allow a rich collection of clustering algorithms to be equivalently applied. Compared to previous related work, our view allows us to couple classification and clustering stages for the estimation and adaptation of the similarity matrix for better performance. That is, instead of focusing separately on classification and clustering we focus on the similarity matrix and use classification for its initial estimation and clustering for its incremental adaptation using several linkage schemes. Coupling of classification and clustering stages can also be seen in (Li and Roth, 2005; Luo et al., 2004; McCallum and Wellner, 2003) in different ways. All report performance improvements when compared to their baseline systems. However, no much work has been done to compare the contribution of the similarity metrics and clustering to coreference resolution in detail and explain why the performance will be improved with the more accurate similarity metrics or the complex clustering. This is the focus of our paper.

3 Methodology

As mentioned earlier, the performance of coreference resolution depends on the coupling between classification and clustering. We will describe our coreference system that improves the similarity matrix through this coupling.

3.1 Classification

Entity-Level Model. In coreference resolution, a similarity metric for a pair of mentions is required to cluster. Here, we consider the learning of similarity metrics (elements of the similarity matrix) as link/no link classification problem of a mention pair, and the confidence of a linking decision from the classifier can be used as the similarity metric of the two mentions under consideration. However, in most of the previous work, the features for classification are extracted by considering the mention-pairs in focus and their local context. Intuitively, there might be several cases that the mention-level features might not supply enough information to make better linking decisions. For example, consider a document section that includes the fragment

"Clinton also touched on the matter of American Edmond Bob who is being tried in a closed court in Russia on charges of spying. The United States believe he is innocent of these charges and are demanding his release on humanitarian grounds. The official said Putin understands our concern."

Assume that "Edmond Bob" and "he" are correctly linked. Using only mention pairs and their local context for making decisions might result in an incorrect and conflicting link of "Putin" and "he". However, this incorrect decision could have been overcome by using the information that "he" has been already linked to another mention "Edmond Bob" to establish a partial entity. Therefore, it becomes less likely to link "he" and "Putin" since the fact that "Edmond Bob" and "Putin" are two different personal names that can be captured through entity-level features. This clearly indicates the necessity of using information beyond mention pairs and their local context.

One way to go beyond the local context of the mention pairs is to take the advantage of the previous linking decisions. Using those decisions one can construct the corresponding partial entity for each mention in the mention-pair in focus. Considering the previous example, there is a link between "he" and "Edmond Bob", which means that there is a partial entity including "he" and "Edmond Bob". Now, when we try to decide on linking "Putin" to "he", we can trace back the previous link decision between "he" and "Edmond Bob". This allows us to compare "Putin" to the another proper name "Edmond Bob". Since the partial entities might contain one or more mentions, it is not computationally feasible to pair each mention to other mentions inside a partial entity to extract features for classification. Therefore, we need to define a single mention, called the canonical mention (Luo et al., 2004), that best represents the partial entity. For each partial entity, we select a mention as the canonical mention according to the following ordered preference list: longest NAME mention, longest NOMINAL mention and longest PRONOUN mention. In doing so, one can easily derive entity-level features from the pair of canonical mentions of the corresponding partial entities.

Feature Extraction. In the preceding section, we briefly talked about the mention-level features. Table 1 shows the set of features extracted in this study. It is an extension of the basic features in (Luo et al., 2004). Note that, due to the availability of linguistic resources and differences in English and Chinese, the corresponding feature sets are different in size and types. We organized source of features into three broad groups: (i) mention_string: the information containing within the mention string, (ii) mention_context: the information within the mention context, (iii) mention_pair: the information related with the mention pair.

The feature set in Table 1 serves as the baseline. Recall that one can also extract entity-level features in accordance with Table 1 using corresponding canonical mention pairs to create the entity-level feature set. Now we have two classification models: (i) Mention-level model (baseline model): Mention-level features in Table 1; (ii) Entity-level model: Baseline

Table 1. The mention-level feature set for classification; the same table is used for both basic and canonical mention pairs

Category	Features	Remark	Language
Mention_head	(1) Spell, Count, POS	Same as in (Luo, 2004)	English & Chinese
	(2) Mention type	The ACE mention type	
	(3) Entity type	The ACE entity type	
	(4) Gazetteer info	Information from gazetteer	
	(5) Low-case spell	Low-case of the head word	English
	(6) Capitalized word	# of capitalized word	
	(7) Definite word	Whether the head word is a definite word	
	(8) Gender, number, possessive, reflexive	Same as in (Luo, 2004)	
Mention_context	(9) Dependent info	The dependent word, pos, and relation	English & Chinese
	(10) Possessive info	Whether there is a possessive indicator	
	(11) Verb info	The nearest verb string	
	(12) Preposition word	Whether there is a preposition word around	
Mention_pair	(13) String match	Same as in (Luo, 2004)	English & Chinese
	(14) Token, sentence, mention distance	Same as in (Luo, 2004)	
	(15) Acronym	Same as in (Luo, 2004)	
	(16) Apposition	Same as in (Luo, 2004)	

features plus entity-level features between the pair of canonical mentions as described in Table 1 (for the features in mention-pair category, we only implement (13) and (14)).

3.2 Clustering

Linkage Schemes. The similarity matrix, defined as a collection of similarity metrics among pairs of all mentions, provides guidance when we try to decide if two clusters, each with a single mention, can be merged. As we progress in clustering we start to have clusters with more than one mention. So, we need to develop a linkage scheme to compute the similarity between two clusters to be used for merging. In this paper, in addition to commonly used linkage schemes, such as maximum, minimum and average linkage schemes, we have developed another linkage scheme, which has been customized for the coreference resolution problem in consideration. Our linkage scheme can exploit entity-level information. We describe it after a brief description of the standard linkage schemes:

Maximum Linkage: The distance of a cluster to another cluster is the maximum of the distances between items of each cluster.

Minimum Linkage: The distance of a cluster to another cluster is the minimum of the distances between items of each cluster.

Average Linkage: The distance of a cluster to another cluster is the average of the distances between items of each cluster.

Longest Canonical Maximum Linkage: Here we combine the canonical mention selection strategy in (Luo et al., 2004) with the linkage scheme proposed in (Daume and Marcu, 2005). It consists of the following steps: (1) Choose the canonical mention for each cluster as in (Luo et al. , 2004), which is briefly described in Section 3.1, (2) For each partial entity, compute the similarity metric of its canonical mention to the other partial entity cluster as described in (Daume and Marcu, 2005), (3) Choose the maximum among the two linkage metrics.

Clustering Schemes. Clustering schemes we describe here are about the order of clustering process given the clusters, independent of linking scheme used. Clustering can be viewed from several different perspectives. The traditional way processes the mentions in the order of left to right, like left2right first-link and left2right best-link methods. The other way is linking the best similar pairs in a bottom-up manner as in agglomerative clustering. Yet another way treats clustering as a graph problem and tries to solve clustering using the graph theory, such as correlation clustering.

Left2right best-link clustering: process the mentions in the order of left to right. For each mention, link it to the most similar previous cluster with the confidence greater than the fixed threshold (0.5 in our algorithm).

Agglomerative bottom-up clustering: initialize each mention as a cluster. Iteratively merge the most similar two clusters until the distance of any two clusters is below a fixed threshold (0.5 in our algorithm).

Unweighted correlation clustering: the graph outputted from the classifier is an un-weighted complete graph with "Link" or "Nolink" tags. Unweighted correlation clustering algorithm tries to find a partition which agrees with the original graph as much as possible on the edge tags. For details, the reader is referred to (Bansal et.al., 2002).

4   Experiments

We report experimental results based on ACE 2005 English and Chinese training data, given the golden mentions. For each language, 20% of data is reserved for development and 80% for training. All the following performances are reported for the development data.

4.1   Classification Evaluation

We select Yamcha toolkit[1] for implementing SVM based classifiers. To avoid the impact of clustering on performance, we used the naïve-clustering algorithm: the mentions are partitioned into disjoint connected groups according to the linking decisions. The results of the two models are shown in Table 2. Here "AF" is the ACE F score and is calculated using the ACE scoring script[2]. As can be easily seen from Table 2, the coreference resolution performance consistently increases with the complexity of the feature set in both languages.

---

[1] http://chasen.org/~taku/software/yamcha/
[2] http://www.nist.gov/speech/tests/ace/ace05/index.htm

Table 2. Performances of mention-level and entity-level classification models

	Mention-level AF (precision/recall)	Entity-level AF (precision/recall)
English	71.6 (91.4/58.9)	82.9 (90.8/76.3)
Chinese	82.9 (91.9/75.6)	90.8 (93.3/88.4)

Table 3. The comparison of different linkage schemes under bottom-up clustering on the baseline classifier

	Max	Min	Average	Longest Canonical Maximum
English	72.4(92.4/59.5)	86.1(86.8/85.5)	87.4(88.9/86.0)	88.6(90.3/86.9)
Chinese	83.3(92.4/75.9)	90.7(91.8/89.6)	91.2(92.5/89.8)	91.4(93.3/89.5)

Table 4. The comparison of clustering schemes on the baseline classifier and longest canonical maximum linkage (ACE F score)

	Left2right best-link clustering	Bottom-up clustering	Correlation clustering
English	88.6	88.6	83.5
Chinese	91.9	91.4	89.1

Table 5. The comparison of the coupling of classification and clustering

	Entity-level classifier + customized clustering	Mention-level classifier + customized clustering
English	87.3	88.6
Chinese	91.8	91.4

It is interesting to note that the improvement of coreference resolution with the entity-level model is almost due to significant increase in recall with marginal drop in precision. With the entity-level features, the entity-level model can capture information more than the mention-level model, effectively increasing the recall without sacrificing much the precision. Also, the relatively larger increase in the recall for English when compared to Chinese indicates that the English coreference resolution benefits from entity-level information more than the Chinese one. Comparing the overall absolute performances, it seems that the coreference resolution is easier for Chinese than for English. This is probably due to two reasons; (i) diverse nature of English data, and (ii) the difficulty of pronoun resolution in English.

4.2 Clustering Evaluation

Linkage Schemes Evaluation. To fairly compare the different linkage schemes described in 3.2, we run the agglomerative (bottom-up) clustering scheme with the similarity metrics derived from the baseline classifier and show the performances in Table 3 with the same format in Table 2. From Table 3, except the maximum linkage scheme, we found that the same phenomenon shows up as in entity-level classification: the improvement of coreference resolution with the entity-level model is almost due to significant increase in recall with marginal drop in precision. This indicates that the linkage scheme can work as the entity-level classifier: capture the entity-level information to improve the linkage similarity that can be viewed as an extension of similarity matrix in clustering. At the same time, the last three linkage schemes seem to achieve the similar performances for English and Chinese. With Student's t test, we found that, for English, "longest canonical maximum linkage" outperform "average linkage" and "minimum linkage" with 95% confidence, and for Chinese, the three linkages really perform similarly.

Clustering Schemes Evaluation. To avoid impact on performance from classification and linkage, we compare the performance variation with clustering schemes using the same classifier (baseline classifier) and the same linkage scheme (Longest Canonical Maximum Linkage). The performances of the three clustering algorithms are shown in Table 4. For both English and Chinese languages, the bottom-up and left2right best-link clustering have shown similar performance, while outperforming the correlation clustering with 95% confidence. Although correlation clustering is a global optimization resolution for clustering, it is unweighted version that we have implemented and it makes use of the hard decisions from the classifier, so there is no chance to improve the imperfect similarity matrix through the linkage schemes and therefore its performance is worst comparing other clustering schemes that can incorporate the linkage schemes.

4.3   Coupling of Classification and Clustering

From the experiments in 4.1 and 4.2, we found that the best coupling of classification and clustering is the combination of the entity-level classification and the customized clustering strategy: longest canonical maximum linkage and agglomerative bottom-up clustering. The performance of the best coupling is shown in Table 5. It is a little surprise that the best coupling does not outperform the combination of the mention-level classification and the customized clustering strategy. With Student's t test, the two coupling perform similar for both English and Chinese with 95% confidence. We are currently exploring the reason for the unexpected performances.

5   Conclusion

We have considered the coreference resolution problem as a clustering problem. We have argued that there are two ways to improve the performance: improved similarity matrix estimation via classification, or incremental adaptation of the similarity matrix in clustering through customized linkage schemes. In this paper, we have done extensive exploration of those phenomena within the context of content extraction as envisioned by the ACE program. We have provided several experimental results that we believe that they will provide useful guidance for coreference resolution.

References

1. Nikhil Bansal, Avrim Blum, and Shuchi Chawla: Correlation clustering. The 43rd Annual Symposium on Foundations of Computer Science (FOCS). (2002).
2. C. Cardie and K. Wagstaff: Noun phrase coreference as clustering. In Proc. of Empirical Methods in Natural Language Processing. (1999).

3. Hal Daume III, Daniel Marcu: A Large-Scale Exploration of Effective Global Features for a Joint Entity Detection and Tracking Model. In Proc. of Human Language Technology Conference. (2005).
4. X. Li and D. Roth, Discriminative Training of Clustering Functions: Theory and Experiments with Entity Identification. In Proc. of the Annual Conference on Computational Natural Language Learning (CoNLL). (2005).
5. Xiaoqiang Luo, Abe Ittycheriah, Hongyan Jing, Nanda Kambhatla and Salim Roukos: A Mention-Synchronous Coreference Resolution Algorithm Based on the Bell Tree. In Proc. Of the Association for Computational Linguistics. (2004).
6. Andrew McCallum and Ben Wellner: Toward Conditional Models of Identity Uncertainty with Application to Proper Noun Coreference. In IJCAI Workshop on Information Integration on the Web. (2003).
7. Josephy F. McCarthy and Wendy G. Lehner: Using Decision Trees for Coreference Resolution. In Proc. Of the International Cofereence on Artificial Intelligent. (1995).
8. Thomas S. Morton: Coreference for NLP Applications. In Proc. Of the Association for Computational Linguistics. (2000).
9. Vincent Ng and Claire Cardie: Improving Machine Learning Approaches to Coreference Resolution. In Proc. Of the Association for Computational Linguistics. (2002).
10. Wee M. Soon, Hwee T. Ng, and Chung Y. Lim: A Machine Learning Approach to Coreference Resolution of Noun Phrases. In Computational Linguistics. (2001).

Parsing with Oracle*

Michal Žemlička

Charles University, Faculty of Mathematics and Physics,
Malostranské nám. 25, 118 00 Praha 1, Czech Republic
michal.zemlicka@mff.cuni.cz

Abstract. Combining two well-known techniques – pushdown automata and oracles – results in a new class of parsers (oracle pushdown automata) having many advantages. It makes possible to combine easily different parsing techniques handling different language aspects into a single parser. Such composition moreover preserves simplicity of design of the combined parts. It opens new ways of parsing for linguistic purposes.

1 Introduction

The standard model of pushdown automaton (PDA, see Def. 5) works with lookahead so that it encodes the lookahead into the states of the PDA (compare e.g. the Figs. 6.7 and 6.8 in [1]). Such model is advantageous for theoretical analysis of automata features but it does not reflect the implementation of PDA in compilers – especially in the case when recursive descent parsing is used. It also does not match the intuition that lookahead analysis can be understood as a process of making decision what move is possible in a given configuration. Hence we decided to create a model that would be able to model many real parsers.

The motivations for oracle pushdown automata are:

1. to build a formal model of the concept of lookahead being in fact rather informal in the literature on parsing,
2. to show that the formalization is fruitful as it refines the intuition and enables to study parser effectiveness problems, and
3. to design a formal model for the study of parser implementations in software engineering and in computational linguistics.

We will discuss a general model (*oracle pushdown automata*) inspired by the oracle from [2].

The concept of the lookahead inspection can be generalized to understand it as an oracle in common sense, i.e. as a (black-box) activity making decisions. The oracle can be implemented e.g. as a finite automaton or as a tool of communication with people or with other automata or other software components being peers in a service-oriented system [3,4]. The concept of oracle can be then used as a theoretical background for the description of some service-oriented systems. The oracle is then one of the services.

---

* This research was partially supported by the Program "Information Society" under project 1ET100300517.

Petr Sojka, Ivan Kopeček and Karel Pala (Eds.): TSD 2006, LNAI 4188, pp. 309–316, 2006.

Let us give an example showing the application of the concept: It can happen that during the parsing of a natural language the parser is unable to parse given text properly and it could be useful to let the user cooperate with the parser (to enter a proper result). If such cases are rare enough, it could be an optimal solution. It could be moreover used for improvement (learning) of the parser via remembering the human decisions in a data store that can be used by the parser. It is also possible that parser can (when necessary) call specialized applications solving specific linguistic issues in the way known from service-oriented systems. These software engineering and computational linguistic issues are topics of a further study.

2 Known Definitions

Although it is probably more common to define pushdown automata in a single definition, we prefer to decompose this definition to smaller parts. Some of the 'partial' notions can later help us to incorporate oracle into the pushdown automaton.

We suppose that it is possible to incorporate the oracle similarly also into other parsers used for linguistic purposes.

Definition 1 (Pushdown machine[1]). *A* pushdown machine *(PDM) is a quadruple* $\mathcal{M} = (Q, \Sigma, \Gamma, \delta)$ *where*

Q *is a finite nonempty set of* states,
Σ *is a finite nonempty set of* input symbols *called* input alphabet,
Γ *is a finite nonempty set of* stack symbols *called* stack alphabet, *and*
δ *is a finite subset of* $Q \times (\Sigma \cup \{\varepsilon\}) \times \Gamma \times Q \times \Gamma^*$ *called* transition function *or the set of* transition rules.

Any element $(q, a, Z, q', \alpha) \in \delta$ *is called a* rule, *and if* $a = \varepsilon$, *it is called an* ε-rule. *The first three components of a rule can be viewed as a precondition and the last two components as a postcondition of the rule. To emphasize it, we can write* $(q, a, Z) \rightarrow (q', \alpha) \in \delta$ *instead of* $(q, a, Z, q', \alpha) \in \delta$.

Definition 2 (Internal configuration, configuration[2]). *Let* $\mathcal{M} = (Q, \Sigma, \Gamma, \delta)$ *be a PDM.*

An internal configuration *of* $\mathcal{M}$ *is a couple* $(q, \alpha) \in Q \times \Gamma^*$, *where q is the current state, and* α *is the string over* Γ^* *composed of the symbols in the stack, the first letter of* α *being the top-most symbol of the stack.*

A configuration *of* $\mathcal{M}$ *is a triple* $(q, u, \alpha) \in Q \times \Sigma^* \times \Gamma^*$, *where u is the input word to be read, and* (q, α) *is an internal configuration.*

Definition 3 (Transition relation, transition, computation[3]). *Let* $\mathcal{M} = (Q, \Sigma, \Gamma, \delta)$ *be a PDM.*

The transition relation *is a relation over configurations defined in the following way: let* $(q, a, Z, q', \beta) \in \delta$ *and let* $c = (q, au, Z\alpha)$ *and* $c' = (q', u, \beta\alpha)$ *be two configurations where a is in* $\Sigma \cup \{\varepsilon\}$, *u is in* Σ^*, *q and q' are in Q, Z is in* Γ *and* α *and* β *are in* Γ^*. *We say*

---

[1] Taken from [5, pages 138–139]; synchronized notation.

[2] Taken from [5, page 139]; synchronized notation.

[3] Taken from [5, page 139]; synchronized notation, slightly modified.

then that there is a transition *between c and c', and we write c ⊢ c'. If a = ε, the transition is called an ε-transition, and if a ∈ Σ, the transition is said to involve the reading of a letter.*

A valid computation is an element of the reflexive and transitive closure of the transition relation. We denote a valid computation starting from c and leading to c' by c $\overset{*}{\vdash}$ c'. A convenient notation is to introduce, for any word x ∈ Σ* the relation on internal configuration, denoted $\overset{x}{\vdash}$ and defined by:

$$(q, \alpha) \overset{x}{\vdash} (q', \alpha') \iff \exists z \in \Sigma^* : (q, xz, \alpha) \overset{*}{\vdash} (q', z, \alpha').$$

We clearly have $\overset{x}{\vdash} \circ \overset{y}{\vdash} = \overset{xy}{\vdash}$.

Definition 4 (Accessible (internal) configuration[4]). *Let $\mathcal{M} = (Q, \Sigma, \Gamma, \delta)$ be a PDM. An internal configuration (q', α') is* accessible *from an internal configuration (q, α) in $\mathcal{M}$, or equivalently, (q, α) is* co-accessible *from (q', α') in M if there is some $u \in \Sigma^*$ such that $(q, \alpha) \overset{u}{\models} (q', \alpha')$. Similarly, a configuration $c' = (q', v, \alpha')$ of $\mathcal{M}$ is said to be* accessible *from a configuration $c = (q, uv, \alpha)$ of $\mathcal{M}$ if $c \overset{*}{\vdash} c'$ in $\mathcal{M}$.*

Definition 5 (Pushdown automaton[5]). *A* pushdown automaton *(a PDA for short) is composed of a pushdown machine $(Q, \Sigma, \Gamma, \delta)$, the* initial state $q_0 \in Q$, initial pushdown symbol $Z_0 \in \Gamma$ *(forming with a word x to be recognized an* initial configuration $(q_0, x, Z_0))$, *and a set $F \subset Q$ of* accepting states. *It is therefore a 7-tuple $(Q, \Sigma, \Gamma, \delta, q_0, Z_0, F)$. The pushdown machine (Q, Σ, Γ, P) is called the* PDM *associated to $\mathcal{A}$.*

For a PDA, an (internal) configuration is accessible *if it is accessible from the initial (internal) configuration, and is* co-accessible *if it is co-accessible from an accepting (internal) configuration.*

A word $x \in \Sigma^*$ is recognized *by a PDA $\mathcal{A} = (Q, \Sigma, \Gamma, \delta, q_0, Z_0, F)$ if there is $q \in F$ and $\alpha \in \Gamma^*$ such that $(q_0, x, Z_0) \overset{*}{\vdash} (q, \varepsilon, \alpha)$.*

There is no transition starting with empty pushdown – hence when the pushdown is empty, the computation terminates. Unless an accepting configuration is reached, the computation terminates with an error.

The language accepted *by a PDA is the set of all words recognized by this PDA. For any PDA $\mathcal{A} = (Q, \Sigma, \Gamma, \delta, q_0, Z_0, F)$ we note $L(\mathcal{A})$ the language recognized by $\mathcal{A}$.*

Language accepted by a pushdown automaton is called pushdown automaton language.

3   Oracle Pushdown Automata

To define oracle pushdown automaton we need to go deeper into the definition of usual pushdown automaton. The following three definitions are derived from Defs. 3, 4, and 5.

Definition 6 (Oracle, authorized transition, authorized computation). *Let $\mathcal{M} = (Q, \Sigma, \Gamma, \delta)$ be a PDM. Let c be a configuration of $\mathcal{M}$. We say, that a transition t of $\mathcal{M}$ is*

---

[4] Taken from [5, page 139]; synchronized notation, extended.

[5] Taken from [5, pages 139–140]; synchronized notation, simplified.

authorized *and can be performed, iff a predicate* $O(\mathcal{M}, c, t)$ *is fulfilled. We call the predicate* oracle. *An authorized transition is called for short* move. *Similarly, authorized transition relation between configurations* c *and* c' *is called* move relation, *we write* $c \longmapsto c'$ *if there is a move between* c *and* c'.

An authorized computation *is an element of the reflexive and transitive closure of the move relation. We denote a valid computation starting from* c *and leading to* c' *by* $c \stackrel{*}{\longmapsto} c'$.

For any word $x \in \Sigma^*$ *we introduce the relation on internal configurations of* $\mathcal{M}$, *denoted* $\stackrel{x}{\Longmapsto}$ *and defined by:*

$$(q, \alpha) \stackrel{x}{\Longmapsto} (q', \alpha') \iff \exists y \in \Sigma^* : (xy, q, \alpha) \stackrel{*}{\longmapsto} (y, q', \alpha').$$

We clearly have $\stackrel{x}{\Longmapsto} \circ \stackrel{y}{\Longmapsto} = \stackrel{xy}{\Longmapsto}$.

A quintuple $\mathcal{M}' = (Q, \Sigma, \Gamma, \delta, O)$ *is called* oracle pushdown machine *(OPDM for short)*.

We say that $\mathcal{M} = (Q, \Sigma, \Gamma, \delta)$ *is a* basic pushdown machine *(or basic PDM for short) of* $\mathcal{M}'$.

Definition 7 (Reachable (internal) configuration). *Let* $\mathcal{M}$ *be an OPDM. An internal configuration* (q', α') *of* $\mathcal{M}$ *is* reachable *from an internal configuration* (q, α) *of* $\mathcal{M}$, *or equivalently,* (q, α) *is* co-reachable *from* (q', α') *if there is some* $u \in \Sigma^*$ *such that* $(q, \alpha) \stackrel{u}{\Longmapsto} (q', \alpha')$. *Similarly, a configuration* (q', v, α') *of* $\mathcal{M}$ *is* reachable *from a configuration* (q, uv, α) *of* $\mathcal{M}$, *or equivalently,* (q, uv, α) *is* co-reachable *from* (q', v, α') *if* $(q, uv, \alpha) \stackrel{*}{\longmapsto} (q', v, \alpha')$.

Definition 8 (Oracle Pushdown Automaton). *An oracle pushdown automaton (an OPDA for short) is an oracle pushdown machine* $(Q, \Sigma, \Gamma, P, O)$, *together with a distinguished initial state* $q \in Q$, *a distinguished initial pushdown symbol* $Z_0 \in \Gamma$ *(forming together with a word* $x \in \Sigma$ *to be recognized an* initial configuration $c_0 = (q_0, x, Z_0)$), *and a set* $F \subset Q$ *of* accepting states. *It is therefore an 8-tuple* $\mathcal{A} = (Q, \Sigma, \Gamma, \delta, O, q_0, Z_0, F)$. *A PDA* $\mathcal{B} = (Q, \Sigma, \Gamma, \delta, q_0, Z_0, F)$ *is said to be the* basic automaton *of* $\mathcal{A}$.

For an OPDA $\mathcal{M}$, *an (internal) configuration of* $\mathcal{M}$ *is* reachable *if it is reachable from the initial (internal) configuration of* $\mathcal{M}$, *and is* co-reachable *if it is co-reachable from an accepting (internal) configuration of* $\mathcal{M}$.

A word $x \in \Sigma^*$ *is* recognized *by an OPDA* $\mathcal{A} = (Q, \Sigma, \Gamma, \delta, O, q_0, Z_0, F)$ *if there are* $q \in F$ *and* $\alpha \in \Gamma^*$ *such that* $(q_0, x, Z_0) \stackrel{*}{\longmapsto} (q, \varepsilon, \alpha)$.

We denote the language accepted *by an OPDA* $\mathcal{A} = (Q, \Sigma, \Gamma, \delta, O, q_0, Z_0, F)$ *being the set of all words accepted by* $\mathcal{A}$ *by* $L(\mathcal{A})$.

There is no transition starting with empty pushdown – hence when the pushdown is empty, the computation terminates. Unless an accepting configuration is reached, the computation terminates with an error.

Language accepted by an oracle pushdown automaton is called oracle pushdown automaton language.

Convention 1. *It is possible to view an OPDA as an ordered pair* $(\mathcal{A}, O)$ *where* $\mathcal{A}$ *is its basic automaton and* O *is its oracle.*

Definition 9 (Parsing situation). *Let* $\mathcal{M} = (Q, \Sigma, \Gamma, \delta)$ *be a PDM. A parsing situation of* $\mathcal{M}$ *is an ordered pair* $(q, Z) \in Q \times \Gamma$ *where q is the current state, and Z is the top-most stack symbol.*

Note 1. In practice we can use different types of the oracle, for example:

1. Just one oracle interacting with the environment (e.g. with other automata, or even with human beings). Such oracles can learn e.g. by remembering the reactions of users handling unexpected constructs. It is a construct that can be used as a modeling tool for the parsing systems having the service-oriented architecture (SOA) [4]. The oracles of this type are important from the software engineering point of view. We shall not research them formally for now.
2. The oracle from Def. 6.
3. A set of configuration-specific oracles.
4. A set of internal-configuration-specific oracles. This case may be useful e.g. for LL(k) parsers for $k \geq 2$.
5. A set of parsing-situation-specific oracles. This oracle corresponds to the "classic" model of PDA.
6. A set of state-specific oracles. It may be useful e.g. for SLL(k) parsers to keep them of reasonable size even for larger k (estimation for standard solution is e.g. in [1]).

These oracle settings can be combined with restrictions on or extensions of the oracle internal memory and/or computing abilities or with restrictions on the access to the unread part of the input (access to the whole unread part of the input or only to some restricted part – e.g. only to k symbols of lookahead).

To support our intuition we can define an oracle function that returns for each configuration (or an internal configuration or a parsing situation or a state) a set of transitions authorized for given configuration.

Definition 10. *Let* $\mathcal{M} = (Q, \Sigma, \Gamma, \delta, O)$ *be an OPDM,* $\mathcal{M}' = (Q, \Sigma, \Gamma, \delta)$ *its basic PDM, and c their configuration. Let us define an* oracle function o *implementing the oracle O:*

$$o(\mathcal{M}', c) = \{t \in \delta | O(\mathcal{M}', c, t)\}$$

Whenever it is clear which automaton is understood, it is possible to omit the first parameter and write just $o(c)$ (or even $O(c)$ whenever it is not necessary explicitly distinguish between functional and predicate form of the oracle).

In practice it is possible to implement the oracle by any computing mechanism – e.g. by invocation of an external application.

Note 2. The oracle concept primarily models intuitive approach used by the parser implementations in compilers and linguistics. The oracle concept allows to optimize parsers and to extend their applicability.

Definition 11 (Deterministic oracle pushdown automaton). *We say that an OPDA $\mathcal{A}$ is* deterministic *(DOPDA for short), if it its oracle authorizes for each configuration at most one transition. Then we can write the values returned by the oracle function as singletons.*

Convention 2. *Let* $\mathcal{M} = (Q, \Sigma, \Gamma, \delta, O)$ *be an OPDM. When the computation of the oracle O depends only on state and part of the pushdown of $\mathcal{M}$ and on a prefix of unread part of the input, we can write prefix of the unread part of input that is used by the oracle for its computation in brackets ('[', ']') behind the symbol to be read, and similarly we can write in brackets the used prefix of the stack behind the symbol on top of the stack.*

In order to simplify the description of the moves near the end of input string we assume that the input string is augmented by $\$^k$ – we use an augmented grammar (see e.g. [6, page 372]).

Note 3. Oracle need not depend on the basic automaton and its current configuration only. It can depend on the interaction with "real world" (for example with users). It need not be deterministic. For this thesis we will restrict ourselves to the deterministic behavior of the oracles.

The k-lookahead oracle function is an oracle function having the property that it depends only on k symbols on input, state, and top of the pushdown.

In the case when the oracle uses only a restricted part of the configuration, it is possible to use as the input of the oracle only this restricted part of the configuration. (Example: SLL(k) parsing – the oracle decides using only the state, top of the stack, and the first k symbols from the unread part of the input.)

Definition 12 (***k*-lookahead configuration**). *Let* $\mathcal{M} = (Q, \Sigma, \Gamma, \delta, O)$ *be an OPDM. We can define to every configuration* $c = (q, w, \alpha)$ *of $\mathcal{M}$ a k-lookahead configuration* $C_k(c) = (q, First_k(w), First_1(\alpha))$.

Example 1. Let us have an OPDA which oracle makes its decision using only k-lookahead configuration

$$C_k = (q, a_1 \ldots a_k, Z).$$

A move of the OPDA from given configuration to the state q', reading the symbol a_1 and replacing the top-most pushdown symbol by the string α will be denoted $(q, a_1[a_2 \ldots a_k], Z) \rightarrow (q', \alpha)$. The case when no symbol is read is written as follows: $(q, [a_1 \ldots a_k], Z) \rightarrow (q', \alpha)$.

Let us look at how different oracles can "work":

Trivial: The oracle 'authorizes' every transition. (Let $\mathcal{M} = (Q, \Sigma, \Gamma, \delta, O)$. Then for any $c = (q, x, Z\alpha)$ be a configuration of $\mathcal{M}$ and $\forall t = (q, b, Z, q', \beta) \in \delta$: $O(\mathcal{M}, c, t)$.) It is, every transition of the PDM is an authorized transition of OPDM. Trivial oracle will be denoted Tr.

Classic: The oracle selects for each configuration at most one move based on state, top of the stack, and exactly the first k symbols from the unread part of the input. It corresponds to classic kinds of deterministic parsing (e.g. SLL(k), SLR(k)). For any OPDM $\mathcal{M}$ and its configurations c and c' it holds that $C_k(c) = C_k(c') \implies o(c) = o(c')$. This oracle is sometimes denoted as k-lookahead oracle.

Lazy: The oracle uses only smallest part of the configuration necessary for the selection of applicable transitions.

Adaptive: The oracle can ask other applications or even users for help when meets unpredicted situation. It remembers the hint for next occurrences of the problem.

Definition 13 (Sibling automata). *We say that two oracle pushdown automata* $\mathcal{A} = (P_{\mathcal{A}}, O_{\mathcal{A}})$, $\mathcal{B} = (P_{\mathcal{B}}, O_{\mathcal{B}})$ *where* $P_{\mathcal{A}} = P_{\mathcal{B}}$ *are siblings. We shall also say that* $\mathcal{A}$ *is a sibling of* $\mathcal{B}$ *and* $\mathcal{B}$ *is a sibling of* $\mathcal{A}$.

Lemma 1. *Let OPDA* $\mathcal{A} = (P, Tr)$. *Then* $\mathcal{A}$ *and* P *go through the same configurations and recognize the same language.*

Proof. In both cases the initial configurations are identical: (q_0, w, Z_0). Tr does not restrict the set of moves used by P. Hence $\mathcal{A}$ can in each configuration use the same set of moves as P do. Both automata must therefore go through the same configurations and recognize the same language.

Definition 14 (Oracle refinement). *Let us have two sibling OPDA* $\mathcal{A} = (P, O)$ *and* $\mathcal{A}' = (P, O')$. *We say that* O *is the* refinement *of* O' *if for every configuration* c *of the basic automaton* P $o(c) \subseteq o'(c)$ *or, equivalently* $O(\mathcal{A}, c, t) \implies O'(\mathcal{A}', c, t)$. *We also say that* $\mathcal{A}$ *is a refinement of* $\mathcal{A}'$.

Note 4. If the oracle can be of arbitrary strength, the language recognized by an OPDA having such oracle cannot be recognized by any PDA.

An example is an oracle O implemented by an oracle function using its own pushdown. It is then possible to construct an OPDA with the oracle O accepting a non-context-free language $a^n b^n c^n$. The basic automaton counts the a's and when it "matches" the b's, the oracle "count" the b's too and then "enforces" the basic automaton to count the same number of c's.

4 Conclusion

We have introduced a generalization of pushdown automata that can enhance the computational power of the original concept. We suppose that the concept of oracle introduced by Turing in [2] can be incorporated successfully also into other computational models. It can enhance these models and allow to decompose the parser into separate parts that can be easier manageable and can handle different tasks.

Using approach proposed here it is possible to combine techniques that specify what constructs conform the language and techniques specifying what constructs do not conform the language at once. Although it probably seems obscure, in [7] it is shown that combination of these approaches is very important and useful.

Other use of oracle pushdown automata is in compiler construction: the oracle can be restricted to lookahead handling to form lookahead automata [8] applicable in top-down parsing. This approach allows the use of only necessary lookahead. It allows to generate significantly smaller parsers – especially for higher language lookaheads (see [8,9]).

The model presented here bridges the gap between theoretical model of pushdown automaton and many real (especially top-down) parsers. The proposed model seems to be useful in solving many theoretical and practical issues. The decomposition of parsers to the basic automaton and oracle simplifies the design, implementation, and maintenance of complex parsers.

References

1. Sippu, S., Soisalon-Soininen, E.: Parsing Theory. Volume II: LR(k) and LL(k) Parsing. Number 20 in EATCS. Springer Verlag, Berlin (1990).
2. Turing, A.M.: Systems of logic based on ordinals. Proceedings of the London Mathematical Society **45** (1939) 161–228.
3. Král, J., Žemlička, M.: Software confederations – an architecture for global systems and global management. In Kamel, S., ed.: Managing Globally with Information Technology, Hershey, PA, USA, Idea Group Publishing (2003) 57–81.
4. Erl, T.: Service-Oriented Architecture: Concepts. Technology, and Design. Prentice Hall PTR (2005).
5. Auterbert, J.M., Berstel, J., Boasson, L.: Context-free languages and pushdown automata. In Rozenberg, G., Salomaa, A., eds.: Handbook of Formal Languages, Berlin, Springer (1997) 111–174.
6. Aho, A.V., Ullman, J.D.: The Theory of Parsing, Translation and Compiling. Volume I.: Parsing. Prentice-Hall, Englewood Cliffs, N.J. (1972).
7. Oliva, K.: Teoretické základy (a širší souvislosti) morfologické disambiguace korpusu lingvistickými metodami (in Czech: Theoretical backgrounds (and a broader view) of morphological disambiguation of corpus using linguistic methods) (2003) Available under
   http://korpus.juls.savba.sk/archive/seminare/2003-04-28/ .
8. Žemlička, M.: Principles of kind parsing – an introduction. Technical Report 2002/1, Charles Univerity, Faculty of Mathematics and Physics, Department of Software Engineering, Prague, Czech Republic (2002).
9. Žemlička, M.: Kindtran – kind transducer (2002)
   http://www.ms.mff.cuni.cz/~zemlicka/KindTran/.

Part III

Speech

"**Speech**: the expression of or the ability to express thoughts and feelings by articulate sounds: *he was born deaf and without the power of speech.*"

NODE (New, Oxford Dictionary of English), Oxford, OUP, 1998, page 1788, meaning 1.

Part III

Speech

Evaluating Language Models Within a Predictive Framework: An Analysis of Ranking Distributions

Pierre Alain, Olivier Boëffard, and Nelly Barbot

IRISA / Université de Rennes 1 - ENSSAT
6 rue de Kerampont, B.P. 80518, F-22305 Lannion Cedex
{pierre.alain, olivier.boeffard, nelly.barbot}@irisa.fr
http://www.irisa.fr/cordial/

Abstract. Perplexity is a widely used criterion in order to compare language models without any task assumptions. However, the main drawback is that perplexity supposes probability distributions and hence cannot compare heterogeneous models. As an evaluation framework, we propose in this article to abandon perplexity and to extend the Shannon's entropy idea which is based on model prediction performance using rank based statistics. Our methodology is able to predict joint word sequences being independent of the task or model assumptions. Experiments are carried out on the English language with different kind of language models. We show that long-term prediction language models are not more effective than the standard n-gram models. Ranking distributions follow exponential laws as already observed in predicting letter sequences. These distributions show a second mode not observed with letters and we propose to give some interpretation to this mode in this article.

1 Introduction

Language models are involved in numerous information processing systems given that the data processed are word sequences. Domains such as speech processing, automatic translation, data mining or natural language interfaces may be concerned by this methodology. Using more or less restrictive assumptions, a language model describes the sequence of words in a sentence.

From a methodological point of view, there are two ways to test the effectiveness of a language model: either by evaluating the model itself with no regard for any applicative context or assuming that it is restricted to a task (as for example a speech recognition system). This latter case means that the performance of the task qualifies the effectiveness of the language model.

The cross entropy between a language model and a test set is the most widely used criterion to evaluate a language model. The less the entropy is, the better is the model. However, the perplexity criterion, based on the cross entropy, suffers a few drawbacks. The probabilistic assumptions is one of them. It's the main reason why experimental procedures require protocols promoting the evaluation of the entire task. But this methodology is as contestable as the former. It is difficult indeed to distinguish, on an entire performance, which is the part of the language model from the rest of the system. Besides, transposing the results acquired from different domains is quite uneasy.

Petr Sojka, Ivan Kopeček and Karel Pala (Eds.): TSD 2006, LNAI 4188, pp. 319–326, 2006.

In order to alleviate this drawback, we propose to adopt an evaluation framework for language models, independent on the task, and to abandon the perplexity criterion. We privilege a framework based upon a statistic on the ranks of prediction, which does not require any assumptions on the models. A predictive framework is not a new way for evaluating language models; Shannon worked on a prediction framework in the beginning of 1950 [1] in order to evaluate the entropy of English letter sequences. His proposal is based on an experimental method framing entropy using a predictive game and considering n-grams. More recently, Cover [2] proposed a predictive model consisting in a gambling estimation to evaluate the entropy of a language. Bimbot *et al.* [3] did extend Cover's experiments to the prediction of words instead of letters. Whatever, Shannon, Cover and Bimbot only showed interest in the prediction of a single letter or a single word.

We propose in this article to extend Shannon's game to the prediction of consecutive words so that long-term prediction models can be evaluated (such as multigram models which can predict many words in a raw). We propose experiments comparing n-gram and multigram and a linguistic analysis of the ranking distributions.

The contents of the paper is organized as follows. Section 2 describes our proposition for estimating a rank of prediction given a l-words sequence. Section 3, we describe the experimental methodology, and results are discussed in section 4.

2   Ranking Prediction

The Shannon's game [1] consists in asking a person to predict a letter from the knowledge of the previous letters. Given a history (the h_{N-1} sequence of $N - 1$ letters in the past), such a methodology provides a rank for each prediction (the 1st rank corresponds to the most probable letter, the 2nd one to the next probable,...). As proposed in [3], we adapt the Shannon's and Cover's principles for predicting words of a natural language. But the proposals of Cover and Bimbot are still suffering the fact that they are based upon estimation of the cross entropy of the language model.

We intend to define a framework which allows a comparison of language models with no regard for assumptions concerning the nature of the model. We also need to define a framework quite independent of the model size (degrees of freedom), which is clearly not the case with the perplexity. In the following, we take interest in the prediction of several consecutive words. We define a predictive or guessing window, of length l, as the prediction of word sequence $W_i\ W_{i+1} \cdots W_{i+l-1}$ knowing its history $h(W_i) = W_1\ W_2 \cdots W_{i-1}$. A language model is asked to provide the rank of prediction of a given test sequence. The less the rank of prediction is, the better the language model is.

However, determining a rank on a l-size window is a combinatorial issue. We propose an exact solution based on a graph representation and using an efficient algorithm for searching the R best paths in this graph.

We are interested here in finding the best guessing sequence of words. This goal is equivalent to find the best path in a graph. Here, the graph is *multivalued*, all edges are *multiedges* corresponding to the histories that the language model can use to make its prediction. Given a predictive window, the rank of the test word sequence $W_i, \cdots, W_{i+l}$ is that of lowest cost path. However, a multi-valued graph can lead to several possible paths for one sequence of test words. To overcome this difficulty, we apply an A^* algorithm to find the best path in a multivaluated graph. We propose pruning heuristics in order to compute the R best paths. The rank of prediction is defined by the number of guesses that the language model has to make in order to reach the test sequence.

We do not have sufficient space in this article to describe the details of an A^* implementation. In particular, we use an admissible pruning function which makes it possible to execute the algorithm in a reasonable time. In this article, we stress the experimental comparison of language models using a predictive framework.

3   Experiments

The experiments were carried out using texts from the year 1987 of the *Wall Street Journal*. The training corpus comprises 500,455 sentences, with a vocabulary of 94,198 words and 11,260,184 occurrences. The selected vocabulary is composed of the 30,000 most frequent words. For these 30,000 words, 11,118,995 occurrences are observed. The test corpus is composed of 50,037 sentences, different from the training corpus, comprising 38,564 different words and 1,127,831 occurrences. The predicting test is conducted on 12,000 windows of two words. These windows are selected by a shift of 7 words starting from the first word of the file. 7 is the maximum number of words given a maximum authorized length of history.

The standard 3-gram models is generated given the training corpus and the selected vocabulary. A cutting threshold is fixed to 1. All the parameters retained in a language model must thus appear at least twice. These 3-gram model contain 1,646,823 parameters (except the backoff coefficients). 2/2-multigram models are built starting from the same 30,000 words vocabulary augmented with a set of fragments. We consider here fragments up to 2-words sequences. Changing the number of fragments implies a modification of the number of parameters of the language model. Given the training corpus, the set of fragments varies from 125,000 (a language model with 2,662,174 parameters) to the totality of the fragments existing in the training corpus and built on the word vocabulary set (1,815,271 fragments and 5,069,602 parameters for the resulting language model). Our experimental framework is more general than the protocols suggested by [4]. Indeed, we incorporate in the model all the possible fragments, as a consequence we do not need to select the more effective subset of fragments given a vocabulary. At the training stage, a cutoff value is set to one [5] in order to keep only joint word sequences present at least twice in the training corpus.

The fact that all the models are built on the same vocabulary guarantees a fixed out-of-vocabulary rate. The experiments were carried out with a 2-words predictive window. This corresponds to the minimal situation where a n/m-multigram can be evaluated against a standard n-gram.

The maximum rank allowed in the A^* algorithm is set to 7,000,000; beyond this rank, the window is declared not predicted by the language model. This maximum rank is determined according to the length of the predicting windows. We could observe on preliminary experiments that the maximum rank reaches the value 659,473 for the standard 3-gram, 659,370 for the variable 3-gram, and 1,814,435 for the full multigram model.

All the experiments require the calculation of an average value of the prediction ranks. These average values are presented within 95% confidence intervals. These confidence intervals are established by re-sampling the empirical distributions (Monte-Carlo methodology

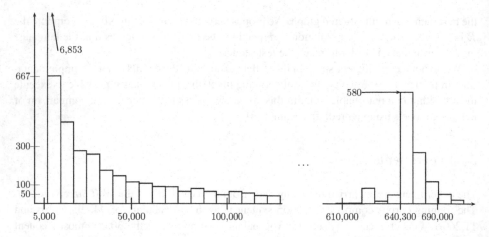

Fig. 1. A distribution of ranks for the 2/2-multigram with 500,000 fragments. The histogram is evaluated using 100 fixe-size bins. Two statistical modes are noticeable.

known as bootstrap). First, we present the results of prediction for the 12,000 windows of the test set. The distributions and average values will make it possible to determine the relative performance of the two classes of models. Then, we will try to analyze the principal characteristics of the events observed on the distributions of ranks. On the one hand, we explain the behavior of the model from a structural point of view and on the other hand we characterize some word occurrences at a linguistic level. The linguistic labels correspond to POS labels annotated automatically by the CLAWS system [6].

4   Results and Discussion

The maximum rank allowed in the A^* algorithm is set to 7,000,000; beyond this rank, the window is declared not predicted by the language model. This maximum rank is determined according to the length of the predicting windows. We could observe on preliminary experiments that the maximum rank reaches the value 659,473 for the standard 3-gram, 659,370 for the variable 3-gram, and 1,814,435 for the full multigram model.

4.1   Comparison of Language Models

Figure 1 is an example of a distribution obtained during the test showing the ranks of prediction for the 2/2 multigram with 500,000 fragments. All the experimental distributions have this same shape. Changes appear on the maximum rank reached and on the average values estimated from these distributions. One can notice that the experimental distributions show two modes. The first mode follows a power law, this mode was already observed by Shannon in his experiments on English letters. We also notice a second mode. We suspect that this mode corresponds to windows predicted with *difficulty*. We will give section 4.2 a more detailed analysis on this fact.

In order to compare average statistics with their confidence intervals, one can either take into account all the terms of the distribution, or limit an estimation of the average to the

Table 1. Average ranks (applying a 10^4 scaling factor) with a 95% interval confidence for the six language models under evaluation. The mean values integrate the two modes

Model	Mean [c.i. ±5%]	# parameters
3-gram	**9.18** [8.82 − 9.52]	1,646,823
2/2-multigram 1.8M	**20.65** [19.69 − 21.53]	5,069,602
2/2-multigram 1M	**13.69** [13.17 − 14.21]	4,254,331
2/2-multigram 500k	**10.21** [9.82 − 10.56]	3,651,436
2/2-multigram 250k	**9.84** [9.47 − 10.19]	3,139,321
2/2-multigram 125k	**9.67** [9.30 − 10.03]	2,662,174

Table 2. Average ranks (applying a 10^4 scaling factor) with a 95% interval confidence for the six language models under evaluation. The mean values integrate only the first mode (ranks under 200,000). The last column shows the contribution of the first mode over the overall probability mass.

Model	Mean [c.i. ±5%]	% Mass
3-gram	**1.65** [1.58 − 1.72]	84.6%
2/2-multigram 1.8M	**1.71** [1.64 − 1.78]	83.2%
2/2-multigram 1M	**1.71** [1.64 − 1.78]	83.3%
2/2-multigram 500k	**1.70** [1.63 − 1.77]	83.3%
2/2-multigram 250k	**1.72** [1.65 − 1.79]	83.3%
2/2-multigram 125k	**1.95** [1.88 − 2.03]	84.6%

first mode. If we consider all the values of an empirical rank distribution, results show that language models with a great number of parameters are not favoured. When a language model tries to guess a hard-predictable window, taking lot of parameters implies that numerous candidates could not be very useful. On the side of rank interpretation, one can wonder whether a language model which predicts a window after 600,000 proposals is more powerful than a model which predicts this same window after 1,800,000 other proposals. We think that there is a threshold from which the prediction is always bad.

Table 1 shows the average ranks obtained from each ranking distributions and integrating both modes. We note that models which use a great number of parameters obtain bad scores. This performance is mainly due to the maximum value attained by these models. Indeed, the 2/2-multigram with 1.8M parameters has a maximum rank at 1,814,435. The same model with 1,000,000 fragments has a maximum rank at 999,015. The three other multigram models have a maximum rank near 670,000. The maximum rank for the 3-gram models is near 660,000. To conclude, the standard 3-gram model obtains the best average rank of prediction. Table 2 shows average ranks with their confidence intervals considering only the first mode on the empirical distributions. During the process of calculating mean values, we only integrate ranks lower than 200,000. The last column of the table shows the mass of this first mode compared to the entire distribution. The 2/2-multigram models with more than one million fragments are not any more penalized by the bad ranks coming with hard-predictable test windows. We notice that the variable 3-gram model remains always a worst predictor, just like the 2/2-multigram with 125,000 fragments. The more the models approach a 2-gram (a 2-gram is a 2/2-multigram without any fragments), the worst the capacity of prediction

Table 3. Percentage of predicted elements for 1,000 predictive windows of two words. For the sake of clarity, we note *mode A* the first mode, and *mode B* the second mode of the empirical distributions.

Model	1st position						2nd position					
	mode A			mode B			mode A			mode B		
history size	0	1	2	0	1	2	0	1	2	0	1	2
3-gram	2%	30%	68%	68%	28%	4%			100%	100%		
2/2-multigram 125k	6%	48%	46%	54%	38%	8%		100%		100%		
2/2-multigram 500k	6%	44%	50%	52%	39%	9%		100%		100%		

Table 4. Percentage of predicted elements of 1,000 predictive windows of two words (word by word, or directly with one fragment)

Model	two words		one fragment	
	mode A	mode B	mode A	mode B
3-gram	100%	100%		
2/2-multigram 125k	22%	100%	78%	0%
2/2-multigram 500k	21%	98%	79%	2%

Table 5. The Most frequent syntactic tags (BNC linguistic tagset (C5)) in both modes for the last history word, and for the two words of the prediction windows

Model	word history		1st position		2nd position	
	mode A	mode B	mode A	mode B	mode A	mode B
3-gram	AT0/CRD	AJ0/CJC	AT0/VVN	AJ0/CJC	AT0/PRP	NN2/NP0
2/2-multigram 125k	NN1/NN2	AT0/CJC	PRP/AT0	AJ0/NN2	AT0/PRP	NN1/NN2
2/2-multigram 500k	NN1/NP0	AT0/CJC	PRP/AT0	AJ0/NP0	PRP/PRF	AT0/PRP

is. All the other models give statistically non significant results. We cannot distinguish them even if we must keep in mind that their numbers of parameters fluctuate in an important way.

4.2 Statistical Mode Analysis

For both modes, tables 3 and 5 give, respectively, a description of the parameters, and the syntactic categories of the predicted words. For the sake of clarity, we note *mode A* the first mode, and *mode B* the second mode of the empirical distributions. All the results are estimated using 1,000 randomly selected prediction windows.

We use the British National Corpus, BNC, linguistic tagset (C5) POS notations: AT0 = *article*, CRD = *Cardinal Number*, AJ0 = *Adjective*, CJC = *Coordinating conjunction*, VVN = *Past participle form of lexical verb*, PRP = *Preposition*, NN{0,1,2} = *Noun, singular or plural*.

For the prediction of the first word (1st position), mode A is mainly characterized by the use of 2-gram and 3-gram built with a noun in the history and an article or a preposition for the head of prediction. Whereas mode B takes some 1-gram with adjective or noun as POS, and some 2-gram made of articles in the history, and a noun in the head. For the prediction of the second word (2nd position), mode A chooses some 2-gram built with an article, or a preposition in the history, and a preposition in the head of prediction. Rather than, mode B uses 1-gram composed of a noun (singular or plural), or an article.

Table 4 shows the difference of prediction length between the models. For example, when a model decides to predict two consecutive words, it does not have to predict a 2nd *position* word and the window is fully predicted in only one guess. For this reason, the multigram models in table 3 do not use a long term history for the prediction of the 2nd position word. On the one hand, if both words occur often together in the learning corpus, the prediction can be done in one state (80% of the multigrams predictions, see table 4); on the other hand, if they are rarely together, a long-term history probability is weaker and then the prediction has to be done in two guesses.

The following sentences illustrate some predictive windows taken at mode B position (the prediction window is located with |):

```
... AS[PRP21] TO[PRP22] SUGAR[NN1] CANE[NN1] AND[CJC] | OTHER[AJO]
PLANTATIONS[NN2] | MR[NNS] VILLEGAS[NPO] OFFERS[VVZ] ONLY[AVO] ...
... COMPOSED[VVN] OF[PRF] REPRESENTATIVES[NN2] FROM[PRP]
FINANCE[NN1] AND[CJC] | CORPORATE[AJO] WORLDS[NN2] | IS[VBZ] ...
```

We conclude by this analysis that mode B corresponds to a ineffective mode for the language model. The language model does not perform well because of the use of a short history. This phenomenon tends to be worsened when the predictive window prediction lengthens. In this case, the language model has to predict a word sequences without taking into account a history. For this reason, ranks become very large by a combinatorial effect (which is N^l if N is the vocabulary size, and l the window size). A comparison of language models based only on the mode A is thus justified.

5   Conclusion

In this article, we presented an extension to Shannon's original game in order to evaluate language models. This evaluation framework relies on rank distributions, and does not require any assumptions on the nature (probabilistic or not) of the language models under comparison. This kind of predictive framework allows a reliable comparison of language models without any assumption about the applicative task.

The results show an unexpected behavior of the ranking distributions. Indeed, the use of this framework with a limited vocabulary (a vocabulary of letters for the Shannon's game) leads to a power law distribution. With our vocabulary of 30,000 words, a new mode appears for bad prediction ranks due to a combinatorial effect. We tried in this article to analyze this *second* mode (the first one is the well known power law distribution). For these bad ranks, the language models use some parameters which are not effective for a predictive task (the unigram model does not have a great knowledge to predict word sequences).

References

1. Shannon, C.: Prediction and entropy of printed english. Bell System Technical Journal **30** (1951) 50–64.
2. Cover, T., King, R.: A convergent gambling estimate of the entropy of english. IEEE Transactions on Information Theory **24** (1978) 413–421.

3. Bimbot, F., El-Beze, M., Igounet, S., Jardino, M., Smaili, K., Zitouni, I.: An alternative scheme for perplexity estimation and its assessment for the evaluation of language models. Computer Speech and Language **15** (2001) 1–13(13).
4. Deligne, S., Bimbot, F.: Language modeling by variable length sequences: theoretical formulation and evaluation of multigrams. In: IEEE International Conference on Acoustics and Speech Signal Processing. (1995) 169–172.
5. Chen, S., Goodman, J.: An empirical study of smoothing techniques for language modeling. Computer Speech and Language **13** (1999) 359–394.
6. Garside, R., Geoffrey, L., Geoffrey, S.: The computational analysis of english. a corpus-based approach. London: Longman. (1987).

Another Look at the Data Sparsity Problem

Ben Allison, David Guthrie, and Louise Guthrie

University of Sheffield, Regent Court, 211 Portobello Street, Sheffield, S1 4DP, UK
b.allison@dcs.shef.ac.uk

Abstract. Performance on a statistical language processing task relies upon accurate information being found in a corpus. However, it is known (and this paper will confirm) that many perfectly valid word sequences do not appear in training corpora. The percentage of n-grams in a test document which are seen in a training corpus is defined as n-gram coverage, and work in the speech processing community [7] has shown that there is a correlation between n-gram coverage and word error rate (WER) on a speech recognition task. Other work (e.g. [1]) has shown that increasing training data consistently improves performance of a language processing task. This paper extends that work by examining n-gram coverage for far larger corpora, considering a range of document types which vary in their similarity to the training corpora, and experimenting with a broader range of pruning techniques. The paper shows that large portions of language will not be represented within even very large corpora. It confirms that more data is always better, but how much better is dependent upon a range of factors: the source of that additional data, the source of the test documents, and how the language model is pruned to account for sampling errors and make computation reasonable.

1 Introduction

In natural language processing, data sparsity (also known by terms such as data sparseness, data paucity, etc) is the term used to describe the phenomenon of not observing enough data in a corpus to model language accurately. True observations about the distribution and pattern of language cannot be made because there is not enough data to see the true distribution. Many have found the phrase "language is a system of very rare events" a notion both comforting and depressing, but fewer have ever seen it as a challenge.

This paper explores the extent to which data sparsity is an issue across a range of test documents and training corpora which vary in size and type. It examines the extent to which the chosen training corpus affects the performance of a task, and how much methods to combat data sparsity (principally smoothing) are responsible for performance. That is, the lower the percentage of a model's parameters which is observed in real language use (the corpus), the higher the percentage of times those parameters must be estimated.

The goal of many language processing tasks is to gather contexts, and build a model of those contexts (e.g. statistical machine translation or automatic speech recognition). To do this, the approach in statistical NLP is typically to gather the necessary information from a corpus, and use the data observed in this corpus to assign a probability distribution. However, as this paper will show, using a very large corpus (1.5 billion words) there are many, many instances in normal language where no probability (or only a zero probability) would be

Petr Sojka, Ivan Kopeček and Karel Pala (Eds.): TSD 2006, LNAI 4188, pp. 327–334, 2006.

assigned to a word sequence using the simple distribution derived from the corpus. The majority of these word sequences are legal, but there is insufficient data to estimate their probability.

To combat this problem, smoothing techniques have been proposed. The intuition behind the most popular of these techniques is to take some probability "mass" away from the sequences that have been seen before, so that some can be assigned to the sequences which have not been seen. More complex smoothing approaches interpolate probabilities for an n word sequence with those for its component $(n-k)$ word sequences; as explained by [2]:

> "if an n-gram has a nonzero count then we use the distribution $\alpha(w_i|w_{i-n+1}^{i-1})$. Otherwise, we backoff to the lower-order distribution $\gamma(w_i|w_{i-n+1}^{i-1})P_{smooth}(w_i|w_{i-n+2}^{i-1})$, where the scaling factor $\gamma(w_i|w_{i-n+1}^{i-1})$ is chosen to make the conditional probabilities sum to one."

This paper quantifies the number of sequences unseen in various documents over a range of corpus sizes (and types), using test documents drawn from a broad range of document types. The question answered is: what percentage of tokens in a new document is unseen in a training corpus? This gives us the number of times that a language model trained in a given domain would have to estimate the probability of an n word sequence without ever having seen that sequence. Clearly, the best language models would minimise the number of times this were necessary. [7] addresses a similar question, considering smaller training corpora and with test documents fixed to those heldout from the training corpus. He investigates the vocabulary size which yields the best word-error rate on a speech recognition task, and shows a correlation between trigram coverage and lower word-error rate.

This paper principally concerns itself with trigram modelling — this is by far the most common n-gram used in modelling, since it is typically considered to provide a good balance between some context and enough repetition to make that context useful. Going beyond this value of n, [3] shows that higher-order models (four-grams and above) suffer so much from data sparseness that they become unusable. In the case of trigrams, the probability of any three word sequence W is estimated by:

$$p(W) = p(w_i|w_{i-2}w_{i-1}) = \frac{count(w_{i-2}, w_{i-1}, w_i)}{count(w_{i-2}, w_{i-1})}$$

This paper also explores the number of bigrams and unigrams from new documents which are found in training corpora of up to 1.5 billion words.

The paper also briefly explores some interesting side effects of measuring the percentage of unseen n-grams in documents of various types. It shows that different types of documents can be separated by the percentage of their tokens which appear in a fixed corpus, and also shows that domain specific corpora are not always necessary - it depends upon the task in question.

One final area the paper considers is the effect that some common techniques for compression of language models has upon the number of unseen trigram sequences. The results using these techniques indicate that huge improvements in storage requirements for models can be achieved for what some might consider an acceptable loss in observed trigram patterns.

It is almost universally accepted that more data is always better; a phrase in the literature is "There's no data like more data" [5], and [4] suggest "having more training data is normally more useful than any concerns of balance, and one should simply use all the text that is available." [1] showed that performance for their chosen task increased as they increased the size of their training corpus, and furthermore showed that a particular method's relative performance on a small training set will not necessarily be replicated if the training corpus grows in size. However, this paper does not seek to question or necessarily affirm these positions; it is concerned with performance not so much on a specific task, but rather with a problem affecting all tasks using corpora to estimate the probability of word sequences. It seeks to show how often one must make up for deficiencies in various corpora by estimating probabilities of unseen events. The method of these estimations, and their relative performances, is examined in other work; here we are concerned with how often they are necessary.

2 Data Used in the Study

2.1 Training Data

Several corpora were used for training:

The BNC – The British National Corpus is a corpus of over 100 million words of modern English, both spoken and written. It is designed to be balanced by domain and medium (where it was intended to be published. It can be considered to represent most common varieties of modern English language.

The Gigaword Corpus – A large archive of newswire text data acquired by the Linguistic Data Consortium. The total corpus consists of over 1.7 billion words from four distinct international sources of English newswire ranging from approximately 1994-2002.

Medline – 1.2 billion words of abstracts from the PubMed Medline project. Medline was compiled by the U.S. National Library of Medicine (NLM) and contains publications in the fields of life sciences and biomedicine. It contains nearly eleven million records from over 7,300 different publications, spanning 1965 – the present day.

2.2 Testing Data

Initial testing data came from three sources, intended to represent a range of language use. For each source, a collection of documents totalling approximately 6,000 words for each source was produced. Sources were as follows:

Newspaper articles – Documents composed of current stories from
    http://www.guardian.co.uk and http://www.thesun.co.uk
Scientific writing – From Einstein's Special and General Theory of Relativity
Children's writing – From http://www.childrens-express.org, a project producing news and current affairs stories by children, for children

Further testing was performed with large sets of data both to clarify results and to observe the phenomenon that data from "strange" sources had appreciably different patterns of trigram coverage.

Newspaper archives – Documents from the Financial Times archive

Anarchist's Cookbook – Documents from the notorious "Anarchist's Cookbook", originally written during the 1960s (although since updated) and comprising articles for small-scale terrorist acts such as drug production, home-explosive creation and identity fraud [6].

MT system output – Google's attempt to translate Chinese news stories. Includes some manual correction of untranslatable (by Google) characters.

Emails – Messages drawn at random from the Enron email corpus [8].

ASR data – Documents consisting of text output from an ASR system.

3 Method

For the purposes of this paper, coverage is defined as the percentage of tokens from an unseen document found at least once in a training corpus. Both type and token percentages were explored, and token coverage is reported here. For this application, the type/token distinction is as follows: in counting tokens, all instances of a specific n-gram will be counted separately towards the final percentage. For types, each unique n-gram will only be counted once.

Training and test corpora were all prepared in the same way – all non-alphabetic characters were removed, and all words were converted to lower case. For bigrams and trigrams, tokens were formed both by allowing and prohibiting the crossing of sentence boundaries. However, it was found that this had a minimal impact on percentage scores, and the results reported here are those allowing sentence-boundary crossing.

4 Results

Figure 1 shows the average token coverage for the initial test documents of unigrams, bigrams and trigrams against the following corpora:

Corpus 1: 150,000 words from the BNC
Corpus 2: 1million words from the BNC
Corpus 3: 26 million words from the BNC
Corpus 4: Whole (100 million words) BNC
Corpus 5: Gigaword (1.5 billion words)

Figure 2 shows how the coverage of more normal documents degrades significantly when the test documents are from a more unusual source (Medline).

Figure 3 shows the way that different document types separate in terms of their coverage statistics. For each type, between 50 and 250 documents were tested. The figure shows the distribution of coverage scores for these different sources. The types of test document used are indicated in the figure, and for a more complete description, see the "Data" section.

Figure 4 shows the effects of the language model compression techniques on coverage of the same documents as the original tests, using both the BNC and the Gigaword as training corpora. The horizontal axis shows the compression technique, and the vertical, the average coverage (of the same original test documents) using this technique. The techniques used are:

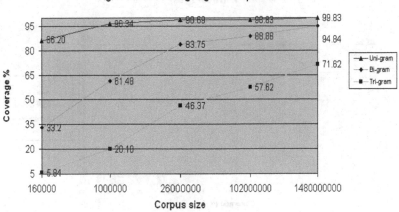

Fig. 1. Sparsity in initial documents

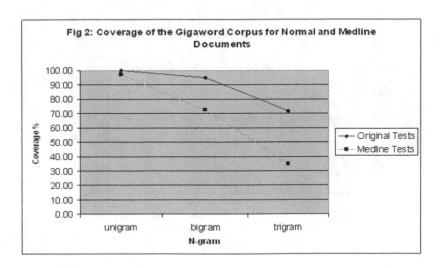

Fig. 2. Gigaword coverage of news and Medline Documents

All trigrams – No compression (as reported above)

Freq 1 – Only trigrams with frequency greater than one are included in the model

Freq 2 – Only trigrams with frequency greater than two are included in the model

Only 50k words – Only trigrams where all three words are one of the 50,000 highest frequency words in the corpus are included in the model

The last two compressions are combinations of the previous ones, e.g. only trigrams with frequency greater than one and all three words are one of the 50,000 highest frequency words in the corpus

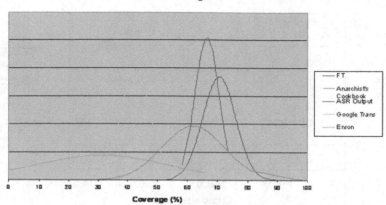

Fig 3: Distribution of Different Document Types by Trigram Coverage

Fig. 3. Distribution of different document types

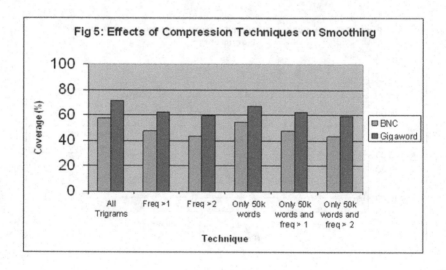

Fig 5: Effects of Compression Techniques on Smoothing

Fig. 4. Effects of Compression Techniques

5   Conclusion

The results of these different experiments have shown how varying conditions in a language modelling/context gathering scenario affects the number of unseen events. The higher the frequency of these unseen events, the more reliant any model in these conditions will be upon its method for dealing with unseen events.

The results show a steady coverage increase as the size of the training corpus increases. The largest corpora considered are over one billion words in size, and the results indicate that one can expect an increase in the coverage up to and beyond this point. Furthermore, they show that in these conditions, with over a billion and a half words of language knowledge at its disposal, a system would still have to estimate the probability of approximately 30% of all legal three word sequences without ever having seen them.

However, some solace can be found in the unigram and bigram coverage rates, which indicate that when a back-off smoothing algorithm must estimate trigram probabilities from bigrams or unigrams, there will be almost no instances where this is not possible due to lack of data. Indeed, 95% of all bigrams can be found in the 1.5 billion word corpus. Where even the bigram is missed, 99.8% of all single words are found within this corpus, meaning the number of times where a word is out-of-vocabulary is tiny. The missed words were either misspellings, colloquialisms which entered language after the corpus creation, or proper nouns. In almost no cases will it be necessary to resort to a last-ditch estimate of a function of the size of the vocabulary.

Various authors have shown a correlation between coverage and language modelling tasks (see [7] for an examination of word-error-rate correlation with coverage in a speech recognition task). However, it is not the purpose of this paper to predict the performance of systems based upon corpora in these conditions, or to evaluate language modelling strategies. Perplexity is not considered here, since it assumes the existence of smoothing approaches in the language model. This paper instead seeks to show the dependency of modelling strategies on their smoothing techniques.

Further results show that the use of domain specific corpora becomes more and more necessary as the n in the n-gram to be modelled increases. Gigaword and Medline do a surprisingly good job of covering one another's unigrams, and arguably do an acceptable job with bigrams. The real unsuitability is evident only when considering trigrams, and one can assume that this phenomenon will grow when considering 4- and 5-grams.

More results show that different document types display different patterns of coverage with respect to a static corpus in the general (large collections), as well as the specific case. These results once again reinforce the hypothesis that, as the domain becomes more unusual with respect to the language model, so the model must more often estimate the probabilities of unseen events. Two of the sources (ASR system output and the Anarchist's Cookbook) are reasonably well approximated by the Gigaword model — both represent well-formed English, if a little unusual, and the ASR system's output is by definition regulated by a language model. The other two sources are less well dealt with by the model — Google's translations clearly represent broken English (as anyone inspecting the system's output will doubtless confirm) and the emails represent direct communication, unlikely to be fitted by a model formed from newswire text.

The last set of results somewhat vindicates compression strategies which throw away infrequent n-grams. The loss in coverage could well be defended in the face of the huge space reduction – from 39 million trigram types for the BNC and 260 million for the Gigaword, down to 3.5 million and 50 million respectively for a moderate ten to fifteen percent drop in coverage. This allows the use of accurate frequency counts obtained from large corpora to be combined with the diminutive size of much smaller resources.

This paper has quantified the reliance of language models on their chosen strategies for estimating probabilities for unseen events. It has shown that in some cases, domain specific corpora are essential, whereas in others they are not so necessary. Finally, it has given quantifiable defence to some techniques for compressing a language model. As data processing capacities increase over time, the paper gives some evidence that fewer and fewer phrases will have to be estimated by smoothing. Hopefully the weakest link in the language modelling chain will become defunct.

References

1. Banko, M., Brill, E., (2001). Mitigating the Paucity of Data Problem. In Proceedings of the Conference on Human Language Technology.
2. Chen, S., Goodman, J., (1998), An empirical study of smoothing techniques for language modeling. Technical report TR-10-98, Harvard University.
3. Jelinek, F. (1991) Up from trigrams!. In Proceedings Eurospeech '91
4. Manning, C., Schütze, H., (1999) Foundations of Statistical Natural Language Processing. MIT Press.
5. Moore, R. (2001) There's No Data Like More Data (But When Will Enough Be Enough?). In Proceedings of IEEE International Workshop on Intelligent Signal Processing.
6. Powell, W. (1970) The Anarchist's Cookbook. Ozark Pr Llc.
7. Rosenfeld, R., (1995), Optimizing Lexical and N-gram Coverage Via Judicious Use of Linguistic Data. In Proceedings Eurospeech '95.
8. Klimt, B. Yang, Y. (2004) Introducing the Enron Email Corpus. Carnegie Mellon University.

Syllable-Based Recognition Unit to Reduce Error Rate for Korean Phones, Syllables and Characters

Bong-Wan Kim[1], Yongnam Um[1], and Yong-Ju Lee[2]

[1] Speech Information Technology and Industry Promotion Center,
Wonkwang University, Korea
{bwkim, umyongnam}@sitec.or.kr
[2] Division of Electrical Electronic and Information Engineering,
Wonkwang University, Korea
yjlee@wonkwang.ac.kr

Abstract. In this paper we propose a new type of syllable-based unit for recognition and language model to improve recognition rate for Korean phones, syllables and characters. We propose 'combined' units for which both Korean characters and syllable units realized in speech are taken into consideration. We can obtain character, syllable and phone sequences directly from the recognition results by using proposed units. To test the performance of the proposed approach we perform two types of experiments. First, we perform language modeling for phones, characters, syllables and propose combined units based on the same text corpus, and we test the performance for each unit. Second, we perform a vector space model based retrieval experiment by using the proposed combined units.

1 Introduction

There are recent approaches to open-vocabulary spoken document retrieval (SDR) that are based on subword-based speech recognition that uses phones or syllables [1,2]. In particular, subword recognition units are significant for Korean recognition since the out-of-vocabulary (OOV) rate will be higher if a word is used as a recognition unit for agglutinative languages such as Korean. However, there is a barrier for improving the capacity of SDR by using subword units: relatively higher error rate obtains though the problem of OOV rate can be avoided if subword units are used. Thus, in this paper we introduce a new syllable-based approach to improving recognition rate for Korean phones, syllables and characters. Since Korean characters and syllable units are interconnected phonologically and morphologically, 'combined' units, for which both Korean characters and syllable units realized in speech are taken into consideration, are proposed for language model and speech recognition unit. The paper is organized as follows. In Sect. 2, we describe the text corpus which is used for training the language model and the speech corpus which is used for training the acoustic model and testing. In Sect. 3, we describe so-called combined units. In Sect. 4, we deal with the results of the experiments, and our conclusion follows in Sect. 5.

2 Text and Speech Corpora

2.1 Text Corpus (KSR-2002-TN) [3]

For the language model we have used this text corpus which was created by the Speech/Language Technology Research Department of the Electronics and Telecommuni-

Petr Sojka, Ivan Kopeček and Karel Pala (Eds.): TSD 2006, LNAI 4188, pp. 335–341, 2006.

cations Research Institute (ETRI). This is the collection of 20M words or 1.4M sentences from the texts of Korean daily newspapers from January 1, 2000 to December 31, 2000.

2.2 Speech Corpora [4]

Speech Database for Korean Dictation (Dict01) – This is a speech corpus created and distributed by the Speech Information Technology and Industry Promotion Center (SiTEC) in Korea. It is the collection of speech of 400 speakers (about 105 sentences per speaker). 20,833 sentences composed of highly frequent 10K words selected from a text corpus of 40M words were used for prompts. The speech data was recorded through the Andrea ANC 750 microphone. In this paper, speech data of 360 speakers (66.95 hours) from this corpus is used for training acoustic models, and speech data of 40 speakers (7.87 hours) is used for testing the performance of recognition units.

Speech Database for Korean Address (Address01) – This is a speech corpus created and distributed by the SiTEC to develop the location based service system such as the navigation system. Prompts contain 2,110 phrases such as addresses and names of apartments and buildings. The speech data of 300 speakers (about 140 phrases per speaker) was recorded through the Labtec Axis-301 microphone. This is used for testing the performance for the proposed units in the retrieval task. Data which contains 4 sets of 2,110 phrases read by 60 speakers (5.98 hours) is used for the tests.

3   Combined Units

In Korean orthography, consonant and vowel symbols of the Korean alphabet are packed into syllable blocks that are composed of initial, medial, and final positions. There are three primary syllable structures: CV, CVC, CVCC. When there is no initial consonant, the symbol 'ㅇ' - indicating a null sound - is used as a placeholder. Thus, consonant symbols always appear in the initial position of the syllable blocks. Although grapheme-to-phoneme correspondences are highly consistent and reliable at the individual symbol level, syllable blocks do not always correspond with spoken syllable boundaries. This is because Korean spelling conventions, or syllable block formations, tend to conform to the word's morphological composition, rather than to their phonetic constituents. For example, the Korean word 알았다 /alas'ta/ is spelled with three syllable blocks: 알 /al/ (representing the morpheme 'know'), 았 /as'/ (representing past tense) and 다 /ta/ (representing declarative ending) even though the word is pronounced as [arat'a] [5]. Thus, resyllabification takes place when concatenated morphemes are realized phonetically in real speech. In this paper we call written syllable block 'character' and phonetically realized syllable 'syllable'.

A Korean syllable is composed of one optional initial consonant, one obligatory nuclear vowel, and one optional final consonant - (C)V(C) in which consonant clusters are not allowed. In the system of Korean characters, 19 graphic types (codes) occur in initials, 21 graphic types (codes) in middles, and 27 graphic types (codes) in finals (in which consonant symbol clusters can occur), and 11,172 combinations of codes are allowed for characters (including characters without finals). In the system of read speech, 18 consonants can occur in initials, 21 vowels in middles, and 7 consonants in finals. 3,192 types of syllables are possible including syllables with or without initial or final consonants, but there are syllable types that appear much less often in Korean texts or speech. The Dictionary of Standard Pronunciation of Korean reports that 1,453 syllable types appear in its 65,973 entry words and the average number of phones per syllable is 2.63 [6].

We have analyzed the text corpus of KSR-2002-TN for language modeling. In the text corpus, 1.14M of word types and 2,033 character types occur, and the number of character types that occur is smaller than the number of possible types. The number of syllables that are produced when the texts are converted into read speech is 1,937, which is not so different from the number of syllables that appear in [6]. Characters or syllables can be used as units for open-vocabulary recognition for SDR since 2K ~ 11K of vocabulary can cover the whole text. Characters have the advantage of keeping the information about the orthography, but they have the disadvantage of worse performance of recognition since they may have multiple pronunciations through resyllabification when they are pronounced. On the other hand, syllables do not have the problem of multiple pronunciations, and they have the advantage that they can be decomposed into phones whenever the phone sequences are needed, but it is hard to recover the information about the orthography before resyllabication directly through them.

We think that both characters and syllables can be taken into consideration beneficially for language model and recognition unit since correspondences between characters and syllables are significant statistically. Thus, in this paper we propose that units for which both characters and syllables are considered should be posited for language model and recognition unit. Such units have the following advantages. First, since syllable and character sequences can be obtained as the result of recognition, they can be used for SDR. Second, phone sequences can be obtained by simple decomposition of the syllables in the results of speech recognition. Thirdly, phone recognition can be improved by modeling in terms of syllables, which are longer than phones. The number of types of combined units that appear in the text corpus of KSR-2002-TN is 6,125.

For the purpose of illustration, LM units for a Korean word 알았다 are given here: phone (a r a d0 D a), syllable (_a _r_a_d0 _D_a), character (알 았 다), and combined unit (알/_a 았/_r_a_d0 다/_D_a). The symbol '_' represents connecting phones in composing syllables, and the symbol '/' represents combining characters and syllables.

In Table 1 are shown the perplexities and OOVs of phones, syllables, characters, and combined units when language models are made up for each unit by using the text corpus of KSR-2002-TN and tested by 20,833 sentences in the Dict01 corpus. Notice that 3 entries for sentence-beginning, sentence-ending, and unknown-word are included for LM entries.

Table 1. Perplexities and OOVs for each language model, trained on KSR-2002-TN and tested on sentences from Dict01 speech database

LM unit	# 1-gram entries	# 2-gram entries	Perplexity	2-gram hit ratio (%)	# OOVs
Phone	47	1,523	12.14	99.71	0 (0.00%)
Syllable	1,940	407,141	50.75	99.87	0 (0.00%)
Character	2,036	346,540	43.98	99.82	1 (0.00%)
Combined unit	6,128	631,781	40.05	99.64	3 (0.00%)

We observe that the size of vocabulary increases for combined unit three times as large as for characters and syllables, but the perplexity for language model decreases rather for combined unit. Characters and syllables have correlations. Although those characters and syllables that do not appear in the training text corpus may appear in the actual speech, the results of the test (around 0% of OOV rate) show that its possibility is not so high.

4 Experimental Results

4.1 Experimental Setup

Softwares – We have used the HTK toolkit for training acoustic models and recognition testing [7], and the CMU-Cambridge Statistical Language Modeling toolkit for language modeling [8].

Phone set – The phone set consists of 46 phones (including silence and short pause). The plosives in the syllable final are modeled differently from those in the syllable initial to distinguish them.

Acoustic Models – Two versions of acoustic model – context independent (CI) and context dependent (CD) models - were built. The speech of 360 speakers from Dict01 was used for training. The CI model has 128 mixtures per state, and the CD model is the crossword triphone which has 16 mixtures per state.

Language Models – We created a 2-gram language model respectively for phone, syllable, character and combined syllable unit from the text corpus by KSR-2002-TN.

4.2 Phone, Syllable and Character Recognition Task

We have performed recognition test for the speech data of 40 speakers (4,160 sentences) from Dict01 which are not used for training. Table 2 shows error rates of each unit. Phone error rates of the syllable, character and combined unit are calculated by using the phone sequences obtained from phone model boundary information of recognition results. Syllable and character error rates of the combined unit are calculated by using the syllable and character sequences obtained by simple decomposition of the recognition results.

The combined unit proposed without regard to the context dependency of the acoustic model shows lower error rate for phones, syllables and characters than other units. The proposed approach shows a 28% relative decrease of phone error rate when using CI acoustic model and a 34% relative decrease when using CD acoustic model, compared to a phone recognizers, and in the case of CD acoustic model its speed of recognition is higher than that of a phone recognizer. With respect to syllables its speed of recognition decreases, but it shows a 10% relative decrease of syllable error rate when using CI acoustic model and a 11% relative decrease when using CD acoustic model. With respect to characters, on the other hand, its speed of recognition is three times higher on the average and it shows a 37% relative decrease of character error rate when using CI acoustic model and a 49% relative decrease when using CD acoustic mode. Thus the proposed unit is shown to be significant for recognition of phones, syllables and characters.

Table 2. Error rate of each unit

Acoustic model	Recognition and LM unit	Error rate (%)				Realtime factor
		Phone	Syllable	Character	Combined unit	
CI Phone	Phone	30.54	-	-	-	0.34
	Syllable	23.99	39.55	-	-	0.63
	Character	29.81	-	58.71	-	4.37
	Combined unit	21.92	35.64	37.15	38.79	1.17
CD Phone	Phone	19.90	-	-	-	1.01
	Syllable	14.39	23.86	-	-	0.53
	Character	19.05	-	44.32	-	1.97
	Combined unit	13.12	21.23	22.72	23.85	0.65

4.3 Retrieval Task

The experiment in this paper was designed for examining the possibility of combining character and syllable information to be of use in the field of open-vocabulary spoken document retrieval system. Our retrieval model is based on the vector space model (VSM) [9]. The model creates a space in which both documents and queries are presented by vectors. Given a query Q and a document D, two T-dimensional vectors q and d are generated, where T is the total number of possible indexing terms. Each component of q and d represents a term frequency. The inner product of q and d is then used to estimate a measure of similarity between the query Q and the document D:

$$S(q, d) = \sum_{t=Q} q(t) \cdot d(t) \ . \tag{1}$$

The indexing terms used in this study are phone N-grams [1], character N-grams and syllable N-grams. 1-gram, 2-gram, and 3-gram are used for phones [2]. Only 1-gram and 2-gram are used for characters and syllables since characters and syllables have more units than phones and thus 3-gram would require too much memory. We have tried to combine the set of phone N-gram, character N-gram and syllable N-gram indexing terms. We have obtained the final (Q, D) relevance scores through a simple linear combination of the three resulting measures of similarity:

$$S_{p,c,s}(q, d) = c_p \cdot \frac{1}{6} \sum_{N=1}^{3} N \cdot S_{p,N}(q, d) + c_c \cdot \frac{1}{3} \sum_{N=1}^{2} N \cdot S_{c,N}(q, d) + c_s \cdot \frac{1}{3} \sum_{N=1}^{2} N \cdot S_{s,N}(q, d), \tag{2}$$

where $S_{p,N}$, $S_{c,N}$ and $S_{s,N}$ represent the relevance score of (1), obtained with the set of N-gram indexing terms of phone, character and syllable. c_p, c_c and c_s are the weights for each relevance score. The value of the weight can be set up empirically. In our experiment we set up the values such that $c_p = 1$, $c_c = 0$ and $c_s = 0$ when only the information about the phones is used and $c_p = 0.2$, $c_c = 0.4$ and $c_s = 0.4$ when the information about both the characters and syllables is used.

Two popular measures for retrieval performance are *Recall* and *Precision*. Recall is a measure of the ability of a system to present all relevant items and precision is a measure of the ability of a system to present only relevant items. The precision and recall rates depend on how many documents are kept to form the n-best retrieved document set. Precision and Recall vary with n, generally inversely with each other. We evaluate the retrieval performance by means of a single performance measure, called *mean average precision* (mAP), which is the average of precision values across all recall points. A perfect retrieval system would result in a mean average precision of 1.0 [10].

10 queries composed of 4 to 8 phones (such as place and building names) were selected to test the performance of combined units, and the relevance score was obtained for each query with the speech data of 60 speakers (a total of 8,247 sentences). The results are shown in Table 3.

Table 3. Retrieval performance of each model

Acoustic model	Retrieval model	mAP
	PH(P)	0.3491
CI Phone	CU(P)	0.4737
	CU(P,C,S)	0.5094
	PH(P)	0.5247
CD Phone	CU(P)	0.6320
	CU(P,C,S)	0.6652

Here, PH(P) is the model which calculates the relevance score based on the recognition results of a phone recognizer and CU(P) is the model which calculates the relevance score based on the phone sequence from the recognition results of the combined unit. CU(P,C,S) is the model which calculates the relevance score using character, syllable and phone information from the recognition results of the combined unit approach. Even when only phone information from the recognition results of the combined unit approach is used, 36% (CI) and 20% (CD) relative increases result in mAP measures than when the recognition results of a phone recognizer is used. In the case of CU(P,C,S), in which the character and syllable information is added in addition to the phone information, additional 10% (CI) and 6% (CD) relative increases result over PH(P) model. This shows that characters and syllables, complementary to phones, are useful for information retrieval. Our experiment was performed with respect to the read speech. However, additional experiments may be required for planned speech and spontaneous speech as well since spoken document retrieval should also be tested with respect to them.

5   Conclusion

In this paper we propose new recognition units to improve the recognition rates for phones, syllables, and characters in Korean. In the proposed approach we combine characters and syllables to compose new units to be used for language model and speech recognition unit since characters and syllables have correspondences due to Korean writing system.

To test the performance of the proposed approach we did two types of experiments. First, we did language modeling for phones, characters, syllables and proposed combined units based on the same text corpus, and we tested the performance for each unit. We observed an average 28% relative decrease of error rate for phones, syllables and characters when the combined unit was used for language modeling and recognition unit. Second, we did the VSM-based retrieval experiment by using the proposed combined unit. Even when only phone information from the recognition results of the combined unit approach is used, a 28% relative increase on the average results in mAP measures than when the recognition results of a phone recognizer are used. When the character and syllable information is added in addition to the phone information, additional 10% (CI) and 6% (CD) relative increases result over the phone recognizer, which shows that characters and syllables, complementary to phones, are useful for information retrieval.

In near future we hope to test the performance of the proposed units through an SDR experiment with respect to planned or spontaneous speech. Other combination technique and hierarchical approach may be considered to perform the fusion of character and syllable information.

Acknowledgements

This work was supported by the Korea Research Foundation Grant funded by the Korean Government (MOEHRD) (the Center for Healthcare Technology Development, Chonbuk National University, Jeonju 561-756, Korea).

References

1. Kenny Ng, *Subword-based Approaches for Spoken Document Retrieval*, Ph.D. Thesis, Massachusetts Institute of Technology (MIT), Cambridge, MA, 2000.
2. Nicolas Moreau, Hyoung-Gook Kim, Thomas Sikora, "Phone-based Spoken Document Retrieval in Conformance with the MPEG-7 Standard," 25th International AES Conference (Metadata for Audio), London, UK, 2004.
3. Speech/Language Technology Research Department in ETRI, http://voice.etri.re.kr.
4. SiTEC (Speech Information Technology and Industry Promotion Center), http://www.sitec.or.kr.
5. Ho-Min Sohn, *The Korean language*, Cambridge University Press, Cambridge, MA, 1999.
6. Korea Broadcasting System, *Dictionary of Standard Pronunciation of Korean*, Emunkak, 1993.
7. HTK (Hidden Markov Model Toolkit), http://htk.eng.cam.ac.uk.
8. CMU-Cambridge Statistical Language Modeling toolkit, http://mi.eng.cam.ac.uk/~prc14/toolkit.html.
9. Gerald Salton, Michael J. McGill, *Introduction to Modern Information Retrieval*, McGraw-Hill, New York, 1983.
10. TREC, Common Evaluation Measures, NIST, 10th Text Retrieval Conference (TREC 2001), Gaithersburg, MD, 2001.

Recognizing Connected Digit Strings
Using Neural Networks

Łukasz Brocki, Danijel Koržinek, and Krzysztof Marasek

Polish-Japanese Institute of Information Technology
Koszykowa 86, 02-008 Warsaw, Poland
{lucas, danijel, kmarasek}@pjwstk.edu.pl

Abstract. This paper discusses the usage of feed-forward and recurrent Artificial Neural Networks (ANNs) in whole word speech recognition. The Long-Short Term Memory (LSTM) network has been trained to do speaker independent recognition of any series of connected digits in polish language, using only the acoustic features extracted from speech. It is also shown how to effectively change the analog network output into binary information on recognized words. The parametrs of the conversion are fine-tuned using artificial evolution.

1 Introduction

Speech recognition is a spatio-temporal problem, i.e. not only is it important to discover different frequency patterns of speech, but also their duration and sequence. Only those classifiers that can combine the two types of information are able to recognize speech. Most modern speech recognition systems are based on the concept of Hidden Markov Models[8][9], however hybrids of neural networks and statistical systems are often used. This paper shows a very simple speech recognition system based solely on a neural network. ANNs are very good classifiers, mostly because the information is spread over a large number of synapses connecting different neurons. This allows them to be robust when the input signal is noisy or distorted. ANNs are used as classifiers in many different problems, however until recently they were not very successful in speech recognition.

The contents of the paper is as follows: in Sect. 2 an overview of different types of neural networks used for speech processing is given. Some common problems with phoneme and word recognition are also discussed. In Sect. 3 the used speech corpus is described. In Sect. 4 signal parametrization and network setup are described. In Sect. 5 it is shown how to convert analog network output to binary information. In Sect. 6 recognition score of this system is given and results are briefly discussed. In Sect. 7 some concluding remarks are given.

2 Neural Networks for Speech Processing

2.1 Phoneme and Whole Word Recognition

Because words consist of many phonemes and their acoustic features are highly dependent on the context, it is hard to train a neural network to recognize such a complicated sequence

Petr Sojka, Ivan Kopeček and Karel Pala (Eds.): TSD 2006, LNAI 4188, pp. 343–350, 2006.

using only the extracted features. This task is simplified by providing the information about the probabilities of phoneme occurrence and their sequence. In this paper, the harder task is attempted which does not use such information. Some phonemes, e.g. isolated vowels, can sometimes be even recognized by a single perceptron, using no context derived information, because the features are stationary throughout the phonemes' duration. Phonemes whose features do change, e.g. plosives like "k" or "t", pose a bigger problem. These phonemes consist of silence at the beginning followed by a plosive burst and some noise at the end, possibly with aspiration. Literature distinguishes two main ways for recognizing time altering sequences using neural networks [2]: by collecting information from several time-frames at each step, or by using only one time-frame, but by applying feedback loops to a neural network, so that short-term memory can be achieved.

2.2 Feed-Forward and Standard Recurrent Networks

To capture the context of a recorded utterance, the amount of frames visible by the multilayer perceptron at any given time is increased. This approach is not always effective, because the increase in context length results in the rapid growth of the network, which, in turn, decreases the generalization and the speed of training. Another problem is that the length of the context the network can learn is constant, depending on the network topology. In speech recognition, the length of the context may depend on the phonemes, their neighborhood and their position in words or phrases. Therefore it is not always known, which makes it hard to determine the topology of the network. To make things even more difficult, speech is often subject to non-linear time warp, which means that speech can be stretched and squashed in the time domain at different places. Solution to this problem cannot be achieved efficiently using the feed-forward network model.

Recurrent neural networks analyze only one frame at a time, however, the feedback loops in the network topology allow them to have short-term memory. There are two main methods for training recurrent neural networks, both based on gradient descent: Backpropagation Through Time (BPTT) [10] and Real Time Recurrent Learning (RTRL) [11]. Both of these have a major flaw: the backpropagated error either increases to infinity or diminishes to zero - it never remains stable [5]. This makes the networks incapable of learning a context longer than several frames. That is why they are sufficient to recognize phonemes, which last around 50 ms. (around 5 frames), but they experience difficulty in recognizing whole words, which often last more than 500 ms (50 frames). That is also why neural networks are used mostly for approximating the posterior probabilities of phonemes, leaving the higher level operations for statistical systems.

2.3 LSTM Recurrent Networks

LSTM (Long Short-Term Memory) neural networks are recurrent neural networks trained using gradient descent methods. Their specific topology ensures that the backpropagated error remains stable. It has been proved that these networks are capable of learning dependencies that are 1000 time frames apart from each other - a feature impossible to achieve using traditional recurrent neural networks.

LSTM networks consist of the so called "memory blocks". Each block contains several gates which directly control special memory cells used to store information. The gates are

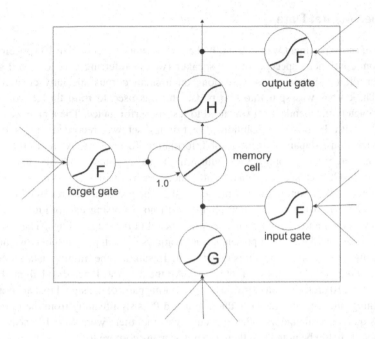

Fig. 1. One memory block of the LSTM neural network. The memory cell input first goes through the activation function $G(x)$, the output of which is multiplied by the output of the input gate. This signal is fed to the memory cell. The memory cell output is then squashed by the activation function $H(x)$ and the result is multiplied by the output of the output gate, after which it is stored as the output of the whole block.

simple sigmoidal units, whose activation function $F(x)$ returns values in the range of $(0, 1)$. The input to the memory cell is multiplied by the output of the input gate, so if the latter is near zero, it will stop any information from reaching the memory cell. Similarly, the output gate will block any information from leaving the memory block. However, if the output values of these gates is near 1, the signal will flow almost unchanged. The forget gate's role is to reset the contents of the memory cell. If the value of this gate is zero, the contents of the memory cell will also be zeroed out. A good analogy to the LSTM memory block is a memory circuit which can execute read, write and reset operations. LSTM is a differentiable version of such a circuit.

Detailed description of LSTM neural networks can be found in [4] and [1]. LSTM has been used for framewise phoneme classification. In [2] it is shown that LSTM is more accurate in this task than other neural network types. LSTM has also been used for whole word recognition. In [3] the application for spoken digit recognition is discussed. The authors of that paper achieved similar results to the state-of-the-art statistical systems based on the principle of Hidden Markov Models. They used a slightly different training method than the one used here and they did not use any post processing to change analog network output to binary information. However, this paper is partially based on their work.

3   Experimental Data

The goal of the experiment was to train the LSTM network to recognize 10 spoken digits in Polish from continuous speech, for any speaker (we are referring here to "word spotting" for spoken digits). Experiments were done on a small corpus specially created for this project. The corpus was split into two parts: one was used to train the network and the other completely independent set was used to test its performance. The signal was sampled at 16 kHz, with 16 bits of resolution. The training set was recorded in a sound-proof studio in the Polish-Japanese Institute of Information Technology. A studio-type pressure microphone was used in combination with a high quality sound card. Speakers where all males aged 19-32. Each speaker spoke 10 utterances, each of which consisted of 20 randomly chosen digits, spoken continuously with no pauses. The test data was recorded on different desktop computers using cheap microphones with no denoising capabilities. Background noise, conversation and computer fans are often heard in these recordings. The test data set consist of voices of 15 males not present in the training set. Each person spoke two utterances giving 40 digits altogether, no pauses in between. To sum up, the training data set consist of 2000 spoken digits and the test data set of 600. All the data was labeled and aligned by hand into 11 classes: 10 digits and an extra class representing parts of the signal that are not speech, e.g. breathing, silence, noise... Since the test data differs significantly from the training data this poses quite a challenge. Another difficulty was that there were only 10 speakers in the training set. It should be noted that there are not as many corpora for Polish language as there are for other languages and access to them is limited. The authors had to prepare the data themselves.

4   Experiments

4.1   Signal Parametrization

The signal was parametrized using MFCC (Mel-Frequency Cepstral Coefficients) [9]. 12 MFCCs, their deltas, the log energy and its delta was used. Altogether this gave 26 features per frame. The size of each frame was 25 ms and it was shifted by 15 ms.

4.2   Network Topology

The network topology was following: 26 inputs, 85 blocks, 2 cells per block. Each block had input, output and forget gates. "Peephole connections" [1] were used. There were 11 output units - 10 units for each of the digit plus one that was to be excited each time non-speech event was observed. The network was fully connected. All units were biased. The output of the memory cell was altered by a squashing function $H(x)$[4]. Because the task of the network was classification, a softmax output layer with cross-entropy error function was used. The error was calculated at each step. Synaptic weights were altered at each step as well. The learning rate was equal to 10^{-7} and the momentum 0.99. The goal of the project was to make a word recognizer, not only a classifier. In other words, the system was supposed to inform us only once when a digit was spoken, preferably in the last frame of the utterance. The output unit cannot be active throughout the duration of the word, because in continuous speech we would not be able to differentiate one long word from two short spoken one by one. Training a network to recognize only the last frame of the utterance would be almost impossible, because the endings of words are hard to define. A good example is the Polish digit 6 which pronounced correctly should sound /S e s' ts'/[1] but when spoken fluently it looses its last phoneme and sounds more like /S e s'/. To be more robust with these sorts of problems units have to be trained to activate during the whole second half of the word. This technique is quite universal, since the network has no problems with learning to recognize words with different endings. Also two digits pronounced continuously one after the other can also be recognized (Fig. 2). Finally the output of the system should be binary instead of real valued like the network output.

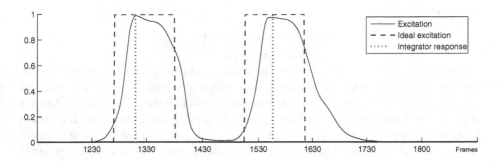

Fig. 2. A part of the network excitation through time of the utterance "zero zero" with no pause between the words is shown. Even though the words are connected, the excitation of the network temporarily diminishes because the network is trained to recognize only the second half of the word.

5   Post Processing

A good method for changing the analog output of the network to binary is to integrate the excitation of each output unit in time. For this purpose an integrator was used, which reads the excitation of a given output unit, processes it and returns a binary value: whether the word was recognized in the given frame or not. The integrator adds the excitations of a neuron through the time-window of length W. If the sum exceeds the threshold X, the integrator returns the value of 1 - the word was recognized. In all other frames the returned value equals 0. Refraction time Y is the the minimum time that must pass after the integrator returned 1, before it can generate the positive value again. Through the refraction period, the integrator returns the value of 0. The second criterion, aside from refraction time, of entering the state where the integrator can recognize again is excitation falling below a certain threshold Z. Both these criteria must be fulfilled in order for the integrator to be able to recognize. This gives four real value parameters: W, X, Y and Z. Evolution Strategy has been used to find the right values of all four parameters. The topic of Evolution Strategies is excellently described in [6] and [7]. It is worth mentioning that the fitness should be calculated on the test data, so that the system works better on the data the network never "saw". The parameters obtained this way seem quite reasonable, e.g. word "zero" had the integration time W equal to 114.797 ms. and the refraction time Y 121.432 ms., which is very close to the half of the length of

---

[1] Transcription is in Polish SAMPA[12].

recordings of this word present in the corpus. Since the network maximizes the second half of each word, these values are actually what we expected.

6   Results

Recognition performance was calculated on the integrator output. False answers are defined as any positive excitation of the integrator in the wrong frame. Theoretically, the integrator can excitate at any given time, however we allow only one excitation per uttreance, and no excitation outside of the utterance. Because of the unique way the integrator works the following formula, similar to the measures of recall and precision, was used to calculate its performance:

$$\frac{good\ answers\ -\ false\ answers}{number\ of\ utterances} \times 100\% \tag{1}$$

The above equation allows negative values, but if this happens, they are clipped to 0%. Since the used corpus was relatively small, high recognition results were easily achieved on training data. Unfortunately, the disparity between the results of the training and test data was large. It is to be noted that the test data was quite different from the training data. If the test data had been recorded in the sound-proof studio, using quality equipment and the number of speakers in the training set had been greater, smaller disparity between the two sets could have been expected.

Table 1. Recognition results of individuals digits.

Word	Pronounciation (Polish SAMPA)[1]	Recognition score (training data)	Recognition score (test data)
0	z e r o	99,7%	97,1%
1	j e d e n	98,6%	90,2%
2	d v a	97,7%	95,5%
3	t S I	97,2%	87,9%
4	t S t e r I	97,6%	96,8%
5	p j e˜ ts'	96,6%	90,7%
6	S e s' ts'	95,3%	92,4%
7	s' e d e m	99,5%	84,3%
8	o s' e m	97,0%	93,7%
9	dz' e v j e˜ ts'	95,5%	93,0%
	Complete system recognition score	97,5%	92,2%

Best results that authors managed to achieve on test set and corresponding results on the training set are displayed in Table 1. It is interesting to note, that the network performed worse on the digits that have common endings. Digits one /j e d e n/, seven /s' e d e m/ and eight /o s' e m/ or five /p j e˜ ts'/ and nine /dz' e v j e˜ ts'/ were often confused. The digit six, even though it is different from all other digits, also performed badly - in this case differences in fluent pronunciation was the problem. Some speakers often skiped the last phoneme, so the whole word sounded like /S e s'/ instead of /S e s' ts'/. The best performing digits were zero /z e r o/ and two /d v a/ due to their uniqueness and length.

Words with common endings are recognized worse than others, because the network maximizes just the second half of each word. Therefore, it seems reasonable to train the second network that would run backwards in time and maximize the first half of each word. One must modify the integrator to make advantage of information from two nets. This modification should further improve recognition score.

7   Conclusion

The obtained results were not too objective, because the recorded corpus was small. The main idea of the project was, however, an unconventional approach to whole word recognition and proving it makes sense. The described experiments show that the LSTM neural networks can be trained to recognize spoken words using only the acoustic information derived from the features obtained by parametrization of the raw signal. None of the higher level units (e.g. phonemes, syllables) had to be used. Also, it is described how to create an integrator that changes the analog output of the neural network into a binary decision of the recognized word. Such hybrid systems do not outperform the state-of-the-art statistical systems. However, they cannot be directly compared, as the former is a result of years of experiments and fixing, but the connectionist approach is fairly new. The authors are quite certain, that this is the first adaptation of this technology to speech recognition for the Polish language.

Acknowledgments

The authors would like to thank Alex Graves for the help and tips in the use of the LSTM for speech recognition. They would also like to thank Michał Szymerski for the help in the manual labeling and alignment of the corpus. Finally, they would like to thank prof. Witold Kosiński, Małgorzata Rzeźnik and Mladen Domazet for their suggestions and corrections. The participation of this paper in the conference was funded by grants ST/SI/07/2006 and ST/MUL/01/2005 awarded by the Minister of Science and Education to the PJIIT.

References

1. Gers, F. (2001) "Long Short-Term Memory in Recurrent Neural Networks", PhD thesis.
2. Graves, A., Schmidthuber, J. (2005) "Framewise Phoneme Classification with Bidirectional LSTM and Other Neural Network Architectures", Journal of Neural Networks, p. 602-610, June/July 2005.
3. Graves, A., Eck, D., Beringer, N., Schmidthuber, J. (2004) "Biologically Plausible Speech Recognition with LSTM Neural Nets", Proceedings of the First International Workshop on Biologically Inspired Approaches to Advanced Information Technology, Bio-ADIT 2004, Lausanne, Switzerland, Jan 2004, p. 175-184.
4. Hochreiter, S., Schmidhuber, J. (1997) "Long Short-Term Memory", Neural Computation, 9(8):17351780.

5. Hochreiter, S., Bengio, Y., Frasconi, P., Schmidhuber, J. (2001). "Gradient flow in recurrent nets: the difficulty of learning long-term dependencies", In Kremer, S. C. and Kolen, J. F., editors. A Field Guide to Dynamical Recurrent Neural Networks. IEEE Press.
6. Michalewicz, Z. (1994) "Genetic algorithms + Data Structures = Evolution Programs", Springer Verlag.
7. Michalewicz, Z., Fogel, D.B. (1999) "How to Solve It: Modern Heuristics", Springer Verlag.
8. Rabiner, L. R. "A tutorial on hidden markov models and selected applications in speech recognition." Readings in speech recognition, pages 267–296, 1990.
9. Young, S. (1995) "The HTK Book", Cambridge University Press.
10. Werbos, P. J. (1990) "Backpropagation through time: what it does and how to do it." Proc. IEEE, 78(10):1550-1560.
11. Williams, R., Zipser, D. (1989) "A learning algorithm for continually running fully recurrent neural networks.", Neural Computation, 1(2):270-280.
12. http://www.phon.ucl.ac.uk/home/sampa/polish.htm

Indexing and Search Methods for Spoken Documents*

Lukáš Burget, Jan Černocký, Michal Fapšo, Martin Karafiát, Pavel Matějka, Petr Schwarz, Pavel Smrž, and Igor Szöke**

Speech@FIT, Faculty of Information Technology, Brno University of Technology
Božetěchova 2, 612 66 Brno, Czech Republic
`speech@fit.vutbr.cz`
`http://www.fit.vutbr.cz/speech/`

Abstract. This paper presents two approaches to spoken document retrieval—search in LVCSR recognition lattices and in phoneme lattices. For the former one, an efficient method of indexing and search of multi-word queries is discussed. In phonetic search, the indexation of tri-phoneme sequences is investigated. The results in terms of response time to single and multi-word queries are evaluated on ICSI meeting database.

1 Introduction

It is very likely that today's success of Google in text search will excite interest in searching also other media. Among these, search in speech is probably the most interesting, as most of human-to-human communication is done by this modality. We can imagine applications for example in meeting processing and eLearning. Search in recordings is also becoming more important with the new US legislation on record-keeping, and there are many security and defense related applications. These techniques are often referred to as "keyword spotting", this term however implies that only one keyword can be searched at a time. Our approach allows for more complex queries, therefore, we prefer to rank it rather under spoken document retrieval (SDR).

Unlike search in text, where the indexing and search is the only "science", SDR is a more complex process that needs to address the following points:

- conversion of speech to discrete symbols that can be indexed and searched—large vocabulary continuous speech systems (LVCSR) and phoneme recognizers are used. Using phoneme recognizer allows to deal with out-of-vocabulary words (OOVs) that can not be handled by LVCSR.
- accounting for inherent errors of LVCSR and phoneme recognizer—this is usually solved by storing and searching in word, respectively phoneme lattices (Fig. 1) instead of 1-best output.

---

* This work was partially supported by EC project Augmented Multi-party Interaction (AMI), No. 506811 and Grant Agency of Czech Republic under project No. 102/05/0278. Lukáš Burget was supported by post-doctoral grant of Grant Agency of Czech Republic No. 102/06/P383.
** The authors are listed in alphabetical order, Jan Černocký `cernocky@fit.vutbr.cz` is the corresponding author.

Petr Sojka, Ivan Kopeček and Karel Pala (Eds.): TSD 2006, LNAI 4188, pp. 351–358, 2006.

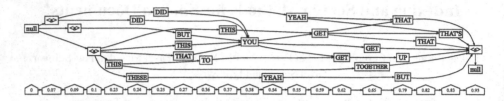

Fig. 1. Example of a word lattice

- determining the confidence of a query—in this paper done by evaluating the likelihood ratio between the path with searched keyword(s) and the optimal path in the lattice.
- processing multi-word queries, both quoted (exact sequences of words) and unquoted.
- providing an efficient and fast mechanism to obtain the search results in reasonable time even for huge amounts of data.

In this paper, we do not deal with pre-processors such as LVCSR system and phoneme recognizer, but concentrate on indexing and search issues. Section 2 reviews the LVCSR-based search with confidence computation and indexing. Section 3 details the technique used for two- and multi-word queries. The phonetic search is covered in section 4 with a tri-phoneme approach to indexing described in section 5. Section 6 presents the experimental results in terms of index sizes and response-times evaluated on 17-hour subset of ICSI meeting database.

2   LVCSR-Based Search

LVCSR lattices (example in Fig. 1) contain nodes carrying word labels and arcs, determining the timing and acoustic (L_a^{lvcsr}) and language model (L_l^{lvcsr}) likelihoods generated by an LVCSR decoder. Usually, each speech record is first broken into segments (by speaker turn or voice activity detector) and each segment is represented by one lattice. The confidence of a keyword KW is given by

$$C^{lvcsr}(KW) = \frac{L_\alpha^{lvcsr}(KW)L^{lvcsr}(KW)L_\beta^{lvcsr}(KW)}{L_{best}^{lvcsr}}, \qquad (1)$$

where the $L^{lvcsr}(KW) = L_a^{lvcsr}(KW)L_l^{lvcsr}(KW)$.

The forward likelihood $L_\alpha^{lvcsr}(KW)$ is the likelihood of the best path through lattice from the beginning of lattice to the keyword and the backward likelihood $L_\beta^{lvcsr}(KW)$ is the likelihood of the best path from the keyword to the end of lattice. For node N, these two likelihoods are computed by the standard Viterbi formulae:

$$L_\alpha^{lvcsr}(N) = L_a^{lvcsr}(N)L_l^{lvcsr}(N) \max_{N_P} L_\alpha^{lvcsr}(N_P) \qquad (2)$$

$$L_\beta^{lvcsr}(N) = L_a^{lvcsr}(N)L_l^{lvcsr}(N) \max_{N_F} L_\beta^{lvcsr}(N_F) \qquad (3)$$

where N_F is a set of nodes directly following node N (nodes N and N_F are connected by an arc) and N_P is a set of nodes directly preceding node N. The algorithm is initialized by setting $L_\alpha^{lvcsr}(first) = 1$ and $L_\beta^{lvcsr}(last) = 1$. The last likelihood we need in Eq. 1: $L_{best}^{lvcsr} = L_\alpha^{lvcsr} = L_\beta^{lvcsr}$ is the likelihood of the most probable path through the lattice.

The **indexing** of LVCSR lattices is inspired by [1]. It begins with the creation of lexicon which provides a transformation from word to a unique number (ID) and vice versa. Then, a forward index is created storing each hypothesis (the word, its confidence, time and nodeID in the lattice file) in a hit list. From this index, a reverse index is created (like in text search) which has the same structure as the forward index, but is sorted by words and by confidence of hypotheses.

Each speech record (ie. meeting) is represented by many lattices. The reverse index tells us, in which lattice the keyword appears and what is it's nodeID in this particular lattice.

In the **search** phase, the reverse index is used to find occurrences of words from query. An important feature of our system is the generation of the most probable **context** of the found keyword—a piece of the Viterbi path from the found keyword forward and backward. For all matching occurrences, the searcher therefore loads into the memory a small part of lattice within which the found word occurs. Then, the searcher traverses this part of lattice in forward and backward directions selecting only the best hypotheses; in this way it creates the most probable string which traverses the found word.

3 Multi-word Queries

A usable system for SDR should support queries of type

`word1 word2 word3`   and   `"word1 word2 word3"`

with the former one representing finding words in random order with optional spaces in between (in opposite to text-search where we work within a document, we specify a time-context) and the later one representing the exact match. Provided the query Q is found in the lattice, we again need to evaluate its confidence $C^{lvcsr}(Q)$. Similarly to Eq. 1, this is done by evaluating the likelihood of the path with all the words w_i belonging to the query and dividing it by the likelihood of the optimal path:

$$C^{lvcsr}(Q) = \frac{L_{rest}^{lvcsr} \prod_i L^{lvcsr}(w_i)}{L_{best}^{lvcsr}}, \tag{4}$$

where L_{rest}^{lvcsr} is the likelihood of the "Viterbi glue": optimal path from the beginning of the lattice to $w_{earliest}$, connections between words, w_i (for unquoted query) and optimal path from w_{latest} to the end of the lattice. In other words L_{rest}^{lvcsr} represents everything except the searched words. We should note, that each time we deviate the Viterbi path from the best one, we loose some likelihood, so that $L^{lvcsr}(Q)$ is upper-bounded by $\min_i C^{lvcsr}(w_i)$—actually the confidence of the worst word in the query.

The same index as for single-word queries (keywords) is used here. Processing of a query involves the following steps:

1. Based on frequencies of words, the least frequent one from the query, w_{lf}, is taken as first and all its occurrences are retrieved.

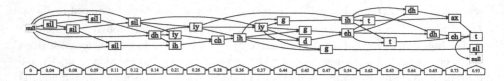

Fig. 2. Example of a phoneme lattice

2. The search proceeds with other words and verifies if they are within the specified time interval from w_{lf} (for non-quoted queries) or joint to w_{lf} (for quoted ones). The internal memory representation resembles again a lattice. In such way, a candidate list is created.
3. The list is pre-sorted by the upper-bound of query confidence, as described above. The list is then limited to the pre-determined number of candidates (usually 10).
4. For these candidates, the evaluation of correct confidence is done according to Eq. 4. While looking for the "Viterbi glue", the Viterbi algorithm is extended before and after the part of lattice containing Q in order to obtain the left and right contexts.

4   Phonetic Search

The main problem of LVSCR is the dependence on recognition vocabulary. The phonetic approach overcomes this problem by conversion of query to string and searching this string in a phoneme lattice (Fig. 2). The lattice has similar structure as word lattice (section 2), phonemes P populate nodes instead of words.

The confidence of keyword KW consisting of string of phonemes $P_b \ldots P_e$ is defined similarly as in Eq. 1 by:

$$C^{phn}(KW) = \frac{L_\alpha^{phn}(P_b)L_\beta^{phn}(P_e) \displaystyle\prod_{P \in P_b \ldots P_e} L_a(P)}{L_{best}^{phn}}, \tag{5}$$

where $L_\alpha^{phn}(P_b)$ is the forward Viterbi likelihood from the beginning of lattice to phoneme P_b, the product is the likelihood of the keyword, and $L_\beta^{phn}(P_e)$ is the likelihood from the last phoneme till the end of the lattice. L_{best} is the likelihood of the optimal path. As phoneme recognition is done without language (phono-tactic) model, the language model likelihoods are replaced by a constant—phoneme insertion penalty (PIP). It plays a role in the computation of $L_\alpha^{phn}(P_b)$, $L_\beta^{phn}(P_e)$ and L_{best}^{phn} and does not intervene in the product giving the likelihood of the keyword. The value of PIP needs to be tuned. The experiments of Szöke et al. [3] have shown that in case the phoneme lattice is dense, it is sufficient to look for an exact match of the searched string and not to take into account substitution, insertion and deletion errors.

5   Indexing Phoneme Lattices

While the indexing of word lattices is straightforward, indexing phoneme lattices is more tricky: in advance, we do not know what we will search for. Yu and Seide in [7] and Siohan and Bacchiani in [8] have chosen indexing sequences of phonemes with variable length, we have however investigated a simpler approach making use of overlapping tri-phonemes and indexing similar to multi-word queries. The use of tri-phonemes was also recommended in [6] as the best balance between number of units and number of units' occurrences in a corpus.

In the indexing phase, tri-phonemes T_i are selected in lattices. For each T_i, its confidence is evaluated by Eq. 5 as if T_i was a keyword. In case this confidence is higher than a pre-determined threshold, the tri-phoneme is inserted into the index.

The search stage consists of the following steps:

1. The searched keyword generates a set of overlapping tri-phonemes. Based on their frequencies in the index, the least frequent one T_{lf}, is taken as first and all its occurrences are retrieved.
2. The search proceeds with other tri-phonemes and verifies that they form a chain in time (with a security margin between adjacent tri-phonemes). Similarly to multi-word queries, the internal memory representation has again the form of lattice. In such way, a candidate list is created.
3. The confidence of keyword is again upper-bounded by the confidence of the worst tri-phoneme. Based on these, the list is pre-sorted and limited to the pre-determined number of candidates (usually 10).
4. For these candidates, we go into the respective phoneme lattices and evaluate the correct confidence using Eq. 5.

We have verified, that in case no thresholds are applied in the index, we obtain exactly the same accuracy of search that in case phoneme lattices are processed directly.

6 Experiments

The evaluation was done on 17 hours of speech from ICSI meeting database [4]. Attention was paid to the definition of fair division of data into training, development and test parts with non-overlapping speakers. We have also balanced the ratio of native/nonnative speakers and balanced the ratio of European/Asiatic speakers.

LVCSR lattices were generated by AMI-LVCSR system [2] and phonetic lattices were generated by a phoneme recognizer based on long-temporal context features with a hierarchical structure of neural nets [5].

The accuracies of different approaches were evaluated by Figure of Merit (FOM), which approximately corresponds to word accuracy provided that there are 5 false alarms per hour in average. In LVCSR-search, the FOM was 67% while for the phoneme-lattice search, we reached FOM of 60%. Detailed results are discussed in [3]—in this experimental evaluation, we have concentrated on response times, and disk footprints that are crucial for real deployment of the system.

The size of audio is 1.8 GB. The number of LVCSR lattices representing this audio is 25815 and they occupy 600 MB. LVCSR index needs 130 MB. Phoneme lattices (branching factor 4) need 2.1 GB of disk and the tri-phoneme index requires 220 MB.

In all tests, we report average time to process one query. The number of hits was set to 10-best in all experiments. The context to retrieve in LVCSR queries was set to ± 10 words and ± 7.5 seconds (whichever is shorter). The processing was done on a AMD Athlon 3200+.

Table 1. The results of LVCSR-based search

Test	time per query [s]
Test17	0.8
Test1	0.2
Quoted2	9.6
Quoted3	33.0
Quoted4	34.0
Unquoted2	1.2
Unquoted3	1.3
Unquoted4	1.8

We made sure that the data to be searched (lattices, indexes) resided on the local hard-disk and that no other CPU/memory consuming processes run on the machine.

The first test in LVCSR-search aimed at single keywords. Two sets were defined: Test17 containing 17 frequent words and Test1 containing words occurring just once in the test set. The total number of different words in Test1 is 2310, but only 50 were used in these evaluations.

The following test aimed at 2- till 4-word *quoted* queries. We have randomly chosen sequences of 2 to 4 words from the transcriptions of the test set and made sure at least one word within each sequence is at least 5 characters long. Examples of such sequences are:

2: "A MATTER", "NOUN PHRASES"
3: "THE DETECTOR TO", "PERSON TO DO"
4: "BUY A TICKET OR", "THE SITUATION OF LETTING"
50 sequences of each length were selected. These tests are denoted Quoted2 ... Quoted4.

In the test of unquoted queries, all tested sequences contained only words with length ≥ 5 characters and we worked again with 2- till 4-word sequences (note that for unquoted sequence, the words can appear in any order). The context (or "document size") was set to 20 words. To define the sets of queries, we have divided the test set into windows containing 10 words, discarded windows with less than 10 words and selected one sequence satisfying the word-length constraint from each window. Then, these sequences were randomized and 50 were selected for each length. Examples of such sequences are:

2: RELEVANT RANGES, WEDNESDAY ACTUAL
3: PERSON LISTENING FIRST, STUDY RIGHT GERMANY
4: TEACHER QUALITY THERE COURSE, TRAIN MODELS SUBTRACTION USING

These tests are denoted Unquoted2 ... Unquoted4.

Table 1 summarizes the response times for LVCSR-based search.

In the tests of phonetic search, only single keywords from sets Test17 and Test1 were looked for. Measurement of response times were done on the same 17h test-set, the results are summarized in Table 2.

We see that in LVCSR search is very fast and that single word and multiple-word unquoted queries require only 1-2 seconds. It is very likely that these figures will extend well to bigger

Table 2. The results of phonetic search

Test	time per query [s]
Test17	10.5
Test1	9.3

archives. The times required for quoted queries are quite prohibitive and we need to suggest optimizations. One of first targets will be the C++ STL library that is used for the creation of the internal lattice structures and which is quite slow.

The response times of phonetic search are longer than in LVCSR, but the search is still usable for the given size of archive. We should note that the comparison of response times for Test17 and Test1 is inverse for LVCSR and phonetic search. This is explained by the nature of the two algorithms: LVCSR can take advantage of rarity of words in Test1—they simply appear less frequently in the index so that the processing is faster. On contrary, phonetic search of items from Test1 takes almost the same time as Test17, as this approach can do no difference between rare and frequent words (actually, it does not have a notion of "word" in both indexing and search).

7   Conclusion

We have presented several techniques of indexing and search in LVCSR and phonetic lattices for spoken document retrieval. They were evaluated on real meeting data from ICSI meeting database. In LVCSR, both one-word and multi-word queries are handled with fast response times, the processing of quoted queries still needs some investigation. In phonetic search, we have verified the functionality of indexing tri-phones derived from phoneme lattices, but speeding up is needed also here.

In our further research, we will investigate direct techniques to derive tri-phoneme indices without lattices—tri-phonemes can actually be seen as keywords and as such pre-detected by a standard acoustic keyword spotting and indexed. We will also investigate the importance of different tri-phonemes for indexing and search and suggest customized pruning thresholds to keep the index size manageable. Finally, our goal is to build and test a system combining LVCSR and phonetic search allowing to search multi-word queries with OOVs.

References

1. Sergey Brin, Lawrence Page: *The Anatomy of a Large-Scale Hypertextual Web Search Engine, Computer Science Department*, Stanford University, 1998.
2. T. Hain et al.: The 2005 AMI system for the transcription of speech in meetings, in *Proc. Rich Transcription 2005 Spring Meeting Recognition Evaluation Workshop*, Edinburgh, July 2005.
3. Igor Szöke et al.: Comparison of Keyword Spotting Approaches for Informal Continuous Speech, in *Proc. Eurospeech 2005*, Lisabon, Portugal, September 2005.
4. A. Janin and D. Baron and J. Edwards and D. Ellis and D. Gelbart and N. Morgan and B. Peskin and T. Pfau and E. Shriberg and A. Stolcke and C. Wooters: The ICSI Meeting Corpus, in *Proc. ICASSP-2003*, Hong Kong, April 2003.

5. P. Schwarz, P. Matějka, J. Černocký: Hierarchical structures of neural networks for phoneme recognition, accepted to ICASSP 2006, Toulouse, France, May 2006.
6. K. Ng: *Subword-Based Approaches for Spoken Document Retrieval*, PhD thesis, Massachusetts Institute of Technology, USA, February 2000.
7. P. Yu and F. Seide: Fast two-stage vocabulary independent search in spontaneous speech, in *Proc. ICASSP 2005*, Philadelphia, 2005.
8. O. Siohan and M. Bacchiani: Fast vocabulary-independent audio search using path-based graph indexing, in *Proc. Eurospeech 2005*, Lisboa, Portugal, 2005.

Analysis of HMM Temporal Evolution for Automatic Speech Recognition and Verification

Marta Casar and José A.R. Fonollosa

TALP Research Center, Dept. of Signal Theory and Communications,
Universitat Politècnica de Catalunya
Jordi Girona, 1-3, 08034 Barcelona, Spain
{mcasar, adrian}@gps.tsc.upc.edu

Abstract. This paper proposes a double layer speech recognition and utterance verification system based on the analysis of the temporal evolution of HMM's state scores. For the lower layer, it uses standard HMM-based acoustic modeling, followed by a Viterbi grammar-free decoding step which provides us with the state scores of the acoustic models. In the second layer, these state scores are added to the regular set of acoustic parameters, building a new set of expanded HMMs. This new paremeter models the acoustic HMM's temporal evolution. Using the expanded set of HMMs for speech recognition a significant improvement in performance is achieved. Next, we will use this new architecture for utterance verification in a "second opinion" framework. We will consign to the second layer evaluating the reliability of decoding using the acoustic models from the first layer. An outstanding improvement in performance versus a baseline verification system has been achieved with this new approach.

1 Introduction

A widely-used type of speech recognition system is based on a set of so called acoustic models that link the observed features of the voice signal with the expected phonetics of the hypothesis sentence. The most usual implementation of this process is probabilistic, namely Hidden Markov Models [1]. A HMM is a collection of states with an output distribution for each state, defined in terms of a mixture of Gaussian densities. These output distributions are generally conformed by the direct acoustic vector plus its dynamic features (namely, its first and second derivatives), plus the energy of the spectrum. These dynamic features are the way of representing the context in HMM, but generally they are only limited to a few subsequent feature vectors and do not represent long-term variations. Thus, although using such augmented feature vectors significantly improves performance, current speech recognition systems still don't provide convincing results when conditions are changeable (noise, speakers, dialects,...).

We propose a two-layer speech recognition architecture dividing the modeling process into two levels and training a set of HMM for each level. References to other layered architectures for speech recognition [2], or meta-models [3], can be found in the literature.

But recognition is not our only goal. Every time a recognized word sequence is considered there is, inherently to it, some degree of uncertainty about its correctness. Therefore, it is necessary to build up a measure of how corresponding to the input utterance is the resulting

Petr Sojka, Ivan Kopeček and Karel Pala (Eds.): TSD 2006, LNAI 4188, pp. 359–366, 2006.

word sequence. From this measure, a decision can be taken on whether the output will be considered as correct or incorrect.

Traditional approaches for evaluating the correctness of recognition results are based on either alternative hypothesis models or an N-best algorithm. Besides, verification can be implemented using a "second opinion" approach [4]. This way, the correctness of the decoded hypothesis is determined by comparing the results of two recognition systems for consensus. One variant of this approach could be using an analysis of the recognition process itself as second opinion. Using the two-layer architecture proposed it can be consigned to the second layer the evaluation of the reliability of the models from the first layer.

This paper is organized as follows: first in section 2 we introduce our proposal for modeling HMM temporal evolution using state scores, and its implementation into a double layer speech recognition system. In section 3 we deal with utterance verification, presenting a second opinion based approach using the layered architecture defined. In section 4 we present the experiments to test the performance of our approach, together with the databases and baseline systems for each task. General conclusions about this work are discussed on section 5.

2   Modeling HMM Temporal Evolution Using State Scores

In standard HMM-based modeling feature vectors depend only on the states that generated them. Context is represented by the dynamic features which, generally, do not model long-term variations. We present a method to incorporate context into HMM by considering the state scores obtained by a phonetic units recognizer. These state scores are obtained from a Viterbi grammar-free decoding, and added to the original HMM, obtaining a set of "expanded" HMM. A similar approach has been used in [5] integrating the state scores of a phone recognizer into the HMMs of a word recognizer, and using state-dependent weighting factors.

2.1   Mathematical Formalism

In standard SCHMM the density function $b_i(x_t)$ for the output of a feature vector x_t by state i at time t is computed as a sum over all codebook classes $m \in M$:

$$b_i(x_t) = \sum_m c_{i,m} \cdot p(x_t|m, i) \approx \sum_m c_{i,m} \cdot p(x_t|m) \qquad (1)$$

In [5] probability density functions are considered which make it possible to integrate a large context $x_1^{t-1} = x_1, \ldots, x_{t-1}$ of feature vectors which have been observed so far, into the HMM output densities. For that purpose, a new hidden random variable l (class label) corresponding to phone symbols is introduced, which is a discrete representation of the feature vectors x_1^{t-1}. Thus, Eq. (1) is expanded and the output probability is defined (see [5]) as:

$$b_i(x_t|x_1^{t-1}) \approx \left[\sum_m c_{i,m} \cdot p(x_t|m)\right] \cdot \left[\sum_l P(l|i)P(l|x_1^{t-1})p(x_t|l)\right] \qquad (2)$$

In our case, we don't want to introduce the modeling of the context for each feature vector into the HMM output densities, but to create a new feature modeling the context. So, a new probability term is defined:

$$b'_i(x_t) = \sum_l P(l|i)P(l|x_1^{t-1})p(x_t|l) \propto \sum_l P(l|i)P(l|x_1^t) \tag{3}$$

This is obtained by applying Bayes' rule to $P(l|x_1^t)$:

$$P(l|x_1^t) = P(l|x_t, x_1^{t-1}) = \frac{p(x_t|l, x_1^{t-1})P(l|x_1^{t-1})}{p(x_t, x_1^{t-1})}$$

And, given that class l is itself a discrete representation of feature vectors x_1^{t-1}, we can approximate $p(x_t|l, x_1^{t-1}) \approx p(x_t|l)$. Also, $p(x_t, x_1^{t-1})$ is a constant in its evaluation across the different phonetic units, so $P(l|x_1^t) \propto p(x_t|l)P(l|x_1^{t-1})$

In Eq.(3), $P(l|i)$ is estimated during the Baum-Welch training of the expanded set of models, and $P(l|x_1^t)$ corresponds to the state scores output obtained by the Viterbi grammar-free decoding step.

We can see that, when combining $b_i(x_t)$ for each spectral feature and $b'_i(x_t)$ for the phonetic unit feature, the joint output densities are equivalent to Eq.(2).

2.2   Implementation

Figure 1 represents the double layer architecture implemented. We use a standard HMM based scheme for the lower layer. Next, the phonetic units recognizer performs a grammar-free decoding, providing us with a new quantification of the input signal.

Different units were tested with the phonetic units recognizer, obtaining best performance working with a semidigit recognizer. Consequently, labels l will represent last states of semidigit models and the density value can be computed as the probability that the current state s_t of a semidigit model is equal to l. Thus, semidigit last state scores output will be the new parameter to be added to the original parameter set.

In the upper layer, the new set of expanded HMM is built, adding the new parameter (state scores probability) to the original features (spectral parameters). This way, five parameters are considered henceforth for further training and decoding. As in [5], we will introduce a weighting factor w to control the influence of the state scores information, regarding the spectral parameters. However, we will work with a global weighting factor for the new parameter (not state-dependent), testing different values in the search of an optimal empirical weight.

3   Utterance Verification Based on the Analysis of HMM Temporal Evolution

To be able to consider a second opinion, it is mandatory to have a certain confidence about its reliability. In our approach we're not using a second independent opinion to validate the output of the system, but analyzing the coherence of the recognition by means of a second

TRAINING

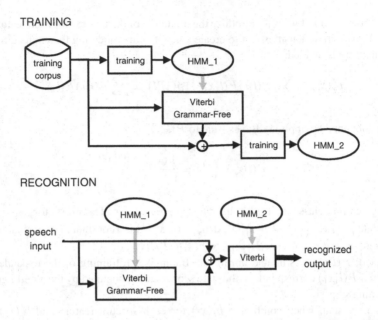

RECOGNITION

Fig. 1. Training and recognition schemes used for the double layer recognition system

decoding. The expanded HMM set built contains both the original spectral parameters plus the state scores parameter that can be seen as a model of the HMM temporal evolution. Therefore, we can compare the output of decoding using the expanded HMMs to that of a first decoding using regular acoustic models. If the two outputs differ, it means the temporal evolution of the models used presents some incoherence and, thus, the outputs are probably wrong (and therefore refused). But if they are equal, they are supposed to be right (and accepted).

The architecture proposed for recognition and verification, represented in figure 2, relies in a double procedure. Once the two decoding outputs are generated, they are compared for consensus and classified following a sentence based criterion as accepted or refused. To evaluate the performance of this decision, sentences have been tagged in four categories: *exact* when correctly accepted by the verification step, *error* when incorrectly accepted, *detected* if correctly refused and *rejected* when incorrectly refused. In order to do this taggin both recognition outputs were previously evaluated classifying the sentences as correct or incorrectly recognized. Then, detected sentences will be those incorrectly recognized only by the first recognizer, rejected the ones incorrectly recognized only by the second, exact sentences those correctly recognized by both decodings, and error sentences the ones incorrectly decoded by both recognizers.

The weighting factor w will have a significant role in the utterance verification performance, as it will imply to give more or less importance to the temporal evolution of HMM states.

The decoded output will be in the shape of a word string conformed by a chain of recognized words. A first string level filtering stage can be performed before comparing the two outputs, making a first acceptance/rejection decision of the hypothesis made by the recognizer. This stage consists on filtering the two decoding outputs using several task-dependent rules (i.e. sentence length, presence of out-of-vocabulary words, etc.). Sentences rejected on this previous basis will be tagged as *garbage*. In the following sections we will present different results for experiments with and without this string filtering stage.

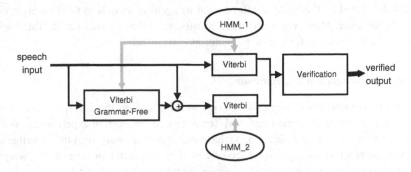

Fig. 2. Recognition and verification scheme of the utterance verification system

4   Evaluation Experiments

4.1   Databases

Experiments have been developed using two different databases. First, the Spanish corpus of the *SpeechDat* and *SpeechDatII* projects [6] has been divided into three sets: a training dataset, a developing dataset (for training the HMM of the second layer), and a testing dataset. This database consists on recordings performed over both fixed and mobile telephone networks, with a total of 4000 speakers for the fixed corpus, and 1066 speakers for the mobile set of recordings.

The results from the experiments using this first testing dataset have been used for selecting the best configuration of the new system and, when necessary, tuning the parameters used. Afterwards, all the models have been tested with an independent database obtained from a real telephone voice recognition application, henceforth DigitVox. It contains 5317 sentences with identity card numbers (8 digit chains) recorded in noisy conditions. Experiments developed using this database will test the independence of our models, thus approaching to similar conditions as those faced when recognizing unknown speakers in a changeable environment.

4.2   Reference Speech Recognition System

Our reference speech recognition system is the semi-continuous HMM based system RAMSES [7]. The main features of this system are:

- Speech is windowed every 10ms with 30ms window length. Each frame is parametrized with the first 14 melfrequency cepstral coefficients (MFCC) and its first and second derivatives, plus the first derivative of the energy.
- Spectral parameters are quantified to 512 centroids, energy to 64 centroids.

- Semidigits are used as HMM acoustic units. 40 semidigit models are trained, plus one noisy model for each digit, modeled each with 10 states. Silence and filler models are also used, modeled each with 8 states.
- For decoding, a Viterbi algorithm is used implementing beam search to limit the number of paths. Frames are quantified to 6 centroids for spectral parameters and 2 for energy.

The HMMs trained by this system will be used as acoustic models in the first layer of our layered architecture. Moreover, recognition results using this original set of HMM will be considered as our baseline for speech recognition experiments.

4.3   Speech Recognition Experiments

Digit chain recognition has been taken as our working task for testing speech recognition performance, as this will be the target task for utterance verification experiments. With the aim of selecting the best configuration, we have performed an analysis of the contribution of the new parameter by building several acoustic models with different state scores' weighting factor w. Table 1 summarizes the results obtained with the DigitVox database.

Table 1. Recognition rates using state scores based expanded models

configuration		Sentence	Word
system	w	recognition rate	recognition rate
baseline	-	93.304 %	98.73 %
layered	1	93.191 %	98.71 %
	0.5	93.605 %	98.80 %
	0.2	93.699 %	98.80 %

Performance obtained by our system slightly overcomes the baseline, specially when weighting the probabilistic state scores contributions for the new models. Still, this new recognition approach should be regarded keeping in mind our main target: obtaining a reliable second opinion for utterance verification.

4.4   Utterance Verification Baseline System

Our system has been compared to a standard verification algorithm relying on phone-based filler models. This method (see [8]) is based in the normalization of the scores output by the recognizer by means of a phone based decoding search. The phone decoding uses a network of unconnected phonemes constrained only by phone sequences characteristic of the language without respect to the current lexicon or language model. Once normalized, these scores can become a measure of an overall goodness of recognition by providing an estimate of the acoustic match of the phone models to the input unconstrained word or word-sequences models.

Phone-based filler models have proved to perform better than other vocabulary independent approaches, as word-based filler models, or anti-models (see [9]). They can be outperformed by more complex solutions like feature transformation models [10] or lattice-based combination models [11], but at the cost of being optimized for each specific recognition task and environment. Our goal, however, is to find a verification solution that doesn't need additional tuning.

4.5   Utterance Verification Experiments

Experiments have been carried out using DigitVox testing database, being completely independent from the one used for training the models and tuning the parameters. This promises verification results not conditioned by an over-training of the parameters neither by adaptation to the speech recordings.

Let us define (as in [12]) the *TRR (True Rejection Rate)* as the rate between the number of incorrect hypothesis detected by the verification system (correctly refused), and the total number of incorrect hypothesis: $TRR = D/I$

Then, the *FRR (False Rejection Rate)* is the rate between the number of correct hypothesis rejected by the system (incorrectly refused) and the total number of correct hypothesis: $FRR = R/C$

In terms of the *TRR* and *FRR* measures, a ROC curve (Receiver Operating Characteristic) [13] is a curve that shows the TRR versus the FRR for every threshold level used, expressing the latest in the x axis. Depending on the curve obtained we can evaluate the performance of the verification system.

By modifying the weighting factor w given to the new parameter in the expanded HMM set we will be modifying the performance of the second decoding. This will be used to obtain different behaviors of the verification system. Figure 3 shows the ROC curve representing TRR vs. FRR values for our both verification systems, with and without the string filtering step.

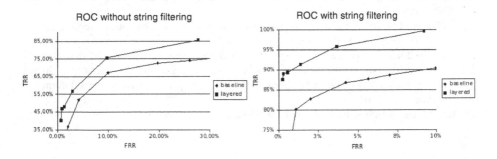

Fig. 3. TRR vs. FRR filtering for both systems

5   Summary

Throughout this paper we present some experiments carried out using a double layer speech recognition and utterance verification approach based on the analysis of HMM temporal evolution.

Speech recognition results using the layered architecture are slightly better than our baseline, but the computational cost increase becomes a drawback. However, when using this layered system with verification purposes following a "second opinion" approach, results become high-flying. Appart from a better TRR vs FRR behavior, our verification approach offers a very performant correct recognition rate for a really low error rate, compared to results obtained by the baseline system.

Acknowledgments

This work has been partially supported by Spanish MCyT under the projects TIC2002-04447-C02 and TIN-2005-08852.

References

1. Huang et al.: Spoken Language Processing. 1st edn. Prentice Hall PTR (2001).
2. Demuynck et al.: Flavor: a flexible architecture for LVCSR. EUROSPEECH (2003).
3. Cox and Dasmahapatra: High-level approaches to confidence estimation in speech recognition. IEEE Trans. on Speech and Audio Processing 10 (2002) 460–471.
4. Hernández-Ábrego and Mariño: A second opinion approach for speech recognition verification. Proceedings of the VIII SNRFAI I (1999).
5. Stemmer et al.: Context-dependent output densities for Hidden Markov Models in speech recognition. EUROSPEECH (2003).
6. Moreno and Winksky: Spanish fixed network speech corpus. SpeechDat Project. LRE-63314 (1999).
7. Bonafonte et al.: Ramses: el sistema de reconocimiento del habla continua y gran vocabulario desarrollado por la UPC. VIII Jornadas de Telecom I+D (1998).
8. Young: Detecting misrecognitions and out-of-vocabulary words. ICASSP I (1994).
9. Jiang and Huang: Vocabulary-independent word confidence measure using subword features. ICSLP (1998).
10. Rahim et al.: Discriminative utterance verification using minimum string verification error (MSVE) training. ICASSP (1996).
11. Schaaf and Kemps: Confidence measures for spontaneous speech recognition. ICASSP II (1997).
12. Sanchis: PhD Thesis. Estimation and application of confidence measures for speech recognition (in spanish). PhD thesis, Universidad Politécnica de Valencia. Departamento de Sistemas Informáticos y Computación (2004).
13. Egan: Signal detection theory and ROC analysis. Academic Press (1975).

Corpus-Based Unit Selection TTS for Hungarian

Márk Fék, Péter Pesti, Géza Németh, Csaba Zainkó, and Gábor Olaszy

Laboratory of Speech Technology
Department of Telecommunications and Media Informatics
Budapest University of Technology and Economics, Hungary
{fek, nemeth, zainko, olaszy}@tmit.bme.hu, pesti@alpha.tmit.bme.hu

Abstract. This paper gives an overview of the design and development of an experimental restricted domain corpus-based unit selection text-to-speech (TTS) system for Hungarian. The experimental system generates weather forecasts in Hungarian. 5260 sentences were recorded creating a speech corpus containing 11 hours of continuous speech. A Hungarian speech recognizer was applied to label speech sound boundaries. Word boundaries were also marked automatically. The unit selection follows a top-down hierarchical scheme using words and speech sounds as units. A simple prosody model is used, based on the relative position of words within a prosodic phrase. The quality of the system was compared to two earlier Hungarian TTS systems. A subjective listening test was performed by 221 listeners. The experimental system scored 3.92 on a five-point mean opinion score (MOS) scale. The earlier unit concatenation TTS system scored 2.63, the formant synthesizer scored 1.24, and natural speech scored 4.86.

1 Introduction

Corpus-based unit selection TTS synthesis creates the output speech by selecting and concatenating units (e.g. speech sounds or words) from a large (several hours long) speech database [1]. Compared to TTS systems using diphone and triphone concatenation, the number of real concatenation points becomes much smaller. Moreover, the database of traditional diphone and triphone concatenation TTS systems is recorded with monotonous prosody whereas the units from a large speech corpus retain their natural and varied prosody. Thus, it becomes possible to concatenate larger chunks of natural speech, providing superior quality over diphone and triphone concatenation.

Corpus-based unit selection TTS systems have already been developed for several major languages. The state-of-the-art Hungarian TTS systems use diphone and triphone concatenation, see for example [2]. These systems allow unrestricted domain speech synthesis, but the speech quality is limited by the non-unit-selection based waveform concatenation technology. In this paper, we describe our ongoing work in developing a corpus-based unit selection TTS for Hungarian. Our first goal was to develop a restricted domain TTS capable of reading weather forecasts. Based on the experience gained, we plan to extend the system to read unrestricted texts.

Section 2 describes the text collection and the design of the text corpus. Section 3 details the recording and labeling of the speech database. Section 4 describes the mechanism of the unit selection. Finally, Section 5 describes the result of a subjective evaluation test comparing the quality of the system to that of earlier Hungarian TTS systems.

Petr Sojka, Ivan Kopeček and Karel Pala (Eds.): TSD 2006, LNAI 4188, pp. 367–373, 2006.

2   Text Collection and Corpus Design

We collected texts of daily weather forecasts in Hungarian from 20 different web sites for over a year. After spell checking and resolving abbreviations, the resulting text database contained approximately 56, 000 sentences composed of about 493, 000 words (5, 200 distinct word forms) and 43, 000 numbers. Almost all of the sentences were statements; there were only a few questions and exclamations. On the average, there were 10 words in a sentence (including numbers). The average word length was slightly over 6 letters because of the frequent presence of longer than average weather related words. Statistical analysis has shown that as little as the 500 most frequent words ensured 92% coverage of the complete database, while the 2, 300 most frequent words gave 99% coverage. The next paragraph describes a more detailed analysis that takes the position of the words within a prosodic phrase into consideration. We have obtained similar results on data collected over only a half year period, thus we assume that these results are mainly due to the restricted weather forecast domain. As Hungarian is an agglutinative language, a corpus from an unrestricted domain requires approximately 70, 000 word forms to reach 90% coverage [3]. The favorable word coverage of the restricted domain allowed us to choose words as the basic units of the speech database.

The next step was to select a part of the speech corpus for recording. We used an iterative greedy algorithm to select the sentences to be read. In each iteration, the algorithm added the sentence that increased word coverage the most. A complete coverage was achieved with 2, 100 sentences. We extended the algorithm to include some prosodic information derived from position data. Sentences were broken into prosodic phrases, using punctuation marks within a sentence as prosodic phrase boundaries. We assigned two positional attributes to each word: the position of the word within its prosodic phrase, and the position of the prosodic phrase (containing the word) within the sentence. Both positional attributes may have three values: first, middle, or last. Our underlying motivation was that words at the beginning and at the end of a prosodic phrase tend to have a different intonation and rhythm than words in the middle of the prosodic phrase. Similarly, the first and the last prosodic phrases in a sentence tend to have a different intonation than the prosodic phrases in the middle of a sentence. We obtained 5, 200 sentences containing 82, 000 words by running the extended algorithm. The sentences contain 15, 500 words with distinct positional attributes and content.

A speech synthesizer using words as units can only synthesize sentences whose words are included in the speech database. In a real application it may occur that words to be synthesized are not included in the database. In order to synthesize these missing words, we have chosen speech sounds to be the universal smallest units of the speech database. As we use speech sounds only as an occasional escape mechanism to synthesize words not included in the speech database, we did not optimize the database for triphone coverage.

3   Speech Database Recording and Labeling

The selected sentences were read by a professional voice actress in a sound studio. We have also recorded 60 short sentences covering all the possible temperature values. The speech material was recorded at $44, 1kHz$ using 16 bits per sample. The recording sessions spanned over four weeks with $2 - 3$ days of recording per week and $4 - 5$ hours of recording per day. The recorded speech material was separated into sentences. The 5260 sentences resulted in a database containing 11 hours of continuous speech. We have extracted the fundamental frequency of the waveforms by using the autocorrelation based pitch detection implemented in the Praat software [4]. Pitch marks were placed on negative zero crossings to mark the start of pitch periods in case of voiced speech and at every $5ms$ in case of unvoiced speech. When concatenating two speech segments, the concatenation points are restricted to be on pitch marks, assuring the phase continuity of the waveform. The fundamental frequency itself is not stored but recalculated from the pitch periods when needed.

The word and speech sound unit boundaries are marked automatically. To mark the sound boundaries in the speech waveform, a Hungarian speech recognizer was used in forced alignment mode [5]. We performed a manual text normalization by expanding numbers, signs, and abbreviations in the textual form of the sentences before and during the recording. The speech recognizer performs an automatic phonetic transcription. The phonetic transcription inserts optional silence markers between words, and takes into account the possible co-articulatory effects on word boundaries. Thus, it provides a graph of alternative pronunciations as input to the speech recognizer. The speech recognizer selects the alternative that best matches the recorded speech, and also returns the corresponding phonetic transcription. The hidden Markov model based speech recognizer was trained with a context dependent triphone model on a Hungarian telephone speech database [6]. The preprocessing carries out a Mel cepstral (MFCC) analysis using a fixed frame size of $20ms$ and a frame shift of $10ms$. The detected sound boundaries are aligned to the closest pitch mark.

We performed a statistical analysis on sound durations using the detected sound boundaries and manually checked sounds with extreme durations. We identified and corrected several sentences where the waveform and the textual content of the sentence did not match, due to mistakes in the manual processing of the database. Apart from that, we have observed some problems concerning the incorrect detection of sound boundaries for unvoiced fricatives and affricates. The problem is likely caused by the use of telephone speech to train the recognizer, because telephone speech does not represent frequencies above $3400Hz$ where unvoiced fricatives and affricates have considerable energy. We plan to correct the problem by retraining the recognizer on the recorded 11 hour long speech corpus.

The word boundaries were marked automatically on the phonetic transcription returned by the recognizer. Separate markers were used for identifying the beginning and the end of each word. Each marker was assigned to a previously detected sound boundary. In some cases, the last sound of a word is the same as the first sound of the following word. If there is a co-articulation effect across word boundaries, only one sound will be pronounced instead of two. In this case, we place the word boundary end/start markers after/before the fusioned sound so as to include the sound in both words. When selecting the waveform corresponding to words starting/ending with such speech sounds, only 70% of the fusioned sound is kept, and their first/last 30% is dropped.

4   Unit Selection

The unit selection algorithm divides the input into sentences and processes every sentence separately. The algorithm follows a two-phase hierarchical scheme [7] using words and speech sounds as units. In the first phase of the algorithm, only words are selected. If a word is missing from the speech database, the algorithm composes it from speech sounds in the second phase. The advantage of the hierarchical scheme is that it makes the searching process faster. We plan to add an intermediate, syllable level to the system, which may work well in case of unrestricted domain synthesis.

The unit selection algorithm identifies the words based on their textual content. A phonetic transcription is also generated and used for identifying the left and right phonetic context of the words. The speech sounds are identified by the phonemes in the phonetic transcription. A list of candidate units with the same textual (or phonetic) content is created for every word (or speech sound) in the sentence (or word) to be synthesized.

The unit selection algorithm uses two cost functions. The target cost captures how well a unit in the speech corpus matches a word (or speech sound) in the input. The concatenation cost captures how natural (or smooth) the transition is between two concatenated units sounds. The number of candidates for a given unit is limited to reduce the search time. If there are more candidates than the limit, only the ones with the lowest target cost are kept. The Viterbi algorithm is used to select the optimum path among the candidates giving the smallest aggregated target and concatenation cost.

In our implementation, the target cost is composed of the following subcosts:

1. The degree of match between the left and right phonetic contexts of the input unit and the candidate. This part of the target cost is zero, if the phonetic contexts are fully matched. We have defined seven phoneme classes for consonants, based on their place of articulation (bilabial, labiodental, dental, alveolar, velar, glottal, nasal) [8]. Consonants within the same class tend to have similar co-articulation effects on neighboring sounds. The target cost is smaller for phonemes in the same class, and becomes bigger if the preceding or following phonemes are from different classes. The target costs between the different phoneme classes are defined in a cost matrix. The weights in the matrix were set in an ad-hoc way. Further optimization may improve the quality of the system.
2. The degree of match between the position of the input word and the position of the candidate within their respective prosodic phrases. The positions can take three values: first, middle, or last. This subcost is only defined for words.
3. The degree of match between the relative positions of the prosodic phrases (containing the input word or the candidate) within their corresponding sentences. This subcost is only defined for words.

The concatenation cost is calculated as follows:

1. Units that were consecutive in the speech database have a concatenation cost of 0, because we cannot have a better concatenation than in natural speech. This motivates the algorithm to choose continuous speech segments from the database.
2. Candidates from the same database sentence have lower concatenation cost than candidates from different sentences. This gives a preference to concatenate units with similar voice quality.
3. Continuity of fundamental frequency (F_0), calculated as the weighted difference between the ending F_0 of the first and the starting F_0 of the second unit.

The various weights of the two cost functions were tuned manually during informal listenings, on test sentences not included in the corpus.

Table 1. Mean opinion scores per sentence. The confidence ($\alpha = 0.05$) took values between 0.04 and 0.09.

sentence number	1	2	3	4	5	6	7	8	9	10	variance
natural	4.83	4.83	4.91	4.88	4.79	4.90	4.86	4.92	4.84	4.84	0.04
corpus-based	4.75	4.28	4.16	3.56	3.59	3.85	4.29	3.63	3.75	3.30	0.44
diphone-triphone	2.52	2.88	2.79	2.56	2.66	2.60	2.44	2.76	2.65	2.46	0.15
formant synthesis	1.25	1.20	1.33	1.26	1.25	1.20	1.26	1.21	1.21	1.20	0.04

5   Subjective Evaluation

We have carried out a subjective listening test to compare the quality of our corpus-based unit selection TTS system to that of a state-of-the-art Hungarian concatenative TTS system [2]. We have also included a Hungarian formant synthesizer [9] in the test to measure the evolution of quality across different TTS generations.

We decided to limit the length of the test to 10 minutes to make sure that the listeners do not lose their interest in the test. Listeners were asked to evaluate the voice quality of the synthetic speech after every sentence heard. Intelligibility was not evaluated, because we do not expect it to be a real problem for weather forecasts. The listeners had to evaluate the quality of the synthesized speech on the following 5-point scale: excellent (5), good (4), average (3), poor (2), bad (1).

The content of the test sentences was matched to the weather forecast application. We chose 10 random sentences from a weather report. The weather report originated from one of the web sites included in the database collection. Thus, the style of the sentences was close to the speech corpus, but the chosen sentences were not included in the corpus. A listener had to evaluate 40 sentences (10 natural, 10 generated by the formant synthesizer, 10 generated by the diphone-triphone synthesizer, and 10 generated by the corpus-based synthesizer) in a pseudo-random order.

The test was carried out via the Internet using a web-interface. This allowed the participation of a large number of test subjects. The average age of the 248 listeners was 22.9 years. Most of them were students. The results from 185 males and 36 females were evaluated, while 27 listeners were excluded because we judged their results as inconsistent. At the beginning of the test, the testers had to listen to an additional $11th$ weather report sentence in four versions. This allowed the listeners to familiarize themselves with the different speech qualities. Each sentence was played only once to reduce the length of the test. According to the listener responses to our questionnaire, most of them carried out the test in a quiet room using average quality equipment.

We excluded testers from further evaluations who gave an 'average (3)' or worse score to natural speech samples at least twice. We supposed that these excluded testers were either guessing, or had difficulty with the playback. According to our preliminary tests, the playback function did not work continuously for large speech files in case of slow Internet connections. Therefore we have converted all speech samples to $22kHz$ and compressed them with a $32kbps$ variable bit rate MPEG1-LIII encoder. We did an informal evaluation with high quality headphones and found no quality difference between the encoded and the original speech samples.

M. Fék et al.

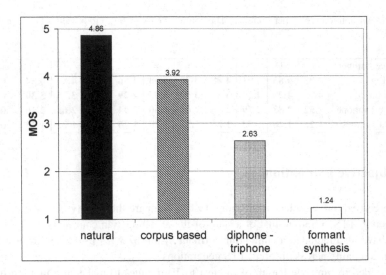

Fig. 1. Mean opinion scores obtained for the different TTS systems. The confidence ($\alpha = 0.05$) took values between 0.02 and 0.03.

Table 2. Relation of the MOS values to the number of real concatenation points in a sentence synthesized by the corpus-based system.

sentence number	1	2	3	4	5	6	7	8	9	10
MOS (corpus-based)	4.75	4.28	4.16	3.56	3.59	3.85	4.29	3.63	3.75	3.30
number of concatenation points	3	4	4	6	9	10	12	14	15	24
number of words	10	11	8	7	10	12	9	15	25	22
number of concatenated words	0	0	0	0	0	0	0	0	0	2

The resulting Mean Opinion Scores (MOS), summarized in Figure 1, show a major quality difference between the different synthesizers. The corpus-based synthesizer outperformed the diphone-triphone concatenation system by 1.3 points, which indicates that we may expect higher user acceptance and more widespread use of the corpus-based system.

We have explored the correlation between perceived quality and the number of real concatenation points in a synthesized sentence. We define the real concatenation point as a point separating two speech segments in the synthesized sentence that were not continuous in the speech database. Table 2 shows the sentences ordered by the number of concatenation points. The best MOS was achieved by the sentence containing the least, i.e. 3 concatenation points. The worst quality was achieved by the sentence containing the most, i.e. 24 concatenation points. The speech quality, however, does not depend consistently on the number of concatenation points. The $7th$ sentence, for instance, has the second best quality but contains more (12) concatenation points than most of the sentences. The correlation between the MOS scores and the number of concatenation points is $-0,68$. Table 2 also shows, that there was only one sentence where it was necessary to use speech sounds as units.

6   Conclusion

In this paper, we have described our ongoing work on a corpus-based unit selection TTS system for Hungarian. We have built an experimental application for synthesizing restricted domain weather forecasts. The quality of the system was evaluated using a subjective listening test. 10 sentences from a weather forecast were synthesized by the corpus-based unit selection system. The sentences were also synthesized by two unrestricted domain TTS systems using non-unit-selection based diphone/triphone concatenation and formant synthesis. The new system outperformed the diphone/triphone concatenation by 1.3 MOS points, and the formant synthesis by 2.7 MOS points. The quality of the experimental TTS system showed a greater variance depending on the input sentence than the other two systems. Some correlation was found between the number of concatenation points in a sentence and its quality. We expect to further improve the quality by introducing fundamental frequency smoothing. Our future plan is to improve the prosody model and the unit selection algorithm to be able to extend the system to general unrestricted TTS synthesis.

Acknowledgments

We would like to thank our colleagues, Mátyás Bartalis, Géza Kiss, and Tamás Bőhm for their varoius contributions. We also thank all the listeners for participating in the test.

This project was funded by the second Hungarian National R&D Program (NKFP), contract number 2/034/2004.

References

1. Möbius, B.: Corpus-Based Speech Synthesis: Methods and Challenges. AIMS 6 (4), Univ. Stuttgart, pp. 87–116., 2000.
2. Olaszy, G., Németh G., Olaszi, P., Kiss, G., Gordos, G.: PROFIVOX - A Hungarian Professional TTS System for Telecommunications Applications. International Journal of Speech Technology, Volume 3, Numbers 3/4, December 2000, pp. 201–216.
3. Németh, G., Zainkó Cs.: Word Unit Based Multilingual Comparative Analysis of Text Corpora. Eurospeech 2001, pp. 2035–2038., 2001.
4. Boersma, P.: Accurate Short-Term Analysis of the Fundamental Frequency and the Harmonics-to-Noise Ratio of a Sampled Sound. IFA Proceedings 17, pp. 97–110., 1993.
5. Mihajlik P., Révész T., Tatai P.: Phonetic Transcription in Automatic Speech Recognition. Acta Linguistica Hungarica, Vol. 49 (3–4), pp. 407–425, 2002.
6. Vicsi, K., Tóth, L. Kocsor, A., Gordos, G., Csirik, J.: MTBA - Magyar nyelvű telefonbeszéd adatbázis (Hungarian Telephone-Speech Database). Híradástechnika, vol. 2002/8., pp. 35–39, 2002.
7. Taylor, P., Black, A., W.,: Speech Synthesis by Phonological Structure Matching. Eurospeech 1999, vol. 2, pp. 623–626, 1999.
8. Olaszy, G.: Az artikuláció akusztikus vetülete – a hangsebészet elmélete és gyakorlata (The Articulation and the Spectral Content—the Theory and Practice of Sound Surgery). in: Hunyadi, L. (ed.): KIF-LAF (Journal of Experimental Phonetics and Laboratory Phonology), Debreceni Egyetem, pp. 241–254, 2003.
9. Olaszy, G., Gordos, G., Németh, G.: The MULTIVOX Multilingual Text-to-Speech Converter. in: G. Bailly, C. Benoit and T. Sawallis (eds.): Talking machines: Theories, Models and Applications, Elsevier, pp. 385–411, 1992.

Automated Mark Up of Affective Information in English Texts

Virginia Francisco and Pablo Gervás

Departamento de Sistemas Informáticos y Programación
Universidad Complutense de Madrid, Spain
virginia@fdi.ucm.es, gervas@sip.ucm.es

Abstract. This paper presents an approach to automated marking up of texts with emotional labels. The approach considers in parallel two possible representations of emotions: as emotional categories and emotional dimensions. For each representation, a corpus of example texts previously annotated by human evaluators is mined for an initial assignment of emotional features to words. This results in a List of Emotional Words (LEW) which becomes a useful resource for later automated mark up. The proposed algorithm for automated mark up of text mirrors closely the steps taken during feature extraction, employing for the actual assignment of emotional features a combination of the LEW resource, the ANEW word list, and WordNet for knowledge-based expansion of words not occurring in either. The algorithm for automated mark up is tested and the results are discussed with respect to three main issues: relative adequacy of each one of the representations used, correctness and coverage of the proposed algorithm, and additional techniques and solutions that may be employed to improve the results.

1 Introduction

The present paper proposes a method for automated tagging of texts with emotions. Before marking text with emotions we have to decide which emotions we are going to deal with. Then we need a corpus of emotional marked text in order to analyse how people mark text and how our program will have to do it. Based on this corpus we obtain a list of "emotional words" and the relation between these words and the emotions we are modelling. Finally, with this relation between words and emotions we model a method for marking up every text.

For the study of emotional texts we need to decide which emotions we are going to model, and how we are going to represent them. There are different methods in order to research emotions [1]: *emotional categories* - based on the use of emotion-denoting words -, *descriptions based on psychology* [2] and *evaluation* [1], *circumflex models* - emotional concepts are represented by means of a circular structure [3], so that two emotional categories close in the circle are conceptually similar of them. - and *emotional dimensions* which represent the essential aspects of emotion concepts: evaluation (positive/negative) and activation (active/passive) are the main dimensions, sometimes they are augmented with the power dimension (dominant/submissive).

Petr Sojka, Ivan Kopeček and Karel Pala (Eds.): TSD 2006, LNAI 4188, pp. 375–382, 2006.

2 Labelling Text with Emotions

There are several issues that need to be taken into account when attempting to mark up a document with emotions: the granularity to be employed, and the particular approach to be used to relate emotions and textual elements.

On deciding the parts of the text which are going to be marked with emotions there are different options [4]: word, phrase, paragraph, chapter,... One of the simplest approaches is to use sentences as the emotional structures. Another solution is to combine the sentences into larger units using an algorithm to summarise the affect of text over multi-sentence regions (winner-take-all scheme, Bayesian networks...).

Existing approaches to emotional mark up can be grouped in four main categories [4]: *keyword spotting* [5] – text is marked up with emotions based on the presence of affect words –, *lexical affinity* – not only detects affective words but also assigns arbitrary words a probability, obtained from a corpus, of indicating different emotions –, *statistical natural language processing* [6] – this method involves feeding a machine learning algorithm a large training corpus of text marked-up with emotions –, *an approach based on large-scale real-world knowledge* [4] – this method evaluates the affective qualities of the underlying semantic content of text –.

The method we are going to use mixes keyword spotting and lexical affinity in the hope that the weaknesses of each individual approach are reduced by their combination. The disadvantages of keyword spotting approach are two: poor recognition of emotion when negation is involved and reliance on surface features. On the other hand the weaknesses of lexical affinity are: it is based only in the word-level, so it can easily have problems with negation; and lexical affinity is obtained from a corpus, which makes it difficult to develop a reusable, domain-independent model.

3 Building Emotion-Annotated Resources

This section deals with the process of building two basic resources for emotional mark up: a corpus of fairy tale sentences annotated with emotional information, and a list of emotional words (LEW). Both the corpus and the list of emotional words are annotated with two methods: using the emotional dimensions (valence, arousal and dominance) and marking its with emotional categories (happy, sad, angry ...). In the following sections we describe in detail how we have obtained the list of emotional words (LEW) and how our approach works.

3.1 Corpus Annotation Method

If we want to obtain a program that marks up texts with emotions, as a human would, we first need a corpus of marked-up texts in order to analyze and obtain a set of key words which we will use in the mark up process. Each of the texts which forms part of the corpus may be marked by more than one person because assignment of emotions is a subjective task so we have to avoid "subjective extremes". To be precise 15 evaluators have marked each of the tales. We obtain the emotion assigned to a phrase as the average of the mark-up provided by different persons. Therefore the process of obtaining the list of emotional words involves two different phases: first people mark up texts of our corpus, then from the marked up texts of the previous phase we obtain emotional words. As a working corpus, we selected 8 popular tales, with different lengths (altogether they result in 10.331 words and 1.084 sentences), written in English. In order to evaluate the tales we have split the experiment in two phases:

- Phase 1: We selected four different tales for each evaluator in order to mark them up with emotional dimensions. Tales are split into sentences and evaluators are offered three boxes for each sentence in which to put the values of the emotional dimensions: valence, arousal and dominance. In order to help people in the assignment of values for each dimension we provide them with the SAM standard [7] which can be seen in the Figure 1.

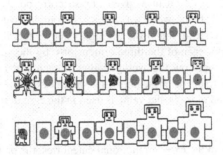

Fig. 1. Dimensional scales according to SAM: valence, arousal and dominance

- Phase 2: The four tales which did not take part in phase 1 are used in this second phase. At this point the mark up of the tales uses emotional categories: happy, sad, anger, surprise ... In order to help them in the assignment of emotional categories we provide a list of different emotional labels.

3.2 Extraction Method for a List of Emotional Words

Based on the tales marked up by human evaluators we obtain a data base of words and their relation with emotional dimensions and categories. There are two different methods of extraction depending on the labeling method: emotional dimensions or emotional categories. For each extraction method, there is a generic part which is common to both, and a specific part which involves handling the particular representation of emotion in each case. The common part can be described as follows.

First we split the text into phrases and we obtain for every phrase the particular representation of the emotional content involved in each case. Phrases are processed with the qtag [1] tagger which for each word returns the part-of-speech (e.g. noun, verb, etc.). Every sentence is divided into words and with every word and its label we carry out the following process:

---

[1] http://www.english.bham.ac.uk/staff/omason/software/qtag.html

- If the label is in the list of stop POS tags we leave it out. Our stop list is composed of labels such as: conjunctions, numbers, determiners ...
- If the label is not in the stop POS tags we proceed to extract the stem of the word using a slightly modified version of the Porter stemming algorithm [8].
- Once we have the stem of the word it is inserted into our data base with the particular representation of the emotional content involved in each case.
- After processing all the tales, we carry out a normalization and expansion process of our list of words. We extend our list with synonyms and antonyms of every word which are looked up in WordNet [9]. The extraction method results in a list of 3.027 emotional words.

Emotional Dimensions. In the case of emotional dimensions, the particular representation of the emotional content involved in a given phrase corresponds to the three emotional dimensions assigned to it. If the word was already in our list we add up the new values to the ones we had. In order to obtain the average value of the dimensions we divide the numeric value we have for each of the three dimensions, by the number of appearances of the word in the texts, to work out the average value of each dimension for each word. For inserting related words into the database, the same values of dimensions as the original word are used for synonyms and the opposite value is used in the case of the antonyms (9- original value).

Emotional Categories. In the case of emotional categories, the particular representation of the emotional content involved in a given phrase corresponds to the emotion assigned to every phrase by most of the evaluators. When we have the stem of the word it is inserted into our word data base with the value 1 in the field of the emotion assigned to the phrase in which the word was. If the word was already in our list we add up 1 to the field of the phrase's emotion. In order to obtain the average value of the emotions we divide the numeric value of each of the emotions by the number of appearances of the word in the texts, to work out the probability of that word indicating the emotions we are studying. For inserting related words into the database, the same probabilities of the original word are used in the case of synonyms case and the opposite probability in the case of antonyms (1- original probability).

4   A Method for Automated Mark Up of Emotions

Our process classifies sentences into emotions. The first step is to perform sentence detection and tokenization in order to carry out our process based on the relation between words and different emotions. We have created two mark-up processes, the first one marks up tales with emotional dimensions and the second one with emotional categories. This process also has a common part for each representation method. The common part of the mark up method is:

- By means of the tagger qtag, mentioned in the previous section, we obtain the tag for every word in the sentence; If the tag associated with the word is in our list of stop POS tags we leave it out.
- We get the stem of the word by means of the modified Porter stemming algorithm mentioned before.

- We look the pair stem-tag up in the lists of emotional words available for the specific representation method. If the word is present we get the particular representation of its emotional content.
- If the word is not in any of the lists available we obtain the hypernyms of the word from WordNet, and we look them up in the available lists; the first appearance of a hypernym is taken and the emotional content associated to the hypernym is associated to our original word. If none of the hypernyms appear in the available lists, the word does not take part in the process.

In order to obtain the value of each of the emotional dimensions of the sentence we look up every word of the sentence and assign to it a value for the three dimensions as given by our lists. Based on these values of the words we obtain the final value of the sentence. For emotional dimensions, the words are looked up first in the list of emotional words (LEW) obtained from the annotation experiments. If the word is not in LEW we look up for it in the ANEW word list [10]. Once all the words of the sentences have been evaluated, we add up the value of each dimension of the different words and assign to the sentence the average value of valence, arousal and dominance, that is, we divide the total value of each dimension by the number of words which have taken part in the process.

In order to obtain the emotion associated to the sentence in the case of emotional categories we look around every word of the sentence in the LEW list and assign to it the probability of carrying the emotions we are studying. Based on these probabilities of the words we obtain the final emotion of the sentence. Once all the words of the sentences have been evaluated, we add up the probability of each emotion of the different words and assign to the sentence the emotion which has a bigger probability.

5   Evaluation

In order to evaluate our work we carried out two different tests. In these tests four tales are going to take part, two of them have been in the corpus we have used to obtain our LEW list and the other two are new tales. This way we will measure on the one hand how well our process marks the tales from which we have obtained our LEW list and on the other hand how well our approach works with tales that have not been involved in our extraction process. The tales which take part in these tests are English popular tales with different number of words (from 153 words and 20 lines to 1404 words and 136 lines). Each of our four tales will be tagged first with the emotional dimensions, and then with the categories.

The data on emotional dimensions we have available for each tale are the values that each dimension takes for each sentence. To evaluate our tagger we have divided the evaluation according to the different dimensions: valence, arousal and dominance. In order to get a measure of our tagger we have take measures first from the evaluators' tales and then from our tagger's tales.

For evaluator's tales we have, as reference data, the values assigned for each dimension and each sentence by the human evaluators. An average emotional score for each dimension of a sentence is calculated as the average value of those assigned to the corresponding dimension by the human evaluators. The deviation among these values is calculated to act as an additional reference, indicating the possible range of variation due to human subjectivity. Figure 2 shows the average deviation of evaluators in each of the tales (C1, C2, C3 and C4).

In the case of tagger's tales for each dimension, if the deviation of the tagger is less or equal to the average deviation among evaluators, we consider that the sentence is tagged correctly. Figure 2 seems to indicate that the tagger is obtaining better results in terms of deviation from the average obtained by humans for the arousal and dominance dimensions, and comparable results in the case of valence. The graph in Figure 3 shows the success percentage – the percentage of sentences in which the deviation of the automatically tagged dimensions from the human average is within the deviations between human evaluators.

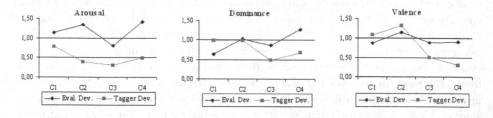

Fig. 2. Evaluator and tagger deviation for different emotional dimensions

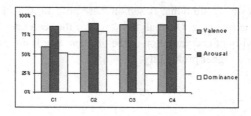

Fig. 3. Success percentage in automated tagging for the different dimensions

The data on emotional categories we have available for each tale are emotional label for each sentence. As we have done for emotional dimensions we have taken measures first from the evaluators' tales and then from our tagger's tales.

For evaluator's tales we have noticed that the percentage of sentences on which the majority of the human evaluators - half of their number plus one - agrees on the assignment of an emotion is very low, around 45%. This is an important data when it comes to interpreting the results obtained by our tagger. A reference value for the emotion of each phrase is obtained by choosing the emotion most often assigned to that sentence by the human evaluators.

In the case of tagger's tales the reference value obtained in the evaluator's tales is used to compare with the results generated by our tagger. The graph in Figure 4 shows the percentages of success obtained for each tale, each sentence has been considered successfully tagged if the emotion assigned by the tagger matched the reference value, and the relationship between the success percentage and the percentage of sentences whose reference value is supported by one more than half the number of evaluators.

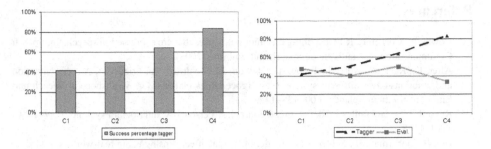

Fig. 4. Success percentage in automated tagging and relation between the success percentage of our tagger and majority-supported evaluators for emotional categories

Once human evaluators had finished with the mark up process they were asked to fill in a questionnaire about the evaluation process. Analysis of the results indicates that human evaluators find it easier to mark up tales with emotional categories than with emotional dimensions. However, if we look at the results we can see that values for different dimensions match reasonably well the categories assigned to sentences in the emotional categories approach.

With respect to the success percentage we can conclude that in both cases the best results are obtained with the tales which took part in our extraction method (C3 and C4). If we compare the results of the two approaches we can see that the best results are obtained with the emotional dimensions approach.

6 Conclusions

The fact that we have considered words in a context instead of individually reduces some of the disadvantages associated with simple keyword spotting, because the same word may have different meanings in different contexts. Some issues related to context still need further work. Negation, for instance, may have the effect of inverting the polarity of the emotional content of words under its scope. We are considering the use of shallow parsing techniques to determine the scope of negations appearing in the sentences, in order to take their effect into account.

With respect to methods based on lexical affinity we have reduced the dependency on a given corpus by resorting to two different data bases: LEW (corpus dependent) and ANEW (corpus independent). We have also complemented our data base of emotional words with synonyms, antonyms, and hypernyms. Nonetheless, we still get better results for the tales used to obtain the LEW corpus than for new tales, so we consider necessary to continue exploring better solutions for this problem.

Aside from these issues requiring improvement, we have observed that very long sentences lead to confusion when assigning emotions. In future versions we will consider a finer granularity for representing sentences. Another problem was the large observable disagreement between human evaluators. This may be reduced by carrying out experiments with a larger number of evaluators.

References

1. Cowie, R., Cornelius, R.: Describing the emotional states that are expressed in speech. In: Speech Communication Special Issue on Speech and Emotion (2003).
2. Alter, K., Rank, E., Kotz, S., Toepel, U., Besson, M., Schirmer, A., Friederici, A.: Accentuation and emotions—two different systems? In: Proceedings of the ISCA Workshop on Speech and Emotion, Northern Ireland (2000) 138–142.
3. Russell, J.: A circumflex model of affect. Journal of Personality and Social Psychology **39** (1980) 1161–1178.
4. Liu, H. Lieberman, H., Selker, T.: A model of textual affect sensing using real-world knowledge. In: Proceedings of IUI, Miami, Florida (2003).
5. Ortony, A., Clore, G., Collins, A.: The cognitive structure of emotions. Cambridge University Press, New York (1988).
6. Goertzel, B., Silverman, K., Hartley, C., Bugaj, S., Ross, M.: The baby webmind project. In: Proceedings of AISB. (2000).
7. Lang, P.: Behavioural treatment and bio-behavioural assessment: Computer applications. In Sidowski, J.B., Johnson, J.H., (Eds.), T.A.W., eds.: Technology in mental health care delivery systems, Norwood, NJ, Ablex Publishing (1980) 119–137.
8. Porter, M.: An algorithm for suffix stripping. In: Readings in information retrieval, San Francisco, CA, USA, Morgan Kaufmann Publishers Inc. A (1997) 313–316.
9. Miller, G.: Wordnet: a lexical database for English. Communications of the ACM **38** (1995) 39–41.
10. Bradley, M., Lang, P.: Affective norms for English words (ANEW): Stimuli, instruction manual and affective ratings. Technical report c-1. Technical report, The Center for Research in Psychophysiology, University of Florida (1999).

First Steps Towards New Czech Voice Conversion System*

Zdeněk Hanzlíček and Jindřich Matoušek

University of West Bohemia, Department of Cybernetics,
Univerzitní 8, 306 14 Plzeň, Czech Republic
zhanzlic@kky.zcu.cz, jmatouse@kky.zcu.cz

Abstract. In this paper we deal with initial experiments on creating a new Czech voice conversion system. Voice conversion (VC) is a process which modifies the speech signal produced by one (source) speaker so that it sounds like another (target) speaker. Using VC technique a new voice for speech synthesizer can be prepared with no need to record a huge amount of new speech data. The transformation is determined using equal sentences from both speakers; these sentences are time-aligned using modified dynamic time warping algorithm. The conversion is divided into two stages corresponding to the source-filter model of speech production. Within this work we employ conversion function based on Gaussian mixture model for transforming the spectral envelope described by line spectral frequencies. Residua are converted using so called residual prediction techniques. Unlike in other similar research works, we predict residua not from the transformed spectral envelope, but directly from the source speech. Four versions of residual prediction are described and compared in this study. Objective evaluation of converted speech using performance metrics shows that our system is comparable with similar existing VC systems.

1 Introduction

Voice conversion is a process which modifies the speech signal produced by one (source) speaker so that it sounds like another (target) speaker. Using VC technique a new voice for speech synthesizer can be prepared with no need to record a huge amount of new speech data.

In this paper we describe some initial experiments on creating a new Czech VC system. In fact, some investigation on VC in Czech has been already performed by Vondra & Vích [9], their system employs linear and nonlinear spectral envelope warping and cepstral speech synthesis. In our work, another approach utilizing linear predictive analysis, probabilistic spectral envelope transformation and residua prediction is researched.

This paper is organized as follows. Sect. 2 describes speech data used in our experiments and methods used for its analysis, synthesis and time-alignment. Sect. 3 deals with spectral envelope transformation and residua prediction techniques. In Sect. 4 methods for objective evaluation of converted speech are presented. Sect. 5 describes results of our first experiments. Finally, Sect. 6 concludes the paper and outlines our future work.

2 Speech Data

For the determination of the transformation between the source and target speaker, speech data from both are required. Though several techniques utilizing different utterances have

---

* Support for this work was provided by the Academy of Sciences of the Czech Republic, project No. 1ET101470416.

been already proposed [8], we decided to employ parallel sentences (equal utterances from both speakers). These utterances have to be time-aligned and the conversion function is derived from the relation between corresponding frames. As unvoiced parts of speech are supposed to be unimportant for the perception of speaker individuality, conversion of voiced segments was performed only. Unvoiced speech was copied without any modification.

2.1 Speech Data Recording

All audio data were recorded under special condition in an anechoic chamber. Together with the audio signal the electroglottographic (EGG) signal was acquired; it is used for pitch-marks detection and voiced/unvoiced decision.

7 speakers (5 men and 2 women) were recorded at 48kHz; however, for our experiments both speech and EGG signal were down-sampled to 16kHz; higher frequencies are supposed to be unnecessary for speaker identity perception. Each speaker read the same 60 phonetically balanced sentences.

2.2 Speech Data Parametrization

The analysis and synthesis of speech is frame-based, i.e. the waveform signal is divided into partly overlapped segments. In voiced speech this process is performed pitch-synchronously; each frame is two pitch period long and the overlap between contiguous frames is one pitch period. Pitch-marks are extracted from the EGG signal. Unvoiced speech is divided uniformly with the period corresponding to average F_0 and overlap equal to half of this period. However, no conversion of unvoiced speech was performed, thus its parametrization is not needed at all.

Utilizing linear predictive analysis, spectral envelope of each frame is described with linear predictive coefficients (LPCs). Then, they are converted into line spectral frequencies (LSFs) which have better interpolation properties. Spectral details are represented by residual signals that are gained by inverse filtering each frame with appropriate LPC-filter.

2.3 Speech Data Alignment and Selection

For finding the correspondence between parallel utterances from both speakers, a modified version of dynamic time warping (DTW) algorithm was proposed. A segmentation produced by a speaker-independent HMM-based speech recognizer is used to restrict the warping function shape. However, as the acquired segmentation is not perfect, a simple manual correction of gross errors was performed.

An example of the warping function restricted by the boundaries between phones is depicted on Fig.1. Regarding the accuracy of the segmentation, we can distinguish two cases. Providing the accurate segmentation, the alignment can be performed within each phone separately (i.e. the warping function passes all points given by corresponding boundaries). However, even the corrected segmentation is not absolutely accurate. Thus the profile of the warping function is not so strongly restricted and it passes the boundary points with a tolerance.

The warping function determines pairs of corresponding frames. Before transformation function estimation some suspicious data are excluded, such as pairs composed of one voiced and one unvoiced frame. Long constant sections (horizontal or vertical) of warping function are discarded too, because they usually signify wrong alignment caused by pronunciation mismatch.

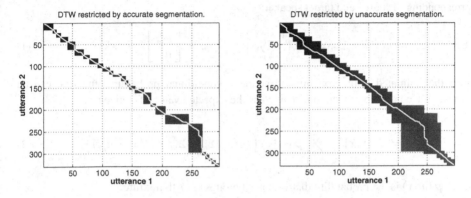

Fig. 1. An example of restricted DTW function. The tolerable area is coloured black.

2.4 Speech Resynthesis

Providing the speech spectrum of voiced frames has been converted (see below), resynthesis of speech signal is performed. The energy of each converted frame is normalized to have the same energy as the source frame. Resulting waveform is built using overlap-add (OLA) method, i.e. frames are weighted with synthesis window, overlapped and add. We employ a triangular synthesis window.

3 Voice Conversion

Supposing the training sentences are time-aligned, a transformation function can be estimated. As noted above, only voiced parts of speech are considered to be transformed; thus all conversion techniques in the following text are automatically related to voiced speech. The conversion is divided into two stages corresponding to the source-filter model of speech production. A conversion function based on GMM is employed for transforming the spectral envelope described by LSFs. Residua are converted using so called residual prediction techniques.

3.1 Spectral Envelope Transformation

Spectral envelope features are represented by LSF parameters. An approach proposed by Stylianou et al. [1] and later improved by Kain et al. [2] was employed. Pairs composed of matching LSF vectors from source and target speaker (x and y respectively) are described by joint probability density function. Thus a GMM is estimated from LSF pairs using expectation-maximization (EM) algorithm, i.e. mean value μ_m, covariance matrix Σ_m and weight α_m are estimated for each mixture m ($m = 1, 2 \ldots M$). However, the EM algorithm has to be modified because the covariance matrixes are close to singular. Hence, a constant diagonal matrix εI ($\varepsilon \approx 10^{-3}$) has to be added in each iteration. For proper initialization of GMM parameters a bisecting K-means algorithm is used.

Mean vectors and covariance matrixes can be divided into blocks according to components corresponding to source and target speaker:

$$\Sigma_m = \begin{bmatrix} \Sigma_m^{xx} & \Sigma_m^{xy} \\ \Sigma_m^{yx} & \Sigma_m^{yy} \end{bmatrix} \qquad \mu_m = \begin{bmatrix} \mu_m^x \\ \mu_m^y \end{bmatrix} \tag{1}$$

From the estimated joint probability function a conditional probability function can be derived. The conversion function is defined as the expected value of y given x:

$$y = E\{y|x\} = \sum_{m=1}^{M} p(m|x)\left(\mu_m^y + \Sigma_m^{xy}\left(\Sigma_m^{xy}\right)^{-1}\left(x - \mu_m^x\right)\right) \tag{2}$$

where $p(m|x)$ is the probability that vector x belongs to m-th mixture.

$$p(m|x) = \frac{\alpha_m \mathcal{N}\left(x|\mu_m^x, \Sigma_m^{xx}\right)}{\sum_{i=1}^{M} \alpha_i \mathcal{N}\left(x|\mu_i^x, \Sigma_i^{xx}\right)} \tag{3}$$

3.2 Residual Prediction

Speaker identity is not completely described by the spectral envelope; some of important speaker characteristics are involved in residual signal (e.g. spectral zeros or nonlinear interaction in the vocal tract). Thus the transformation of residual signal should improve perception of speaker individuality.

Although the source-filter model is based on assumption that spectral envelope and residual signal are independent, Kain at al. [4] demonstrated that some correlation exists and thus the residual signal can be predicted from the shape of the spectral envelope. Later, techniques of residual prediction were developed by Sündermann et al. (e.g. [6] and [7]).

The prediction is usually performed from the transformed spectral envelope. A relation between spectral envelope and residual signal of target speaker is estimated from training sentences. However, we decided for another approach. We try to estimate the residual signal directly from spectral envelope of source speaker. Providing that time-alignment of parallel training sentences is correct, our motivation is following:

– The spectral envelope transformation is defined in terms of mean value. Thus, transformed envelope partially losts its natural variability. Prediction from such an envelope leads to extra signal smoothing. Anyway, the residuum is (indirectly) predicted from the source envelope; thus direct prediction should result in lower signal degradation.
– In the case that both envelope and residuum are converted directly from source speech, transformation can be divided into two independent modules.

Although no comparative study has been accomplished so far, our approach seems to be a promising alternative to the standard one.

Residual GMM-Codebook Method (RGCM). In the transformation, LPCs from source speech are converted to cepstral coefficients v_n. The probability distribution of these single cepstral vectors is estimated; again EM algorithm is employed. A typical target speaker's residual magnitude spectrum $\hat{r}_q$ for each GMM component q $(q = 1 \ldots Q)$ is determined as a weighted average of all residual magnitude spectra r_n $(n = 1 \ldots N)$. The weights correspond to the posterior probabilities $p(q|v_n)$

$$\hat{r}_q = \frac{\sum_{n=1}^{N} r_n p(q|v_n)}{\sum_{n=1}^{N} p(q|v_n)} \tag{4}$$

The phase spectrum for each GMM component is determined as

$$\hat{\phi}_q = \phi_{\hat{n}} \quad \text{where} \quad \hat{n} = \arg\max_{n=1\ldots N} p(q|v_n) \tag{5}$$

Thus, we remember one magnitude and one phase target spectral vector for each source GMM component.

During transformation, magnitude residuum is predicted from the source cepstral vector v_i as a weighted sum over all GMM components:

$$\tilde{r}_i = \sum_{q=1}^{Q} \hat{r}_q p(q|v_i) \tag{6}$$

Phase spectrum is selected from the component $\tilde{q}$ with the highest value of posterior probability

$$\tilde{\phi}_i = \hat{\phi}_{\tilde{q}} \quad \text{where} \quad \tilde{q} = \arg\max_{q=1\ldots Q} p(q|v_i) \tag{7}$$

Residual Class-Codebook Method (RCCM). We have proposed a new method for residual estimation where cepstral coefficients of source speech are grouped into classes using a bisecting K-means algorithm. Thus each class q $(q = 1 \ldots Q)$ is represented by its centroid $\bar{v}_q$. Analogous to previous method, one residual magnitude spectrum and one phase spectrum are computed and stored for each class. The same equations can be used, but all posterior probabilities $p(q|v_n)$ or $p(q|v_i)$ must be replaced with the following weights

$$w(q, v_n) = \frac{d(\bar{v}_q, v_n)^{-1}}{\sum_{i=1}^{Q} d(\bar{v}_i, v_n)^{-1}} \quad \text{or} \quad w(q, v_i) = \frac{d(\bar{v}_q, v_i)^{-1}}{\sum_{j=1}^{Q} d(\bar{v}_j, v_i)^{-1}} \tag{8}$$

where $d(x, y)$ is the Euclidean distance between x and y.

Residual Selection Methods (ERSM & RRSM). A disadvantage of both previous methods is averaging of magnitude spectrum. As a result, converted speech losts its natural variability. In ERSM method all target residua from the training stage all stored in the table together with corresponding (time-aligned) source LSFs and their deltas. During the transformation stage the feature vector with minimum distance from the source one is found in the table and the corresponding residuum is selected. Then the sequence of selected residua is smoothed to avoid sudden jump changes and other artifacts in resulting speech.

In the last proposed method (RRSM), source residua (instead of LSFs and their deltas) are stored in the table together with corresponding (time-aligned) target residua.

4 Evaluation

For objective evaluation another speech data from both speakers are needed which were not used in training process. An error between two sequences of time-aligned LSF vectors can be computed using Euclidean distance between corresponding vectors. We denote $s(n)$, $t(n)$ and $\hat{t}(n)$, $n = 1 \ldots N$, source, target and transformed LSFs respectively. We introduce inter-speaker error $d(s(n), t(n))$ and transformation error $d(t(n), \hat{t}(n))$. For judging the quality of spectral envelope transformation so-called LSF performance index P_{LSF} [4] is defined as

$$P_{LSF} = 1 - \frac{\sum_{n=1}^{N} d(t(n), \hat{t}(n))}{\sum_{n=1}^{N} d(t(n), s(n))} \tag{9}$$

For more complex assessing of the conversion performance, Euclidean distance directly between spectral vectors, so-called spectral distortion (SD), is computed. Then a SD performance index P_{SD} [4] and a variation of signal-to-noise ratio P_{SNR} [5] can be defined (Eq. 10 and 11).

$$P_{SD} = 1 - \frac{\sum_{n=1}^{N} SD\left(T(n), \hat{T}(n)\right)}{\sum_{n=1}^{N} SD(T(n), S(n))} \tag{10}$$

$$P_{SNR} = 20 \log_{10} \frac{\sum_{n=1}^{N} |T(n)|}{\sum_{n=1}^{N} SD\left(\hat{T}(n), T(n)\right)} \tag{11}$$

$S(n)$, $T(n)$ and $\hat{T}(n)$, $n = 1 \ldots N$, are source, target and transformed magnitude spectra respectively. Unequal lengths of pitch-synchronously segmented frames could be sources of possible problems or ambiguities within SD calculation. Thus, corresponding frames have to be normalized to equal length. However the result heavily depends on the used type of interpolation. In our experiments cubic spline interpolation was employed.

In all aforementioned performance indexes, higher values indicate a better VC performance.

5 Experiments and Results

This section deals with the first results of the proposed methods. Since all data has not been processed so far, only two exemplary conversions are demonstrated here. 40 sentences has been used for training and 10 sentences for evaluation.

Table 1. Evaluation of LSF transformation - performance indexes P_{LSF}

Mixture count	F → M	M → F	Both
5	0.233	0.397	0.315
10	0.261	0.399	0.330
20	0.253	0.389	0.321
30	0.258	0.390	0.324
50	0.258	0.390	0.324

In Table 1 results of LSFs transformation experiments are presented. Various numbers of GMM components were used. It seems to be useless to set the number of mixtures above 10. Probably the spectral space is described well enough and more components are non-effective (their weights are close to zero).

Although the conversion function in both directions were derived from one joint GMM, performance indexes differ markedly. This could be caused by a different speech style of both speakers. This fact could complicate the comparison of competitive VC systems.

In Table 2 residual prediction techniques are compared. In all cases the same envelope transformation (based on GMM with 10 components) was employed. Within RGCM method the number of GMM mixtures was 20; analogously, 20 classes were used in RCCM. In column denoted NONE, no residual prediction was performed, i.e. source residua were directly used in transformed speech. The values in this column are markedly lower, thus benefit of residual prediction is obvious. Moreover, the results indicate that our proposed method (RCCM) is better than others.

Table 2. Evaluation of spectral detail transformation - P_{SD} and P_{SNR}

	RGCM	RCCM	ERSM	RRSM	NONE
P_{SD} (F → M)	0.331	0.361	0.331	0.329	-0.022
P_{SD} (M → F)	0.323	0.382	0.333	0.295	0.066
P_{SD} (both)	0.327	0.372	0.332	0.312	0.022
P_{SNR} (F → M)	5.250	5.911	5.018	4.997	-1.168
P_{SNR} (M → F)	1.683	3.711	2.307	1.250	-0.884
P_{SNR} (both)	3.467	4.811	3.663	3.124	-1.026

6   Conclusion and Future Work

First steps in developing a new Czech voice conversion system were presented in this paper. An envelope transformation based on GMM was described. Four methods of residual transformation, that predict target residua directly from the source speech, were proposed. An objective evaluation of converted speech hints that our system is comparable with similar existing VC systems (e.g. [4] or [5]).

In our future work we will aim at improving the performance of conversion and also the quality of resynthesized speech. A subjective evaluation based on listening tests will be performed. Residual prediction techniques from the converted envelope and from source speech will be properly compared as well.

References

1. Stylianou, Y., Cappé, O., Moulines, E.: Continuous Probabilistic Transform for Voice Conversion. IEEE Transactions on Speech and Audio Processing, Vol. 6, No. 2 (1998) 131–142.
2. Kain, A., Macon, M. W.: Spectral Voice Conversion for Text-to-Speech Synthesis. Proceedings of ICASSP'98 (1998) 285–288.
3. Kain, A., Macon, M. W.: Design and Evaluation of Voice Conversion Algorithm Based on Spectral Envelope Mapping and Residual Prediction. Proceedings of ICASSP'01 (2001).

4. Kain, A.: High Resolution Voice Transformation. Ph.D. thesis, Oregon Health & Science University, Portland, USA (2001).
5. Gillett, B., King, S.: Transforming Voice Quality. In Proceedings of Eurospeech '03 (2003) 1713–1716.
6. Sündermann, D., Bonafonte, A., Ney, H., Höge, H.: A Study on Residual Prediction Techniques for Voice Conversion. In Proceedings of ICASSP '05 (2005) 13–16.
7. Sündermann, D., Höge, H., Bonafonte, A., Duxans, H.: Residual Prediction. In Proceedings of ISSPIT '05 (2005).
8. Ney, H., Sündermann, D., Bonafonte, A., Höge, H.: A First Step towards Text-Independent Voice Conversion. In Proceedings of Interspeech '04 (2004) 1173–1176.
9. Vích, R., Vondra, M.: Voice Conversion Based on Nonlinear Spectrum Transformation. In Proceedings of 14th Czech-German Workshop (2004) 53–60.

Are Morphosyntactic Taggers Suitable to Improve Automatic Transcription?

Stéphane Huet, Guillaume Gravier, and Pascale Sébillot

IRISA
Campus de Beaulieu, F-35042 Rennes Cedex, France
{shuet, ggravier, sebillot}@irisa.fr

Abstract. The aim of our paper is to study the interest of part of speech (POS) tagging to improve speech recognition. We first evaluate the part of misrecognized words that can be corrected using POS information; the analysis of a short extract of French radio broadcast news shows that an absolute decrease of the word error rate by 1.1% can be expected. We also demonstrate quantitatively that traditional POS taggers are reliable when applied to spoken corpus, including automatic transcriptions. This new result enables us to effectively use POS tag knowledge to improve, in a postprocessing stage, the quality of transcriptions, especially correcting agreement errors.

1 Introduction

Automatic speech recognition (ASR) systems globally use little knowledge about language. Very often, linguistic knowledge is limited to the learning of probabilities of word sequences on a corpus. However, as ASR systems act on natural language, linguistic knowledge should improve the quality of transcription. Some language models (LM) already integrate linguistic knowledge such as syntactic structures of utterances [1], topics of the document to transcribe [2,3] or parts of speech (POS) [4]. A part of speech is a grammatical property of a word, or a group of words, in a given sentence (*e.g.* nouns, verbs, prepositions, conjunctions, *etc.*) often along with morphological information (gender, number, conjugation, *etc.*). The knowledge of these categories is generally included in LM thanks to class-based N-gram models [5]. Formally, if we denote by C_i the set of possible POS tags for a word w_i, the probability of the word sequence $w_1^n = w_1, \ldots, w_n$ is obtained as follows:

$$P(w_1^n) \approx \sum_{c_1 \in C_1, \ldots, c_n \in C_n} \prod_{i=1}^{n} P(w_i|c_i) P(c_i|c_{i-N+1}^{i-1}) \tag{1}$$

The interpolation of a class-based N-gram models with a word-based N-gram model generally results in a negligible decrease of the word error rate (WER) of transcription and different improvements have been proposed. For example, probability can be estimated by considering that the POS tags of the words w_i to recognize are directly incorporated in the production of the ASR systems and are not only an intermediate result [6]. This approach evaluates the probabilities thanks to more accurate calculations than in (1) but leads to a dramatic increase of the number of events to consider.

In all these approaches, POS tags, *i.e.*, morphosyntactic information, allow to build LMs which are further used in the transcription process. As experiments have resulted in a limited

Petr Sojka, Ivan Kopeček and Karel Pala (Eds.): TSD 2006, LNAI 4188, pp. 391–398, 2006.

improvement with respect to word-based N-gram LMs, we propose to investigate on the use of POS tags in a postprocessing stage to correct some errors. In the first part of our work, we study automatic transcriptions and show that the proportion of errors that could be corrected by the knowledge of POS information is significant. We then demonstrate the ability of automatic taggers to deal with spoken language and with transcription errors. We finally evaluate several approaches to use POS tag information to rescore the N-best sentence candidates produced by our ASR system. Our experiments show that a majority of gender and agreement errors are corrected. However, new errors are also introduced, thus resulting in a marginal decrease of the WER.

2   Typology of Transcription Errors

In order to evaluate the potential contribution of POS taggers for automatic speech transcription, we first analyze closely a short excerpt of an automatic transcription in order to measure the proportion of errors that can be corrected by POS knowledge.

The ASR system used in our experiments, designed by IRISA and ENST for the transcription of broadcast news shows in the French language, aims at producing a word graph using a three pass strategy[1]. In a first pass, a large word graph is generated using context-independent acoustic models and a trigram LM. The second pass aims at rescoring the 1,000 best paths of the first pass word graph after expansion by a 4-gram LM. Finally, the third pass is similar to the second one but uses speaker adapted acoustic models, where MLLR adaptation is carried out using the second pass output. A smaller word graph is also generated by the third pass, with about 80 word boundaries per second. To get rid off segmentation problems, we consider in this work a manual segmentation by utterances, where an utterance is actually a breath group. On the ESTER [7] broadcast news corpus, the overall word error rate on the entire corpus is 22.4 % while the word graph error rate is 13.9 %. However, in this section, we analyze the transcription errors on a subset of 6,500 words of the entire corpus, where the WER is 17.8 %.

Among the transcription errors we observed, three groups stand out. Some errors are caused by a "drift" of the ASR system, generally explained by either a bad acoustics or a misrecognition of named entities which are out of vocabulary. These errors seem to be out of the scope of POS-based techniques. Fortunately, they only affect a restricted part of the analyzed extract. The second set of errors is related to ungrammatical transcriptions (Fig. 1) which can in particular be caused by short grammatical words like "a" ("has"), "à" ("at"), "de" ("of"), or "et" ("and"), that are sometimes missing or wrongly inserted in the transcription hypotheses. We also find tense and mood errors for verbs, with a too systematic prevalence for the present indicative tense. Among these errors, some are rectifiable using POS knowledge since the tagging of utterances can produce absurd POS sequences, such as three consecutive prepositions. Nevertheless, this criterion must be cautiously used, because of repetitions which naturally appear in spoken language. The third set represents errors most probably rectifiable by POS, i.e., erroneous gender and number agreements. These errors are particularly numerous, affecting a seventh of the utterances. Most of these errors come from the fact that, in the French language, the plural and singular forms, or the masculine and

---

[1] The authors would like to thank François Yvon for providing them the LM and the tagged lexicon.

```
REF: bush ** SAIT donc QU' il faudra coopérer
HYP: bush s' EST donc ** il faudra coopérer
```

Fig. 1. Ungrammatical utterance

```
REF: c' est un monstre injuste envers sa soeur si DÉVOUÉE
HYP: c' est un monstre injuste envers sa soeur si DÉVOUÉ
```

Fig. 2. Example of agreement error

feminine forms of many words are homophone. There are also many homophone confusion between the various tenses of verbs. Among these errors, 70 are rectifiable without inspecting dependencies between consecutive utterances (Fig 2); their correction would result in an absolute decrease of 1.1 % of the WER. Through the report of the main decoding errors, it therefore appears that POS knowledge is a valuable information to improve transcription quality.

3   Behavior of Taggers

The previous section showed the interest of POS taggers to correct some transcription errors by focusing on the possible sequences of POS. However, to use this technique, taggers must reliably operate on spoken corpora, produced by annotators or by ASR systems. It is this property that is evaluated in this section.

Morphosyntactic taggers aim at associating the most likely tag with each word or word group, in the word sequence to study. These tools are normally applied on written corpora. To quantitatively evaluate them, a text is manually tagged by annotators and tags are compared one by one with those automatically produced. In comparison to written corpora, spoken corpora transcribed by human listeners have been seldom studied [8]. Oral output has however characteristics, such as repetitions, revisions or fillers, that may complicate tagging. POS tagging of the automatic transcription of planned speech is an even more complex task as the text is segmented in breath groups rather than in sentences, and lacks punctuation and, in the case of our ASR system, capital letters.

In order to make the use of POS easier to decode speech, we decided to build our own morphosyntactic tagger. The remainder of this section first describes the protocol used to build this tagger, before evaluating its behavior on transcribed speech. We measure the quality of the tagging output on a test corpus and compare the results with those obtained by a standard tagger for the French language.

3.1   Tagger Design

The taggers conceived for written documents use linguistic rules or automatically extract statistic information from voluminous data. Given that programs based on statistical calculations produce satisfactory results for written documents and do not require to manually write numerous contextual rules, we built our tagger by solely using statistical methods. Another reason for this choice is the ability of statistical taggers to provide scores for a sequence of tags.

With this intention in mind, we established a 200,000-word training corpus representing a 16-hour extract from the ESTER corpus. The manual transcriptions, originally containing capital letters and punctuations, were tagged by the Cordial software[2]. We manually corrected the tagging, before removing all capital letters and punctuation marks to obtain a format similar to the one of the text produced by our ASR system. We used a tagged pronunciation lexicon to know all the possible POS for each word. We chose our morphosyntactic tags to distinguish the gender and the number of adjectives and nouns, and the tense and the mood of verbs, which led to a set of 80 tags. This set is very similar to the ones proposed in school grammars and directly inspired by Cordial's one.

Our morphosyntactic tagger is based on a class-based N-gram model to find the tags sequence:

$$\hat{c}_1^n = \arg\max_{c_1^n} \prod_{i=1}^{n} P(w_i|c_i) P(c_i|c_{i-N+1}^{i-1}) \tag{2}$$

for a word sequence w_1^n. Adjustments on a development corpus led us to choose a $N = 7$ order and an unmodified Kneser-Ney smoothing. To evaluate the effect of segmentation on the quality of tagging, we proceeded with two trainings, by segmenting the training corpus by sentence and by utterance.

3.2 Tagging Evaluation

To get a quantitative measure of the quality of tagging for manually produced transcriptions (REF), segmented by sentence[3] or utterance[4], or for transcriptions automatically produced by the decoder (HYP), we manually tagged a 1-hour broadcast news from the French radio station France-Inter. This broadcast, incorporating 11,300 words, will be referred to as GOLD in the sequel. The automatic tagging of REF was evaluated by counting the number of shared tags with GOLD. The measure of the quality of tagging was problematic for HYP, for which we measured a WER of 22 %, since words differ from those of GOLD. It was thus impossible to form a reference tagging for HYP as there does not exist any valid POS for the words of ungrammatical utterances. We give two measures of the quality of the tagging of HYP: the percentage of correctly recognized and tagged words among all the words of GOLD, and the percentage of correctly recognized and tagged words among all the correctly recognized words in HYP (this latter number is given in brackets in Table 1).

The results obtained by our tagger on the test corpora are given in the two first lines of Table 1, by combining all the possible segmentations of the training and test corpora. These results establish that tags are globally correct, including for the automatic transcriptions for which recognition errors were likely to jeopardize the tagging of correctly recognized words. This is quite surprising since we did not resort to specific methods to deal with the particularities of spoken language, apart from the use of an oral corpus to estimate the

---

[2] Distributed by the *Synapse Développement* corporation.

[3] Defined according to the punctuation present in manual transcription.

[4] Breath group defined according to silent pauses.

Table 1. Evaluation of taggers (in percentages)

	REF / sentence	REF / utterance	HYP
training corpus / sentence	91.42	91.09	72.60 (91.83)
training corpus / utterance	91.50	91.42	72.99 (92.32)
Cordial	88.69	88.61	70.75 (89.48)

tagger probabilities. However, this robustness is due to the fact that taggers locally assign possible tags and that many words are unambiguous. Therefore, even if the transcription is partially erroneous, unambiguous words correctly recognized helps keeping the tagger on tracks. Besides, the results show that training from the segmentation by utterance produces the best results, which led us to prefer this kind of segmentation later on.

Besides, by inspecting errors done during POS tagging, we noticed some could be considered as acceptable. For example, the distinction between the POS "past participle" and "adjective" are in a high majority of cases questionable. We also observed that numerous errors are caused by a wrong tokenization of our tagger. For instance, while "*états-unis*" ("*united states*") was tagged as a proper name in GOLD, automatic tagging led to recognize on the one hand "*états*" ("*states*") as a noun and on the other hand "*unis*" ("*united*") as an adjective. Among the 966 errors observed for the tagging of REF segmented by utterance, 42 were caused by confusions between past participle and adjective, 216 by wrong tokenization, 124 by confusions between common nouns and proper names and 10 by words unknown by the tagger.

Finally, we compared the performances of our tagger with those of Cordial, probably the best tagger available for written French, which has already produced good results on a spoken corpus [8]. The last line of Table 1 shows the results. Our tagger yields results comparable to those obtained with Cordial, and even better. On this particular corpus, the Cordial tagger does perform poorly compared to results obtained with it on written documents, usually above 95 % correct. This is explained by the particularities of the automatic transcriptions, for which Cordial was not specifically conceived. The lack of capital letters is particularly problematic since Cordial relies on this information to detect proper names. By ignoring all the errors caused by confusion between proper names and common names, the percentage of correctly assigned tags rises to 93.52 % for the test corpus segmented by utterance, while, according to the same criterion and on the same test data, the performances of our tagger only improve up to 92.55 %.

This sequence of experiments shows that the tagging of automatic transcription *is* reliable, assertion which was only a hypothesis before. Our tagger leads to results that allow us to use it to score the quality of the decoding. In the following section, we present experiments on using POS knowledge in a postprocessing step to reevaluate N-best candidate sentences.

4   Contribution of Tagging to Transcription

To exploit the knowledge of POS during speech decoding, we used our tagger to score each hypothesis found for an utterance. For each candidate sentence w_1^n, the most likely corresponding tag sequence c_1^n is computed according to (2) before evaluating a score function given by

```
REF: à L'  AMÉNAGER avant qu' elle ne soit DÉTRUITE
COR: à LA MÉNAGER avant qu' elle ne soit DÉTRUITE
HYP: à LA MÉNAGER avant qu' elle ne soit DÉTRUIT
```

Fig. 3. Example of an utterance where transcription agreement errors were manually corrected

$$\log P(c_1^n) = \sum_{i=1}^{n} \log P(c_i|c_{i-N+1}^{i-1}) \ . \tag{3}$$

This score aims at reordering the list of the hypotheses produced by the ASR system for each utterance.

To validate our approach, we first tested the behavior on the 70 agreement errors found on the limited corpus analyzed in section 2. For each utterance containing one of these errors, we evaluate the score function (3) on three versions of the utterance: the reference transcription (REF), the automatic transcription (HYP) and the automatic transcription where agreement errors have been manually corrected (COR). Figure 3 shows the three versions for an example utterance. The motivation for this first experiment is to verify that the POS score function is able to correctly rank the three versions of the utterance, with the higher score on REF and the lower on HYP. We observed that, for the 63 analyzed utterances, score was higher on COR than on HYP for 46 of them and was higher on REF than on HYP for 41. These results establish therefore that, in a majority of cases, this score allows to correct agreement errors and is likely to reduce the WER.

We then used the POS score function to reorder the list of 100-best hypotheses produced for 4 hours of French broadcast news. The 100-best list has an oracle word error rate of 14.2 % while the initial WER is 22.0 %. When reranking the N-best lists based only on POS score, the WER increases significantly from 22.0 % to 26.2 %. Therefore, we decided to combine the POS score with the acoustic score and the LM score.

ASR is, in practice, usually expressed as a search of w_1^n from the acoustic input y_1^n, *i.e.*,

$$\hat{w}_1^n = \arg\max_{w_i^n} \ log P(y_1^n|w_1^n) + \alpha \ log P(w_1^n) + \gamma \ n \tag{4}$$

where α is the LM scale factor and γ a word insertion penalty term. To introduce POS scores, we extended the maximization (4) to

$$\hat{w}_1^n = \arg\max_{w_i^n} \ log P(y_1^n|w_1^n) + \alpha \ log P(w_1^n) + \beta \ log P(c_1^n) + \gamma \ n \ . \tag{5}$$

$P(w_1^n)$ is computed by a 4-gram LM on words while $P(c_1^n)$ is determined by a 7-gram LM on POS tags.

We observed a slight decrease of the WER down to 21.4 % with this method. Figure 4 reports the WER without the POS score (*i.e.*, $\beta = 0$) and with the POS score after optimization of β. In both cases, γ is fixed for α and β to enable the lowest possible WER. The results show that for all α, tagging score leads to a very slight but consistent decrease of the WER. We generally noticed that agreement errors were corrected. For instance, an utterance transcribed as "*le messin disputent aujourd'hui*" ("*the inhabitant of Metz play today*") was correctly rectified in "*le messin dispute aujourd'hui*" ("*the inhabitant of Metz*

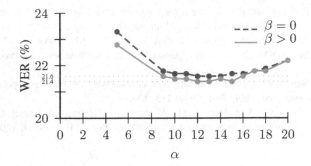

Fig. 4. WER as a function of the LM scale factor α, with ($\beta > 0$) and without ($\beta > 0$) POS information

plays today") but a few new errors appear like the correct transcription *"les visages de Jacques Chirac et Jean-Marie Le Pen apparaissent"* (*"the faces of Jacques Chirac and Jean-Marie Le Pen appear"*) erroneously rectified in *"les visages de Jacques Chirac et Jean-Marie Le Pen apparaît"* (*"the faces of Jacques Chirac and Jean-Marie Le Pen appears"*).

POS knowledge brings restricted information in relation to word-based LM, although both methods are complementary as the consistent reduction of the WER proves it.

5 Future Works

In this paper, we have shown that a significant proportion of transcription errors for the French language concerns agreement errors and can be corrected by POS knowledge. We have quantitatively proved that taggers can be used on spoken corpora transcribed by annotators or obtained by ASR systems. This allows us to exploit POS tagging to improve transcriptions. Our experiments show that POS taggers are suitable to correct some agreement errors, even if it globally only results in a slight decrease of the WER. To better those first results, instead of operating on the N-best hypotheses produced by an ASR system, we plan to rescore all the homophones of the best hypothesis found [9]. Besides, we want to investigate other sets of POS tags for our tagger.

References

1. Chelba, C., Jelinek, F.: Structured language modeling. Computer Speech and Language **14** (2000) 283–332.
2. Khudanpur, S., Wu, J.: A maximum entropy language model to integrate n-grams and topic dependencies for conversational speech recognition. In: Proc. of ICASSP. (1999).
3. Iyer, R., Ostendorf, M.: Modeling long distance dependence in language: Topic mixtures versus dynamic cache models. IEEE Transactions on Speech and Audio Processing **7** (1999) 30–39.
4. Maltese, G., Mancini, F.: An automatic technique to include grammatical and morphological information in a trigram-based statistical language model. In: Proc. of ICASSP. (1992).
5. Brown, P., Della Pietra, V., deSouza, P., Lai, J., Mercer, R.: Class-based n-gram models of natural language. Computational Linguistics **18** (1992) 467–480.

6. Heeman, P.: POS tags and decision trees for language modeling. In: Proc. of the Joint SIGDAT Conference on Empirical Methods in Natural Language Processing and Very Large Corpora. (1999).
7. Galliano, S., Geoffrois, E., Mostefa, D., Choukri, K., Bonastre, J.F., Gravier, G.: The ESTER phase II evaluation campaign for the rich transcription of French broadcast news. In: Proc. of Eurospeech. (2005).
8. Valli, A., Véronis, J.: Étiquetage grammatical de corpus oraux : problèmes et perspectives. Revue française de linguistique appliquée **4** (1999) 113–133.
9. Gauvain, J.L., Adda, G., Adda-Decker, M., Allauzen, A., Gendner, V., Lamel, L., Schwenk, H.: Where are we in transcribing French broadcast news? In: Proc. of Eurospeech. (2005).

Fast Speaker Adaptation Using Multi-stream Based Eigenvoice in Noisy Environments

Hwa Jeon Song[1] and Hyung Soon Kim[2]

[1] Research Institute of Computer Information and Communications
Pusan National University, Geumjeong-gu, Busan 609-735, Korea
hwajeon@pusan.ac.kr
[2] Department Electronics Engineering, Pusan National University
Geumjeong-gu, Busan 609-735, Korea
kimhs@pusan.ac.kr

Abstract. In this paper, the multi-stream based eigenvoice method is proposed in order to overcome the weak points of conventional eigenvoice and dimensional eigenvoice methods in fast speaker adaptation. In the proposed method, multi-streams are automatically constructed by a method of the statistical clustering analysis that uses the information acquired by correlation between dimensions. To obtain the reliable distance matrix from the covariance matrix in order to divide full dimensions into the optimal number of streams, MAP adaptation technique is employed on the covariance matrix of training data and the sample covariance of adaptation data. According to vocabulary-independent word recognition experiment with several car noise levels and supervised adaptation mode, we obtained 29% and 31% relative improvements with 5 and 50 adaptation words at 20dB SNR in comparison with conventional eigenvoice, respectively. We also obtained 26% and 53% relative improvements with 5 and 50 adaptation words at 10dB SNR, respectively.

1 Introduction

When there is a mismatch between training and testing environments, speaker adaptation techniques have been shown to be effective ways to reduce acoustic mismatches in automatic speech recognition systems. Among the typical adaptation methods such as maximum a posteriori (MAP) adaptation [1], maximum likelihood linear regression (MLLR) adaptation [2], and eigenvoice adaptation [3], MLLR is effective for limited adaptation data and can also reduce the mismatch between training and testing environments by bias term as well as rotation term in a transformation matrix in model space. However, it exhibits severe performance degradation when the amount of adaptation data is very small, that is, in rapid speaker adaptation.

Eigenvoice adaptation is more advantageous than the MLLR and MAP approaches, when the amount of adaptation data is extremely small. However it shows almost no additional improvement with increased amounts of adaptation data. While dimensional eigenvoice method proposed in [4] shows an additional improvement when using sufficient adaptation data, it cannot guarantee the desired performance when the amount of adaptation data is not sufficient.

Petr Sojka, Ivan Kopeček and Karel Pala (Eds.): TSD 2006, LNAI 4188, pp. 399–406, 2006.

In this paper, we propose the multi-stream based eigenvoice method as a means to overcome the weak points of conventional eigenvoice and dimensional eigenvoice. In the proposed method, statistical clustering analysis is used to divide the full dimensions of the feature vector into multiple streams based on the information acquired by correlation between dimensions. We also generalize the proposed method by combining with the bias compensation method in [5].

In Section 2, eigenvoice speaker adaptation is briefly described. In Section 3 our proposed method, multi-stream based eigenvoice method, is described. Section 4 shows a comparison of the experimental results of the conventional methods and of the proposed method. Finally, Section 5 provides a conclusion.

2   Eigenvoice Based Fast Speaker Adaptation

2.1   Eigenvoice

Eigenvoices are eigenvectors that are orthogonal to each other and contain the most important components of variation among reference speakers in a training DB. Eigenvoice adaptation represents the model parameter of a new speaker with the weighted sum of K eigenvoices as

$$\hat{\mu} = \mathbf{e}(0) + \sum_{j=1}^{K} w(j)\mathbf{e}(j). \tag{1}$$

where $\mathbf{e}(0)$ is the mean reference supervector, and $w(j)$ is the weight of $\mathbf{e}(j)$, eigenvoice j. The weight $w(j)$ of eigenvoices can be estimated by maximum likelihood eigendecomposition (MLED) [3] using the adaptation data of a new speaker.

2.2   Dimensional Eigenvoice

According to dimensional eigenvoice method [4,5], the speaker space is divided into D subspaces in which the dimension of each sub-space is one, where D denotes the full dimension of observation vector. In this method, since K weights of eigenvoices are estimated for each observation vector dimension, total number of parameters to be estimated is $D \times K$. Therefore, the location of a new speaker estimated by dimensional eigenvoice in speaker space can be estimated more precisely than that by conventional eigenvoice when using sufficient adaptation data.

3   Multi-stream Based Eigenvoice for Fast Speaker Adaptation

The dimensional eigenvoice method cannot guarantee the desired performance when the amount of adaptation data is insufficient [4]. This is because the number of parameters that should be estimated in the dimensional eigenvoice method is more than that of the eigenvoice method. In [4], it is assumed that the dimensions of the observation vectors are independent of each other in the dimensional eigenvoice method. However, this assumption does not hold in a real situation. Therefore, clustering among the dimensions that have high correlations with each other is more reasonable than the dimensional eigenvoice method and the number of estimated parameters is decreased in comparison with that of dimensional eigenvoice method. The weights estimated by using the information from correlation between dimensions are more reliable than those of dimensional eigenvoices.

3.1 Multi-stream Based Eigenvoice

We propose a multi-stream based eigenvoice adaptation. A stream in this paper means a group of dimensions with high correlation among them. Equation (2) is an example of multi-stream based eigenvoice method in which the number of streams is 3.

$$
\begin{bmatrix} \mu_1 \\ \mu_2 \\ \mu_3 \\ \mu_4 \\ \mu_5 \\ \mu_6 \\ \mu_7 \\ \mu_8 \\ \vdots \\ \mu_D \end{bmatrix}
\begin{aligned} &= w^{(1)}(1)\begin{bmatrix} e_1(1) \\ e_2(1) \end{bmatrix} + \cdots + w^{(1)}(K)\begin{bmatrix} e_1(K) \\ e_2(K) \end{bmatrix} \\ &= w^{(2)}(1)\begin{bmatrix} e_3(1) \\ e_4(1) \\ e_5(1) \\ e_6(1) \end{bmatrix} + \cdots + w^{(2)}(K)\begin{bmatrix} e_3(K) \\ e_4(K) \\ e_5(K) \\ e_6(K) \end{bmatrix} \\ &= w^{(3)}(1)\begin{bmatrix} e_7(1) \\ e_8(1) \\ \vdots \\ e_D(1) \end{bmatrix} + \cdots + w^{(3)}(K)\begin{bmatrix} e_7(K) \\ e_8(K) \\ \vdots \\ e_D(K) \end{bmatrix} \end{aligned}
\tag{2}
$$

where $w^{(r)}(k)$ is the k-th eigenvoice weight of r-th stream. It should be noted that dimensions clustered in each stream and the dimensionality of each stream are not fixed.

In multi-stream based eigenvoice, observation dimensions are split into N_{SS} disjunct clusters such as $\{C_1, C_2, \cdots, C_r, \cdots, C_{N_{SS}}\}$ and the mean vector of r-th stream in state s and mixture m can be generalized as follows:

$$
\left\langle \hat{\mu}_m^{(s)} \right\rangle_{C_r} = \left\langle e_m^{(s)}(0) \right\rangle_{C_r} + \sum_{k=1}^{K} w^{(r)}(k) \left\langle e_m^{(s)}(k) \right\rangle_{C_r} + \left[\sum_{d \in C_r} b^{(r)}(d) \langle i(d) \rangle_{C_r} \right]_{opt}.
\tag{3}
$$

where $1 \leq r \leq N_{SS}, 1 \leq k \leq K, 1 \leq d \leq D$. $<\cdot>_{C_r}$ denotes r-th stream and C_r is a set of dimensions clustered in r-th stream. In (3), the bias compensation method proposed in [5] is also applied where $i(d) = [\delta(d-1), \cdots, \delta(d-D)]^T$ is the D-dimension basis vector for bias compensation and $\delta(\cdot)$ denotes the Kronecker delta function. $w^{(r)}(k)$ and $b^{(r)}(d)$ are weights of the k-th eigenvoice and d-th basis unit vector in r-th stream, respectively. If $N_{SS} = 1$, (3) becomes the conventional eigenvoice method, whereas if $N_{SS} = D$, (3) becomes the dimensional eigenvoice method. And the bias compensation term can be optionally included in (3). That is, 'opt' in (3) denotes an optional term.

3.2 Clustering Analysis

In this paper, we introduce statistical clustering analysis that can automatically divide full dimensions into multiple streams. We will focus on a linkage method among agglomerative hierarchical procedures. Linkage methods are suitable for clustering items, as well as variables. However, this is not true for all hierarchical agglomerative procedures. We also briefly describe single linkage, complete linkage and average linkage in turn. The followings are the steps in the agglomerative hierarchical clustering algorithm for grouping N objects.

– Agglomerative hierarchical clustering algorithm [6]

Step 1: Start with N clusters, each containing a single entity and an $N \times N$ symmetric matrix of distances (or similarities) $\mathbf{D} = \{d_{ik}\}, 1 \leq i, k \leq N$.

Step 2: Search the distance matrix for the nearest (most similar) pair of clusters. Let the distance between "most similar" clusters U and V be d_{UV}.

Step 3: Merge clusters U and V. Label the newly formed cluster (UV). Update the entries in the distance matrix by (a) deleting the rows and columns corresponding to clusters U and V and (b) adding a row and column giving the distances between cluster (UV) and the remaining clusters.

Step 4: Repeat Steps 2 and 3 a total of N-1 times. (All objects will be in a single cluster after the algorithm terminates.) Record the identity of clusters that are merged and the levels (distances or similarities) at which the mergers take place.

3.3 Single Linkage

The single linkage algorithm uses the minimum distance (or nearest neighbor) in step 3 of the agglomerative hierarchical clustering algorithm.

$$d_{(UV)W} = \min \{d_{UW}, d_{VW}\}. \tag{4}$$

Here the quantities d_{UW} and d_{VW} are the distance between the nearest neighbors of clusters U and W and clusters V and W, respectively.

3.4 Complete Linkage

The complete linkage algorithm uses the maximum distance in step 3 of the agglomerative hierarchical clustering algorithm.

$$d_{(UV)W} = \max \{d_{UW}, d_{VW}\}. \tag{5}$$

Here the quantities d_{UW} and d_{VW} are the distance between the most distant members of clusters U and W and clusters V and W, respectively.

3.5 Average Linkage

The average linkage algorithm uses the average distance in step 3 of the agglomerative hierarchical clustering algorithm.

$$d_{(UV)W} = \frac{\sum_i \sum_k d_{ik}}{N_{(UV)} N_{(W)}}. \tag{6}$$

Here d_{ik} is the distance between object i in the cluster (UV) and object k in the cluster W, and $N_{(UV)}$ and N_W are the number of items in clusters (UV) and W, respectively.

4   Experimental Results

Our task domain is vocabulary-independent isolated word recognition in noisy environment using supervised adaptation mode. Korean phonetically optimized words (POW) DB [7] is used to construct the speaker independent (SI) model and speaker dependent (SD) models in the training session. Only a portion of the POW DB (40 males) is used in this experiment. The speech data is sampled at 16 kHz and segmented into 20 ms frames at every 10 ms. We use 36-dimensional observation vectors including 12 MFCCs, their deltas and double deltas.

Our baseline system uses triphone models of continuous mixture density HMM. Each HMM has three states and the number of mixtures per state is one. We tied the states using the tree-based clustering method. The total number of tied states is 4,050. A set of 40 SD models is constructed by MLLR followed by MAP adaptation from the SI model. To obtain eigenvoices, we apply principal component analysis (PCA) to 40 SD models. We use 30 eigenvoices for the adaptation. The dimension of the supervector L is 145,800 when the number of mixture per state is one.

The Korean phonetically balanced words (PBW) DB, provided by SiTEC (Speech Information Technology and Industry Promotion Center) in Korea, and built in an environment different from the training DB, is devoted to adaptation and evaluation. We perform supervised mode adaptation experiments for the 10 male speakers. From 452 different words spoken by each speaker, we use 50 words for the adaptation and 400 words for the evaluation. Additionally, car noise, also provided by SiTEC, is artificially added to the PBW DB to evaluate the performance of the proposed method in a noisy environment. To add car noise at a desired signal-to-noise ratio (SNR) such as 10dB or 20dB, the ITU recommendation P.56 [8] is applied by using the corresponding ITU software. Noise was recorded in a car running at 100 km/h on a highway.

In this paper, we conducted the experiments with multi-stream based eigenvoice method using average linkage. Fig. 1 shows the block diagram of clustering analysis using adaptation data. To use the linkage algorithm, we first converted the correlation coefficient matrix into a distance matrix by the Gower method [6] as follows:

$$d_{ik} = \sqrt{2(1 - s_{ik})}. \tag{7}$$

where d_{ik} and s_{ik} are the distance component and the correlation coefficient between the i-th and the k-th dimension, respectively.

The groups (or streams) with the correlation among dimensions are constructed based on the distance matrix by clustering analysis. In this paper, we also used the MAP adaptation technique to obtain the covariance matrix for clustering as shown in Fig. 1. The covariance matrix obtained from adaptation data only is not reliable because the amount of data is insufficient. Hence, the final covariance matrix is obtained by MAP adaptation using the covariance matrix of the POW DB from the training session and that of the adaptation data.

The performance of the multi-stream based eigenvoice method, in noisy environments, using average linkage which is shown higher and more reliable performance than other linkage methods is shown in Table 1. The threshold value (*TH*) for merging the dimensions is automatically determined by using the combination of the mean and standard deviation of distances obtained in step 3 from the distance matrix as follows:

$$TH = \bar{m} + \frac{\gamma \cdot \sigma}{T}. \tag{8}$$

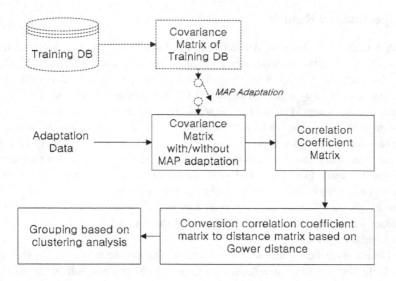

Fig. 1. Procedure of clustering analysis using adaptation data

where T is the number of adaptation utterances and γ is a weighting factor,

$$\bar{m} = \frac{1}{D-1} \sum_{n=1}^{D-1} d^n_{(UV)W}, \qquad \sigma^2 = \frac{1}{D-1} \sum_{n=1}^{D-1} (d^n_{(UV)W} - \bar{m})^2. \tag{9}$$

is the same as in (4-6), and superscript n in $d^n_{(UV)W}$ denotes the n-th clustering step. D denotes the dimensionality of the observation vector. It should be noted that the addition of standard deviation σ with a large value to the mean $\bar{m}$ according to γ results in the increase of the number of streams. In this paper, we used $\gamma = 1$.

The multi-stream based eigenvoice method (MEV in Table 1) proposed in this paper shows 29% relative improvement with 5 adaptation words and a 31% relative improvement with 50 adaptation words at 20 dB SNR in comparison with the performance of conventional eigenvoice method. MEV also shows a 26% and a 53% relative improvement with 5 and 50 adaptation words at 10 dB SNR, respectively.

In the case of the proposed methods, the performance is severely degraded when the number of utterances is one. Hence, we set the constraint that $N_{SS} = 1$ in (3) when the number of adaptation utterances is one.

The results of multi-stream based eigenvoice method with bias compensation in (3) are also shown in Table 1. According as SNR decreases, it is shown that the multi-stream based eigenvoice method with bias compensation (MEV&EC in Table 1) is more effective than MEV since the mismatch between training and testing environment is reduced by bias compensation vector.

Table 1. Word recognition rates(%) of various methods at several SNR levels. (EV : eigenvoice; DIM_EV: dimensional eigenvoice; EV&EC: eigenvoice with bias compensation; MEV: multi-stream based eigenvoice; MEV&EC: multi-stream based eigenvoice with bias compensation).

Adaptation Scheme	SNR	Number of Adaptation Words							
		0	1	5	10	20	30	40	50
EV			97.30	98.00	98.15	98.15	98.23	98.15	98.18
DIM_EV			0.00	92.65	98.48	98.80	98.88	98.83	98.80
EV&EC	Clean	95.78	97.80	98.55	98.63	98.73	98.78	98.83	98.85
MEV			97.30	98.35	98.43	98.68	98.78	98.90	98.85
MEV&EC			97.80	98.58	98.70	98.88	98.85	98.93	98.83
EV			96.65	97.73	97.90	98.00	98.03	97.93	98.03
DIM_EV			0.00	91.83	98.48	98.80	98.88	98.73	98.83
EV&EC	20dB	93.23	96.75	98.28	98.23	98.28	98.28	98.33	98.33
MEV			96.65	98.38	98.45	98.48	98.65	98.58	98.65
MEV&EC			96.75	98.20	98.65	98.70	98.65	98.53	98.75
EV			92.33	94.45	94.20	94.58	94.78	94.83	94.68
DIM_EV			0.00	87.40	97.28	98.18	98.20	98.23	98.18
EV&EC	10dB	80.18	93.70	96.18	96.28	96.43	96.38	96.50	96.45
MEV			92.33	95.88	97.43	97.28	97.75	97.58	97.50
MEV&EC			93.70	96.43	97.53	97.43	98.03	97.65	97.65

5   Conclusions

In this paper, we proposed the multi-stream based eigenvoice method as an effective method to combine the conventional eigenvoice method and dimensional eigenvoice method. Dimensional eigenvoice method is a special case of multi-stream based eigenvoice method. While the robust estimation of parameters in dimensional eigenvoice method requires sufficient amount of adaptation data, in multi-stream based eigenvoice method, the higher performance than those of conventional methods was obtained regardless of amount of adaptation data because the optimal number of estimation parameters was automatically determined according to amount of adaptation data. Statistical clustering analysis was used to divide the full dimensions of a feature vector into multiple streams. We applied the MAP adaptation technique based on the covariance matrix of training data and the sample covariance of adaptation data to obtain the final covariance matrix for clustering.

Our proposed method is also generalized by including bias compensation concept to reduce the mismatch between training and testing environment. That is, speaker adaptation and environment compensation in speaker space are simultaneously conducted by multi-stream based eigenvoice method with bias compensation. Experimental results in this paper show that our proposed method is very useful for fast speaker adaptation in noisy environments.

Acknowledgement. This paper was performed for the Intelligent Robotics Development Program, one of the 21st Century Frontier R&D Programs funded by the Ministry of Commerce, Industry and Energy of Korea.

References

1. Lee, C. H., Lin, C. H., Juang, B. H.: A study on speaker adaptation of the parameters of continuous density hidden Markov models. IEEE Trans. Signal Processing, vol. 39, no. 4, (1991) 806–814.
2. Leggetter, C. J., Woodland, P. C.: Maximum likelihood linear regression for speaker adaptation of continuous density hidden Markov models. Computer Speech and Language, vol. 9, no. 1, (1995) 171–185.
3. Kuhn, R., Jungua, J. C., Nguyen, P., Niedzielski, N.: Rapid speaker adaptation in eigenvoice space. IEEE Trans. Speech and Audio Processing, vol. 8, no. 6, (2000) 695–707.
4. Park, J. S., Song, H. J., Kim, H. S.: Performance improvement of rapid speaker adaptation based on eigenvoice and bias compensation. In: Proc. EuroSpeech, (2003) 1481–1484.
5. Song, H. J., Kim, H. S.: Simultaneous Estimation of Weights of Eigenvoices and Bias Compensation Vector for Rapid Speaker Adaptation. In: Proc. ICSLP, (2004).
6. Johnson, R. A., Wichern, D.W.: Applied Multivariate Statistical Analysis. 4th edn. Prentice-Hall, (1998).
7. Lim, Y., Lee, Y.: Implementation of the POW (Phonetically Optimized Words) algorithm for speech database. In: Proc. ICASSP, vol. 1, (1995) 89–91.
8. ITU recommendation P.56 : Objective measurement of active speech level. (1993).

Phonetic Question Generation Using Misrecognition

Supphanat Kanokphara and Julie Carson-Berndsen

School of Computer Science and Informatics
University College Dublin, Ireland
{supphanat.kanokphara, julie.berndsen}@ucd.ie

Abstract. Most automatic speech recognition systems are currently based on tied state triphones. These tied states are usually determined by a decision tree. Decision trees can automatically cluster triphone states into many classes according to data available allowing each class to be trained efficiently. In order to achieve higher accuracy, this clustering is constrained by manually generated phonetic questions. Moreover, the tree generated from these phonetic questions can be used to synthesize unseen triphones. The quality of decision trees therefore depends on the quality of the phonetic questions. Unfortunately, manual creation of phonetic questions requires a lot of time and resources. To overcome this problem, this paper is concerned with an alternative method for generating these phonetic questions automatically from misrecognition items. These questions are tested using the standard TIMIT phone recognition task.

1 Introduction

One of the main advantages of statistical speech recognition systems is that they are assumed to not to require a lot of language-specific linguistic knowledge; once an annotated corpus is available as acoustic training data, the system can be trained to build models from that data. However, since most current speech recognition systems are based on context-dependent Hidden Markov models (HMM), this requires a large number of context-dependent units to be trained. Unfortunately, no single corpus (or even multiple corpora) can possibly contain such a large number of units.

In order to alleviate this problem and strike a balance between the number of context-dependent units and the limited acoustic training data, tree-based state tying is commonly employed [1], which allows parameters that exhibit similarity to be shared between context-dependent units. The level of similarity is determined automatically from a phonetic decision tree.

For reasonable modeling, these shared parameters are constrained by a set of phonetic questions. These questions aim to determine the similarity of the contexts and often rely on the phonetic judgments of a human expert who can determine whether the contexts refer to similar contexts based on phonetic categories such as consonant, vowel or labial. In other words, this requires language-specific linguistic knowledge. To reduce the manual effort in the question construction procedure, there have been attempts to automatically generate questions for tree-based state tying systems [2,3] and [4].

Even though these automatic systems differ, they have one thing in common; they generate phonetic questions by defining phone classes which have some similar properties. This is

Petr Sojka, Ivan Kopeček and Karel Pala (Eds.): TSD 2006, LNAI 4188, pp. 407–414, 2006.
© Springer-Verlag Berlin Heidelberg

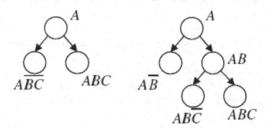

Fig. 1. Decision tree with or without intersection class question

reasonable since experts also manually transcribe phonetic questions by mean of phone similarities. As a result, phonetic questions from automatic systems are usually as good as or only slightly worse than phonetic questions defined by experts. However, the benefit from automatic systems is significant. Phonetic questions can be generated quickly. This is useful for fast development of new language speech recognition systems.

Phone recognizers normally use the Viterbi search to map a sequence of phones to a speech utterance. Since the recognition result is not always perfect, misrecognized phones are inevitable. The motivation of this paper comes from the assumption that if a phone recognizer wrongly hypothesizes a phone as another phone, these confusable phones should have some level of similarity. Hence, these confusable phone classes can be used to generate phonetic questions.

According to [4], it is quite obvious that including combinations (intersections) of two or more classes in the phonetic question set yields higher system accuracy. This can be illustrated in Fig. 1. The node in the left tree is clustered with class BC while the nodes in the right tree are clustered with class B and C. Both trees yield the same results, which are the classes ABC. However, the difference is that the right tree must generate the classes $A\overline{B}$ and $AB\overline{C}$, , which may not be suitable classes for tying. To generate all possible class combinations, another tree cluster is introduced. This tree is different from the conventional decision tree. Decision trees choose a class to cluster optimally depending on the likelihood score. This tree requires no likelihood score. It clusters all classes orderly. Decision trees stop clustering earlier when the criteria are met. This tree clusters each class until there is only one member in that class or there are no more classes left for clustering and therefore all possible class intersections can be generated.

Systematically, the paper is organized as follows. Section 2 lists a number of techniques for generating confusable phone classes. Section 3 shows how to generate class intersections from confusable phone classes. Section 4 shows the experimental result while section 5 draws the conclusion and future works.

2   Misrecognition

In this paper, confusable phone classes are generated using phone substitution errors hypothesized by context-independent acoustic models (phone deletion and insertion are ignored). Although the idea of using confusable phone classes as phonetic questions appears reasonable, the weak point of this approach is the same as other automatic phonetic question

Table 1. Example of misrecognition table

phones	/a/	/b/	/c/	/d/
a	10	1	0	0
b	3	12	1	0
c	0	2	20	5
d	0	0	0	6

generation systems, namely that the quality of phonetic questions greatly depends on the quality of speech used to generate the questions. In order to fully use confusable phone classes as phonetic questions, a number of techniques are applied to reduce this error.

Firstly, all confusable classes are used directly. This is the simplest use of misrecognition. However, this may be risky because of out-of-class misrecognition errors. The second technique is called count-limited misrecognition. This technique comes from the assumption that the number of phones that are misrecognized out of class should be small and if the number of misrecognized phones is less than the threshold, that phone should not be counted in the class. Finally, a "cross constraint" technique is tested. For this technique, only two-way misrecognitions are accepted. For example, if "p" is recognized as "b" and "b" is recognized as "p", "p" and "b" are in the same class. However, if "a" is recognized as "l" while "l" is not recognized as "a", "a" and "l" are not in the same class.

3 Generation of Class Intersections

After the misrecognition classes are obtained, the class intersections can be generated by combining all of these classes. The concept of generating class intersections is simple. The algorithm starts from a class and cluster with other classes until there is only one member in the class or no more classes left for intersection. To clearly explain this, let us assume that a phone recognizer misrecognized phones as shown in Table 1. The number in each cell indicates how many times a row phone is recognized as a column phone. For example, "a" can be recognized as /a/ ten times, /b/ one time, /c/ and /d/ zero time. Classes from this table are (from each column) {"a", "b"}, {"a", "b", "c"}, {"b", "c"} and {"c", "d"}. {"a", "b"} means both "a" and "b" can be recognized as /a/. {"a", "b", "c"} means "a", "b" and "c" can be recognized as /b/ and so on. Then, {"b"} and {"c"} classes can be generated from the class intersections /b/&/c/ and /c/&/d/, respectively.

The algorithm to generate these class intersections is as follows.

1. Read each column from the misrecognition table.
2. List all classes with the phones where the number of recognition is higher than a threshold, e.g. from Table 1 /a/ {"a", "b"} (threshold = 0), etc.
3. Add a special class called the /A/ class to the class list. This class contains all phones in the table ({"a", "b", "c", "d"} in this case).
4. Use /A/ class as the root node of the tree.
5. For each column
   (a) List all classes in the column. This includes /A/ class.
   (b) For each activated leaf node in the tree.

    i. Split the node according to class list constructed in step 5.1.

    ii. For each split node

        A. Find the intersection of classes between the node and its parent node. For example, node /c/ can split to /c/&/d/ node.

        B. If the node contains the empty set, deactivate the node.

        C. If the node contains the same phones as any node in step 5.2.1, deactivate the node.

6. All leaf nodes are confusable phone classes.

Fig. 2 shows the algorithm procedure. The black node indicates a deactivated node. In the figure, the node is deactivated according to step 5.2.2.3.

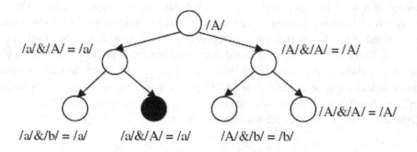

Fig. 2. Decision tree with or without intersection class question

4   System Overview

4.1   Phone Recognition System

The phone recognition system used in this paper has been constructed using HTK[5]. All speech files are parameterized into 12 dimensional PLP, 0th cepstrums and their deltas and accelerations (39 length front-end parameters). Flat start training is then used for model initialization according to the gender-dependent phones. The transitions of male and female phones are tied together for robustness. Each model contains 5 states and the covariance matrices of all states are diagonal (left-right model with no skip state).

After context-independent HMMs have been trained, they are expanded to context-dependent HMMs using a cross-word network. Phonetic decision trees are then used to cluster the context-dependent HMM states into classes according to phonetic questions generated from the system in section 3. These classes are tied and trained together. From the context-dependent HMMs, the number of model mixtures is increased by 1 and the models are trained. This process continues until the number of mixtures is 10.

All training processes are estimated using the maximum likelihood algorithm. The number of training iterations after each change is determined automatically in line with [6]. The language model is trained from the phone sequences of the training set using back-off bigrams. For the recognition process, the Viterbi algorithm is used without any pruning factor.

4.2   The Corpus

The experiments use the standard TIMIT corpus [7] consisting of 6300 sentences, 10 sentences spoken by each of 630 speakers from 8 major dialect regions of the U.S., of which 462 are in training set and 168 are in the testing set. There is no overlap between the training and testing sentences, except 2 dialect (SA) sentences that were read by all speakers. The training set contains 4620 utterances (326 males and 136 females) and the testing set contains 1680 (112 males and 56 females). The core test set, which is the abridged version of the complete testing set, consists of 192 utterances, 8 from each of 24 speakers (2 males and 1 female from each dialect region). In this paper, SA sentences are eliminated from the training set because they occur in both the training and testing sets. In this paper both core and complete test sets are used for evaluation. Automatic phonetic questions are generated from the misrecognition of the training set. In this paper, TIMIT original phone set is converted into traditional 39 phone set [8] before training.

4.3   Cheat Phonetic Question Set

To ensure that the quality of manually generated phonetic questions is sufficiently good (not an unfair experiment as a result of using poor quality handmade phonetic questions), a set of questions is first transcribed by a phonetician. These phonetic questions are constructed based on phone classes from a number of different sources [1,9] and [10]. A number of phonetic questions are removed from the question set by trial-and-error until the highest system accuracy is obtained. This trial-and-error process is tested with the TIMIT core test set. This *cheat phonetic question set* is used as a baseline in this paper. This is called cheat phonetic question set because it is adjusted optimally for TIMIT core test set. Note that in reality, cheat phonetic questions are not possible to be generated because the test set is unknown. Therefore, the accuracy of general models should be lower than the models trained from cheat questions.

Table 2. Misrecognition types

Type	Core	Complete	# questions
direct	73.5	n/a	80,476
1-limited	73.2	n/a	24,008
cross constraint	73.8	73.8	23,852
baseline	74.4	74.0	868

5   Experiment

The experiment in this paper is separated into two phases. The first phase tests a number of techniques as described in Sect. 2. The best technique is then selected and passed to the second phase. In the second phase, the models for generating misrecognition are altered. In the first phase all misrecognitions are generated from simple context-independent models while in the second phase, misrecognitions are generated from more complex models.

5.1 Phase One

Firstly, we tried to find the best misrecognition technique for generating phonetic questions. In this phase, misrecognitions are trained from context-independent models. This test is performed on the TIMIT core and complete test sets. Table 2 shows experimental results according to three misrecognition types in Sect. 2. According to the table, among the three types of misrecognition, "cross constraint" is the best (73.8% on core test set and 74.0% on complete test set). On core test set, the accuracy from "cross constraint" misrecognition is still lower than phone recognition which is trained by cheat phonetic question set (74.4%). However, the accuracy of the models trained by cheat question set drops when they are tested with complete test set. This is because cheat phonetic question set is adjusted only for core test set. In contrast, the accuracies of the models trained by "cross constraint" misrecognition are the same on both core and complete test set. This means that the quality of phonetic questions generated from the system is good enough and it is less susceptible to the change of test set or corpus than the manual phonetic questions.

For "count-limited", since the accuracy when the threshold is one is worse than zero ("direct" in Table 2), no more tests are performed for a higher threshold. Also, because the results of "direct" and "1-limited" are worse than "cross constraint", the tests are performed only on core test set.

In this phase, the accuracy of the models trained from the cheat question set is still better than the accuracy of the models trained from misrecognition. With the analyzing the number of questions, the number of questions from misrecognitions are higher than the number of cheat questions. This means that in questions generated from misrecognitions, there are a lot of out-of-class errors. We hypothesize that if the models for misrecognition are better, the number of out-of-class errors should be reduced. In the next phase, we will improve the system accuracy by using better models for misrecognition.

Table 3. Strategies to improve model quality for misrecognition

Type	Complete	# questions
backing-off	74.0	1,264
second	74.0	1,640

5.2 Phase Two

Two strategies for increasing model quality are proposed. The first strategy is to use backing-off context-dependent models. Backing-off is very simple context-dependent generalization technique. This technique requires no phonetic questions for context-dependent generalization. When insufficient data for training a model exists, that model backs-off and some less informative but trainable model is used instead. For example, if a triphone has only a few examples in the training data, a biphone should be used. If a biphone is still not trainable, a monophone should be used. With this strategy, it is possible to insure that all models are well trained. The disadvantage of this strategy, however, is that the difference between more and less informative models is too large when a backing-off occurs.

From the above reason, the models generated from backing-off technique are worse than the ones generated from tree-based state tying. However, the misrecognitions generated from backing-off context-dependent models are better than the ones generated from context-independent models.

In this phase, only test on complete test set is shown. The accuracy of the models trained from "backing-off" increases up to 74.0% which is equal to the accuracy of the models trained from cheat questions. This indicates that better models can generate better misrecognition. Moreover, the quality of the questions generated from misrecognition are as good as cheat manual questions.

We also want to know that if we use the models trained above to generate misrecognitions again, use these misrecognitions to generate questions and train the models again from regenerated questions, is the result better? In Table 3, "second" shows the accuracy from these models. The accuracy is the same as "back-off". This means that the models are saturated and no more improvement can be obtained. So there is no need to repeat these steps again. Moreover, "back-off" is slightly better than "second" since the number of questions from "second" is higher than the number of questions from "back-off".

6   Conclusion

An alternative way to automatically generate phonetic questions has been presented. This technique employs misrecognitions to generate classes where each class is assumed to have similar properties. Then phonetic questions are generated from these class combinations. The quality of these questions is proved by the recognition result. The accuracy of the models trained from these questions is as good as the accuracy of the model trained from cheat questions. These questions are, however, more consistent than handmade questions which rely on judgment of human experts (for example, for the same TIMIT corpus, there are disagreements in linguistic classes between [9] and [10]). These questions are also more easily implemented in any new language without language specific linguistic knowledge since misrecognition-based question generation is an automatic process.

Acknowledgements

This material is based upon works supported by the Science Foundation Ireland for the support under Grant No. 02/IN1/I100. The opinions, findings and conclusions or recommendations expressed in this material are those of the authors and do not necessarily reflect the views of Science Foundation Ireland.

References

1. Odell, J.J.: The Use of Context in Large Vocabulary Speech Recognition. Ph.D. Thesis. Cambridge University, Cambridge (1995).
2. Beulen K., Ney H.: Automatic Question Generation for Decision Tree Based State Tying. In Proc. ICASSP, Vol. 2 (1988) 805–809.
3. Singh, R., Raj, B., Stern, R. M.: Automatic Clustering and Generation of Contextual Questions for Tied States in Hidden Markov Models. In: Proc. ICSLP, Vol. 1 (1999) 117–1202.
4. Willett, D., Neukirchen, C., Rottland, J. and Rigoll, G.: Refining Tree-Based Clustering by Means of Formal Concept Analysis, Balanced Decision Trees and Automatically Generated Model-Sets. In: Proc. ICASSP, Vol. 2 (1999) 565–568.

5. http://htk.eng.cam.ac.uk/.
6. Tarsaku, P. and Kanokphara, S.: A Study of HMM-Based Automatic Segmentations for Thai Continuous Speech Recognition System. In Proc. the Symposium on Natural Language Processing, (2002) 217–220.
7. Garofolo, J.S., Lamel, L.F., Fisher, W.M., Fiscus, J.G., Pallett, D.S., Dahlgren, N.L.: DARPA TIMIT Acoustic-Phonetic Continuous Speech Corpus CDROM, NIST (1993).
8. Lee, K.F. and Hon, H.W.: Speaker-Independent Phone Recognition Using Hidden Markov Models. IEEE Trans. Acoust., Speech, Signal Processing, 37(11) (1989) 1641–1648.
9. Kanokphara, S. and Carson-Berndsen, J.: Feature-Table-Based Automatic Question Generation for Tree-Based State Tying: A Practical Implementation. In Proc. Int. Conf. on Industrial and Engineering Applications of Artificial Intelligence and Expert Systems, (2004).
10. Chang, S., Greenberg, S. and Wester, M.: An Elitist Approach to Articulatory-Acoustic Feature Classification. In: Proc. Eurospeech, (2001) 1725–1728.

Speech Driven Facial Animation Using HMMs in Basque

Maider Lehr[1], Andoni Arruti[2], Amalia Ortiz[1], David Oyarzun[1], and Michael Obach[1]

[1] VICOMTech Research Centre
Mikeletegi Pasealekua, 57, 20009, Donostia - San Sebastián, Spain
{mlehr, aortiz, doyarzun, mobach}@vicomtech.es
http://www.vicomtech.es
[2] University of the Basque Country, Signal Processing Group,
Manuel de Lardizabal Pasealekua, 1, 20018, Donostia - San Sebastián, Spain
andoni.arruti@ehu.es

Abstract. Nowadays, the presence of virtual characters is less and less surprising in daily life. However, there is a lack of resources and tools available in the area of visual speech technologies for minority languages. In this paper we present an application to animate in real time virtual characters from live speech in Basque. To get a realistic face animation, the lips must be synchronized with the audio. To accomplish this, we have compared different methods for obtaining the final visemes through HMM based speech recognition techniques. Finally, the implementation of a real prototype has proven the feasibility to obtain a quite natural animation in real time with a minimum amount of training data.

1 Introduction

In human-machine interactive interfaces, in order to obtain a communication as intuitive and comprehensible as possible, there is a clear trend to merge different possibilities of presenting information, in particular, speech and facial animation. In multimedia environments, using both audio and animation is a natural and efficient way of communicating. the information appears more reliable if animation is synchronized with sound. Due to this fact, it is usual to see virtual characters in many aspects of our everyday life.

In order to synchronize the character's lip animation with its speech, the phonetic content is needed, that is to say, phonemes and their duration. If the sound is synthesized from written text, this information is generated by the speech synthesizer. There are many applications that merge these two technologies (animation and speech synthesis) in order to create friendly interfaces [1,2,3,4]. Nevertheless, if the animation is generated from audio, the character has a much more natural appearance because its voice comes from a real person, but we have to perform audio analysis to obtain the phonetic information needed. Most of the research done on this type of application concerns English [5,6]. The presence of minority languages in the area of virtual characters is very limited. This is obviously due to the lack of both resources and tailored technology.

In this paper, we study the development of a system capable to produce the suitable data to animate faces from natural voice in Basque using open source technologies. We believe that using open source technologies such as HTK or Sphinx may help diminish the digital gap between majority and minority languages. Specifically, we used HTK Toolkit [7] (based on HMM methods) to discover the best approach to obtain a synchronous animation in real

Petr Sojka, Ivan Kopeček and Karel Pala (Eds.): TSD 2006, LNAI 4188, pp. 415–422, 2006.

time from speech in Basque, using the minimum amount of resources possible. The output of our speech analysis had to be a match between a set of visemes (visual representation of the phoneme) and phonetic data, corresponding to the lip visualization of the virtual character for each frame of the animation. The final application obtained after different analyses and studies was tested in a prototype. The outcome of this test allowed us to use this application to synchronize the animation with on-line audio in real time.

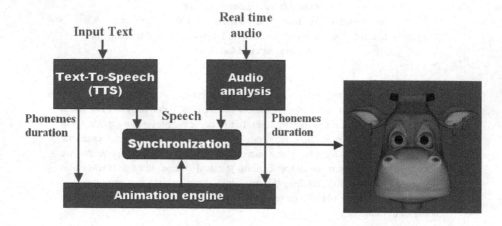

Fig. 1. Animation of the virtual character

2   Technical and Methodological Issues

The purpose of this study is to provide the Basque community with services and facilities not available at the moment. To accomplish this, we have to fulfill the following tasks:

- Research and decide on a method to obtain the suitable data from the speech signal in Basque.
- Synchronize the original voice with the animation from the information provided by the tool developed in the previous analysis.
- Test the performance of these techniques in real-time applications.

2.1   Recognition System

In this part we analyse some approaches to develop the recognition system. First, we describe the methods used and then, we show the results.

Development Approaches. As has been already mentioned, the goal of the project was to obtain the suitable data to animate the lips of the virtual character in real time. To obtain these data, we performed a set of tests using HTK Toolkit. Resources for Basque, such as corpora are scarce and, at present, no open source oral database in the language is available. Therefore, in order to train and test the HMMs, we recorded 250 sentences in Basque, 150 for training and 100 for testing. We added another 50 sentences and used the total amount to create the bigram model. Recordings were done using a Sennheiser desktop microphone

(16 kHz/ 16bits/ mono). Recording conditions were not optimal in regards to noise level. The audio files were recorded in a working room with people speaking and with other types of noises, such as steps or street sounds. During training, feature extraction was performed over 25 ms segments every 10 ms. The Basque version of SAMPA was used as phoneme set for the recognizer. Monophone models were created, which consisted of non-emitting start and end states and 3 emitting states (except from the short pause model) using single Gaussian density functions (due to the small amount of training data). The states are connected left-to-right with no skips. For training, we initially set the mean and variance of all the Gaussians of all the models to the global mean and variance of the complete data set. These models were then trained iteratively using the embedded Baum-Welch re-estimation and the Viterbi alignment. The short pause model was added only after a few training cycles. The resulting single Gaussian monophone system was tested using a Viterbi decoder.

Mel Frecuency Cepstral Coefficients (MFCC) vs. Reflection Coefficients (LPREFC). In this environment, we analysed two types of parameterization. One of them was based on MFCCs and the other was based on LPREFCs. MFCCs handle acoustical features of speech sounds and are based on human auditory perception. In this case, the utterances in all data sets were encoded in Mel Frecuency Cepstral Coefficient vectors. Each vector contained the parameterized static vector plus the delta coefficients, as well as the acceleration coefficients. This resulted in 39 dimensional feature vectors. LPREFCs are model based coefficients. We used them to perform the LP analysis. They are closely related to the vocal tract shape. Since the vocal tract shape can be correlated with the phoneme being pronounced, LP analysis can be directly applied to phoneme extraction. 18 reflection coefficients were calculated plus the delta coefficients and the acceleration coefficients. This resulted in 54 dimensional feature vectors.

Complete phoneme set vs. phoneme clusters. For each type of parameterization, we tested two recognition configurations depending on the recognition unit. The first approach used the whole phoneme set to be recognized and a model was created for each phoneme. The resulting set contained 26 phonemes. In contrast, the second approach consisted on grouping the phonemes on the basis of their visual representation. Since different phonemes share the same visual representation, we obtained a set of 16 models to define, as shown in Table 1[1].

---

[1] The examples of the table are in unified Basque (Euskara Batua).
apeza: priest/ begia: eye/ ama: mother/
denda: shop/ ekarri: bring/ gaia: topic/ arrunta: common/ dirua: money/
atso: old woman/ txikia: small/ atzo: yesterday/
zoroa: mad/ xoxoa: blackbird/
hasi: start/
afaria: dinner/
etorri: come/
ijito: gipsy/
neska: girl/ ñabar: mixed/
lana: work/
iluna: dark/
hemen: here/
ipar: north/
oso: very/
umore: humour/

Table 1. Phoneme to viseme mapping

Visemes	Phonemes	Examples
1	p, b, m	apeza, begia, ama
2	d, k, g, rr, r	denda, ekarri, gaia, arrunta, dirua
3	ts, tS, tz	atso, txikia, atzo
4	z, S	zoroa, xoxoa
5	s	hasi
6	f	afaria
7	t	etorri
8	x	ijito
9	n, J	neska, ñabar
10	l	lana
11	L	iluna
12	a	ama
13	e	hemen
14	i	ipar
15	o	oso
16	u	umore

Experimental Results. The following table[2] illustrates the results obtained for the two types of parameterization. These results represent the number of visemes recognized by the system. In the case of the phoneme clusters this result is obtained directly. However, in the case of the complete phoneme set we mapped the phone transcriptions of the reference text (the text to recognize) and the text recognized to obtain the viseme recognition rate. The phonemes that have the same visual representation were mapped to the same symbol.

Table 2. Experimental results (viseme recognition rate)

Parametrization	All phoneme set	Phoneme clusters
Mel-Frecuency Cepstrum coefficients	76.45% (Acc:70.76%)	71.32% (Acc:65.28%)
Reflection coefficients	65.33% (Acc: 58.64%)	60.56% (Acc: 54.14%)

Parameterization based on MFCCs. As was mentioned earlier, two different approaches were explored with respect to the recognition module. In the one case, each phoneme was represented by one model. In the other case, each model represented a cluster of phonemes sharing the same visual representation. We compared the results of both approaches and the

[2] Acc.(%): represents correct labels, taking into account insertions.

outcome clearly showed that grouping phonemes on the basis of visemes was not the best approach. The error rate was about 5% worse (the same results were obtained in [9,10]). This was somehow predictable, since MFCC parameterization is closely related to speech acoustic features. The corresponding MFCC parameterization vectors of the phonemes of the same cluster can be very different from each other.

Parameterization based on LPREFCs. Additionally, another type of parameterization was used to test if another type of parameters was more suitable for grouping the phonemes by their visual representation. In particular, the reflection coefficients were used, since they are not so strongly tied with the acoustic features of the voice. These coefficients use information from the formants and perhaps could be more efficiently correlated with the visual representation of the speech signal. In this case also, we first used the complete set of phonemes to be recognized and, later, generated phoneme clusters. Results show that this parameterization is not suitable either to perform valid recognition based on phoneme clusters. In this case, the results obtained using phoneme clusters were around 4% worse than the results obtained using the complete phoneme set.

MFCC vs. LPREFC. The results obtained using MFCCs were better than the results obtained using LPREFC, both for the configuration of the complete phoneme set and the configuration of phoneme clusters. In both cases the error rate was around 11% worse for LPREFCs. Thus, the use of the parameterization based on LPREFCs did not improve phoneme cluster-based recognition.

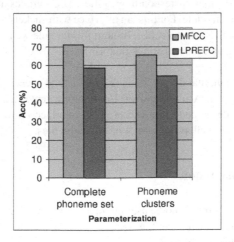

Fig. 2. Experimental results

2.2 Prototype

The application captures the speech signal from the input through a sound card and identifies the appropriate phonemes. As phonemes are recognized, they are mapped to their corresponding visemes. The virtual character is then animated in real time and synchronized with the speaker's voice. The application developed in this paper consists of three modules (Figure 3) (in this paper we concentrate on the component for extracting the mouth shape information from speech signal):

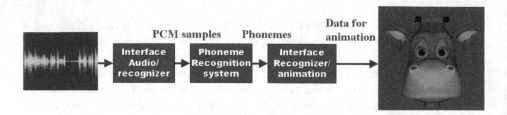

Fig. 3. Diagram of the application developed

- The phoneme recognition system. This module was described in the previous section.
- The module that sends the input audio to the recognition system. Once the off-line recognition system has been developed, it has to be connected with on-line audio, so that the recognizer generates the phonemes corresponding to the speech waveform in real time. To develop this interface we used the ATK API [8].
- The communication interface between the recognition system and the animation platform. Once the phonemes corresponding to the audio samples are recognized, they are sent to the animation module. For this, an interface with sockets was developed, based on the TCP/IP communication protocol. Through this module we fed the animation module with the recognized unit for realistic animation.

It should be noted, though, that due to the lack of sufficient speech data in Basque, the end user must train the system. A minimum of 150 training sentences is needed. In order to facilitate this task, we developed an interface. This interface allows the user to select the sound recording device as well as the format of the audio files.

3   Results and Discussion

Our software fits in today's multi-modal user interactive systems, for which talking characters are an essential part. The present paper focused on obtaining a useful and usable application in the television domain, where virtual presenters are more and more common. The overall aim was to create a quiz type TV program for children using a virtual character. This character is presently running in a popular Basque TV (EiTB) program, in which children answer questions and interact with the said character. In this case, a cow. Results are satisfactory for this first version.

The virtual character is in a virtual environment. The animation reacts to the caller's answers, therefore needs to run in real time. Lip animation runs as the actress who dubs the virtual character in the program speaks into the microphone. This voice is sent in real time to the software developed in this work. The software analyses the stream and generates the data to synchronize the lips with the audio. This information is interpreted by the animation engine.

4 Future Work

The results we obtained with the presented recognition application are not accurate enough. However, real time animation obtained is satisfactory.

As a next step, it would be interesting to develop a rich audio-visual database for Basque. With a rich audio database, we could eliminate the training requirement. Besides, with this corpus we could study other possibilities in HTK, such as triphone configuration or a configuration with multiple mixture components. The corpus would also give us information about the structure and grammar of Basque language and more clues as to the reasons for poor performance results. We could determine if the bad results are due to a lack of data or to another reason. Moreover, if the database contained visual information, it would be possible to perform recognition using both audio and visual features. With a more accurate recognition analysis, we could expand the domain in which the software could be used. It would be integrated in applications such as lip reading for hearing-impaired people or to simply improve comprehension when audio quality is low. Combining audio and animation as means of communication, in noisy environments or when bandwidth is limited, the chances of successful communication increase.

On the other hand, it is interesting to perform a deeper study of the possibilities of the ATK API. We use this API as the interface to communicate live audio with the recognition system. However, its present performance is not as robust as we would like.

We also noted a great dependency between the application and the microphone used. This is another issue that we should address.

Acknowledgments

This research is the result of the collaboration in R&D project with Baleuko and Talape (Basque companies in television and film production). We want to express our acknowledgements for the opportunity of evaluating our research in a live diary TV program and also in public events with children.

References

1. Ezzat, T., Poggio, T.: MikeTalk: A Talking Facial Display Based on Morphing Visemes. Proc. Computer Animation Conference, Pennsylvania (1998).
2. Hill, D., Pearce, A., Wyvill, B.: Animating speech: an automated approach using speech synthesis by rules. The Visual Computer **3** (1988) 277–289.
3. Magnenat-Thalmann, N., Primeau, E., Thalmann, D.: Abstract muscle action procedures for human face animation. The Visual Computer **3** (1988) 290–297.
4. Lewis, J., Parke, F.: Automated lip-synch and speech synthesis for character animation. Proc. CHI87, ACM, New York (Toronto, 1980) 143–147.

5. Goldenthal, W., Waters, K., Van Thong, J.M., Glickman, O.: Driving Synthetic Mouth Gestures: Phonetic Recognition for FaceMe. Proc. Eurospeech, Rhodes, Greece (1997).
6. Massaro, D., Beskow, S., Cohen, M., Fry, C., Rodriguez, T.: Picture My Voice: Audio to Visual Speech Synthesis using Artificial Neural Networks. AVSP, Santa Cruz, California (1999).
7. Young, S., Kershaw, D., Odell, J., Ollason, D., Valtchev, V., Woodland, P.: The HTK Book. http://htk.eng.cam.ac.uk/.
8. Young, S.: The ATK Real-Time API for HTK. http://htk.eng.cam.ac.uk/.
9. Lee, S., Yook, D.: Viseme Recognition Experiment Using Context Dependent Hidden Markov Models. IDEAL, Manchester, UK (2002).
10. Dongmei, J., Lei, X., Rongchun, Z., Verhelst, W., Ravyse, I., Sahli, H.: Acoustic viseme modelling for speech driven animation: a case study. MPCA, Leuven, Belgium (2002).

Comparing B-Spline and Spline Models for F0 Modelling

Damien Lolive, Nelly Barbot, and Olivier Boëffard

IRISA / Université de Rennes 1 - ENSSAT
6 rue de Kerampont, B.P. 80518, F-22305 Lannion Cedex
damien.lolive, nelly.barbot, olivier.boeffard@irisa.fr
http://www.irisa.fr/cordial/

Abstract. This article describes a new approach to estimate F_0 curves using B-spline and Spline models characterized by a knot sequence and associated control points. The free parameters of the model are the number of knots and their location. The free-knot placement, which is a NP-hard problem, is done using a global MLE (Maximum Likelihood Estimation) within a simulated-annealing strategy. Experiments are conducted in a speech processing context on a 7000 syllables french corpus. We estimate the two challenging models for increasing values of the number of free parameters. We show that a B-spline model provides a slightly better improvement than the Spline model in terms of RMS error.

1   Introduction

Intonational speech models are widely used in the speech technology field. Text-to-Speech synthesis, TTS, is certainly the speech technology which cannot circumvent the use of such a model. During the past years, TTS systems tried to predict melodic curves from text messages and speaking styles. More recently these models were used in order to find an optimal sequence of acoustic units. Under this new paradigm, a search strategy relies on both acoustic and prosodic features [1]. Although intonation is a combination of numerous factors, this article focuses on the fundamental frequency, F_0, which is the most prominent. F_0 contours, extracted from the speech signal, represent the vibration of the vocal folds over time. A wide range of publications have reported on efforts in modelling F_0 evolution. We can particularly cite MoMel [2], Tilt [3], as well as Sakai et Glass's work [4] which use regular spline functions.

In this article, we propose a B-spline stylization that incorporates local regularity notion without affecting the overall shape of the F_0 curve estimated using a least squares criterion. In [5], a comparison between interpolant splines and B-splines ability to model F_0 is presented using the quadratic distance. Here, we compare the B-spline stylization to a regression spline stylization estimated according to the least squares criterion. The parameters of both models are the number of knots and their placement. In order to conduct the experiments, we choose the syllable as the minimal support of a melodic contour. Of course, the proposed stylization methodology does not make this assumption. A Monte-Carlo type algorithm (Simulated-Annealing) is implemented to circumvent the combinatorial complexity of the free-knot placement which allows to catch contour irregularities. We also discuss the behavior of this algorithm for both models.

Petr Sojka, Ivan Kopeček and Karel Pala (Eds.): TSD 2006, LNAI 4188, pp. 423–430, 2006.

In section 2, we recall the definition of B-spline and spline models. The free-knot placement problem is tackled in section 3 using a Monte-Carlo type algorithm. In section 4, the experimental protocol is described and the results are given in section 5.

2 B-Spline Model

In this section, we introduce the spline functions and their generalization to B-spline curves which have the ability to model open curves with variable local regularity.

Let us consider an interval $[a, b]$ and its subdivision into $l + 1$ sub-intervals: $a = u_0 < \ldots < u_{l+1} = b$. A spline of degree m associated to (u_i) is a polynomial function of degree m inside each sub-interval and belongs to the class of functions C^{m-1}, which are $(m-1)$ times continuously differentiable, on $[a, b)$. The l transition points $u_1, \ldots, u_l$ are called the internal knots. The set of splines of degree m associated to (u_i) is a linear space of dimension $m + l + 1$.

Splines are widely used to smoothly fit a sequence of observations. A well-known application in speech field is the MoMel algorithm which aims to provide melodic contour representation using a quadratic spline. It estimates a sequence of n target points which constitute the stationary points of a spline of degree 2. The points u_i are given by the abscissas of the n target points and their $n - 1$ median points. Therefore, the quadratic spline is associated to $l = 2n - 3$ internal knots and is characterized by the $2n$ constraints due to the n points to interpolate with an horizontal tangent.

The linear space of splines associated to (u_i) admits a basis of B-spline functions. In order to define them, we rename the internal knot sequence to $t_{m+i} = u_i$, for i from 1 to l, to which we add the external knots $t_0 = \ldots = t_m = a$ and $t_{m+l+1} = t_{2m+l+1} = b$. We denote $\mathbf{t}$ the vector containing the internal and external knots and the B-spline functions are then recursively defined:

- for $i = 0, \ldots, 2m + l$, the B-splines of degree 0 are given by $B_0^i(t) = \mathbf{1}_{[t_i, t_{i+1})}(t)$
- for $i = 0, \ldots, m + l$, the B-splines of degree m are given by

$$B_m^i(t) = \frac{t - t_i}{t_{i+m} - t_i} B_{m-1}^i(t) + \frac{t_{i+m+1} - t}{t_{i+m+1} - t_{i+1}} B_{m-1}^{i+1}(t)$$

where quotients equal zero if $t_i = t_{i+m}$ or $t_{i+1} = t_{i+m+1}$.

Consequently, a spline function of degree m can be written as a linear combination of B-spline functions of same degree. Spline generalization to B-spline curve allows duplicated knots, the knot multiplicity corresponding to the number of times it appears in $\mathbf{t}$. This way, a B-spline curve of degree m on $[a, b[$ associated to a knot vector $\mathbf{t}$ can be written as a linear combination of B-spline functions of degree m where the coefficients $c_0, \ldots, c_{m+l}$ are called control points. The B-spline curve is also defined at the abscissa b by continuity extension. We denote the parameter vector of a B-spline curve on $[a, b]$ by $\theta^l = (t_{m+1}, \ldots, t_{m+l}, c_0, \ldots, c_{l+m})$ and the matrix representation of a B-spline curve g_{θ^l} is given by

$$g_{\theta^l}(x_j) = \sum_{i=0}^{m+l} c_i B_m^i(x_j) = (\mathbf{Bc})_j \tag{1}$$

where $x_0, \ldots, x_{N-1}$ are elements of $[a, b]$, $\mathbf{B}$ is the matrix containing $B^i_m(x_k)$ as (k, i)-th entry and $\mathbf{c}$ is the column vector of the control points.

The knot effect on the curve $g_{\theta l}$ is mainly controlled by its multiplicity. If we consider an internal knot t_i, greater its multiplicity m_i is, lower is the regularity of the curve at t_i. More precisely, if $g_{\theta l}$ belongs to $\mathcal{C}^{m-1}$ between two consecutive knots, it belongs to $\mathcal{C}^{m-m_i}$ at knot t_i. For instance, if $m_i = m - 1$ the curvature of the B-spline curve changes at t_i, if $m_i = m$ the curve cannot be differentiated at t_i and if $m_i > m$, it is not continuous at t_i. Thus, a B-spline curve permits to catch the main fluctuations and discontinuities of an observed curve and a spline function is a particular case of smooth B-spline curve.

In this paper, the goal is to estimate the optimal B-spline curve which fits a set of melodic contour measures. The optimization criterion is the least squares error criterion which permits to obtain a global approximation of the set of data, whereas an interpolation approach gives a good local approximation in the neighborhood of the target points. In [4], melodic contours are modeled by a sum of natural cubic splines estimated by a least squares criterion including a roughness penalty and the strong fluctuations of the data are then ignored.

Let an increasing sequence (x_j) of N values and a vector $\mathbf{F_0} = (F_0(x_j))$ of melodic contour measures, we fix $t_0 = t_m = x_0$ and $t_{m+l+1} = t_{2m+l+1} = x_{N-1}$. For a given internal knot vector $\mathbf{t}^*$, we derive the B-spline curve $g_{\theta l}$ of degree m associated to $\mathbf{t}$, i.e. its control points, which minimizes the quadratic error with the observations. According to (1), the optimal control points are given by

$$\widehat{\mathbf{c}} = \arg\min_{\mathbf{c}} ||\mathbf{F_0} - \mathbf{Bc}||_2^2 = \left(\mathbf{B}^T \mathbf{B}\right)^{-1} \mathbf{B}^T \mathbf{F_0} \tag{2}$$

if the matrix $\mathbf{B}^T \mathbf{B}$ is invertible, i.e. when the columns of $\mathbf{B}$ are linearly independent. That is to say $\mathbf{t}$ must not have knots with multiplicity order greater than $m + 1$ to avoid null columns of $\mathbf{B}$. Besides, the number N of lines of $\mathbf{B}$ has to be really greater than the number of columns in order to differentiate the columns of $\mathbf{B}$, i.e. $N \gg m + l + 1$.

3 A Free-Knot Optimization Process

In section 2, we have presented B-spline and spline models associated to a knot vector. Besides, for a given knot vector, we have derived the B-spline curve which best fits a set of F_0 measures using a quadratic distance. Now, we are searching for the optimal knot vector in function of the internal knot number l.

3.1 The Free-Knot Placement Problem

Let us denote $(F_0(x_j))$ a set of N observations of a melodic contour where (x_j) is an increasing sequence. We want to determine, given a number of internal knots l, the optimal knot vector $\mathbf{t}$ using a least squares criterion, that is to say

$$\widehat{\mathbf{t}} = \arg\min_{\mathbf{t}} \left\| \mathbf{F_0} - \mathbf{B} \left(\mathbf{B}^T \mathbf{B}\right)^{-1} \mathbf{B}^T \mathbf{F_0} \right\|_2^2 \tag{3}$$

where the matrix $\mathbf{B}$ depends on the knot vector $\mathbf{t}$, such as $t_0 = t_m = x_0$ and $t_{m+l+1} = t_{2m+l+1} = x_{N-1}$. We have chosen to localize the knots at observation places $x_0, \ldots, x_{N-1}$, thus the knots can be considered as integer values.

Before choosing the best methodology to find $\hat{\mathbf{t}}$, we need to have a look over the search space difficulty. We have conducted a first informal experiment where we try to roughly characterize the search space. For $l > 2$, we notice a chaotic behavior of the error surface. So, we obviously cannot apply classical gradient search technics. We conclude this preliminary experimental work by the necessity of a global optimization to avoid the numerous local minima of the error surface.

3.2 Simulated-Annealing Optimization

In this section, we propose a global optimization algorithm to answer the free-knot optimal placement using a Simulated Annealing procedure. Simulated Annealing, SA, optimization mimics the process of metal crystallizing from the liquid phase back to the solid phase while its temperature slowly decreases. SA initiates a Metropolis Monte Carlo simulation at a high temperature. A relatively large percentage of the random steps that result in an increase in the energy will be accepted. After a sufficient number of Monte Carlo steps the temperature is decreased. The Metropolis Monte Carlo simulation is then continued. This process is repeated until the final temperature is reached. SA algorithm simulates the previous scenario and consists of a pair of nested loops. The outer-most loop sets the temperature and the inner-most loop runs a Metropolis Monte Carlo simulation at that temperature. The cooling schedule does not depend on the function to be optimized. Unlike a greedy strategy which always take the best possible step from any configuration, SA can take a bad step and can overcome to be stuck in a local minimum.

The main difficulty concerns the relation between the model parameters and the random distributions of the SA algorithm [6]. After several tuning experiments, we propose the following description:

1. SA samples a vector $\mathbf{r}$ in $\{1, \ldots, N - 2\}^l$.
2. We define $\mathbf{v}$ a vector such that $v_i = x_{r_i}$.
3. An internal knot vector $\mathbf{t}^*$ is defined by sorting the coordinates of $\mathbf{v}$.
4. A knot vector $\mathbf{t}$ is defined by adding $(m + 1)$ times x_0 and x_{N-1} to the extremities of $\mathbf{t}^*$.
5. For i covering the knot vector $\mathbf{t}$, we merge with t_i the knots that follow t_i if the distance between them and t_i is less than 5% of the interval $[x_0, x_{N-1}]$. We then replace, in $\mathbf{t}$, the merged knots by the value t_i to increase its multiplicity. This process is then applied to the first knot $t_{i'}$ such that its distance from t_i is greater than 5% of the interval $[x_0, x_{N-1}]$. This step is repeated until the whole vector is treated.

During the optimization, the SA algorithm randomly chooses a knot vector and tries to calculate the cost function for the proposed solution. When all the possible merges were realized, if the sorted knot vector contains knots with multiplicity order higher than $m + 1$, this vector is rejected. In that case, SA generates another knot vector. Little by little, SA will converge to correct solutions while optimizing the cost function.

For spline functions, if the knots number is too high, the vector that SA must generate is very constrained: the knots are distinct integers. In this case, the number of rejected knot vectors and the ratio between the number of incorrect and correct vectors are very high. In such a situation, SA does not succeed in adjusting the distributions of the parameters and does not converge to a correct solution. Even if the constraints are so important that SA does not seem well adapted, it is in fact a limit case of functioning. Practically, only a very restricted set of solution vectors are concerned.

4   Experimental Protocol

The objective is to compare the modelling qualities of B-spline and spline models. The knots of the models are estimated using the algorithm described in section 3.2. We now present the methodological hypothesis of the experiments realized to compare the models.

The speech corpus used in these experiments is a French one made of approximately 7000 syllables randomly extracted from a 7000 sentences corpus. The acoustic signal was recorded in a professional recording studio; the speaker was asked to read the text. Then, the acoustic signal was annotated and segmented into phonetic units. The fundamental frequency, F_0, was analyzed in an automatic way according to an estimation process based primarily on the autocorrelation function of the speech signal. Next, an automatic algorithm was applied to the phonetic chain pronounced by the speaker so as to find the underlying syllables. We choose the syllable as the minimal support of a melodic contour. Our objective is to measure the performance of the unsupervised stylisation of melodic contours using different decision criteria.

For l internal knots, the estimated model $\widehat{\theta}^l$ depends on $(2l + m + 1)$ parameters, and if this number is greater than the number N of F_0 values, it is more economical to memorize the curve. The curves having different lengths, we normalize the number of parameters in order to calculate the means of comparable D.F. number (Degree of Freedom) for all the curves. More precisely, we divide the parameter number of a B-spline model by the number of points of the curve. A normalized D.F. number equal to 1 will then correspond to the whole curve, i.e. to a full model.

The proposed experiments use mean values calculation of the RMS error - Root Mean Square error - of the models. These ones are formulated as 99% confidence intervals calculated with Bootstrap methodology.

5   Experiments and Results

Figure 1 gives an example of melodic contour estimation for each model. The estimation of the models is realized using 4 internal knots. The presented melodic contour has a discontinuity at abscissa 9. To reflect it, the B-spline model contains a knot of multiplicity 4. As for the spline model, the best it can do is to put 4 knots around the discontinuity. We can notice the more important modelling capacity of B-splines for curves with variable local regularity. In terms of RMS error, the B-spline and spline models give respectively $0.59Hz$ and $4Hz$.

To be able to compare splines and B-splines for equal degrees of freedom (D.F.), we have studied the evolution of the RMS error in function of the D.F. number for each model. The obtained curve (figure 2) permits to measure the parameter number impact on the estimated models quality. The normalized D.F. number varies from 0 to 1. All syllables of the corpus are taken into account in this figure. When D.F. number increases, RMS error decreases. However, for splines (dashed curve), when normalized D.F. number is close to 1, RMS error increases. It is a limit case of functioning of SA. Indeed, as the knots are integers and the knots cannot be merged for splines, the number of valid vectors is small. In this particular case, the algorithm does not converge to a solution. To counter this problem, we would choose a different structure of the knot vector by representing shifts between knots. This structure

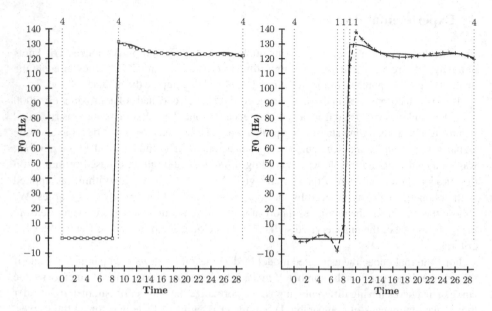

Fig. 1. Estimation of a syllable for each model. The original curve is represented with a solid line. The estimated curves for the B-spline model (left) and spline model (right) are dashed curves. The estimation is realized using 4 internal knots, i.e. 0.41 normalized D.F. The knot places are presented with vertical dotted lines.

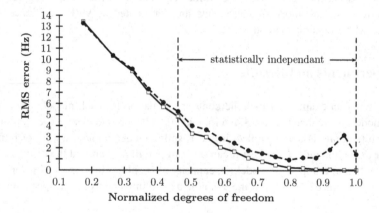

Fig. 2. Evolution of the RMS error 99% confidence intervals in function of the normalized degrees of freedom (D.F.) for B-splines (solid line) and splines (dashed line). The normalized D.F. axis is divided into 20 equilibrated classes, this way each point of the curves represent the same number of values.

would decrease the number of rejected knot vectors and thus increase SA performance in limit cases. Moreover, the RMS error curve for B-splines (solid line) regularly decreases through the normalized D.F. value 1. The knot vector for B-splines, which permits the merging of knots, is less constrained than for splines. In this case, the SA algorithm does not have any difficulty to find a good solution.

Table 1. Normalized D.F. number for each model and corresponding RMS error 99% confidence intervals

norm. D.F.	0.17	0.26	0.32	0.37	0.42	0.46	0.50	0.54	0.59	0.63
splines	13.31	10.38	9.16	7.35	6.13	5.32	4.03	3.67	2.88	2.47
	±0.50	±0.46	±0.40	±0.38	±0.34	±0.33	±0.30	±0.26	±0.21	±0.20
B-splines	13.46	10.35	8.98	7.06	5.74	4.87	3.32	3.02	2.08	1.71
	±0.46	±0.43	±0.43	±0.41	±0.36	±0.33	±0.26	±0.23	±0.21	±0.19

norm. D.F.	0.67	0.71	0.75	0.79	0.84	0.88	0.92	0.96	1.00
splines	1.81	1.56	1.26	0.97	1.17	1.15	1.88	3.19	1.46
	±0.16	±0.15	±0.12	±0.11	±0.18	±0.19	±0.32	±0.41	±0.28
B-splines	1.11	0.82	0.51	0.27	0.23	0.11	0.10	0.05	0.06
	±0.15	±0.12	±0.09	±0.06	±0.05	±0.03	±0.03	±0.01	±0.02

On the first part of the curves, we observe that the two models are equivalent. The knot number being low, it is normal that B-splines and splines have equivalent performances. With a small number of knots, the merging of knots for B-splines does not ameliorate the results. On the one hand, a small number of knots implies that the merging is not applied frequently, and on the other hand, when the merging is applied, the improvement is not so visible. However, when the normalized D.F. number increases, B-splines give better results and their RMS error decreases faster than for splines.

Table 1 presents the details of the 99% confidence intervals on the RMS error in function of the normalized D.F. From a value of 0.5 normalized D.F., both models are statistically independent and the B-spline model is more efficient than the spline one. Moreover, from this value of normalized D.F., both models reach the F_0 JND threshold of $4 Hz$ and give a mean compression rate of approximately 50%. In [7], it has been shown that MoMel leads to 6Hz of mean RMS error in the best case.

6   Conclusion

This article describes a new approach to estimate F_0 curves using B-spline and Spline models characterized by a knot sequence and associated control points. The free parameters of the model are the number of knots and their location. A SA algorithm is used to estimate the optimal free-knot placement. Next, we have compared the two presented models. Experiments conducted on a corpus of French show that B-spline model gives better results than spline one. Nevertheless, in a speech processing context, the spline model enables to reach the F_0 JND threshold with a relatively high compression rate (50%) which is sufficient in practice. As for the B-splines, that are more general than splines, they take explicitly into account the discontinuities of melodic contours. Moreover, SA algorithm is more stable with the B-spline model because of its more limited number of constraints.

References

1. Raux, A., Black, A.: A unit selection approach to f0 modeling and its application to emphasis. In: Proc. ASRU Conf. (2003) 700–703.
2. Hirst, D., Cristo, A.D., Espesser, R.: Levels of representation and levels of analysis for the description of intonation systems. In M. Horne (Ed.), Prosody: Theory and Experiment, Kluwer Academic Pusblisher **14** (2000) 51–87.
3. Taylor, P.: Analysis and synthesis of intonation using the tilt model. J. Acoust. Soc. America **107** (2000) 1697–1714.
4. Sakai, S., Glass, J.: Fundamental frequency modeling for corpus-based speech synthesis based on statistical learning techniques. In: Proc. ASRU Conf. (2003) 712–717.
5. Barbot, N., Boeffard, O., Lolive, D.: F0 stylisation with a free-knot b-spline model and simulated-annealing optimization. In: Proc. Eurospeech Conf. (2005) 325–328.
6. Ingber, L.: Adaptive simulated annealing (asa): lessons learned. Control and Cybernetics **25** (1996) 33–54.
7. Mouline, S., Boeffard, O., Bagshaw, P.: Automatic adaptation of the momel f_0 stylisation algorithm to new corpora. In: Proc. of ICSLP. (2004).

Environmental Adaptation with a Small Data Set of the Target Domain

Andreas Maier, Tino Haderlein, and Elmar Nöth

University of Erlangen Nuremberg, Chair for Pattern Recognition,
Martenstr. 3, 91058 Erlangen, Germany
Andreas.Maier@informatik.uni-erlangen.de

Abstract. In this work we present an approach to adapt speaker-independent recognizers to a new acoustical environment. The recognizers were trained with data which were recorded using a close-talking microphone. These recognizers are to be evaluated with distant-talking microphone data. The adaptation set was recorded with the same type of microphone. In order to keep the speaker-independency this set includes 33 speakers. The adaptation itself is done using maximum a posteriori (MAP) and maximum likelihood linear regression adaptation (MLLR) in combination with the Baum-Welch algorithm. Furthermore the close-talking training data were artificially reverberated to reduce the mismatch between training and test data. In this manner the performance could be increased from 9.9 % WA to 40.0 % WA in speaker-open conditions. If further speaker-dependent adaptation is applied this rate is increased up to 54.9 % WA.

1 Introduction

Gathering training data is a time-consuming and expensive task. Therefore, most speech recognizers are highly specialized to a single recognition task. In most cases the data were collected using a close-talking microphone. However, in real task environments this constraint is often not met. For example car navigation systems often rely on hands-free speaking systems. Close-talking recognizers are not suitable for this task.

We present two techniques in order to adjust a recognizer to a new environment. The first one is MAP and MLLR adaptation [1] in combination with the Baum-Welch algorithm. Therefore, new in-task-domain adaptation data has to be collected. However, the amount of data which is needed for adaptation is much smaller than for training. Since transliterating the new data is even more expensive supervised and unsupervised adaptation are presented in comparison. This procedure is similar to [2]. The second technique is based on the idea to reduce the acoustical mismatch between close-talking training data and the distant-talking evaluation data by producing a "general" reverberation which is convolved into the signal. For training and evaluation we employed the AIBO [3], the Verbmobil [4], and the Fatigue [5] databases which are presented in the following.

2 Databases

2.1 AIBO Database

The AIBO Database contains emotional speech of children. In a Wizard-of-Oz experiment children in the age of 12 to 14 years were faced the task to control a Sony AIBO^{TM} robot [6] by voice. In total 51 pupils (21 male and 30 female) of two different schools were recorded in German language. The whole scenery was recorded by a video camera in order to document

Petr Sojka, Ivan Kopeček and Karel Pala (Eds.): TSD 2006, LNAI 4188, pp. 431–437, 2006.

the experiment and a head-mounted microphone (*ct*). From the sound track of the video tape a second version of the AIBO corpus was extracted: a distant-talking version (*rm*) was obtained. In this manner no second manual transliteration was necessary because the transcription of the distant-talking and the close-talking version is the same. The distance between the speaker's position and the video camera was approximately 2.5 m. In total 8.5 hours of spontaneous speech data were recorded. The resulting utterances contain 3.5 words each on average. This corpus with 12,858 utterances in total was split into a training, a validation, and a test set with 8,374, 1,310, and 3,174 utterances, respectively. The size of the vocabulary is 850 words plus 350 word fragments. The category-based 4-gram language model which was used for all evaluations was trained on the transcription of the training set and has a perplexity of 50 on the test set.

2.2 Verbmobil (VM)

The Verbmobil (VM) database is a widely used speech collection. We use a German subset of the whole corpus which was already investigated in [7]. The scenario of the corpus is human-human communication with the topic of business appointment scheduling. It contains in total 27.7 hours of continuous speech by 578 speakers of which 304 were male and 274 were female. The size of the vocabulary is 6825 words. On average each of the 12,030 utterances contains 22 words. The size of the training and the test set is 11,714 and 268 utterances, respectively. In order to keep the consistency with earlier experiments the size of the validation set was kept at 48 utterances (cf. [4]). The language model which is employed for the recognition is a category-based 4-gram model which was trained on the transcription of the training data. Its perplexity on the Verbmobil test set is 152.

2.3 Fatigue (FAT)

In order to do an evaluation of the Verbmobil recognizers in acoustical mismatch the Fatigue database which is presented in [5] was used. In this experiment the impact of fatigue on the concentration of participants was investigated. Therefore 3 male and 3 female persons were kept awake a whole night. Among other tasks like playing computer games these six speakers had to read texts which were partially taken from the transcription of the Verbmobil database. The vocabulary and the language model stays the same as in the case of the Verbmobil database. However, this procedure reduces the perplexity of the language model since the test utterances were in the training set of the language model. The perplexity of the 4-gram language model on the Fatigue test set is only 88. The position of the speaker was in front of a microphone array with 15 microphones where 13 were arranged in a linear order. For this work only the central microphone number 7 is used (FAT-Mic7). The distance between the speaker's mouth and the microphone array was approximately 70 cm. The size of the room was 4.5 m × 4.3 m × 3.2 m. This database serves as a reverberated version of parts of the Verbmobil database. So no changes to the recognizer were required.

3   Applied Methods

3.1   Artificial Reverberation

Artificial reverberation is used to create disturbances which resemble those caused by reverberation in a real acoustic environment. It is applied to the signal directly before the

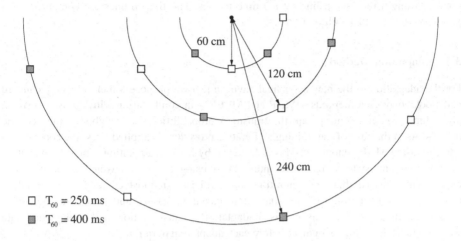

60 cm

120 cm

240 cm

□ T_{60} = 250 ms
■ T_{60} = 400 ms

Fig. 1. Recording positions for the impulse responses used in this work (black dot: microphone; squares: assumed speaker positions)

feature extraction. So the robustness of the features to reverberation can be improved. The idea is to convolve the speech signal with impulse responses characteristic for reverberation in typical application scenarios e.g. a living room. Thus a reverberated signal can be computed. These impulse responses can be measured in the proposed target environment or generated artificially. For the case of this paper impulse responses have been measured in a specific environment. In current research the artificial reverberation was found to improve the robustness of speech recognizers to acoustic mismatches [5,8]. In both papers the training data is reverberated using the same twelve impulse responses from assumed speaker positions shown in Fig. 1. The responses differ in the distance, the angle, and the reverberation time T_{60}. The reverberation time is defined as the time that passes until the signal decays to 10^{-6} of its initial sound energy. This corresponds to a reduction of 60 dB. Each response is applied to $\frac{1}{12}$ of the training data. In this manner training data is created which covers a broad variety of possible reverberation.

3.2 Recognizer Specifications

The acoustic models of this work are state-tied polyphone models, which are also called semi-continuous Hidden Markov Models (SCHMM). 500 mixture components are shared between all states in the codebook. In addition each state has a weight for each density. In the training the codebook is initialized by the identification of Gaussian mixtures. The transition probabilities between the states are determined by ten iterations of the Baum-Welch algorithm. Then the codebook is re-estimated. The Baum-Welch algorithm and the codebook re-estimation is repeated in an alternating manner for ten times.

As features the commonly used Mel Frequency Cepstrum Coefficients (MFCC) are employed. We use 12 static features: the spectral energy and 11 cepstral features. Furthermore 12 dynamic features are calculated as an approximation of the first derivative of the static features using a regression line over 5 time frames. The time frames are computed for a period of 16 ms with a shift of 10 ms.

3.3 Adaptation Method

For the adaptation to the new acoustical environment we propose a method using standard codebook adaptation methods – MAP and MLLR – in combination with the Baum-Welch algorithm in order to interpolate the transition probabilities and weights of the acoustic models. As in the case of the training an iterative procedure is applied. First the codebook is adjusted using MAP adaptation. This is followed by MLLR adaptation. Then the transition probabilities and state weights are interpolated using the Baum-Welch algorithm. The experiments showed that three iterations are sufficient in most cases. For this kind of adaptation a transliteration of the adaptation data is necessary and hence the method is supervised. In order to do unsupervised adaptation a transliteration of the adaptation data was generated using the recognizer before each adaptation iteration.

4   Experiments and Results

4.1   AIBO Database

Since the distant-talking data of the AIBO database is very noisy and the distance is quite far the recognition on this data set is poor. The plain close-talking recognizer achieves only 9.9 % word accuracy (WA) on the distant-talking evaluation set although the accuracy on the *ct* test set was 79.0 % WA. Training with the distant-talking data achieves 51.1 % WA. This can be seen as an upper boundary for this recognition task. First the effect of artificial reverberation on the adaptation was investigated. Table 1 shows the results which were obtained using only codebook adaptation with MAP followed by MLLR. In this experiment half of the room microphone training data was used for adaptation. *ct* denotes the plain AIBO close-talking recognizer while *ct rv* denotes the recognizer which was trained using only artificially reverberated data. The combination of both was beneficial especially when supervised adaptation was performed. The best results were achieved when half of the training data were reverberated while the other half stayed as is (*ct-2*). Unsupervised adaptation could achieve reasonable recognition rates.

Table 1. Recognition rates with different sets of artificially reverberated training data with the AIBO recognizer using half of the room microphone data for adaptation

training set	baseline	word accuracy	
		MAP+MLLR adaptation	
		supervised	unsuper- vised
close-talking (ct)	9.9 %	29.6 %	22.1 %
reverberated (ct rv)	19.4 %	32.9 %	28.4 %
ct + ct rv	16.0 %	33.5 %	27.7 %
$\frac{1}{2}$ ct + $\frac{1}{2}$ ct rv (ct-2)	18.4 %	34.3 %	29.7 %

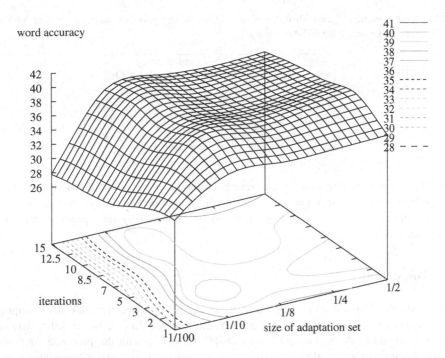

Fig. 2. Supervised Baum-Welch adaptation in combination with MAP and MLLR adaptation of the *AIBO ct-2* recognizer with the *AIBO rm* training set. The word accuracies were obtained with a 4-gram language model.

For the case of the *ct-2* training set more investigations concerning the size of the adaptation data and the number of iterations during the adaptation process were done. Fig. 2 shows the results obtained with different sizes of the adaptation data and an increasing number of iterations. As can be seen three iterations of this process seem to be enough. Furthermore $\frac{1}{10}$ of the training data – approximately 30 minutes of speech data – are enough to estimate the new parameters robustly. So the recognition rate can be increased to 40.0 % WA. The best result was obtained with half of the room microphone training data (41.0 % WA). If this method is applied in an unsupervised manner 36.5 % WA can be achieved.

4.2   Verbmobil and Fatigue Database

A similar experiment was done with the Verbmobil database for training and the Fatigue database as test set. The recognizer's accuracy on the close-talking version of the Fatigue test set is 86.9 % WA. Then training was done using the close-talking microphone data (*ct*) and artificially reverberated data (*ct rv*). These recognizers were evaluated using the Fatigue database distant-talking center microphone. Since only six speakers are available in the Fatigue database the adaptation was done in a leave-one-speaker-out (LOO) manner. So adaptation was done using five speakers while evaluation was done with the respectively missing sixth speaker. Thus adaptation data and test data were disjoint. The results displayed

Table 2. Recognition rates with different sets of artificially reverberated training data with the Verbmobil recognizer on the FAT-Mic7 test set

training set	word accuracy	
	baseline	MAP + MLLR supervised
close-talking (ct)	47.4	57.9
reverberated (ct rv)	71.4	68.8
$\frac{1}{2}$ ct + $\frac{1}{2}$ ct rv (ct-2)	69.2	66.7

in Table 2 show the effect of artificial reverberation in combination with MAP and MLLR adaptation. As can be seen that the adaptation improves the baseline recognizer. However, neither the *ct rv* nor the *ct-2* recognizers can be improved by this speaker-independent adaptation technique.

5   Discussion

Using MAP and MLLR adaptation and artificial reverberation in a difficult task can improve the recognition a lot. However, many speakers are required. In case of the AIBO database the recognition could be improved from 18.4 % to 40.0 % with the proposed adaptation method using just about 30 minutes of adaptation data (*ct-2* recognizer). However speaker-independent adaptation is not always sensible. The adaptation of the recognizers which were trained using artificially reverberated training data could not achieve further improvement. This is due to the lack of speaker-independency. The five adaptation speakers could not provide speaker-independent adaptation data superior to the artificial reverberation. In addition the respective sixth left out speaker was always of the opposite gender than the majority of the adaptation speakers (3 male and 3 female speakers). So environmental adaptation could only be provided with the plain close-talking (*ct*) recognizer. The use of artificial reverberation, however, was always beneficial.

Further experiments showed that additional speaker-dependent adaptation yields even more improvement on both recognition tasks. In this manner the upper boundary of 51.1 % WA on the AIBO rm task can be broken. So 54.9 % WA on the AIBO database are achieved with the previously adapted recognizer. The speaker-dependent adaptation of the AIBO rm recognizer – and hence the the new upper boundary – is only slightly better with 57.9 % WA. For the Verbmobil database no upper boundary can be determined. Again speaker-dependent adaptation improves the recognition further to 76.1 % WA.

6   Summary

In this paper we showed that speaker-independent adaptation to a certain acoustical environment is possible using a small set of in-task-domain training data. We used three databases in our experiments: the AIBO, the Verbmobil, and the Fatigue database.

Furthermore we added artificial reverberation to the close-talking signal in order to reduce the acoustical mismatch between training and test data. For the adaptation of the codebook we used MAP and MLLR adaptation. The transition probabilities and the state weights were adjusted using the Baum-Welch algorithm.

On the AIBO distant-talking recognition task a total improvement from 9.9 % WA to 40.0 % WA could be done using only about 30 minutes of adaptation data in supervised condition. In unsupervised condition 36.5 % WA could be achieved. However, this kind of speaker-independent adaptation is only sensible if the adaptation set includes enough speakers to keep the constraint of speaker-independency as could be shown with the Fatigue test set. The reverberated version could recognize 71.9 % WA while the speaker-independent adaptation yielded only 68.8 % WA. Speaker-dependent adaptation is suitable for further processing. So 54.9 % WA on the AIBO database and 76.1 % WA on the Fatigue database could be achieved.

References

1. M. Gales, D. Pye, and P. Woodland, "Variance compensation within the MLLR framework for robust speech recognition and speaker adaptation," in *Proc. ICSLP '96*, Philadelphia, USA, 1996, vol. 3, pp. 1832–1835.
2. E. Bocchieri, M. Riley, and M. Saraclar, "Methods for task adaptation of acoustic models with limited transcribed in-domain data," in *Proc. ICSLP '04*, Jeju Island, Korea, 2004, pp. 326–329.
3. A. Batliner, C. Hacker, S. Steidl, and E. Nöth, "'You stupid tin box' - children interacting with the AIBO robot: A cross-linguistic emotional speech corpus," in *Proc. of the 4th International Conference of Language Resources and Evaluation '04*, Lisbon, Portugal, 2004, pp. 171–174.
4. W. Wahlster, *Verbmobil: Foundations of Speech-to-Speech Translation*, Springer–Verlag, New York, Berlin, 2000.
5. T. Haderlein, E. Nöth, W. Herbordt, W. Kellermann, and H. Niemann, "Using Artificially Reverberated Training Data in Distant-Talking ASR," in *Proc. Text, Speech and Dialogue; 8th International Conference, TSD 2005; Karlovy Vary, Czech Republic, 2005*, Berlin, Heidelberg, 2005, vol. 3658 of *Lecture Notes in Artificial Intelligence*, pp. 226–233, Springer–Verlag.
6. Sony, "AIBO Europe – Official Website," 2005, http://www.aibo-europe.com.
7. G. Stemmer, *Modeling Variability in Speech Recognition*, Ph.D. thesis, Chair for Pattern Recognition, University of Erlangen-Nuremberg, Germany, 2005.
8. A. Maier, C. Hacker, E. Nöth, and H. Niemann, "Robust parallel speech recognition in multiple energy bands," in *Pattern Recognition, Proceedings of the 27th DAGM Symposium*, Berlin, Heidelberg, 2005, vol. 3663 of *Lecture Notes in Computer Science*, pp. 133–140, Springer–Verlag.

Current State of Czech Text-to-Speech System ARTIC*

Jindřich Matoušek, Daniel Tihelka, and Jan Romportl

University of West Bohemia, Department of Cybernetics,
Univerzitní 8, 306 14 Plzeň, Czech Republic
jmatouse@kky.zcu.cz, dtihelka@kky.zcu.cz, rompi@kky.zcu.cz

Abstract. This paper gives a survey of the current state of ARTIC – the modern Czech concatenative corpus-based text-to-speech system. All stages of the system design are described in the paper, including the acoustic unit inventory building process, text processing and speech production issues. Two versions of the system are presented: the single unit instance system with the moderate output speech quality, suitable for low-resource devices, and the multiple unit instance system with a dynamic unit instance selection scheme, yielding the output speech of a high quality. Both versions make use of the automatically designed acoustic unit inventories. In order to assure the desired prosodic characteristics of the output speech, system-version-specific prosody generation issues are discussed here too. Although the system was primarily designed for synthesis of Czech speech, ARTIC can now speak three languages: Czech (both female and male voices are available), Slovak and German.

1   Introduction

This paper gives a survey of the current state of the text-to-speech (TTS) system ARTIC. ARTIC (Artificial Talker in Czech) has been built on the principles of concatenative speech synthesis, i.e. it primarily consists of three main modules: acoustic unit inventory (AUI), text processing module and speech production module [1]. Moreover, it is a corpus-based system; to our knowledge ARTIC is the only Czech TTS system using large carefully prepared corpora [2] as the ground for the automatic definition of speech synthesis units and the determination of their boundaries and also for unit selection technique. The block diagram of the ARTIC TTS system is shown in Fig. 1.

The paper is organised as follows. Section 2 briefly describes the phonetic inventory used in our system. Section 3 deals with the acoustic units actually employed in the system and the process of their automatic preparation. In Sections 4.1 and 4.2 two versions of our system are presented. Finally, Section 5 concludes the paper and outlines our future work.

2   The Phonetic Background

Phonemes, or phones respectively, are the basic phonetic units that represent the spoken speech of each language. Naturally, the phonetic inventories constitute a ground of each speech synthesis system. In our system we currently use 41 "basic" phones. The set of phones is shown in Table 1.

---

* Support for this work was provided by the Academy of Sciences of the Czech Republic, project No. 1ET101470416, and the Grant Agency of the Czech Republic, project No. 102/05/0278.

Petr Sojka, Ivan Kopeček and Karel Pala (Eds.): TSD 2006, LNAI 4188, pp. 439–446, 2006.
© Springer-Verlag Berlin Heidelberg 2006

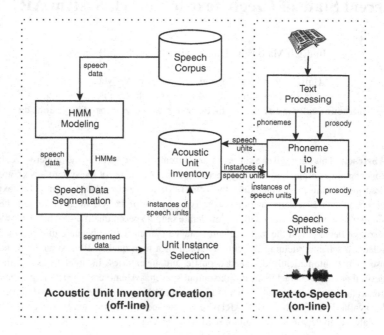

Fig. 1. A simplified scheme of the Czech text-to-speech system ARTIC

Table 1. Czech phonetic inventory used in our TTS system (in SAMPA [4] notation)

Basic Set	Vowels	[a], [a:], [e], [e:], [i], [i:], [o], [o:], [u], [u:]
	Diphthongs	[o_u], [a_u], [e_u]
	Plosives	[p], [b], [t], [d], [c], [J\], [k], [g]
	Nasals	[m], [n], [J]
	Fricatives	[f], [v], [s], [z], [Q\], [P\], [S], [Z], [x], [h], [j]
	Liquids	[r], [l]
	Affricates	[t_s], [d_z], [t_S], [d_Z]
Allophones		[F], [N], [?], [G], [r=], [l=], [m=], [@]

In addition to the basic set of phones, some significant allophones could be also utilised (see the the row "Allophones" in Table 1). Currently we use glottal stop [?] as it was shown to improve the quality of the synthesised Czech speech [3]. The nasal allophones [N] and [F] are employed very often as well. Two symbols representing pause are utilised too: the short inter-word pause and long silence. The former is very important for speech synthesis as it handles the word-to-pause or pause-to-word coarticulation and helps to maintain the correct speaking rate during speech synthesis. The latter is used mainly for modelling both the leading and trailing silences presented in the utterances of the source speech corpus. On the whole, 46 phone-like units are currently used in our system.

It is generally known that context independent phones are not suitable for speech synthesis tasks because they do not respect the phonetic features of the adjacent phones. Using phones without any complementary information about their neighbours would result in hardly intelligible synthetic speech that would suffer from phone-to-phone coarticulation problems. In speech synthesis systems more precise acoustic unit inventories (AUIs), which respect the phone-to-phone coarticulation phenomenon, are used. These inventories enrich the phone set either by adding the information about the neighbours (the case of context dependent phones, so called triphones) or by shifting the phone boundaries so that the signal of an resulting acoustic unit partly covers the signals of more phones (in the case of diphones two halves of adjacent phones are captured). In our system both approaches are used. In the single unit instance system, described in Section 4.1, triphones are exclusively employed. On the other hand, in the multiple unit instance system presented in Section 4.2 both diphones and triphones can be used (currently, there is a slight preference for diphones). Some experiments with other unit types (e.g. halfphones or syllables [5]) were also conducted.

3   Acoustic Unit Inventory Creation

In concatenative corpus-based speech synthesis the source speech corpus forms the basis the speech synthesis system is built on. For our purposes, two speech corpora were designed very carefully in order to contain phonetically balanced sentences [2]. They comprise 5,000 to 10,000 sentences (about 13 to 18 hours of speech). Each sentence is described by linguistic and signal representations of speech. As for linguistics, both orthographic and phonetic transcriptions of each sentence are used. Speech signals are represented by their waveforms and their spectral properties are described by vectors of mel frequency cepstral coefficients (MFCCs). In the current system 12 MFCCs plus normalised energy together with corresponding first, second and third differential coefficients (52 coefficients in total) are used.

Due to the very large corpora, automatic techniques have been searched for in order to create AUI. We have designed a statistical approach (using three-state left-to-right single-density model-clustered crossword-triphone hidden Markov models, HMMs) to the automatic construction of AUI of Czech language. As a result, all the speech available in the corpus was segmented into phones, or triphones respectively. Knowing the unit boundaries, AUI can be relatively easily built from the segmentation scheme (either using single or multiple instances per each speech unit) by collecting features needed in speech synthesis (e.g. speech samples or parameters, pitch-marks [2], duration, F0, etc.). The automation of the whole AUI process allows us also to control the size of the resulting AUI (by tuning up the clustering process, see Section 4.1 and/or working with single/multiple unit instances). Several experiments with the baseline segmentation system were carried out in order to find as precise segmentation as possible, e.g. the removal of the unit boundaries offset caused by HTK (the hidden Markov model toolkit) parameterization mechanisms [6], glottal stop modelling [3], various speech parameterization schemes [7], various HMM initialisation methods [6], correction of pause alignments [1], etc. When some pre-segmented data are available (by an expert in acoustic phonetics, preferably, or by a speaker-independent speech recognition system run in forced-alignment mode), a more accurate HMM initialisation method, so-called bootstrap, could be utilised to get slightly better segmentation results, and/or to use them to adjust the automatic segmentation [1]. Our segmentation system achieves the segmentation accuracy of 96 % (in tolerance region 20 ms) or 86 % (in tolerance region 10 ms) when compared to the reference manual segmentation [6].

4   Speech Synthesis System

Two versions of speech synthesis system are currently supported: single unit instance system and multiple unit instance system. Each version has its pros and cons. The single unit instance system uses a compact acoustic unit inventory (there is only one instance of each speech unit present in the inventory) and thus it is suitable for low-resource devices (mobile phones, pocket PCs, etc). On the other hand, the multiple unit instance system takes more instances of each speech unit into account and selects the optimal instances dynamically during synthesis runtime. Consequently, the resulting synthetic speech is of a higher quality, but at the expense of enormous memory requirements. More details will be explained in the following subsections.

Text processing forms an important part of a text-to-speech system. The input text is typically a subject of a thorough analysis and processing. The task of text processing module is then to get a unique phonetic representation of the written text. A punctuation-driven sentence clauses detection is performed to estimate the structure of a synthesised utterance. Since the input text generally contains "non-standard words" (abbreviation, acronyms, numbers and numerals written as figures, dates, hours, currency amounts etc.), so-called text normalisation based on a tagger performing context-dependent morphological disambiguation of each word is implemented in ARTIC [8]. Then, a detailed rule-based phonetic transcription takes care of the conversion from the normalised written (i.e. orthographic) to the pronunciation (i.e. phonetic) form. Finally, the acoustic units actually used in the system (i.e. triphones or diphones) are derived from the fundamental phonetic representation.

4.1   Single Unit Instance System

In the single unit instance system each triphone is represented and synthesised using a single instance. However, "pure" triphones could not be used directly in speech synthesis – their number is enormous (in the case of 46 phones it is 97,336 triphones) and a substantial part of them need not appear in the speech corpus even if a sophisticated sentence selection procedure is employed. There are also a number of triphones which appear very rarely in the corpus. For these reasons, it is good to cluster the set of all triphones and obtain a set of clusters with "similar" triphones present in each cluster. In our system, decision-tree based clustering of similar models of corresponding triphone HMMs has been utilised within the framework of the automatic speech segmentation process mentioned in Section 3 to define the set of clustered triphones. The clustered triphones are then the basic speech units used later in speech synthesis.

After the clustering and the final segmentation are done, many instances of each speech unit exist in the acoustic unit inventory. Unlike the multiple unit instance system, an off-line unit instance selection scheme was proposed to select a single, "most representative" instance per each speech unit. The selection scheme is based on a statistical analysis of all unit instances available in the segmented speech corpus (outliers are removed and the instance with the highest segmentation score is selected [9]).

Having a single instance of each speech unit, there is a need to modify the signals of the representative instances in order to meet the characteristics of the synthesised utterance, mainly the prosodic and spectral features. A modified OLA technique (both in time and frequency domain) is employed for these purposes and also for the concatenation of the modified units into the resulting synthetic speech. Some experiments with a harmonic/noise-based speech signal generation method were also conducted, especially in the context of the reduction of the AUI storage requirements [10].

The intelligibility and naturalness of synthetic speech is highly influenced by its supraseg-mental features – i.e. prosody. In the case of the single unit instance system, an explicit prosody estimator/generator is needed.

The prosody model used with the single unit instance system (called data-driven prosody model) is conceptually similar to the approach of concatenative synthesis (enriched with a unit selection approach): it concatenates elementary prosody units derived from real speech data contained in a specially designed and annotated prosody corpus (unlike the rule-based model used in the previous versions of our TTS system [1]). The prosody units can have either one representative for a parametrisation of a specific portion of a text, or more representatives and a prosody generation module chooses the best fitting one according to a particular criterion, as it is analogically in a TTS unit selection approach.

The data-driven model comprises of two basic components – prosodic structures and a surface prosodic characteristics generator. Prosodic structures formally describe the linguistic functions of certain prosodic phenomena in terms of derivation trees produced by a generative prosodic grammar [11]. In other words it can be called a formal suprasegmental phonology where each word of a sentence is described by its distinctive features based on the position of the word within a certain prosodic structure (i.e. derivation tree). Prosodic structures consist of abstract units such as prosodic clauses, prosodic phrases, prosodic words, prosodemes, semantic accents. Each word is thus described by its relation to these units – so called description array.

The surface prosody generator is a classifier assigning each description array occurred in training data with a cadence – an intonation (and rhythmic) scheme (pattern) fitting into an interval of a single prosodic word. A cadence inventory is constructed using a suitable agglomerative clustering algorithm over vectors representing sampled F0 contours of prosodic words occurring in the training data. The classifier uses a mapping from the space of possible description arrays to the space of cadences while the so called relation of prosodic homonymy [12] solves cases when the particular description array is not in the training data and thus it is "unobserved" from the point of view of the model.

This classifier is solved and implemented quite satisfactorily (yet not the case for the prosodic homonymy and synonymy formalisation and detection, which still need to be thoroughly explored) and the current research in the field of prosody is focused mainly on a parser producing the prosodic structures of input sentences. Currently we use only a rule-based prosodic parser but an HMM-based and a probabilistic grammar-based parser are being developed and tested.

The prosodic structures – as a universal system of prosody formalisation – are also to be used as a symbolic prosody description in the system with multiple unit instances (described further in the text) where no explicit surface prosody modifications are carried out.

4.2 Multiple Unit Instance System

In the recent years we have started to deal with the multiple unit instance approach (mostly known as unit selection), and the first fully working version of the unit selection module has lately been integrated into the ARTIC TTS system.

Contrary to many other unit selection systems, our unit selection is driven by the target specification described only at a high-level by symbolic features (so-called deep structure). Consequently, no explicitly set low-level prosodic contours described in Section 4.1 (so-called surface structure) are required here [13]. Although one can object that the use of low-level features is advantageous for the control of the global prosodic character of the synthesised phrase, our results show that it is not so important. Moreover, this treatment allows us to avoid the necessity of the prosodic and spectral modifications of the selected candidate sequence, which cause the most significant degradations of speech quality (as shown in [14]).

The whole idea of the symbolic-driven unit selection is based on the fact that although it is possible to generate very natural explicit contours of prosodic characteristics (see section 4.1) used to drive TTS, it is very hard (if at all possible) to generate such explicit prosody which would guarantee the basic requirement for unit selection – to select adjacent units from an original phrase in the corpus if the phrase appears at the input of TTS. Moreover, our experience suggests that it is not straightforward to find a sequence of units which is both natural-sounding and following the explicit contours. Therefore, we try to adapt the concepts of *prosodic synonymy* and *homonymy* to our approach of unit selection. We expect these concepts to mimic the prosodic style of the original speaker on their own. Our preliminary results, described further, seem to suggest that our suppositions have been correct.

We carried out informal listening tests in order to evaluate the quality of the speech synthesised using the first version of the unit selection [13]. They were divided into 3 groups, the first comparing the unit selection and single unit instance versions, using a 7-point CCR test (3 for unit selection much better, 2 unit selection better, ..., -3 single candidate much better). The second test was a modified MOS evaluating naturalness (5 for completely natural, 4 almost natural, ..., 1 completely artificial), and the last test was used to assess the similarity of synthesised and natural phrases. The results, computed as the average of assessments produced by 14 – mostly lay – listeners, were very encouraging. The unit selection version was assessed as *much better* (average score 2.66) in the CCR test (while using the same corpus for the building of both systems!). The level of naturalness was evaluated as *almost natural* (score 3.95) in the MOS test, and the prosody style was perceived as *equal to the original* in 77% of evaluations (more details about the tests and their evaluations could be found in [13]).

5   Conclusion and Future Work

An overview of the current state of the text-to-speech system ARTIC was given in the paper. All substantial aspects of the system were outlined here. Two versions of the system were presented, each of them being suitable for different tasks. Having low demands on memory (up to 10 MB) and yielding the moderate output speech quality, the single unit instance system could be mainly used in low-resource devices (mobile phones, pocket PCs, etc.).

On the other hand, a noticeably higher quality at the expense of the markedly increased computational requirements (hundreds of megabytes of RAM are required) could be obtained by the multiple unit instance system. As such, the multiple unit instance version is suitable for servers or powerful PCs.

After two Czech voices (male and female) were built on the principles described above, two other languages (Slovak [15] and German [16]) have been successfully implemented within the framework of ARTIC TTS system. Our text-to-speech system has been recently applied also in the area of audiovisual speech synthesis – the first computer 3D Czech talking head with realistic face animations was designed [17].

In our next work we will continuously aim at improving the quality of the synthetic speech produced by our TTS system. Beside other aspects (e.g. enhanced prosody generation or dynamic unit selection) a substantial attention will be paid to the improvements in the quality of the automatically designed acoustic unit inventories. We will focus mainly on the increase of the accuracy of the automatic segmentation of speech, and on minimising the size of the inventories while maintaining the quality of the resulting speech. Research in the field of the automatic voice conversion, which will enable to change the voice the system "speaks" with no need to record a huge number of new speech data, has been launched recently as well.

References

1. Matoušek, J., Romportl, J., Tihelka, D., Tychtl, Z.: Recent Improvements on ARTIC: Czech Text-to-Speech System. Proc. ICSLP, vol. III. Jeju Island, Korea (2004) 1933–1936.
2. Matoušek, J., Psutka, J., Krůta, J.: On Building Speech Corpus for Concatenation-Based Speech Synthesis. Proc. Eurospeech, vol 3. Ålborg, Denmark (2001) 2047–2050.
3. Matoušek, J., Kala, J.: On Modelling Glottal Stop in Czech Text-to-Speech Synthesis. Proc. TSD. Springer, Berlin (2005) 257–264.
4. Czech SAMPA. http://www.phon.ucl.ac.uk/home/sampa/czech-uni.htm.
5. Matoušek, J., Hanzlíček, Z., Tihelka, D.: Hybrid Syllable/Triphone Speech Synthesis. Proc. Interspeech. Lisboa, Portugal (2005) 2529–2532.
6. Matoušek, J., Tihelka, D., Psutka, J: Automatic Segmentation for Czech Concatenative Speech Synthesis Using Statistical Approach with Boundary-Specific Correction. Proc. Eurospeech. Geneva (2003) 301–304.
7. Matoušek, J., Tihelka, D., Psutka, J: Experiments with Automatic Segmentation for Czech Speech Synthesis. Proc. TSD. Springer, Berlin (2003) 287–294.
8. Kanis, J., Zelinka, J., Müller, L.: Automatic Numbers Normalization in Inflectional Languages. Proc. SPECOM. Moscow (2005) 663–666.
9. Donovan, R. E., Woodland, P. C.: A Hidden Markov-Model-Based Trainable Speech Synthesizer. Computer Speech and Language 13:223–241 (1999).
10. Tychtl, Z.: Phase-Mismatch-Free and Data Efficient Approach to Natural Sounding Harmonic Concatenative Speech Synthesis. Proc. EUSIPCO. Wien, Austria (2004) 1027–1030.
11. Romportl, J., Matoušek, J.: Formal Prosodic Structures and their Application in NLP. Proc. TSD. Springer, Berlin (2005) 371–378.
12. Romportl, J.: Structural Data-Driven Prosody Model for TTS Synthesis. Proc. Speech Prosody, vol II. Dresden, Germany (2006) 549–552.
13. Tihelka, D.: Symbolic Prosody Driven Unit Selection for Highly Natural Synthetic Speech. Proc. Eurospeech. Lisbon (2005) 2525–2528.

14. Tihelka, D., Matoušek, J.: The Analysis of Synthetic Speech Distortions. Proc. Czech-German Workshop on Speech Processing, Czech Academy of Sciences. Prague (2004) 124–129.
15. Matoušek, J., Tihelka, D.: Slovak Text-to-Speech Synthesis in ARTIC System. Proc. TSD. Springer, Berlin (2004) 155–162.
16. Matoušek, J., Tihelka, D., Psutka, J., Hesová, J.: German and Czech Speech Synthesis using HMM-Based Speech Segment Database. Proc. TSD. Springer, Berlin (2002) 173–180.
17. Krňoul, Z., Železný, M.: Realistic Face Animation for a Czech Talking Head. Proc. TSD. Springer, Berlin (2004) 603–610.

Automatic Korean Phoneme Generation Via Input-Text Preprocessing and Disambiguation

Mi-young Kang[1,2,3], Sung-won Jung[1,2], Hyuk-chul Kwon[1,2], and Aesun Yoon[1,3]

[1] Pusan National University, Korean Language Processing Laboratory, Research Institute of Computer Information and Communication
[2] Pusan National University, Department of Computer Science Engineering
[3] Pusan National University, Department of French
Jangjeon-dong Geumjeong-gu, 609-735 Busan, S. Korea
{kmyoung, swjung, hckwon, asyoon}@pusan.ac.kr

Abstract. This paper proposes an Automatic Korean Phoneme Generator (AKPG) that can be adapted to various natural language processing systems that handle raw input-text from users such as the Korean pronunciation education system. Resolving noise and ambiguity is a precondition for correct natural language processing. In order to satisfy this condition, the AKPG, as a module of an NLP system, combines linguistic and IR methods. Preprocessing modules are incorporated into the AKPG to handle spelling-errors that render correct phoneme generation impossible. In addition, the preprocessing modules convert alphanumeric symbols into Korean characters. Finally, in order to remove part-of-speech (POS) ambiguities and those of homographs with the same POS, homograph collocations are collected from a large corpus using the IR method. In addition, those homographs are integrated into dependency rules for partial parsing.

1 Introduction

The most natural communication method is vocal communication. Thus, many studies have endeavored to develop text-to-speech (TTS) systems, for Korean language as for many other languages. Several TTS for Korean are commercially available [2,8]. Speech synthesis is based on phonemes, the **distinctive sounds** of a particular language system. Those phonemes are converted from text. For text-to-phoneme conversion, (a) a dictionary-based approach, which uses a pre-constructed pronunciation specification for each word, or (b) a rule-/knowledge-based approach, which generates the pronunciation by applying phonological rules or heuristics, are generally adopted. As Korean is a strongly agglutinative language, a Korean word can be composed of one or several concatenated morphemes of different linguistic features. Thus, using only the dictionary-based approach, it is difficult to cope with data sparseness. Adopting only the rule-based approach is not promising either, because many Korean words, which have originated from Chinese, show, compared to original Korean words, irregular phonological phenomena. Therefore, several studies on Korean TTS have combined the two approaches: the dictionary-based approach, for handling exceptional pronunciation cases and the rule-/knowledge-based approach, for dealing with cases to which general phonological rules can be applied.

Petr Sojka, Ivan Kopeček and Karel Pala (Eds.): TSD 2006, LNAI 4188, pp. 447–454, 2006.

However, correct text-to-phoneme conversion is impossible when there are spelling and spacing errors in the input-text. Firstly, many spelling errors occur in Korean, due to the gap between underlying phonemic form and articulated surface form. Korean spelling is sensitive to morpho-phonological rules, and vice versa, because Korean is a phonemic writing system. Secondly, Korean words are delimited by spaces, the constraints of which are prescribed by Korean normative grammar. The violation of those constraints induces linguistic errors and ambiguities. Thus, morpho-phonological rules, which are sensitive to linguistic, are erroneously applied and therefore fail to be converted into correct phoneme. Furthermore, the correct conversion of text to phonemes is impossible without disambiguating homographs. Several studies have proposed word sense disambiguation (WSD) methods using the dictionary-based approach, n-grams, Bayesian classifiers, and decision tree, among others. Whereas several studies and customized systems for Korean have resolved homographs of different POS, they failed in resolving homographs of the same POS.

In order to implement an efficient Automatic Korean Phoneme Generator (KPG), this paper processes the input-text and elaborates disambiguation modules while combining the dictionary-based approach and the rule-/knowledge-based approach.

2   Korean Orthographic and Morpho-Phonological Characteristics

Korean orthography is closely related to phonological units, that is, to phonemes. The Korean alphabet, Hangeul, is firstly a phonemic writing system. Each Korean phoneme corresponds to a letter. Those letters are placed in a defined position within a square shape. Thus, Korean has an orthography based on syllables. Six syllable structures (i.e. character structures) are possible in a syllable square:[1] V, CV, VC, CVC, VCC, and CVCC. For example, the letters ㄱ(k), ㅏ(a), and ㄴ(n), are placed in the square 간 under the structure CVC.

Korean phonological rules can be classified as follows:

(1)   those that are related to orthography, because the sound changes occur between phonemes, which correspond to Korean letters, and

(2)   those that provide variants, and, thus, are not related to orthography.

The following are representative phonological rules, which are related to Korean orthography. In *neutralization* just seven consonants, /p/, /t/, /k/, /l/, /m/, /n/, /ŋ/, can appear in the syllable-final position. The stops are neutralized as a homorganic lenis stop, and affricates and fricatives as a coronal lenis stop [t]. This phenomenon implies implosion at the same time.

In *tensification*, lenis, including /p/, /t/, /k/, /ts/ and s, are changed into fortis including [p'], [t'], [k'], [ts'] and [s'], respectively, in the post-obstruental position.

---

[1] Throughout this paper, Korean characters are transcribed into International Phonetic Alphabet. In addition, the symbols and abbreviations used for simplification in this paper are as follows.
|: separation; #: spacing (word bound); ·: syllable bound; -/+: morphological bound; *: unacceptable form; [ ]: phonetic representation; / /: phonological representation; < >: Part-of-speech tag(s) and/or its meaning between ''; ( ): Korean letter or character; ADV: adverb; C: consonant; END: verbal ending; N: noun; POST: postposition; V: vowel

(3)   Sample derivation of neutralization rule: /ipʰ (잎)/ <N 'leaf > → [ip (입)]

In *tensification*, lenis, including /p/, /t/, /k/, /ts/ and s, are changed into fortis including [p'], [t'], [k'], [ts'] and [s'], respectively, in the post-obstruental position.

(4)   Sample derivation of tensification rule within a single morpheme: /mok·ki(목기)/ <N'a wooden container'> → [mok̚·k'i(목끼)]

By *liaison*, a consonant in coda is resyllabified as the onset of the next syllable before an initial-vowel syllable.

(5)   Sample derivation of liaison rule in an inflected form: /apʰ (앞) + -ɯn(은) / <N 'front' + POST> → [a·pʰ ɯn(아픈)]

Besides, the following phonological rules, which produce non-phonemic variants, are not related to orthography, and thus are not sensible to orthography. *Lenis stop voicing* is the phenomenon by which lenis stops /k/, /t/, /p/, /ts/ are changed into [g], [d], [b], [dz], respectively; in *Flapping*, liquid /l/ is changed into [r] in the onset-syllable position between vowels; in *Palatalization*, phonemes such as /n/, /l/, /s/ are changed into variants such as [ɲ], [ʎ], [ɕ], respectively; and in *Rounding*, the fricative /s/ is changed into [ʃ].

The **phonological rules are concerned with linguistic bounds** such as (a) the phonological phrase bound (the maximal scope of phonological rule application), (b) the phonological word bound (a word, as a spacing unit including a single morpheme, inflected form, or compound form), (c) the morphological bound (regarding whether the morpheme is of a major class or a minor class) [2]. Spacing errors often involve the phonological word bound. In addition, according to a change of spacing, syntactic and semantic interpretations, and pronunciation, differ as well. For example, tensification occurs in (6), whereas it has no effect in (7), because, due to spacing, the /p/ in question is not a part of an inner-word structure. When the next syllable is of a major category, the *neutralization* applies first, before *liaison*, within a phonological word.

(6)   /kuk(국)/ <N 'soup'> + /pap(밥)/ <N 'rice'> → [kuk̚·p'ap̚] <'boiled rice soup'>

(7)   /kuk(국)/ <N 'soup'> # /pap(밥)/ <N 'rice'>/→ [kuk̚] # [pap̚] <'soup (and) rice'>

3   Ambiguities in Converting Korean Text to Phonemes

Besides spelling errors and spacing errors, correct text-to-phoneme conversion requires that ambiguities also be resolved.[8] distinguishes seven major types of homo-graphs with their samples in English: (a) different POS, (b) same POS, (c) certain proper names that are homographs with common nouns in capitalized contexts, (d) roman n merals (e) fractions/dates (f) years/quantifiers and (g) abbreviations This classification corresponds mostly to that of Korean homographs, with slight differences. Contrary to Indo-European languages where the usage of capital letters in writing is a grammatical element ,Korean ,having its own alphabet system, presents no capitalization problem. In addition, the types (d) to (g), related to Arabic numerals and text symbols, reveal more complications in Korean than in other languages. Korean numerals show various variants. Their automatic transliteration for Korean TTS is very complicated because their distribution is largely dependent on context In

---

[2] The content of words, such as nouns, verbs, adjectives, and adverbs, are classified as major categories, and grammatical morphemes, such as noun suffixes, verbal pre-endings, verbal endings, and others, as minor categories.

addition, the usage of text symbols such as dashes or hyphens ('-'), tildes ('~'), periods ('.'), among others, covers a wide range of areas, and thereby causes semantic and phonetic ambiguity. In order to remove those ambiguities, a transliteration system, which automatically converts Arabic numerals and text symbols into Korean alphabet strings, were implemented, and integrated into the present system.[4]

Type (a) corresponds to the majority of homographs in Korean. A Korean word can be composed of one or several concatenated morphemes of different linguistic features, which are equivalent to phrases in English. Many homographs are formed while inflecting concatenating grammatical morphemes to a stem. We can subcategorize the following types.

(8) Homographs of different POS with only differences of space

　　a. /puk(북)/ <N'north'> + /-pota(보다)/ <POST> → [puk̚·p'oda] 'better than the north'
　　b. /puk(북)/ <N'north'> # /pota(보다)/ <ADV> → [pu k̚ # poda]

The homograph in (8) is closely related to the word spacing. According to the Korean spacing constraints, a postposition or an affix should be attached to the noun or a verb without a space, whereas an adverb appears with a space on both of its sides. The homonym *poda* can be a postposition in (8)*a* as well as an adverb in (8) *b*. Its grammatical categories are defined by spacing, by analyzing the syntactic features of its contexts.[3] Compared to Type (a), Type (b) is the trickiest in TTS, as it is in other NLP, because the system needs to process semantic analysis and parsing. The following section explains how our system implemented this disambiguation module.

4   Text-Preprocessing and Extraction Homographs' Collocations

In order to resolve spelling/spacing errors that produce serious errors in text-to-phoneme conversion and disambiguate homographs, this system provides a text processing module based on partial parsing that proceeds on the basis of the asymmetric relationship between words.

Text-preprocessing using partial parsing Partial parsing manages the governing relationship using words that were previously incorporated into the knowledgebase as having a high probability of containing spelling errors for spell-checking [5]. The orientation of the parsing to detect and correct grammatical and semantic errors, in our system, is constructed with respect to this 'word potentially involved in a word-spacing error' (WPI). The partial parsing is triggered when this WPI is detected. Partial parsing proceeded from the selected WPI until its target (i.e., a word that formed a collocation with it), or no other possible targets, are found. The homograph disambiguation module with partial parsing provided four possible checking directions *a posteriori*: those using right-hand parsing and left-hand parsing, and those combining two parsing directions such as undetermined direction parsing and conditionally determined direction parsing (see [5] for further details).

This method can be directly applied in disambiguating homographs with different POS (See (8)) while treating them as WPI. However, in order to apply this module to those with the same POS, their collocations need to be collected through indirect methods, because there are no means to collect them starting directly from homographs with the same POS.

---

[3] We can find research discussing the slightly different phenomena in Thai. [Tesprasit V. *et al.*] Contrary to Korean, Thai uses a space to separate clauses rather than to separate words. The homograph is treated with word boundary recognition.

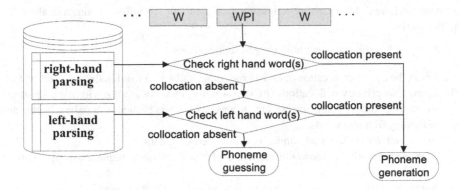

Fig. 1. Text preprocessing and phoneme generation for homographs based on partial parsing

Collocation extraction In extracting **seed-collocations**, a machine-readable dictionary, the *Standard Korean Dictionary* (hereafter *SKD*),[4] is used. The dictionary offers phonetic symbols (if a word entry does not provide a phonetic symbol, the Korean general phonology, for example liaison, is applied). Although the dictionary offers homographs that are distinguished by vowel length, this paper does not deal with them. There is no vowel-length feature in contemporary Korean, because there are no distinctive differences in vowel length for younger speakers of the standard dialect [3]. Apart from the homographs with vowel length differences, about 230 pairs of homographs, which show pronunciation differences between (a) non post-obstruental *tensification* or /n/-*insertion*, and (b) general phonological rules. Thus, the **distinction of Korean homographs with the same POS** can be regarded as a **binary distinction**. This starts from the fact that each of the words has the same spelling but can be distinguished into two categories according to the pronunciation difference.

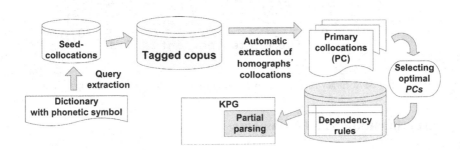

Fig. 2. Construction of knowledge base for disambiguation of homographs

The seed-collocations are used as input-queries to collect homographs' primary collocations, using the extraction algorithms (9), from the tagged corpus, composed of one year's

---

of worth of Korean broadcasting scripts comprising about 1.6 million nouns and about 0.3 million verbs.

(9) Algorithm for extracting homographs' collocations

a. Let *SC* be a seed-collocation of each homograph, and *e* be a word in the seed-collocation.
b. Extract, as primary collocations (*PCs*), ±4 nouns or verbs from *e* within a sentence in the tagged corpus, while eliminating stop words such as pronouns, auxiliary verbs, and extremely frequent words.
c. Iterate *step b* over the total number of *e* in a seed-collocation.
d. Measure the distinctive power of each *PC* for homograph disambiguation using functions *F*, and sort those powers.
e. Iterate *Step b* to *Step d* until no more *e* in seed-collocations remains.

The function *F* is simply the frequency of each *PC* collected based on an *SC*. In general, Chi-square and mutual information are used as *F*; however, the frequency shows the best result in our experiment. Using the total number of *PCs* promises neither higher accuracy nor efficiency. Because of their size, noise can easily be produced. Therefore, this study determines the *PCs* of high-distinctive power. By augmenting *PCs* gradually by 1%, from the top 1% to the top 10%, the accuracy of disambiguating is measured on the test-data *T*, which is composed of 2,093 sentences constructed by gathering, from web pages, four to ten sample sentences according to the frequency of each homograph pair. The best accuracy is observed with the top 4% of *PCs*, as shown in Fig. 3. Those top 4% are integrated in dependency rules for the partial parsing module as collocations.

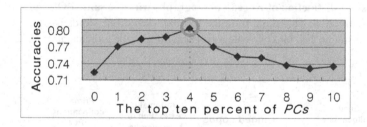

Fig. 3. Accuracy according to percentage of collocations per homograph

5   Experimentation and Comments

We evaluated our system by comparing it with current TTS systems, the 'VoiceWare' and 'CoreVoice' TTS systems, which have been deemed the best TTS systems for Korean. We used the same test data and measured the accuracy of the three systems in generating the correct phonemes for homographs. Table 1 shows the accuracy of Voiceware and Corevoice compared with our system. The result shows that our KPG outperforms the other systems by an average of about 8.8%, using only base-line collocations for partial parsing, and by about 16.9% while expanding those collocations using the top 4 % of *PCs*. The KPG's architecture is shown in Fig. 4.

Table 1. Experimental results for customized TTS systems and KPG on disambiguation

Systems		Correct	Incorrect	Accuracy
CoreVoice		1,338	755	63.93%
VoiceWare		1,325	768	63.31%
KPG	Base-line: with SC	1,516	577	72.43%
	With expanded PCs	1,685	408	80.51%

The performance of KPG in generating phonemes from Korean-character texts is given in Table 2. From the result, the amelioration was observed by using the text-preprocessing module in converting raw texts composed of articles and novels to phonemes. About 31.43% of the orthographic errors, spelling and spacing errors, were removed, and the phoneme generation performance was improved by 2.42%.

Table 2. Experimental results for KPG on raw data

	Total words	Correct words	Error words	Accuracy
Without preprocessing module	10,131	9,756	374	96.30%
With preprocessing module	10,147	10,017	130	98.72%

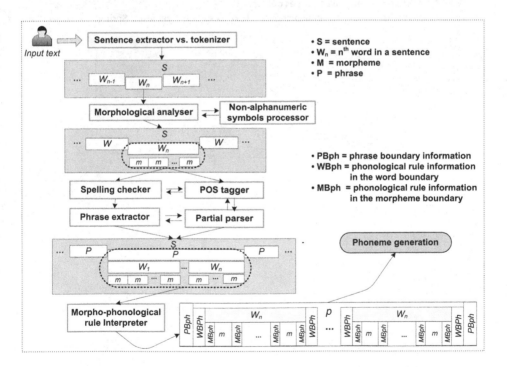

Fig. 4. KPG with text-preprocessing and disambiguation based on partial parsing

Acknowledgments

This work was supported by the Korea Research Foundation Grant. (KRF-2004-037-D00018).

References

1. BELEW R.K.: Finding Out About, Cambridge University Press (2000).
2. CoreVoice: http://corevoice.com/.
3. Ingram, C. L. and Park, S.G.: Cross-language vowel perception and production by Japanese and Korean learners of English, Journal of Phonetics, 25 (1997) 343–370.
4. Jung, Y.I., Lee, D.H., Nam, H.S., Yoon, A. and Kwon, H.C.: Learning for Transliteration of Arabic-Numeral Expressions Using Decision Tree for Korean TTS, Proc. InterSpeech2004-ICSLP, Vol. 3 (2004) 1937–1940.
5. Kang, M.Y., Yoon, A., and Kwon, H.C.: Improving Partial Parsing Based on Error-Pattern Analysis for Korean Grammar-Checker, TALIP, Vol 2-4, ACM (2003) 301–323.
6. Resnik, P. and Yarowsky, D.: Distinguishing Systems and Distinguishing Senses: New Evaluation Methods for Word Sense Disambiguation, Natural Language Engineering 5-2 (1997) 113–133.
7. Taylor, I. and Taylor, M.: Writing and Literacy in Chinese, Korean and Japanese. John Benjamins Publishing Company (1995).
8. VoiceWare: http://www.voiceware.co.kr.
9. Yarowsky, D.: Homograph Disambiguation in Text-to-speech Synthesis, Springer Verlag (1996) 157–172.

Robust Speech Detection
Based on Phoneme Recognition Features

France Mihelič and Janez Žibert

Faculty of Electrical Engineering, University of Ljubljana
Tržaška 25, Ljubljana, SI-1000, Slovenia
{france.mihelic, janez.zibert}@fe.uni-lj.si

Abstract. We introduce new method for discriminating speech and non-speech segments in audio signals based on the transcriptions produced by phoneme recognizers. Four measures based on consonant-vowels and voiced-unvoiced pairs obtained from different phonemes speech recognizers were proposed. They were constructed in a way to be recognizer and language independent and could be applied in different segmentation-classification frameworks. The segmentation systems were evaluated on different broadcast news datasets consisted of more than 60 hours of multilingual BN shows. The results of these evaluations illustrate the robustness of the proposed features in comparison to MFCC and posterior probability based features. The overall frame accuracies of the proposed approaches varied in range from 95% to 98% and remained stable through different test conditions and different phoneme recognizers.

1 Introduction

Speech/non-speech segmentation is the task of partitioning audio streams into speech and non-speech segments. While speech segments can be easily defined as regions in audio signals where somebody is speaking, non-speech represent everything which is not speech and as such consist of one or a combination of data from various acoustical sources, e.g. music, machine noises, etc.

A good segmentation of continuous audio streams to speech and non-speech has many practical applications. It is usually applied as a pre-processing step in real-word systems for automatic speech recognition (ASR) [9] like broadcast news transcription [2], automatic audio indexing and summarization [4], audio diarization [8] and all other applications where efficient speech detection helps to greatly reduce computational complexity and generate more understandable and accurate outputs. In our work we were focused on speech/non-speech segmentation of broadcast news (BN) data.

The most commonly used features for discriminating speech, music and other sound sources are Mel-frequency cepstrum coefficients (MFCCs) [6]. Although MFCC coefficients were originally designed to model the short-term spectral information of speech events, they were successfully applied in speech/non-speech discrimination systems [2] in a combination with Gaussian mixture models (GMMs) or hidden Markov models (HMMs).

These representation and approaches are focused on acoustic properties of data, which are manifested either in time and frequency or spectral (cepstral) domain. All representations tend to characterize speech in comparison to other non-speech sources (mainly music). Another view of speech produced and recognized by humans is to see it as a sequence of

Petr Sojka, Ivan Kopeček and Karel Pala (Eds.): TSD 2006, LNAI 4188, pp. 455–462, 2006.

recognizable units. Speech production could be thus considered as a state machine, where the states are phoneme classes.

2   Phoneme Based Recognition Features

We extended the idea of Williams and Ellis [11], where they proposed a novel approach of extracting features for speech and music discrimination based on posterior probability features derived from phoneme recognizer. The obtained features – entropy and dynamism – features were later successfully applied in speech/music segmentation of BN data [1].

In our work we explored higher-level features derived directly from a phoneme recognition output.

Typically, the output of a phoneme (speech) recognizer is the most likely sequence (hypothesis) of pre-defined speech units together with time boundaries. The recognition result could thus be interpreted as a representation of a given signal. Since the phoneme recognizer is designed for speech signals it is expected that it will exhibit characteristic behavior when speech signals will be passed through and all other signals will result in uncharacteristic behaviors.

We decided to determine features from broader groups of phonemes to be language independent and not much influenced on speech recognition errors. We selected consonant-vowel (CV) pairs and voiced-unvoiced (VU) regions of speech.

After analysis of behaviors of phoneme recognizers on different speech and non-speech data conditions, we decided to extract following features based on time duration and changing rate of basic units:

- *Normalized time duration rate* of consonant-vowel (CV) or voiced-unvoiced (VU) pairs, defined in CV case as

$$\frac{|t_C - t_V|}{t_{CVS}} + \alpha \cdot \frac{t_S}{t_{CVS}} \tag{1}$$

where t_C is the overall time duration of all consonants recognized in signal window of time duration t_{CVS}, and t_V is the time duration of all vowels in t_{CVS}. The second term denotes the portion of silence units (t_S) represented in a recognized signal measured in time duration. α serves to emphasize the amount of silence regions in signal and has to be $0 \leq \alpha \leq 1$. In VU case the above expression (1) stays the same whereas unvoiced phonemes replace consonants, voiced substitute vowels and silences are the same. Note that in CV case: C means consonant, V vowel, S silence, while in VU case: V means voiced, U unvoiced, S silence.

- *Normalized CV (VU) speaking rate*, defined in CV case as

$$\frac{n_C + n_V}{t_{CVS}} \tag{2}$$

where n_C and n_V are the number of C and V units recognized in signal in the time duration t_{CVS}. Speaking rate in general heavily depends on speaking style. To reduce this effect, we decided not to count S units.

– *Normalized CVS (VUS) changes*, defined in CV case as

$$\frac{c(C, V, S)}{t_{CVS}} \tag{3}$$

where $c(C, V, S)$ counts how many times C, V and S units exchange in signal in the time duration t_{CVS}.

– *Normalized average CV (VU) duration rate*, defined in CV case as

$$\frac{|\bar{t}_C - \bar{t}_V|}{\bar{t}_{CV}} \tag{4}$$

where $\bar{t}_C$ and $\bar{t}_V$ represent average time duration of C and V units in a given segment of a recognized signal, while $\bar{t}_{CV}$ is the average duration of all recognized (C,V) units in the same segment.

All proposed features measure properties of recognized data on segments of a processing signal. Segments should be large enough to provide reliable estimations. Typical segment sizes used in our experiments were chosen between 2.0 and 5.0 seconds.

Fig. 1 shows phoneme based features in action. In this example CV features were produced by two different language phoneme recognizers. One was built for Slovenian language (darker line), the other (brighter line) used for recognizing English language. This example was extracted from a Slovenian BN show. The data in Fig. 1 consist of different portions of speech and non-speech. Speech segments are built from clean speech produced by different speakers and in a combination with music, while non-speech is represented by music and silence parts. As can be seen from Fig. 1 each of this feature has a reasonable ability to discriminate between speech and non-speech data, which was also later confirmed by our experiments. Furthermore, features computed from English language recognizer, and thus in this case used on foreign language, exhibit nearly the same behavior as features produced by Slovenian phoneme decoder.

3 Speech/Non-speech Segmentation

In our segmentation experiments we followed the approach presented in [1] designed for speech/music segmentation. The basic idea was to use hidden Markov models (HMMs) to perform segmentation and classification simultaneously.

The base building blocks of the system were GMMs. They were trained via the EM algorithm in a supervised way. Since we experimented with several different representations of audio signals, the number of models used in classification was different as well as number of mixtures in GMMs.

We built a fully connected network consisted of N HMM models, where N was the number of GMMs used for classification. Each HMM was constructed by simply concatenating internal states associated with the same probability density function represented by one GMM. In this way a minimum duration was imposed to each HMM. All transitions inside each model and between models were set manually. Additionally, we experimented with different probability weights to favor one or another model to achieve optimum results on evaluation data. In a segmentation process the Viterbi decoding was used.

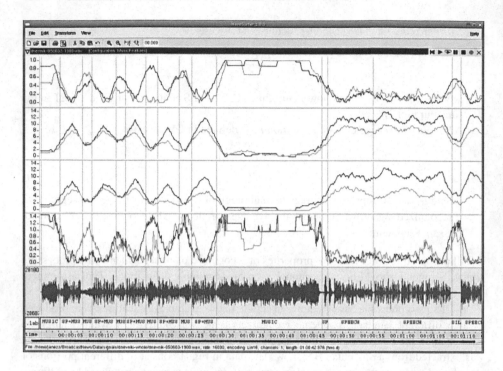

Fig. 1. Phoneme based CV features. First pane (from top to bottom) shows normalized CV time duration, second CV speaking rate, third normalized CVS changes and fourth normalized average CV duration rate. All panes consist of two lines. Darker line represents features obtained from phoneme based speech recognizer build for Slovenian language, while brighter line displays features obtained from English phoneme recognizer. Bottom pane displays audio signal with corresponding manual transcription.

4   Evaluation Experiments

Our main goal was to compare different approaches and representations of audio signals in speech/non-speech discrimination of BN shows.

As a baseline system for speech/non-speech classification MFCC features representation in a combination with HMM classifier was chosen.

The second group of experiments were based on entropy-dynamism features, which was already successfully applied in speech/music discrimination and segmentation tasks [11]. The parameters were set according to [1].

Proposed CVS (VUS) phoneme based features were obtained from two phoneme recognizers. One was built on Slovenian data trained from three speech databases [5]. We will refer it as Si-recognizer. The second was built from TIMIT database [3] and referred as En-recognizer. Both phoneme recognizers were based on the language-dependent monophone HMM models using MFCC with Δ and $\Delta\Delta$ features. The CVS (VUS) features were calculated from (1) - (4). In classification the feature vectors were produced on frame-by-frame basis. Hence, we used fixed window length of 3.0 s with frame rate of 100 ms in all experiments. In (1) α was set to 0.5.

As was mentioned in previous sections classifications were made by GMMs. In all cases we used the models with diagonal covariance matrices. In the case of MFCC and entropy-dynamism features two models for detecting speech were employed: broadband speech and telephone speech models, and two models for detecting non-speech data: music and silence. All models were trained on the training parts of the evaluation databases. The number of mixtures in GMMs was set to 128 in MFCC case, while in entropy-dynamism case just 4 mixtures were trained (in [1] just 2-mixture GMMs were applied). In CVS (VUS) case only two models were used: speech and non-speech. Here, GMMs with 2 mixtures were constructed. In the HMM classification case the minimum duration constraint was set to 1.4 s for all cases. All transition probabilities (including self-loop transitions) inside HMM were fixed to 0.5.

In all cases we set threshold probability weights of speech and non-speech models in the classification system to optimize the performance of a segmentation on an evaluation dataset.

4.1 Audio Databases and Evaluation Measures

We performed wide-range experiments on three different databases.

The first database consists from 3 hours of two entertainment shows in Slovenian language and Italian language. This database was constructed to serve as an evaluation dataset for setting open parameters in test experiments.

The rest two sets are SiBN [12] and COST278 BN [13] BN databases. They consist from BN shows comprised mainly of speech data interleaved with short segments of non-speech events. SiBN database currently involves 33 hours of BN shows in Slovenian language from one TV station. In the contrast the COST278 BN database consists of data from 9 different European languages and 14 different TV stations.

Data from both BN datasets were divided into training, evaluation and test parts. The training part includes one show from each dataset of overall duration of 3 hours. Tests experiments were performed individually on 30 hours of SiBN and on 25 hours of COST278 BN data.

All results were obtained in terms of frame level accuracy. We calculated three different statistics: the percentage of true speech identified as speech, the percentage of true non-speech identified as non-speech, and the overall percentage of speech and non-speech identified correctly (overall accuracy).

4.2 Evaluation Data Experiments

Evaluation dataset was used to set all thresholds and open parameters of representations and models to obtain optimal performance on the evaluation data. The performances of several different classification methods are shown in Fig. 2. The overall accuracies are plotted against combination of non-speech and speech treshold probability weights. For each classification method the best possible pair of speech and non-speech weights were chosen where the maximum overall accuracy was achieved.

As can be seen from Fig. 2 all segmentation methods based on phoneme based CVS (VUS) features perform stable in the whole range of operating points of probability weights. The overall accuracy ranges between 92% and 95%. On the other side MFCC and entropy-dynamism features were more sensitive to different operating points MFCC representations

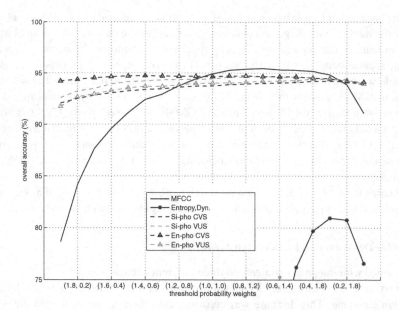

Fig. 2. Setting the optimal threshold weights of speech and non-speech models to maximize overall accuracy of different representations and approaches. (*MFCC*) – 12 MFCC features with energy and first delta coefficients modeled by 128 mixture GMMs. (*Entropy, Dyn.*) – entropy and dynamism features modeled by 4 mixture GMMs, (*Si-pho CVS, Si-pho VUS, En-pho CVS, En-pho VUS*) phonemes feature representations based on CVS and VUS phoneme groups obtained from Slovenian (Si) and English (En) phoneme recognizers.

achieved the maximum accuracy slightly above 95% at operating point (0.8,1.2). Around this point it performed better than CVS (VUS) based segmentations. Entropy-dynamism features did not perform as well as CVS (VUS) and MFCC features and were even more sensitive to different operating points of probability weights.

4.3   Test Data Experiments

We made two groups of experiments. In the first group (first values in Table 1) we built classifiers from GMM models estimated from training dataset, set the optimal threshold probability weights of speech and non-speech models on evaluation dataset. Values in round brackets denote results obtained from non-optimal models using equal threshold probability weights, i.e. no evaluation data was used in these experiments.

Although SiBN and COST278 BN databases consist of different types of BN data, the classification results given in Table 1 reveal the same performance of different methods on both datasets. This is due to the fact that the same training data and models were used in both cases. Furthermore, it can be concluded that the representations of audio signals with CVS (VUS) features performed better in comparison to MFCC and entropy-dynamism based representations. The advantage of using the proposed phonemes based features becomes even more evident when they are compared in terms of speech and non-speech accuracies. In

Table 1. Speech/non-speech classification results on SiBN and COST278 dataset. Values in brackets denote results obtained from non-optimal models using equal threshold probability weights.

Features Type	SiBN dataset			COST278 dataset		
	Speech	Non-Speech	Accuracy	Speech	Non-Speech	Accuracy
MFCC	97.9 (96.4)	58.7 (72.3)	95.3 (94.8)	98.7 (97.8)	44.0 (54.2)	94.6 (94.6)
Entropy, Dyn.	99.3 (89.9)	55.8 (93.8)	96.5 (90.1)	99.6 (83.1)	37.4 (84.7)	95.0 (83.2)
Si-pho, CVS	98.2 (97.6)	91.1 (93.0)	97.8 (97.3)	96.6 (95.6)	76.9 (79.3)	95.1 (94.3)
Si-pho, VUS	98.1 (97.7)	88.7 (90.1)	97.5 (97.2)	97.2 (96.6)	72.2 (74.3)	95.3 (95.0)
En-pho, CVS	98.5 (98.4)	88.2 (88.8)	**97.8**(97.7)	97.9 (97.8)	71.1 (71.6)	**95.9**(95.8)
En-pho, VUS	97.5 (96.7)	90.0 (92.9)	97.0 (96.4)	96.8 (96.6)	72.4 (74.3)	95.0 (95.0)

general, there exists a huge difference between CVS (VUS) and MFCC, entropy-dynamism representations in correctly identifying non-speech data with relatively small loss of accuracy in identifying speech data. This resulted in almost all cases of CVS (VUS) features to increase overall accuracy in comparison to other features. Another important issue reveal the results in round brackets. In almost all cases the overall accuracies are lower than in an optimal case, but there exists huge discrepancies in detecting speech and non-speech segments. While in case of CVS (VUS) features the differences between optimal and non-optimal results (of speech and non-speech accuracies) are not so large, there exist huge deviations in MFCC and entropy-dynamism case, especially in terms of non-speech accuracy. This is a direct consequence of stability issues discussed in previous section (see Fig. 2).

When comparing results inside CVS (VUS) representations there cannot be found any substantial differences in classifications. The results from Si-phones and En-phones confirm that the proposed measures are really independent of different (language) phoneme recognizers.

5   Conclusion

To sum up, the results speak in favor of the proposed phonemes based features. This can be explained by the fact that our features were designed to discriminate between speech and non-speech, while MFCC and posterior probability (entropy, dynamism) based features were developed for speech processing of audio data. Another issue is concerning stability and thus robustness of the evaluated approaches. For MFCC and entropy-dynamism features performance of the segmentation depends heavily on the training data and conditions, while the classification with CVS (VUS) features in a combination with GMM models performed reliable on all evaluation and test datasets.

References

1. Ajmera, J., McCowan, I., Bourlard, H.: Speech/music segmentation using entropy and dynamism features in HMM classification framework. Speech Communication 40(3) (2003) 351–363.
2. Graff, D.: An overview of Broadcast News corpora. Speech Comm. – special issue on Broadcast News Processsing 37(1) (2002) 15–26.

3. Garofolo, J.S., Lamel, L.F., Fisher, W.M., Fiscus, J.G., Pallett, D.S., Dahlgren, N.L.: DARPA TIMIT acoustic-phonetic continuous speech corpus. U.S. Dept. of Commerce, NIST, Gaithersburg, MD (1993).
4. Magrin-Chagnolleau, I., Parlangeau-Vallès, N.: Audio indexing: what has been accomplished and the road ahead. In: Proceedings of Joint Conference on Information Sciences, (JCIS 2002). Durham, North Carolina (2002) 911-914.
5. Mihelič F., et al.: Spoken language resources at LUKS of the University of Ljubljana. International Journal of Speech Technology 6(3) (2003) 221–232.
6. Picone, J.W.: Signal modeling techniques in speech recognition. Proceedings of the IEEE 81(9) (1993) 1215–1247.
7. Reynolds, D.A., et al.: Beyond Cepstra: Exploiting High-Level Information in Speaker Recognition. In: Proceedings of the Workshop on Multimodal User Authentication, Santa Barbara, California (2003) 223–229.
8. Reynolds, D.A, Torres-Carrasquillo, P.A.: Approaches and Applications of Audio Diarization. In: Proceedings of the International Conference on Acoustics, Speech, and Signal Processing (ICASSP2005), Philadelphia, USA (2005).
9. Shafran, I., Rose, R.:Robust speech detection and segmentation for real-time ASR applications. In: International Conference on Acoustics, Speech, and Signal Processing (ICASSP2003), Hong Kong (2003)432–435.
10. Siegler, M., Jain, U., Raj, B., Stern, R.: Automatic Segmentation, Classification and Clustering of Broadcast News Data. In: Proceedings of the DARPA Speech Recognition Workshop, Chantilly, VA, USA (1997) 97–99.
11. Williams, G., Ellis, D.P.W.: Speech/music discrimination based on posterior probabilities. In: Proceedings of ES 99, Vol. 2, Budapest, Hungary (1999) 687–690.
12. Žibert, J., F. Mihelič, F.: Development of Slovenian Broadcast News Speech Database. In: Proceedings of the International Conference on Language Resources and Evaluation (LREC 2004), Lisbon, Portugal (2004) 2095–2098.
13. Žibert J., et al., The COST278 Broadcast News Segmentation and Speaker Clustering Evaluation - Overview, Methodology, Systems, Results. In: Proceedings of Interspeech 2005, Lisbon, Portugal (2005) 629–632.

Composite Decision by Bayesian Inference in Distant-Talking Speech Recognition

Mikyong Ji, Sungtak Kim, and Hoirin Kim

SRT Lab., Information and Communications University
119, Munjiro, Yuseong-gu, Daejeon, 305-732, Korea
{lindaji, stkim, hrkim}@icu.ac.kr

Abstract. This paper describes an integrated system to produce a composite recognition output on distant-talking speech when the recognition results from multiple microphone inputs are available. In many cases, the composite recognition result has lower error rate than any other individual output. In this work, the composite recognition result is obtained by applying Bayesian inference. The log likelihood score is assumed to follow a Gaussian distribution, at least approximately. First, the distribution of the likelihood score is estimated in the development set. Then, the confidence interval for the likelihood score is used to remove unreliable microphone channels. Finally, the area under the distribution between the likelihood score of a hypothesis and that of the $(N+1)^{st}$ hypothesis is obtained for every channel and integrated for all channels by Bayesian inference. The proposed system shows considerable performance improvement compared with the result using an ordinary method by the summation of likelihoods as well as any of the recognition results of the channels.

1 Introduction

The state-of-the-art speech recognizers can achieve high recognition accuracy when close-talking microphones are used. However, in distant-talking environments, the performance is significantly degraded due to a variety of causes such as the distance between the sound source and the microphone, the position of the microphone, the direction of the speaker, the quality of the microphone, etc.

To cope with these problems, microphone array-based speech recognizers have been widely applied to improve not only the quality of the speech but also the recognition performance [1,2,3]. The simplest beamforming processing using the delay-and-sum principle has been successfully used. However, it is difficult to estimate time-delay accurately in noisy and reverberant environments [4]. While the use of the microphone array can capture only one-directional acoustic information, the use of the spatially distributed multiple microphones can capture spatial acoustic information in a room [5]. In addition, the latter makes the arrangement of microphones in a room easier than the former.

In this paper, we propose methods to improve the performance of the distant-talking speech recognition by producing a composite decision from the recognition results with multiple microphones. In the work, the distribution of the likelihood score is assumed to be a Gaussian density function. Its distribution is estimated, the confidence interval for the likelihood score is found to extract unreliable results, and the area under the distribution

Petr Sojka, Ivan Kopeček and Karel Pala (Eds.): TSD 2006, LNAI 4188, pp. 463–470, 2006.

between the likelihood score of the hypothesis and that of the $(N + 1)^{st}$ hypothesis is computed per channel. Eventually, it is merged into a composite result by Bayesian inference.

The remainder of the paper is organized as follows. In Section 2, we introduce methods to combine the recognition results by simultaneously recorded speech inputs into a composite one, and Section 3 describes the experimental results and the performance evaluation. Finally, we conclude and describe future works in Section 5.

2   Integration by Bayesian Inference

Speech inputs recorded simultaneously through two or more microphones are separately recognized per recognizer and their results are combined into the best scoring hypothesis by the integration module in Fig. 1. Given the speech inputs, $X_1, X_2, \ldots, X_C$ obtained by multiple microphones, the best hypothesis should be chosen to maximize $P(W|X_1, X_2, \ldots, X_C)$. If we assume that the speech inputs from different channels are conditionally independent given a hypothesis and each hypothesis has an equal prior probability $P(W) = 1$, this can be further simplified by Bayesian inference as

$$\overline{W} = \arg\max_{W} p(W|X_1, X_2, \cdots, X_C) = \arg\max_{W} \prod_{i=1}^{C} p(X_i|W) \qquad (1)$$

where C is the number of microphones.

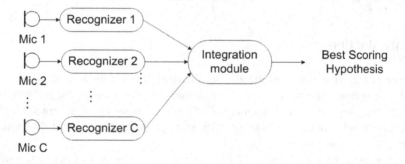

Fig. 1. System architecture

The relation between the best hypothesis and the multiple speech inputs is described into a Bayesian network shown in Fig. 2.

2.1   Integration by Likelihoods

If we take the logarithm of Eq. (1), which is simplified by Bayesian inference, the equation is represented as follows:

$$\overline{W} = \arg\max_{W} \sum_{i=1}^{C} \log p(X_i|W). \qquad (2)$$

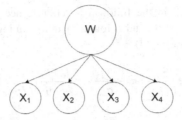

Fig. 2. Bayesian Network

The best hypothesis can be determined by the sum of the log likelihoods whose hypotheses are the same among the recognition results by multiple channels. That is, the best rescoring hypothesis is identified as a composite recognition result.

2.2 Reliable Channel Selection by Confidence Interval

The result of measurements is often accompanied by a confidence interval to determine an interval that has a high probability of containing the true value [6,7]. Thus, if we say we are $(1-\alpha) \bullet 100\%$ confident between $-l_0$ and l_0 for the parameter l, it is described by

$$P(-l_o < l < l_o) = 1 - 2\alpha \qquad (3)$$

where α is a number between 0 and 1. In other words, there is only an $\alpha\%$ chance that l will be less than $-l_0$ and an $\alpha\%$ chance that will be larger than l_0. In this paper, the confidence interval for the log likelihood score of the hypothesis, $\log p(W|X_c)$ is computed. The lower limit is employed to remove an unreliable channel of which the likelihood of the best hypothesis lies under the upper tail area in Fig. 3.

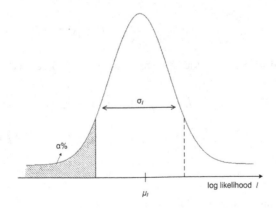

Fig. 3. Confidence interval

The log likelihood score $log\ p(W|X_c)$ is assumed to follow a Gaussian distribution with mean μ_l and variance σ_l^2. Afterwards, the distribution is estimated. The detail about the estimation will be described in the following section. Since there is no closed form to integrate the Gaussian PDF, the bound is found by transforming into the standard Gaussian function and using its table in Eq. (4).

$$P\left(\frac{-l_o - \mu_l}{\sigma_l} < \frac{l - \mu_l}{\sigma_l} < \frac{l_o - \mu_l}{\sigma_l}\right) = 1 - 2\alpha. \tag{4}$$

2.3 Integration Using Area Under Density Curve Between Hypotheses' Scores

We assume that the log likelihood score l follows a Gaussian distribution and the conditional observation distribution of $l|\mu$ is Gaussian with mean μ and variance σ^2, which is assumed known. Then, its density is as follows:

$$p(l|\mu) \propto e^{-\frac{1}{2\sigma^2}(l-\mu)^2}. \tag{5}$$

The part that doesn't depend on the parameter μ is the same for all parameter values; if we ignore the constant of proportionality, it can be represented by Eq. (5). Suppose that the prior probability for the parameter μ is a flat prior density ($f(\mu) = 1$). The shape of the posterior for μ is given by

$$p(\mu|l) \propto p(\mu) \cdot p(l|\mu) \propto e^{-\frac{1}{2\sigma^2}(\mu-l)^2}. \tag{6}$$

On the other hand, if we have the Gaussian distribution with mean m and variance s^2 for μ, the shape of the posterior is

$$p(\mu|l) \propto e^{-\frac{1}{2\sigma^2 s^2/(\sigma^2+s^2)}\left(\mu - \frac{(\sigma^2 m + s^2 l)}{\sigma^2 + s^2}\right)^2}. \tag{7}$$

The update of the PDF of μ can be simplified by Eq. (8).

$$m' = \frac{\sigma^2}{\sigma^2 + s^2} \times m + \frac{s^2}{\sigma^2 + s^2} \times l, \quad (s')^2 = \frac{\sigma^2 s^2}{\sigma^2 + s^2}. \tag{8}$$

Consequently, the distribution for the next observation l_{n+1} is described by

$$p(l_{n+1}|l_1, l_2, \cdots, l_n) = \int p(l_{n+1}, \mu|l_1, l_2, \cdots, l_n) d\mu$$

$$= \int p(l_{n+1}|\mu) \times p(\mu|l_1, l_2, \cdots, l_n) d\mu \tag{9}$$

$$\propto e^{-\frac{1}{2(\sigma^2 + s_n^2)}(l_{n+1} - m_n)^2}$$

where we are ignoring the part that does not involve μ.

$$p(l) \propto e^{-\frac{1}{2(\sigma^2 + s^2)}(l-m)^2}. \tag{10}$$

Instead of using the log likelihood score of the hypothesis itself from the recognition result directly as in Section 2.1, the proposed method estimates the distribution of the likelihood score, $p(l)$ and the area under the distribution between the log likelihood score of the hypothesis and the $(N + 1)^{st}$ hypothesis is computed in Eq. (11).

$$A^c(W) = P(L^c(W^{N+1}) < l < L^c(W)) = \int\limits_{L(W^{N+1})}^{L(W)} p(l)dl \qquad (11)$$

where l is the log likelihood score, W^{N+1} is the $(N + 1)^{st}$ hypothesis in the N-best list, $L^c(W^{N+1})$ is the log likelihood score of the $(N + 1)^{st}$ hypothesis given the speech input by microphone c, X_c, and $p(l)$ is the PDF of the likelihood score. That is, the area under the distribution between the log likelihood score of a hypothesis and that of the $(N + 1)^{st}$ hypothesis is computed per channel input and it is integrated into Bayesian inference introduced in Eq. (1). The composite result is decided by Eq. (12).

$$\overline{W} = \arg\max_W \sum_{c=1}^C A^c(W). \qquad (12)$$

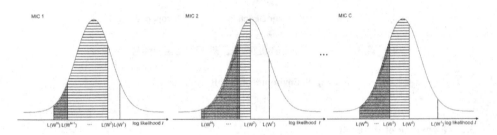

Fig. 4. Area under the distribution between the log likelihood of each hypothesis and that of the $(N + 1)^{st}$ hypothesis for each microphone input

3   Experiments

3.1   Experimental Setup

For the experiments, we use Korean POW (phonetically optimized word) 3848 database. It consists of 3848 different words which are divided to 8 sub-sets and each speaker uttered one of 8 sub-sets. The total number of speakers is 80 (40 males and 40 females). To show the effectiveness of the proposed system, only 268 words among the database are selected. As shown in Fig. 5, the selected 268 words are recorded again by using a loudspeaker at 5 positions marked in a room where four microphones are installed at the four corners to face its center. The speech inputs through four microphones were sampled by 16 KHz. Also, the five kinds of music without vocal sound were recorded by four channels in the same environment in Fig. 5 and added per channel to make noisy database.

We use MFCCs, their corresponding delta and acceleration coefficients as the feature vectors. A pre-emphasis filter $H(z) = 1 - 0.97z^{-1}$ is used before framing and each frame is multiplied with a 20 ms Hamming window, shifted by 10 ms.

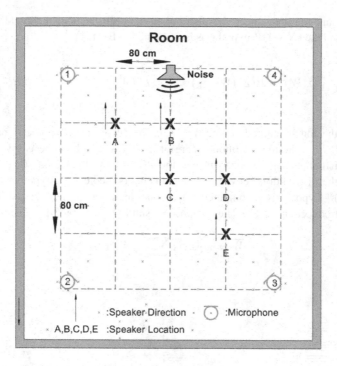

Fig. 5. Environment of DB Collection

3.2   Experimental Results

For performance comparison, we applied four different integration methods to multiple recognition results: integration by the magnitude of the likelihood (ML), by the summation of the likelihoods (BN_L), by the area under the likelihood density curve (BN_D), and by applying a confidence interval in order to remove unreliable channels ahead of the BN_D (BN_DC). Table 1 shows the baseline recognition results by the speech inputs through four multiple microphones. Table 2 and 3 represent the recognition results per location and they are followed by four different composite recognition results. Table 4 describes the error reduction rate (ERR) of BI_DC over other integration methods. ORACLE is the maximum reachable word accuracy. It describes whether the correct word is included in the N-best lists for integration.

Table 1. Recognition accuracy of the baseline system (%)

CH SNR	MIC1	MIC2	MIC3	MIC4
Clean	88.35	73.57	83.86	89.67
10 dB	81.49	83.33	82.28	82.33
5 dB	60.08	66.98	66.19	61.89
0 dB	22.72	32.40	30.63	23.98

As shown in the experimental results, the composite recognition result is improved compared with an individual output by each microphone. The performance improvement was significant when the integration by the area under the likelihood density curve was applied and it was applied after removing unreliable channels with a confidence interval even more. As N got increased, the Word Error Rate was decreased by only small amount.

Table 2. Performance comparison of integration methods (Clean, N=1, %)

LOC CH	LOCA	LOCB	LOCC	LOCD	LOCE	AVG
MIC1	89.29	88.81	91.59	85.85	86.23	88.35
MIC2	73.23	66.63	86.52	70.27	71.22	73.57
MIC3	77.34	84.03	85.18	86.42	86.33	83.86
MIC4	86.71	90.44	91.11	91.59	88.53	89.67
ML	85.47	87.28	88.24	90.25	88.81	88.01
BI_L	87.28	89.01	91.87	89.58	88.43	89.23
BI_D	90.25	90.73	91.40	91.30	91.01	90.94
BI_DC	90.44	90.73	91.40	91.59	91.11	91.05
ORACLE	95.89	95.89	96.85	96.37	95.79	96.16

Table 3. Performance comparison of integration methods (Music noise 5 dB, N=1, %)

LOC CH	LOCA	LOCB	LOCC	LOCD	LOCE	AVG
MIC1	64.05	56.50	62.43	59.18	58.22	60.08
MIC2	72.08	64.44	69.02	66.06	63.29	66.98
MIC3	69.50	63.67	68.45	65.87	63.48	66.19
MIC4	66.44	59.75	62.43	61.66	59.18	61.89
ML	72.47	63.96	68.64	65.68	64.63	67.08
BI_L	71.89	65.49	68.36	66.54	64.15	67.29
BI_D	74.19	67.50	71.32	67.78	65.68	69.29
BI_DC	74.67	67.69	71.70	67.88	65.58	69.50
ORACLE	82.03	77.06	80.50	77.25	76.00	78.57

Table 4. ERR of BI_DC over other integration methods (%)

Method SNR	Best Channel	ML	BI_L	BI_D
Clean	21.26	37.30	26.26	2.11
10 dB	16.07	6.85	12.13	1.32
5 dB	21.74	21.06	19.59	2.26
0 dB	-1.30	22.01	16.38	1.27

4   Conclusion

The integrated system to produce a composite speech recognition output has been proposed and it is shown that the integration of the recognition results from spatially distributed microphones is effective in distant-talking speech recognition. After we assume that the likelihood score follows a Gaussian distribution, the area under the distribution between hypotheses is computed and combined into the best scoring hypothesis. When this proposed method is applied after removing unreliable channels, the best performance is achieved. However, the distribution of the likelihood score should be estimated in advance; it is still useful from the viewpoint that it can greatly contribute to the performance improvement in distant-talking speech recognition to realize hands-free applications.

In this paper, we considered one-directional noise source, and restricted the number of distributed microphones to four. Thus, diverse experiments are required to confirm the effectiveness of our system.

References

1. Hughes, T. B., Kim, H., Dibiase, J. H., Silverman, H. F.: Using A Real-Time, Tracking Microphone Array as Input to an HMM Speech Recognize. Proc. of ICASSP, Vol. 1. (1998) 249–252.
2. Yamada, T., Makamura, S., Shikano, K.: Hands-free Speech Recognition with Talker Localization by a Microphone Array. Trans. of Information Processing Society of Japan, Vol. 39. No. 5. (1998) 1275–1284.
3. Takiguchi, T., Nakamura, S., Shikano, K.: HMM-Seperation Based Speech Recognition for a Distant Moving Speaker. IEEE Trans. on Speech and Audio Processing, Vol. 9. No. 2. (2001) 127–140.
4. Yamada, T., Nakamura, S., Shikano, K.: Distant-Talking Speech Recognition Based on a 3-D Viterbi Search Using a Microphone Array. Trans. on Speech and Audio Processing, Vol. 10. No. 2. (2002) 48–56.
5. Shimizu, Y., Kajita, S., Takeda, K., Itakura, F.: Speech Recognition Based on Space Diversity Using Distributed Multi-Microphone. Proc. of ICASSP, Vol. 3. (2000) 1747–1750.
6. Bolstad, W. M.: Introduction to Bayesian Statistics. John Wiley & Sons, Hoboken New Jersey (2004).
7. Neapolitan, R. E.: Learning Bayesian Networks. 2nd edn. Pearson Prentice Hall, Upper Saddle River New Jersey (2004).

Speech Coding Based on Spectral Dynamics

Petr Motlíček[1,2], Hynek Hermansky[1,2,3],
Harinath Garudadri[4], and Naveen Srinivasamurthy[4]

[1] IDIAP Research Institute
Rue du Simplon 4, CH-1920, Martigny, Switzerland
motlicek@idiap.ch, hynek@idiap.ch
[2] Faculty of Information Technology, Brno University of Technology,
Božetěchova 2, Brno, 612 66, Czech Republic
[3] École Polytechnique Fédérale de Lausanne (EPFL), Switzerland
[4] Qualcomm Inc., San Diego, California, USA
{hgarudad, naveens}@qualcomm.com

Abstract. In this paper we present first experimental results with a novel audio coding technique based on approximating Hilbert envelopes of relatively long segments of audio signal in critical-band-sized sub-bands by autoregressive model. We exploit the generalized autocorrelation linear predictive technique that allows for a better control of fitting the peaks and troughs of the envelope in the sub-band. Despite introducing longer algorithmic delay, improved coding efficiency is achieved. Since the described technique does not directly model short-term spectral envelopes of the signal, it is suitable not only for coding speech but also for coding of other audio signals.

1 Introduction

Intelligibility of the coded speech depends on proper estimation of parameters related to the short-term spectral envelope. Due to inertia of the air-mass in vocal tract cavities, the speech spectral envelope is relatively smooth and the speech signal is short-term predictable. This is used with advantage in techniques such as Linear Prediction (LP) and most of current speech coding techniques employ LP that approximates the envelope of the short-term power spectrum of speech by a spectrum of an all-pole (autoregressive) model. The LP-based speech coding techniques rely on the source-filter model of speech production and usually fail for any other kind of audio signals (several speakers, music, speech with some background, . . .). See e.g., [1] for an excellent and comprehensive review.

Classical speech analysis techniques assume short-term signal stationarity. The input signal is divided into short-term frames (10–30 ms), each containing relatively stationary signal and each being processed independently by techniques such as LP that yield vectors of short-term features. Speech dynamics is represented by a sequence of these vectors, each vector representing a particular configuration of the vocal tract.

However, vocal organs and their neural control mechanism have their own inertia too and subsequently the evolution of vocal tract shapes is also largely predictable. Thus, in terms of efficiency, it might be desirable to capitalize on this predictability and to encode longer temporal context (several hundreds of milliseconds) rather than processing every (10–30 ms) temporal vectors independently. This is supported by recently reported efficiency of a

Petr Sojka, Ivan Kopeček and Karel Pala (Eds.): TSD 2006, LNAI 4188, pp. 471–478, 2006.

new generation of modulation spectrum based audio coding techniques [2]. While such an approach obviously introduces longer algorithmic delays, the efficiency gained may justify its deployment in many evolving communications applications.

In this paper, we introduce a new audio coding technique that employs autoregressive modeling applied for approximating the instantaneous energy (Hilbert envelope) of critical-band sized sub-band signals. Unlike in [2], much longer temporal segments (around 1000 ms) are processed at a time. We also propose several initial attempts for proper reconstruction of the audio signal from such encoded Hilbert envelopes.

2   Encoding

2.1   Frequency Domain Linear Prediction

Hilbert envelope (squared magnitude of an analytic signal) can be parameterized by Frequency Domain Linear Prediction (FDLP) [3] that represents frequency-domain analogue of the well-known time-domain Linear Prediction (LP) [4]. Just as LP fits an all-pole model to the power spectrum of the input signal, FDLP fits an all-pole model to the squared Hilbert envelope of the signal.

To get an all-pole approximation of the Hilbert envelope, first the Discrete Cosine Transform (DCT) is applied to a given audio segment. Next, the autocorrelation LP technique is applied to the DCT transformed signal. The Fourier transform of the impulse response of the resulting all-pole model approximates the Hilbert envelope of the signal. The whole technique of deriving all-pole models of sub-band Hilbert envelopes is similar to the technique applied in [3].

2.2   Derivation of Parameters of Temporal Envelopes in Frequency Sub-bands

In the proposed coding technique, the signal is divided into 1000ms long non-overlapping temporal segments which are transformed by DCT into the frequency domain, and later processed independently. FDLP technique is applied to every sub-segment of the DCT transformed signal that represent the frequency range of the sub-band. We get the approximations of Hilbert envelopes in sub-bands.

N_{BANDs} Gaussian functions (N_{BANDs} denotes number of frequency sub-bands) equally spaced on the Bark scale, with standard deviation $\sigma = 1$bark, are projected on the linear (Hertz) frequency scale and used as weighting windows on the DCT transformed signal. Therefore, the weighting windows are asymmetric and their width and spacing increases with frequency. The Bark scale from Perceptual Linear Prediction (PLP) analysis [5] is applied.

FDLP applied on each sub-segment from windowed DCT segment yields the approximation of the sub-band Hilbert envelope. The order of the all-pole model that in the case of FDLP controls temporal resolution of the technique depends on the length of the processed signal frame and is chosen experimentally. A graphical representation of the whole technique is given in Fig. 1.

2.3   Spectral Transform Linear Prediction

Well-known properties of LP that would normally apply to power spectra of the signal (such as better fitting of peaks than dips) apply in the case of FDLP to Hilbert envelopes. In order

CODER:

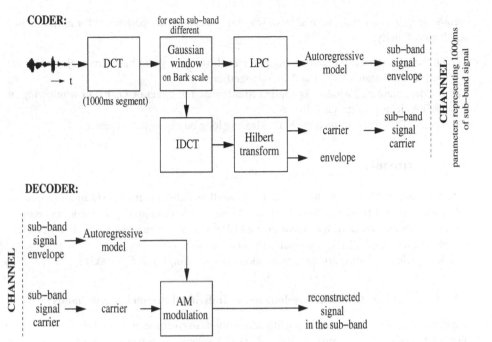

Fig. 1. Graphical scheme of the whole technique for one frequency sub-band

to control the balance between modeling peaks and dips of the envelope, Spectral Transform Linear Prediction (STLP) technique [6] is used.

3   Decoding

FDLP approximates squared Hilbert envelope of the sub-banded temporal trajectory $x_k(t)$ (k determines the sub-band, t is time variable). Estimated Hilbert envelope $a_k(t)$ yields information about modulation of the signal in the particular sub-band. To reconstruct the signal, an additional component, the carrier $c_k(t)$, is required. This carrier is then modulated by the estimated envelope (see e.g., [7] for mathematical explanation).

$a_k(t)$ is approximated by FDLP and described by parameters of the resulting all-pole model. We have so far no explicit method to parameterize $c_k(t)$. However, some attempts for its efficient coding are discussed later in this paper.

3.1   Decoder

A general scheme of the decoder, also given in Fig. 1, is relatively simple and follows backwards the steps performed on the encoder. The decoding operation is also applied on each (1000ms long) input segment independently.

First, the signal $c_k(t)$ that represents Hilbert carrier is generated. The temporal envelope $a_k(t)$ is created from transmitted all-pole model coefficients. Temporal trajectory $x_k(t)$ is created so that $c_k(t)$ is modulated by $a_k(t)$. All these steps are performed for all frequency sub-bands. Finally:

1. Obtained temporal trajectories $x_k(t)$ for each frequency sub-band are projected to the frequency domain by DCT and added together.
2. A "de-weighting" window is applied to alleviate the effect of Gaussian windowing of DCT trajectory in the encoder.
3. Inverse DCT is performed to obtain 1000ms long output signal (segment).

4   Experiments

When the original temporal envelope $a_k(t)$ as well as Hilbert carrier $c_k(t)$ in all frequency sub-bands are fully preserved, the encoding scheme described in previous sections is lossless. This is analogous to classical residual-excited LP vocoder, where using the unmodified error signal for excitation of LP system yields the original signal.

All experiments were performed with audio signals sampled at $F_s = 8$kHz.

4.1   Representing Temporal Envelope in the Individual Frequency Sub-bands

We chose $N_{BANDs} = 15$ which roughly corresponds to partition of one sub-band per 1bark. The FDLP estimated Hilbert envelope of each frequency sub-band is described by Line Spectral Frequencies (LSFs). The order of the all-pole models (the same for all sub-bands) was found by informal listening experiments. For coding the 1000ms long audio segments, the order of the model was set to $N_{LSFs} = 20$. We have used scalar quantization with $N_{BITs} = 4$ bits per LSF, which seems to be sufficient (quantization noise is not audible).

When using conventional autocorrelation all-pole method for deriving the FDLP all-pole models, the Hilbert envelope peaks seem overemphasized and the decoded signal sounds reverberant. This is especially true when low model order is used. STLP can de-emphasize the peaks and thus significantly reduces this reverberation. In our experiments, we use STLP compression factor $r = 0.1$.

4.2   Decoding

In order to reconstruct an input audio signal in the decoder, we need to restore the carrier $c_k(t)$ in each frequency sub-band and to modulate this carrier by the envelope estimated using FDLP. In the first experiments we were dealing with rather effortless approaches producing output signal of *synthetic* quality on very low bit-rates.

1. Generating unvoiced speech: In the simplest approach, the carrier $c_k(t)$ can be substituted by a band-passed white noise. The applied band-pass represents frequency response of the Gaussian window that was applied in the analysis. Since we do not use (and therefore do not need to transmit) any information about the original $c_k(t)$, the bit-rate of the transmission R is given only by the rate necessary for the transmission of the quantized all-pole models. The resulting signal sounds obviously unvoiced (whispered) but is clearly intelligible.

2. Generating voiced speech: First, we have experimented with spectral components located at the frequencies that are integral multiples of some fixed fundamental frequency $F0$.

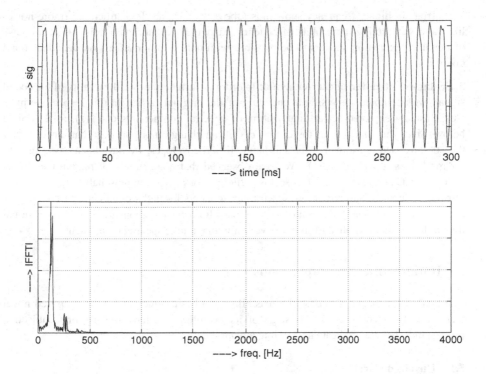

Fig. 2. Temporal trajectory and its spectral representation of $c_k(t)$ for $k = 2$. The frequency of the strongest spectral component is about 112Hz, which corresponds to the center bin of the 2nd sub-band.

However, as shown in Fig. 2, for voiced signal segments, especially in lower frequency bands, the carrier signal $c_k(t)$ appears to be well structured. Magnitude spectrum of Fourier Transform (FT) of $c_k(t)$ typically contains one dominant spectral component located close to the central frequency of the corresponding sub-band. Therefore, in order to introduce some voiced quality into the reconstructed signal, we tried to substitute $c_k(t)$ by a cosine with the corresponding frequency.

Another (computationally more expensive) approach is to estimate several additional strong spectral components using a "peak-picking" algorithm and to transmit just the corresponding frequencies to regenerate $c_k(t)$ in the decoder.

Subjectively, all these approaches introduce some voicing quality into the resulting audio signal, however, the reconstructed signal sounds quite unnatural and machine-like, similar to buzzy character of speech coded by a simple fixed-pulse excited vocoder without any voicing decision. However, the decoded speech appears clearly intelligible.

Finally, we have informally observed that a simple but possibly sufficient voice detector can be built on peaks and troughs of temporal envelope $x_k(t)$ in any of the low frequency sub-bands (up to $k = 5$). Since the voiced speech segments typically have dominant spectral energy concentration at lower frequencies, peaks of the envelope in lower sub-bands indicate voicing. Informal experiments with mixed excitation based on this criterion appear promising for improving the coded speech quality.

Carriers in higher frequency sub-bands (above $k = 5$) are less structured (more noise-like) and substituting these higher-frequency carriers by a band-pass noise as in the case of unvoiced excitation appears to be possible with only a minor effects on decoded signal quality.

3. Scalar quantization of carrier signal: In order to further improve the quality of the coded signal, we attempted some simple encoding of the original carrier. In this respect we have so far mainly explored scalar quantization of spectral components of $c_k(t)$, as described below. Since the character of the carrier $c_k(t)$ can change more quickly than once during the 1000ms used in estimating the sub-band Hilbert envelopes, we have been working with 200ms long segments of $c_k(t)$. We have observed that quantization of magnitudes by as little as 2 bits and phases by 3 bits seems sufficient for preserving reasonable signal quality. Further, it appears that only a few spectral components located around center frequency of corresponding frequency sub-bands are necessary for a carrier reconstruction. Yet additional thresholding can be applied to suppress very low magnitude spectral components.

5   Initial Subjective Impressions

The goal of this paper is to describe feasibility and basic principles of the proposed novel technique. However, even at this stage of its evolution, we have already first subjective impressions that may indicate its possible advantages.

5.1   Unvoiced Carrier

First experiments were aimed at finding proper approximations of temporal envelopes $a_k(t)$ by FDLP and thus we used only random noise carriers. The sufficient intelligibility was achieved at bit-rates $R = 1.2$kbps (with parameters $N_{BANDs} = 15, N_{LSFs} = 20, N_{BITs} = 4$). The algorithm provides subjectively much more natural signal than LPC10 standard with only noise excitation at the bit-rate around 2.1kbps. Although the reconstructed signal sounds whispered, it is clearly intelligible. Therefore, we applied this parameterization of temporal envelopes in all subsequent experiments focused on parameterization of the carrier $c_k(t)$.

In addition, other informal experiments indicate that preserving as few as 5 important frequency sub-bands seem not to degrade an intelligibility of reconstructed speech. This means that bit-rates around 400bps are achievable.

5.2   Voiced Carrier

Fixed-frequency carrier: The same bit rate of $R = 1.2$kbps can be obtained when $c_k(t)$ is substituted by cosine signal with frequency equal to center bin of corresponding sub-band. This substitution is suitable for fully voiced audio segments. Then magnitude spectra of $c_k(t)$ especially for low frequency bands contain one strong spectral component. The reconstructed signal is well audible but contains strong tonal artifacts.

Estimating frequencies of the carrier: Simple "peak-picking" algorithm performed on top of spectral magnitudes can reduce these artifacts. Subjectively the best results were achieved with scalar quantization of spectral components of $c_k(t)$. Then, especially periodic audio signals (e.g., music) can be encoded into few kbps (around 5kbps), preserving good quality.

Mixed carrier: Reconstructed signal can be noticeably improved when combining the two source-models together.

6 Discussion and Conclusions

This paper describes first experiments with novel audio codec based on spectral dynamics. Although the algorithm introduces rather large algorithmic delays, we believe the technique can find many possible applications.

Here, we have described only preliminary experiments focused mainly on the approximation of temporal envelopes and proposed simple methods how to encode the carrier.

Among possible advantages of this coding technique compared to classical state-of-the art methods based on short-term frames belongs:

- Exploiting predictability of temporal evolution of spectral envelopes of speech spectra allows for efficient transmission and/or storage of intelligible speech.
- The technique is based on independent processing of individual frequency sub-bands. It is therefore inherently suitable for exploiting non-equal frequency resolution of human hearing.
- The technique is not directly based on source-filter model of speech production, thus it is also potentially suitable for coding of non-speech sounds.
- The well structured character of the sub-band carrier signals (discussed in Section 4.2) suggests a potential for its efficient coding, thus allowing for encoding of high-quality audio. Some simple carrier coding schemes have been discussed in this paper, other are a topic of our current interest.
- Though not extensively discussed in this paper, it is straightforward to control the algorithmic delay, the quality of reconstructed sound, the resiliency to drop-outs, and the final bit-rate, making the codec suitable for variable bandwidth channels.
- The reconstruction is based on linear addition of contributions from different frequency sub-bands. Possible loss of data (e.g., due to drop-outs in the transmission) may merely mean loss of data from some sub-bands and some change in the signal quality but does not significantly affect signal intelligibility.

Acknowledgments

This work was partially supported by grant from ICSI Berkeley, USA. It was also carried out in the framework of the Swiss National Center of Competence in Research (NCCR) on "Interactive Multi-modal Information Management (IM)2" as well as DARPA through the "EARS (Effective, Affordable, Reusable Speech-to-Text)" project.

References

1. A. S. Spanias. "Speech Coding: A Tutorial Review", *in Proc. of IEEE*, Vol. 82, No. 10, October 1994.
2. M. S. Vinton, L. E. Atlas. "A scalable and progressive audio codec", *in Proc. of ICASSP*, Vol. 5, pp. 3277–3280, Salt Lake City, USA, May 2001.

3. M. Athineos, H. Hermansky, D. P. W. Ellis. "LP-TRAP: Linear predictive temporal patterns", *in Proc. of ICSLP*, pp. 1154–1157, Jeju, S. Korea, October 2004.
4. J. Makhoul. "Linear Prediction: A Tutorial Review", *in Proc. of IEEE*, Vol. 63, No. 4, April 1975.
5. H. Hermansky. "Perceptual linear predictive (PLP) analysis for speech", *J. Acoust. Soc. Am.*, pp. 1738–1752, 1990.
6. H. Hermansky, H. Fujisaki, Y. Sato. "Analysis and Synthesis of Speech based on Spectral Transform Linear Predictive Method", *in Proc. of ICASSP*, Vol. 8, pp. 777–780, Boston, USA, April 1983.
7. S. Schimmel, L. Atlas. "Coherent Envelope Detector for Modulation Filtering of Speech", *in Proc. of ICASSP*, Vol. 1, pp. 221–224, Philadelphia, USA, May 2005.

Detecting Broad Phonemic Class Boundaries
from Greek Speech in Noise Environments

Iosif Mporas, Panagiotis Zervas, and Nikos Fakotakis

Wire Communications Laboratory, Electrical and Computer Engineering Department
University of Patras, 261 10 Rion, Patras, Greece
Tel: +30 2610 997336; Fax: +30 2610 997336
{imporas, pzervas, fakotaki}@wcl.ee.upatras.gr

Abstract. In this work, we present the performance evaluation of an implicit approach
for the automatic segmentation of continuous speech signals into broad phonemic
classes as encountered in Greek language. Our framework was evaluated with clear
speech and speech with white, pink, bubble, car and machine gun additive noise.
Our framework's results were very promising since an accuracy of 76.1% was
achieved for the case of clear speech (for distances less than 25 msec to the actual
segmentation point), without presenting over-segmentation on the speech signal. An
average reduction of 4% in the total accuracy of our segmentation framework was
observed in the case of wideband distortion additive noise environment.

1 Introduction

Annotation of speech signals to phoneme, diphone or syllable-like level is essential for tasks
such as, speech recognition [1], construction of language identification models [2], prosodic
database annotation, and in speech synthesis assignments such as formant and unit selection
techniques [3]. Since, segmentation of speech signals is a time-consuming and tedious
task which can be carried out only by expert phoneticians, several automated procedures
have been proposed. Speech segmentation methodologies can be classified into two major
categories depending on whether we possess or not knowledge of the uttered message.
These categories are known as explicit and implicit segmentation methods [4], respectively.
Regarding explicit approaches, the speech waveform is aligned with the corresponding
phonetic transcription. On the other hand, in implicit approaches the phoneme boundary
locations are detected without any textual knowledge of the uttered message. Although
explicit approaches achieve better accuracy than implicit, the requirement of prior phoneme
sequence knowledge makes them inappropriate for real life applications, such as language
identification tasks.

In the area of automatic speech segmentation extensive research has been conducted.
Aversano et al. [5], proposed a segmentation method based on the critical-band perceptual
analysis of preprocessed speech that fed a decision function and reported an accuracy of
73,58% within a range of ± 20 msec. Suh and Lee [6], proposed a structure, based on multi-
layer perceptron and reported a 15msec phoneme segmentation performance of 87% with
3,4% insertion rate in speaker dependent mode. Svendsen and Kvale [7] proposed a two-stage
boundary detection approach consisted of an acoustic segmentation of speech followed by an

Petr Sojka, Ivan Kopeček and Karel Pala (Eds.): TSD 2006, LNAI 4188, pp. 479–484, 2006.

HMM based phonemic segmentation, and reported an accuracy of 80-85% for four languages and a range of 20 msec. Svendsen and Soong [8] presented an accuracy of 73% within three frames, based on a constrained-clustering vector quantization approach. Grayden and Scordilis [9] proposed a Bayesian decision surface for dividing speech into distinct obstruent and sonorant regions and applied to each of them specific rules; an 80% of accuracy was reported with an insertion rate of 12%. In [10] Essa proposed an approach taking advantage of the visual clues at each pitch period for the detection of the voiced phoneme boundaries. In conclusion, Pellom and Hansen [11] evaluate an HMM based explicit segmentation approach in a variety of additive noise environments. Since most real life applications operate in noise environments we focus in the evaluation of our implicit, pitch-synchronous method of detecting broad phonemic class boundaries from speech signals with additive noise.

In this paper, we present results for the task of automatic speech segmentation to broad phonemic classes in additive noise environments. In section 2 we describe the utilized method at length and we present the speech data used for the evaluation. Finally in section 3, the evaluation results are presented and discussed.

2   Method Description and Speech Corpora

Our method depends on the hypothesis that the voiced parts of a speech signal are composed of periodic fragments produced by the glottis during vocal-fold vibration [12], so since the articulation characteristics are almost constant in the middle of a voiced segment, each of these fragments will differ from its adjacent ones at the co-articulation regions. The above contemplation leads to segmentation of the speech waveform to voiced phoneme segments and unvoiced intervals. Since in Greek language each unvoiced interval consists of one or two phonemes [13], the unvoiced phoneme sequence can be recognized by using a language model adapted on the adjacent recognized by the acoustic model voiced phonemes, in order to extract the corresponding phoneme sequence, as illustrated in Figure 1.

For this purpose, we initially segment the speech signal into voiced and unvoiced intervals, using Boersma's algorithm [14]. This method uses the short-term autocorrelation function r_x of the speech signal:

$$r_x(\tau) \quad \equiv \int x(t)x(t+\tau)dt \tag{1}$$

The pitch is determined as the inverted value of τ corresponding to the highest of r_x. Threshold values for silence, voiced and unvoiced detection are introduced in order to extract the corresponding intervals. After distinguishing voiced and unvoiced regions, voiced speech is segmented to fragments determined by the pitchmarks location. Subsequently, a moving average smoothing is applied to each fragment for the task of abrupt local irregularities reduction. Ultimately, we utilize an evaluation algorithm for the measurement of the distance between adjacent smoothed fragments. In that way we detect the co-articulation points, which correspond to the voiced phoneme boundaries.

For the extraction of pitchmarks we used the point process algorithm of Praat [15]. The voiced intervals are determined on the basis of the voiced/unvoiced decisions extracted from the corresponding F_0 contour. For every voiced interval, a number of points (glottal pulses) are found. The first point, t_1, is the absolute extremum of the amplitude of the sound

$$t_1 = \max[t_{mid} - T_0/2, t_{mid} + T_0/2] \tag{2}$$

where t_{mid} is the midpoint of the interval, and T_0 is the period at t_{mid}, as can be interpolated from the pitch contour. Starting from time instant t_1, we recursively search for points t_i to left until we reach the left edge of the interval. These points must be located between t_{i-1}-1.2$T_0(t_i$-1) and t_i-1-0.8$T_0(t_i$-1), and the cross-correlation of the amplitude of the environment of the existing point t_{i-1} must be maximal. Between the samples of the correlation function parabolic interpolation has been applied. The same procedure is followed and for the right of t_1 part of the particular voiced segment. Though the voiced/unvoiced decision is initially taken by the pitch contour, points are removed if the correlation value is less than 0.3. Furthermore, one extra point may be added at the edge of the voiced interval if its correlation value is greater than 0.7.

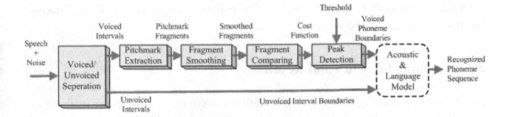

Fig. 1. Block diagram of the proposed framework

2.1 Voiced Phoneme Boundary Detection

Voiced phoneme boundaries are observed into speech regions that are marked with heavy co-articulation phenomena. Since the manner of articulation is almost constant during each specific phoneme, fragments lying in the same phoneme and away from the co-articulation regions have similar amplitude evolution, while frames located in such regions will have different contours while the articulation behavior changes.

For the task of calculating the difference between the amplitude contour of each fragment and its adjacent ones, we employed the dynamic time warping (DTW) algorithm [16], which computes the distance path between each pair of neighboring fragments of speech that are determined by the pitchmarks. Thus, a cost function is computed for each pair of adjacent fragments, as a measure of similarity between adjacent fragments of the speech waveform.

$$CostFunction(i) = DTW(fragment(i), fragment(i+1)) \qquad (3)$$

Local maxima of the function are equivalent to the phoneme boundaries of an utterance, since the warping path between adjacent fragments is longer.

As a final step, peaks of the cost function are detected. To decide which of the peaks correspond to candidate segment boundaries a threshold operational parameter, *Thr*, is introduced. For each peak we calculate the magnitude distances from its side local minimums. The minimum of the two resulted magnitude distances is compared to *Thr*. For values higher to *Thr* the corresponding fragment is considered to contain a detected boundary, otherwise is ignored. Finally, each detected boundary is assumed to be located on the middle sample of the prior chosen fragment.

2.2 Speech Corpora

The validation of our implicit voiced-phoneme segmentation technique for was carried out with the exploitation of two databases: WCL-1 [17] and NOISEX-92 [18].

As regards WCL-1, is generic domain phonetically and prosodically balanced corpus of Greek speech annotated on phonemic level. It is consisted of 5.500 words, distributed in 500 paragraphs. Newspaper articles, paragraphs of literature and sentences were used, in order to cover most of the contextual segmental variants. The database was phonetically annotated by expert phonetician. For the high quality narrow phonetic transcriptions, the SAMPA alphabet adapted for Greek was employed.

NOISEX-92 database includes recordings of various noises such as voice babble, factory noise, high-frequency radio channel noise, pink noise, white noise. In addition, there are provided various military noises, as fighter jets, destroyer noises, tank noise and machine gun noise. Finally, car noise is provided.

3 Experimental Setup and Results

For the task of evaluating our speech segmentation framework, we conducted experiments in both un-noisy and noisy environments practicing different thresholds. A segmentation point is defined as correctly-detected only if its distance from the actual annotation point is less than t msec. In order to measure the performance of our method we introduce accuracy metric and over-segmentation. Accuracy is defined as the percentage of the number of the correctly-detected segmentation points P_c to the total number of the real-boundary points P_t,

$$Accuracy = P_c/P_t \cdot 100\% \tag{4}$$

where the real boundary points are the boundaries of the voiced phonemes and the boundaries of the unvoiced intervals. Since in implicit approaches, where our method falls, detected segmentation points are not equal to the true ones, an effective way of measuring the reliability of a segmentation method is over-segmentation. Over-segmentation is defined as the ratio of the number of the detected segmentation points P_d to the total number of the true segmentation points P_t,

$$OverSegmentation = P_d/P_t \tag{5}$$

In the experiments we have focused on improving accuracy while keeping the over-segmentation factor close to the value of one. As a result, a vast variety of threshold values was tested for several smoothing factors. Additionally, we investigated the accuracy of our procedure for t=25msec. An empirical way for selecting practically optimal values for the free parameters such as the smoothing factor and the threshold was used for the case of noise absence. In that way, we were able to optimize the accuracy of our method. The best obtained result through the optimization procedure was 76,1%, without presenting over-segmentation, for a smoothing factor equal to 80 and $Thr = 2, 5 \times 10^{-4}$, (Over-Segmentation < 1,05).

The next step to our experimental procedure was the evaluation of our segmentation schema in several additive noise environments. For this task we selected white noise, Gaussian white noise, voice babble, noise in pilot cockpit, tank noise, HF radio channel noise, car noise, pink noise and machine gun noise. Sentences from the WCL-1 database were corrupted by the various noise conditions at a global SNR of 10 dB. The method's accuracy under noise conditions was tested using the practically optimal values of the parameters as were obtained from the un-noisy environment experiments ($S = 80$, $Thr = 2,5 \times 10^{-4}$). The achieved results are tabulated in Table 1, were it is clearly presents that our method performs equally well in noise environments with high frequency, as well as with wideband distortion characteristics, like HF radio channel noise or Gaussian white noise respectively. Method's accuracy reduces significantly in the case of machine gun noise since it is described by high colored energy distribution characteristics. It distorts the waveform contour in a degree that smoothing effort to recover the compared fragments' contour performs poorly.

Table 1. Speech segmentation accuracy for additive noise environments (SNR=10 dB)

ADDITIVE NOISE	ACCURACY
No noise	76,10%
Gaussian white noise	72,30%
White noise	72,07%
Pink noise	71,05%
Speech in background (voice babble)	70,58%
Noise in pilot cockpit (F-16)	70,13%
HF radio channel noise	69,95%
Tank noise (Leopard, M109)	69,89%
Car noise (Volvo 340)	69,47%
Machine gun	59,11%

4 Conclusions

In this work, we have implemented and evaluated a speaker independent method for automatic broad phoneme class segmentation of speech signals using the knowledge of pitchmark locations in un-noisy and noisy environments. Segmentation experiments without noise showed an accuracy of 76,1%. On the other hand, the method demonstrated robustness for wideband distortion noise characteristics. Given the fact that the textual message of the speech utterance in not necessary for the extraction of the boundary locations as well as its robustness to noisy environments, makes it appropriate for applications that require automatic broad annotation of speech in real environment conditions.

References

1. Young S., Kershaw D., Odell J., Ollason D., Valtchev V., P. Woodland P., "The HTK Book", Revised for HTK Version 3.0, July 2000.
2. Zissman M., "Comparison of four Approaches to Automatic Language Identification of Telephone Speech", IEEE Trans. Speech and Audio Proc., SAP-4, pp. 31–44, Jan. 96.
3. Dutoit, T., "An Introduction to Text-To-Speech Synthesis", vol. 3, Text, Speech and Language Technology. Kluwer Academic Publishers, 1997.
4. van Hemert J., "Automatic Segmentation of Speech", IEEE Transactions on Signal Processing, vol. 39, no. 4, April 1991.

5. Aversano G., Esposito A., Esposito A., Marinaro M., "A new text-independent method for phoneme segmentation", In Proc. of 44th IEEE Midwest Symp. Circuits and Systems, vol. 2, pp. 516–519, 2001.
6. 6. Suh Y., Lee Y., "Phoneme segmentation of continuous speech using multi-layer perceptron", In Proc. of ICSLP '96, pp. 1297–1300, 1996.
7. Svendsen T., Kvale K., "Automatic alignment of phonemic labels in continuous speech", In Proc. of ICSLP '90, Kobe, Japan, 1990.
8. Svendsent T., Soong F. K., "On the automatic segmentation of speech signals", In Proc. of ICASSP '87, pp.77-80, Dallas, April 1987.
9. Grayden D., Scordilis M., "Phonemic segmentation of fluent speech", In Proc. of ICASSP 1994, pp. 73–76, 1994.
10. Essa O., "Using prosody in automatic segmentation of speech", In Proc. of 36th ACM Southeast Regional Conference, 1998.
11. Pellom B., Hansen J., "Automatic segmentation of speech recorded in unknown noisy channel characteristics", Speech Communication, 25, pp. 97–116, 1998.
12. Reddy, D., R., "Pitch Period Determination of Speech Sounds", Communication of the ACM, vol. 10, pp. 343–348, 1967.
13. Tsagalidis A., http://www.media.uoa.gr/language/.
14. Boersma, P., "Accurate short-term analysis of the fundamental frequency and the harmonics-to-noise ratio of a sampled sound", In: Proc. of IFA, 17: 97–110, 1993.
15. Boersma, P., Weenink, D., Praat: doing phonetics by computer, (2005). Retrieved from http://www.praat.org/.
16. Deller J., Proakis J., Hansen J., "Discrete-time processing of speech signals", MacMillan Series for Prentice-Hall Publishers, New York, 1993.
17. Zervas P., Fakotakis N., Kokkinakis G., "Development of a prosodic database for Greek speech synthesis", In Proc. of SPECOM 2005, pp. 603–606, Patras, Greece, 2005.
18. Varga, A., Steenneken, H., J., M., Tomlinson, M., and Jones, D., The NOISEX-92 study on the effect of additive noise on automatic speech recognition, 1992.

A System for Information Retrieval
from Large Records of Czech Spoken Data*

Jan Nouza, Jindřich Žďánský, Petr Červa, and Jan Kolorenč

SpeechLab, Technical University of Liberec, Hálkova 6 461 17 Liberec 1, Czech Republic
{jan.nouza, jindrich.zdansky, petr.cerva, jan.kolorenc}@tul.cz

Abstract. In the paper we describe a complex multi-level system that serves for automatic search in large records of Czech spoken data. It includes modules for audio signal segmentation, speaker identification and adaptation, speech recognition and full-text search. The search can focus both on key-words and key-speakers. The transcription accuracy is about 79 % (for broadcast programs), search accuracy about 90 %. Due to its distributed platform, the system can operate in almost real-time.

1 Introduction

After great success of applying full-text search technology to extract information from electronically available documents, the focus of IT research is moving towards mining in acoustic and video (multimedia) data [1]. Many important facts can be found in broadcast spoken programs (news, commentaries or debates), as well as in movies, sport and cultural documents. However, these multimedia sources must be transcribed into text form before any search for key-words or key-speakers or topics can be started. Recent advances in automatic speech recognition (ASR) made this audio-to-text transcription possible, though its robustness is still a relevant research issue.

Much attention was devoted namely to the search in broadcast news. The earliest systems developed for information retrieval (IR) in this domain occurred around year 2000, see e.g. [2]. Later, ASR techniques were applied also to other types of voice data, such as historical archives of spoken documents [3] or testimonies processed within the MALACH project [4]. Large progress in mining speech data was reported namely for English [1,2,3] though systems for other languages, like French, are also available [5]. Great majority of the IR systems employ the classic approach where speech is transcribed into sequences of words that are directly used as searched items. An alternative method, presented e.g. in [6], consists in translation of speech signal into phonetic lattices that serve as basis for a later search within arbitrary vocabulary.

In this paper we present a system for word-oriented search in automatically transcribed records of Czech spoken documents. It is based on our ATT (Audio Transcription Toolkit) platform developed during the last 2 years. Since it uses a general, very large lexicon covering about 99 % (frequency ranked) Czech lexical inventory, it is suited for a broader range of tasks. In the following, we mention at least those classified by our collaborating partners as highly important:

---

* This work was supported by the Czech Grant Agency (GACR grant no. 102/05/0278).

Petr Sojka, Ivan Kopeček and Karel Pala (Eds.): TSD 2006, LNAI 4188, pp. 485–492, 2006.

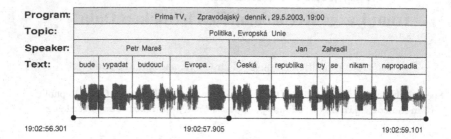

Fig. 1. Hierarchical segmentation of spoken documents

Continual monitoring of TV and radio stations. Here, the interested parties do not insist on perfect transcription of broadcast stream because they know it would need additional human work. Rather, they prefer a formatted text output that is suitable for fast search and allows immediate audio check of found items. An additional demand is to identify speech segments spoken by a particular person.

Searching for specific key-words in regularly broadcast programs. Some clients want to monitor specific TV and radio programs and to search for only a small number of key-words that are a-priori known.

Aligning human-made transcription to audio records of speech. This is the case namely in situations were a formal text record may slightly differ from what was actually spoken (due to artifacts of spontaneous speech) and where this difference may be a source of disputation (e.g. records of parliament talks). Here, the task consists in getting direct access to the audio signal associated with any word or any sentence in the transcription and allowing its easy acoustic check.

2   Task Overview

In general, this project is aimed at automatic search in large spoken data sets (processed off-line) or long acoustic streams (accessed on-line).

In contrast to full-text search in documents, which are already organized into articles, paragraphs, sentences and words, acoustic data is much more complex in its nature. Therefore, one of the key problems in speech data indexing is proper partitioning of the signal. In case of broadcast stream, the most natural segmentation follows the scheme depicted in Fig. 1.

At the highest level, the record is partitioned into individual programs (e.g. news, movies, advertisement, etc). Their identification usually makes no problem because we can use additional information provided by broadcasters in form of program codes and time stamps. At the next level, spoken data is grouped into parts that deal with the same topic. The identification of the topic is a complex task, especially in case of broadcast news where one topic can be covered be several contributions presented by various speakers. Since it utilizes linguistic information, it can be performed as one of the final steps in the data transcription process. In this paper this level is not solved. On the signal level, the first segmentation

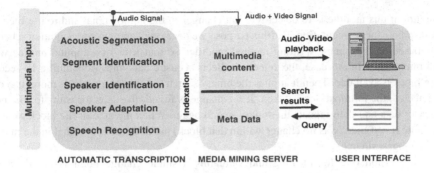

Fig. 2. Modules and functions of spoken data mining system SPOKEMIN

step consists in identifying those time instants where signal changes significantly its long-span character. Usually, these moments correspond to speaker turns, channel switches or speech/non-speech borders. If the segment between two adjacent change points is speech, its data is processed as one signal block (utterance) belonging to a single speaker. It is sent to speaker and speech recognition modules that return back information about speaker identity and speech content. The latter has form of a sequence of words, which are the lowest-level elements of transcription. Program names, topics, speaker info and text, together with their time stamps, make the search space for the information retrieval system.

3   System Architecture

In this section we describe real system called SPOKEMIN (SPOKEn Data MINing) developed in our lab in 2005–2006. A diagram showing its modules and functions is depicted in Fig. 2.

3.1   Signal Processing

The system can process acoustic data that are either stored in previously recorded files or that come directly from on-line sources, such as a microphone, TV/radio card or internet stream broadcasting. The acoustic models in the speech/speaker recognition modules request that the processed data are sampled at 16 kHz rate into 16 bits.

Speech parameterization is done as the first operation applied to the signal. To save time and memory, the signal is processed only once and the resulting features (or their subsets) are used in all modules, i.e. for signal segmentation as well as for speaker and speech recognition. Feature vectors are composed of 40 numbers, classic 39 MFCC parameters and 1 frame energy. Cepstral Mean Subtraction is applied to static MFCCs only after segmentation is done, i.e. for each segment separately.

3.2   Signal Segmentation

The aim of this module is to detect relevant changes in the audio signal and to use them as break-points for segmentation. For this purpose we developed an own segmentation scheme. It is based on the binary splitting method modified so that it can be applied on-line with minimum delay. In our case, the detector collects acoustic data and waits until a 10-second long block is available. Then it applies the binary search for change-points. If more than one is detected, the leftmost one is taken. If no change is found, the detector waits for the next block of data and then repeats the binary search again. When the size of the block exceeds 1 minute (i.e. if there was no change within that block) the detector cuts signal in the middle of the longest silence.

The decision rule for locating and validating a single change point is based on the maximum likelihood approach which was found more accurate then the commonly used techniques based on the Bayesian Information Criterion, as it was shown in [7].

3.3   Speech/Non-speech Detection, Speaker and Gender Identification

This module makes classification of segments into several broader classes. These are: silence (low background noise), noise (loud noise, jingles, music, etc), male and female voice. All these categories are represented by GMMs (Gaussian Mixture Models). The same representation is used also for speakers included in the speaker database. Currently, it includes models of some 300 subjects, mainly TV and radio speakers and top politicians. For each of them we collected at least 75 seconds of speech for training the GMMs and for speaker adaptation purposes. This training data was collected during a longer period (2003–2006) in order to get robust models.

A speech segment is matched to the GMMs using a 2-level classification scheme. On the first level, speech/non-speech separation and speaker ordering is performed by employing 256-mixture GMMs. On the second level, which is applied for speech segments only, speaker verification is done by comparing the best speaker model with a male or female Universal Background Model (UBM). As result, each segment gets one the following labels: non-speech, male, female or a person's name from the speaker list. Moreover, N-best list from the first level is also stored for later use.

3.4   Speaker Adaptation

It is well-known that adaptation of acoustic models to the voice characteristics of individual speakers can improve speech recognition in significant way. Our system utilizes two types of adaptation techniques. For the persons in the speaker database, speaker adapted (SA) models were prepared off-line by a special module that is based on a combination of MAP and MLLR techniques. These SA models are used for those speakers who passed successfully through the verification process. For the rejected ones, a special SA model is computed on the fly by properly mixing the model parameters of the N-best speaker list. For details, see [8].

3.5   Speech Decoding and Transcription

The transcription of the utterance is performed by a speech recognition module. It employs our own LVCSR decoder optimized for large (100K+) vocabularies [9]. The recent version

```
BLOCK=4       BEGIN=36970       LENGTH=2970       IDENTITY=<Daniel_Takáč> <Male>
RAWTEXT=<36970|37100|> <37100|37460|vládní> <37460|37900|představy>
<37900|37960|o> <37960|38430|šetření> <38430|38940|kritizují>...
```

Fig. 3. Example of the SPOKEMIN's transcription format

of the lexicon contains about 312K entries mapped onto some 340K pronunciation base-forms. The lexicon is made of the most frequent Czech words, word-forms and multi-word expressions. It was shown previously that the OOV (out-of-vocabulary) rate for the lexicon of this size was about 1 % for most spoken data [9]. The language model (LM) is based on bigrams estimated from a corpus of some 3.5 GB of Czech text. Acoustic models, in our case 41 phoneme and 7 noise models, are 3-state, 100-mixture HMMs, whose parameters were estimated on a 50-hour speech training database made of broadcast, microphone and telephone records.

Speech transcription is performed by a Viterbi decoder whose goal is to determine the most probable sequence (with unknown length N) of words W from lexicon V together with their time positions (represented by ending times t_n) according to eq. (1):

$$W = \arg\max_{w_n \in V, N, 0 < t_n < T} \left(\sum_{n=1}^{N} \ln(L(w_n|\mathbf{x}(t_{n-1}) \dots \mathbf{x}(t_n))) + \beta \ln(P(w_n|w_n - 1)) \right) \quad (1)$$

where $L()$ denotes likelihood of word w_n for acoustic observation vectors $\mathbf{x}$ in time span t_{n-1} to t_n, $P()$ is the bigram value for word w_n following w_{n-1} and β is LM factor.

The output of the speech recognition module has form depicted in Fig. 3. For each segment (block) it gives its start time and length (measured in milliseconds from the recording start), segment label identification (usually the speaker's name and gender) and a sequence of recognized tokens. (This raw text is further post-processed in a module that cares about capitalization and punctuation.)

3.6   Search in Transcriptions

The above text transcriptions serve for search. In the recent system's version, a query is defined by typing the searched word or its sub-string into the form of the IR interface that is depicted in Fig. 4. The search engine finds all occurrences of the items and makes their time-ordered list. Any of the listed items can be checked visually by reading the transcription of the given segment and acoustically by listening to the whole segment or to the found word only. (Later, also video replay will be available.)

3.7   Implementation

One of the most importing features of an IR system is its operating speed and response time. Much care was devoted to speeding up the operation of all the modules, namely the speech decoder. After many optimizations of the code, now it is able to process an utterance in time which is usually shorter than 2xRT (two times duration of the speech) on a PC with a Pentium 3 GHz HT processor. Moreover, the ATT platform was designed to run in distributed

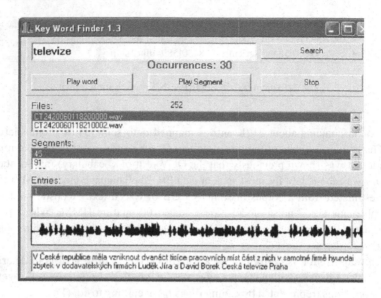

Fig. 4. Interface to the search engine operating over the transcriptions

environment. It means that after the signal is segmented each segment can be processed on a separate machine. Our experience show that if 3 and more client PCs are connected within the ATT network, the transcription time gets shorter than the duration of the processed records.

4   Performance Evaluation

The system and its modules have been exposed to many evaluation tests. In this chapter we mention at least the most relevant ones. The test data used in the experiments were 3 complete programs recorded from CTV 1 station in December 2005. Two of them were main evening news called "Události" (Dec. 9 and 12), the other was "Večerník" of Dec. 7. They were recorded as whole, i.e. with initial and final jingles as well as with opening and intermediate headlines spoken on music background. Three shows with total length of 62 minutes were split into 430 segments (from these 16 contained no speech). Their reference transcriptions included 9760 words. From them, 109 (1.12 %) were OOV words.

4.1   Speech Recognition Results

In the first set of experiments we compared different types of acoustic models employed in speech recognition. Speaker-independent (SI) models served for establishing baseline results (see Table 1.). In the next test we employed gender-dependent (GD) models according to the identified speaker's gender. The other 2 experiments measured the impact of the speaker adaptation (SA) techniques. In the first test, off-line prepared SA models were used for the verified speakers, the unknown and rejected ones were backed up by the GD models. In the second test, SA models were computed even for the group of the rejected speakers after

Table 1. Word error rate and real time factor for different acoustic models

Acoustic model	SI	GD	GD + SA	SA
WER [%]	24.55	22.80	21.93	21.43
xRT	2.45	2.35	2.23	2.15

employing the unsupervised SA technique mentioned in paragraph 3.4. From Table 1 we can observe that the application of the best scheme yielded 3.43 % absolute reduction of WER when compared to the baseline. Moreover, using the speaker-fitted models had positive effect also on faster recognition as shown in the lower row of Table 1.

4.2 Segment Classification Results

In the second set of experiments, the performance of the segment classification was evaluated. Table 2 presents the results in very detailed way, when explicitly showing all situations of correct and wrong decisions. We can see that most wrong decisions happened when a known speaker (one of the 300 people in the speaker database) did not pass the verification stage but he/she was assigned to the proper gender group. (Detailed analysis showed that the correct speaker was usually the first one on the ordered list, which is a fact that still can be utilized in practical search tasks.) Another interesting observation is that 5 of 16 non-speech segments were labeled as speech. Often this was caused in situations where laugh or cough occurred in these segments.

4.3 Search Results

In Table 3 we present some results from search experiments. We chose a small set of words that were often used in media searching, such as VIP subjects and institutions, company and country names, etc. Our set of 10 entities was composed to cover both short (monosyllabic) key-words as well as longer items. In the analyzed TV programs they occurred 124 times in total. Statistics saying how many times they were found at correct places and how often they were omitted or wrongly identified is shown in Table 3. It should be noted that both the types of incorrect search were often caused by confusions between acoustically very close morphological derivations of the same word (e.g. "policie" and "policii" are two forms equivalent two one English word "police"). Anyway, we can see that about 90 % of all searched words were found correctly in the broadcast programs. Similar performance was observed also for other types of spoken data, e.g. parliament debates, which is shown also in Table 3.

Table 2. Automatic classification of segments into speaker, gender and non-speech groups

Audio segment with	Correctly recognized	Wrongly recognized as				
		KM	KF	UM	UF	NS
Known male - KM	104	1	0	68	0	0
Known female - KF	57	0	2	0	26	0
Unknown male - UM	115	4	0	x	1	0
Unknown female - UF	31	0	2	3	x	0
Non-speech - NS	11	2	1	1	1	x

Table 3. Search results for 10 key-words retrieved from different spoken data streams

key-word	62-minute record of TV broadcast				120-minute file of parliament speech			
	Total occur.	Correctly found	not found	Wrongly found	Total occur.	Correctly found	Not found	Wrongly found
televize	30	29	0	1	2	0	0	2
policie	17	15	2	0	0	0	0	0
soud	15	13	1	1	2	2	0	0
Hyundai	12	8	4	0	0	0	0	0
zákon	11	11	0	0	52	48	2	2
Polsko	10	9	1	0	0	0	0	0
premiér	9	9	0	0	1	0	0	1
president	9	8	1	0	0	0	0	0
ministr	8	7	1	0	13	12	0	1
Klaus	3	3	0	0	1	0	0	1

5 Conclusions and Further Work

System SPOKEMIN is capable of automatic monitoring of Czech spoken data, transcribing its content and allowing a full-text search in the transcriptions. It can operate on-line with a delay shorter than several tens of seconds. It supports parallel processing distributed to a cluster of PCs, which allows for off-line processing of speech records in times that are shorter than their duration. Its recent version has been in trial use in a media mining company since March 2006. First experience shows that the system saves a lot of human work. In near future, its capabilities will be extended towards more advanced search options and a link to video files (e.g. for TV news).

References

1. Semantic Retrieval of Multimedia. IEEE Signal Processing Magazine. March 2006.
2. Makhoul J. et al: Speech and Language Technologies for Audio Indexing and Retrieval. Proc. IEEE, vol. 88, no. 8, pp. 1338–1353, 2000.
3. Zhou B., Hansen J.H. L.: Speechfind: An Experimental On-line Spoken Document Retrieval System for Historical Audio Archives. Proc. of ICSLP 2002, Denver.
4. Byrne W. et al.: Aut. recognition of spontaneous speech for access to multilingual oral history archives. IEEE Trans. on SAP vol. 12, no. 4: pp. 420–435.
5. Favre B., Bechet F., Nocera P.: Mining Broadcast News Data: Robust Information Extraction from Words Lattices. Proc. of EuroSpeech 2005. Lisbon, Sept. 2005.
6. Kurimo M., Turunen V., Ekman I: An Evaluation of a Spoken Document Retrieval Baseline System in Finnish. Proc. of ICSLSP 2004. Jeju, October 2004.
7. Žďánský J.: Methods for Speaker Detection Change Identification in Audio Signal. PhD thesis (in Czech). Technical University in Liberec. October 2005.
8. Červa, P., David, P., Nouza, J.: Acoustic Modeling Based on Speaker Recognition and Adaptation for Improved Transcription of Broadcast Programs. Proc. of Specom 2005, October, 2005, Patras, Greece, pp. 183–186.
9. Nouza, J., Žďánský J., David, P., Červa, P., Kolorenc, J., Nejedlova, D.: Fully Automated System for Czech Spoken Broadcast Transcription with Very Large (300K+) Lexicon. Proc. of Interspeech 2005, Lisboa, Portugal, pp. 1681–1684.

A Structure of Expert System for Speaker Verification*

Aleš Padrta and Jan Vaněk

University of West Bohemia, Department of Cybernetics,
Univerzitní 8, 306 14 Plzeň, Czech Republic
apadrta@civ.zcu.cz, vanekyj@kky.zcu.cz

Abstract. A structure of an expert system for speaker verification is introduced in this article. According to the previous research, the birth of the essential ideas leading to expert system is indicated. At first, the specifics of the speaker verification task are discussed. Then, the expert system based on the combination of the rules and an oriented graph is introduced. Finally, the benefit of this approach is tested on small knowledge base, which is focused on the signal processing. The results of performed experiments show that the proposed expert system is capable to improve the performance of the verification, although the knowledge base is really small.

1 Introduction

Many experiments with configuration of particular modules were performed throughout the development of the speaker verification system [1]. The results of the experiments with the signal-processing module [2] show that an optimal configuration vary for specific conditions and it dramatically affects the performance of the verification system. Analogical situations can be found for the other modules of verification system. A human expert is capable of choosing the most suitable configuration of the module for the current conditions.

Each verification trial has specific conditions – for example the signal quality, the length of the utterance, the emotional state of the speaker, and the language or the topic of the utterance. Artificial corpora are the only exceptions. Thus, a suitable configuration of all modules is different for each verification trial. The selection of the most suitable configuration cannot be done by human beings because of the huge amount of the verification trials. A fully automatic selection can be realized by an expert system with the appropriate knowledge base.

Our expert system for speaker verification is introduced in this article. At first, the specific procedures used in speaker verification systems are discussed in Section 2. Consequently, the appropriate structure of the expert system for speaker verification is proposed in Section 3. Next, Section 4 is devoted to the description of experiments and their results. Finally, the conclusions are given in Section 5.

2 Characteristic Procedure for Speaker Verification

All systems for speaker verification consist of some subsystems, which are mutually independent, but they are tied together [3,4]. Each subsystem belongs to one of three

---

* Support for this work was provided by the Academy of Science and the Grant Agency of the Czech Republic, projects no. 1QS101470516 and GACR 102/05/0278.

Petr Sojka, Ivan Kopeček and Karel Pala (Eds.): TSD 2006, LNAI 4188, pp. 493–500, 2006.

basic groups [5]: the preprocessing and signal processing subsystems, the data modeling subsystems, and the verification subsystems.

The characteristic sequence of particular subsystem in speaker verification systems is depicted in Figure 1. At first, the utterance is transformed to the set of the feature vectors. A preprocessing of the signal is usually included in corresponding subsystem to suppress undesirable effects. This transformation is denoted as signal processing. Consequently, the set of feature vectors is used to create a model of appropriate speaker. The corresponding subsystem is generally employed in training phase only. In some cases, when the verification is based on model comparison, the model is also created from the test feature vectors. The subsystems from the third group use the outputs of the subsystems from previous groups to perform the last step, the verification.

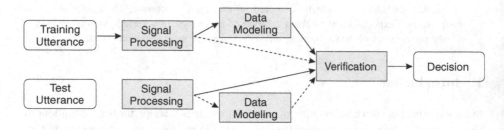

Fig. 1. The sequence of subsystems for speaker verification

Each subsystem can be implemented in many ways. The instance of subsystem is denoted as a module. When a verification system employ more than one verification module, then one more subsystem is needed. The combination subsystem [6] is used for gathering the outputs of the verification modules into a single decision.

The prior experiments [2] have confirmed the dependence of the signal processing module on the noise and the channel distortion. Next, the dependence of GMM complexity on the amount of training data has been demonstrated [7]. The verification based on an universal background model can be improved by selecting the UBM according to the gender of the speaker [8] or other conditions of recording [9]. In the future research, more dependencies will be certainly discovered. Thus a configuration, which corresponds to the actual operating conditions, is needed for high-quality function of the appropriate module.

Each verification trial is different from the other ones, i.e. it has different operating conditions. As a consequence, the configuration of the verification system should be modified for each trial. The human experts have the appropriate knowledge to create a suitable configuration. Unfortunately, they are not capable to make a huge amount of the mentioned modification.

We analyzed the above mentioned facts and come to the hopefully solution – a fully automatic expert system, which contains appropriate knowledge base and is capable to configure and call the particular modules of the speaker verification system.

3   Expert System for Speaker Verification

3.1   Architecture Proposal

The architecture of the desired expert system depends on the characteristics of the speaker verification task. The following architecture come from the information, which were discussed in the previous section.

At first, it is necessary to represent the sequence of particular modules during verification trial. The sequence of the modules in Figure 1 can be easily represented by an oriented graph. The nodes of the graph correspond to the appropriate modules and the edges determine the succession of the nodes.

The proposed oriented graph for the expert system is denoted as

$$\overrightarrow{G} = \overrightarrow{G}(N, E, \widehat{E}), \tag{1}$$

where $N = \{n_1, \ldots, n_I\}$ is a set of the nodes, $E = \{e_1, \ldots, e_J\}$ is a set of the data-edges, and $\widehat{E} = \{\widehat{e_1}, \ldots, \widehat{e_{\widehat{J}}}\}$ is a set of the informative-edges. An informative edge represents the succession of nodes only, while a data-edge transports some data between the modules in addition.

The topology of the graph is sometimes trial-dependent. In some cases, it is better to choose another proper module instead of the change of configuration. Therefore a life condition c_j is assigned to each data-edge e_j, $j = 1, \ldots, J$ in addition to the source node s_j and the target node t_j. If the condition c_j is not fulfilled then the edge e_j does not exists. The edge e_j is denoted as

$$e_j = e_j(c_j, s_j, t_j). \tag{2}$$

Next, the expert knowledge for the particular modules configuration needs to be stored. The knowledge can be easily represented by expert rules. Each rule is related to some module. Therefore a set of expert rules $R_i = \{r_1(i), \ldots, r_{K_i}(i)\}$ is assigned to each node n_i, $i = 1, \ldots, I$ in addition to module m_i. The node n_i is denoted as

$$n_i = n_i(m_i, R_i). \tag{3}$$

Each rule $r_k(i)$, $i = 1, \ldots, I$, $k = 1, \ldots, K_i$ consists of the conditional part $c_k(i)$ and the action part $a_k(i)$

$$r_k(i) = r_k(i)(c_k(i), a_k(i)). \tag{4}$$

If the condition $c_k(i)$ is fulfilled then the the action part $a_k(i)$ is activated, i.e. the value of some attribute of the module m_i is changed.

The evaluation of the conditional part $c_k(i)$ usually requires an information from other modules $m_{i'}$, $i' \neq i$. Thus the module $m_{i'}$ has to be evaluated prior to the module m_i. This relationship is represented by informative-edges $\widehat{e_{\widehat{j}}}$, $\widehat{j} = 1, \ldots, \widehat{J}$. These informative-edges are not trial-dependent, so the life condition is fruitless. The informative edge $\widehat{e_{\widehat{j}}}$ is denoted as

$$\widehat{e_{\widehat{j}}} = \widehat{e_{\widehat{j}}}(\widehat{s_{\widehat{j}}}, \widehat{t_{\widehat{j}}}). \tag{5}$$

The above specified architecture of the expert system allows the selection of the particular modules, the definition of the modules evaluation sequence, and the configuration of the modules according to the actual verification trial.

3.2   Verification Trial Progress

The initial conditions of all verification trials are the same – two utterances are available. In our proposed expert system, initial conditions are represented by nodes n_1 and n_2. Appropriate modules m_1 and m_2 represent the mentioned utterances. The subsequent process originates from these nodes, thus no edge ends in nodes n_1 or n_2 (see Figure 2).

On the opposite side of the graph exists one terminal node n_I. According to the discussion in Section 2, the appropriate module m_I contains the verification result. The verification process ends in node n_I, so no edge begins in it.

Several restrictions exist for the graph topology between initial nodes n_1, n_2 and terminal node n_I

- Oriented loops are prohibited.
- If an attribute of the module $m_{i'}$ is a part of the condition $c_k(i)$, $k = 1, \ldots, K_i$, then an oriented path from the node $m_{i'}$ to the node m_i must exist. This oriented path can consist of both type of edges – data or informative ones.
- If an attribute of the module $m_{i'}$ is a part of the life condition c_j, $j = 1, \ldots, J$, then an oriented path from the node $m_{i'}$ to the node s_j must exist. This oriented path can consist of both type of edges – data or informative ones.

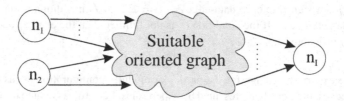

Fig. 2. Characteristic topology of the graph for verification trial

The following algorithm is used for the evaluation of the verification trial. Two sets are defined to distinguish already evaluated nodes and edges from the non-evaluated ones. The set A contains the non-evaluated components, while the set B contains the evaluated components.

1. Initialization
    - All nodes n_i, $i = 1, \ldots, I$ are inserted into set A.
    - All data-edges e_j, $j = 1, \ldots, J$ are inserted into set A.
    - All informative-edges $\widehat{e_{\widehat{j}}}$, $\widehat{j} = 1, \ldots, \widehat{J}$ are inserted into set A.
2. Activation of accessible nodes
    - The node n_i in the set A is accessible, if all input edges of this node are in the set B
    - Activation of node n_i include following steps:
        • Create an instance of the module m_i
        • Read the default configuration of module m_i.
        • Configure the module according to the rules $r \in R_i$.
        • Execute the module – process the signal, create model, etc.

- • Move node n_i to set B.
  - All accessible nodes are activated in this step.
3. Expansion of accessible edges
   - The edge in the set A is accessible, if its source node is in the set B. The life condition has to be fulfilled for data-edges.
   - The expansion of the edge involve the shift of the edge from the set A to the set B.
   - All accessible edges are expanded in this step.
4. Terminal condition
   - If there was no shift from the set A to the set B, the algorithm ends. Otherwise move to the step 2.

At first look, the activation of the node n_I is better terminal condition. A deeper analysis shows that an infinite loop of algorithm can occur in the case of improperly designed graph when this terminal condition is used.

4 Experimental Setup

In order to check the suitableness of the proposed structure of the expert system, a verification system based on the proposed architecture was created. It contains a small knowledge base focused on the signal processing.

4.1 Description of System

The configuration of the signal processing modules depends on the noise level and the channel distortion of the utterances [2]. Based on this knowledge, four signal processing modules were created. Each of them is suitable for a different operating conditions:

SP_1 – suitable for the clean utterances
SP_2 – suitable for the utterances contaminated by an additive noise
SP_3 – suitable for the utterances damaged by a channel distortion
SP_4 – suitable for the utterance damaged by a channel distortion and an additive noise together

In order to choose the proper signal processing module, the information about the noise level and the channel distortion in the current utterance are required. The followings modules are used for this purpose:

D_1 – the noise level detector, it estimates the minimal SNR of the utterances.
D_2 – channel distortion detector, it estimated the channel difference between test utterance and train utterance.

The appropriate knowledge of the human expert turned into the rules can be denoted as

$$\text{if } ((D_1 > 10.0) \wedge (D_2 < 0.295)) \text{ then use } SP_1 \tag{6}$$

$$\text{if } ((D_1 < 10.0) \wedge (D_2 < 0.370)) \text{ then use } SP_2 \tag{7}$$

$$\text{if } ((D_1 > 10.0) \wedge (D_2 > 0.295)) \text{ then use } SP_3 \tag{8}$$

$$\text{if } ((D_1 < 10.0) \wedge (D_2 > 0.370)) \text{ then use } SP_4 \tag{9}$$

The corresponding topology of the graph is depicted in Figure 3. The corresponding modules m_1 and m_2 represent the two utterances, which should be compared. The modules m_3 and m_4 contain the detector D_1 and D_2 respectively. Modules m_5 and m_6 perform signal processing of training data and test data respectively. The sets R_5 and R_6 represent the knowledge expressed by rules (6), (7), (8), and (9). Module m_7 create a GMM from the training data. Module m_8 performs the verification based on UBM. The selection of the proper UBM is controlled by the set R_8 based on the rules (6), (7), (8), and (9). In order to keep the correct sequence of modules, some informative edges were added.

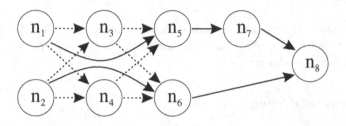

Fig. 3. Topology of the experimental expert system. Dashed line = informative edges; Solid line = data edges.

4.2   Speech Data

The utterances from 100 speakers (64 male and 36 female) were used in our experiments. They were recorded in the same way as in the [10]. Each speaker read 24 sentences that were divided into three parts: 21 sentences of each speaker were used for training of the GMM of the speaker, 2 sentences were used for the construction of the background model, and 1 sentence was used for the tests.

Five test sets were prepared for testing different operational conditions. They were denoted as set 1 to set 5. Each test set represents one typical distortion of the signal. These distortions were as follows:

Set 1 – Original data from the close talk microphone were used.
Set 2 – The noise with SNR from 15 to 20 dB was added to the original data.
Set 3 – Channel distortion is applied on the original data.
Set 4 – Both noise and channel distortion like B and C were added.
Set 5 – All above mentioned sets were merged into one set.

The training data for the speaker model and the universal background model are the original ones without modifications.

4.3   Experimental Results

Five verification systems were used to recognize the tests marked as Set 1 - Set 5. These systems differ in the employed signal processing only. At first, four systems, which always used one of the signal processing SP_1 - SP_4, were tested. Then, the proposed expert system utilizing the knowledge base focused on the signal processing was used.

The results of all verification systems for the particular tests are displayed in Table 1. The performance of the verification is expressed by Equal Error Rate. The best results are emphasized for each test set.

Table 1. Overview of the experimental results

Signal	Results [EER]				
processing	Set 1	Set 2	Set 3	Set 4	Set 5
SP_1	**2.36%**	23.76%	9.72%	31.47%	16.83%
SP_2	9.59%	16.32%	9.59%	16.86%	13.09%
SP_3	6.03%	20.73%	**7.72%**	20.93%	13.74%
SP_4	4.73%	**10.79%**	7.81%	19.18%	10.63%
Expert system	**2.36%**	10.96%	8.72%	**15.66%**	**9.43%**

It can be seen that the systems using one signal processing work well in suitable operating conditions. When the operating conditions change, other signal processing is the best one. This fact is utilized by the expert system, which try to choose the optimal signal processing for the current operating conditions.

The used knowledge base allows to distinguish between the particular sets quite well, but a non-optimal signal processing was assigned to some trials, mostly from the set 3. The result of the set 4 indicate that the improper assignment to the set can sometimes improve the performance, because the operating conditions worth more than the membership of some set. This information can be used to improve the detectors in the future.

5 Conclusions

An architecture of the expert system for speaker verification was introduced in this article. The suitable representation of the expert knowledge was selected according to the specific procedures of the speaker verification task. The proposed approach based on the combination of the rules and an oriented graph was tested by the knowledge base focused on the signal processing. The results of the experiments shows that the proposed expert system is suitable for speaker verification. Although the used knowledge base was really small, the EER was improved by 1.2%. More improvements can be achieved by the knowledge base extension and inclusion of more modules. The architecture of the proposed expert system hold the line.

References

1. Vaněk, J., Padrta, A.: *Introduction of Improved UWB Speaker Verification System*, Proc. of Text Speech and Dialogue 2005, Karlovy Vary, Czech Republic.
2. Vaněk, J., Padrta, A.: *Optimization of Features for Robust Speaker Recognition*, In Speech processing. Prague : Academy of Sciences of the Czech Republic, 2004. pp. 140–147. ISBN 80-86269-11-6.
3. Schalk, H., Reininger, H., Euler, S.: A System for Text Dependent Speaker Verification - Field Trial Evaluation and Simulation Results, Eurospeech 2001, pp. 783–786, 2001.

4. David, P.: Presentation of Real-time System for Automatic Speaker Identification and Verification, The 7th World Multiconference on Systemics, Cybernetics and Informatics, pp. 372–376, 2003.
5. Liou, H.-S., Mammone, R.: A Subword Neural Tree Network Approach to Text Dependent Speaker Verification, ICASSP 95, pp. 357–360, 1995.
6. Farrel, K. R.: Text Dependent Speaker Verification Using Data Fusion, ICASSP 95, pp. 349-352, 1995.
7. de Veth, J., Bourland, H.: Comparison of Hidden Markov Model Techniques for Speaker Verification, ESCA 94, 1994.
8. Heck, L., Genoud, D.: Integrating Speaker and Speech Recognizers: Automatic Identity Claim Capture for Speaker Verification, Proc. 2001: A Speaker Odyssey, The Speaker Recognition Workshop, Crete, Greece, June 2001.
9. Heck, L., Weintraub, M.: Handset-Dependent Background Models for Robust Text Independent Speaker Recognition, ICASSP 97, pp. II-1071-1074, 1997.
10. Radová, V., Psutka, J.: UWB_S01 Corpus – A Czech Read-Speech Corpus, Proc. ICSLP 2000 Beijing China (2000) 732–735.

Automatic Online Subtitling
of the Czech Parliament Meetings*

Aleš Pražák, J.V. Psutka, Jan Hoidekr, Jakub Kanis, Luděk Müller, and Josef Psutka

University of West Bohemia, Department of Cybernetics,
Univerzitní 8, 306 14 Plzeň, Czech Republic
{aprazak, psutka_j, hoidekr, jkanis, muller, psutka}@kky.zcu.cz

Abstract. This paper describes a LVCSR system for automatic online subtitling (closed captioning) of TV transmissions of the Czech Parliament meetings. The recognition system is based on Hidden Markov Models, lexical trees and bigram language model. The acoustic model is trained on 40 hours of parliament speech and the language model on more than 10M tokens of parliament speech trancriptions. The first part of the article is focused on text normalization and class-based language model preparation. The second part describes the recognition network and its decoding with respect to real-time operation demands using up to 100k vocabulary. The third part outlines the application framework allowing generation and displaying of subtitles for any audio/video source. Finally, experimental results obtained on parliament speeches with recognition accuracy varying from 80 to 95 % (according to the discussed topic) are reported and discussed.

1 Introduction

There is a lot of hearing impaired people who have only limited access to the information contained in acoustic signal of mass media. There are some projects for their assistance, such as TV subtitles (closed captions), but their cost is high and applicability is quite limited. The goal of our work is to use recent advances in the field of automatic speech recognition (ASR) for offline automatic subtitle generation and even for live broadcasting.

Currently, we have developed the system for the automatic online generation of subtitles for tasks with a vocabulary limited by a specific domain, such as parliament speeches. The whole system consists of three modules. The first module provides the speech signal acquisition from the source media and its delivery to the second module - a large vocabulary continuous speech recognition (LVCSR) system. LVCSR system results are then passed to the third module that provides their post-processing and subtitles displaying.

2 Language Model

By law, the shorthand records of all Czech Parliament meetings are available for public use on the Internet. These shorthand records are amended to avoid slips of the tongue and to meet grammatical rules.

---

* Support for this work was provided by the Academy of Science of the Czech Republic, project no. 1QS101470516.

Petr Sojka, Ivan Kopeček and Karel Pala (Eds.): TSD 2006, LNAI 4188, pp. 501–508, 2006.

2.1 Text Normalization

The language model training text contains many non-standard (NS) words: abbreviations, acronyms, numbers written as figures, dates etc. A conversion of NS words to their standard forms (digit sequences, abbreviations and acronyms to the full word forms) is called text normalization.

The text normalization for languages with a low degree of inflection, such as English, is easier, because the most conversions are unambiguous. However, in highly inflectional languages, such as Czech or other Slavic languages, one NS word can be converted to several standard forms, each of which has the same meaning, but represents different morphological categories (gender, case and number). The morphological meaning of NS word is given by its context in a whole sentence. The method proposed in [1] solves the task of finding the right standard form for a given NS word. This method is based on a tagger performing context-dependent morphological disambiguation of each word in a given sentence.

Our system for text normalization has two modules. The first module ensures the NS word detection and classification and the second module the conversion itself. The detection and classification is based on regular expressions. We distinguish 17 different types of NS words, for example cardinal or ordinal number, fraction, date, hours, abbreviation, currency amount, percentage etc. The detected NS words are then converted to their standard form by the second module. The conversion is algorithmic and uses the method proposed in [1]. The NS word is converted to the basic form and then the right standard form is created using morphological information given by the tagger.

The accuracy of the NS word conversion is about 90 % (see [1]) and that is cause why some manual correction has to follow. The implementation of automatic text normalization with the manual correction accelerates process of the text normalization more then ten times in comparison with full manual text normalization.

2.2 Language Model Classes

Currently, we have about 10 M tokens of normalized Czech Parliament speech transcriptions (Chamber of Deputies only) from two electoral periods. The texts from different electoral periods differ only in the deputies and government members. To be able to automatically subtitle parliament meetings of any (including future) electoral period, the names of all representatives (deputies and government members) of that period have to be added to the system vocabulary.

We have created a language model with five classes for representative names and surnames in different grammatical cases. The language model was trained in two steps.

Firstly, the known names of representatives were automatically inflected to all grammatical cases. This inflection was based on specific rules for different cases and different inflectional patterns. Seven patterns for male names and four patterns for female names cover over 99 % of all Czech names. The representative names in the training text were then replaced by the tags corresponding to the name case. Unfortunately, different grammatical cases can have the same morphological form (especially female names), so manual classification of ambiguous morphological forms is still necessary.

In the second step, the names of representatives and their phonetic transcriptions were inflected in the same manner and added to five classes trained from the tags. The first class contains names and surnames in the first grammatical case, the second class in the second and fourth case, the third class in the third and sixth case and the fourth class in the seventh grammatical case. In addition to multi-word `"name_surname"`, also `"surname"` was added to the class in proportion to their occurrence ratio in the training text. The last fifth class contains reverse multi-words `"surname_name"` in the first grammatical case.

In this way, the class-based language model can be used for any electoral period with known representatives.

3 LVCSR System

The large vocabulary continuous speech recognition (LVCSR) system developed at the Department of Cybernetics, University of West Bohemia is the main module of the whole subtitling system.

3.1 Acoustic Processing

The digitization of an analogue signal at the input of the LVCSR system is provided at 44.1 kHz sample rate and 16-bit resolution format. The aim of the front-end processor is to convert continuous acoustic signal into a sequence of feature vectors. Several tests were performed in order to determine the best parameterization of the acoustic data. We have made experiments with MFCC and PLP parameterizations (see [2] for methodology). The best results were achieved using 27 filters and 12 PLP [3] cepstral coefficients with both delta and delta-delta sub-features. Therefore one feature vector contains 36 coefficients. Feature vectors are computed at a rate of 100 frames per second.

Each individual basic speech unit is represented by a three-state HMM with a continuous output probability density function assigned to each state. At present, we use 8 mixtures of multivariate Gaussians for each state. The choice of appropriate basic speech unit with respect to the recognition network structure and its decoding will be discussed in the following section.

3.2 Recognition Network

Our LVCSR system uses the lexical tree (phonetic prefix tree) structure for representation of acoustic baseforms of all words of the system vocabulary.

In a lexical tree, the same initial portions of word phonetic transcriptions are shared. This can dramatically reduce the search space for a large vocabulary, especially for inflectional languages, such as Czech, with many words of the same word stem. The automatic phonetic transcription is applied to all words of the system vocabulary and resulted word baseforms for all pronunciation variants are added to the lexical tree. The phonetic transcription of foreign words and phonetic exceptions can be defined separately.

For better word pronunciation modeling, we use triphones (context dependent phonemes) as basic speech units. By using a triphone lexical tree structure, the in-word triphone context can be easily implemented in the lexical tree. However, the full triphone cross-word context leads to fan-out implementation by generation of all cross-word context triphones for all tree leaves. For example, the lexical tree based on a 40000-word vocabulary from a Czech newspaper corpus and phonetic alphabet comprising 44 phonemes contains 15 cross-word context triphones to each 1 in-word triphone on average. This solution results in enormous memory requirements and vast computational demands. To respect the requirement of the real-time operation we have proposed an approximation of the triphone cross-word context.

One of the approaches uses monophones (context independent phonemes) on the word boundaries - in the root and leaves of the lexical tree. This brings the necessity of training two acoustic models and smoothing their monophone and triphone likelihoods. To cope with this, we can use the same triphone state likelihoods and merge the states of all triphones of the same monophone with one given context. As the system vocabulary is limited, not all right and left cross-word contexts have to be modeled and consequently not all triphones have to be used. This approach results in so-called biphones that represent merged triphone states with only one given context - right in the root and left in the leaves. The biphone likelihood is computed as the mean of the likelihoods of merged triphone states. The proposed biphone cross-word context represents a better approximation than a simple replacement of triphones by monophones on the word boundaries. In addition, this approach increases neither the recognition network complexity nor the decoding time, but only the duration of offline recognition network creation.

3.3   Recognition Network Decoder

Since the bigram language model is used, a lexical tree copy for each predecessor word is required. The trigram language model which requires more lexical tree copies (for each two predecessor words) does not lead to improvement adequate to its more complex implementation.

The lexical tree decoder uses a time-synchronous Viterbi search with token passing [4] and effective beam pruning techniques applied to re-entrant copies of the lexical tree. Since the beam pruning is used inside and also at the level of the lexical tree copies, sudden increase of hypotheses log-likelihoods occurs due to application of language model probabilities at time of word to word (lexical tree to lexical tree) transitions. Fortunately, early application of the knowledge of the language model can be carried out by factorizing language model probabilities along the lexical tree. In the lexical tree, more words share the same initial part of their phonetic transcriptions and thus only the maximum of their language model probabilities is propagated towards the root of the lexical tree during the factorization. The normalization of factorized probabilities is also applied along different word lengths. In addition, a linear transformation of language model log-likelihoods (with language model weight and word insertion penalty) is carried out. This allows the optimal weighting of language and acoustic models. The probability factorization is performed in time of lexical tree copy creation.

To deal with the requirement of the real-time operation, an effective method for managing lexical tree copies is implemented. An algorithm controls lexical tree to lexical tree (word to word) transitions and lexical tree copies creation/discarding. The number of lexical tree copies decoded in real-time is limited, so there is only a small number of examined hypotheses with different word histories at one time. The control algorithm keeps only the most perspective hypotheses and avoids their undesirable alternations, which protects the decoding process from time consuming creation of lexical tree copies. The algorithm also manages and records tokens (comprising time indexes and log-likelihoods) passed among lexical tree copies in order to identify the best path at the end of the decoding. To support a word graph generation for speech understanding or another post-processing, not only the best, but several (n-best) word to word transitions are stored. For word graph portability, HTK Standard Lattice Format (SLF) [5] is used to store the word graph.

The proposed LVCSR system implementation handles tasks up to 100k words in real-time.

4   Application Framework

The implementation of speech signal acquisition and subtitle displaying is platform dependent. Our implementation on Microsoft Windows system is based on Microsoft DirectX technology [6].

The application framework consists of two DirectShow filters [7] one-way connected to each other. Thus, there are two detached DirectShow filters – one for audio and one for video stream. This solution is independent of the source media and can be used for digital records via cascade of DirectShow filters as well as for TV signal acquired by Windows Driver Model (WDM) capturing filters.

The speech signal from any media type supported by the system is acquired by our audio DirectShow filter. From this filter that does no signal transformation the speech signal is passed directly to the LVCSR system engine running in the separate thread. The recognized word sequence is forwarded via system pipes to the subtitle displayer implemented as a video DirectShow filter. Since the real-time recognition alternates the recognized word sequence, only its changes are forwarded. DirectShow filter implementation allows user to set its behavior. The delay between two changes sent to the subtitle displayer can be tuned. This affects the delay of subtitle completion and thus its readability.

To increase subtitle readability, the full word forms representing numbers are converted back to the digit sequences, i.e. the procedure opposite to the text normalization described above. The number value, order of magnitude and morphological categories are added to all numbers in the system vocabulary and used to convert full word forms to the digit sequences. The algorithm has to find boundaries between numbers in the continuous sequence of words representing numbers, to convert them back to their numeric symbols correctly. Furthermore, a simple speech detector based on one-state speech and silence models is used to detect the most probable sentence endings.

Recognized subtitles are incorporated to the source video stream by our video DirectShow filter. Each video frame, transparent subtitle bitmap is combined with the source bitmap. To reach maximum readability of the subtitles, two or three scrolling rows are displayed. Subtitles font anti-aliasing and shadowing effects are implemented too. All subtitle proportions are relative to the source media format. Filter properties, such as subtitle font type, size, and color are adjustable by the user.

Since the two developed DirectShow filters perform no format conversions, their filter priorities have to be set to very high level to use automatically by most player applications for each source media type. Because the system pipes are used for filter communication, recognized subtitles can be displayed alternatively by another application. This allows using proposed application design for the automatic online generation of subtitles also for pure audio signal, i.e. signal without video stream.

Fig. 1. Online subtitling of TV transmission of parliament speech

5   Experiments

The subtitling of the Czech Parliament meetings is a very suitable task to prove the concept of the automatic online subtitling, because the vocabulary is limited by a specific domain.

5.1   Acoustic Model

The acoustic model was trained on 40 hours of parliament speech records with manual transcription. We used 42 Czech phonemes. As the number of Czech triphones is too large, phonetic decision trees were used to tie states of Czech triphones. Now, subtitling of the Czech Parliament meetings works with 3729 different HMM states. The acoustic model is speaker and gender independent.

5.2   Language Model

The bigram back-off language model with Good-Turing discounting was trained on about 10M tokens of normalized Czech Parliament transcriptions (Chamber of Deputies only) from two electoral periods. The SRI Language Modeling Toolkit (SRILM) [8] was used for training. Only words, which occurred in the training text with frequency higher than two were added to the system vocabulary.

5.3   Test Data

Five different parliament speech test records, half an hour each, were chosen for the testing. The language model does not contain transcriptions of these records.

The first test record (TR1) concerns the privatization and the floods. The meeting chair stutters a lot. The second test record (TR2) is a read announcement of the Minister of Health (woman). The third test record (TR3) is a discussion on employees and entrepreneurs. The fourth test record (TR4) applies to discussion of budget and appeal of the Ukraine president Juschenko about piety for famine victims. The meeting chair stutters a lot. The last test record (TR5) is voting only.

The OOV word rate is relatively high, due to high ratio of slips of the tongue (33 %). OOV word rate, test record perplexity and experimental results are introduced in Table 1.

Table 1. Experimental results

Test record	OOV word rate	Test record perplexity	Recognition correctness	Recognition accuracy
TR1	2.35 %	360	90.81 %	86.81 %
TR2	2.50 %	1357	87.48 %	83.91 %
TR3	2.46 %	419	85.14 %	82.47 %
TR4	3.42 %	201	85.04 %	79.35 %
TR5	0.47 %	27	94.93 %	94.28 %
TR1 - TR5	**2.37 %**	**294**	**88.18 %**	**84.67 %**

6   Conclusion

The subtitles of the Czech Parliament meetings generated online by our continuous speech recognition system are easily readable and did not reduce original audio information. The most mistakes are caused by OOV words, other mistakes are caused mainly by missing prepositions and wrong endings of flexible words.

The subtitling system is usable for any electoral period with known deputies and government members. The recognition accuracy depends on a discussed topic, but it does not fall below 80 % for conventional speeches.

References

1. Kanis, J., Zelinka, J., Müller, L.: Automatic numbers normalization in inflectional languages. In: 10th International Conference SPEECH and COMPUTER (SPECOM 2005), Patra, Greece, 2005.
2. Psutka, J., Müller, L., Psutka, J. V.: Comparison of MFCC and PLP Parameterization in the Speaker Independent Continuous Speech Recognition Task. In: 7th European Conference on Speech Communication and Technology (EUROSPEECH 2001), Aalborg, Denmark, 2001.
3. Hermansky, H.: Perceptual linear predictive (PLP) analysis of speech. J. Acoustic. Soc. Am. 87, 1990, pp. 1738–1752.
4. Young, S. J., Russell, N. H.: Token Passing: A Simple Conceptual Model for Continuous Speech Recognition Systems. Cambridge University Engineering Dept., Technical Report No. 38, 1989.

5. Young, S. J., et al.: The HTK Book. Entropic Inc., 1999.
6. Linetsky, M.: Programming Microsoft DirectShow. Wordware Publishing, 2001.
7. Pesce, M. D.: Programming Microsoft DirectShow for Digital Video and Television. Microsoft Press, 2003.
8. Stolcke, A.: SRILM - An Extensible Language Modeling Toolkit. In: International Conference on Spoken Language Processing (ICSLP 2002), Denver, USA, 2002.

Character Identity Expression in Vocal Performance of Traditional Puppeteers

Milan Rusko[1] and Juraj Hamar[2]

[1] Institute of Informatics of the Slovak Academy of Sciences, Bratislava
Milan.Rusko@savba.sk
[2] Department of Aesthetics, Faculty of Philosophy of the Comenius University, Bratislava
Hamar@internet.sk

Abstract. A traditional puppeteer generally uses up to a dozen different marionettes in one piece. Each of them impersonates a character with its own typical voice manifestation. It is therefore very interesting to study the techniques the puppeteer uses to change his voice and their acoustical correlates. This study becomes even more interesting when a traditional style exists that has been respected by the puppeteers for more than a century. Thus we decided to make use of the fact that there are records available of several pieces played by Bohuslav Anderle (1913-1976) and we recorded parts of the same plays played by his son, Anton Anderle (1944), supplemented by his verbal description of personality features of the characters that the actor tries to express in their voices. A summary of variety of characters one puppeteer has to master is given and the psychological, aesthetic and acoustic-phonetic aspects of their personalities are discussed. The main goal of the paper is to present a classification of voice displays of characters, techniques of voice changes, and their acoustic correlates.

1 Introduction

Motto: "Academies of sciences and arts should record to a gramophone disc the pathetic speech of the folk puppeteers – at least the oldest ones – before they are gone." [1]

It is well known, that expressive speech synthesis, speaker recognition, speaker verification and other areas of automatic speech processing can profit from using the experience of psychology, aesthetics, phonetics and phonology in speech research. All these disciplines can help to better understand a phenomenon we decided to explore – intentional change of voice by the speaker. There are two interesting special approaches to the research on intentional voice changes and voice imitation:

The first one we have called **"One voice – several speakers"**, is used to study voice imitation, and the second approach, that we call **"One speaker – several voices"**, studies actor's voice when representing different characters.

This paper describes preliminary steps of our research following the second approach. A puppeteer who switches among a dozen of voices representing personalities of his characters seems to be an ideal object of such a research.

1.1 Marionette Theatre in Slovakia and the Anderle Family

A history of the folk puppet theatre in Slovakia goes back to the time of the Austro-Hungarian monarchy. The first written evidence of a puppet show in Bratislava is from the year 1609. The

Petr Sojka, Ivan Kopeček and Karel Pala (Eds.): TSD 2006, LNAI 4188, pp. 509–516, 2006.

greatest puppeteers often mastered 40–50 plays. The whole repertoire was generally played with one set of 15 - 20 puppets. The movement (animation) and voice (declamation) of all the puppets was generally realized by one puppeteer. Sometimes also other family members helped him with performances.

a)   b)

Fig. 1. a) Bohuslav, Vladimír, and Anna Anderle on their way to a next stop, 1943**b)** Anton Anderle on the backstage, 1994

More than twenty puppeteers were active in the inter-war period in Slovakia; but the communist regime has soon ruined this rich tradition. The only traditional folk puppeteer which is still performing today is Anton Anderle (*1944) who is a follower of the third generation of the famous Anderle family. His father Bohuslav Anderle (1913–1976) was a well known puppeteer who was able to perform 40 pieces.

As a talented boy Anton rehearsed the same plays which his father played at a big puppet theatre. In the seventies he tape-recorded his father's puppet pieces. After 1989 Anton has started playing the old father's repertoire again. At present Anton Anderle's theatre is one of the most popular traditional puppet theatres in Europe.

2   Personality – Character Identity

It is very difficult to separate speech features reflecting personality from those that express emotions, affect and attitude. We are aware of the fact that these four parts of expressiveness are in close correlation and that they share the same acoustic means. It is therefore unlikely to find a clear one-to-one relation between personality features and the acoustic features that represent them.

2.1   Traditional Psychological Classification of Personality Dimensions

In psychology research the Five Factor Model of personality is often being used [2,3]. The five factors are considered to be the basis of the personality space:

Table 1. Five Factor Model of personality with description and examples

Personality dimension	Our code [values]	Description	High level [1] (example adjectives)	Low level [-1] (example adjectives)
Neuroticism	**N [1,0,-1]**	Tendency to experience negative thoughts	Sensitive Nervous Insecure Emotionally distressed	Secure Confident
Extraversion	**E [1,0,-1]**	Preference for and behaviour in social situations	Outgoing Energetic Talkative Social	Shy Withdrawn
Openness to experience	**O [1,0,-1]**	Open minded-ness, interest in culture	Inventive Curious Imaginative Creative Explorative	Cautious Conservative
Agreeableness	**A [1,0,-1]**	Interactions with others	Friendly Compassionate Trusting Cooperative	Competitive
Conscientiousness	**C [1,0,-1]**	Organized, persistent in achieving goals	Efficient Methodical Well organized Dutiful	Easy-going Careless

2.2 Parameters of Voice Quality

A particular voice setting is usually described in terms of the degree of deviation from a "neutral" setting. The neutral setting is defined as a normal position relative to possible adjustments [4].

Using Laver's classification scheme [4] it is possible to describe voice qualities.

2.3 Actor's Classification, Aesthetic Concept, and Realization

Personal characteristic of the traditional characters of the folk puppet theatre is a complex of three interconnected levels: semantic, optical and auditive. The semantic level characterizes the character as to its function in the play. The optical layer represents all components of visual representation of a puppet (face, costume, material and animation). The auditive layer includes speech, music and all the sounds generated by actor and his puppets.

For deeper understanding of the actors notion of personality of his characters, we asked Anton Anderle to characterize their personality and to explain the techniques he uses to change his voice. The actor based the description on both psychological features of the character and the acoustic-phonetic means to express them.

3   Available Speech Data

At present we have two basic types of recordings available. The first one is a set of eight complete puppet plays played by Bohuslav Anderle. The second part of the database consists of parts of pieces that were played by Anton Anderle in 2006 to demonstrate the typology of voices. The actor's natural voice and 21 voices of different characters have been recorded. This studio-quality record lasts about one hour.

Examples of the voices can be found at http://ui.sav.sk/speech/voices.htm.

Table 2. Laver's classification scheme representing particular voice settings with our simple code

Suprelaryngeal Settings	Code	Laryngeal Settings	Code
Longitudinal axis:	**LP**	**Simple phonation types:**	**MV**
Labial	**LD**	Modal voice	**F**
Labial protrusion	**RL**	Falsetto	**W**
Labiodentalization	**LL**	Whisper	**C**
Laryngeal		Creak	
Raised larynx			
Lowered larynx			
Latitudinal axis settings:	**CR**	**Compound phonation types:**	**WV**
Labial	**LS**	Whispery voice	**WF**
Close rounding	**TA**	Whispery falsetto	**CV**
Lip-spreading	**BA**	Creaky voice	**CF**
Lingual tip-blade	**RA**	Creaky falsetto	**WC**
Tip articulation	**DT**	Whispery creak	**WCV**
Blade articulation	**PA**	Whispery creaky voice	**WCF**
Retroflex articulation	**P**	Whispery creaky falsetto	**BV**
Tongue-body	**V**	Breathy voice	**HV**
Dentalized	**PH**	Harsh voice	**HF**
Palato-alveolarized	**LPH**	Harsh falsetto	**HWV**
Palatalized	**CJP**	Harsh whispery voice	**HWF**
Velarized	**OJP**	Harsh whispery falsetto	**HCV**
Pharyngealized	**PJP**	Harsh creaky voice	**HCF**
Laryngopharyngealized	**RJP**	Harsh creaky falsetto	**HWCV**
Mandibular		Harsh whispery creaky voice	**HWCF**
Close jaw position		Harsh whispery creaky falsetto	
Open jaw position			
Protruded jaw position			
Retracted jaw position			
Velopharyngeal settings:	**N**	**Overall muscular tension settings:**	**TV**
Nasal	**DN**	Tense voice	**LV**
Denasal		Lax voice	

Table 3. Classification of the characters based on several elementary semantic opositions

Criteria	One pole	code	Second pole	code
Sex	Male	**XM**	Female	**XF**
anthropological view	human	**HH**	Non-human	**HN**
Age	Old	**AO**	Young	**AY**
morality	Positive	**MP**	Negative	**MN**
Aesthetics	Tragical	**ET**	Comical	**EC**
Reflexion of ethnic	Our	**RO**	Foreign	**RF**
Social status	Noble	**SN**	Low	**SL**

Table 4. A shortened overview of the classification of basic types of voices given by the actor supplemented with our judgement of their personality dimensions (in code), speech quality description and its code, as well as some additional remarks

Name of the character	Actor's concept	Pers. code	Speech quality	Sp.Q code	Semantic features; other notes
Actor	Neutral, natural	E1, O1, A1	Middle pitched	MV	XM, HH;
Persian shah's daughter (Faust)	Young, gentle, judicious, relaxed, womanly, kindly, well-mannered	N-1, O1, A1	calm falsetto, low vocal effort	F	XF, HH, AY, MP, SN; The same as **Donna Caroline** (*Don Juan*)
Žabinka – Gašparko's wife (more pieces)	Hysterical, funny	N1, O-1,	Falsetto, resonant, sharp	RL, F	XF, HH, AY, MP, EC, RO, SL; Higher speech rate
Countess (Belengardo)	Angry, assertive, provocative, shrill	N1, E1, A-1	Falsetto, higher vocal effort	F	XF, HH, AO, MN, SN, Very high speech rate
Angel (Faust)	insisting	A1, C1	Falsetto, lower vocal effort	TV	XF, HN, MP; Special (urging) falling intonation contours
Faust (Faust)	Scholar, philosopher, serious	O1, C1	Modal effort, middle pitch	MV	XM, HH, AO, ET, SN; natural voice, pathetic
Gašparko (all pieces)	Funny, cheeky, lier	N1, E1, O1	Higher to modal pitch, raised larynx	RL, TV	XM, MP, EC, RO, SL; Lisping (s-š, c-č) Chatty, High sp. rate.
Belengardo (Belengardo)	Intriguant, self-assured, energetic, loud, self-confident,	E1, A-1, C1	higher throat res., wide mouth opening, hoarse	LS	XM, HH, AO, MP, SN;
King Meraldus (Turkish Island)	noble, serious, good, clever	N-1, A1, C1	Low pitched, thoroughly articulated	CR LP	XM, HH, AO, MP, SN;
Wagner (lacquey) (Faust)	agreedable, peaceful	N-1, O-1, C1,	Low pitched,	LL, CR, LV	XM, HH, AO;
Mefistofeles (Faust)	Devilish, rigid	A-1, C1	exaggerated, low, husky,	LL	XM, HN, MN;
Škrhola (Two godfathers)	Lionhearted, able, vigorous, optimistic	E1, A1	Wide (smiling) mouth, strong voice, throat resonance.	LS	XM, HH, AO, MP, EC, RO, SL;
Trčko (Two godfathers)	Dull, a little bit simple-minded,	N1, E-1	Middle pitched, nasal	N	XM, HH, AO, EC, RO, SL; muttering
Spirit of Don Avenez (Don Juan)	Mysterious, threatening, frightening	N-1, C1	Breathy, low pitched	LL, BV,	XM, HN, ET, SN; low speech rate vowels strongly elongated.
Gypsy (Jánošík)	Subservient,	E1, C-1	Denasalization (m-b, n-d), lower register,	DN, BV	XM, HH, AY, RF SL; rising intonation contours instead of declining one.
Jew (Comeback to home)	cunning	E1, A-1, C1	creaky, less voiced with modal pitch and not loud	WCV	XM, HH, RF, SL; influenced by Jidish (jewish dialect) –

4   Acoustic Analysis

Longer sections of the particular voices for analyses were obtained by concatenation of the utterances spoken by the individual character. The fundamental frequency as a representative of pitch and register was measured by autocorrelation of the LP residual and also from cepstrum. The spectral tilt that is a correlate of loudness and vocal effort was derived from long time average FFT spectrum. Breathy and creaky voice qualities can be measured on glottal pulses. We computed them by Discrete LP inverse filtering using Aparat [5]. A set of parameters is then measured from which the Normalized Amplit. Quotient is considered to be the most robust [6].

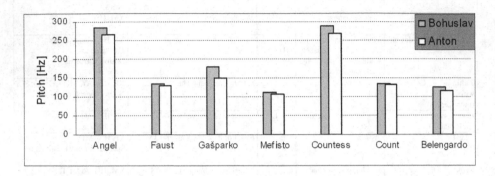

Fig. 2. Comparison of average fundamental frequency measured on longer speech utterances shows that the assignment of average F0 to the individual characters is very consistent with these actors

The full analysis of the results obtained by acoustical measurements, prosody analysis, statistical and cluster analysis of the material is out of scope of this paper and it will be published in our following works.

The following step in our research is to annotate the whole speech material orthographically to be able to use automatic signal annotation tools. Then we will be able to carry out measurements giving statistically verified results. We will try to record full versions of the plays in the interpretation of Anton Anderle. Experiments with "hyper-expressive" unit-selection synthesizer based on the database of recordings of puppet theatre performances can be one of the next steps.

5 Conclusion

This work represents an effort towards better understanding of the auditive display of personality dimensions. A special approach that studies intentional changes in the voice of a puppet player to present personalities of the individual characters is presented.

We have collected a speech material and created a database. We have adopted Five Factor Model of personality dimensions known from psychology and Laver's classification scheme of the characteristics of voice quality. We added a semantic classification of the characters based on several elementary semantic oppositions. Together with a simple code for all three classification schemes it was possible to accomplish a description of all the characters from the puppet pieces.

We believe this research will contribute to the knowledge on acoustical aspects of personality which, together with emotions, affect and attitude belong to the main objects of expressive speech synthesis research.

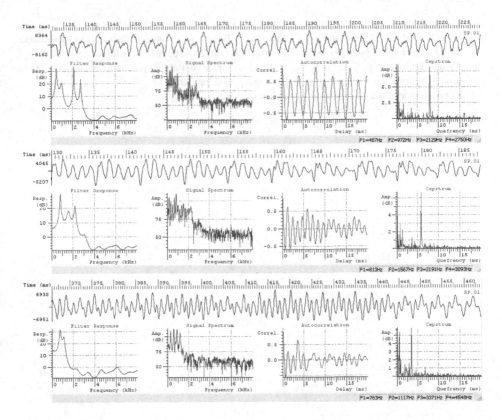

Fig. 3. Comparative measurement of vowel a from the same word uttered by low pitched voice Mefisto (top), neutral Faust (center) and falsetto voice Angel (bottom), uttered by B. Anderle. The LP filter response shows the formant positions. Dominant harmonics are evident from the signal spectrum. Autocorrelation function reflects the degree of periodicity and the dominant peak in cepstral function indicates the pitch period.

Acknowledgement

This work was funded by the Ministry of Education of the Slovak Republic, task number 2003 SP 20 028 01 03 and by the Slovak Agency for Science, VEGA, grant No. 2/2087/22.
    The SFS software package [7] was used for some of the analyses (see Fig. 3.).

References

1. Veselý Jindřich: Don Juan..., Národopisný věstník českoslovanský, XXII, No. 2–3, 1929, pp. 80–181.
2. Digman, J. M., Personality structure: Emergence of the five factor model, *Annual Revue of Psychology*, 41, 1990, pp. 417–440.
3. McRae, R. R.; John, O. P.; 1992 "An introduction to the five-factor model and its applications", *Journal of Personality* 60, pp. 175–215.

4. Laver J., *The gift of speech*, Edinburgh University Press., Edinburgh, UK., (1991).
5. Airas M., Pulakka H., Bäckström T., Alku P., A Toolkit for Voice Inverse Filtering and Parametrisation, *Proceedings of Interspeech 2005*, Lisbon, Portugal, 2005, pp. 2145–2148.
6. Alku P., Bäckström T., Vilkman E., Normalized amplitude quotient for parametrization of the glottal flow, J. Acoust. Soc. Am., vol. 112, no. 2, August 2002, pp. 701–710.
7. http://www.phon.ucl.ac.uk/resource/sfs/

A Dissonant Frequency Filtering for Enhanced Clarity of Husky Voice Signals

Sangki Kang and Yongserk Kim

SW Lab., Telecommunication R&D Center,
Telecommunication Network Business,
Samsung Electronics Co., Korea
{sangki.kang, yskimasi}@samsung.com

Abstract. In general, added noise in clean signal reduces intelligibility and degrades the performance of speech processing algorithms used for the applications such as speech compression and recognition. In this paper, a new voice clarity enhancing method using a dissonant frequency filtering (DFF) (especially $C\sharp$ and $F\sharp$ in each octave band when reference frequency is C) combined with noise suppression (NS) is proposed. The proposed method targets for speakers whose intelligibility became worse than normal under both noisy and noiseless environments.

The test results indicate that the proposed method provides a significant audible improvement for speakers whose intelligibility is impaired and especially for the speech contaminated by the colored noise. Therefore when the filter is employed as a pre-filter for enhancing the clarity of husky voice where several types of noises are also exploited, the output speech quality and clarity can be greatly enhanced.

1   Introduction

Degradation of quality or intelligibility of speech caused by the acoustic background noise is common in most practical situations. Therefore, the problem of removing the uncorrelated noise component from the noisy speech signal, that is, speech enhancement, has received considerable attention for several decades. There have been numerous studies on the enhancement of the noisy speech signal. [1,2,3,4,5,6,7]. They can be grouped into three categories as follows: The first category contains speech enhancement algorithms based on the short-time spectral estimation such as the spectrum subtraction [1] and Wiener filtering [2,3] techniques. The algorithms in the second category are the comb filtering and the adaptive noise canceling technique which exploit the quasi-periodic nature of the speech signal [4,5,6]. The third category contains algorithms that are based on the statistical model of the speech signal and utilize the hidden Markov model (HMM) or the expectation and maximization (EM) algorithm [7].

In this paper, we propose a novel speech enhancement scheme using filtering of a dissonant frequency (especially $C\sharp$ and $F\sharp$ in each octave band when reference frequency is C) combined with noise suppression [9] for speakers whose speech became less intelligible under the noisy and noiseless environment.

Petr Sojka, Ivan Kopeček and Karel Pala (Eds.): TSD 2006, LNAI 4188, pp. 517–522, 2006.

2   A Dissonant Frequency Filtering Combined with Noise Suppression

According to the standard musicology, a musical interval is defined as being *consonant* if it sounds pleasant or restful. *Dissonance*, on the other hand, is the degree to which an interval sounds unpleasant or rough. Dissonant intervals generally feel tense and unresolved. For example, $C\sharp$ and $F\sharp$ belong to the dissonant sounds when the reference frequency is C. Among them, $F\sharp$ is known as "the Devil's interval" in music [10]. So $C\sharp$ and $F\sharp$ needs to be eliminated to make speech less annoying and more pleasant. The dissonant frequency filtering (DFF) method is one of the candidates that eliminate the annoying sounds. It is also well known that NS algorithms can be exploited to enhance perceptual voice clarity.

In this paper, we exploit the two types of algorithms in series to enhance the performance of the respective algorithms. To achieve performance improvement, it is important to accurately estimate the fundamental frequency that determines the performance of the dissonant frequency filtering. Therefore, we also adopt an improved fundamental frequency estimation algorithm [8]. The proposed method can be summarized as follows:

First, the noisy input signal is processed using a noise suppression algorithm. Second, the resulting signal is transformed into frequency domain using Fast Fourier Transform (FFT) and then the fundamental frequency is estimated [8]. Next, filtering of the dissonant frequency based on the obtained the fundamental frequency (pitch) is performed.

The dissonant frequencies such as F_{d1} and F_{d2} corresponding to above $C\sharp$ and $F\sharp$ relative to a fundamental frequency F_0 are defined as

$$F_{d1} = F_0 \times 2^{n+\frac{1}{12}}, \quad n = 0, 1, \cdots, 7, \tag{1}$$

$$F_{d2} = F_0 \times 2^{n+\frac{6}{12}}, \quad n = 0, 1, \cdots, 7, \tag{2}$$

where F_{d1} and F_{d2} are the dissonant frequencies, F_0 is the fundamental frequency obtained by the improved fundamental frequency estimation using parametric cubic convolution [8] and n which represents the octave band varies from 0 to 7 on condition that F_{d1} and F_{d2} are less than the half of sampling frequency. The dissonant frequencies F_{d1} and F_{d2} will be filtered out if the following condition is satisfied as

$$F_0 \times 2^{n+\frac{1}{24}} < F_{d1} < F_0 \times 2^{n+\frac{3}{24}}, \quad n = 0, 1, \cdots, 7, \tag{3}$$

$$F_0 \times 2^{n+\frac{11}{24}} < F_{d2} < F_0 \times 2^{n+\frac{13}{24}}, \quad n = 0, 1, \cdots, 7, \tag{4}$$

where each range corresponds to a half tone or a semitone.

A simple filtering algorithm is employed in this paper. If speech shows a peak in the region defined above, that peak will smeared out, that is, the magnitude in that region is reduced to be lowered than the neighboring magnitude while its phase is kept. Finally, the inverse Fourier Transform of filtered signal is carried out. The block diagram of the above method is illustrated in Fig.1.

3   Experimental Results

The database for more reliable performance evaluation consists of 30 speech files collected from 10 speakers (6 males and 4 females) whose intelligibility is manipulated to be worse than normal speakers, each one delivering 3 Korean sentences. All utterances were sampled at 8kHz with 16-bit resolution. FFT window size was 1024-point. Noise types considered in our experiments include white Gaussian noise, babble noise and car noise recorded inside a car moving approximately at a speed of 80 km/h. We obtained the noisy speech by adding noise to clean speech with the noise power being adjusted to achieve SNRs =5, 10, and 15 dB. The noise suppression algorithm in IS-127 [9] is adopted. In order to evaluate the performance of the proposed enhancement scheme, MOS (mean opinion score) tests were conducted. Total 20 listeners participated in the test. During the testing period, all subjects used a high-quality handset as a listening device in a quiet room. The recordings in each presentation were played randomly. The listeners were asked to give a score ranging from 1 (Bad) to 5 (Excellent) according to the perceived quality. The simulation results are presented in Table 1 and Figures 2 and 3. The simulation results indicate that the proposed method provides a significant gain especially in a husky voice corrupted with babble noise.

Table 1. MOS results of subjective measures of enhanced voice clarity without and with noise suppressor

Noise types	SNR	Unprocessed	Processed by DFF	Processed by NS+DFF
White	5dB	2.11	2.36	2.96
Gaussian	10dB	2.23	2.57	3.08
noise	15dB	2.46	2.76	3.29
Babble	5dB	2.13	2.52	3.06
noise	10dB	2.26	2.75	3.32
	15dB	2.44	2.97	3.63
Car	5dB	2.26	2.54	2.87
noise	10dB	2.35	2.64	3.12
	15dB	2.54	2.77	3.24

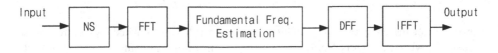

Fig. 1. Voice clarity improvement scheme

4   Conclusion

In this paper, we proposed a new voice enhancing method utilizing a dissonant frequency filtering as well as a noise suppression algorithm. The simulation results indicate that the

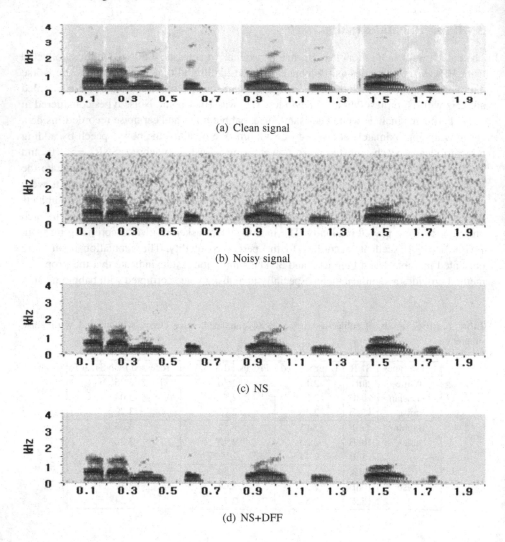

(a) Clean signal

(b) Noisy signal

(c) NS

(d) NS+DFF

Fig. 2. Spectrogram of enhanced husky voice signal (5 dB white noise)

proposed method improves the intelligibility of speech contaminated by colored noise. Therefore when the filter is deployed as a pre-filter, the resulting quality and clarity of husky voice can be greatly enhanced.

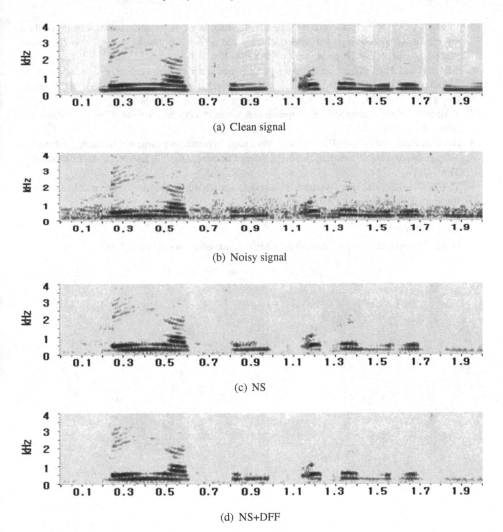

Fig. 3. Spectrogram of enhanced husky voice signal (5 dB babble noise)

References

1. S.F. Boll: Suppression of acoustic noise in speech using spectral subtraction. IEEE Trans. Acoust., Speech, Signal Processing, vol. ASSP-29, April (1979) 113–120.
2. J.S. Lim and A.V. Oppenheim: All-pole modeling of degraded speech. IEEE Trans. Acoust., Speech, Signal Processing, vol.ASSP-26, June (1978) 197–210.
3. J. Hansen and M. Clements: Constrained iterative speech enhancement with application to speech recognition. IEEE Trans. Acoust., Speech, Signal Processing, vol. ASSP-39, no. 4, April (1991) 21–27.
4. M.R. Samber: Adaptive noise canceling for speech signals. IEEE Trans. Acoust., Speech, Signal Processing, vol.ASSP-26, Oct. (1978) 419–423.

5. J.S. Lim, A.V. Oppenheim, and L.D. Braida: Evaluation of an adaptive comb filtering method for enhancing speech degraded by white noise addition. IEEE Trans. Acoust., Speech, Signal Processing, vol. ASSP-26, no. 4, April (1991) 354–358.

6. S.F. Boll and D.C. Pulsipher: Suppression of acoustic noise in speech using two microphone adaptive noise cancelation. IEEE Trans. Acoust., Speech, Signal Processing, vol. ASSP-28, no. 6, Dec. (1980) 752–753.

7. Y. Ephraim: Statistical-model-based speech enhancement systems. Proc. of IEEE, vol. 80, no. 10, Oct. (1992) 1526–1555.

8. Hee-Suk Pang, SeongJoon Baek, Koeng-Mo Sung: Improved fundamental frequency estimation using parametric cubic convolution. IEICE Trans. Fundamentals, vol. E83-A, no. 12, (2000) 2747–2750.

9. TIA/EIA/IS-127: Enhanced variable rate codec, speech service option 3 for wideband spread spectrum digital systems. (1997).

10. Jonathan Tennenbaum: The foundations of scientific Musical Tunning. FIDELIO Magazine, Vol. 1 No. 1, (1991–92).

11. D. M. Howard and J. Angus: Acoustics and Psychoacoustics. Focal Press (1996).

Post-processing of Automatic Segmentation of Speech Using Dynamic Programming

Marcin Szymański and Stefan Grocholewski

Poznan University of Technology, Institute of Computing Science
ul. Piotrowo 2, PL-60 965 Poznań Poland
mszymanski@cs.put.poznan.pl

Abstract. Building unit-selection speech synthesisers requires a precise annotation of large speech corpora. Manual segmentation of speech is a very laborious task, hence there is the need for automatic segmentation algorithms. As it was observed that the common HMM-based method is prone to systematical errors, some boundary refinement approaches, like boundary-specific correction, were introduced.

Last year, a dynamic programming fine-tuning approach was proposed, that combined two sources information, boundary error distribution and boundary MFCC statistical models. In this paper we verify the usefulness of incorporating several other data, boundary energy dynamics models and the signal periodicity information.

1 Introduction

In the process of constructing speech recognition and synthesis systems it is essential that the proper set of prerecorded utterances is available. It should additionally contain full annotation, including the sequence of phoneme labels and subsequent unit durations (which identify the transition time points). The accuracy of phoneme boundaries may not be crucial in case of recognition systems, however errors in segmentation seriously affect the quality of the obtained *synthesis* systems.

Manual segmentation of speech is a very labor-intensive process, moreover it should be performed by an expert (usually in phonetics) and it is prone to inconsistencies. The simplest idea is to implement an algorithm which will do this task automatically. We assume that the phone sequence is known in this task (in contrast to the phoneme recognition problem), either directly or in the form of a convertable orthographic transcription. Obviously, the obtained automatic boundary points will not be faultless.

The basic algorithmic solution of the segmentation is to run a HMM recognizer in *forced alignment* mode. The segmentation can now be considered a special case of recognition, where the word– and model-net are the simple concatenation of units, corresponding to the imposed phonetic transcription of an utterance. The standard recognition for HHM's involves finding the most likely state sequence via the dynamic Viterbi decoding:

$$\hat{s}_1^T = \arg\max_{s_1^T} p(y_1^T|s_1^T)p(s_1^T)$$

where s_1^T is a state sequence and T is a length of the observation sequence y_1^T.

Petr Sojka, Ivan Kopeček and Karel Pala (Eds.): TSD 2006, LNAI 4188, pp. 523–530, 2006.

For segmentation, where the sequence s_1^T is known *a priori*, the model boundaries are returned as a supplemental result of the Viterbi decoding or can be obtained in a *backward-pass*. This approach is already well studied (see e.g. [8]).

The important limitation of HMM's application to speech processing is its ignoring the probability densities (pdf's) of phoneme duration. Since the state transition probability in standard HMM is represented by one constant value, the state duration have an implicit geometric probability density, which most probably is inadequate as the duration model. For this reason, the observed phoneme duration is often modeled. In general, this can be viewed as a conversion from the Markov chain approach into the *segment models* [6]. Segment-based recognition involves finding

$$(\hat{N}, \hat{a}_1^N) = \arg \max_{N, a_1^N} \{ \max_{l_1^N} p(y_1^T | l_1^N, a_1^N) p(l_1^N | a_1^N) p(a_1^N) \}$$

where a_1^N is a N-length phone sequence and l_1^N denote a vector of respective segment lengths. As far as the segmentation is concerned, only the model duration sequence (l_1^N) is searched for.

The above state-chain based methods are primarily designed for speech recognition, not segmentation, and thus have the following drawbacks:

- the results they return are discretized according to the given frame-rate (usually 10 ms), while in the segmentation task we expect higher precision;
- statistical models of acoustic observations (represented by MFCC vectors) contained in each HMM state are trained on longer fragments of phoneme segments, while models trained on near-boundary observations only seem to be more appropriate for the segmentation task.

Moreover, it was observed that the Viterbi decoding tends to make systematical errors for certain boundary classes, e.g. transitions from speech to silence are often located ca. 20 ms before reference annotation.

For those reasons a refinement stage is required, in which "coarse" boundary points obtained from state-chain method are fine-tuned. The simple solution, boundary-specific correction (BSC), as proposed in [5], consists in calculating the mean error for each of 100 boundary classes (the phonetic alphabet was split into 10 clusters) and subtracting such estimate from every transistion case in a test set. In [1], the regression-trees (CART) were used instead of a partition into 100 classes; this method was reimplemented as the baseline of our work.

The BSC/CART method, however, applied the fine-tuning "blindelly", i.e. it did not consider the underlying acoustic contents of a wavefile in place of a transition. Thus, in [7], two sources of information were combined: the boundary-specific error distribution and a boundary acoustic observation distribution (MFCC parameters were simply used for that purpose). The method used dynamic programming to obtain the final segmentation. In a following extension, the duration distributions were also incorporated into this method.

As we see the ability to combine several differently calculated signal features as the main advantage of the above approach, in this paper we try to extend it by the parameters, which are beyond the standard MFCC vectors used for speech recognition and may carry some important clues for the precise location of the phoneme transition points. These are, namely, filterbank-based energy and the maximum signal autocorrelation coefficient.

The rest of this paper is organized as follows: Section 2 introduces the baseline boundary correction algorithms, Section 3 introduces the dynamic programming method together with the newly-incorporated parameters; in Section 4 the experimental results are presented. The paper is concluded in Section 5.

2   Boundary-Specific Correction with Regression Trees

The boundary-specific statistical correction (BSC) was introduced in [5]. The average error of the automatic segmentation result compared to manual reference annotation is computed for each type of boundaries. For the test set, each individual boundary b_i is corrected by shifting the transition point by its boundary-specific mean deviation:

$$\hat{b}_i = b_i - \mu_{C(b_i)}$$

In [5], Czech phonemes were divided into 10 clusters, reflecting their phonetic and acoustic features. As each boundary is described by its left and right context, this resulted in a total of 100 types of boundaries.

As an extenstion of BSC, a regression tree (CART) based method was proposed in [1]. A single binary decision tree is constructed by choosing questions on a phonetic context of an examined transition. The tree is applied to the testing data by moving the boundaries by the time found in a specific leaf of the tree.

In [7], the CART technique was re-implemented for Polish, using ca. 40 contextual questions. The tree was trained with a minimum of 70 supporting units in each leaf.

3   Dynamic Boundary Correction

This section introduces the DBC approach, which combines several sources of information (incl. the boudary-specific error estimates, boundary acoustic observation and duration distributions) in a single boundary-refinement method.

3.1   Correction Ranges

It should be noted that the DBC algorithm performs the optimisation considering acoustic data near the fine-tuned boundary only, in contrast to state-chain (e.g. HMM) based systems that perform the segmentation "globally". For this reason, in the post-processing stage, the transition points will only be shifted along the adjacent segments (left and right) of the particular boundary, in order to preserve the boundaries to unrestrictedly migrate along the utterance (ignoring the HMM stage results). This may be equivalent to the assumption that the state-based segmentation stage does not introduce gross errors (a gross error occurs when an automatically obtained boundary passes beyond one of the adjacent segments of a reference manual transcription [4]; this kind of error is considered the most harmfull in case of unit-selection synthesis). It should be noted that the assumption does not mean that the number of gross errors cannot change during the fine-tuning stage.

3.2   Time Discretization (Tuning Precision)

The presented methods are mainly oriented for the use within unit-selection synthesis. As the segment transitions obtained from one of these methods can become concatenation points during the synthesis, one may try to avoid *some* of the negative effects (e.g. cracks) of linking two clips with unmatched soundwave levels by placing the potential transition points on *rising zero crossings.*[1]

In the ideal case an algorithm would deliver results with a high precision, even to the level of one sample. However, such a measurement is unreachable because of asynchronicity of speech. Thus, the potential boundary points are spread in ca. 1 to 5 ms intervals.

The method first searches all rising zero-crossings throughout the wavefile. To assure that at least one potential boundary point appears within each 5 ms, it also allows a falling zero crossing to be used as a boundary, where necessary. If still no zero crossings are found within 5 ms or more, as many as needed potential transition points are spread regularly along such a period. Finally, wherever three zero-crossing points appear within 1 ms, the middle one is discarded.

The drawback of this approach is that it requires a calculation of MFCC or any other desired parameter vectors at a few hundred or more potential boundary points along each utterance. In experiments, the time required for this calculation exceeded the actual dynamic optimisation time. This issue needs to be addressed.

3.3   Information Sources

Boundary-specific error distribution. Boundary-specific segmentation error information used in DBC is, in contrast to the BSC/CART method, not limited to the mean error. The individual errors are collected from the training set (a signed difference between state-chain stage result and a reference transition point) and clustered with a maximum likelihood criterion, yielding a statistical model of the boundary-specific segmentation error:

$$ln \; P_{\mathrm{BSE}}(b_i - t \mid C(b_i))$$

For modeling, the error distribution single Gaussian pdf's are usually used. The example values of this cost-function are demonstrated in Fig. 1.

Boundary cepstral information. To introduce the acoustic information into the refinement stage, in [7], the boundary MFCC observations were collected from the training set, as demonstrated in Fig. 2. The MFCC+Delta+Acc vectors are calculated for two intersecting Hamming windows (plus 4 windows at each side required for the derrivative calculation); the window length and frame distance were the same as in the baseline segment model stage, i.e. 25 ms and 10 ms, respectively. The above examples were clustered according to the context to form decision trees; finally, normal distribution mixtures were estimated for the clusters.

---

[1] Authors are aware that some synthesis systems, e.g. BOSS[3], crossfade the adjacent units. However, the presented potential-boundary rule is not incompatible with them. On the other hand, some systems may require or expect boundaries to be pitch-synchronized; this is not yet supported in our method.

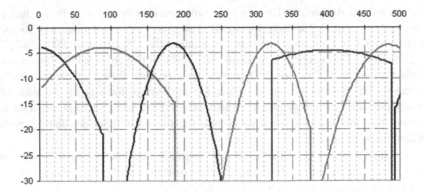

Fig. 1. Log probability of placing subsequent boundaries at a particular moment in time inside a 500 ms fragment of an example utterance, considering the state-based segmentation results and a boundary-specific error distribution.

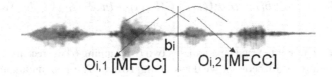

Fig. 2. Boundary acoustic information aquisition.

On evaluation, the left-side and right-side observation likelihood are combined using the formula:

$$ln\ P_{\text{MFCC}}(O_t \mid b_i) = ln\ P(O_{t,1} \mid C(b_{i,1})) + ln\ P(O_{t,2} \mid C(b_{i,2}))$$

The example values of this function are demonstrated in Fig. 3.

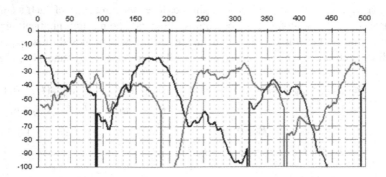

Fig. 3. Log probability of placing boundaries at a particular point inside a fragment of an example utterance, based on the MFCC boundary likelihood.

Boundary energy dynamics. The energy information is collected in a similar manner to the Sec. 3.3 and Fig. 2. However, the signal is first divided into 4 frequency bands; the respective filter transition frequencies are, approximately, (75,320), (320,800), (800,2700) and (2700,7000). The energy is then calculated for each of two cross-fading Hann windows. The window length is 8 ms and the frame distance is 4 ms. Four log energy values plus delta and accelaration coefficients constitute a feature vector for each of two sides of the boundary (actually, for the derivative estimation, we need more adjacent windows to be processed, but only the two that overlap *over* the transition point are directly used for boundary observations).

Such training data is clustered based on maximum likelihood using triphone context questions (with a minimum of 60 examples in every leaf). Finally, the diagonal covariance normal distribution is estimated for each cluster.

This forms the energy-based cost function, used during an evaluation (i.e. boundary fine-tuning). It then combines the left-side and right-side observation likelihood into the single formula:

$$ln\ P_{\text{En}}(O_t \mid b_i) = ln\ P(O_{t,1} \mid C(b_{i,1})) + ln\ P(O_{t,2} \mid C(b_{i,2}))$$

Signal periodicity. For the signal periodicity, two overlapping 64 ms rectangle windows are formed (the relative shift between windows being 16 ms). The maximum auto-correlation coefficient was used as the only feature (the 'shift', for which it is searched for, changes between 2.5 ms and 13 ms, which correspond to 77–400 Hz). With the delta coefficient it contitutes a 2-element feature.

The rest of the training data processing is done analogously to the previous subsections. As a result we get a boundary cost-function, $ln\ P_{\text{A-cor}}(O_t \mid b_i)$.

3.4   Dynamic Programming Formulae

The cost of placing a boundary b_i at the potential transition point occuring at time t depends on a sum of several elements: $ln\ P_{\text{BSE}}(b_i - t \mid C(b_i))$ and acoustical cost functions, MFCC-, energy- and correlation-based. A simple, local maximization of such a sum could theoretically lead to "swapping" two consequitive boundary points, thus implicating negative duration segments. For this reason, a dynamic algorithm was proposed (now expanded by two additional costs), in which $\phi_{i,t}$ denotes a likelihood of placing a boundary b_i at t:

$$\phi_{1,t} = w_{\text{BSE}} \times ln\ P_{\text{BSE}}(b_1 - t \mid C(b_1)) + w_{\text{MFCC}} \times ln\ P_{\text{MFCC}}(O_t \mid b_1)$$
$$+ w_{\text{En}} \times ln\ P_{\text{En}}(O_t \mid b_1) + w_{\text{A-cor}} \times ln\ P_{\text{A-cor}}(O_t \mid b_1)$$
$$\phi_{i,t} = w_{\text{BSE}} \times ln\ P_{\text{BSE}}(b_i - t \mid C(b_i)) + w_{\text{MFCC}} \times ln\ P_{\text{MFCC}}(O_t \mid b_i)$$
$$+ w_{\text{En}} \times ln\ P_{\text{En}}(O_t \mid b_i) + w_{\text{A-cor}} \times ln\ P_{\text{A-cor}}(O_t \mid b_i) + max_{0 \leq u < t}(\phi_{i-1,u})$$

where w are weight coefficients (any of them being zero means that the corresponding feature is ignored).

The optimal solution is obtained in the algorithm's backward pass.

3.5   Duration Model Version

A final extention of the above method consists in incorporating the duration likelihood of a left-side segment of a examined boundary into the formula:

$$\phi_{i,t} = w_{\text{BSE}} \times ln\, P_{\text{BSE}}(b_i - t \mid C(b_i)) + w_{\text{MFCC}} \times ln\, P_{\text{MFCC}}(O_t \mid b_i)$$
$$+ w_{\text{En}} \times ln\, P_{\text{En}}(O_t \mid b_i) + w_{\text{A-cor}} \times ln\, P_{\text{A-cor}}(O_t \mid b_i)$$
$$+ max_{0 \leq u < t}(\phi_{i-1,u} + ln\, P_{\text{DUR}}(t - u \mid b_i, 1))$$

It is assumed here that a phrase starts and ends with a silence segments (possibly of a zero duration). As silence segments were not subject to the duration modeling, the presented extention does not change the formula of $\phi_{1,t}$.

4   Experimental Results

In the experiments we use a part of Polish Corpora [2] database. It consists of a total of 5 hours of speech, inside 28 folders of 365 separate short sentences each. Hence, we deal with a speaker-independent segmentation.[2] The baseline HMM models were trained for the MFCC target rate of 10 milliseconds, while the manual segmentation was done with a 5 ms precision.

The tests were performed in 7-fold cross-validation, repeated 3 times. The developement of the segmentation method is demonstrated in Table 1. For each version we calculate the number of gross error and the Root Mean Square Error. All BSC and DBC methods were applied as a refinement stage to the segmentation result obtained from the segment-model approach.

Table 1. Developement of the segmentation method

Method	%Gr.E.	RMSE[ms]	Method	%Gr.E.	RMSE[ms]
Viterbi dec.	0.051	17.75	DBC+Dur+En	0.016	13.76
Segment model	0.032	17.15	DBC+Dur+Acor	0.019	13.88
BSC/CART	0.031	14.81	DBC+En+Acor	0.032	14.53
DBC	0.031	14.62	DBC+Dur+En+Acor	0.015	13.76
DBC+Duration	0.021	13.91			

The results show that the largest accuracy boost was obtained by the introduction of the CART-based correction technique. Dynamic programming extentions constitute a smaller improvement, but incorporating the duration modeling again reduces both error measures. Also, the energy dynamic parameters prove to carry some evidence of where the particular boundary lies. As for autocorrelation, it failed to yield a worthwhile accuracy boost except for the gross errors in one case.

---

[2] It may be noted that the database was designed to contain as much different diphones as possible; this might have influenced the statistical models used in this work.

5 Conclusions

We have presented an extended approach for fine-tuning the transition points obtained from a state-chained based algorithm. This final segmentation stage succesfully combines the error distribution information and boundary MFCC and energy observation models in a dynamic programming algorithm. The main drawback of the approach is the time required for the observations aquisition; although the calculation time is not crucial in case of the segmentation task, we think that there is the need for a more effective method for calculation of acoustic likelihood at potential boundary points.

Regarding other segmentation-related future plans, we plan to design a confidence measure, that would decide which boundaries should be inserted manually by human expert *prior* to the automatic stages and which would be succesfully annotated by the latter (in that case, the segmentation algorithm considers the inforced expert boundary points and does not change them). The objective of this semi-automatic approach is to reduce the trade-off between the human labor and the segmentation accuracy. For instance, the confidence measure may try to minimize a number of gross errors; having this number very close to zero allows to make an assumption from Section 3.1.

References

1. Adell J., Bonafonte A. (2004) Towards phone segmentation for concatenation speech synthesis *Proc. 5th Speech Synthesis Workshop*, pp. 139–144, Pittsburgh.
2. Grocholewski S. (1997), CORPORA – Speech Database for Polish Diphones, *Proc. Eurospeech'97*, pp. 1735–1738.
3. Klabbers E, Stoeber K, Veldhuis R, Wagner P, Breuer S (2001) Speech Synthesis Development Made Easy: The Bonn Open Synthesis System *Proc. Eurospeech 2001*, pp. 521–525.
4. Kvale K. (1993), *Segmentation and Labelling of Speech*, Ph.D. Thesis, Inst. for Teleteknikk, Trondheim.
5. Matousek J., Tihelka D., Psutka J. (2003), Automatic Segmentation for Czech Concatenative Speech Synthesis Using Statistical Approach with Boundary-Specific Correction, *Proc. Eurospeech 2003*, pp. 301–304, Geneva.
6. Ostendorf M., Digalakis V.V., Kimball O.A. (1996), From HMM's to Segment Models: A Unified View of Stochastic Modeling for Speech Recognition, *IEEE Trans. on Speech and Audio Proc.*, Vol. 4, No. 5, September 1996.
7. Szymański M., Grocholewski S. (2005), Dynamic programming method for fine-tuning the boundary points in automatic segmentation of speech, *Proc. Speech Analysis, Synthesis and Recognition Workshop*, Krakow, Poland.
8. Taylor P.A., Isard S.D. (1991) Automatic phone segmentation, *Proc. Eurospeech*, pp. 709–711, Genova.

Diphones vs. Triphones in Czech Unit Selection TTS*

Daniel Tihelka and Jindřich Matoušek

University of West Bohemia, Department of Cybernetics,
Univerzitní 8, 306 14 Plzeň, Czech Republic
dtihelka@kky.zcu.cz, jmatouse@kky.zcu.cz

Abstract. When we started to deal with the unit selection technique in ARTIC TTS, the question of the choice of the unit type used within the system was being dealt with. Although the basic version of our TTS system is based on triphones, we decided on the use of diphones in unit selection – mainly due to our concerns about the susceptibility of the unit selection technique to segmentation inaccuracies, and due to a limited experience with the overall system behaviour. However, we also planned to examine the possibilities of the use of triphones. As the first version of our unit selection is being built at present, this paper will examine whether the use of diphones can bring a significant advantage over the use of triphones, and whether there is a clear reason why one type of units behaves better than the other.

1 Introduction

Diphones and triphones (also known as context-dependent phones) belong among the units most intensively used in TTS systems. Although diphones are mainly connected with the beginnings of the expansion of modern concatenative speech synthesis, they were overcome by triphones in the field of "single unit instance" TTS (also called single candidate), as speech concatenated from triphones is more intelligible [1,2]. However, the resurrection of diphones begun when the unit selection (also multiple unit instance) technique started to be intensively developed, e.g. in [3,4].

The potential advantages and disadvantages of diphones and triphones can be summarized as follows:

- There is a smaller number of diphones, resulting in a higher number of candidates of each unit and in larger space that must be searched in the selection procedure. On the other hand, the selection algorithm, if well-tuned, is supposed to have a greater chance of finding a good sequence of candidates.
- The larger number of triphones also brings a larger number of uncovered units (those not occurring) in a corpus of a fixed size.
- The concatenation of triphones in spectrally varying regions at phone boundaries can "mask" the failures of concatenation cost measure. Contrary to this, the measure of the cost in spectrally stable regions in phone centres is supposed to be prone to those failures.
- The segmentation accuracy (usually done automatically using HTK – which is also our case – or DTW) is not so important in the case of diphones, as the shift into the middle of the phone signal bypasses the need of precise segmentation [3].

* This research was supported by the Grant Agency of the Czech Republic, project no. GACR 102/06/P205, and by the Academy of Sciences of the Czech Republic, project no. 1ET101470416.

Petr Sojka, Ivan Kopeček and Karel Pala (Eds.): TSD 2006, LNAI 4188, pp. 531–538, 2006.

To see if there is a clear confirmation of these assumptions, we used the same conditions (which basically means the same corpus and selection algorithm) to generate synthetic speech using both diphones and triphones. The use of other alternative units in unit selection TTS, such as halfphones [5], has not been examined yet, although it is also part of our future plans.

This paper is organized as follows. The following section presents a short description of our unit selection, Section 3 presents the distribution of units in the corpus, and Section 4 illustrates the behaviour of the MFCC trajectories in the corpus. The comparison of both unit types is carried out in Section 5, where listening tests are used to evaluate the overall quality of synthetic speech, and Section 6 displays the courses of costs used in unit selection. Finally, in Section 7 the speed of the selection is measured for the given units, and Section 8 summarizes the findings.

2   Introduction of Our Unit Selection

For the experiments in this paper we used the first version of unit selection, described details in in [6] and incorporated in our TTS ARTIC [7]. The unit selection module was originally designed for the use of diphones, so slight generalization of the module has been carried out in order to work with both diphones and triphones[1].

The prosody of synthesized phrases is driven by target cost, described solely on the symbolic level (without any explicit definition of F_0, duration and/or energy). In this way, the prosody of the generated phrase emerges on the basis of this symbolic description, and it is not known until the phrase is synthesized. To ensure overall smoothness, Euclidean distance from F_0 and MFCC, both measured at the unit boundaries and z-score normalized, is computed in concatenation cost. The selected sequence of candidates is then concatenated together in the time domain without any signal modification, smoothing and/or post-processing (except a small weighted overlap at the candidate boundaries).

Naturally, the important question is whether those features are appropriate for unit selection and whether there is a way of building features according to the essence of human perception. However, this is the task of our parallel research, aiming to answer those questions.

3   The Power of Unit Sets

The same speech corpus was used for all the experiments presented in this paper. It consists of 5,000 phrases (about 12.5 hours of recorded speech), recorded by a non professional female speaker with some radio-broadcasting experience, in a consistent news-like style [8]. It was automatically segmented, using the HTK toolkit, into so-called *clustered triphones* [9] – units where a clustering process assigns one triphone label to several different triphones in the corpus.

---

[1] Let us note here that the term *unit* will describe a different triphone or diphone label, whereas the term *candidate* will mean one particular token of a corresponding unit in a corpus. SAMPA alphabet is used in all unit labels.

The segmentation into clustered triphones was directly used to derive the diphones – the phones (given by the clustered triphone boundaries) were cut in the middle and two inter-phone neighbouring halves were connected together. The numbers of the original clustered triphone and derived diphone candidates are shown in Table 1.

As there are naturally many more clustered triphones than diphones, we have defined *generalized triphone* in order to have triphones comparable to diphones in the set potency, and thus to be able to observe the influence of the different character of concatenation points. To generalize the triphones, we classified both left and right context phones into the following phonetic categories (on the basis of phonetics and signal similarity) – *vowels* (marked by V), *liquids* plus *fricative* [j] (marked by L), *nasals* (marked N), *voiced plosives* (P), *unvoiced plosives* plus pauses and glottal stop (p), *voiced* (F) and *unvoiced fricatives* (f), and *voiced affricates* which, however, where considered either as *voiced fricative* in the left context, or *voiced plosive* in the right context, and similarly for *unvoiced affricates*. Naturally, there is a possibility of more precise division (especially of vowels), yet the aim was to approximate the diphones, and the more categories exist, the closer to clustered triphones we are. The correct coarticulation handling relies on the context-related target sub-cost in the unit selection. The frequency plot of unit candidates, sorted according to the frequency, is then shown in Figure 1.

Table 1. The power of sets of units; *number of units* means the number of different unit labels in the corpus, *total candidates* is the sum of all tokens of the units in the corpus; *avg., median, min* and *max candidates* values are computed from all candidates. Symbol # denotes short (inter-phrase) pause.

	diphones	clust. triphones	gen. triphones
number of units	1,528	7,106	1,081
total candidates	432,783	437,782	437,782
avg. candidates	283	61	405
median candidates	59	32	131
min candidates	1[#-g]	15 [?-a+o]	15 [F-Z+P]
max candidates	5,006[j-e]	1,539 [p-r+o:]	8,712 [V-v+V]

4   Mel Frequency Cepstral Coefficients (MFCC)

We will now look at the MFCC coefficients which are used, or examined, for the measure of concatenation cost by unit selection systems, e.g. [3,10,11]. In Figure 2, the course of trajectories of MFCCs through several phones are shown. To illustrate different cases, two words were chosen from different parts of our corpus – one representing trajectories through a sequence of voiced phones, and one for the trajectories in the sequence of unvoiced phones. The MFCCs were computed for 24ms window and 10ms framerate, and as there are 12 z-score normalized coefficients in each vector, the individual trajectories are shifted not to overlap. The vertical lines, moreover, mark the phone boundaries as obtained during the segmentation of the corpus; the diphone boundaries are exactly in the middle of the phone segments.

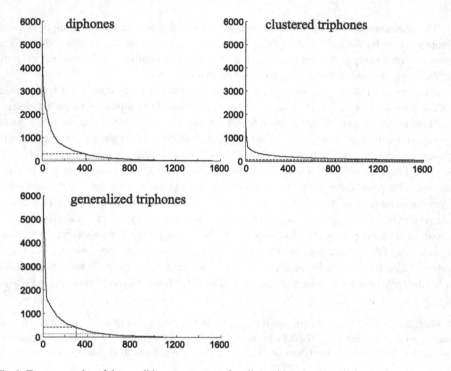

Fig. 1. Frequency plot of the candidate occurrences for all considered units. All figures have the same x and y scale, the mean value is marked by dashed line, the median by dotted line.

It may be seen that there is no observable discontinuity at the phone boundaries (this tendency was observed in most of the examined cases). It seems that the window of 24ms is enough to smoothen the spectrally varying regions. The point to be discussed is whether the simple Euclidean distance of MFCCs (even computed from a much lower window) is appropriate for the measure of concatenation smoothness – for example when HMM are used for automatic segmentation, more sophisticated treatment of the MFCCs must be used to obtain reasonable accuracy.

5   Listening Tests

The aspect determining the quality of the unit selection module is the naturalness of the generated phrases. Therefore, we asked 9 listeners, all without any known hearing problems, to listen to 3 versions of 10 short phrases (from 2 to 4 seconds) and sort them on the basis of overall quality (i.e. the minimum of artificial artefacts such as prosodic lapses, speed vibrations, machine-like sounds, discontinuous or unintelligible segments, etc.). The best phrase was then marked by number 1, the second best by 2, and the worst by 3. To avoid guessing, listeners were allowed to use the same mark for versions with very similar quality, but if two versions were marked by 1, the third took mark 3. The number of individual marks, and the average mark were then computed for all three versions, and are presented in Table 2.

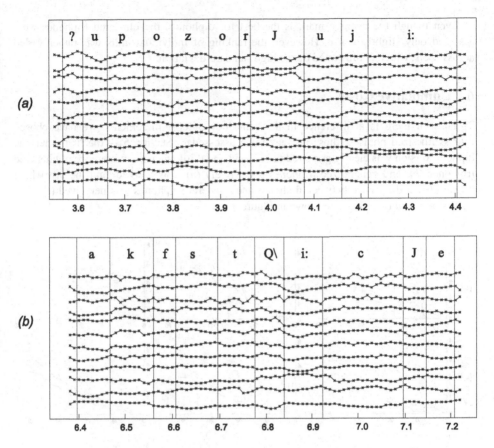

Fig. 2. The fragment of the trajectories of z-score normalized vectors of MFCCs in 2 natural phrases. The (*a*) chart shows the trajectories of the sequence of voiced phones, the (*b*) shows the courses for the sequence of unvoiced phones. The phone boundaries are depicted by vertical lines.

Table 2. The evaluation of the listening tests. The table shows the total number of individual assessments given to the phrases synthesized using the considered units; the average mark and its standard deviation are computed from those assessments.

	diphones	clust. triphones	gen. triphones
number of 1 marks	43	42	24
number of 2 marks	30	34	17
number of 3 marks	17	14	49
average mark	1.71	1.69	2.28
std. deviation	0.77	0.73	0.86

Even though the average mark is the best for diphones, the clustered triphones were assessed only slightly worse. However, the ranking of individual units was rather varied across users, which is illustrated by the high standard deviation.

6   Cumulative Costs

To show if there is a difference in the behaviour of cost increments, we have chosen four synthesized phrases (those also used and assessed in Section 5) – the first when the diphone version was clearly preferred (*a*), second and third when the preference of clustered triphones (*b*), and generalized triphones respectively (*c*), was marked, and the last where no significant difference between diphones and clustered triphones was perceived (*d*). The curves of cumulative costs are shown in Figure 3.

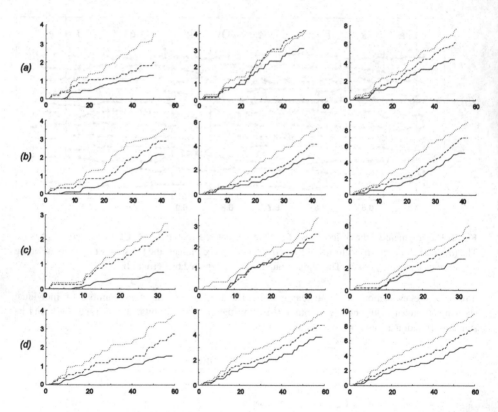

Fig. 3. The course of cumulative costs for synthetic phrase where diphones (*a*), clustered triphones (*b*) or generalized triphones (*c*) were preferred, and the phrase were diphones and clustered triphones did not significantly differ (*d*). The costs computed for diphones are drawn by a solid line, for clustered triphones by a dashed line, and for generalized triphones by a dotted line.

It is interesting that the lowest cost increments are still for diphones, although they were not assessed as the best by the listeners. The key point is whether it is simply the lower number of triphone candidates which causes the more frequent target mismatch and the lower concatenation suitability (using the given measures), or whether the features used are not adequate enough for the listeners' perception. Therefore, we are carrying out parallel research aiming to treat the unit selection idea in agreement with the phenomena of human perception.

7   Speed of Selection Algorithm

A very important aspect, from the point of view of practical usage, is the response of the unit selection TTS, i.e. how fast it can generate phrases. The approximate comparison of the unit selection module speed for the considered units is given in Table 3. We measured the time of 61 phrases (of different lengths) generation, and the averages of 4 measures gave the total times in the table. Let us note that our unit selection implementation has not been fully optimized yet.

Table 3. The comparison of unit selection speed for given type of units. The overall length of all synthesized phrases is approximately 8 minutes. The *total time* is the overall time of the algorithm run, the *ratio* is the proportion between the time of the selection run and the time of playing the phrases.

	diphones	clust. triphones	gen. triphones
total time	5m 36s	0m 20s	9m 45s
ratio	0.7	0.04	1.22

8   Conclusion

The paper attempts to show that there is no clear answer to the question whether diphones are more suitable than triphones for unit selection TTS. In addition, it tries to point out some neglected aspects of the approach.

A significant advantage of the use of triphones is the speed, given by the lower number of candidates per unit. Moreover, although the lower number of candidates gives a lower chance of finding the "right" candidate (using the given measure), the triphones were assessed only as slightly worse than diphones. Therefore, further analysis using the methodology described in [12] is planned to try to reveal under what circumstances the triphones fail.

Our main long-term attention remains focused on the general aspects of the unit selection approach, such as the design of features in agreement with human perception, the handling of symbolic prosody specification incorporating the idea of prosodic synonymy and homonymy [6], and further analysis of the behaviour of the approach.

References

1. Matoušek, J., Tihelka, D., Psutka, J.: Influence of Variable-Length Speech Units on Quality of Synthetic Speech Signal. Proceedings of NORSIG 2002. Norway (2002).
2. Hon, H.-W., Acero, A., Huang, X., Liu, J., Plumpe, M.: Automatic generation of synthesis units for trainable text-to-speech systems. Proceedings of ICASSP '98, vol. 1. Seattle (1998) 2293–2296.

3. Clark, R.A.J., Richmond, K., King, S.: Festival 2 – Build Your Own General Purpose Unit Selection Speech Synthesizer. Proceedings of ISCA Speech Synthesis Workshop. Pittsburgh (2004) 173–178.
4. Beutnagel, M., Conkie, A., Syrdal, A.K.: Diphone Synthesis using Unit Selection. Proceedings of 3rd ESCA/COCOSDA Speech Synthesis Workshop. Jenolan Caves, Australia (1998) 231–236.
5. Conkie, A.: A robust unit selection system for speech synthesis. Proceedings of Joint Meeting of ASA/EAA/DAGA in Berlin. Berlin, Germany (1999).
6. Tihelka, D.: Symbolic Prosody Driven Unit Selection for Highly Natural Synthetic Speech. Proceedings of Interspeech 2005 – Eurospeech. Lisbon (2005) 2525–2528.
7. Matoušek, J., Romportl, J., Tihelka, D., Tychtl, Z.: Recent Improvements on ARTIC: Czech Text-to-Speech System. Proceedings of ICSLP 2004, vol. III. Jeju Island, Korea (2004) 1933–1936.
8. Matoušek, J., Psutka, J., Krůta, J.: On Building Speech Corpus for Concatenation-Based Speech Synthesis. Proceedings of Eurospeech 2001, vol 3. Ålborg (2001) 2047–2050.
9. Matoušek, J., Tihelka, D., Psutka, J.: Automatic Segmentation for Czech Concatenative Speech Synthesis Using Statistical Approach with Boundary-Specific Correction. Proceedings of Eurospeech 2003. Geneva (2003) 301–304.
10. Stylianou, Y., Syrdal, A.K.: Perceptual and Objective Detection of Discontinuities in Concatenative Speech Synthesis. Proceedings of ICASSP, vol. 2. Salt Lake City (2001) 837–840.
11. Vepa, J., King, S.: Join Cost for Unit Selection Speech Synthesis. In Text to Speech Synthesis: New Paradigms and Advances, Chapter 3. Prentice Hall PTR (2004) 35–62.
12. Tihelka, D., Matoušek, J.: Revealing the most Significant Deterioration Factors in Single Candidate Synthetic Speech. Proceedings of SPECOM 2005. Greece (2005) 171–174.

Silence/Speech Detection Method
Based on Set of Decision Graphs*

Jan Trmal, Jan Zelinka, Jan Vaněk, and Luděk Müller

University of West Bohemia, Department of Cybernetics,
Univerzitní 8, 306 14 Plzeň, Czech Republic
{jtrmal, zelinka, vanekj, muller}@kky.zcu.cz

Abstract. In the paper we demonstrate a complex supervised learning method based on a binary decision graphs. This method is employed in construction of a silence/speech detector. Performance of the resulting silence/speech detector is compared with performance of common silence/speech detectors used in telecommunications and with a detector based on HMM and a bigram silence/speech language model. Each non-leaf node of a decision graph has assigned a question and a sub-classifier answering this question. We test three kinds of these sub-classifiers: linear classifier, classifier based on separating quadratic hyper-plane (SQHP), and Support Vector Machines (SVM) based classifier. Moreover, besides usage of a single decision graph we investigate application of a set of binary decision graphs.

1 Introduction

A silence/speech detection is an inseparable part of speech signal processing problems. Silence/Speech Detectors (SSD) are used to reduce data bandwidth demands, in voice compression algorithms, serves in noise adaptation techniques and in adaptation techniques in general. A high-quality SSD should be able to perform well under different operational conditions, in presence of a noise and independently on speaker.

Different signal processing algorithms can have very distinct requirements on a SSD. In general, both false positive errors (marking a non-speech signal as a speech signal) and false negatives (marking a speech signal as a non-speech signal) are targets of minimization. However, some applications can give priority to false negatives reduction (for example Voice Activity Detectors (VAD) used in telecommunication speech codecs), some applications prioritize false positives (for example adaptive echo cancellation algorithms and speaker verification tasks), some applications prefer only to recognize silence between complete sentences and not to recognize pauses between words (such as speech recognition tasks).

In this paper we describe methods based on construction of decision graphs i.e. hierarchical ordered set of classifiers. We use different sub-classifiers (linear classifiers, quadratic classifiers and SVM based classifiers) and compare their performance to the prevalent GMM classifier and to the detectors from telecommunication environment.

---

* Support for this work was provided by the Grant Agency of Academy of Sciences of the Czech Republic, project No. 1ET101470416 and by the Ministry of Education of the Czech Republic, project No. MŠMT LC536.

Petr Sojka, Ivan Kopeček and Karel Pala (Eds.): TSD 2006, LNAI 4188, pp. 539–546, 2006.

2 Sub-classifiers

The first described sub-classifier is a SVM based classifier. The SVM is a set of supervised learning methods for classification and regression. Usually, these methods use a transformation of a input vector to a vector with (much) higher dimensionality. The transformed data are supposed to be linearly separable.

A special method for the purpose of training the linear classifier is used. Resulting classifier is represented by the maximum margin hyper-plane, i.e. hyperplane separating two clusters and being equally distant from each of them. Quadratic optimization problem must be solved for finding this hyper-plane.

Given training vectors $\mathbf{x}_i \in R^n$, $i = 1, \dots N$, vectors of supposed classifier decisions $y \in R$, such that $y_i \in \{-1, +1\}$, and some non-linear transformation $\phi(\mathbf{x})$, the C-SVM solves the following problem:

$$\min_{w,b,\xi} \frac{1}{2}\mathbf{w}^T \mathbf{w} + C \sum_{i=1}^{N} \xi_i \tag{1}$$

subject to

$$y_i(\mathbf{w}^T \phi(\mathbf{x}_i) + b) > 1 - \xi_i$$
$$\xi_i \geq 0 \; i = 1 \dots N$$

This formulation is the primary problem of Quadratic Programming (QP). It is necessary to explicitly transform the data and use these transformed data. This fact can be prohibiting (so-called "curse of dimensionality"), so an alternative formulation is used. This alternative formulation is obtained by transforming the problem into its dual formulation.

The dual formulation is

$$\max_{\alpha} \; -\frac{1}{2}\sum_{i=1}^{N}\sum_{j=1}^{N} y_i y_j \Phi(\mathbf{x}_i, \mathbf{x}_j)\alpha_i \alpha_j + \sum_{j=1}^{N} \alpha_j \tag{2}$$

subject to

$$\sum_{i=1}^{N} \alpha_i y_i = 0$$
$$0 \leq \alpha_i \leq C \qquad \forall i \in \{1, \dots, N\}$$

where $\Phi(\mathbf{x}_i, \mathbf{x}_j) = \phi(\mathbf{x}_i)^T \phi(\mathbf{x}_j)$ is a kernel function. A kernel function is a function fulfilling conditions stated in Mercer's Theorem and can be interpreted (in this context) as a dot product of its input vectors transformed into some high-dimensional space. The classifier resulting from the dual problem has a form

$$y(\mathbf{x}) = \text{sign} \sum_{i=1}^{N} \alpha_i \Phi(\mathbf{x}, \mathbf{x}_i) \tag{3}$$

The dual QP formulation uses an implicit mapping of the input vectors. We do not provide the function transforming the input feature vectors, all we have to do is to supply some function representing the dot product in that resulting space.

Training of SVM often requires solution of a very large QP optimization problem. Although for solving QP general algorithms could be used, there exist special algorithms for the SVM training. These algorithms exploit the special structure of the SVM QP problems. Probably the most used algorithm is the Sequential Minimal Optimization (SMO). SMO breaks the large QP problem into a series of the smallest possible QP problems. These small QP problems are solved analytically, so the time-consuming iterative numerical QP optimization is avoided. The amount of memory required for SMO is linear in the training set size which allows SMO to handle very large training sets. For more detail see [2].

The second described classifier is a quadratic classifier which dissects the feature vector space with a quadratic hyper-plane. This classifier is motivated by a probabilistic approach where a feature vector $\mathbf{x}$ is classified as a class $y \in \{-1; +1\}$ and PDF $p(\mathbf{x}|y)$ is approximated by a normal distribution with diagonal covariance matrices. The implemented quadratic separating hyper-plane is of the following form:

$$\sum_{i=1}^{n} a_{2,i} \cdot x_i^2 + \sum_{i=1}^{n} a_{1,i} \cdot x_i + a_0 = 0, \tag{4}$$

where $a_{i,j}$ and a_0 are parameters of the hyper-plane.

The third sub-classifier is a linear classifier which is the consequence of the equality of the covariance matrices.

We used a Genetic Algorithm (GA) to find the optimal parameters estimation for the linear and the quadratic classifier. An initial result which serves as a population initialization is computed as a linear hyper-plane separating two feature vectors belonging to different classes randomly selected from the training set. The mutation operator modifies some randomly chosen parameter by addition of a random number having the PDF with zero mean and fixed variance. The crossover operator was not used.

3 Telecommunication Silence/Speech Detectors

In most cases, the silence/speech detectors used in the telecommunication environment were designed as simple rule-based systems which are driven by a set of features and flags obtained during the speech parameterization and compression. The purpose was to preserve the low complexity of voice codecs. They must be able to operate reliably even under marginal condition with respect to different environments, different speakers and different languages.

Their primary purpose was to enable the bandwidth saving effect through the means of discontinuous transmission (DTX) and to enable some basic adaptation of algorithms to a background noise, but the false positives were given priority over speech cut-offs. Often, a simple hangover scheme is included into the standard to ensure transmission of the undetected parts of speech.

We tested four commonly different VAD used. The first one belonging to G.729 coding is the historically oldest. The G.729 coding is still used today and is connected with Voice over IP technologies. There exists standards defining voice coding and transmission at 8 kbps, 6.4 kbps and 11.8 kbps.

The three other VAD are of similar age and belong to the Adaptive Multi-Rate technology (AMR). AMR speech codec is a mandatory codec for the third generation mobile phone systems (3GPP) and is supposed to be widely used in cellular systems. The AMR-WB codec works with signal sampled 16 kHz, while the "plain" AMR works with 8 kHz sampled speech signal.

All mentioned codecs use the Algebraic-Code-Excited Linear Prediction technique (ACELP). They partially differ in the codebook searching strategy. For details, see [8].

4 Binary Decision Graphs

A binary decision graph (BDG) for classification is an acyclic graph, whose each leaf has assigned a probability distribution of classification, and each non-leaf node has assigned a YES-NO question. The higher accuracy of classification and the lower number of nodes are the main contributions in comparison with a binary decision tree. The BDG construction algorithm tries to find the BDG having the lowest error rate on the training data. In our experiments we restricted the number of nodes and we limited the maximal accuracy to avoid overtraining.

There are two basic approaches to BDG construction. The first approach is to transform a binary decision tree into a BDG. The goal is not only to maximize the accuracy but we also try to minimize number of nodes. Thus, the transformation converts a binary decision tree into a BDG with the same or higher accuracy and simultaneously tries to reduce the number of nodes as much as possible. The transformation consists in a sequence of several relatively elementary operations such as nodes merging and nodes deletion.

The second approach to BDG construction is to construct a BDG directly. A simple algorithm implementing this approach is the modification of top-down binary decision tree construction algorithm and works as follows:

1. Start with a set of all examples at the root node.
2. While the number of nodes is lower than the selected threshold and the accuracy is lower than the selected threshold do:
   (a) Apply the transformation.
   (b) Select some leaf node n with the set of examples M.
   (c) Evaluate all possible questions for node n, choose the optimal (or suboptimal) question q and associate it with the node n.
   (d) According to the question q, divide the set of examples M into the sets M_{YES} and M_{NO} and make two new successor nodes: node n_{YES} with the set of examples M_{YES} and the node n_{NO} with the set of examples M_{NO}.
3. Apply the transformation.

There are two crucial points in the BDG construction algorithm. The first one is the question evaluation and the suboptimal question searching algorithm. A question is relevant only if $|M_{YES}| > 0$ and $|M_{NO}| > 0$. The suboptimal question searching algorithm concedes only a relevant question. In our experiments we used three kinds of classifiers (linear, quadratic and SVM based) and we used only one kind at a time.

Our question evaluation function E evaluating a question q is defined:

$$E(q, TS) = \sum_{i=1}^{n_E} c_i \cdot E_i(q, TS),$$ (5)

where TS is the training set, E_i is the i-th partial evaluating function and manually fixed c_i is the weight of function E_i. Besides entropy we used the relative number of corrected classification error estimation as a partial evaluating function. The weights of these partial evaluating functions are higher than weights of the other simpler partial evaluating functions.

We apply a genetic algorithm as a (sub)optimal question searching algorithm for linear and quadratic classifiers, and we apply a grid search algorithm for SVM based questions.

The second point is the selection of a leaf node which will be expanding later. Our algorithm tries to expand all leaf nodes and selects the leaf node of which expansion corrects most errors.

In addition to one single BDG, we utilized a set of BDG. Each BDG in the set is constructed from a unique part of the training set. Unique parts can be selected in a fully random manner or can be determined by some automatic clustering method. We utilized the second alternative. Our implemented clustering is a simple non hierarchical k-means algorithm. The influence of the number of clusters k on the overall performance is considered in section Experiments and Results.

5 HMM Based Silence/Speech Detector

An HMM based SSD is a modified HMM based speech recognition system. Hence, we can distinguish three parts of the HMM based SDD.

The first part is an acoustic model. The acoustic model consists of models of phonemes or more differentiated units such as triphones, i.e. phones situated between two specific phones. The acoustic model in our HMM based speech detection consists of only two models: model of silence and model of speech. Both models permit generation of exactly one segment. The output probability density function in each state is approximated by Gaussian Mixture Model (GMM) with diagonal covariance matrices. The number of mixtures in GMM is given in the experimental results in the Section 6. In our experiment we gradually increased the number of mixtures by one and saved and tested the particular models.

The second part is a pseudo-language model which is implemented as a pseudo-word net. We use a n-gram based pseudo-language model. The model is based on language having only two words: "silence" and "speech". In our experiments we compared the zerogram, unigram and bigram based pseudo-language models. The detector based on the zerogram pseudo-language model makes a decision in accordance with GMM models only. The unigram model uses information about a priori probability of the speech and silence. The bigram model is more complicated and use four transition probabilities. All the a-priori probabilities were computed from the training part of the data.

6 Experiments and Results

In our experiment we used the Czech high-quality speech corpus [6]. In the first experiment we tested the telecommunication SSD. We downsampled the test recordings because the corpus contains recordings sampled at 44.1 kHz and the detectors operate at signals sampled at 8 kHz and 16 kHz respectively.

Table 1. Comparison of performance of detectors used in the telecommunication SSD

	G.729	AMR/2	AMR/1	AMR-WB
mean	85.1 %	89.22 %	89.22 %	85.51 %
max	94.9 %	98.96 %	98.96 %	98.38 %
min	39.9 %	56.69 %	56.69 %	49.23 %

In all following experiments, the MFCC feature vectors were used. In the second experiment the method based on BDG with linear sub-classifiers was considered. In the experiment we studied the influence of the maximal number of nodes m in one BDG and the number of clusters k on the accuracy of the silence/speech classification. The results of the second experiment are in Table 2. In the first column, i.e. for $m = 1$, only an a priori information for each cluster is applied. In the second column, i.e. for $m = 3$, only one sub-classifier of given kind is used in each cluster.

Table 2. The results of classification by means of sets of BDG with linear sub-classifiers

k	$m = 1$	$m = 3$	$m = 10$	$m = 20$	$m = 30$
1	78.73 %	96.41 %	96.98 %	97.03 %	97.03 %
10	92.36 %	96.50 %	97.11 %	97.21 %	97.22 %
100	95.44 %	96.91 %	97.26 %	97.30 %	97.32 %
200	95.39 %	97.04 %	97.26 %	97.28 %	97.29 %
300	95.92 %	96.96 %	97.20 %	97.22 %	97.23 %

The results of the third experiment where the method based on BDG with quadratic sub-classifiers was considered are slightly better as shown in the Table 3. Also, the overtraining effect is not so noticeable.

Table 3. The results of classification by means of sets of BDG with quadratic sub-classifiers

k	$m = 1$	$m = 3$	$m = 10$	$m = 20$	$m = 30$
1	78.73 %	96.85 %	96.95 %	97.03 %	97.03 %
10	92.36 %	96.37 %	97.15 %	97.35 %	97.37 %
100	95.44 %	96.91 %	97.40 %	97.41 %	97.44 %
200	95.39 %	97.17 %	97.43 %	97.45 %	97.47 %
300	95.92 %	97.17 %	97.36 %	97.40 %	97.41 %

Table 4. The results of classification by means of sets of BDG with SVM sub-classifiers

k	$m = 1$	$m = 3$	$m = 10$	$m = 20$
1	78.73 %	93.84 %	96.05 %	96.85 %
10	92.36 %	96.37 %	97.02 %	96.83 %
100	95.44 %	96.67 %	97.39 %	96.94 %

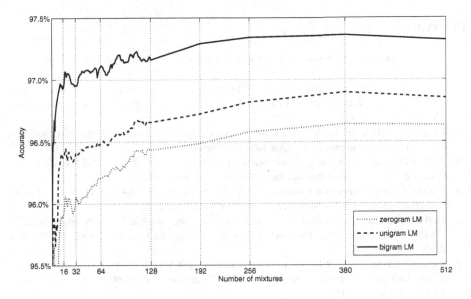

Fig. 1. Performance of the HMM Based Silence Detector

As we already mentioned, we used also the SVM classifier. However, we were not able to train the SVM classifiers using the whole set M during the node n expansion, because the process of training of SVM was exceedingly time consuming. To resolve this, each time when the number of input feature vectors was higher than some empiricaly chosen number Q, we had chosen exactly Q feature vectors in a fully random manner from the set M. This can be the reason of the worse performance (compare results).

In the last experiment the HMM based SSD was considered. The results are shown in Figure 1. As can be seen from the figure, the pseudo-language modeling is a beneficial option. With the increase of n in n-gram models the accuracy increases. The best result (97.36 %) has been obtained for 380 mixtures with the bigram pseudo-language model.

7   Conclusion

The speech detection still cannot be declared as a solved problem. After all, the highly accurate silence detection problem is comparable to a speech recognition problem. Our experiments have shown that there exists a wide performance gap between methods which are expected to provide stable results across many mutually different operating environments while keeping low computational demands and methods which are constructed using algorithms which are computationally somewhat more expensive and targeted to operate in defined environment.

In the future, we intend to develop a robust real-time SSD for dialog systems. Another aim is to apply the decision based methods in audio-visual speech recognition system as a posteriors estimation algorithm.

References

1. Vapnik, V.: Statistical Learning Theory, John Wiley & Sons, Inc., New York, (1999). ISBN 0-471-03003-1.
2. Platt, J.: Using Sparseness and Analytic QP to Speed Training of Support Vector Machines, in Advances in Neural Information Processing Systems 11, M. S. Kearns, S. A. Solla, D. A. Cohn, eds., MIT Press, (1999).
3. Voice Activity Detector for Adaptive Multi-Rate speech traffic channels, GSM 06.94 version 7.1.1 Release 1994 Telecommunications Standards Institute (1994).
4. AMR Wideband speech codec; Voice Activity Detector (VAD), 3GPP TS 26.194 version 6.0.0 Release 6. European Telecommunications Standards Institute (1994).
5. VAD for Coding of Speech at 8 kbit/s Using Conjugate-Structure Algebraic-Code-Excited Linear-Prediction (CS-ACELP) – ITU-T Recommendation G.729 Annex B.
6. Müller, L.; Psutka, J.: Building robust PLP-based acoustic module for ASR applications. In SPECOM 2005 proceedings. Moscow: Moscow State Linguistic University, 2005. pp. 761–764. ISBN 5-7452-0110-X.
7. Radová V.; Psutka J.: UWB_S01 Corpus: A Czech Read-Speech Corpus, Proceedings of the 6th International Conference on Spoken Language Processing ICSLP2000, Beijing 2000, China. Volume IV., pp. 732–735.
8. Chu, W. C., Speech Coding Algorithms: Foundation and Evolution of Standardized Coders, John Wiley and Sons, Inc., New Jersey, USA, 2003, ISBN 0-471-37312-5.
9. Šmídl, L.; Prcín, M.; Jurčíček F.: How to Detect Speech in Telephone Dialogue Systems. In: Proceedings of EURASIP Conference on Digital Signal Processing for Multimedia Communications and Services ECMCS 2001, Hungary, Budapest, 2001, on CD-ROM. (ISBN 963-8111-64-X).
10. Cornu, E.; Sheikhzadeh H.; Brennan R. L.; Abutalebi H. R. et al: ETSI AMR-2 VAD: Evaluation and Ultra Low-Resource Implementation. In: International Conference on Acoustics Speech and Signal Processing (ICASSP'03), 2003, available at www.amis.com/tech_resources/dsp_technology_papers/ICASSP2003_VAD.pdf

Prosodic Cues for Automatic Phrase Boundary Detection in ASR

Klára Vicsi and György Szaszák

Budapest University for Technology and Economics
Dept. for Telecommunication and Mediainformatics, Budapest, Hungary
{vicsi, szaszak}@tmit.bme.hu
http://alpha.ttt.bme.hu/speech/

Abstract. This article presents a cross-lingual study for Hungarian and Finnish about the segmentation of continuous speech on word and phrasal level based on prosodic features. A word level segmenter has been developed which can indicate the word boundaries with acceptable accuracy for both languages. The ultimate aim is to increase the robustness of Automatic Speech Recognizers (ASR) by detection of word and phrase boundaries, and thus significantly decrease the searching space during the decoding process, very time-consuming in case of agglutinative languages, like Hungarian and Finnish. They are however fixed stressed languages, so by stress detection, word beginnings can be marked with reliable accuracy. An algorithm based on data-driven (HMM) approach was developed and evaluated. The best results were obtained by time series of fundamental frequency and energy together. Syllable length was found to be much less effective, hence was discarded. By use of supra-segmental features, word boundaries can be marked with high correctness ratio, if we allow not to find all of them. The method we evaluated is easily adaptable to other fixed-stress languages. To investigate this we adapted the method to the Finnish language and obtained similar results.

1 Introduction

Supra-segmental features are an integral part of every spoken language utterance. These can provide cues to the linguistic structure of the speaker's message, emotional state or communicative intent. Intonation, stress, rhythm, etc. can help to signal the syntactic structure of utterances into larger discourse segments and provide additional information for human speech processing. Using supra-segmental features in automatic speech recognition to increase its robustness is a tendency again. Some trials were conducted in the mid-eighties. But it has not yet been possible to exploit such knowledge in an automatic speech recognition system [1], [6]. This relative failure, according to Philippe Langlais [2] is mainly due to three types of difficulties:

- Significant contextual variability of prosodic knowledge (type of speech, speaker, structure and content of sentences, nature of the environment, etc.;
- Complexity of relations between prosodic information and various linguistic organization levels of a message;
- Problems encountered with accurate measurement of prosodic parameters, and their possible integration on a perceptual level.

Petr Sojka, Ivan Kopeček and Karel Pala (Eds.): TSD 2006, LNAI 4188, pp. 547–554, 2006.

The solution has been much more successful in the field of speech synthesis. For example, J. Venditti and J. Hirschberg summarised the current state of knowledge in intonation and discourse processing for American English [10]. They described an intonation-discourse interface which can be used in speech technology, mainly for speech synthesis.

In a number of recent works certain researchers have focused on temporal information for the detection of speech landmarks, again in American English [8]; A. Salomon, C.Y. Espy-Wilson, and O. Deshmukh for example, used the above method in [7] as the front end of an HMM-based system for automatic noisy speech recognition. Other researchers used multiple cues for detection of phrase boundaries in continuous speech, and integrated these into speech recognition systems [3], [4].

Speech production is a continuous movement of the articulating organs, producing a continuous acoustic signal. In human speech processing, linguistic content and phonological rules help the brain to separate syntactic units, such as sentences, phrases (sections between two intakes of breath), or even words. In our experiments we examined how words can be automatically separated in continuous speech in fixed stress languages such as Hungarian and Finnish (both of these languages belong to the Finno-Ugrian language family). These two languages are highly agglutinative, so they are characterised with longer average word length than English and also with a relatively free word order. Due to this, almost all words have some stress (a stronger or a slighter stress depending on the syntactical structure), normally on the first syllable (fixed stress), except in case of conjunctions or articles. This means that the word-level intonation units which we dealt with during our experiment are composed from a word, stressed on the first syllable, together with unstressed conjunctions or articles, if any exists. These word level intonation units are shorter than prosodic phrases. Hence, forward in this article we will strictly use the expression "word unit", and the boundaries of these units will be called "word boundaries".

In our experiment we measured fundamental frequency, energy and time course. These parameters (all or some of them) are necessary for the realisation and perception of stress in the Finno-Ugrian language family.

2   Methodology

For stress classification a HMM-based statistical method was used. Hungarian BABEL [5] and Finnish Speech Database [11] continuous read speech databases were used for the examination. The databases were segmented on prosodic level by an expert: word, phrase and sentence boundaries were also marked. For Hungarian 1600 sentences from 22 speakers and for Finnish 250 sentences from 4 speakers were used.

2.1   Acoustic Pre-processing

Fundamental frequency (Hz) and energy level (dB) were measured. Syllable duration was found to be problematic to measure exactly without using speech recognizer output, hence it was discarded. For the determination of fundamental frequency, autocorrelation method was used. In addition, a median filtering of the fundamental frequency sequence was applied in the following way: fundamental frequency F_i at the ith frame was obtained after median filtering:

$$F_i = med\{F_{i-3}, F_{i-2}, F_{i-1}, F_i, F_{i+1}, F_{i+2}, F_{i+3}\} \tag{1}$$

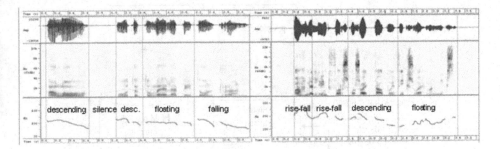

Fig. 1. Examples for the trained prosodic curve types. Time function, spectrogram of the speech signal are shown, below the prosodic labels with F_0 contour on Hungarian speech data.

Frame rate was chosen to be 25.6 ms. The E_i energy values, again with a frame rate of 25.6 ms, were calculated with an integration time of 100 ms using the standard equation:

$$E_i = \frac{1}{M+1} \sum_{n=i-\frac{M}{2}}^{i+\frac{M}{2}} s_n^2 \tag{2}$$

where M is the number of samples pro 100 ms, s is the speech signal.

2.2 Data-Driven Approach

For the determination of word units and their boundaries, the HMM method was applied using F_0, energy level parameters and their first and second order deltas. This type of examination needs a speech database, segmented on prosodic level, to train prosodic pattern HMM models. Databases were segmented by audio-visual segmentation method by an expert relying on fundamental frequency and energy cues. Prosodic phrase segment boundaries were marked so that they overlap with word boundaries. Since Hungarian is a highly agglutinative language, the average word length is relatively high, so prosodic structure often represents even word boundaries.

A set of 6 different Hidden Markov Models was constructed. We trained 6 different models that represent 5 types of prosodic (intonation) curves which are descending, falling, rising, floating and rise-fall. In other words, we interpreted intonation on syntagmatical or on word level. The 6th model is a silence model. Training examples for different prosodic curves are presented in Fig. 1 between cursors.

The block diagram of the training procedure of HMMs is shown in Fig. 2. Speech is pre-processed acoustically as described above, F_0 and energy data are computed, which are then used to train prosodic HMMs. By word level segmentation, these HMMs are used to recognize prosodic patterns on pre-processed input data. The prosodic model itself may be of interest in the future, but for the moment, we use only the boundaries of these "intonation" units for the evaluation.

We have also adapted this data-driven approach for Finnish language, using the same 6 prosodic models as for Hungarian. Training strategy for Finnish was the same as for

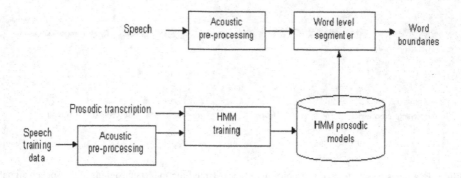

Fig. 2. Block diagram of the training procedure

Hungarian. We have made some cross- and multilingual experiments with Hungarian and Finnish. In this case, we used prosodic HMM models trained on one language to segment speech on the other language. We also trained a hibrid Hungarian-Finnish multilingual prosodic segmenter by including training data from both languages. Again, we used the same strategy discribed above (see Fig. 2).

2.3 Evaluation

To evaluate results, the obtained prosodic segmentation is compared with the original one. We use two measures to present our results. First one is correctness, which denotes whether a unit boundary predicted by our algorithm was correct or not. Please note, that as all prosodic unit boundaries were placed on word boundaries, correctness also shows the rate of correct detection of word boundaries:

$$Corr[\%] = \frac{C_{correctly\ marked\ word\ boundaries}}{C_{all\ marked\ word\ boundaries}} * 100 \qquad (3)$$

where C refers to the count of word boundaries. Our second measure is effectiveness, which says how many word boundaries were found at all:

$$Eff[\%] = \frac{C_{correctly\ marked\ word\ boundaries}}{C_{all\ word\ boundaries\ in\ reference\ transcription}} * 100 \qquad (4)$$

This second measure is expected to be less than 100% , hence not all words in speech are emphasized, and some words in syntagms share their "intonation" curve. We accept a marked (word) boundary to be correct if it is within a tolerance interval. This tolerance interval was set to [t-50, t+50] for time t, allowing a deviation of 50 ms from real word boundary.

For speech recognition tasks, correctness is more critical then effectiveness, because if a word boundary is predicted it should be detected correctly (we require a ratio at least around 80%). Of course, the higher the effectiveness the more robust the system, but we cannot permit this at the expense of lower correctness.

3   Results

By training of the HMM prosodic recognizer, the first task was the optimization of main HMM parameters. This means mainly to find the optimal number of states. Since intonation phrases are longer than phonemes - modeled usually with 5 state models by 10 ms frame rate - the number of states for prosodic models can be changed between 9 and 15. By our applied frame rate of 25.6 ms, 9 state models require a minimal phrase length of 230 ms. Minimal phrase length for 15 state models is 380 ms, which is a typical value for Hungarian according to our examinations. The optimal number of states was found to be 11.

Only 6 dimensional observation sequences (F_0, energy and their first and second order deltas) were used, 2, or at most 4 Gaussian components sufficed to describe output distribution of each state. Note, that the first and the last states are non-emitting ones [9].

HMM parameters fixed, we have tried two acoustic pre-processing alternatives: in the first case we used only F_0 or only Energy data with appended first and second order deltas; in the second case we used as input data F_0 and Energy, and to both of them first and second order deltas were appended. In Table 1 results are presented as a function of the acoustic pre-processing parameters. The best results were obtained when fundamental frequency-type parameters were used together with energy-type parameters.

Table 1. Correctness and effectiveness of boundary determination of word units with different acoustical pre-processing

Used parameter(s)	Language	Training corpus	Corr / Eff [% / %]
$F_0+dF_0+d^2F_0$	Hungarian	14 persons	67.4 / 58.4
$E+dE+d^2E$	Hungarian	14 persons	67.7 / 66.6
$F_0+dF_0+d^2F_0+$			
$E+dE+d^2E$	Hungarian	14 persons	**76.5 / 53.0**

We have also tested several training strategies for the constructed HMMs. During the examination, a 14 speaker data set was used for training and 18 speakers for testing. First the size of the training material was changed. The training set was reduced to 4 persons and finally to one person, while the test set consisted of the same 18 speakers in all cases. If the HMMs were trained on few speakers, these speakers were selected carefully in order to ensure a relatively accurate training corpus. Results are shown in Table 2.

Table 2. Correctness and effectiveness of boundary determination of word unit with HMM for different training settings

Used parameter(s)	Language	Training corpus	Corr / Eff [% / %]
$F_0+dF_0+d^2F_0$	Hungarian	1 person	77.1 / 49.6
+	Hungarian	4 persons	**77.4 / 57.2**
$E+dE+d^2E$	Hungarian	14 persons	76.5 / 53.0

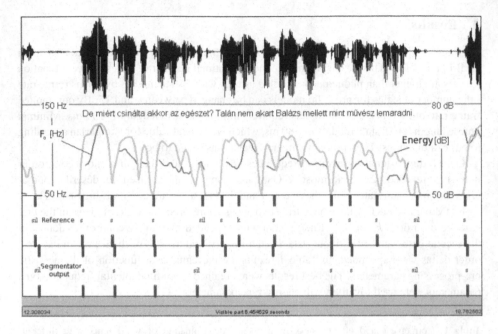

Fig. 3. HMM provided word level segmentation (down) versus expert-made hand segmentation (up) on a passage of 3 Hungarian sentences: [s] denotes word boundaries, [sil] silence

Surprisingly, there is no relevant difference in correctness if fewer speakers are involved in the training corpus. Effectiveness, however, depends very much on the number of speakers, and to achieve effectiveness over 50% at least four speakers' data should be used for training. If only F_0 or energy patterns are used, effectiveness is excellent, but we have 10% reduction in correctness. The overall best result was 77.4% correctness with 57.2% effectiveness, obtained with HMMs trained on 4 speakers' F_0 and energy data.

The developed system can be convenient for automatic segmentation of word units. An example is presented in Fig. 3 of how the developed segmentation technics work on word level. Time function of the speech signal, F_0 and energy contour are visible on the screen, while at the bottom the first row contains an expert-made hand segmentation taken as reference, the second row illustrates the output obtained by automatic prosodic segmentation. Segmentation accuracy means the correctness of determination of word unit boundaries.

Results obtained for Finnish with the same data-driven method as for Hungarian are presented in Table 3. We can note a considerable fall in correctness, while effectiveness is high. The reason for this may be that Finnish speech is much slower than Hungarian, and Finnish words often contain long plosive sounds where F_0 and energy contour show a very similar behaviour to the one they have on real word boundaries. As a result, many more word boundaries can be found than in Hungarian, but we can also detect some in-word secondary emphasis, which explains the lower correctness.

Cross-lingual prosodic word boundary segmentation results for Finnish and Hungarian are presented in Table 4. It can be seen that segmentation of Finnish speech with models trained on a Hungarian database gives nearly the same result as the Finnish models. On the other

Table 3. Correctness and effectiveness of boundary determination of word unit with HMM for Finnish language compared to Hungarian

Used parameter(s)	Language	Training corpus	Corr / Eff [% / %]
$F_0+dF_0+d^2F_0+$	Finnish	4 persons	69.2 / 76.8
$E+dE+d^2E$	Hungarian	4 persons	77.4 / 57.2.6

Table 4. Results of direct cross-lingual word boundary segmentation for Finnish and Hungarian

HMM models (trained on)	Test data (tested on)	Corr / Eff [% / %]
Hungarian (4 speakers)	Hungarian	77.4 / 57.2
Hungarian (4 speakers)	Finnish	67.1 / 52.1
Finnish (4 speakers)	Finnish	69.2 / 76.8
Finnish (4 speakers)	Hungarian	70.7 / 52.3
FI+HU (4+4 speakers)	Hungarian	75.0 / 68.2
FI+HU (4+4 speakers)	Finnish	69.7 / 83.7

hand, segmentating Hungarian data with Finnish models yields 70.7% correctness, which is somewhat better than on Finnish data (67.1%). This is probably due to the sparseness of Finnish data.

Generally this means that a prosodic word boundary segmenter well trained with a Hungarian database can be applied for automatic segmentation of unknown Finnish speech material and vice versa. Naturally hand-made correction is necessary. Using multi-lingual training strategy ensures a considerably more effective prosodic segmantation performance for Hungarian, by preserving a good correctness ratio.

4   Conclusion

Our prosodic segmenter based on measuring fundamental frequency and energy level functions gave promising results. Word boundaries can be marked with acceptable correctness, even if we are not able to find all of them. Two measurements, correctness and effectiveness, were used to describe the behaviour of this prosodic segmentation system. The method we evaluated is easily adaptable to other fixed-stress languages.

Word boundaries are found with acceptable correctness and effectiveness for fixed-stress languages like Hungarian and Finnish. In case of Finnish, we obtained results comparable with Hungarian, with lower correctness and higher effectiveness, which may be the result of the difference between the two languages, and also of data sparseness in the Finnish database.

Moreover, these results ensure that integration of a prosodic recognizer into a CSR system can help reduce the searching space and thus improve speech recognition performance. The importance of this searching space reduction is great in recognition of agglutinative languages such as Hungarian and Finnish, where the possible number of words may be more than one million. In this domain further investigations are needed.

Cross- and multi-lingual prosodic word boundary segmentation study of Finnish and Hungarian shows similarity between the two languages at word level prosody: i.e. segmentation of Finnish speech with models trained on Hungarian data give nearly the same result as models trained on Finnish data. By segmentation of Hungarian speech with models trained on Finnish correctness is similar to the one obtained by models trained on Hungarian data, and effectiveness is improved. These similarities are of course well known from the prosodic description of the two languages.

Summarizing the results of our experiments, it is clearly worth continuing research in this field. We believe that examination of other fixed-stress languages would be useful. We have presented one means of showing how it is possible to use prosodic information, but there may be several solutions. A practical result emerged from these experiments: this prosodic recognizer can also be used as a word-level automatic segmenter for Hungarian and Finnish languages.

Acknowledgements

We would like to thank Toomas Altosaar (Helsinki University of Technology) for his kind help and his contribution to the use of the Finnish Speech Database. The work has been supported by the Hungarian Research Foundations OTKA T 046487 ELE and IKTA 00056.

References

1. Di Cristo: Aspects phonétiques et phonologiques des éléments prosodiques. Modèles linguistiques Tome III, 2:24-83. (1981).
2. Langlais, P. and Méloni, H.: Integration of a prosodic component in an automatic speech recognition system. 3rd European Conference on Speech Communication and Technology. Berlin, pp. 2007-2010. (1993).
3. Mandal, S., Datta, A. K. and Gupta, B.: Word boundary Detection of Continuous Speech Signal for Standard Colloquial Bengali (SCB) Using Suprasegmental Features. FRSM (2003).
4. Peters, B.: Multiple cues for phonetic phrase boundaries in German spontaneous speech. Proceedings 15th ICPhS. Barcelona CA: ICPhS, pp. 1795–1798. (2003).
5. Roach, P.: BABEL: An Eastern European multi-language database. International Conference on Speech and Language Processing. Philadelphia. (1996).
6. Rossi , M.: A model for predicting the prosody of spontaneous speech (PPSS model). Speech Communication, 13:87–107. (1993).
7. Salomon, A., Espy-Wilson, C.Y. and Deshmukh, O.: Detection of speech landmarks. Use of temporal information. The Journal of the Acoustical Society of America 115:1296–1305. (2004).
8. Yang, L.: Duration and pauses as phrase and boundary marking indicators in speech. Proceedings 15th ICPhS. Barcelona, CA: ICPhS, pp. 1791–1794. (2003).
9. Young, S., Evermann, G., Kershaw, D, Moore, G., Odell, J., Ollason, D. et al.: The HTK Book (for version 3.3). Cambridge: Cambridge University, pp. 22–131. (2005).
10. Venditti, J. and Hirschberg, J.: Intonation and discourse processing. Proceedings 15th ICPhS. Barcelona, CA: ICPhS, pp. 107–114. (2003).
11. Vainio, M., Altosaar, T., Karjalainen, M., Aulanko, R., Werner, S.: Neural network models for Finnish prosody. Proceedings of ICPhS 1999. San Francisco, CA: ICPhS, pp. 2347–2350. (1999).

Dynamic Bayesian Networks for Language Modeling

Pascal Wiggers and Leon J.M. Rothkrantz

Man-Machine Interaction Group
Delft University of Technology
Mekelweg 4, 2628 CD Delft, The Netherlands
p.wiggers@tudelft.nl, l.j.m.rothkrantz@tudelft.nl

Abstract. Although n-gram models are still the de facto standard in language modeling for speech recognition, it has been shown that more sophisticated models achieve better accuracy by taking additional information, such as syntactic rules, semantic relations or domain knowledge into account. Unfortunately, most of the effort in developing such models goes into the implementation of handcrafted inference routines. What lacks is a generic mechanism to introduce background knowledge into a language model. We propose the use of dynamic Bayesian networks for this purpose. Dynamic Bayesian networks can be seen as a generalization of the n-gram models and HMMs traditionally used in language modeling and speech recognition. Whereas those models use a single random variable to represent state, Bayesian networks can have any number of variables. As such they are particularly well-suited for the construction of models that take additional information into account. In this paper language modeling with belief networks is discussed. Examples of belief network implementations of well-known language models are given and a new model is presented that models dependencies between the content words in a sentence.

1 Introduction

The task of a stochastic language model is to assign a probability to every sentence in a language. Using the chain rule of probability theory this is often reformulated as the task of predicting the next word in a sentence based on the previous words. The most common language models: n-grams, are based directly upon this principle and predict the next word based on a limited history of typically two or three preceding words. Despite their simplicity those models are surprisingly powerful as their locality makes them quite robust while at the same time they capture much of the local syntactic and semantic constraints in language. Nevertheless, a number of more sophisticated models have been introduced that do perform better than n-grams, all of which use additional knowledge of some sort. The knowledge used ranges from syntax [1] over semantic similarities between words [2] to knowledge of the application domain [3]. Although one might expect that the information used in different models is at least to some extend complementary, there have been only a few attempts to combine them [4]. Also there are many other pieces of information that are potentially useful for language modeling that can be explored, as an example one can think of the type of text or conversation at hand [5]. The structure and vocabulary of read text differs a lot from that of a spontaneous conversation, a fact typically dealt with by training different models for different types of data. Indeed there is little else one can do with the flat-structured n-grams.

Petr Sojka, Ivan Kopeček and Karel Pala (Eds.): TSD 2006, LNAI 4188, pp. 555–562, 2006.

We presume that the main reason that the area of knowledge-rich language models is largely unexplored is the lack of a unifying framework. Work in this domain typically proceeds along the following lines: a feature that might be useful in language modeling is identified, a probabilistic model that includes this feature is formulated and then most of the effort goes into deriving and implementing the algorithms needed to train the model and do inference with it. Although all of these models can be classified as probabilistic language models their already complex algorithms are highly specialized and therefore difficult to integrate.

In this paper we argue that dynamic Bayesian networks, that have proven themselves in artificial intelligence and recently also in speech recognition [6], can provide us with a framework that allows for rapid development and validation of knowledge-rich language models.

2   Related Work

A wide variety of language models have been developed that use other knowledge than the preceding words. Trigger-based models [2] use semantic relations between words. They are based on the notion of coherence of a text: words have a tendency to occur together with related words. This is implemented in the model as words triggering related words. Multispan language models model semantic similarity between words and the history using information retrieval techniques that calculate similarities between vectors associated with words and histories [7]. Another group of language models exploit coherence by modeling the topic of conversation [5,8,9].

A recent development are the so-called structured language models (SLMs) introduced by [1] that use syntactic information to model dependencies between words by formulating probabilistic parsers as generative language models [10,11]

Finally, some models use knowledge of an application domain to get more accurate word probabilities. In [3] travel frequencies between railway stations are used to better predict station names in a train table dialog system.

3   Dynamic Bayesian Networks

Bayesian networks originated in artificial intelligence as a method for reasoning with uncertainty based on the formal rules of probability theory [13]. Bayesian networks are represented as directed acyclic graphs of which the nodes are random variables and the arcs indicate conditional independence of the variables, i.e. the absence of an arc between two variables signifies that those variables do not (directly) depend upon each other. Thus a belief network is a factored representation of a joint probability distribution over all variables. The joint distribution is given by:

$$\prod_V P(V|Parents(V))$$ (1)

Dynamic Bayesian networks model processes that evolve over time. They consist of slices that specify the relations between variables at a particular time, implemented as a Bayesian

Network and a set of arcs that specify how a slice depends on previous slices. Dynamic Bayesian networks (DBNs) can be seen as a generalization of both n-gram models and hidden Markov Models. The difference being that HMMs use only one variable to represent the state of the model, whereas a DBN can use any number of variables. Several efficient inference algorithms have been developed for DBNs [12]. Training is typically done with an instance of the EM algorithm.

DBNs have already found their way to speech recognition, [6,14] have used DBNs to include articulatory information in acoustic models, as well as to model relations between observation features. Several types of DBNs have been used to construct multi-modal recognizers that integrate speech recognition and automatic lip-reading [15]. They have also been applied to dialog act classification [16].

4 Language Modeling with DBNs

Although DBNs have been used into speech recognition their use in language modeling and more general in natural language processing remains rather limited. We might presume that this is because other techniques such as grammars and weighted finite state transducer are more generally known in those areas. Finite state transducers can once again be seen as a special kind of belief network. In this section we will show how several well-known language models can be formulated as DBNs.

4.1 *N*-Grams

Fig. 1 shows the basic DBN representation of a trigram. It simply consists of a word variable in every time slice connected to its two predecessors. However, there are a number of issues we have to deal with. For n-grams one will typically use dummy states to indicate the start

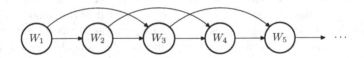

Fig. 1. Trigram Bayesian network

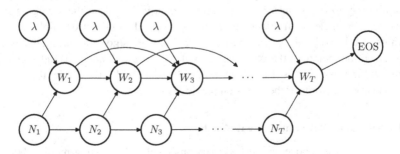

Fig. 2. Interpolated trigram

and the end of a sentence, where the start symbol is repeated several times to allow the use of trigrams for the first two words. The same can be done in DBNs, but there are better ways. To deal with the first two words a variable (N) is introduced that simply counts the words upon which the word distribution is conditioned. Now for the first and second slice special distributions $P_{first}(W)$ and $P_{second}(W|W)$ are used, from the third slice on the standard trigram is used. Another binary variable (EOS) is added that signals the end of a sentence. This variable is needed to make sure that the model is a proper language model, in the sense that the probabilities it assigns to all sentence in the language will sum to one rather than all sentences of a particular length. The n-gram counterpart of this is a sink state that transitions with probability one to itself. The counter can be conditioned on the end-of-sentence variable to let it restart for every sentence, thus ensuring that the first words of a sentence do not depend on the last words of the previous sentence. To keep the figures clear, we will not draw counter and end-of-sentence nodes in the remaining figures in this paper, but all of the models that will be discussed do include those variables.

Fig. 2 on the preceding page shows yet another variable: λ, this is a so-called switching variable with three states that is used to implement smoothing. Depending on the value of λ, the current word does either not depend on it predecessors at all, only on the previous word, or on the previous two words. As λ is a hidden node, the result is a mixture of distributions, essentially implementing deleted interpolation:

$$P_\lambda(W_t|W_{t-1}, W_{t-2}) = \lambda_1 P(W_t) + \lambda_2 P(W_t|W_{t-1}) + \lambda_3 P(W_t|W_{t-1}, W_{t-2}) \quad (2)$$

A well-known variation on n-gram models are skipping models in which a word does not depend on its direct predecessors but on words earlier in the history. Obviously, one can construct such models with DBNs by adding appropriate arcs to the model.

4.2 Class-Based Language Models

Class-based language models group words into classes in order to generalize to unseen words and to gather more reliable statistics. N-gram probabilities over classes are used to predict the class of a word which is then used to predict the word itself. [17] introduced class-based models with part-of-speech (POS) classes. Fig. 3 on the next page shows the DBN counterpart of hidden POS-model, the POS-tags are added to the model as a hidden variable (P) that is connected in time. Compared to n-grams, class-based models achieve better generalization and a smaller parameter set at the cost of less fine-grained modeling, to get the best of both worlds class-based models and n-grams are often combined through interpolation. This is particularly easy to accomplish in a DBN as is shown in Fig. 4 on the facing page which combines a POS-model with a trigram. There is no need to derive or implement special algorithms for this model, the general purpose belief network algorithms are all that is needed.

We can further improve the class-based model by also adding first and second order relations on the class level as is depicted in Fig. 4. Additionally we can let the class nodes depend on previous words or the words on previous tags.

4.3 Dependencies Between Content Words

The models discussed above are all DBN versions of already existing models, but we can also add other variables to the models to obtain new language models. For example it seems

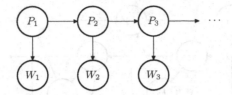

Fig. 3. Hidden class-based POS-model

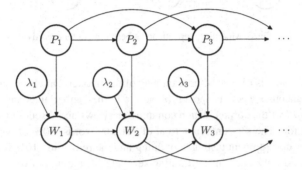

Fig. 4. POS-trigram

reasonable to assume that it is useful to model relations between content words in a sentence, as these will often relate to each other. This cannot be modeled with n-grams as the number of function words that separate the content words varies. Fig. 5 shows a belief network that can model such relations. A lemma variable (L) is added that takes as its states the lemmas of all content words. We decided on using lemmas rather than the content words themselves to alleviate data sparseness somewhat. When the model moves to the next slice it will first predict the POS-tag, from which follows if the word is a function word or a content word (implemented by the binary variable F). In case of a function word the word is predicted as usual based on its POS-tag and the previous words without using the lemma. The lemma in this slice will simply be a copy of the previous lemma, this way the last content lemma seen is memorized. If the POS-tag indicates a content word, the lemma will be predicted based on the previous lemma and is subsequently used in the prediction of the word.

5 Experiments

To experiment with belief network models we have implemented tools for the construction and training of belief networks as well as for recognition and inference (forward, forward-backward, Viterbi algorithms and slice-by-slice prediction). Unlike existing toolkits, these tools are targeted specifically at speech and language processing, which means that they can deal efficiently with variables that can take a large number of states, e.g. the number of words in the vocabulary, and distributions that are typically sparse. Other features include parameter tying and backing-off of distributions, as well as methods for pruning and fast approximate inference.

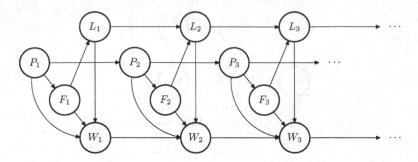

Fig. 5. Modeling dependencies between content words

We trained all models discussed here on part of the Spoken Dutch Corpus (CGN [18]), a corpus of spontaneous speech as spoken by adults in the Netherlands and in Flanders. We used subset *comp-f* of the corpus, which contains interviews and discussions broadcasted on radio and television. The set contains a total of 790.269 words, 80% of which we used for training, 10% for development testing and tuning and the remaining 10% for evaluation. All words that occured only once in the training set were treated as out-of-vocabulary words, resulting in a vocabulary size of 17833 words, 10470 lemmas and 257 POS-tags. The POS-tags include details such as number, degree and tense. Table 1 gives the perplexity of n-gram and POS models on our evaluation set.

Table 1. Perplexity results

language model	perplexity
interpolated bigram	296.49
interpolated trigram	280.76
interpolated trigram with POS-tags	245.39
lemma dependencies	258.44

It shows that the model that uses both word trigrams as well as POS-classes has a much lower perplexity than a simple interpolated trigram. This result is in correspondence with what one would expect from literature. The perplexity of the model using content lemmas is lower than that of n-gram models, but it does not do as well as the models with POS-tags added, this might have to do with the small size of the data set, the distribution over lemmas is extremely sparse, we therefore expect the model to improve if more training data is used.

6 Conclusions

In this paper we proposed the use of dynamic Bayesian networks for language modeling and showed how several well-known language models can be realized as belief networks. The main goal of our work is to explore the usefulness of higher knowledge sources such as syntax and semantics, domain knowledge and user characteristics in language modeling and speech recognition. We belief that Bayesian networks provide an ideal tool for such a task as they make it possible to define new models in a declarative way by simply specifying the variables involved together with the network structure without the need for special-purpose inference routines. Using a single framework to experiment with different models has the additional advantage that it is easier to compare models.

A language model that takes dependencies between content words into account was presented. The model does better in terms of perplexity than a standard trigram model but was not able to outperform a trigram model with POS classes on our data set, probably because the data set was rather small. We plan to repeat the experiments on a substantially larger dataset. In addition we want to use those models for rescoring of lattices output by a speech recognizer.

Acknowledgements

We would like to thank Rogier van Dalen for providing the metapost code for the figures in this document.

References

1. C. Chelba, F. Jelinek, Exploiting Syntactic Structure for Language Modeling. In Proc. of the 36th Annual Meeting of the ACL, August 1998.
2. R. Rosenfeld, A Maximum Entropy Approach to Adaptive Statistical Language Modeling. Computer, Speech and Language 10, 187–228, 1996.
3. P. Wiggers, L.J.M. Rothkrantz, Using Confidence Measures and Domain Knowledge to Improve Speech Recognition, Proceedings of Eurospeech 2003, Geneva Switserland, September 2003.
4. J. Goodman, A Bit of Progress in Language Modeling, Computer Speech and Language, October 2001, pages 403–434.
5. R. Iyer, M. Ostendorf, Modeling Long Distance Dependence in Language: Topic Mixtures vs. Dynamic Cache Models, Proc. ICSLP '96, Philadelphia, PA, 1996.
6. G. Zweig, Speech Recognition with Dynamic Bayesian Networks, Ph.D. Thesis, Computer Science Division, University of California at Berkeley, 1998.
7. J. R. Bellegarda, A Multispan Language Modeling Framework for Large Vocabulary Speech Recognition, IEEE Transactions on Speech and Audio Processing, Vol. 6, No. 5, September 1998.
8. D. Gildea, T. Hoffman, Topic-Based Language Models using EM, Eurospeech 1999, Budapest.
9. R. Zhang, A. I. Rudnicky, Improve Latent Semantic Analysis based Language Model by Integrating Multiple Level Knowledge, in proc. of ICSLP 2002, Denver, Colorado.
10. B. Roark, Probabilistic Top-Down Parsing and Language Modeling, Computational Linguistics, Volume 27, Number 2.
11. E. Charniak, Immediate-Head Parsing for Language Models, Meeting of the Association for Computational Linguistics", pages 116-123, 2001.
12. K. Murphy, Dynamic Bayesian Networks: Representation, Inference and Learning, Ph.D. Thesis, University of California, Berkeley, 2002.
13. J. Pearl, Probabilistic Reasoning in Intelligent Systems - Networks of Plausible Inference, 1988, Morgan Kaufmann Publishers, Inc.
14. J. Bilmes, Natural Statistical Models for Automatic Speech Recognition, Ph.D. Thesis, Dept. of EECS, CS Devision, U.C. Berkeley 1999.

15. A. V. Nefian, L. Liang, X. Pi, X. Liu, K. Murphy, Dynamic Bayesian Networks for Audio-Visual Speech Recognition, EURASIP Journal on Applied Signal Processing 2002:11, 1–15.
16. S. Keizer, Reasoning under Uncertainty in Natural Language Dialogue using Networks, Ph.D. Thesis Twenty University, 2003. 96.
17. F. Jelinek, Self-organized language modeling for speech recognition. In Alex Waibel and Kai-Fu Lee, editors, Readings in Speech Recognition, 1990, Morgan Kaufman Publishers, Inc. San Mateo, Ca.
18. I. Schuurman, M. Schouppe, H. Hoekstra, T. van der Wouden. CGN, an Annotated Corpus of Spoken Dutch. In Proceedings of the 4th International Workshop on Linguistically Interpreted Corpora (LINC-03). 14 April, 2003. Budapest, Hungary.

Part IV

Dialogue

"**Dialogue**: a discussion between two or more people or groups, especially one directed towards exploration of a particular subject or resolution of a problem: *interfaith dialogue*."

NODE (New, Oxford Dictionary of English), Oxford, OUP, 1998, page 509.

Feature Subset Selection Based on Evolutionary Algorithms for Automatic Emotion Recognition in Spoken Spanish and Standard Basque Language

Aitor Álvarez, Idoia Cearreta, Juan Miguel López, Andoni Arruti, Elena Lazkano, Basilio Sierra, and Nestor Garay

Dept. of Computer Science and Artificial Intelligence,
Computer Science Faculty (University of the Basque Country)
Manuel Lardizabal 1, E-20018 Donostia (Gipuzkoa), Spain
e-mail: aalvarez031@ikasle.ehu.es

Abstract. The study of emotions in human-computer interaction is a growing research area. Focusing on automatic emotion recognition, work is being performed in order to achieve good results particularly in speech and facial gesture recognition. In this paper we present a study performed to analyze different Machine Learning techniques validity in automatic speech emotion recognition area. Using a bilingual affective database, different speech parameters have been calculated for each audio recording. Then, several Machine Learning techniques have been applied to evaluate their usefulness in speech emotion recognition. In this particular case, techniques based on evolutive algorithms (EDA) have been used to select speech feature subsets that optimize automatic emotion recognition success rate. Achieved experimental results show a representative increase in the abovementioned success rate.

1 Introduction

Human beings are eminently emotional, as their social interaction is based on the ability to communicate their emotions and perceive the emotional states of others [3]. Affective computing, a discipline that develops devices for detecting and responding to users emotions [27] is a growing research area [35]. The main objective of affective computation is to capture and process affective information with the aim of enhancing the communication between the human and the computer. Within the scope of affective computing, the development of affective applications is a challenge that involves analyzing different multimodal data sources. In order to develop such applications, a large amount of data is needed in order to include a wide range of emotionally significant material. Affective databases are a good chance for developing such applications, either for affective recognizers or either for affective synthesis. In this paper different speech paralinguistic parameters have been calculated for the analysis of the human emotional voice, using several audio recordings. This recordings are stored in a bilingual and multimodal affective database. Several works have already been done in which the use of Machine Learning paradigms take a principal role.

2 Related Work

As previously mentioned, affective databases provide a good opportunity for training affective applications. This type of databases usually record information such as images,

Petr Sojka, Ivan Kopeček and Karel Pala (Eds.): TSD 2006, LNAI 4188, pp. 565–572, 2006.

sounds, psychophysiological values, etc. There are some references in the literature that present affective databases and their characteristics. [4] carried out a wide review of affective databases. Other interesting reviews are the ones provided in [12] and [19]. Most references found in literature are related to English, while other languages have less resources developed, especially the ones with relatively low number of speakers. This is the case of Standard Basque. To our knowledge, the first affective database in Standard Basque is the one presented by [25]. Concerning to Spanish, the work of [30] stands out. Several studies have been realized about the different features used in human emotional speech analysis [5,32]. However, the studies related to languages such as Standard Basque and Spanish are not numerous. In one hand, the works by [14] and [24] can be emphasized on Spanish language; on the other hand, the study presented by [25] related to Standard Basque is remarkable. The number of voice features analysed varies among the studies, but basically most of these are based in fundamental frequency, energy and timing parameters, like speech rate or mean phone duration. The use of Maching Learning paradigms takes a principal role in some works that can be found in literature. [7] presented a good reference paper. The Neural Networks Journal recently devoted special issue to emotion treatment from a Neural Networks perspective [36]. The work by [4] is related with this paper in the sense of using a Feature Selection method in order to apply a Neural Network to emotion recognition in spoken English, although both the methods to perform the FSS and the paradigms are different. In this line it has to be pointed out the work by [11] which uses a reduced number of emotions and a greedy approach to select the features.

3 Study of Automatic Emotion Recognition Relevant Parameters Using Machine Learning Paradigms

3.1 RekEmozio Database

The RekEmozio database was created with the aim of serving as an information repository for performing research on user emotion. The aim when building the RekEmozio resource was to add descriptive information about the performed recordings, so that processes such as extracting speech parameters and video features could be carried out on them later. Members of different work groups involved in research projects related to RekEmozio performed several processes for extracting speech and video features; this information was subsequently added to the database. The emotions used were chosen based on Ekman's six basic emotions [8], and neutral emotion was added. The characteristics of the RekEmozio database are described in [20]. A normative study of affective values in the RekEmozio database has been performed with the aim of finding out which recordings obtained better emotion recognition rates with experimental subjects [19]. Validation of the RekEmozio database attempts to extract recordings with relevant affective information in order to assist in the development of affective applications applied to local culture and languages. In this particular case, only recordings in which emotion detection success rate was over 50% were used in later work.

3.2 Emotional Feature Extraction

For recognition of emotions in speech, the most important question is which features should be extracted from the voice signal. Previous studies show us that it is difficult to find specific voice features that could be used as reliable indicators of the emotion present in the speech [17]. In this work, RekEmozio database audio recordings (stereo wave files, sampled at 44100 Hz) have been processed using standard signal processing techniques (windowing, Fast Fourier Transform, auto-correlation,...) to extract a wide group of 32 features which are described below. Supposing that each recording in database corresponds to one single emotion, one global vector of features has been obtained for each recording, using some statistical operations. Parameters used are global parameters calculated over entire recordings. Selected features are described next (in italics):

- **Fundamental Frequency F0**: Is the most common feature analyzed in several studies [5,32]. For F0 estimation we have used Sun algorithm [34] and statistics are computed: *maximum, minimum, mean, range, variance, standard deviation* and *maximum positive slope in F0 contour.*
- **RMS Energy**: The mean energy of speech quantified by calculating root mean square value (RMS) and 6 statistics *maximum, minimum, mean, range, variance* and *standard deviation.*
- **Loudness**: *absolute loudness* based on Zwicker's model [9].
- **Spectral distribution of energy**: Each emotion requires a different effort in the speech and it is known that the spectral distribution of energy varies with speech effort [5]. Effortful speech, like anger or surprise tends to contain relatively greater energy in low and mid spectral bands than the speech that does not need as much effort, like sadness or neutral. We have computed energy in *low band*, between 0 and 1300 Hz, *medium band*, between 1300 and 2600 Hz and *high band* from 2600 to 4000 Hz [15].
- **Mean Formants and Bandwidth**: Energy from the sound source (vocal folds) is modified by the resonance characteristics of the vocal tract (formants). Acoustic variations dues to emotion are reflected in formants [2]. We have computed the *first three mean formants*, and their corresponding *mean bandwidths.*
- **Jitter**: Defined as the *perturbation in vocal chords vibration.* Its estimation is based on the model presented by [31].
- **Shimmer**: *Perturbation cycle to cycle of the energy.* We based its estimation on the previously calculated absolute loudness.
- **Speaking Rate**: Progress has been made on a simple aspect of rhythm, the alternation between speech and silence [5]. We divided the speaking rate estimation in 6 values based on their duration with respect to the whole elocution: *duration of voice, silence, maximum voice, minimum voice, maximum silence* and *minimum silence.*

3.3 Machine Learning Standard Paradigms Used

In the supervised learning task, we have defined a classification problem where the main goal is constructing a model or a classifier able to manage the classification itself with acceptable accuracy. With this aim, some variables are to be used in order to identify different elements, the so called predictor variables. In the present problem, each sample is composed by the set of 32 speech related values, while the label value is one of the seven emotions identified. We briefly introduce the single paradigms used in our experiments. These paradigms come from the family of Machine Learning (ML). A state of the art description and deep explanation about FSS methods can be found in [13] and [18].

Decision Trees. A decision tree consists of nodes and branches to partition a set of samples into a set of covering decision rules. In each node, a single test or decision is made to obtain a partition. The starting node is usually referred as the root node. In each node, the goal is selecting an attribute that makes the best partition between the classes of the samples in the training set [21] and [22]. In our experiments, two well-known decision tree induction algorithms are used, ID3 [28] and C4.5 [29].

Instance-Based Learning. Instance-Based Learning (IBL) has its root in the study of nearest neighbor algorithm [6] in the field of Machine Learning. The simplest form of nearest neighbor (NN) or k-nearest neighbor (k-NN) algorithms simply stores the training instances and classifies a new instance by predicting the same class its nearest stored instance has or the majority class of its k nearest stored instances have, respectively, according to some distance measure as described in [37]. The core of this non-parametric paradigm is the form of the similarity function that computes the distances from the new instance to the training instances, to find the nearest or k-nearest training instances to the new case. In our experiments the IB paradigm is used, a inducer developed in the $\mathcal{MLC}$↔project [16] and based on the works of [1] and [38].

Naive Bayes Classifiers. The Naive-Bayes (NB) rule [23] uses the Bayes theorem to predict the class for each case, assuming that the predictive genes are independent given the category. To classify a new sample characterized by d genes $X = (X1, X2, \ldots, Xd)$, the NB classifier applies the following rule:

$$C_N - B = \arg\max_{c_j \in C} \ p(c_j) \prod_{i=1}^{d} p(x_i|c_j)$$

where $c_N - B$ denotes the class label predicted by the Naive-Bayes classifier and the possible classes of the problem are grouped in $C = \{c_1, \cdots, c_l\}$. A normal distribution is assumed to estimate the class conditional densities for predictive genes. Despite its simplicity, the NB rule has obtained better results than more complex algorithms in many domains.

Feature Subset Selection by Estimation of Distribution Algorithms. The basic problem of ML is concerned with the induction of a model that classifies a given object into one of several known classes. In order to induce the classification model, each object is described by a pattern of d features. Here, the ML community has formulated the following question: are all of these d descriptive features useful for learning the "classification rule"? On trying to respond to this question, we come up with the Feature Subset Selection (FSS) [18] approach which can be reformulated as follows: given a set of candidate features, select the "best" subset in a classification problem. In our case, the "best" subset will be the one with the best predictive accuracy. Most of the supervised learning algorithms perform rather poorly when faced with many irrelevant or redundant (depending on the specific characteristics of the classifier) features. In this way, the FSS proposes additional methods to reduce the number of features so as to improve the performance of the supervised classification algorithm. FSS can be viewed as a search problem [13], with each state in the search space specifying a subset of the possible features of the task. Exhaustive evaluation of possible feature subsets is usually unfeasible in practice due to the large amount of computational effort required. In this way, any feature selection method must determine the nature of the search process. In the experiments performed, an Estimation of Distribution Algorithm (EDA) [26] has been used which has the model accuracy as fitness function. To assess the goodness of each proposed gene subset for a specific classifier, a wrapper approach is applied. In the same way as supervised classifiers when no gene selection is applied, this wrapper approach estimates, by the 10-fold crossvalidation [33] procedure, the goodness of the classifier using only the variable subset found by the search algorithm.

4 Experimental Results

The above mentioned methods have been applied over the crossvalidated data sets using the $\mathcal{MLC}$++ library [16]. Each dataset corresponds to a single actor. Experiments were carried out with and without FSS in order to extract the accuracy improvement introduced by the feature selection process. Tables 1 and 2 show the classification results obtained using the whole set of variables, for Standard Basque and Spanish languages respectively. Each column represents a female (Fi) of male (Mi) actor, and mean values corresponding to each classifier/gender is also included. Last column presents the total average for each classifier. Results don't seem very impressing; ID3 best classifies the emotions for female actresses, both Standard Basque and Spanish, while C4.5 outstands for Standard Basque male actors and IB for Spanish male actors.

Table 1. 10-fold crossvalidation accuracy for Standard Basque Language using the whole variable set

	Female				Male					Total
	F1	F2	F3	mean	M1	M2	M3	M4	mean	
IB	35,38	48,79	35,23	39,80	44,17	49,32	36,89	40,91	42,82	41,52
ID3	38,71	45,45	44,70	**42,95**	46,67	46,97	43,26	51,14	47,01	45,27
C4.5	41,52	52,20	35,00	42,90	60,38	53,26	45,08	49,47	**52,04**	**48,13**
NB	42,95	45,76	37,65	42,12	52,20	44,09	36,21	41,44	43,48	42,90

Table 2. 10-fold crossvalidation accuracy for Spanish Language using the whole variable set

	Female						Male						Total
	F1	F2	F3	F4	F5	mean	M1	M2	M3	M4	M5	mean	
IB	34,55	43,64	54,55	54,55	38,18	45,09	25,45	33,64	51,82	47,65	33,64	**38,44**	**38,40**
ID3	36,36	52,73	49,09	47,27	42,73	**45,63**	20,91	30,91	40,91	47,27	40,00	36,00	36,81
C4.5	30,91	50,00	46,36	43,64	42,73	42,72	29,09	31,82	46,36	42,73	35,45	37,09	36,36
NB	38,18	42,73	49,09	40,00	42,73	42,54	24,55	30,91	49,09	45,45	34,55	36,91	36,27

Results obtained after applying FSS are more appealing, as can be seen in Tables 3 and 4. There, classifier IB appears as the best paradigm for all the categories, female and male, and Standard Basque and Spanish languages. Moreover, the accuracies outperform the previous ones in more than 15%. It must also be highlighted that FSS improves the well classified rate for all the ML paradigms.

Table 3. 10-fold crossvalidation accuracy for Standard Basque Language using FSS

	Female				Male					Total
	F1	F2	F3	mean	M1	M2	M3	M4	mean	
IB	63,03	68,03	59,32	**63,46**	72,65	67,35	60,98	62,80	**65,94**	**64,88**
ID3	62,73	60,48	65,45	62,88	72,65	61,97	56,52	62,65	63,44	63,20
C4.5	60,23	65,98	60,00	62,07	71,82	62,8	60,08	63,56	64,56	63,49
NB	64,47	64,55	48,94	59,32	74,55	62,5	62,73	60,00	64,94	62,53

Table 4. 10-fold crossvalidation accuracy for Spanish Language using FSS

	Female						Male						Total
	F1	F2	F3	F4	F5	mean	M1	M2	M3	M4	M5	mean	
IB	61,82	66,36	75,45	71,82	68,18	**68,72**	42,73	57,27	69,09	63,64	60,91	**58,72**	57,63
ID3	59,09	66,36	66,36	60,00	61,81	62,72	42,73	51,82	66,36	61,82	60,00	56,54	53,63
C4.5	57,27	62,73	64,55	65,45	63,64	62,72	43,64	56,36	65,45	64,55	56,36	57,27	54,36
NB	54,55	59,09	68,18	65,45	60,00	61,45	40,91	48,18	64,55	59,09	51,82	52,91	52,00

5   Conclusions and Future Work

Affective databases have been very useful for developing affective computing systems, being primarily used for training affective recognition systems. RekEmoziodatabase, either validated or not, is being used to training some automatic recognition systems applied to the localization where authors make their research. In the future, new voice features related to emotions will be taken into account, with the aim of to improve the current results. This paper describes how results obtained by Machine Learning techniques applied to emotion classification can be improved automatically selecting the appropriate subset of classifying variables by FSS. The classification accuracies, although not very impressive yet, are clearly improved over the results obtained using the full set of variables. Still, an analysis of the features selected by FSS is required as an effort to extract meaningful information from that set. Merging or combining information from multiple sources by means of a multiclassifier model [10] could help to obtain better classification accuracies.

Acknowledgements

The involved work has received financial support from the Department of Economy of the local government "Gipuzkoako Foru Aldundia" and from the University of the Basque Country (in the University-Industry projects modality).

References

1. Aha, D., Kibler, D. & Albert, M.K. (1991). *Instance-Based learning algorithms*, Machine Learning **6**, 37–66.
2. Bachorowski, J.A., Owren, M. J. (1995) *Vocal expression of emotion: Acoustic properties of speech are associated with emotional intensity and context*, Psychological Science 6 219–224.

3. Casacuberta, D. *La mente humana: Diez Enigmas y 100 preguntas (The human mind: Ten Enigmas and 100 questions)*. Océano (Ed), Barcelona, Spain (2001) ISBN: 84-7556-122-5.

4. Cowie, R., Douglas-Cowie, E., Cox, C. *Beyond emotion archetypes: Databases for emotion modelling using neural networks*. Neural Networks 18 (2005) 371–388.

5. Cowie, R., Douglas-Cowie, E., Tsapatsoulis, N., Votsis, G., Kollias, S., Fellenz, W., Taylor, J.: Emotion recognition in human-computer interaction (2001).

6. Dasarathy, B.V.: Nearest Neighbor (NN) Norms: NN Pattern Recognition Classification Techniques. IEEE Computer Society Press (1991).

7. Dellaert, F., Polzin, T., Waibel, A.: Recognizing Emotion in Speech. In Proc. of ICSLP (1996).

8. Ekman, P., Friesen, W.: Pictures of facial affect. Consulting Psychologist Press, Palo Alto, CA (1976).

9. Fernández, R.: A Computational Model for the Automatic Recognition of Affect in Speech. Massachusetts Institute of Technology (2004).

10. Gunes, V., Menard, M., Loonis, P., Petit-Renaud, S.: Combination, cooperation and selection of classiers: A state of the art. International Journal of Pattern Recognition, 17 (2003) 1303–1324.

11. Huber, R., Batliner, A., Buckow, J., Noth, E., Warnke, V., Niemann, H.: Recognition of emotion in a realistic dialogue scenario. In Proc. ICSLP (2000) 665–668.

12. Humaine: Retrieved March 10, 2006, from `http://emotion-research.net/` (n.d.).

13. Inza, I., Larrañaga, P., Etxeberria, R., Sierra, B.: Feature subsetselection by Bayesian network-based optimization. Artificial Intelligence 123 (2000) 157–184.

14. Iriondo, I., Guaus, R., Rodríguez, A., Lázaro, P., Montoya, N., Blanco, J. M., Bernadas, D., Oliver, J.M., Tena, D., Longhi, L.: Validation of an acoustical modelling of emotional expression in Spanish using speech synthesis techniques. In: SpeechEmotion (2000) 161–166.

15. Kazemzadeh, A., Lee, S., Narayanan, S.: Acoustic correlates of user response to errors in human-computer dialogues. Proc. IEEE ASRU, (St. Thomas, U.S. Virgin Islands), December (2003).

16. Kohavi, R., Sommerfield,D., Dougherty,J.: Data mining using MLC++, a Machine Learning Library in C++, International Journal of Artificial Intelligence Tools 6 (4) (1997) 537–566 `http://www.sgi.com/Technology/mlc/`.

17. Laukka, P.: Vocal Expression of Emotion. Discrete-emotions and Dimensional Accounts. Acta Universitatis Upsaliensis. Comprehensive Summaries of Uppsala Dissertations from the Faculty of Social Sciences, 141, 80 pp. Uppsala (2004) ISBN 91-554-6091-7.

18. Liu, H., Motoda, H.: Feature Selection for Knowledge Discovery and Data Mining. Kluwer Academic Publishers (1998).

19. López, J.M., Cearreta, I., Fajardo, I., Garay, N.: Evaluating the validity of RekEmozio affective multimodal database with experimental subjects. Technical Report EHU-KAT-IK-04-06. Computer Architecture and Technology department, University of the Basque Country (2006).

20. López, J.M., Cearreta, I., Garay, N., López de Ipiña, K., Beristain, A.: RekEmozio project: bilingual and multimodal affective database. Technical Report EHU-KAT-IK-03-06. Computer Architecture and Technology department, University of the Basque Country (2006).

21. Martin, J.K.: An exact probability metric for Decision Tree splitting and stopping, Machine Learning 28(2/3) (1997).

22. Mingers, J.: A comparison of methods of pruning induced Rule Trees, Technical Report. Coventry, England: University of Warwick, School of Indutrial and Business Studies, (1988).

23. Minsky, M.: Steps towards artificial intelligence. Proceedings of the IRE, 49 (1961) 8–30.

24. Montero, J.M., Gutiérrez-Arriola, J., Palazuelos, S., Enríquez, E., Aguilera, S., Pardo, J.M.: Emotional speech synthesis: from speech database to tts. Proceedings of the 5th International Conference of Spoken Language Processing. Sydney, Australia (1998) 923–926.

25. Navas, E., Hernáez, I., Castelruiz, A., Luengo, I.: Obtaining and Evaluating an Emotional Database for Prosody Modelling in Standard Basque. Lecture Notes on Artificial Intelligence, Vol 3206. Springer-Verlag, Berlin (2004) 393–400.

26. Pelikan, M., Goldberg, D.E., Lobo, F.: A Survey of Optimization by Building and Using Probabilistic Models. Technical Report 99018, IlliGAL (1999).
27. Picard, R.W.: Affective Computing. MIT Press, Cambridge, MA (1997).
28. Quinlan, J.R.: Induction of Decision Trees, Machine Learning 1 (1986) 81–106.
29. Quinlan, J.R.: C4.5: Programs for Machine Learning, Morgan Kaufmann. Publishers, Inc. Los Altos, California (1993).
30. Rodríguez, A., Lázaro, P., Montoya, N., Blanco, J.M., Bernadas, D., Oliver, J.M., Longhi, L.: Modelización acústica de la expresión emocional en el español. Procesamiento del Lenguaje Natural, No. 25, Lérida, España (1999) 159–166. issn: 1135-5948.
31. Rothkrantz, L.J.M., Wiggers, P., van Wees, J.W.A., van Vark, R.J.: Voice stress analysis. Proceedings of Text, Speech and Dialogues 2004 (2004).
32. Schröder, M.: Speech and Emotion Research: An overview of research frameworks and a dimensional approach to emotional speech synthesis. Ph.D. thesis, PHONUS 7, Research Report of the Institute of Phonetics, Saarland University (2004).
33. Stone, M.: Cross-validation choice and assessment of statistical procedures. Journal Royal of Statistical Society 36 (1974) 111–147.
34. Sun, X.: Pitch determination and voice quality analysis using subharmonic-to-harmonic ratio http://mel.speech.nwu.edu/sunxj/pda.htm (2002).
35. Tao, J., Tan, T.: Affective computing: A review. In: J. Tao, T. Tan, R. W. Picard (eds.): Lecture Notes in Computer Science, Vol. 3784 – Proceedings of The First International Conference on Affective Computing & Intelligent Interaction (ACII '05). Beijing, China (2005) 981–995.
36. Taylor, J.G., Scherer, K., Cowie, R.: Neural Networks, special issue on Emotion and Brain. Vol. 18, Issue 4 (2005) 313–455.
37. Ting, K.M.: Common issues in Instance-Based and Naive-Bayesian classifiers, Ph.D. Thesis, Basser Department of Computer Science. The Univesity of Sydney, Australia (1995).
38. Wettschereck, D.: A study of distance-based Machine Learning Algorithms, Ph.D. Thesis, Oregon State University (1994).

Two-Dimensional Visual Language Grammar*

Siska Fitrianie and Leon J.M. Rothkrantz

Man-Machine-Interaction Group, Delft University of Technology
Mekelweg 4 2628CD Delft, The Netherlands
{s.fitrianie, l.j.m.rothkrantz}@ewi.tudelft.nl

Abstract. Visual language refers to the idea that communication occurs through visual symbols, as opposed to verbal symbols or words. Contrast to a sentence construction in spoken language with a linear ordering of words, a visual language has a simultaneous structure with a parallel temporal and spatial configuration. Inspired by Deikto [5], we propose a two-dimensional string or sentence construction of visual expressions, i.e. spatial arrangements of symbols, which represent concepts. A proof of concept communication interface has been developed, which enables users to create visual messages to represent concepts or ideas in their mind. By the employment of ontology, the interface constructs both the syntax and semantics of a 2D visual string using a Lexicalized Tree Adjoining Grammar (LTAG) into (natural language) text. This approach captures elegantly the interaction between pragmatic and syntactic descriptions in a 2D sentence, and the inferential interactions between multiple possible meanings generated by the sentence. From our user test results, we conclude that our developed visual language interface could serve as a communication mediator.

1 Introduction

Skills at interpreting visual symbols play an important part in humans' learning about the world and understanding of language. Words are also composed by symbols, of course. There are nonverbal symbols that can provide essential meanings with their succinct and eloquent illustrations. Humans respond to these symbols as messages, though often without realizing exactly what it is that has caused us to reach a certain conclusion. Such symbols are often visual, though they can be auditory or even tactile. The research described in this paper concentrates on visual nonverbal symbols. In particulary, it focuses on exploring such symbols to represent concepts, i.e. objects, actions, or relations.

According to [15], human communication involves the use of concepts to represent internal models of humans themselves, the outside world and of things with which the humans are interacting. In earlier work, we have investigated a languange independent communication using visual symbols, i.e. icons [8], based on signs and symbols, which are understood universally [15]. As a proof of concept, an iconic interface has been developed in a specific domain. It is applied on a communication interface on PDAs in crisis situations. In such situations, wired communication could be disabled by the breakdown of the infrastructure or information overload and speech communication is difficult due to noisy

---

* The research reported here is part of the Interactive Collaborative Information Systems (ICIS) project, supported by the Dutch Ministry of Economic Affairs, grant nr: BSIK03024.

Petr Sojka, Ivan Kopeček and Karel Pala (Eds.): TSD 2006, LNAI 4188, pp. 573–580, 2006.
© Springer-Verlag Berlin Heidelberg 2006

environments. Visual language has been used successfully in human-computer interaction, visual programming, and human-human communication. Words are easily forgotten, but images stay in our minds persistently [6]. Therefore, icons can evoke a readiness to respond for a fast exchange of information and a fast action as a result [14]. Furthermore, a direct manipulation on the icons allows us to have a faster interaction [11].

A visual (communication) language uses a set of spatial arrangements of visual symbols with a semantic interpretation that is used in carrying out communication [3]. This language is based upon a vocabulary of visual symbols where each symbol represents one or more meaning, which are created according to the metaphors appropriate for the context of this type of languages. The sentence structure of a visual language is different from a sentence in spoken language [12]. The spoken language is composed by a linear ordering of words, while a visual language has a simultaneous structure with a parallel temporal and spatial configuration, e.g. the sign language syntax for deaf people [1], comic illustrations [4], diagrams. Based on this, we propose a two-dimensional syntax structure that enables a visual language sentence constructed in a 2D way.

2   Related Work

The approach described in this paper basically is inspired by Deikto, a game's interaction language [5]. The creator aimed at producing the smallest language capable of expressing the concepts used in the story world. A sentence in Deikto is represented by a connected acyclic graph, where a predecessor element explains its successor. A graph element can be a lexicon or another clause. To help the players, the game provides hints of what lexicon(s) can be selected based on its word class. Deikto follows a rigid grammar by assigning each verb the parts of the sentence in its dictionary definition. This revolving verb approach is supported by Fillmore's case grammar [7] and Schank's conceptual dependency theory [17]. In case grammar, a sentence in its basic structure consists of a verb and one or more noun phrases. Each phrase is associated with the verb in a particular case relationship. The conceptual dependency defines the interrelationship of a set of primitive acts to represent a verb. The approach employs rules and a set of primitive acts, e.g. ATRANS: transfer possession of an object. Instead of using the word class (e.g. subject, verb, object), both approaches use thematic roles, e.g. agent, patient, instrument, etc, to define a sentence structure.

VIL, a one-dimensional visual language application [13], is designed to allow people to communicate with each other by constructing sentences solely relying on icons. The system is based on the notion of simplified speech by reducing a significant complexity. It is also inspired by the case concept of Fillmore and the verb classification of Schank.

In the following sections we will give an overview of the 2D visual language we propose. Further, we will concentrate on the visual sentence construction and conversion to text or speech as well as a proof of concept visual language interface we have developed. Finally, we also present our test results.

3   Two-Dimensional Visual Language

According to [1], the syntax analysis of the visual language does not reduce to classical spoken sentence syntax. There exists a set of "topic" and "comment" relations, in which a comment explains a topic. Therefore, in our two-dimensional syntax structure, a sentence is constructed in an acyclic-graph of visual symbols, i.e. icons (see fig. 1(b)). Conventional textual syntax structures are not considered 2D, since the parser processes them as 1D streams of symbols.

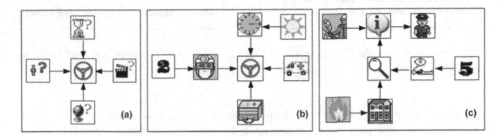

Fig. 1. Examples of visual language sentences: (a) hints for the verb "drive" and (b) a simple sentence: "Two paramedics drove an ambulance to the hospital at 15.00" and (c) a compound sentence: "The firefighter informs the police that he will search five victims in the burning building"

A visual symbol can be connected by an arrow to another symbol, in which the former explains the latter symbol. Each symbol represents concepts or ideas. The sentence may be constructed from any part, however as soon as a verb is selected, the structure of the sentence will be determined. We define a case for every symbol in our vocabulary. For example: the symbol "paramedic" contains number, location, status, name, as attributes of the case. Particulary for symbols that represent verbs, based on the theory of [7,17], we define a case of every verb and follow the frame syntactic analysis used for generating the VerbNet [10]. For example: the case of the verb "drive" contains agent, theme, location, time.

To help the user, attributes of each selected visual symbol's case on a 2D sentence are displayed (see fig. 1(a)). As the icon is deselected, the hint will disappear to reduce the complexity. A hint symbol can be selected and replaced by a visual symbol that is grammatically correct to form a sentence. The approach gives a freedom to users to fill in the parts of a sentence, but at the same time the system can restrict the choices of symbols which lead to a meaningful sentence. A user may attach symbols that are not given by the hint by inserting a new node on a specific node on the sentence. This means that the new node explains the selected node. Our developed grammar allows a compound sentence construction, which can be done by inserting another verb on a verb node of the sentence (see fig. 1(c)) or noun phrase conjunction.

4   Knowledge Representation

Visual symbols have no meaning outside of their context. A visual symbol can be interpreted by its perceivable form (syntax), by the relation between its form and what it means (semantics), and by its use (pragmatics) [2]. The relation between visual symbols and words can have an ambiguous meaning. We tackled this by creating a verbal context that can link both

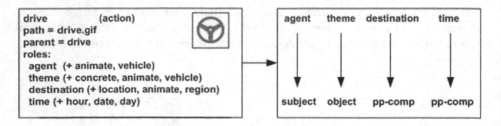

Fig. 2. Schematic vie of the two components of a verb lexical definition: semantic types and linking to syntactic arguments

visual and verbal thoughts together to form a symbol that can be remembered and recalled. An ontology is employed to represent context that binds verbal and visual symbols together.

We employ the ontology to store information of the vocabulary, i.e. visual symbols that represent nouns, pronouns, proper-nouns, adjectives, and adverbs, and their properties (i.e. attributes of a case). The ontology provides a natural way to group its elements based on their concepts and provides the system information about their semantic description, e.g. symbols of "firefighter" and "paramedic" are grouped under "animate" and a symbol of "ambulance" is under "vehicle". In particularly for verb symbols, based on [10], a lexeme has one or more sense definitions, which consist of a semantic type with associated thematic roles and semantic features, and a link between the thematic roles and syntactic arguments. The definition also defines required and optional roles. Figure 2 shows a case for the verb "drive".

5   Lexicalized Tree Adjoining Grammar by Visual Symbols

Each visual symbol provides only a portion of the semantics of a visual language sentence. The meaning of a 2D sentence with more than just one symbol can still be represented by the same set of symbols, but it turns out to be very difficult to determine the sentence meaning. The syntax of interactions between concepts (that are represented by visual symbols) enriches progressively the semantic of the sentence. The only thing that can be automatically derived from the semantics of the symbols in a visual language sentence is a fixed word or phrase belonging to these symbols.

Based on [16], we assign our vocabulary with Lexicalized Tree Adjoining Grammar (LTAG) [9]. Figure 3(a) shows the example of our TAG trees vocabulary. For this purpose, we exploit XTAG grammar [18] that presents a large existing grammar for English verbs. Mapping our VerbNet-based syntactic frames to the XTAG trees greatly increases the robustness of the conversion of 2D visual language sentences to natural language text/speech.

Based on the case of every symbol in a 2D sentence, a parser processes a 2D stream of symbols and maps the thematic roles of them into the basic syntactic tree on the VerbNet-based vocabulary. Presumably, transformation of VerbNet's syntactic frames are recoverable by mapping the 2D sentence onto elementary trees of TAG tree families. For this purpose, the parser exploits the system's ontology to have the syntactic argument of every symbol in

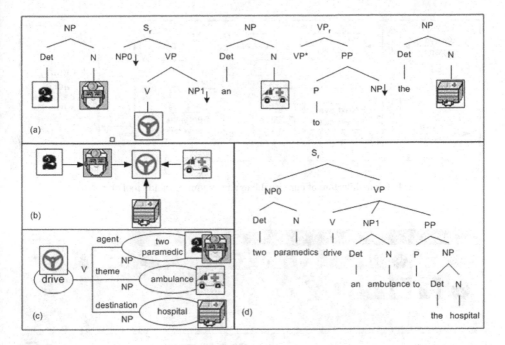

Fig. 3. Conversion to natural language text: (a) examples of the iconized TAG elementary trees, (b) example of a 2D sentence: "Two paramedics drove an ambulance to the hospital", (c) example of mapping the thematic roles to the basic syntactic tree defined by the case of the verb "drive", and (d) example of a parse tree as the results of mapping the basic syntactic tree to the TAG trees

the sentence. Figure 3 shows an example of parsing a 2D sentence using LTAG. We specify the semantics of a 2D sentence in two ways. First, our developed ontology offers a simple syntax-semantics interface for every symbol. As shown in fig. 2, each verb case has restricted the choice of symbols to form the sentence, i.e. by associating thematic roles to semantics features. The meaning of a TAG tree is just the conjunction of the meanings of the elementary trees used to derive it, once appropriate case elements are filled in. Finally, the VerbNet structure provides an explicitly constructed verb lexicon with syntax and semantics. By this way, the syntax analysis and natural language construction can be done simultaneously.

6   Reporting Crisis Situations

Our visual language communication tool was designed for reporting observations in a crisis situation. A user can arrange an acyclic graph of visual symbols, i.e. icons, as a realization of his/her concepts or ideas. Besides supporting a fast interaction by converting the message into natural language, the tool also can be combined with any language application, e.g. a text to speech synthesizer, a language translator, etc, through a socket network. The current prototype provides a speech synthesizer to read aloud the resulted natural language text with correct pronunciations. Figure 4 shows the architecture of our developed tool.

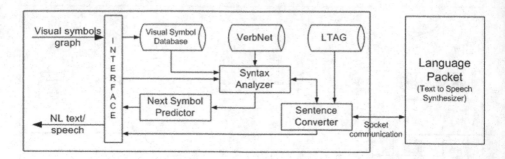

Fig. 4. The architecture of our visual language communication tool on a PDA

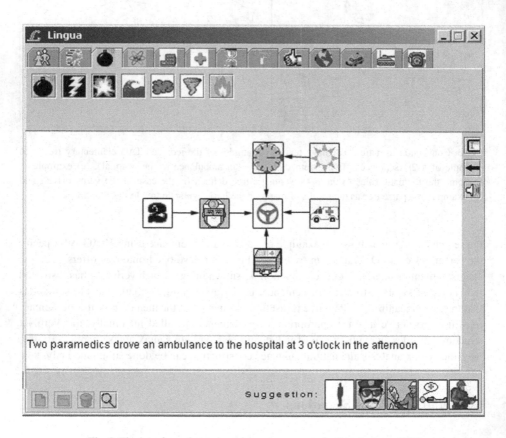

Fig. 5. The interface of our visual language communication tool on a PDA

Figure 5 shows the interface of our visual language communication tool. On the interface, visual symbols are grouped in clusters based on their concept. The interface provides a next-symbol predictor to help users to find their intended symbols fast. It predicts which symbols are most likely to follow a given segment of a visual symbol graph based on its syntax structure. When a user selects one of the suggestions, it is automatically inserted into the graph to replace a selected hint symbol. The probability of the prediction of a visual symbol is estimated with n-grams language modelling. To compute the multi-grams model, our tool collects the data during the interaction. The interface provides a real time distinctive appearance of which visual symbols can be selected next according to syntactical rules. To construct a message, a user can select visual symbols from the menu or from the prediction window. If the user changes the input graph, the resulted text will be refreshed.

7 Evaluation

We performed a similar user test as reported in [8]. It aimed to assess whether or not users were still capable to express their concepts in mind using the provided visual symbols in a 2D way. The test also addressed the usability issues on interacting with 2D sentence constructions on the visual language interface. Eight people took part in the test. The tasks were created using images of real crisis situations. The participants were asked to report what they might experience, by creating 2D visual language sentences on the interface. While performing the task, they were asked to think aloud. There were no incorrect answers, except if any task was not performed at all. All activities were recorded and logged for analyses purposes.

The experimental results showed that our target users were able to compose 2D visual language messages to express their concepts and ideas in mind. The users used some time to find another concept when they could not find a relevant concept from the provided visual symbols to represent their message. Although adaptation time was needed to recognize some icons, the results also indicated that the hints given while creating 2D-icon string helped the user to compose a complete report.

8 Conclusion

A two-dimensional visual language grammar, as the continuation of our research [8], has been developed. The idea is inspired by a game's language interaction, Deikto [5]. A sentence can be created using a spatial arrangement of visual symbols, i.e. icons. To support a natural visual language sentence construction, the arrangement may not be in a linear order. We combine LTAG syntax and VerbNet frames so that we can analyze the syntax and semantics of visual sentences and convert them to text/speech simultaneously and easier. The approach naturally and elegantly captures the interaction between the graph structure of the visual sentences and the tree structure of LTAG syntax, and the inferential interactions between multiple possible meaning generated by the sentences.

An experimental visual language interface has been developed that is applied for reporting observations in a crisis situation. Our target users could express their concepts and ideas solely using a spatial arrangement of visual symbols. However, future work should be done to gather data about how people might create visual messages in their real life and how they experience this. Therefore, the 2D visual language grammar can cover all possible message constructions.

References

1. Bevelier D., Corina D. P. and Neville H.J.: Brain and Language: a Perspective from Sign Language. Neuron, Cell Press. **21** (1998) 275–278.
2. Chandler D.: Semiotics, the Basic. Routledge (2001).
3. Chang S.K., Polese G., Orefice S., and Tucci M.: A Methodology and Interactive Environment for Iconic Language Design. International Journal of Human Computer Studies. **41** (1994) 683–716.
4. Cohn N.: Visual Syntactic Structures, Towards a Generative Grammar of Visual Language. http://www.emaki.net/essays/ (2003).
5. Crawford C.: Erasmatron. http://www.erasmatazz.com (2005).
6. Frutiger A.: Sign and Symbols, Their Design and Meaning. New York: van Nostrand Reinholt (1989).
7. Fillmore C.J.: The Case for Case. in Universals in Linguistic Theory, Ed. by Emmon Bach and Robert Harms. New York: Holt, Rinehart and Winston (1968).
8. Fitrianie S. and Rothkrantz L.J.M.: Language-Independent Communication using Icons on a PDA. Text, Speech and Dialogues. Lecture Notes in Artificial Intelligence. Springer. **3658** (2005) 404–411.
9. Joshi A. K., Levy L., and Takahashi M.: Tree Adjunct Grammars. Journal of the Computer and System Sciences. **10** (1975) 136–163.
10. Kipper-Schuler K.: VerbNet: A Broad-Coverage, Comprehensive Verb Lexicon. Ph.D. thesis proposal, University of Pennsylvania (2003).
11. Kjeldskov J. and Kolbe N.: Interaction Design for Handheld Computers. In: Proc. of APCHI '02. Science Press. China. (2002).
12. Lester P. M.: Visual Communication: Images with Messages, 4th Ed. Wadsworth/Thompson, Belmont, CA (2006).
13. Leemans N.E.M.P.: VIL, A Visual Inter Lingua. Doctoral Dissertation, Worcester Poly-technic Institute, USA (2001).
14. Littlejohn S.W.: Theories of Human Communication, 5th Ed. Wadsworth (1996).
15. Perlovsky L. I.: Emotions, Learning and Control. In: Proc. of Intl. Symposium: Intelligent Control, Intelligent System and Semiotics (1999).
16. Ryant N. and Kipper K.: Assigning Xtag Trees to VerbNet. 7th International Workshop on Tree Adjoining Grammar and Related Formalisms (TAG+7). Vancouver, Canada (2004).
17. Schank R.: Computer Models of Thought and Language. W. H. Freeman. San Francisco (1973).
18. XTAG Research Group: A Lexicalized Tree Adjoining Grammar for English. Technical Report IRCS-01-03. IRCS, University of Pennsylvania (2001).

Are You Looking at Me, Are You Talking with Me: Multimodal Classification of the Focus of Attention

Christian Hacker, Anton Batliner, and Elmar Nöth*

University of Erlangen-Nuremberg,
Chair for Pattern Recognition (Informatik 5)
Martensstraße 3, D-91058 Erlangen, Germany
hacker@informatik.uni-erlangen.de

Abstract. Automatic dialogue systems get easily confused if speech is recognized which is not directed to the system. Besides noise or other people's conversation, even the user's utterance can cause difficulties when he is talking to someone else or to himself ("Off-Talk"). In this paper the automatic classification of the user's focus of attention is investigated. In the German SmartWeb project, a mobile device is used to get access to the semantic web. In this scenario, two modalities are provided - speech and video signal. This makes it possible to classify whether a spoken request is addressed to the system or not: with the camera of the mobile device, the user's gaze direction is detected; in the speech signal, prosodic features are analyzed. Encouraging recognition rates of up to 93 % are achieved in the speech-only condition. Further improvement is expected from the fusion of the two information sources.

1 Introduction

In the SmartWeb-Project [1] a mobile and multimodal user interface to the Semantic Web is being developed. The user can ask open-domain questions to the system, no matter where he is: carrying a smartphone, he addresses the system via UMTS or WLAN using speech [2]. In this paper we present an approach to automatically classify whether speech is addressed to the system or e.g. to a human dialogue partner or to the user himself. Thus, the system can do without any push-to-talk button and, nevertheless, the dialogue manager will not get confused. To classify the user's focus of attention, we take advantage of two modalities: speech-input from a close-talk microphone and the video stream from the front camera of the mobile phone are analyzed on the server. In the speech signal we detect *On-Talk* vs. *Off-Talk* using prosodic information, that means, we investigate, whether people use different speech-registers when addressing a system (On-Talk) and when addressing a human dialogue partner. In this paper, all linguistic information is neglected. In the video stream we classify *On-View* when the user's gaze direction is towards the camera. In deed, the users usually look onto the display of the smartphone while interacting with the system, because they receive visual feedback, like the n-best results, maps, or pictures. *Off-View* means, that the user does not look at the display at all.

---

* This work was funded by the German Federal Ministry of Education and Research (BMBF) in the frame of SmartWeb (Grant 01 IMD 01 F, http://www.smartweb-project.de). The responsibility for the content lies with the authors.

Petr Sojka, Ivan Kopeček and Karel Pala (Eds.): TSD 2006, LNAI 4188, pp. 581–588, 2006.

Table 1. Three databases, words per category in %: On-Talk, read (ROT), paraphrasing (POT), spontaneous (SOT) and other Off-Talk (OOT)

	# Speakers	On-Talk	ROT	POT	SOT	OOT [%]
SW$_{spont}$	28	48.8	13.1	21.0	17.1	-
SW$_{acted}$	17	33.3	23.7	-	-	43.0
SK$_{spont}$	92	93.9	1.8	-	-	4.3

After a short literature survey, recently recorded databases are described in Sect. 3. In this paper, acted and spontaneous speech is compared. Features to analyze On-Talk and On-View are described in Sect. 4; results of the classification are given in Sect. 5. A discussion of the results, an analysis of prosodic features and a motivation of the fusion of both modalities is given in Sect. 6.

2   Related Work

In [3] On-Talk and On-View are analyzed for a Human-Human-Robot scenario. Here, face detection is based on the analysis of the skin-color; to classify the speech signal, different linguistic features are investigated. The assumption is that commands directed to a robot are shorter, contain more often imperatives or the word "robot", have a lower perplexity and are easy to parse with a simple grammar. However, the discrimination of On-/Off-Talk becomes more difficult in an automatic dialogue system, since speech recognition is not solely based on commands. Oppermann et al. [4] describe such a corpus collected in a Wizard-of-Oz experiment in the context of the SmartKom project (cf. SK$_{spont}$ in Sect. 3). Unfortunately, only a small part of the data is labeled as Off-Talk. For this database, results of On-/Off-Talk classification using prosodic features and part-of-speech categories are given in [5]. It could be shown that the users indeed use different speech registers when talking to the system, when talking to themselves, and when reading from the display. Video information was not used, since in the SmartKom scenario the user was alone and nearly always looking onto the display while talking.

To classify the user's gaze direction, face-tracking algorithms like in [6] did not seem to be appropriate, since in our scenario the face ought to be lost, if the user does not look onto the display anymore. A very fast and robust detection algorithm to discriminate two classes (face/no face) is presented by Viola and Jones [7]. It is based on a large number of simple Haar-like features (cf. Sect 4). With a similar algorithm five facial orientations are discriminated in [8]. As features, different pairs of pixels in the image are compared.

3   Corpora

For the SmartWeb-Project two databases containing questions in the context of a visit to a Football World Cup stadium in 2006 have been recorded. Different categories of Off-Talk were evoked (in the SW$_{spont}$ database[1]) or acted (in our SW$_{acted}$ recordings). Besides *Read*

---

[1] Designed and recorded at the Institute of Phonetics and Speech Communication, Ludwig-Maximilians-University, Munich.

Off-Talk (ROT), where the candidates had to read some possible system response from the display, the following categories of Off-Talk are discriminated: *Paraphrasing Off-Talk* (POT) means, that the candidates report to someone else what they have found out from their request to the system, and *Spontaneous Off-Talk* (SOT) can occur, when they are interrupted by someone else. We expect ROT to occur simultaneously with On-View and POT with Off-View. All SmartWeb data has been recorded with a close-talk microphone and 8 kHz sampling rate.

Recordings of the SW_{spont} data took place in situations that were as realistic as possible. No instruction regarding Off-Talk were given. The user was carrying a mobile phone and was interrupted by a second person. This way, a large amount of Off-Talk could be evoked. Simultaneously, video has been recorded with the front camera of the mobile phone. Up to now, speech of 28 speakers has been annotated (0.8 hrs. of speech). This data consists of 2541 words; the distribution of On-/Off-Talk is given in Tab. 1. The vocabulary of this part of the database contains 750 different words. As for the video data, up to now 27 speakers recorded in different environment (indoor, outdoor, weak and strong backlight) have been annotated. These 4 hrs. video data that also contains non-speech segments consist of 76.1 % On-View, 15.5 % Off-View and 1.6 % without face; the rest was not well-defined.

We additionally recorded acted data (SW_{acted}, 1.7 hrs.) to investigate which classification rates can be achieved and to show the differences to realistic data. Here, the classes POT and SOT are not discriminated and combined in *Other Off-Talk* (OOT, cf. SK_{spont}). First, we investigated the SmartKom data, that have been recorded with a directional microphone: Off-Talk was uttered with lower voice and durations were longer for read speech. We further expect that in SmartWeb nobody using a head-set to address the automatic dialogue would intentionally confuse the system with loud Off-Talk. These considerations result in the following setup: The 17 speakers sat in front of a computer. All Off-Talk had to be articulated with lower voice and, additionally, ROT had to be read more slowly. Furthermore, each sentence could be read in advance so that some kind of "spontaneous" articulation was possible, whereas the ROT sentences were indeed read utterances. The vocabulary contains 361 different types. 2321 words are On-Talk, 1651 ROT, 2994 OOT (Tab. 1).

In SmartKom (SK_{spont}), 4 hrs. of speech (19416 words) have been collected from 92 speakers. Since the candidates were alone, no POT occurred: OOT is basically "talking to oneself" [5]. The proportion of Off-Talk is small (Tab. 1).

4 Feature Extraction

The most plausible domain for **On-Talk vs. Off-Talk** is a unit between the word and the utterance level, such as clauses or phrases. In the present paper, we confine our analysis to the word level to be able to map words onto the most appropriate semantic units later on. However, we do not use any syntactic and semantic classes, but only prosodic information. The spoken word sequence which is obtained from the speech recognizer in SmartWeb is only required for the time alignment and for a normalization of energy and duration based on the underlying phonemes. In this paper, we use the transcription of the data assuming a recognizer with 100 % accuracy; lower accuracy decreases Off-Talk classification rates only to a small extend, as preliminary experiments have shown.

In most cases of the described acted data and in many cases of the other data, indeed, one can *hear* if the addressee is a machine or a computer; features could be loudness,

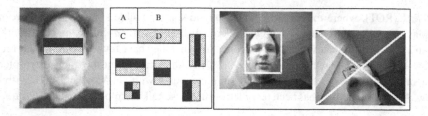

Fig. 1. Face detection after Viola and Jones [7]. Left to right: The best feature, wavelet features and their calculation, results from our task (On-View and Off-View).

accentuation, intonation, or rate-of-speech. For the automatic classification we use a highly redundant set of 100 prosodic features. These features are calculated for each word, and, additionally, for some of the neighboring words to encode information from the context. A short description of the features and abbreviations used in Tab. 2 and 3 is given in the following: 30 features are based on the energy (*Ene*) of the signal, e.g. maximum, minimum, mean (*Max, Min, Mean*), absolute value (*Abs*), or the position of the maximum (*MaxPos*). Further 25 features are calculated from the fundamental frequency f_0, e.g. *Max, Min* as above and the position of onset (beginning of voiced region), offset, and the extrema (*OnsetPos, OffsetPos, MaxPos* etc.). The reference point for all position-features is the end of the current word. 29 more features are calculated to characterize duration (*Dur; AbsSyl* is normalized with the number of syllables), and 8 to describe pauses (*Pau*) before and after the current word. Filled pauses contain non-words. Eight features are calculated for the whole turn, i.e., they have the same value for each word: 4 are based on jitter and shimmer, the rate-of-speech, and one feature is based on the f_0, energy and duration, respectively (*Global*). A detailed overview of prosodic features is given in [9].

For the classification of **On-View vs. Off-View** it is sufficient in our task, to discriminate frontal faces from the rest. Thus, we employed a very fast and robust algorithm described in [7]. The face detection works for single images; up to now, no use of context information is implemented. The algorithm is based on simple Haar-like wavelets; the most significant feature is shown in Fig. 1, left: The integral of the light area is subtracted from the integral of the dark area. All wavelets (up to scaling and translation) are shown in Fig. 1 in the middle. The integral of the quadrangle spanned by each pixel and the origin is calculated in advance. Then the area D can be easily computed from $(A+B+C+D)-(A+B)-(A+C)+A$. From many possible features, up to 6000 are selected with the ADABOOST algorithm; a hierarchical classifier speeds up the detection [7]. In this paper we use 176×144 grayscale images, 7.5 per second; faces are searched in different subimages, greater than half the image, and scaled to 24×24. Fig. 1, right, shows On-View and Off-View of a mobile phone user.

5   Experimental Setup and Results

In the following all databases are evaluated with the LDA-classifier and leave-one-speaker-out validation. All results are measured with the class-wise averaged recognition rate CL-N ($N = 2, 3, 4$) to guarantee robust recognition of all N classes (unweighted average recall). In the 2-class task we classify On-Talk vs. rest; for $N = 3$ classes we discriminate On-

Table 2. On-Talk vs. OOT: Best single features and classification rate CL-2 in %. The dominant feature group is emphasized. " > 1": values are greater for On-Talk.

SW_{spont}	On-T. / OOT	CL-2
EneMax	> 1	61
EneGlobal	> 1	60
EneMean	> 1	60
PauFilledBefore	< 1	54
JitterSigma	> 1	54
EneAbs	> 1	54
f_0Max	> 1	53
ShimmerSigma	> 1	53
JitterMean	> 1	53
PauBefore	< 1	53

SW_{acted}	On-T. / OOT	CL-2
EneGlobal	> 1	68
EneMax	> 1	68
RateOfSpeech	> 1	65
$f_0Global$	> 1	65
EneMean	> 1	63
ShimmerSigma	> 1	63
f_0Max	> 1	61
EneAbs	> 1	61
f_0Min	< 1	60
ShimmerMean	> 1	60

Table 3. Best single features for On-Talk vs. ROT (cf. Tab. 2)

SW_{spont}	On-T. / ROT	CL-2
EneGlobal	> 1	60
DurAbs	< 1	58
$f_0MaxPos$	< 1	58
$f_0OnsetPos$	> 1	57
DurGlobal	> 1	57
EneMaxPos	< 1	56
EneMean	> 1	56
EneAbs	< 1	56
$f_0OffsetPos$	> 1	55
$f_0MinPos$	< 1	53

SW_{acted}	On-T. / ROT	CL-2
DurGlobal	< 1	86
EneMaxPos	< 1	73
DurAbs	< 1	71
EneMean	> 1	71
$f_0MaxPos$	< 1	69
EneMax	> 1	69
DurAbsSyl	< 1	68
$f_0OnsetPos$	> 1	68
$f_0MinPos$	< 1	65
RateOfSpeech	> 1	62

Talk, ROT and OOT (= SOT ∪ POT); the $N = 4$ classes On-Talk, ROT, SOT, POT are only available in SW_{spont}. First, we evaluated for each corpus the single best features (classifiers with 1 feature, each). To discriminate e.g. On-Talk and OOT, all ROT words were deleted. The top-ten best features can be found in Tab. 2; for the task On-Talk vs. ROT features are ranked in Tab. 3. The column CL-2 shows higher rates for SW_{acted} than for SW_{spont}, best results are achieved for On-Talk vs. ROT (SW_{acted}).

Tab. 4 shows results based on all 100 features for different databases. Again, best results are obtained for the acted data: 81 % CL-2 and even higher recognition rates for three classes, whereas chance would be only 33 % CL-3. For SK_{spont} higher rates are achieved than for SW_{spont}. All results could be improved when the 100-dimensional feature vectors are normalized per speaker (zero-mean and variance 1): Tab. 4, right, shows the results when we assume that mean and variance (independent whether On-Talk or not) of all the speaker's prosodic feature vectors are known in advance. This is an upper bound for the results that can be reached with adaptation. The results for SW_{acted} rise drastically to 93 % CL-3; for the other corpora a smaller increase can be observed. For SW_{spont} 4 classes could be discriminated with 50 % CL-4. Here, POT is the problematic category that is very closed to all other classes

Table 4. Results on audio (100 prosodic features) and video

| | audio | | | audio, normalized | | | video |
	CL-2	CL-3	CL-4	CL-2	CL-3	CL-4	CL-2
SW$_{spont}$	65.3	55.2	42.0	66.8	56.4	49.8	76.5
SW$_{acted}$	80.8	83.9	-	92.6	92.9	-	-
SK$_{spont}$	72.7	60.0	-	74.2	61.5	-	-

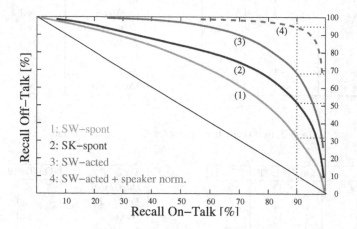

Fig. 2. ROC-Evaluation On-Talk vs. Off-Talk for the different databases

(35 % recall only). If we train with acted data and evaluate with SW$_{spont}$, we achieve 63 % CL-2, the other way round 86 % on SW$_{acted}$. The drop is surprisingly small, however, this does not hold for the 3-class task: rates for ROT are very low.

Fig. 2 shows the ROC-evaluation for all databases. In a real application it might be more "expensive" to drop a request that is addressed to the system than to answer a question that is not addressed to the system. If we thus set the recall for On-Talk to 90 %, every third Off-Talk word is detected in SW$_{spont}$ and every second in SK$_{spont}$. For the SW$_{acted}$ data, the Off-Talk recall is nearly 70 %; after speaker normalization it rises to 95 %.

As for the **On-View** classification, we evaluate our data frame based with a freely available classifier[2]. For On-View vs. {Off-View ∪ No-Face} 77 % CL-2 are achieved. For 6 of 27 speakers CL-2 was smaller than 60 %; the reason seems to be strong backlight. However, for 12 speakers recognition rates of more than 80 % were achieves, for the seven best even 94 – 98 %. We expect, that classification rates will rise, if the results are averaged over words or sentences.

6   Discussion

As expected, results for spontaneous data were worse than for acted data (Sect. 5). However, if we train with SW$_{acted}$ and test with SW$_{spont}$ and vice versa, the drop is just small. There

---

[2] http://sourceforge.net/projects/opencvlibrary/

is hope, that real applications can be enhanced with acted Off-Talk data. Next, we want to reveal similarities in the different databases and analyze single prosodic features.

Most relevant features to discriminate **On-Talk vs. OOT** (Tab. 2) are the higher energy values for On-Talk, as well for the SW_{spont} data as for the acted data. Also jitter and shimmer are important. The range of f_0 is larger for On-Talk which might be caused by an exaggerated intonation when talking to computers. For SW_{acted} global features are more relevant (acted speech is more consistent), in particular the rate-of-speech that is lower for Off-Talk. Instead, for the more spontaneous SW_{spont} data pauses are more significant (longer pauses for OOT). To discriminate **On-Talk vs. ROT** (Tab. 3) duration features are highly important: the duration of read words is longer. In addition, the duration is modeled with *Pos*-features: maxima are reached later for On-Talk (e.g. caused by a continuation rise within asyndetic listing). Again, energy is very significant (higher for On-Talk). Most features show for both databases the same behavior but unfortunately there are some exceptions, probably caused by the instructions for the acted ROT: *DurGlobal* is in SW_{acted} smaller for On-Talk, and in SW_{spont} (and SK_{spont}) for ROT. To distinguish **ROT vs. OOT**, the higher duration of ROT is significant as well as the wider f_0-range. ROT shows higher energy values in SW_{spont} but only higher absolute energy in SW_{acted} which always rises for words with longer duration.

For the SK_{spont} corpus, similarities with SW_{spont} could be observed for On-Talk vs. ROT. In the other cases, in particular jitter and shimmer become more important. Since OOT means "talking to oneself" (very low voice) in SK_{spont} the classification rate with energy increases.

Using all 100 features, best results are achieved with SW_{acted}. The classification rates for the SK_{spont} data are worse, but better than for the SW_{spont} data since there was no Off-Talk to another Person (POT). Thus, we are going to analyze the different SW_{spont} speakers. Some of them yield very poor classification rates. It will be investigated, if it is possible for humans to annotate these speakers, without any linguistic information. Further, we expect, that classification rates will rise if the analysis is performed turn-based. Also the turn-based average from the video classifier is expected to result in more robust scores. Last but not least, the combination of both modalities will increase the recognition rates, since especially POT, where the user does not look onto the display, is hard to classify from the audio signal. The multimodal classification of the focus of attention will result in *On-Focus*, the fusion of On-Talk and On-View. Additional linguistic features (bag-of-words or part-of-speech features) could further rise the accuracy.

7   Concluding Remarks

In this paper, a set of 100 prosodic features was analyzed; we classified from the audio signal whether the user speaks to the system or not. Very high classification rates up to 93 % are achieved for acted speech. A significant improvement was obtained by speaker normalization. Since On-View could be classified robustly from the video signal, a fusion of both modalities will increase recognition in the future. Further applications could be to control a car radio very robustly with On-Talk (acted speech is easy to learn), whereas most of the time the driver speaks to other occupants or to himself. For human-machine dialogues, e.g. with an avatar, additionally video information can be used. An application could be assisted living for the elderly, where the On-Talk module permanently listens for a potential command to control telephone, TV, and household appliances.

References

1. Wahlster, W.: Smartweb: Mobile Application of the Semantic Web. GI Jahrestagung 2004 (2004) 26–27.
2. Reithinger, N., Bergweiler, S., Engel, R., Herzog, G., Pfleger, N., Romanelli, M., Sonntag, D.: A Look Under the Hood - Design and Development of the First SmartWeb System Demonstrator. In: Proc. ICMI, Trento (2005).
3. Katzenmaier, M., Stiefelhagen, R., Schultz, T.: Identifying the Addressee in Human-Human-Robot Interactions Based on Head Pose and Speech. In: ICMI. (2004).
4. Oppermann, D., Schiel, F., Steininger, S., Beringer, N.: Off-Talk – a Problem for Human-Machine-Interaction. In: Proc. European Conf. on Speech Communication and Technology, Aalborg (2001).
5. Batliner, A., Zeissler, V., Nöth, E., Niemann, H.: Prosodic Classification of Offtalk: First Experiments. In: Proc. TSD, Berlin, Springer (2002) 357–364.
6. Deutsch, B., Gräßl, C., Bajramovic, F., Denzler, J.: A Comparative Evaluation of Template and Histogram Based 2D Tracking Algorithms. In: Pattern Recognition, 27th DAGM Symposium, Berlin, Springer (2005) 269–276.
7. Viola, P., Jones, M.J.: Robust Real-Time Face Detection. Int. J. Comput. Vision 57(2) (2004) 137–154.
8. Baluja, S., Sahami, M., Rowley, H.A.: Efficient Face Orientation Discrimination. In: IEEE International Conference on Image Processing, Singapore (2004).
9. Batliner, A., Fischer, K., Huber, R., Spilker, J., Nöth, E.: How to Find Trouble in Communication. Speech Communication 40 (2003) 117–143.

Visualization of Voice Disorders
Using the Sammon Transform

Tino Haderlein[1], Dominik Zorn[2], Stefan Steidl[2], Elmar Nöth[2], Makoto Shozakai[3],
and Maria Schuster[1]

[1] University of Erlangen-Nuremberg, Department of Phoniatrics and Pedaudiology
Bohlenplatz 21, 91054 Erlangen, Germany
Tino.Haderlein@informatik.uni-erlangen.de
http://www5.informatik.uni-erlangen.de
[2] University of Erlangen-Nuremberg, Chair for Pattern Recognition (Informatik 5)
Martensstraße 3, 91058 Erlangen, Germany
[3] Asahi Kasei Corporation, Speech Recognition Department
Atsugi AXT Main Tower 22F, 3050 Okata, Atsugi-shi, Kanagawa 243-0021, Japan

Abstract. The Sammon Transform performs data projections in a topology-preserving manner on the basis of an arbitrary distance measure. We use the weights of the observation probabilities of semi-continuous HMMs that were adapted to the current speaker as input. Experiments on laryngectomized speakers with tracheo-esophageal substitute voice, hoarse, and normal speakers show encouraging results. Different speaker groups are separated in 2-D space, and the projection of a new speaker into the Sammon map allows prediction of his or her kind of voice pathology. The method can thus be used as an objective, automated support for the evaluation of voice disorders, and it visualizes them in a way that is convenient for speech therapists.

1 Introduction

Today, automatic speech processing can do much more than simply recognizing speech input. Based on speech, it is possible to find out a user's identity, his or her emotional state, or speech quality. This wide field of possible applications has its basis in the high information load of natural speech that extends far beyond the bare meaning of the spoken word. Still, a field that has been less considered, is the possible benefit to medical or clinical purposes with respect to diagnosis support. There are several scenarios concerning disorders or diseases where methods from speech recognition could be applied successfully for objective analysis. The origins of voice disorders are various, ranging from injuries, inflammation, palsy or neoplasms of the larynx to misuse of the voice or side effects from other diseases. In the USA between 5% and 10% of the population suffer from such disorders [1]. These numbers give an impression of the extent of the problem and the costs connected with it and show that it might be very helpful for speech therapists to get some automated and objective support for the evaluation and classification of pathologic voices or speech. If the results of such an automatic evaluation are merely a sequence of numbers based upon cepstral features, for example, this will be of no help for the technically uneducated medical personnel. Therefore, the goal of our work is to provide a graphical visualization of a small number of features which are extracted from a high number of "technical" features by some adequate dimension

Petr Sojka, Ivan Kopeček and Karel Pala (Eds.): TSD 2006, LNAI 4188, pp. 589–596, 2006.

reduction. Another important aspect is the ability of comparing a new speaker's disorder to an existing database of previous speakers.

We created an analysis framework for different kinds of voice disorders as a front-end for traditional speech recognition techniques. The basis of the distance measure between different speakers are the Hidden Markov model parameters of a speech recognition system that are changed when the recognizer is adapted to the current test speaker. Our interest does not focus on recognition or accuracy purposes in the first place (still these can be addressed), but to gain insight into severity and mutual relations of voice disorders. The results of the recognizer adaptation are presented graphically. A mapping technique, the so-called *Sammon* mapping [2], allows the graphical representation of abstract data, unveiling underlying structures and configurations. This method of mapping data is actually not new, but it has never been applied to this concrete problem. Recordings of hoarse speakers and laryngectomized persons were available for testing.

In Sect. 2 the underlying speech recognition system will be described, Sect. 3 defines the distance measure for HMMs needed by the Sammon mapping that will be introduced in Sect. 4. The test data is described in Sect. 5, the results can be viewed in Sect. 6. Section 7 gives a conclusion and a short outlook.

2   Interpolated Semi-continuous HMMs

The features computed to express the differences between speakers are obtained from the adaptation of a speech recognizer to the current test speaker. Our recognizers are based on semi-continuous Hidden Markov Models (SCHMMs). Unlike discrete HMMs, continuous HMMs represent the output probabilities of their states by continuous probabilistic functions. This improves the recognition results but also heavily increases the number of model parameters. SCHMMs address this problem by sharing a common set of output densities in all states. Each HMM state incorporates these densities by a specific vector of weights. We use the interpolation method from [3] to adapt the output weights of an existing speaker-independent recognizer to individual speaker characteristics with a small amount of adaption data. Unlike in usual acoustic voice evaluation, we do not only use a single, sustained vowel, but a standard text uttered by the respective speaker (see Sect. 5). In this way, we achieve a set of speaker-adapted recognizers. Then we use the output weights of each recognizer for the mapping procedure. The original recognizer was trained on 27 hours of normal laryngeal speech.

This method of feature extraction seems to be rather expensive, but previous unpublished experiments at our institute showed that the features usually used in speech recognition, like cepstral coefficients, are not suitable for this task.

3   A Distance Metric for Semi-continuous HMMs

The Sammon mapping (Sect. 4) is a non-linear transformation preserving data topology. This topology is represented within the matrix of respective utterance distances. The quality and information quantity of a Sammon map is fully determined by this metric and not by the mapping itself. Thus, it is extremely important to have a suitable distance metric. On the other hand, the distance metric can be chosen without any mathematical restrictions like linearity etc. This is the great advantage of the Sammon Transform against other dimension reduction operations, like PCA.

In our case, we need a good distance calculus for speaker-adapted SCHMMs in order to get the distance between a pathologic voice and the normal voices represented by the baseline recognizer, or between two pathologic voices. We propose a distance measure computed from the distances of the respective elementary SCHMMs of different speaker-dependent speech recognizers. The arithmetic mean of these model distances serves as the final result. So the problem reduces to calculating the distance of the states of two SCHMMs. Distance calculation has to use the interpolation weights but still take into consideration the densities from the recognizer codebook containing the Gaussian output densities. This is due to the varying information load which can be considered higher for densities with low and lower for those with a high variance. If a simple Euclidean distance of the weight vectors were used, this information would get lost and the quality of the distance metric would diminish. The codebook itself is static and common to all speakers.

The basic distance metric is an HMM state distance which is computed in two steps, one for the mean vector of each codebook density and a second one for its covariance matrix.

3.1 Distance of Mean Vectors

Concerning the mean value of the output densities for each HMM state, the approach is straightforward. For each state i of a model p the mean vector $\vec{m}_{ik}(p)$ of each codebook density k is scaled with the corresponding output weight $c_{ik}(p)$ as introduced in [3]:

$$\hat{\vec{m}}_{ik}(p) = c_{ik}(p) \cdot \vec{m}_{ik}(p) \tag{1}$$

Given two HMMs named p and q, the standard Euclidean distance can now be computed between $\hat{\vec{m}}_{ik}(p)$ and $\hat{\vec{m}}_{ik}(q)$ which are both of dimension R:

$$\text{MEAN}d_{ik}(p,q) = \sqrt{\sum_{r=1}^{R} (\hat{m}_{ik,r}(p) - \hat{m}_{ik,r}(q))^2} \tag{2}$$

It represents the distance in the mean vectors of the scaled density k of state i between the two HMMs.

3.2 Distance of Covariance Matrices

There are various distance metrics for matrices. For the distance of covariance matrices of two codebook densities we use the Euclidean distance of corresponding weighted column vectors and interpret their arithmetic mean as covariance distance. Analogous to (1), each vector $\vec{v}_{ik,\rho}(p)$ of column ρ of the covariance matrix is scaled with the corresponding interpolation weight c_{ik}:

$$\hat{\vec{v}}_{ik,\rho}(p) = c_{ik}(p) \cdot \vec{v}_{ik,\rho}(p) \tag{3}$$

As the dimension of a codebook density is R, the covariance matrix is of the size $R \times R$, i.e. there are R pairs of corresponding column vectors $\hat{\vec{v}}_{ik,\rho}(p), \hat{\vec{v}}_{ik,\rho}(q)$ to be processed. For each pair the Euclidean distance is:

$$\text{COVA}d_{ik,\rho}(p,q) = \sqrt{\sum_{r=1}^{R}(\hat{\bar{v}}_{ik,\rho r}(p) - \hat{\bar{v}}_{ik,\rho r}(q))^2} \qquad (4)$$

In order to produce a single distance value for two corresponding densities out of the R results $\text{COVA}d_{ik,\rho}(p,q)$ from the column vectors, their arithmetic mean serves as final covariance distance $\text{COVA}d_{ik}(p,q)$ for one codebook density k:

$$\text{COVA}d_{ik}(p,q) = \frac{\sum_{r=1}^{R}\text{COVA}d_{ik,\rho}(p,q)}{R} \qquad (5)$$

Finally $\text{MEAN}d_{ik}(p,q)$ and $\text{COVA}d_{ik}(p,q)$ are combined to one density distance:

$$d_{ik}(p,q) = \frac{\text{MEAN}d_{ik}(p,q) + \text{COVA}d_{ik}(p,q)}{2} \qquad (6)$$

In general, $\text{MEAN}d_{ik}(p,q)$ is much smaller than $\text{COVA}d_{ik}(p,q)$. Therefore, the introduction of weights for both values is subject of future work.

3.3   Single State and HMM Distance

The calculations in (1) to (6) are performed for all of the K Gaussian output densities of a state i. In the end, the resulting set of K density distances $d_{ik}(p,q)$ obtained from (6) is averaged and provides a single state distance $d_i(p,q)$:

$$d_i(p,q) = \frac{\sum_{k=1}^{K} d_{ik}(p,q)}{K} \qquad (7)$$

In the same way, the HMM distance δ_{pq} between models p and q can be obtained by normalizing the sum of all N state distances:

$$\delta_{pq} = \frac{\sum_{i=1}^{N} d_i(p,q)}{N} \qquad (8)$$

The HMM distance in (8) is computed for each pair of elementary HMMs, thus filling up a matrix $\mathbf{D}$ holding the speaker distances. This matrix is symmetric, so for n utterances $\frac{n^2-n}{2}$ distances have to be calculated. Limiting the amount of HMM state densities K taken into consideration to some K' when calculating the state distance can reduce computation time. For $K - K' \ll K$ the effect on the resulting HMM distance is negligible.

4   Sammon Mapping

The Sammon mapping performs a topology-preserving reduction of data dimension. It minimizes a stress function between the topology of the low-dimensional Sammon map and the high-dimensional original data. The latter topology is defined by the distances between utterances or speakers, as defined in Sect. 3. The low-dimensional Sammon map is usually visualized as 2-D or 3-D image. With respect to [4], we call a Sammon map a *cosmos*, while a mapped utterance inside a cosmos is called a *star*.

The heart of Sammon's method is its special error function E, yielding a stress factor between the actual configuration of stars in m-dimensional target domain and the original data in d-dimensional space ($m < d$):

$$E = \frac{1}{\sum_{p=1}^{n-1} \sum_{q=p+1}^{n} \delta_{pq}} \sum_{p=1}^{n-1} \sum_{q=p+1}^{n} \frac{(\delta_{pq} - \nu_{pq})^2}{\delta_{pq}} \qquad (9)$$

δ_{pq} denotes the distance between HMMs with number p and q, as in (8), ν_{pq} is the distance between stars $s(p)$ and $s(q)$ in the cosmos map. E is within $[0, 1]$, where $E = 0$ means a lossless projection from d- to m-dimensional space. Due to (9), utterances forming clusters in original space will tend to cluster also in destination space. The same holds for utterances being far apart from each other. In order to achieve the final map we apply standard steepest descent to (9).

5 Speech Data

Each test person read the German version of the "North Wind and Sun" passage which is a phonetically rich text with 108 words (71 disjunctive). It is often used in speech therapy in German speaking countries. Dependent on the degree of voice pathology, a speech sample of approx. 35 sec to 3 min duration was thus recorded and then used for the speaker-dependent adaptation of the SCHMMs by recomputing the codebook mixture weights as described in Sect. 2.

We applied the mapping to four different corpora. Firstly, a group of 18 male laryngec-tomees was investigated. Their larynx had been removed because of laryngeal or hypopha-ryngeal cancer. These speakers use tracheoesophageal substitute voice, i.e. a shunt valve between the trachea and the pharyngoesophageal segment allows to divert the expiratory air stream into the esophagus and causes voicing by tissue vibrations there. Additionally various voice and speech properties, such as hoarseness, intelligibility, pitch, speech effort etc., were evaluated by five experienced raters on a five-point scale. For a more detailed description of this data set and its recording environment see [5].

The second speaker group were 9 female and 9 male chronically hoarse speakers.

Finally, two sets of normal non-pathologic speakers were used as control groups. The first subgroup contains 18 elderly, male persons, they were chosen in order to form an age-matching control group for the laryngectomees. They were recorded in the same environment as the pathologic voices [5]. The second subgroup consisted of 9 young males and 7 females forming an age-matching group with respect to the training speakers of the baseline recog-nizer.

Table 1 shows more details concerning the speaker groups.

6 Mappings of Voice Disorders

Figure 1 shows a mapping of all available speakers into a single 2-D cosmos. It is clearly visible that the different speaker groups were almost completely separated into different areas. In addition, the genders of the hoarse and young reference speakers were separated.

Table 1. The speaker groups

group	#speakers	avg. age	duration
Laryngectomees	18 (18m, 0f)	64.2	21.5 min
Hoarse speakers	18 (9m, 9f)	47.6	18.4 min
Normal sp. (old)	18 (18m, 0f)	65.4	15.5 min
Normal sp. (young)	16 (9m, 7f)	n/a ($\approx$25)	12.5 min

The degree of voice pathology is growing from right to left, with the hoarse speakers located between the laryngectomees and the normal speakers. The speakers' pitch is growing from the top to the bottom of the cosmos. However, which voice properties are arranged in which direction by the Sammon Transform, is dependent on the data and not known in advance. This phenomenon was already reported in [4] where a cosmos map was suggested to have an unlimited number of axes. Most of them represent complex properties of the data and are thus difficult to describe.

Figure 2 shows an example for the visualization of human and automatic evaluation results which were mapped to a 2-D cosmos of the laryngectomized speakers. The intensity of the stars in the left mapping represents the speech effort rated by the human experts. On the right side the intensity reflects the word accuracy achieved on an SCHMM recognizer (cp. [5]) for each speaker. A strong correlation can be seen between both graphics. Speakers with high effort values are likely to have a low recognition rate and vice versa.

Another experiment was on projecting an unknown speaker into an already existing cosmos of well-known and previously evaluated cases of pathologic voices. If this is possible, then a pre-computed cosmos of various voice disorders can serve as a reference, and the new speaker's degree or even the type of pathology can be determined by the position where the recording is projected into the map. We have slightly modified Sammon's mapping method, so that the existing map stays unchanged and only the new star's coordinates are evaluated based on (9). As an example, Figure 3 shows two maps of the 18 laryngectomized speakers. The map to the left was computed all at once whereas inside the map to the right the marked star has been projected into the cosmos of the 17 remaining speakers. There is no visible difference between both maps. However, the rising mapping error which cannot be reduced if the rest of the map is kept static, will result in more incorrect projections, if a higher number of stars is projected.

7   Conclusions and Outlook

We believe that voice characteristics are present in the observation probabilities of semi-continuous HMMs. The weights of these HMMs after adaptation to a single speaker serve as input data for the Sammon Transform. It performs a topology-preserving dimension reduction and allows the visualization of high-dimensional feature spaces. Different voice disorders and their extend were clearly separated in 2-D space, and their relations to normal speakers became visible. The projection method allows to insert an unknown speaker into an existing cosmos map with a negligible error. This can serve as an objective and automatic diagnostic support for medical personnel, including adequate visualization of the results.

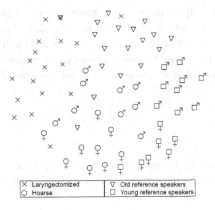

Fig. 1. Cosmos of all speaker groups and their arrangement by the Sammon Transform

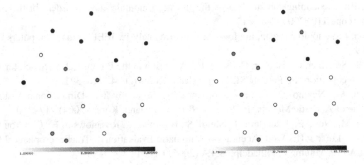

Fig. 2. Cosmos of 18 laryngectomized speakers; *Left:* Distribution of average speech effort rated by 5 human experts. Dark stars mark speakers with high effort. *Right:* Distribution of word accuracy from an automatic speech recognizer. Dark stars mark speakers with low recognition rate. A comparison of both maps shows that recognition performance can be a good indicator for speech effort.

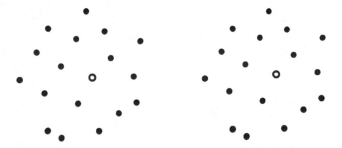

Fig. 3. *Left:* A cosmos of laryngectomized speakers computed all at once. The marked star will be removed and re-projected. *Right:* The star has been re-projected into the map. Its position can be considered identical.

The method can also help to improve the automatic recognition of people with voice disorders, e.g. in dialogue systems. The basis for this idea is a pool of robust prototype recognizers trained on speech with different disorders. When confronted with a new speaker, the system would project the speaker into a cosmos of the prototype recognizers, determine the disorder and select the "closest" recognizer or combine a set of several close recognizers for further processing.

Acknowledgments

This work was partially funded by the German Cancer Aid (Deutsche Krebshilfe) under grant 106266. The responsibility for the contents of this study lies with the authors.

References

1. Ruben, R.: Redefining the survival of the fittest: communication disorders in the 21st century. Laryngoscope **110** (2000) 241–245.
2. Sammon, J.: A nonlinear mapping for data structure analysis. IEEE Trans. Computers **C-18** (1969) 401–409.
3. Steidl, S., Stemmer, G., Hacker, C., Nöth, E.: Adaption in the Pronunciation Space for Non-Native Speech Recognition. In: Proc. ICSLP, Jeju Island, Korea (2004) 318–321.
4. Shozakai, M., Nagino, G.: Analysis of Speaking Styles by Two-Dimensional Visualization of Aggregate of Acoustic Models. In: Proc. ICSLP, Jeju Island, Korea (2004) 717–720.
5. Schuster, M., Nöth, E., Haderlein, T., Steidl, S., Batliner, A., Rosanowski, F.: Can You Understand Him? Let's Look at His Word Accuracy – Automatic Evaluation of Tracheoesophageal Speech. In: Proc. ICASSP. Volume I., Philadelphia, PA (2005) 61–64.

Task Switching in Audio Based Systems

Melanie Hartmann and Dirk Schnelle

Telecooperation Group
Darmstadt University of Technology
Hochschulstraße 10
D-64283 Darmstadt, Germany
{melanie, dirk}@tk.informatik.tu-darmstadt.de

Abstract. The worker on the move has an ever-increasing need to access information, such as instructions on how to process with a task. The use of audio to convey that information and for interaction has many advantages over traditional hands&eyes devices, especially if the user needs his hands to perform a task. In this paper, we focus on a task model stored in a workflow engine. The execution of a task is often interrupted by external events or by the user who wants to suspend a task or switch to another one. If the user wants to resume the task he has to be aware of his current position in the workflow. Due to the transient nature of speech, he does not have the possibility to review what he has done before in audio-only systems. In this paper, we present a novel approach, based on psychological theories, to assist the user to get back into the context of an interrupted task. The usability of this recovery concept was successfully tested in a user study.

1 Introduction

The future workplace will get more and more complex and lead to an ever-increasing need to deliver information to workers, such as manuals or instructions on how to proceed with a task. The use of audio to convey that information and for interaction has many advantages over traditional devices like a PDA, especially in those environments, where the user needs his hands and eyes to perform the actual task.

In this paper, we focus on tasks that can be described in a workflow definition language. The execution of a task is often interrupted by external events or by the user who wants to suspend the task or switch to another task. If the user wants to resume the task, he has to be aware of his current position in the workflow. Due to the transient nature of speech, he does not have the possibility to review what he has done before if he is dealing with audio-only systems. The user has to know how he can ask for information about the current state of the process, which leads to a decreased usability especially for novice users. In this paper we present a novel approach to assist the user to get back into the context of an interrupted task.

2 Why Is Task Switching a Problem?

Before answering that question, we give a short overview of the terminology being used in this paper.

Petr Sojka, Ivan Kopeček and Karel Pala (Eds.): TSD 2006, LNAI 4188, pp. 597–604, 2006.

We regard a **task** as an arbitrary sequence of actions which belong together and share a common goal. A **task switch** is the process of stopping or pausing the execution of a task for the benefit of a second task. A task switch decomposes in its components *start, interrupt, resume* and *end*. An **interruption** of a task is defined by Corragio [1] as a discrete event that breaks continuity of cognitive focus on the primary task. An interruption can be caused by an external source (e.g. another person), by the user himself or by our system in the following referred to as task-handler (e.g. by informing the user about an incoming email).

If the user wants to resume a task, he has to restore its context. At this point several challenges are faced:

- How much information is needed to help the user resuming the task?
- Which information is necessary for the resumption?
- How should the user interact with the task-handler considering the transient and invisible nature of speech?

In order to determine the relevant information for getting back into the context of a task, we refer to some basic psychological assumptions stating that goals are crucial for the problem solving process [2]. In order to achieve a goal it often has to be decomposed into subgoals. Having achieved the subgoals, the cognitive system has to evaluate if it can now continue with the corresponding supergoal. Therefore, this supergoal has to be readily available in memory. Goals are assumed to be in a stack-like cognitive structure, ensuring that the items belonging to the control flow reside in memory. The newest goal on the stack directs the behavior [3,4]. In this cognitive architecture, goals are sources of activation without requiring active maintenance or rehearsal and they are linked associatively to other goals via task constraints. Our approach bases on the cognitive architecture ACT-R (*Adaptive Control of Thought, Rational*, [3]), which consists of a set of inter-related mechanisms to simulate and explain human cognition. Its basic processing assumption states that, when the central cognition queries the memory, it returns the most active item in memory (corresponding to the newest goal), which then directs the behavior. Hence, our system has to assist the user to activate all relevant items needed to perform the current task.

3   Related Work

To our knowledge there is hardly any research on how to help the user resuming a task, especially in the audio domain. In this chapter, we present an interface developed by Franke, Daniels and McFarlane [5] and discuss its relation to our approach.

They developed a "spoken dialog interface system for a radio-based human-software agent military logistics task" that contains context review mechanisms. For that purpose, the user is provided with special commands to query the interface about aspects of the previous task. This can be general queries like *"Where was I?"* and also specific questions, e.g. *"Which supplies were ordered?"*. Additionally, the user can request a full progress review of the interrupted task.

In comparison to our work, Franke et al. focus on rather simple and short tasks, in a specific application area with very formal standardized military communication, whereas we want to develop a more general approach, which can be used for every workflow description in order to be independent of the application domain. With Franke's approach, the user has to be trained which questions he can use to get the information he wants. We cannot act on this assumption in our work, surely the user has to know some basic commands, but he has to be able to quickly find his way through the task without having much experience. Additionally, Franke et al. do not vary the amount of repeated information, e.g. depending on the elapsed time, because they only cope with short tasks and short interruptions, whereat only few information accumulate. In contrast, we most likely deal with a larger amount of data which would be too annoying to listen to, if the interruption was not really disruptive. Thus we have to adapt the presented amount to the current situation.

4   Concept

We assume that a workflow has one main goal (e.g. *Repairing a car*) which can be split into several subgoals (*Error diagnosis* and *Fix part*). These can in turn consist of some subgoals (*disassemble*, *clean* and *reassemble*). Each subgoal can thereby be associated with a subtask of the workflow or a workflow step.

Further, we suppose that it is sufficient for short interruptions to restore the context of the current subtask, because the higher level goals are better encoded and are therefore not affected that much by retention loss. If the interruption takes longer, the user also needs help to restore the higher level goals, thus more information has to be presented.

In this section, we present how we determine the amount of required information, how the knowledge about the current task is obtained and stored and how the user can interact with our system.

4.1   Determining Amount of Required Information

In order to determine how much information the user needs for resuming a task, we need to estimate the adverse effect of the interruption. Therefore, we identified several factors divided in four categories that have an impact on the disruptive effect of an interruption. These factors are rated on a uniform scale and its weighted sum estimates the adverse effect of the interruption.

- Characteristics of the primary task: cognitive load at the point of interruption [6,1,7]
- Characteristics of the interruption and its announcement: e.g. interruption frequency and predictability [1,8]
- Characteristics of the interrupting task: duration and interference with the interrupted task [1,7,9,10]
- Characteristics of the user: involvement in ongoing task and expertise [10]

4.2   Knowledge Representation

As mentioned before, a task consists of several subtasks and thus subgoals. If a goal of a task is activated, it activates all individual propositions of the task. In contrast, a single proposition (e.g. a workflow step) mainly activates the propositions it is directly linked to. Thus the priming effect of a goal is superior to the one of a workflow step. An experiment conducted by Trafton et al. [11] also indicated that being aware of the current goals is more important than remembering the current position. This shows the importance of being aware of the current goals and subgoals. Additionally, the user needs to know what he has done at last (position information). However, the goals are sometimes not explicitly stated. In this case we can only help the user with the repetition of the shared history (position information), which induces the priming of the user's goals. The goal and position information is stored hierarchically. Thereby, the goal-items describe the aims of the task in different granularities and the position-items what the user has already done. Figure 1a illustrates such a goal-hierarchy in form of a tree which contains all possible goals during a shopping task. The steps of the task are represented by its leaves. The relevant information for a given step consists of all goals located between the root of the goal-hierarchy (the task's goal) and the node corresponding to the step. The position items are specified by all already achieved goals that are directly linked to a goal on this path. Figure 1a points out the relevant goal and position items for the step *enter credit card number*. In order to aid the user in resuming a task it is sufficient to store these relevant information items (adapted to the user's situation) in a goal-stack as can be found in Figure 1b. The order of elements in the stack is determined by the breadth-first search of the corresponding goal-tree.

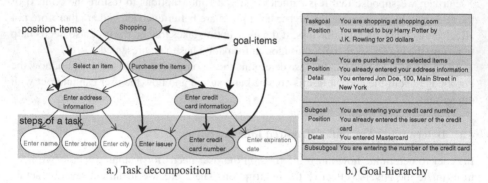

a.) Task decomposition   b.) Goal-hierarchy

Fig. 1. Example of a goal-hierarchy using the example of a shopping process with highlighted goal and position items for the point of entering the credit card number

How much information (goal and position information) is really repeated is determined by the factors listed in the previous section. If the user needs very few information, the system only provides him with the last position information, because we can assume that higher goals are still sufficiently activated or that at least the presentation of some cues (like the current position) suffices to reactivate them. If the user lacks little more information, the system starts at a higher level goal and repeats all underlying goal and position information. Every item can also feature some detail information, which are read with the corresponding item and must never be repeated alone. Every goal and subgoal marks a starting point in the goal-stack at which the system can start reading the information. However, only the last position item can act as a starting point, because we think that the last performed action is sufficient to prime the higher goals for short interruptions.

The stored data cannot only be used to help the user to get back into the context of the interrupted task, it can also aid the user orienting himself during the performance of the task. For that purpose, we simply have to provide him with the possibility to ask for this information. Further, we can use the same storage structure for some additional information which might be useful during the task execution, e.g. the content of the shopping cart. This allows for an easy and uniform way of providing the user with additional information about the current task.

We specified an XML-structure (*RecoveryXML*) to store the goal-stack. It contains several so-called information containers. The most important one is the position-container. This container consists of the goal and the position information. Further containers can be used to provide the user with additional information as mentioned before. The information which is stored in the RecoveryXML file is derived from the task's workflow description (specified in XPDL [12]) during the task execution. The goal and position information has to be added as extended attributes of the workflow activities and their transitions.

4.3 Interaction

We provide the user with the possibility to skip the repetition and to ask for more information if he is not satisfied with the represented amount. The same interaction is supported when he requests data about his current position or any other available information during the task execution. This provides a consistent way of interacting with the system during the whole performance of the task.

5 User Study

We conducted a user study to test the usability of our recovery concept. We measured the performance of users when they resume an interrupted task and when they are thereby supported by the repetition of different amounts of information. We divided the participants into three groups that were supported by different amounts of repeated information. We intended to find out whether the amount of information has an influence on the user's performance and on the user experience. Further, we aimed at determining how much information should be repeated for being helpful and without being annoying. In this section, we present the setup of our user study and its results.

5.1 Test Setup

For the user study we used a shopping task consisting of two parts: searching and purchasing. In order to search an item the user had to navigate in a category tree where the books and CDs, which can be bought, represent the leaves. To purchase the selected items, the user had to enter his credit card information, a billing and a shipping address.

Each user got interrupted once in every subtask (search, purchase) and had to perform a memorization task. For the task resumption some context information about the task was read to the user before the workflow continued at the point where it was interrupted. Thereby, the amount of information depended on the recovery strategy the user was assigned to. The recovery strategies used were:

ALL Repeat all information collected from the shopping task so far
LAST ITEM Repeat only the last stored information item
NONE The shopping task continues without giving any additional information (control group)

Finally, the users filled out a questionnaire regarding their subjective feedback on the system.

5.2 Results

We found that the repetition of information really led to a decreased users' response time after the interruption and that most users rated the repetition as very helpful (the mean rating was 4.65 with 0 meaning "not helpful at all" and 6 "very helpful"). Further, we noted that the users who received the maximum amount of information were surprisingly not annoyed by its repetition. In this section, we present these results in more detail.

Response Times. We compared the response times (resumption lags) of the various groups using a one-way analyze of variance (ANOVA) to test whether the response time after the interruption was shorter for the participants in the ALL- and LAST ITEM-group than for members of the NONE-group. The results are illustrated in Figure 2. The differences for the various groups were significant for the search-part ($F(2, 25) = 5.1, MSE = 12.7, p = 0.014(< 0.05)$) and marginal significant for the purchase-part ($F(2, 24) = 3.1, MSE = 12, p = 0.064(< 0.1)$). The result cannot be due to the duration of the attention-switch, because we played a jingle indicating the restart of the shopping task to compensate this effect.

a.) Search   b.) Purchase   c.) Amount of information.

Fig. 2. Results of the user study: a.) and b.) show the response times after an interruption (average: average response time over all groups during the whole search or purchase part), c) shows the users' rating of the amount of repeated information

Amount of Repeated Information. We asked the participants to judge the amount of repeated information in order to test whether the members of the ALL-group rated the amount of repeated information as more annoying than the members of the LAST ITEM-group, whereby 0 meant "not enough information" and 6 "too much information". The result is shown in Figure 2 (group ALL: $M = 3.20, SD = 1.31$; group LAST ITEM: $M = 3.33, SD = 0.95$). The results are counter to our expectations, both groups found the amount of repeated information very suitable and we could not detect any differences between the groups.

This result is rather surprising because the users of the ALL-group perceived about 23s of repeated information for the search-part and 38s for the purchase-part (for comparison 4s and 3s for the members in the LAST ITEM-group). It is doubtful that these ratings persist, when the participants use the shopping process more frequently, but this has to be proved in further user studies

6   Summary and Outlook

In this paper we presented a novel approach to manage knowledge about performed tasks in order to help the user getting back into the context of an interrupted task. We assume that goals are the most important information to be remembered for resuming a task. We specified an XML-structure called RecoveryXML that stores all relevant information about the state of a task focusing on information about the current goals and about the current position in the workflow. The RecoveryXML structure is retrieved from the task's workflow description. In order to determine how much information the user needs in which situation, we took a closer look at the factors that make an interruption disruptive and used them to estimate the deleterious effect of the interruption.

Finally, we conducted a user study to prove the usability of our recovery concept and found that the repetition really helped users to resume a task.

In order to provide the user with the right amount of information, we have to test and refine our estimation of the disruptive effect of an interruption by conducting further user studies.

Our recovery concept is not limited to the usage in task-oriented workflows. It can also be helpful for the orientation in structured texts. In order to transfer our concept to the reading of text, we have to re-define the meanings of goal- and position items. Goals correspond to headings or the currently read sentence. The position items comprise the last paragraph, a text-summary for the currently read section and the already read headings (like for workflows only those items are of interest that are directly linked to the "goal-path"). A detail-item can optionally be appended to each heading. It can contain a summary of the corresponding chapter. In order to retrieve the recovery file automatically from the text's structure, we have to be able to summarize the texts automatically or find another way to speed up the repetition, for example using techniques like SpeechSkimmer [13]. This expansion to structured text can be useful for many application areas, for example for museum guides or for searching and jumping in audio-documents. In the latter case, the user is not aware of the context of the search term or the position he jumped to. Our system can help him by reading some relevant information to him, like headings or summaries, to understand the context.

Acknowledgments

Thanks a lot to SAP Research Palo Alto for supporting our research. Special thanks to Frankie James, her comments were very useful and helped to conduct the user study.

References

1. Corragio, L.:   Deleterious Effects of Intermittent Interruptions on the Task Performance of Knowledge Workers. In: 18th international conference on information systems. (1990).
2. Anderson, J.: Cognitive Psychology and Its Implications. Worth Publishers (2004).
3. Anderson, J., Lebiere, C.: The atomic components of thought. Erlbaum (1998).

4. Newell, A.: Unified theories of cognition. Harvard University Press (1990).
5. Franke, J., Daniels, J., McFarlane, D.: Recovering Context after Interruption. In: 24th Annual Meeting of the Cognitive Science Society. (2002).
6. Miyata, Y., Norman, D.: Psychological issues in support of multiple activities. In: User Centered System Design. (1986).
7. Latorella, K.: Effects of the modality on interrupted flight deck performance: Implications for data link. In: Human Factors and Ergonomics Society. (1998).
8. Cohen, S.: Aftereffects of stress on human performance and social behavior: a review of research and theory. In: Psychological Bulletin, 88. (1980).
9. Altmann, E., Trafton, J.: Memory for goals: an activation-based model. In: Cognitive Science 26. (2002).
10. Edwards, M., Gronlund, S.: Task interruption and its effects on memory. In: Psychology Press Ltd. (1998).
11. Trafton, J., Altmann, E.: Preparing to resume an interrupted task: Effects of prospective goal encoding and retrospective rehearsal. In: International Journal of Human-Computer Studies, 58. (2003).
12. WfMC: Process Definition Interface - XML Process Definition Language. In: WfMC Specification. (2005).
13. Arons, B.: A system for interactively skimming recorded speech. In: ToCHI. (1997).

Use of Negative Examples
in Training the HVS Semantic Model

Filip Jurčíček[1], Jan Švec[2], Jiří Zahradil[2], and Libor Jelínek[2]

[1] Center of Applied Cybernetics, University of West Bohemia
Pilsen, 306 14, Czech Republic
`filip@kky.zcu.cz`
[2] Department of Cybernetics, University of West Bohemia
Pilsen, 306 14, Czech Republic
`honzas@kky.zcu.cz, jzahrad@kky.zcu.cz, jelinekl@kky.zcu.cz`

Abstract. This paper describes use of negative examples in training the HVS semantic model. We present a novel initialization of the lexical model using negative examples extracted automatically from a semantic corpus as well as description of an algorithm for extraction these examples. We evaluated the use of negative examples on a closed domain human-human train timetable dialogue corpus. We significantly improved the standard PARSEVAL scores of the baseline system. The labeled F-measure (LF) was increased from 45.4% to 49.1%.

1 Introduction

A corpus for semantic parsing usually consists of utterances (word sequences) and its semantic annotation (semantic parse trees). In such corpus, there are positive and negative examples which can be used for training statistical models.

A positive example is a pair of a word and its semantic annotation. A positive example says that some word has some (concrete) semantic annotation. A negative example, similarly to a positive example, is a pair of a word and its semantic annotation; however, it says about a word that it does not have a semantic annotation. A negative example gives us much less information than a positive example because we have to collect several negative examples to replace one positive example.

In this paper, the statistical semantic parsing is a search of the sequence of concepts $S = c_1, c_2, \ldots, c_T$ that has the maximum aposteriori probability $P(S|W)$ for the word observation $W = w_1, w_2, \ldots, w_T$. The search can be described as

$$S^* = \underset{S}{\mathrm{argmax}}\, P(S|W)$$
$$= \underset{S}{\mathrm{argmax}}\, P(W|S)P(S) \tag{1}$$

where $P(S)$ is the semantic model and $P(W|S)$ is the lexical model.

In Section 2, we describe the HVS model with the baseline initialization of a lexical model. Section 3 details both positive and negative examples and the way how to collect negative examples and a new initialization of the lexical model. In Section 4, we provide experimental results. Finally, Section 5 closes this paper.

Petr Sojka, Ivan Kopeček and Karel Pala (Eds.): TSD 2006, LNAI 4188, pp. 605–612, 2006.

2   The HVS Model

The hidden vector state (HVS) model is an approximation of a pushdown automaton. A *vector* state in the HVS model represents a stack of a pushdown automaton, which keeps information that spans over several words.

The semantic information matching every word in an utterance is described by a sequence of concepts from a leaf to a root of a semantic annotation (see Fig. 1). If we place concepts along the way from the leaf to the root to a vector, than a derivation tree can be transformed to a sequence of these vectors. We imposed a hard limit on the maximum depth of a stack equal to four. For example, the word *Prague* is described by the vector state [STATION, TO, DEPARTURE, EMPTY].

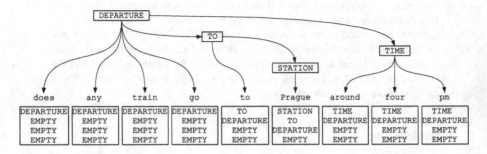

Fig. 1. An example of a full semantic parse tree with the corresponding stack sequence

The transitions between vector states are modeled by stack operations: popping 0 to 3 concepts from a stack, pushing a new concept onto a stack, and generating a word. The first two operations belong to the semantic model which is dgiven by:

$$P(S) = \prod_{t=0}^{T+1} P(n_t|c_{t-1}[1, 4]) \cdot$$
$$\cdot P(c_t[1]|c_t[2, 4]) \qquad (2)$$

where n_t is the vector state shift operation and takes values in range $0, \ldots, 4$, and c_t at word position t is a vector state of 4 concepts, i.e. $c_t = [c_t[1], c_t[2], c_t[2], c_t[4]]$, where $c_t[1]$ is a preterminal concept dominating the word w_t and $c_t[4]$ is a root concept. The probability $P(n_t|c_{t-1}[1, 4])$ represents a model for popping 0 to 3 concepts from a stack. The variable n_t defines the number of concepts which will be popped of a stack. If $n_t = 0$, it relates to growing a stack by one concept. If $n_t = 1$, it relates to replacing preterminal concept $c_t[1]$ by a new concept. If $n_t > 1$, it relates to popping n_t concepts and pushing a new concept. For example, the transition from the vector state represented by the seventh block in Figure 1 is made by popping two concepts TO and STATION and pushing a new concept TIME ($n_6 = 2$). The probability $P(c_t[1]|c_t[2, 4])$ represents a model for pushing a new concept $c_t[1]$ onto a stack. The concept $c_t[1]$ is given the rest of a stack $c_t[2, 4]$.

The lexical model performs the last operation, generation of a word. The lexical model defined as

$$P(W|S) = \prod_{t=0}^{T+1} P(w_t|c_t[1,4])$$

(3)

The word w_t is given $c_t[1,4]$. For more details about the HVS model see [1].

2.1   Training Data

The HVS model is possible to train using simple semantics. For the sentence *"Does any train go to Prague around four pm?"*, the corresponding semantics is DEPARTURE(TO(STATION), TIME). Dialogue annotators have to define semantics that represents each utterance, but they need not provide a full parse tree[1]. In Fig. 1, you can see a full parse tree of the example above. To train the HVS model, we eased the Czech human-human train timetable (HHTT) dialogue corpus version DEC-2005. The corpus was described in [2].

Table 1. A sample dialogue with semantic annotation (a literal translation from Czech to English)

Speaker	Semantics	Literal English translation
operator	GREETING	the information please
user	GREETING	hello
	DEPARTURE(TIME, TRAIN_TYPE, TO(STATION))	I have a question how can I go today by regional train to <*station*> staryho plzence </*station*>
operator	OTHER_INFO	well we do not have many connections here
	TIME, TIME	now one goes at eight sixteen if you catch it after that only at eleven ten
user	TIME	at eleven ten
	ACCEPT(TIME, FROM(STATION))	it is not so bad at eleven ten from <*station*> hlavniho </*station*> yeah
	CLOSING	yeah well OK

2.2   Baseline Model

We divided training of the HVS model into three parts: 1) initialization of the semantic and lexical models, 2) estimation of the semantic and lexical models, 3) smoothing of the semantic and lexical models.

We initialized probabilities $P(w_t|c_t[1,4])$, $P(n_t|c_{t-1}[1,4])$, and $P(c_t[1]|c_t[2,4])$ uniformly. In the case of the lexical model, we wanted probability of a word w given a vector state $c[1,4]$ to be the same for all words ($P(w|c[1,4]) = 1/|V|$ $\forall w \in V$, where V was a word lexicon).

To estimate the semantic and lexical models, we used the expectation-maximization (EM) algorithm because HHTT corpus did not provide fully annotated treebank data. We implemented the linear interpolation smoothing [3] into our model. We smoothed all three probabilities $P(n_t|c_{t-1}[1,4])$, $P(c_t[1]|c_t[2,4])$, and $P(w_t|c_t[1,4])$.

---

[1] A full parse tree defines not only a tree structure but also alignment of words to leafs of the tree.

3   Initialization of the Lexical Model

In comparison with section 2.2, we propose a different initialization based on using negative examples which are collected automatically from a corpus. First, we describe positive examples. Second, we detail negative examples and their automatic extraction from a corpus. Futher, we describe suitable utterances for negative examples extraction. Finally, we present the novel initialization of the lexical model.

3.1   Positive Examples

A positive example is a pair of a word and a vector state. A positive example says a word w is possible to generate by a vector state $c[1, 4]$. For the utterance from the Fig. 1 *"Does any train go to Prague around four pm?"* with the semantic annotation DEPARTURE(TO(STATION), TIME), a positive example could be a pair (*Prague*, [STATION, TO, DEPARTURE, EMPTY]). Because we do not have full semantic parse trees with vector states aligned to words, the utterance with its semantic annotation contains others positive examples with the word *Prague*, for instance (*Prague*,[TIME, DEPARTURE, EMPTY, EMPTY]).

To determine a probability of the word *Prague* given $c[1, 4]$, the EM algorithm must estimate probability over all possible alignments of words in an utterance with a semantic annotation. However, we could make it easier for the EM algorithm if we knew, for example, that the vector state [TIME, DEPARTURE, EMPTY, EMPTY] cannot generate word like *Prague*. As a result, the EM algorithm would have less possible alignments.

3.2   Negative Examples

A negative example, similarly to a positive example, is a pair of a word and a vector state. However, a negative example says a word w is *not* possible to generate by a vector state $c[1, 4]$. In other words, negative examples are pairs of words and vector states $c[1, 4]$ that do not appear in the same utterances. For instance, the utterance *"Does any train go at five pm?"* with semantic annotation DEPARTURE(TIME) implies that the word *go* is not generated by a vector state different to [STATION, TO, DEPARTURE, EMPTY]. As a result, the pair (*go*, [STATION, TO, DEPARTURE, EMPTY]) could be a negative example.

We analyzed 38 concepts in the corpus, and we found four concepts suitable for negative examples extraction : STATION, TRAIN_TYPE, NUMBER, and TIME. In other words, we search for pairs of any word and a concept form STATION, TRAIN_TYPE, NUMBER, and TIME.

3.3   Selection of Utterances for Negative Examples Extraction

Not all utterances are ideal for extraction of negative examples, for instance the utterance *"Weather is pleasant in Prague today."* with semantic annotation OTHER_INFO. If we used the utterance for extracting negative examples, we would have to conclude that the word *Prague* cannot be generated by the vector state [STATION, . . .] because the concept OTHER_INFO does not dominate the concept STATION.

To avoid selecting improper utterances for negative examples extraction, we use only utterances containing concepts: ACCEPT, ARRIVAL, DELAY, DEPARTURE, DISTANCE, DURATION, PLATFORM, PRICE, and REJECT because these concepts can dominate concepts STATION, TRAIN_TYPE, NUMBER, and TIME. For example, from the utterance *"What is price of a ticket from Prague at six pm"* with semantics PRICE(FROM(STATION), TIME), we can induce that in the utterance there are not words representing concept TRAIN_TYPE. The algorithm in Fig. 2, finally, describes the process of collecting negative examples from a corpus. For more details about mentioned concepts see [2].

```
concepts = [ACCEPT, ARRIVAL, DELAY, DEPARTURE, DISTANCE,
            DURATION, PLATFORM, PRICE, REJECT]

dominatedConcepts = [STATION, TRAIN_TYPE, NUMBER, TIME]

for every utterance in trainingSet:
  if utterance.semantics contains a concept from concepts:
  # use the utterance as a source of negative examples

    for every concept in utterance.semantics:
      if concept in dominatedConcepts:
        # use words as negative examples
        negativeExamples[concept].append(utterance.words)
```

Fig. 2. Algorithm to extract negative examples

3.4   Application of Negative Examples

Because negative examples say that a word cannot be generated by a concept, we modify the initialization of the lexical model to utilize negative examples. We still initialize the lexical model uniformly; however, at the same time, we *disable* generation of some words according to collected negative examples. See following equations:

$$
x(w, c[1,4]) = \begin{cases} \epsilon & \text{if } (w, c[1,4]) \text{ is a negative example,} \\ 1/|V| & \text{otherwise} \end{cases}
$$

$$
P(w|c[1,4]) = \frac{x(w, c[1,4])}{\sum_{\overline{w} \in V} x(\overline{w}, c[1,4])} \quad \forall c[1,4] \quad \forall w \in V \tag{4}
$$

where ϵ is enough small value, V is a word lexicon.

We found that it is better to use non-zero value for ϵ because negative examples are not errorless. For example, we need only one wrongly annotated utterance to generate fatal negative example (*Prague*, [STATION, ...]). Consequently, we want to preserve the ability of the lexical model to generate all words because the EM algorithm can overcome a wrong negative example.

4 Experiments

We tested our model on semantic annotations from HHTT corpus version DEC-2005. Currently, the corpus consists of 862 dialogues completely annotated with semantic annotation. Both operators and users are annotated. The corpus has 13769 utterances in total. The vocabulary size is 2667 words. There are 38 semantic concepts in the corpus. In our experiments, the dialogues were randomly divided into training data (619 dialogues - 9928 utterances, 72%), development data (69 dialogues - 1108 utterances, 8%), test data (174 dialogues - 2733 utterances, 20%).

We evaluated our experiments using the standard PARSEVAL measures [4]; labeled precision (LP), recall (LR), and labeled F-measure (LF), which are computed as follows:

$$LP = \frac{\# \, of \, correct \, concepts \, in \, P}{\# \, of \, concepts \, in \, P} \cdot 100\%$$

$$LR = \frac{\# \, of \, correct \, concepts \, in \, P}{\# \, of \, concepts \, in \, T} \cdot 100\%$$

$$LF = \frac{2 \cdot LP \cdot LR}{LP + LR} \cdot 100\%$$

where P is the candidate parse tree (our estimated the most propable parse), T is the corresponding correct parse tree from the corpus. A concept in P is *correct* if there exists a concept in T of the same label that spans the same words. We used the *evalb* program from Satoshi Sekine and Michael John Collins[2] to compute these scores. We tested whether the observed differences in PARSEVAL measures are significant at $p = 0.01$ using a stratified shuffling test with one million trials from Dan Bikel[3].

4.1 Validation

To determine the effect of negative examples on the initialization of the lexical model, we evaluated different initializations of the lexical model on our development data. We evaluated the effect separately for each concept NUMBER, TIME, STATION, and TRAIN_TYPE. Table 2 compares the results of the baseline system with uniformly initialized lexical model.

Table 2. PARSEVAL scores on the development data

	LP	LR	LF	p-value
baseline	43.7	51.3	47.2	
NUMBER	43.6	51.2	47.1	> 0.01
TIME	43.6	45.7	44.6	< 0.01
STATION	46.9	53.8	50.1	< 0.01
TRAIN_TYPE	44.8	51.2	47.6	> 0.01
NST	48.7	54.4	51.4	< 0.001

---

[2] http://nlp.cs.nyu.edu/evalb
[3] http://www.cis.upenn.edu/~dbikel/software.html

The use of negative examples for the initialization of the lexical model for the concept NUMBER seems to lower the PARSEVAL scores; however, the difference was not statistically significant.

The use of negative examples for the initialization of the lexical model for the concept TIME significantly lower the PARSEVAL scores. As a result, the concept TIME was excluded from futher experiments.

The use of negative examples for the initialization of the lexical model for the concept STATION significantly improves the PARSEVAL scores.

The use of negative examples for the initialization of the lexical model for the concept TRAIN_TYPE seems to improve the PARSEVAL scores; however, the difference was not statistically significant.

Finally, we tested the initialization of the lexical model using the concepts NUMBER, STATION, and TRAIN_TYPE together (NST) (see Table 2, the row NST). These results are statistically significant on the development data.

4.2 Test Data Results

Table 3 shows the results of the baseline initialization of the lexical model using uniform initialization and the initialization of the lexical model using negative examples for the concepts NUMBER, STATION, and TRAIN_TYPE (NST). We report results for both test and development data. The use of negative examples for the initialization of the lexical model for the concepts NUMBER, TRAIN, and TRAIN_TYPE significantly improve PARSEVAL scores.

Table 3. PARSEVAL scores on the test and the development data

	Test data				Development data			
	LP	LR	LF	p-value	LP	LR	LF	p-value
baseline	42.2	49.2	45.4		43.7	51.3	47.2	
NST	46.6	51.9	49.1	< 0.001	48.7	54.4	51.4	< 0.001

5 Conclusion

This paper has presented the use of negative examples in training the HVS model. We identified suitable utterances for extraction of negative examples. We found three concepts NUMBER, STATION, and TRAIN_TYPE for which the initialization using negative examples of the lexical model significantly improves the PARSEVAL scores. The labeled F-measure (LF) was increased from 45.4% to 49.1%.

In the future work, we want futher exploit different ways of initialization of the lexical model.

Acknowledgment

This work was supported by the Ministry of Education of the Czech Republic under project 1M0567.

References

1. He, Y., Young, S.: Semantic processing using the hidden vector state model. Computer Speech and Language **19:1** (2005) 85–106.
2. Jurcicek, F., Zahradil, J., Jelinek, L.: A human-human train timetable dialogue corpus. In: Proceedings of 9th European Conference on Speech Communication and Technology, Lisboa, Portugal (2005).
3. Jelinek, F.: Statistical Methods for Speech Recognition. MIT Press, Cambridge, MA, USA (1997)
4. Black, E., Abney, S., Flickinger, D., Gdaniec, C., Grishman, R., Harrison, P., Hindle, D., Ingria, R., Jelinek, F., Klavans, J., Liberman, M., Marcus, M., Roukos, S., Strzalkowski, S.T.: A procedure for quantitatively comparing the syntactic coverage of english grammars. In: Proceedings of the 1990 DARPA Speech and Natural Language Workshop, Pacific Grove, CA (1991) 306–311.

Czech-Sign Speech Corpus
for Semantic Based Machine Translation*

Jakub Kanis[1], Jiří Zahradil[2], Filip Jurčíček[1], and Luděk Müller[1]

[1] University of West Bohemia, Department of Cybernetics
Univerzitní 8, 306 14 Pilsen, Czech Republic
{jkanis, filip, muller}@kky.zcu.cz
[2] SpeechTech s. r. o, Pilsen, Czech Republic
jiri.zahradil@speechtech.cz

Abstract. This paper describes progress in a development of the human-human dialogue corpus for machine translation of spoken language. We have chosen a semantically annotated corpus of phone calls to a train timetable information center. The phone calls consist of inquiries regarding their train traveler plans. Corpus dialogue act tags incorporate abstract semantic meaning. We have enriched a part of the corpus with Sign Speech translation and we have proposed methods how to do automatic machine translation from Czech to Sign Speech using semantic annotation contained in the corpus.

1 Introduction

Pursuant to the law *155/1998 Sb.* the Sign Speech (SS) means Czech Sign Language and Signed Czech. The article 4 specifies the Czech Sign Language (CSE) as follows:

- Czech Sign Language is a basic communication facility of the deaf people in the Czech Republic.
- Czech Sign Language is a natural and adequate communication system. It is composed by the specific visual-spatial resources, i.e. hand shapes (manual signals), movements, facial expressions, head and upper part of the torso positions (non-manual signals). Czech Sign Language has basic language attributes, i.e. system of signs, double articulation, productiveness, peculiarity and historical dimension, and has stable lexical and grammatical structure.

The article 5 specifies the Signed Czech (SC) as follows:

- Signed Czech is an artificial language system, which facilitates communication between deaf and hearing people.
- Signed Czech uses grammatical resources of the Czech language, which is simultaneously loudly or unloudly articulated. The signs of the Czech Sign Language according to the individual Czech words are showed together with the articulation.

* Support for this work was provided by the Grant Agency of Academy of Sciences of the Czech Republic, project No. 1ET101470416.

Petr Sojka, Ivan Kopeček and Karel Pala (Eds.): TSD 2006, LNAI 4188, pp. 613–620, 2006.

The CSE is usually used for communication between deaf people while SC is used in communication between deaf and hearing people. For example the majority of Czech TV programs for deaf people are performed in SC. Since the last time, there are programs performed in CSE too. This lack of using CSE is given by a status of the CSE before year 1989. The CSE before year 1989 was an unofficial language, using only by a deaf community. Only an oral method in combination with the SC was used for teaching deaf children. A linguistic research of sign languages started after year 1960 in the world, when W. Stockoe published his book Sign Language Structure. The Stokoe's book was the first work, which has studied the sign language from a linguistic point of view. The linguistic research of the CSE started in 90's. There exists no official form of the CSE and the language and the signs are various in different regions. And of course, like in others sign languages, there exists no written form of the CSE used by deaf people. From this reasons there is no comprehensive work about CSE syntax, but first studies show that the CSE shares some syntactic structures with others sign languages.

The using of written language instead of spoken language is wrong idea in the case of Deaf. This is because the Deaf have problems with majority language understanding when they are reading a written text. The majority language is the second language of the Deaf and its acquiring is only particular. Thus majority language translation to the sign speech is important for better Deaf orientation in the majority language speaking world. Currently human interpreters provide this translation, but their service is expensive and not always available. The machine translation systems with graphical avatar (artificial human figure) as output represent the solution, which cannot fully replace interpreters. But it can help in everyday communication.

There are two main approaches in area of machine translation (MT): linguistic and data oriented machine translation. A majority of existing translation systems is based on linguistic oriented approach, for example [1] system for translation from English to British Sign Language (BSL), [2,3,4] systems for translation from English to American Sign Language (ASL) and [5] system for translation from Polish to Polish Sign Language (PSL). The systems based on data oriented approach appear recently too, for example [6] statistical based system for translation from German to German Sign Language (DGS) and [7] example based system. The main problem of the data oriented approach is acquisition of training data – bilingual corpus. In this paper we describe the creation of Czech-Sign Speech corpus suitable for data oriented machine translation.

We have chosen an existing train timetable dialogue corpus (TTDC) [8] as a base of our Czech Sign Speech corpus. The choice of this corpus has a lot of advantages. Firstly, the TTDC is a record of a spontaneous telephone communication between operator and user, so the corpus covers a whole well-defined task. Secondly, every dialog is carefully transcribed to the Czech. Thirdly, the dialogs are provided with dialog act and semantic annotation. Fourthly, the TTDC is the corpus of a telephone spontaneous speech, results acquired from its can be used in real-life and telephone applications. It opens the world of telephone communication for deaf users. Fifthly, the same corpus can be used for training of complete system translating from the spoken language to the sign language (a speech recognizer on one side and a translation system and graphical avatar on the second side). In next sections we describe the TTDC and its extension by Sign Speech translation of dialogs in detail.

2   Train Timetable Dialogue Corpus

The corpus was collected in a train timetable information center. It was recorded since April, 2000 to September, 2000. There were 6584 calls collected, from which 6353 calls (dialogues) were transcribed. Callers were mainly Czechs.

The audio part of corpus contains 106 hours of speech. Corpus uses orthographic transcription because it is more suitable for transcription of Czech spontaneous speech [9]. Spontaneous Czech contains words and usages not found either in standard written or in formal spoken Czech. From another point of view, the corpus consists of 81543 turns. Each turn starts with a speaker change. The size of the vocabulary of the whole corpus is about 12k words, and there are almost 600k tokens in it. The operator's vocabulary (5839 words) is smaller than user's vocabulary (9485 words). While a dialogue has 6 user's turns on average, the first user's turn contains 35% of user's tokens in the dialogue on average. Each turn was divided into segments that allow assigning of one dialogue act to each utterance segment.

2.1   Dialogue Act Tagging Scheme

TTDC corpus [8] is annotated by dialogue acts with additional structured semantic tags. It uses dialogue act tagging scheme slightly inspired by DAMSL (Dialogue Act Markup in Several Layer) [11] but strongly based on DATE (Dialogue Act Tagging for Evaluation) scheme [12]. The corpus uses three dimensional annotations (1) DOMAIN, (2) SPEECH-ACT, (3) SEMANTICS. The corpus has annotated whole dialogues utterances - both user's and operator's as a contrast to DATE, which was originally designed just for evaluation of dialogue systems, therefore annotation was present only at system's responses.

2.2   Data Dimensions

According to [8] TTDC tag set suppresses some disadvantages of his successors and boosts their advantages. In general, semantic annotation *normalizes* dialog utterances and therefore we believe that this annotation can help in the task of machine translation from spoken Czech to SS. We briefly describe the DOMAIN, the SPEECH-ACT, and the SEMANTIC dimensions of TTDC tag set in the following section.

DOMAIN Dimension. This dimension assigns every utterance to three areas of conversational action: **Task, Communication, Frame**. The first area of DOMAIN is the task domain, which is train timetable inquiry answering. The second area is managing communication channel, it manages the verbal channel and provides evidence what has been understood. Finally, the third area is a situation frame, which refers to an apology or an instruction contained in a sentence. This domain is not as frequent in human-human dialogs as in human-machine dialogs.

Automatic sign language translation can use domain information to focus on task sentences and handle the communication problems in correct sign-specific form.

SPEECH-ACT Dimension. This dimension refers to an utterance's communicative goal, independently on an utterance form. This dimension differentiates utterances that have the same value of the SEMANTICS dimension. For instance, the SPEECH-ACT dimension values REQUEST-INFO and PRESENT-INFO can refer to the same value in the SEMANTICS dimension, e.g. DEPARTURE(TIME, FROM(STATION)). TTDC scheme use namely these speech acts: request-info, present-info, verify, verify-neg, offer, acknowledgment, status-report, explicit-confirmation, implicit-confirmation, instruction, apology, opening, closing and speech-repair.

In SS translation domain, we are planning to use extracted information about utterance segments to for example sentence type resolution.

SEMANTIC Dimension. This dimension captures task relevant information from each utterance. In train timetable inquiry answering task domain; the goal of communication is to determine information needed to answer an inquiry, e.g. a departure train station or time of desired departure. In the sentence "Is there any train to Pilsen at eight am", the semantics is REQUEST=departure, TO=Pilsen, and TIME=eight am. The extracted semantic concepts should be also sufficient for machine translation. Semantic annotation has preserved the hierarchical structure of an utterance, but it stills prevailed simplicity. Although, the semantic layer generalizes sentences, this generalization is precious and because of vocabulary reduction it makes machine translation process simpler. Another possibility is to conditioning translation with respect to semantic annotation.

There are two main semantic concepts defined in TTDC. DEPARTURE is a concept for an utterance that represents question about departure of a particular train (answer is usually exact time when the train leaves a particular train station) and ARRIVAL is similar concept for arrival to particular station. Each of previous semantic concepts is allowed to have 27 non-terminal leaves (concepts): FROM, TO, THROUGH, IN_DIRECTION, TRAIN_TYPE, TIME, and few rare concepts: BACK, DELAY, DISTANCE, DURATION, GREETING, PRICE, PERSON, AREA, WAIT, etc. Nearly all concepts can be nodes in hierarchical semantic tree, as there are very weak constraints on their possible relations in natural spoken language.

Totally, we have 1000 dialogues semantically (manually) annotated, that means 16645 dialogue acts and 1202 of them are unique. The corpus consists of totally 26472 semantic tokens (concepts) with hierarchical binding. See annotation sample in Table 1.

3   Sign Speech Translation

3.1   Process of Translation

There exist no formal written forms of the SS, thus the main problem in SS corpus building is a choice of the appropriate written forms. In the first stage of corpus building we decide to extend the TTDC corpus by Signed Czech translation of dialogues. The SC sentence has the same grammatical structure like Czech sentence and uses the signs of CSE corresponded to the individual Czech words. The SC sentence in written form can be simply represented by a sequence of CSE signs. Every CSE sign is represented by a unique string. To speed up the manual translation process we have extended the annotation tool DAE, proposed in [8].

Table 1. A sample: part of dialogue including SC translation and semantic annotation

Speaker	DA Semantics	Czech Sentence SC Translation
operator	comm,opening NIL	informace prosím *informace/1 _/2*
user	comm,opening NIL	dobrý den *dobrý_den/1,2*
	task,request-info DEPARTURE(TIME, TRAIN_TYPE, TO(STATION))	já mám prosbu jakpak jedou dneska osobní vlaky ňák dopoledne do starýho_plzence *já/3 potřebovat/4,5 kdy/6 jet/7 dnes/8 osobní_vlak/9,10 _/11 dopoledne/12 do/13 starý/14 plzeň/14 malý_věc/14*
operator	frame,status-report NIL	no tak tam už moc na výběr nemáte *_/1 _/2 _/3 už/4 moc_hodně/5 _/6 výběr/7 ne/8*
	task,present-info TIME, TIME	teďka jede v osm šestnáct jestli stihnete potom až v jedenáct deset *teď/9 jet/10 v_ve/11 osm_hodin/12 šestnáct/13 jestli/14 stihnout/15 potom/16 až/17 v_ve/18 jedenáct_hodin/19 deset/20*
user	comm,implicit-conf TIME	až v jedenáct deset *až/1 v_ve/2 jedenáct_hodin/3 deset/4*
	task,acknowledgment ACCEPT(TIME, FROM(STATION))	a to by tak ňák stačilo těch jedenáct deset z hlavního *_/5 _/6 _/7 _/8 _/9 stačit/10 _/11 jedenáct_hodin/12 deset/13 z_ze/14 důležitý/15*
	task,request-info VERIFY(TRAIN_TYPE)	jo a dá se tam vzít kočárek *_/16 _/17 moci/18 _/19 tam/20 vzít/21 _/22*

This software, including our extension, is distributed under GPL license and is available for download at project webpage [13].

Every translator uses the same CSE dictionary to ensure a consistence of translations. We use a text version of the most extensive CSE dictionary [14] (this dictionary contains 3063 signs). We have added two special signs into the dictionary. The first is used in the case that some Czech word is not translated in the corresponded SC sentence. And the second is used for the words, which need to be finger-spelled. This dictionary is a part of our annotation tool DAE. And the translator can choose only the signs from this dictionary in translation process of dialogues.

We use an explicit alignment too. The translator has to match every Czech word with one or more signs in SC sentence. The one sign can be match with more Czech words too. For example SC sentence (English literal translations of original SC sentence): *"good_morning I need when go regional_train to old pilsen small_thing"* corresponds to Czech sentence: *"good morning I have a question how can I go today by regional train to old_pilsen"* . Here on one hand the Czech words *good* and *morning* correspond to one sign *good_mornig* and other hand the word *old_pilsen* corresponds to three signs *old* , *pilsen* and *small_thing* . The explicit alignment has some advantages. We can simply check if the translator translates all words from Czech sentence (i.e. every Czech word has to be assigned at least one sign). And we can straightly create a bilingual dictionary, which is phrase based (one or more Czech words can corresponds to one or more signs).

3.2 Direct Translation System Based on Explicit Alignment

The bilingual dictionary with phrases can be used as a simple direct translation system. If there are more possible translations for one word/phrase we choose the most probable possibility. We have collected 800 dialogues in SC since May 2006. We have used 720 dialogues for dictionary creation and the rest 80 dialogues for testing. The statistical data and results are in Table 2.

Table 2. The result of direct translation system

	Training data	Testing data
no. of sentences	10241	1188
no. of distinct words	3557	1019
no. of distinct signs	658	368
no. of running words	-	8122
no. of OOV words	-	221(2.72%)
SER[%]	-	50.5
WER[%]	-	14.0

Where SER is sentence error rate, it is a ratio of bad sentence translations to a number of all translated sentences. And WER, word error rate, is similarly a ratio of bad word translations to a number of all translated words.

3.3 Semantic Based Machine Translation

The dialog act and semantic annotation of TTDC corpus can be used in different ways for machine translation. Firstly, this annotation can be considered to be an Interlingua for Czech and Sign Speech. The interlingual representation of text is independent of a source language. How we can see in Figure 1, there is the same semantic tree for Czech sentence and its SC translation. The MT system then works as follows: the source language text is converted to the interlingual representation first and then the target language text is generated from this language-independent, interlingual representation. Secondly, the SPEECH-ACT dimension of dialog act annotation can be used for the sentence type resolution. For example in CSE is important to distinguish if the question is yes/no- or wh- type of question, because every type uses other non-manual signals.

4 Conclusions and Future Work

In this paper we have described the first stage of a Sign Speech corpus building and a simple direct translation system based on phrase bilingual dictionary. The SS corpus is based on the existing TTDC corpus. The TTDC corpus is a dialogue corpus with a dialog act and a semantic annotation. In the first stage of SS corpus building we have added the Signed Czech translation of dialogues. To speed up the manual translation process we have extended the annotation tool DAE, proposed in [8]. Every translator uses the same CSE dictionary [14]

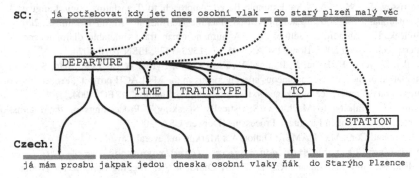

SC: já potřebovat kdy jet dnes osobní vlak – do starý plzeň malý věc

DEPARTURE

TIME   TRAINTYPE   TO

STATION

Czech:

já mám prosbu jakpak jedou dneska osobní vlaky ňák do Starýho Plzence

English: please I have a question, do we have today
any connections today ehm to Starý Plzenec.

Fig. 1. Semantic annotation of Czech and SC sentence

with two special signs added (signs for 'no translation' and 'finger-spelling'). Every translator has also to decide the explicit alignment between a Czech sentence and the SC translation. We have created a simple translation system based on this explicit alignment. The sentence error rate of proposed system is 50.5%. This quite good result is given mainly by a strong linguistic similarity of both languages (SC uses the grammatical resources of Czech).

We plan to add CSE dialogues translations to the corpus in the second stage of the corpus building. We can use the same CSE dictionary and annotation tool (with necessary modifications). The written form of CSE will be more complicated than the written form of SC. Especially if we want to describe a spatial component of CSE. Our main goal is to design the CSE written form, which would be suitable for CSE synthesizer.

References

1. Marsahll, I., Safar, E., "Sign Language Generation using HPSG", In Proceedings of the 9th International Conference on Theoretical and Methodological Issues in Machine Translation, TMI-2002, Japan. 2002.
2. Speers, d'A.L., "Representation of American Sign Language for Machine Translation", Ph.D. Dissertation. Department of Linguistics, Georgetown University.
3. Zhao, L. et al., "A Machine Translation System from English to American Sign Language", Association for Machine Translation in the Americas. 2000.
4. Huenerfauth, M., "A Multi-Path Architecture for Machine Translation of English Text into American Sign Language Animation", In Proceedings of the Student Workshop at the Human Language Technology conference / North American chapter of the Association for Computational Linguistics annual meeting (HLT-NAACL 2004). Boston, MA, USA. 2004.
5. Suszczanska, N., Szmal, P., Francik, J., "Translating Polish Texts into Sign Language in the TGT System", 20th IASTED International Multi-Conference Applied Informatics AI 2002. Innsbruck, Austria. 2002, pp. 282–287.
6. Bungeroth, J., Ney, H., "Statistical sign language translation", In: Streiter, Oliver / Vettori, Chiara (eds): LREC 2004, Workshop proceedings : Representation and processing of sign languages. Paris: ELRA (2004) - pp. 105–108.

7. Morrissey, S., Way, A., "An Example-Based Approach to Translating Sign Language", 2nd International Workshop on Example-Based Machine Translation – At MT Summit X. 2005.
8. Jurčíček, F., Zahradil, J., Jelínek, L., "A human-human train timetable dialogue corpus", In Interspeech Lisboa 2005. Bonn: ISCA, 2005. pp. 1525–1528. ISSN 1018-4074.
9. Psutka, J., Ircing P., Hajic, J., Radova, V., Psutka, J.V., Byrne, W., and Gustman, S., "Issues in annotation of the Czech spontaneous speech corpus in the MALACH project", Proceedings of the International Conference on Language Resources and Evaluation, LREC, 2004.
10. Young, S., "Talking to Machines (Statistically Speaking)", Proceedings of the International Conference on Spoken Language Processing, Denver, USA, 2002.
11. Allen, J. and Core, M., "DAMSL: Dialog Act Markup in Several Layer", http://www.cs.rochester.edu/research/cisd/resources/damsl, 1997.
12. Walker, M., and Passonneau, R., "DATE: A Dialogue Act Tagging Scheme for Evaluation of Spoken Dialogue Systems", IEEE Trans. Speech and Audio Proc., 7(6):697–708, 1999.
13. Jurčíček F., Kanis J., Zahradil, J., "DAE, Annotation tool project page", http://ui.zcu.cz/projects/dae/, 2006.
14. Langer, J., Ptáček, V., Dvořák, K., "Znaková zásoba českého znakového jazyka", Univerzita Palackého v Olomouci, Olomouc 2004.

Processing of Requests in Estonian Institutional Dialogues: Corpus Analysis

Mare Koit[1], Maret Valdisoo[1], Olga Gerassimenko[1], Tiit Hennoste[1,2], Riina Kasterpalu[1], Andriela Rääbis[1], and Krista Strandson[1]

[1] University of Tartu, J. Liivi 2,
50409 Tartu, Estonia
{mare.koit, maret, olga.gerassimenko, tiit.hennoste,
riina.kasterpalu, andriela.raabis, krista.strandson}@ut.ee
http://www.cl.ut.ee

[2] University of Helsinki, P.O. Box 9, 00014 Helsinki, Finland
tiit.hennoste@helsinki.fi
http://www.helsinki.fi/university/

Abstract. The paper analyses, how an information operator processes a customer's requests. The study is based on the Estonian dialogue corpus. Our further aim is to develop a dialogue system (DS) which interacts with a user in Estonian and recognises, interprets and grants a user's requests automatically. There are two main classes of computational models of the interpretation of dialogue acts – cue-based and inferential-based. In this paper, we try to combine these two approaches. The corpus analysis demonstrates that a number of linguistic cues can be found which can be used by a DS for recognising requests in Estonian. The DS will use linguistic cues in order to recognise a dialogue act type. After that, a frame of the act will be activated and filled in in order to interpret (understand) the act and to generate a responding act. A simple regular grammar is used for the dialogue management.

1 Introduction

Telephone services that rely on spoken dialogue systems are now being introduced at a large scale for information retrieval and transaction, e.g. flight, train and bus schedule systems, help desks, smart-home systems or navigation systems [8].

Our goal is to build a DS which interacts with a user over telephone by giving information in Estonian and following norms and rules of human-human communication. An analysis of actual dialogues is needed in order to find out the ways of using questions and requests by humans and their formal features depending on language and culture which can be used for the automatic recognition.

In a previous work [3] Estonian institutional dialogues have been analysed with the purpose of finding out the linguistic features that can be used in automatic recognition of questions. In this paper, we will analyse requests, differentiating them from questions. Our aim is to design a processing cycle of requests which can be then implemented in a DS.

There are two main classes of computational models of the interpretation of dialogue acts [6] – cue-based and inferential-based. In this paper, we try to combine these two approaches. First, the DS will use linguistic cues in order to recognise a dialogue act type. After that, a

Petr Sojka, Ivan Kopeček and Karel Pala (Eds.): TSD 2006, LNAI 4188, pp. 621–628, 2006.

frame of the recognised act will be activated and filled in in order to interpret (understand) the act and to generate a response.

The paper is organized as follows. In section 2 we give an overview of our empirical material. Section 3 clarifies the notion of a request as compared to questions. In section 4 we first discuss some linguistic cues of requests found as a result of the corpus analysis and secondly, determine a frame of a request. Section 5 investigates the structure of a dialogue which begins with a customer's request and discusses a dialogue model. In section 6 we will make conclusions.

2   Corpus Used

Our study is based on the Estonian dialogue corpus EDiC [3]. The corpus contains 871 human-human spoken dialogues, including 715 calls. Dialogue acts are annotated in dialogue transcripts using a typology which departs from conversation analysis [5]. This is a DAMSL-like dialogue act set with some differences [4]. There are about 120 dialogue acts in the typology. The acts are divided into two big groups – adjacency pair (AP) acts (e.g. request–giving information) and single (non-AP) acts (e.g. acknowledgement), cf. [3]. Names of dialogue acts consist of two parts separated by a colon: the first two letters give abbreviation of the name of an act-group, e.g. DI – directives, FR – free reactions. The third letter is used only for AP acts – the first (F) or second (S) part of an AP act; 2) full name of the act, for example, DIF: REQUEST, DIS: GIVING INFORMATION, FR: ACKNOWLEDGEMENT. The act names are originally in Estonian. A software tool (corpus workbench) is being worked out that simplifies the corpus analysis [9]. For this paper, 144 calls (almost 20,000 tokens) were selected from EDiC. Four dialogue types are represented (Table 1).

Table 1. Overview of the corpus

Dialogue type	Number of dialogues	Number of tokens	Number of customer's requests
Directory inquiries	60	4,384	55
Calls to travel agencies	36	12,104	33
Calls to outpatients' offices	26	2,422	22
Ordering a taxi	22	1,028	19
Total	144	19,938	129

3   What Is a Request?

In our typology of dialogue acts, a difference between directives and questions is made [4]. The main difference is formal – questions have special explicit formal features in Estonian (interrogatives, intonation, specific word order). No such features exist for directives. Other information-requests (and directive-actions in sense of DAMSL) are considered as directives in our typology. For example, *Can you tell me X?* is an open yes/no question but *Tell me X* is a request (a directive). We consider only customers requests here. We divide requests into two groups on the basis of the reaction expected from the addressee. The first group is formed by information requests – a customer needs certain information, e.g. a phone number. The other group is requests that expect an action by the addressee (to book a time to a doctor's reception, to send a taxi).

In our corpus, a customer's requests are information requests in directory inquiries and calls to travel agencies (e.g[1] *ma=taks teada 'Ee Kaubamaja ilusa'longi telefoninumbrit.* / I'd like to know the phone number of the beauty salon of the E department store). The requests that expect an action occur in calls to an outpatients' office or in ordering taxi (*ma 'sooviksin dotor doktor 'Nublu jurde: 'aega 'kahekümnendaks 'juuliks.* / I'd like to get a reception time to doctor Nublu on July, 20). Still, the action is always accompanied by giving information: the operator informs a customer if he is (un)able to perform the action and/or has performed it (*doktor 'Nublu on 'puhkusel asendus'arst on.* / doctor Nublu has holidays, a substituting doctor is here). If a customer who calls an outpatients' office or taxi service needs information then she usually forms a question (not a request).

4 How to Interpret a Request?

There are two main classes of computational models of the interpretation of dialogue acts [6]. The first class is called cue-based. These models consider interpretation as a classification task and solve it by training statistical classifiers on labeled examples of dialogue acts. The second class of models implements the inferential approach.

In this paper, we will propose a combination of a cue-based and inferential model. We use a cue-based model in order to determine a dialogue act type, and then an inferential model in order to interpret the act.

4.1 Linguistic Cues

Our first aim is to find out lexical and syntactic cues of customer's requests in Estonian institutional calls. To do so, we analyse the occurrences of verbs. The number of requests which do not contain a verb is 16 in our corpus. The 113 remaining requests include a verb (a predicate). As the corpus analysis demonstrates, a limited number of verbs (16) occur in a customer's requests. The most frequent (Table 2) are *soovima* (to wish, here: I'd like) and *paluma* (to ask, here: please) – 60 occurrences (46% of requests). In addition, *tahtma* (to want) and *ütlema* (to tell) are used in 21 cases (16%). These four verbs make up 62% of all usages. Five more verbs are used 3–6 times (altogether 22 times). The remaining 7 verbs are used in 1–2 cases.

Some modes and persons of verbs are preferred in requests [1]. The verbs can be divided into two groups. In the first group, the imperative is used in order to form a request (*ütle* 'tell', *pane* 'put', *anna* 'give', *vaata* 'look'). 13 requests (11% of requests with a verb) are expressed by those verbs.

In the second group of verbs, the first person conditional or indicative is used (*ma soovin/tahan/palun/võtan* 'I wish/want/ask/take'). 80 requests are formed in this way. 73 requests (65%) include a verb in the conditional. The conditional has a certain morphological

---

[1] Transcription of conversation analysis [5] is used in the examples, cf.
http://www.cs.ut.ee/~koit/Dialoog/EDiC

Table 2. Number of the most frequent verbs and their modes in customer's requests

Verb	Mode			Total
	indicative	conditional	imperative	
soovima 'to wish' (here: I'd like)	2	33		35
paluma 'to ask'	12	13		25
tahtma 'to want'	3	10		13
ütlema 'to tell'			8	8
võtma 'to take'		6		6
vaja olema 'to be needed'		5		5
huvitama 'to be interested'	1	3		4
panema 'to put' (here: to book)	1	1	2	4
Total	19	71	10	
				100

feature (*-ks-*) in Estonian which can be used as a significant cue for the automatic recognition. 21 requests (11%) contain a verb in the indicative.

The conditional is generally related to a request, adding politeness [1]. Still, some requests include a verb in the indicative. The indicative is a universal form of declarative acts. In our corpus, it is frequently used only in the case of the verb *paluma* 'to ask' (here: please). This word is used also as a polite formula in Estonian, therefore its meaning includes politeness and it functions as a softener of a directive utterance.

Another cue for recognising requests is the position of a verb in an utterance. Our analysis demonstrates that a verb starts an utterance in 44 cases (39%). Another group is formed by the utterances which begin with the pronoun *mina* 'I' (38 cases). In addition, 21 utterances begin with a particle, conjunction or adverb: *et* 'that', *aga* 'but', *äkki* 'maybe', *palun* '[I] ask' (here: please). A verb occupies the second position in the utterance.

We can sum up by saying that there are certain cues in Estonian which are used for recognising requests: 1) certain verbs, 2) certain forms – conditional and (rarely) imperative. Verb semantics determines whether a verb can be used in a request.

An experiment was carried out to confirm the following hypothesis: if the computer finds the verb form in the conditional then the utterance is probably a request (only the verbs found in the requests in our analysed corpus were considered). It can be mentioned that 81% of utterances that include one of these verbs in the conditional are requests in our analysed corpus. For the experiment, a test corpus was compiled (505 dialogues from EDiC; 57,585 tokens). The corpus workbench [9] was used to analyse the test corpus. The results are promising – 78% of utterances that include a verb in the conditional are a customer's requests (180 utterances, 140 requests). Still, as the total number of a customer's requests is 466 in the test corpus, additional cues should be implemented to recognise them. (We exclude questions from our current analysis because other cues, different from verbs, are used for their recognition.)

4.2 Frame of Request and Semantic Grammar

After the type of a dialogue act is determined, a frame of the act can be activated by the DS. The next task is to fill in the slots of the frame. In the descriptions of dialogue acts we represent two types of knowledge. The static (declarative) part of the frame forms the structure of the corresponding act, and the dynamic (procedural) part includes the procedures of reasoning processes which underlie the interpretation of the act and the generation of the responding act (cf. Figure 1).

```
Request (A, B, D)
I. Static part
Precondition: A believes that B is able to do D
Goal: B knows that A wants B to do D
Body: A informs B that A wants B to do D
Consequence: B knows that A wants B to do D

II. Dynamic part
Generation procedures (implemented by A):
Inform B that A wants B to do D
Interpretation-generation procedures (implemented by B):
(1) (to do D+) give information
(2) inform A that D cannot be done (+ argument)
```

Fig. 1. Frame of request (A – author, B – addressee, D – action)

The reaction expected from the addressee can be either giving information or performing a physical action (which is accompanied with giving information about its results). The idea of adjacency pairs [5] of dialogue acts is implemented in the frame – if the first part of an AP is a request (by A) then the second part (by B) can be giving the requested information (maybe after an action is done, e.g. a taxi is sent), or informing A that B is unable to do D.

Semantic grammars can help the DS to understand which action a customer expects (cf. [7]). For example, if the DS performs the role of a taxi operator then the semantic grammar can be represented as a frame which includes the slots 'address', 'customer's name', 'time' etc. In the case of a receptionist of an outpatients' office it is necessary to fill in the slots 'patient's name', 'his/her ID code', 'doctor's specialty', 'doctor's name', 'reception time' etc.

5   How to Grant a Request?

Let us go back to the corpus analysis. In the following we will analyse only these dialogues that start with a customer's request (after an introductory part). The number of such dialogues in our analysed corpus is 96. The remaining dialogues (a customer starts with a question) will not be considered here.

There are three possible continuations of the dialogue after a customer's request: (1) the operator's grant follows immediately, (2) the operator initiates an information-sharing sub-dialogue, (3) the customer initiates a sub-dialogue. The first continuation is typical in directory inquiries and calls for taxi – the needed action is performed and information is given immediately in 29 and 12 cases respectively. All the calls to an outpatients' office, on the contrary, belong to type (2) – an operator always initiates a sub-dialogue asking several data about the patient (name – 9 cases, ID code – 5 cases, time – 9 cases, Ex. 1).

(1)

C(ustomer): tervist, (.) mina sooviksin (.) neuroloogi juurde e aega kinni [panna.] DIF: REQUEST

I would like to go to a neurologist the next week

O(perator): jah, isikukood palun=h. /* information-sharing */

yes, ID code, please

(.)

C: oot oodake palun.

wait please

In calls to a travel agency, a customer receives an answer immediately if the request cannot be performed (6 cases). An operator initiates a sub-dialogue in 10 cases, and a customer does it in 8 cases (after the operator's acknowledgement *jah?* 'yes' which signals that the operator is expecting a specification of the request).

Various bits of information are specified by the operator. In calls to an outpatients' office there are, for example, name, specialty of the doctor, reception time, personal data of the patient. In travel agency dialogues – number and age of travelers, time and duration of the trip, etc.

It is quite typical for travel agency dialogues that a customer starts with a general request (*I would like to travel to Norway*), and then goes over to an information-sharing (typically question–answer) sub-dialogue specifying the request. The customer asks different questions about the trip (date, duration, price, accommodation, abatements, etc.). In that way, the initial (too general) request will not be granted by the operator directly; however a sequence of answers to questions can be considered as a grant of the request. Such behavior is cooperative – the customer's first (general) request determines a domain (the DS can activate a suitable frame), after which details will be specified in a sub-dialogue.

Beside information-sharing, clarification sub-dialogues occur in our analysed dialogues. In conversation analysis, such sub-dialogues are called repairs [5]. A repair typically begins with a question offering answer, and its function is clarification or reformulation in Estonian institutional dialogues [3] (Ex. 2).

(2)

O: ja 'hind tuleb kuskil: oleneb=siis milline kompanii 'kinnitab, 'viisteist tuhat nelisada kaheksa'kümend kuni kaheksateist tuhat kaheksasada kuus'kümend.

and the price is depending on the company fifteen thousand four hundred and eighty until eighteen thousand eight hundred and sixty

C: edasi=tagasi. RPF: REFORMULATION /* clarification */

there and back

O: edasi=tagasi noore 'hind on=siin. RPS: REPAIR

there and back, the price for young

The results of the corpus analysis suggest that the regular grammar on Figure 2 can be taken as a basis of the dialogue manager (cf. [7]).

```
dialogue ::= (request (information-sharing)* grant
              (clarification)*)+
grant ::= giving_information | missing_information | other
```

Fig. 2. Dialogue grammar

6   Conclusion and Future Work

Our study has shown that a customer's requests are formed in Estonian institutional dialogues by using a limited number of verb forms as predicates. The verb semantics determines its possible usage.

The DS recognises a user's dialogue act on the basis of linguistic cues found in the utterance. Then it activates a frame of the act and fills in its slots. The act frame predicts how to generate the response. A dialogue grammar is used for the dialogue management and indicates possible ways of dialogue processing. The DS can initiate sub-dialogues. For example, the DS starts with an analysis of a user's general request and then asks adjusting questions in order to explain her exact goal. Our analysis demonstrates that a customer typically starts with a general request in calls to an outpatients' office, and then the operator asks questions (in an information-sharing sub-dialogue), in order to collect the data needed for granting the request. On the other hand, such behavior gives an opportunity to the DS to reduce problems of speech recognition (information is collected step-by-step).

Several experiments have been carried out at our university in automatic recognition of dialogue acts. Neural networks (learning vector quantization and multilayer perceptron) and decision trees have been tested [2]. Two simple web-based dialogue systems which interact with a user in Estonian have being implemented in cooperation with the Laboratory of Phonetics and Speech Technology at the Tallinn University of Technology. The first DS gives information of flights which depart from the Tallinn Airport, and the second – of theatre performances. Text-to-speech synthesis is integrated into the first DS, and both speech recognition and text-to-speech synthesis will be included into the second.

Our next aim is to test the linguistic cues found in the corpus analysis by using transformation-based machine learning.

Acknowledgement

This work is supported by Estonian Science Foundation (grant No 5685).

References

1. Erelt, M. (ed.) Estonian Language. // Linguistica Uralica Supplementary Series vol 1. Estonian Academy Publishers, Tallinn, 2003.
2. Fishel, M. Dialogue act recognition in Estonian using artificial neural networks. // Proc. of the 2nd Baltic Conference on Human Language Technologies, Tallinn, 2005, 231–236.
3. Hennoste, T., Gerassimenko, O., Kasterpalu, R., Koit, M., Rääbis, A., Strandson, K. and Valdisoo, M. Questions in Estonian Information Dialogues: Form and Functions. // Text, Speech and Dialogue. 6th International Conference TSD 2005. Ed. V. Matousek, P. Mautner. Springer, 2005, 420–427.

4. Hennoste, T., Koit, M., Rääbis, A., Valdisoo, M. Developing a Dialogue Act Coding Scheme: An Experience of Annotating the Estonian Dialogue Corpus. // LREC 2004 Satellite Workshop Compiling and Processing Spoken Language Corpora. Ed. Nelleke Oostdijk, Gjert Kristoffersen, Geoffrey Sampson. Lisboa, Portugal, 40–47.
5. Hutchby, I., Wooffitt, R. Conversation Analysis. Principles, Practices and Applications. Polity Press, 1998.
6. Jurafsky, D., Martin, J. H. An introduction to natural language processing, computational linguistics, and speech recognition. Prentice Hall, 2000.
7. Minker, W., Bennacef S. Speech and Human-Machine Dialog. Boston/Dordrecht/London: Kluwer Academic Publishers, 2004.
8. Möller, S. Quality of Telephone-based Spoken Dialogue Systems. Springer 2004
9. Treumuth, M. A software tool for the Estonian Dialogue Corpus. // Proc. of the second Baltic Conference on Human Language Technologies. Tallinn, 2005, 341–346.

Using Prosody for Automatic Sentence Segmentation of Multi-party Meetings

Jáchym Kolář[1,2], Elizabeth Shriberg[1,3], and Yang Liu[1,4]

[1] International Computer Science Institute, Berkeley, CA, USA
[2] Department of Cybernetics, University of West Bohemia in Pilsen, Czech Republic
[3] SRI International, Menlo Park, CA, USA
[4] University of Texas at Dallas, TX, USA
{jachym, ees, yangl}@icsi.berkeley.edu

Abstract. We explore the use of prosodic features beyond pauses, including duration, pitch, and energy features, for automatic sentence segmentation of ICSI meeting data. We examine two different approaches to boundary classification: score-level combination of independent language and prosodic models using HMMs, and feature-level combination of models using a boosting-based method (BoosTexter). We report classification results for reference word transcripts as well as for transcripts from a state-of-the-art automatic speech recognizer (ASR). We also compare results using the lexical model plus a pause-only prosody model, versus results using additional prosodic features. Results show that (1) information from pauses is important, including pause duration both at the boundary and at the previous and following word boundaries; (2) adding duration, pitch, and energy features yields significant improvement over pause alone; (3) the integrated boosting-based model performs better than the HMM for ASR conditions; (4) training the boosting-based model on recognized words yields further improvement.

1 Introduction

Standard automatic speech recognition systems output only a raw stream of words, leaving out important structural information such as punctuation. Punctuation, in particular that associated with sentence boundaries, is crucial to human readability. Sentence boundaries also benefit various natural language processing techniques (e.g., machine translation, information extraction and retrieval, text summarization) which are typically trained on formatted input such as text. Previous efforts in sentence segmentation have studied the role of both lexical and prosodic features, in data from news broadcasts (mostly read speech) and from spontaneous telephone conversations (two-party conversations) [1,2,3,4,5,6,7,8,9]. Work on multi-party meetings has been more recent, and has generally examined the use of prosody for sentence segmentation using only pause information, for example [10,11,12]. In this paper we explore the use of prosodic features beyond pauses, including duration, pitch, and energy features, for automatic sentence segmentation of a large set of data from the publicly available ICSI meeting corpus [13].

Petr Sojka, Ivan Kopeček and Karel Pala (Eds.): TSD 2006, LNAI 4188, pp. 629–636, 2006.
© Springer-Verlag Berlin Heidelberg 2006

2   Method

2.1   Speech Data and Experimental Setup

The ICSI meeting corpus [13] contains approximately 72 hours of multichannel conversational speech data. For the sentence segmentation experiments herein, we used 73 out of the total 75 available meetings (two meetings were excluded because of their very different character from the rest of the data). The 73 meetings were split into a training set (51 meetings, 539k words), a development set (11 meetings, 110k words), and a test set (11 meetings, 102k words). The test set contains unseen speakers, as well as speakers appearing in the training data as it is typical for the real world applications.

A crucial step when performing sentence segmentation of spontaneous speech is to define the notion of a "sentence", since spontaneous utterances do not consist of sentences as defined in written text. Although the original manual transcripts of the ICSI corpus do contain punctuation, the punctuation is highly inconsistent. Transcribers were instructed to focus on transcribing words as quickly as possible; there was not a focus on consistency or conventions for marking punctuation. As a result, different transcribers used different approaches to punctuation annotation. We used instead punctuation marks from a project on annotation of dialog acts in the same corpus [14,15]. In this annotation pass, labelers carefully annotated both dialog acts and their boundaries, using a set of segmentation conventions for the latter.

For training and testing our models we have used both forced alignment of reference transcripts and ASR output. Recognition results were obtained using the state-of-the-art SRI CTS system [16], which was trained using no acoustic data or transcripts from the analyzed meeting corpus. To represent a completely automatic system, we used automatic speech/nonspeech segmentation. Word error rates for this difficult data are still quite high, the used ASR system performed at 38.2% (on the whole corpus). To generate the "reference" sentence boundaries for the ASR words, we aligned the reference setup to the ASR hypotheses with the constraint that two aligned words may not occur further apart than a fixed time. The possible sentence boundaries for ASR output were then merged from corresponding aligned words from the reference. Since the ASR hypotheses tend to miss short backchannels that are usually followed by a sentence boundary, sentence boundaries are less frequent (in our data 13.9%) than in reference conditions (15.9%).

2.2   Prosodic Features

We developed a database of 270 prosodic features describing pause, pitch, duration, and energy information in the vicinity of each word boundary, inspired by [2,17]. Features were extracted directly from the automatically aligned speech signal, so that no hand-labeling of prosody (such as ToBI) was necessary in model training. A number of features were highly correlated, differing only in the normalization approach. To reduce the feature space, we combined similar features into groups, and then selected the features from each group that were most frequently used in a first set of decision trees. We then used the resulting smaller set of 40 features to train the models reported in this paper.

Pause features consisted of the pause duration after the current, previous, and following words. Duration features included the duration of vowels, final rhymes, and whole words, aiming mainly to reflect the phenomenon of preboundary lengthening. We used raw durations as well as duration features normalized using phoneme duration statistics from the whole database. Pitch features included features describing minimal, maximal and mean values, f_0 slopes, and differences and ratios of values across word boundaries. These features were extracted both from raw f_0 value and from a f_0 contour stylized by a piece-wise linear function. Energy features were represented by maximal, minimal, and mean frame-level RMS values, both raw and per-channel normalized. Statistics showing which prosodic feature were used by our models are provided at the end of Section 3.

2.3 Classifiers

We report results obtained using two different approaches: (1) a combination of independent language and prosodic models in an HMM framework, and (2) a boosting-based algorithm (BoosTexter) that uses one integral model containing both lexical and prosodic features.

HMM Approach. The approach for sentence boundary detection from speech that has received the most attention in recent years is a hidden Markov model (HMM) [1,2,5]. This approach provides a convenient way for combining lexical and prosodic features and is computationally efficient. In the HMM, the word/event pairs correspond to states, and the words as well as other (in our case prosodic) features correspond to observations. That is, the words appear both in the states and in the observations, with the transition probabilities given by the N-gram language model. Transition probabilities are estimated using standard N-gram techniques from text data, in which sentence boundaries are marked by a special tag (which is for training purposes treated in the same way as other word tokens). The HMM observation likelihoods are estimated by converting posteriors obtained by a prosodic classifier into likelihoods, under the assumption that prosodic features depend only on the events, and not on the words.

After several simplifications [2,5], to combine prosodic and lexical scores we use the relation

$$P(e_i|F, W) \propto P(e_i|W) \left(\frac{P(e_i|f_i)}{P(e_i)} \right)^{\lambda} \tag{1}$$

where e_i and f_i stand for i-th event (type of boundary, in our case "sentence boundary" or "no boundary") and vector of prosodic features, respectively, and W and F for the sequences of words and prosodic features, respectively. λ is an exponential scaling factor estimated using held-out data, which allows us to weight the relative contributions from the two models.

In past work, the most popular classifiers for estimating posteriors $P(e_i|f_i)$ have been decision trees, since they handle features with undefined values, combine continuous and categorical features, and are easily human-readable and interpretable. When training a sentence boundary classifier, we have to deal with the problem of imbalanced data [18], since sentence boundaries occur only at approximately 16% of all word boundaries in our corpus. The skewed distribution of training data may cause decision trees to miss out on inherently valuable features that are dwarfed by data priors. One solution to this problem is to train classifiers on data downsampled to equal class priors. To take advantage of all available data, we apply ensemble sampling instead of simple downsampling. Ensemble sampling is performed by randomly splitting the majority class into int(N) nonoverlapping subsets, where N is the ratio between the number of samples in the majority and minority classes. Each subset is joined with all minority class samples to form int(N) balanced sets to train classifiers. It is also advantageous to employ bagging [19], which decreases classifier variance by averaging results obtained by multiple classifiers. The classifiers are trained from different datasets sampled with replacement from the original training set. A combination of these two methods (applying bagging on ensemble samples) makes up *ensemble bagging*, which we used in our experiments.

Boosting-Based Approach. The HMM approach has also a couple of disadvantages. The combination of prosodic and lexical models makes strong independence assumptions, which are not typically met in actual language data. Moreover, the HMM training maximizes the joint probability of data and hidden events, but a criterion more closely related to classification error is the posterior probability of the correct hidden variable assignment given the observations. To overcome these drawbacks, models based on maximum entropy [4,6] or conditional random fields [9] have been proposed in past work. These models provide a more principled way to combine prosodic and overlapping lexical features. In this work, we explore a different approach, by integrating prosodic and lexical features into one model based on boosting. We provide some detail here on the approach, since it has not been described for this task in previous work.

The principle of boosting is to combine many weak learning algorithms to produce an accurate classifier. The algorithm generates weak classification rules by calling the weak learners repeatedly in series of rounds. Each weak classifier is built based on the outputs of previous classifiers, focusing on the samples that were formerly classified incorrectly. This general method can be basically combined with any classifier. We used an algorithm called BoosTexter, that combines weak classifiers having a basic form of one-level decision trees using confidence-rated predictions [20]. The test at the root of each tree can check for the presence of a word N-gram, or for a value of a continuous feature. This allows a straightforward combination of lexical and prosodic features.

For training the classifier, we have used exactly the same set of prosodic features as was used for prosodic classification using decision trees. We have added the following N-gram features (w_0 denotes the word before the classified boundary, w_1 the word after the boundary, and so on) – unigrams: w_0, w_1, bigrams: w_0w_1, $w_{-1}w_0$, trigrams: $w_{-1}w_0w_1$, $w_0w_1w_2$, and a binary feature indicating whether the word before the boundary is identical with the following word.

3   Experimental Results and Discussion

Our experimental results testing both approaches in reference and ASR conditions are summarized in Table 1. As an evaluation metric we use a "boundary error rate" described by

$$E = \frac{I + M}{N_W} \ [\%] \tag{2}$$

where I denotes the number of false sentence boundary insertions, M the number of misses, and N_W the number of words in the test set. For each system, we report error rates using

Table 1. Sentence boundary detection error rates (defined as count of false alarms and misses divided by the total number of words [%]) for different models (HMM trained on reference, BoosTexter trained on reference /TrREF/ and BoosTexter trained on recognized words /TrASR/) and test conditions (REFerence and ASR), numbers within parentheses correspond to relative reductions over chance error rate

		HMM approach	BoosTexter-TrREF	BoosTexter-TrASR
REF	chance	15.92 (0.0)	15.92 (0.0)	N/A
	LM	7.47 (53.1)	7.73 (51.4)	N/A
	pause	8.96 (43.7)	8.78 (44.8)	N/A
	all prosody	8.06 (49.4)	8.28 (48.0)	N/A
	LM+pause	5.89 (63.0)	5.88 (63.1)	N/A
	LM+all prosody	5.77 (63.8)	5.78 (63.7)	N/A
ASR	chance	13.85 (0.0)	13.85 (0.0)	13.85 (0.0)
	LM	9.43 (31.9)	9.59 (30.8)	9.48 (31.6)
	pause	8.97 (35.2)	8.85 (36.1)	8.82 (36.3)
	all prosody	8.30 (40.1)	8.31 (40.0)	8.35 (39.7)
	LM+pause	7.03 (49.2)	6.84 (50.6)	6.81 (50.8)
	LM+all prosody	7.00 (49.4)	6.67 (51.8)	6.58 (52.5)

lexical features alone, pause durations alone (including both pause duration at the boundary, and at the previous and following word boundaries), all prosodic features alone, lexical features plus pause durations, and lexical features plus all prosodic features. We also present chance performance, or the performance achieved by classifying every word boundary as the class having the highest prior probability (which is "no sentence boundary" in our case). Note that chance performance differs for reference versus ASR conditions as described in Section 2.1. To enable a comparison of relative gain from each set of features for both conditions, we also report the relative error reduction with respect to chance error.

Results for the reference condition (REF) indicate that the language model alone performs better than the prosodic model alone, and either model is outperformed by a combination model. The gain from additional prosodic features (beyond pause) is larger when lexical information is not accessible. However, when combining with the lexical model, there is a significant gain from adding prosodic features beyond pauses, both for the HMM (0.12% absolute, 2.0% relative, $p < 0.01$) and for BoosTexter (0.10% absolute, 1.7% relative, $p < 0.01$). Results using both approaches are very similar for the reference condition.

Results for the ASR condition show that recognition errors cause more degradation for lexical than for prosodic features. Note that while degradation is expected for lexical features, it is not the case that prosodic features should be completely robust to word error: some prosodic features depend on phone or word boundary information for extraction or normalization. The level of degradation for individual models is also visible from values of the exponential weight λ (optimized on development data), which is used for combining the prosodic and language models in the HMM. For the reference condition, the optimal value was 0.8 (giving a slightly higher weight to the lexical model), while for the ASR condition it was 1.1 (actually giving a higher weight to the prosodic model).

An interesting observation is that the BoosTexter model using both prosodic and textual features proved to be more robust to recognition errors than the HMM. Note that for the

Table 2. Prosodic feature usage (percentage of total feature usage) for groups of prosodic features

group	total usage	two most frequently used features from each group
pause	24.8	pause after current word(16.1), pause after previous word(5.7)
duration	48.9	word duration(9.3), last rhyme normalized duration(5.5)
pitch	21.4	first slope of following word(3.6), min f_0 of last voic. region(3.2)
energy	4.9	mean RMS following word(2.3), min of voiced norm RMS (1.5)

language model and prosody alone, boosting does not help. However, when using both prosodic and lexical cues, it yields some gain over the HMM. This fact supports the hypothesis that it is advantageous to more tightly integrate prosodic and textual features. We tried training BoosTexter on recognized rather than reference words, to see how training on data more matched to the test data (i.e., containing many word errors) would affect performance. As shown, this approach outperforms the approach of training on reference in the case of boosting, but not when using the HMM. Finally, there was a significant gain from adding prosodic features beyond pauses. For the best BoosTexter model the gain was 0.23% absolute and 3.4% relative, significant at $p < 0.001$.

To explore which prosodic features were useful in this task, we analyzed prosodic decision trees from the HMM approach, because they are much easier to interpret than the resulting BoosTexter model. We used the measure "feature usage" [2], which counts how many times (by token) each feature is queried in a decision tree. Results were averaged over all trees generated during ensemble bagging. The statistics for each group of features as well as the best features from each group are listed in Table 2. The statistics show that the most frequently used features were pause duration after the current word, raw word duration, pause after the following word, and normalized duration of the last rhyme in the word. Sums of usages of features from the four basic groups show that those most frequently queried in decision trees were duration features, followed by pause, pitch, and energy features.

4   Summary and Conclusions

We explored the use of prosody including pauses, duration, pitch, and energy features, for automatic sentence segmentation of a large set of data from the ICSI meeting corpus. We have examined two different approaches to the boundary classification: HMM and a boosting-based classifier BoosTexter. Results indicate that (1) information from pauses is important, including pause duration both at the boundary, and at the previous and following word boundaries; (2) adding duration, pitch, and energy features yields a further significant improvement; (3) an integrated boosting-based model performs better than an HMM for ASR conditions; (4) training the boosting-based model on recognized words yields additional improvement.

From this work, we conclude that prosody can make an important contribution to meeting understanding, via helping to find boundaries of sentences or dialog acts. Features beyond pauses are worth exploring in future work, as are modeling techniques that can tightly integrate prosodic and lexical features. Finally, for corpora in which state-of-the-art ASR performance is still rather poor, it may be useful to train models on recognized rather than reference words.

Acknowledgments

The authors thank Dilek Hakkani-Tur and Gokhan Tur for help with the boosting software, and Ozgur Cetin for generating ASR output. This work was supported by the European Union 6th FWP ISR Integrated Project AMI (FP6-506811), the DARPA CALO project (NBCHD-030010), NSF project IIS-0121396, DARPA Contract No. HR0011-06-C-0023, and by the Academy of Sciences of the Czech Republic (project No. 1QS101470516). The views expressed are those of the authors, and not the funding agencies.

References

1. Stolcke, A., Shriberg, E., Bates, R., Ostendorf, M., Hakkani, D., Plauche, M., Tur, G., Lu, Y.: Automatic Detection of Sentence Boundaries and Disfluencies Based on Recognized Words. In: Proc. ICSLP 98, pp. 2247–2250, Sydney (1998).
2. Shriberg, E., Stolcke, A., Hakkani-Tur, D., Tur, G.: Prosody-based Automatic Segmentation of Speech into Sentences and Topics. In: Speech Communication, vol. 32, no. 1–2, p. 127–154 (2000).
3. Warnke, V., Kompe, R., Niemann, H., Nöth, E.: Integrated Dialog Act Segmentation and Classification Using Prosodic Features and Language Models. In: Proc. EUROSPEECH 97, pp. 207–210, Rhodes, Greece (1997).
4. Huang, J., Zweig, G.: Maximum Entropy Model for Punctuation Annotation from Speech. In: Proc. ICSLP 2002, pp. 917–920, Denver (2002).
5. Kim, J.H., Woodland, P.: A Combined Punctuation Generation and Speech Recognition System and Its Performance Enhancement Using Prosody. In: Speech Communication, vol. 41, no. 4, pp. 563–577 (2003).
6. Liu, Y., Stolcke, A., Harper, M., Shriberg, E.: Comparing and Combining Generative and Posterior Probability Models: Some Advances in Sentence Boundary Detection in Speech. In: Proc. EMNLP, Barcelona, Spain (2004).
7. Liu, Y., Shriberg, E., Stolcke, A., Hillard, D., Ostendorf, M., Peskin, B., Harper, M.: The ICSI-SRI-UW Metadata Extraction System. In: ICSLP 2004, Jeju, Korea (2004).
8. Kolář, J., Švec, J., Psutka, J.: Automatic Punctuation Annotation in Czech Broadcast News Speech. In: Proc. SPECOM 2004, St. Petersburg, Russia (2004).
9. Liu, Y., Stolcke, A., Shriberg, E., Harper, M.: Using Conditional Random Fields for Sentence Boundary Detection in Speech. In: Proc. ACL pp. 451–458, Ann Arbor (2005).
10. Ang, J., Liu, Y., Shriberg, E.: Automatic Dialog Act Segmentation and Classification in Multiparty Meetings. In: Proc. IEEE ICASSP-2005, pp. 1061–1064, Philadelphia (2005).
11. Ji, G., Bilmes, J.: Dialog Act Tagging Using Graphical Models. In: Proc. IEEE ICASSP-2005, pp. 33–36, Philadelphia (2005).
12. Zimmermann, M., Stolcke, A., Shriberg, E.: Joint Segmentation and Classification of Dialog Acts in Multiparty Meetings. In Proc.: IEEE ICASSP-2006, Toulouse, France (2006).
13. Janin, A., Baron, D., Edwards, J., Ellis, D., Gelbart, D., Morgan, N., Peskin, B., Pfau, T., Shriberg, E., Stolcke, A., Wooters, Ch.: The ICSI Meeting Corpus. In: Proc. IEEE ICASSP-2003, pp. 364–367, Hong Kong (2003).
14. Dhillon, R. et al.: Meeting Recorder Project: Dialog Act Labeling Guide. ICSI Technical Report TR-04-02, International Computer Science Institute, Berkeley (2004).
15. Shriberg, E. et al.: The ICSI Meeting Recorder Dialog Act (MRDA) Corpus. In: Proc. SIGDIAL, Cambridge, MA, USA (2004).
16. Zhu, Q., Stolcke, A., Chen, B., Morgan, N.: Using MLP Features in SRI's Conversational Speech Recognition System. In: Proc. INTERSPEECH 2005, pp. 2141–2144, Lisboa (2005).

17. Buckow, J., Warnke, V., Huber, R., Batliner, A., Nöth, E., Niemann, H.: Fast and Robust Features for Prosodic Classification. In: Proc. TSD'99 Marienbad, pp. 193–198, Springer Verlag, Berlin (1999).
18. Liu, Y., Shriberg, E., Stolcke, A., Harper, M.: Using Machine Learning to Cope with Imbalanced Classes in Natural Speech: Evidence from Sentence Boundary and Disfluency Detection. In: Proc ICSLP 2004, Jeju, Korea (2004).
19. Breiman, L.: Bagging Predictors. In: Machine Learning 24(2), pp. 123–140 (1996).
20. Schapire, R.E., Singer, Y.: BoosTexter: A Boosting-based System for Text Categorization. In: Machine Learning, 39(2/3), pp. 135–168 (2000).

Simple Method of Determining the Voice Similarity and Stability by Analyzing a Set of Very Short Sounds

Konrad Lukaszewicz[1] and Matti Karjalainen[2]

[1] Institute of the Biocybernetics and Biomedical Engineering PAS
ul. Ks. Trojdena 4, Warsaw, Poland
konrad.lukaszewicz@ibib.waw.pl
[2] Helsinki University of Technology
Laboratory of Acoustics and Audio Signal Processing
Otakaari 5 A Espoo, FI-02015 TKK, Finland
matti.karjalainen@tkk.fi

Abstract. This paper presents a simple method of determining the voice similarity by analyzing a set of very short sounds. A large number of pitch-length sounds were extracted from natural voice signals from different realizations of open vowels 'a' and 'o'. The voice similarity was defined as the sum of single elementary similarities of short sound pairs. This method is oriented to the microphonemic speech synthesis based on waveform concatenation, and it could help to limit the time needed for database collection. This simple and low computational load speech synthesis method can be applied in small portable devices and used for the rehabilitation of speech disabled people.

1 Introduction

Many available speech synthesizers can produce very natural voice. The quality of voice cannot however be considered without relationship to application. Usually each application has its own needs, and the expected quality necessary for a particular application can vary [2,6]. Nowadays, the largest group of people, who are using synthetic speech daily, is the blind community. Usually they use speech for the communication with computer user interface. Then the quality of speech is not so important as its flexibility and quick response.

For people who have lost their voice, the verbal communication becomes one of the most important problems. The speech synthesizer can in this case be used as speech prosthesis. The synthetic speech used by speech disabled people has to fit individual voice characteristics. This demand needs the collection of a specific database for each individual person. Currently the time and effort that is needed to collect a full set of required data for speech synthesis is too long to be applied for each patient separately.

The microphonemic method of speech synthesis [4,5] belongs to the group of the concatenative speech synthesizers. The synthetic speech signal is generated by concatenation of short (typically pitch size) waveform elements. Modification of the length and size of each sound element and smoothly connecting them can generate high quality speech signal where the individual speech features are maintained. The database used for the microphonemic speech synthesizer consists of a large number of sound elements, which represent all the diphonems in the particular language. The length of each element is typically a pitch period.

Petr Sojka, Ivan Kopeček and Karel Pala (Eds.): TSD 2006, LNAI 4188, pp. 637–643, 2006.

One of the main problems related to designing a microphonemic speech synthesizer is the collection of the necessary sound set. To limit the number of data elements and time needed to collect the whole set, the number of different realizations of each phoneme has to be defined. The higher the number covered by the database, the better quality of synthetic speech can be obtained, but this will increase the size of the database and the time needed to collect it. On the other hand, the speech synthesizer used as speech prosthesis for a patient after tracheotomy should have personal features of the original voice of the patient.

Considering the sound elements of pitch period size, a similarity measure is defined. The similarity has been determined by analyzing the auditory spectrum of short elementary sounds. In our analysis the stability of articulation of the Polish vowels 'a' and 'o' was assessed. A sound element of single pitch length has been taken from the middle part of each realization of the vowel. Totally 346 short sound elements of vowel 'a' and 215 of vowel 'o' were collected for each voice. Four different voices were tested.

The algorithm of sound similarity presented here can be used to determine the number of substantially different realizations of each vowel for the natural voice. While a few databases were collected and are ready for synthesis of different voices, a new particular voice can be obtained by modification of another one in the existing database. This algorithm can be used for choosing the most suitable one for the modification database. A modified database, which includes vowels most similar to a particular voice, could give synthetic speech of better quality.

2   Auditory Tests

The elementary (pitch length) sounds were collected from 47 different words of a speaker. The Polish vowel 'a' was tested. The extracting point was placed at the middle point of the vowel realization. The beginning and the end of the selected signal were placed at zero-crossing points to obtain a smooth connection in the concatenation. The collected elements were standardized in length and amplitude by multiplying with a trapezoidal window to increase the pitch or by adding a short silence for decreasing the pitch. So all played sounds had the same length and amplitude.

By concatenating each stored element 40 times, 47 different steady-state sounds were generated. The duration of each sound was about 0.3 sec. To test the similarity, pairs of two sounds were played and compared. The first sound was always the same while the second one was changed.

In the auditory test for each listener, 47 pairs were played. The listener could hear each pair as many times as he needed in order to make the decision whether the played sounds were similar or not, i.e., a binary decision. 22 tests were performed by 7 different listeners.

The first pair was made of two identical sounds, thus in each test the result for comparison of the first pair was always positive. Some sounds were determined by the listeners as being more similar to the source sound (sound number 1) than the other ones (Table 1). If we look at the histogram of similarity (Fig. 1) we can see that the sounds 6, 11, 20, 33 and 45 are the most similar ones. On the vertical axis the number of positive decision was placed, while the horizontal axis describes the sound number that was compared with the sound number one.

Table 1. Results of the auditory test: similarity of sounds pairs determined by the listeners

Sound	Similarity %	Sound	Similarity %	Sound	Similarity %
1-1	100.0	1-17	4.55	1-33	54.55
1-2	4.55	1-18	4.55	1-34	0.0
1-3	9.09	1-19	22.73	1-35	18.19
1-4	0.0	1-20	45.45	1-36	0.0
1-5	31.82	1-21	9.09	1-37	36.36
1-6	81.82	1-22	18.19	1-38	4.55
1-7	18.19	1-23	16.64	1-39	0.0
1-8	9.09	1-24	16.64	1-40	16.64
1-9	4.55	1-25	0.0	1-41	0.0
1-10	16.64	1-26	0.0	1-42	0.0
1-11	68.18	1-27	31.82	1-43	16.64
1-12	4.55	1-28	36.36	1-44	4.55
1-13	0.0	1-29	36.36	1-45	68.18
1-14	0.0	1-30	4.55	1-46	4.55
1-15	27.27	1-31	16.64	1-47	4.55
1-16	31.82	1-32	9.09		

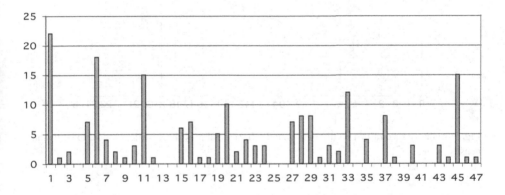

Fig. 1. Auditory test results as a histogram

3   Comparison by Auditory Spectrum

Even when the elementary sounds were extracted from utterances of one speaker and very similar context (the sounds were extracted from the same triphone CVC), the listeners noticed significant differences. The perceptual differences can be computationally estimated by using proper auditory models. We have applied an auditory spectrum algorithm that warps the Fourier spectrum to the Bark scale and the magnitude scale to loudness density (also called specific loudness) [3,7]. Considering the auditory spectra of similar and different pairs we can see large differences in the spectral patterns. Figures 2 and 3 present the auditory spectra of two sound pairs. Fig. 2 shows the auditory spectra of two similar sounds, while Fig. 3 presents auditory spectra of two different sounds.

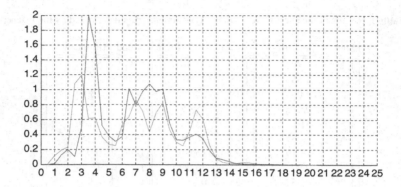

Fig. 2. Auditory spectra of two similar sounds. Horizontal axis: Bark scale; vertical axis: loudness density [sone].

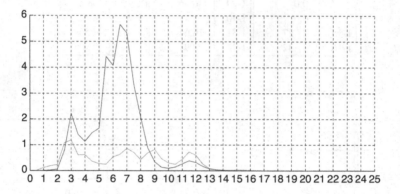

Fig. 3. Auditory spectra of two different sounds; Horizontal axis: Bark scale, vertical axis: loudness density [sone]

4   Similarity Determination Algorithm

For finding the similarity of two elementary sounds the auditory spectra were considered. For comparing the pattern of energy in the spectrum a set of 17 parameters was defined: number of the energy bands, the total loudness in each band, the position of each energy band and the center of [1] gravity for each band. To define the beginning and the end of an energy band, the positions of local minima were searched for. Related to auditory resolution, a minimum in auditory spectrum was searched for as any range of drop in energy that is wider than 2 Barks on the critical band scale [1]. The width of a minimum region was then set to 1 Bark around the minimum. The position of the center of gravity for each band was defined as the first moment calculated for each band separately.

These parameters were used to compare the auditory spectra of the sounds pairs. The sounds were similar if: the numbers of bands were the same, the positions of the bands were at the same region, the total loudness of each band was at the same level and the positions of the centers of gravity were at the same frequency regions. Additional adjustment was applied to "tune" the algorithm to match the auditory tests result.

5   Parameter Histograms

Each one of the recorded voices comes form a different speaker. Considering some of these defined above parameters we can notice that the vowel realizations can be very different even for a single speaker. In the histogram of Fig. 4, the numbers of bands detected for four different voices are presented. That information can be used for constructing the database for the microphonemic voice synthesizer. For example for speaker "HAN" the vowel 'a' in most cases has three or two bands. Those realizations of vowel 'a' could be determined as representative ones for this particular voice.

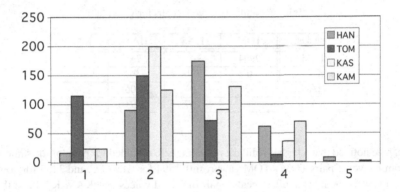

Fig. 4. Histogram of numbers of bands (horizontal axis) in vowel 'a' for four different voices

Another example is the positions of the centre of gravity. Figure 5 presents the centre of gravity position of the first band for one voice in vowel 'a'.

6   Voice Similarity

The algorithm defined above was used to test the similarity between four different voices: TOM, KAS, HAN and KAM. From each voice, 346 microphonems for vowel 'a' (from the middle part of the vowel) and 215 microphonems for vowel 'o' (from the middle part of the vowel) were collected. The similarity of voice pairs was calculated as the sum of the single tests results. In the single test, the similarity of a short sound pair was calculated. The result of each test was 1 when the sounds in the pair were similar and 0 if the sounds in the pair were different. In each pair of two short signals the first was taken from the first voice and the second one from the second voice. Thus, for each pair of voices the total number of tests was 346x346 = 119025 for vowel 'a' and 215x215 = 46225 for vowel 'o'. The numbers of positive result of the single tests for each pair of voices were placed in Tables 2 and 3.

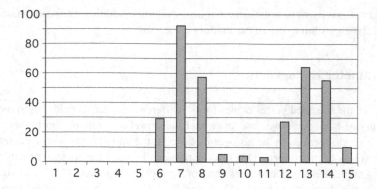

Fig. 5. Histogram of the position of centre of gravity (horizontal axis: Bark scale) of the first band in vowel 'a' for speaker "TOM"

Table 2. Similarity of voice pairs for vowel 'a'

Speaker	TOM	KAS	HAN	KAM
TOM	2994	0	73	1
KAS	0	790	9	167
HAN	73	9	1006	59
KAM	1	167	59	1028

It can be noticed that a higher similarity results were obtained for pairs of the same voices. For example voice pairs TOM - TOM gave result 2994 for vowel 'a' and 3463 for vowel 'o'. For both vowels the most similar speaker pair of tested voices was KAM-KAS and the most different one TOM-KAS. Considering each voice we can notice that analyzing the vowel 'a' and vowel 'o' we have obtained similar results. The most similar voice for voice TOM was HAN and the next similar voices were KAM and KAS. The same order of voice similarity was received when the vowel 'o' was considered.

7   Discussion

Using this simple method of sound comparison we can notice how many different realizations of each vowel we can meet in a particular voice. The feature histograms show the most common forms of each vowel for a particular voice. It can be noticed that for example in

Table 3. Similarity of voice pairs for vowel 'o'

Speaker	TOM	KAS	HAN	KAM
TOM	3463	1	312	8
KAS	1	689	6	342
HAN	312	6	1765	5
KAM	8	342	5	909

voice HAN the most common number of energy bands for vowel 'a' was 3 while for voice KAS it was 2. By analyzing the auditory spectrum we can determine how stable a voice is and how similar it is to another one. According to the tests it looks like for one speaker each of the tested vowels (e.g. 'a' and 'o') can be represented by two different realizations. In the tested voices it covered 80 % of all realizations of vowels 'a' and 'o'. The voice similarity algorithm could be used to complete a generic database, which can be used for synthesis of a few similar voices. The database for one voice could be modified by exchange of the vowels and some voiced consonants to obtain another individual sounding voice. In this case the most significant realizations (for a particular speaker) of each vowel have to be applied as the database modification elements.

8   Conclusion

The presented method of analyzing voices requires low computational effort and is based on very short sound signals that are typical for the microphonemic synthesis method. The presented results show that it is possible to compare two voices by analyzing sets of short signals extracted from many different points of a single subject's utterance.

References

1. Chistovich L. A., "Central Auditory Processing of Peripheral Vowel Spectra," J. Acoust. Soc. Am. 77 (3), March 1985, pp. 789–805.
2. Karjalainen M., Laine U. and Toivonen R., "Aids for the Handicapped Based on SYNTE 2 Speech Synthesizer," Proc. IEEE ICASSP'80, Denver 1980, pp. 851–854.
3. Karjalainen M., "A New Auditory Model For The Evaluation of Sound Quality of Audio Systems," Proc. IEEE ICASSP'85, Tampa 1985, p. 608–611.
4. Lehtinen L. and Karjalainen M., "Individual Sounding Speech Synthesis by Rule Using the Microphonemic Method," Proc. Eurospeech'89, Paris 1989, p. 180–183.
5. Lukaszewicz K. and Karjalainen M., "Microphonemic Method of Speech Synthesis," IEEE, ICASSP'87, Dallas 1987, p. 1426–1429.
6. Wloskowicz D., Lukaszewicz K. and Radecki K., "Implementation of Synthetic Speech in a Phone Communication System for Deaf-mute People," Polish J. Med. Phys. & Eng. 1999, Vol. 5, No. 1 (15), Warszawa 1999, p. 33–39.
7. Zwicker E. and Fastl H., Psychoacoustics–Facts and Models. Springer Verlag, 1990.

Visualization of Prosodic Knowledge Using Corpus Driven MEMOInt Intonation Modelling*

David Escudero-Mancebo and Valentín Cardeñoso-Payo

University of Valladolid, Valladolid 47014 Spain
descuder@infor.uva.es,
http://www.infor.uva.es

Abstract. In this work we show how our intonation corpus driven intonation modelling methodology MEMOInt can help in the graphical visualization of the complex relationships between the different prosodic features which configure the intonational aspects of natural speech. MEMOInt has already been used successfully for the prediction of synthetic F0 contours in the presence of the usual data scarcity problems. Now, we report on the possibilities of using the information gathered in the modelling phase in order to provide a graphical view of the relevance of the various prosodic features which affect the typical F0 movements. The set of classes which group the intonation patterns found in the corpus can be structured in a tree in which the relation between the classes and the prosodic features of the input text is hierarchically correlated. This visual outcome shows to be very useful to carry out comparative linguistic studies of prosodic phenomena and to check the correspondence between previous prosodic knowledge on a language and the real utterances found in a given corpus.

1 Introduction

The study of intonation in speech technology is important because it brings information about the structure of the message and about the pragmatics of the discourse. The research field of intonation modelling has grown significantly during the last two decades due mainly to its interest in text-to-speech applications. Despite this fact, the state of the art in intonation modelling is still characterized by a diversity of paradigms and approaches, revealing a lack of consensus. In this context the availability of tools shedding light in the many aspects that are a matter of discussion is important. This article presents a methodology for modelling intonation devised attending to two main goals: to be efficient in text-to-speech applications and to offer contrastable information about some of the controversial aspects in this field of research.

The availability of large speech corpora is the main reason for the spectacular advance in the quality of nowadays text-to-speech systems [1]. The high degree of naturalness is achieved by training learning procedures that use the data of the corpus. Although this approach is acceptable from an engineering point of view, results can be frustrating from a scientific point of view: a neural network permits to learn intonation from corpus, but it is not obvious to transfer the knowledge of the neural network to a book on phonetics. Here

---

* This work has been partially sponsored by Spanish Government (MCYT project TIC2003-08382-C05-03) and by Consejeria de Educacion (JCYL project VA053A05).

Petr Sojka, Ivan Kopeček and Karel Pala (Eds.): TSD 2006, LNAI 4188, pp. 645–652, 2006.

we defend a methodology that is efficient in learning intonation from corpus and for visually displaying the information obtained from the corpus so that it is possible to contrast results with previous observations or theoretical models.

The problem of intonation modelling consists of finding a matching between the prosodic features of the intonation units found in the text, and the corresponding F0 contours patterns (see [4] for a review). This problem is difficult because of the high number of prosodic features affecting intonation: accent, type of sentence, structure of the sentence, emotions, social culture of the speakers. Furthermore, there is not a consensus about the best technique to use to parameterize the F0 contours: Tilt[15], Fujisaki[9], templates[14]. . . . The correspondence between the prosodic features and the acoustic parameters is also a matter of discussion where many different approaches have been tested: neural networks[11], decision trees [15], regression trees[2], rules[3]. We have to add to these difficulties the intrinsic variability of intonation where speakers can utter the same sentence in many different ways. As a result, even huge corpora get undersized, so that it is necessary to devise a strategy to cope with data scarcity. Here we propose a technique that assumes all these difficulties, modelling and representing the intonation in terms of the prototypical patterns and its variability observed in the corpus and displaying the relationship of these aspects with respect to the prosodic factors affecting them.

The proposed technique is called MEMOInt, and it is based on a combination of agglomerative clustering and sequential feature selection [16]. The combination of both techniques permits to train efficiently intonation models from corpus useful to predict synthetic intonation and also to display as a decision tree the information of the corpus as it has been show in [8][5] Here we show MEMOInt capabilities to display graphically the prosodic information of the corpus. In section 2 we review the MEMOInt fundamentals; in section 3 the experimental results and in 3.2 the results on visualization.

2   MEMOInt: Methodology for Modelling Intonation

Figure 1 describes schematically the fundamentals of MEMOInt. In this section we focus on the modelling stage to explain the procedure that outputs the visual information mentioned above.

In corpus based modelling intonation the corpus is considered a set $C = \{IU_i, \quad 1..N\}$, where IU_i is each of the N units of intonation identified in the corpus. Every IU is a duple $IU = (PF, AP)$. $IU.AP$ are a set of acoustic parameters that represent the form of the F0 contour of IU. $IU.AP$ are obtained automatically from the F0 contours in the parameterization stage. On the other hand, $IU.PF$ are a set of prosodic features that represent the prosodic function of IU. They reflect different aspects of intonation like accent, grammatical structure of the sentences, size of the intonation units, emotions, type of sentence etc. Those features are to be extracted automatically from text or manually labeled in the corpus.

MEMOInt applies an agglomerative clustering process following an inter-class maximum similarity criterion that is justified because merging together classes of IU with similar AP is acceptable as they can be perceived the same. Due to the final use of the models in text-to-speech, the agglomerative process must stop when the prediction capabilities of the new

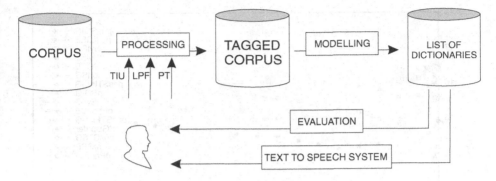

Fig. 1. Functional scheme of MEMOInt. The CORPUS is processed to obtain the TAGGED CORPUS which is the input of the modelling stage producing the LIST OF DICTIONARIES. The capabilities of the list of dictionaries are evaluated and it can also be use by a TTS system. The parameters of MEMOInt are: Type of Intonation Unit (TIU), List of Prosodic Features (LPF), Parameterization Technique (PT).

configuration after merging classes predicts worst than the previous one. (see [5] and [8] for details)

The agglomerative process determines the correspondence between AP and PF. By keeping track of the different values of the PF merged, it is built an index to assign a class in the final configuration to any PF combination. This can be used in text-to-speech where PF is driven by text and AP can be used to generate a synthetic F0 contour. Let us call *dictionary* to the combination of the index, made of a sequence of PF, and the clustering associated to it.

The more the number of PF involved, the worst the scarcity problem. To cope with it, we follow sequential learning so that different clusters are constructed by using different number of PF. In every step MEMOInt selects the PF which inclusion implies better prediction results. As result we obtain N different dictionaries (as many as PF considered). Given any combination of PF we select the cluster that predicts more accurately the sample according to the observations in the training stage (see [8] for details).

The sequential selection of PF allows either to obtain a ranking of importance of different PF or to test new alternatives. The list of dictionaries provides a way to draw a decision tree which gives easy to contrast visual information, which illustrates the intonation patterns of the corpus, as we show in the following sections.

3   Experimental Results

3.1   Building of the Dictionaries

For the experimental validation of the clustering technique, we have used an intonation corpus which contains more than 700 sentences (4363 intonation units) recorded by a professional actress in studio conditions[1]. High quality F0 contours were obtained using a laringograph device. Sentences has been segmented and labelled following a semiautomatic process. We

---

[1] Gently provided to us by the research group TALP of the Polythecnic University of Catalonia, Spain.

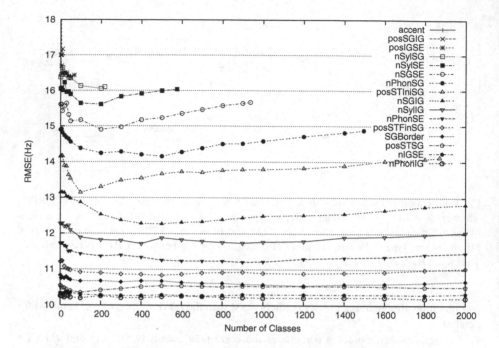

Fig. 2. Building the list of dictionaries: each curve represents the effect of adding dictionary D_i to the list of dictionaries LD_i, $(i = 1, \ldots, N_{pf})$. The name of the PF added to build D_i is the legend of the curve. Each curve represents the prediction error of the training samples as a function of the number of classes at each step of agglomeration, starting at the right end with the maximum number of classes for that set of PF. The optimal number of classes for dictionary D_i corresponds to the minimum of the associated curve.

selected only the declarative sentences, which represent about 95% of the whole corpus. The sentences have been segmented into different types of intonation units: intonation groups (IG), stress groups (SG) and syllables (see [12] for a definition of this units). In this study the basic unit of reference has been the SG, defined as the combination of a stressed syllable of a word plus the preceding and following one. The acoustic parameters are the control points of the Bézier curves of degree 3 fitting the F0 contours in the intonation units (more details in [7]). The following prosodic features were considered: type of sentence typeSE (1 value), position of the tonic syllable in the first SG posSTiniSG (3 values) and in the last one posSTfinSG (3 values), number of IGs nIGSE (5 values), SGs nSGSE (6 values), syllables nSylSE (6 values) and phonemes PhonSE (6 values) in the sentence, number of stress groups nSGIG (6 values), syllables nSylIG (6 values), and phonemes nPhonIG (6 values) in the IG, position of the IG in the sentence posIGSE (7 values), position of the SG in its IG posSGIG (6 values), SGBorder indicating the configuration of the SG, number of syllables nSylSG (9 values) and phonemes nPhonSG (6 values) in the SG, position of the stressed syllable posSTSG (3 values). For the experiments, the corpus was split into 3 subsets: modelling, training and testing sets.

We use the centroid to represent the samples of each class in the clusters. The Euclidean distance between the respective centroids of the classes was used as the inter-class similarity

Table 1. Description of the dictionaries in terms of number of classes and number of samples per class

List of Dictionaries LD7	D1	D2	D3	D4	D5	D6	D7
Number of eligible classes	2	4	17	30	26	21	24
Number of grouped classes	2	5	40	111	83	80	190
Initial number of nlasses	2	10	68	230	631	1068	1795
Mean number of samples per class	1235	494	113	42	35	32	16
Mean intra-class dispersion (Hz)	37	33	31	26	21	20	17

metric to guide the merging process. The prediction error is computed as the distance between the points of the real F0 contour and the points of the corresponding synthetic one. This distance is measured using the recommended RMSE and Pearson Correlations [10].

Figure 2 monitors the building process of the list of dictionaries. Error values were obtained by averaging the prediction error over the set of SG in the training corpus. The quality of the obtained results is comparable with the one obtained following other approaches of the state of the art (see [8] for objective and subjective tests). Table 1 shows the impact of the agglomerative process in the final number of representative classes. Note that for every type of intonation unit, there is a serial of dictionaries to select one: some of the classes are never used. This reduction of classes is helpful to simplify the representation of the clusters that is presented in the following section.

3.2   Visualization of Intonation Patterns

Figure 3 shows a tree-like graphical representation of the classes in the list of dictionaries (only a selection). Each node represents a class in the clusters. For every class, we show the Bezier curve representing the F0 profile of the centroid and the standard deviation of each control point. The graph at each node provides a visual representation of the prototypical F0 patterns of the IU belonging to that class.

The classes belonging to the level i are the selected classes for dictionary D_i. Only classes which have been effectively used for prediction and contain more than 10 samples have been represented. The labels of tree branches give the values of the PF. The path going from the root to a given node provides one of the sequences of prosodic features which correspond to the node class.

This tree representation differs from a conventional regression tree in many aspects. Here the same class could appear in different nodes if more than one PF combination indexes it. Furthermore, the parent-child relationship does not imply the splitting of the samples of the parent node. Here the hierarchy is determined by the PF and the contents of the nodes by the agglomerative process. The tree is an easy to read representation of the information of the dictionaries. The input is an array of PF and the output is the corresponding class. The criterion to select the output is to choose the most accurate class in the tree: the closer to the root node the less accurate node. Thus, if the input is the array of PF (noAccent, GAFinal, GEFinal, a) the output is the class C4_75; and if the input is (accent, GAFinal, GEFinal, a), the output is C1_6. Navigating the tree, it is observed the impact of the corresponding PF with respect to the shape of the prototypical F0 pattern.

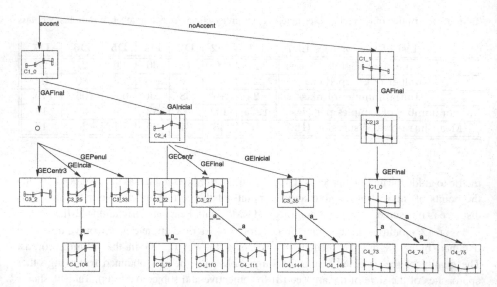

Fig. 3. Models of the dictionary represented as a decision tree. We have selected a part of the whole tree. X scale is normalized. Y scale is 100–220Hz.

The visualization of the information in the tree allows us to contrast some of the assessments found in the bibliography about Spanish Intonation. In [6], an overview of the proposals of several authors can be found. Here we review the main assessments and we contrast them with plots in figures 3.

- **Prominence** (or relative importance of the stress group with respect to the others) was labelled in the corpus with the prosodic feature accent. Observations of the intonation of the corpus projected in figure 3 permits to assess that this feature is the most relevant one attending to the shape of the F0 patterns. This is reflected in the fact that this feature has been selected the first one among all the prosodic features taken into account when the learning procedure previously detailed has been applied. Furthermore, the tree shows that the classes in the branches corresponding to the prominent part (accent value) are characterized by higher F0 values in contrast with the patterns appearing in the unaccented branch (noAccent value). This observation is in consonance with the Phonetics theory that gives to the F0 feature the function of focusing different parts of the sentences.

- **Prosodic structure of the stress group**: Sosa[13] observed that the prototypical patterns associated to the Spanish stress groups are $L * +H$ pattern and the less frequent $H*$ one (using TOBI notation). This fact can be observed in the tree where $L * +H$ patterns appear in C4_104, C4_76, C4_110, C4_144, C4_146. The pattern $H*$ appears in the class C4_111. Apparently C4_111 does not differ significantly from the other classes, but it must be taken into account that the duration is normalized so that the peak of the F0 contour is coincident with the stressed syllable without any temporal displacement as it occurs in the $L * +H$ classes already mentioned (note that nSilGA has 4 possible values: _a_, _a, a_, a), where _ means un-stressed syllable and a means stressed one).

- **Junctures or prosodic boundaries** are very important to arrange the structure of the discourse. The boundaries use to precede or even to substitute the pauses. They are characterized by an abrupt jump in the tendency of the F0 contour. The typical pattern is a rising one called *anticadencia* that can be observed in classes C3_25, C4_104. The patterns in C3_2 and C3_33 are known exceptions called *semicadencia* in the Spanish Phonetics literature (see [12]).
- **Final boundary**: affecting the last part of the F0 contour. Typical final juncture of declarative sentences is $L * +L\%$. This pattern is clearly seen in figure 3 in classes C1_0, C4_73, C4_74, C4_75. This final part of the F0 contours has associated the distinctive function to discriminate the type of sentence. When the corpus is enriched with interrogative and exclamative sentences it is expected that the patterns with the prosodic feature values GAFinal and GEFinal will be determinant.

Finally, we remark that the visualization of figure 3 will surely let experts to get more conclusions about the intonation phenomena, although a thorough discussion of this is out of the scope of the present paper.

4 Conclusions and Future Work

In this communication we have shown the application of MEMOInt to visualize the prosodic information of a given corpus. The classes of F0 patterns correspond with the observations of different authors in Spanish phonetics. The decision tree permits to track the relationship between the typical F0 movements and the set of input prosodic features causing those movements. The observations driven from the tree corroborate the observations found in the bibliography. This converts MEMOInt in a tool to shed light in the many aspects to reveal in this field of research.

Next step in our research will be to measure the capabilities of MEMOInt to analyze the prosodic structure of the utterances with respect to the grammatical structure of the sentence. Furthermore, we expect to use the decision tree to compare the intonation of different corpora.

References

1. A. Aaron, E. Pitrelli, and J. F. Pitrelli. Conversational computers. *Scientific American*, June:64–70, 2005.
2. P.D. Aguado, K. Wimmer, and A. Bonafonte. Joint extraction and prediction of fujisaki's intonation model parameters. In *Proceedings of EuroSpeech 2005*, 2005.
3. J. Allen, M. S. Hunnicutt, and D. Klatt. *From Text to Speech: The MITalk System*. Cambridge University Press, 1987.
4. A. Botinis, B. Granstrom, and B. Moebius. Developments and Paradigms in Intonation Research. *Speech Communications*, 33:263–296, July 2001.
5. V. Cardeñoso and D. Escudero. A strategy to solve data scarcity problems in corpus based intonation modelling. In *Proceedings of ICASSP 2004*, 2004.
6. D. Escudero. *Modelado Estadístico de Entonación con Funciones de Bézier: Aplicaciones a la Conversión Texto Voz*. Ph.D. thesis, Dpto. de Informática, Universidad de Valladolid, España, 2002.

7. D. Escudero and V. Cardeñoso A. Bonafonte. Corpus based extraction of quantitative prosodic parameters of stress groups in spanish. In *Proceedings of ICASSP 2002*, Mayo 2002.
8. D. Escudero and V. Cardeñoso. Optimized selection of intonation dictionaries in corpus based intonation modelling. In *Proceedings of Eurospeech*, September 2005.
9. H. Fujisaki and K. Hirose. Analysis of voice fundamental frequency contours for declarative sentences of Japanese. *Journal of Acoustics Society of Japan*, 5(4):233–242, 1984.
10. D. J. Hermes. Measuring the perceptual similarity of pitch contours. *Journal of Speech, Language, and Hearing Research*, 41:73–82, February 1994.
11. O. Joskisch, H. Mixdorff, H. Kruschke, and U. Kordon. Learning the parameters of quantitative prosody models. In *Proceedings of ICSLP 2000*, 2000.
12. T. Navarro-Tomás. *Manual de Entonación Española*. Madrid, Guadarrama, 1944.
13. J. M. Sosa. *La Entonación del Español*. Cátedra, 1999.
14. R. Sproat. *Multilingual Text-to-Speech Synthesis*. Kluwer, 1998.
15. P. Taylor. Analysis and Synthesis of Intonation using the Tilt Model. *Journal of Acoustical Society of America*, 107(3):1697–1714, 2000.
16. A. Webb. *Statistical Pattern Recognition*. Wiley, 2nd edition, 2002.

Automatic Annotation of Dialogues Using n-Grams*

Carlos D. Martínez-Hinarejos

Departamento de Sistemas Informáticos y Computación
Universidad Politécnica de Valencia, Camino de Vera, s/n, 46071, Valencia, Spain
cmartine@dsic.upv.es

Abstract. The development of a dialogue system for any task implies the acquisition of a dialogue corpus in order to study the structure of the dialogues used in that task. This structure is reflected in the dialogue system behaviour, which can be rule-based or corpus-based. In the case of corpus-based dialogue systems, the behaviour is defined by statistical models which are inferred from an annotated corpus of dialogues. This annotation task is usually difficult and expensive, and therefore, automatic dialogue annotation tools are necessary to reduce the annotation effort. An automatic dialogue labeller technique that is based on n-grams is presented in this work. Its different variants are evaluated with respect to manual human annotations of a dialogue corpus devoted to train queries.

1 Introduction

A dialogue system [1] is commonly defined as a computer system that interacts with a user using dialogue in order to solve a certain problem. Tasks such as ticket reservation or timetable consultation [2] are common examples of dialogue system applications.

To define the behaviour of a dialogue system, the most common method is to acquire a corpus of dialogues that is related to the task that the system must carry out. In this process of acquisition, a set-up known as Wizard of Oz [3] is used. The dialogue system behaviour is defined from the set of acquired dialogues. Two main alternatives have been used in the system behaviour definition: rule-based [4] and corpus-based (or statistical) [5]. The rule-based approach needs an expert to design and update the rules when there are new tasks. However, in the corpus-based approach, the behaviour is determined by statistical models that are automatically inferred.

The problem with the corpus-based approach is the need for huge amounts of data (in this case, dialogues), which must be conveniently annotated to estimate the parameters of the statistical models. One of the most widely used annotation approaches is Dialogue Act (DA) labelling [6]. In this approach, every turn is annotated with one or more DA, which represents the function from a dialogue viewpoint of the annotated segment. A segment (usually known as an utterance) is a sequence of words that constitutes a basic meaningful unit in terms of dialogue.

The annotation of the corpus implies the definition of the set of DA and the annotation rules [7] as well as the corpus annotation. The annotation process is very time-consuming. Therefore, the development of automatic techniques for annotating dialogues would be very useful in the development of corpus-based dialogue systems.

---

* Work partially supported by the Spanish project TIC2003-08681-C02-02.

Petr Sojka, Ivan Kopeček and Karel Pala (Eds.): TSD 2006, LNAI 4188, pp. 653–660, 2006.

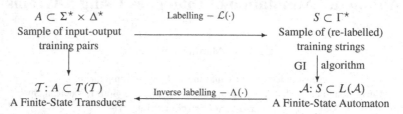

Fig. 1. General scheme for the GIATI technique. Σ, Δ and Γ are the input, output, and extended set of symbols, respectively. A and S are the initial sets of aligned and re-labelled samples. $L(\mathcal{A})$ and $T(\mathcal{T})$ represent the languages derived from $\mathcal{A}$ and $\mathcal{T}$, respectively. $\mathcal{L}$ and Λ are the labelling and inverse labelling functions.

In this work, an automatic annotation technique based on n-grams is presented. This technique is based on a former Stochastic Finite-State Transducer (SFST) inference technique, which is mainly used in Machine Translation. The SFST inference technique and its n-gram version is described in Section 2. In Section 3, the dialogue task and corpus are presented. In Section 4, the experimental framework is described and the results are summarised. In Section 5, conclusions and future work lines are presented.

2   Inference of Stochastic Finite-State Transducers

The first step in the process of automatic labelling is the construction of the n-gram labeller. The construction of this n-gram is based on a SFST inference technique known as GIATI[1] [8,9]. GIATI is a general SFST inference technique, which is based on a re-labelling process of input-output pairs of sentences. This re-labelling process depends on the alignments [10] between the input and the output symbols. A smoothed n-gram is inferred from the re-labelled corpus. This n-gram is transformed into the final SFST by inverting the labelling process. The general scheme for the GIATI technique is presented in Figure 1. In our case, we skip the transformation of the n-gram into a SFST, avoiding the problems caused by the n-gram smoothing, which is difficult to incorporate into a SFST. In any case, the key point in this technique is the appropriate selection of the re-labelling process (and its inverse).

The particular application of GIATI to the dialogue case is much easier. In this case, the input symbols are the words of the turn, and the output symbols are the associated DA. The alignment between input and output pairs is defined by aligning the last word of each segment with the corresponding DA and leaving the rest of the words in the turn with an empty alignment. With this alignment strategy, the resulting alignment is linear, i.e., there are no cross-inverted alignments. This fact facilitates the selection of the re-labelling scheme. One fact we must point out is that this technique is independent of the language and the application the dialogue covers. In any case, both the words of the language and the DA labels are treated as generic sets of symbols, which makes the application of the technique independent of these factors. A preliminary application of GIATI to dialogue annotation that covered these points was presented in [11].

---

[1] GIATI is the acronym for Grammatical Inference and Alignments for Transducer Inference.

I would like to know the fare leaving from Madrid on next Monday   .
                                                    ↓   ↓
                              (U:Question:Fare:Origin)   (U:Question:Fare:Day)

I would like to know the fare leaving from Madrid@(U:Question:Fare:Origin) on next Monday
.@(U:Question:Fare:Day)

Fig. 2. An example of re-labelling for one user turn. The upper part shows the alignment between the words and the DA. The lower part shows the result of the re-labelling.

In this work, the re-labelling scheme is as follows:

- If a word w is not aligned with any DA, then the new label is the same word w.
- If a word w is aligned with a DA d, then the new label is $w@d$, where @ is a special joining symbol that is not present in Σ nor in Δ.

Figure 2 shows an example of re-labelling with this scheme.

The inference process is performed after the re-labelling step. This process usually computes a smoothed *n*-gram, where *n* is a parameter. It is supposed that the greater the *n*, the more specific the *n*-gram is for the training data. The resulting *n*-gram computes the probabilities of all the sequences of *n* words in the re-labelled training data (i.e., for the word w, several re-labelled words such as w, $w@d_1$, $w@d_2$, $w@d_3$, etc. could be derived, and the *n*-gram is computed for these re-labelled words).

An equivalent Stochastic Finite-State Automaton (SFSA) can be computed from the smoothed *n*-gram. The resulting SFSA can be transformed into a SFST by applying the inversion of the re-labelling. The SFST can process an unlabelled dialogue using a classical Viterbi parsing. The SFST output will provide the corresponding DA labels for each segment. In our case, the SFST transformation is avoided by implementing a Viterbi algorithm that works directly with *n*-grams.

This Viterbi implementation takes the words in the current turn as input and performs a tree beam-search. The *i*th level in the tree corresponds to the sequence of the first *i* words of the turn. Each node in the tree corresponds to a sequence of words and its corresponding outputs, along with the probability of the sequence. Therefore, when taking the next word, all the nodes in the previous level branch into k child nodes, where k is the number of outputs

Vocabulary: a, b, c, $c@o_1$, $c@o_2$, d, e, $e@o_3$
Input sentence: a c d e b

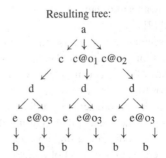

Fig. 3. An example of the Viterbi tree search

Table 1. Statistics from the complete DIHANA annotated corpus

Feature	Total	User	System	Feature	Total	User	System
Number of turns	15413	6280	9133	Avg. segments by turn	1.5	1.5	1.5
Number of segments	23542	9712	13830	Number of DA	248	153	95

that the current word has associated to it. The probability of a child node is calculated from the probability of its parent and the probability of the new n-gram sequence (which results from concatenating the parent's n-gram and the current word with its output). In the last level, the node with the highest probability is chosen, and the final output is obtained by going up the tree and retrieving the corresponding sequence of words and outputs. One example of tree expansion is shown in Figure 3 for a generic set of symbols.

3   Dialogue Corpus

In this work, automatic annotation is applied to a dialogue corpus acquired for the DIHANA project [12]. The goal of the DIHANA project is the construction of a modular speech dialogue system, which is devoted to the consultation of timetables and fares for Spanish trains nation-wide. The acquisition of this dialogue corpus was performed using the classical Wizard of Oz (WoZ) technique [3]. In this acquisition process, the behaviour of the Wizard was clearly defined by a set of rules (WoZ strategy). The acquired corpus consisted of 900 different speech dialogues. For this acquisition, 225 volunteers were recruited; most of them were not aware that they were speaking to a human Wizard.

The acquisition process was based on the definition of scenarios for each acquisition. A scenario is defined by an objective, which may or may not have restrictions that the user must follow (e.g., name of the departure town). The objective of a scenario is the set of data items that should be known by the user at the end of the dialogue. Each volunteer performed four different scenarios, each of which corresponded to a different type of objective. No other restrictions (neither lexical nor syntactical) were imposed on the volunteer in the acquisition apart from the scenario objectives.

The resulting corpus of speech dialogues consisted of about five and a half hours of speech signal. On average, each dialogue had seven user turns and ten system (Wizard) turns. The final vocabulary size was 980 words. The whole set of transcribed dialogues was annotated with DA by a team of human experts. The annotation scheme used defined a DA as a three-level label [7].

Every segment of every turn was annotated with one of these labels, which also included an identifier for the speaker (either user or system). The first level of the label corresponded to the intention of the segment (query, statement, response,...). The second level corresponded to the repository of information that was implicit in the segment (i.e., the set of data used or modified in the segment, according to the intention given by the first level). The third level indicated the specific data (but not the specific values) provided in the segment. The first level could only take a single value, but both the second and third level could take zero, one, or several values. The set of possible values is presented in Table 2, where the *Nil* value represents the empty value for both the second and third levels.

This manual annotation process was performed by applying a set of rules which was refined in several steps [7]. An example of an annotated dialogue is shown in Figure 4 (the original dialogue was in Spanish). Some statistics from the final annotated dialogue corpus are presented in Table 1.

S1: Welcome to the information system about trains . How can I help you ? *(S:Opening:Nil:Nil)*
 U1: To obtain the times from Valencia *(U:Question:Departure-time:Origin)* to Sevilla *(U:Question:Departure-time:Destination)* this Saturday . *(U:Question:Dep-time:Day)*
S2: I am going to consult times for trains departing Valencia destination Sevilla on Saturday , 10th of April of 2004 . *(S:Confirmation:Dep-time:Dest,Day,Org)* Wait a moment , please . *(S:Waiting:Nil:Nil)*
S3: The only train for that route is a Garcia-Lorca which leaves at 11:30 in the morning and arrives at 8:18 in the evening . *(S:Answer:Dep-time:Arr-time,Dep-time,Num-trains,Train-type)* Do you want more information ? *(S:Consult:Nil:Nil)*
U2: Yes , to obtain the fare . *(U:Question:Fare:Nil)*
S4: The fare of that train in tourist class is 41.50 euros for a one-way ticket . All return tickets have a 20 percent discount . *(S:Answer:Fare:Class,Fare)* Do you want more information ? *(S:Consult:Nil:Nil)*
U3: No . *(U:Closing:Nil:Nil)*
S5: Thanks for using this service . Have a nice trip . *(S:Closing:Nil:Nil)*

Fig. 4. Example of a manually annotated dialogue

These annotated dialogues can be used to develop statistical dialogue models [5,13]. The main drawback of the statistical models is the need for huge amounts of annotated data. Therefore, the technique described in Section 2 can speed up the annotation process and, consequently, the development of statistical models. The next section describes the experiments and the assessment of the technique for the DIHANA corpus.

4 Experiments and Results

Some experiments were performed using the DIHANA corpus in order to assess the quality of the automatic annotation technique. The first step was the division between training and test dialogue sets. As this technique was supposed to be applied to a set of dialogues that was larger than the current annotated set, the training set was chosen so that it was smaller than the test set. In this case, the training set was made up of the 204 dialogues annotated in the first stage of the definition of the annotation rules and the test set was made up of the remaining

Table 2. Labels defined for each level.

First level	Second level	Third level
Opening, Closing, Undefined, Not-Understood, Waiting, Consult, Acceptance, Rejection, Question, Confirmation, Answer	Nil, Dep-time, Arr-time, Fare, Org, Dest, Day, Train-type, Service, Class, Trip-time	Nil, Dep-time, Arr-time, Fare, Org, Dest, Day, Train-type, Service, Class, Trip-time, Order-num, Num-trains, Trip-type

Table 3. Training and test corpus statistics

Feature	Training corpus			Test corpus		
	Total	User	System	Total	User	System
Number of turns	3577	1472	2105	11836	4808	7028
Number of segments	5376	2212	3164	18170	7504	10666
Number of DA	169	102	67	234	146	88
Vocabulary size	632	485	319	913	757	379

696 dialogues of the complete corpus. The statistics for the training and test corpora are presented in Table 3. As was expected, the training set did not cover all the possible DA and words present in the test set.

Some of the DA and the words that were present in the test set were not present in the training set. To deal with this drawback, some preprocessing had to be applied to the training corpus before applying the n-gram inference:

1. All the training dialogues had to be categorised. The applied categorisation included towns, dates, hours, fares, train types, and ticket classes.
2. All the words were labelled with an identifier for the speaker of the turn they belonged to. This ensures that user words are labelled with user DA, and that system words are labelled with system DA.

GIATI was applied after these preprocessing steps. The re-labelling process used the scheme described in Section 2. Three different n-grams, $n = 2, 3, 4$ were inferred on the re-labelling corpus. In all these inferences we maintained the following: the SLM toolkit was used [14]; the vocabulary was composed of all the words present in the re-labelled corpus; and the smoothing technique was the Good-Turing discounting [15].

The annotation was performed in two different ways: turn by turn, or dialogue by dialogue. For the application of these n-grams, an implementation of the Viterbi parsing algorithm was carried out as described in Section 2. For this parsing process, the input was the categorised turns of the test dialogues, and the output were the annotated dialogues. Some dialogues remained unlabelled after the n-gram parsing due to memory management problems (the

Table 4. SER and DAER results for the test set of dialogues using different n-grams

Measure / n-gram	Turn by turn			Dialogue by dialogue		
	2-gram	3-gram	4-gram	2-gram	3-gram	4-gram
Unlabelled turns	22 (0.2%)	20 (0.2%)	20 (0.2%)	205 (1.7%)	55 (0.5%)	9 (0.1%)
Mean Time/Dialogue (secs)	24	38	52	26	31	41
SER	8.2%	7.4%	7.6%	9.5%	7.2%	6.9%
DAER	43.0%	30.3%	29.7%	40.9%	27.3%	26.0%
DAER (1st+2nd)	39.5%	26.9%	26.3%	37.3%	23.6%	22.3%
DAER (1st)	25.8%	12.2%	11.3%	24.1%	10.9%	10.0%
DAER (2nd)	35.1%	24.7%	24.1%	33.7%	21.5%	20.1%
DAER (3rd)	17.5%	11.2%	11.3%	19.2%	11.9%	11.4%

search space was too large, even when beam-search was used). The annotated turns were compared with the reference using two measures:

- Segmentation Error Rate (SER): percent of turns incorrectly segmented by the *n*-gram labelling.
- DA Error Rate (DAER): similar to Word Error Rate (WER) but with DA; the obtained DA sequence is compared with the reference DA sequence, counting the number of insertion (I), deletions (D) and substitutions (S) necessary to transform the first one into the second one, along with the correct matches (C). DAER is calculated using the formula $\frac{I+D+S}{C+D+S}$.

Because of the three-level structure of DA labels, DAER was computed in several ways: for the three levels together (the whole label); for the first and second levels together; and for the first, the second and the third level separately. These alternative DAER take into account the possibility of correcting only part of the label and not the whole label. The results for SER and DAER (along with the number of unlabelled turns and the time per dialogue) are presented in Table 4.

From the results shown in Table 4, it is clear that the described method performs relatively well, allowing a significant reduction of the human effort in the annotation task. At the segmentation level, only very few turns must be corrected. At the DA level nearly 3/4 of the turns were correct using 4-gram and the dialogue by dialogue approach, which implies a great savings in time when annotating the dialogues (correcting DA is less time-consuming than annotating from scratch). Also worth noting is the high accuracy achieved at individual levels (which implies that only one part of the DA label will have to be corrected) and the small mean time used to annotate each dialogue.

5 Conclusions and Future Work

This paper presents a technique based on *n*-grams that are automatically inferred from a small set of annotated dialogues. This allows the annotation of a set of unlabelled dialogues. Although the technique is not error-free, the obtained annotation saves time and effort in the annotation process, as only a reduced set (nearly one quarter) of dialogue turns has to be re-labelled. This technique offers the possibility of labelling larger corpora with less effort and, consequently, having more data for inferring better probabilistic dialogue models in less time.

Future work is directed towards several improvements and variants of the automatic annotation process. The use of higher order *n*-grams should be explored, even though it might lead to the inference of "overfitted" labellers, which only perform well on the training examples.

Another application that should be explored is the use of the technique on other annotation schemes (e.g., dialogues annotated with the current state of the data) to assess the validity of this method. In addition, the application of this method to other dialogue corpora with different complexities is necessary in order to find the possible limitations of the technique in complex domains and evaluate the amount of data that is needed to obtain good *n*-grams models.

It would also be interesting to consider the possibility of performing incremental labelling (i.e., the *n*-gram is used to annotate a smaller set of dialogues, which after being corrected are incorporated into the training part in order to reduce the total number of errors). This possibility becomes very interesting when changing the domain or when the set of DAs is only partially defined at the beginning of the annotation task. Implementation issues are also important in future research, especially reducing the space complexity in Viterbi decoding.

Acknowledgements. The author would like to thank the team of expert labellers for their excellent work in the manual annotation process, David Picó for providing the GIATI figure and the anonymous reviewers for their comments and suggestions.

References

1. Kuppevelt, J.V., Smith, R.W.: Current and New Directions in Discourse and Dialogue. Volume 22 of Text, Speech and Language Technology. Springer (2003).
2. Aust, H., Oerder, M., Seide, F., Steinbiss, V.: The philips automatic train timetable information system. Speech Communication **17** (1995) 249–263.
3. Fraser, M., Gilbert, G.: Simulating speech systems. Computer Speech and Language **5** (1991) 81–99.
4. Gorin, A., Riccardi, G., Wright, J.: How may i help you? Speech Communication **23** (1997) 113–127.
5. Stolcke, A., Coccaro, N., Bates, R., Taylor, P., van Ess-Dykema, C., Ries, K., Shriberg, E., Jurafsky, D., Martin, R., Meteer, M.: Dialogue act modelling for automatic tagging and recognition of conversational speech. Computational Linguistics **26**(3) (2000) 1–34.
6. Searle, J.R.: Speech acts. Cambridge University Press (1969).
7. Alcacer, N., Benedí, J., Blat, F., Granell, R., Martínez, C.D., Torres, F.: Acquisition and labelling of a spontaneous speech dialogue corpus. In: Proceeding of 10th International Conference on Speech and Computer (SPECOM), Patras, Greece (2005) 583–586.
8. Picó, D., Tomás, J., Casacuberta, F.: GIATI: A general methodology for finite-state translation using alignments. In: Statistical, Structural and Syntactical Pattern Recognition. Proc. of the Joint IAPR Intternational Workshops SSPR 2004 and SPR 2004. Volume 3138 of Lecture Notes in Computer Science. Springer-Verlag, Lisboa, Portugal (2004) 216–223.
9. Casacuberta, F., Vidal, E., Picó, D.: Inference of finite-state transducers from regular languages. Pattern Recognition **38**(9) (2005) 1431–1443.
10. Brown, P.F., Pietra, S.A.D., Pietra, V.J.D., Mercer, R.L.: The mathematics of statistical machine translation: Parameter estimation. Computational Linguistics **19**(2) (1993) 263–311.
11. Martínez-Hinarejos, C.D., Casacuberta, F.: A pattern recognition approach to dialog labelling by using finite-state transducers. In: Proceedings of 5th. IberoAmerican Symposium on Pattern Recognition, Lisbon, Portugal (2000) 669–677.
12. Benedí, J.M., Varona, A., Lleida, E.: Dihana: Dialogue system for information access using spontaneous speech in several environments tic2002-04103-c03. In: Reports for Jornadas de Seguimiento - Programa Nacional de Tecnologías Informáticas, Málaga, Spain (2004).
13. Martínez-Hinarejos, C.D., Casacuberta, F.: Evaluating a probabilistic dialogue model for a railway information task. In Sojka, P., Kopeček, I., Pala, K., eds.: Proceedings of the 5th International Conf. on Text, Speech and Dialogue—TSD 2002. Lecture Notes in Artificial Intelligence LNCS/LNAI 2448, Brno, Czech Republic, Springer-Verlag (2002) 381–388.
14. Rosenfeld, R.: The cmu-cambridge statistical language modelling toolkit v2. Technical report, Carnegie Mellon University (1998).
15. Church, K.W., Gale, W.A.: A comparison of the enhanced good-turing and deleted estimation methods for estimating probabilities of english bigrams. Computer Speech and Language **5** (1991) 19–54.

PPChecker: Plagiarism Pattern Checker in Document Copy Detection*

NamOh Kang[1], Alexander Gelbukh[2], SangYong Han[1,**]

[1] School of Computer Science & Engineering,
Chung-Ang University, South Korea
kang@archi.cse.cau.ac.kr, hansy@cau.ac.kr
[2] National Polytechnic Institute, Mexico
gelbukh@gelbukh.com
http://www.gelbukh.com

Abstract. Nowadays, most of documents are produced in digital format, in which they can be easily accessed and copied. Document copy detection is a very important tool for protecting the author's copyright. We present PPChecker, a document copy detection system based on plagiarism pattern checking. PPChecker calculates the amount of data copied from the original document to the query document, based on linguistically-motivated plagiarism patterns. Experiments performed on CISI document collection show that PPChecker produces better decision information for document copy detection than existing systems.

Keywords: Document Copy Detection, Plagiarism Pattern.

1 Introduction

Availability of Internet and easy access to electronic texts makes it easy for many users to share information and to create new documents. However, it also gives convenient environment to malicious plagiarists. This is a serious problem for information sharing. While it is not resolved it will make authors reluctant to share their documents and will reduce the chances for the users to access valuable information.

For protecting the author's copyright, many kinds of intellectual property protection techniques have been introduced: copy prevention, signature and content-based copy detection, etc. Copy protection and signature-based copy detection can be very useful to prevent or detect copying of a whole document. However, these techniques have some drawbacks that make it difficult for users to share information and can not prevent partial copying of a document [1].

Huge amount of digital documents is made public day to day in Internet. Most of them are not supported by either copy prevention technique or signature-based copy detection technique. This increases the necessity of content-based copy detection technique. So

---

* This research was supported by the MIC (Ministry of Information and Communication), Korea, under the Chung-Ang University HNRC-ITRC (Home Network Research Center) support program supervised by the IITA (Institute of Information Technology Assessment).
** Corresponding author.

Petr Sojka, Ivan Kopeček and Karel Pala (Eds.): TSD 2006, LNAI 4188, pp. 661–667, 2006.
© Springer-Verlag Berlin Heidelberg 2006

far, many document copy detection(DCD) systems based on content-based copy detection technique have been introduced, such as COPS, SCAM, CHECK, etc. A typical DCD system registers many original documents, compares them with the query document suspected to be plagiarized, and determines the probability of plagiarism. These systems have an advantage of finding the originality of a total or partial copy of a document. However, most DCD systems mainly focus on checking for the possibility of copying between original documents and a query document. They do not give any evidence of plagiaristic sources to the user. In this paper, we describe the plagiarism pattern checking system(PPChecker) that provides evidence information for plagiarism-like style.

The paper is organized as follows. In Section 2, we present some related work. Section 3 explains the system design components used in PPChecker. In section 4, we describe the architecture of PPChecker. In section 5, the experimental result of the system performance is shown. Finally, Section 6 draws conclusion and depicts the future work.

2   Related Work and Motivation

2.1   Content-Based DCD Systems

Document copy detection has been actively researched since 1990s. Many systems for document copy detection have been introduced, such as COPS, SCAM, CHECK, SSK, MDR, etc.

COPS [2] was developed in frame of the Stanford Digital Library Project. It performs comparison between the registered documents and a given query document by a sentence unit. COPS shows very good result in comparing exactly equal sentences, but it can not detect partial sentence overlaps. Shivakumar et al. developed SCAM [1] to improve COPS. SCAM uses document word frequency to detect copying. It can find partial overlaps, but comparison of documents sharing many words misleads it.

CHECK [3] extracts structural information and keywords from documents and uses them to check the overlap. It is limited to structured documents. Semantic Sequence Kernel (SSK) [4] first finds out semantic sequences in documents and then uses a kernel function to calculate their similarity. It is good on comparison between non-reworded documents.

Match Detect Retrieval (MDR) system [5] uses string-matching algorithms based on suffix trees to identify the overlap between a suspicious document and candidate documents. It is very powerful for finding exact copy. However, constructing suffix tree for a suspicious document is very expensive, and this system is very weak at detecting modified documents.

WCopyfind [6] uses phrases with six or more words as a comparing unit. It counts the number of words from matching phrases and calculates plagiarism rate as a ratio of the number of matching words and the total number of words in the document. WCopyfind could find a partial overlap, but the user should set an adequate word number in a phrase.

2.2   Plagiarism Patterns

Plagiarism pattern research has not reached its maturity. It is hard to find a scientific classification of plagiarism, except for Karen Fullam et al.'s plagiarism patterns and their variants [7].

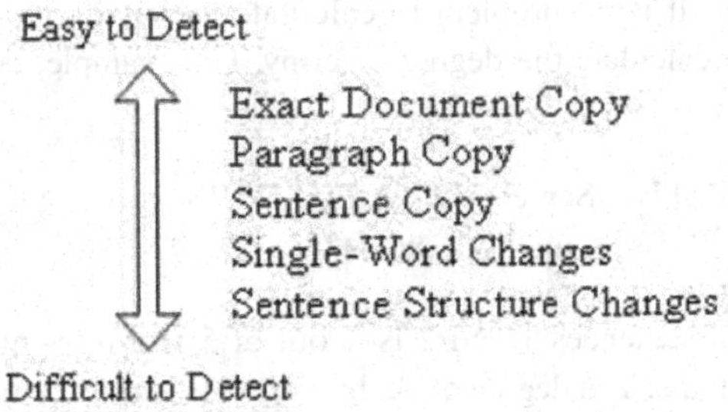

Easy to Detect

↑
| Exact Document Copy
| Paragraph Copy
| Sentence Copy
| Single-Word Changes
↓ Sentence Structure Changes

Difficult to Detect

Fig. 1. The plagiarism patterns and their levels of sophistication

Figure 1 illustrates that it is easier to find an exact copy of the units such as document, paragraph, or sentence than to find the subtle forms of them such as word changes and structure changes.

So far, many DCD systems have been focused at detecting the overlap between documents using various comparing units. However, they do not consider plagiarism patterns. In this paper, we introduce a DCD system based on plagiarism patterns.

3 System Design Components

Comparing unit(chunking unit), overlap measure function, and plagiarism decision function crucially affect the performance of a DCD system. In this section, we consider each of these factors in our system PPChecker.

3.1 Comparison Unit

A DCD system breaks documents down into comparing units(chunking units) for checking the possibility of copying. There are many options to choose comparing unit, such as sentence, paragraph, word, or whole document. For example, COPS uses sentences, SCAM uses words, and CHECK uses paragraphs as comparing unit.

The adopted comparing units affect the accuracy of a DCD system. Selecting large comparing units decreases the necessary number of comparisons but makes it difficult to find partial copy. On the other hand, smaller comparing units increase the number of comparisons and therefore reduce the system's speed. However, it is easy to catch partial copying of the information based on the local similarity.

In this paper, we select sentence as the comparison unit. Sentences form paragraphs or the whole document. Comparison of sentences is a good metric to calculate local similarity. The goal of PPChecker is to provide the user with plagiarism pattern information of the query document. Karen Fullam's research [7] also shows that sentence is a good unit to extract plagiarism pattern information on query document.

3.2 Overlap Measure Function

Overlap measure function is used to determine copying information of the comparing units extracted from documents. Traditionally, many DCD systems use vector space model or cosine similarity model. It is no problem to calculate the similarity between two objects, but it is not enough to calculate the degree of copy. For example, consider the following sentences:

Sentence 1: "A B C D E"   Sentence 2: "A B C D F"
Sentence 3: "G H"   Sentence 4: "G H"

The overlap between sentences 1 and 2 is 4 out of 5 words. Sentence 3 and 4, have a perfect overlap of two items. The degree of such overlap is very important to detect copying: the larger overlap the more evidence of plagiarism. The overlap between the sentences 1 and 2 is two times greater than the overlap between of sentence 3 and sentence 4. So, in the former case overlapping value should be higher than in the latter case. However, the sentences 1 and 2 give 0.8 and the sentences 3 and 4 give 1.0 in cosine similarity. Moreover, the cosine similarity can not give any information of plagiarism. In this research, we suggest the overlap measure function which can quantify the overlap between comparing units and give information about plagiarism.

Let S_o is a part of the original document and S_c of the query document. The similarity $Sim(S_o, S_c)$ can be calculated as follows.

$$S_o = \{w_1, w_2, w_3, \ldots, w_n\}, \ S_c = \{w_1, w_2, w_3, \ldots, w_m\}.$$

$$Comm(S_o, S_c) = S_o \cap S_c, \ Diff(S_o, S_c) = S_o - S_c.$$

$$Comm(S_o, S_c) = S_o \cap S_c, Diff(S_o, S_c) = S_o - S_c.$$

$$Syn(w) = \{The \ synonym \ of \ w\}.$$

$$SynWord(S_o, S_c) = \{w_i | w_i \in Diff(S_c, S_o) \cap Syn(w_i) \in S_o\}.$$

$$WordOverlap(S_o, S_c) = \frac{|S_o|}{|Comm(S_o,S_c)|+\alpha \times |SynWord(S_o,S_c)|}, \ \alpha \text{ is weight value.}$$

$$SizeOverlap(S_o, S_c) = \sqrt{|Diff(S_o, S_c)| + |Diff(S_c, S_o)|}.$$

$$Sim(S_o, S_c) = |S_o| \times (1/(e^{WordOverlap(S_o,S_c)-1} + SizeOverlap(S_o, S_c))).$$

Calculation of $Sim(S_o, S_c)$ gives not only similarity between S_o and S_c but also the plagiarism information. The following table 1 shows how to decide plagiarism patterns.

The proposed overlap measure function can not distinguish between an exact copy and changing structure of a sentence. For distinguishing them, it is necessary to check the word order in sentences.

Table 1. Plagiarism patterns and their decision parameters

Plagiarism pattern	Decision parameters
Sentence copy exactly	$WordOverLap(S_o, S_c) = 1, SizeOverlap(S_o, S_c) = 0$
Word insertion	$SizeOverlap(S_o, S_c) \neq 0, Diff(S_o, S_c) > 1$
Word removal	$SizeOverlap(S_o, S_c) \neq 0, Diff(S_c, S_o) > 1$
Changing Word	$1 < WordOverlap(S_o, S_c) < \infty, SizeOverlap(S_o, S_c) = 0$
Changing Sentence	$WordOverlap(S_o, S_c) = 1, SizeOverlap(S_o, S_c) = 0$

3.3 Plagiarism Detection

Sentence level overlap and plagiarism pattern information can be calculated by using overlap measure function. However, the decision on whether a document is copied or not is made basing on its global copy information. This information is very useful to generate ranking information to be supplied to the user when many documents are checked for the possibility of copying. In PPChecker, the global copying degree of the query document is calculated by gathering sentence level information in paragraph or document unit. If all sentences of a paragraph or a document pass a given threshold value, some weight value is used to calculate the global degree of copying.

4   The Architecture of PPChecker

The architecture of PPChecker is shown in Figure 2. All original documents are stored in the document data base. When the query document is received, the system divides it and the original documents into comparing units-sentences. These sentences are then used to calculate the overlap and the plagiarism information in *local_similarity_extractor* function (see below) by using the overlap measure function defined in Section 3.2. The extracted information is used to calculate the degree of copying from each other in original documents, and the ordered information is supplied to the user.

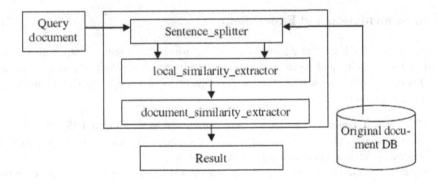

Fig. 2. The architecture of PPChecker

The algorithm used in PPChecker is as follows:

Algorithm 1

<u>Input:</u>

$Document\_DB = \{D_1, D_2, D_3, \ldots, D_n\}$
and each $D_1 = \{S_{i1}, S_{i2}, S_{i3}, \ldots, S_{im}\}$
$QueryDocument = QS_1, QS_2, QS_3, \ldots, QS_t$

Output:
_____

Decreasing ordered document list in document similarity value

for $i = 1$ to n

for $j = 1$ to t

localsimilarity $[1..j] = 0$;

for $k = 1$ to m

if $|Comm(S_{ik}, QS_j)| \geq \frac{|S_{ik}|}{2}$ // then $\frac{|S_{ik}|}{2}$ is selected threshold value

localsimilarity $[j] = \max$ {localsimilarity $[j]$, $Sim(S_{ik}, QS_j)$ }

end

end

if all similarities in document is over than threshold value

docsimilarity $[i] = D_w \times \sum_n localsimilarity[n]$

else if all similarities in a paragraph is over than threshold value

docsimilarity $[i] = \sum_l localsimilarity[l] + P(\_)w \times \sum_m localsimilarity[m]$

else

docsimilarity $[i] = \sum_l localsimilarity[l]$

// P_w and D_w are Paragraph_weight and Document_weight,

// respectively.

end

return sort(docsimilarity)

5   Implementation and Experiment

PPChecker was implemented under Windows XP using the language C#. It uses Porter stemmer for stemming and WordNet for finding synonyms. To evaluate the system, we use the CISI document collection set. For the experiment, we generated the test document set from CISI as follows.

1. 11 relevant documents related to a specific query were selected from CISI set.
2. One document was selected as the original document. The other 10 documents were selected as candidate documents for plagiarism test.
3. Some text extracted from the original document was transformed (exact copy, changing synonyms, changing sentence structure) and was inserted into the candidate documents for plagiarism detection to make a plagiarized document.
4. The plagiarized documents were returned into the CISI document set. Selected original document was removed from the CISI document set and became the query document.

As a baseline, we implemented a DCD system based on word similarity of the whole document (WD_System) and of a sentence (WS_System). We measured quality in terms of R-precision; $R = 10$.

In case of exact copy detection and exchanging synonyms, PPChecker give better results than other systems. For changed sentence structure, PPChecker and WS_System give similar results. This shows that in case of checking for changed structure of sentence, information on the words and the synonyms is not necessary to detect the possibility of copying.

Table 2. Copy detection test ($R = 10$)

		WD_System	WS_System	PPChecker
Test 1	Exact copy	2	6	8
	Synonym	2	6	8
	Structure change	1	5	4
Test 2	Exact copy	1	7	9
	Synonym	1	6	7
	Structure change	1	3	3
Test 3	Exact copy	1	6	8
	Synonym	0	4	7
	Structure change	0	3	4

6   Discussion and Future Work

The experimental results show that PPChecker produces more precise results in exact copy detection and copy with changing for synonyms. PPChecker's overlap measure function is more useful than normalized comparison value such as cosine similarity. Consideration of plagiarism pattern information produced in comparison helps to make a more precise decision.

In our experiments, only the documents registered in document database could be used to detect plagiarism. However, nowadays huge amount of documents are open for access in Internet and thus vulnerable to plagiarism. Thus research on using Internet as document database is necessary in the future.

PPChecker uses WordNet for checking word synonymy. If we use a domain-specific ontology for this, precision could be improved. Finally, research on plagiarism patterns is to be continued due to its crucial importance for document copy detection.

References

1. Shivakumar, N. and Garcia-Monlina, H.: SCAM: A Copy Detection Mechanisms for Digital Documents. In: Proceedings of International Conference on Theory and Practice of Digital Libraries, Austin, Texas. June 1995.
2. Brin, S., Davis, J., and Garcia-Molina, H.: Copy Detection Mechanisms for Digital Documents. In: Proceedings of ACM SIGMOD Annual Conference, San Jose, CA, May 1995.
3. Si, A., Leong, H., and Lau, R.: CHECK: A Document Plagiarism Detection System. In: Proceedings of ACM Symposium for Applied Computing, pp. 70–77, Feb 1997.
4. Bao Jun-Peng, Shen Jun-Yi, Liu Xiao-Dong, Liu Hai-Yan,and Zhang Xiao-Di.: Document Copy Detection Based On Kernel Method. In: 2003 International Conference on Natural Language Processing and Knowledge Engineering Proceedings.
5. Krisztian Monostori, Arkady Zaslavsky,and Heinz Schmidt: Document Overlap Detection System for Distributed Digital Libraries, Proc. of the 5th ACM conference on DL, 2000, pp. 226–227.
6. Louis Bloomfield: http://plagiarism.phys.virginia.edu, The Plagiarism Resource Site Charlottesville, Virginia.
7. Karen Fullam, Jisun Park: Improvements for Scalable and Accurate Plagiarism Detection in Digital Documents, 2002.
8. Narayanan Shivakumar, Hector Garcia-Molina: Building a Scalable and Accurate Copy Detection Mechanism, 1st ACM Int. Conference on Digital Libraries (DL '96), March. 1996. pp. 160–168.
9. Finkel, R., Zaslavsky, A. Monostori, K., and Schmidt, H.: Signature Extraction for Overlap Detection in Documents. In: Proceedings of Australasian Computer Science Conference, 2002.

Segmental Duration Modelling in Turkish

Özlem Öztürk[1] and Tolga Çiloğlu[2]

[1] Electrical and Electronics Engineering Department
Dokuz Eylul University, Izmir, Turkey
ozlem.ozturk@eee.deu.edu.tr
[2] Electrical and Electronics Engineering Department
Middle East Technical University, Ankara, Turkey
ciloglu@metu.edu.tr

Abstract. Naturalness of synthetic speech highly depends on appropriate modelling of prosodic aspects. Mostly, three prosody components are modelled: segmental duration, pitch contour and intensity. In this study, we present our work on modelling segmental duration in Turkish using machine-learning algorithms, especially *Classification and Regression Trees*. The models predict phone durations based on attributes such as current, preceding and following phones' identities, stress, part-of-speech, word length in number of syllables, and position of word in utterance extracted from a speech corpus. Obtained models predict segment durations better than mean duration approximations (∼0.77 *Correlation Coefficient*, and 20.4 ms *Root-Mean Squared Error*). In order to improve prediction performance further, attributes used to develop segmental duration are optimized by means of *Sequential Forward Selection* method. As a result of Sequential Forward Selection method, phone identity, neighboring phone identities, lexical stress, syllable type, part-of-speech, phrase break information, and location of word in the phrase constitute optimum attribute set for phoneme duration modelling.

1 Introduction

Prosody refers to characteristics of speech such as intonation, timing, stress, loudness, and other acoustical properties imposed by articulatory, emotional, mental, and intentional states of the speaker. One of the most prominent components of prosody is considered as timing or duration. Duration can be defined as the time taken to utter an acoustic unit such as phoneme, syllable, etc. In this study, it is aimed to predict the phoneme durations of a Turkish sentence given its written form so that resultant phoneme durations resemble those of natural speech. Such information are needed in Text-to-Speech (TTS) systems. TTS is used in many areas such as information retrieval, language education, and reading machines for visually impaired. Without appropriate prosody models, synthetic speech is perceived as monotonous, boring and less intelligible.

Various methods exist for building duration models [1]-[13]. Those that combine linguistic expert knowledge with manual analysis of quite limited amount of data are generally known as *rule-based* approaches. Rule-based heuristic systems such as Klatt's duration modelling system [8] which assigns a percent increase or decrease to the inherent duration of the segment which is specified as one of its distinctive properties are case-dependent and hence, exhibit less flexibility.

State-of-the-art is dominated by *corpus-based* approaches [1]-[7][9]-[13]. They have appeared due to the increasing computational power and availability of large corpora.

Petr Sojka, Ivan Kopeček and Karel Pala (Eds.): TSD 2006, LNAI 4188, pp. 669–676, 2006.

Corpus-based (data-driven) approaches utilize large text and speech corpora to map linguistic features such as phonetic context, number of words in sentence, number of syllables in word to timing of synthetic speech. Corpus-based modelling involves machine learning techniques such as Artificial Neural Networks (ANN) [3][5][6][12], and Classification and Regression Trees (CART) [1][4][7][9][10] to reveal the relation between timing of speech and linguistic features.

In this study, a CART based method is used to map linguistic features to phoneme durations. CART is a predictive model that can be viewed as a tree. It is a popular nonparametric supervised learning method. In CART, each branch of the tree represents a choice and the leaves of the tree represent best predictions. CART provide *interpretability* so that underlying dynamics between input space and outputs can be clearly identified. They can also be applied to any data and requires less parameter tuning [14].

For phoneme duration modelling, a collection of attributes is defined such as phoneme identity, left/right context, lexical stress, part-of-speech, and etc. Relevancies of attributes affecting phoneme duration in Turkish are determined by means of statistical analysis. Using CART, durational attributes are mapped to phoneme durations. The performance of the mapping is evaluated by objective measures such as correlation coefficient (CC), mean absolute error (MAE), and root-mean squared error (RMSE). In order to increase phoneme duration prediction performance, Sequential Forward Selection (SFS) method is applied to the feature set so that optimal performance is achieved.

Focusing on the most influencing research, an overview of different approaches to duration modelling is given in the Introduction. Section 2 introduces the text and speech databases used in feature extraction and model development. Section 3 introduces attributes used for phoneme duration modelling. Phoneme duration modelling studies are presented and corresponding results are discussed in Section 4. Last section comprises final conclusions and future directions.

2   Speech Database

Speech corpora design is a fundamental issue to be handled for developing appropriate prosody, in particular, duration models. A speech database can be built randomly or by means

Table 1. SAMPA symbols of the phonemes in speech corpus and their frequencies

Phoneme	Frequency	Phoneme	Frequency	Phoneme	Frequency	Phoneme	Frequency
a	4028	gj	372	n	2522	t	1214
a:	187	h	331	N	111	tS	387
b	902	i	3031	o	1090	u	1356
c	696	1	1730	2	353	u:	61
d	1647	i:	102	o:	16	v	264
dZ	520	1:	27	2:	1	w	120
e	3114	j	1349	p	307	y	693
e:	68	k	948	r	2450	y:	10
f	171	l	1152	s	1069	z	512
g	112	5	1154	S	523	Z	91
G	470	m	1594				

of optimizing the units acoustically or with respect to their textual properties. Databases built randomly may not be adequate to provide sufficient variability of acoustical units. The text database used in the recordings was optimized to provide phonetic variability with the help of a simple greedy algorithm. Resulting speech files are annotated with respect to SAMPA [15] units first by forced alignment then by manual corrections. No allophonic variations are used for the vowels and the consonant 'r' but allophones of 'g', 'k', 'n', and 'l' are used. Long vowels are distinguished from their short counterparts. Resulting speech corpus contains 36855 phonemes. The lists of phonemes and their frequency in the speech corpus are given in Table 1. Phoneme duration distribution of the corpus approximates gamma distribution.

3 Feature Set

Various durational attributes have been used in the literature for duration modelling. Attributes used in various studies are listed in Table 2.

Features that are considered to affect phonetic duration in Turkish are determined and extracted from both speech and text corpus. Each phone in the database is assigned a feature vector describing the phone and the values of its attributes. The attributes and their values used in this study can be divided into two groups as categorical and numerical.

Categorical Features

- *Identity*: The phonetic description of current, preceding and following phonemes. Each phoneme can take one of 42 SAMPA symbols and each preceding/following phoneme can be either one of 42 SAMPA or *silence*.
- *Lexical Stress*: There exist two levels for lexical stress: Accented (A) or Not-Accented (NA). A segment is associated with an A if the vowel of the parent syllable is stressed and an NA otherwise.
- *Position in Syllable*: A three level representation is used to code phoneme position in syllable: Nucleus (N), Onset (O) and Coda (C).
- *Syllable Type*: Two levels are used to denote parent syllable types: Heavy (H) and Light (L).
- *Part-of-Speech*: Each phoneme in the database is annotated with the major POS tag of the parent word such as NOUN, PRONoun, VERB, QUEStion, INFinitive, POSTPronoun, CONJunction, ADVerb, ADJective, CompoundNOUN, or EXClamation. These tags are obtained through a morphological analysis procedure.
- *Phrase Break Information*: Speech corpus has been evaluated perceptually several times and major perceptual breaks in the utterances are marked manually. The marks mainly correspond to the speaker's breath takings. The feature is represented by three levels: Segment takes a Phrase Initial (PI) value if it immediately follows a phrase break, a Phrase medial (PM) value if there is no phrase break engagement and a Phrase Final (PF) if a phrase break immediately follows the segment.

Numerical Features

- *Syllable Position in Word*: Syllables of the same word are counted from the left starting from 1. The database contains words of at most 10 syllables; however, there is no words that contain 9 syllables.

Table 2. Features used in several studies

Languages	Attributes	Segments
Czech [1]	current/previous/next-phone-identities, syllable/word/phrase-lengths-in-phones,phone-position-in-syllables-from-beginning/end, phone-position-in-word-from-beginning/end and word-position-in-phrase	Phoneme
English [2]	number-of-phones-in-the-syllable, nature-of-syllabic-peak, position-in-tone-group, type-of-foot,stress and word-class	Syllable
Spanish [5][6]	phone-identity, contextual-phones, stress, stress-in-the-syllable, syllable-beginning-with-vocal, diphthong,phone-in-a-function-word, phrase-type, position in phrase and number-of-units-in-the phrase	Phoneme
Catalan [7]	vowel-identity, stress, sentence-position, post-vocalic-phone-class and manner-of-articulation	Phoneme
Hindu and Telugu [9]	segment-identity, segment-features,previous/next-segment-features, parent-syllable-structure,position-in-parent-syllable,parent-syllable-initial/final,parent-syllable-position-type,number-of-syllables-in-parent-word, position-of-parent-syllable,parent-syllable-break-information, phrase-length-in-number-of-words,position-of-phrase-in-utterance, and number-of-phrases-in-utterance	Phoneme
German [11]	segment-identity, segment-type, word-class, position-of-phrase-in-utterance,phrase-length-in-number-of-words,position-of-word-in-phrase, word-length-in-number-of-syllables,position-of-syllable-in-word,stress, segment-position-in-syllable, segmental-context,segmental-context-type	Phoneme
Japanese [13]	current/preceding/following-phone-identities,left/right-prosodic-context, accent-status, syllable-structure and special-morpheme-status	Vowel

- *Word/Syllable Position in Sentence*: Words/Syllables are counted from left starting from 1. The longest sentence contains 19 words and 45 syllables. All phonemes of the parent word take the same value.
- *Word Length*: Each phoneme of the same word is annotated with the total number of syllables in that word. The attribute values are numeric and ranges from 1 to 10.
- *Total number of Words (Syllables) in Sentence (Word)*: Each phoneme of a sentence is represented by the total number of words (syllables) in the sentence (word). The value of the feature changes in between 3 and 19.
- *Number of Words from (to) the Preceding (Following) Phrase Break*: The attributes identify the number of words between the parent word and the preceding (following) phrase break counting from 0.
- *Number of Syllables from (to) the Preceding (Following) Phrase Break*: This attribute is almost the same as the number of words from the preceding phrase break attribute counting from 0.

4   Phoneme Duration Modelling and Sequential Forward Selection

Experiments for developing duration models are performed with the REPTree algorithm of WEKA [14]. Vowel and consonant durations are predicted at the same time. Prediction performance of each experiment is evaluated using MAE, RMSE, and CC.

The speech database is split into two subsets: training dataset is used to develop duration models and test dataset is used to evaluate the performance of the model on unseen data. The test set consists approximately 20% of the database and the remaining phonemes constitute the training set. The total number of instances in the training and test sets are 29527 and 7328, respectively.

Each attribute described in Section 3 is evaluated by means of tree building method to observe the individual affects on phoneme duration. *Phoneme Identity* is considered to be the discriminating attribute; hence corresponding results are used as a reference (baseline) for the rest of the experiments. Individual performances of the attributes in terms of CC, MAE and RMSE are given in Table 3. As illustrated in the table, *Phoneme Identity* (1) is the best predictor of all attributes. *Preceding/Following Phoneme Identities* (2-3) turn out to be the second best predictors. However, such kind of an evaluation does not give an idea about the relative relevance of the attributes when all combinations are considered.

Table 3. Individual prediction performances of attributes. Results are given in increasing RMSE order.

Index	Attribute	CC	MAE (ms)	RMSE (ms)
1	Phoneme Identity	0.5958	18.2003	25.7872
2-3	Preceding/Following Phoneme Identities	0.53	20.8325	27.1914
5	Position in Syllable	0.3106	23.3704	30.5724
12	Phrase Break Information	0.2641	24.3414	30.9329
17	Number of Syllables to Fol. Phrase Break	0.2443	24.5178	31.0977
6	Syllable Type	0.1473	24.4769	31.7265
14	Number of Words to the Fol. Phrase Break	0.1381	24.8184	31.7601
10	Total Number of Syllables in Word	0.1212	24.5606	31.8327
7	Syllable Position in Word	0.1218	24.4285	31.8344
9	POS	0.0873	24.7954	31.9577
16	Number of Syllables from the Prev. Phrase Break	0.0713	24.6631	31.9872
8	Word Position in Sentence	0.0539	24.7744	32.0196
15	Syllable Position in Sentence	0.0386	24.7759	32.0445
13	Number of Words from the Prev. Phrase Break	0.0234	24.7784	32.0597
4	Lexical Stress	0.0193	24.7751	32.0604
11	Total Number of Words in Sentence	0	24.7806	32.0658

In order to evaluate relative importance of each attribute, models using all possible attribute combinations are to be developed. For a set of N attributes the total number of combinations is $2^N - 1$. Discarding *Phoneme Identity*, since it is the discriminating attribute, and considering *Preceding/Following Phoneme Identities* as a single attribute, the number of independent variables to predict phoneme duration turns out to be 15. Therefore, $2^{15} - 1 = 32767$ experiments have to be performed to uncover the relation between the phoneme durations and the chosen attributes which is too much time consuming. Therefore, the best attribute set is determined by means of SFS method. SFS can be viewed as a greedy procedure which starts with an empty or pre-selected set of attributes and adds more attributes as the resulting learning algorithm's performance is improved. Model performances obtained at each step of SFS are given in Table 4.

674   Ö. Öztürk and T. Çiloğlu

Table 4. Prediction error performances obtained with SFS

SFS Level	Attributes	CC	MAE (ms)	RMSE (ms)
1	1	0.5958	18.2003	25.7872
3	1, 2-3	0.7576	15.1605	20.9321
4	1, 2-3, 6	0.7706	14.7089	20.44
5	1, 2-3, 6, 12	0.7744	14.6039	20.2937
6	1, 2-3, 6, 9, 12	0.7772	14.5887	20.184
7	1, 2-3, 4, 6, 9, 12	0.7798	14.5613	20.0792
8	1, 2-3, 4, 6, 9, 12, 14	0.7806	14.5574	20.0456
9	1, 2-3, 4, 6, 9, 12, 14, 7	0.7807	14.5607	20.0478
17	All	0.7718	14.6678	20.4236

Table 4 shows that considering a set of eight attributes provides better performance measures than a set containing nine elements. Hence, attribute selection is ended at that point and the optimum predictor set is composed of *Phoneme Identity*, *Preceding/Following Phonemes Identities*, *Lexical Stress*, *Syllable Type*, *POS*, *Phrase Break Information*, and *Number of Words to the Following Phrase Break*. It should also be noted that when all attribute set is considered, resultant performances are worse than those obtained by using optimum attribute set.

5   Concluding Remarks and Future Directions

Within the scope of this study, phoneme duration modelling in Turkish is performed. To this aim, attributes that may affect phoneme duration in Turkish are defined and extracted from the developed speech and text corpora. Model development is performed using tree building by means of a self-learning algorithm. Learning algorithm is run on the training set and its performance is evaluated on test dataset, hence resulting performances can be regarded as the models real performance on unseen data. SFS method is applied to find an optimal set of attributes to build a regression tree. Resulting model performance is comparable to those reported in literature. Some of the reported performances are listed in Table 5.

Table 5. CART modelling performances reported in literature

Language	CC	RMSE (ms)
Czech [1]	0.79	20.3
Korean [4]	0.73	26
Hindu [9]	0.7526	27.14
Telugu [9]	0.8014	22.86
Korean [10]	0.847	20.45

According to our observations on tree-based modelling of phoneme durations in Turkish, neighboring phonemes turn out to be the most influential attributes on phoneme duration. Regarding this fact, it is aimed to develop an appropriate speech corpus to provide sufficient representatives of triphones and a restricted number of pentaphones to predict phoneme durations. Although development of such a corpus is a heavy burden, resulting system will not require learning algorithms but rather simple statistics such as mean value.

Another point of concern is that one of the main causes of prediction error is the inevitable inconsistency in the segmentation of phonemes. Consequently, although it is known to be a difficult task, research on devising objective consistency measures in phoneme (or some other suitable unit) segmentation is considered to be an essential future work.

Acknowledgements

We are grateful to Eren Akdemir, Turgay Koç, and Yücel Özbek for their support in segmenting the speech corpus. This study is supported by METU Research foundation (BAP-2005-03-01-06).

References

1. Batůšek, R., (2002), *A Duration Model for Czech Text-to-Speech Synthesis*, in Proceedings of Speech Prosody 2002, Aix-en-Provence, France, pp. 167–170.
2. Campbell, N., (2000), *Timing in Speech: A Multi-Level Process*, in M. Horne (ed), Prosody: Theory and Experiment, Kluwer Academic Publishers, Dordrecht, pp. 281–335.
3. Chen, S. H., Hwang, S. H., Wang, Y. R., (1996), *A Mandarin Text-to-Speech System*, in Computational Linguistics and Chinese Language Processing, Computational Linguistic Society of R. O. C., vol. 1, no. 1, pp. 87–100.
4. Chung, H., (2002), *Duration models and the perceptual evaluation of spoken Korean*, in Proceedings of Speech Prosody, Aix-en-Provence, France, pp. 219–222.
5. Cordoba, R., Vallejo, J. A., Montero, J. M., Gutierrez-Arriola, J., Lopez, M. A., Pardo, J. M., (1999), *Automatic Modeling of Duration in Spanish Text-to-Speech System Using Neural Networks*, in Proceedings of EUROSPEECH, Budapest, Hungary, pp. 1619–1622.
6. Cordoba, R., Montero, J. M., Gutierrez-Arriola, J, Vallejo, J. A., Enriquez, E., Pardo, J. M., (2002), *Selection of the Most Significant Parameters for Duration Modeling in a Spanish Text-to-Speech System Using Neural Networks*, Computer Speech and Language, Elsevier Ltd., Vol. 16, pp. 183–203.
7. Febrer, A., Padrell, J., and Bonafonte, A., (1998), *Modeling Phone Duration: Application to Catalan TTS*, in Proceedings of 3rd ESCA/COCOSDA Workshop on Speech Synthesis, NSW, Australia, pp. 43–46.
8. Klatt H. D., (1987), *Review of Text-to-Speech Conversion for English*, in Journal of the Acoustical Society of America, vol. 82, pp. 737–793.
9. Krishna, N. S., Murthy, H. A., (2004), *Duration Modeling of Indian Languages Hindi and Telugu*, in Proceedings of 5th ISCA ITRW on Speech Synthesis, Pittsburgh, USA, pp. 197–202.
10. Lee, S. and Oh, Y. W., (1999a), *Tree-Based Modeling of Prosodic Phrasing and Segmental Duration for Korean TTS Systems*, in Speech Communication, Elsevier Ltd., Vol. 28, pp. 283–300.
11. Möbius, B. and van Santen, J. P. H., (1996), *Modeling Segmental Duration in German Text-to-Speech Synthesis*, in Proceedings of International Conference on Spoken Language Processing, Philadelphia, USA, Vol. 4, pp. 2395–2398.
12. Sreenivasa, K. R., Yegnanarayana, B., (2004), *Modeling Syllable Duration in Indian Languages Using Neural Networks*, in Proceedings of International Conference on Acoustics, Speech and Signal Processing, Quebec, Canada, pp. 313–316.

13. Venditti, J. J., van Santen, J. P. H., (1998), *Modeling Vowel Duration for Japanese Text-to-Speech Synthesis*, in Proceedings of the International Conference on Spoken Language Processing, Sydney, Australia, paper 0786.
14. Witten, H. I. and Frank, E., (1999), *Data Mining: Practical Machine Learning Tools and Techniques with Java Implementations*, Morgan Kauffman Publishing.
15. Wells, J. C., *SAMPA for Turkish*, http://www.phon.ucl.ac.uk/home/sampa/turkish.htm, Last accessed: October 2005.

A Pattern-Based Methodology
for Multimodal Interaction Design

Andreas Ratzka and Christian Wolff

Institute for Media, Information and Cultural Studies, University of Regensburg, D-93040
Regensburg, Germany
`{Andreas.Ratzka, Christian.Wolff}@sprachlit.uni-regensburg.de`

Abstract. This paper describes a design methodology for multimodal interactive
systems. The method suggested is meant to serve as a foundation for the application
of robust software engineering techniques in the field of multimodal systems. Starting
from a short review of current design approaches we present a high level view of the
design process for multimodal systems, highlighting design issues related to context of
use factors. Our proposal is discussed in the context of a multimodal organizer which
serves as our showcase application. The design of multimodal systems brings together
a broad variety of analysis methods (task, context, data, user). The combination of
modalities as well as the different interaction devices imply a high degree of freedom
as far as design decisions are concerned. Therefore, a (simple) unification of existing
approaches towards interface design like GOMS (task analysis) or Buergy's interaction
constraint model for context analysis is not sufficient. We employ the design pattern
approach as a means of guiding the analysis and design process. Design patterns are
discussed as a general modeling tool as well as a possible approach towards designing
multimodal systems.

1 Introduction

Current literature on multimodal interaction describes the potential of multimodality in
terms of increased adaptability, robustness and efficiency [21]. Grasso et al. point out the
potential of combining the advantages of direct manipulation and speech interaction [14].
However, this potential can only be exploited if the design follows basic principles of software
ergonomics such as those of ISO 9241-10. Given the high complexity of flexible multimodal
interactive systems, the designer needs more than ever support to achieve these, partially
conflicting, goals while preserving the maintainability of the project.

There are some well-known approaches towards modeling and prototyping multimodal
systems such as RDPM [10,23], focusing on task specification, rapid prototyping and Wizard-
of-Oz-testing. Unfortunately, they rely on a hard-coded mapping between task and concrete
interaction. Furthermore, they usually disregard modality specific aspects as well as context
of use modeling.

At the same time theoretical frameworks, such as modality theory [3,4], TYCOON [19],
CARE [11] and others [20,31] constitute a solid basis for multimodal system design, but
ignore context of use modeling and issues of rapid application design. An exception are [5]
and [6] which present a collection of modality claims. These claims are built into a decision
support system which gives advice on the use of speech in multimodal or unimodal interactive

Petr Sojka, Ivan Kopeček and Karel Pala (Eds.): TSD 2006, LNAI 4188, pp. 677–686, 2006.

systems. However this work has been restricted to speech due to the high complexity of the domain.

Other approaches, such as the Interaction Constraints Model [8] provide frameworks for comprehensive context of use analysis, but skip detailed design issues of multimodal interaction. The Unifying Reference Framework [9] describes common properties of model-based design methodologies, but none of the approaches analysed in that work addresses multimodality.

Our method attempts to overcome this shortcoming and addresses the design of context adequate multimodal interaction styles. The resulting framework may serve as a foundation for the application of robust software engineering techniques in the field of multimodal systems.

In Section 2 we present multimodal design issues derived from context of use factors and discuss reasonable modality combinations and modality allocation for data output. Section 3 presents current approaches towards multimodal design for a showcase prototype of a multimodal organizer, followed by a suggestion for a high level view of a comprehensive design approach for multimodal systems. In Section 4 we discuss the potential role of design patterns [1,7,32] for the multimodal design process in more detail, presenting some examples for pattern candidates. Finally, Section 5 discusses open questions and directions for further research, which will lead to elaborating software engineering methods for multimiodal interfaces.

2 Multimodal Design Issues

Multimodal interaction provides a greater spectrum of design choices than traditional interaction styles. This requires more sophisticated recognition technologies as well as methods for data fusion. Fusion means that input via different modalities (such as speech and pen gestures) is interpreted in combination. Furthermore, fusion allows for so called mutual disambiguation, that is, in case of recognition ambiguity, incompatible hypotheses can be rejected more easily.[1]

At the same time, the developper of a multimodal application is confronted with greater modelling challenges. He has to design input grammars that consider not only the variety of possible user utterances but also the combination of different input modalities.

When designing system output, the developper has to keep in mind the context of use of the application (e.g. automotive, desktop or mobile) and the underlying user activities which determine whether the user's visual or auditory perception channels are available to interaction with the system. Mobile applications which can be used in different situations should provide freedom of choice between several interaction styles.

Our work focuses on the combination of WIMP-[2] and speech-based interaction. The interaction space typically includes keyboard input, pointing (or haptic) input, speech input, graphical output and speech output.

In some cases, traditional interaction such as speech based dialogue (speech input and speech output) or WIMP (keyboard and pointing input and graphical output) styles might

---

[1] A comprehensive overview about multimodal interactive systems can be found in [2] and [21].

[2] *Window, icon, menu, pointing device.*

be most appropriate. WIMP-interaction on the one side can be enhanced with speech input, speech output, or both. Speech interaction on the other side can be enhanced with keyboard input, graphical output, or pointing input combined with graphical output.

Multimodality requires the presence of two modalities at either input or output or both sides, e.g.

- speech and pointing input combined with graphical feedback,
- speech input combined with graphical and speech feedback,
- pointing input combined with graphical and speech feedback, or even
- speech and pointing input combined with graphical and speech feedback.

Modality combinations should fulfill certain requirements in order to be a reasonable design choice (view [21], [25]):

- They provide increased speed, robustness and/or flexibility in man machine interaction.
- They allow man machine interaction in situations where ordinary interaction styles fail.
- They don't contradict human communication abilities.

Reeves et al. [25] warn against inappropriate design solutions for multimodal systems which would lead to confusion and increased cognitive load.

In general, design options for input and output modalities have become more diverse recently as multimodal systems move away from the traditional office application / desktop PC setting, including more diverse devices (PCs, PDAs, mobile phones, interactive systems in cars etc.).

In terms of data input the user can (or must) decide which modality to use. On the contrary, when it comes to data output, the system has to select the most appropriate channel. Multimodal interactive systems can output data via sound (e.g. speech) or graphically, while other modalities like haptic output play a minor role and are typically reserved for simple (but potentially critical) notification functions.[3] The optimal configuration depends on the context of use: whether the output of sound is disturbing, whether the user can be expected to look at the standard display is largely determined by task, user preferences, and environmental factors.

In some cases, the aspects influencing modality choice can be derived from the task specification or device configuration: For a car navigation system or an organizer plugged into a car's handsfree set, speech interaction or head-up displaying techniques fit best. In other cases, user behavior can give hints on the appropriateness of interaction channels: If the user is talking to the system, it can be inferred that speech interaction is not discouraged by the situation. If the user performs pointing actions, it can be concluded that he is currently looking at the display. Furthermore, gaze-trackers and sensors detecting lighting and noise level can be employed to retrieve situative aspects.

Finally it is desirable that the user himself can configure the interaction style, selecting detailed, terse or no speech output at all. This imposes some metacommunicative complexity, as these configuration options have to be self descriptive.

---

[3] Example: Vibrating steering wheels in driver assistance systems in cars.

3   Methodological Support for Multimodal Design

Before discussing our suggestion for a comprehensive approach towards a multimodal design methodology, we will briefly sketch our prototyping domain and discuss a short task analysis for this type of application.

3.1   Experimental Setting

We have chosen the scenario of a multimodal organizer as it comprises sufficiently complex task and context of use aspects. Multimodal organizers typically include applications like email, voicemail, date definition, addressbook lookup routines etc. System output encompasses the display of date and message lists, contact lists, message texts, or calendar entries. User input may consist of the selection of list items, input of names, texts, dates or the specification of search criteria and list filters. System output may be motivated by immediately preceding user input, but this is not the case when the system notifies the user about incoming e-mails or forthcoming events.

Traditionally, the central design step for interactive systems starts with a detailed task analysis. This may be done at different levels of abstraction – from keystroke level analysis and process algebraic notations such as CTT, MDL, HTA, TKS or UAN to high level use case modeling as employed in UML-based software engineering methods (cf. [12,22]). In the following we give some informal examples of typical tasks in our setting at an intermediate level of detail.

1. **Get New Messages** – The system displays a list or a feature table of messages (emails, voicemails, dates etc.). The user may select an item in order to retrieve the content, detailed information or in order to trigger further processing (forwarding, replying etc.). In case of lengthy tables, the user may sort the list or provide filter or search criteria in order to restrict the list size.
2. **Create New Message** – The user has to provide receivers (To:, Cc: and Bcc:) and probably date and site information (in the case of a dating message) and the message text. The newly created message can be independent or based on a previously received message (reply or forward). Furthermore, the message can contain additional data or attachments.
3. **Message Filtering and Notification** – The user can specify filtering and notification options if he wants to be notified about email messages from certain persons or mailing lists or if he wants to filter them out. When notification is activated the user wants to get informed about incoming messages and forthcoming events.

3.2   A High-Level Design Process for Multimodal Systems

While many models and methods have been suggested for the design of interactive systems (cf. [27,29], or [33], to name just a few), there is no accepted reference model for the design of multimodal systems. As discussed in Section 2, the higher degrees of freedom in designing multimodal systems lead to a more complex design process. We suggest the model shown in Figure 1 as a first and necessarily rather high-level approach. It encompasses the following design steps:

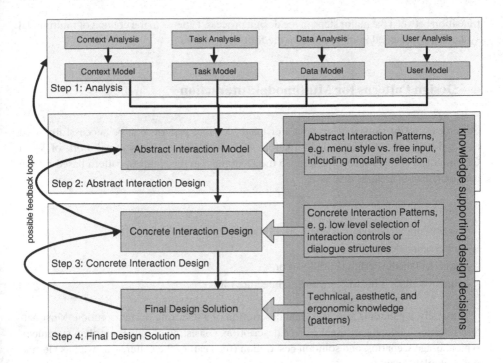

Fig. 1. High-level Design Process for Multimodal Systems

- Analysis: Context, Tasks, Data, and the User are introduced as the basic dimensions for analysis; well known methods taken from software engineering as well as interaction design research can be used in this step (e. g. task analysis methods or data modeling tools like UML[4]).
- Abstract Interaction Design: The model parameters resulting from step one serve as input for an abstract interaction design, including decisions on choice of modality, basic dialogue structures, and display layout issues.
- Concrete Interaction Design: The abstract design model is mapped to a concrete interaction model which means that actual interaction elements are selected, dialogue structures are instantiated and a fine-grained layout is worked out.
- Final Design Solution: The last transformation step involves checking available design guidelines as well as decisions on aesthetic and stylistic aspects (e. g. speaker characteristics for speech synthesis or the selection of a visual skin compatible with the application context and users).

The model has two major functions: First, it allows for an integration of existing analysis and design approaches, as many single steps in the model touch well-known issues in software engineering. Second, the basic structure of the model is meant to make explicit where design patterns containing decision-relevant knowledge can be used for easing the

---

[4] *Unified Modeling Language.*

transition between the major steps in the design process. Patterns in the context of multimodal systems are discussed in more detail in the following chapter.

4   Design Patterns for Multimodal Interaction

Starting from Christopher Alexander's original idea that patterns can be successfully used as a guidance in complex design situations [1], and based on the seminal work of Ward Cunningham who introduced patterns in the IT domain in the eighties, pattern based-design has flourished in areas as diverse as

- architecture [1],
- object-oriented modeling (the work of the "Gang of Four", cf. [13]),
- interaction design [7],
- web and media design ([32], [34]) or
- the overall IT infrastructure and architecture [30].

Basically, a pattern is a semi-formal description of a recurring design solution. Most pattern libraries follow the original pattern description, consisting of name, problem statement, typical usage scenarios, and solution description (the heart of the pattern), as well as alternative and related patterns.

The very idea of a pattern as an experience-driven knowledge structure suggests that patterns be based on well established design decisions and experiences. Regarding the lack of experience in multimodal interaction design, this can hardly be accomplished, as there is no comprehensive body of (successful) multimodal applications yet from which patterns might be derived. On the other hand, patterns for interaction design have been successfully introduced at a time when the same situation was prevalent. We further believe that the semi-formal structure of patterns makes them a promising tool for modeling novel application types like multimodal systems. We have started work on a pattern collection for multimodal interaction which is unfinished yet and requires further validation. However, it is a good starting point capable of generating more detailed requirements for a comprehensive design methodology.

Looking at existing pattern libraries like the one presented by [32] for Web Design, it is obvious that for each application domain major criteria for classifying patterns are necessary (e. g. pattern granularity). We suggest that patterns for multimodal design be classified according

- to the design step in which they can be applied (see fig. 1),
- to their pattern granularity (a "coarse" pattern may describe global dialogue structures, whereas a fine-grained pattern might describe properties of a specific control or data presentation mode in a single dialogue step), and
- to the interaction direction (input / output patterns).

In the following, we present some examples for multimodal design patterns.

4.1 Modality Hint (Abstract Interaction Design)

Problem The user is interacting via speech, but system output might be easier represented via graphical output. The system does not know whether the user is able to perceive graphical output or not.

Use when The user has been using speech, indicating that the situation does not discourage sound-based interaction. The system can derive visual attention neither from task nor from device configuration nor from interaction history.

Solution The system gives a spoken hint like: "look at the display or say: read me the list". The user can select the output modality via speech or a graphical input element displayed at a consistent position of the screen.

4.2 Patterns for Notification Output (Abstract Interaction Design)

Alert

Problem An important event occurs, but the user's attention is not directed towards (standard) system output.

Use when You are developing an application which involves user notification about important events. The user should get informed without delay. A disruption of the user in his primary tasks has no severe implications.

Solution Use ambient modalities in order to notify the user. When the user's direction of gaze or hand position can be anticipated because of the primary task, visual and haptic notification techniques might be appropriate as well.

Non-disruptive Notification

Problem An event occurs, but the user's attention has to be directed to an important, potentially safety critical activity. The user wants to decide himself when to retrieve new information.

Use when You are developing an application which involves user notification about events. The application scenario (either the task or the situation) involves safety critical activities or requires high concentration.

Solution Use output modalities of high spatial selectivity, such as graphics or (for blind users) haptics. The information should be displayed at a consistent place. If there might be a lot of information to be notified about, the user should be given a standardised command for retrieving it. The presence of new information should be indicated at a consistent place on the display.

4.3 Design Patterns for Data Input (Concrete Interaction Design)

Multimodal Menu

Problem Speech menus allow, just as graphical menus, the selection of interaction options. A broad and flat structure is typically recommended for graphical menus [26, p. 249] [16,17]. In speech menus, such a structure results in lengthy prompts, slowing down interaction. Speech interaction hence demands narrower and deeper menus.

Use when The user should get the opportunity to select an alternative.

Solution In multimodal interaction situations the user can be presented a menu visually and perform selections via speech. The visual part of the menu should remain broad and flat. The items at one menu level should be split up into groups that can be given self-explaining names. The speech feedback uses these names in order to introduce additional levels into the speech-based menu which is narrowed (but deepened) that way. The speech menu items are played back only if the user himself is currently using speech.

Multimodal Form. Forms are, besides menus, the second basic interaction style prominent both in WIMP and in speech applications. The user can enter data into different slots, so called form items.

Problem When the user interacts solely via speech, detailed speech prompting is necessary. When the user interacts via pointing and typing or pointing and speaking speech prompting might be inappropriate.

Use when The user has to fill-in data slots in order to get the task done.

Solution When the user selects a form item via speech, the system uses speech to prompt for further input. At the same time, the graphical menu item is selected. When a pointing device has been used for selection, speech prompts are avoided. Whenever the speech recogniser fails to understand the user input, this problem has to be reported via speech. If recognition has occured with low confidence or the recognition result is ambiguous, verification and disambiguation should be performed multimodally, via speech and popup-dialogues, giving the user the opportunity to switch to a more robust modality for error correction.

5   Conclusion and Future Work

We have identified a basic methodology for multimodal system design and defined a starting set of design patterns based on the task analysis of a multimodal organizer. Future work will extend the pattern collection and result in design support for application developers. Additional criteria for pattern classification and generation have to be identified. We have already analysed literature on modality theory [3,4,5,6,31] and context of use analysis [8,9], both presented in [24]. We are going to investigate how the pragmatics of dialogue moves or interaction moves [18] can help in deciding modality allocation and thus be a basis for further design patterns.

Beyond a pattern collection, this will include notational support, helping the designer to work efficiently due to reusable components. In this context we have to verify whether a statechart-based approach, like the one for GUI-design presented by [15], could be applied to multimodal interaction design as well.

References

1. Alexander, C., Ishikawa, S., Silverstein, M., Jacobson, M., Fiksdahl-King, I., Angel, S.: A Pattern Language. Oxford University Press (1977).
2. Benoît et al. Audio-visual and Multimodal Speech Systems. Audio-visual and Multimodal Speech Systems. Handbook of Standards and Resources for Spoken Language Systems – Supplement Volume (2000).

3. Bernsen, N. O.: Modality Theory: Supporting Multimodal Interface Design. Proc. ERCIM (1993).
4. Bernsen, N. O.: A toolbox of output modalities. Representing output information in multimodal interfaces. WPCS-95-10. Centre for Cognitive Science, Roskilde University (1995).
5. Bernsen, N. O.: Towards a tool for predicting speech functionality. In: Speech Communication 23, (1997) 181–210.
6. Bernsen, N. O.: Multimodality in language and speech systems – from theory to design support tool. In: Granström, B., House, D., and Karlsson, I. (Eds.): Multimodality in Language and Speech Systems. Dordrecht: Kluwer Academic Publishers (2002) 93–148.
7. Borchers, J. O.: A Pattern Approach to Interaction Design. AI & Society Journal of Human-Centred Systems and Machine Intelligence 15, 4, Springer (2001) 359–376.
8. Bürgy, C.: An Interaction Constraints Model for Mobile and Wearable Computer-Aided Engineering Systems in Industrial Applications. Doctoral Dissertation, University of Pittsburgh, Pennsylvania, USA (2002).
9. Calvary, G., Coutaz, J., Thevenin, D., Limbourg, Q., Bouillon, L., Vanderdonckt, J.: A unifying reference framework for multi-target user interfaces. Interacting with Computers 15, 3 (2003) 289–308.
10. Cenek, P., Melichar, M., Rajman, M.: A Framework for Rapid Multimodal Application Design. Proc. of TSD'05 Karlovy Vary, Czech Republic, Springer (2005) 393–403.
11. Coutaz, J., Nigay, L., Salber, D., Blandford, A., May, J., Young, R. M.: Four Easy Pieces for Assessing the Usability of Multimodal Interaction: The CARE Properties. Proc. Interact'95, Chapman & Hall, London (1995) 115–120.
12. Dittmar, A.: More Precise Descriptions of Temporal Relations within Task Models. In: P. Palanque and F. Paternò (Eds.): DSV-IS 2000, LNCS 1946, Springer (2001) 151–168.
13. Gamma, E., Helm, R., Johnson, R., Vlissides, J. Design Patterns: Elements of Reusable Object-Oriented Software. Addison-Wesley (1995).
14. Grasso, M. A., Ebert, D. S., and Finin, T. W.: The integrality of speech in multimodal interfaces. ACM Trans. Comput.-Hum. Interact. 5, 4 (1998) 303–325.
15. Horrocks, I.: Constructing the User Interface with Statecharts. Addison-Wesley (1999).
16. Kiger, J. I.: The depth/breadth trade-off in the design of menu-driven user interfaces. International Journal of Man-Machine Studies, 20 (1984) 201–213.
17. Landauer, T. K., and Nachbar, D. W.: Selection from alphabetic and numeric menu trees using a touch screen: Breath, depth, and width. Proc. CHI'85, Human Factors in Computing Systems, ACM, New York (1985), 73–78.
18. Larsson, S.: Using a type hierarchy to characterize reliability of coding schemas for dialogue moves. Gothenburg Papers in Computational Linguistics (1998).
19. Martin, J.-C.: Towards "intelligent" cooperation between modalities. The example of a system enabling multimodal interaction with a map. Proc. IJCAI-97 Workshop on Intelligent Multimodal Systems, Nagoya, Japan (1997).
20. Nigay, L., Coutaz, J.: A Design Space For Multimodal Systems: Concurrent Processing and Date Fusion. Proc. INTERCHI'93, ACM Press, NY, USA (1993).
21. Oviatt, S., Cohen, Ph., Wu, L., Vergo, J., Duncan, L., Suhm, B., Bers, J., Holzman, T., Winograd, T., Landay, J., Larson, J., Ferro, D.: Designing the User Interface for Multimodal Speech and Pen-based Gesture Applications: State-of-the-Art Systems and Future Research Directions. In: *Human Computer Interaction* 15(4), (2000) 263–322.
22. Pribeanu, C., Limbourg, Q., Vanderdonckt, J.: Task Modelling for Context-Sensitive User Interfaces. In: C. Johnson (Ed.): DSV-IS'01, LNCS 2220, Springer (2001) 49–68.
23. Rajman, M., Bui, T.H., Rajman, A., Seydoux, F., Trutnev, A., Qurteroni, S.: Assessing the usability of a dialogue management system designed in the framework of a rapid dialogue prototyping methodology. Acta Acustica united with Acustica, the journal of the European Acoustics Association (EAA) 90 (2004) 1096–1111.

24. Ratzka, A.: Combining Modality Theory and Context Models. To appear in: Proc. PIT 2006, Springer (2006).
25. Reeves, L. M., Lai, J., Larson, J.A., Oviatt, S., Balaji, T.S., Buisine, S., Collings, P., Cohen, P., Kraal, B., Martin, J.-C., McTear, M., Raman, T., Stanney, K.M., Su, H., Wang Q.Y.: Guidelines for multimodal user interface design. In: Communications ACM 47(1), (2004) 57–59.
26. Shneiderman, B.: Designing the User Interface: Strategies for Effective Human-Computer Interaction. Reading, Mass.: Addison-Wesley (1997).
27. da Silva, P. P.: User Interface Declarative Models and Development Environments: A Survey. In: P. Palanque and F. Paternò (Eds.): DSV-IS'00, LNCS 1946, Springer (2001), 207–226.
28. Souchon, N., Limbourg, Q., and Vanderdonckt, J.: Task Modelling in Multiple Contexts of Use. In: P. Forbrig et al.(Eds.): DSV-IS'02, LNCS 2545, Springer (2002) 59–73.
29. Trætteberg H.: Model-based User Interface Design. Ph.D. Thesis, Department of Computer and Information Science, Norwegian University of Science and Technology (2002).
30. Trowbridge, D., Cunningham, W. et al. Describing the Enterprise Architectural Space. Microsoft Corporation, June 2004.
31. Vernier, F., Nigay, L.: A Framework for the Combination and Characterization of Output Modalities. DSV-IS '00, Springer (2000) 35–50.
32. Van Welie, M., and van der Weer, G. C.: Pattern Languages in Interaction Design: Structure and Organization. Proc. Interact '03 (2003).
33. Wilson, S., Johnson P., Kelly, C., Cunningham, J., and Markopoulos P.: Beyond Hacking: a Model Based Approach to User Interface Design. Proc. HCI'93 (1993).
34. Wolff, Ch.: Media Design Patterns. In: Eibl, M., Womser-Hacker, Ch. & Wolff, Ch. (Eds.). Designing Information Systems. Constance: UVK (2005) 209–217.

A Pattern Learning Approach to Question Answering Within the Ephyra Framework

Nico Schlaefer[1], Petra Gieselmann[1], Thomas Schaaf[2], and Alex Waibel[1,2]

[1] Interactive Systems Labs, ITI, Universität Karlsruhe
Am Fasanengarten 5, 76131 Karlsruhe, Germany
{nico, petra}@ira.uka.de
[2] Interactive Systems Labs, Carnegie Mellon University
407 S. Craig Street, Pittsburgh, PA 15213
{tschaaf, waibel}@cs.cmu.edu

Abstract. This paper describes the Ephyra question answering engine, a modular and extensible framework that allows to integrate multiple approaches to question answering in one system. Our framework can be adapted to languages other than English by replacing language-specific components. It supports the two major approaches to question answering, knowledge annotation and knowledge mining. Ephyra uses the web as a data resource, but could also work with smaller corpora. In addition, we propose a novel approach to question interpretation which abstracts from the original formulation of the question. Text patterns are used to interpret a question and to extract answers from text snippets. Our system automatically learns the patterns for answer extraction, using question-answer pairs as training data. Experimental results revealed the potential of this approach.

1 Introduction

Question answering is a form of information retrieval that deals with natural language questions. The main goal is to retrieve explicit answers to questions rather than whole documents. This task has already been addressed by various systems following both linguistic and statistical approaches and has been intensively investigated in the Text REtrieval Conference (TREC) [1].

In this paper, we describe the Ephyra framework for open-domain question answering which allows to efficiently implement and combine new techniques for question analysis and answer extraction. Ephyra can easily be integrated in different NLP applications, such as dialog management, and it can be adapted to other languages. As part of this framework, we developed a pattern matching approach. Ephyra automatically learns text patterns that can be applied to text passages for answer extraction. The system is trained on question-answer pairs and uses conventional web search engines to fetch text snippets suitable for pattern extraction. A second set of patterns is used to interpret questions. The interpretation of a question abstracts from its original formulation but yet preserves its semantics. The pattern matching approach has a high precision but a relatively low recall. Therefore, we combined it with a number of backup techniques for query formation and answer selection that are used when this approach fails. Since the focus of this paper is on the pattern matching approach, we do not discuss the backup techniques in detail.

Petr Sojka, Ivan Kopeček and Karel Pala (Eds.): TSD 2006, LNAI 4188, pp. 687–694, 2006.

Section 2 gives an overview of related work on question answering and pattern learning. In Section 3, we introduce the Ephyra framework. Section 4 is about our pattern matching approach. Section 5 gives experimental details and results of the pattern matching approach combined with backup techniques. Section 6 is a conclusion and an outlook on future work.

2   Related Work

Many of today's question answering systems, such as AnswerBus [2] or AskMSR [3], use a common architecture that comprises the following three modules: query formation, search and answer selection. Ephyra also consists of these three modules on the top level and some of its backup techniques (e.g. answer type testing and query reformulation) are based on these systems.

Lin et al. introduced the idea of combining knowledge annotation and knowledge mining techniques in a single framework [4]. Knowledge annotation allows to extract answers for frequent question classes from semi-structured sources such as web sites or web services, while knowledge mining applies statistical methods to unstructured sources such as the entire web. Ephyra supports these two paradigms and adds learning techniques on top of that.

The LAMP question answering system [5] follows a pattern mining and matching approach. It uses manually created text patterns to classify a question and to extract a key phrase, which is an object or event that the questions asks about. A second set of patterns is learned automatically and is used to extract answers from search results. The approach is limited to a single key phrase, and thus questions such as "How many calories are there in a Big Mac?" (cf. TREC8, question 56) cannot be handled because of the two key phrases "calories" and "Big Mac". Another shortcoming of LAMP is the relatively small set of 22 question classes. We introduce a more general approach to question interpretation that supports multiple key phrases and that distinguishes more classes to ensure that the right property of the key object is retrieved.

3   The Ephyra Framework

Ephyra is a modular framework that can easily be extended by integrating additional techniques. The system is also adaptable to other languages, which was achieved by separating language-specific from language-independent code and by defining patterns that are specific for the English language in separate resource files. The overall architecture is shown in Figure 1.

The question normalization component applies a number of normalization steps to the question string. It drops punctuation and quotation marks and modifies verb constructions in order to ensure that the question meets the premises of the following components.

A query generator transforms the question string into one or more queries. Ephyra comprises a query generator that builds a simple "bag of words" and a more sophisticated one that rephrases the question, anticipating the format of an answer. The question interpreter is part of our pattern learning approach (see Section 4.1). Our framework can be extended by simply plugging in additional query generators.

The queries are handed over to the search module, which comprises two types of searchers. Knowledge miners use conventional IR systems to query unstructured sources (e.g. Google

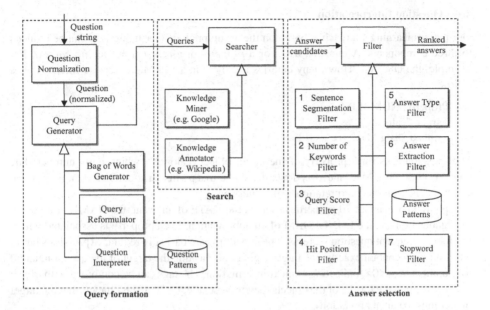

Fig. 1. Overview of the Ephyra Architecture

to search the web). Knowledge annotators allow to integrate resources such as web sites or web services that provide semi-structured information (e.g. the CIA World Factbook). To incorporate an additional knowledge source, one can simply create a new searcher.

Finally, the search results are processed by a set of filters. A filter usually checks the results for a specific feature and promotes those results that are promising with respect to that feature. For instance, the answer type filter promotes answers that are of the expected type (such as *date* or *location*). In addition, a filter can create new results from the existing ones (e.g. by breaking down a text snippet into sentences) and it can drop candidates that are unlikely to answer the question. The answer extraction filter also belongs to our pattern learning approach (cf. Section 4.2). By adding an additional filter, a new feature for answer evaluation or extraction can be integrated.

4   A Pattern Learning Approach

The Ephyra system uses two types of text patterns in the query formation and answer selection components described previously.

- *Question patterns* are applied to question strings to interpret the questions and to transform them into queries.
- *Answer patterns* are used to extract answers from relevant text snippets and to rank them.

While the question patterns need to be specified manually, Ephyra can automatically learn answer patterns, using question-answer pairs as training data.

4.1 Question Interpretation

Our pattern learning approach is based on the assumption that each question can be reduced to three components: A question asks for a *property* of a *target* in a specific *context*. For example, the question "How many calories are there in a Big Mac?" can be interpreted as follows:

- Property: NUMBER
- Target: "calories"
- Context: "Big Mac"

The question asks for a property of the target object "calories", which is its number. The context object "Big Mac" narrows down the scope to a particular food. Together, these three components form the interpretation of the question.

Ephyra knows about 70 properties such as the DATE of an event, the NAME of a person or organization and the LONGFORM of an abbreviation. Each property is associated with a number of frequent question patterns. These patterns are basically regular expressions but in addition, they contain exactly one target tag <T>, indicating the target of the question, and 0 to *n* context tags <C>, indicating context information. The tags can be combined with *object types* to restrain the format of the objects they represent (e.g. <T_ABBR> means that the target object must be an abbreviation).

Ephyra interprets a question by sequentially applying all the question patterns. If the question matches a pattern, Ephyra knows the property the question asks for and the substrings of the question corresponding to the <T> and <C> tags are extracted as target and context objects. In our example, the question could be interpreted with a pattern `"how many <T> are (there )?(in|on|at) <C>"` belonging to the property NUMBER.

The classification of questions based on properties is reasonable, since it ensures that there are just enough classes to retrieve the right aspect of a target. Obviously, it is not feasible to cover all properties that a question could possibly ask for, but this is also not necessary because a question can usually be interpreted in more than one way. For instance, the question "What is the name of the wife of Bill Clinton?" can be interpreted as follows:

- Property: WIFE, Target: "Bill Clinton"
- Property: NAME, Target: "wife of Bill Clinton"

The first interpretation is the preferable one because the target is simple and it supports synonyms such as "spouse". But even without a property WIFE, the question can still be handled with the more general property NAME.

The interpretations are transformed into search engine queries. The query string is the concatenation of the target object and all context objects in quotation marks plus additional keywords in the question. In our example, Ephyra would build the string `"calories" "Big Mac"`. The query strings are then used to fetch text snippets from the Google and Yahoo search engines.

4.2 Answer Extraction

Each of the properties is also associated with a set of answer patterns. These patterns are used to extract answer candidates from text snippets that contain the target and context objects of the question. The format of the answer patterns is similar to the question patterns described in the previous section. An answer pattern contains a target tag <T>, an arbitrary number of context tags <C> and a property tag <P>. In addition, each pattern is assigned a confidence value that estimates the reliability of answers extracted with that pattern.

Ephyra replaces all occurrences of target or context objects in a text snippet by the respective tags (<T> or <C>) and successively applies the answer patterns for the particular property to the text snippets. Whenever a snippet matches a pattern, the part of the snippet that corresponds to the <P> tag is extracted. In our example, the snippet "One Big Mac contains 560 calories and 32 grams of fat" is transformed into "One <C> contains 560 <T> and 32 grams of fat". The pattern "contains <P> <T>" can then be used to extract the property "560". If the extracted string does not occur in the set of answer candidates found so far, a new candidate is created and its initial score is set to the confidence measure of the pattern. Else, the score of the existing candidate is simply incremented by that confidence value. This mechanism results in a ranked list of answer candidates with more promising candidates coming first.

4.3   Pattern Learning

Initially, the properties and question patterns need to be specified manually. Ephyra can then automatically learn answer patterns, using question-answer pairs as training data: At first, the answer patterns are extracted from text snippets. Secondly, the patterns are assessed and patterns that are unreliable or too specific are dropped.

Properties and question patterns. We determined the properties and question patterns by analyzing the questions from the TREC9 question answering track (700 questions). Firstly, we derived simple patterns by replacing the target and context objects in the questions with the respective tags. Then we generalized the question patterns by adding synonyms and alternative formulations. To avoid ambiguous patterns, we associated some of the <T> and <C> tags with *object types* to put restraints on the target and context objects (cf. Section 4.1). For instance, these are some question patterns for the property NUMBER:

```
how many <T> are there
how many <T> are (there )?(at|in|on) <C>
what is the number of <T> (at|in|on) <C>
```

Extraction of answer patterns. The Ephyra system can be trained on question-answer pairs. We used the questions and answers from the TREC9 QA track, the same training set used to identify the properties and question patterns. At first, the questions in the training set are interpreted by applying the question patterns. Questions that cannot be interpreted are discarded. For each interpretation, a tuple consisting of a target, an arbitrary number of context objects and the answer (i.e. the property) is generated. It is possible to selectively add tuples for properties that are not sufficiently covered by the training data.

Ephyra then uses the tuples to query the Google and Yahoo search engines and fetches the text snippets from the search results. In our running example, the query string is: "calories" "Big Mac" "560". The answer is included in the query because we are interested in snippets that contain both the target and the property. All occurrences of target, context and property objects in the snippets are replaced by the tags <T>, <C> and <P> respectively. For example, the snippet "One Big Mac contains 560 calories and 31 grams of fat" is transformed into "One <C> contains <P> <T> and 31 grams of fat". Now the answer patterns can be extracted from the snippets. This is done by applying the following two regular expressions (similar to the patterns used in [5]):

- `\B<T>\B(.*?)\B<P>\B\s*(\W|\w+)`
- `(\W|\w+)\s*\B<P>\B(.*?)\B<T>\B`

An answer pattern is basically a regular expression that covers a target tag <T>, a property tag <P> and any characters in between these tags. In addition, it covers one word or special character preceding or following the <P> tag (depending on whether the <P> tag comes before or after the <T> tag). In our example, the second of the above regular expressions would extract the answer pattern "`contains <P> <T>`".

Assessment of answer patterns. Since this approach can result in a huge amount of patterns and thus in a poor response time, Ephyra assesses the answer patterns and drops patterns that are too specific or unreliable. Again, the starting point is a set of question-answer pairs (we reused the TREC9 data). Similarly to the previous step, Ephyra interprets the questions and generates query strings from the interpretations and answers. It then queries the search engines, fetches the snippets and replaces all occurrences of target and context objects by the <T> and <C> tags.

The algorithm then applies each of the previously learned answer patterns to all the snippets for the respective property and judges the extracted answers. For each answer pattern a, the algorithm records how often it could be used to extract a correct answer ($correct_a$) and how often it extracted a wrong answer ($incorrect_a$). Furthermore, for each property p, the total number of snippets is recorded ($snippets_p$). These values are used to compute the following two measures:

$$Confidence_a = \frac{correct_a}{correct_a + incorrect_a}, \quad Support_a = \frac{correct_a}{snippets_p}$$

These measures are then compared to thresholds. Patterns with a low confidence are considered to be unreliable and are dropped. A low support value means that a pattern is too specific and thus it is also dropped. We chose the thresholds to represent a good compromise between response time, precision and recall. The confidence values are reused to judge answers (see Section 4.2).

5   Experimental Details and Results

We evaluated Ephyra on the 200 TREC8 questions. For each question, our system returned a ranked list of up to five answers. These answers were judged manually by means of the patterns provided by TREC. Table 1 summarizes the results. Our system first tried to answer a question using knowledge annotation, then pattern matching, and if this approach failed it tried the backup techniques. The precision is the percentage of questions with at least one correct answer. The MRR (Mean Reciprocal Rank), as used in the TREC8 evaluation [6], takes the rank of the first correct answer into account.

Table 1. Performance of Ephyra on the TREC8 questions

	Questions	# Correct	Precision	MRR
Knowledge annotation	4	3	0.75	0.75
Pattern learning	96	55	0.57	0.40
Backup	99	47	0.47	0.32
All	200	105	0.53	0.36

The results are encouraging, showing that the pattern learning approach has a high precision, but on the other hand a relatively low recall. Therefore, the combination with backup techniques is reasonable. The confidence scores of the answers are good indicators for their reliability and can be used to merge them with answer candidates from other approaches. The pattern learning approach also has the benefit of mainly returning exact answers instead of sentences or sentence fragments. We only used about 700 questions to derive the properties and to generate the question and answer patterns and thus we assume that the performance of our approach can be improved substantially by increasing the amount and quality of the training data.

6   Conclusion and Outlook

We introduced the Ephyra question answering system, a modular framework that allows to combine multiple approaches to question answering in a single system. Ephyra can be integrated in other NLP applications and is adaptable to languages other than English. Based on this framework, we developed a new approach using text patterns to interpret questions and to extract answers from text snippets. The patterns for answer extraction are learned automatically. We find the concept of the interpretation of a question (comprising a target, context information and a property) promising. The interpretation is largely formulation-independent and thus questions and answers may use different terms. In contrast to previous approaches, multiple key phrases within a question are supported. Furthermore, the classification of questions based on properties results in just enough classes to ensure that the right aspect of a target is retrieved.

However, the answer patterns used by our approach are quite specific and thus require a redundant source. Currently, we are exploring how more sophisticated linguistic techniques such as phrase chunking and named entity tagging can be deployed to derive more generic patterns from the patterns returned by our learning algorithm. We believe that in this way the recall can be improved significantly and at the same time the number of patterns can be reduced. These NLP techniques could also be used to extract the target and context objects from a question, which would allow to automatically learn additional question patterns.

Acknowledgement

This work was supported in part by the DFG as part of the SFB 588 and by the European Commission under project CHIL (contract #506909).

694   N. Schlaefer et al.

References

1. Voorhees, E., Buckland, L.: The 14th Text REtrieval Conference Proceedings (2005).
2. Zheng, Z.: Answerbus question answering system. Proceedings of the Human Language Technology Conference (2002).
3. Brill, E., Lin, J., Banko, M., Dumais, S., Ng, A.: Data-intensive question answering. Proceedings of the 10th Text REtrieval Conference (2001).
4. Lin, J., Fernandes, A., Katz, B., Marton, G., Tellex, S.: Extracting answers from the web using knowledge annotation and knowledge mining techniques. Proceedings of the 11th Text REtrieval Conference (2002).
5. Zhang, D., Lee, W.: Web based pattern mining and matching approach to question answering. Proceedings of the 11th Text REtrieval Conference (2002).
6. Voorhees, E., Tice, D.: The TREC-8 question answering track evaluation. Proceedings of the 8th Text REtrieval Conference (1999).

Explicative Document Reading
Controlled by Non-speech Audio Gestures

Adam J. Sporka[1], Pavel Žikovský[2], and Pavel Slavík[1]

[1] Czech Technical University in Prague, Faculty of Electrical Engineering,
Department of Computer Science and Engineering,
Karlovo náměstí 13, 121 35 Praha 2, Czech Republic
{sporkaa, slavik}@fel.cvut.cz
[2] Musical Acoustics Research Centre, Music Faculty,
Academy of Performing Arts in Prague,
Malostranské nám. 13, 11800 Praha 1, Czech Republic
pavel.zikovsky@hamu.cz

Abstract. There are many situations in which listening to a text produced by a text-to-speech system is easier or safer than reading, for example when driving a car. Technical documents, such as conference articles, manuals etc., usually are comprised of relatively plain and unequivocal sentences. These documents usually contain words and terms unknown to the listener because they are full of domain specific terminology. In this paper, we propose a system that allows the users to interrupt the reading upon hearing an unknown or confusing term by a non-speech acoustic gesture (e.g. "uhm?"). Upon this interruption, the system provides a definition of the term, retrieved from *Wikipedia, the Free Encyclopedia*. The selection of the non-speech gestures has been made with a respect to the cross-cultural applicability and language independence. In this paper we present a set of novel tools enabling this kind of interaction.

1 Introduction

Text-to-speech sythesis (TTS) has become an established means of implementation of the output speech modality in various user interfaces. Its primary use is to mediate textual information in situations where the users may not or can not use their vision. Typical applications of TTS, besides various telephony applications, include systems presenting information to the visually impaired [8] or to the people in eyes-busy situations, such as drivers or pilots.

An important subset of these applications is reading of text documents. The TTS is frequently used for the low-cost rendering of audio books, such as in project Gutenberg [2]. Audio books are stored in a non-interactive compressed audio format (MP3, OGG, etc.) and accessed by means of common personal MP3 players. This use of TTS resembles radio drama broadcasts.

However, a similar approach could be used for accessing technical documents for the purpose of annotating unknown terms for the user so they may proceed through the material without switching to a dictionary or encyclopedia.

Technical texts, such as papers, manuals, technical reports, etc. are generally well-structured documents with the primary purpose to provide an objective and unequivocal

Petr Sojka, Ivan Kopeček and Karel Pala (Eds.): TSD 2006, LNAI 4188, pp. 695–702, 2006.

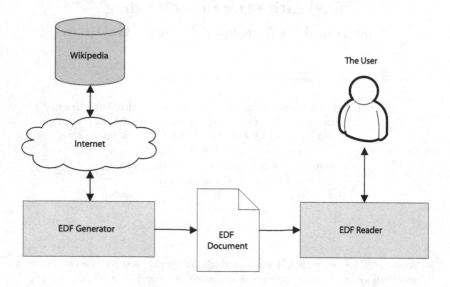

Fig. 1. Context of the system

description of a subject. However, this is different than in the case of books of fiction that many times use language that is not domain-specific or specialized. Technical documents contain numerous technical terms, that may be unknown to the reader, especially in the case when the reader's expertise does not entirely cover the subject of the document.

In our paper, we propose a system that combines the TTS with a non-speech input acoustic modality. The non-speech input is based on use of sounds other than speech, such as humming or whistling [7,5]. This interaction style has been investigated previously in [3] or [4]. In our system we use it for user-initiated switching between reading the document and explication of the terms contained in it.

Our system makes use of non-speech gestures which are short melodic patterns produced by humming. In general, each gesture may be assigned a system command which is executed upon the completion of the gesture. Our set of non-speech gestures is based on common non-verbal vocalizations that occur during general conversation.

Our system allows the user to interrupt the reading in the moment of miscomprehension of the text (see section 2.2), to which the system reacts by explaining the term in question. The user may stop the explanation of the term once they are sure they understood its definition. The system then resumes the reading, starting with the sentence that contained the explained term and thus allowing the user to regain the context of the text.

Another contribution of our paper is the method of automatic annotation of technical documents which fetches the explanations of all terms contained in the document.

The overall scheme of the system is shown in Figure 1. Our system is targeted to mobile autonomous systems working both on- and off-line. Therefore all explications have to be pre-fetched into a single document structure. We have defined such a structure and call it *Explicative Document Format.*

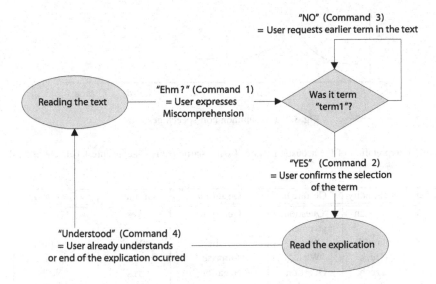

Fig. 2. User interface state diagram

2   System Description

Our system is based on an audio-only user interface, consisting of two modalities: A speech modality, used to transfer the text information to the user, and a non-speech gestures modality, used to control the reading process by the user.

The control mechanism has the following three states: reading the text, selection of the term for explanation, and explaining the term. The structure of control mechanism is explained in Figure 2. A female voice was used for reading the document whereas a male voice was employed to read the definitions.

2.1   Design of Non-speech Gestures

To determine a suitable set of non-speech audio gestures, we observed the occurence of non-speech sounds in common speech. This allowed us to identify four most frequent non-speech gestures, as shown in Fig. 3.

Subsequently, we have performed a semantic study of these gestures. The goal of the study was to determine their meaning as percieved by representatives of different cultures.

We have created a simple questionnaire whereby each participant of the study was asked what was the most obvious and natural interpretation of each of the four gestures in their own language and culture. The results of this study are summarized in Table 1.

The results show an agreement of meaning with most of the gestures as being understood by the participants from wide range of cultures. Gesture a was most frequently understood as an expression of a question. The common understanding of gesture b varied and therefore we decided not to use this gesture in our system. The gesture c was generally understood as agreement while the gesture d meant a disagreement for all participants. Considering these results, we decided for the assignment of the commands to the gestures as shown in Table 2.

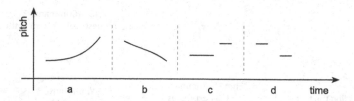

Fig. 3. Set of common non-speech gestures

Table 1. Interpretation of the acoustic gestures by the participants. The gesture labels corresponds to those in Figure 3.

Part.	Nationality	Gesture *a*	Gesture *b*	Gesture *c*	Gesture *d*
A	Austrian	"Question, agreement."	"Question."	"Yes."	"No."
B	Columbian	"Yes."	"Question."	"Yes."	"Negation."
C	Czech	"What?"	"Surprise."	"Agreement."	"Disagreement."
D	Czech	"Question."	"Negation."	"Yes."	"No."
E	Czech	"Question."	*N/A*	"Yes."	"No."
F	French	"What?"	"I don't think so."	"Yes."	"No."
G	German	"Question, agreement."	"Question."	"Yes."	"No."
I	Iranian	"What?"	"Interesting!"	"Yes."	"No."
J	Italian	"Surprise."	"Disagreement."	"Agreement."	"Disagreement."
K	Romanian	"Confusion."	"Part. satisfaction."	"Good."	"Bad."
L	Slovak	"What do you mean?"	"I don't think so."	"Agreement, willingness."	"Disagreement."
M	USA	"Don't know."	*N/A*	"yes"	"no"

2.2 Reaction Time upon Term Miscomprehension

From the user interface state diagram shown in Figure 2 it is clear that the usability of the system would be affected by the reaction time upon miscomprehension of a term, i.e. the time that passes between the user hears a term they do not understand and they express their miscomprehension.

We have carried out a brief experiment that was to answer the following question: "Upon a miscomprehension of a term, what is the common reaction time of the users after which they are likely to report the miscomprehension?"

There were seven participants of this experiment (1 female, 6 male). Only fluent English speakers were asked to participate.

Table 2. Assignment of gestures

Gesture *a* ("What?")	Command 1 (Explain!)
Gesture *c* ("Yes")	Command 2 (Yes)
Gesture *d* ("No")	Command 3 (No)
Gesture *a* ("Yes")	Command 4 (Understood)

Each participant was asked to listen to a technical text in English language, read by a TTS. The text was not presented in a visual form. Upon encountering a term the participant for some reason had not understood, he or she were asked to notify the experimenter by raising hand. After this notification, the playback of the text was interrupted. The participant was asked to state, what term was not understood. The experimenter highlighted the term in the text and made note in the text of when the user made the notification. Afterwards, the playback of the text was resumed.

For each miscomprehension, the reaction time in words has been recorded. 5 to 10 instances of miscomprehension were recorded for each participant. The Microsoft Mary voice, available in the standard installation of the Microsoft Windows XP Professional, was used as the text-to-speech engine [1].

The results are shown in table 3. The average reaction time was most usually between 2 and 4 words. In some extreme cases, the delay was as many as 8 words. However, immediate responses and responses after a single word were noted in 22% of all records.

2.3 Explicative Document Format

In order to be able to operate in off-line conditions, our Explicative Document Format (EDF) has been designed to describe both main text and definitions of all terms in the document. Therefore, the EDF has two principal parts—the original text with tags around terms, and the explanatory parts, where all explications are stored.

Each definition has a unique identifier, which is used to link the terms in the text with their respective definitions. Figure 4 shows a short example of an EDF document. As the term which can be misunderstood can be longer than a word, the form of the tags has been designed in order to allow an overlapping structure. This fact disallowed us to use an XML-based format, as it does not allow the tag overlapping.

3   The Prototype Implementation

3.1   Creating The EDF Documents

To automate the creation of EDF documents we created a tool called EDF-WiKi, which scans the text for all possible terms, and attempts to fetch the explanations of the terms from the

Table 3. Reaction time upon a miscomprehension. D – reaction time (in words).

Subject	Gender	Age	EN Fluency	Culture	$\overline{D}$	SD(D)
B	M	50	near-native	Columbian	3.8	1.9
C	M	24	fluent	Czech	2.2	1.3
D	M	31	fluent	Czech	2.3	1.4
E	M	23	fluent	Czech	2.1	1.4
G	M	27	near-native	Greek	2.9	2.2
I	F	22	fluent	Iranian	3.0	2.4
M	M	40	native	US	1.9	1.5
Overall	—	—	—	—	2.8	1.9

Wikipedia [9] and creates the whole output document. From user point of view, the EDF-WiKi is straightforward: User opens a document and presses the button "EDF it!". After all the information is retrieved from Wikipedia server, the program asks for a filename to save the EDF document.

From the programming point of view, the problem looks as follows: First, the document is scanned for all terms with length between certain number of characters (we used 4) and certain word count (we used 2; because of information retrieval time increases exponentially with the length of terms). For each term we remember it's position in the text. Subsequently, the retrieval of all terms from Wikipedia is attempted. If Wikipedia answers that it does not know the particular term, the term is omitted, as it is probably common word. Finally, tags are inserted to the original text and explications are appended at the end of the document. The algorithm is more clearly shown in Figure 5.

3.2   EDF Documents Reader

The EDF reader is the run-time environment of our system. It is the implementation of the interaction paradigm, as described in section 2, allowing the user to access the documents in the EDF format.

Its prototype has been implemented in MS VC++ 6.0. Microsoft Speech API 5.1 [1] has been used to control the TTS. To detect the pitch of the humming, we have tested several techniques, such as zero-crossings, analysis of the FFT, and autocorrelation methods. For our purposes, we found the autocorrelation, as described in [6], to be the most efficient method.

4   The User Evaluation

In the user evaluation sessions, we asked four users (3 male, 1 female) to get acquainted with our system and use it for a while. We have used different *Wikipedia articles* that were not related to the participants' fields of expertise. Each participant has been presented one article of about 600 words of length. When finished, we asked the following questions:

1. *Can you imagine the use of such a system while driving?* All users answered positively this question.

```
[1*Lorem [2*[3*ipsum*2]*1] dolor*3] sit amet, consectetuer
adipiscing elit. Morbi rutrum ...

|1*lorem ipsum. Sed eros leo, interdum sed, ullamcorper vel, porttitor a,
arcu. Aenean rhoncus ornare nisi. Nullam tempor nibh at est nonummy
placerat.
|2* ipsum. Proin venenatis placerat lectus. Proin porttitor quam sed
arcu. Sed laoreet lorem vitae felis. Maecenas elementum urna in magna.
|3* ipsum dolor. Cras nec pede. Sed mattis pellentesque metus. Cras
nisl. Vivamus a est nec nisi facilisis convallis. Vivamus luctus felis
sed augue. Proin pharetra ante sed justo. Quisque nec dui.
```

Fig. 4. Example of the EDF format. [1* ... start of a tag, *1] ... end of a tag, |1* ... start of a definition.

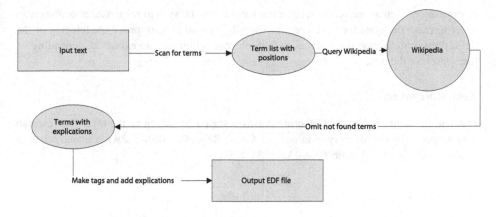

Fig. 5. EDF Generation Pipeline

2. *What other uses of this system you can think of?* Two users suggested the use of non-speech gestures for web navigation. One user suggested the adaptation of this system as a interactive manual for maintenance of machinery. Another user suggested a combination with the speech recognition.
3. *What benefits do you find in use of the non-speech gestures?* Three users answered that they found the non-speech gesture control intuitive. These users also reported that they found the set of gestures easy to use. One user expressed a concern that the non-speech gestures would interfere with the output speech modality.
4. *When using our system, did you find the explanation of the terms provided relevant?* Two users answered that in some cases the information presented was not that clear to them as the system gave an explanation that was not relevant to the use of the term in particular context. However, this is may be attributed to the data source [9] rather than to the interaction method itself.

The system was positively accepted by the users. All users were able to use the system only after a short explanation of its function. The non-speech gestures proved to be a viable modality for this particular application.

5 Conclusion

In this paper we have presented a system, which allows the user to listen to a technical text and ask for explanations of incomprehensible terms. The control of the system is performed by means of the non-speech acoustic gestures.

To control our system we have chosen a set of non-speech gestures according to the results of our study. The selected set of the non-speech gestures proved to be a natural way to input basic commands, such as agreement or disagreement. Our study has also proved that the selected gestures are cross-culturally applicable. From our experience, this control paradigm has a low cognitive load and can be used even during complex actions such as driving, etc.

The performed usability test proved a good usability of the whole system as well as the control by the sound gestures themselves. In future, we would like to track individual user performance (such as the reaction time, etc.) and adapt the system responses accordingly in order to make the system even more user friendly, as well as to improve the fetching of the definitions from free on-line sources so that relevant definitions are extracted, depending on the context of the text.

Acknowledgment

Our sincere thanks belong to Catherine Forsman for proofreading of the text. The research was supported by the Ministry of Education, Czech Republic (MŠMT ČR), research program MSM 6840770014 and project No. 1M6138498401.

References

1. Microsoft Speech Application Program Interface (SAPI) Version 5.0. Online, retrieved 20 Mar 2006. http://www.microsoft.com/speech.
2. Project Gutenberg. Online, retrieved 20 Mar 2006. http://www.gutenberg.org/.
3. P. Hämäläinen, T. Mäki-Patola, V. Pulkki, and M. Airas. Musical computer games played by singing. In T. I. Evangelista G., editor, *Proc 7th Intl Conf on Digital Audio Effects, Naples, Italy*, pages 367–371, 2004.
4. T. Igarashi and J. F. Hughes. Voice as sound: using non-verbal voice input for interactive control. In *UIST '01: Proc 14th Annual ACM Symp on User Interface Software and Technology*, pages 155–156, New York, NY, USA, 2001. ACM Press.
5. A. J. Sporka, S. H. Kurniawan, and P. Slavík. Acoustic control of mouse pointer. *Universal Access in Information Society*, 4(3):237–245, 2006.
6. L. R. Rabiner. On the use of autocorrelation analysis for pitch detection. *IEEE Transactions on Acoustics, Speech, and Signal Processing*, ASSP-25(1):24–33, February 1977.
7. A. J. Sporka, S. H. Kurniawan, and P. Slavík. Non-speech operated emulation of keyboard. In *Designing Accessible Technology*. Springer-Verlag (London), 2006.
8. P. Žikovský, T. Pěšina, and P. Slavík. Processing of logical expressions for visually impaired users. In *Proceedings of TSD 2004, Lecture Notes in Artificial Intelligence LNCS/LNAI 3206*, pages 553–560. Springer-Verlag (Berlin), 2004.
9. Wikimedia Foundation, Inc. *Wikipedia, the free encyclopedia.* http://www.wikipedia.org.

Hybrid Neural Network Design and Implementation on FPGA for Infant Cry Recognition

Israel Suaste-Rivas[1], Alejandro Díaz-Méndez[1], Carlos A. Reyes-García[1],
and Orion F. Reyes-Galaviz[2]

[1] Instituto Nacional de Astrofísica Óptica y Electrónica, México
{isuaste, ajdiaz, kargaxxi}@inaoep.mx
[2] Instituto Tecnológico de Apizaco, México
orionfrg@yahoo.com

Abstract. It has been found that the infant's crying has much information on its sound wave. For small infants crying is a form of communication, a very limited one, but similar to the way adults communicate. In this work we present the design of an Automatic Infant Cry Recognizer hybrid system, that classifies different kinds of cries, with the objective of identifying some pathologies in recently born babies. The system is based on the implementation of a Fuzzy Relational Neural Network (FRNN) model on a standard reconfigurable hardware like Field Programmable Gate Arrays (FPGAs). To perform the experiments, a set of crying samples is divided in two parts; the first one is used for training and the other one for testing. The input features are represented by fuzzy membership functions and the links between nodes, instead of regular weights, are represented by fuzzy relations. The training adjusts the relational weight matrix, and once its values have been adapted, the matrix is fixed into the FPGA. The goal of this research is to prove the performance of the FRNN in a development board; in this case we used the RC100 from Celoxica. The implementation process, as well as some results is shown.

1 Introduction

In this paper we describe the implementation in hardware of a general pattern classifier based on a neural network architecture which uses fuzzy sets in the form of linguistic properties. The idea of using a relational neural network as a pattern classifier was taken from the general classifier presented by Pedrycz [1]. Later on, Reyes [2] designed a Fuzzy Relational Neural Network (FRNN) for automatic speech recognition. The FRNN is based on fuzzy sets for the input and the structure of the neural network, its operation is divided in two main parts, the first one for learning and the second one for testing. By taking the same architecture, we decided to implement the FRNN in FPGAs and to verify it on the infant cry recognition problem. The FRNN system, implemented in software, has been tested on an infant cry recognition problem in previous works [3,4]. This problem is attractive because the crying in babies is a primary communication function, governed directly by the brain; any alteration on the normal functioning of the babies' body is reflected in the cry [5]. Based on the information contained inside the cry's wave, the infant's physical state can be determined, and even some physical pathologies may be detected, mainly those related to the central nervous system. If any of these pathologies could be detected in the early stages of life, they could be attended and, perhaps, avoided by the opportune application of treatments and therapies.

Petr Sojka, Ivan Kopeček and Karel Pala (Eds.): TSD 2006, LNAI 4188, pp. 703–709, 2006.

2   Infant Cry

Similar to Automatic Speech Recognition (ASR), the Automatic Infant Cry Recognition (AICR) process is basically a problem of pattern processing. In AICR the acoustical processing is first performed. At this stage the crying signal is analyzed to extract the more important acoustic features in time domain. The crying wave is filtered to eliminate irrelevant or undesirable information like noise, channel distortion, and other particular signal characteristics. Although data are reduced when removing repetitive components, the relevant information for pattern classification is preserved in an optimal way. Some of the more usual simple techniques for signal processing are: Linear Prediction Coding, Cepstral Coefficients, Pitch, Intensity, among others [6]. A vector can represent the set of obtained characteristics, and each vector may represent a pattern. This pattern is then compared with the knowledge the classification model has, so it can perform pattern classification.

3   The Fuzzy Neural Network

Fuzzy neural network models attempt to benefit with the advantages of the neural networks and the fuzzy set theory properties. Neural networks have the ability to discover underlying regularities in the task domain; they also have a high computational rate due to their inherent parallelism [2]. Besides, fuzzy set theory provides flexibility to work with vague data and ambiguous information, the kind of information that is present in daily life problems. In order to enable a system to handle real-life situations, the concept of fuzzy sets should be incorporated into the neural network. The neural network used consists of two layers, the input layer and the output layer. The input layer is formed by a set of Nn neurons, with each of them corresponding to one of the N linguistic properties assigned to each of the n input features. In the output layer there are l neurons, where each node corresponds to one of the l classes. There is a link from every node in the input layer to every node in the output layer. All the connections, instead of regular weights, are described by means of fuzzy relations $R: X \times Y \rightarrow [0, 1]$ between the input and output nodes.

3.1   The Learning Phase

The learning phase collects information from the training patterns which will be useful in the next phase. This phase has three modules: the Linguistic Feature Extractor (LFE), the Desired Output Estimator (DOE), and the Neural Network Trainer (NNT). The LFE takes the training samples, from the original input vectors, and each input feature is transformed in membership values to each of the assigned linguistic properties. Thus a vector containing n features can be transformed in a $3n$, $5n$, or $7n$_dimensional vector. The new resulting vector is called Linguistic Properties Vector (LPV).

The DOE is in charge of computing the membership values of each sample to each class of the problem. The resulting vector is called Desired Vector (DV). Then, the LPV and the DV are used by the Neural Network Trainer.

1. *The Linguistic Feature Extractor*: Each input feature can be represented as a vector of membership values to each of the linguistic properties low, medium, and high

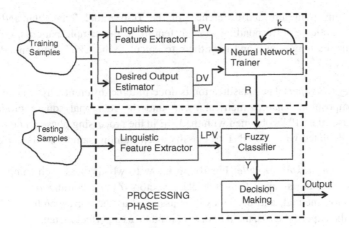

Fig. 1. Automatic Infant Cry Recognizer's architecture

for a $3n$_dimensional vector, very low, low, medium, high, and very high for a $5n$_dimensional vector, or very low, low, more o less low, medium, more o less high, high, and very high for a $7n$_dimensional vector. To calculate this membership values some different membership functions can be used: the Trapezoidal membership function, the Triangular function and the symmetric Gaussian membership function, among others.

2. *The Neural Network Trainer*: The used neural network model is based on the fuzzy neural structure proposed by Reyes in [2]. The Neural Network Trainer takes both LPV and DV vectors as the basis for training the network. The input vector is clamped to the input layer and the desired output vector is clamped to the output layer during training. The outputs of the network are computed to obtain the error at the output layer. The error is represented by the distance between the actual output and the target output. The objective of the training process is to minimize this error. During each learning step, once the error has been computed, the trainer adjusts the relationship values or weights of the corresponding connections, either until a minimum error is obtained or a given number of iterations is completed. The output of the NNT is a relational matrix containing the knowledge needed to further map the unknown input vectors to their corresponding class during the classification process. The relational neural network, the learning process in a Fuzzy Neural Network and the updating parameters are explained in detail in [2].

3.2   The Processing Phase

Once the learning phase is completed, the information collected is used to classify unknown patterns; the processing or classification phase is in charge of performing that task. The modules that form the processing phase are the Linguistic Feature Extractor (LFE), the Fuzzy Classifier (FC), and the Decision Making Module (DMM). The LFE is similar to the one described in the learning phase. The only difference is that, in the classification phase, the LFE does not calculate new parameters to be applied by the membership functions. The LFE in this phase takes the values of the radius and central points of the Pi function, or the maximum, minimum and difference for the Trapezoidal, Triangular and Gaussian membership functions, corresponding to each feature in the sample patterns, collected by the LFE in the learning phase, and uses them to calculate the LPV's corresponding to the testing patterns.

1. *The Fuzzy Classifier*: The classification is done in three different ways, namely $max - min$ composition, max-geometrical mean and the relational square product. Each method uses the LPV's obtained with the LFE in the processing phase and the relational matrix calculated with the NNT to classify each training sample to its corresponding class.
2. *The Decision Making Module*: Finally, to know to which class each sample belongs, the highest value is taken from the class vectors $Y(y_j)$, coming from the selected classification method, and the index j is assigned as the corresponding class. If j is equal to the expected class, the output is computed as a perfect match.

This module keeps account of the number of accurate matches for each class, calculates the percentage of good matches per class, and the overall accuracy percentage. The DDM is also in charge of forming the confusion matrix corresponding to the selected classification method.

4 Hardware Implementation

The board RC100, from Celoxica, is an important piece in this work due to the fact that the FRNN was implemented in it. This board contains two programmable logic circuits [7]: XILINX Spartan II FPGA and a CPLD (Complex Programmable Logic Device) XILINX XCR3128XL which is used to configure the FPGA Spartan II through the parallel port by the memory FLASH. The software required for the implementation was Handel-C [8]. Fig. 2 shows the block diagram of the FRNN's implementation process. This process is divided in two main parts; first, the corresponding to training is done in a computer, and once the relational matrix has been trained it is fixed in the FPGA.

In Fig. 3, we can see the schematic design used for the hardware implementation. After training in the computer, the first task executed is the loading of the fuzzy relational matrix: $R(x_i, y_j)$, where $x_{i...(n-1)}$ indicates the row in which the current value can be found, and $y_{j...l}$ refers to the class the input vector belongs to. Next, the input vector (X_i) is read, which represents a pattern with n elements, in this vector $X_i = n$ contains the label of the corresponding vector's type of cry. The fuzzy relational matrix and the input vectors are saved in the flash RAM in different address locations. Both values, $R(x_i, y_j)$ and X_i, are stored in registers and they are processed by the *min* comparator, with which we obtain the minimum value between the input vector and the present relational weight. The result is placed in the register *min* $x_{i,j}$, which is compared with the threshold U_j, using the *max* comparator, where the maximum value is chosen and saved in the register *max* x. This new value is compared with the previous one and the larger of both is selected. In the case of the first input value, this is compared with zero. The same operation is repeated until the $n - 1$ values, from vector X_i for class y_j, have been processed.

Finally the result obtained is called $Y(y_j)$. A multiplexor decides the place where $Y(y_j)$ is going to be located in the appropriate register $Neuron_{(j...l)}$, at last, the result is sent

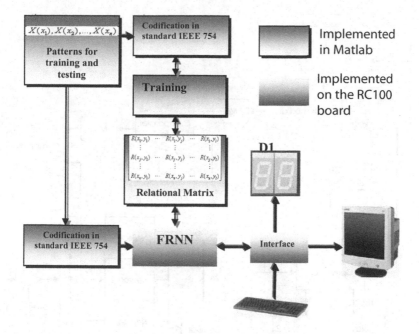

Fig. 2. Block diagram of the complete FRNN

to the screen without decodification. If $X_i = n$ the value is placed in a decimal encoder and sent to the Display 1 of the RC100 board for its visualization, this is the right label of the processed sample and indicates the class the sample belongs to. The same operation is repeated until $Y(y_j = l)$. When this condition occurs, the obtained values for each $Y(y_j)$ are compared, and the last block of the FRNN makes a decision after which the result is sent to Display 1 (previously decodified). Now, in the screen we can see in Spanish the name of the output class, depending on which was the class neuron with the higher activation level. The operation frequency is given by a clock of 20 MHz, and the total number of clock cycles the FRNN requires to process each input vector is 64,365, which is equivalent to 3.2 miliseconds. Nonetheless, we can see the result in the screen only after 122 milliseconds, due to the time the FPGA takes to refresh the monitor screen. In order to validate performance of the FRNN in the FPGA, these results are compared with the ones obtained in the Matlab simulation, where approximately every 2.5 seconds the result for a single input vector, using the already trained FRNN, is obtained. The system was tested on an infant cry recognition problem, in which the objective was to classify the cry samples as belonging to the normal, deafness or asphyxia class. The samples used were recorded by medical doctors who, at the end of each sample, added the label of the class the sample belongs to. Each original sample is divided in one second segments, from which Linear Prediction Coding (LPC) features are extracted through an acoustical analysis stage. In total we have 1020 one second samples of the three classes of infant cry; normal, asphyxia, and deafness. From them, 816 are used for training and the remaining 204 are kept apart for testing. In Table 1 some of the results obtained with the FRNN on the board RC100 are shown. As it can be seen, in the presented case, we obtain 94.6% of accuracy which is the same obtained by using Matlab's simulation.

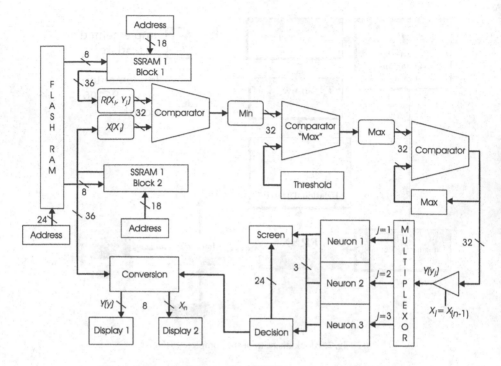

Fig. 3. Schematic diagram of the FRNN implemented on the FPGA

Table 1. Confusion Matrix of the FRRN using seven triangular membership functions

Type of Cry	Samples	Confusion Matrix			Classification
		Normal	Deaf	Asphixia	
Normal	72	68	4	0	
Deaf	64	0	64	0	
Asphixia	68	3	4	61	
Total	204				94.6078%

5   Conclusions

When the Fuzzy Relational Neural Network (FRNN) was implemented in Matlab, using 10 Principal Component Analysis (PCA) and 7 triangular membership functions, the results obtained were around 94.6% correctly classified, which encouraged to its hardware implementation. The acoustical features extraction method selected for this implementation was the LPC, because its calculation is simpler than the calculation of Mel Frequency Cepstral Coefficients (MFCC), on the hardware implementation. The results obtained when implementing the FRNN in the Celoxica's RC100 development board were of 94.6%, which is the same that the one obtained when using Matlab. The present implementation requires the separate training of the FRNN, before being fixed to the FPGA. During testing, the input vectors should be previously processed in the computer, for the extraction of the acoustical features. This operation must be performed on the same hardware board in the future. With our experiments we could show that a classifier like the FRNN could be effective to implement a hardware system devoted to the recognition or classification of Infant Cry, to help the early diagnosis of pathologies in recently born babies.

References

1. Pedricz, W.: Neuro computations in relational systems. IEEE Trans. On Pattern Analysis and Intelligence, vol. 13, No 3., pp. 289–296. (1999).
2. Reyes, C. A.: On the design of a fuzzy relational neural network for automatic speech recognition. Doctoral Dissertation, The Florida State University, Tallahassee, Fl (1994).
3. Suaste, I., Reyes, O., Diaz, A., Reyes C.: A Fuzzy Relational Neural Network for Pattern Classification. Proceedings of CIARP, Puebla, México, pp. 358–365. (2004).
4. Suaste, I., Reyes, O., Diaz, A., Reyes C.: Implementation of a Linguistic Fuzzy Relational Neural Network for Detecting Pathologies by Infant Cry Recognition. Proceedings of IBERAMIA, Puebla, México, pp. 953–962. (2004).
5. Wasz-Höckert O., Lind J., Vuorenkoski V., Partenen T., Valanne E.: The infant cry: a spectrographic and auditory analisis Clin. Dev. Med. 29, pp. 1–42 (1968).
6. Orozco, J., Reyes, C.A.: Mel-frequency cepstrum coefficients extraction from infant cry for classification of normal and pathological cry whit feed-forward neural networks. Proceedings of ESANN, Bruges, Belgium. (2003).
7. RC100 User Manual:
   http://www.celoxica.com/support/view_article.asp?ArticleID=376
   Celoxica. Version 1.2. United Kingdom, (2001).
8. Handel-C. Language Refence Manual:
   http://www.celoxica.com/methodology/handelc.asp Celoxica Ltd. Version 1.2. United Kingdom, (2001).

Speech and Sound Use in a Remote Monitoring System for Health Care

Michel Vacher, Jean-François Serignat, Stéphane Chaillol, Dan Istrate,
and Vladimir Popescu

CLIPS-IMAG, UMR CNRS-UJF-INPG 5524
BP53, 38041 Grenoble Cedex9, France
Michel.Vacher@imag.fr
http://www-clips.imag.fr/geod/User/michel.vacher

Abstract. Ageing affects the economic and social foundations of societies at world level. Health care has to respond to the challenge that population ageing presents. Medical remote monitoring needs human operator to be assisted by means of smart information systems. Physiological and position sensors give numerous data, but speech analysis and sound classification can give interesting additional information about the patient and may help in decision-making. The entire analysis system is composed of parallel tasks: signal detection and channel selection, sound/speech classification, life sound classification and speech recognition. The multichannel sound processing allows us to localize the source of sound in the apartment and to select appropriate signal segments for analysis. Recognized key words indicative of a distress situation are extracted from sentences. Key words and classification results are sent to the medical remote monitoring application through network. An adapted speech corpus was recorded in French and used for evaluation purposes.

1 Introduction

It is well known that ageing is emerging as an important concern for the most developed countries, but in the 21st century rapid ageing will progressively become a global phenomenon [1]. In the developed countries, older people will constitute 33% of their population—but 37% in Europe—in 2050 as opposed to 19% today, and the median age will increase by 9 years, reaching 46 years in 2050. In this context the central challenge of health and long-term care policies is to provide full access to high-quality services for all, while ensuring the financial sustainability of these services, meeting the growing demand for health and care services, related to the significant growth of 80 years and over old people. Progress in aids and assistive technologies might be a cost-efficient way to support the supply of informal care and care provisions.

Therefore, effective medical monitoring from a remote location requires that a smart information system is used to alert a human operator of patient distress. Presently, physiological and position sensors give a variety of data, but do not take into account distress calls or fall sounds. This is why speech analysis and sound classification can give interesting additional information on the patient and may help the decision-making.

In this paper we describe the speech/sound analysis part of a multichannel smart system:

– speech is analyzed in order to extract informative key words,

Petr Sojka, Ivan Kopeček and Karel Pala (Eds.): TSD 2006, LNAI 4188, pp. 711–718, 2006.

– sounds are detected and identified among several predefined sound classes.

This system is a part of a medical remote monitoring project with the aim of detecting abnormal patient behaviour at home in the context of residential health care [2]. The medical monitoring system not described in this article uses the sound system and sensors to make its decision: medical sensors (oxymeter, tensiometer, thermometer and actimeter), various sensors (infrared sensors and door contacts). The input of the smart sound system is composed of data collected by the means of 5 to 8 microphones (one per room).

The sentence uttered by the patient may give valuable information on the state of the patient:

– a distress case: "Help me!", "Doctor!",
– a normal state: "Coffee is cold!", "The door is open!".

In the same way, each sound produced in the apartment is indicative of:

– a patient's activity: the patient is locking the door, ...
– the patient's physiology: he is having a cough, ...
– a possible distress situation for the patient: a scream or a glass breaking is suddenly appearing.

If the system has a good ability to recognize speech and to classify such sounds, it will be possible to know if the patient needs help.

2   System Organization

The general organization of the system is shown in Figure 1. Wireless microphones (SENNHEISER eW500) are used because of their small dimensions and of their omnidirectional characteristics. Each receiver (32 MHz frequency band) is connected to a channel of the acquisition card. The sound synchronisation system is made up by the *sound/speech system* and the *speech recognition system* as shown in Figure 2. These two components are running as independent applications on the same computer, they are synchronized through

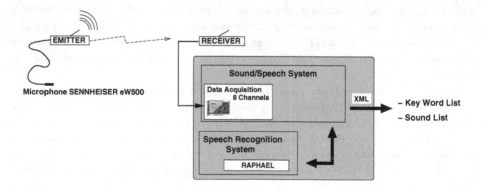

Fig. 1. Global System Organization

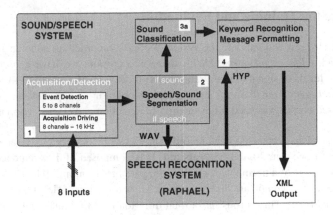

Fig. 2. Sound Flow-Chart

a file exchange protocol. The first stage of the *sound/speech system* is the acquisition and detection module, it is not described in this article. The acquisition card has 8 differential inputs and a maximal sampling rate of 200 ksamples/s. The sampling frequency was fixed at 16 kHz. This value is usual in speech recognition. The acquisition module was evaluated via Receiver Operating Curves giving *missed detection rate* as function of *false detection rate*. The Equal Error Rate (EER) is 0% above +10 dB of SNR and 6.5% at 0 dB. After the detection step, the signal has to be sent only to the appropriate stage: *speech recognition system* or *sound classifier*. This decision-making, speech/sound segmentation, is achieved by the second stage. It is very important to send non linguistic sound to the classifier and not to the recognizer.

At the end the useful extracted information is sent by the keyword recognition and message formatting stage through the network using XML format. Useful information is: time and date, name of the room, classification result (sound or speech, recognized keywords, class of the life sounds). Figure 3 shows an example of results coded in XML format in case of speech recognition in the kitchen: the logarithmic likelihood was −20.2 for "No Speech", −17.2 for "Speech", therefore the sound event was classified as *"parole"* (speech) and sent to the speech recognizer RAPHAEL, developed in our laboratory. The recognized sentence was in French *"un docteur vite"* (a doctor quickly).

```
<appli:segmentation description="appli audio">
<pièce>Cuisine</pièce>
<horodate>1-12-2005 à 15:19:20</horodate>
<résultat>parole</résultat>
<information>Probabilité de son=-20.2018, Probabilité de parole=-17.2258</information>
</appli:segmentation>
<appli:reconnaissance description="appli audio">
<pièce>Cuisine</pièce>
<horodate>1-12-2005 à 15:19:20</horodate>
<résultat>un docteur vite</résultat>
</appli:reconnaissance>
```

Fig. 3. Result Sample in the case of Speech

3   Corpus for Training and Evaluation

In order to train, test and validate the system we have recorded an adapted *speech corpus* in French and a *life sound corpus*. With these two corpora we have generated a noised corpus with 4 levels of signal to noise ratio (SNR=0 dB, +10 dB, +20 dB, +40 dB). The HIS (*"Habitat Intelligent pour la Santé"*) noise was recorded in an experimental test apartment [3]. This noised corpus was used for evaluation of detection and classification modules.

Speech corpus. This corpus has been recorded at CLIPS laboratory by 21 speakers (11 men and 10 women) between 20 and 65 years old. It is composed of 126 sentences in French: 66 are characteristic of a normal situation for the patient: "Bonjour" (Hello), "Où est le sel" (Where is the salt)... and 60 are distress sentences: "Au secours" (Help), "Un médecin vite" (A doctor quickly)... This corpus has a total duration of 38 minutes and is constituted by 2,646 audio files in wave format.

Life sound corpus. The every day life sounds are divided into 7 classes corresponding to 2 categories: *normal* sounds related to usual activities of the patient (door clapping, phone ringing, step sounds, dishes sounds, door lock), *abnormal* sounds related to distress situations (breaking glasses, screams). This corpus contains recordings made at CLIPS laboratory (15%), files of "Sound Scene Database in Real Acoustical Environment" [4] (70%) and files from a commercial CD (15%). 20 types of sounds were selected with 10 to 300 repetitions per type.

4   Speech/Sound Segmentation System

4.1   Segmentation

A Gaussian Mixture Model (GMM) method is used in order to separate speech from life sounds [5], [6]. There are other possibilities : Hidden Markov Model (HMM) [8], Bayesian method, etc. GMM has been chosen because with other methods similar results have been obtained, however at the cost of higher complexity. The segmentation system cannot use 1 s windows like in [6], [7] because the audio signal can be as short as 36 ms. A preliminary step before signal classification is the extraction of acoustic parameters. LFCC (Linear Frequency Cepstral Coefficients) and normalised energy as additional parameter are used. The bandwidth of the filters is constant and leads to a good resolution at high frequencies; life sounds are better discriminated with LFCC from speech by using high frequency components than with MFCC (MEL Frequency Cepstrum Coefficients), MEL scale. For each frame, the energy is normalised with respect to the average energy in the frames of the complete signal and may be, this way, less dependent on experimental recording conditions.

The speech/sound segmentation with a GMM method supposes that the distribution of acoustic parameters for a sound class may be modeled with a sum of Gaussian models after a training step (K-means followed by Expectation Maximisation in 20 steps). The BIC (Bayesian Information Criterion) is used in this paper in order to determinate the optimal number of Gaussian models. It selects the model through the maximization of integrated likelihood: $BIC_{m,\kappa} = -2L_{m,\kappa} + v_{m,\kappa}\ln(n)$, where $L_{m,\kappa}$ is the logarithmic maximum of likelihood, equal to $f(x|m,\kappa,\hat{\theta})$ (f is integrated likelihood), m is the model and κ the

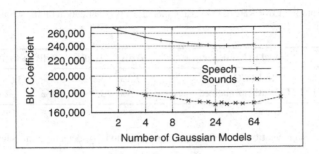

Fig. 4. BIC Coefficient Evolution as Function of Gaussian Model Number

component number of the model, $v_{m,\kappa}$ is the number of free parameters of model m and n is the number of frames. The minimum of BIC indicates the best model.

The BIC has been calculated for the speech class and for the life sound class with various number of Gaussian models. Results are given in Figure 4 for speech (continuous line) and for life sounds (dashed line): a number of 24 Gaussian models seems to be a good choice.

4.2 Evaluation

The analysis window was set to 16 ms (2^8 samples, sample rate fixed to 16 kHz) with an overlap of 8 ms. The segmentation between speech and sound was evaluated with a "cross-validation" protocol: training is achieved with 80% of the corpus, and each file of the 20% remaining is tested according to the models. Training is performed with pure sounds and testing with sounds mixed with HIS noise at 0, +10, +20 and +40 dB levels. Cutting is made to insure that no test is done on a model trained with the same speaker or the same sentence.

Speech/sound discrimination performances are evaluated through the segmentation error rate (SER) which represents the ratio between the misclassified sounds and the total number of sounds to be classified. In Table 1 the segmentation results are presented for LFCC parameters coupled or not with normalized energy. The best results are achieved for LFCC with energy: the Segmentation Error Rate is 4% above +10 dB and 14.5% at 0 dB.

Detection and Segmentation stages. For global system evaluation we have built a test set containing a mixture between real noise (recorded in the test apartment), 22 sentences (2 different speakers) and 23 life sounds. The noise level is constant and SNR is equally distributed between +10 dB and +40 dB by signal level variation. The duration of the test file is 3,600 s (1 hour).

The detection module has extracted 44 audio signals, whereas one signal has been missed. The classification results for the 44 extracted signals are given in Table 2. Speakers, sentences and life sounds of the test set are put out for training like in the cross-validation protocol.

The best results are obtained with LFCC parameters. Normalized energy is not relevant because this feature remains too dependent on experimental recording conditions, although it is less dependent than non normalized energy. Loss of performances for SNR between +40 dB and +10 dB is about 2%.

Table 1. Segmentation Error Rate (24 Gaussian models), cross-validation on the whole corpus (Speech & Life Sounds)

Signal to Noise Ratio	0 dB	+10 dB	+20 dB	+40 dB
16 LFCC alone	17.3%	5.1%	3.8%	3.6%
16 LFCC with normalized energy	14.5%	3.9%	3.9%	4%

Table 2. Global Segmentation Error Rate (24 Gaussian models), detection and segmentation on 45 audio signals

Features	16 LFCC only	16 LFCC with normalised energy
Error Rate	6.7%	8.9%

5   Speech Recognition System

5.1   RAPHAEL

For Speech Recognition, the autonomous system RAPHAEL is used [9]. The language model of this system is a medium vocabulary statistical model (around 11,000 words). This model is obtained by using textual information extracted from the Internet as described in [10] and from "Le Monde" corpora. It is then optimized for the distress sentences of our corpus. In order to insure a good speaker independence, the training of the acoustic models of RAPHAEL has been made with large corpora recorded with near 300 French speakers: respectively 80 speakers (BREF80 corpus), 120 (BREF120 [11]) and 100 (BRAF100 [12]).

The synchronisation with the sound/speech system is achieved via a file exchange protocol. As soon as the requested wave file has been analysed by RAPHAEL, it is deleted and the hypothesis found is stored in a hypothesis file. Another wave file from the queue may be then analysed.

5.2   Evaluation and First Results

It is very important that the key words related to a distress situation are well recognized. The speech recognition system has been evaluated with the sentences from 5 speakers of our corpus (630 tests). For normal sentences and in 6% of the cases, an unexpected distress key word is introduced by the system and leads to a *False Alarm Sentence*. For distress sentences and in 16% of the cases, the distress key word is not recognized but missed: this leads to a *Missed Alarm Sentence*. This often occurs in isolated words like "Aïe" (Ouch) or "SOS" or in French syntactically incorrect expressions like "Ça va pas bien" (I am not feeling very well). The language model has to be optimized in a suitable way and the dictionary of the speech recognizer to be completed in order to obtain lower error rates.

6   Sound Classification

GMM and HMM are well suited for sound classification [6,8]. For this framework the life sound corpus has been supplemented with a new class (object falls). The preliminary results are given in Table 3. The analysis window was set to 16 ms with an overlap of 8 ms. The classification was achieved with a "cross validation-protocol". We used LFCC features with derivatives of first and second-order. The optimal number of Gaussian models was determined using the BIC criterion: a number of 12 Gaussian models is appropriate for the GMM method with the 8 sound classes of our corpus. For the HMM method, we use 3 state HMM, each state of a class being described by 12 Gaussian models.

HMM seems to give best results for SNR$\geq$+10 dB and we are working to improve these first results.

Table 3. Classification Error Rate (%) using 12 Gaussian models

Signal to Noise Ratio	0 dB	+10 dB	+20 dB	+40 dB	$\geq$+50 dB
GMM	23.6	15.4	16.5	10.2	3.2
HMM	29.7	12.6	10.8	9	2

7 Conclusions and Perspectives

In this paper we have presented a sound processing system designed to work in the framework of a medical remote monitoring application. An adapted French speech corpus with distress and normal sentences has been recorded and used for evaluation purpose. The system detects sound events, identifies the type of sounds among speech and life sounds. This step may be used under realistic conditions with moderate noise: +10 dB SNR. In the case of speech, a French speech recognizer is initiated, then distress key words or calls for help may be extracted from the recognized sentences. Therefore, this system is able to extract new additional information from speech and sounds: the behaviour of the patient is best known and this may be very useful for the medical monitoring system to make a decision in a distress case.

Acknowledgements. This work is a part of the DESDHIS-ACI "Technologies for Health" project of the French Research Ministry. This project is a collaboration between the CLIPS ("*Communication Langagière et Interaction Personne-Système*") laboratory, in charge of the sound analysis, and the TIMC ("*Techniques de l'Imagerie, de la Modélisation et de la Cognition*") laboratory, charged with the medical sensors analysis and data fusion.

References

1. European Commission: Europe's response to World Ageing. Promoting economic and social progress in an ageing world. A contribution of the European Commission to the Second World Assembly on Ageing. 18 March (2002).
2. V. Rialle, J.B. Lamy, N. Noury, L. Bajolle: Remote monitoring of patients at home: A Software Agent approach. Computer Methods and Programs in Biomedicine. **72**, 3 (2003) 257–268.
3. G. Virone, N. Noury and J. Demongeot: A System for Automatic Measurement of Circadian Activity in Telemedicine. Proc. IEEE Transactions on Biomedical Engineering, **49** (2002) 1463–1469.

4. Real World Computing Partnership: CD – Sound Scene Database in Real Acoustical Environments (1998–2001).
5. D. Reynolds: Speaker Identification and Verification using Gaussian Mixture Speaker Models. Workshop on Automatic Speaker Recognition, Identification and Verification, Martigny, Switzerland (1994) 27–30.
6. J. Pinquier, C. Senac and R. Andre-Obrecht: Speech and music classification in audio documents. proc. IEEE Int. Conf. on Acoustics, Speech and Signal Processing, **4** (2002) 4164.
7. L. Lu, H.J. Zhang and H. Jiang: Content analysis for audio classification using feature extraction matrix. proc. IEEE Transaction on Speech and Audio Processing, **10**, 7 (2002) 504–516.
8. T. Yamada and N. Watanabe: Voice Activity Detection using non-Speech Models and HMM Composition. Workshop on Hands-free Speech Communication, Tokyo, Japan (2001).
9. M. Akbar et al.: Parole et traduction automatique : le module de reconnaissance RAPHAEL. Proc. COLING-ACL'98, Montréal, Quebec, **2** (1998) 36–40.
10. D. Vaufreydaz et al.: Internet Documents—a Rich Source for Spoken Language Modeling. Proc. IEEE Workshop ASRU '99, Keystone-Colorado, USA (1999) 277–281.
11. J.L. Gauvain, L.F. Lamel, M. Eskenazi: Design considerations and text selection for BREF, a large French read-speech corpus Proc. ICSLP '90, Kobe, Japan (1990) 1097–1100.
12. D. Vaufreydaz et al.: A New Methodology for Speech Corpora Definition from Internet Documents Proc. LREC 2000, 2nd Int. Conf. on Language Resources and Evaluation, Athens, Greece (2000) 423–426.

Author Index

Abraham, Ajith 159
Alain, Pierre 319
Allison, Ben 327
Álvarez, Aitor 565
Arruti, Andoni 415, 565

Barbot, Nelly 319, 423
Batliner, Anton 581
Bejček, Eduard 21
Benešová, Václava 29
Boëffard, Olivier 319, 423
Bojar, Ondřej 29
Bolshakov, Igor A. 37
Brazdil, Pavel 45
Brocki, Łukasz 343
Buccella, Augustina 229
Burget, Lukáš 351

Cardeñoso-Payo, Valentín 645
Carson-Berndsen, Julie 407
Casar, Marta 359
Casillas, Arantza 165
Cearreta, Idoia 565
Cechich, Alejandra 229
Černocký, Jan 351
Červa, Petr 485
Chaillol, Stéphane 711
Chen, Ying 301
Choi, Key-Sun 119
Çiloğlu, Tolga 669
Colas, Fabrice 45

De Pauw, Guy 197
de Schryver, Gilles-Maurice 197
Díaz-Méndez, Alejandro 703

Escudero-Mancebo, David 645

Fakotakis, Nikos 479
Fapšo, Michal 351
Fék, Márk 367
Ferrández, Óscar 53
Fitrianie, Siska 573
Fonollosa, José A.R. 359
Francisco, Virginia 375

Fresno, Víctor 165
Fukutomi, Satoshi 127

Galicia-Haro, Sofia N. 37
Garay, Nestor 565
Garudadri, Harinath 471
Gelbukh, Alexander 61, 661
Gerassimenko, Olga 621
Gervás, Pablo 375
Gieselmann, Petra 687
Godlewski, Grzegorz 213
Graliński, Filip 69
Gravier, Guillaume 391
Grocholewski, Stefan 523
Guthrie, David 327
Guthrie, Louise 327

Hacioglu, Kadri 301
Hacker, Christian 581
Haderlein, Tino 431, 589
Hamar, Juraj 509
Han, SangYong 159, 661
Hanzlíček, Zdeněk 383
Hartmann, Melanie 597
Hennoste, Tiit 621
Hermansky, Hynek 471
Hlaváčková, Dana 79
Hócza, András 87
Hoidekr, Jan 501
Hoirin, Kim 463
Holan, Tomáš 95
Horák, Aleš 79
Hovy, Eduard 3
Hudlicka, Eva 13
Huet, Stéphane 391
Hwang, Soonhee 261

Isahara, Hitoshi 119
Istrate, Dan 711
Izquierdo-Beviá, Rubén 173

Jelínek, Libor 605
Jung, Sung-won 447
Jung, Youngim 261
Jurčíček, Filip 605, 613

Kadlec, Vladimír   79
Kang, Mi-young   447
Kang, NamOh   661
Kang, Sangki   517
Kanis, Jakub   501, 613
Kanokphara, Supphanat   407
Karafiát, Martin   351
Karjalainen, Matti   637
Kasterpalu, Riina   621
Kim, Bong-Wan   335
Kim, Hyung Soon   399
Kim, Jong-Bok   103, 111
Kim, Yongserk   517
Klimeš, Václav   135
Kocsor, András   87
Koit, Mare   621
Kolář, Jáchym   629
Kolorenč, Jan   485
Koržinek, Danijel   343
Kozareva, Zornitsa   143
Kuboň, Vladislav   151
Kwon, Hyuk-chul   261, 447

Lazkano, Elena   565
Le, Cuong Anh   189
Lee, Yong-Ju   335
Lehr, Maider   415
Lolive, Damien   423
Lopatková, Markéta   151
López, Juan Miguel   565
Lukaszewicz, Konrad   637

Maier, Andreas   431
Marasek, Krzysztof   343
Martínez, Raquel   165
Martínez-Barco, Patricio   53, 173
Martínez-Hinarejos, Carlos D.   653
Matějka, Pavel   351
Matoušek, Jindřich   383, 439, 531
Mihelič, France   455
Mikyong, Ji   463
Möllerová, Petra   21
Montalvo, Soto   165
Montes-y-Gómez, Manuel   293
Montoyo, Andrés   143
Moreno-Monteagudo, Lorenza   173
Motlíček, Petr   471
Mporas, Iosif   479
Müller, Luděk   501, 539, 613
Muñoz, Rafael   53

Němec, Petr   181
Németh, Géza   367
Nguyen, Minh Le   189
Nguyen, Thanh Tri   189
Nöth, Elmar   431, 581, 589
Nouza, Jan   485
Nunes, Maria das Graças Volpe   269

Obach, Michael   415
Oh, Jong-Hoon   119
Olaszy, Gábor   367
Ortiz, Amalia   415
Oyarzun, David   415
Ozeki, Kazuhiko   127
Öztürk, Özlem   669

Padrta, Aleš   493
Palomar, Manuel   53
Palomar Sanz, Manuel   229
Pesti, Péter   367
Piasecki, Maciej   205, 213
Plátek, Martin   151
Podveský, Petr   237
Pognan, Patrice   151
Popescu, Vladimir   711
Pražák, Aleš   501
Psutka, Josef   501
Psutka, J.V.   501
Ptáček, Jan   221

Rääbis, Andriela   621
Ratzka, Andreas   677
Reyes-Galaviz, Orion F.   703
Reyes-García, Carlos A.   703
Roger, Sandra   229
Romportl, Jan   439
Rothkrantz, Leon J.M.   555, 573
Rusko, Milan   509

Schaaf, Thomas   687
Schlaefer, Nico   687
Schnelle, Dirk   597
Schuster, Maria   589
Schwarz, Petr   351
Sébillot, Pascale   391
Semecký, Jiří   237
Serignat, Jean-François   711
Shimazu, Akira   189
Shin, Kwangcheol   159
Shozakai, Makoto   589
Shriberg, Elizabeth   629

Sidorov, Grigori   61
Sierra, Basilio   565
Slavcheva, Milena   245
Slavík, Pavel   695
Smrž, Pavel   351
Song, Hwa Jeon   399
Songwook, Lee   253
Specia, Lucia   269
Sporka, Adam J.   695
Srinivasamurthy, Naveen   471
Steidl, Stefan   589
Štěpánek, Jan   277
Straňák, Pavel   21
Strandson, Krista   621
Suárez, Armando   173
Suaste-Rivas, Israel   703
Sungtak, Kim   463
Švec, Jan   605
Szaszák, György   547
Szöke, Igor   351
Szymański, Marcin   523

Takagi, Kazuyuki   127
Terol, Rafael M.   53
Tihelka, Daniel   439, 531
Trmal, Jan   539
Tugwell, David   285

Um, Yongnam   335

Vacher, Michel   711
Valdisoo, Maret   621
Vaněk, Jan   493, 539
Vázquez, Sonia   143
Vera-Félix, José Ángel   61
Vicsi, Klára   547
Villaseñor-Pineda, Luis   293
Villatoro-Tello, Esaú   293

Wagacha, Peter W.   197
Waibel, Alex   687
Wiggers, Pascal   555
Wolff, Christian   677

Yamagata, Kiwamu   127
Yang, Jaehyung   103
Yang, Liu   629
Yoon, Aesun   261, 447

Žabokrtský, Zdeněk   95, 221
Zahradil, Jiří   605, 613
Zainkó, Csaba   367
Žďánský, Jindřich   485
Zelinka, Jan   539
Žemlička, Michal   309
Zervas, Panagiotis   479
Žibert, Janez   455
Žikovský, Pavel   695
Zorn, Dominik   589

Lecture Notes in Artificial Intelligence (LNAI)

Vol. 4188: P. Sojka, I. Kopeček, K. Pala (Eds.), Text, Speech and Dialogue. XIV, 721 pages. 2006.

Vol. 4180: M. Kohlhase, OMDoc – An Open Markup Format for Mathematical Documents [version 1.2]. XIX, 428 pages. 2006.

Vol. 4155: O. Stock, M. Schaerf (Eds.), Reasoning, Action and Interaction in AI Theories and Systems. XVIII, 343 pages. 2006.

Vol. 4149: M. Klusch, M. Rovatsos, T.R. Payne (Eds.), Cooperative Information Agents X. XII, 477 pages. 2006.

Vol. 4139: T. Salakoski, F. Ginter, S. Pyysalo, T. Pahikkala, Advances in Natural Language Processing. XVI, 771 pages. 2006.

Vol. 4133: J. Gratch, M. Young, R. Aylett, D. Ballin, P. Olivier (Eds.), Intelligent Virtual Agents. XIV, 472 pages. 2006.

Vol. 4130: U. Furbach, N. Shankar (Eds.), Automated Reasoning. XV, 680 pages. 2006.

Vol. 4114: D.-S. Huang, K. Li, G.W. Irwin (Eds.), Computational Intelligence, Part II. XXVII, 1337 pages. 2006.

Vol. 4108: J.M. Borwein, W.M. Farmer (Eds.), Mathematical Knowledge Management. VIII, 295 pages. 2006.

Vol. 4106: T.R. Roth-Berghofer, M.H. Göker, H. A. Güvenir (Eds.), Advances in Case-Based Reasoning. XIV, 566 pages. 2006.

Vol. 4099: Q. Yang, G. Webb (Eds.), PRICAI 2006: Trends in Artificial Intelligence. XXVIII, 1263 pages. 2006.

Vol. 4095: S. Nolfi, G. Baldassare, R. Calabretta, D. Marocco, D. Parisi, J.C. T. Hallam, O. Miglino, J.-A. Meyer (Eds.), From Animals to Animats 9. XV, 869 pages. 2006.

Vol. 4093: X. Li, O.R. Zaïane, Z. Li (Eds.), Advanced Data Mining and Applications. XXI, 1110 pages. 2006.

Vol. 4092: J. Lang, F. Lin, J. Wang (Eds.), Knowledge Science, Engineering and Management. XV, 664 pages. 2006.

Vol. 4088: Z.-Z. Shi, R. Sadananda (Eds.), Agent Computing and Multi-Agent Systems. XVII, 827 pages. 2006.

Vol. 4087: F. Schwenker, S. Marinai (Eds.), Artificial Neural Networks in Pattern Recognition. IX, 299 pages. 2006.

Vol. 4068: H. Schärfe, P. Hitzler, P. Øhrstrøm (Eds.), Conceptual Structures: Inspiration and Application. XI, 455 pages. 2006.

Vol. 4065: P. Perner (Ed.), Advances in Data Mining. XI, 592 pages. 2006.

Vol. 4062: G. Wang, J.F. Peters, A. Skowron, Y. Yao (Eds.), Rough Sets and Knowledge Technology. XX, 810 pages. 2006.

Vol. 4049: S. Parsons, N. Maudet, P. Moraitis, I. Rahwan (Eds.), Argumentation in Multi-Agent Systems. XIV, 313 pages. 2006.

Vol. 4048: L. Goble. J.-J.C.. Meyer (Eds.), Deontic Logic and Artificial Normative Systems. X, 273 pages. 2006.

Vol. 4045: D. Barker-Plummer, R. Cox, N. Swoboda (Eds.), Diagrammatic Representation and Inference. XII, 301 pages. 2006.

Vol. 4031: M. Ali, R. Dapoigny (Eds.), Advances in Applied Artificial Intelligence. XXIII, 1353 pages. 2006.

Vol. 4029: L. Rutkowski, R. Tadeusiewicz, L.A. Zadeh, J.M. Zurada (Eds.), Artificial Intelligence and Soft Computing – ICAISC 2006. XXI, 1235 pages. 2006.

Vol. 4027: H.L. Larsen, G. Pasi, D. Ortiz-Arroyo, T. Andreasen, H. Christiansen (Eds.), Flexible Query Answering Systems. XVIII, 714 pages. 2006.

Vol. 4021: E. André, L. Dybkjær, W. Minker, H. Neumann, M. Weber (Eds.), Perception and Interactive Technologies. XI, 217 pages. 2006.

Vol. 4020: A. Bredenfeld, A. Jacoff, I. Noda, Y. Takahashi (Eds.), RoboCup 2005: Robot Soccer World Cup IX. XVII, 727 pages. 2006.

Vol. 4013: L. Lamontagne, M. Marchand (Eds.), Advances in Artificial Intelligence. XIII, 564 pages. 2006.

Vol. 4012: T. Washio, A. Sakurai, K. Nakajima, H. Takeda, S. Tojo, M. Yokoo (Eds.), New Frontiers in Artificial Intelligence. XIII, 484 pages. 2006.

Vol. 4008: J.C. Augusto, C.D. Nugent (Eds.), Designing Smart Homes. XI, 183 pages. 2006.

Vol. 4005: G. Lugosi, H.U. Simon (Eds.), Learning Theory. XI, 656 pages. 2006.

Vol. 3978: M. Hnich, M. Carlsson, F. Fages, F. Rossi (Eds.), Recent Advances in Constraints. VIII, 179 pages. 2006.

Vol. 3963: O. Dikenelli, M.-P. Gleizes, A. Ricci (Eds.), Engineering Societies in the Agents World VI. XII, 303 pages. 2006.

Vol. 3960: R. Vieira, P. Quaresma, M.d.G.V. Nunes, N.J. Mamede, C. Oliveira, M.C. Dias (Eds.), Computational Processing of the Portuguese Language. XII, 274 pages. 2006.

Vol. 3955: G. Antoniou, G. Potamias, C. Spyropoulos, D. Plexousakis (Eds.), Advances in Artificial Intelligence. XVII, 611 pages. 2006.

Vol. 3949: F. A. Savacı (Ed.), Artificial Intelligence and Neural Networks. IX, 227 pages. 2006.

Vol. 3946: T.R. Roth-Berghofer, S. Schulz, D.B. Leake (Eds.), Modeling and Retrieval of Context. XI, 149 pages. 2006.

Vol. 3944: J. Quiñonero-Candela, I. Dagan, B. Magnini, F. d'Alché-Buc (Eds.), Machine Learning Challenges. XIII, 462 pages. 2006.

Vol. 3930: D.S. Yeung, Z.-Q. Liu, X.-Z. Wang, H. Yan (Eds.), Advances in Machine Learning and Cybernetics. XXI, 1110 pages. 2006.

Vol. 3918: W.K. Ng, M. Kitsuregawa, J. Li, K. Chang (Eds.), Advances in Knowledge Discovery and Data Mining. XXIV, 879 pages. 2006.

Vol. 3913: O. Boissier, J. Padget, V. Dignum, G. Lindemann, E. Matson, S. Ossowski, J.S. Sichman, J. Vázquez-Salceda (Eds.), Coordination, Organizations, Institutions, and Norms in Multi-Agent Systems. XII, 259 pages. 2006.

Vol. 3910: S.A. Brueckner, G.D.M. Serugendo, D. Hales, F. Zambonelli (Eds.), Engineering Self-Organising Systems. XII, 245 pages. 2006.

Vol. 3904: M. Baldoni, U. Endriss, A. Omicini, P. Torroni (Eds.), Declarative Agent Languages and Technologies III. XII, 245 pages. 2006.

Vol. 3900: F. Toni, P. Torroni (Eds.), Computational Logic in Multi-Agent Systems. XVII, 427 pages. 2006.

Vol. 3899: S. Frintrop, VOCUS: A Visual Attention System for Object Detection and Goal-Directed Search. XIV, 216 pages. 2006.

Vol. 3898: K. Tuyls, P.J. 't Hoen, K. Verbeeck, S. Sen (Eds.), Learning and Adaption in Multi-Agent Systems. X, 217 pages. 2006.

Vol. 3891: J.S. Sichman, L. Antunes (Eds.), Multi-Agent-Based Simulation VI. X, 191 pages. 2006.

Vol. 3890: S.G. Thompson, R. Ghanea-Hercock (Eds.), Defence Applications of Multi-Agent Systems. XII, 141 pages. 2006.

Vol. 3885: V. Torra, Y. Narukawa, A. Valls, J. Domingo-Ferrer (Eds.), Modeling Decisions for Artificial Intelligence. XII, 374 pages. 2006.

Vol. 3881: S. Gibet, N. Courty, J.-F. Kamp (Eds.), Gesture in Human-Computer Interaction and Simulation. XIII, 344 pages. 2006.

Vol. 3874: R. Missaoui, J. Schmidt (Eds.), Formal Concept Analysis. X, 309 pages. 2006.

Vol. 3873: L. Maicher, J. Park (Eds.), Charting the Topic Maps Research and Applications Landscape. VIII, 281 pages. 2006.

Vol. 3864: Y. Cai, J. Abascal (Eds.), Ambient Intelligence in Everyday Life. XII, 323 pages. 2006.

Vol. 3863: M. Kohlhase (Ed.), Mathematical Knowledge Management. XI, 405 pages. 2006.

Vol. 3862: R.H. Bordini, M. Dastani, J. Dix, A.E.F. Seghrouchni (Eds.), Programming Multi-Agent Systems. XIV, 267 pages. 2006.

Vol. 3849: I. Bloch, A. Petrosino, A.G.B. Tettamanzi (Eds.), Fuzzy Logic and Applications. XIV, 438 pages. 2006.

Vol. 3848: J.-F. Boulicaut, L. De Raedt, H. Mannila (Eds.), Constraint-Based Mining and Inductive Databases. X, 401 pages. 2006.

Vol. 3847: K.P. Jantke, A. Lunzer, N. Spyratos, Y. Tanaka (Eds.), Federation over the Web. X, 215 pages. 2006.

Vol. 3835: G. Sutcliffe, A. Voronkov (Eds.), Logic for Programming, Artificial Intelligence, and Reasoning. XIV, 744 pages. 2005.

Vol. 3830: D. Weyns, H. V.D. Parunak, F. Michel (Eds.), Environments for Multi-Agent Systems II. VIII, 291 pages. 2006.

Vol. 3817: M. Faundez-Zanuy, L. Janer, A. Esposito, A. Satue-Villar, J. Roure, V. Espinosa-Duro (Eds.), Nonlinear Analyses and Algorithms for Speech Processing. XII, 380 pages. 2006.

Vol. 3814: M. Maybury, O. Stock, W. Wahlster (Eds.), Intelligent Technologies for Interactive Entertainment. XV, 342 pages. 2005.

Vol. 3809: S. Zhang, R. Jarvis (Eds.), AI 2005: Advances in Artificial Intelligence. XXVII, 1344 pages. 2005.

Vol. 3808: C. Bento, A. Cardoso, G. Dias (Eds.), Progress in Artificial Intelligence. XVIII, 704 pages. 2005.

Vol. 3802: Y. Hao, J. Liu, Y.-P. Wang, Y.-m. Cheung, H. Yin, L. Jiao, J. Ma, Y.-C. Jiao (Eds.), Computational Intelligence and Security, Part II. XLII, 1166 pages. 2005.

Vol. 3801: Y. Hao, J. Liu, Y.-P. Wang, Y.-m. Cheung, H. Yin, L. Jiao, J. Ma, Y.-C. Jiao (Eds.), Computational Intelligence and Security, Part I. XLI, 1122 pages. 2005.

Vol. 3789: A. Gelbukh, Á. de Albornoz, H. Terashima-Marín (Eds.), MICAI 2005: Advances in Artificial Intelligence. XXVI, 1198 pages. 2005.

Vol. 3782: K.-D. Althoff, A. Dengel, R. Bergmann, M. Nick, T.R. Roth-Berghofer (Eds.), Professional Knowledge Management. XXIII, 739 pages. 2005.

Vol. 3763: H. Hong, D. Wang (Eds.), Automated Deduction in Geometry. X, 213 pages. 2006.

Vol. 3755: G.J. Williams, S.J. Simoff (Eds.), Data Mining. XI, 331 pages. 2006.

Vol. 3735: A. Hoffmann, H. Motoda, T. Scheffer (Eds.), Discovery Science. XVI, 400 pages. 2005.

Vol. 3734: S. Jain, H.U. Simon, E. Tomita (Eds.), Algorithmic Learning Theory. XII, 490 pages. 2005.

Vol. 3721: A.M. Jorge, L. Torgo, P.B. Brazdil, R. Camacho, J. Gama (Eds.), Knowledge Discovery in Databases: PKDD 2005. XXIII, 719 pages. 2005.

Vol. 3720: J. Gama, R. Camacho, P.B. Brazdil, A.M. Jorge, L. Torgo (Eds.), Machine Learning: ECML 2005. XXIII, 769 pages. 2005.

Vol. 3717: B. Gramlich (Ed.), Frontiers of Combining Systems. X, 321 pages. 2005.

Vol. 3702: B. Beckert (Ed.), Automated Reasoning with Analytic Tableaux and Related Methods. XIII, 343 pages. 2005.

Vol. 3698: U. Furbach (Ed.), KI 2005: Advances in Artificial Intelligence. XIII, 409 pages. 2005.

Vol. 3690: M. Pěchouček, P. Petta, L.Z. Varga (Eds.), Multi-Agent Systems and Applications IV. XVII, 667 pages. 2005.